CHILD WELFARE SERVICES

CHILD WELFARE SERVICES

Third Edition

ALFRED KADUSHIN, Ph.D.

Julia Lathrop Professor of Social Work
University of Wisconsin, Madison

Macmillan Publishing Co., Inc.
New York

Collier Macmillan Publishers
London

Preliminary Edition copyright © 1965 by Alfred Kadushin. First Edition © copyright
1967, and Second Edition copyright 1974 by Alfred Kadushin

Macmillan Publishing Co., Inc.
866 Third Avenue, New York, New York 10022

Collier Macmillan Canada, Ltd.

Library of Congress Cataloging in Publication Data

Kadushin, Alfred.
    Child welfare services.

    Includes bibliographies and indexes.
    1. Child welfare—United States.   I.   Title.
HV741.K26   1980   362.7'0973   79–13416
ISBN 0–02–361810–8

Printing: 2 3 4 5 6 7 8   Year: 1 2 3 4 5 6

To Sylvia; to Goldie; to Raphael—with love.

PREFACE

This book is a comprehensive study of the principal child welfare services. It begins by defining child welfare, placing it as a field of practice within social work, and presents a scheme for the categorization of child welfare problems in terms of role theory. It goes on to provide a historical perspective on how and why child welfare services developed and to describe the current socioeconomic context in which they operate. Separate chapters are devoted to each of the principal supportive, supplementary, and substitutive child welfare services: family service and child guidance clinics, the social insurance, aid to families of dependent children, protective services, day care, homemaker service, foster care, adoption, institutional child care. Each chapter includes material on the historical development of the service, the situations for which the service is appropriate, scope of the service, process in offering the service, evaluation of the service, problems encountered by the service, and trends in offering the service.

A chapter on child welfare services in other countries provides an international perspective on the practice of child welfare in the United States. The final chapter is concerned with the sociology of the child welfare worker—characteristics, career routes, occupational problems, and satisfactions.

A special effort has been made to include as much of the relevant research as possible and to supplement material from casework with material available from other practice methods.

The book is directed to the student of social work both at the undergraduate level and at the graduate level. Undergraduate students—whether they plan to work in a social agency after graduation or to go on to a graduate school of social work—will find the material in the text useful preparation. Graduate students enrolled in child welfare seminars or taking courses that are concerned, in part, with child welfare problems will find this a useful, systematic, and detailed review of child welfare services.

The text, then, can appropriately be used at both the undergraduate and the graduate levels. The first two editions have been widely used for courses at both levels.

The book is also directed to the child welfare worker currently employed in social agencies. The volume is designed to offer both fully trained professional workers and those with limited professional training a systematic review of the substantive knowledge available concerning child welfare services and to provide a synthesis of widely scattered material for the busy practitioner.

Finally, the book is designed to give the reader a broad knowledge of child welfare services rather than to develop skills for working directly with people who present child welfare problems. The primary purpose of the text is to teach about child welfare—the *what* and the *why*—rather than to teach the *how* of doing child welfare work. It is directed toward developing a knowledge about, concern for, and understanding of child welfare services rather than oriented toward developing technical, professional skills required in treating clients. It is important to note that "knowing" about a field of social work practice is a necessary pre-requisite for effective "doing" and "treating." Charlotte Towle aptly notes:

> Students must have knowledge with which to think. Feeling as a professional per-son must come to feel is developed through, and in response to, knowledge. Understanding comes about through knowledge that has been integrated through emotional acceptance, which permits the faculties of knowing and thinking to function in the doing. The nature of doing will, therefore, reflect integration or lack of integration of knowledge.[1]

The presentation is primarily descriptive and expository, concerned with explicating current child welfare practices—how child welfare services actually operate rather than how they should operate. Admittedly, what *is* is a far cry from what *should be*. The detailed material on each of the particular services presented in the text makes it clear that American society has failed large num-bers of its children and that child welfare services have relatively low priority in the allocation of national resources. Ours has not been, and is not likely to be, a filiocentric society. Although the needs and rights of children are a matter of great concern within the individual family unit, this concern has not been re-flected in public policy.

The congressionally appointed Joint Commission on Mental Health of Chil-dren, making its report to the nation in 1970 after three years of study, categor-ically states that "this nation, the richest of all world powers, has no unified national commitment to its children and youth. The claim that we are a child-centered society . . . is a myth. Our words are made meaningless by our actions. . . ." [2]

The finding was repeated by a prestigious committee of the National Acad-emy of Sciences that, in reviewing the situation, concluded, "existing govern-ment programs are not adequately meeting the needs of America's children and families." [3]

Essential data for planning child welfare services are not available at the national level and often not at the state level. Inequities are imposed on children by virtue of the accident of where they live. Some communities spend consider-ably more on child welfare services than do other communities. No determined effort to reduce such inequities, which has been made in education, is being at-tempted in child welfare.[4]

Through the detailed exposition on services, this book also makes clear that in many significant respects the field of child welfare social work has failed large numbers of America's children. In general the field is oriented toward crisis, rescue, and remedy rather than toward prevention and planning. It is reactive rather than proactive, responding primarily in an *ad hoc* manner to emergency situations rather than planning long-term policies. It serves only a limited per-centage of America's children and is concerned with life at the margins of society

[1] Charlotte Towle, *The Learner in Education for the Professions* (Chicago: University of Chicago Press, 1954), p. 358.

[2] *Crisis in Mental Health: Challenge for the 1970's,* Report of the Joint Commission on the Mental Health of Children (New York: Harper and Row, Publishers, 1970), p. 2.

[3] National Academy of Sciences. *Toward a National Policy for Children and Families* (Washington, D.C.: The Academy, 1976).

[4] Michael Kirst, Walter Garms, and Theo Oppermann. *State Service for Children: An Ex-ploration of Who Benefits, Who Governs* (Palo Alto, Calif.: Stanford University, 1978, mimeo).

rather than at the center. Services are offered to the few who have limited problems and considerable strengths rather than to the many who have multiple problems and few resources.

The tendency is for "different agencies to respond disconnectedly to a series of discrete crises," so that service to any one family is poorly coordinated. Much of the basic policy in child welfare is founded on intuition and tradition rather than on empirical research and precise information. There is little follow-up and disciplined evaluation of results.

But the text also attempts to make clear the factors that help to explain, although they do not excuse, the failures of society and of the agencies, and to point out the very real achievements of child welfare social work. As a consequence of the efforts of the individual child welfare worker and the agencies under whose auspices he or she practices, we have rescued for life a sizable number of children. We have found families, protection, care, and physical and emotional support for children who would otherwise have endured greater suffering and pain—if they had lived at all. This is the measure of the victory we have achieved, and it is a record of which we can justifiably be proud.

Since the publication of the previous edition in 1974, there have been significant changes in child welfare services programs and significant changes in the national context in which child welfare services are implemented. The present edition reflects those changes.

In addition, intensified concern about permanence, deinstitutionalization, child abuse and neglect, and the diversion of status offenders from the courts to the child welfare system and increased court involvement in child welfare decisions have suggested the need for updating. The recent rapid increases in divorce, the employment of mothers, teenage pregnancies, and single-parent families and the changing relationships between the sexes and changing attitudes toward parenthood also were important in suggesting the need for revision.

There is a less receptive attitude toward new social welfare programs, including child welfare, than was the case at the time of the first two editions, and there is a greater resistance to adequate support of existing programs. Social welfare competes with new high-priority problems, such as energy and conservation, for increasingly scarce tax dollars. The changing climate of opinion suggests that there are limited possibilities in the coming period of a new thrust analogous to the New Deal, the New Frontier, and the Great Society programs. There is currently less confidence, less hope in the ability of government and government policy to solve social problems.

There is currently a great concern with accountability, "production" of results, "cost-benefit analysis," and the "biggest bang for the buck." Systems analysis specialists and management consultants are displacing professional social workers as key decision makers in some program operations. There is a greater, and perhaps desirable, tendency to be critical about the objectives of social programs and what they can accomplish and are accomplishing.

All statistics in the book have been updated. Students and teachers who used previous editions of the book indicated the need for greater selectivity in citing statistics and research results. The problem of selectivity becomes more difficult because there has been a rapid acceleration of research relevant to child welfare services during the past ten years, much of which should be called to the reader's attention.

Keeping the text within reasonable limits required some deletions as more current material was added. Content on the social insurance and the social assistance programs was summarized and combined in a single chapter. The number of illustrative vignettes, unfortunately, had to be reduced.

A word of explanation needs to be offered for what is excluded from the book. Services to the delinquent child and to the physically handicapped and mentally retarded child have not been discussed. The material on these services is considered in more specialized texts and is so vast that even a condensed review would have made this book immoderately long and prohibitively expensive. Also, these services have a frame of reference different from that of the services discussed. As Jenkins pointed out:

> Services to the delinquent child must involve detailed consideration of the "legal structure and court apparatus." Services to the physically handicapped and mentally retarded have traditionally been of primary concern to the health and education professions respectively. The traditional child welfare agencies operate in these areas only tangentially.[5]

A more recent national study of social services to children specifically excluded "services to juvenile delinquents or handicapped children" from its definition of child welfare services.[6]

Decisions about what to include and what to omit were difficult to make. Dramatic case history material vitiates somewhat the scholarly posture of the text. Yet, as a practicing social worker and social work educator, the author has great respect for the affective components of teaching-learning that are communicated through case histories, and so these have been included when appropriate.

The list of people to whom I am indebted is extremely long. It includes teachers and supervisors, students and clients, friends and adversaries, co-workers and colleagues in the United States, the Netherlands, and Israel. It includes the many teachers and students who, having used earlier editions of the text, gave me their very constructive suggestions for revision. And it includes the National Institute for Mental Health, the Children's Bureau, the University of Wisconsin Graduate School, and the Silberman Fund, from whom I have received research grants to support the studies that have increased my understanding of child welfare. To name one is to slight another, yet some must be named:

Professor David Fanshel, School of Social Work, Columbia University and Professor Joan F. Shireman, School of Social Work, University of Illinois; Professor Charles Zastrow, School of Social Work, University of Wisconsin, Whitewater; Professor Benson Jaffee, School of Social Work, University of Washington—who read and perceptively commented on portions of the manuscript; Dr. Abraham Lurie, Director of Social Services, Hillside Hospital, New York, a friend of many years with whom I have often discussed social work problems to my invariable enlightenment; and my wife, Sylvia, who has helped me, beyond calculable measure.

A. K.

[5] Shirley Jenkins, *Priorities in Social Services: A Guide for Philanthropic Funding*. Vol I: *Child Welfare in New York City* (New York: Praeger Publishers, Inc., 1971), p. 25.

[6] Ann W. Shyne and Anita G. Schroeder, *National Study of Social Services to Children and Their Families* (Rockville, Md.: Westat, Inc., 1978), p. 14.

CONTENTS

1 CHILD WELFARE: ORIENTATION AND SCOPE   1

2 PERSPECTIVES ON CHILD WELFARE SERVICES   33

3 SUPPORTIVE SERVICES   75

4 SUPPLEMENTARY SERVICES: SOCIAL INSURANCE   115

5 PROTECTIVE SERVICES   151

6 HOMEMAKER SERVICES   235

7 DAY-CARE SERVICE   267

8 SUBSTITUTE CARE: FOSTER FAMILY CARE   313

9 THE UNMARRIED MOTHER AND THE OUT-OF-WEDLOCK CHILD   413

10 SUBSTITUTE CARE: ADOPTION   465

11 THE CHILD-CARING INSTITUTION   583

12 CHILD WELFARE SERVICES IN OTHER COUNTRIES   631

13 THE SOCIOLOGY OF THE CHILD WELFARE WORKER   673

Index   701

CHILD WELFARE SERVICES

1 CHILD WELFARE: ORIENTATION AND SCOPE

INTRODUCTION

The term *child welfare* in a general sense has very broad connotations. If we include under the term every activity that either directly or indirectly promotes the welfare of children, we would end by including most of the significant activities engaged in by society.

The sanitary engineer working toward the organization of a physically healthier environment for children, the traffic engineer working toward the reduction of automobile accidents, the research scientist studying congenital anomalies, and the military specialist guarding the country from attack—all promote the welfare of children, and thus these activities may be subsumed under a general definition of *child welfare*. Carstens (1937) notes that "child welfare has in the course of time acquired a significance that is so broad and vague that it has come to be applied to almost every effort in social and community work that is likely to benefit children" (p. 64 *).

SOCIAL WORK

A more specific and more meaningful definition of child welfare is based on the fact that society has granted to the profession of social work responsibility for helping to resolve many of the problem situations encountered by children. In its narrower sense, *child welfare* is regarded as a field of social work practice. Because it is of the genus *social work*, it shares the characteristics of the genus. To clarify the nature of child welfare, therefore, we must attempt to delineate the normative characteristics of social work. The following illustration may be of help.

Nine years ago Mrs. F., then unmarried, gave birth to a boy and placed him in the home of a childless married couple whom she knew well. She then left town. Her friends raised the boy as their own, although they never legally adopted him. When Mrs. F. married, she told her husband of her out-of-wedlock

---

* References are to be found at the end of each chapter.

1

child, and he agreed to accept the boy into the family. Mrs. F. visited her friends to tell them of her marriage and of her husband's decision to have the child live with them. Her friends, who had become very much attached to the boy, were reluctant to give him up.

Mrs. F. consulted a lawyer, who agreed to help her establish her legal rights and privileges. However, he felt that aspects of the problem other than the legality of Mrs. F.'s claim to the boy needed to be considered. How would it affect him to be removed from the home in which he was loved and accepted and to be placed in another that was unfamiliar? How would her own marriage be affected? And how would her friends feel when they were suddenly deprived of a child whom they had for a long time regarded as their own? These were not questions with which the lawyer was, by training, competent to deal. These were questions involving social relationships, marital relationships, parent–child relationships, and the social institution of marriage and the family. To help Mrs. F. clarify, for herself, the possible social effects of a decision based on her legal rights alone, the lawyer referred her to a social worker.

The inclusion of the word *social* in the title of the profession reflects the social worker's primary concern with the relation of the individual, the group, or the community to the social environment. Early in the profession's history, Mary Richmond (1922) defined *social work* as "those processes which develop personality through adjustments consciously effected individual by individual between man and his social environment" (pp. 98–99). The United Nations Secretariat defines *social work* as an "activity designed to help towards a better mutual adjustment of the individual and his social environment" (Friedlander, 1961, p. 5). The Woman's Bureau of the U.S. Department of Health, Education, and Welfare (1952) notes that "social work is uniquely concerned with the individual in relation to outer social realities in which he is involved and the satisfactions he gets from them."

Witmer and Kotinsky (1952) note that the "profession that takes as its particular task the job of helping individuals, one by one, or in groups, to deal with difficulties they encounter in operating in accordance with the requirements of a social institution is social work . . ." (p. 359). Perlman (1953) similarly states that the "person in interaction with some problematic aspect of his social reality is the focus of the social caseworker's concern" (p. 130).

The Model Statute Social Workers' License Act defines *social work* as the "professional activity of helping individuals, groups, or communities enhance or restore their capacity for social functioning and for creating societal conditions favorable to this goal" (*National Association of Social Workers' News*, May 1970, p. 7).

A special issue of *Social Work* (September 1977), the principal journal of the National Association of Social Workers, reports the proceedings of a national conference explicitly concerned with attempting to define the nature and direction of social work. Although there are differences in detail throughout the proceedings, there is repeated emphasis on the distinctive concern of social work with social functioning, social problems, social needs, social roles, social policy, social institutions, and social well-being.

Because social behavior is carried out primarily in the performance of social roles, there have been attempts to define *social work* in terms of social role performance. Thus Boehm (1959) defines *social work* as the profession that seeks to enhance the social functioning of individuals singly and in groups by activities focused upon their social relationships which constitute the interaction between man and his environment. The focus of activities is the professional intervention in that aspect of man's functioning only which lies in the realms of social relationships or of social role performance [p. 54].

In another article, Boehm (1960) notes that

social work is concerned with enhancing of social functioning of those activities considered essential for the performance of the several social roles which each individual, by virtue of his membership in social groups, is called upon to carry out. . . . Social work intervenes as the interaction (between the individual and the social structure) manifests itself in problematic social relationships.

And in 1977 a National Conference on Social Welfare task force once again focused on social role as the unique and differentiating concern of social services in its definition of *social services* as "those activities purposely and critically used to assist, to develop, and to maintain the ability of individuals and families to cope with the social roles and requirements necessary for productive participation in society" (p. 24).

Physical disease results in the need for the application of specific remedial measures designed to alleviate or cure the disease. Similarly, disabilities in the enactment of social roles require the application of specific remedial measures designed to help people to enact social roles in a more effective manner. Such treatment is made available through the profession of social work.

Other professional groups, notably sociologists, are also interested in the phenomenon of social functioning. However, social work is distinguished from sociology because it is a technology. As a technology, social work is concerned with, and responsible for, helping to "achieve controlled changes in natural relationships via relatively standardized procedures which are scientifically based" (Greenwood, 1955, p. 24).

Basic sciences study particular phenomena, and what is learned may be applied by technologists. For example, the doctor, as technologist, uses the findings of the biologist, the engineer uses the findings of the physicist, and the social worker uses the findings of the sociologist. The doctor repairs a tumorous brain, the engineer shapes the metal to support a bridge, the social worker uses knowledge of family interaction to help a conflicted family become a harmonious family.

The sociologist, as a social scientist, seeks only to understand the world of the client. The social worker, as a technologist, seeks to change it.

One might object, however, that, like the social worker, guidance counselors, marriage counselors, clinical psychologists, and psychiatrists are also technologists seeking to effect change in problem situations. Although this is true, there is a difference in responding to these problems that points to the distinction between social work and these other technologies.

Every situation that social workers, counselors, psychologists, and psychiatrists encounter is a psychosocial situation—the result of man's interaction with his social environment. However, the principal concerns of social work have been, and are, the social antecedents, concomitants, and consequences of the problem situation. The principal concerns of the counselor, the psychologist, the psychia-

trist have been the psychological aspects. The social worker is primarily concerned with the psychoSOCIAL situation; the counselor, psychologist, and psychiatrist are traditionally more concerned with the PSYCHOsocial situation.

Admittedly the analysis is not neat and valid for the social worker offering
"psychotherapy" in, let us say, a child guidance clinic. The activity of such a
social worker is not clearly distinguishable from that of a clinical psychologist
or psychiatrist. Here we have the beginnings of another profession that unites
the "psychotherapists," however diverse their formal professional affiliation
(Henry, 1971; Kraft, 1968). Furthermore, in seeking to help clients with seemingly similar psychosocial problems, these different professional groups give different emphases to the variety of therapeutic possibilities available.

Since every difficulty is psychosocial, help can be directed either toward the
person or toward the social situation. Thus one can make an effort to help the
person cope with the situation, or he may work to change the situation so that
it is easier to cope with; one can help to make the person more capable or the
situation more "copeable."

All those interventions that focus on the client's adjustive and adaptive capacity and seek to effect changes in the client's functioning through the psychic
interaction between client and professional are known as *psychotherapies*. All
those interventions that focus on the social situation, the social context of the psychosocial problem, and seek to ameliorate or change the social situation in favor
of the client or to remove the client from a stressful social environment are known
as *sociotherapies*. In some measure, all approaches are based on some combination of psychotherapy and sociotherapy. However, social workers have greater
access to, and more frequently employ, sociotherapeutic resources. This is particularly true in child welfare services, for the child client has few personal
resources that might be exploited for change, and his almost total dependency
on his environment makes sociotherapeutic resources—homemakers, day care,
foster homes, adoptive homes, institutions, and so on—the therapeutic resource
of choice.

When a particular kind of social problem, or a difficulty in social role performance, is sufficiently recurrent and widespread, a social agency is organized
to help people who encounter this particular problem, and a specialized field
of social work is thus institutionalized. For instance, physical illness requiring
hospitalization is a recurrent problem that has more than physical consequences:
it disrupts family relationships, requiring the reallocation of social roles and the
introduction of social role substitutes within the family. If a mother is hospitalized, someone else must perform her activities in the home. In the hospital, the
mother temporarily assumes a new social role—that of a patient. If she is to make
optimum use of the hospital facilities, she has to relate effectively to the hospital,
which is a medical institution with a social structure. Medical social workers have
the responsibility of helping people to deal with the social concomitants of illness.

Similarly, psychiatric social workers have the responsibility of helping people adjust to the social antecedents, concomitants, and consequences of the recurrent problem of mental illness. School social workers help children who have
difficulty in enacting the social role of pupil or in relating to a social institution
—the school system. The social worker in corrections has the responsibility of
helping the individual with the problems that arise from contact with the legal
institutions of society. The social worker in public assistance has the responsibil-

ity of helping the client in his role as a wage earner and with the social antecedents, concomitants, and consequences of the family's relationship to the economic institutions of our society.

CHILD WELFARE AS A FIELD OF
SOCIAL WORK PRACTICE

It might be noted that for a variety of historical and political reasons, social
work, as a profession, is concerned with only a limited number of the great
variety of existing social roles and related social problems. The social roles and
social problems relating to child welfare are clearly designated as among those
for which social work has responsibility. The authority and permission for social
workers to act in relation to these problems has been sanctioned by the community, the client group served, and the profession, which has historically recognized social work in child welfare as a specialized field of practice.

Child welfare services are a more clearly defined domain than most other
fields of social work practice. It is one of the few major "employment arenas
in which social workers may be said to substantially lead, manage, guide and
control the system for which they are responsible" (Morris, Anderson, 1975, p.
160). For instance, interviews with a random sample of 250 householders in four
western communities indicated that their image of social work was most clearly
defined in terms of child welfare activities and functions. Asked to identify the
practice setting in which they expected to find social workers employed, respondents listed foster care agencies, adoption agencies, and family counseling
agencies among the first four agencies most frequently listed. The most frequent
single function identified by respondents as being characteristic of social work
related to "helping troubled children" (Condie et al., 1978).

Child welfare is a specialized field of social work practice, and like each
of the other specialized fields of practice, it is concerned with a particular set
of significant social roles and with their effective implementation. The recurrent
problems with which child welfare is concerned are related to the specific relationships between parents and children. According to the Child Welfare League
of America, child welfare involves providing social services to children and
young people whose parents are unable to fulfill their child-rearing responsibilities or whose communities fail to provide the resources and protection that
children and families require. Child welfare services are designed to reinforce,
supplement, or substitute the functions that parents have difficulty in performing and to improve conditions for children and their families by modifying existing social institutions or organizing new ones. A child welfare service, like any
social service, is an "organized formalized way of dealing with a social problem"
(Turitz, 1967, p. 248), the social problem in this instance arising from difficulty
in the parent–child relationship.

A special field of practice arises from the need for specialized knowledge
and specialized methods of intervention to deal with clusters of related problems.
In order to provide efficient and effective service, agencies and their staffs focus
on special problem areas and thus come to constitute a specialized field of practice. The term *child welfare* as used here applies, then, to a particular set of
social problems that become the responsibility of a group of professionals, the

child welfare social workers, who attempt to help in the prevention or amelioration of problems in the social role functioning of the parent–child network.

Child welfare, broadly defined, has to do with the general well-being of all
children and with any and all measures designed to promote the optimal development of the child's bio-psycho-social potential in harmony with the needs
of the community. Child welfare services, as a field of social work practice, are
more narrowly focused. Such services are concerned with particular groups of
children and their families. They are "specific services, provided to specific populations by specific types of agencies" (Neel, 1971, p. 25). In defining child
welfare service as a field of social work practice, the Child Welfare League of
America notes that these "are specialized social welfare services which are primarily concerned with the child whose needs are unmet within the family and/or
through other social institutions" (Council on Social Work Education, 1959,
p. 5).

If a child is incorporated in a family system where his needs are adequately
met, there is no need for intervention of child welfare services. Only if there is
some dysfunction in the parent–child network, for whatever reason, is service
intervention called for. Child welfare services are thus alternatives to the normative familial arrangements for the care, protection, and nurturing of children. The
child welfare network is mobilized either when a breakdown of the child care
system has taken place or when there is danger that such a breakdown might
take place. At this point, child welfare services have both the responsibility and
the authority to intervene in such situations to effect change.

The approach suggesting that child welfare services are responsible primarily in those situations in which the usual normative social provisions are failing
to meet the child's needs adequately is generally called a *residual* or *minimalist*
orientation to social services. The *residual* conception of social welfare sees social
services as appropriate when the normal institutional arrangements for meeting
crucial social needs break down.

The contrasting *institutional* or *developmental* orientation suggests that
child welfare services are social utilities, like public schools, libraries, and parks
(Wilensky, Lebeaux, 1958; Kahn, 1962). Such services, then, should be made
available to all children in all families and should be appropriately helpful to
all. Child welfare services, rather than being only for the "poor, the troubled, the
dependent, the deviant and the disturbed," should also be directed to "average
people under ordinary circumstances" to meet "normal living needs" (Shorr, 1974;
Kahn, Kammerman, 1975, 1976). Rather than defining the adequate family as
the family that needs no help from the social services, the presumption is that
every family might need such help, that in a complex world no family is entirely
self-sufficient. A series of recent comprehensive formulations of suggested national policy programs regarding families and children unanimously urges adoption of such an orientation on the part of child welfare services (National Academy of Sciences, 1976; Moronay, 1976; Kenniston, 1977; Rice, 1977).

We are struggling here with the differences between what actually is and
what ought to be. However desirable it might be for child welfare services to
be offered universally in response to the needs of all families, the fact is that
only residual services are currently offered. Although the field is striving toward
the "institutional" orientation of services that are available to all, because of limited resources the priority is given to meeting the needs of the deprived, the

disadvantaged, the dependent, and the vulnerable. Aside possibly from day-care service, the clientele of child welfare service agencies is composed largely of social casualties.

It is hoped that people will turn to social work agencies, and to child welfare agencies in particular, to enhance social functioning. Just as the World Health Organization has defined *health* as the "state of complete physical, mental, and social well-being, not merely the absence of disease or infirmity," adequate social functioning might be defined as the state of optimum satisfaction in social relationships, rather than merely the absence of problems in social functioning.

The fact, however, is that most individuals come to social agencies only when they are in trouble. Hence, realistically, we are justified in focusing on problems in social role implementation and performance; we are justified in focusing on the unmet, or inadequately met, needs of children. It might further be noted that federal legislation embodying definitions of child welfare service is primarily residual in orientation, identifying particular groups of children in whose behalf the legislation is enacted. Thus the Social Security Act of 1935 identified child welfare services as being for the "protection and care of homeless, dependent and neglected children and children in danger of becoming delinquent." Although the 1962 Amendment to the Social Security Act talks of "protecting and promoting the welfare of children," it defines child welfare services as "social services which supplement or substitute for parental care and supervision" so as to ensure protection and care for "homeless dependent or neglected children" and children of working mothers and "prevent or remedy" such problems as "abuse, exploitation or delinquency of children."

A recent detailed design of a *System of Social Services for Children and Families* (1978) prepared for the Federal Administration for Children, Youth and Families defined clients of child welfare agencies in residual terms. The design notes that such clients "are the children, youth and their families . . . for whom the traditional measures of the community—the school, churches, the extended family group—have been found to be unavailable, inappropriate or inadequate. Therefore, these children, youth and their families must turn to the children and family social service system for treatment to ameliorate or solve their problem" (U.S. Department of Health, Education, and Welfare, Children's Bureau, 1978, p. 3).

The aim of this book is to describe the residually oriented activities that child welfare services actually do perform. The institutionally oriented programs that, in the best of all possible worlds, should be implemented must, unfortunately, be left to another book.

It might be argued that the orientation toward child welfare services presented here does violence to the reality of the child's living situation. Our attention, it is argued, should not be focused narrowly on the parent–child relationship but on the total family configuration. One might do better to be concerned with family welfare, of which child welfare is a specialized aspect (Sampson, 1962; Shulze, 1955). It is frequently noted that "good family welfare is the best child welfare."

The social system of the family might be seen as consisting of three principal, interrelated subsystems—the marital-pair system, the parent-child system, and the system of sibling relationships (Pollak, Brieland, 1961, p. 322). Difficulty in any one of the three subsystems is very likely to produce problems in the related subsystems. But if a conflict between husband and wife is not reflected to any significant degree in the parent–child subsystem, then marital counseling might be more helpful than child welfare services. And one might further argue that although children live within the family, they have special needs, and that the child welfare specialists have developed a particular understanding of these needs and the services required to meet them.

SOCIAL ROLES

Because child welfare services focus on malfunctions in role enactment within the parent–child relationship, it might be helpful at this point to discuss the concept of *social role* and to clarify the specific role responsibilities inherent in the parent–child role network. A role is the prescribed behavior and attitudes that a person occupying a particular status is expected to assume. As Sarbin (1954) says, "A role is a pattern of attitudes and actions which a person takes in a social situation" (p. 224). Linton (1945) states it somewhat more technically:

> The term *role* is used to designate the sum total of the culture patterns associated with a particular status. It thus includes the attitudes, values, and behavior ascribed by society to any and all persons occupying the status. . . . Insofar as it represents overt behavior, a role is the dynamic aspect of status, what the individual has to do in order to validate his occupation of the status [p. 77].

Similarly, Kluckhohn notes (quoted in Parsons, Shils, 1954):

> The set of behaviors which ego is expected to perform by virtue of his position as father, mother, or child is called a social role. A man in his role as father is expected to behave in certain ways; a woman in her role as mother in certain other ways; and each child according to age, sex, and birth order in still other ways. A role is thus a series of appropriate and expected ways of behaving relative to certain objects by virtue of a given individual's status in a given social structure or institution [p. 350].

As Bernard (1957) puts it, "A role, figuratively speaking, is a job description" (p. 43). It is a job description to be followed by the person performing the "job" of parent or child, and it includes not only the statement of the expected behavior but also the statement of the expected accompanying emotion. It prescribes that the parent not only feed the child but also love him; it prescribes that the child not only obey the parent but also respect him. Nevertheless society sanctions a variety of patterns of behavior as well as different levels of adequacy in role performance (Geismer, Ayers, 1959).

> An important feature of a large proportion of social roles is that the actions which make them up are not minutely prescribed and that a certain range of variability is regarded as legitimate. Sanctions are not invoked against deviants within certain limits [Parsons, Shils, 1954, p. 24].

Sanctioned alternatives, however, fall within prescribed limits. Generally, alternative modes of behavior will be sanctioned as long as the responsibility of the role is successfully discharged. For example, spanking and withdrawal of attention are both acceptable modes of disciplining a child, but physical brutality is not acceptable because it conflicts with one of the principal purposes of the role of parenthood: care and protection of the child. As Brim says (1957), "role prescriptions include the behavior believed in the society to be the instrumental means to the achievement of some desired result" (p. 346).

The role prescription, therefore, will change with changes in society's conception of the purpose of the role. A society that asks parents to prepare the child to live obediently under an authoritarian regime will require forms of behavior in discharging the responsibilities of parenthood different from those required by a society that asks parents to prepare the child to live as a participating member of a democracy (Wolfenstein, 1953). Different subcultural groups in a given society may have differing conceptions of parenthood, so that the role prescription of the white middle-class parent may be different from that of a lower-class black parent (Bronfenbrenner, 1958).

Unlike some other social roles, such as church member, for instance, the parental role, around which a good deal of one's life is organized, demands a high level of involvement and commitment. It can be given up only at considerable emotional, social, and legal cost. On the other hand, it is enacted under conditions of limited visibility. How the parent cares for the child, disciplines the child, or interacts with the child is not generally visible to the community.

Role enactment requires interaction with others; it involves a set of complementary expectations concerning the individual's own actions and those of others with whom he interacts—his counterparts. For the parent, the nature of his counterpart, the child, is always changing, so that the parental role prescription needs constantly to be revised. The parent of the young child is required to meet the child's dependency needs, but the same parent must change his behavior to meet the child's growing need for independence in adolescence. Recognizing that the role prescriptions for parent and child vary with time and with subcultural groups, and that each role description carries with it acceptable alternatives, let us attempt to delineate the normative aspects of role behavior for parent and child in our society.

The Parental Role

The acceptable behavior associated with the performance of a given role includes rights (the behavior expected by us from our reciprocals—the husband from the wife, the child from the parent) as well as obligations (the behavior that others expect us to perform toward them—the husband to the wife, the parents to the child). One person's rights in the role set are the other person's obligations.

What is the parent expected to do and feel in relation to his child in acceptably discharging his parental role?

1. He is expected to provide an income that will permit him to meet the needs of the child for food, clothing, shelter, education, health care, and social and recreational activities.

2. He is expected to provide for the emotional needs of the child—to pro-

vide love, security, affection, and the emotional support necessary for the healthy emotional development of the child.

3. He is expected to provide the necessary stimulation for normal intellectual, social, and spiritual development if the family believes this to be important. The parent should see that a school is available and that the child goes to school, that a peer group is available and that the child is encouraged to play, that religious training is available and that the child is encouraged to participate.

4. He must help to socialize the child. Socialization is the process of inducting "new recruits" into the social group and teaching them the behavior that is customary and acceptable to the group. The parent, in other words, has the responsibility for changing a biological organism into a human being.

5. He must discipline the child and keep him from developing patterns of behavior and attitudes disapproved of by the society.

6. He must protect the child from physical, emotional, or social harm.

7. He must present a model for the identification of sex-linked behavior.

8. He must help to maintain family interaction on a stable, satisfying basis so that an effort is made to meet the significant needs of all the members of the family. The parent must help to resolve discomforts, frictions, and dissatisfactions and must meet emotional needs with accepting, affectionate responses.

9. He must provide a fixed place of abode for the child and provide a clearly defined "place" for him in the community. Thus the child comes to know who he is and to whom he belongs and ultimately comes to achieve a stable self-identification.

10. The parent stands as an intermediary between the child and the outer world, defending the child's rights in the community and protecting the child from unjust demands by the community. Because the parental responsibility for socialization of the child is now shared with many community agencies, parents find that their role requires making "decisions concerning which agencies should do the job for them and which ones should be allowed to exercise influence. Parents are necessarily culture brokers for their children before the age of consent; they encourage and facilitate access to some parts of culture, censor others and unconsciously or ambivalently screen out still others in response to their own preferences and sensibilities" (Benson, 1968, p. 53).

The parents are the principal emotional support system available to the child. They provide the child with comfort, praise, empathic understanding, sympathy, and affection. They are a source of unconditional positive regard for the child in sensitive response to his individualized needs.

Providing care, emotional support, direction, and guidance over the period of the child's dependency, the parent provides the child with the sense of permanence and associated stability and continuity in relationships needed for healthy development.

These role functions are applicable to the parental pair, although efforts have been made elsewhere to differentiate the distinctive role responsibilities of father and mother (DuVall, 1946; Slater, 1961; Zelditch, 1955).

The recent trend is in the direction of male–female equalitarian sharing of the various behaviors and functions, duties and prerogatives associated with the role of the parent. Although for the largest percentage of the population the traditional allocation of the various aspects of the parental role still obtains, in a small but growing percentage of the population the father carries more of the traditional mother's responsibilities and the mother carries more of the traditional father's responsibilities (Nye, 1976). Previously crystallized normative role prescriptions are currently in transition.

Instead of the separate and distinct cultural expectations of behaviors, attitudes, and values associated with the mother's role and another set associated with the father's role, there is a movement toward an undifferentiated set of parental behaviors, attitudes, and values that is shared and implemented, without gender distinction, by both parents. Not only are the duties and privileges of the father and the mother undergoing change, with reassignment or greater sharing of responsibilities, but there is also a reformulation of the respective responsibilities between parents and the community, with the community assuming more responsibility for child care, for example, through day-care or early education programs.

Parenthetically, this analysis seems to imply that the nuclear family of father, mother, and children is the only acceptable family structure. Actually, however, it merely identifies the role responsibilities that must be implemented if the child's needs are to be adequately met. The role responsibilities can be implemented by a woman in a single-parent family acting as both mother and father, by a father in a single-parent family acting as father and mother, or by different members in a communal family who each discharge different role functions, or by a couple in a "married" homosexual or lesbian relationship. The family need not necessarily be nuclear, or monogamous or heterosexual or continuous. It is conceivable that the child's needs can be adequately met in a variety of different family structures in which the necessary role tasks are implemented by a variety of allocations of task assignment. If, however, the role arrangements established to meet the child's needs fall short in any one of the variety of different family forms, child welfare services would be the appropriate source of help. It might be said, however, that variant family forms, other than the single-parent family, such as, for instance, the communal family, statistically affect only a very limited number of children. Nor does the analysis suggest any fixed allocation of functional assignments within the parental role pair. Aside from breast feeding, none of the parental role activities is specifically and invariably gender-related. Male and female members of the parental pair—or male and female members of communal groups—can assign any child-nurturing and child-rearing role tasks to any person without reference to gender.

The Child's Role

The child's role is inevitably somewhat more limited. As Sarbin (1954) notes, "assignment of tasks imposed by a particular role must be appropriate to the physical and intellectual capacity of the role participants." Totally or partially dependent, the child is limited in physical and mental capacity and possesses a limited repertoire of skills. Nevertheless the status of child carries with it a set of obligations, and these are reciprocal to the parental roles:

1. If the parental role requires that the parent teach the child the appropriate attitudes and values of the society, the role of the child demands that he learn these attitudes and values and that he act in accordance with them and in accordance with the prescription for his age and sex.
2. If the parent's role is to discipline the child when he engages in inappropriate behavior, the child's role is to accept such discipline, to obey the parent, and to make the necessary changes in his behavior. The child is required to display the behavior that is acceptable to the family, to the peer group, and to the community.
3. The child is expected to meet some of the emotional needs of his parents by responding affectionately to them, confiding in them, and respecting them. The child is expected to act in a manner that will reflect credit on his parents and elicit praise for them in the community.
4. The child must cooperate with the parent in the parent's efforts to protect him from danger and harm and to meet his physical, emotional, and educational needs. The child is required to eat the food offered, to go to the school provided, and to refrain from activity likely to be physically, socially, or emotionally damaging.
5. The child has some responsibility for maintaining family unity and reducing family tensions by cooperating and sharing with other members of the family and by showing loyalty to members of the family group.
6. The child is required to perform whatever appropriate chores are asked of him and to care for whatever clothes, toys, and furniture the parents have provided.

The older child also has some responsibility in performing three different, significant roles: as a child in the family unit, as a pupil in the school system, and as a friend in his peer group. The listing relates primarily to the role of the child in the family unit. However, problems in the performance of his role as a pupil or persistent disturbance in his relationship with his peer group may create problems in parent–child relationships.

The Community's Role

Although less visibly and apparently than either the parent or the child, the community is an authentic component of the parent–child network. The community, represented by the state, is a parent, beyond the biological parent, to all children. This is the meaning of the concept of *parens patriae.* As such, the community has some rights and obligations in implementing its role in the parent–child network. When the community fails to implement its role effectively, we have another group of situations requiring the intervention of child welfare services.

The community fulfills its "parental" obligations by exercising its regulatory and legislative powers in protecting children and providing the resources they need for proper biological and psychosocial development. The community protects children by licensing day-care centers and providing legal sanctions against child labor, neglect and abuse of children, truancy, and the sale of alcohol, tobacco, and pornography to minors. Through legislation establishing adequate programs for social insurance, income maintenance, health care, public welfare agencies, schools, and recreational facilities, the community provides resources that enable the child to meet his needs. A community that fails to function adequately in behalf of its children becomes a legitimate focus of social action on the part of child welfare services.

PROBLEMS OF ROLE FUNCTIONING: PARENT–CHILD NETWORK

Most children live in a reasonably well-established family group, in which both parents and children are effectively discharging their respective role requirements.

As Le Masters (1970) notes, "in a well-organized family, the major roles have been identified, assigned, and are performed with some degree of competence," having been understood and accepted (p. 50). However, the community must still provide school facilities, health facilities, clean water, a decent sewerage system, adequate police protection, and so on. These services, required by normal children in normal families, are not child welfare services as we have defined them here.

Child welfare services are those services required when parents or children are either incapable of implementing or unwilling to implement (or both) their respective role requirements, or when a serious discrepancy arises between the role expectations of the community and the individual's performance. We can now categorize recurrent problems of role implementation and fulfillment that might require the intervention of child welfare social work services (alternative categorizations are available in social work literature: Chescheir, 1979; Atherton, 1971a; Atherton, 1971b; Maas, 1957; Perlman, 1962):

1. Parental role unoccupied.
2. Parental incapacity.
3. Parental role rejection.
4. Intrarole conflict.
5. Interrole conflict.
6. Child incapacity and/or handicap.
7. Deficiency of community resources.

Parental Role Unoccupied

The most obvious difficulty results when the position of parent is unoccupied. The role may never have been occupied, as is true of the paternal role in the truncated family system of the unmarried mother and the illegitimate child; death, separation, or divorce may leave the role of the father or the mother —or sometimes both—permanently unfilled; long hospitalizations, military service, or imprisonment may leave the role of the parent temporarily vacant. In all these cases, some essential requirements for the normal operation of the parent–child system remain unmet. As long as the role is unfilled, the child is not incorporated in an adequately functioning family and is likely to be deprived. This, then, is an area of concern for child welfare services.*

* Some of the brief illustrations that follow originally appeared in *The New York Times* Annual Listing of "100 Neediest Cases," submitted by New York social work agencies. © 1964 by The New York Times Company. Reprinted by permission. Additions have been made from later years and other sources.

Role Unfilled—Death of Mother

Gregory C., thirty-seven, a factory clerk, is devoted to his motherless children—Pete, twelve; Violet, ten; Rose, nine; and Billy, seven—and is determined to keep them together.

Eight months ago Mr. C.'s wife died of cancer. He tried to carry on alone, asking a neighbor to care for the children after school until he returned from work. But the double burden of running the home and providing for his family became overwhelming. Relatives suggested that he divide the children among them, but the children, terrified, begged their father not to send them away.

Upset and confused as to how to proceed in caring for his children, Mr. C. came to an agency.

Role Unfilled—Death of Father

Mrs. Lillian C., thirty-seven, came to the agency for help with her two boys—Ben, sixteen, and Tommy, eleven. While their mother went to work, both boys were playing truant regularly from school. Tommy would idle about the house, awaiting her return. Ben loitered on street corners with a gang of boys and was becoming unmanageable.

During the past five years, Mrs. C. has had little time for the children. When her husband died ten years ago, she managed on their small savings supplemented by financial help from her brother. But this help stopped when her brother suffered business reverses, and Mrs. C. had to take a job as cashier to make ends meet. Constantly fatigued by the need to be both mother and father to her children, she became hopeless and bitter. She often told her sons that they were being "cheated by life."

Role Unfilled—Physical Illness

Ordinarily, Jack R., ten, and his brothers—William, seven, and Saul, five—are punctual pupils, neatly though poorly dressed, and attentive in class. But recently they began to be tardy and were frequently absent. Jack fell behind in his work; the younger boys were unruly; all three looked unkempt.

When teachers finally enlisted the agency's aid, the social worker found that the boy's mother, Mrs. Janet R., twenty-nine, had been hospitalized for several weeks with asthma, and the boys and their father, Henry R., thirty, were trying to carry on alone. Mr. R., who works long hours as a store clerk, spent nights and weekends doing heavy chores while Jack handled the light tasks and supervised his brothers. But the lunches Jack prepared were skimpy; he couldn't keep up with the dishwashing and the baths and the marketing.

The doctors say it may be several months before Mrs. R. can return home. Mr. R. and the boys would make any sacrifice to remain together, but they cannot manage alone any longer.

Role Unfilled—Imprisonment

Larry V. is ten and normally active and boisterous. He looks like his father. His mother's great fear is that he will follow in his father's footsteps. Mr. V. recently was sentenced to a prison term for mugging. Mrs. Dorothy V., thirty-five, is so ashamed of her husband's criminal record that she has cut herself off from friends and neighbors. She has also become unduly strict with Larry, disciplining him severely and setting inflexible rules about homework and bedtime. The result is that he has grown increasingly rebellious, which has been very upsetting to Mrs. V. The family has been receiving public assistance.

Role Unfilled—Mental Illness

Mrs. Sylvia P., thirty, was lost when she came to the agency several months ago. Last winter her husband Milton, thirty-three, a salesman, suddenly became quarrelsome and erratic. He was dismissed from his job and soon after was committed to a mental institution.

To support her children—George, nine, and Sue, five—Mrs. P. went to work as a file clerk. But she had to move into an overcrowded apartment with her sister and her ailing mother, both of whom complained endlessly about the children's noise. George became restless and disobedient. Both he and Sue were disturbed by their father's absence, and Mrs. P., ashamed, answered their questions evasively. The children became such a problem that Mrs. P. asked the agency for help.

Role Unfilled—Illegitimacy

A year ago, Betty N., twenty-four, was happy and secure. Now she faces the problem of caring for an illegitimate child.

Betty's fiancé, Stephen S., twenty-five, entered medical school two years ago. A year later, Betty was graduated from college and began to teach, saving for their wedding day. Last summer she became pregnant. Stephen offered financial help for an abortion, but he refused to marry her, saying it would hurt his career. Betty broke off with him.

Betty's parents have agreed to pay for her confinement but they have refused to provide for the baby and have urged her to give it up for adoption. Torn by indecision, Betty came to the agency.

Role Unfilled—Migration

Paul's father, after a long period of unemployment, recently decided to try his luck elsewhere. Because he was uncertain about the job possibilities in Chicago, he decided to go without the family. He left Appalachia six months ago and is still looking for steady work. Paul, ten, misses his father, with whom he used to hunt and fish frequently. He is becoming depressed and his school work suffers as a result.

Parental Incapacity

Inadequate role implementation sometimes results from incapacity. The role incumbent may be physically present and want to fulfill his role requirements but may be incapacitated by physical, mental, or emotional inadequacy or by lack of training or knowledge. A physically handicapped mother may find it difficult to meet the demands of an active, healthy youngster. A mentally deficient mother may be incapable of learning the essential routines of child care. A mother who is herself emotionally immature cannot meet the dependent needs of her infant child. Some parents, deprived in their own childhoods, may have come to parenthood without adequate education or marketable job skills and without having learned essential child-care skills from *their* parents. Sometimes addiction to drugs or alcohol may render a parent incapable of providing adequate physical and emotional care for his children. In all of these cases, because the role of the parent is inadequately implemented and the child suffers, child welfare services are an appropriate remedial resource.

Role Incapacity—Illness

Frank F. and his wife Rose, both thirty-six, have been married for fifteen years. They have lived from crisis to crisis, but now it has become too much for them. Mr. F. is a laborer; his earnings have never adequately covered the family's needs. Mrs. F. is diabetic; the care of three children leaves her suffering chronic fatigue. She upbraids her husband for being a bad provider. He lashes out at her for being a poor manager. They quarrel bitterly and endlessly.

The continual tension is reflected in the children: Mark, fourteen, refuses to play with other children; Frances, eleven, often cannot eat; Therese, eight months old, cries constantly. Their pastor suggested that they seek the help of a social agency.

Role Incapacity—Physical Handicap

Mrs. Belle H., thirty-two, is crippled in body but not in spirit. A year ago Mrs. H. was stricken with polio and had to be hospitalized. Her husband Victor, thirty-four, sent ten-year-old Shirley to live with relatives. Sylvia, four, was placed in a foster home.

Two months ago Mrs. H. was brought home in a wheelchair, with both legs useless and one arm partially paralyzed. Believing it would aid her rehabilitation, her doctors advised that the family be reunited, and the children are now home again.

Mrs. H. goes to a clinic for therapy several times a week and eventually will recover partial use of her limbs. Now, however, her handicap prevents Mrs. H. from adequately caring for her children.

Role Incapacity—Ignorance

Peter's mother was making a small but constant error, out of ignorance, that had serious effects on his health. It was noticed at the well-baby clinic that he was not gaining any weight and that his color was poor. When, at the request of the authorities, the situation was investigated, it was found that Peter's mother had been using teaspoonfuls instead of tablespoonfuls in making up his formula.

Role Incapacity—Emotional Immaturity

Kathy is only eleven, but she bears a burden far beyond her years. Her mother, Mrs. Maureen L., forty, is an alcoholic. Her father, George, forty-one, works nights in a factory and takes little interest in his family, which includes, besides Kathy, George, Jr., eight; Louis, seven, and Peter, six. For the past two years Kathy more and more has had to do the housework and care for the children. When her mother disappears, as often happens, Kathy does the marketing and cooking. When her mother has fits of weeping, Kathy anxiously tries to "mother" her, too.

Recently Kathy began to show signs of the strain she is under. She daydreamed in school. She lied to her teacher. She took money from her mother's purse to spend on classmates. Mr. L., alarmed, came to the agency.

Role Incapacity—Mental Retardation

Tommy is four, a bright, sturdy, normal little boy with a quick smile. But he needs help, because his parents are mentally retarded.

Tommy's parents grew up in institutions; there they received enough training to be self-sufficient. His father, who is twenty-eight, works as a dishwasher and is able to support his family adequately. But his unpredictable attitudes confuse Tommy. When Tommy misbehaves, sometimes his father scolds him, sometimes he laughs at him. Tommy's mother is bewildered by her lively son and is unable to understand or anticipate his actions. He refuses to mind her and lacks the most rudimentary training. It was on the advice of a clinic nurse that she sought the agency's help.

Role Incapacity—Drug Addiction

Ruth, eight, and Jimmy, six, frequently have had to beg food from the neighbors. Their parents are drug addicts, and the children are frequently neglected for long periods of time, when the parents are on drugs. The apartment is barren of furniture and the children poorly clothed, since all of the limited family income goes to support the habit. Mr. C. finds it difficult to hold a steady, adequately paying job. Neglect and deprivation are beginning to affect the health of the children adversely.

Role Rejection

Inadequate role implementation sometimes results from role rejection. For many people parenthood is a voluntarily assumed role; for others, however, parenthood is an involuntary burden resulting from a biological accident. There is, on the part of these parents, a conscious or unconscious rejection of the parental role, which results in varying degrees of failure in role performance. These parents are apt to be indifferent, neglectful, or abusive. Some totally abandon the role of parents by deserting their families. The child suffers, or is apt to suffer, as a result of rejection of the parental role, and child welfare services are consequently required to protect the child.

Role Rejection—Neglect and Abandonment

Nancy is almost five. She is headstrong and defiant; she tears her dolls apart and bites other children when she quarrels with them. Her sleep is disturbed by nightmares during which she cries out for her "Mummy."

Nancy's parents, an unstable couple in their twenties, were never happy in their marriage. They quarreled constantly, and frequently separated for long periods. Four months ago they left Nancy with a friend, saying they expected to be out late that night. But next day the friend received a letter saying they were leaving town and could no longer provide for Nancy. They asked that she be taken to the agency.

Role Rejection—Abandonment

Freddy is a brown-haired, chubby little boy almost three years old. At times he is sweet and affectionate; at others, for no apparent reason, he throws himself on the floor of his boarding home kicking and pounding. Often he wakes in the night screaming.

Shortly after Freddy was born, his mother asked the welfare department to place him for adoption. She said that he was illegitimate and that his father had deserted her. Before her story could be checked, she disappeared. Recently a court determination of abandonment was made, and the welfare department turned Freddy over to the agency for adoption.

Role Rejection—Neglect

Mrs. Yvonne E., thirty-one, was sentenced to sixty days in the county jail Wednesday on charges of neglect of children.

The E. case came to the attention of the police department's crime prevention bureau July 22, after a neighbor summoned police. An investigation at about 4 A.M. showed that Mrs. E.'s four children were alone in the apartment. The floors were strewed with decayed food and mildewed clothing; windows were broken and insects infested the bedding; food in the refrigerator was covered with insects, and the children were attempting to fry a spoiled, uncleaned fish. Toilet facilities in the apartment were plugged.

Role Rejection—Physical Abuse

A little girl with both eyes swollen nearly shut heard a judge describe her mother as "a savage," as he sentenced the mother to one year in the house of correction.

Mrs. Barbara F., twenty-one, admitted pummeling the child, Darlene, three, with her fists and striking her time after time with her shoes and belt. Asked whether she loved the child, Mrs. F., a waitress, replied, "I didn't think much of her from the day she was born." Police were called Tuesday after a baby-sitter, Mrs. Minnie J., noticed that the child's face, legs, back, and stomach were severely bruised.

Role Rejection—Desertion

Steve is only nine. Last year he was an A pupil. This year he has tried so hard to look after his mother and his baby sister Anne, two, that he is failing.

Steve's father, Mr. Malcolm P., thirty-three, a bookkeeper, and Steve's mother, Mrs. Lois P., quarreled incessantly because Mr. P. squandered his money on gambling. Sometimes he would stay away from home for days at a time; six months ago he deserted his wife and children, though continuing to send money for their support.

Mrs. P. grew so ill and despondent that she neglected her home and children. Steve stayed up nights to do the housework and took on much of Anne's care. When Mr. P. delayed sending money for their support, Steve searched in vain for a part-time job as errand boy. But at school he could not concentrate. His teacher, learning of the home situation, advised Mrs. P. to consult the agency.

Intrarole Conflict

Inadequate role implementation sometimes results from problems of conflict in role definition or intrarole conflict. The mother and the father may disagree strongly as to who is supposed to do what for, and with, the child. The mother may expect the father to help her care for the child; the father may define his role more narrowly as primarily that of a provider.

Intrarole conflict may result from the seemingly incongruent demands imposed by the parental role, which requires that one love the child yet discipline him, indulge him yet deprive him, free him yet restrict him. Or conflict may result from differing interpretations of role behavior by the various reference groups with which the person is affiliated; the parents may expect one kind of behavior from their adolescent child whereas his peer group may define expected behavior in quite another, and conflicting, way. Some parents and children may define their reciprocal roles differently. The frequently cited generation gap refers, in essence, to problems of intrarole definition.

Some parents fail to perceive clearly the requirements of the role, or society may have failed to define the role clearly. In periods when the role of parent is changing, it is not clear how the parent should behave or what is expected of him. Furthermore, even though parental roles generally might be clearly defined, specific aspects of the role might be ambiguous. For instance, the division of parental energy and time between the child's needs and the parent's own needs may be a matter over which society itself is undecided. The problems deriving from these conflicts impede effective implementation of parental role, and the child therefore suffers.

Intrarole Conflict—Definition of Role

Mr. and Mrs. F. were advised by an elementary-school teacher to apply for help at a child guidance clinic. Paul, their eight-year-old son, was doing poorly in his studies and frequently displayed disruptive behavior in the classroom. He shouted, fought with other children, and was difficult to discipline.

In talking with the caseworker, Mr. and Mrs. F. revealed that the problem of disciplining Paul was a matter of considerable friction between them. Mr. F. had grown up in a home that emphasized strict obedience, respect for elders, and prompt physical punishment for lapses in behavior. He believed that parents should order and children should obey. Mrs. F. felt uncomfortable with this approach. Her tendency was to be more permissive, to allow more latitude, and to permit the children to "express themselves rather than be squelched." As a consequence of this difference, neither parent took responsibility for disciplining Paul. Each would make an attempt at it when emergencies arose, but neither one felt that he had full right to try his own approach because the marital partner so strongly disagreed with it.

Interrole Conflict

Inadequate role implementation may result when the parental role conflicts with another social role. According to Werble (1960):

> When the expectations between the vital social roles occupied by a single actor are inconsistent, contradictory, or mutually exclusive so that compliance with one set of role expectations necessarily entails noncompliance with another set of role expectations, we have the problem of role conflict [p. 30].

The occupational role often conflicts with the duties and obligations of the parental role. The father, who is away from the home a great deal because of the demands of his job, faces such a conflict, just as the working mother faces a conflict between her role as a mother and her role as an employee. Also, the demands on a man in his role as son to his own parents may conflict with the demands made on him as a father to his children. The conflicting demands made by different role requirements stemming from the variety of positions people occupy simultaneously in a complex society may result in the inadequate implementation of the parental role. In such situations, the child is deprived, and the intervention of child welfare services is appropriate.

Role Conflict—Working Mother

Mrs. W. needed to work and enjoyed her job. Her husband's income as a postal clerk could not meet the needs of a growing family of six children—five girls and a boy. Mrs. W. decided to go to work when it seemed clear that the family was becoming more and more heavily indebted. But two of the children—Mike, two and one-half, and Ruth, three and one-half—were still at home and needed her, and even the school-age children seemed to react negatively to her absence from home. Mrs. W. wasn't sure that being a salesclerk, when she should be a mother, was the best choice to make. Besides, a good deal of her energy was being absorbed in making arrangements with all sorts of people to care for the preschool children during the time she was at work. Concerned about the situation, Mrs. W. came to the agency to discuss her conflicts.

Role Conflict—Mother/Daughter

During the last four months Mrs. R. had been more of a stranger than a mother to her three children—Nancy, five; Joan, seven; and William, eleven. Mrs. R.'s father, seventy-six, suffered a heart attack about six months ago. A widower, he was living alone in a six-room house that the family had owned for the last thirty years. He refused to go to an institution, and Mrs. R., an only child, was very worried that he might overextend himself and suffer another sudden heart attack. As a result, she made an effort to visit him daily and care for him. She left in the morning and did not come home until the children were asleep. Mr. R. had been trying to care for the family in his wife's daily absence. Although she recognized that her children were suffering as a result of the family's disorganization occasioned by the care of her father, she felt great guilt if she neglected her duties as a daughter.

Problems can arise not only as a consequence of role coverage or role inadequacy or role rejection but also while such consequences are developing. Thus, in addition to the problem that results for role coverage when a parent divorces and leaves the home, the very process of divorce and disengagement itself may be a source of problems. Children may be affected adversely by the process of change. Child welfare social work may appropriately be assigned responsibility in helping parents and children through the divorce process or the dying of a terminally ill parent.

Child Incapacity and/or Handicap

Inadequate role implementation also results from excessive demands on the role incumbents. The physically handicapped or emotionally disturbed child is incapable of performing the role normally required of a child. Such a child imposes on its parents a burden of care, of specialized knowledge, of patience and control beyond that which any society can normally expect of them, and the possibility of adequately meeting the needs of such a child is reduced. The child's failure to meet the expectations of the parents robs them of the emotional satisfactions that are the rewards of fulfilling their many parental obligations and duties and makes it even more difficult for them to perform the parental role adequately. In such cases, the provision of child welfare services is appropriate.

Excessive Demand—Epilepsy

Anne is only six, but she knows that she is different, that her parents quarrel constantly over her, and that her older brother and sister are ashamed of her. Anne is an epileptic.

Anne's father, Jacob L., thirty-eight, a municipal clerk, has never accepted his daughter. He reminds his wife Lillian, thirty-five, that he never wanted a third child. He complains that Anne takes too much of Mrs. L.'s time. Mrs. L., in turn, accuses him of making Anne's condition worse by his refusal to share the parental burden. The L.'s sense of shame has affected the other children: Joseph, thirteen, shies away from the outside world; Dana, ten, is a behavior problem at school.

Excessive Demand—Mental Deficiency

For years Samuel and Martha W. couldn't understand why their youngest child, Ethel, five, was so different from her four brothers and sisters, ranging in age from seven to fourteen. She could not talk or respond to speech; she had no control over her body functions; yet she was strong and active and kept hurting herself. Ethel is a severely retarded child.

The care of Ethel, on top of the problem of caring for her four children on the meager income of Mr. W., forty-eight, a peddler, became too much for Mrs. W., forty-three. A social worker, disturbed by signs of neglect the other children showed at a free summer camp, visited the home and persuaded Mrs. W. to take Ethel to the agency.

Excessive Demand—Emotional Disturbance

During the past two years, Billy, seven, has been unable to sleep more than four or five hours a night. He wakes up during the night screaming and covering his eyes as though he sees something that frightens him. He strikes and bites his brothers and sisters and is destructive of neighbors' property. Billy tends to play by himself, carrying on an intelligible conversation with his toys. He has temper tantrums that last for hours. His behavior is disrupting the entire family and the neighbors are beginning to complain.

Despite their best efforts, Mr. and Mrs. S. seem incapable of dealing with their son's behavior. They are exhausted by their attempts to help him and frustrated and upset because they do not know what to do next. They feel their failure all the more keenly because they have proved themselves to be reasonably adequate parents in dealing with their other children—Kathy, nine; Frank, fourteen; and Sylvia, three. Billy, however, is too much for them to contend with.

Excessive Demand—Brain Injury

Mrs. Janice C., twenty-seven, and her husband Michael, thirty-one, a machinist, face a sorrowful decision. Doctors say their youngest child, three-year-old Susan, must be put in an institution, but they cannot bear to part with her.

Susan is a victim of a progressive brain disease that is expected to take her life within a few years. Mrs. C. is expecting another child, and she finds Susan's care increasingly heavy. Susan cannot sit up by herself or control her movements. She hits her head repeatedly on her crib and high chair, which are carefully padded, and needs constant watching. Moreover, the other two C. children—Lorraine, seven, and Alice, six—resenting the attention given their handicapped sister, are becoming defiant and unruly.

In addition to role inadequacy, the child may generate problems in his relationship with his parents by rejecting his role much as the neglecting parent rejects his role. The child who plays truant from school rejects his role as pupil; the child who runs away from home rejects his role as child in the family; the child who isolates himself from contacts with other children rejects his role as member of the peer group.

Child Role Rejection

Jim, twelve, was picked up by the police after having slept all night at the Greyhound bus stop. This is the third time during the past three months that Jim has tried to run away from home. He indicated, when questioned, that he doesn't get along with his family, he doesn't feel as if he belongs in his family, and he wants to be on his own.

There can be problems in the parent–child network that derive from child interrole conflict. The demands of the role of friend in the peer group may conflict with the roles of pupil at school or child in the family.

Child Interrole Conflict

Louis, eleven, and his parents are persistently in conflict about his performance of chores in the home. He is expected to keep his room clean, mow the lawn, cooperate with doing the dishes. More often than not he fails to do these chores. Louis is a very active member of a little-league team and a hockey team. He says that if he is not going to let his team down, he needs to spend a lot of time practicing with them. He forgets to do the things around the house because he has the team on his mind. If he did the things his parents always keep at him for doing, he would have less time for practice.

Deficiency of Community Resources

Inadequate role implementation sometimes results from deficiencies in community resources. For instance, a father will find it difficult to implement the income maintenance aspects of the parental role if there are no jobs available. As Spiegel (1960) points out, "Insofar as role activities require technical instruments, equipment, furniture, props, customs, climate and other appropriate physical facilities (including money), a lack or insufficiency of these instrumental prerequisites interferes with role transactions" (p. 369). When adequate employment opportunities, schools, recreational facilities, or health services are lacking, or when social and racial discrimination, overcrowding, and social disorganization are characteristic of the community, parents may find it difficult to implement their roles. The atmosphere of the community needs to be free of the stigma of racial and class discrimination if the parents are to be expected to raise their child with a sense of dignity and self-acceptance. The problems may result not only from the lack of available resources but also from the lack of access to them by particular groups. If discrimination operates to keep some kinds of jobs closed to nonwhites, women, former offenders, former alcoholics, or those who have been mentally ill, the problem for these groups is a deficiency in environmental resources, which adversely affects family role enactment. Efforts to change community conditions that adversely affect social functioning are part of the responsibility of child welfare services.

Community Deficiency—Inadequate Housing

Mr. and Mrs. R. are very much concerned about the threat to their children's healthy development presented by the neighborhood in which they live. Mr. R. has worked steadily for the past fifteen years as an elevator operator in a large office building. They have been living in the same apartment house for the past twenty years. So far they have been able to rear their children—George, sixteen; Alice, twelve; and Susan, seven—without any serious problems. However, the neighborhood in which they live has been rapidly deteriorating. Several women in the apartment house are openly engaged in prostitution. The neighborhood barbershop and candy store are the hangouts for dope pushers, numbers runners, and pornography salesmen. They would like to move out of the neighborhood but cannot find any apartment as large as the one they now occupy at a rental they can afford. Despite their best efforts at being adequate parents, they feel that the counterinfluence of some of the neighborhood elements may negatively affect the behavior of their oldest boy, George, in particular.

Community Deficiency—Unemployment

The men stand around idly on Main Street. There is nothing else to do. Three months ago the local mine, in which most of them have worked for the better part of their employable lives, closed down. The vein was giving out and it was no longer profitable for the mine company to continue operations. Three hundred men were suddenly thrown out of work, and the town industries and services have been able to absorb only a small fraction of this large body of unemployed men. For the rest there remain limited savings, unemployment insurance for a limited period, and then, no one knows exactly what. As miners, as wage earners, these men had been able to support their families. Now there are no jobs available, and they worry about how they might continue to care for their children.

The variety of problems in role enactment described is neatly summarized by Bartlett (1961) when she says that:

the condition with which child welfare services are primarily concerned is the deficiency in these provisions resulting from (1) incapacity of parents, (2) extraordinary needs of certain children, and (3) limitations of opportunities and resources [p. 43].

Recent studies confirm the contention that the social problems outlined in this section are, in fact, the primary concerns of child welfare agencies (Shyne, Schroeder, 1977; Haring, 1975; Packman, 1968). Such studies attempted a nationwide "census" of the circumstances that resulted in applications for service from child welfare agencies. Findings were that problems in parental role coverage resulting from death, divorce, separation, desertion, imprisonment, and illegitimacy; inadequate parental role performance owing to physical and/or mental illness; parental role rejection manifested in neglect and/or abuse of the child; and inadequate enactment of the child's role owing to emotional or physical disability accounted, in aggregate, for most of the reasons someone, either the family or the community, had called for the help of a child welfare social worker. Environmental circumstances—financial need or inadequate housing—were listed as the most important reasons for service in a very limited percentage of the cases, although they were a contributing reason in a much larger percentage of the cases.

The problems encountered by child welfare agencies change with changes in the society. Earlier in the century, many of the cases that came to the child welfare agencies reflected intergenerational and intercultural conflict. The parents, often recent immigrants speaking no English, brought to the parent–child relationship a definition of the parental role that had been shaped in the context of the Old World, whereas the children defined their expectations in terms of the American experience. Currently, however, child welfare agencies encounter problems of intergenerational conflict resulting from the different definitions of parent–child roles caused by a fast-changing culture. The over-thirty parent reflects attitudes and convictions very different from those of his child, and the conflict is expressed in bitter battles about hair length, marijuana, sex, work habits, and so on. A decade ago, parental incapacity arising from alcoholic addiction was a problem frequently encountered by child welfare agencies; today, parental incapacity is often caused by drug addiction.

Whereas fifty years ago child welfare agencies were frequently concerned with children of recently arrived immigrant parents facing difficulties of adjustment to a new and strange world, fifty years from now child welfare agencies may be concerned with families in which the parental role of the father is unfilled because he is away on an interplanetary trip that is scheduled to take three to five years to complete.

Problems of role enactment may be the result of social pressures or psychological pressures, or both. In some instances, the most significant component of the problem is a personal pathology; in others, it is the pathology of society. A black man with limited education has difficulty in obtaining and holding an adequate job. Living on a limited income in crowded, substandard housing, he may be led by the pressure of the social situation to desert his family. A middle-class engineer living on a decent regular income in a comfortable suburb may also desert his family because he feels tied down, hemmed in, anxious, and depressed. In both instances, the role of parent has been abandoned, although for very different reasons. As far as the child is concerned, the etiology of the problem matters little. What does matter is that something must be done to fulfill the obligations of the rejected position. Each situation may present a unique combination of psychological and social factors resulting in a particular kind of problem.

Some problems are more susceptible to solution through community organization. Others are more susceptible to solution through the involvement of the client in group activity. Still others are more susceptible to solution through work with the individual client. It might sometimes be helpful to use a combination of approaches.

For instance, the working mother of a preschool child must arrange for child care while she is on the job. If the community lacks day-care services and the problem is of concern to a sufficiently large number of women in the community, social workers would then employ the method of community organization in an effort to establish a day-care center.

Sometimes, however, even if a day-care facility is already available in the community, a mother may be anxious about the effects of temporary role substitution on her relationship with her child. The caseworker might discuss with the mother her feelings about relinquishing her maternal role for some part of each day and her anxieties regarding the child's reaction to day care and might help her make a reasoned decision with which she will be comfortable.

Child welfare social work is not synonymous with case work although this is, admittedly, the method of helping most frequently employed. Any and all methods—casework, group work, community organization, social action—are employed, alone and in combination, that can be applied appropriately in effecting some positive change in, and for, the client or the client group. Social system change, social reform, is as much a responsibility of child welfare social work as is client symptom change; prevention is as appropriate as rescue–therapy–rehabilitation. These diverse approaches are complementary in this as well as in other fields of social work practice.

Further, the formulation does not suggest that any one method has to be defined in a particular way. Casework in child welfare can be defined as a method that includes brokerage and advocacy activity in the client's behalf, and its psychotherapeutic interventions might as legitimately employ a behavioral modification as a psychoanalytic or a Rogerian nondirective approach.

CATEGORIES OF CHILD WELFARE SERVICES

Child welfare services, whether designed to help on the level of community action, group involvement, or individual contact, can be categorized as supportive, supplemental, or substitutive. These categories are not mutually exclusive, and they sometimes tend to overlap.

Supportive services include child guidance clinics, the family service agency programs, and the work of child protective agencies. Supportive services are the first line of defense in dealing with actual or incipient problems in child welfare, when the family and the parent–child relationship system are structurally intact but subject to stress. If the stress is permitted to continue, it might result in a structural break: divorce, separation, desertion, and so on. Supportive services are designed to use the family's own strength to work toward a reduction of strain in the parent–child relationship system.

The child who is disobedient, rebellious, and incorrigible may be beyond the normal parent's capacity to socialize. In such a case, the child guidance clinic may effectuate sufficient change in the relationship between parent and child so that the child becomes more responsive to the parent's teachings.

Casework services offered by family service agencies on behalf of the child support, reinforce, and strengthen the parents' efforts to discharge their parental responsibilities adequately. And, in dealing with marital friction that would ultimately have deleterious effects on the child, the family agency is offering another supportive service.

Protective services, offered by child welfare agencies for children who have been grossly neglected or abused, are primarily supportive services designed to develop and strengthen any and all factors in the situation that would enable the parents to enact their roles in a more socially acceptable manner.

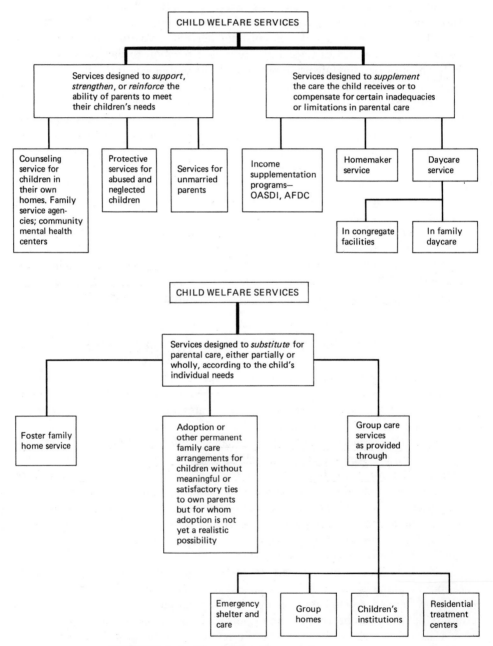

FIGURE 1-1. The child welfare services system.

Supplementary services are the second line of defense, called upon when a parent–child relationship is seriously impaired because a significant aspect of the parental role is inadequately covered but the family configuration is such that, with supplementation, the child can continue to live at home without harm. Financial maintenance programs of all kinds—assistance as well as insurance—are, in effect, supplementary services. Financial maintenance programs act *in loco parentis* as far as the income-producing responsibilities of the parents are concerned. Homemaker programs and day-care programs are also supplementary, for both are designed to supplement the mother's enactment of child-care functions.

Substitute services are the third line of defense and are used when the situation is so damaging as to require either a temporary or a permanent dissolution of the parent–child relationship system. A substitute family is offered the child in a foster home, an adoptive home, or an institution. The substitute family may be similar in structure to the normal family, as in the case of the foster family or the adoptive home, or it may be different, as in the case of the institution—the orphan asylum, the residential treatment home, the training school for delinquents, the institution for the physically, emotionally, or mentally handicapped, and so on. The substitution may be temporary (as in the case of a foster home) or permanent (as in the case of an adoptive home). The institution may be employed either as a temporary or as a permanent family substitute. In all substitute family-care arrangements, the natural parent of the child yields almost total responsibility to somebody else for the performance of the parental role in relation to the child.

Figure 1–1 schematically summarizes the services that are the concern of the child welfare services system.

Validation of the fact that these services constitute the essential core concerns of child welfare agencies is substantiated by a recent detailed review of the activities of public child welfare services in twenty-five states (U.S. Health, Education, and Welfare, Children's Bureau, 1976, pp. 103–104). In all states, substantially all of the following services were found to be among the services offered as child welfare services: social services for children in their own home; protective services; day-care services; homemaker services; foster-family care; social services for unmarried parents; adoption services; shelter care for children in emergency; group home services; institutional care for children.

The child welfare service system, then, is a network of public and voluntary agencies in social work practice that specialize in the prevention, amelioration, or remediation of social problems related to the functioning of the parent–child relationship network through the development and provision of specific child welfare services: services to children in their own home, protective services, day care, homemaker service, foster-family care, services to the unwed mother, adoption services, and institutional child care.

PLAN OF THE BOOK

The plan of the book is to present a detailed review of each of these broad categories of supportive, supplementary, and substitute services and to examine the specific programs that fall into one or another of these categories: child guidance, family services, protective service, income maintenance programs, day-care service, homemaker service, foster care, adoption, and institutional care.

In the case of each of the services, we shall present material regarding the following content areas:

1. General historical background.
2. Situations for which the service is appropriate.
3. Scope of the service.
4. Processes in offering the service.
5. Evaluation.
6. Problems regarding the service.
7. Trends in offering the service.

Before presenting a discussion of each of the specific child welfare services, we have included a chapter on the historical and current context of child welfare. This material is designed to provide a frame of reference for the discussion that follows. Following the chapters on each of the services, there is a chapter on child welfare practices in other countries that provides an international perspective on our problems and the way we meet them.

Because readers of the book are likely to be interested in child welfare as a career and because the professional subculture of the child-welfare social worker affects the services offered, the final chapter is a discussion of the sociology of the child welfare worker: demography, recruitment, career line, value orientations, occupational problems, and so on.

SUMMARY

Child welfare is defined as a special field within the profession of social work. Social work is concerned with man in relation to his social situation. As a technology, it is responsible for effecting changes in some problem aspect of the client's enactment of his social roles. It may effect such changes by preventing the likelihood of the impairment of social role enactment, by enhancing social role performance, or by helping to restore the capacity to implement social roles effectively.

As a specialized field within social work, child welfare is concerned with the antecedents, concomitants, and consequences of a particular social milieu: the parent–child relationship network and the enactment and implementation of parental roles and child roles.

The recurrent problems for which child welfare has been given some responsibility include those deriving from roles left vacant because of death, hospitalization, illegitimacy, imprisonment, and so on; roles inadequately implemented because of illness, handicap, ignorance, and so on; role rejection, as in cases of abandonment, abuse, and neglect; intrarole conflict; interrole conflict; problems resulting from the child's inability to implement his role; and problems resulting from deficiencies in community resources.

In meeting such problems, child welfare has developed a number of services. These may be grouped as supportive services (family service, child guidance clinics, and protective services), supplementary services (insurance and income maintenance programs, homemaker programs, and day-care programs), and substitutive services (foster-family care, adoptions, and institutional child care).

BIBLIOGRAPHY

ATHERTON, CHARLES R., et al. "Locating Points for Intervention." *Social Casework,* **52** (March 1971a) 131–141.

———, et al. "Using Points for Intervention." *Social Casework,* **52** (April 1971b) 223–233.

BARTLETT, HARRIETT. *Analyzing Social Work Practice by Fields.* New York: National Association of Social Workers, 1961.

BENSON, LEONARD. *Fatherhood: A Sociological Perspective.* New York: Random House, Inc., 1968.

BERNARD, JESSIE. *Social Problems at Midcentury.* New York: Holt, Rinehart & Winston, Inc., 1957.

BOEHM, WERNER. *Objectives of the Social Work Curriculum of the Future.* New York: Council on Social Work Education, 1959.

———. *The Training of Psychotherapists.* Ed. by Nicholas Dellis and Herbert Stone. Baton Rouge: Louisiana State University Press, 1960.

BRIM, ORVILLE. "The Parent–Child Relation as a Social System's Parent and Child Roles." *Child Development,* **28** (September 1957).

BRONFENBRENNER, URIE. "Socialization and Social Class Through Time and Space," in *Readings in Social Psychology.* Ed. by E. E. Maccoby et al. New York: Holt, Rinehart & Winston, Inc., 1958.

CARSTENS, C. C. "Child Welfare Services," in *Social Work Yearbook.* New York: Russell Sage Foundation, 1937.

CHESCHEIR, MARTHA W. "Social Role Discrepancies as Clues to Practice." *Social Work,* **24** (March 1979), 89–94.

CONDIE, DAVID C., et al. "How the Public Views Social Work." *Social Work,* **23** (January 1978), 47–54.

COUNCIL ON SOCIAL WORK EDUCATION. "Child Welfare," in *Description of Practice: Statements in Fields of Social Work Practice.* New York: Council on Social Work Education, 1959, mimeo.

DUVALL, EVELYN M. "Conception of Parenthood." *American Journal of Sociology,* **52** (1946).

FRIEDLANDER, WALTER. *Introduction to Social Welfare,* 2nd ed. Englewood Cliffs, N.J.: Prentice-Hall, Inc., 1961.

GEISMER, L. L., and BEVERLY AYERS. *Patterns of Change in Problem Families.* St. Paul, Minn.: Family-Centered Project, Greater St. Paul Community Chest and Councils, Inc., 1959, Appendix A.

GREENWOOD, ERNEST. "Social Work and Social Science—A Theory of Their Relationship." *Social Service Review,* **29** (March 1955).

HARING, BARBARA L. *1975 Census of Requests for Child Welfare Services.* New York: Child Welfare League of America, 1975.

HENRY, WILLIAM E., et al. *The Fifth Profession; Becoming a Psychotherapist.* San Francisco: Jossey-Bass, Inc., 1971.

KAHN, ALFRED. "The Social Scene and Planning of Services for Children." *Social Work,* **7** (July 1962b).

KAHN, ALFRED S., and SHEILA B. KAMERMAN. *Not for the Poor Alone.* Philadelphia: Temple University Press, 1975.

————. *Social Services in the United States: Policies and Programs*. Philadelphia: Temple University Press, 1976.

KENISTON, KENNETH. *All Our Children—The American Family Under Pressure* (Report of the Carnegie Council on Children). New York: Harcourt Brace Jovanovich, 1977.

KRAFT, IVOR. *Toward a New Conception of Social Work in American Society*. Cleveland: School of Applied Social Services, Case Western Reserve University, January 1968. Mimeo.

LE MASTERS, ERSEL E. *Parents in Modern America*. Homewood, Ill.: The Dorsey Press, 1970.

LINTON, RALPH. *The Cultural Background of Personality*. New York: Appleton-Century-Crofts, 1945.

MAAS, HENRY. "Behavioral Science Basis for Professional Education: The Unifying Conceptual Tool of Cultural Role," in *Proceedings of the Interdisciplinary Conference*. Washington, D.C.: Howard University, School of Social Work, May 1, 1957.

MORONEY, ROBERT M. *The Family and the State: Considerations for Social Policy*. New York: Longman, Inc., 1976.

MORRIS, ROBERT, and DELWIN ANDERSON. "Personal Care Services: An Identity for Social Work." *Social Service Review*, 49 (June 1975), 157–174.

NATIONAL ACADEMY OF SCIENCES. *Toward a National Policy for Children and Families*. Washington, D.C.: National Academy of Sciences, 1976.

NATIONAL ASSOCIATION OF SOCIAL WORKERS. "Special Issue on Conceptual Frameworks." *Social Work*, 22 (September 1977).

NATIONAL CONFERENCE ON SOCIAL WELFARE. *The Future for Social Services in the United States—Final Report of the Task Force*. Columbus, Ohio: National Conference on Social Welfare, 1977.

NEEL, ANN F. "Trends and Dilemmas in Child Welfare Research." *Child Welfare*, 50 (January 1971), 25–32.

NYE, F. IVAN. *Role Structure and Analysis of the Family*. Beverly Hills, Calif.: Sage Publications, 1976.

PACKMAN, JEAN. *Child Care: Needs and Numbers*. London: George Allen & Unwin, Ltd., 1968.

PARSONS, TALCOTT, and EDWARD SHILS (Eds.). *Toward a General Theory of Action*. Cambridge, Mass.: Harvard University Press, 1954.

PERLMAN, HELEN HARRIS. "Social Components of Casework Practice," in *Social Welfare Forum*. New York: Columbia University Press, 1953.

————. "The Role Concept and Social Casework: Some Explorations. II: What Is Social Diagnosis?" *Social Service Review*, 36 (March 1962).

POLLAK, OTTO, and DONALD BRIELAND. "The Midwest Seminar on Family Diagnosis and Treatment." *Social Casework*, 42 (July 1961).

RICE, ROBERT M. *American Family Policy—Content and Context*. New York: Family Service Association of America, 1977.

RICHMOND, MARY. *What Is Social Casework?* New York: Russell Sage Foundation, 1922.

SAMPSON, JEROME. "Is Child Welfare a Specialty?" and the discussion by Zitha Turitz that follows. *Child Welfare*, 41 (November 1962).

SARBIN, THEODORE. "Role Theory," in *Handbook of Social Psychology*. Ed. by Gardner Lindzey. Cambridge, Mass.: Addison-Wesley Publishing Co., Inc., 1954.

SCHORR, ALVIN L. (Ed.). *Children and Decent People*. New York: Basic Books, Inc., 1974.

SHULZE, SUSANNE, et al. "Symposium: Developing Generic and Specific Knowledge Through the Study of Children Services." *Child Welfare* (April–May 1955).

SHYNE, ANN W., and ANITA G. SCHROEDER. *National Study of Social Services to Children and Their Families*. Rockville, Md.: Westat, Inc., August, 1978.

SLATER, PHILIP. "Parental Role Differentiation." *American Journal of Sociology,* 47 (November 1961).

SPEIGEL, JOHN. "The Resolution of Role Conflict Within the Family," in *A Modern Introduction to the Family.* Ed. by Norman Bell and Ezra Vogel. New York: The Free Press, 1960.

TURITZ, ZITHA. Quoted in Helen Hazen, "Distinctive Aspects of Child Welfare." *Child Welfare* (July 1957).

———. "Development and Use of National Standards for Child Welfare Services." *Child Welfare,* 46 (May 1967), 245–253.

UNITED NATIONS, DEPARTMENT OF ECONOMICS AND SOCIAL AFFAIRS. *Training for Social Work—An International Survey.* New York, 1950.

———. *Parental Rights and Duties Including Guardianship.* New York, 1968.

U.S. DEPARTMENT OF HEALTH, EDUCATION, AND WELFARE, CHILDREN'S BUREAU. *Child Welfare Services in 25 States—An Overview.* Washington, D.C.: Government Printing Office, 1976.

U.S. DEPARTMENT OF HEALTH, EDUCATION, AND WELFARE, CHILDREN'S BUREAU. *System of Social Services for Children and Families—Detailed Design.* Washington, D.C.: U.S. Government Printing Office, 1978.

U.S. DEPARTMENT OF LABOR, WOMEN'S BUREAU. *The Outlook for Women in Social Work—General Summary.* Social Work Series Bulletin, No. 235-8. Washington, D.C.: Government Printing Office, 1952.

WERBLE, BEATRICE. "The Implications of Role Theory for Casework Research," in *Social Science Theory and Social Work Research.* Ed. by Leonard Kogan. New York: National Association of Social Workers, 1960.

WILENSKY, HAROLD, and CHARLES LEBEAUX. *Industrial Society and Social Welfare.* New York: Russell Sage Foundation, 1958.

WITMER, HELEN L., and RUTH KOTINSKY (Eds.). *Personality in the Making.* New York: Harper & Row, Publishers, 1952.

WOLFENSTEIN, M. "Trends in Infant Care." *American Journal of Orthopsychiatry,* 23 (1953).

ZELDITCH, MORRIS. "Role Differentiation in the Nuclear Family," in *Family: Socialization and Interaction Process.* Ed. by Talcott Parsons and Robert Bales. New York: The Free Press, 1955.

2 PERSPECTIVES ON CHILD WELFARE SERVICES

FACTORS IN THE DEVELOPMENT OF CHILD WELFARE SERVICES

The social problems that are the proper concern of child welfare are as old as mankind. The orphaned, the illegitimate, the abandoned, and the handicapped child have always been with us. In the first section of the first book of the Bible, Genesis, we encounter a problem of sibling rivalry in the conflict between Cain and Abel and concern on the part of the parents, Adam and Eve, about the trouble in their family. Yet professional social work is less than a century old. The question arises, then: How were the problems of child welfare handled before this network of services was developed? Several significant factors help to explain the emergence of the field of child welfare social work:

1. The development of a humanitarian ideology and the growing rejection of previously acceptable solutions.
2. Economic and political changes that reinforced and supported changes in ideology.
3. The increased specialization of social institutions.
4. The increase in scientific knowledge.
5. The "discovery" of childhood.
6. The rise in status of the family and the child.
7. Changes in the "arithmetic of child production."

Ideology and Alternative Solutions

Child welfare services are one part of the total social system. It is to be expected, then, that such services reflect the nature of the economy, the family organization, and the position of the child in the particular society. Each society deals differently with the problems of children and families. Children have always been responded to with some ambivalence: wanted and welcomed under certain circumstances, yet an inevitable burden and inconvenience with whom scarce resources had to be shared. Children evoke resentment and hostility as

33

well as love and affection. Potential child welfare problems have been dealt with by contraception, abortion, infanticide, and abandonment.

One general solution to the problems of child welfare is to eliminate them at their source. Dead children present only a very limited problem—that of disposal. And children who are never conceived do not present even this small problem. So the first line of defense against the development of problems in child welfare is contraception. The solution is an ancient one, but one that has always aroused controversy. Judiciously applied, it prevents the problem presented by unwanted children. Indiscriminately applied, however, it threatens the continued existence of the group.

Himes (1936) summarized his detailed historical study of contraception by noting that

> contraception, as only one form of population control, is a social practice of much greater historical antiquity, greater cultural and geographical universality, than commonly supposed, even by medical and social historians. Contraception has existed in some form throughout the entire range of social evolution—that is, for at least several thousand years. The desire for, as distinct from the achievement of, reliable contraception has been characteristic of many societies widely removed in time and space [p. xii].

Egyptian papyri, dating from 1850 B.C., that give contraceptive prescriptions and instructions are part of the elaborate documentary evidence in support of the thesis (Himes, 1936, p. 61). Primitive contraceptive measures were mechanical in nature. Often, however, they took the form of strong social sanctions regarding the spacing of children. Thus, parents were forbidden to have intercourse during the time that the child was being nursed—which might extend over a two- or three-year period.

If contraception failed, as it often did, there were socially sanctioned resorts to abortion or infanticide. Thus, in a study of some 350 societies, Devereaux (1976) found abortion practiced in almost all. In some forty of these societies, the practice was approved wholly or conditionally, or was regarded with neutral tolerance (pp. 361–371). Lecky (1869) notes, with reference to abortion, that "no law in Greece or in the Roman Republic or during the greater part of the Empire condemned it" (p. 22).

If abortion failed, or if it was not applied in time, infanticide, particularly in selective instances, was then resorted to in dealing with child welfare problems at their source.

Lecky (1869) also points out that "infanticide was almost universally admitted among the Greeks, being sanctioned and in some cases enjoined upon what we should now call the 'greater happiness principle,' by the ideal legislations of Plato and Aristotle and by the actual legislations of Lycurgus and Solon" (p. 27). Reviewing the relevant, and sometimes contradictory, source material, Hands (1968) concludes that "there can be little doubt that the Hellenistic age, with its high incidence of poverty, witnessed infant exposure on a large scale" (p. 69). In the Roman Empire, Lecky (1869) notes, "Pagan and Christian authorities were united in speaking of infanticide as a crying vice of the Empire and Tertullian observed that no laws were more easily, or more constantly evaded, than those which condemned it" (p. 29). And Sumner (1959) indicates that "For the masses, until the late days of the Empire, infanticide was at most a venial crime" (p. 319).

The author of a recent historical survey of infanticide notes that it "has from time immemorial been the accepted procedure for disposing not only of deformed or sickly infants but of all such newborns as might strain the resources of the individual family or the larger community. . . . It was thought altogether natural that proletarians, poverty stricken and hopeless, should [thus] protect themselves from further responsibility" (Langer, 1974, pp. 354–355). (See also Williamson, 1978.) Stone (1977) suggests that:

> There is a long history of fairly generalized infanticide in western Europe going back to antiquity, when it seems to have been extremely common. How far it remained a common deliberate policy for legitimate children in the Early Modern period is still an open question, although it is suggestive that as late as the early eighteenth century in Anjou, priests were instructed to warn their congregations in a sermon every three months of the mortal sin of killing an infant before baptism [pp. 473–74].

Reviews of the more limited literature available from the Far East show the same procedures to have been widely utilized there in maintaining a balance between available resources and mouths to be fed. A Chinese official speaking of Shonsi province in the mid-1860s says:

> I have learned of the prevalence of female infanticide in all parts of Shonsi. . . . The first female birth may sometimes be salvaged with effort but the subsequent births are usually drowned. There are even those who drown every female baby without keeping any. . . . This is because the poor worry about daily sustenance . . . and the rich are concerned over future doweries [Ho, 1967, p. 60].

A British official reporting in 1856 on the situation in one section of India said, "Infanticide is not only occasionally practiced here but uniformly and universally and unblushingly acknowledged" (Panigrahi, 1972, p. 37).

Infanticide often took the form of abandonment. The parents who were unable to care for their child left him to be found and accepted by others who could. If the child was not found or if no one accepted him, nature took its course and neither the family nor the society was further concerned with the child. Parents unable to care for a child, but still concerned over his fate, might choose to abandon him in a well-frequented spot to assure his being found. Thus, in Rome, children were brought to a "column near the Vilabrium, and these taken by speculators who educated them as slaves or very frequently as prostitutes" (Lecky, 1869, p. 30).

The abandonment of infants was resorted to for a long time throughout Europe. Caulfield (1931), analyzing the situation in eighteenth-century England, contends that "dropping [abandoning] of infants was an extremely frequent occurrence during this period and was accepted by all classes without comment" (p. 31). McCloy (1946), in a detailed study of social welfare problems in eighteenth-century France, notes that "one of the saddest features of eighteenth-century French history was the wholesale abandonment of infants by their parents"

(p. 238). The frequently told tale of Hansel and Gretel is, in effect, a story of attempted abandonment; the motivation of the stepmother may be primarily psychological (the rejection of the children of the former wife), but the father accedes to her plan to "lose" them because there is not enough food for both parents and children.

One historian reviewing late Roman and early medieval history notes, "The gains for children in this period appear mainly theoretical and only dimly perceived by most parents. . . . Repeated prohibitions by civil and religious authorities seemed to avail little against such grim acts as infanticide, abortion, sale of children and abandonment" (Lyman, 1973, p. 95).

Another historian, reviewing the period between the ninth and thirteenth centuries in western Europe, indicates that since the poor "were most directly and constantly at the mercy of the demonic cycles of famine, malnutrition, disease and death," their "children were by far the most common victims of parental negligence and despair, of abandonment, exposure and even infanticide, which must be counted among the major threats to young life in this period" (McLaughlin, 1973, p. 119).

The tour—the revolving box built into the front of the church in which the parent placed the child to be received by the church—permitted the anonymous abandonment of children. By 1830 there were some 230 tours throughout France, with 336,297 infants legally abandoned from 1824 to 1833.

Although abandonment is a private solution that may leave the community with the problem of providing for the unwanted child, it proved to be a public solution as well. The mortality rates for abandoned children were much higher than the already high rates for nonabandoned children. In Elizabethan England many parents were

> too poor to support their children at all and parish records contain numerous entries concerning the desertion of unwanted children who were found dead on the roads from exposure and starvation—a practice which continued among the poorer classes up to the nineteenth century [Pinchbeck, Hewitt, 1969, p. 22].

As late as 1873 the "medical register of New York reported 122 infants found dead in streets, alleys, rivers and elsewhere" (Radbill, 1968, p. 10).

Abandoned children placed in foundling hospitals died at such a rate that although it is likely that the existence of such facilities decreased the number of infanticides, it "may be questioned whether they diminished the number of deaths" (Lecky, 1869, p. 37). The abandoned children dying in the various hospitals in France, notes McCloy (1946), "probably varied at the frightful rate of 50 to 80 percent, by cities" (p. 248). Such resources for abandoned children may be subject to Mead's (1962) accusation (in another context) that they were "only a prolonged, ritualized method of disposing of the infant for whom nobody wishes to care."

Jonas Hanway, an eighteenth-century English child welfare researcher of parish workhouses, which received young children for institutional care, made efforts to follow up the history of each child placed. He found that in many parishes "the mortality of all children received was 80 to 90 percent or, if you please, upon those received under twelve months old, 99 percent" (Caulfield, 1931, p. 140).

A French doctor, Villerme, suggested that children's foundling homes should bear the inscription "here one kills children at public expense."

The London Foundling Hospital, established in 1741 to "prevent the frequent murders of poor miserable infants at their birth" and "to suppress the inhuman custom of exposing newborn infants to perish in the streets," was soon overwhelmed with abandoned children:

> Instead of being a protection to the living the institution became, as it were, a charnel house for the dead. . . . In the period between 1766 and 1786 there were 37,600 children admitted to the Foundling Home in Moscow; of that number 1000 were eventually sent out and some 6100 were still housed there in 1786. This meant that some 30,000 children (of the 37,600) were lost! [Dunn, 1973, p. 390]. [See also Fairchilds, 1978, p. 84.]

Another report notes that "in the years 1817–20 the number of foundlings in charge of the Paris Hospital (and interestingly about a third of them children of married couples) was about equal to a third of all babies born in Paris during that period. Of the 4779 infants admitted in 1818, 2370 died in the first three months" (Langer, 1974, p. 359). It was justifiable, then, to call institutionalization of abandoned children "legalized infanticide."

Among the poor, another solution was the selling of children:

> In the days of the Later Roman Empire, the spectacle of children being sold became a sight so common that various regulatory measures against it were passed. The Justinian Code of 534 contained a provision by which a father whose poverty was extreme was allowed to sell his son or daughter at the moment of birth, and repurchase the child at a later date [Bossard, Boll, 1966, p. 493].

The motives for these expedients indicate the relationship between these "preventive solutions" and potential problems in child welfare. Devereaux (1976) states, in reviewing the motives for abortion, "Economic factors play a tremendously important role in the motivation for abortion. . . . Anyone familiar with the tremendous economic burden which primitive women carry and with the great poverty of many groups [will understand this]" (p. 13). Miller (1928) notes the relationship of abortion and infanticide in primitive societies to available food supply: "The child must enter the world only when his presence will not crowd or necessitate unwanted economy"; thus infanticide and abortion "are means of restoring the equilibrium between human numbers and natural resources" (p. 30). Sumner (1959) notes that these practices are "primary and violent acts of self-defense by parents against famine, disease, and other calamities of overpopulation which increase with the number which each man and woman has to provide for" (p. 313). Hobhouse (1951) concurs: "To primitive man having a severe struggle for existence, the advent of a new mouth to feed is often a serious matter. Hence infanticide is not an uncommon practice in the uncivilized world and coincides with genuine and even devoted attachment to the child if once allowed to live" (p. 339).

Infanticide and abandonment resulted more frequently from hardness of life than from hardness of heart. "Urgent want and the sterility of the niggardly earth" were the reasons advanced by the people of Radash Island who allowed each woman only three children, requiring her to kill each succeeding child

(Payne, 1916, p. 37). Bossard (1966) notes this same motive for Greek support of infanticide when he repeats the story of the Greek father who, when asked, "Why do you expose your child?," answered, "Because I love the children I have" (p. 614). Hands (1968) points out that "after Emperor Constantine and Theodosius had forbidden the practice of infant exposure, it became necessary to admit the parents' right in extreme cases of poverty to sell a new-born child" (p. 71).

Poverty of resources is only one of the motives. If caring for the child is likely to be difficult, abortion or infanticide might be employed. If, for instance, the mother dies in childbirth, the child, too, may be killed:

> In Australia the infant is buried alive with its mother or killed and burnt with her corpse. The Semang of the Malay Peninsula wrap mother and child in one shroud, the child being placed on the mother's breast with its face downward. . . . Among the Chiloctin Indians of Canada the death of a mother during delivery leads to burying the child in its cradle with the mother [Miller, 1928, pp. 39–40].

Somewhat similarly, the illegitimate child was aborted or killed not only because of the shame attendant upon the birth of a bastard but also because the mother would have found difficulty in caring for and rearing him (Devereaux, 1976, pp. 245–289). A child conceived in an incestuous union was also likely to be aborted because his birth would present a social problem. The 1890 edition of the *Encyclopaedia Britannica* notes that "The modern crime of infanticide shows no symptoms of diminution in the leading nations of Europe. In all of them it is closely connected with illegitimacy in the class of farm and domestic servants" (quoted in Bakan, 1971, p. 42).

By the same token, deformed or defective children are done away with in some societies. This obviates, once again, a problem in child welfare that is likely to result from the failure of a child to perform adequately the expected social role. "Among the Indians on the Amazon River, the child was exposed to a test for a right to survival, as all infants immediately after birth were submerged in a stream, but the deformed child was never pulled out again" (Miller, 1928, p. 48). Sumner (1959) quotes Seneca as referring to the "killing of defective children as a wise and unquestioned custom," and Seneca is seconded by Pliny in this (p. 319). Aristotle, too, thought that defective children should be put to death, and the exposure of sickly children among the Spartans is well known. The Roman Twelve Tables clearly stipulated that deformed children were not to be given care (Bennett, 1923).

Twins present a special problem because such a birth doubles the burden of care and the number of mouths to be fed. Hence, twin births often result in infanticide in some societies. For the same reason, children born while an older child is still very dependent may be killed because the simultaneous burden of child care is too great. Thus, among the Pima, ". . . if a woman gets pregnant while lactating, she aborts by pressure on the belly. The unborn is sacrificed to the interests of the previous baby 'which the mother loved more because she could see it'" (Devereaux, 1976, p. 310).

Plato's idea was that "men over fifty-five and women over forty should not procreate," and if they did, the child should be aborted or killed, because older parents are not likely to live long enough to see their children become indepen-

dent. The prevention of childbearing by older parents obviates the problem of
dependent orphans.

The child who was difficult to care for because of the death of the father
was also a candidate for infanticide as a solution: "In the Hellenistic law of
Egypt, after the death of the husband, a marriage-contract is annulled and the
widow is empowered to expose her expected child" (Cameron, 1932, p. 108).

Thus the principal candidates for infanticide and abandonment were most
likely to be those children who presented the greatest problems in child care: the
physically deformed and mentally retarded children and children of illicit, irregular, difficult or impermanent relationships. Such children and such situations
are candidates for child welfare services today. Because there were no child welfare services until relatively recently, other alternatives, such as infanticide or
abandonment, were employed. A gradually changing ideology regarding the
care of dependents, the handicapped, and the deprived, however, made these
solutions progressively more unacceptable.

Concern for the needs of the less privileged, less capable members of society is not a modern phenomenon: the Code of Hammurabi and the Old Testa-
ment provide humanitarian admonitions about caring for people in need. "Greece
in the age of Plato provided funds for soldiers' orphans and free medical service
for poor children. The famous *pueri alimentarii* in Rome at the period of the
Empire was a special semigovernmental service for the charitable maintenance
of the children of indigent citizens" (Seligman, 1930, p. 375).

Concern for the dependent and the deprived became one of the central
values of Christianity. Christianity preached the sanctity of all human life—even
that of the fetus in the womb. This meant that both infanticide and abortion were
crimes. The child was guaranteed the right to life and the resources to sustain life.
Reinforcing and supplementing these theological presuppositions was the humanitarian ideology of the Enlightenment, which provided a secular foundation
for the rights of the child.

As a result, some of the previous solutions to child welfare problems—infanticide, for instance—became ideologically inadmissible. But, when society
makes such solutions unacceptable, it must provide alternative solutions. At this
point, the necessity for child welfare service becomes evident. This relationship
is revealed in the history of Western Europe and is noted by Sumner (1959),
who says that as a "corollary of the legislation against infanticide, institutions to
care for foundlings came into existence" (p. 319). In fact, Constantine, influenced by Christian teaching, in A.D. 315 promulgated a law "to turn parents from
using a parricidal hand to their new-born children and to dispose their hearts to
the best sentiments. . . . If a father brings a child saying he cannot support it,
someone should supply him without delay with food and clothing" (Payne, 1916,
p. 264).

The Church became the protector of parentless children, accepting those
children whose parents could not provide for them. As early as A.D. 325, the
Council of Nicaea prescribed that xenodochia be established in each Christian
village—institutions that had the responsibility of aiding the sick, the poor, and
abandoned children (Constantelos, 1968).

There were some early beginnings of organized child welfare services in
medieval Europe. The first asylum for abandoned infants was established in
Milan in 787, and in 1160 Guy de Montpellier established the Order of the Holy

Spirit for the care of foundlings and orphans. However disastrous the outcomes, as we have noted above, the foundling homes were an organized attempt to provide an alternative to infanticide and haphazard abandonment.

The objective that prompted the establishment of the London Foundling Hospital in 1741 accurately reflects the rationale for the establishment of institutions for children everywhere. The objective, as stated in the hospital's charter, was to "prevent the murders of poor miserable children at their birth and to suppress the inhuman custom of exposing new-born infants to perils in the streets and to take in children dropped in churchyards or in the streets or left at night at the doors of church wardens or overseers of the poor."

Trexler (1973) notes that Pope Innocent III "instituted the hospital of the Santo Spirito in Rome because so many women were throwing their children into the Tiber" (p. 99).

In 1712 Peter the Great decreed that Russian monasteries must act as "orphan nourishers" and that "unwed mothers [must] deposit their infants in these asylums through specially built windows which shielded them from the gaze of the receiver instead of 'sweeping these babies into unsuitable places' " (Madison, 1963, p. 84).

Gradually more and more institutions, hospitals, and asylums became available in which to house abandoned and neglected children. A variety of alternative measures arose that predate professional social work: resources such as the workhouse for children, "outdoor relief" (relief outside an institution through a cash grant or the like) for parents who were unable to care for their children, and an elaborate system of "binding out" or apprenticeship training entered into while the child was still very young.

The point, however, is that when a society rejects abortion, infanticide, and abandonment as solutions, it must assume the responsibility to care for the child whose life it has saved. This, then, suggests the need for developing the services and resources that constitute the field of child welfare.

Economic and Political Changes

A humanitarian attitude toward the child cannot prevail if the economic situation is unfavorable. Even after the attitude of the Christian church toward children became dominant, instances of child abandonment and child neglect rose during periods of economic distress. Sumner (1959) observes that "in reality nothing put an end to infanticide but the advance in the arts [increased economic power] by virtue of which parents can provide for their children" (p. 321).

The Industrial Revolution, by increasing the productive capacity of all adults, made it possible for them to care for a greater number of dependent children. Society could now afford to support and care for physically handicapped children, mentally defective children, and dependent children whose own parents were unable to care for them.

In analyzing the relationship of the productivity of adults to the needs of the child population, Bossard (1966) notes, "The status of childhood, as reflected in school, work, and child-care standards of all kinds, represents in large measure the relative size of the nonproductive and productive groups and the capacities of the latter to serve the former" (pp. 590–591).

Political factors also increased the need for some community-supported institution to deal with child welfare problems. Social institutions evolve in order to perform a useful function in society, and to permit society to operate more effectively and with less conflict. Child welfare services meet the needs of children, but they also reduce the threat of social disequilibrium. Humanitarian and ethical considerations are often secondary to the need to maintain social stability by providing the necessary social arrangements (in this case, the child welfare services) to deal with problems of social dysfunctioning that did affect a significant number of children (Atherton, 1969). Failure to provide child welfare service entails a possible increase in the number of children who might become delinquent or develop physical and/or mental illness and therefore constitute both a threat to, and a burden on, society.

Finally, the enfranchisement of nonpropertied classes gave political power to a growing number of poor parents who needed the help of the community in implementing their parental role. Ignoring the needs and demands of this growing group of voters would present an internal political threat.

Failure to provide child welfare services poses an external threat that derives from the dependence of modern nation states on a citizen army for national security. In World Wars I and II, very sizable percentages of men in the United States and Britain were found to be physically, mentally, or emotionally unfit for service, partly as a result of childhood deprivation.

Specialization of Social Institutions

Another factor in the development of child welfare services is the increasing specialization of social institutions and the change, or loss, of functions of some institutions. One such institution is the neighborhood.

Over a long period of history, most people lived in small rural groups where they grew up together, knew one another intimately, and kept contact with neighboring families over a number of generations. The extended family, including collateral relatives as well as nonrelated but familiar members of the community, assumed some responsibility for maintaining children whose parents were unable to fulfill their role obligations. Problems of child welfare were frequently solved through mutual aid. In underdeveloped countries today, where the organization of communal life resembles that of Europe hundreds of years ago, mutual aid from neighbors and kin is still a frequent source of help. In such societies "there are plenty of orphans but no orphanages." A recent report by the United Nations Children's Fund, describing the effects of urbanization in underdeveloped countries, notes that poverty, hunger, and disease are often a traditional part of the child's life in the rural community, "but there, at least, the child has his natural protection and will seldom be abandoned by the community even if his parents die. In the new environment of the urban slums things are quite different." The impersonal relationships of the city replace the personal relationship of the rural community and require the introduction of child welfare organizations (Sicault, 1963, p. 23).

In an urban society, siblings often live at a distance from each other and from their parents and grandparents. Nor is the obligation of mutual support as firmly sanctioned—the obligations to one's nuclear family take clear precedence over those to the extended family.

The early parish group, too, was a closely knit primary group—the unifying factor being the sharing of significant beliefs. The parish "was a mutual aid group, the members of which looked out for each other especially during the era of persecution" (Queen, 1922, p. 576). The parish group has lost much of this cohesiveness, and even if it had not, the secularization of modern society would exclude many people from such aid.

The feudal system, with its elaborate structure of rights and obligations, was a more formally contractual kind of mutual aid. As de Schweinitz (1947) says:

> under feudalism there could, at least in theory, be no uncared-for distress. The people who today would be in the greatest economic danger were, in the Middle Ages, presumably protected by their masters from the most acute suffering. . . . Insurance against unemployment, sickness, old age was theirs in the protection of their high lords [p. 2].

Mutual aid was also a feature of another kind of primary group—the occupational family: the guild, which operated as an extended family to protect its members from risks to security. When guilds were small and their members knew one another intimately, they felt a responsibility for one another's welfare and made provisions for the care of the widows and children of deceased fellow members. Queen (1922) points out that, for guild members:

> there was a close community of interest and a sharing of the daily experiences of life. The guild itself was just a primary group with intimate personal relations. . . . This being the case, it was quite natural that we should find the guilds assumed responsibility for the bereaved widows and orphans of their members, educated the latter, and, if they were girls, provided them with dowries [p. 282].

Ultimately all the institutions that had assumed responsibility for dealing with child welfare problems diminished their involvement in such problems or else found that social change made previous solutions untenable. With the growth of an urbanized population, with the growing mobility of the population attendant upon industrialization, the "neighborhood" is less apt to denote a primary group, so that mutual aid through this source becomes less certain. Both the guilds and their modern counterparts—trade unions, professional associations, merchants' and manufacturers' associations—were institutionalized around a primary function other than child welfare. As this primary function—concern with the problems of the occupation—became more complex, the institutions became less concerned with secondary, nonessential functions. The church's religious function took precedence over its eleemosynary concerns, especially after the Reformation, which reduced the resources available to the church generally and, consequently, the resources that it could make available for charitable purposes. Steinbicker (1957) notes that "poor relief was the first ecclesiastical institution to be secularized after the religious revolt."

These changes meant that a new institution had to be developed to deal with child welfare problems. The diminished interest and capacity of institutions like the neighborhood, the extended family, the guild, and the church in dealing with child welfare problems created a need for child welfare social work, which was designed to fill the gap.

The neighborhood, the extended family, the church, and the occupational group still contribute to helping with child welfare problems. Such resources exist side by side with the more formal professional resources and services, and they are frequently explored by the individual before he approaches the professional services. However, only child welfare social work is explicitly concerned with child welfare problems as its primary, specific, institutional responsibility.

At the same time that many social institutions are disencumbering themselves of concern for the child, one institution—the nuclear family—has developed a more specialized concern for the child. As the modern family loses some of its traditional functions—production, protection, recreation, and so on—the problems and satisfactions of child rearing are becoming its principal business. It is a common enterprise, which for many is the principal ingredient of marriage. With such specialization in family function, children become of increasing importance.

The Scientific Revolution

Advances in scientific knowledge have not only increased the productivity of each worker so that fewer productive adults can support a larger number of dependents, but they have also made possible the development of a science of child welfare. Greater scientific concern with the problems of child development and the results of such studies have intensified the importance of childhood. Freud was among the first to call attention to the crucial importance of childhood in shaping human destiny, and his work was followed by a host of other studies, examining and clarifying the effects of childhood experiences. The years of childhood began to assume greater importance and significance vis-à-vis other periods of life.

The Freudian emphasis on childhood was supported by other scientific advances—particularly the Darwinian theories on man's origin and evolution. The genetic point of view—which stresses continuity in development, points to the importance of beginnings, and insists that the past is structured in the present— became a solidly accepted concept. Childhood assumed an unprecedented importance.

But such studies, and the growth in knowledge that resulted from such studies, did more than heighten the importance of childhood; they also gave rise to a new profession. Professions develop in response to a human need, but the attempt to meet the need can be professionalized only if there is a scientific body of knowledge available to form the basis for professional action. The studies regarding childhood and children became the basis for such journals as *Child Development, Child Welfare; Courrier, The International Journal of Child Welfare, Children Today*—none of which existed one hundred years ago. Ultimately this material is codified and organized so that courses are taught, textbooks are written, and educational programs are developed for the training of professionals in specialties concerned with various aspects of childhood. Thus the expansion and elaboration of special knowledge concerned with welfare services for children made possible a professional field of specialization in child welfare.

The Discovery of Childhood

The recognition of childhood as a distinct period of life is so widely accepted that it is difficult to realize that it was not always so. Biological differences, of course, forced a recognition of the child as a being distinct from the adult. But childhood was believed to be a short period "of transition which passed quickly and was just as quickly forgotten" (Aries, 1962). Throughout most of history, life has been exceedingly short for most people and "maturity" had to be reached early in life. It might be remembered that Romeo was not yet sixteen, and Juliet not yet fourteen, when their fervent, tragic romance was in flower. When the average life span did not exceed thirty years, childhood could not be prolonged. "Conscious of the brevity of life . . . parents were eager to introduce their sons and daughters into the adult world at the earliest possible moment" (Pinchbeck, Hewitt, 1969, p. 198).

The economic position of the family and of society was such that the individual had to become self-supporting as quickly as possible. Children began to earn their living at six or seven years of age. According to a statute enacted in England in 1535, "Children under fourteen years of age, and above five, that live in idleness and be taken begging may be put to service by the government of cities, towns, etc., to husbandry; or other crafts of labor" (quoted in Bremner, 1970, p. 64). William Blake, the poet, began working in a silk mill in 1764, when he was seven years old. An advertisement in *The Baltimore-Federal-Gazette* of January 4, 1808, stated, "This [Baltimore Cotton] manufactory will go into operation this month, where a number of boys and girls from eight to twelve years of age are wanted" (quoted in Trattner, 1970, p. 27).

Stone (1977) notes that in the sixteenth and seventeenth centuries children "lower down the social scale left home at between seven and fourteen to begin work as domestic servants, laborers, or apprentices but in all cases living in their masters' houses rather than at home or in lodging" (p. 107) and "that the period of close parent–child bonding was a relatively short one at all levels of society" (p. 116)—and, one might add, that the responsibility of parents for the care of dependent children was relatively short in duration. This brevity of childhood would limit the development of child welfare problems (also see Shorter, 1977, p. 26).

Older people in small English villages, recounting their childhood as they lived it in the latter part of the nineteenth century, note how early in life childhood ended for them: "The children helped in their own way. We started field work when we were five or six. . . . I was living in Deplen when I first started ploughing. I was fifteen years old and I had been at work for seven years. . . . I lost my father when I was nine so I had to think about work" (Blythe, 1969).

The definition of the term *child* has been, and is, quite elastic. In the past, the end of childhood as a period of dependency came very much earlier than it does today. As children very early in life became responsible for self-support, "childhood effectively ended at the age of seven or, at the latest, nine" (Pinchbeck, Hewitt, 1969, p. 42).

For a long time, there was no distinctive child dress; it was merely adult dress in miniature, so that there was little symbolic demarcation of childhood and children were very early absorbed into the world of adults.

Aries (1962) says that:

> in medieval society, the idea of childhood did not exist. . . . The idea of childhood is not to be confused with affection for children: it corresponds to an awareness of the particular nature of childhood, that particular nature which distinguishes the child from the adult, even the young adult. In medieval society, this awareness was lacking [p. 128].

Just as there is a relationship between greater concern for children and the development of a more productive economy, so there is a relation between the development of modern education and the idea of childhood. The view of childhood as an important and significant period evokes a need for a formal, highly developed system of education, which, in turn, reinforces and supports the idea of the distinctiveness of childhood. Age grading becomes part of the way of categorizing people in society.

Changes in family living arrangements, from households that included the many relatives of the extended family to the household that excluded all except the nuclear family, contributed to the enhancement of concern for the child. Pinchbeck (1969) argues that:

> Just as the institutional development and acceptance of formal education with the consequent isolation of the child from adult society was a prerequisite of the emergence of modern sociological and psychological concepts of childhood, so also the gradual isolation and individualization of the family as a social and psychological entity ultimately contributed to the same end. The ties between parent and child were necessarily strengthened in a family reduced to parents and children [p. 307].

The Status of the Family and the Child

The status of the child is closely related to the status of the family as an institution vis-à-vis other institutions through which people seek the satisfaction of basic needs. The family is, for the child, the only significant social institution to which he is related for the first years of his life.

The family, although always an institution of importance, came to be overshadowed by other institutions to which adults owed allegiance. The church, the state, the peer group, the army, the guild, the occupation—all have frequently taken priority over the family; and men have devoted their primary attention, energy, and concern to these other areas of their lives.

Aries (1962), in talking about the family in the Middle Ages, indicates that it fulfilled a function—it ensured the transmission of life, property, and names— but it did not penetrate very far into human sensibility (p. 411). According to Aries (1962), the medieval family "existed in silence: it did not awaken feelings strong enough to inspire poet or artist. We must recognize the importance of this silence—not much value was placed on the family" (p. 364).

More recently, however, the family has become the significant center of our lives. Religion, occupation, the friendship of peers, the state—all are subservient to the family. We invest more of ourselves in the family than in almost any other social institution. The fact that family—and the nuclear family at that—has assumed such central importance in our lives results in an increase in the importance of the child, who is a member of this, but of no other, significant social institution.

Changes in the Arithmetic of Child Production

Another important factor that affects the status of the child is what Bossard (1966) has aptly termed the *arithmetic of production:* the relationship between birthrate and child mortality rates. For a long time in the history of mankind, many children were born and many died. Parents expected that a high percentage of the children they conceived would be with them only a short period of time:

> In the late 17th and early 18th centuries about half of the recorded children of French peasantry were dead by the age of ten and between half and two-thirds by the age of twenty. In the cities, conditions were worse still, and in London in 1764 forty-nine percent of all recorded children were dead by the age of two and sixty percent by the age of five [Stone, 1977, p. 68].

Throughout most of European history parent–child relationships were not very intense and were of relatively short duration: "The family was a loose association of transients constantly broken up by the death of parents or children or the early departure of the children from the home" (Stone, 1977, p. 81).

In a society where a parent's relationship with his own children was casual, distant, and brief, with little emotional intensity, it is not very likely that the community will invest very much in providing for the needs of children in general. The segment of society composed of children had low priority in public consciousness and conscience: "The omnipresence of death coloured affective relations at all levels of society by reducing the amount of emotional capital available for prudent investment in any single individual, especially in such ephemeral creatures as infants" (Stone, 1977, p. 65). "Indifference was a direct and inevitable consequence of the demography of the period" (Aries, 1962, p. 39).

To invest emotionally in children was to invite problems, for one was so often doomed to see the child die. If one was to hope to retain psychological stability, he had to maintain an attitude of restrained attachment toward children. Because the child was a transient in the family and because, even if he survived, the period of his childhood was short, anything peculiarly identified with childhood was relegated to secondary importance. The family was adult-centered, adult-directed, and adult-oriented. Mitchell (1970), noting these factors, concludes that:

it is probable that the modern concept of parental love is of comparatively recent origin, and that throughout most of history interest in, and affection for, infants and young children has been at a much more superficial level. . . . If parents were thus unable to develop deep feelings of affection towards their offspring, they would be unlikely to entertain such sentiments toward the children of their neighbors [p. 301].

Hence it was difficult to get public support for child welfare services to meet the needs of the children of the community.

With advances in sanitation, in public health, and in medicine and with the greater availability of more effective contraceptive measures, fewer children were conceived, but those who were conceived had better chances of surviving. One could allow himself to develop a deep feeling for the few children he had, with confident hope that such love would not inevitably be followed by sorrow and pain at the child's untimely death. And because children came to be, for many, the results of careful and restricted planning, they were apt to be highly valued when they were born.

Legal Status of the Child

The legal status of the child has changed over time, making explicit and re-inforcing the more favorable position of the child in society. At one time, chil-dren had the status of chattel: "The child's position in the average family of the masses was for centuries roughly in this order: father, cattle, mother, child" (Despert, 1965, p. 15). Hunt (1969) points out that comparing children to ani-mals was "an image that appears throughout seventeenth-century literature on children. In a total sense the small child was an intermediate being, not really an animal (although he might often be compared to one) but on the other hand not really human either" (p. 125).

Early European legal systems gave little, if any, recognition to the rights of the child. The amphidroma ceremony in ancient Athens, performed on the fifth day after birth, symbolized the actual social birth of the child. Before then, the child, alive but not actually a member of the community, could be disposed of. The Roman concept of *patria potestas* gave the father almost abso-lute power over his children. In early Germanic law, the child was under the *Munt* of the father, which gave the father authoritative control. Neither the Roman nor the Germanic code made explicit the obligations of the father to main-tain and protect the child. Parents in pre-Revolutionary France could obtain a *lettre de cachet* permitting imprisonment of a disobedient child, and the Napole-onic Code clearly defined the subordinate position of the child.

With the gradual acceptance of the rights of the child, parental authority has come to be defined "as a series of rights and obligations on the part of both parents which are to be exercised for the good of the child and which are bal-anced by a sense of correlative rights and obligations on the part of the child" (United Nations, 1968, p. 11). Parental power, previously exercised in domina-tion over the child in the interests of parents, is now more likely to be regarded as a trust to be employed in the best interests of the child.

The very real change in attitude toward the status of children is exemplified by the fact that in November 1954 the United Nations General Assembly unanimously adopted and proclaimed a Declaration of the Rights of the Child, which affirms the rights of the child to have special protection and to enjoy opportunities and facilities that will enable him to develop in a healthy and normal manner; to have a name and a nationality from his birth; to enjoy the benefit of social security, including adequate nutrition, housing, recreation, and medical services; to grow up in an atmosphere of affection and security, and, wherever possible, in the care and under the responsibility of his parents; to receive special treatment, education, and care if he is handicapped; to be among the first to receive protection and relief in times of disaster; to be protected against all forms of neglect, cruelty, and exploitation; and to be protected from practices that may foster any form of discrimination. The 1970 White House Conference on Children affirmed these rights (U.S. White House Conference, 1970b).

In the 1970s, stimulated in part by the civil rights and the women's movements, there emerged a "children's rights" movement. A literature became available (Gottleib, 1973; Wilkerson, 1973; Harvard Educational Review, 1973; Gross, Gross, 1977; Vardin, Brody, 1979). Laws were codified and specific organizations developed, such as the Children's Defense Fund, concerned with championing children's rights. The American Civil Liberties Union publishes a monthly newsletter concerned with children's rights—the *Children's Rights Report*. And 1979 was designated by the United Nations as the Year of the Child.

Legal changes reflect attitudinal changes toward children. During the last five hundred years society has gradually become more child-oriented, there has been an emotional intensification in the relationship between parents and children, and the child has come to be perceived as a person in his own right rather than being viewed for his instrumental contribution to family functioning:

> While a residual affection between mother and child—the product of a biological link—has always existed, there was a change in the priority which the infant occupied in the mother's rational hierarchy of values. Whereas in traditional society the mother had been prepared to place many considerations—most of them related to the desperate struggle for existence—above the infant's welfare, in modern society, the infant came to be most important [Shorter, 1975, p. 5].

All of these factors—ideological changes, changes in productivity, the specialization of institutions, the discovery of childhood, the arithmetic of child production, the changing status of children—have contributed to the development of a special system, the child welfare services system. This system has developed gradually, and some kind of child welfare was practiced long before an identifiable occupational group was assigned this particular responsibility. Community efforts took the form of the *pueri alimentarii* of ancient Rome, almshouses, and the "outdoor" poor relief granted to indigent people living in their own homes. For instance, outdoor poor relief in the late eighteenth century in New York City was offered in response to recurrent problems of child welfare: "husband in prison . . . husband has broke his leg . . . a house full of small children . . . husband at sea . . . husband bad fellow . . . sick and distressed . . . her husband has abandoned her and she has broke her arm" (quoted in Mohl, 1971, p. 25). And side by side with these public efforts to relieve distress and want, we have always had the private acts of goodwill by benevolent individuals and the activities of organized voluntary groups. Thus Hands (1968) notes the distribution of corn and oil and cash in ancient Greece and Rome through the auspices of wealthy benefactors, and in early-nineteenth-century New York City child welfare problems were ameliorated by such private benevolent groups as the Society for the Relief of Poor Widows with Small Children, the Female Assistance Society, the Orphan Asylum Society, the New York Society for the Prevention of Pauperism, and the Humane Society. (The latter, incidentally, dealt with a social situation that no longer presents a problem for child welfare—the imprisonment of a father for debt.)

Professional child-welfare workers were preceded by such gifted and dedicated "amateurs" as Saint Vincent de Paul, who fought during the reign of Louis XIII for the establishment of institutions for abandoned children; Vives, who in 1525 wrote *On the Relief of the Poor*, the first modern textbook on social work in public welfare; Thomas Carom, who in 1739 energized London into building a hospital for foundlings; Lord Ashley, Earl of Shaftesbury, who tirelessly fought for passage of the Factory Acts, limiting the worst abuses of child labor in nineteenth-century England; Florence Kelly, who performed similar yeoman service for American children; and Dr. Bernado and Charles Loring Brace, who nightly collected the abandoned, homeless, parentless children off the streets of nineteenth-century London and New York, respectively.

It would be difficult to measure the influence these individuals had on stimulating a sense of greater community responsibility for services for children. But having noted that the profession of social work and the formal organization of a network of child welfare services was preceded by a variety of preprofessional "social work" efforts to deal with child welfare problems, efforts that existed alongside such responses as contraception, abortion, infanticide, abandonment, child labor, and neighborly mutual aid as procedures for dealing with such problems, it might also be noted that the reverse situation exists today. Alongside the formal system of professional child-welfare services, society currently employs many of the classical solutions in dealing with child welfare problems. A rich network of neighborly, volunteer mutual aid exists side by side with the formal agency resources responding to child welfare problems. When a single car accident in Mount Kisko, New York, killed two women and critically injured four others, it left twenty young children permanently or temporarily motherless. Neighbors volunteered to help with baby-sitting and child care and to collect funds for the families (Grehen, 1960).

Ethnic- and church-group mutual aid societies continue to act as family surrogates in times of stress or need. The immigrant *Landsmanshaft* organizations are examples of these mutual aid approaches. They continue today in attenuated forms, affected adversely by growing assimilation.

On a larger scale, the informal network of child care in the black community, existing side by side with the formal agency-care system, is another example of the continuation of earlier historical methods of dealing with child welfare problems before the development of social work. Records of this kind of care go back to the 1860s "in the attention ex-slaves gave to black children orphaned by the sale and death of their parents by parental desertion and wartime dislocation" (Gutman, 1977, p. 224). Analyzing the 1970 census, Royster (1975) concluded that "informal caring for children is more prevalent in the black community—the overall proportion for categories of children under 19 living with heads of families other than their own parents is much higher for blacks than it is for whites" (p. 3-3). As a result, many children are kept out of the formal child-welfare–foster-care system, and the informal system competes with the formal agency system for potential foster parents.

On the other hand, the ancient procedure of child abandonment as a personal solution to child welfare problems is still frequently employed. An adoption worker in Pakistan, reporting on the work of his agency in 1977, says, "Ours is a voluntary organization which looks after parentless children found abandoned in dustbins, on street corners and at hospitals" (Ispahani, 1977, p. 45).

Even infanticide exists as a twentieth-century procedure for dealing with child welfare problems at the source. A government policy of euthanasia in Nazi Germany sanctioned the deliberate killing of defective children; "idiot and malformed children" were killed by "doses of morphine, chloride, and luminol" at the children's institutions to which they had been sent (Mitscherlich, 1949, p. 114). A court trial in 1963 in Liège, Belgium, was concerned with the "mercy killing" of a child born deformed as a result of the mother's having taken Thalidomide (a tranquilizer) during her pregnancy. The family had prevailed upon their doctor to prescribe a lethal dose of a sleeping drug, and the family and the doctor were charged with homicide. During the trial the city of Liège officially sanctioned a referendum of the local population: of those who voted, 16,732 approved the infanticide, while only 938 disapproved. The doctor and the family were acquitted (Gallahue, 1963).

A research report published in 1973 noted that of 299 consecutive deaths in a special-care nursery for seriously malformed infants, 43 (14 per cent) were related to the withholding of treatment (Duff, Campbell, 1973). In these instances it had been decided that even if the children could be maintained alive, which was doubtful in many instances, such very defective infants would have "little or no hope of achieving meaningful humanhood" (see also Kohl, 1978).

The most important of the classical measures currently applied to potential child-welfare problems are contraception and abortion. Contraception has widespread community acceptance, and abortion is legal in some countries, illegal but openly tolerated in others, illegal and not tolerated in still others, but common everywhere.

The revolution in attitudes toward publicly supported contraception programs in the United States had moved along rapidly enough so that in mid-1972 most of the fifty states had affirmed the right of unmarried women eighteen years of age or older to birth control information and services. In twenty-three states they had this right without parental consent at still younger ages (Paul et al., 1976).

The current widespread support for family-planning facilities is indicated by the fact that whereas public expenditures for such programs were close to zero in 1965, by 1975 such expenditures amounted to $186 million (Kahn, Kamerman, 1976, p. 400). Such facilities served 3.8 million women during that year.

Between 1973, when the U.S. Supreme Court legalized abortion, and 1978 some 5 million abortions were performed in the United States. Many of the abortions were financed by public funds through the Medicaid program.

THE AMERICAN EXPERIENCE

In view of the crucial factors that determine the status of children and the valuation of the child, American child-centeredness becomes explicable. The American ethos is grounded not only in the Judeo-Christian tradition but more particularly in the Humanist tradition of the Enlightenment. A humanitarian concern for the dependent and the underprivileged is congruent with our tradition. A highly industrialized nation, the United States is in an economic position to implement its philosophical attitude. Our pragmatic, secular orientation has resulted in a widespread acceptance of contraceptive measures and the idea of family planning. This attitude, along with our highly developed medical and public health resources, has resulted in the kind of arithmetic of child production associated with high valuation of the child. Our respect for scientific research has led to acceptance, however ambivalent, of the teachings of child-care experts—all of whom have a vested professional interest in heightening the status of childhood.

Some particular aspects of the American experience further help to explain the great emphasis on the child in America. In a nation of immigrants, the experience of parents—related to another time and another place—tends to be discounted. Indeed, parents often had to turn to their children for help in learning the language and customs of their adopted country. The reversed teacher–learner relationship between parent and child favors the child.

Even with the slowing down of immigration, some of this attitude remains in the tradition and is reinforced by rapid social change, which, in the context of what Kingsley Davis has called the "de-accelerating" rate of socialization, implies that the parent's knowledge and solutions are not always applicable to the problems faced by his children. They are solutions made for another time—as though the parent were an immigrant in his own country. Once again, the tendency is to derogate the parents somewhat and to increase the valuation of the child. Upward social mobility also has the effect of derogating parental experience in favor of the child's knowledge.

In a tradition-oriented society, the past is revered, and its custodians— parents and grandparents—are respected. In a society oriented toward change, the emphasis is on the future, and hopes, ambitions, and attention are lavished on the child as the future toward which we strive. That orientation of the American culture reinforces the importance of children and childhood, and our positive regard for the individual and for individual development makes the child, not the family, the vehicle for fulfilling the future and reaping its rewards.

The democratic tradition, of necessity, is reflected in family organization. It is difficult for the ethos to sanction autocracy within the family. The tendency toward congruence presses the family in the direction of democratization of internal relationships, suggesting, within the limits of practicability and biological competence, a greater voice for children in the family and less domination of children by parents.

The family that has production as one of its key functions can permit only limited democracy. Somebody has to be "boss" of a productive unit to ensure that the necessary work will be done smoothly, efficiently, effectively. When the family becomes primarily a unit of consumption, family organization can support a greater measure of democracy. This is one of the changes that has taken place in most American families within the last fifty years. With such change has come the possibility of a more democratically organized family and a concomitant enhancement of the status of children.

These are some of the special factors, unique to the American experience, that have reinforced the growing importance of children and childhood over a period of time. These special considerations give American culture a filiocentric orientation conducive to the development of child welfare services.

THE CURRENT CONTEXT OF CHILD WELFARE SERVICES

Introduction

A historical overview gives us some perspective on the factors that have stimulated changes in child welfare resources and services, but it is also helpful to consider the changes currently taking place in American society that may influence the need for child welfare services.

Historical trends are both more revealing and more relevant than annual statistics, which, because they are ephemeral and soon outdated, will be cited here only sparingly, and for illustrative purposes. Throughout, *children* refers to individuals eighteen years of age or younger; *nonwhite* includes Indian and Oriental, as well as black children (black children make up about 95 per cent of this group). Most of the statistical data, specific details of which the student might wish to check for himself, are derived primarily from recent government publications (U.S. Department of Commerce, 1972, 1975, 1977a, b, 1978; Snapper, Ohms, 1978) and from a limited number of specialized nongovernment publications (Ross, Sawhill, 1975; National Council of Organizations for Children and Youth, 1976). Additional specific references are cited where appropriate.

The Child Population

In 1977 there were some 64.25 million children in the United States—30 per cent of the total population of 218 million Americans. *The trend is toward a decrease in the proportion of children to total population.* By contrast, in 1960, 36 per cent of the population of the country was composed of children eighteen years of age or younger.

These figures reflect *the trend toward lower birthrates during the 1965–1975 decade.* This was true for both white and nonwhite women. The birthrate among nonwhite women, however, was still somewhat higher than that among whites. As a consequence, the median age of the nonwhite population was younger than that of the white group. A larger proportion of the total population of nonwhites, therefore, was concentrated in the younger age groups. This meant a somewhat disproportionate nonwhite population of risk for child welfare services.

The decline in birthrates during the 1960s (interrupted only by a temporary upturn in 1969–1970) grew sharper during the early 1970s.

From 1970, when the birthrate—the number of births per 1,000 population—was 18.4, the birthrate dropped to 14.7 in 1976, the lowest in our history and below the replacement level for zero population growth.

The extent to which childbearing has fallen becomes dramatic when it is realized that it took only 35 million fecund women to bear 4.7 million children in 1957, whereas it took 48 million fecund women to bear 3.2 million babies in 1976.

The number of children under five decreased from over 20 million in 1960 to about 15.2 million in 1977—a decline of 25 per cent. This unprecedented decrease is the more remarkable because it occurred at a time when the number of young adults of childbearing age had increased sharply (Grier, 1971).

The high birthrate in the post-World War II decade produced about 5 million more potential mothers in 1970 than there had been in 1960. An "echo baby boom" had been anticipated as a consequence. Instead the beginning of the 1970s was marked by a "baby bust" or a "birth dearth." Hospitals all over the country began to reduce obstetrical services in the early 1970s in response to the falling birthrates.

Although high unemployment rates during the 1970s may have been a temporary factor in the declining birthrates, the greater availability of adequate family-planning technology, coupled with a decrease in the number of children desired, may be a permanent feature of our national life.

Recent reports have shown a significant drop in the number of children women desire. In 1965 women expected to have, on the average, three children; by 1977, the expected average had dropped to closer to two.

The trend is toward postponement of marriage and childbirth and toward a modest increase in intentional childlessness. Between 1970 and 1976, the proportion of population twenty-five to twenty-nine years old who had never married increased from about 19 per cent to 25 per cent among men and from 10.5 to 14.8 among women. Although many of the men and women delaying marriage and childbirth are likely ultimately to marry and have children, for some the decision to defer marriage and childbirth may imply a decision not to marry and to remain childless.

Further, marrying later in life suggests that this group has less married reproductive time available to have children, so that late marriage is likely to result in low birthrates.

There is an apparent increase in intentional childlessness. Whereas in 1960 only 20 per cent of ever-married women under twenty-five (the age by which most women have their first child) were childless, by 1975 the figure had increased to 32 per cent. The percentage of women under thirty who indicated in surveys that they expected to have no children, although small, had grown considerably in the 1960s and 1970s: from 1.7 per cent in 1964 to 4.6 per cent in 1975 (Silka, Kiesler, 1977).

Intentionally childless marriages are becoming a more acceptable option. The National Organization for Non-Parents is widely disseminating studies that show that some 10 per cent of parents regret having children and that married couples are happier when childless. One of the organization's slogans, from the prophet Isaiah, is "Thou hast multiplied the nation but not increased the joy." A series of recent books presents the case for remaining childless (Peck, 1971; Silverman, Silverman, 1971; Peck, Senderowitz, 1974; Whelan, 1975). The decrease in the number of children in the population is, however, largely the result

of more people's waiting and having fewer children, only a very small component of the decrease being attributable to couples who choose to have none. In
1975 less than 5 per cent of married women indicated that they planned not to
have any children. With the more widespread availability of birth control,
backed by abortion, women are more likely to have only the number of children they want. In support of their determination to limit family size, a surprisingly large number of Americans have been sterilized: "By 1975 nearly half of
couples married 10–24 years were surgically sterilized" (Westoff, Jones, 1977,
p. 157).

If other factors remain constant, therefore, the demand for child welfare
services may decline during the coming decade as a consequence of these factors,
which suggest continued low birthrates.

The teenage population during the 1975–1985 decade will decrease as the
bulge of teenagers born during the high-birthrate years of the late 1960s moves
out of adolescence, replaced by a smaller teenage group reflecting the lower
birthrate of the early 1970s. The teenage group is a group that requires many
different kinds of social services, so that a reduction in the proportion of this
age group in the total population will be reflected in some reduction in the pressure of demand for services.

Countering the reduction in demand for service resulting from the decreased number of young children and teenagers, the group of female adults
between twenty and twenty-nine, which yields a disproportionately high percentage of applicants for child welfare services, including Aid to Families of
Dependent Children, will increase by some 34 per cent between 1970 and 1985
—from 15 million to about 20 million, reflecting the higher birthrates of the late
1960s. During this period, this birth group will be marrying, having children in
and out of wedlock, divorcing and separating, and contributing to the number
of single-parent families.

Furthermore, although there will be a smaller total pool of children in 1980
for which services might be needed, a growing proportion of the smaller pool is
apt to require services because of increases in a variety of family factors resulting
in family disruption. Therefore there may be a continuing and, speculatively,
even a greater need for child welfare services in the 1980s.

The trend is toward a more favorable child-dependency ratio. The largest
proportionate increase in population projected between 1970 and 1980 is in the
twenty–thirty-nine age group, from 26 per cent to 31.6 per cent of the total population. This is the age population of productive adults who will be working, producing, and paying taxes. At the same time, the proportion of the population that
consists of younger, dependent children will be smaller in the immediate future.

The projected increase in the proportion of the population consisting of
productive adults coupled with the decrease in the proportion of the population
consisting of young children results in a more favorable child-dependency ratio
—proportionately fewer dependent children being cared for by a proportionately
larger population of productive adults. When the ratio of dependent children
to productive adults is low—when there is a favorable child-dependency ratio—
the community is in a more advantageous economic position to provide adequate
services for those children who need them.

Between 1970 and 1976, because of the decrease in the proportion of children in the population, the overall dependency ratio decreased. This ratio is the

number of dependents in the population—children under eighteen and senior citizens over sixty-five—to every one hundred adults between the ages of eighteen and sixty-four. In 1970 the dependency ratio was 78.2, and it was 69.4 in 1976. Reduction in the dependency ratio was dampened by the fact that the group of older dependents is increasing at the same time that the population of children is decreasing, having increased from some 20 million in 1970 to some 23 million in 1976.

The allocation of resources to care for dependent groups in the population is primarily a political decision that follows a country's economic capacity. There is, currently, intensified competition for the increasingly limited tax dollar. In this competition, demographic trends might ultimately have crucial significance. A declining percentage of the population consists of children; a growing percentage of the population consists of the aged. The aged, as contrasted with children, not only have the vote but are organized effectively politically. It is likely, then, that in any shoot-out for the more limited tax funds available in the future, the needs of the dependent aged may take precedence over the needs of the population of dependent children and may affect adequacy of funding for child welfare services.

The Unwanted Child

We owe the child the right to be conceived and born as a wanted child if we are to reduce the need for child welfare services. The deliberate decision to conceive implies readiness to have a child and favorable conditions for his reception. An unwanted pregnancy may reflect unfavorable child-care conditions and, hence, increases the probability of need for child welfare services. Family planning involves not only limiting the number of children but also timing their arrival to coincide with the family's readiness to welcome a new member.

There currently appears to be more effective family planning among all groups in the population, although a higher percentage of unwanted pregnancies occurs among nonwhites and the poor (Okada, Gillespie, 1977).

The illegitimately conceived child, like the deformed child, runs a high risk of being unwanted and constitutes a higher than normal potential need for child welfare services. Making contraceptive information and devices available to the unmarried helps reduce the risk of illegitimate children. And programs of abortion on demand are already beginning to have some impact on the number of illegitimate births.

As a consequence of the greater availability of family-planning counseling, genetic counseling, and abortions, the *trend is in the direction of a greater number of children being wanted at birth.*

Unwanted marital fertility has continued to decline, so that by 1973 fewer than 9 per cent of births to married women were unplanned: "The largest percentage of unwanted births was reported to poor blacks—23 percent—but this group showed the steepest decline in unwanted fertility of all the poverty status and racial groups examined" (Weller, Hobb, 1978, p. 172). This decline reduces the number of children who tax their families' capacity to care for them and who consequently constitute a potential demand for child welfare services.

The use of abortion with programs of amniocentesis—determination of genetic defects in the fetus—has resulted in the reduction of the number of children with congenital anomalies and hence a reduction in the need for child welfare services. Before 1968 such centers did not exist; by 1976 there were some 140 such facilities throughout the United States (*New York Times,* December 4, 1977).

Infant and Child Mortality

Once he is conceived as a wanted child, we owe the child the right to life. *The trend has been toward a steady decrease in infant and child mortality.* Infant mortality rates have declined steadily from 26 per thousand live births in 1960 to 15 in 1977. Nevertheless, our mortality rate was higher than those of fifteen other industrialized countries in 1975–1976. The United States slipped from eighth place in 1955 to sixteenth in 1977 (see Table 2–1). Countries with lower infant mortality rates included the Scandinavian countries, the Netherlands, Japan, the United Kingdom, Australia, France, and West Germany.

Although the infant mortality rate among nonwhites in the United States is declining, it is still consistently higher than the rate among whites, so that the chances of a nonwhite child's dying in its first year are twice as high as those of a white child. In this case, race is a less significant factor than poverty, the lack of adequate prenatal and postnatal medical care available to the poor, and

TABLE 2–1. Infant Mortality Rate: Selected Countries in Rank Order

		Year	*Mortality Rate*
1.	Sweden	1976	8.7
2.	Japan	1975	10.1
3.	Denmark	1975	10.4
4.	Czechoslovakia	1975	10.4
5.	Finland	1976	10.5
6.	Netherlands	1976	10.5
7.	Switzerland	1975	10.7
8.	Norway	1975	11.1
9.	France	1975	11.3
10.	West Germany	1975	11.3
11.	Singapore	1976	11.6
12.	Spain	1975	12.1
13.	England–Wales	1976	14
14.	Australia	1976	14.3
15.	Scotland	1976	14.8
16.	United States	1976	15.1
17.	New Zealand	1975	16
18.	Austria	1976	18.3
19.	Israel	1975	22.9
20.	Poland	1976	23.8
21.	USSR	1974	27.7

Demographic Yearbook 1976, 28th Issue (New York: United Nations, 1977), Table 14, pp. 305–308.

limited access to contraceptive information and devices that would permit more desirable spacing of pregnancies. In fact, the infant mortality rate among poor whites in the United States is still higher than that among equivalent populations in many other countries. If the United States were ranked on the basis of infant mortality rates among whites alone, it would still have a less favorable ranking than thirteen other countries. The high proportions of births to mothers under twenty, among whom the risk of low-birth-weight infants and infant mortality is higher, was an additional factor contributing to our low comparative standing (Wegman, 1977).

Family Disruption: Divorce, Desertion, Illegitimacy

Once guaranteed the right to life, we owe the child the opportunity to grow up in an intact home under the care of both a father and a mother. The loss of either or both parents increases the risk of the need for child welfare service. *The trend of family disruption arising from the death of a parent has been downward.*

Marrying at the median age of 21.6 in 1977 and bearing few children, the modern mother is likely to complete her childbearing phase earlier in life. This, coupled with an increase in life expectancy for both sexes, means that most parents will live through the full period of dependency of their children. Thus there has been a steady decrease in the absolute and relative numbers of orphans— from 6.5 million in 1920 (some 16 per cent of the child population) to 3.4 million orphans in 1977 (some 5 per cent of the child population).

Maternal mortality, as one cause of partial orphanhood, has also been decreasing. Although decreasing along with white maternal mortality rates, the rate of maternal mortality among nonwhites was about three times higher than that among whites in 1975. Although life expectancy for both whites and nonwhites has increased, the nonwhite child is more likely than a white to lose a parent as a result of death. By 1976 life expectancy was 69.7 years for white males and 77.3 for white females, but only 64.1 years for nonwhite males and 72.6 years for nonwhite females. The difference, however, is narrowing.

Although death of parents is less frequently a cause of family disruption, there is an increase in other significant forms of family disruption. *The trend is toward an increase in divorce, in desertions, and in illegitimacy.* All of these trends increase the potential need of child welfare services.

In the two decades following the end of World War II, divorce rates stabilized. Since 1965, however, there has been a steady rise, from 2.5 per thousand in 1965 to 5.1 per thousand in 1978. The number of divorces granted increased from 479,000 in 1965 to 1,122,000 in 1978. Of greater immediate significance for increasing the need for child welfare services is the fact that more and more often children tend to be involved in divorce actions. During the 1965–1975 decade, the number of children involved in divorce more than doubled, reaching over 1 million children by 1975. Although previously more marriages than families were dissolving as a result of divorce, the reverse is currently true. In 1950, 56 per cent of the divorces involved childless marriages; in 1973 this was true of only 40 per cent of the divorces. Every divorce involving a child precipitates a situation in which child welfare services may be called upon to meet the unfilled paternal roles. Some percentage of these children regain a father on remarriage of the mother, but many continue to grow up in a single-parent home.

> The phenomenal upswing of divorce in this country has been stimulated by the growing acceptance of the principle that divorce is a reasonable and at times a desirable alternative to an unhappy marriage. While the negative sanctions have lessened, so too have the legal and economic constraints involved in obtaining divorces [Norton, Glick, 1976, p. 12].

No-fault divorce had been adopted by 1974 in twenty-three states and residence requirements had been shortened. The greater availability of free legal services and simplified and destigmatized divorce proceedings have made divorces less prohibitively expensive. All the preceding have reduced barriers that previously inhibited divorce. These legal and ideological changes are reinforced by the reduction in economic constraints to divorce as families have fewer children and more women achieve independence through employment. There is evidence that the divorce rate is slowing down to a more traditional upward pace. The growth in the divorce rate has slowed considerably in comparison with the period between 1967 and 1973, when the annual rate of increase was 11.5 per cent. There was little change in the divorce rate between 1973 and 1978. And even those people who get divorced do not reject marriage but merely their marital partner: 80 per cent of divorced people remarry, "a triumph of hope over experience," as Samuel Johnson once said.

Separations and desertions affect almost as many children as divorce, although statistical data are difficult to compile. Marital disruption is more frequent among urban families, among low-income groups, and among nonwhites. Desertion, traditionally the "poor man's divorce," may run as high as 400,000–500,000 each year (Freed, Foster, 1969).

Although blacks had a higher divorce rate than whites in 1977, the proportional increase between the two groups during the seventeen years from 1960 to 1977 was very similar: the ratio for blacks had risen 160 per cent and for whites 136 per cent.

Income is inversely related to family disruption: as income goes down, family disruption goes up. The higher disruption rate for black families, then, is tied to the fact that a disproportionate percentage of the black population have low incomes.

Another factor of significance for child welfare services is the *trend toward a continued gradual increase in the number of illegitimate * births*. In 1977, 515,700 out-of-wedlock births were reported based on information from thirty-eight states and the District of Columbia. This number constituted 16.5 per cent

---

* The Juvenile Rights Project of the American Civil Liberties Union has suggested the terms *marital* and *nonmarital* child to replace *legitimate* and *illegitimate,* which have negative connotations. A marital child is one whose parents were married at the time of the child's birth or whose parents later "legitimized" the child by marriage or court order. Although I am in full sympathy with the point of view expressed, the use of *legitimate* and *illegitimate* in statistics and literature is so standard and the terms are used with such specific meaning that a changeover here would only result in confusion. I have therefore regretfully retained the traditional terms but use the less invidious term *out of wedlock* where this can be done without changing the meaning of the statistic or the quotation.

of all live births during that year. In contrast, in 1965, there had been 291,200 births out of wedlock, 7.7 per cent of all live births. Because these figures are affected by the total number of unmarried fecund women in the population and the variations in the total number of live births, the number of children per 1,000 unmarried women aged fifteen to forty-four is perhaps a more accurate measure of change. This rate indicates a gradual change from 23.5 in 1965 to 26 in 1977. The rate in 1977 was, in fact, lower than in 1970, when it was 26.4.

Child welfare services are, however, concerned with the increasing numbers of illegitimate children born. Of particular concern is the rise in both the numbers and the rate of out-of-wedlock births in the teenage population—the age group that might have the greatest difficulty in caring for such children. In 1976 about one out of every ten white women fifteen to nineteen years old had a premarital pregnancy (Zelnick, Kantner, 1978).

For the age group at greatest risk for the need for child welfare services, the fifteen- to nineteen-year-olds, the illegitimacy rate increased for white women between 1971 and 1975 but decreased for black women. For 1,000 white unmarried teenage women, the rate increased from 10.3 in 1971 to 12.1 in 1975; for black women the rate decreased from 99.1 to 95.1 during the same period (Zelnik, Kantner, 1978, p. 19).

There is a significant difference in the incidence of illegitimacy among whites and nonwhites, although the difference is narrowing. In 1950 the rate was nearly twelve times higher among nonwhites than among whites. Since 1960 the rate among whites has increased, whereas that among nonwhites has decreased, so that by 1975 the latter was only about 6.4 times higher than the former. (The historical, social, and economic reasons for these differences are discussed in Chapter 9). Figure 2–1 recapitulates some of the vital statistics.

The trend is toward an increase in the percentage of children growing up in a one-parent home. However, the great majority of American children grow up in an intact home under the care of two parents. As a matter of fact, during the past one hundred years, decreases in parental death during childhood dependency have offset the increases in divorce, desertion, and illegitimacy. Consequently, the child today has a better chance of growing up in an unbroken home than a child born in 1870. The short-range trend, however, is toward a clear, sharp increase in one-parent homes (Bane, 1976a, b).

In 1960 some 91 per cent of all American children lived in a two-parent home. In 1977 only 79.2 per cent of all children under eighteen were growing up in a home with both parents, and one child in every six was living in a single-parent family.

Between 1970 and 1977 female-headed family households increased by 37 per cent, while husband–wife households increased by 6 per cent. The increase in single-parent families has been most rapid among young families with young children, among low-income families, and among nonwhite families.

If the rate of single-parent families has increased more rapidly than the increase in husband–wife families, the rate of increase of single-parent families with children under six has increased even more rapidly.

Black women heading families were younger than white women in this status. In 1977 the median age of black women heading families was 38.7 as compared with a median age of 44.7 for white women. White women were more likely to be heads of families as a result of divorce or widowhood; black women

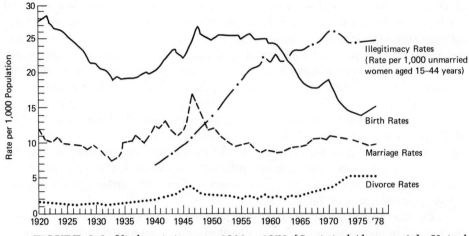

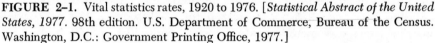

FIGURE 2–1. Vital statistics rates, 1920 to 1976. [*Statistical Abstract of the United States, 1977.* 98th edition. U.S. Department of Commerce, Bureau of the Census. Washington, D.C.: Government Printing Office, 1977.]

were more likely to be in this position because they had never been married. Hispanic women heading families were as young as black women and became heads of families for similar reasons.

In talking about those children who did not live with two parents in 1977, we are talking about some 14 million children—10.5 million children living in a single-parent family headed by a mother, 900,000 children living in a single-parent family headed by a father, and some 3 million children living in foster homes, in institutions, or with relatives.

In this, too, the white child has an advantage: in 1977 about 84.8 per cent of all white children—but only 46.1 per cent of black children—were growing up in a two-parent home. Black children living with neither parent were more frequently cared for by grandparents than was true for white children living with neither parent—8.5 per cent of black children under three as contrasted with 1.6 per cent of white children under three (U.S. Bureau of the Census, April 1978, Table 4, p. 26).

Because such statistics are cross-sectional—counting children at some particular time—they underestimate the percentage of children who are likely to be affected by a family disruption at any time during their childhood.

As a consequence of high rates of marital dissolution due to divorce, separation, desertion, and, to a much more limited extent, death, plus the continuing high rates of illegitimacy, it is estimated that in the near future, only a bare majority (55–60 per cent) of all children will grow up in traditional two-parent households in continuous, permanent, undisrupted contact with both of their biological parents (Bane, 1976, p. 110).

It might be noted that although in 1976 some 80 per cent of all children were living in a two-parent family, only 67 per cent were living with their two biological parents. Thirteen per cent of the children were living with a step-parent in a reconstituted family following divorce or the death of one parent or following the marriage of an unwed mother to a man who was not the father of the child (Carter, Glick, 1976, p. 41).

Income is a very significant factor in family disruption, although race plays some part (Billingsley, 1969; Cutright, 1971; Farley, Hermalin, 1971; Hill, 1972): "The effects of income level . . . [are] about five times as strong as the effects of race. Female-headed families are five times more characteristic of poor families than of black families" (Ten Houton, 1970, p. 153). Among whites and nonwhites, "the percentage of families headed by a woman moves steadily downward as family income rises" (Stein, 1970, p. 5). But because the percentage of female-headed families is higher among nonwhites at every income level, the factor of race would seem also to be significant. It should be noted, however, that Glick (1978) estimates that "probably one-fourth to one-third of the difference between black families and white families reported as maintained by a woman could be explained by the much larger [census] undercount by black men than for white men" (p. 4).

The evident importance of these statistics is that a child in a one-parent home, or a child without parents, is a greater than normal risk for the need of child welfare services. The increase in the number of such families increases the likelihood of demand for such services.

The single-parent family is achieving acceptance as a "normal," nonpathological child-rearing environment and as a respectable family form. The increase in the percentage and number of children living in single-parent households makes them progressively less atypical and more statistically "normal." As previously noted (Chapter 1) there is no inherent pathology in the single-parent family form (Kadushin, 1970; Herzog, Sudia, 1973). However, it is a more difficult arrangement to carry off successfully, if only because the single-parent family is much more likely to be economically deprived.

There is a clear relationship between low family income and the single-parent family structure. If there is some question as to whether single parenthood is a hazard to the emotional and psychological development of children, there is a greater certainty that children in single-parent female-headed families face economic disabilities.

Fifty per cent of female-headed families with children under 18 had incomes below the officially defined poverty level in 1977. By contrast, this was true of only 8.5 per cent of husband–wife families with children under 18. In addition, the dual-parent family has more assured status in our country; the laws and the mores have been developed largely in support of this kind of family structure; two parents provide the possibility of division of labor that makes the job of parenting less exhausting; and the presence of two parents diminishes the possibility of an excessively intense parent–child relationship and provides an extra buffer between one parent and the child in time of crisis. In addition, the dual-parent family provides a greater variety of role models with whom the child can identify in a highly cathected relationship, and it provides a backup parent in the case of the loss or the incapacity of one parent. In our society at the present time, the nuclear, monogamous, heterosexual family, whatever its faults and shortcomings, seems to be the context in which adequate, committed, and continuous long-term care of children, involving frequent, regular, consistent, and positive parent–child interaction, seems most probable and feasible. Other variant (not deviant) arrangements—single-parent families, communal families, sequential monogamous families—are possible but more difficult contexts for providing for the needs of both parents and children.

Whatever the reasons, the fact of the matter is that single-parent households are currently represented disproportionately in the case loads of child welfare agencies, suggesting a heightened need for service on the part of such families. The 1975 Census of Requests for Child Welfare Services (Haring, 1975) indicates that 41 per cent of the 1,924 families for whom services were requested during a one-week period were single-parent families—38 per cent headed by a woman, 3 per cent headed by a man (Haring, Table 8, p. 14). In a study of child welfare services offered to children in their own home (Sherman et al., 1973), 53 per cent of the sample of families studied were single-parent families—52 per cent mother-headed, 1 per cent father-headed (Table 3.1, p. 31). A nationwide study of clients of family service agencies found that "single parent families are disproportionately heavy users of family service" (Beck, Jones, 1973, p. 17).

Of the 1,800,000 children estimated to have received social services from public agencies in 1977, 45 per cent were in single-parent homes (Shyne, Schroeder, 1978, p. 9). In 1976 16.4 per cent of all families were single-parent families. The percentage of single-parent families in the child-welfare-agency case loads is then clearly disproportionate to the percentage of such families in the general population.

The 1975 recipient-characteristic study of families receiving assistance through the Aid to Families of Dependent Children (AFDC) showed that 80 per cent of all such families were single-parent families headed by a woman (Oberheu, 1977, p. 2). One can counter the statistic that 80 per cent of all AFDC recipient families are single-parent families headed by a woman by noting that only 35 per cent of single-headed families are receiving assistance. However, that 35 per cent is a much higher figure than the percentage of two-parent families receiving assistance.

All of this is not to suggest that problems requiring child welfare services are inevitable for the single-parent family, only that they are more likely.

Poverty: A Factor in the Need for Child Welfare Services

Poverty is another factor that increases the potential need for child welfare services. The family living on the edge of poverty faces stresses that increase the probability of failure in parental role performance and the probability of family disruption. We owe the child the right to be wanted, the right to life, and the right to grow up in the loving care of both a father and a mother; we owe him, further, the right to grow up in a family that has sufficient resources to meet his basic needs. *The trend over the past decade has been toward a reduction in the percentage and number of children living in poverty.*

It is difficult to define poverty. There is a controversy over whether poverty can be defined in absolute terms or whether it is a subjective, individual sense of deprivation. Even if one accepts the idea that poverty can be defined in absolute terms, there is still the problem of deciding what standard measures can be applied to calculate the level of income actually needed by a family (Merriam, 1968; Orshansky, 1969). During the 1960s, the federal government used a poverty index that is widely accepted and that has been periodically adjusted in response to rises in the cost of living. By 1979 the poverty index for a nonfarm family of four was $6,700.

In 1959 it was estimated that some 16 million children—about 25 per cent of all American children—were living in poverty. Ten years later, in 1969, some 10.5 million children—about 15.8 per cent of all American children—were living in poverty.

Although some substantial reductions had been made in the percentage of the population living in poverty during the 1959–1969 decade, between 1969 and 1977 there was little change. In 1977, 11 million children were living in poverty—17 per cent of all children under 18. If we weren't losing the war against poverty, we weren't winning it either in the 1970 decade.

Reduction in the poverty population during the period did not result from any substantial redistribution of income in the United States.

Between 1950 and 1975, there had been some redistribution of income, but it was slight. The income of the lowest 20 per cent of the population in 1950 was 4.5 per cent of the total aggregated income, the income of the highest 20 per cent was 42.7 per cent of the total. By 1977 these figures were 5.2 per cent for the lowest 20 per cent of the population and 41.5 per cent for the highest 20 per cent. The gap between the poor and the affluent in America remains almost as wide as ever.

The poverty population of the United States is, in large measure, a population of children and adults in single-parent female-headed family units, and disproportionately nonwhite. Not all groups shared equally in the benefits from the war against poverty achieved between 1959 and 1969. The principal victories during the 1960s were won for the white family headed by a male. Nonwhite families and families headed by a woman made fewer gains; nonwhite families headed by a woman made fewer still. Finally, although the number of people below the poverty line dropped by almost 40 per cent, to 24 million, from 1959 to 1969, the decline for whites was about 25 per cent more rapid than that for nonwhites.

However, over the seventeen-year period 1960–1977, gains were made for both black and white children. The 19.2 per cent of white children who had been living in poverty in 1960 was reduced to 11.3 per cent in 1977; whereas 65.6 per cent of black children had been living in poverty in 1960, the 1977 figure was 40.4 per cent—lower than in 1960 but still four times higher than the white rate.

Nonwhite workers are still heavily overrepresented in low-income groups, and the unemployment rate for blacks was, throughout the decade, nearly double that for whites. Because they hold poorer-paying jobs and are subject to higher rates of unemployment, nonwhite families have lagged substantially behind white families in income. Although blacks constituted some 12 per cent of the population, they made up about 33 per cent of the total population in poverty in 1977.

Poverty is related to some of the other contingencies that tend to increase the likelihood that a family will require child welfare services. Divorce, separation, widowhood (when there are young children in the family), and unmarried motherhood involve not only a problem in family organization resulting from the loss of a father figure but also a great probability of a sharply reduced family income. One of the growing pockets of poverty in the United States is that of the family headed by a woman.

Over time, the single-parent family has become an increasing proportion of all the families at lower income levels. Not only are such families increasing in number, but two-parent families move out of poverty more rapidly than one-parent families, leaving behind a greater concentration of such families and their children in the lower income group. In 1959 only one fifth of all poor children were found in female-headed households; by 1977 slightly over half of all poor children were concentrated in such families.

Median family income of male-headed black families has lagged consistently behind the median family income of male-headed white families. And median family income for female-headed families lagged significantly behind the median income for male-headed families, white or black. In 1976 the median income of a white family headed by a male was $16,501; of a black family headed by a black male, $13,137. During the same year, the median family income for a family headed by a white female was $8,226; that for a family headed by a black female was $5,069.

Controlling for level of education still shows a difference between the income of black and white males. White men who had completed high school had a median income of $10,463 in 1975. Black men with the same amount of

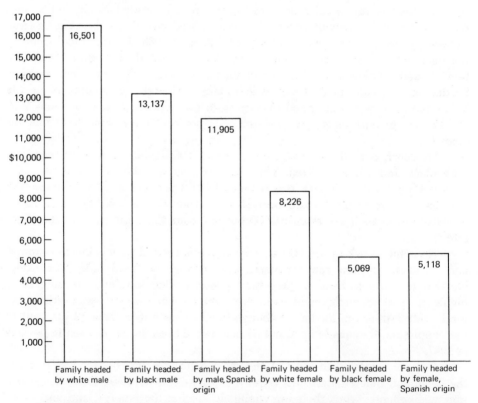

FIGURE 2–2. Median family income by head of family and race, 1976. The richest families are likely to be families headed by a white male; the poorest families are likely to be families headed by a black female. [*Population Profile of the United States, 1977.* U.S. Department of Commerce, Bureau of the Census Series P-20, No. 324, April 1978.]

schooling had a median income of $7,468. There is a similar disparity in income between white and black males who had completed three or more years of college education (Coleman, 1977, p. 18).

Because there are many more white than non-white children in the country, although most nonwhite children are poor, most poor children are white. In terms of the actual numbers of children affected, poverty is a problem for whites, particularly for the white child living in a family headed by a female. In 1977 three were 6 million white children living in poverty and 3.8 million black children living in poverty.

The large family, like the nonwhite family and the family headed by a woman, is apt to be poor. Native American children and children of Spanish origin are also apt to be poor.

Starting in the mid-1970s, census data began to include material on people of "Spanish origin" as a separate category. Such data were not available earlier. There were 11.3 million persons of Spanish origin in the population in 1977— 6.5 million persons of Mexican origin; 1.7 million of Puerto Rican origin; 700,000 of Cuban origin; and 2.3 million of Central or South American or other Spanish origin. In general, children in families of Spanish origin were not as well off as white children, but they are less disadvantaged than black children. Children under eighteen composed a larger percentage of this group (42.3 per cent) than the percentage of children in the white or black group, so that the median age of this group was younger—21.7 years, as compared with 23 for the black population and 30 for the white population.

Persons of Spanish origin, comprising 4.5 per cent of the population of the United States, had 4,766,800 children under eighteen in 1977. Median family income was slightly higher than that of the black population, but lower than the median income of white families (see Figure 2–2). Some 23 per cent of these families lived below the poverty level. There were more female-headed families among this group than was true for the white population, but fewer such families as compared with the black population.

Working Mothers

Although many mothers work because they want to, most mothers—particularly mothers of pre-school-aged children—work because they have to. The lower the family income, the more likely it is that the mother will be working. *The trend has been toward an increase in working mothers, particularly mothers of preschool children.*

This poses a problem of interrole conflict—the role of mother versus the role of employee—and dictates the need for some temporary substitute child-care service for the dependent child. In 1960 20 per cent of mothers with children under six were working; by 1978, 41 per cent of such mothers were employed. This meant that over 6.5 million preschool children shared their mothers with employers. (A more detailed analysis of the working mother is included in Chapter 8.)

The participation of mothers in the labor force has some benefits, however. It increases the income level of many families, thus permitting the families to meet the needs of children more adequately; it also moves the child-dependency ratio in a favorable direction because it results in an expansion of the work force and an increase in the country's productivity.

Labor-force participation rates of Hispanic women were lower than for either whites or blacks. They were more likely to have younger dependent children in the home. There may be less of a tradition of out-of-home employment for this group.

The rapid change of the American family from a single-wage-earner family to a family of both husband and wife as wage earners has implications for the need for child welfare services. As a result of the increase in the number of working mothers, many families have moved out of poverty, have been able to provide more adequately for children, and have built up a cushion of resources enabling the family to deal with transient cases without requiring agency service. In 1977 median annual income for a husband–wife-wage-earner family was $17,570. This compares with a median income of $14,543 for a husband-only wage-earner family.

However, increases in the rate and number of working mothers with children under six increase the need for child day-care services. Increases in the number of mothers in the labor force affect child welfare services in another way as well. Withdrawing from traditional neighboring and volunteering roles in favor of paid employment increases the demands on formal, organized child welfare agencies.

Minority-Group Status: A Factor in the Need for Child Welfare Services

Being nonwhite is a major factor increasing the probability that child welfare services may be needed. Every applicable social indicator reveals the relative disadvantage of the nonwhite American. Among nonwhites, infant and maternal mortality rates, illegitimacy rates and family disruption rates, and unemployment rates are higher. The percentage of nonwhites living in poverty is higher than that of whites, as is the percentage of young children whose mothers are working and the percentage who live in dilapidated, substandard housing. Illiteracy rates are higher among nonwhites, as are high-school dropout rates, crime rates, and rates of victimization from crime. The incidence of disabling illnesses is higher among nonwhites; the percentage of children under seventeen who have never seen a dentist is higher. Life expectancy is also lower; median income is lower; lifetime earnings are lower; level of education achievement is lower; frequency of accessibility to adequate medical care is lower; accessibility to higher-status jobs is lower; home ownership is lower; the percentage of the group covered by any kind of health insurance is lower (U.S. Department of Commerce, 1975).

As a consequence of their disadvantaged position, the nonwhite population provides a disproportionately large group of recipients of all of the welfare services and a disproportionately large group needing such services.

Table 2–2 recapitulates some of the statistical changes in 1960–1977 that are significant for child welfare services. For purposes of comparison, statistics for whites and blacks are reported separately. The figures generally show improvement for both whites and blacks, but they also reveal the comparatively more favorable situation of the white population.

TABLE 2–2. Trends Relevant to Child Welfare Services

Relevant Factor	Years	White	Black
Birth rate (per 1,000 population)	1960	22.7	32.1
	1965	18.3	27.6
	1970	15.5	25.2
	1976	13.8	21.1
Infant mortality (per 1,000 live births)	1960	22.9	43.2
	1965	21.5	40.3
	1970	17.4	31.4
	1977	13.3	23.5
Maternal mortality	1960	26	97.9
(per 100,000 live births)	1965	21	83.7
	1970	14.4	55.9
	1975	9.1	29
Life expectancy at birth	1960	70.6	63.6
(Total: male and female)	1965	71	64.1
	1970	71.7	65.3
	1976	73.5	68.3
Median annual family income	1960	$ 5,835	$3,233
	1965	$ 7,251	$3,994
	1970	$10,236	$6,541
	1977	$16,740	$9,560
Percentage of population	1960	18	56
below poverty level	1965	13	47
	1970	10	32
	1977	8.9	29
Unemployment rates (annual average)	1960	4.9	10.2
	1965	4.1	8.1
	1970	4.5	8.2
	1977	6.2	13.1
Illegitimacy rate (per 1,000 unmarried	1960	9.2	98.3
women 15–44 years of age)	1965	11.6	97.6
	1970	13.8	86.6
	1976	12.7	78.1
Divorce (per 1,000 total population;	1960	2.2	
not available by race)	1965	2.5	
	1971	3.7	
	1977	5.1	
Percentage of mothers in labor force	1966	24	40
(with children under 6)	1971	29	47
	1976	35.5	53.2

TABLE 2–2. (Continued)

Relevant Factor	Years	White	Black
Own children living with	1960	92	75
both parents as a percentage of	1965	91	71
all children in the racial group	1970	87	57
	1977	84.8	46.1
Number and percentage of children	1960	55,476,000	8,723,000
in population of racial group		35.8%	42.0%
	1970	51,062,000	9,509,000
		31.1%	42.1%
	1977	53,641,000	9,398,000
		29.1%	38.4%
Percentage of children in families	1960	19.2	65.5
below poverty level	1965	14.4	57.3
	1970	9.7	39.6
	1976	11.3	40.4

CHANGING VALUES

Statistical trends regarding the number of children at risk and trends regarding the social contingencies that directly affect the number of children possibly needing child welfare services are very important factors helping us to understand the context in which such services are offered. Of importance, too, is the nature of ideological changes.

We are currently undergoing a change in attitudes toward parenthood that may affect the context in which child welfare services are offered. The concern with zero population growth and the movement for changes in the status of women have diminished the prestige formerly accorded the status of parent. Parenthood is no longer unanimously and enthusiastically applauded, and having more than two children may shortly be regarded as socially irresponsible, if not actually illegal.

With fewer children and increased life expectancy, women are currently finding that only a relatively small percentage of their productive years is devoted to the full-time maternal role. The average woman may be a full-time mother for about ten years, and as she is capable of being fully productive for a period of some thirty to thirty-five years, the woman who has dedicated herself to motherhood finds herself with either a part-time job or no job at all for a good part of her life. This fact supports and reinforces the orientation of the women's movement and the population control groups toward a deemphasis on motherhood and a search for alternative lifestyles for women. Currently the idea of parenthood as an important, significant life goal is open to question and debate, and childless marriages are more acceptable than they once were. The greater availability and acceptance of contraceptive devices backed up by legalized abortion help to reinforce these changes in ideology.

There is currently a greater acceptance of a wider variety of child-rearing contexts and less consensus that the nuclear family is the most desirable. The report of the 1970 decennial conference on children points to the "wide diversity of family forms"—nuclear family, extended family, single-parent family, commune —and supports acceptance of "differential family forms" according to their appropriateness and effectiveness in particular situations. The report noted that "There is a need to make visible the increased variability in family forms and to recognize the right of individuals to live in any family form they feel will increase their options for self-fulfillment" (U.S. White House Conference on Children, 1970a, p. 232).

There is a growing acceptance, too, of the idea that the responsibility for rearing a child is shared by the parents and the community. The idea of joint responsibility leads to a greater acceptance of day-care centers and other community-centered arrangements for progressively earlier implementation of the partnership.

There has been an increase in concern about offering adequate service to black families and black children on the part of the child welfare agencies during the past decade, in sharp contrast to the earlier disinterest documented by Billingsley and Giovannoni (1972) in their historical review of services to black children. This change resulted partially from the migration of the black population from southern rural centers to northern urban centers, where more adequate services are found, and from the relative decrease in demand for services on the part of white families and children. The major cause, however, lies in the ideological shifts that resulted from the Civil Rights movement of the 1960s, which focused attention on the problems of all minority groups. Institutional racism, as manifested in policies of child welfare services, came under critical review and led to recommendations for policy changes.

SUMMARY

This chapter has been concerned with developing a historical perspective on child welfare services and attempting to place child welfare services within the current context of American society. A number of factors were discussed to help explain the fact that although child welfare problems have been encountered throughout history, only recently has a special institution such as social-work child welfare services been organized. Among the factors discussed were the following:

1. The inadmissibility of previous solutions and changes in ideology.
2. The greater productivity of the community in making possible the support of a large group of dependents.
3. The increased specialization of social institutions.
4. The "discovery" of childhood.
5. Changes in the arithmetic of production.
6. The increased status of the family and the child.
7. The scientific revolution and the development of a science of child rearing.

The American experience presents some special considerations that heighten the tendency to elevate the status of the child and increase the concern for his needs. The immigrant status of most parents and the strong future orientation in the United States help to emphasize this filiocentric trend.

Among current trends in American society of relevance to child welfare services, the following aspects were discussed:

1. Recent relative decreases in the size of the child population.
2. The changes in child-dependency ratios occasioned by the changing demography.
3. Changes in the life cycle of the family and their effect on childhood dependency.
4. Continued decreases in infant, child, and maternal mortality, and increases in life expectancy.
5. The family disruption caused by the increase in divorce rates, increases in the number of children affected by divorce, increases in illegitimacy rates, and reduction in death rates of the parents. Other factors related to changes in family functioning, such as the increase in the number of working mothers, were also discussed.
6. The prevalance of poverty in the United States, particularly among families headed by a woman and among nonwhite families.
7. Membership in a minority group as a factor in increasing the risk of need for child welfare services because of higher rates of family disruption (through divorce, separation, death, illegitimacy), lower family income, and fewer employment opportunities.
8. Ideological changes regarding childless marriages, family planning, abortion, and the nature of the family.

BIBLIOGRAPHY

ARIES, PHILIPPE. *Centuries of Childhood.* New York: Alfred A. Knopf, Inc., 1962.

ATHERTON, CHARLES R. "The Social Assignment of Social Work." *Social Service Review,* 43, 4 (December 1969), 421–429.

BAKAN, DAVID. *Slaughter of the Innocents—A Study of the Battered Child Phenomenon.* San Francisco: Jossey-Bass, Inc., 1971.

BANE, MARY JO. *Here to Stay: American Families in the 20th Century.* New York: Basic Books, Inc., 1976a.

———. "Marital Disruption and the Lives of Children." *Journal of Social Services,* 32 (1976b), 103–116.

BECK, DOROTHY F., and MARY A. JONES. *Progress on Family Problems—A Nationwide Study of Clients' and Counselors' Views of Family Agency Service.* New York: Family Service Association of America, 1973.

BENNETT, H. "The Exposure of Infants in Ancient Rome." *Classical Journal,* 13 (1923), 341–351.

BILLINGSLEY, ANDREW. "Family Functioning in the Low. Income Black Community." *Social Casework,* 50, 10 (December 1969), 563–572.

———, and JEANNE M. GIOVANNONI. *Children of the Storm—Black Children and American Child Welfare.* New York: Harcourt Brace Jovanovich, Inc., 1972.

BLYTHE, RONALD. *Akenfield—Portrait of an English Village.* New York: Delta Paperbook, 1969.

BOSSARD, JAMES H. S., and ELEANOR S. BOLL. *The Sociology of Childhood,* 4th ed. New York: Harper & Row, Publishers, 1966.

BREMNER, ROBERT H. (Ed.). *Children and Youth in America—A Documentary History*, Vol. 1, pp. 1600–1865. Cambridge, Mass.: Harvard University Press, 1970.

CAMERON, A. "The Exposure of Children and Greek Ethics." *The Classical Review*, **46** (1932), 105–114.

CARTER, HUGH, and PAUL C. GLICK. *Marriage and Divorce—A Social and Economic Study*, rev. ed. Cambridge, Mass.: Harvard University Press, 1976.

CAULFIELD, ERNEST. *The Infant Welfare Movement of the Eighteenth Century*. New York: Paul Hocker, 1931.

COLEMAN, SINCLAIR. *Income Disparities Between Black and White Americans*. Washington, D.C.: Superintendent of Documents, 1977.

CONSTANTELOS, DEMETRIOS J. *Byzantine Philanthropy and Social Welfare*. New Brunswick, N.J.: Rutgers University Press, 1968.

CUTRIGHT, PHILLIP. "Income and Family Events: Marital Stability." *Journal of Marriage and the Family*, **33**, 2 (1971).

CUTRIGHT, PHILLIP. "Components of Change in the Number of Female Family Heads Aged 15–44: United States, 1940–1970." *Journal of Marriage and the Family*, **36**, 1974, 714–721.

DE SCHWEINITZ, KARL. *England's Road to Social Security*. Philadelphia: University of Pennsylvania Press, 1947.

DESPERT, J. LOUISE. *The Emotionally Disturbed Child—Then and Now*. New York: Robert Brunner, 1965.

DEVEREAUX, GEORGE. *A Study of Abortion in Primitive Societies*, rev. ed. New York: International Universities Press, 1976.

DUFF, RAYMOND S., and A. G. M. CAMPBELL. "Moral and Ethical Dilemmas in the Special-Care Nursery." *The New England Journal of Medicine*, **289** (Oct. 25, 1973), 890–94.

DUNN, PATRICK P. "The Enemy Is the Baby: Childhood in Imperial Russia." *History of Childhood*, ed. Lloyd deMause. New York: Psychohistory Press, 1973.

FAIRCHILDS, CISSIE C. *Poverty and Charity in Aix-en-Provence 1640–1789*. Baltimore: Johns Hopkins University Press, 1974.

FARBER, BERNARD. *Guardians of Virtue—Salem Families in 1800*. New York: Basic Books, Inc., 1972.

FARLEY, REYNOLDS, and ALBERT I. HERMALIN. "Family Stability: A Comparison of Trends Between Black and White." *American Sociological Review*, **36**, 1 (February 1971).

FREED, DORIS J., and HENRY H. FOSTER. "Divorce American Style." *Annals of the American Academy*, **38**, 3 (May 1969), 71–88.

GALLAHUE, JOHN. "Tragedy at Liege." *Look* (March 12, 1963), 72–78.

GLICK, PAUL C. "Living Arrangements of Children and Young Adults." *Journal of Comparative Family Studies*, **7** (Summer 1976), 322–333.

———. *The Future of the American Family*. Washington, D.C.: Statement to Select Committee on Population, U.S. House of Representatives, May 1978.

GOTTLIEB, DAVID (Ed.). *Children's Liberation*. Englewood Cliffs, N.J.: Prentice-Hall, Inc., 1973.

GREHEN, FARRELL. "Mothers, Martyrs of the Speed Age." *Life* (January 18, 1960), 16.

GRIER, GEORGE. *The Baby Bust: An Agenda for the 70's Special Report*. Washington, D.C.: The Washington Center for Metropolitan Studies, 1971.

GROSS, BEATRICE, and RONALD GROSS. *The Children's Liberation Movement*. Garden City, N.Y.: Anchor Books, 1977.

GUTMAN, HERBERT S. *The Black Family in Slavery and Freedom, 1750–1925*. New York: Vintage Books, 1977.

HANDS, A. R. *Charities and Social Aid in Greece and Rome*. Ithaca, N.Y.: Cornell University Press, 1968.

HARING, BARBARA L. *1975 Census of Requests for Child Welfare Services.* New York: Child Welfare League of America, 1975.

Harvard Education Review, "The Rights of Children" (A Special Issue). Part I, Vol. 33 (November 1973); Part II, Vol. 34 (February 1974).

HERZOG, ELIZABETH, and CECELIA SUDIA. "Children in Fatherless Families," pp. 141–232, in *Review of Child Development Research.* Ed. by Bettye M. Caldwell and Henry N. Ricciuti. Chicago: University of Chicago Press, 1973.

HILL, ROBERT B. *The Strengths of Black Families.* New York: Emerson Hall Publishers, 1972.

HIMES, NORMAN E. *Medical History of Contraception.* Baltimore: The Williams & Wilkins Co., 1936.

HO, PING-TI. *Studies on the Population of China 1368–1953.* Cambridge, Mass.: Harvard University Press, 1967.

HOBHOUSE, L. T. *Morals in Evolution.* London: Chapman & Hall, Ltd., 1951.

HUNT, DAVID. *Parents and Children in Seventeenth-Century France.* New York: Basic Books, Inc., 1969.

ISPAHANI, BEGUM G. "Pakistan." *Adoption and Fostering,* 90, 4 (1977), 45–46.

KADUSHIN, ALFRED. "The Single Adoptive Parent—An Overview of the Research." *Social Service Review,* 44 (September 1970), 263–271.

KAHN, ALFRED J., and SHEILA B. KAMERMAN. *Social Services in the United States: Policies and Programs.* Philadelphia: Temple University Press, 1976.

KOHL, MARVIN (Ed.). *Infanticide and the Value of Life.* Buffalo, N.Y.: Prometheus Books, 1978.

LANGER, WILLIAM L. "Further Notes on the History of Infanticide." *History of Childhood Quarterly.*

———. "Infanticide: A Historical Survey." *History of Childhood Quarterly,* 1 (1974), 353–365.

LECKY, WILLIAM E. *History of European Morals,* Vol. 2. New York: Appleton-Century-Crofts, 1869.

LYMAN, RICHARD B. "Barbarism and Religion: Late Roman and Early Medieval Childhood." *The History of Childhood,* ed. Lloyd deMause. New York: The Psychohistory Press, 1973.

MADISON, BERNICE. "Russia's Illegitimate Children Before and After the Revolution." *Slavik Review,* 22 (1963), 82–95.

McCLOY, SHELBY T. *Government Assistance in Eighteenth-Century France.* Durham, N.C.: Duke University Press, 1946.

McLAUGHLIN, MARY MARTEN. "Survivors and Surrogate Children and Parents from the Ninth to the Thirteenth Century." *The History of Childhood,* ed. Lloyd deMause. New York: The Psychohistory Press, 1973.

MEAD, MARGARET. "A Cultural Anthropologist's Approach to Maternal Deprivation," in *Deprivation of Maternal Care.* Geneva: World Health Organization, 1962.

MERRIAM, IDA C. "Income and Its Measurement," in *Indicators of Social Change.* Ed. by Eleanor B. Sheldon and Wilbert E. Moore. New York: Russell Sage Foundation, 1968.

MILLER, NATHAN. *The Child in Primitive Society.* New York: Brentanos, 1928.

MITCHELL, R. G. "Children in Society," in *Child Life and Health.* Ed. by Ross S. Mitchell. London: J. & A. Churchill Ltd., 1970.

MITSCHERLICH, ALEXANDER. *Doctors of Infamy.* New York: Abelard-Schuman, Ltd., 1949.

MOHL, RAYMOND. *Poverty in New York 1783–1825.* New York: Oxford University Press, Inc., 1971.

NATIONAL ACADEMY OF SCIENCES. *To Word a National Policy for Children and Families.* Washington, D.C.: National Academy of Sciences, 1976.

NATIONAL COUNCIL OF ORGANIZATIONS FOR CHILDREN AND YOUTH. *America's Children 1976—A Bicentennial Assessment.* Washington, D.C.: National Council of Organizations for Children and Youth, 1976.

NORTON, ARTHUR J., and PAUL C. GLICK. "Marital Instability: Past, Present and Future." *Journal of Social Issues,* 32 (January 1976), 5–22.

OBERHEU, HOWARD D. *1975 Recipient Characteristics Study, Part 1: Demographic and Program Statistics.* Washington, D.C.: Government Printing Office, 1977.

OKADA, LOUISE M., and DUFF G. GILLESPIE. "The Impact of Family Planning Programs on Unplanned Pregnancies." *Family Planning Perspectives,* 9 (July–August 1977), 173–176.

ORSHANSKY, MOLLIE, "How Poverty Is Measured." *Monthly Labor Review,* 92 (February 1969), 37–41.

PANIGRAHI, LOLITA. *British Social Policy* and *Female Infanticide in India.* New Delhi: Munshira M. Manoharla 1, 1972.

PAUL, EVE W., HARRIET F. PILPEL, and NANCY F. WECHSLER. "Pregnancy, Teenagers and the Law." *Family Planning Perspectives,* 8 (January–February 1976), 16–21.

PAYNE, GEORGE H. *The Child in Human Progress.* New York: G. P. Putnam's Sons, 1916.

PECK, ELLEN. *The Baby Trap.* New York: Bernard Geis Associates, Inc., 1971.

PECK, ELLEN, and JUDITH SENDEROWITZ. *Pronatalism—The Myth of Mom and Apple Pie.* New York: Thomas Y. Crowell, 1974.

PINCHBECK, IVY, and MARGARET HEWITT. *Children in English Society,* Vol. 1: *From Tudor Times to the Eighteenth Century.* London: Kegan Paul, Trench, Trubner & Co., 1969.

QUEEN, ALFRED S. *Social Work in the Light of History.* Philadelphia: J. B. Lippincott Co., 1922.

RADBILL, SAMUEL X. "A History of Child Abuse and Infanticide," in *The Battered Child.* Ed. by Ray E. Helfer and C. Henry Kempe. Chicago: University of Chicago Press, 1968.

ROSS, HEATHER L., and ISABEL V. SAWHILL. *Time of Transition—The Growth of Families Headed by Women.* Washington, D.C.: The Urban Institute, 1975.

ROYSTER, EUGENE C. *Barriers to Foster Care in the Black Community.* Lincoln University, Pa.: Lincoln University, Department of Sociology, June 30, 1975. Mimeo, 235 pp.

SELIGMAN, EDWIN R. (Ed.). *Encyclopedia of Social Science,* Vol. 3. New York: The Macmillan Company, 1930.

SHERMAN, EDMUND A., MICHAEL H. PHILLIPS, BARBARA HARING, and ANN W. SHYNE. *Services to Children in Their Own Homes—Its Nature and Outcome.* New York: Child Welfare League of America, 1973.

SHORTER, EDWARD. *The Making of the Modern Family.* New York: Basic Books, Inc., 1975.

SHYNE, ANN W., and ANITA G. SCHROEDER. *National Study of Social Services to Children and Their Families.* Rockville, Md.: Westat, Inc., August, 1978.

SICAULT, GEORGES (Ed.). *The Needs of Children.* New York: The Free Press, 1963.

SILKA, LINDA, and SARA KIESLER. "Couples Who Choose to Remain Childless." *Family Planning Perspectives,* 9 (January–February 1977), 16–25.

SILVERMAN, ANNA, and ARNOLD SILVERMAN. *The Case Against Having Children.* New York: David McKay Co., Inc., 1971.

SNAPPER, KURT J., HARRIET H. BARRIGA, FAYE H. BAUMGARNER, *and* CHARLES S. WAGNER. *The Status of Children—1975.* Washington, D.C.: Social Work Research Group, George Washington University, 1975.

SNAPPER, KURT, and JOANNE S. OHMS. *The Status of Children, 1977.* Washington, D.C.: Government Printing Office, 1978.

STEIN, ROBERT L. "The Economic Status of Families Headed by Women." *Monthly Labor Review,* 93 (December 1970), 3–10.

STEINBICKER, CARL R. *Poor Relief in the Sixteenth Century.* Washington, D.C.: Catholic University Press, 1957.

STONE, LAWRENCE. *The Family, Sex and Marriage in England, 1500–1800.* New York: Harper & Row, Publishers, 1977.

SUMNER, WILLIAM G. *Folkways.* New York: Dover Publications, Inc., 1959.

TEN HOUTEN, WARREN D. "The Black Family: Myth and Reality." *Psychiatry,* 33, 2 (May 1970), 145–173.

TRATTNER, WALTER I. *Crusade for the Children.* Chicago: Quadrangle Books, Inc., 1970.

TREXLER, RICHARD C. "Infanticide in Florence: New Sources and First Results." *History of Childhood Quarterly,* 1 (Summer, 1973), 98–110.

————. *Demographic Yearbook, 1976,* 28th Issue. New York: United Nations, 1977.

U.S. BUREAU OF THE CENSUS. *Marital Status and Living Arrangements, March, 1977.* Washington, D.C.: Government Printing Office, 1977.

U.S. DEPARTMENT OF COMMERCE. *Census of Population, 1970. General Social and Economic Characteristics—Final Report U.S. Summary.* Washington, D.C.: Government Printing Office, 1972.

————. *The Social and Economic Status of the Black Population in the United States, 1974.* Washington, D.C.: Government Printing Office, July 1975.

————. *Population Profile of the United States: 1976.* Washington, D.C.: Government Printing Office, 1977a.

————. *Social Indicators, 1976.* Washington, D.C.: Government Printing Office, December 1977b.

————. *Statistical Abstract of the United States, 1978,* 99th ed. Washington, D.C.: Government Printing Office, 1978.

VARDIN, PATRICIA, and ILENE N. BRODY (Eds.). *Children's Rights: Contemporary Perspectives.* New York: Teachers College Press, 1979.

WEGMAN, MYRON E. "Annual Summary of Vital Statistics—1976." *Pediatrics,* 60 (December 1977), 797–804.

WELLER, ROBERT H., and FRANK B. HOBBS. "Unwanted and Mistimed Birth in the United States, 1968–1973." *Family Planning Perspectives,* 10 (May–June 1978), 168–172.

WESTOFF, CHARLES F., and ELISE P. JONES. "Contraception and Sterilization in the United States, 1965–1975." *Family Planning Perspectives,* 9 (July–August 1977), 153–158.

WHELAN, ELIZABETH M. *A Baby?—Maybe.* New York: Bobbs-Merrill Co., 1975.

WILKERSON, ALBERT E. *The Rights of Children: Emergent Concepts in Law and Society.* Philadelphia: Temple University Press, 1973.

WILLIAMSON, LAILA. "Infanticide: An Anthropological Analysis," in *Infanticide and the Value of Life.* Ed. by Marvin Kohl. Buffalo, N.Y.: Prometheus Books, 1978.

ZELNIK, MELVIN, and JOHN F. KANTHER. "First Pregnancies to Women Aged 15–19: 1976 and 1971." *Family Planning Perspectives,* 10 (January–February 1978), 11–20.

3 SUPPORTIVE SERVICES

INTRODUCTION

The first line of defense in child welfare services is to support, reinforce, and strengthen the ability of parents and children to meet the responsibilities of their respective statuses. Supportive services are designed for children living in their own homes. In these instances, both parents are generally present and show some willingness and capacity to enact their roles effectively. However, there may be difficulties in the parent–child relationship as a result of parent–child conflict or as a reflection of marital conflict.

We start with supportive services because it is, logically, the first service to use when a family needs help with a parent–child problem. We always act on the supposition that until proven otherwise, the best place for the child is in his own home, cared for by his own parents. Supportive services are an exemplification of this orientation.

In making use of such services, the family remains structurally intact. The child can remain, and be maintained, in his own home despite some malfunction in the parent–child relationship system. In offering supportive services, the agency does not take over the responsibility for discharging any of the role functions of either parent or child. The service always remains external to the family's social structure. Supportive service is different from supplementary services, for instance, where some significant aspect of the role is performed by some other parental figure, such as a homemaker, or by some social institution, such as the income maintenance programs.

The two principal agencies offering supportive services are the family service agencies and the child guidance clinics. The family service agencies intervene more frequently through service to the parent; the child guidance clinic, through service to the child. Both agencies hope to effect changes that will enable parents and child to live together with greater satisfaction and less friction. The aim is to lessen the danger of family disruption by improving the social functioning of family members.

The work of family service agencies and child guidance units is one significant component of services to children in their own homes, designed ultimately so that the child can continue to live in his own home.

HISTORICAL BACKGROUND

The family service agency has its origins in the Charity Organization Societies that were established in the United States during the 1880s. Such societies were organized to coordinate the activities of the many private charities serving the poor. Operating without a full awareness of one another's activities, they often served the same client in a haphazard, contradictory manner.

Until the beginning of the Great Depression in the 1930s, such agencies primarily served an economically deprived clientele, and the problems brought to the agency were those that were closely related to economic need (Cloward, Epstein, 1964). The service revolved around offering, and helping the client to use, concrete resources, prominent among which were cash relief grants. At the same time, there was emphasis on helping the poor through the personal influence and interest of the social worker—"not alms alone, but alms and a friend" was thought to be the most desirable approach. Such an approach can be viewed as a precursor of the use of a personal relationship in helping, the principal approach of the family service agency and the guidance clinic of today.

When government agencies assumed primary responsibility for relief grants, both the characteristics of the clientele and the kinds of primary problems brought to the family service agencies began to change. More and more insistently, the agencies defined their function as that of providing help with emotional problems in interpersonal relationships and family adjustment, parent–child problems, and marital problems. By the 1950s, this change in emphasis had been successfully interpreted to the community. As a result, the current clientele is more nearly representative of the general composition of the community, as parent–child and marital problems exist at every socioeconomic level. The problems for which clients currently seek help are now more likely to be concerned with child welfare.

The Family Service Association of America is the national coordinating organization to which almost all of the family service agencies belong. It was established in 1911 as the National Association of Societies for Organizing Charity. In response to changing clientele and ideology, its name was changed in 1930 to the Family Welfare Association of America, and again in 1946 to the Family Service Association of America.

The supportive nature of the family service agency is clearly outlined in the stated aims of the organization. The Family Service Association of America (1953) declares that "the central purpose of the family service agency is to contribute to harmonious family interrelationships, to strengthen the positive values in family life, and to promote healthy personality development and satisfactory social functioning of various family members" (p. 3).

The second principal child welfare supportive service, the child guidance clinic, has a different history. The forerunner of the modern clinic originated in a concern with the problem of juvenile delinquency. In 1909 Dr. William Healy, working under the aegis of the Juvenile Court of Cook County, Illinois, began a study of juvenile offenders. He attempted to apply some of the newer concepts of psychiatric service derived from Freud's discoveries, and he made explicit efforts to individualize the juvenile offender. In 1917 Dr. Healy's facility, later known as the Institute for Juvenile Research, received state support, and his work was extended to a wider group of emotionally disturbed children, whether delinquent or not. The attempt to individualize each child involved a fourfold approach: "a medical examination to analyze the child's physical assets and abilities, psychological tests to estimate his intellectual capacity, psychiatric interviews to determine his attitudes and the character of his mental life," and a study of the child's developmental history and social situation (Witmer, 1940, p. 47). Thus Healy's approach considered not only the physical and psychological factors in development but the social factors as well, and the dynamic interaction between parents and children as causative factors in the child's disturbed behavior. This fourfold approach characterizes the guidance clinic today.

The pioneer work of Healy was widely disseminated as a result of the sponsorship of demonstration clinics by the National Committee for Mental Hygiene in the early 1920s.

The first demonstration clinic was established in 1922 in St. Louis, with a staff consisting of a psychiatrist, a psychologist, and a social worker. Additional clinics were set up in six cities throughout the country: Norfolk (Virginia), Dallas, Minneapolis, Los Angeles, Cleveland, and Philadelphia. Two traveling clinics were established, operating from three to six months in each city, in an effort to demonstrate the value of such a service and to encourage the community to set up a permanent clinic.

To implement the demonstration, the Commonwealth Fund also set up a program for the training of child guidance workers at the New York School of Social Work. The school established special courses in child guidance and established a psychiatric clinic, the Bureau of Child Guidance, New York City, which was used as a training center for social workers.

Before the demonstration experiment was terminated in 1927, it had established the feasibility and need for such a facility for all children who presented emotional problems. By 1928 a Directory of Psychiatric Clinics for Children in the United States, published by the Commonwealth Fund, listed 470 clinics in thirty-one states offering service to 40,000 children during that year (Harper, 1940, p. 332).

The premise on which the child guidance clinic approach was based was that delinquency was only one manifestation of parent–child difficulties; that emotional disturbances among children, of which delinquency was merely a symptom, resulted from a malfunction in the relationship between parent and child during the early period in the child's development; and that the child's behavior was purposive and was a response to these developmental difficulties and a reflection of the fundamental problem. If such behavior were to be studied in sufficient detail, with a perceptive knowledge of the critical aspects of child development, one could arrive at an understanding of why the child was behaving in this way. Because the behavioral problem was a response to something that had gone wrong in the relationship between parents and children, one needed to understand and change not only the child's behavior but the parents' behavior as well.

And although the central concern of child guidance clinics was the child, it soon became an axiom of clinic practice that "for every problem child, there is a problem parent." Thus the parent, as well as the child, became an object of concern. The delinquent child shared problems of parent–child relationships with other children, many of whom manifested the results of such disorders in a way that was more disturbing to themselves than to others. There was a movement, then, toward helping all children with problems rather than the delinquent child only. A study of the activities of these clinics indicates that many of the supposedly modern innovations in practice, such as the community mental-health orientation, advocacy, and brokerage were integral aspects of this early service (Levine, Levine, 1970).

In summary, one might note that the family service agency is a direct descendant of those agencies in the community controlled and administered by social workers. The guidance clinic was fathered by psychiatry and the mental hygiene movement, mothered by the courts and the Commonwealth Fund, and had social work as a godfather. The development of community mental health centers throughout the country under the Community Mental Health Centers Act of 1963 provided an additional significant resource for both outpatient and inpatient care of children needing psychiatric service. Each center is designed to serve a limited population (75,000–200,000) and is readily accessible to the community it serves. As more community mental health centers are organized, the child guidance clinic tends to cease to be a discrete entity and becomes one unit of a comprehensive community mental-health program.

SITUATIONS IN WHICH SUPPORTIVE AGENCIES ARE THE APPROPRIATE RESOURCE

Any kind of difficulty in the implementation of parent–child roles is appropriate for supportive family service. The parent who has difficulty in disciplining his children, who derives little satisfaction from parenthood, who is concerned about his child's peer-group relationships or school performance, a family torn by sibling conflict, an unsatisfactory marital situation to which the children are reacting by disorders in behavior—all supposedly can profit from regular, periodic interviews with a family agency caseworker.

It is difficult to make a clear-cut distinction between the problem that is appropriate for referral to family services and that appropriate for the child guidance unit in a mental health center. The family service agency is more apt to offer service in those situations in which parents have problems to which the child is responding; the child guidance unit is more apt to offer service in those situations in which children have problems to which the parents are responding. The circularity of the problem configuration is evident in this statement and the consequent confusion as to where the distinction, if any, lies. Historically, family service has been concerned with the problems of the family, and through this concern became interested in treating the child; and child guidance clinics were concerned with the problems of children, through which they came to be concerned with the problems of parents.

Because the community mental health center performs a function similar to that of family service agencies and serves a similar clientele, some efforts have been made to distinguish one agency from the other. One study notes that the family service agency relates more closely to social agencies and that mental health centers, or clinics, relate more to medical facilities and personnel. Referring sources saw the clinic as the appropriate place to refer problems that were "psychiatric in nature," and they saw problems of "interpersonal relationships and environment" as more appropriate for referral to family service agencies (Hill, Lehman, Slotkin, 1971). Somewhat similarly, another study (Rothman, Kay, 1978) showed that the profession of social work had more prominence in the family-service agency system as compared with the community mental-health center system.

Studies of the operations of particular family service agencies substantiate the fact that problems regarding parent and child roles are among those for which clients most frequently seek help (Fanshel, 1958, pp. 36–37). Nationwide studies confirm that parent–child difficulties constitute a high proportion of the problems that bring families to a family service agency. In 1970, 42 per cent of family agency clients presented a problem of "parent–child" relationship at intake, 26 per cent listed a problem of "child rearing or child care," 14 per cent were concerned with the "personality adjustment of a child under thirteen." Clients presented more than one problem, but the three major areas were personality problems, marital problems, and parent–child problems (Beck, Jones, 1973). Interpersonal adjustment problems are generally given higher priority at intake than situational problems (employment, housing, and the like).

The presenting problem is the "ticket of admission" to an agency. For the child guidance clinics, set up to help the child, the presenting problem is generally formulated in terms of the child's deficiencies in role implementation. These most frequently include problems in relation to school or difficulties in learning; delinquent or predelinquent behavior, such as fighting, stealing, firesetting, running away, and truancy; neurotic problems, such as night terrors, excessive shyness, phobias, enuresis, soiling, depression, and withdrawal; sexual problems; and psychosomatic difficulties.

The strain imposed on parent–child relationships by the persistence of these kinds of problems is obvious. Any child who consistently presents any of these behaviors is not effectively carrying out his role.

Both the child guidance clinic and the family service agency attempt to deal with families in trouble by direct treatment of the child, but the family agency is more likely to try to help the child through help to the parents. Family service agencies, however, do accept responsibility for direct casework with children who have problems, and there is no significant difference between the cases coming to the family service agency and those coming to the child guidance clinic. The more severely disturbed children are, however, more likely to be referred to the child guidance clinic, if only because of the presence of a psychiatric consultant on the clinic team.

SCOPE

The yearly report questionnaire requested of member agencies by the Family Service Association of America (FSAA) indicates that there were, in 1975, some 300 agencies affiliated with the national organization employing some 4,500 professionally trained staff and serving 500,000 families and over 2 million individuals a year. In addition to the 300 family service agencies affiliated with the FSAA, it is estimated that there are some additional 700 voluntary agencies, a sizable percentage of which are sectarian, serving family-service agency functions.

In 1976, 280 family service agencies throughout the country offered service to 559,000 different families. Of these families, 66 per cent had more than one in-person interview and 19 per cent had six or more interviews (Family Service Association of America, 1977, p. 15).

In 1976, of the 2,300 mental health clinics in the United States, an estimated 200 were child guidance clinics. Of the 268,000 children seen at these facilities in 1976, only 40 per cent received any treatment; 160,800 received no more than a diagnostic workup (Goldsmith, 1977, p. 892).

Some 10 per cent of clients seen at community health centers are children and adolescents with behavior disorders (Rothman, Kay, 1977, p. 14). Adolescents (ten to fourteen) were the age group most frequently served, and twice as many boys as girls received service.

Family service at the start of the 1970 decade was essentially an urban service; rural areas remain essentially without such services. Clients were most frequently referred by friends and relatives, less often through social workers, teachers, or physicians.

Agencies in 1970 were serving a slightly higher proportion of disadvantaged families than they did in 1960. In 1970 some 51 per cent of agency client families were of lower or upper-lower socioeconomic status.

Despite the decided effort of family service agencies to indicate their readiness to serve black families, there was almost no increase in the use of family service by members of the black community between 1960 and 1970. Nevertheless black clients were served by family agencies in nearly double their proportion to the general population. Of family agency clientele in 1970, 2.4 per cent were of Spanish origin and 0.3 per cent American Indian (Beck, Jones, 1973, p. 85).

Overall, young families with an above-average number of children, families that might be anticipated to face considerable stress, are the principal users of family service. They are often substantially below the general population in family income (Beck, Jones, 1973, p. 3).

The children needing help at clinics and family service agencies are difficult to define, and the numbers needing such help are difficult to estimate. The phrase *emotionally disturbed child* is ambiguous, open to a variety of interpretations. Attempts have been made to estimate (either by a comprehensive survey of a particular area or through interviews with teachers) the number of children who might be characterized as emotionally disturbed. The 1978 Report of the President's Commission on Mental Health summarizes such studies by noting that "Surveys of general populations show that the overall prevalence of persistent and socially handicapping mental health problems among children aged 3 to 15 years is about 5 to 15 percent" (Vol. 2, p. 39).

PROCESS IN SUPPORTIVE SERVICES

Casework Service Approach

Many parents concerned about the behavior of their children do not see the relevance of mental health clinics or the family service agency to the problems they face. Detailed interviews with a stratified sample of eight hundred families drawn from the general population in Westchester County, New York, and supplemented by data provided by the schools was used by reviewing psychiatrists to determine that a "third of the 800 children in the sample were judged to be moderately or severely impaired" (Lurie, 1974, p. 110). Only a very limited number of the parents had actually sought professional help for their child's problems. Many parents tended to view these behavioral problems as a "phase" the child was going through and found it repugnant to define such problems as requiring professional help.

A small percentage of families come to the family agency or clinic after reading or hearing about the work of such agencies through mass communication media—newspapers, radio, television, and so on; these may be regarded as self-referred applicants. More frequently, however, applicants are referred by friends, other social and health agencies, schools, courts, and physicians.

Once the initial contact has been made, the agency and the applicant get acquainted with one another. The agency learns the general nature of the applicant's problems and determines if it is the appropriate agency for helping the applicant. The applicant learns something about how the agency operates and determines if he wants the kind of help the agency has to offer, in the way the agency offers it. If both applicant and agency agree that parents are having a problem with their children and would like to have the help of the agency in dealing with it, and if the agency feels it can be of help, the applicant becomes a client.

Clients and agency workers often see the nature of the problem situation somewhat differently, clients more frequently ascribing their principal problem to environmental stress: inadequate income, unemployment, poor job opportunities, an unsafe neighborhood, drug use in the neighborhood, lack of day care, and discrimination. Nevertheless, the principal service requested by clients and given by the agency is counseling. In a limited number of cases, financial assistance, day care, or homemaker service is offered. About 30 per cent of the clients are referred to other agencies so that the agency performs a steering function.

If the applicant continues as a client with the agency, an effort is made to get a clearer picture of the problem through a social study. The clinic is more apt than the family agency to offer psychological examinations, as well as an interview between staff psychiatrist and child. In both agencies, however, interviews are held with parents and children, as well as with other members of the community who have some knowledge of the child. The social study covers the developmental history of each of the family members, the developmental history of the family as an entity, and the current relationships and patterns of interaction among family members.

Based on the information developed in the social study, an assessment is made of the nature of the difficulty and its principal factors. Once again, the assessment in the clinic is likely to be more highly formalized than in the family service agency, involving a meeting in which the various professionals who have seen the parents and the child discuss their view of the family. The diagnosis is then used for planning a treatment program. The goals of casework treatment, as described by the FSAA (1953), are to

1. Support or maintain the client's current strength by helping him mobilize the capacity and resources to meet his current life situation.

2. Modify the client's attitudes and patterns of behavior by increasing his understanding of himself, his problems, and his part in creating them.

"The focus of the agency's help is on the specific reality problems that the family is facing and on the ways of reducing pressure and relieving undue hardship. . . . The effect of treatment in both categories is to reduce social and emotional pressures and to increase the client's capacity for satisfactory social functioning" (pp. 7–8). Both parent and child, as a result of such treatment, can more effectively implement their respective roles and reduce the possibility of family disruption.

Treatment is based on interviews between parents and caseworker and/or child and caseworker in the family agency. In the clinic, although the parent is most likely to see a caseworker, the child may be seen by either staff caseworker, staff psychologist, or staff psychiatrist. Interviews with the child are supplemented by sessions in which the child communicates his problems and his reaction to his problems through the medium of play therapy.

Because it is recognized that the supportive service, the first line of defense in child welfare, is somewhat amorphous, it might be best to amplify this description of process with the following case study.

Mrs. S., a woman with professional background in a field allied to psychology, came to us with her concern about David, age 5. David was a bed wetter, was refusing to attend kindergarten, and when he did go caused so much trouble by his absolute refusal to conform that his teacher described him as "the worst and most difficult pupil" in a class of 52 children. He could not get along with children of his own age, whom he either attacked or from whom he withdrew. The family consisted of Mr. and Mrs. S., a couple in their early thirties, David, and his younger sister, Rita, age 2.

In the first interview Mrs. S. had no trouble at all in presenting the facts of her situation and her view of the problem in a very poised and intelligent manner. Her interpretation, however, lay very much outside herself. For the first two years of David's life, Mr. S. had been overseas in the armed services. Mrs. S. had moved back to her own parents, who were in good financial circumstances. David had been greatly spoiled by his grandfather and an uncle, Mrs. S.'s married brother, ten years her senior, himself childless and very fond of David, who visited frequently and showered him with expensive gifts. Although soon after Mr. S.'s return to civilian life the S.'s moved into their own apartment, Mr. S.'s relationship to his son was not satisfactory, according to Mrs. S. In a slightly critical and yet triumphant manner, she described how her husband rather awkwardly forced himself on his son and seemed unable to establish a natural relationship with him. The visits and gift-bringing of Mrs. S.'s older brother were still continuing, accompanied by the uncle's rather dramatic show of affection for David, with which Mr. S., an undemonstrative person, felt unable to compete. While his brother-in-law's visits were a continuous source of irritation to Mr. S. and Mrs. S. herself recognized that they were not helpful to the family's attempts to grow into a more cohesive unit, Mrs. S. saw no way of changing this situation, since she felt she could not deprive her childless brother of the satisfaction that the relationship to David gave him.

This material came out easily from Mrs. S., who seemed to have it on the tip of her tongue. Only when the counselor asked specifically about her own relationship to David did she begin to talk less fluently and with less poise. While Mrs. S.

had made very conscious attempts at giving time and attention to David, which we gathered he was constantly seeking, a note of annoyance crept into her voice as she described his demands, as if she were somewhat resentful of them. When she described playing games with David, a picture of a really competitive situation emerged in which Mrs. S. would get annoyed every time David won, or when he came out ahead of her in solving a puzzle and then tried to help her finish hers. It was hard for the listener to imagine that this was a description of a mother and a child doing things together; it sounded much more like a relationship between contemporaries.

When Mr. S. was seen subsequently, he gave the impression of a man who lived somehow in the shadow of Mrs. S.'s family. Since his return to civilian life he had been working for his father-in-law and his brother-in-law. While he resented his economic dependence on them and their interference with David, he felt quite powerless to bring about any change. He compared his own reticence in showing feeling with the demonstrativeness of his in-laws, and blamed them for standing between him and his son. Like his wife, Mr. S. could not as yet acknowledge his own part in the difficulty, and needed to hold others responsible. Discussion with Mrs. S. during subsequent interviews gradually moved into the area of her relationship to her brother, who, being ten years older, had always made her "feel very inconsequential." She had always felt that he, as the son, had been favored by her mother, and this had left her with a feeling that being a girl did not really amount to much. Fearing a complete loss of love, Mrs. S. could not afford to let herself know her feelings of resentment toward her mother and brother. In her need to keep her feelings hidden, she always met her mother's continuous criticism by trying to please her and conform to her standards.

It now became painfully clear to Mrs. S. how this had affected her relationship to David, whose needs as a child she had not been entirely free to meet. For example, she had begun to toilet train David—one of whose problems was bedwetting—at an extremely early age, because this was her mother's concept of child rearing and she did not dare oppose it in spite of her professional knowledge that this was harmful to the child. Her inability to assume any control over her brother's relationship to David also began to take on a different meaning for Mrs. S. She realized that her feeling of guilt toward her brother, because of her acknowledged hostility to him, had in a way paralyzed her and driven her to let him have more of David than was his right.

Mrs. S. was now much freer to consider her relationship with her husband. She began to grasp how much she had tried to dominate him since his return from the war. She had encouraged him to move to New York City (his roots and ties were elsewhere), to take a job in her father's business, and to take on her friends, thus leaving very little room for him to find himself again after the war experience. She had not helped him with his need to form a relationship to David, and had really found some satisfaction in the fact that David clung to her and was pushing Mr. S. away. In her relationship to David, too, there had been rivalry, since in Mrs. S.'s concept of the relationship of male and female, either the man dominated the woman and made her feel little or the woman controlled and dominated the man.

For Mrs. S. it was very meaningful that from the first moment the counselor, who was a woman, treated him as the man in the family, whose opinion and feelings were very important, and whose active participation in contact was considered essential if David was to be helped. Having felt weak in his silent struggle with his wife, her family, and even his son, Mr. S. immediately gained strength from this attitude on the part of the counselor. The counselor helped Mr. S. to recognize his tendency to withdraw whenever he needed to reveal himself to another person. His reaction was directly linked to his problem with his son, who, he felt, had been taken away from him by his in-laws as a result of their demonstrative ways. Deeply touched by the counselor's recognition of his pain over this, Mr. S. related his pattern of withdrawal to his own background, describing a most ineffectual father and a cold mother who showed her contempt of her husband and of men in general in an unmistakable manner. His wife's domination over him seemed to have brought out the fear that he was destined to suffer his father's fate. He was resentful but unable to express this feeling, since he feared that any show of anger toward his wife might lead her to leave him. He felt he had little to offer her, particularly after his return from the war when he had to make a new beginning.

As a result of sharing his deep sense of inadequacy with the counselor and finding that exposure of these very painful feelings had not crushed him, an emotional change occurred in him which, in his relationship to the agency, found its tangible expression in his decision to take over payment of the fee for the interviews, for which until then his wife had carried responsibility. At home Mr. S. was increasingly able to let his wife know his feelings and thoughts; and Mrs. S., who herself had achieved greater freedom to relate to her husband on a more realistic, mature basis, discovered what an interesting companion Mr. S. really was. In relation to the outside world, the couple felt a unity such as they had never felt before. Suddenly they could quite comfortably handle the question of visits and gift-bringing with Mrs. S.'s brother and experienced much satisfaction in finding that they were able to do this in a natural, matter-of-fact way that was not offensive to the brother and left them without a sense of guilt.

As Mr. and Mrs. S. gained more security in their relationship as husband and wife, they found a way of handling David that gave him the possibility of identification with his father so necessary to a sense of security at his particular age level. As Mrs. S. came to see David as a five-year-old child rather than as another male competitor, she found herself able to meet his demands in a realistic manner. Her attitude became more loving and had in it firmness and consistency, whereas formerly she had swung from one extreme to another in her handling of him. For Mr. S. the realization that he was important to his son and that he as the father had something very special to offer him was possible only because of his increased respect for himself as a man. He was quite startled to find how much the child responded to him when he approached him spontaneously, without his previous fear of being pushed away. David stopped bed-wetting completely and, not needing to cling to his mother any more, was free to form more positive relationships with children of his own age. The school reported tremendous improvement in the child [pp. 75–79].*

The S. family might have been offered equally effective service at a child guidance clinic. The approach to the family would have been essentially similar, except that the guidance clinic record might have included more direct contact and work with the child. The similarity in approach derives from the fact that the family service agency and the child guidance clinic have the same basic set of presuppositions regarding the treatment of parent–child relationship problems:

---

* From Elsa Leichter, "Parent–Child Relationship Problems—Participation in Treatment by Both Parents," in Robert Gomberg and Frances Levinson (Eds.), *Diagnosis and Process in Family Counseling* (New York: Family Service Association of America, 1951). By permission of the publisher.

1. Children have problems because of some serious imbalance in their affectional relationship with their parents.
2. Because the problem is the result of faulty interaction between parent and child, it is best not to seek to help either the child or the parent *alone;* it is best if both participants in the interactional process are helped to effect some change in the way they relate to each other. Simultaneous treatment of both parents and child is therefore desirable.
3. Behind the parents' difficulties in acting in an accepting manner toward their children lies some disorder in their relationship with their own parents. Consequently, helping the parents to implement their roles more effectively requires some exploration of their own developmental histories.
4. People can change as they become more aware of the reasons that they behave as they do. One aim of treatment is to help both parents and child to develop more conscious recognition of the purposes their behavior serves. Having become aware of the purposiveness of their behavior, they are in a better position, supposedly, to control and/or change their behavior. It is for this reason that the therapist seeks to establish an atmosphere of psychological safety and acceptance. In response to such conditions, parents and children can risk expressing thoughts and feelings that they may be hiding from themselves, as well as from others. The mother can openly say, for the first time perhaps, that she does often hate her child because it is less dangerous, less likely to lead to rejection, to express this feeling here than elsewhere:

If a client can be helped to understand why he behaves as he does or to recognize and understand the origin of the neurotic tactics that continually defeat him, he will gradually abandon the inappropriate behavior and substitute therefore more rational tactics in the management of his life. Increased self-understanding is regarded as inherently good and as a means toward the end of good psychological health [Hobbs, 1962, p. 741].

5. One might help parents and children to effect changes in behavior by offering the therapist as a pattern for identification and emulation. The therapist exemplifies the "good" parent in his attitudes toward the child and his behavior. The parent in treatment is presented, through the therapist, with an illustration of an emotionally healthier approach toward children. If the relationship between parent and therapist is a positive one, the parent seeks to "imitate" the therapist as a person he admires and respects: "Individuals frequently accept guidance from those they love. They model themselves after them and seek to win their approval" (Witmer, 1946, p. 45).
6. Children who need the help of supportive services often are reacting to negative parental attitudes: rejection, indifference, punitiveness. Consequently they have learned to regard all adults as potentially hurtful. The clinic offers a corrective emotional experience in which the child encounters an adult who explicitly contradicts the anticipated indiscriminating generalization that the child is making from his parents to all adults. Good supportive casework is carefully designed to make it possible for a client to learn to be close to another person without getting hurt. In ex-

periencing this knowledge, the child is able to divest the symbol of "adult" of its anxiety-producing potential. For the child, the satisfying, trustful, confident human relationship developed with the therapist is ultimately generalized to other adult figures. Having learned to "trust" himself to risk a loving relationship with one adult without having been hurt and rejected, the child is more likely to risk a similar relationship with his parents. He develops a feeling of security with the people who are emotionally of utmost importance to him: his parents.

Because they share the same preconceptions, the treatment approaches of the child guidance clinic and the family service agency in dealing with parent–child relationship problems are often indistinguishable. However, there are differences in the way treatment is administered. The family service agency is staffed by social workers, with a psychiatrist frequently acting as part-time consultant. The clinic is more frequently under the directorship of a psychiatrist and includes psychiatrists as active members of the treatment team, in addition to social workers and clinical psychologists. Hence, although at the family service agency social workers see both parents and children for treatment, in the clinic the psychiatrist frequently treats the child while the social worker treats the parents. There are a variety of other patterns, however, in the allocation of responsibilities among psychiatrists, psychologists, and social workers in the clinic.

Until fairly recently, the approach of the child guidance clinic and the family service agency was based almost exclusively on principles from psychoanalytic psychology. Currently there is more interest in and utilization of approaches based on behavioral-modification learning theory. Such an approach to children's problems postulates that disturbed or maladaptive behavior is learned behavior. Treatment therefore consists of "unlearning" the maladaptive response. The focus is on the undesirable behavior itself, the "symptom," rather than on resolving any internal condition that is manifested in the symptom. The behaviorist denies that there is any internal conflict sustaining the behavior that might be perceived by others as a symptom.

Behavioral modification procedures are focused on helping clients to act differently in the expectation that they will then feel differently about their situation. The more traditional kinds of family service and child guidance psychotherapies are focused on helping clients feel differently in the anticipation that they then will act differently.

The difference between the two approaches is a difference in seeing the child's behavior as an expression of underlying conflict or as a learned response that must be inhibited or extinguished. There is less concern with "diagnosis" because the "etiology" of the problem is not important. There is more concern with an exact definition of the particular behavior that needs to be changed and with the source and nature of those "reinforcements" that encourage continuation of the undesirable behavior.

Laws of learning can then be applied not only to the elimination of undesirable learned behavior but also to the acquisition of new and desirable patterns of behavior.

The behavior was learned and is sustained by the current activities of people in a position to reward and/or punish such behavior, generally the parent.

Behavioral modification therapy therefore frequently involves instructing the parents so that they support desirable behavior through prompt and appropriate rewards and/or discourage undesirable behavior by nonreinforcement or by appropriate and prompt punishment.

Various techniques have been developed, such as counterconditioning or reciprocal inhibition, operant conditioning, modeling, and aversion therapy, and these have been applied to a wide variety of children's problems: hyperactivity, temper tantrums, phobias and tics, bed-wetting, retardation, childhood psychosis, delinquency. Some of the techniques have been "translated" for social workers, and their applicability to social work situations has been made explicit (Jehu, 1967; Thomas, 1967; Fisher, Gochros, 1975; Gambrill, 1977; Schwartz, Goldiamond, 1977; Wodarski, Bagrozzi, 1979).

The following is an account of the use by social workers of desensitization procedures in treating a school phobia. The child had been treated at the clinic through the use of traditional psychotherapeutic approaches over a period of six months, but no improvement had been noted.

Jimmy, ten, was referred to the child guidance clinic because he was unable to go to school. A month prior to the referral he had suffered a bronchial infection, following which the Christmas holiday season occurred. After that, the youngster refused to return to school, in spite of efforts by the parents, the teacher, and the principal. The patient stated that when he thought about going to school in the morning he became frightened and often vomited. His previous school attendance record was excellent, as was his school work performance. Jimmy was described as being high-strung, sensitive, and preoccupied with high-level performance. As therapy progressed, secondary problems began to arise, consisting of avoidance of friends and peers. Apparently, Jimmy could not find adequate excuses for being out of school, and as his friends telephoned or visited the home, he became quite anxious and finally refused any contact with peers at all. The patient indicated that he did not feel that he could assert himself and that he did not feel as worthwhile as his brother or sister.

The patient described many arguments at home involving everyone in the family. He indicated that he would not be overly concerned if his father moved out of the house, but if his mother left, it would be quite different. "If she goes, the whole family would fade away. We would have to go to another home. . . . If it did happen, it would be horrible. I wouldn't know what would happen to myself or anyone else. The family would be just all messed up, and I'd go crazy." This concern about losing his mother was evidenced at other times; for example, the patient also stated that if his mother went to the store, he often imagined that she might get hit by a car. Or even when mother took him to the store with her, Jimmy would stay in the car and begin to think that there might be a robbery and that she might get shot. Other factors that seemed related to his concerns were: (1) Jimmy got lost as a small child and remembered how terribly frightened he was; (2) five years previously, when his mother was working, he had worried a good deal about her; (3) his mother often used the phrase, "Someday I'll be dead, and you'll wish you had me. You'll want help, and I won't be there." And, in referring to school, she often said, "One of these days when you get home, I won't be here."

After approximately six months of traditional therapy, shortly before school was to start, the patient indicated that he was nervous about trying to go back to school, but indicated that he felt "bigger" than he had felt six months previously.

He also stated that he felt he knew himself better and felt more confident. There appeared to be a good relationship between Jimmy and the therapist. On the day he was to return to school, the patient could not take the step out of the home, and again he panicked.

The desensitization procedure in this case was carried out in the school environment. The school officials were informed of the procedure, and they cooperated fully with the therapist. Jimmy was told that each day the therapist would accompany him to school, and that together they would approach the school gradually. Since it was known that he could tolerate going by the school in a car, the first step consisted of Jimmy and the therapist sitting in the car in front of the school. The other steps were as follows: (2) getting out of the car and approaching the curb; (3) going to the sidewalk; (4) going to the bottom of the steps of the school; (5) going to the top of the steps; (6) going to the door; (7) entering the school; (8) approaching the classroom a certain distance each day down the hall; (9) entering the classroom; (10) being present in the classroom; (11) being present in the classroom with the teacher and one or two classmates; (12) being present in the classroom with a full class. This procedure was carried out over twenty consecutive days, including Saturdays and Sundays [p. 148].*

At the end of the twenty-day period, Jimmy remained in school. A two-year follow-up study has indicated that there have been no subsequent manifestations of the phobia.

The authors of the report, both social workers, explain the success of the program on the basis of reciprocal inhibition. They paired a pleasant stimulus, contact with the workers (with whom Jimmy had a good relationship), with an anxiety-provoking stimulus, the school. The pleasure, the presence of the therapist, weakened the anxiety provoked by the school, ultimately resulting in the gradual diminution of such anxiety. Although other, more complex, psychodynamic factors were involved (fear of separation from his mother, hostile wishes that his mother would be injured, and the guilt and anxiety aroused by such wishes), dealing with the behavior, in and of itself, seemed to effect the change desired by both the family and the child.

Learning-theory approaches, it is argued, are particularly efficacious with children for the following reasons:

1. The world of "significant others" is more restricted in the case of a child and hence can be more easily controlled.
2. Those closest to the child in a position of authority, the parents, have not only the potential for controlling the child's environment but also the desire to do something about changing the child's behavior. Consequently their cooperation in therapy can be enlisted.
3. Parents, as the most significant figures in the child's life in most frequent contact with the child, are the principal and most potent dispensers of reinforcement and punishment.
4. Maladaptive behaviors for which children are referred often include the specific, well-defined behaviors—temper tantrums, bed-wetting, phobias— most amenable to behavior therapy approaches.

* From William P. Garvey and Jack R. Hegrenes, "Desensitization Techniques in the Treatment of a School Phobia," *American Journal of Orthopsychiatry, 36,* 1 (January 1966). Copyright © 1966, the American Orthopsychiatric Association, Inc. Reproduced by permission.

5. In children, learned patterns of behavior have been recently acquired and are not so firmly established as in adults, and behavior more recently learned may be more easily unlearned.
6. There is less ethical objection to controlling and "manipulating" the child's environment than is true for the more independent adult, and there is less objection to establishing behavioral goals for children.

Such an approach might also be more effective for those clients, generally lower-class, who are uncomfortable in a nondirective relationship centered on "talk," concern with "self-actualization," and a search for "meanings." The drop-out rate of such clients might be reduced by an approach that offers specific directives for action.

Behavioral modification therapists have actively recruited and trained the parents as co-therapists. The parents are trained to respond to the child's behavior in a manner designed to effect changes in the child's behavior in terms of learning theory (McPherson, Samuels, 1971). The following is an account of the way one mother was enlisted as therapist for her child:

> The child in this study was a four-year-old boy, Peter S. He is the third of four children in a middle-class family. Peter had been brought to a clinic because he was extremely difficult to manage and control. His mother stated she was helpless in dealing with his frequent tantrums and disobedience. Peter often kicked objects or people, removed or tore his clothing, called people rude names, annoyed his younger sister, made a variety of threats, hit himself, and became very angry at the slightest frustration. He demanded attention almost constantly, and seldom cooperated with Mrs. S. [Hawkins *et al.*, 1966, p. 100].

Clinic personnel observing the mother–child interaction in the home noted the frequency of manifestations of nine specific objectionable behaviors. Included among these were "throwing objects," "biting his shirt or arm," "pushing his sister," "removing or threatening to remove his clothing," and so on.

> The mother was informed of the nine objectionable behaviors which would be treated. She was shown three gestural signals which indicated how she was to behave toward Peter. Singal "A" meant she was to tell Peter to stop whatever objectionable behavior he was emitting. Signal "B" indicated she was immediately to place Peter in his room and lock the door. When signal "C" was presented she was to give him attention, praise, and affectionate physical contact. Thus, every time Peter emitted an objectionable behavior, Mrs. S. received a signal from the clinician instructing her on her response [p. 102].

On the basis of such programmed learning, the mother developed a changed pattern of interaction with Peter, and the mother, as "therapist," applied the behavioral responses designed to effect changes in Peter's behavior. Use of parents as therapists is called *filial therapy*.

Filial therapy is defined as "planned intervention adhering to psychotherapeutic practices in which parent and child interact under the supervision of a therapist for the purposes of achieving behavior and/or personality changes in the child, the parent, or both" (Reisinger, Ora, Frangia, 1976, p. 104).

Rather than attempting to act directly to change the behavior of the child, the worker trains the parent to engage in behavior modification intervention. Such training might take place in the agency or, more frequently, in the client's home. The worker may interact with the child in the playroom of the agency while the parent watches, using the worker as a model.

As contrasted with the usual dyadic helping relationship of worker and client, the filial therapy relationship is a triadic one, the worker acting as a consultant to the parent, who is the mediator actually involved in effecting change in the child, who is the client. Filial therapy is feasible because the behavioral modification procedures are specific and action-oriented and can be quickly taught to the parent.

A number of reviews of the clinical experience and research related to filial therapy (Johnson, Katz, 1973; Tarormina, 1974; Reisinger, Ora, Frangia, 1976; O'Dell, 1974; McCauley, McCauley, 1977) indicate that although such interventions have achieved successful outcomes, there are also problems, such as initiating parent involvement in such programs and maintaining parental interest and parental persistence in application of the procedures. Such programs require the ability to plan and to persevere with some persistence and consistency in implementing the treatment program and the time and the energy to devote to monitoring the program. All of this requires a well-organized, systematic person with the ability and will to structure his life—a tall order for many harassed parents.

Workers might call the parents each week to discuss progress and to encourage continuation in the program. The encouragement and praise of the worker for the parent's efforts when tabulations of behavior frequencies are turned in to the worker and when other evidence of involvement in the program is presented also act to reinforce the parents' continuation of the program.

There are additional questions with regard to the maintenance over time of changed behavior, and the extent to which the parent can generalize behavior learned in one context to contact with the child in other contexts or with regard to other problems.

Critics of the behavioral modification approach raise the question of whether or not the mechanical "rat psychology" conception of man's behavior and the "manipulative" nature of the procedure is compatible with the humanistic ideology of social work (Bruck, 1968). The response in the still-continuing debate is the evidence: the parents and children who are living together more satisfactorily as a result of these procedures and the fact that the approach brings to social work a degree of precision and scientific vigor that it previously lacked (Carter, Stuart, 1970).

Task-centered casework (Reid, Epstein, 1972, 1977; Reid, 1978) is a third explicitly defined approach that stands midway between psychotherapeutic casework and behavior modification in its degree of focus and structure and the extent of concern with behavior as opposed to feelings. In the task-centered approach, the worker helps a client to define clearly the problem with which help is wanted, formulating specific, partial tasks to resolve the problem, formulating an explicit contract, assigning a limited period of time for completion of the tasks, and focusing worker–client effort on task achievement. Ewalt (1977) reports the successful application of such an approach in a child guidance clinic. As a consequence of interest in behavior modification and task-centered approaches, social work in supportive services is currently more goal-oriented, more concerned with behavior and somewhat less with feeling states, more focused and more specific in selecting target problems as objectives for change, more explicit in arrangements with the clients via contracts, more accepting of defined time limitations on the duration of contact with the client, and more directive in helping the client achieve more structured, objectifiable goals within time limits.

Group Service Approach ✓

Both family service agencies and child guidance clinics have adopted a group approach in helping families with parent–child relationship problems. The group may supplement the individual casework service; often, however, this may be the only form of help offered a family. The supportive service agencies have developed two different kinds of programs employing a group approach: family-life education programs and group counseling or group treatment programs.

Family life education is defined by the FSAA as "a process by which people are helped through group discussion to broaden their understanding of family relationships. . . . The aim of such education is the prevention of unhappy family relationships and the strengthening and enrichment of family life." The family life education program of family service agencies is implemented through lectures by agency social workers to community groups, leadership of parent discussion groups, formal institutes on child care and parent–child relationships, and participation in radio and television programs on family life education. A few larger family service agencies have staff members who are assigned full-time responsibility for family life education programs. The meetings may be initiated by the agency, but frequently the agency is asked to provide a group leader and a program for groups of parents in various community organizations—PTA groups, women's service groups, and so on.

The group counseling service is frequently difficult to distinguish from the ongoing family-life education program. Both kinds of groups consist of limited numbers of parents who come together with some regularity to discuss parent–child relationship problems with the help of a skilled leader provided by the agency. Some distinguishable differences, however, have been identified.

The counseling groups are viewed by the agency "as a special controlled environment which offers a corrective emotional experience—a re-education living experience to the client" (Conrad, 1959, p. 124). The family life education programs have an educational rather than therapeutic function, so that content and discussion emphasize normal family relationships and rational procedures in dealing with normal problem situations. Group counseling services, unlike parent education services, seek to dissolve pathology in the parent–child relationship.

The group counseling program is likely to include parents who are seriously disturbed and who face serious problems. Family life education programs usually involve clients who are educable, who are free to interact with the educational content in a rational manner, and who are fully conscious of why they accept or reject the material being discussed. Group counseling programs, on the other hand, usually involve clients who, because of emotional conflicts of some consequence, are not fully conscious of why they react negatively or overenthusiastically to the material being discussed.

Parent life education is based on the assumption that difficulties in parent–child relationships often arise from limited experience and lack of knowledge rather than as a result of any personality difficulty. Group counseling programs assume that the parent has some personality difficulty.

The difference in composition of the two kinds of groups also determines differences in the activity of the social worker or the discussion leader. In the family life education programs, the leader is an educator–expert on parent–child relationships and is responsible for presenting to the group what research and experience have determined as the best approach in meeting parental problems. In the group counseling sessions, the discussion leader is more apt to be permissive, noncommittal, and neutral.

The family life education program has an orderly progression of meetings, the leader setting out in advance what is, in effect, the syllabus of a course in parent education. The syllabus, however, is kept flexible so as to give group members the opportunity of modifying it to reflect their preferences. The content of the group counseling meetings is less structured, being designed primarily in response to the changing emotional needs of the group. The emphasis is on emotional expressiveness and spontaneity, and the leader acts so as to reward such responses rather than more intellectual, more conventional responses.

Educational group leaders are more apt to be task-oriented and are concerned with communicating a body of content. Group counselors are apt to be concerned less with a specific task than with establishing and maintaining an atmosphere conducive to relaxation and full discussion with a minimum of defensiveness. Here the interaction among group members is the primary vehicle for helping parents to effect changes in their relationships with their children.

The group counseling meetings are frequently a later adjunct to the casework services being received by the family. In family life education programs, on the other hand, parents who display a need for more intensive, more individualized contact through group discussions are referred for casework services.

There are significant similarities between the two kinds of groups. Both tend to concern themselves with recurrent situations that occasion difficulties for parents and children: questions about "eating, sleeping, toilet training, the handling of aggression, the question of discipline, how to deal with sibling rivalry, how to handle sex curiosity . . . the child's reactions to disturbing experiences, such as death in the family" (Pollak, 1953, p. 200).

Both the family life educator and the group counselor must establish an atmosphere conducive to effective interaction—a warm, psychologically safe, affectively positive atmosphere. In both groups, the leader plays the role of stimulating, expediting, and guiding discussion. In both groups, the leader must have a permissive, accepting, reassuring manner.

Both kinds of groups tend to draw on the living experiences of the parents with their children and to involve the emotional as well as the intellectual participation of the group members. Out of a sharing of common experiences and involvement with the content should come a greater understanding and capacity for parenthood.

The parent education programs sponsored by supportive service agencies have a preventive as well as supportive intent. Brim points out that parents to-day are less likely to have been socialized to the parental role through traditional channels (Brim, 1959, pp. 17–18). Because the grandmother, the experienced parent, does not often live with the new mother, she is not in a position to demonstrate and supervise child-rearing practices. Even if the grandmother could do this, the development of scientific knowledge regarding child rearing has supplanted traditional approaches. Science supposedly makes available more desirable ways of rearing children than does tradition. Consequently, parent edu-cation programs are designed as formal channels of communication between the expert–scientist and the modern parent. The aim in many of the programs is to help parents "achieve the ability to accept themselves, to discover their own strength, and to develop the ability to find their own answers in handling their children" (Brim, 1959, p. 103).

Both in the individual interviews and in the group meeting, it is hoped that the parents will gain increased understanding of children's needs in general and of the needs of their child in particular, some further understanding of the parental role, and increased self-awareness about their reactions to their child and the effects of their behavior on the child. With increased understanding, increased self-awareness, and the support of the caseworker and/or the group may come the necessary changes in their relationship with the child that will re-sult in greater satisfaction in the parental role. The aim is to develop greater self-confidence in the parents, to make them feel more at ease and more relaxed in their role as parents. This result in itself is believed to create a healthier cli-mate for child development. Parents in the group may identify with a more ther-apeutic approach to children as exemplified in the attitude of the group leader.

When the group is organized, its purpose is discussed with individuals and with organizations asking for a group leader in behalf of their members. An ef-fort is made to clarify expectations. Individuals may not be admitted to a group if they are so disturbed as to behave in a way that will disrupt the group. For some parents, however, the group approach is the approach of choice. This is based on some advantageous characteristics of the group approach, such as the following:

1. The group counseling situation may make acceptance of a treatment relationship easier for some clients. The focus of attention is wider in a group, and the relationship with the social worker is not so embarrass-ingly intense and threatening as it is in a casework situation.
2. In the group, negative feelings toward the worker, the agency, and the child can often be more easily expressed because of the "safety in numbers."
3. The fear of overdependency on the worker, excited in the one-to-one interview relationship, is less intense in the group.
4. Suggestions for changes in child care may be more easily accepted by some parents in the group situation than in individual interviews. Mem-bers of the group identify with one another and tend to help each other find solutions to similar problems. Criticism that would not ordinarily be accepted without resentment may often be accepted from a fellow group member.
5. The parent, in exchanging experiences with others facing similar prob-

lems, is stimulated to verbalize his often negative feelings about his child with less anxiety and comes to view his behavior more objectively.

6. The parent's anxiety is reduced as he comes to realize that his child and his reaction as a parent are not as atypical as he had supposed. Hearing from other parents that they too have similar difficulties is reassuring.

7. The parent derives value from sharing experiences regarding possible solutions to problem situations. The repertoire of possible solutions available to each group member is increased as those offered by other members are added to those that the group develops in discussing parent–child problems.

Child guidance clinics have developed family life education programs designed to introduce groups of parents to the use of behavioral approaches. Although the success of these programs has been limited, the definite, precise procedures give the parents a sense of control and relief from feelings of hopelessness about their children's disturbing behavior (Rose, 1972, 1977).

Behavioral modification approaches have also been used to treat children in the context of peer groups (Rose, 1969).

Family service agencies offer group education programs to families who are not having any difficulty but who want to learn procedures for more effective parenting to prevent problems from developing. Group education programs are designed as preventive interventions. Their objective is to teach parents about child development and child behavior so as to enable them to do a more effective job of parenting.

The curriculum of such family life education programs is often built around programs of parent training such as the Parent Effectiveness Training program developed by Gordon (1975) or the behavioral modification manuals by Becker (1971) or Patterson (1971). Through such educational programs, agencies help parents to feel more confidence in their parenting skills, to develop a greater understanding and tolerance of children's behavior, and to build skills in the reflective communication of feeling, leading to a cooperative resolution of parent–child conflicts. The importance of increasing reciprocal supportive behavior and decreasing defensive behavior is stressed.

Active, emphatic listening, reflective responding, behavorial contracting, and conflict-negotiating procedures are among the kinds of concrete specific skills that are designed to be taught to parents in such programs. In addition, they are taught skills in praising, ignoring, behaving consistently, communicating, and making positive affective statements ("I liked the way you did that").

An effort is made to teach the parent more careful observation of the behavior that presents a problem in the parent–child relationship, to pinpoint the specific nature of the behavior, and to record it accurately. In each instance, an effort is made to define behavior specifically: *hyperactivity* may translate into the number of times the child leaves the table during the course of a meal; *disobedience* may translate into the number of times the child refused to make his bed or clear the table; *dawdling* into the time it takes for the child to get out of bed and get dressed after awakening; *aggressiveness* into the number of hits exchanged by a brother and sister between three and eight o'clock on a school day.

Changes in parental behaviors are also defined in specific terms: "not hitting the child when the child talks back to the parent," "not calling the child derogatory names," "talking to the child at mealtime," and so on.

Money has been used as a program incentive. The parents pay an initial $50 for admission to the program. For the completion of each homework assignment, each data sheet form, and so on, some money is returned. If the parents complete all of the requirements, the partial repayments add up in the end to a refund of the initial fee paid.

In 1976, 79 per cent of family service agencies were offering some kind of family life education program, the most frequently offered special service in addition to individual counseling. Social workers in such agencies were using a wide variety of intervention procedures in offering help to clients. Sixty per cent or more of agency workers had training in transactional analysis, behavioral modification, gestalt therapy, sex therapy, family group treatment, parent effectiveness training, or multiple impact therapy. Behavior modification and family group therapies were the most frequently employed interventions (Family Service Association of America, 1977).

Family Therapy Approach

There has been a strong trend toward the use of family therapy in dealing with parent–child problems. Family service agencies as well as child guidance clinics have participated in this trend. Both agencies are using (1) joint-interview casework sessions in which a married couple meets with a caseworker and (2) family interviews (casework sessions that include the couple and one or more other members of the nuclear or extended family). The change in focus over time has been from treating the child, to treating the child and the mother, to treating the child and both parents, to treating the family unit of which the child is a member.

Family therapy is based on "dynamically oriented interviews with the whole family," viewed as a behavioral and social system. It focuses on the family as an integrative unit, as a special entity greater than the sum of individual family members. The assumption is that the child is what he is because the family is what it is and that if the child is to change, the family must change, too. As the child does not get "sick" alone, he will not get well alone. Meeting with the family rather than with individual members permits the worker to obtain a more accurate and more relevant diagnostic understanding of the family. Rather than being told about family interaction, he can observe directly the patterns of leadership and control, the allocation of roles, the pattern of intrafamily communication, the nature of conflict, the operation and effectiveness of mutual defenses, the nature of family alliances and rejections, the extent and nature of existing strengths. Intrapersonal problems can be observed as they become visibly manifested in interpersonal encounters.

In family interviewing what one parent conceals the other reveals. What the parents hide together the child blurts out. What one member expresses in a twisted prejudiced way is corrected by another when certain anxiety-filled material is touched on. The family may engage in a silent pact to avoid these areas. But sooner or later such denials are broken through. Family life by its very nature is inimical to the guarding of personal secrets [1, p. 94].

Through the family interview, "the worker and all participating family members are directly and mutually exposed to each other's impact with the result that the worker is placed in an especially strategic position for intervening directly in the system" (Couch, 1969, p. 280). The worker can stimulate new patterns of interaction, can directly encourage expression of feeling, and at the same time can provide a safe context for the expression of such feeling and offer protection to the family member against whom negative feelings might be expressed. He can demonstrate, for family observation, new ways of relating to each other. In the presence of all, the "worker legitimizes new norms and expands members' perceptions of the range of permissible and worthwhile behavior, thus stimulating all [family members] simultaneously to modify basic norms controlling their family interaction" (Couch, 1969, p. 284).

Community Organization Approach

In addition to casework and group work, the family service agencies offer a supportive service to parents and children through their community organization activity. These agencies call attention to problems in the community that are likely to have an adverse effect on parent–child relationships and attempt to mobilize the community to remedy such situations. Child guidance clinics, too, have operated on the community level to develop a more receptive and understanding attitude on the part of community leaders toward parent–child relationship problems and to develop better coordination of services to the families presenting such problems.

The 1970 decade witnessed a decided oscillation in approaches to the problems faced by supportive agency clientele. In 1970–1971, there had been a very decided shift in the balance between casework and alternative methods in family-service agency approaches to problems presented by clients. Not only was there a shift in the modality of service, but there was an associated shift in the population to which principal service efforts were to be directed—from middle-class white to lower-class white and nonwhite.

The most notable example of this change in emphasis was the announcement in February 1971 by the Community Service Society of New York that it planned to terminate "123 years of family casework and individual counseling." The Community Service Society, established in 1848 as the Association for Improving the Conditions of the Poor, is the oldest and largest family service agency in America. The society explained the policy change by noting that casework and individual counseling "had proved inadequate for the poor who face overwhelming problems in the slums." The general director of the society noted that "If the individual is to be helped, someone has to deal with the complex of social ills that bears on the individual, not just the individual himself. Instead of starting out by saying that 'the individual is the client,' we're going to say the 'community is the client' " (The New York Times, January 29, 1971). As an alternative, the society planned to work directly with existing neighborhood groups to deliver services, to exert pressure on government agencies, and to coordinate existing public and private programs.

Similarly, on January 4, 1972, the National Conference of Catholic Charities, one of the largest of the nationwide denominational agencies, announced that the "organization planned to supplement its traditional social services [which included supportive family services] with a new focus on political activism" (*The New York Times*, January 5, 1972).

The announcement by the Community Service Society of its abandonment of casework as its principal operative approach in helping the client was, however, only a more dramatic and extreme example of a shift previously debated and adopted by the Family Service Association of America. In 1969 the organization adopted a program of family advocacy. This involved helping families

> develop effective strategies to deal with the systems that are failing to meet their needs, secure a fair share of existing resources and services as well as develop new ones. First priority at this time will be given to high risk families suffering most acutely from the impact of racism, dehumanization, poverty, and injustice—the Family Service Association of America will begin with an attempt to adapt Family Service to the needs of the poor and nonwhite communities [Family Service Association of America, 1969].

Patrick V. Riley, Assistant General Director of the FSAA, defined the changed approach as dealing "with institutional systems rather than with individuals" (Riley, 1971, p. 374). Family service agencies are encouraged by the policy statement to become involved in local social action in behalf of clients—to move from "case to cause" (Manser, 1973).

By the middle of the 1970s, the pendulum had begun to swing back somewhat. The Community Service Agency, which had signaled its intention to abandon individual casework in favor of community action and development, reversed its orientation a few years later. In 1973 a new director was appointed who supported multifaceted approaches that included individual counseling as one of the principal options. Apparently a community action and community development approach had been more difficult to implement than had been anticipated.

In the previous edition of this book, published in 1974, it was noted at this point that:

> At the present writing, while there is considerable pious, rhetorical support for the change in emphasis, and some beginning limited action, most social workers, in most family service agencies, continue day by day to do the work illustrated in this chapter. They are painfully and conscientiously working with conflicted parents and children on an individual family counseling basis to support, strengthen, and reinforce whatever positive aspects there are in the relationship, so that the family can live together with slightly less aggravation, and slightly more satisfaction. This is, after all, an eminently worthy endeavor for which no one needs to apologize.
>
> Given the continuing if not the exclusive need for some kind of casework—individual counseling, the problem then becomes one of increasing the effectiveness of the therapeutic technology of the supportive services caseworker. One way

this is being attempted is through the use of radically different approaches to helping, such as behavioral modification as noted above.

This quotation, in general, describes the situation as it exists at the time of this writing in 1978. The shift in the early part of the decade toward greater concern with community action and systems change has left a legacy, however, in terms of more explicit interest and activity around advocacy on behalf of children. In response to resolutions adopted by the 1970 White House Conference on Children, a Federal Office of Child Advocacy has been established. Many states have attempted to develop an organizational structure for programs of child advocacy, coordinating the efforts of private and public agencies and citizens' groups. The child advocate is concerned with the interests and welfare of children, monitoring the local situation to ensure that children's rights are secured and that their needs are met. The activity implies "intervention on behalf of children in relation to those services and those institutions which impinge on their lives" (Kahn, Kamerman, McGowan, 1972, p. 11). The orientation of advocacy programs suggests a conscious concern with changes in all the institutions, in addition to the family, that may affect a child's life:

> The most common targets of family service advocacy are the systems involving education, public welfare, health, housing, and employment. The actions range from seeking changes in operating policies and practices that can be readily achieved at the local level to seeking to influence public attitudes to seeking to change state or federal legislation or administration policy [Riley, 1971, p. 379; Paul, Neufeld, Pelosi, 1977].

A nationwide census in 1976 of 273 member agencies of the Family Service Association of America indicated that only 28 per cent of the reporting agencies were involved in any advocacy activity. Only 8 per cent of the agencies had a full-time advocacy staff member (Family Service Association of America, 1977).

A national overview of child advocacy, *Child Advocacy Programs, 1975* (National Center for Child Advocacy, 1976), lists a total of about 130 programs throughout the entire country. Although the study indicates that this is not an exhaustive list, it was apparently all that a fairly intensive census effort by the National Center for Child Advocacy was able to uncover. The descriptions of the program activities indicate that rather traditional programs are being offered by these agencies, some of which have been in existence for some time: providing public education, offering consultation, reviewing legislation. In a limited number of instances, groups were involved in proposing legislation and supporting, lobbying, and advising legislators and in organizing support for children's causes (McGowan, 1978).

EVALUATION OF SERVICE

Individual Treatment

The extent to which the counseling services offered by supportive service agencies help in resolving the client's problem is not clear. There is the broad question of the effectiveness of counseling and psychotherapeutic procedures generally and beyond that the question of the comparative effectiveness of the different therapeutic approaches.

A heightened concern with accountability regarding agency service during the 1970s has led to an intensified evaluation of results. As a consequence, there has been a considerable proliferation of research and discussion with regard to this question. Only a limited amount of this material is directly concerned with supportive services, although almost all of it is indirectly relevant because even when it is not focused on treating parent–child relationship problems, it tests the therapeutic interventions that are being used in such treatment. Given the complexity of the issues, the diversity of the results obtained, and the limited space that can be devoted here to the highly specialized questions raised, we can add only some general pointers and warn the reader to proceed with caution and skepticism.

Earlier studies of family service agencies tended to be equivocal in the evaluation of results (Kogan et al., 1953; Ripple, 1957, 1964; Meyer et al., 1965; Geismar, Krisberg, 1966, 1967; Kuhl, 1969). In general, more often than not, modest positive results were achieved for more than half of the clients served. Solutions were easier to find for specific external problems than for problems requiring personality change.

On three different occasions, Levitt (1957, 1963, 1972) summarized the studies evaluating results of child guidance clinic service. In each instance, he arrived at the general conclusion that the effectiveness of psychotherapy in dealing with emotional illness in children is yet to be proved. He pointed out that a favorable outcome was more likely in cases with identifiable behavioral symptoms like enuresis and school phobia and least likely in cases of delinquency and acting out.

A limited number of more recent studies of family service agencies by Sherman et al. (1973), Beck and Jones (1973), Sainsbury (1975), and Dailey and Ives (1978) tend to support these general conclusions. For instance, the Child Welfare League studied the supportive services offered to children in their own home (Sherman, Phillips, Haring, Shyne, 1973). The group of children studied had been referred to child welfare agencies for possible foster-care placement. A careful review of the situation resulted in a decision on the part of the worker to maintain the child in his own home and to work with the family toward amelioration of their problems. Four child-care agencies and some 185 families were involved in the study. The problems involved neglect and abuse, the need for day care, and emotional–behavioral problems manifested by either the parent or the child. Most families received multiple services, which almost always included casework counseling either as the primary service or in addition to financial assistance, day care, homemaker service, medical and/or psychiatric service, vocational training, and job placement.

The mother's emotional functioning, and care of the child were among the most frequent and most important subjects discussed during casework counseling. The predominant approach used in the casework counseling was support—the expression by the worker of emotional "reassurance, understanding, encouragement or sympathy with the client's feeling, situation and efforts to cope with the situation" (p. 138). Support was twice as frequently employed as the technique ranked second in frequency of use, namely, "directive" action defined as the workers' attempts "through advice, recommendations or suggestions to promote or discourage particular client behaviors and course of action" (p. 138).

About two thirds of the families independently interviewed by research workers "had a positive perception of the helpfulness or effectiveness of the service." Children showed more positive changes than their parents, although the focus of service was on the parents. Parents showed positive changes in the areas of child-training methods, emotional care of the child, and parent–child relationships.

A more extensive study by Beck and Jones (1973) was based on information from all clients who came to family service agencies during one week in the spring of 1970. Two hundred and sixty-six family service agencies throughout the country reported on some 3,600 cases involving about 13,000 persons who came for service during that week. A high percentage of such cases coming to family service agencies involved parent–child problems.

Of the original group of 3,600 cases, about 1,900 were followed up after case closing, most often through a detailed personal interview. Using a structured interview outline, the interviewer attempted to find out about clients' dissatisfaction and satisfaction with the service and about changes in family functioning that the client attributed to the agency. At the same time, the caseworker responsible for service to the family was interviewed separately by the researchers to determine his view of the effects of service. The measures of change were, then, the subjective assessment by clients and workers, independently sharing their perceptions of the results of service.

Focusing on only those cases in which a parent–child relationship problem or a child-rearing problem was presented, the interviewers found that both caseworkers and parents reported improvement in about 63 per cent of the families. Of the children involved in these cases, 35 per cent showed improvement: "There was a marked association of counselor–client relationship with outcomes. With minor exceptions . . . this was found to be twice as powerful a predictor of outcomes as any other client or service characteristic covered by the study, and more *powerful* than all client characteristics combined" [emphasis in original] (Beck, Jones, 1973, p. 8).

As ratings for worker–client relationships move from "unsatisfactory" to "very satisfactory," change scores showed a substantive and consistent increase at a level that is statistically highly significant. There is available a critical review of this research and the researchers' response (Schuerman, 1975; Beck, Jones, 1976).

There is some controversy about the effectiveness of social work intervention generally, and more specifically about the more traditional, psychoanalytically oriented casework. Fisher (1976), reviewing a variety of studies concerned with the testing of casework interventions, concluded that traditional casework procedures are generally not helpful and may, in some instances, be harmful. The critical comments on his conclusion by social work researchers included in the text tend to suggest that his summation is open to question (see also Gurman, 1974; Wood, 1978).

In contrast, the claim is made that behavior modification approaches are likely to be considerably more effective than traditional casework approaches in helping with the wide variety of parent–child problems that come to the attention of the supportive service agencies.

Behavior modification procedures have been employed with some measure of success with relatively mild problems of deportment, persistent disobedience in the home and in school, fighting with siblings and peers, and food fads, through more serious problems of stealing, fire-setting, serious aggression, sexual deviations, enuresis, phobic disorders, shyness and withdrawal, to the most serious problems of autism and childhood schizophrenia (Kazdin, Wilson, 1978, pp. 24–27).

Much of the behavior modification literature does present studies of successful change in children's behavior as a result of such intervention without any evidence of symptom substitution. Even studies contrasting the effects of such intervention with nontreated or differently treated control groups—as reported, for instance, by Christopherson et al. (1976) for a child guidance clinic population—show behavior modification as more effective. When additional tests of effectiveness are made, however, such as assessment of outcomes by a variety of procedures and follow-up assessment of maintenance of the change over time, the impact of behavior modification appears to be less potent than anticipated (Kent, O'Leary, 1976; Patterson, 1975).

Efforts have been made to test the comparative effectiveness of the two approaches to treatment broadly described in this chapter, namely, traditional psychotherapeutic casework and behavior modification. One of the more rigorously designed of such research efforts was by Sloane et al. (1975). The general conclusion was that both procedures are more effective than no treatment at all, and both are almost equally efficacious, the behavior modification approach being modestly more effective with some types of cases. An effort by Luborsky, Singer, Luborsky (1976) to answer the question of comparative effectiveness by reviewing the results of eighteen different studies with controlled comparisons showed behavior therapy to be superior to other psychotherapies in six comparisons and to be no different in twelve.

Reviewing over seventy studies comparing behavior modification procedures with alternative nonbehavioral methods, Kazdin and Wilson (1978) conclude that such competitive exercises are not particularly helpful. It is clear, whatever the box score, that behavior modification methods are generally useful in regard to many parent–child relationship problems, that a wide variety of diverse methods of behavior modification methods have been developed and are being refined so as to increase the probability of their enhanced effectiveness, that they are at least equally effective as alternative nonbehavioral methods and have the clear advantage of being more efficient. Instead of a concern with competitive comparison, the focus should be on defining what procedure is effective with what problem under what circumstances. Such a search should be conducted in a context that is receptive to any answer that is empirically supported by well-defined outcome measures of magnitude of change, desirability of change, consumer satisfaction, and cost effectiveness.

The fact that behavior modification therapists generally establish a positive relationship with clients points to another problem in evaluating the comparative effectiveness of different procedures. A variety of common "nonspecific effects" may be more important in accounting for the changes effected than the specifically differentiated procedures themselves: the placebo effect of hope and faith in the procedure communicated by the therapist; the Hawthorne effect resulting from the concern, attention, and interest of the therapist, no matter what is done; and the suggestions and expectations that are inherent in every approach (Russell, 1974; Shapiro, 1976).

Doing some violence to the details, the overall conclusion suggested by reviews of the psychotherapy outcome research might be summarized by the statement that some treatment is better than none, that the effect of treatment is modestly positive, and that the specific nature of the treatment may be less significant than the common "nonspecific effects." This statement echoes the general conclusion of President Carter's Commission on Mental Health (1978). Reviewing over five hundred studies of psychotherapy, they concluded:

> that the accumulated weight of evidence has shown that psychotherapy, at least in most situations, has a *detectable* positive effect among those treated. While treated patients often improve a great deal during psychotherapy, so do many control patients; relative to these changes, the *added* benefit from psychotherapy, while detectable, is modest. . . . The form of therapy has shown surprisingly little general relationship to effectiveness [emphasis in original] [Vol. 4, pp. 1750–1751].

The conclusion that the effect of individual psychotherapy is positive but modest may also be applicable to group treatment approaches, although there are few studies regarding such interventions that employ controls.

Wells, Dilkes, and Burkhardt (1977) reviewed the results of eighteen family-therapy outcome studies from 1950 to 1970 following an earlier review by Wells, Dilkes, and Trivelli (1972). They note that "only two studies demonstrated any real degree of satisfactory methodology" (p. 512). A recapitulation of results showed an "overall success rate for family therapy with children and adolescents (combining 'improved' and 'some improvement' categories) of 79 percent" (p. 512).

Comparing success rates for individual therapy and marital and family therapy in a review of some seventy-five studies, Gurman and Kniskern (1978) found group approaches to be more effective than individual therapy.

PROBLEMS

1. Many families who need, and can use, supportive services are reluctant to apply for them. Some of this reluctance arises from lack of knowledge of the availability of the services and may disappear with better dissemination of information. More frequently, however, parents fail to see the agencies as a resource that can help them resolve parent–child difficulties.

2. Another problem is that, having come, many clients drop out before obtaining the full benefit of the contact. A nationwide study of family service clients showed that about 40 per cent of all cases were closed because the client was unwilling, or failed, to continue contact. Child guidance clinics face a similar problem: dropout rates have been estimated at between 35 and 45 per cent.

Part of the difficulty is that the parents assume that the child will be "straightened out." The suggestion that the parents' behavior is contributing to the child's difficulty and that they must involve themselves in treatment is contrary to their expectations and is viewed as a threat. In place of advice and a prescription, they are invited to engage in a process of self-examination. Their expectation is that the clinic will deal directly and primarily with the child and that the child will be required to change (Maas, Kahn, 1955). Families also drop out because they see little change in the child's behavior as a consequence of agency contact (Farley, Peterson, Spanos, 1975).

Paralleling the reports on dropouts from individual casework, studies of dropouts from family therapy show that similar variables operate. Middle-class families in which the decision to accept help was shared between husband and wife were more likely to remain in family therapy than were lower-class families in which the couple were ambivalent about therapy or in which the husband maintained a highly authoritarian attitude (Slipp, Ellis, Kressel, 1974).

3. The reluctance to contact the supportive service agency and the drop-out rate of those who do come suggest a third problem: the casework-counseling approach of these agencies may not be either appropriate or acceptable to a group of potential clients and may have to be supplemented with a more active approach in which the client and the worker "do" things together and in which direct "advice" on parent–child relationships is prescribed.

A study by Mayer and Timms (1970) based on interviews with working-class clients of the Family Welfare Association in London, a British family service agency, suggests some of the reasons for the higher dropout rate among lower socioeconomic groups. Although the worker was concerned with determining and dealing with the "causes" of the problem, the working-class client was concerned with doing something about the problem directly. Each assumed that the other shared his view of what they were doing together. Thus the client soon became puzzled and frustrated by the worker's behavior. The research suggests that the worker would do well to make his assumptions and methods clear to the client.

4. Available research also indicates that it is difficult for people to find their way through the maze of social services or even to obtain the simple facts regarding their availability. Low-income people who might need the services most are often least likely to know about them and least capable of dealing with the red tape surrounding them. In many sections of the country, moreover, no supportive services are available; in others, such services are heavily duplicated. Professionally trained personnel, therefore, may be inefficiently deployed.

5. The problem of "boundaries" also plagues supportive service agencies: Where does the family service agency end and the child guidance clinic begin? The child is part of the family; the disturbed child is still a child and a member of the family. To treat the child apart from the family is as illogical as to treat the family apart from the child. As a result of this ambiguity, some family service agencies and some children's agencies have merged to form family and children's agencies.

6. Family service agencies have continuing problems in finding adequate funding. Between 1966 and 1976 there was a reduction in the support for family service agencies received from United Ways and sectarian federations and an increase in funding from governmental sources. Despite the fact that support from government increased from 12 to 29 per cent as the source of agency funding, the largest percentage of such support (51 per cent) still came from United Ways and sectarian federations. Only 8 per cent of family-service agency funds came from client fees for casework counseling (Family Service Associations of America, 1977, pp. 6–7).

TRENDS

The preceding discussion noted that there is a trend toward more frequent employment of behavioral modification approaches by supportive agencies, a greater emphasis on a family-centered approach and the use of group procedures, and a shift in the balance between casework and community organization approaches to the client's problems.

1. The trend has been toward widening the responsibilities for supportive service to American families. Successive policy changes on the part of public welfare programs, particularly Aid to Families of Dependent Children (AFDC), have made the agencies responsible for offering supportive services to low-income families in the community.

Title XX, the recently adopted social services amendments to the Social Security Acts, makes such social services available to a broader public than AFDC recipients through county departments of public welfare. Comprehensive mental health centers also accept some responsibility for offering supportive services to the family.

2. A variety of new agencies now include family counseling as part of a complex program of social services. The Neighborhood Service Centers were established in response to the geographical inaccessibility of established agencies, the fragmented nature of their services, and their "formality." The traditional agencies are characterized as "too big, too distant, too self-serving—formal, impersonal, officious"; the neighborhood service center, on the other hand, is seen as "informal, personal, integrated" (O'Donnell, Sullivan, 1969, p. 1). The centers are located in low-income neighborhoods, often as storefront operations. They are open on weekends, informal in their intake procedures, and staffed in part by local residents.

The recency and rapidity of development of multiservice neighborhood centers can be grasped from the fact that in 1970 there were 2,500 such centers, 62 per cent of which had been established since 1964. The centers, located in low-income neighborhoods, serve a disproportionately great number of low-income clients (O'Donnell, Reid, 1971).

A supportive function is included among the stated goals of the community service center. Among the objectives of the center is to "maintain and improve parental functioning—to help parents to carry their responsibility for nurturing the health, education, growth and development of their children" (U.S. Department of Health, Education, and Welfare, 1970, p. 14). The multiservice neighborhood center stresses efforts to determine what the "consumer" wants from the agency. The shift in terminology from *client* to *consumer* is in itself a significant exemplification of a change in relationship between the agency and those who use the agency service fostered by the multiservice neighborhood centers. There is also a more explicit emphasis on the agency's responsibility for social action, community organization, and advocacy in behalf of neighborhood residents.

Despite the determined efforts of such agencies to be more responsive to the needs of local residents, preliminary studies show that they face many of the administrative problems that plague the more traditional agencies. The tendency is to solve these problems by making intake selective and by working toward specialization of service within the agency (Kirshner, 1966; Perlman, Jones, 1967; O'Donnell, Sullivan, 1969).

As Kahn (1976) says in reviewing the results of studies of such programs, "Despite all the complaints about service fragmentation and inadequacy to which they were the intended response, most of the more ambitious multi-service centers have offered little more than centralized intake. . . . They have seldom created a case integration service" (p. 34). Furthermore, although many multi-service centers were established with the intent of breaking with the casework orientation of traditional agencies, most centers find that their central activity is counseling—"trying to change the client or at least dealing with his problems"— rather than community action (O'Donnell, Reid, 1972, p. 7). This is, perhaps, a testimonial to the technological and political difficulties inherent in systems change and a suggestion that despite social work's best intentions, it may continue to stress individual casework.

Parent–child development centers, created by the Office of Economic Opportunity in 1970 and subsequently funded by the Office of Child Development of the Department of Health, Education, and Welfare, are also competing with the family service agency. Serving low-income families with young children, the parent–child centers include family counseling and family-life education as part of their service (Costello, Binstock, 1971).

The network of alternative agencies—hot-line crisis switchboards, drop-in centers, free clinics, and runaway houses—provides mental health support services. There is currently greater appreciation of the value of mobilizing the natural support system available to families through informal contacts with relatives, friends, and neighbors. The trend toward encouraging the development of self-help groups is a response to this approach.

Family service agencies are active in providing consultation to self-help groups, most frequently to Parents Without Partners and to Parents Anonymous, a self-help group of abusing parents.

3. There is increasing evidence that brief, preplanned service may be as effective as extended services in dealing with parent–child problems (Reid, Shyne, 1969; Reid, Epstein, 1972, 1977), and there is a trend toward the more frequent use of this approach. Reviewing the effects of brief, planned service in a family service agency, Reid and Shyne (1969) found improvement in about 81 per cent of the cases presenting parent–child relationship problems. Similarly, a four-year evaluation, using multiple measures of outcome, of a large-scale, brief therapy program at a psychiatric center for children and adolescents showed the procedure to be highly efficient and effective (Leventhal, Weinberger, 1975). Lower expenditures of casework time and effort yielded results as good as or better than more extended contact. Similar results have been obtained in experiments in child guidance clinics (Shaw, 1968; Barten, 1971).

Explanations for this finding relate to the fact that short-term treatment requires the explicit formulation of specific, limited goals that structure the joint activity of worker and client, and that awareness of time limitations may focus greater worker–client effort on problem solving.

As L. Parad (1971) points out, the largest percentage of clients coming to family service agencies and child guidance clinics have always continued only for a very limited number of interviews. However, a prolonged, intensive contact was thought to be most desirable and less "superficial." Currently the change is not as much a change in the percentage of clients coming for a limited number of interviews as it is a change in the attitude of professionals toward the desirability and utility of the short contact. There is growing acceptance of the therapeutic value of a limited contact and more deliberate planning for such contacts by professionals.

The whole push toward accountability and the more effective use of agency time, along with a greater acceptance of the behavior modification approaches, has resulted in a greater concern in supportive service agencies with doing specifically defined activities within time limits. Consequently we hear more about "contracting" (worker and client making contracts about what they hope to accomplish), "casework by objectives," "task-centered casework," and "planned short-term treatment." The emphasis is on making explicit the problems that will be worked on, the steps that will be taken to help the family, and the specific time limits in which change is to be accomplished.

4. The trend toward deliberate, consciously planned short contact is supported by a trend toward the more frequent use of "crisis intervention" approaches by supportive agencies (Rapoport, 1962). Crisis intervention derives from the concept of psychosocial equilibrium. When a stressful situation is encountered by the client—a member of the family falls ill, a man retires, another child is born, a job is lost, and so on—the previously established family equilibrium is disturbed, and if the disturbance is beyond the family's coping capacity, a crisis develops. During the period of crisis, "defenses are lowered—motivation is heightened, due to the discomfort of the anxiety created by the disequilibrium. . . . Thus, the individual is usually more amenable to help during crises and a minimum of therapeutic effort may have maximal therapeutic effect" (Parad, 1971, p. 139). If the agency intervenes at the point of crisis to help the family deal with the crisis, the contact is generally of short duration, terminating when some kind of equilibrium is restored.

In some innovative programs, crisis intervention has been implemented by intensive contact with the family. The social worker enters the home and stays for periods of four or five hours a number of times a week over an extended period, offering support to the family with the objective of preventing the foster-care placement of a child. The worker's case load is two families a month (Kinny, Madsen, Fleming, Haapala, 1975).

5. Because some clients are reluctant to make use of the agency, there is a trend toward what is sometimes termed *aggressive* or *assertive* casework. This involves a more active attempt to identify—generally through the help of the schools—those families in the community that are likely to be in trouble. Once the families are identified, the agency takes the initiative in going to them, telling them of the services that are available, and actively attempting to invite their use of the services. The agencies that have adopted such an approach have explored other, less traditional ways of helping families deal with parent–child relationship problems. Similarly, group work agencies—settlement houses, community centers, and so on—are reaching out to problem youths in their area who would never go near the agency. "Detached workers" move out of the agency and frequent local candy stores or poolrooms, getting acquainted with the neighborhood gangs and offering their help.

More frequently now family service agencies are establishing district or outpost offices to make service more geographically accessible.

6. Special projects have been developed by supportive service agencies to help families with particular needs. The Community Service Society of New York City has a Single Parent Family Project. Recognizing the special situation of single parents, the project conducts weekly discussion groups and a year-round calendar of parent and child outings and events, the costs of which are subsidized by the agency. Other agencies provide a hot-line service for single parents who feel a need to talk to someone about some crisis in their relationship with their children.

7. There has been a trend toward allowing greater choice of agency service through "purchase of care." Public agencies in need of counseling for their clients might arrange to purchase such service from a family service agency or a child guidance clinic. The client might then be permitted to select the agency of his choice, and the public welfare agency, having negotiated a contract with the voluntary agency, would pay for the needed service (Winogrand, 1970; Vorwaller, 1972; Manser, 1972).

In 1976 three quarters of the Family Service Association of America member agencies had purchase-of-service contracts with a public agency, generally involving Title XX funds.

8. The growing concern with the numbers of children in foster homes and institutions has resulted in a recent intensified interest in services to children in their own homes (Maybanks, Bryce, 1979). A variety of experimental programs have been developed in an effort to maintain children in their own homes and reduce the risk of substitute care placements. These will be discussed more fully in Chapter 8.

SUMMARY

The first line of defense in meeting child welfare problems is the supportive service. The family service agencies and child guidance clinics are available to support, strengthen, and reinforce the family in dealing with conflicts in the parent–child relationship network. In offering such help, supportive services remain outside the family social system.

Family service agencies have their origin in the charity organizations that sought to make charity more scientific and effective. Child guidance clinics have their origin in attempts to deal with juvenile delinquency. Family service agencies come to child welfare through treatment of the parent; the child guidance clinics have always been concerned directly with the child.

Both child guidance clinics and family service agencies are unevenly distributed throughout the country and serve a relatively small percentage of the population. It is estimated that all the child guidance clinics and family service agencies in the nation do not serve more than a half million children a year.

Workers in both agencies seek to create a therapeutic relationship with the parent and/or the child. The relationship is used as a source of influence, a source of identification, and the basis for a corrective emotional experience.

Evaluation studies tend to suggest that the service is helpful, but available research does not establish this helpfulness at statistically significant levels.

Among the problems faced by supportive agencies are high dropout rates resulting in inefficient use of service; reluctance to use the service on the part of many who need it; the inapplicability of a psychotherapeutic approach to the supportive agency client; the limited availability of supportive service; and overlap between the responsibilities of family service agencies and guidance clinics.

Among the trends identified were a greater emphasis on community organization–social action approaches and a decreased emphasis on casework, more frequent use of behavioral modification procedures, an increase in the diversity of agencies offering supportive services, changes in the service delivery systems, the greater acceptance of "aggressive" social work, the greater acceptance of family group therapy and brief treatment procedures, and the growth of purchase-of-care arrangements.

BIBLIOGRAPHY

ACKERMAN, NATHAN. *Treating the Troubled Family.* New York: Basic Books, Inc., 1966.

BARTEN, HARVEY B. *Brief Therapies.* New York: Behavioral Publications, 1971.

BECK, DOROTHY F. "Research Findings on the Outcome of Marital Counseling." *Social Casework* (March 1975), 153–181.

————, and MARY A. JONES. "Debate with Authors." *Social Service Review,* 3 (June 1976), 312–331.

BECKER, WESLEY C. *Parents and Teachers: A Child Management Program.* Champaign, Ill.: Research Press, 1971.

BRIM, ORVILLE, JR. *Education for Child Rearing.* New York: Russell Sage Foundation, 1959.

BRUCK, MAX. "Behavior Modification Theory and Response: A Critical Review." *Social Work,* 13, 2 (April 1968), 43–55.

CARTER, ROBERT D., and RICHARD B. STUART. "Behavior Modification Theory and Practice: A Reply." *Social Work,* 15, 1 (January 1970).

CHRISTOPHERSEN, EDWARD R. *et al.* "The Family Training Program: Improving Parent–Child Interaction Patterns," pp. 36–56, in *Behavior Modification Approaches to Parenting,* Eric J. Mash, Lee C. Handy, and Leo A. Hamerlynck, Eds. New York: Brunner/Mazel, 1976.

CLOWARD, RICHARD, and IRWIN EPSTEIN. *Private Social Welfare's Disengagement from the Poor: The Case of Family Adjustment Agencies.* 1964. Mimeo.

CONRAD, GERTRUDE. "The First Eighteen Months of Group Counseling in a Family Service Agency." *Social Casework,* 40, 3 (March 1959).

COSTELLO, JOAN, and ELEANOR BINSTOCK. *Review and Summary of a National Survey of the Parent–Child Center Program.* Office of Child Development, U.S. Department of Health, Education, and Welfare. Washington, D.C.: Government Printing Office, 1971.

COUCH, ELSBETH H. *Joint and Family Interviews in the Treatment of Marital Problems.* New York: Family Service Association of America, 1969.

DAILEY, WILDA J., and KENNETH IVES. "Exploring Client Reactions to Agency Services." *Social Casework* (April 1978), 233–245.

EWALT, PATRICIA L. "Psychoanalytically Oriented Child Guidance Setting," pp. 27–34, in *Task Centered Practice*. Ed. by William Reid and Laura Epstein. New York: Columbia University Press, 1977.

FAMILY SERVICE ASSOCIATION OF AMERICA. *Scope and Methods of the Family Service Agency*. New York: Family Service Association of America, 1953.

————. *Summary of Family Advocacy Program November 26, 1969*. Mimeo. New York: Family Service Association of America, 1969.

————. *Agency Program and Funding—1976*. New York: Family Service Association of America, December 1977.

FANSHEL, DAVID. *An Overview of One Agency's Casework Operation*. Pittsburgh: Family and Children's Service, October 1958.

FARLEY, WILLIAM O., KIM D. PETERSON, and GERALD SPANOS. "Self Termination from a Child Guidance Center." *Community Mental Health Journal*, 11 (1975), 325–34.

FISHER, JOEL. *The Effectiveness of Social Casework*. Springfield, Ill.: Charles C Thomas, 1976.

FISHER, JOEL, and HARVEY L. GOCHROS. *Planned Behavior Change: Behavior Modification in Social Work*. New York: The Free Press, 1975.

GAMBRILL, EILEEN D. *Behavior Modification—Handbook of Assessment, Intervention and Evaluation*. San Francisco: Jossey-Bass, Inc., 1977.

GARVEY, WILLIAM P., and JACK R. HEGRENES. "Desensitization Techniques in the Treatment of a School Phobia." *American Journal of Orthopsychiatry*, 36 (January 1966), 147–152.

GEISMAR, LUDWIG L. "Implications of a Family Life Improvement Project." *Social Casework*, 52, 7 (July 1971), 455–465.

————, and JANE KRISBERG. "The Family Life Improvement Project," Part I. *Social Casework*, 47, 9 (November 1966), 563–570. Part II. *Social Casework*, 47, 10 (December 1966), 663–667.

————. *The Forgotten Neighborhood*. Metuchen, N.J.: Scarecrow Press, 1967.

GOLDSMITH, JEROME. "Mental Health Services for Children," pp. 891–897, in *Encyclopedia of Social Work*, John B. Turner, Editor in Chief. New York: National Association of Social Workers, 1977.

GORDON, THOMAS. *P.E.T.--Parent Effectiveness Training*. New York: New American Library, 1975.

GURMAN, ALAN S. "The Efficacy of Therapeutic Intervention in Social Work: A Critical Reevaluation." *Journal of Health and Social Behavior*, 15 (June 1974), 136–140.

GURMAN, ALAN S., and DAVID P. KNISKERN. "Research on Marital and Family Therapy: Progress, Perspective and Prospect," in *Handbook of Psychotherapy and Behavior Change*, 2nd ed. Ed. by S. L. Garfield and A. E. Bergin. New York: John Wiley & Sons, Inc., 1978.

HARPER, AMOS, *et al*. *American Charities and Social Work*, 4th ed. New York: Thomas Y. Crowell Company, 1940.

HASENFELD, YEHESKEL. "Organization Dilemmas in Innovating Social Services: The Case of Community Action Centers." *Journal of Health and Social Behavior*, 12 (September 1971), 208–216.

HAWKINS, ROBERT P., *et al*. "Behavior Therapy in the Home: Amelioration of Problem Parent–Child Relations with the Parent in a Therapeutic Role." *Journal of Experimental Child Psychology*, 4 (1966), 94–107.

HILL, WILLIAM G., JOSEPH B. LEHMANN, and ELIZABETH J. SLOTKIN. *Family Service Agencies and Mental Health Clinics*. New York: Family Service Association of America, 1971.

HIRSCH, JOSEPHINE S., JACQUELYNNE GAILEY, and ELEANOR SCHMEL. "A Child Welfare Agency's Program of Services to Children in Their Own Homes." *Child Welfare* (March 1976), 193–204.

HOBBS, NICHOLAS. "Sources of Gain in Psychotherapy." *American Psychologist,* **17** (November 1962).

HUBER, HERMAN, and FRANK LYNCH. "Teaching Behavioral Skills to Parents—A Preventive Role for Mental Health." *Children Today* (January–February 1978), 8–10.

JEHU, DEREK. *Learning Theory and Social Work.* London: Kegan Paul, Trench, Trubner & Co., 1967.

JOHNSON, CLAUDIA, and ROGER C. KATZ. "Using Parents as Change Agents for Their Children: A Review." *Journal of Child Psychology and Psychiatry,* **14** (1973), 181–200.

KAHN, ALFRED S. "Service Delivery at the Neighborhood Level: Experience, Theory and Fads." *Social Service Review* (March 1976), 23–56.

KAHN, ALFRED, SHEILA KAMERMAN, and BRENDA McGOWAN. *Child Advocacy—Report of a National Baseline Study.* New York: Columbia University School of Social Work, 1972.

KAZDIN, ALAN E.; WILSON, G. TERENCE. *Evaluation of Behavior through Therapy: Issues, Evidence and Research Strategies.* Cambridge, Mass.: Ballinger Publishing Co., 1978.

KEITH, PAT M. "Perceptions of Participants in a Family Life Education Program." *Social Casework* (February 1978), 116–119.

KENT, RONALD N., and K. DANIEL O'LEARY. "A Controlled Evaluation of Behavior Modification with Conduct Problem Children." *Journal of Clinical and Consulting Psychology,* **44,** 4 (1976), 586–596.

KINNY, JILL M., BARBARA MADSEN, THOMAS FLEMING and DAVID A. HAAPALA. "Home Builders: Keeping Families Together." *Journal of Consulting and Clinical Psychology,* **45** (1975), 667–73.

KIRSCHNER ASSOCIATES. *A Description and Evaluation of Neighborhood Centers—A Report for the Office of Economic Opportunity.* December 1966.

KOGAN, LEONARD, *et al. A Follow-up Study of the Results of Social Casework.* New York: Family Service Association of America, 1953.

KUHL, P. H. *The Family Center Project: Action Research on Socially Deprived Families.* Copenhagen: The Danish Institute of Social Research, Publication 35, 1969.

LEFF, ROBERT. "Behavior Modification and the Psychosis of Childhood: A Review." *Psychological Bulletin,* **69,** 6 (June 1968), 396–409.

LEVENTHAL, THEODORE, and GERALD WEINBERGER. "Evaluation of a Large Scale Brief Therapy Program." *American Journal of Orthopsychiatry,* **45,** 1 (January 1975), 119–133.

LEVINE, MURRAY, and ADELINE LEVINE. *A Social History of Helping Services—Clinic, Court, School, and Community.* New York: Appleton-Century-Crofts, 1970.

LEVINGER, GEORGE. "Continuance in Casework and Other Helping Relationships: A Review of Current Research." *Social Work,* **5** (July 1960).

LEVITT, EUGENE. "The Results of Psychotherapy with Children: An Evaluation." *Journal of Consulting Psychology,* **21** (1957).

———. "Psychotherapy with Children: A Further Evaluation." *Behavioral Research Therapy,* **1** (1963).

———. "Research on Psychotherapy with Children," in *Handbook on Psychotherapy and Behavior Change—An Empirical Analysis.* Ed. by Allen E. Bergin and Sol L. Garfield. New York: John Wiley & Sons, Inc., 1972.

LUBORSKY, LESTER, BARTON SINGER, and LISE LUBORSKY. "Comparative Studies of Psychotherapies: Is It True That 'Everybody Has Won and All Must Have Prizes?'" pp. 3–22, in *Evaluation of Psychological Therapies.* Ed. by Robert L. Spitzer and Donald F. Klein. Baltimore: Johns Hopkins University Press, 1976.

LURIE, OLGA. "Parents' Attitudes Toward Children's Problems and Toward Use of

Mental Health Services." *American Journal of Orthopsychiatry,* **44** (January 1974), 109–20.

MAAS, HENRY, and ALFRED KAHN. "Sociocultural Factors in Psychiatric Clinic Services for Children." *Smith College Studies in Social Work* **25** (February 1955).

MANSER, ELLEN (Ed.). *Family Advocacy—A Manual for Action.* New York: Family Service Association of America, 1973.

MANSER, GORDON. "Implications of Purchase of Service for the Voluntary Agencies." *Social Casework,* **53**, 6 (June 1972), 335–341.

MASH, ERIC J., LEE C. HANDY, and LEO A. HAMERLYNCK. *Behavior Modification: Approaches to Parenting.* New York: Brunner/Mazel, 1976.

MAYBANKS, SHEILA, and MARVIN BRYCE. *Home Based Services for Children and Families.* Springfield, Ill.: Charles C Thomas, 1979.

MAYER, JOHN E., and NOEL TIMMS. *The Client Speaks—Working Class Impressions of Casework.* London: Kegan Paul, Trench, Trubner & Co., 1970.

McCAULEY, ROGER, and PATRICIA McCAULEY. *Child Behavior Problems—An Empirical Approach to Management.* New York: Free Press, 1977.

McGOWAN, BRENDA G. "The Case Advocacy Function in Child Welfare Practice." *Child Welfare,* **57** (May 1978), 275–284.

McPHERSON, SANDRA B., and CYRILLE R. SAMUELS. "Teaching Behavioral Methods to Parents." *Social Casework,* **52**, 3 (March 1971), 148–153.

MEYER, HENRY S., *et al. Girls at Vocational High.* New York: Russell Sage Foundation, 1965.

NATIONAL CENTER FOR CHILD ADVOCACY, OFFICE OF CHILD DEVELOPMENT, U.S. DEPARTMENT OF HEALTH, EDUCATION, AND WELFARE, *Child Advocacy Program, 1975.*
Washington, D.C.: Government Printing Office, 1976.

O'DELL, S. "Training Parents in Behavior Modification: A Review." *Psychological Bulletin,* **81** (1974), 418–423.

O'DONNELL, EDWARD L., and OTTO M. REID. "The Multiservice Neighborhood Center—Preliminary Findings from a National Survey." *Welfare in Review,* **9**, 3 (May–June 1971), 1–8.

————, and OTTO M. REID. "The Multiservice Neighborhood Center—Neighborhood Challenge and Center Response." *Welfare in Review,* **10** (1972), 1–7.

O'DONNELL, EDWARD L., and MARILYN M. SULLIVAN. "Service Delivery and Social Action Through the Neighborhood Center—A Review of Research." *Welfare in Review,* **7**, 6 (November–December 1969), 11–12.

PARAD, LIBBIE. "Short-Term Treatment: An Overview of Historical Trends, Issues and Potentials." *Smith College Studies in Social Work,* **51** (February 1971), 119–146.

PATTERSON, GERALD R. *Families—Applications of Social Learning to Family Life.* Champaign, Ill.: Peacock Press Co., 1971.

PATTERSON, G. R. *The Aggressive Child: Victim and Architect of Coercive System,* in L. A. Hamerlynck, E. J. Marsh, L. C. Handy, Eds., *Behavior Manifestation and Families.* New York: Brunner/Mazel, 1975.

PAUL, JAMES L., G. RONALD NEUFELD, and JOHN W. PELOSI, Eds. *Child Advocacy Within the System.* Syracuse, N.Y.: Syracuse University Press, 1977.

PERLMAN, ROBERT, and DAVID JONES. *Neighborhood Service Centers.* U.S. Department of Health, Education, and Welfare. Washington, D.C.: Government Printing Office, 1967.

POLLAK, G. "Family Life Education, Its Focus and Techniques." *Social Casework,* **34** (May 1953).

PRESIDENT'S COMMISSION ON MENTAL HEALTH. *Task Panel Reports,* Vols. 2–4. Washington, D.C.: Government Printing Office, 1978.

RAPOPORT, LYDIA. "The State of Crises: Some Theoretical Considerations." *Social Service Review*, 26 (1962).

REID, WILLIAM J., and ANN W. SHYNE. *Brief and Extended Casework*. New York: Columbia University Press, 1969.

———, and LAURA EPSTEIN. *Task-Centered Casework*. New York: Columbia University Press, 1972.

———, and LAURA EPSTEIN. *Task Centered Practice*. New York: Columbia University Press, 1977.

REID, WILLIAM J. *The Task Centered System*. New York: Columbia University Press, 1978.

REISINGER, JAMES J., JOHN P. ORA, and GEORGE W. FRANGIA. "Parents Are Change Agents for Their Children." *Journal of Community Psychology*, 4 (1976), 103–123.

RICE, ROBERT M. *Family Listening Post*. New York: Family Service Association of America, 1977.

RILEY, PATRICK V. "Family Advocacy—Case to Cause and Back to Case." *Child Welfare*, 40, 7 (July 1971), 374–383.

RIPPLE, LILLIAN. "Factors Associated with Continuance in Casework Service." *Social Work*, 2 (January 1957).

———. *Motivation Capacity and Opportunity—Studies in Casework Theory and Practice*. Social Service Monographs, 2nd Series. Chicago: School of Social Service Administration, University of Chicago, 1964.

ROSE, SHELDON. "A Behavioral Approach to Group Treatment of Parents." *Social Work*, 14, 3 (July 1969), 21–29.

———. *Treating Children in Groups*. San Francisco: Jossey-Bass, Inc., 1972.

———. *Group Therapy: A Behavior Approach*. Englewood Cliffs, N.J.: Prentice Hall, 1977.

ROTHMAN, JACK, and TERRENCE KAY. "Community Mental Health Centers and Family Service Agencies." *Social Work Research and Abstracts*, 13 (Winter 1977), 10–16.

RUSSELL, ELBERT W. "The Power of Behavior Control: A Critique of Behavior Modification Methods." *Journal of Clinical Counseling*, 30 (1974), 11–136.

SAINSBURY, ERIC. *Social Work with Families*. Boston: Routledge and Kegan Paul, 1975.

SCHUERMAN, JOHN R. "Do Family Services Help? A Critical Review." *Social Service Review*, 49 (September 1975), 363–375.

SCHWARTZ, ARTHUR, and ISRAEL GOLDIAMOND. *Social Casework: A Behavioral Approach*. New York: Columbia University Press, 1975.

SHAPIRO, ARTHUR K. "The Behavior Therapies: Therapeutic Breakthrough or Latest Fad?" *American Journal of Psychiatry*, 133 (February 1976), 154–159.

SHAW, ROBERT, et al. "A Short-Term Treatment Program at a Child Guidance Clinic." *Social Work*, 13, 3 (July 1968), 81–90.

SHERMAN, EDMUND A., et al. *Service to Children in Their Own Homes—Its Nature and Outcome*. New York: Child Welfare League of America, 1973.

SLIPP, SAMUEL, SARAH ELLIS, and KENNETH KRESSEL. "Factors Associated with Engagement in Family Therapy." *Family Process*, 13, 4 (December 1974), 413–427.

SLOAN, BRUCE, et al. *Psychotherapy Versus Behavior Therapy*. Cambridge, Mass.: Harvard University Press, 1975.

TAVORMINA, JOSEPH B. "Basic Models of Parent Counseling: A Critical Review." *Psychological Bulletin*, 81, 11 (1974), 827–835.

THOMAS, EDWIN J. (Ed.). *The Socio-Behavioral Approach and Applications to Social Work*. New York: Council on Social Work Education, 1967.

U.S. DEPARTMENT OF HEALTH, EDUCATION, AND WELFARE. *Toward a Comprehensive Service Delivery System Through Building the Community Service Center*. Washington, D.C.: Government Printing Office, 1970.

VORWALLER, DARREL J. "The Voluntary Agency as a Vendor of Social Services." *Child Welfare*, **51**, 7 (July 1972), 436–442.

WELLS, RICHARD A., THOMAS C. DILKES, and NINA T. BURCKHARDT. "The Results of Family Therapy: A Critical Review of the Literature." *Family Process*, **11** (1972), 189–207.

WERRY, J. S., and J. P. WOLLERSHEIM. "Behavior Therapy with Children: A Broad Overview." *American Academy of Child Psychiatry Journal*, **6**, 2 (April 1967), 346–370.

WINOGRAND, IRIS R. (Ed.). *Purchase of Care and Services in the Health and Welfare Fields*. Proceedings of the First Milwaukee Institute on a Social Welfare Issue of the Day. Milwaukee: University of Wisconsin, 1970.

WITMER, HELEN. *Psychiatric Clinics for Children*. London: Commonwealth Fund, 1940.

WODARSKI, JOHN, and DENNIS BAGAROZZI. *Behavioral Social Work*. New York: Human Sciences Press, 1979.

WOOD, KATHERINE M. "Case Work Effectiveness: A New Look at the Research Evidence." *Social Work* (November 1978), 437–484.

4 SUPPLEMENTARY SERVICES: SOCIAL INSURANCE AND PUBLIC ASSISTANCE

INTRODUCTION

Family service agencies and child guidance clinics, in helping with problems of child welfare, primarily operate to strengthen and reinforce the parents in discharging their parental roles, but they do not in any way attempt to assume the parents' responsibility. The service remains, in effect, outside the family system. Supplementary services, on the other hand, enter into the social system of the family. They are designed to discharge some part, however limited, of the role responsibility of the parent. For the period of time that the supplementary service is offered, the family embodies the biological parent(s) and the supplementary parent in the guise of the agency. Supplementary services include the income maintenance programs, day care, and homemaker service.

There is an overlap between the supplementary services and the supportive services. As one aspect of their role is supplemented, the parents are able to discharge others more competently. Where the parental role is left permanently vacant because of death, illegitimacy, desertion, divorce, or separation, or is temporarily unfilled because of imprisonment, military service, illness, or unemployment, serious dislocation of the parent–child system takes place and necessitates some arrangement for role supplementation.

One of the principal roles of the parent is to provide for the child and ensure his healthy development. In our money economy, this means that the family must have a cash income, and the responsibility for implementing the wage-earner role is generally delegated to the father, although the mother may supplement his income. Income maintenance programs are designed to act *in loco parentis*—in place of parents or as supplementary parents—as far as this specific aspect of parental role responsibility is concerned.

Unemployment, disability, or death of the wage earner may result in the loss of family income. Workman's compensation, unemployment insurance, and the Old Age, Survivors', and Disability Insurance (OASDI) are social insurance programs that provide for income maintenance for the family faced with such situations. Public assistance programs—general assistance and the Aid to Families of Dependent Children program—cover some of the contingencies provided for by the social insurances and for others as well. Thus assistance may be granted

115

to families left fatherless through desertion, separation, divorce, imprisonment, or illegitimacy.

Both the insurance and the assistance programs are pertinent to social work because they are concerned with the consequences of failure in the adequate implementation of a social role; they are concerned with situations in which the normal institutional arrangements of a family cannot provide the income to meet the needs of the child. Because both kinds of programs are concerned with situations that directly affect children, these programs can be regarded as pertinent to the field of child welfare. Because both programs are concerned with the same general problem, the maintenance of family income, we are discussing both in the same chapter.

SOCIAL INSURANCE AND PUBLIC ASSISTANCE

The insurance programs and the assistance programs are distinguishable on the basis of the following significant considerations. The insurance programs, unlike the assistance programs, are financed by the employee–beneficiary and the employer or by the employer alone, and the right to benefits derives from participation in the program.

The money spent in meeting the obligations of the public assistance programs, however, comes from general tax revenues, so that all citizens pay to support the program. The right to public assistance is not clearly acknowledged. The claim to benefits is based more on the ethical premise that every citizen in need has a legitimate claim on the community. Eligibility for social insurance is based on the existence of a particular contingency: death, unemployment, or accidental injury. The recipient's financial situation is not a question of concern, so that an unemployed millionaire might receive unemployment insurance.

Eligibility for the assistance programs, on the other hand, is based on verification that a particular situation exists and on verification of need. Death of a father covered by OASDI would qualify his family for insurance benefits, but to qualify for assistance benefits the family would have to prove need as well.

Because the assistance programs are based on need, the process of determining eligibility must involve a detailed study of the intimate family situation. The eligibility study in the insurance program normally concerns itself only with a more objective, factual consideration of the family situation.

The major social insurance programs all grow out of job connection. People are covered by the program by virtue of their employment, and their benefits are determined, to a considerable extent, by the time on the job and the amount of money earned. But many families face temporary or permanent interruption of income or inadequacy of income, even though the family head has not been in insured employment. We therefore need income maintenance programs that are not job-related. The public assistance programs, unlike the existing social insurance programs, are not related to employment.

Social insurance differs from social assistance, then, in the following ways:

1. It is work-related.
2. There are no means tests.
3. It is contributory.

4. It is compulsory.
5. Benefits are clearly defined by law.

The social insurance program includes some of the basic elements of any insurance: there is protection against a defined hazard through group pooling of contributions and sharing of risks, with benefits payable as a matter of legal right in the event that the defined hazard—death, disability, retirement, unemployment—actually occurs.

Unlike private insurance programs, the social insurances are compulsory, and benefits are not directly related to the extent of contribution, so that those who contribute less may derive proportionately greater benefits than those who contribute more. The benefit formulas are weighted in favor of the lower-income wage-earners.

Social insurance is concerned with adequacy as well as equity and has income redistribution consequences (Ozawa, 1976; Danziger, 1977).

Workman's Compensation

Workman's compensation is the oldest form of social insurance in the United States. It provides money benefits and medical care to an injured worker, and cash benefits to the family of workers who are killed. In order to be eligible, the worker must have sustained an injury "arising out of, and in the course of, employment." Thus the program provides some measure of income to the worker —and, through the worker, to his children—when injury on the job temporarily or permanently prevents him from fulfilling the role of wage earner.

The first state workman's compensation laws were adopted in 1911, when ten states passed such legislation. By 1948 workman's compensation laws had been passed in all states.

The programs are administered by the states and, except for a program for its own workers, the federal government is not involved. Consequently, the programs vary from state to state. In all states, only the employer contributes to the program.

The importance of the program might be gauged from the fact that over the last twenty years, the number of disabling work injuries has averaged around 2 million each year. The number of children affected by the programs through injuries sustained by the family wage-earner, therefore, is likely to run even higher.

Because the state programs are so differently organized, overall statistics on the workman's compensation program are difficult to compile. As a result, it is not possible to state accurately how many children might be affected by the operation of the program. The fact that in 1976 some $9.4 billion were paid to beneficiaries in cash and medical benefits indicates the importance of the program to the income maintenance of individuals and their families.

Unemployment Insurance

Unemployment represents a second great hazard to family income maintenance and results in the inability to perform adequately in the role of parent. If the role requires the father to be a wage earner, the community must provide sufficient opportunities to enact this aspect of the role. If this is not possible, supplementation must be provided. Unemployment insurance is one form of supplementation.

Unemployment insurance is a state-administered program designed to replace part of the income lost by unemployment through the payment to unemployed workers of specific amounts of money for a limited period (Schottland, 1970, p. 81). It is sustained, generally, by employer contributions based on a payroll tax. The federal government supervises the program through the Bureau of Employment Security of the U.S. Department of Labor.

Wisconsin, in 1932, was the first state to enact an unemployment insurance program. By 1937 all states had developed such a program.

Neither unemployment insurance nor workman's compensation replaces the wage earner's income at the level each of the programs had hoped to achieve. Workman's compensation seeks to replace two thirds of the worker's wage loss; unemployment insurance, one half.

The situation is improved somewhat for families with children when the program provides for an increase of benefits for dependents. In 1974 such supplementation was provided in seventeen states for families drawing workman's compensation; by eleven states, for families drawing unemployment insurance. Such a provision increases the total level of income available to the family when the father is unemployed or without income because of a work-related injury.

The number of beneficiaries of unemployment insurance in 1977, under the state unemployment insurance programs, was 17 million. How many of these beneficiaries had children, and how many children were involved, is not known. One might reasonably assume that a considerable number of the claimants were heads of families with dependent children. The amount of benefits paid in 1977 under these state programs was $12.2 billion, which indicates the extent to which the program contributes to sustaining family life.

Old Age, Survivors', and Disability Insurance

The most important insurance program affecting children is the Old Age, Survivors', and Disability Insurance program. As originally established in the Social Security Act in 1935, the program was primarily designed to provide old-age pensions. A person who had worked for a stated period of time in covered employment could, upon reaching the age of sixty-five, retire and receive a monthly benefit. But if he died before he reached the retirement age, there was no provision for continuing payments to his surviving dependent wife and children.

In 1939 the Act was amended to include provisions for payments to surviving dependents; at this point, the program developed very considerable significance for child welfare. Whereas previously a mother and children faced with the loss of family income as a result of the death of the father had no recourse other than Aid to Dependent Children, such a family was now entitled to benefits under the insurance program. As more and more workers were covered, and as more families became eligible for payments in case of the death of the father, a shift from the assistance to the insurance programs became evident. For instance, whereas death of the father accounted for 37 per cent of the cases on

Aid to Dependent Children in 1942, in 1975 such a contingency was a factor in only 3.7 per cent of the cases.

The 1939 amendments, which changed an old-age pension program to an old-age pension and survivors' program, still left a sizable group of children unprotected. These were the dependents of the wage earner who became permanently and totally disabled and whose family was consequently without income. If disability were the result of injury on the job, income maintenance responsibility for the family would, at least for a time, be assumed by workman's compensation. But, as noted, even the workers covered by such compensation had no claim and no security if the injury or disability was sustained away from the job.

In 1956, by the narrowest of margins, Congress amended the program to provide for disability insurance benefits to a disabled worker and his dependents. What had started as an Old Age Insurance program (OAI) had, by virtue of the survivors' insurance features, became an Old Age and Survivors' program (OASI), and then had been expanded to an Old Age, Survivors', and Disability program (OASDI).

If an insured worker dies, reaches retirement age, or is disabled, his children are entitled to benefits on his social security account if they are under eighteen years of age, unmarried, and dependent on the parent.

Children who were living with their grandparents for the year immediately before the grandparent retired, became disabled, or died are entitled to benefits from the grandparents' account. A child who was receiving benefits under his biological parents' account can now continue to receive benefits even after adoption. Furthermore, an adopted child is entitled to benefits on the account of his adopted parents. The illegitimate child is covered "if the father was supporting the child or had a legal obligation to do so." Benefit payments continue until the age of twenty-two for those children who remain in school as full-time students. If the child reaches the age of twenty-two in the middle of the semester or quarter, benefits will be continued till the end of the term. However, no benefits are paid the mother of a child if the only child at home is beyond eighteen years of age.

A dependent child not in school ceases to be eligible for benefits when he reaches his eighteenth birthday or if he marries before the age of eighteen. A disabled child over twenty-two drawing benefits because of a disability incurred before his twenty-second birthday will face discontinuation of benefits if he refuses, without good cause, to accept vocational rehabilitation services. A child receiving benefits because of the father's disability will have such benefits terminated if and when the worker is rehabilitated and returns to work.

If an insured worker dies, reaches retirement age, or is disabled, his wife is entitled to insurance benefits if she is caring for a child entitled to benefits on his father's social security account. The wife's benefits are one half of her husband's primary insurance amount.

The fact that a child's mother is divorced from the insured worker does not affect the child's right to benefits from the father. If the mother remarries, the child is still entitled to benefits from the first father's account.

The children of a mother who is covered under the program and becomes disabled can draw benefits as a consequence of her disability. If she dies, her children can draw survivors' benefits on her record. Benefits to children based on the mother's earning record provide a very important protection for the single-parent family headed by a woman. This additional income is also of considerable importance to the two-parent family if the father must employ someone to help care for dependent children after the mother's disability or death. In December 1977, 653,000—about 13 per cent of all child beneficiaries—were receiving benefits on their mothers' work record.

Of particular concern for children is the section in the OASDI legislation that provides that if the dependent child of a worker covered under the program becomes totally disabled prior to his twenty-second birthday, the child can draw monthly benefits indefinitely. In this case, the mother caring for the child can also draw monthly benefits. This is of particular concern to severely retarded children, who are likely to remain dependent throughout life. These children can draw benefits indefinitely. The mother of such a child is also eligible for monthly payments for as long as the child is in her care, regardless of her age or her child's age. Thus the parents of the mentally retarded child have some assurance of continued support for the child beyond their death. Benefits for physically or mentally disabled children are not paid until the eligible parent retires, dies, or is himself disabled.

> Henry B. is twenty-nine years old and severely mentally retarded. He was alone and helpless after the sudden death of his parents in an automobile accident.
>
> Henry B. was the only handicapped child in a family of six children. He had been mentally retarded since birth and had always been entirely dependent on other people to care for him. At the time his parents died, he was the only child still living with them. One of his sisters wanted to take him into her home, but she and her husband couldn't afford the extra expense involved.
>
> When the social security representative got in touch with this daughter about her father's social security, he explained that Henry might be eligible for childhood benefits as a survivor of his father. Henry's sister applied on his behalf. He was accepted as eligible for benefits because his disability was incurred long before he reached twenty-two.
>
> With the social security benefits, the sister and her husband are able to take care of Henry in their home.

The child's benefits, in over 90 per cent of the cases, are paid to the mother, who is given the responsibility of managing the child's benefits in his behalf. If the mother is not available or is unfit to manage the funds responsibly, or if the child is not living with his mother, designating a responsible representative payee may become a problem. A special unit, the Welfare Branch of the Division of Claims Policy, Bureau of Retirement and Survivors' Insurance, has been organized to help deal with such problems. Its local offices may work with local child welfare agencies in evaluating the acceptability of representative payees. If the child is institutionalized, the institution may be designated as the payee. Some institutions apply the benefits toward the cost of child care but, as the child grows older, may designate some part of the benefits as savings for the child. For a child in foster care, the agency or the foster parents may be the payee, depending on the agency's recommendations.

To recapitulate, OASDI affects children by providing continued income in certain situations. These are listed in order of the number of children affected. The number of children listed as receiving benefits as a result of each contingency is, in round figures, for December 1977.

1. Children receiving benefits because an insured parent died: 2.9 million.
2. Children receiving benefits because an insured parent was disabled: 1.5 million.
3. Children receiving benefits because an insured parent reached retirement age: 680,000.
4. Children over eighteen receiving benefits because an insured parent was dead, disabled, or retired and they themselves incurred a disability before their eighteenth birthday: 404,000. (In the large majority of instances such persons were mentally deficient or suffering from cerebral palsy, epilepsy, or schizophrenic disorders.)

In 1977 the amount of money granted for the support of children who benefited from the program was about $8 billion. As of December 1977 there were 5 million children receiving benefits under the OASDI program. Some 580,000 widowed mothers were receiving benefits because they were caring for dependent children of OASDI beneficiaries. About 870,000 youngsters between the ages of eighteen and twenty-two were attending school full time and continuing to draw benefits. The amount of such "stipend" support for this group amounted to $1.7 billion. Monthly benefit payments enabled these young people to remain in school. The total yearly amount that such beneficiaries draw as full-time students is greater than all of the scholarship money made available through all of the colleges and universities in the United States.

Benefit levels for the worker and his or her dependents are based on the length of time the worker has been in the program and the amount of salary the worker was receiving. Each dependent is entitled to a benefit that is some percentage of the primary benefit computed for the worker: in the case of death, 75 per cent of the primary benefit; 50 per cent in the case of retirement or disability. But however the benefit is computed, there is a maximum that a family can receive. The imposition of a family maximum does an injustice to large families. Because of the maximum family benefit, "When the total of the individual monthly benefits payable to all beneficiaries in the family exceeds the maximum, each dependent's benefit is proportionately reduced to bring the total within the maximum" (Ozawa, 1974). The second child in a two-child family is getting a proportionately larger benefit than the fourth child in a four-child family. Benefits per child decrease as family size increases.

The tremendous implications of the OASDI program for children are made clear in the following updated and abridged version of an article by economist Sylvia Porter:

Social Security Is Amazing Aid to Young Widow *

A young father of three infants was killed in a freak accident in our community the other day, leaving not only a heartbroken widow but also an empty bank account. While we were discussing with the neighbors how to ease at least her financial tragedy, I volunteered, "One 'good' angle is the fortune she'll get from Social Security from now on. It'll run into tens of thousands of dollars in cash."

The cash stake of this young widow and her infants, as I figured it out with the

---

* Our thanks to the Madison, Wisconsin, office of the Social Security Administration for providing the updated figures.

local Social Security Administration, comes to about $290,000. What's more, this inheritance is free of income and sales taxes.

Her husband would have had to accumulate a nestegg of more than $200,000 and would have had to invest it at 4 percent tax-free to duplicate in part what she is now going to get.

In our neighbor's case the father had been fully insured at the top Social Security salary level of $17,700 a year. His infants are one, two, and three years old. Now:

On application, his widow will get a lump sum death payment. This amounts to $255 (and is generally regarded as a burial expense payment).

His infants and their mother will get a pension of $1,198.30 a month until the oldest child is eighteen. Assuming that she does not remarry during the fifteen-year period, this adds up to $215,694.

For twelve months, she and her two children still under eighteen will get a monthly pension of $1,198.30. This amounts to $14,379.60 over the year.

For twelve months, she and her child still under eighteen will get a monthly pension of $1,027.20. This amounts to $12,326.40 over the year. Total benefits would be $242,400 over a seventeen-year period if the children don't go to school.

If the children continued school (all three) until age twenty-two the payments would be as follows:

Lump Sum	$ 255.00
(17 years) widow and three children (family maximum)	$242,400.00
(2 years) three students (family maximum)	$ 28,759.20
(1 year) two students (no family maximum)	$ 12,326.40
(1 year) one student (no family maximum)	$ 6,163.20
Total amount to be paid in monthly benefits including the lump-sum burial expense	$289,903.80

This would be a total amount paid until the youngest child no longer qualifies as student (at age twenty-two). Then if the widow did not remarry and started to collect unreduced benefits (82.9 percent at age 62 projected to age seventy-four) she would collect $567.70 per month or $6,812.40 per year. If she collected for twelve years this would mean another additional $81,748.80, which added to $289,903.80 totals $371,652.60.

This was the benefit situation for such a family in 1978. The case described is a demonstration of the current program at its very best. The level of payments listed is the maximum benefit to which a family is entitled under the program. However, many workers have not been in the program long enough (at least ten years) or worked at high enough salaries (in 1978 at least $17,700) so that they and their families can be entitled to maximum benefits.

Ball (1978) gives other examples of the value of social security to the families of wage earners in the program at different earning levels: "A worker earning the male median earnings for 1977 who died at age 35 in that year leaving a wife age 32 and two small children age 3 and 5 would have left his family the Social Security equivalent of an estate worth $129,265. . . . For the worker earning at the federal minimum wage, the comparable amount would be $79,163" (p. 131).

Because this protection increases automatically as wages or prices go up, as has been noted, it is estimated that by January, 1982 the value of the protection available to families in the same situation as those cited "would be $142,163 for the worker earning the median wage . . . and, $87,950 for the worker earning the Federal minimum wage" (Ball, 1978, p. 131).

The lump-sum death benefit payment, designed to meet burial expenses, was the maximum amount payable. It may be less in other cases, for the death benefit payment is equal to three times the primary insurance amount, but in no case does it exceed $255.

The level of OASDI benefits has been increased periodically. The formula for computing benefits has been revised, and minimum levels of benefits and maximum allowable benefits have been raised. The average monthly benefit for a child of a deceased worker was $51 in 1960; this benefit had increased to about $166 in 1977. The average mother's monthly benefit was $123 in 1960; this had increased to about $174 in 1977.

Black children are more dependent for support on the OASDI program than are white children. The most notable difference between racial groups in the way the program affects them lies in the proportion of child beneficiaries. Whereas 14 per cent of all white beneficiaries are children, 31 per cent of all black beneficiaries are children. Black workers are less likely to benefit from retirement because they die younger than whites, but they are more likely to benefit from disability because they are more likely to be employed in hazardous jobs. Thus blacks more than whites benefit most from those provisions of the OASDI program designed to protect the younger population of widowed mothers and children. However, the average monthly benefits of black widowed mothers and children were considerably lower than those of whites, "and the gap has narrowed only slightly since 1960" (Thompson, 1975, p. 30). The fact that black families are larger than white families means the greater likelihood that black family benefits will be subject to family maximums. The more important consideration resulting in differences in black–white benefit levels are the length of time in covered employment and levels of wages while in covered employment. Also, because fewer minority children go to college, fewer of them receive extended benefits through age twenty-two.

OASDI is of particular value to young families in which there has not yet been an opportunity to build up reserves and in which the father has not yet attained his full wage-earning potential (Guillot, 1971).

A study by Mallon (1975) showed that "Social Security benefits paid to young widows with children was [sic] an important source of support for them. They keep a large number out of poverty" (p. 18).

Because of social security benefits, families of widows with children are somewhat better off than families headed by divorced or separated women. However, about 40 per cent of families headed by a widow are poor.

TRENDS AND PROBLEMS: SOCIAL INSURANCE

The trend in the insurance programs is toward liberalization, which takes the form of increasing coverage of previously excluded groups.

Since the inception of the program, more and more children have been affected, not only because of the fundamental changes in the nature of the program itself but also because more groups of fathers have been included in the program. By 1978, 95 out of every 100 workers and their dependents were covered by OASDI. Some of the excluded groups—such as federal employees, policemen and firemen in many states, and railroad workers—are covered by special retirement systems. The trend is more pronounced in the OASDI program than in the workman's compensation program or the unemployment insurance program. However, all programs exclude some employed workers, so that some dependent children still lack the assurance of continued income if the parent dies, is injured at work, or loses his job. Currently, some part-time workers and some self-employed groups are not covered by OASDI.

Coverage is also extended by liberalized definitions of eligibility for benefits. Thus until 1965 an illegitimate child was eligible for OASDI benefits only if the state in which he resided recognized his rights to inheritance. As a result, some illegitimate children in some states were ineligible. The 1965 amendments established a nationwide definition of eligibility: an illegitimate child is eligible "if the father was supporting the child or had obligation to do so."

Liberalization also takes the form of including contingencies not previously covered by the program. For instance, workman's compensation was broadened to make specific provisions for the coverage of occupational diseases.

Despite this extension, there are specific recurrent contingencies, affecting large groups in the population, that are not provided for by any program. Illness, for example, not only results in the loss of a wage but also imposes a burden on an already depleted family income; yet we have no national program of health insurance.

Liberalization of the insurance programs also takes the form of providing increased benefits over longer periods of time. The OASDI program has gone further toward increasing the beneficiaries' real income than either the workman's compensation or the unemployment insurance programs. But despite such liberalization, the adequacy of current levels of payment is open to question. Although the principal purpose of all the social insurance programs is to provide a minimum level of income when the principal wage-earner is removed from the labor market as a result of specific contingencies, the level at which the family is to be maintained is a matter of controversy. At present, average benefits run higher than public assistance payments for comparable situations but lower than the amounts required to meet the needs of a modest but adequate city worker's family budget as computed by the U.S. Department of Labor.

Also, those families that most need social security are apt to be least adequately protected. Because social insurance programs relate benefits to earnings, they are apt to be of less help to those children whose fathers' earnings were inadequate throughout his working life. The inequity is mitigated somewhat by a "floor of protection" that guarantees a minimum benefit to the family of even the lowest eligible wage-earner.

Also, social insurance is supplemented in many instances by employee group life insurance and collective bargaining agreements that provide paid sick leave and pension plans. But in these cases, too, the families with the lowest earnings are least likely to be protected by the more adequate programs. Efforts are being made to make benefits more adequate.

Starting in 1975, provision was made for the adjustment of social security benefits in response to increases in the cost of living. The adjustment involves automatic cost-of-living benefit increases equivalent to the increases in the Consumer Price Index if there is at least a 3 per cent movement in the index and Congress has taken no action to adjust pension levels. Thus social security, as currently administered, offers inflation-proof protection.

Another inequity is created by the payroll taxes paid by the worker to finance his social security: the low-income worker tends to contribute a larger proportion of his wages than the higher-paid worker does. As a regressive tax, imposed at an equal rate at all earning levels, the social security tax is perhaps the heaviest tax burden faced by low-income families. Thus a married man with a $7,600 income and five children would have owed no income tax in 1977 using the standard deductions. However, he would have paid some $445 in social security tax.

Although widely debated, there is still no recognition in the social security system of the work of the homemaker, who contributes her labor but draws no salary. This type of "employment" is not covered under social security (U.S. Senate, 1975, pp. 35–36). There is a trend, however, toward reducing gender-related inequities in the program. For instance, the U.S. Supreme Court moved toward equalizing benefits for men and women in 1975 in the Weisenfeld case. Previously, although women with children could obtain benefits if their husbands retired, died, or were disabled, men could not obtain similar benefits on the account of their working wives unless they could prove that prior to their wife's retirement, death, or disability, they were dependent on her earnings for more than 50 per cent of their support. Stephen Weisenfeld applied for benefits after the death of his wife, who had been employed as a schoolteacher. Denied benefits by the social security office, Weisenfeld, who had been left with the care of an infant son, appealed the ruling. The Supreme Court decided in his favor in overturning the gender-based distinction of the Social Security Administration's eligibility requirements. As a consequence of the Supreme Court decision, women employees will now generate as much protection for their surviving husbands and children as did the male employee for his surviving spouse and children.

The 1977 legislation made it easier for divorced women to obtain benefits on the account of their ex-spouse. Previously it was required that a woman be married to a man for twenty years before she was eligible for benefits if she remained unmarried subsequent to the divorce. The 1977 legislation reduced this requirement to ten years of marriage before divorce. There are, however, still no benefits for husbands on the account of the ex-wives.

Starting in 1976, the social security system began to face a fiscal crisis resulting from a variety of converging factors. In that year, the system paid out $4 billion more than it took in. With an aging population, there is a change in the ratio of beneficiaries to contributors—from four working contributors to each beneficiary in 1965 to an anticipated one working contributor for each beneficiary in 2039. Prolonged high levels of unemployment in the 1970s decreased the number of working contributors; a rapid increase in the number of disability beneficiaries, continuing inflation, increasing outlays, and the general maturing of the program, making more people eligible for benefits, were additional factors.

There are still problems to which the programs are indifferent. For example, the noneconomic consequences the child suffers from the injury, death, disability, or unemployment of the father are not regarded as the concern of the social insurance programs, nor are the programs intended to meet this gap. Thus mothers and children are left to struggle with a variety of social problems without assistance. A detailed study of blue-collar families following the death of the father indicated the emotional disruption to which the surviving children were subjected: "The study findings indicate the need for improved and expanded nonfinancial counseling resources to aid the families and particularly the children of recently deceased workers" (Glasser, 1970, p. 10). Casework rehabilitation services (see Chapter 5) have been associated with assistance programs but not with insurance programs, and as a result, Kahn (1965) notes a difference in the image of the families who are the clients of these two different programs. The family receiving insurance is regarded as a "normal" family capable of solving all its problems except income maintenance; the assistance family is regarded as a less capable family requiring casework services as well as income.

The distinction becomes less and less tenable, if it ever was valid, as an increasingly larger proportion of the population comes under insurance coverage. Certainly it is reasonable to suppose that all families with dependent children, eligible for benefits because of the injury, disability, or death of the father, are likely to face some serious social problems that derive from the need to reallocate social responsibilities within the family system.

INCOME MAINTENANCE: AID TO FAMILIES OF DEPENDENT CHILDREN

Introduction

Social insurance programs provide coverage for only a limited number of situations that are likely to result in a problem of income maintenance. They do not provide protection for the following:

1. A child whose father is ill and partially disabled.
2. A child whose father is unemployed for a long period of time and is not eligible for unemployment insurance or has exhausted his benefits.
3. A child whose father has deserted or is divorced or separated from his wife.
4. A child whose father is imprisoned.
5. A child who is illegitimate.
6. A child whose father is dead but was not, while alive, covered by OASDI.
7. A child whose father is dead, retired, or permanently disabled but whose OASDI benefits are below subsistence level for the family.

A supplementary program is needed to provide for these families. The principal program available to fill this gap is the Aid to Families of Dependent Children—the AFDC program.

In discussing the differences between assistance and insurance programs, we noted that the assistance programs attempt to individualize the needs of the client. In doing this, the agency becomes aware of and takes responsibility for helping with other social problems that the family faces because the social roles of father and husband are vacant or inadequately fulfilled.

Historical Background

The precursor of the AFDC program in this country was the "mothers' pension" program, which was a public assistance rather than a true pension program. Earlier in our history, the problem that most frequently resulted in unfilled paternal roles was the death of the wage earner. The mothers to be assisted were generally widows. The solution, it was felt, lay not with public aid to the family but with reallocation of roles within the family. Children moved up early in life to assume the income maintenance responsibility of the father. The solution was tied to the public acceptance of child labor. Before World War I, many families were supported by two wage earners, but the second wage earner was often a child under sixteen years of age.

The adoption of more rigorous legislation against child labor by the states in the early years of the twentieth century, and by the federal government in 1917, made such a "solution" more difficult and intensified the need for alternatives, such as a mothers' pension program.

Even during the period when it was acceptable for children to work, some widows or deserted mothers had children who were too young to work. In such instances, public outdoor relief and private charity were so inadequate that the children were frequently removed to an institution or a foster home. One of the earliest mothers' pension laws, that of Illinois, passed in 1911, "was proposed by Judge Merritt W. Pinkney, of the Cook County Juvenile Court, because he found himself continually asked to take children from poor, but competent, mothers and commit them to institutions" (Abbott, 1949, Vol. 2, p. 230).

The trend toward such pensions was further influenced by the growing acceptance of the idea of adequate schooling for all children. The relationship between compulsory school laws and mothers' aid is indicated by the fact that as a state raised the age for compulsory school attendance, the age limits of eligible children in the mothers' aid programs were raised accordingly.

Another significant impetus came from the "child-saving" movement of the late nineteenth and early twentieth centuries (Platt, 1969). The movement focused on social control and the prevention of delinquency, but it also stressed the relationship between family life and delinquency and encouraged the preservation of the family. Assistance to "fit and proper parents" in maintaining the home for the child was therefore encouraged as a delinquency prevention procedure.

As a result of the widespread concern with such situations, ten years after the adoption of the first mothers' pension law in 1911, forty states had such legislation. By the time of the Great Depression, Alabama, Georgia, and South Carolina were the only states that did not have a mothers' aid pension program (Leff, 1973).

In the programs instituted before the Great Depression, few states extended coverage to children of unmarried, divorced, or deserted mothers. Most restricted coverage to the children of widows or of incapacitated fathers. The laws were frequently administered by the courts, chiefly the juvenile courts; the age limit of the children to be assisted and the amount of aid varied from state to state. The laws were permissive, so that many counties authorized to grant such aid did not actually do so. This was particularly true in the states that did not share the expenses of the program with local communities. In some states (Arkansas, Mississippi, and New Mexico), although legislation had been passed, the programs were largely inoperative: "Not only was coverage sporadic but in the prosperous 1920's maximum grants were at subsistence or less than subsistence levels" (Coll, 1969, p. 79). Over 95 per cent of the assisted mothers were white and about 85 per cent were widows (U.S. Children's Bureau, 1931, pp. 395–96).

The Great Depression imposed a growing burden on the program, which eventually resulted in the virtual collapse of many. Growing demand for federal participation in the mothers' pension program culminated with the passage of the Social Security Act in 1935. This included provisions for the formal establishment of federal grants to the states for Aid to Families of Dependent Children as one of three categories of public assistance established in Title IV of the Act.

The AFDC program, according to the Social Security Act, is set up to aid "needy" children under eighteen years of age who have been "deprived of parental support or care by reasons of the death, continued absence from the home, or physical or mental incapacity of the parents." In 1961 Congress added another condition for eligibility: dependency due to the unemployment of the father (AFDC-U).

A pregnant mother may receive aid for herself and the unborn child. In 1975, 53,450 unborn children, 0.7 per cent of all children in the program, were being assisted.

States may choose to provide coverage for only some of these contingencies. For example, by the end of 1977, only twenty-seven states had extended coverage to dependent children because of the father's unemployment. Opposition to the measure has stemmed from the fact that although the federal government is ready to participate, some part of the expense of the program will have to be borne by the states. In some states, it was felt that the problem of the unemployed father was not sufficiently severe to warrant inclusion of another category in the AFDC program.

The states can also restrict eligibility in any category. For instance, the definition of *unemployment* varies from state to state. In those states that have passed implementing legislation for AFDC-U, some exclude seasonal workers, the self-employed, and so on. The definition of *physical or mental incapacity of the parent* can vary so as to exclude, in some states, parents who might be eligible in another state. Some states have a waiting period of three months in cases of desertion before the family is eligible, to eliminate cases where the father deserts but returns home within a relatively short period of time. States may set the age of the child who is eligible for help so that one state gives aid to needy children under twenty-one, whereas another state might offer aid only to needy children under eighteen. Differences in eligibility requirements would disqualify a family in one state that would be eligible for benefits in another state. Eligibility differences include such areas as the age limits for dependent children, aid to an unborn child, suitable-home requirements, the income level at which a family is eligible, the duration of waiting periods in cases of desertion, imprisonment or disability, limits on the value of personal property.

Whatever the problem—death, desertion, separation, divorce, incapacity, unemployment—and however it is defined, the child and the family are not eligible unless they are "needy." However, the determination of "need" is left to the state. *Need* is defined as the gap between the total cost of living essentials set by the state and the family's income from all sources.

To identify the gap, a budget is computed that includes the essentials of living: food, rent, a clothing allowance, and fuel. If the income of the family, from all sources, is equal to or greater than the budget computed, the family is deemed not to be in need. If the family's income is less than the computed budget, the family is eligible for assistance, and the amount of the grant is equal to the difference between the income and the computed budget. In addition to providing for the budgeted items, the agency pays the medical and pharmaceutical expenses for members of the family. (These are paid directly to the doctor and the pharmacist.) The family is also eligible for food stamps and may be eligible for day-care help. Items included in the budget and the level of liberality with which budgets are computed vary from state to state.

In 1976 only nineteen states paid up to the full amount of computed need. Some states set a maximum to be paid, even if it is below the estimated level of need. Other states offer a fixed percentage of the estimated need standard.

Thus, although the state standard of need for a family of four (one needy adult and three children) in October 1976 was $240 in Alabama, the actual assistance granted was $170. In Indiana, the state standard was $363, and the assistance granted was $250. In Maryland, the comparable figures were $314 and $242 (Assistance Payments Administration, 1977, p. 237).

In summary, then, AFDC is an assistance program financed by federal, state, and local governments. Federal requirements, enforced through the sanction of grants-in-aid, have resulted in some basic uniformity in the program throughout the United States, but because the program is administered by the states, there is still considerable variation from state to state.

Situations in Which AFDC Is an Appropriate Resource

The situations in which AFDC is an appropriate resource are limited by the eligibility requirements of the program. Table 4–1 indicates the major crisis situations that have led to the application for AFDC and the percentage of families that have applied because of the particular contingency. The data are for the month of May 1975 (Social Security Administration, 1977, p. 31).

TABLE 5–1. Families Receiving AFDC (1975)

	Status of Father	*Percentage of Families Receiving AFDC*
A.	Father absent from home	83.3
	1. Not married to mother	31
	2. Separated	28.6
	3. Divorced	19.4
	4. In armed forces	.3
	5. Other reason	4
		83.3 subtotal
B.	Father incapacitated	7.7
C.	Father unemployed	3.7
D.	Father deceased	3.7
E.	Deprived of mother's but not father's support	1.6
		100.0

Because "need" is also a requirement, it is not surprising that in most of the cases, the families had been living at a marginal economic level for a long time and that many parents had come from homes in which income was marginal. There was thus little opportunity to build economic reserves against crises precipitated by death, desertion, incapacity, and so on.

Scope

In July 1978 there were a total of about 10.5 million persons receiving assistance under the AFDC program. This number includes about 7.3 million children plus their "caretakers"—generally their mothers. The program is therefore by far the largest single public welfare program in the United States affecting children. It is perhaps the only public welfare program affecting children that is available in every county of the United States. It is estimated that since its inception, the program has helped over 100 million children to remain and grow up in their own homes. At any given time, about 10 per cent of all of the children in the United States are receiving AFDC, and about one out of every five children has received financial assistance and services under the AFDC program at some time or another during his life.

Processes in the AFDC Program

Intake and Eligibility

A statistically typical family—the Jones family—consisted of a mother about twenty-seven years old and two children, one under six years of age and one over six years of age. The mother had a tenth- or eleventh-grade education and was not likely to be employed. The family lived in an urban area, and because in 1975, 50.2 per cent of all AFDC recipients were white, there was a slightly better than even chance that Mrs. Joyce would be white. The father was absent from the home rather than being dead or present in the home but incapacitated or unemployed.

Mrs. Jones did not apply for assistance immediately after trouble struck, but made an effort to remain independent by utilizing the family's limited personal and financial resources (Greenleigh, 1960; Burgess, Price, 1963). In a little more than five months, Mrs. Jones exhausted those resources and applied to the Department of Public Welfare in the county where she resided.

Upon application, Mrs. Jones was asked to fill out an application form, which requested information about the composition of the family, birth dates, marriage dates, employment history, school attendance of the children, rent and utilities information, family assets, insurance, pensions, automobiles, savings, home ownership, and so on. At the same time, a separate application was completed for food stamps asking similar kinds of information.

Meeting with an eligibility worker, Mrs. Jones had the opportunity of asking questions about the program and was informed about the agency eligibility procedures and the right to appeal agency decisions in a fair hearing.

The first interview focused on her "presumptive" eligibility and reviewed the general factors in her situation that determined her eligibility. Having been deserted or divorced or separated and having two children under the age of eighteen, all attending school, Mrs. Jones was presumed eligible for assistance under the program. However, every state has a number of other eligibility requirements that must be satisfied. Because this was an assistance program, Mrs. Jones had to prove that the family was in need—that its income, from whatever source, was less than the standard budget computed by the state. If there was some income (let us say that Mrs. Jones was receiving some support from her divorced husband) but the amount was $20 a month less than the computed budget, she would be eligible for the difference and would receive a total AFDC grant of $20. If Mrs. Jones had an insurance policy of sizable cash surrender value, it would have to be converted, as would any valuable real property. This would apply, however, to few applicants. Generally, an applicant is permitted to keep a car or a phone only if it is necessary for transportation or health.

If it were established that Mrs. Jones's income, from all sources, was short of the basic budget, there would still be additional considerations before the family's eligibility would be acknowledged. If Mrs. Jones was applying because her husband deserted her, she would be required to charge him with abandonment so that legal efforts could be made to obtain support. And if Mrs. Jones was in a position to take a job without injuring her health or neglecting her home or children, the agency might require her to find work as a condition of offering assistance. If Mrs. Jones had relatives who were legally responsible for and capable of supporting her, she might be denied assistance.

Because one of the children was under six, Mrs. Jones was not required to register at the employment-service office for job training and placement under the WIN (Work Incentive) program. If all the children in the family were six years of age or older, she would have been required to do this. If Mr. Jones was at home, he would have been required to register for job training and/or placement even though the child was under six.

After the first office interview, a visit to the home would generally be made. Mrs. Jones would be required to produce documentary proof of eligibility: birth certificates proving the children's ages and establishing the fact that she was indeed their mother, her marriage certificate, her lease or mortgage papers, rent receipts, tax records, insurance policies, driver's license, court records on support payments or alimony, bank passbooks, wage receipts, physician's statements on parental illness or disability, and so on. Mrs. Jones was encouraged to take the initiative in providing the documentation necessary to support the application, but if for any reason she had difficulty in obtaining any of the documents, the caseworker stood ready to help her.

Her eligibility, once established, had to be periodically reaffirmed. Any change in the client's situation—if the husband returned, if the mother remarried, if the absent father started making payments, if money was earned by Mrs. Jones or any of the children—had to be reported immediately to the agency so that the budget could be revised accordingly.

In many jurisdictions, Mrs. Jones would have been required to fill out a form each month indicating any changes in family composition or in income. At the end of a year, if the family was still receiving assistance, there would be a more comprehensive reapplication procedure. Eligibility was therefore a continuing concern of the program administrators.

If Mrs. Jones could satisfy all of the conditions of eligibility, her children were less than eighteen years of age (or less than twenty-one years of age if attending school), her husband was absent from the home, the family was in need as defined by the state, she had charged her husband with abandonment, and if necessary, she was ready to accept suitable employment, how much assistance could she hope to receive if she was receiving no income from any source?

Each agency has a budget sheet based on data supplied by home economists. A food budget is computed for each child and for the parent. The food budget varies with the age of the child, so that the budget for a fifteen-year-old boy is greater than that for a five-year-old boy. Rent is included on an as-paid basis, although some of the states set a limit on how much they will allow. Clothing allowances are included although these, too, vary with age. Fuel and electricity are also included, as well as some basic household items, which vary from state to state.

In addition to the basic grant for essential needs—food, clothing, rent, utilities—states also provide for special needs items granted on the basis of a determination of the recipient's individual situation. Because such grants involve considerable worker discretion in assessing the individual's unique circumstances, most states have adopted a simplified consolidated budget that includes such special items on a flat grant basis.

Although the amount computed for the assistance budget is very modest, in many states the family does not receive even that amount, as already noted. Some states have set a maximum on the amount of money they will grant a family, regardless of need, so that not all AFDC families are granted the amount required to meet the budget as computed by the agency.

The average national monthly financial payment per recipient in December 1978 was $85. Mrs. Jones, as head of the average AFDC family, would have received for herself and her two children a total monetary grant of about $255 a month or about $3,000 a year. The "poverty index," established by the federal government, described a city family consisting of mother and 2 dependent children as "in poverty" if their income in 1978 was less than about $4,650 per year. The Jones family, living on their average AFDC income, would then have been below the poverty level. Some of the gap could be reduced by medical assistance and food stamps, in addition to the monthly grant.

AFDC recipients are given a Medicaid card that enables them to obtain medical service. Cost for the service is not charged to the recipient but billed to the program, which pays the doctor, the dentist, the pharmacist, and so on.

By 1980 every state except Arizona had a Medicaid program. States differ in the levels of adequacy of the medical assistance offered and in determining who is eligible for such assistance.

In many states, Medicaid is restricted to AFDC families. In other states, non-AFDC persons are eligible if they can establish the fact that they are medically indigent—that is, have incomes that would make it difficult to meet their medical expenses.

A recipient who leaves AFDC can remain eligible for Medicaid for an additional four months.

Because obtaining Medicaid is difficult for a low-income family not receiving AFDC, this is a valuable aspect of AFDC eligibility—one that acts as an inducement to apply for AFDC and a deterrent to leaving the program.

All AFDC families are eligible for food stamps. In using the food stamp program, recipients can double the purchasing power of the food dollar. The food stamp program has become an increasingly important asset to low-income and near low-income families with children. In 1961 it was a small pilot program designed primarily to sell surplus commodities. By 1971 it had become an income support program for all in need, the working poor as well as the nonworking poor. It has become a nationwide, minimum-income guarantee program with similar eligibility rules and benefit levels throughout the country. In July 1974 it was mandated for all counties in the United States, so that it became a standardized, universally available program.

The equalizing influence that food stamp programs have on income maintenance budgets from state to state despite differences in AFDC grant levels is illustrated by the fact that "for participating families in the South in 1973, the food bonus was almost half the size of their total cash income, while in the northeast it was slightly more than one-tenth" (Bell, 1977, p. 253). The program is administered by the U.S. Department of Agriculture and is operated by the state welfare agencies. The appropriation for the program is open-ended. All AFDC families are automatically eligible.

In 1968 less than 2 million people were involved in the food stamp program. By 1977 16 million recipients were receiving a total aid of about $5 billion annually. The program is a means-tested program: eligibility is determined by a social worker who reviews the details of household income with the applicant. The stamps can be used only for purchase of products for human consumption. The stamp bonus is revised periodically in response to increases in the cost-of-living index. The Food Stamp program has been termed a "mini negative income tax."

In 1978 the food stamp program was simplified and made more accessible to low-income families who might not have had the ready cash available to buy the food stamps. For such families, stamps were provided directly without any exchange of cash.

Allowing for the addition to family income from these in-kind benefits, the living of AFDC families is a marginal subsistence. The total income—money plus in-kind benefits—still leaves most AFDC families with an income below poverty level.

Thus, having overcome the barrier of eligibility, the Jones family had to contend with an even more formidable hurdle: the continuing problem of survival on the grant allotted. Mrs. Jones could improve her position by working part time. Allowance is made for lunches, equipment, clothing needed for work, transportation, and child care, so the sum covering these expenses would not be deducted from her grant. Some states are very liberal and others are restrictive in computing the work expenses that they will disregard in determining the assistance payments. Having accepted employment, Mrs. Jones was able to increase the family income. The first thirty dollars of her earnings and one-third of the remainder were excluded from the computation of her budget. This change in procedure, adopted in 1967, is designed as a work incentive. Any earnings of children who were full- or part-time students would not be counted in computing the grant.

In addition to money, medical or remedial care, and food or food stamps, a fourth kind of assistance comes in the form of social services. Every study points to the fact that the AFDC families have multiple problems: child-care problems, personal and family problems, health problems, family-planning problems, economic problems, home management problems, housing problems, and so on (Greenleigh, 1960, 1964; Langer *et al.*, 1969; Eisenberg *et al.*, 1975).

Financial need itself has several consequences. The family with a limited income has fewer real choices in planning life in the present and in the future; its range of social and recreational activities is limited. Members of such families feel less adequate, more vulnerable, more submissive than others; they lose their sense of self-esteem and self-respect. Some feel a sense of isolation from others, a fear of rejection as "freeloaders," and "welfare chiselers" (Stuart, 1975).

There are some problems that the AFDC family shares with many families on all income levels (problems of emotional disturbances in children and marital maladjustment) and some it shares with other low-income family groups (problems of housing, medical care, money management). Some, however, are more-or-less peculiar to the AFDC family and therefore may require the special understanding and the special help of the social worker.

One of the principal social problems faced by the AFDC family is the fact that it is, in 80 per cent of the cases, a fatherless family. The primary effect of fatherlessness and husbandlessness on the family group is, of course, the necessity of adjusting to living on a reduced income (see Chapter 2). It is the loss of income that causes the family to apply for AFDC. But the absence of the father–husband has consequences in addition to the loss of income. Other aspects of the paternal role are uncovered or inadequately covered, and the children might suffer as a result. It is for help with such varied problems that social service is offered to the AFDC family.

Of course, not all AFDC families need or want social services. Some can and do manage without such help, so an adequate monthly check is all they need from the agency.

Social Service in the AFDC Program

Service, in AFDC, has been defined as purposeful help provided to individuals and families with financial and social difficulties to find and effectively use resources in themselves and in the community. It is an attempt to motivate the client to do something constructive about his situation, to help him decide what he wants to do, to assist him in doing it, and to support and encourage him in his efforts. In the context of child welfare social work, it means maintaining and strengthening the ability of the parents to implement their role responsibilities in the physical, social, and emotional care, protection, and support of their children.

The worker may attempt to help mother and children with any of the consequences of fatherlessness. He may attempt to help with maintaining ties with the absent father, with effecting a reconciliation between the parents, or with getting the absent parent to agree to some support payments. The worker may help with these or with any other problems the family might face. A report summarizes a project in which service is given to AFDC families by trained case-workers, working with a limited case-load:

Primarily what the workers did in their contacts was to provide a learning experience in which people were helped to deal more effectively with practical aspects of daily living. Although most of the families presented serious and complicated problems, the worker helped family members concentrate their sometimes limited capacities on solving one small and tangible problem at a time—one which had possibility of successful solution.

Examples are help in consolidating debts and budgeting income, in getting children to school on time, in securing more adequate housing, in planning regular meals, in preparing for employment, and especially in getting medical care when needed. The latter was something most clients could see as of practical and immediate advantage to themselves. Moreover, adequate medical care helped restore physical energy badly needed to deal successfully with other problems.

Besides its practical benefits, this kind of help in coping with everyday problems gave people experience in how it felt to be successful, and in how to use orderly methods of going about something in at least one specific area in their lives. Since "nothing succeeds like success," such experience, with the continuing help of the worker over a period of time, proved a considerable incentive for people to come to grips successively with other unsatisfactory aspects of their lives [State of California, n.d., pp. 36–37].

As Meier (1961) says, "the best way to help a person *feel* more adequate is to help him *be* more adequate" (p. 20).

The worker helps by consistently demonstrating interest in the client's problems. The assumption is that the client will respond to the interest and concern of the worker, that the interest reflects the worker's evaluation of the client as a person of worth and importance, that this interest and concern can be best expressed—at least initially—by meeting the critical needs of the client.

In helping the family, it is necessary that personalized counseling be supplemented by the employment of what has been termed *hard services:* helping the family by providing "social utilities" such as homemaker service, day care, sheltered workshop experience, and job placement. Personalized counseling is further supplemented by help with access to necessary medical and dental care.

The objectives of AFDC social services are stated in the legislation in general terms: to "strengthen family life and enhance family stability, so that children may have a home life conducive to healthful physical and emotional growth and development; to maximize the level of personal and social functioning; to help the recipients realize their full capacity for self-support and independent living." The justification for providing service has been more frequently stated and more receptively presented in terms of helping the recipient become self-supporting than in terms of any intrinsic value to the family. Although services may help improve the quality of life of the family on welfare, the primary intent of legislative support for these social services is to reduce the number of families on welfare. Consequently, the services emphasized by Congress are related to employment and dependency reduction: job training, job placement, day care, and family planning.

Termination of Assistance

The average family received assistance for about 24–30 months in 1975. AFDC is, then, for most families a temporary expedient rather than a way of life. However, in 1975 about 21 per cent of AFDC families had been receiving assistance for three or more years. Families requiring assistance because of desertion, divorce, or illegitimacy received assistance for longer periods of time than was true for families needing assistance because of incapacity of the father.

Most cases were closed because the family's economic circumstances improved. However, many cases are closed because the family is no longer eligible for assistance, though still in need. The youngest child, for instance, may have reached eighteen years of age, or the father may no longer be technically incapacitated. Most of the families on AFDC (77 per cent) in 1975 had not previously applied for or received aid.

As a result of a longitudinal study of AFDC families, Rein and Rainwater (1977) found that some 80 per cent of such families have a short- or medium-term welfare career. Help from the program is needed as a consequence of some kind of family crisis—divorce, desertion, unemployment—and an effort is made to get off the program as soon as the crisis is resolved. Of course, families may cycle through the program again in response to a later crisis.

The studies show that the most important determinant of how long a family stays on welfare is how long the family has been on welfare. The longer the time a family has been receiving assistance, the less likelihood there is that the family will be terminating support.

In summary, then, our typical client, Mrs. Jones, a twenty-seven-year-old mother with two children in need because the husband was out of the home, would have struggled along for about five months before applying for assistance. Having applied and been found eligible, she would have received a financial grant of about $255 per month plus medical assistance, food stamps, and social service help. She would have received assistance for a period of about twenty months and then would have gone off the program because, through some change in her situation, she was no longer in need.

Group Approaches in the AFDC Program

The group approach has been used to supplement casework activities with AFDC clients: "Group services are defined as those social services of staff directed towards helping clients cope better with problems through a group experience" (Montilius, 1967, p. 5).

Much of the time-consuming, repetitive information that needs to be presented to the client at the point of application might be advantageously presented to a group of prospective AFDC clients.

The following is an excerpt from a group discussion by AFDC mothers about a recurrent problem—explaining the father's absence to the children:

Mrs. Pierce said sometimes you had to think about yourself and find out what you thought about different kinds of things. She said it was after the third group meeting, when we had been talking about what you tell your children about their father, and she didn't agree with everything that was said at that meeting. She said that she knew it was right to tell the children or anybody else the truth, but she didn't see any reason to make the children feel badly by telling them that their father and she didn't live together any more. She said as she thought about herself and why she felt this way, she began to wonder if it wasn't because it would be harder on her than it was on her children. She had decided that you don't take the easy way out for you, but tell your children the truth when they ask and let it go at that. Miss Watson said, "But nobody ever gave me an answer to my question, since my children's father and I weren't married!" Mrs. Pierce expressed agreement and said that was true, and Miss Elliott nodded and they all looked at me.

I said perhaps there wasn't a specific answer to Miss Watson's and Miss Elliott's problem, but is the truth any different for one than for the other? Can we make a mistake right by denying it? All nodded in agreement and we talked about the fact that one cannot make a wrong right, but we can move on from that mistake and be different, if we recognize and face the mistake.

Mrs. Thompson said, "You know what? I've told my kids that their father and I have had a disagreement and that is why we aren't living together." She explained that the children seemed to understand and accept this, and laughingly told the story of her little boy who asked her later, "When are you two going to get over your disagreement?" [Youngman, 1965, p. 29].

Sometimes groups have been formed around specific problem situations. In one instance, a group of mothers interested in making application for employment interviews discussed civil service testing and child care for the working mother. In another instance, the group grew out of the problems a number of different mothers were encountering with their teenage daughters. In another instance, group meetings were held for mothers who had a delinquent child in a training school; the meetings were oriented around helping the mothers to understand the child and helping them to prepare for his return home.

The literature detailing the activities of such groups rarely includes material on the formal evaluation of the results. The reports occasionally include details of self-evaluation by members of the group.

Navarre and Glasser (1969) employed a control group in evaluating the experimental effects of group services offered eighty-nine AFDC mothers whose children had school-related problems. Group sessions were designed to help the mothers develop skills in problem solving and to apply these skills in dealing with the parent–child interactions concerning school problems. The control group consisted of seventy-three AFDC mothers with similar problems who attended no group meetings or only one of the meetings. A comparison of the experimental group of mothers (most of whom had attended six group meetings) and the control group showed that the mothers offered group treatment had significantly improved their attitudes of responsibility toward their children's adjustment in school, task performance, and decision making in the home and had lower generalized anxiety levels. The children of the mothers in the experimental group showed significant improvement in classroom conduct, but there was no difference on such measures as academic motivation, grades, or school attendance.

Separation of Income Maintenance and Services and Title XX

At one time, both the eligibility–income maintenance task and the social service responsibilities were handled by one worker assigned to a family in the AFDC program. This arrangement was significantly altered in the early 1970s when the federal government mandated a separation of the social services from the determination of eligibility and the provision of financial assistance. The principal objectives of AFDC—"to provide financial assistance to children in their own home" and "to maintain and strengthen family life"—are divided and assigned to different administrative units, one concerned with financial assistance, the other concerned with "strengthening and maintaining family life" through the provision of social services. Separation, which is designed to give the clients greater freedom to use or refuse social services, also requires them to initiate the request for service, rather than the request's being part of the application for assistance. Entry into social services requires another decision and special action on the part of the client.

Almost all families make their initial contact with the AFDC program through a request for financial assistance processed by the income maintenance unit. The eligibility form is primarily concerned with data relating to establishing eligibility for financial assistance. In eighteen states, there are one or two questions asking the applicant if social services are needed or providing a check-list of social services, which the applicant may request. Other states have separate forms concerned with the social services that are available and in which the applicant might be interested. In many states, however, the bridge between the income maintenance section and the social services section of the AFDC program is less explicitly established (Citizens Committee for Children of New York, 1978, p. C1).

Even in those states that formally call the client's attention to the availability of social services on the income maintenance application form, access to the needed social services operates ineffectively, as indicated by a study (Citizens Committee for Children of New York, 1978) in New York City based on observation of the procedure and interviews with workers, administrators, and clients. Income maintenance workers rarely called clients' attention to the social service question, rarely questioned clients on their possible need for and interest in such services, and rarely attempted to motivate clients to request such services if need for them became evident. Social service help and needs were peripheral and marginal functions and concerns. Consequently, few AFDC families asked about, or were referred to, the social services unit. This was true not only at the time of application but also in subsequent contacts when the assistance maintenance workers interviewed the family for recertification of their eligibility. Throughout the time the family is related to the agency, social services have little visibility and limited availability. In general, "families have slight chance to learn about available social services, few opportunities to discuss service needs and options and little help in getting service" (Citizens Committee for Children in New York, 1978, p. 33). The assumption is that if the clients do not explicitly request social services, they do not need them—an assumption that might be regarded as an abdication of agency responsibility.

An experiment that randomly assigned new AFDC applicants to a variety of different service-delivery conditions showd that the separation of services, which requires that the client initiate a request for social services, results in lessened use of such services (Piliavin, Gross, 1977).

Although all AFDC families are eligible for social services, a study of the 3,420,000 families in the program in 1975 showed that only 44 per cent of the families received one or more services during a one-year period. The services most frequently provided were related to health (23 per cent of the families), family planning (17.2 per cent), home management, family-life instruction (12 per cent), education and training (12 per cent), and child care (10.8 per cent).

Of the 8 per cent of families with members having problems with alcohol or addictive drugs, only about one in five received related services (Oberheu, 1979, p. 1). Less than 4 per cent of all AFDC families received protective services, legal services, or foster-care services.

These findings confirm fears expressed earlier by researchers who had investigated clients' reactions to the services offered by workers before the separation of services. The researchers noted that separation of services and requiring that the client take the initiative in requesting services might "exacerbate the already difficult problem of failing to distribute social services among the very poor" and might "have the effect of cutting off a reasonable valuable service that most clients . . . seem to like" (Handler, Hollingsworth, 1969, pp. 417–418). In response to the diminished concern with the social services used by the clients, there is some talk of reintegrating the two aspects of the program. Recent federal changes now permit the reintegration at the option of the state.

One worker who is in continuous contact with the family and becomes familiar with the needs and problems of the family—initially from a review of the family's financial situation and subsequently in periodic visits to the family —is seen as an advantageous service to the client (Bernstein, Meezan, 1975).

Before 1975 the social service component of the AFDC program was an integral part of the program. In 1975 Title XX of the Social Security Act—Grants to States for Services—was signed into law as part of the Social Security Amendment Act. It established a new pattern governing federal- and state-supported social service programs. All previously legislated sections of the Social Security Act relating to social service were in effect repealed and replaced by Title XX.

Federal money is added to state expenditures to pay for social services up to a limit of $2.9 billion of federal money.

Title XX was the result of an effort to redefine the place of social services in the welfare system and to determine those social services that would receive federal support and the conditions under which support would be offered.

Title XX removed social services from the public assistance titles of the Social Security Act and gave it free-standing status, funded through a separate grant structure.

All AFDC families are eligible for Title XX social services.

Unlike previous federal–state social-service funding efforts, Title XX eligibility for service is not tied to whether or not a client is a current, former, or potential recipient of assistance. It is tied to income, so that low-income, intact families not eligible for AFDC would be eligible for federally supported services. All families with income levels up to 115 per cent of the state median income level, adjusted to family size, are eligible for service. However, those families whose income is between 80 and 115 per cent of the state median income level must pay some fee based on a graduated scale. Protective services and information referral services are exempt from the fee charge. To give some idea of coverage, it might be noted that 115 per cent of the median income in Wisconsin for a family of four in 1975 was $16,128; 80 per cent of median was $11,219. However, few members of the general public are aware of and make use of the service.

Evaluation

Evaluation of Aims Achieved

The principal stated aims of the program are to provide the child with the following:

1. The economic support and services he needs for health and development.
2. The opportunity to grow up within his own family.
3. A share in the life of the neighborhood and the community.
4. An education that will help him to realize his capacities.

In a great measure, many of these aims have been achieved by the program. However inadequate the grants, the program has provided a basic income for children who might otherwise have had none and has made it possible for children to live in their own homes under the care of their own mothers, instead of being divided among relatives, being left without supervision, or being sent to foster homes. In the forty-five years since the inception of the program, the program has been the means of keeping together the families of 100 million children: "Without this assistance, it is certain that many of these families would have dissolved completely and the children would possibly have suffered permanent emotional and even physical damage" (Blackwell, Gould, 1952).

Maintained at home in their own families, these children have also been afforded the opportunity to share in the life of the neighborhood and the community. A sizable percentage of the children have participated in community youth organizations and activities.

The educational goal has been achieved: "The evidence clearly demonstrates that, as a group, these children have already gone much further than their parents" (Mugge, 1964, p. 11). However, it appears that the educational achievement of AFDC children, as a group, is lower than that of their peers.

Studies of AFDC families show that there appears to be very little basis for viewing the AFDC family as disorganized or severely deviant—the families as a whole present a profile of functioning that is quite stable. Relatively few AFDC families have been charged with child neglect or abuse, and the level of delinquency of AFDC children is similar to that of their peers.

The fact is that since its establishment in 1935, the AFDC program has distributed billions of dollars to families caring for millions of children who would otherwise have been seriously deprived. In one study, which asked mothers who had left the welfare program what they thought it had done for them, over half said, "it provided basic economic security; it prevented the family from breaking up" (Handler, Hollingsworth, 1971, p. 188).

The basic objective of the AFDC program is to meet the fundamental economic needs of children and their caretakers, rather than to make any explicit attempt to solve the problem of poverty or to redistribute wealth. It does mitigate the extent of poverty and provides the assurance of a basic, if frequently inadequate, income, making the difference between deprivation and modest subsistence.

PROBLEMS

1. One of the problems faced by the AFDC program is that it is badly in need of reform, but efforts to change the program have not yet been successful. Criticism of the AFDC program has come from taxpayers, recipients, social workers, citizens' groups, and government officials at every level.

The working poor regard the program as discriminatory because it excludes them from assistance. The program thus provides an incentive to family disruption because a father earning low, intermittent wages could ensure a steady, improved income for his family by deserting and making his family eligible for AFDC.

Clients and social workers, on the other hand, feel that the amount of aid is too low—in most states, well below the official poverty level. Clients regard the eligibility test as demeaning.

Each one of a series of government commissions and task forces appointed to study the program has called for fundamental changes in the nature of the program and a uniform national standard of assistance implemented by federal grants based on one eligibility requirement: need.

In addition to the proposals to revise and amend the welfare system, serious consideration has been given to abolishing the current programs and substituting a guaranteed annual income, a negative income tax, or a children's allowance scheme.

President Nixon introduced a modified version of the negative income tax approach in the Family Assistance Plan (Burke, Burke, 1974). This failed to receive congressional approval, and President Carter, inheriting the problem, introduced his own comprehensive welfare reform, The Better Jobs and Income Program, to provide a basic, federally guaranteed minimum income to all families nationwide. This was also rejected.

At the end of 1979, the possibilities for comprehensive welfare reform legislation seemed to be problematic. Instead, partial and incremental measures to meet some of the most pressing problems seemed to have a better chance of passage.

In May of 1979 President Carter proposed a modest welfare reform program that included some of the essential incremental features. It included provisions for 400,000 new public service jobs and training slots for workers in low-income families. It mandated an increased minimum benefit level of welfare payments and food benefits equal to 65 per cent of the poverty level, a step that would raise benefits for 800,000 families in thirteen states. The national minimum benefit would be $4,654 for a family of four and AFDC for the unemployed would be a required program in all states. The "earned income tax credit," the reverse income tax to low-income wage earners, was to be expanded (*New York Times*, May 24, 1979). If it is passed by Congress, the program will become operative in fiscal 1981–82 and is expected to increase the cost of the income maintenance program by about $6 billion.

2. A continuing problem for the AFDC program is likely to relate to unrealistic public expectations of major reductions, through employment, in the number of families receiving assistance. Our experience with the Work Incentive program since 1967 and the results of studies of the background of AFDC recipients should reduce these expectations.

Available data indicate that the AFDC recipient's potential for self-support is such that only a very modest percentage will be able to move off the program. The studies show that there are real and significant barriers to the employability of the 3 million adults on the AFDC program who care for 8 million children. Employment potential is associated with such factors as educational level, previous job experience, employment skills, physical and mental health status, some general competence in handling personal affairs, and conditions in the local labor market. The dilemma is that those who score high on all of these factors do not need much help and effectively use whatever service they do need. Those who score low need a great deal of help but cannot make effective use of the services available.

In reality, if the recipient's situation and capacity had permitted independence, he would not be on assistance, unless one assumes that the typical recipient does not want to work. Yet every study that tests this assumption concludes that there is little difference between the welfare population and the rest of the community regarding readiness and willingness to work.

The Work Incentive program requires a careful review of the AFDC case load in a search for all employables, followed up by work training and job placement, with day care provided for the young children of employable mothers. As of 1978 the program had had very limited success.

Reviewing the most significant studies of the employment program for AFDC recipients, Goodwin (1977) found that only a limited number of eligibles were found suitable either for training or for employment referral; only a limited number of those trained or referred to jobs actually found steady work; and an even smaller number of those who found steady work earned enough to move off welfare (pp. 2, 35). Given chronic moderate-to-high levels of unemployment and given the low wages that most AFDC parents might earn if employed, Goodwin questions the feasibility of a work requirement for AFDC eligibility as a solution to the problems of families needing assistance. Nevertheless the studies do show that if we cannot justifiably expect to reduce sharply the number of AFDC recipients, a concentrated effort at training and placement can lead to a modest increase in the job possibilities available to some.

In 1967, 15 per cent of welfare recipients worked; in 1975, 16 per cent were actually employed: 10 per cent full time, 6 per cent part time. The problem appears to be the lack of enough steady jobs at the level of skills that the AFDC recipient can offer and paying enough to cover the basic living needs of the family.

3. The AFDC program, as the largest and most expensive of the various public assistance programs, faces the problems that result from a negative public wage. Support for the program is hesitant and ambivalent. While accepting communal responsibility for children who need support, people are less willing to support the adult caregiver. The earlier mothers' aid program primarily offered support to children whose wage-earning parent had died. Death and disability are respectable and acceptable reasons for dependency. But death and disability account for only a small percentage of the children who require AFDC support. Less acceptable reasons, such as desertion, divorce, separation, and out-of-wedlock pregnancies, are the principal circumstances in which help is required. The public has a tendency to evaluate adult AFDC recipients as a socially undesirable group.

The attitude toward the program is also influenced by the strong feelings generated by racial conflict (Kallen, 1971). It is true that blacks form a disproportionately large percentage of AFDC recipients. Although they constituted approximately 11 per cent of the population, they made up 44.3 per cent of all families receiving AFDC in 1975. It might be noted, however, that the groups striving for full membership in American society have always constituted a larger percentage of those obtaining public welfare. At one time, this was true of the

Irish immigrant group, of the Italian immigrant group, and so on. The Know-Nothing movement, which had as one of its cardinal tenets restrictive immigration, pointed to the indigency of immigrants as an argument in favor of such a proposal.

Periodic exposures of "chiseling" and "fraud" adversely affect the image of the program. More detailed studies tend to indicate that although there is some fraud, much of what appears to be fraud is the result of errors and the administrative complexity of the program rather than a consequence of deliberate dishonesty (*The New York Times,* December 21, 1973). A distinction needs to be made between *error rate* and *fraud rate*. *Error rate* refers to grants that should not have been made resulting from errors in documentation and calculation for which the worker is primarily responsible. *Fraud rate* refers to grants that have been inappropriately made as a consequence of deliberate client misrepresentation. The two sources of error are frequently cited as one statistic and erroneously perceived as reflecting the level of fraud.

The fact that real need occasions the request for aid in the largest percentage of instances is demonstrated when such programs are eliminated or made very restrictive. In one instance where a county program of general assistance was discontinued, responsibility for family maintenance was shifted to other programs. A follow-up study noted that "in some form, the community has paid, and is still paying, maintenance costs for most of these families since the needs of the families and the children have continued" (U.S. Department of Health, Education, and Welfare, 1964, p. 17). There was a 54 per cent increase in money owed landlords, grocers, doctors, and so on during the fifteen-month period after curtailment of aid, and the medical needs of dependent children went unmet. The report concludes that the community "has been irreparably damaging its children during the vital growing years, thereby perpetuating, rather than alleviating, problems confronting the community" (*The New York Times,* November 10, 1963).

Studies of the effects of denying assistance to families because the mother had a second child out of wedlock did not have the anticipated effect of reducing further similar pregnancies. On the contrary, depriving families of public assistance increased their vulnerability to out-of-wedlock pregnancies (Bell, 1965, pp. 70, 183), while depriving the children in the family of much-needed aid (Chilton, 1969, p. 22).

4. There is a problem regarding the effects of AFDC on marriage and family disruption. The contention is that the program is an inducement to fathers to leave home, given the assurance that the family will continue to be supported, perhaps even more adequately and more steadily, by AFDC. The research findings regarding this contention appear to be ambiguous. Analyzing the relevant statistical data, Honig (1973) and Moles (1976) found limited and equivocal support for this proposition.

In an interview study of 450 AFDC mothers in New York City who were asked if the availability of welfare influenced the client's decision to separate from her husband, 14 per cent women said that it had. However, a detailed study of the situation as revealed in the interviews indicated that most often the separation was justified (Bernstein, Meezan, 1975, p. 88): "In the overwhelming majority of cases the married life of the AFDC women and their children was marked by a high degree of tension, of misery and brutality, and the results of alcoholism and narcotic addiction. In a phrase, it was generally an impossible situation" (p. 6). Family dissolution here is motivated by the same reasons as in nonwelfare groups (Klausner, 1978, p. viii).

A review of the more significant studies that had been completed by 1978 comes to the conclusion that AFDC defers marriage and that it "facilitates rather than precipitates disruption by providing women with a source of support outside of marriage" (MacDonald, Sawhill, 1978). The authors pointed out that factors other than the availability or lack of availability of AFDC were more potent in determining the decision to marry or not to marry, to break up or to continue a marriage.

It has been suggested that providing income maintenance payments to intact low-income families would counter the incentive for the father to leave so that the family might be eligible for AFDC. Recent research, however, suggests that this tactic may not have the results anticipated. Martial dissolution was monitored in negative-income-tax experiments conducted in New Jersey, Washington, and Colorado in the early 1970s. In these projects, families were randomly assigned to experimental and control groups, and the experimental group of families was guaranteed an income for a three-year period. In all three experiments, marital dissolution was larger in the experimental guaranteed-income group than in the control group (Bradbury, 1977, p. 75; Bishop, 1977, p. 33; Hannan, Tuma, Groenveld, 1978). Assured of an income at some level of adequacy and not solely dependent on the husband–father for support, more women may feel free to discontinue an unsatisfactory relationship.

The effect on family disruption varied with the size of the grant. At lower levels of guaranteed income, family disruption was increased, but at higher guaranteed income levels, there was little difference in disruption rates between the experimental families receiving such assistance and control families.

Guaranteed income did result in a very modest decrease in work effort on the part of men, and somewhat more for women, principally to gain more time for child care.

5. There is a conflict between the general aims of the program, the nature of program administration, and the level of assistance grants. The question has been raised as to whether the program, which offers assistance at a level that barely meets minimum need, is not self-defeating: "While adequate assistance grants do not automatically insure rehabilitation of clients, inadequate assistance definitely makes rehabilitation more difficult" (Tuttle, 1963, p. 70).

No amount of social service can substitute for inadequate assistance. Under such conditions it is difficult to implement the rehabilitative aims of the program. However, increasing the adequacy of support both in money grants and in in-kind assistance to AFDC families increases the inequity imposed on low-income intact families. Families with fathers living at home employed at low-level salaries are not eligible for help despite the fact that their level of living may be even less adequate than that of AFDC families. This is merely one contingency illustrating a more general problem: that much of the program is a necessary compromise between contradictory objectives requiring choices among competing goals. The goals of maintaining work incentives and keeping family disruption to a minimum contradict the desire to provide adequate levels of assistance.

Increasing the incentive to work by permitting the recipient to keep more of his or her earnings—that is, increasing the level of income "disregarded"—increases the number of people potentially eligible for assistance and increases the cost of the program. Increasing the incentive to work thus conflicts with the need to keep the cost of the program within limits and tends to make the program economically expansive and politically unpopular.

Careful monitoring of fraud and in respecting clients' dignity by reducing agency intrusivenesss are contradictory objectives. Directing grants more precisely to those in the greatest need requires identification of those in need through a means test and thus runs counter to the objectives of not stigmatizing the recipient. Individualizing the client situation, treating those who are different differently and those who are in similar circumstances similarly, competes with the objective of making administrative procedures simple and efficient: "It is the tension among and in some cases the inconsistency of these desired characteristics that makes restructuring and reform so difficult to attain" (Haveman, 1974, page x).

TRENDS

We have already noted some recent trends in the program, including the separation of the social service and the income maintenance aspects of the program; the development of a free-standing, separately funded social services program through Title XX; and the continuing interest in elimination of the AFDC program through the substitution of a more comprehensive welfare program.

More recent developments suggest additional trends:

1. There is currently greater concern about developing effective programs for ensuring the continuing support of children by fathers not living at home as a result of divorce, desertion, or out-of-wedlock pregnancy. The success of special "support recovery" programs by such states as New York and California (*The New York Times*, March 21, March 30, 1975) resulted, in 1975, in an amendment to the Social Security Act that required all states to establish an effective support recovery program by July 1977 or lose 5 per cent of their share of federal grants for social service. A parent-locator service was established in the Department of Health, Education, and Welfare, and various federal government files—social security, income tax, and so on—were made available to aid in the search for missing, nonsupporting parents.

2. There has been a trend toward greater control and monitoring of application and eligibility procedures to reduce fraud, inaccuracy, and increases in cost. The use of longer, more detailed eligibility forms, photographic identification cards for recipients, the matching of social security and civil service files with recipient files to verify information, and the development of specially trained eligibility units are in line with such a trend. While reducing errors, these procedures also have the effect of making access to help more difficult for some clients (Cunningham, 1977).

There is a trend toward the purchase of service by the AFDC program. Instead of providing the services the client may need, the welfare agency contracts for the purchase of such services from another agency or private organization. Day-care services, homemaker services, and family-planning services are often contracted for and purchased on this basis (U.S. Department of Commerce,

1971). The trend has been toward developing greater specificity in purchase-of-care procedures and tightening controls to ensure that the public welfare agency is actually getting what it contracted for.

SUMMARY

Because the social insurance programs cover only a limited number of the contingencies that result in income loss for the family, further income maintenance programs in the form of public assistance are necessary.

The assistance program directly affecting children is Aid to Families of Dependent Children. A precursor of the program, developed by the individual states earlier in the twentieth century, was known as the mothers' aid or mothers' pension program. The development of such a program was encouraged by the passage of legislation prohibiting child labor and by legislation making school attendance compulsory. During the Great Depression, the bankruptcy of state programs resulted in the acceptance by the federal government of responsibility for support, and the Social Security Act in 1935 provided for grants to the state for a program of assistance to dependent children.

Currently, the AFDC is a program in which service is offered directly to the recipient by the county, supervised by the state, and supported by local, state, and federal funds. The federal government, in administering its grants-in-aid reimbursement, has set certain minimum requirements with which the states, requesting reimbursement, must comply. Such requirements protect the recipient and establish some broad uniform standards. However, essential details of the program are left to the discretion of the individual states, and there is considerable variation in the program from state to state.

The program is designed to provide an income for children who are "needy" because their fathers are absent from the home, disabled, or unemployed. "Need" is determined by the state and is defined as the difference between an assistance budget for the family, computed by the local agency, and family income from all sources.

In December 1977, the program, available in every county in the United States, offered assistance to 8 million children and some 3 million parents. The typical AFDC family consisted of a mother and three children and required assistance because of family disruption (divorce, desertion, separation). The family had attempted to maintain itself without recourse to assistance for a period of some five months and could expect to be on assistance for a little over two years. During its time on assistance, the family would have attempted to live on a budget below the amount determined as the "poverty index" level for a family of that size.

In addition to the problem of living on a limited income, most AFDC families have additional problems of health, housing, and child care. The largest percentage of the children face the problem of living in a family without a father.

The program has succeeded in its major aim of maintaining dependent children in their own homes under the care of their mothers. It is less successful in keeping the children in school through high school graduation. Although AFDC children are ahead of their parents educationally, they are behind their non-AFDC peers.

Widespread efforts have been made to supplement casework with a group approach to AFDC families. The following problems are identified as a matter of concern to the program:

1. There is a need for general reform of the program to provide an adequate minimum income to all families in need. Recent legislative attempts toward such change were reviewed in this chapter.
2. The general public may have unrealistic expectations concerning a sharp drop in the number of welfare recipients as a consequence of training and employment programs.
3. The negative public image of the program has reduced public willingness to provide the program with the resources it needs.
4. There are conflicts within the program concerning its attitude toward the father who is away from the home.
5. There is a disparity between the aims of the program and the levels of assistance it provides.

The following trends were discussed:

1. Continuing interest in the reform of the AFDC program.
2. Concern about support payments from the absent father and a legislative mandate to implement support payments.
3. More rigorous monitoring and control of applicant eligibility.
4. Public agencies' contracting for the purchase of services from voluntary agencies to meet client needs.

BIBLIOGRAPHY

ABBOTT, GRACE. *The Child and the State.* Chicago: University of Chicago Press, 1949, 2 vols.

ASSISTANCE PAYMENTS ADMINISTRATION, SOCIAL SECURITY ADMINISTRATION. *Characteristics of State Plans for Aid to Families of Dependent Children.* Washington, D.C.: Government Printing Office, 1977.

BALL, ROBERT M. *Social Security—Today and Tomorrow.* New York: Columbia University Press, 1975.

BELL, WINIFRED. *Aid to Dependent Children.* New York: Columbia University Press, 1965.

———. "AFDC: Symptom and Potential," pp. 221–265, in *Jubilee for Our Times.* Ed. by Alvin L. Schorr. New York: Columbia University Press, 1977.

BERNSTEIN, BLANCHE, and WILLIAM MEEZAN. *The Impact of Welfare on Family Stability.* New York: Center for New York City Affairs, New School for Social Research, June 1975.

BISHOP, JOHN. *Jobs, Cash Transfers and Marital Instability: A Review of the Evidence.* Madison, Wis.: Institute for Research on Poverty, 1977.

BLACKWELL, GORDON, and RAYMOND GOULD. *Future Citizens All.* Chicago: American Public Welfare Association, 1952.

BRADBURY, KATHERINE. *The Effects of Welfare Reform Alternatives on the Family.* Madison, Wis.: Institute for Research on Poverty, 1971.

BURGESS, M. ELAINE, and DANIEL O. PRICE. *An American Dependency Challenge.* Chicago: American Public Welfare Association, 1963.

BURKE, VINCENT J., and VEE BURKE. *Nixon's Good Deed—Welfare Reform.* New York: Columbia University Press, 1974.

BURNS, EVELINE M. *The American Social Security System.* Boston: Houghton Mifflin Company, 1949.

CALIFORNIA STATE DEPARTMENT OF SOCIAL WELFARE. *A Study of Marin County, California.* Sacramento, California: State of California Department of Social Welfare, n.d.

CHILTON, RONALD. "The Consequences of Florida's Suitable Home Law—A Case of Ineffective Intervention." *Welfare in Review,* **7,** 5 (September–October 1969), 17–22.

CITIZENS COMMITTEE FOR CHILDREN OF NEW YORK. *Social Services—Short Shrift for 600,000 Children.* New York: Citizens Committee for Children of New York, April 1978.

COLL, BLANCHE D. *Perspectives in Public Welfare—A History.* Social and Rehabilitation Service, U.S. Department of Health, Education, and Welfare. Washington, D.C.: Government Printing Office, 1969.

CONGRESSIONAL BUDGET OFFICE. *Welfare Reform, Issues, Objectives and Approaches.* Washington, D.C.: Government Printing Office, 1977.

CUNNINGHAM, MARY. "Eligibility Procedures for AFDC." *Social Work,* **22** (January 1977), 21–26.

CUTRIGHT, PHILLIPS. "AFDC, Family Allowance and Illegitimacy." *Family Planning Perspectives,* **2,** 4 (October 1970), 4–9.

DANZINGER, SHELDON. "Income Redistribution and Social Security: Further Evidence." *Social Service Review,* **51** (March 1977), 179–184.

EISENBERG, JEANNE G., THOMAS LANGER, and JOANNE GERSTEN. "Differences in the Behavior of Welfare and Non-Welfare Children in Relation to Behavioral Characteristics." *Archives of the Behavioral Sciences,* No. 48, Oct. 1975 (whole number).

GLASSER, MELVIN, et al. *Survivors' Benefits and Blue Collar Workers.* Lexington, Mass.: D. C. Heath & Company, 1970.

GOODWIN, LEONARD. *Do the Poor Want to Work?* Washington, D.C.: The Brookings Institution, 1972.

——. *The Work Incentive (WIN) Program and Related Experiences—A Review of Research and Policy Implications.* Washington, D.C.: Government Printing Office, 1977.

GREENLEIGH, ARTHUR. *Addenda to Facts, Fallacies, and Future: A Study of the Aid to Dependent Children Program of Cook County, Illinois.* New York: Greenleigh Associates, Inc., 1960.

GREENLEIGH ASSOCIATES, INC. *Public Welfare: Poverty, Prevention, or Perpetuation.* New York: Greenleigh Associates, Inc., 1964.

GUILLOT, ELLEN E. "Congress and the Family: Reflection of Social Processes and Values in Benefits in OASDI." *Social Service Review,* **45,** 2 (June 1971), 173–182.

HANDLER, JOEL, and ELLEN J. HOLLINGSWORTH. "The Administration of Social Services and the Structure of Depending—The View of AFDC Recipients." *Social Service Review,* **43** (December 1969).

HANDLER, JOEL, and ELLEN JANE HOLLINGSWORTH. *The "Deserving Poor"—A Study of Welfare Administration.* Chicago: Markham Publishing Co., 1971.

——. *Reforming the Poor—Welfare Policy, Federalism and Morality.* New York: Basic Books, Inc., 1972.

HANNAN, MICHAEL T., NANCY B. TUMA, and LYLE P. GROENVELD. *The Effects of Negative Income Tax Programs on Marital Stability: A Summary and Discussion of*

Results from the Seattle-Denver Income Maintenance Experiments. Menlo Park, Calif.: Center for the Study of Welfare Policy, S.R.I. International, October 1978.

HAVEMAN, ROBERT H., and WATTS, HAROLD W. "Social Experimentation as Policy Research: A Review of Negative Income Tax Experiments," in *Evaluation Studies Review Annual,* Vol. 1. Ed. by Gene Glass. Beverly Hills, Calif.: Sage Publications, 1976.

HONIG, MARJORIE. "The Impact of Welfare Payment Levels on Family Stability." *Studies in Public Welfare,* No. 12, 37–53.

JANOWITZ, BARBARA S. "The Impact of AFDC on Illegitimate Birth Rates." *Journal of Marriage and the Family,* 38 (August 1976), 485–494.

KAHN, ALFRED. "Social Services in Relation to Income Security." *Social Service Review,* 39 (December 1965).

KALLEN, DAVID J., and DOROTHY MILLER. "Public Attitudes Toward Welfare." *Social Work,* 16, 4 (July 1971), 83–90.

KLAUSNER, SAMUEL Z. *Six Years in the Lives of the Impoverished—An Examination of the WIN Thesis.* Philadelphia: Center for Research on the Acts of Man, 1978.

LANGER, THOMAS, et al. "Psychiatric Impairment in Welfare and Nonwelfare Children." *Welfare in Review,* 7, 3 (March–April 1969), 10–21.

LEFF, MARK H. "Consensus of Reform: The Mothers' Pension Movement in the Progressive Era." *Social Service Review,* 47 (September 1973), 397–417.

MacDONALD, MAURICE, and ISABEL V. SAWHILL. "Welfare Policy and the Family." *Public Policy,* 26, 1 (Winter 1978), 89–119.

MALLAN, LUCY B. "Young Widows and Their Children: A Comparative Report." *Social Security Bulletin,* 38 (May 1975), 3–21.

MEIER, ELIZABETH. "Casework Services to ADC Families." *Public Welfare,* 19 (1961).

MOLES, OLIVER C. "Marital Dissolution and Public Assistance Payments Variations Among States." *Journal of Social Issues,* 32, 1 (1976), 87–101.

MONTELIUS, MARJORIE. *Working with Groups—A Guide for Administration of Group Services in Public Welfare.* Washington, D.C.: Government Printing Office, 1967.

MUGGE, ROBERT. "Education and AFDC." *Welfare in Review,* 2 (January 1964).

NAVARRE, ELIZABETH, and PAUL GLASSER. *Group Work Practice with AFDC Mothers—An Evaluation Study.* Ann Arbor, Mich.: School of Social Work, University of Michigan, April 1969. Mimeo.

OZAWA, MARTHA N. "Income Redistribution and Social Security." *Social Service Review,* 50 (June 1976), 209–223.

———. "Children's Right to Social Security." *Child Welfare,* 53, (December 1974), 619–631.

PILIAVIN, IRVING, and ALAN E. GROSS. "The Effects of Separation of Services and Income Maintenance on AFDC Recipients." *Social Service Review,* 51 (September 1977), 390–406.

PLATT, ANTHONY. *The Child Savers—The Invention of Delinquency.* Chicago: University of Chicago Press, 1969.

REIN, MARTIN, and RAINWATER, LEE. "How Large Is the Welfare Class?" *Challenge* (September–October 1977), 20–23.

ROSS, HEATHER, and ISABELL SAWHILL. *Time of Transition.* Washington, D.C.: The Brookings Institution, 1975.

RUGGLES, PATRICIA, and CAROL ZUCKERT. "Social Security Student and Former Child Beneficiaries Aged 18–21." *Social Security Bulletin,* 37 (March 1974), 26–34.

SCHOTTLAND, CHARLES I. *The Social Security Program in the U.S.,* 2nd ed. New York: Appleton-Century-Crofts, 1970.

SECRETARY, U.S. DEPARTMENT OF HEALTH, EDUCATION AND WELFARE. *Reports of the Quadrennial Advisory Council on Social Security.* Washington, D.C.: Government Printing Office, 1975.

SOCIAL SECURITY ADMINISTRATION. *Aid to Families of Dependent Children. 1975 Recipient Characteristics Study,* Part I: *Demographic and Program Statistics.* Washington, D.C.: Department of Health, Education, and Welfare, 1977.

STUART, ARCHIBALD. "Recipient Views of Cash Versus In-Kind Benefits." *Social Service Review,* 49 (March 1975), 79–91.

THOMPSON, GAYLE B. "Blacks and Social Security Benefits—Trends, 1960–73." *Social Security Bulletin,* 38 (April 1975), 29–40.

TUTTLE, ELIZABETH. *Narrative Report of the Special ADC Project.* Cuyahoga County Welfare Department, Cleveland, Ohio, January 1963.

U.S. CHILDREN'S BUREAU. "Mothers' Aid 1931." Reprinted in *Children and Youth—A Documentary History.* Ed. by Robert H. Bremner. Cambridge, Mass.: Harvard University Press, 1971.

U.S. DEPARTMENT OF HEALTH, EDUCATION, AND WELFARE. "Study of Effect of Relief Curtailment in an Ohio County." *Social Security Bulletin,* 27 (February 1964).

U.S. SENATE. "Women and Social Security: Adapting to a New Era." Washington, D.C.: Government Printing Office, 1975.

YOUNGMAN, LOUISE. "Social Groupwork in the AFDC Program." *Public Welfare,* 23 (January 1965).

5 PROTECTIVE SERVICES

INTRODUCTION

It is difficult to classify protective services neatly as either supportive, supplementary, or substitutive. Protective services are called upon in a variety of situations, characterized by a similar factor: neglect, abuse, or exploitation of a child. The protective service agency is organized around the nature of the problem and uses a wide variety of services—supportive, supplementary, and substitutive—in trying to help the family deal with it. The agency may seek to protect the child by strengthening the home (*supportive*), by supplementing the parent's own efforts to care for the child (*supplementary*), or by removing the child from the home and placing him in another home (*substitutive*). Initially, however, activity is directed toward maintaining the neglected or abused child in his own home. Consequently, protective services may be classified as among the services to children in their own home.

DEFINITION

The Children's Division of the American Humane Association, the national body coordinating the work of protective agencies, defines *protective service* as a specialized child-welfare "service to neglected, abused, exploited, or rejected children. The focus of the service is preventive and nonpunitive and is geared toward rehabilitation through identification and treatment of the motivating factors which underlie" the problem (DeFrancis, 1955, p. 2). Protective service is

> based on law and is supported by community standards. Its purpose is protection of children through strengthening the home or, failing that, making plans for their care and custody through the courts. . . . [It is] a service on behalf of children undertaken by an agency upon receipt of information which indicates that parental responsibility toward those children is not being effectively met [Canadian Welfare Council, 1954, p. 8].

The problems with which the protective agencies are concerned arise from gross parental inadequacy in role performance and from active role rejection. The parent may be present but incapable of caring for the child, or unwilling to do so. Under the concept of *parens patriae*, the state has an obligation, as a "parent" to all children, to defend the rights of the child. The problem, however, is to avoid "infringing on the rights of the general parent population while simultaneously insuring the rights of a specific child" (Boardman, 1963, p. 8). One might, how-

151

ever, say that parental rights derive from parental obligations. When these obligations and responsibilities are unfulfilled, the corresponding rights may be abrogated. Currently, the right of the parent to the control of his child is regarded as an inherent natural right subject to the protection of due process. The natural right is not regarded as absolute; it is in the nature of a trust.

With the concept of *parens patriae*, a third party is introduced into the parent–child relationship, providing the child with some assurance of outside protection and support.

There is a growing acceptance of children as separate entities entitled not only to having their needs met but also to having their rights respected. In recognizing children's rights, society has moved from a perception of children as belonging to their parents to seeing children as belonging to themselves in the trust of their parents.

With the growing recognition of the separate rights of children, there is less readiness to grant the assumption that parents always have the child's best interest in mind and that parents and children invariably share a community of interest.

The judicial power of the community to intervene in behalf of the child against the parent "has rarely been challenged; only its *extent* has been questioned" (Simpson, 1962, p. 353). The justification for community intervention is based on the need for community self-preservation. The continuity of the group rests with its children. Any danger to the life of the child threatens this continuity. Thus intervention in cases of neglect and abuse is merely an extension of the community's need to intervene against infanticide. More immediately, however, the community's justification for intervention lies in the fact that neglect or abuse of the child is likely to result in an expense to the community: the maltreated child may need care or medical attention at community expense; the maltreated child is less apt to grow up to be a self-sustaining adult.

The humanitarian justification goes beyond these considerations: a child should not be abused, neglected, or exploited; he has a right to expect protection and care.

It is often suggested that the privacy of urban living makes imperative a more formal, legalized expression of this concern (Garbarino, 1977). Jules Henry (1963), an anthropologist, notes:

> In a primitive culture, where many relatives are around to take an active interest in one's baby, where life is open, or in large households, where many people can see what a mother is doing and where deviations from traditional practice quickly offend the eye and loosen critical, interested tongues, it is impossible for a parent to do as he or she pleases with his child. In a literal sense, a baby is often not even one's own in such societies, but belongs to a lineage, clan, or household—a community—having a real investment in the baby. It is not private enterprise. The almost total absence of the social regulation of parent–child relations in our private-enterprise culture is a pivotal environmental factor making it necessary to institutionalize community concern in an agency offering protective service [p. 332].

All agencies concerned with child welfare may be said to be protective agencies. In the more specialized use of the term, the *protective agency* is an agency that is given special responsibility in cases of child abuse, exploitation, and neglect. Such agencies are often delegated some specific authority, usually by charter, to act for the community in its collective expression of concern for children.

Some have questioned the distinctiveness and uniqueness of the protective service agencies. It is pointed out that all agencies have a responsibility to intervene when a child is abused or neglected, that authority is inherent in all social work, and that the protective agency, in petitioning for court action, has no greater mandate than any other agency (Sandusky, 1964). Nevertheless, the fact is that other agencies in the community tend to attribute to the protective service agency greater responsibility for problems of abuse and neglect.

Kahn (1963) aptly notes that "the protective responsibility is lodged in the whole community" and that all the agencies serving children are, in aggregate, responsible for "protecting" children so as to ensure all their rights. However, the protective service agency does have a special function: "The protective service moves into action only when socially defined minimums are not met or where children are in clear and present danger" (p. 325). And Boehm (1964) indicates that the protective service agency itself "appears to accept the role of 'agency of last resort'" (p. 46).

This may in fact be desirable, because it permits a clear delineation of function, giving one agency the responsibility for court action, freeing the "family agency to continue to concentrate on those families who are motivated to seek service and to refer others elsewhere. . . . The family agency can continue to be perceived as a source of help, not a source of threat" (Rein, 1963, p. 66).

HISTORICAL BACKGROUND

In earlier periods of history, the child was regarded as a chattel of his parents. In its most unrestricted expression, this attitude gave the parents the right to kill the child at birth, to sell him, to exploit his labor, or to offer him as a sacrifice to a deity. Although almost every community restricted and regulated such rights to some extent, until recently parental power over the child was subject to relatively few limitations.

Acceptable, sanctioned procedures for disciplining the child differ with the culture and the times. The Biblical injunction in Proverbs 23:13–14 might be regarded as sanctioning what might today be termed child abuse: "Withhold not correction from the child for if thou beatest him with the rod he shall not die; thou shalt beat him with the rod and shalt deliver his soul from Hell."

In one of the earliest (English) handbooks on the upbringing of the young, parents were advised:

> If thy children rebel and will not bow them low
> If any of them misdo, neither curse nor blow
> But take a smart rod and beat them in a row
> Till they cry mercy and their guilt well know
> [Pinchbeck, Hewitt, 1969, p. 157].

Henry IV of France, whom "contemporaries regarded as an especially easygoing father" (Hunt, 1970, p. 138), wrote to those caring for his young son:

I have a complaint to make: you do not send word that you have whipped my son. I wish and command you to whip him every time that he is obstinate or misbehaves, knowing well for myself that there is nothing in the world which will be better for him than that. I know it from experience, having myself profited, for when I was his age I was often whipped [Hunt, 1970, p. 135].

Given the assumption that the child was born naturally sinful, failure to discipline not only resulted in spoiling the child but further endangering the soul.

Children being killed, abandoned, or punished are common themes in the classic literature about children read to children: "Hush-a-bye Baby," "Hansel and Gretel," "The Pied Piper of Hamelin," "Jack and the Beanstalk," "The Little Old Lady Who Lived in a Shoe," "Snow White and the Seven Dwarfs."

In recapitulating the history of childhood, DeMause (1974) says that:

The evidence which I have collected on methods of disciplining children leads me to believe that a very large percentage of the children born prior to the eighteenth century were what would be today termed "battered children." Of over two hundred statements of advice on child rearing prior to the eighteenth century which I have examined, most approved of beating children severely and all allowed beating in varying circumstances except three [p. 40].

Until the early part of the twentieth century, parents were allowed to exploit the labor of their children. A Manchester merchant, testifying in the nineteenth century at a hearing regarding child labor, noted that if a proposed bill safeguarding the health of children in factories were passed, "parents would conceive it a loss of the British birthright, that of control of a parent over his child" (Housden, 1955, p. 47).

In a general way, the neglected child has always been an object of concern in America (Folks, 1902, pp. 167–169). But the agencies concerned with child protection trace their origin to the dramatic case of Mary Ellen in 1875. The child was cruelly beaten and neglected by a couple with whom she had lived since infancy. There seemed no appropriate legal measure available to protect her. Community leaders, concerned with the situation, appealed to the Society for the Prevention of Cruelty to Animals. This organization brought Mary Ellen to the attention of the court as an "animal" who was being mistreated. Because the law did protect animals from abuse, the complaint was accepted, protection was granted Mary Ellen, and her guardians were sent to prison. As a result of this case, a Society for the Prevention of Cruelty to Children was organized.

The organization of the New York County Society for the Prevention of Cruelty to Children in 1875 was a signal for the development of similar societies elsewhere: San Francisco, Boston, Rochester, Baltimore, Buffalo, and Philadelphia. Many of the Societies for the Prevention of Cruelty to Children were originally organized as separate voluntary agencies; others were organized as subdivisions of the existing agencies concerned with the protection of animals, because "there was acquiescence in the view of the fundamental similarity of protective work for children and of animals" (McCrea, 1910, p. 138). Over the course of time, some of these agencies have merged with social agencies concerned with child welfare, while others have maintained their separate identity. The American Humane Association, originally organized for the protection of animals, established a children's division in 1887 to coordinate the activities of the various voluntary protective service associations that were developing throughout the country. By 1900, 161 such societies had been established throughout the United States (Folks, 1902, p. 173).

The work of these agencies centered on "child rescue." The agency "uncovered" the cases of children who were neglected, abused, or exploited, and worked to remove the children from their homes. The emphasis was on legal action, and the agency agitated for and supported efforts to enact legislation for the protection of children and to enforce these laws. Thus, as Sandusky (1964) notes, "such agencies performed a law enforcement function primarily rather than a social service function" (p. 579).

The New York Society placed agents in all magistrate courts to investigate cases involving abuse and neglect. Agents of the society were given the power of arrest, and interference with the work of the agent was deemed a misdemeanor. Agents were given considerable police power under legislative authority.

Almost from the start, however, another orientation, less legalistic and more social, was evident. It suggested that the primary rationale of protective services was to help the parents, not to punish them; to keep the family together, rather than to disrupt it. It is a difference between seeing the protective service agency as a law enforcement agency and seeing it as a social agency.

However, despite the fact that the current definitions of protective services express a social work rather than a legal emphasis ("protection of the child through strengthening of the home"; "preventive, nonpunitive service geared toward rehabilitation"), the two points of view are inherent in the operations of all agencies. What has been achieved is a greater stress on one, rather than the elimination of either.

The rapid development of protective agencies in the late nineteenth and early twentieth centuries was followed by a period of very limited growth. Impetus was given by the 1960 Golden Anniversary White House Conference on Children and Youth, which recommended that the states enact legislation authorizing communities to charge a specific social agency with responsibility for receiving complaints regarding child neglect and for providing services to the children and the parents involved. Further development of protective services resulted from the 1962 amendments to the Social Security Act, which required each state to develop a plan to extend child welfare services—protective services among them—to every political subdivision of the state.

By 1966 a nationwide survey indicated that protective services under public welfare auspices were reported to exist in forty-seven states. However, it was noted "that much of what was reported as child protective services was in reality nonspecific child welfare services or nonspecific family services in the context of a financial assistance setting" (DeFrancis, 1967, p. vii). The survey showed a long-term decline of such services under voluntary agency auspices. The public agency, particularly the local department of public welfare, was more and more frequently given the responsibility for offering such services. However, there was no clearly identifiable, specially designated protective-services unit in many of the public welfare agencies.

With the adoption of the new social services title to the Social Security Act—Title XX—protective service was made mandatory. By 1978 protective services were provided universally in all fifty states. Some 8 per cent of the total $2.5 billion of federal Title XX funds was being allocated to protective services.

The late 1960s and the 1970s showed an almost explosive growth of interest in the problem of the child requiring protection, the emphasis being given to child abuse. This interest resulted from the focus of medical attention on the "battered child."

A national survey reported by Kempe (1962) of children hospitalized because of abuse uncovered some 302 cases. This led to a Children's Bureau conference on the battered child, which was followed within a very short period of time by the adoption of legislation in state after state requiring the reporting of child abuse. As Paulsen (1966) notes, "Few legislative proposals in the history of the United States have been so widely adopted in so little time" (p. 46).

The rediscovery of child abuse in the 1960s came as a result of the activities of pediatric radiologists, pediatricians, and psychiatrists (Pfohl, 1977; Antler, 1978). Consequently the resurgence of interest in child abuse has a more distinctly medical orientation as contrasted with the almost exclusively social work orientation of an earlier period.

A federal Child Abuse Prevention and Treatment Act was passed in January 1974. This act provides for direct assistance to the states to help them develop child abuse and neglect programs. The act further provides for the support of research in the area of child abuse and neglect and establishes a National Center for Child Abuse and Neglect within the Children's Bureau, Office of Child Development, U.S. Department of Health, Education, and Welfare. The center supports research and acts as a clearinghouse for information on public and private programs in the area of child protection. Congress authorized $15 million in 1974 to finance implementation of the act, increasing this amount to $25 million each for fiscal years 1976 and 1977.

In the fall of 1972, another agency, the National Center for the Prevention and Treatment of Child Abuse and Neglect, was established with the help of federal funds at the University of Colorado Medical Center. It publishes a child protection newsletter, engages in research on child protection, and provides training for professionals concerned with abuse and neglect. A review of its activities, however, suggests a focus on abuse, with limited attention to neglect.

In 1978 the Child Abuse Prevention and Treatment Act was extended, and an implementing authorization of $25 million was provided for 1978 and 1979 and increased to $30 million for 1980 and 1981.

In order for states to qualify for federal assistance under revisions of the Child Abuse Prevention and Treatment Act, the state statutes on abuse must protect all children under age 18; cover mental injury, physical injury, and sexual abuse; include neglect reports and abuse reports; guarantee confidentiality of records; guarantee legal immunity for reporters; and provide for a guardian *ad litem* for children whose cases come to court. Many states have revised their legislation so as to be eligible for federal funds for their protective services program.

The tremendous expansion of activity regarding the maltreatment of children, with a particular focus on child abuse, is exemplified by the fact that in 1978 an annotated bibliography on child abuse was published listing 2,009 citations of published material, the majority published later than 1970 (Kalisch, 1978). Of necessity, then, the material in this chapter is highly abbreviated and selective.

DISTINCTIVE ASPECTS

The state is, ultimately, a parent to all children. When the natural parents neglect, abuse, or exploit the child, the state has the legal right and responsibility to intervene to protect him. The state delegates this authority to the protective service agency, so that, in effect, the agency functions as an arm of the state and operates with legal sanctions. In such situations, not only does the protective service agency have the right to intervene, they have the duty to intervene. All social agencies have an obligation to concern themselves with any situation of danger or potential danger to children, but the protective service agency has an explicitly delegated responsibility to intervene in such situations.

It follows, therefore, that protective services may be initiated on the basis of a request by someone other than a member of the family. In the case of services discussed earlier, client participation is voluntary; in the case of protective services, client involvement may be involuntary. Protective services deal with those instances of failure in parental role performance in which the parent is unaware of the need for service or is unwilling and/or unable to avail himself of the services that the community has provided.

Once involved, the agency cannot withdraw until the child is clearly no longer in danger. Just as the family is not permitted to decide whether or not they want the agency's help, the community does not permit the agency to decide whether or not it should offer the service: "The agency cannot leave a client free to accept or reject its services; nor can it withdraw only because the parent has refused or is unable to take help" (Canadian Welfare Council, 1954, p. 8).

The agency's responsibility of staying with the situation as long as danger to the child exists is illustrated in the following case:

> Neighbors complained that a young mother was seriously neglecting her four-month-old daughter, the first and only child. When the child welfare worker visited the home, she found the baby looking very pale and listless and apparently not in good physical condition. She persuaded the mother to take the baby to a clinic, where the child was found to be seriously malnourished and to have a severe diaper rash. On her next visit to the home, the worker found that the mother had apparently done nothing to carry out the doctor's instructions. As the worker talked to the mother about her lack of care and the seriousness of the baby's condition, the mother ordered her out of the house. The worker agreed to go, but explained that she would have to continue her responsibility for seeing that the baby had more adequate care even to the point of filing petition at court, if necessary [Sandusky, 1960, p. 24].

Because the agency operates on the basis of delegated authority, it may invoke legal sanctions, if necessary, to protect the child and his rights. Although all agencies have the right to petition the court for the protection of the children with whom they are concerned, the protective agencies are viewed by themselves, by other agencies, and by the client group as the agency having a special responsibility for invoking such sanctions.

SITUATIONS IN WHICH PROTECTIVE SERVICES ARE APPROPRIATE

The situations in which protective agencies intervene are those in which the parent is unable and/or unwilling to enact the parental role effectively, and his failure constitutes an actual danger to the normal physical, emotional, and social development of the child. The statutory definitions of maltreatment suggest the different kinds of situations. Although definitions of what is involved in such situations differ from state to state, they generally include most of the following (Katz, Howe, McGrath, 1975):

1. Physical abuse.
2. Malnourishment; poor clothing; lack of proper shelter, sleeping arrangements, attendance, or supervision. Includes "failure to thrive" syndrome, which describes infants who fail to grow and develop at a normal rate.
3. Denial of essential medical care.
4. Failure to attend school regularly.
5. Exploitation, overwork.
6. Exposure to unwholesome or demoralizing circumstances.
7. Sexual abuse.
8. Somewhat less frequently the definitions include emotional abuse and neglect involving denial of the normal experiences that permit a child to feel loved, wanted, secure, and worthy.

These general situations, in effect, break down into two major categories: physical and sexual abuse, and neglect of one kind or another. Infanticide is the ultimate abuse; abandonment is the ultimate neglect. Efforts are made to maintain such distinctions by noting some of the differences in the nature and the etiology of abuse and neglect.

Some regard such distinctions as spurious and false, noting the supposedly frequent overlap of abuse and neglect. Preference is for a unitary term. In place of the abused child or the neglected child, the *maltreated child* or the *endangered child* is the term of choice.

The model Child Protective Services Act defines an abused or neglected child as one "whose physical or mental health or welfare is harmed or threatened with harm by the acts or omissions of his parents or others responsible for his welfare."

Physical Abuse

Physical abuse refers to beating a child to the point where he sustains some physical damage. The line between physical abuse and harsh parental discipline is difficult to define. As Arnold (1962) says, "forms of punishment considered proper, and even wholesome, in Elizabethan or Victorian days would be considered as abuse today" (p. 3). Silver (1969) raises the question of limits: "For example, if a parent punishes a child with a belt, is it after the fourth slash with the belt that parental rights end and child abuse begins; is it after the belt raises a welt over two millimeters that it becomes abuse versus parental rights?" (p. 804).

The problem is to distinguish discipline that is "legitimate violence" toward children from abuse that is excessive and inappropriate and hence unacceptable violence toward children.

Attempts have been made to distinguish discipline from abuse and excessive punishment from inappropriate punishment and bizarre punishment from sadistic punishment. Discipline is more clearly related to the child's behavior; it has a clearly corrective purpose. The discipline is appropriate to and commensurate with the child's behavior that the parent is seeking to change. Whereas many parents spank, the abuser "overspanks," with great regularity and great severity. In contrast with abuse, discipline is manifested in a context of loving concern for what is best for the child rather than in response to the needs of the parent.

Some definitions of abuse are narrow in scope, restricting abuse to actual serious injury sustained by the child, threat of injury or minor injury being excluded. Some definitions are far broader in scope, such as Fontana's (1971) definition of maltreatment, which includes any treatment by which a child's potential development is retarded or completely suppressed by mental, emotional or physical suffering whether it is negative (as in deprivation of emotional or material needs) or positive (as in verbal abuse or battering).

Some definitions stress the fact that the behavior is deliberate, with intent to harm the child. Other definitions give intent less consideration on the supposition that what is happening involves a danger to the child, whether it is intentional or not.

The definition of abuse is sometimes determined by the extent of injury to the child. If discipline is so harsh that as a result the child is bruised, abuse has taken place. It is noted, however, that "bruises" come in all shapes, sizes, and forms, some bruises being relatively minor. There would be little doubt, however, that the following examples, reported by local newspapers, would generally be considered physical abuse:

> A five-year-old girl wandered innocently onto a porch after being instructed not to do so. She was kicked back into the house, thrown across the room and hit on the head and face with a skillet.
> The father of a nine-month-old boy blackened his son's eyes, burned his face, hands, and neck, and fractured his skull [Bryant, 1963, p. 126].

A national newspaper survey of published reports of physical abuse conducted by the Children's Division of the American Humane Association revealed that children were beaten

> with various kinds of implements and instruments. The hairbrush was a common implement used to beat children. However, the same purpose was accomplished with deadlier impact by the use of bare fists, straps, electric cords, T.V. aerials, ropes, rubber hose, fan belts, sticks, wooden spoons, pool cues, bottles, broom handles, baseball bats, chair legs, and, in one case, a sculling oar. Less imaginative, but equally effective, was plain kicking with street shoes or with work shoes.

Children had their extremities—hands, arms, and feet—burned in open flames as from gas burners or cigarette lighters. Others bore burn wounds inflicted on their bodies with lighted cigarettes, electric irons, or hot pokers. Still others were scalded by hot liquids thrown over them or from being dipped into containers of hot liquids. . . .

What kinds of injuries were inflicted on them?

The majority had various shapes, sizes, and forms of bruises and contusions. There was a collection of welts, swollen limbs, split lips, black eyes, and lost teeth. One child lost an eye.

Broken bones were common. Some were simple fractures; others, compound. There were many broken arms, broken legs, and fractured ribs. Many children had more than one fracture. One five-month-old child was found to have thirty broken bones in his little body [DeFrancis, 1963, p. 6].

In some instances, cruelty is episodic. Sometimes, however, an abused child has suffered abuse before.

The dramatic material cited, although valid, tends to present a distorted picture of the actualities of child abuse. It focuses on the battered child, the child subjected to substantial injury.

While the terms *battered child* and *abused child* are often used interchangeably, there is a clear distinction in terms of severity of injury. The term *battered-child syndrome* was originally applied to a hospitalized population of children, generally very young, who were so severely injured as to require medical attention. Statistically the more typical *abused child* is a child older than four years, who has sustained mostly minor, sometimes moderate, physical injury that has not required medical attention of any kind.

Summarization of statistics from state reports in 1976 compiled by the National Center on Child Abuse and Neglect showed that 72 per cent of the abused children required no medical treatment, the injury being, most frequently, bruises and welts. Only 6 per cent of abused children required any hospitalization, and the fatality rate was 0.5 per cent. Among the abused children, 65 per cent were six years of age or older, and 17 per cent were under two years of age. Boys were more frequently abused than girls, but this was true only for children up to age ten or eleven. Girls were more frequently reported abused from ages eleven to seventeen. The change results from the inclusion of sexual abuse in the statistic—a type of abuse that is reported much more frequently with females as victims and is concentrated in older children (American Humane Society, 1978).

The picture of the abusive family, according to the 1976 abuse report statistics collected by the National Clearinghouse, is that of a low-income family with three or fewer children. The families were disproportionately mother-headed, single-parent families (35 per cent) and disproportionately nonwhite (20 per cent). There was evidence of "family discord" and stress due to "insufficient income" in many of the families. Natural parents were most frequently the abusers, being the perpetrators in 87 per cent of the cases. Fathers were somewhat more often the abusers (55 per cent) than the mothers (45 per cent). The parents had limited education and employment skills, less than 3 per cent being college graduates and less than 7 per cent being in a profession (American Humane Society, 1978, Appendix II).

Friends, neighbors, and relatives were the most frequent source of child abuse reports, with law enforcement agencies, schools, social agencies, and medical agencies being other sources of reports. Social agencies carried the major responsibility for helping the parents and the children after abuse was reported. In 78 per cent of the cases, the children remained in their own homes. "Casework counseling" was most frequently the service offered. This service, offered to more than half the families, contrasted with much more limited use of other services: foster care in 10 per cent, day-care and homemaker services in 3 per cent of the cases.

Although abuse is found in all socioeconomic groups, it is most frequently reported among the poor. Surveys such as those by Gil (1970) and Thompson (1974) and data from demonstrations projects (Holmes, 1977) further find a disproportionate number of nonwhites among the abuse sample. This finding may be an artifact of reporting; it may be a function of the heavier emphasis on physical discipline among lower-class groups; or it may be a consequence of the fewer opportunities for temporary "escape" from children—through baby-sitters, an evening out, a vacation weekend—among the poor (Billingsley, Giovannoni, 1970).

Selective sources of referral tend to accentuate the skewed class affiliation of reported abusers. Public hospitals and clinics, police, and welfare agencies are much more frequently sources of abuse reports than are either private hospitals or family physicians. Low-income people are in contact with the first institutions; middle-class and upper-class people more frequently make use of the private, voluntary sources of help.

Reviewing some of the research on the socioeconomic characteristics of abuse and neglect families, Pelton (1978) concluded that after allowing for justifiable explanations of discrepancies in reporting, lower socioeconomic groups are disproportionately represented among maltreaters, so that child abuse is not, in fact, a "classless" phenomenon. Although child abuse takes place at all class levels, proportionately more child abuse takes place among lower-class families. After allowing for the effect of differential reporting, some component of the disproportionate frequency of abuse is a consequence of the greater situational stress faced by lower-class families and their more limited opportunities for escaping from such stress. However, the fact that many lower-class families living under comparable stress do not abuse their children suggests that personality and attitudinal factors account for some percentage of the explanation of abuse.

Neglect

Child neglect may be regarded as another kind of problem. The parent who abuses or cruelly mistreats the child is guilty of a crime of commission; neglect is more frequently a problem of omission. The ultimate in neglect, of course, is child abandonment. The abandoned child is, by virtue of his abandonment, a client of the protective service agency. In less egregious instances, the child is found to be living in filth, malnourished, without proper clothing, unattended, and unsupervised.

The neglectful parent may be rejecting his parental role; more frequently, however, he is merely inadequate in performing it—and he is suffering along with the child.

A woman charged with child neglect described her third-floor cold-water flat to the judge at a hearing:

> It is an awful place to live. The wallpaper is in strips, the floor board is cracked. The baby is always getting splinters in his hands. The bathroom is on the floor above and two other families use it. The kitchen is on the first floor. I share it with another woman. I have no place to keep food. We buy for one meal at a time [Hancock, 1963, p. 5].

The following instances detail the social worker's description of situations encountered in investigating complaints of neglect:

> The family of ten is living in two rooms. The plaster is falling down; window panes were out; the plumbing leaked. The wind howled through cracks and it was bitterly cold. Two young children with frostbitten hands and feet were removed from this home to a hospital [Hancock, 1963, p. 10].
>
> What I saw as I entered the room was utter, stark, disorganization. The room was a combined kitchen–dining room. At the other end of the room two scrawny, owl-eyed frightened children—a girl of about four and a boy of three—stared silently at me. Except for thin cotton undershirts, they were stark naked. They had sore crusts on their legs and arms. They were indescribably dirty, hair matted, body and hands stained and covered with spilled food particles. Sitting on a urine-soaked and soiled mattress in a baby carriage behind them was a younger child—a boy about two.
>
> The floor was ankle deep in torn newspapers. There were feces in about a half-dozen spots on the floor and the air was fetid and saturated with urine odor.
>
> There were flies everywhere. What seemed like giant roaches were crawling over the paper-strewn floor. The kitchen sink and gas stove were piled high with greasy and unwashed dishes, pots, and pans [DeFrancis, 1958, p. 11].

The police are frequently the first to be involved, and police patrol-car reports often detail cases of neglect:

> Responded to a complaint concerning three children, ages two to six, left alone in a parked car for several hours. Observation indicated that the children were dirty and unkempt, cold and hungry, poorly clothed, and in need of medical care [Swanson, 1961, p. 44].

Neglect also refers to consistently inadequate supervision or control of the child. Such complaints might read "A ten-year-old girl smokes and goes with her mother to bars"; "seven- and eight-year-old boys are encouraged to drink and smoke and walk around the house undressed"; "children are wild and undisciplined, parents seem unable, or unwilling, to control them and they run around the neighborhood like little savages, destroying property and terrorizing the smaller kids" (Rein, 1963, p. 41).

In this general category, one might also include educational neglect and medical neglect. In such cases, the parents make no effort to see that the child attends school or to provide the medical care he needs: "One child was covered with sores but not brought to the doctor. In another case, a mother refused the medical advice for follow-up care after a serious illness" (Rein, 1963, p. 44).

Medical neglect is illustrated in the following instance:

Someone noticed that Sally's (two years old) eye was closed and badly swollen and when nothing seemed to be done about it, he rang up the police, who told the protective agency. When the worker called on her, Sally's mother told him she thought the little girl had run into the end of her brother's toy pistol when they were playing in the garden. She added that she had been bathing the eye to see that it would be all right. The worker asked permission to call a doctor who took one look at Sally and said, "Hospital." There they decided that an immediate operation was necessary. Her father gave his consent and they removed Sally's eye to find that the trouble had not been caused by her running into anything but by an air-gun dart which had entered the eye and had lain there for twenty days. If the operation had been delayed, the hospital believed that the infection would have spread to her other eye and then probably she would have been blind for life [Allen, Morton, 1961, p. 48].

The nationwide clearinghouse report (American Humane Society, 1978) compiled on the basis of reports from individual states showed that in 1976 physical neglect was by far the most frequent kind of neglect reported (64 per cent), medical neglect (10 per cent) and educational neglect (7 per cent) occurring less frequently. In 19 per cent of the cases, emotional neglect was reported. The child was abandoned in about 6 per cent of the cases. "Lack of supervision" was frequently cited as associated with neglect.

Children at all age levels were reported neglected, although there was a heavier weighting of such reports for children under eight years of age. Males and females were equally neglected.

Larger families, of four or more children, were more frequently associated with neglect than with abuse. Neglectful families were even more disproportionately single-parent families (57 per cent) with very limited income, 60 per cent having annual incomes of less than $5,000 in 1976. These families were reported as facing a heavy burden of stress associated with single parenthood, insufficient income, inadequate housing, and social isolation. Given the association of poverty and deprivation and neglect, it is not unexpected that nonwhite families and Spanish-surnamed families were disproportionately represented in the neglect reports.

Natural parents were, in almost all cases, the "perpetrators" of neglect, female parents being more frequently cited than male parents in consequence of the high percentage of neglectful families that were single-parent, female-headed families.

Social agencies were primarily responsible for offering service to families reported as neglectful, casework counseling being the service most frequently offered. In 85 per cent of the cases, the child remained in his own home.

Emotional Neglect

A parent may provide adequate physical care for the child and yet manifest his rejection by starving or abusing the child emotionally. Deprivation of affectional support can be as harmful as denial of physical needs.

The Child Abuse Prevention and Treatment Act adopted in 1974 provides assistance to state child-abuse and neglect programs under certain conditions. One condition is that the states comply with the federal law's definition of child abuse and neglect as a "unified term" that "covers physical or mental injury, sexual abuse, negligent treatment or maltreatment of children under 18 years of age by a caretaker who is responsible for the child's welfare under circumstances which indicate that the child's health or welfare is harmed or threatened." To be eligible for assistance states are constrained to include mental injury—emotional abuse—as a reportable condition. By 1979 thirty-two states included mental injury in their abuse laws.

Emotional neglect is difficult to define in the precise terms required by law, and its consequences are equally difficult to establish conclusively. Despite this, an increasing number of states have included the idea of such maltreatment in protective services legislation. Such statutes might refer to the child's "emotional health," " mental well-being," "emotional maladjustment," "emotional impairment," or "mental injury" as requiring intervention without a further definition of the terms used. Some statutes specified the parental behavior associated with emotional maltreatment, such as "denial of parental love or adequate affectional parental association" (Idaho).

Over twenty years ago, Mulford (1958) defined *emotional neglect* as "the deprivation suffered by children when their parents do not provide opportunities for the normal experiences producing feelings of being loved, wanted, secure, and worthy which result in the ability to form healthy object relationships" (p. 21).

Some model statute formulations list some specific behavior indicative of emotional maltreatment. Thus the suggested American Bar Association Juvenile Justice standard notes that emotional maltreatment is "evidenced by severe anxiety, depression or withdrawal or untoward aggressive behavior or hostility toward self or others." Given as an additional indication of justification for community intervention is the fact that "the parents are unwilling to provide treatment for such a child" (Wald, 1975, p. 1019).

National Clearing House on Child Neglect and Abuse defines emotional neglect on its nationwide report form

> as failure to provide the child the emotional nurturing or emotional support necessary for the development of a sound personality, as for example subjecting the child to rejection or to a home climate charged with tension, hostility and anxiety—producing occurrences which result in perceivable problems in children.

The Federal Standards on the Prevention and Treatment of Child Abuse and Neglect, published in 1978 by the Children's Bureau, National Center on Child Abuse and Neglect, further defines mental injury as

> an injury to the intellectual or psychological capacity of a child as evidenced by an observable and substantial impairment in his/her ability to function with his/her normal range of performance and behavior with due regard to his/her culture [pp. 111–15].

Although there is general agreement on the difficulty of writing an acceptable legal definition of emotional maltreatment, there is an equally solid consensus that children do suffer from emotional neglect and abuse—even when they are adequately cared for physically.

As one court decision noted, "Children are entitled not only to food, clothing and shelter but to guidance, advice, counsel and affection, understanding and sympathy and when there are not accorded them . . . that would constitute serious and severe neglect" (quoted in Gesmonde, 1972, p. 108).

Young (1964) cites various examples of emotional abuse:

> Parents stated bluntly that they hated their children. Some expressed an open wish to kill them or a hope that they would die. Others remarked that they had never liked them, never wanted them. A parent frequently referred to his son as "crazy," the "idiot" or a child was told repeatedly that he was "dumb." In other cases a parent emphasized how physically ugly a child was or called him the "criminal."

The following is a case of emotional abuse called to the attention of a protective service agency:

> Judy's misery was exacerbated by the fact that she was the only child in her family to be treated badly, her two- and four-year-old brothers having a good family life with all the normal treats, outings, and sweets. But not only did she have none of these things, but when her father came home from work she had to leave the room instantly and play either in the kitchen or upstairs in her unheated bedroom. She was never allowed in the same room as her father, even if this meant her being sent to bed as early as five o'clock and never allowed to watch television or sit down to a meal with the rest of the family.
>
> The father made no pretense about his hatred and repudiation of the child, although he admitted that he had no reason to suspect that she wasn't his own. This case came to light because a teacher realized that the child was becoming rude and was bullying the other children to an exceptional degree [Allen, Morton, 1961, p. 113].

The literature lists other examples of emotional abuse that highlight the question of definition. Thus Walters (1975) says:

> If John brings home a report card with five A's and one C, the typical response of middle class parents is not "how well you have done" but "why did you get the C?" This constitutes emotional abuse. Low grades frequently prompt middle class parents to set curfew hours and enforced study time and to limit dating, and their children experience feelings of guilt and worthlessness. This constitutes emotional abuse [p. 37].

As the example illustrates, the greatest concern in including emotional maltreatment as a basis for action is that it may lead to unwarranted intervention in family functioning. There is difficulty in distinguishing between emotional abuse and general ineffective parenting that has possible damaging consequences for the child's emotional development.

Intervention may further restrict parental autonomy on the basis of discretionary action by social workers and judges based on ambiguous definitions of potentially harmful situations for children. For these reasons, and because the emotional consequences of parental behavior are difficult to predict, some argue (Wald, 1975) that intervention for emotional maltreatment is justified only if clear damage to the child can be demonstrated as a result of repeated habitual damaging behaviors toward the child on the part of the caretaker.

Emotional abuse may be established when a child who is emotionally disturbed is not provided treatment by the parent or when the parent refuses to accept treatment for himself.

Expert testimony and standardized psychological tests might help objectively establish the extent of the child's emotional and/or psychological impairment. Improvement of the child's emotional adjustment upon removal from the home might experimentally establish the validity of parental emotional maltreatment.

Sexual Abuse

By 1979, forty-two states had listed sexual abuse as a reportable manifestation of child abuse.

Sexual abuse includes not only sexual intercourse, genital or anal, and oral–genital contact, it also includes masturbation, fondling, and exposure. Here again a clear, unambiguous definition is not available. As Wald (1975) notes, it clearly involves "intercourse accomplished with or without the use of threats . . . but it may be difficult to distinguish from appropriate displays of affection and fondling" (p. 1024). A broad definition that includes "any sexual liberties taken by an adult with a child" makes it difficult to determine the limits of permissible agency intervention.

At some point, hugging, kissing, touching, and fondling as expressions of parental warmth toward the young child become inappropriate. At what point this kind of activity becomes tinged with incestuous components is difficult to determine. In discussing the studies relating to incest, Rosenfeld (1977) notes that one criterion defining the boundaries of acceptable affectionate interaction is that "There is no attempt by the parents to satisfy their adult genital–sexual needs through the child" (p. 233).

In the largest percentage of instances with which protective services agencies have become concerned, the problem involves sexual contact between father and daughter (Sgroi, 1975, p. 20; Sarafino, 1979, p. 131). In a more limited number of situations, the stepfather or the mother's boyfriend has sexually abused the daughter. Rarely is there a case of mother–son sexual abuse. Violence and coercion are involved in a small minority of cases (Schultz, 1973, p. 149). The abuser, then, in most instances is not a stranger, and the close and often affectional relationship between child and adult has provided the opportunity for such activity.

The relationship of the sexual abuser to the child is such that the abuser has access to the child and the opportunity for private, intimate contact. Most often, sexual abuse takes place in the child's home. The child is often pressured rather than physically forced to participate (Burgess *et al.*, 1977). The child is often socially and psychologically dependent on the abuser, lending potency to the pressure applied. The child is almost invariably female and the abuser male. There is a very wide age range of sexually abused children, from very young children to late teenagers, but the preponderant number of reports involve teenagers.

The potency of incest taboos which inhibit sexual activity between biologically related parents and children and between biologically related siblings is attenuated in the relationship between step-parents and their children and step-siblings. With increases in divorce and remarriage a larger number of children live in step-relationship context and consequently a larger number of children are at risk of sexual molestation within the family unit.

Those who have experience in treating this problem (Tormes, 1968; Sgroi, 1975; Walters, 1975; Giaretto, 1976) generally agree that the incident that finally comes to community attention is not an isolated event but part of a long-term series of sexual encounters at various levels between father and daughter.

What has been going on for some time may come to light as the child grows older, develops a growing sense of the inappropriateness of the activity, may develop fears of becoming pregnant, and may find the sexual affair with the parent interfering with the development of peer-group heterosexual relationships. The average age of sexually abused children is between eleven and fourteen years.

Nationally collected statistics showed that 1,975 cases of sexual abuse were reported nationwide in 1976, accounting for some 13 per cent of the validated reports of child abuse. Most frequently the sexual abuse involved "molestation" (29 per cent), reports involving incest being second in frequency (20 per cent) (American Humane Society, 1978, Table 4.6). The largest percentage of reports were of "sexual abuse—unspecified."

Because both the social and the legal penalties for sexual abuse are severe, and because there are no overt, observable signs of the abuse that might be evident to others, as in the case of physical abuse, there is a greater likelihood of underreporting this kind of abuse (Finkelhor, 1978). Reporting sexual abuse presents the child with a serious problem of divided loyalties between his or her own needs for protection and safety and the consequences for the parent and the family resulting from disclosure. As a consequence, estimates of incidence are considerably higher than numbers of reported abuse (Sarafino, 1979).

In 1978 "The National Center on Child Abuse and Neglect estimated that the annual incidence of sexual abuse of children is between 60,000 and 100,000 cases per year" (U.S. Department of Health, Education, and Welfare, 1979, p. 3).

In a limited number of cases, physical abuse may be associated with sexual abuse. Physical damage to the vagina or the anus may be involved, particularly in very young children. In some instances, children have contracted venereal disease as a consequence, so that Connecticut requires that all cases of venereal disease in children under thirteen be reported to a protective service agency.

Exposure to Unwholesome or Demoralizing Conditions

Children living with parents who engage in prolonged, severe alcoholism, prostitution, criminal activity, and drug addiction are also considered in danger. Such behavior on the part of the adult, which is "morally injurious to the child," is illustrated in the following reports:

Mother had intercourse with several men in the same room in which the three young children slept.

Mother and father were found in a drunken stupor when [the social] worker arrived and neighbors reported that parents frequently engaged in prolonged drinking bouts.

The child may be living in an illegal environment, such as a house of prostitution or a gambling establishment, or the child may be living in an environment that is likely to contribute to his "moral degradation and/or delinquency." An example is that of a "mother and teenage girl living above a bar where the only entrance to the apartment is between a bar and a pool hall" (Wilson, p. 5).

Exploitation

The child may be forced to work at unreasonable tasks for unreasonably long hours. Often this work is in contravention of child labor laws; sometimes, although technically legal, the work load suggests neglectful exploitation. In either instance, the child is denied an opportunity for normal recreational activities and other opportunities for social and intellectual development. Exploitation also involves encouraging the child to beg, to steal, or to engage in prostitution for the benefit of the parents.

CULTURAL AND INSTITUTIONAL CONTEXT OF MALTREATMENT

This presentation of situations that require intervention has been focused on parents or parental surrogates and on the care, or lack of care, of the child in his own home. There are, however, other kinds of contexts that present dangers of abuse and neglect of children.

The level of violence in society generally, and in mass communication media, suggests an acceptance of the use of force in settling interpersonal disputes. The general acceptance of, and acquiescence in, corporal punishment as a disciplinary procedure calls attention to the collective sanction of possible abuse. Although there is some dispute about whether lower-income families are more predisposed to the use of corporal punishment than middle-class families (Ehrlanger, 1974), studies show that the largest majority of parents of all classes see such disciplinary measures as acceptable (Stark, McEvoy, 1970; Blumenthal et al., 1975). Reports from ten thousand middle-class respondents to a national survey conducted in 1977 indicated that 77 per cent thought "children should be disciplined by physical punishment whenever necessary" (Better Homes and Gardens, 1978, p. 66).

Interviews with a random group of one hundred mothers attending a well-baby clinic indicated that one third of the mothers whose children were less than one year of age had physically punished the child. One fourth of the mothers with children under six months of age had already started "spanking" the child (Korsch et al., 1965, p. 1883). Collective consensual norms permit parents to justify the use of corporal punishment, which runs the risk of becoming abuse.

One can similarly point to collective neglect in the failure to provide adequately for all children in the community.

Collective neglect might be defined as a persistent failure on the part of the community to take action to provide adequate child-care resources despite the clearly established deprivation suffered by a significant group of children in the community. The community is guilty of neglect when it fails to provide adequate housing, adequate levels of public assistance, adequate schooling, adequate health services, or adequate recreational services, or when it allows job discrimination or makes no effort to control an open display of vice, narcotics traffic, and other illegal activity. Malnutrition in children that results from inadequate welfare grants can be regarded as an example of collective neglect.

Neglect on the part of community in immunizing children against disease may have incapacitating and even fatal consequences for children. In 1977 the U.S. Immunization Survey estimated that 15.5 million children were not fully protected against polio; 9.3 million children were not protected against diphtheria, pertussis, and tetanus; 13.8 million were not protected against measles; and 26.4 million remained susceptible to mumps (*New York Times*, April 7, 1977). The protective service agencies have as great a responsibility to protect the child from community neglect as they have to protect him from parental neglect.

At yet another level, one can identify abuse and neglect perpetrated by a variety of agencies in society charged with the temporary care of the child. Schools, children's institutions, and day-care centers have been charged with what has been termed *institutional maltreatment* (National Center on Child Abuse and Neglect, 1978b). Institutional maltreatment has been documented in studies such as those by James (1970), Wooden (1976), and the office of the Comptroller General (1977).

The extent of abuse in child care institutions is a matter of some debate. By 1978 30 states required reporting of any evidence of abuse in such institutions. A nationwide study of such reports (Rindfleisch, 1978) indicated they were limited in number. However, institutional abuse is of sufficient concern so that the National Center on Child Abuse and Neglect (1978) gave protection of children in residential institutions special emphasis in granting funds for research and demonstration projects in 1979 and 1980.

Corporal punishment in the schools is a frequently cited example of institutional maltreatment (Duncan, 1973; Maurer, 1974). In 1977, when the U.S. Supreme Court sanctioned corporal punishment in the schools if certain guidelines were observed, only two states had laws that prohibited such disciplinary procedures. Some thirty-three states either allowed or specifically endorsed corporal punishment in the schools (Hyman *et al.*, 1977).

A task force study by the National Education Association (1972) found that 67.5 per cent of the elementary-school teachers questioned supported corporal punishment in the schoools.

In the case of Ingraham *v.* Wright, the Supreme Court ruled "that spanking by schoolteachers did not violate the Constitution's 8th Amendment ban against cruel and unusual punishment even if the spanking is severe, 'excessive' and medically damaging." The decision was a recognition of the teacher's common-law privilege to inflict reasonable corporal punishment (*The New York Times*, April 20, 1977).

SCOPE

The number of children reported abused is thought to be merely the "tip of the iceberg." Estimates of the actual number of children abused vary widely, from 60,000 (Kempe, 1974) to 500,000 (Light, 1973) to 1.5 million children (Fontana, 1973) abused in a year. After a careful review of state statistical reports, Cohen and Sussman (1975) estimated a total of 41,104 cases of confirmed abuse in 1972. Nagi (1975), after an equally conscientious effort, estimated 167,000 cases of confirmed abuse in 1972 (p. 16).

More dramatically, Gelles (1978) attempted to determine the frequency of abuse by interviews with a national probability sample of 2,143 respondents. From a list of eighteen behaviors they might have engaged in when they had a disagreement with one of their children, respondents selected the behavior actually employed. Based on the responses in the sample interview and extrapolating the results to the total population of children between three and seventeen, Gelles concluded that between 1.4 and 1.9 million children "were vulnerable to physical violence in 1975" (p. 587).

Summarizing a review of the literature on incidence rates of abuse and neglect, Holmes (1978) found that "They are widely divergent and often questionable in their accuracy" (p. 128).

We know only of those cases of abuse that are reported. These are the cases in which services can be offered. All states legally require reporting by professionals of any case of suspected abuse. As the requirement for reporting has become more widely known, and as people have become more familiar with the procedures, reports of abuse have increased.

In 1973 a National Clearinghouse on Child Abuse and Neglect * was established under the auspices of the American Humane Association, with funding from the Office of Child Development, Children's Bureau. The annual reports from the Clearinghouse provide the most accurate and detailed statistics concerning child abuse and neglect currently available from the states. Clearinghouse data are available on a standard report form from 28 states and child abuse and neglect statistics are collated from information provided by other states based on their own state report procedures. This nationwide collation of statistics indicated that there were a total of 512,494 child abuse and neglect reports in 1977, the most recent report available in late 1979. Reports of neglect were twice as frequent as those of abuse. However, some reports were of both neglect and abuse, with parents being reported for both kinds of maltreatment. Separating abuse and neglect reports from reports that include both is difficult. Consequently, the relative incidence of, and number of children affected by, each form of maltreatment is difficult to determine.

The comparative statistics indicate the greater incidence of neglect, as compared with abuse. The discrepancy is actually greater than presented here because some states contributing to the Clearinghouse data do report abuse but not neglect, leading to an underestimation. In those instances where we have comparative statistics regarding the relative prevalence of abuse and neglect, the number of neglected children exceeds the number of abused children in the ratio of 3 to 1, or better (Polansky, 1974, pp. 18–19).

Child abuse has received considerably more attention during the past few years than has child neglect. More tax dollars have been made available, more innovative programs have been developed and supported, and more training programs for workers have been formulated in the area of child abuse than in the

---

* This group is now called the National Study on Child Neglect and Abuse Reporting.

area of child neglect. The Library of Congress lists a special subcategory for child abuse but not for child neglect. Reporting of abuse was mandatory in many states before mandatory reporting of neglect was legislated.

The neglect of child neglect is somewhat surprising, given that more children are likely to be affected by neglect than by abuse.

Although the priority given abuse in protective service concerns is often justified on the basis of the greater possible damage to the child, little consideration has been given to the fatal dangers of neglect. For instance, *The New York Times* (July 11, 1979) reported that "two small sisters were killed yesterday when a fire broke out in the apartment in the Crown Heights section of Brooklyn. . . . The two dead girls were identified as one year old Eileen and two year old Wendy Morten. . . . The children were alone in the apartment at the time of the blaze, fire officials said," in the care of their five-year-old sister. The same paper reported that "every week in New York City, on the average, at least two small children fall from an open window. Most are injured seriously; many die" (March 14, 1978).

It is difficult to estimate the total number of deaths and injuries sustained by children over the course of a year that result from neglect of the child's health and safety by negligent or indifferent parents.

PROCESSES IN PROTECTIVE SERVICES

Case Finding and Intake

An effort has been made to encourage parents who have maltreated their children, or who feel that they might maltreat them, to request agency services voluntarily. Posters and spot radio and TV announcements indicate the availability of parental-stress hotline services that the parent may call. Such services are accessible in many communities seven days a week, twenty-four hours a day. The service offers supportive listening, advice, and reassurance to a parent who is about to "lose his cool with a kid" or to a parent who has just abused a child and wants to talk about his feelings with an interested, accepting person.

Hotline notices posted on bulletin boards in shopping centers and in public toilets, and used in radio and TV spot announcements may read:

Parental Stress Hotline

Sometimes feel you're going to blow your top? Can't cope any longer? The kids are getting to you? You want help? CALL _____ 24 hours a day, 7 days a week.

Do you know of a child who is being abused? Want to let somebody know about it? CALL _____ 24 hours a day, 7 days a week.

Hotlines thus serve both to help the abusive parents and to detect cases of actual or potential abuse.

The abusive or neglectful parent does not generally voluntarily apply for agency service. Case finding and the initiation of contact result from the action of other individuals or community agencies.

Currently, initiation of services frequently results from the legal requirement

s. The laws require that professionals aware of cases of
_____ them to an agency authorized to take action. Originally the
_____ reporting of "nonaccidental physical injury." The conditions
_____ orting were subsequently widened to include neglect, sexual
_____ d emotional or mental injury. An effort has been made in the
_____ e reporting statutes to give a more specific definition of the condi-
_____ require reporting. The trend has been to increase the maximum age of
_____ protected by the legislation to eighteen years.

The list of professsionals required to report is constantly being expanded. It includes, among others, doctors, nurses, social workers, school personnel, day-care-center personnel, legal personnel, and dentists.

Although some states require reporting by "any person" having "reasonable cause to believe" that abuse has taken place, additional states encourage, but do not require, such reporting (Education Commisssion to the States, 1977).

The agencies to which reports are to be made are generally the public welfare agencies or the legal agencies of the community. The laws grant civil and criminal immunity to the professionals required to make such reports, provide penalties for failure to report, and sometimes provide for follow-up. The abuse-reporting laws are essentially a case-finding device that helps the community to identify the abusive family and the abused child.

Upon receiving a complaint "made in good faith" of possible maltreatment, the agency is obligated to investigate the situation. Some complaints are identified as "summer neglect," "spite neglect," and "crisis neglect." *Summer neglect* refers to the increase in complaints during summer, when, with windows open, people can hear what goes on next door; *spite neglect* refers to complaints made by relatives, spouses, or neighbors who call the agency as a way of seeking revenge on the parent; and *crisis neglect* refers to the sudden increase of calls to the agency when the newspapers report a case of a serious injury or the death of a child because of mistreatment (Rein, 1963, p. 73).

National survey data indicate that upon investigation, some 47 per cent of abuse reports and 55 per cent of neglect reports are "not validated" (American Humane Society, 1978, p. 11). This means that despite the worker's conscientious exploration of the situation, he cannot find sufficient evidence of abuse or neglect. Continued service is more likely if referral has been made by a community agency rather than by a private individual because agencies are not likely to make a referral unless there is some substance to the complaint (Boehm, 1964). Reports of abuse are more likely to be substantiated than reports of the more ambiguously defined neglect. Reports from law enforcement agencies are most likely to be substantiated (Groenveld, Giovannoni, 1977).

Regulations require that the investigation be made within a short time after receipt of the complaint so that a child in possible danger may be protected. Such an investigation might start with a check of any previously recorded protective service data on the family. Investigation must be done expeditiously, before bruises or welts disappear. Sometimes color photos of injuries are taken to provide a permanent record.

When a complaint is initiated by an individual, the agency accepts the responsibility not only for investigating the situation but also for helping the person who makes the complaint. Some people may feel guilty about having made the report or about "interfering" in the affairs of another family; consequently, they need reassurance that their communication will be held in confidence.

The first contact by the agency is generally made with the person, or the agency, who has initiated the complaint. If the situation seems to warrant further exploration, contact is initiated with the family against which the complaint has been made. Many agencies suggest that the initial contact with the family be by letter (Brombaugh, 1957, p. 14). The letter, it is argued, identifies the agency, gives a general explanation of the service and the community's concern, suggests that help is needed, and gives the parent a chance to react in privacy and to consider what to do. Other agencies prefer to make an unannounced visit. Henry's (1958) study of the effects of such a procedure demonstrates that this approach does not necessarily have the negative consequences usually anticipated by social workers.

Whether the contact is initiated by letter or by an unannounced visit, the approach is direct and frank. It involves a clear statement by the agency that it has learned that the child is in potential danger and that, representing the community, it would like to enlist the aid of the parents in determining what is happening. The focus of the inquiry is not on the investigation of the truth or the falsity of the allegation, which would put the parents on the defensive. The focus is on what should be done—by agency and parents together—for the optimum benefit of the child. Protective service agencies prefer to "evaluate" rather than "investigate"—and this is an important attitudinal difference: an investigation may be conducted without involving the client; an evaluation implies a joint process, with the parents' active participation. Although in one sense this is an investigation of the situation, in another and more productive sense it is an offer of help to the family.

The parents are not given the right to refuse an exploration: "We accept the parent's right to make his own decision, but we question the wisdom of having him base it solely on his impulse to resist help and not include his wish to help his child" (Lane, 1952). The agency does not regard its approach as an intrusion but as a demonstration of concern and an active implementation of its desire to be helpful to both parents and children. As one client noted, "what they do here is protect parents from being cruel to their children" (Bishop, 1964, p. 83). Where resistance is anticipated or previously experienced, and in situations that present some physical danger to the worker, an officer can be assigned to accompany the worker.

The caseworker tries to get an accurate and objective picture of the situation. He is concerned with specifics: "the dates and times when the children have been left alone unattended for hours at a time; when they have been absent from school without sufficient reason; when the parents have been intoxicated and unable to function adequately as parents" (Henry, 1958, p. 5). Such details will be required as evidence if and when a petition is made to the court, but even more important, they can be used as a basis for discussing with the parents why the community, as represented by the agency, is concerned about the situation and why the parents themselves should be concerned. Getting evidence of neglect and/or abuse and establishing a relationship with the client are not antithetical procedures. Obtaining such information is, in effect, part of the social-study step in the casework process—a prerequisite for diagnosis and treatment—

that is helpful in establishing a relationship. Almost always an effort is made to see the child in behalf of whom the complaint was initiated.

The worker asks to see the child so as to examine any visible physical injuries and to talk to the child, if he or she is old enough, about what happened. The worker looks for teeth missing, black and blue marks and other skin discolorations, scabs covering cuts that are healing, rope burns, pinch marks, scratches, and difficulties the child might display in walking or using his or her hands. Where the worker is uncertain about the extent or nature of injury sustained by the child, a pediatric examination might be required. This may need to be scheduled despite the opposition of the parents. Once again, this requires the use of authority in protecting the child. The worker may supplement the visit by talking to relatives and friends who have knowledge of the situation. This is done only after informing the family that such contacts are planned.

The agency does not disclose to the client the identity of the complainant, because they do not feel it is helpful. However, Varon (1964) suggests that this compounds one of the psychological problems faced by the client: feeling impotent and helpless in the face of social forces that "victimize" him and over which he has no control, he is made to feel more vulnerable and more impotent by an "anonymous" complaint against which he cannot contend. The worker must be aware that the initial contact is apt to arouse the hostility, the guilt, and the defensiveness of parents, for their adequacy as parents is being called into question, their authority over their children is in danger, and the autonomy of the family is being threatened. The parents must be given an opportunity to ventilate their hostility.

Benjamin (1958) has aptly described the prescribed effective professional approach in protective service situations:

> Protective service should reach out to the negligent parents with feeling for them as troubled people, with discernment that life may not have given them sufficient opportunities to develop their capacities for parenthood, and with sympathetic understanding for their inability to cope with their problems alone. Kindness and acceptance should form the basis for every helping relationship. However, understanding is not enough for helping negligent parents. Since they are often disorganized, at times confused or belligerent and destructive in their attitudes, it takes firmness to stop them. . . . Expectations clearly and strongly stated in specific terms give direction to the unorganized client, lift him out of confusion, and help him partialize problems that might otherwise be overwhelming. . . . Implied in the concept of expectation is a concern for the other person and respect for his potential ability to accept his responsibility [pp. 12–17].

The approach is based on a number of assumptions:

1. The parents are not deliberately or perversely willful in their behavior; neglect, abuse, and exploitation are not the result of happenstance but are responses to the difficulties, social and/or personal, that the parents face. The behavior toward the child is symptomatic of some serious difficulty in the parents' and/or the family's situation.
2. There is, consequently, a cause for such deviant behavior that, if understood, might be subject to change; people can, and do, change with the help of the agency.

3. The parents themselves are unhappy about the situation. However resistant and defensive they may be to the community's intervention in the family's life, they welcome, in some measure, the opportunity to see if they can effect changes.
4. For the good of the child, the family, and the community, the first efforts should be directed at helping the parents make the changes that would permit the child to remain in his own home without danger.

It may, however, be difficult to communicate these assumptions successfully to the client group. Varon (1964), in interviews with thirteen former clients of a protective service agency and fifty of their nonclient neighbors, discovered that the agency was generally perceived as investigatory and punitive: "Only a fraction of the former clients interviewed appeared able to conceptualize something as complex as authority that is simultaneously coercive and benevolent" (p. 57).

The basic approach—one that combines acceptance and firmness, an attempt to understand rather than to judge, and respect for the parents as people while in no way condoning their behavior—is illustrated in the following case:

The C. family was referred to the child welfare agency by a hospital which treated the six-year-old boy, Wade, for a broken arm suffered in a beating by his mother. Mr. C. began the first interview with the [social] worker by saying, "I want to say directly at the beginning that I approve of all my wife has done." He said the neighbors were prying into his business and they were "neurotic about the whole affair." Mrs. C. agreed with him.

Mr. C. then tried to deflect the conversation from the beating of the child by talking about the neighbors' interference in the past. The worker listened attentively but brought the subject back to the beating by saying that he could see they had had some trouble with their neighbors but the report of serious abuse of the children was the main concern now. Both parents said they whipped the children because they believed in firm discipline and they challenged the worker's right to question this. Mr. C. again attempted to avoid the subject of Wade's beating by describing at length how strict his parents had been with him. Mrs. C. said the children had "evil in them" which had to be controlled.

The worker said he could understand how Mr. and Mrs. C. felt about his being there. He granted that the parents had the right to discipline their children, but pointed out that when a child is injured "the community wants to find out what the problems are and try to help the family. That's why I am here."

Mr. C. maintained that there was not any problem. He began talking about one of the other children's difficulties in school, and with Mrs. C. went into a long tirade about "young teachers" not being firm enough with youngsters.

Again the worker brought the conversation back to the C.'s own disciplinary practices by saying that children had to be dealt with firmly, but the injury of a child was a serious matter. He added, "I can understand that one may be so upset he has trouble controlling himself." Mrs. C. hesitatingly said, "I was so upset and too angry," and broke into tears. The worker replied that, if together they could try to understand why Mrs. C. gets so upset, perhaps the behavior would not continue [Sandusky, 1960, p. 24].

Interviewing parents, children, and other members of the household who might know about the situation is supplemented by relevant information obtained through careful observation.

Efforts have been made to quantify and objectify the specific elements and circumstances that a worker might watch for in determining neglect. Thus Polansky *et al.* (1978) have developed and revised a Childhood Level of Living Scale, which lists the items associated with possible neglect. The scale is applicable to children between the ages of four and seven years and includes items regarding evidence of the mother's positive care and concern for the child ("mother uses good judgment about leaving the child alone in the house"; "buttons and snaps of child's clothing are frequently missing and not replaced"); the state of repair of the house ("floor covering prevents tripping hazard"); the quality of household maintenance ("the roof or ceiling leaks"); the quality of health care and grooming ("poisonous or dangerous sprays and cleaning fluid are stored out of children's reach"); emotional care ("mother fails to comfort child when he is upset"); inconsistency of discipline and coldness ("child is often ignored when he tries to tell the mother something").

Coombes *et al.* (1978) have developed a similar inventory, including indicators of both abuse and neglect.

The decision to provide continuing service is based on such factors as repetitiveness of the parents' harmful behavior, the degree of guilt expressed, the acceptance of "blame," and the nature of the situation that triggered the incident. The following incidents indicate different responses to these factors:

A hospital reported that a nine-year-old had been brought to the Emergency Room for treatment of a fractured wrist. The mother admitted that the father had caused the injury. The child was treated on an out-patient basis.

An appointment letter was sent to the parents, and both came to the office. Both parents readily admitted what happened. The mother was working, the father was resting after coming home from work. A policeman came to the door with the boy, explaining that he had just caught him on the railroad tracks. The father became upset for various reasons: the shame of having a policeman bring his boy home, knowledge that his son had disobeyed home rules and the law, and anxiety for the injuries that could have occurred if a train had come. The father had a finger missing which made him even more sensitive to the loss of a limb. The father grabbed the boy to discipline him with a belt, they struggled, and somehow in the process the wrist was broken.

The father expressed appropriate guilt for hurting the boy, as he certainly had no intention of breaking his wrist. It was clear that he rarely used a belt, and both parents felt they had pretty good children. There was no expression of any family problems. In this situation, there was no need to protect the child, and the parents were not asking for help with any other problems. Therefore there was no role for continued social work intervention. A letter was sent to the reporting hospital explaining the disposition, with a copy to the parents.

A hospital reported the admission of a twenty-month-old boy with multiple old fractures, numerous scars, head wound, and a hematoma on the back. The mother said he fell down the stairs, and that he was an "evil" child. She entered a hospital the following day to deliver her third child.

A visit was made to the mother in the hospital. She denied any trauma, and gave no recognition to the seriousness of his injuries. She was told that the matter would be presented to the Court before the child's discharge. She did not object, but did verbalize that she didn't want the child removed from her.

In subsequent visits it was determined that the newborn and older child received adequate care and were not abused. The mother was unable to talk about the abused child, and often sat silently with tears rolling down her face.

A trial was held in Family Court, where medical testimony was presented. The mother offered no objections, although she continued to deny the abuse.

The child was placed in a foster care home as soon as he was ready for discharge and continued service was provided to the mother by the social worker in that department.*

Workers employ criteria of the consistency, the pervasiveness, and the duration of abuse in deciding whether to press for the child's removal. If the parent is concerned, contrite, and ready to accept help, this circumstance argues against removal. If there is somebody other than the abusive parent in the home willing to help restrain the abuser's impulsivity and impatience, or if there is a family-network support system that can be mobilized, this also argues against removal.

Diagnosis

The voluminous literature on child maltreatment includes findings from surveys, clinical studies, demonstration projects, and analyses of record material and report forms. There have been several efforts to review and summarize this literature (Parke, Colmer, 1975; Holmes, 1977; Polansky, Holly, Polansky, 1974; Spinetta, Rigler, 1972; Maden, Wrench, 1977; Allen, 1978). We will attempt to highlight the findings without necessarily citing the specific studies except where the research was particularly noteworthy, generally because a control population of nonabusers was included in the study design.

Some tentative efforts have been made to identify the distinctive attributes of the parents who neglect or abuse their children. However, one of the principal conclusions reached by Young (1964) in her study of the records of 180 families referred for neglect or abuse is that the two groups of parents may have little in common (p. 135) and that neglect and abuse may be different diagnostic groupings.

The picture is further complicated by the fact that within both the abuse and the neglect groups, there are subgroups that have little in common with each other diagnostically, except for the fact that ultimate behaviors toward the child are similar. Merrill (1962) lists four types and Delsordo (1963) describes five types of child abuse. Zalba (1967) defines six types, Gil (1970) suggests seventeen types, and Walters (1975) lists ten types.

Gelles (1973) notes that of nineteen traits listed by various researchers supposedly identifying the personality of the child abuser, there was agreement on only four traits by two or more authors, the other fifteen traits being identified by only one author.

Analogous to complex entities such as "juvenile delinquency" and "unwed parenthood," abuse and neglect behavior are a result of a convoluted configuration of psychological, social, and situational factors that result in heterogeneous patterns and make valid generalizations very difficult.

* From Ellen Thompson and Norman Paget, *Child Abuse: A Community Challenge.* Buffalo, N.Y.: Henry Stewart Publishing Co., 1971, pp. 42–44. By permission of the publisher.

Summarizing the results of a review of the available research, Allen (1978) noted that:

> there is no such thing as a "typical example of abuse" which represents the majority of cases, nor is there one factor conclusively present and relevant to all cases. Instead, the research picture suggests that violence is the end product of a complex interaction of individual environmental and interpsychic factors in which the relationship between all these influences varies with the individual [p. 68].

Although the findings from clinical and empirical research are complex and often contradictory, there is some low-level consistency in the configuration of factors frequently associated with abuse. These include a history of abuse and/or rejection in childhood; low self-esteem; a rigid, domineering, impulsive personality; social isolation; a record of inadequate coping behavior; poor interpersonal relationships; high, unrealistic expectations of children; and lack of ability to empathize with children.

It is suggested that abusive parents are strict disciplinarians who have rigid expectations regarding child behavior without empathy with a child's needs, feelings, or individuality. The parent is seen as "owning" the child, as being solely responsible for molding the child and as having a sense of righteousness in making autonomous decisions as to what is best for the child. These parents tend to regard the behavior of even small children as willful, deliberate disobedience. Strict discipline is then perceived as justified because the child is consciously disobeying the parent.

Abusive parents may show a tendency to role reversal, in which the parents turn to their children for nurturing and protection (Morris, Gould, 1963). The child is seen as a source of gratification; when the parent is disappointed and frustrated by the failure of the child to meet his needs, he reacts with hostility toward the child. The failure of the child to meet the parent's needs is seen as willful and deliberate behavior and reactivates the parent's own disappointment in his parents when he was a child.

Abusive parents are seen as having limited ability to tolerate frustration and delays in gratification. They have a low boiling point and, as a consequence of low self-esteem, react impulsively and intensely to even minor provocations.

Abuse, like attempted suicide, may be a cry for help: "Parents who neglect and batter their children are actually speaking their parental incapacities in action language and are asking to be stopped in behaving the way they do" (Morris, Gould, 1963, p. 56). As Kaufman (1957; 1963) notes, such parents, being unconsciously afraid of their own aggression, may feel some security in finding someone who wants to stop this destructive force.

A small percentage of parents is assessed as frankly sadistic, taking positive pleasure in abuse. Another small percentage is psychotic and engages in abuse in response to a distorted perception of reality. An additional small percentage consists of sociopaths who react aggressively to even the most ordinary frustrations. It is estimated that these groups in aggregate make up some 10 per cent of the total group of abusers.

Although it is generally agreed that only a limited percentage of abusive parents are psychotic, a review of studies concerned with the general psychological functioning of abusive parents "sustains the conclusion that abusive parents exhibit considerable psychological dysfunction compared with control groups" (Maden, Wrench, 1977, p. 209).

Smith (1975) compared the parents of 134 hospitalized infants and children under five years of age with those of fifty-three nonabused hospitalized children. The abusive parents showed considerably more psychopathology, personality disorders, criminality, and low intelligence than the control nonabusive parents.

Baher et al. (1976) studied twenty "battering" parents and twenty control parents matched on the basis of age of child, age of parent, type of living accommodations, ordinal position of child, and social class. Data were derived from the use of standard intelligence tests, the Cattell sixteen-factor personality inventory, and a parents' attitude inventory. There was little difference in intelligence scores between the two groups. Abusive parents were rated as being more aggressive and more reserved and detached, and they manifested poorer emotional control. Male abusers tend to present a history of a variety of antisocial behaviors.

The fact that a high percentage of reported abusers are young may suggest stress associated with parental immaturity and with youthful marriage and parenthood before being ready for such experiences.

Clinical and research reports persistently point to a poor relationship between the marital pair in the abusive family. Not only are the participants denied support from each other in dealing with their problems, but the conflicted relationship is a source of additional stress and tension predisposing the parents toward aggression displaced onto the child.

Social isolation from relatives, friends, and neighbors and a low rate of affiliation with and participation in community institutions and organizations seem to be problems presented by a high percentage of abusers. As a consequence, they lack an effective social-support network. They have a higher rate of residential mobility than nonabuser controls (Lauer et al., 1974), and being new neighbors often intensifies their tendency toward isolation.

Perhaps the most repetitive finding is that abusers have themselves experienced abuse as children. This finding has achieved the status of an axiom. As a consequence of his experience, the child learns to employ violence in parent–child interaction. He takes the abusive parent as a role model and patterns his own subsequent parental behavior accordingly. The outcomes are consistent with learning theory. The outcomes are also consistent with child development theory. Having been abused and rejected as children, having lacked a stable, consistent love relationship in childhood, these parents have experienced inadequate gratification of early affectional and dependency needs. In response to this deprivation, these parents are themselves still children—in their narcissism, their selfishness, their dependency, their impulsiveness—in short, in their immaturity. The idea of intergenerational transmission of maltreatment is thus consistent with theoretical suppositions regarding the effects of emotional deprivation in infancy, which suggests that the deprived child, not having been loved, is incapable in adulthood of loving others.

The idea of intergenerational abuse is theoretically attractive not only because it is consient with learning, modeling, and socialization concepts but because it permits the social worker to approach the parent with a greater feeling of acceptance. The abusive parent is not to blame. He, too, is a victim of his own childhood experience.

As one worker says, "One way I overcome my personal dislike for the way the parent has treated the child—or has allowed a child to be treated—is to view the parent as a child, or as a very childlike adult who was probably abused as a child" (Arvanian, 1975, p. 94).

Although these considerations explain and support the contention that abuse is intergenerationally transmitted, Jayaratne (1977), in reviewing the relevant data, finds little empirical support for the proposition. Following a similar review of the research, Holmes (1977) noted that:

> While there is general agreement that abusive parents were themselves treated with hostility and lacked nurturant care in childhood, there is virtually no empirical substantiation of the often repeated view that abused parents were themselves actually abused as children. [Furthermore] in the absence of normative data, it is impossible to determine the extent to which a childhood characterized by hostility and lack of nurturance is particularly characteristic of abusive parents [p. 143].

An atypical group of disturbed, multiproblem families, however, do clearly show, on genealogical examination, intergenerational recurrence of abuse (Oliver, 1977). Some comparisons of abusive parents with a sample of nonabusive parents show that abusive parents generally have had less favorable relationships with their own parents (Melnick, Hurley, 1969; Schneider, Helfer, Pollock, 1972; Bedger, 1976; Green, 1976; Smith, 1976). In all instances, however, sizable percentages of abusive parents had positive developmental experiences, and sizable percentages of nonabusive parents had unfavorable parent–child experiences.

Attempts to tie the experience of abuse as a child with delinquency as an adult based on reports from delinquents similarly show that a large percentage of delinquents report having been abused. However, the relationship appears to be less firmly substantiated if, starting with the records of abused children, one tries to determine how many subsequently showed delinquent behavior. The records of five thousand abused and neglected children in eight New York State counties showed, a dozen or more years later, only 19 per cent with a history of delinquency (Steele, 1976, pp. 20–21).

The preponderance of research efforts concerned with trying to formulate a diagnostic understanding of maltreatment has focused on the parent or the parent surrogate.

There is a beginning effort to look at the interaction of parent and child rather than at the parent alone in attempts to understand the abuse situation. It is suggested that abuse is the result of the interaction of behaviors of both the child and the parent. Neither is totally responsible, nor is either totally innocent (Friedrich, Boriskin, 1976).

The abuse event is the result of a bidirectional, reciprocal relationship. Some children are more difficult to care for and hence are more likely to evoke aggressive responses. Different children tend to evoke different responses from parents.

It is suggested that from the very start, the child is far from being a passive member of the parent–child dyad, that the child's behavior is both a response to and a stimulus for subsequent parental behavior, that often the child initiates and shapes the nature of the interaction, and that the child conditions parental

behavior, selectively rejecting some parental interventions and selectively reinforcing others. Such an orientation suggests that although it is true that parents
produce children, there may be much truth in the assertion that children also
produce parents.

Studies of temperamental differences in children as evidenced immediately
after birth confirm every parent's observation that some children provoke more
aggressive reactions than others. Those researchers who have done the most
detailed study of infant temperamental differences at birth conclude that:

> the characteristics of the child may foster and reinforce a specific direction of
> parental attitudes and practices. It is easy to mother a normally active, positively
> responsive, highly adaptive, routine accepting child whose mood is predominantly
> cheerful. It is quite another matter to maintain the same positive maternal re-
> sponses to a highly active, poorly responsive, non-adaptive arrhythmic child whose
> mood is expressed by a preponderance of crying [Thomas, 1963].

As Gelles (1972) notes, the "role of the victim in intrafamily violence is an
important and active one. The actions of the victim are vital intervening events
between structural stresses that lead to violence and the violent acts themselves"
(p. 155). This statement may help explain why some abusive parents are not
abusive with all children but only with a selected child.

Johnson (1968), in a detailed study of 101 abused children, found that most
of the children "were hard to care for." Some were subject to severe temper
tantrums; some had feeding, toilet-training, or speech problems; some were mentally retarded. About 70 per cent of the group showed "physical or developmental deviation before the injury was reported." The younger children in the
group were described by the child welfare workers as "whiny, fussy, listless,
chronically crying, restless, negativistic, unresponsive"; the older children as
gloomy, impertinent, and sullen (pp. 149–150). Gil (1970) notes that 24.5 per
cent of the child abuse cases registered in the national study he conducted
checked as a factor the "persistent behavioral atypicality of the child; e.g., hyperactivity, high annoyance potential" (p. 127).

A study that compared 255 abused children with 108 nonabused children
from similar kinds of families showed the abused children to be more frequently
below average in intelligence, less physically attractive, and more likely to be
either "extremely sluggish" or "overactive" (Fergusson, Fleming, O'Neill, 1972,
pp. 284–285).

A detailed study of sixty abuse cases at the Downstate Medical Center,
Brooklyn, New York, noted that abused children manifested major psychological,
neurological and cognitive defects when compared with non-abused, normal
controls. Abused children were reported by mothers to be more self-destructive
and more aggressive, both at home and in school. A larger number of abused
children required more attention than their siblings. The mother's perception of
the abused child as the most aggressive and demanding of her offsprings made
this child vulnerable to scapegoating (Green, Gaines, Sangrund, 1974; Green,
1976).

Reidy (1975) compared the level of aggressiveness of twenty physically
abused children with sixteen neglected children and twenty-two normal children
referred from neighborhood day-care centers. The children were matched in

terms of age and socioeconomic background and race. Their aggressive fantasies were rated on the basis of responses to the Thematic Apperception Test (TAT). Their aggressive behavior was rated by teachers observing the child in free play. The abused children expressed significantly more fantasy aggression in responding to the TAT than either the neglected children or the normal controls. The abused children used significantly more aggressive behavior in the free-play situation and were judged by the teachers to be more significantly aggressive as compared with the two other groups of children. Although differences in the level of aggressive fantasy and behavior of the abused children was clearly demonstrated by the study, the question of whether the atypical level of aggression was the result of abuse or the "cause" of abuse was not resolved.

The child who is the result of an unwanted pregnancy, illegitimacy, or "forced" marriage is noted as a high risk for abuse in a number of different studies (Nurse, 1964; Elmer, 1971; Fergusson, Fleming, O'Neill, 1972).

Comparing abused children with their nonabused siblings, Lynch (1976) found that the abused child was more likely to have been subjected to an abnormal pregnancy and delivery, neonatal separation, and postnatal illness than his sibling controls. Low birth weight is associated with subsequent abuse in a number of studies.

Maden and Wrench (1977, p. 202), recapitulating in tabular form the results of twenty studies relating to low birth weight, congenital defects, and birth complications as associated with child abuse, show a statistically significant relationship in at least seven studies.

Two different explanations are presented for the fact that premature babies are apparently at high risk for abuse. First their greater frailty and hence increased need for sensitive care make the mothering of such babies a more taxing yet, perhaps, a less rewarding task because the infant may be less attractive physically and less rewarding psychologically. Second, the frequent placement of such children in special-care units separates mother and child and results in the failure of an early bonding in the relationship.

When asked to identify those factors that, in their experience, are related to child abuse, social workers, child protective workers, psychologists, nurses, and educators highlighted the fact that both parent and child factors are involved (Gillespie, Seaberg, Berlin, 1977). Items relating the social-situational aspects and individual personality aspects of both abuser and abusee were listed. When rank-ordered in terms of importance, individual personality factors of the abuser and the child were given primary emphasis. These included "Hostile-aggressive low frustration tolerance" of caretaker, "caretaker's inability to cope," "inappropriate performance expectations of child," and for the child, "child defiant of caretakers," "excessive demands of child on caretaker," "hyperactive child," and "child unresponsive to caretakers" (p. 346).

In response to these considerations, it might be suggested that the child's hyperactivity, aggressiveness, apathy, mental deficiency, and so on were the result of abuse rather than an initial contributory element. One might say, along with Bakan (1971), that "the abuse of a child creates a child who invites abuse" (p. 111). In the absence of a longitudinal study that provides detailed data on children before they are abused as compared with postabuse functioning, we are left with some nagging doubts as to the sequence. The research does suggest, however, that certain kinds of child characteristics and behavior, whatever the "cause" of their genesis, are likely to be associated with instigation of abuse.

There are contradictory findings regarding abuse as related to the child's ordinal position, some researchers finding the first-born child more frequently abused, others finding the youngest child more susceptible to abuse, others finding ordinal position not significant (Maden, Wrench, 1977, p. 199).

Some see child abuse not as a parent–child problem but as a family problem. Abuse suggests some dysfunction in the total family configuration, with all family members contributing to the abuse in some measure, and all members affected by it. The total family configuration, it is suggested, then requires treatment (Beezley, Martin, Alexander, 1976).

Beyond the parent, the child, and the family, the situational stresses resulting from environmental deprivations contribute to maltreatment. Garbarino (1976) compared the child abuse rates of fifty-eight New York State counties and the socioeconomic differences among the counties. Using U.S. Census data, he found that where unemployment was higher, income levels lower, and education levels and opportunities less adequate, the abuse rates were higher. Counties with a disproportionately large number of "economically depressed mothers often alone in the role of parent attempting to cope in isolation without adequate resources and facilities for their children" (p. 183) were more likely to show higher rates of maltreatment. Low family income and working mothers were highly correlated with maltreatment. The conclusion was that environmental stress did have an impact on child maltreatment.

Clinical data and national survey data (American Humane Society, 1978) on the stresses faced by families referred for maltreatment indicate that the client of the protective service agency is often a woman struggling alone to raise a family of larger than average size on a poverty-level income and in a slum area. The maltreating parent is frequently exhausted, mentally distressed, emotionally deprived, socially isolated, and economically impoverished. The understandable response to these conditions—the exhaustion, frustration, failure of hope, apathetic indifference, and despair that come from living day after day on the edge of poverty, amidst squalor—plays a part in the parents' inability to mobilize themselves to care for the child. Such situational stresses provide a fertile soil for neglect. As Meier (1964) says, "The grinding harassments of constantly doing without the things that are needed, and the small daily discouragements and disappointments that poverty-stricken parents suffer, deplete the energies of parents and render them less able to meet the social and emotional needs of their children" (p. 172).

Although there is general agreement that a stressful living situation—that is, low income; inadequate, crowded housing; unemployment or intermittent employment, and discrimination—is associated with maltreatment, it is unclear why most other parents in the same population living with the same stresses do not abuse their children.

In comparing abusive with nonabusive parents, and controlling for social class, Smith (1975) found that there was little difference in the adequacy of housing and financial resources among the two groups. He concluded that "personality disorders . . . are more important than environmental factors in contributing to child abuse" (p. 207) and that "constitutional personality differences are more fundamental than financial factors in the causation of baby battering" (p. 209). In comparing abusers with nonabusers from the same population where both groups were living in a stressful deprived environment, the abusers were more likely to have had a history of disordered childhood development and subsequent personal difficulties in social functioning than the nonabusive controls (Holmes, 1977, p. 148).

Situational stress is an incremental load imposed on psychological stress, increasing the total stress overload to which the individual is subjected and with which he has to cope. A psychosocial explanation that combines both the social stresses, which might act as the "triggering context" for abuse, and the psychological factors, which predispose the caretaker to resort to abuse as a selective response in dealing with child management problems, appears to be a more valid interpretation than either exclusively, psychologically, or sociologically focused explanations.

Maltreatment might then be understood as the end result of interaction among three major sets of variables: (1) a parent who has the potential for abuse, (2) a child who may be somewhat different and/or difficult and who fails to respond in a manner expected by his parents, and (3) a crisis situation, which triggers the abusive act. The probability of abuse is increased by social isolation, which reduces the ready availability of help and support from other people; cumulative situational tensions that lower tolerance for stress; and a community context that sanctions interpersonal violence.

The following case illustrates the complexity of contributing factors:

> Larry, age twenty-seven, is a quiet, shy, unassuming little man who works as a welder's assistant. Since childhood, he has been plagued by a deep sense of inferiority, unworthiness, and unsureness of himself in his work and in all human relations. There is also a deep resentment, usually very restrained, against a world which he feels is unfair. . . . Larry does not recall either mother or father spanking, as a routine, but there were constant verbal attacks and criticism. He felt that neither of his parents, particularly his mother, really listened to him or understood his unhappiness and his need for comfort and consideration.
>
> While he was in the army, Larry and Becky planned to marry. She was to come to where he was stationed, and they were to be married at Christmas time. He waited all day at the bus station, but she never appeared. Sad and hopeless, he got drunk. Months later, a buddy told him she had married somebody else the first of January. He saw her again a year later when home on leave. She had been divorced; so they made up and got married. She had a child, Jimmy, by her first marriage. . . . They have had three more children of their own. Mary, age four, is liked very much by both parents. . . . David, age two-and-a-half . . . is "a very fine, active, alert, well-mannered little boy." He is quite responsive and both parents like him and are good with him. Maggie, four-and-a-half-months old, was thought by both parents to be "a bit different" from birth. She seemed to look bluer and cried less strongly than their other babies and was also rather fussy. . . . Maggie was admitted to the hospital with symptoms and signs of bilateral subdural hematoma. She had been alone with her father when he noticed a sudden limpness, unconsciousness, and lack of breathing. He gave mouth-to-mouth respiration, and she was brought to hospital by ambulance. There was a history of a similar episode a month before when Maggie was three-and-a-half months old; when alone with her father she had become limp, followed by vomiting. . . .

The circumstances of the attack were as follows: Larry's boss told him that his job was over. The construction contract had been suddenly cancelled and there was no more work. Feeling discouraged, hopeless, and ignored, Larry went home, shamefacedly told Becky he had lost his job, and asked her if she wanted to go with the children to her family. Saying nothing, Becky walked out of the house, leaving Larry alone with Maggie. The baby began to cry. Larry tried to comfort her, but she kept on crying so he looked for her bottle. He could not find the bottle anywhere; the persistent crying and his feelings of frustration, helplessness, and ineffectuality became overwhelming. In a semiconfused "blurry" state he shook Maggie severely and then hit her on the head. Suddenly aware of what he had done, he started mouth-to-mouth resuscitation; then Becky came home and Maggie was brought to the hospital [Steele, Pollock, 1974, pp. 119–20]. *

In this case, Larry, whose history predisposed him to feelings of insecurity and rejection, enters into a marriage in which his position is uncertain and finds himself the father of a child who is difficult to care for and makes heavy demands on parental patience. These factors provide the potential for abuse, which is then precipitated by a crisis situation during which the child acts in a way that increases the already considerable momentary stress, becoming the immediate target for all past and present frustrations.

It is recognized that thus far, much of the discussion has focused on maltreatment rather than making a clear distinction between abuse and neglect. This approach reflects some of the tendency in the literature to discuss both together as well as the fact that some critical diagnostic factors are common to both kinds of maltreatment. At this point, we will distinguish abuse from neglect.

Polansky and his co-workers (1970, 1971, 1972; Polansky, Borgman, and De Saix, 1972) identified clusters of behavior typical of some neglectful mothers. One group of neglectful mothers, manifesting an "apathy–futility syndrome," were "socially withdrawn, physically slow, or immobilized, generally ineffectual." Another group were "childishly impulsive," dependent on others for guidance and approval, and unable to control tension or excitement.

Billingsley (1969) attempted to sort out the characteristics that distinguish the neglectful parent and the abusive parent from the adequate parent and further to distinguish the neglectful parent from the abusive parent. Billingsley selected parents who had been identified by protective service agencies as abusive or neglectful and matched them with parents who had been identified by visiting nurses or AFDC caseworkers as adequate. Intensive interviews with the mothers were conducted by second-year students of a graduate school of social work, who were not told to which group the mothers belonged. Information was elicited concerning the mothers' social and family background, their current social situation and social functioning, and their child-rearing practices. Interviews were supplemented, in some instances, by psychological tests such as the Minnesota Multiphasic Inventory, the Barron Ego-Strength Scale, the California Psychological Inventory, and IQ tests.

Although such factors as "family structure, family stability, and patterns of parental role dominance" did not tend to be associated with different levels of

* From Henry C. Kempe and Ray E. Helfer, *The Battered Child*. Chicago: University of Chicago Press, 1974. By permission of The University of Chicago Press.

maternal adequacy, the mothers who did not mistreat generally reported a "more emotionally satisfying relationship with their parents and were more likely to have had continuous experiences with at least one individual who provided an adequate model for the kind of identity formation which would foster superego development" (p. 149).

Comparisons of the three groups of families in terms of alcoholism, mental disorder, and sexual promiscuity of the mother revealed that:

> Whatever the disorder, it was least often observed in adequate families, next often in neglected families, and most often in abusive families—thus the impression that abusive parents demonstrate a higher incidence of intrapsychic and behavior disorders is supported by this [sic] data. . . . Neglectful families are not without observable intrapsychic distress, but less often exhibit such disorder than do abusive families. . . . Further, families who mistreat their children in general are more apt to exhibit such disorder than those who do not [p. 142].

"However, it is clear that the personalities of the neglectful women and the abusive women have different underlying mechanisms." The women who abuse their children are seriously disturbed individuals, "suspicious, withdrawn, socially alienated, prone to impulsivity and the projection of blame, generally presenting more psychotic tendencies" (p. 150). The picture of the neglectful mother is more diffuse, showing poor socialization and general neurotic tendencies, which are in part a reaction to external stresses.

Some frequently encountered characteristics of abusive parents further suggest the dominance of psychological factors over social factors in the explanatory configuration of abuse as contrasted with neglect. There is often an absence of guilt (McHenry, 1963; Morris, Gould, 1963; Young, 1964) and a tendency toward social isolation with little concern as to what "others" think (Scherer, 1960; Young, 1964; Elmer, 1967; Holter, Friedman, 1968; Moore, 1970).

Frequently, one child becomes the target for abuse, as though he represented, symbolically, some conflict for the parent. Boardman (1962), studying hospitalized abused children, indicates that "because in almost all cases only one child is the victim, hospital members believe that the child has become a symbol of some kind to the adult" (p. 45). The child who is abused may therefore be the victim required for the maintenance of the psychic stability of the family. Removal of the child, without any modification of the family's emotional configuration, may result in the substitution of another victim.

Respondents associated with hospitals, courts, schools, and social agencies were asked to list the characteristics that, in their experience, were associated with abuse and neglect situations. They gave economic factors greater importance in neglect than in abuse (Nagi, 1977, p. 51). Although abuse, like neglect, is more heavily concentrated among the lower socioeconomic classes, it is more randomly distributed throughout the population. Such a finding is congruent with an explanation of abusive behavior as being based more heavily on personality factors.

In summary, protective services present a problem for data assessment or diagnosis in that there are no "typical" abusive or neglectful parents. Causation is multiply determined and includes factors relating to the developmental history and personality of the maltreating parent, interacting with a particular child, in a stressful situational context in a culture that sanctions violence as a response to interpersonal problems.

The diversity of interacting variables may reflect further the fact that all parents are potential child maltreaters. All children impose heavy physical, emotional, social, and economic burdens on the parents. Along with parental love, there is resentment.

Neglect and *abuse* are terms used to describe a wide variety of behaviors that have in common only certain effects on the child. No single cause can explain such behavior. However, abuse may be more often a response to psychological stress, whereas neglect may be more often a response to social stress. Neglect generally results from acts of omission, abuse from acts of commission. Giovannoni (1971) carried the distinction a bit further: "abuse constitutes an exploitation of the rights of parents to control, discipline and punish their children while neglect represents the failure to perform parental duties including those of supervision, nurturance and protection" (p. 649).

Sexual abuse is perceived as quite a different diagnostic entity from physical abuse and neglect. A clear delineation of the special identifying characteristics of the sexual abuser of the child is yet to be achieved, partly because the rubric includes a variety of different behaviors from fondling to oral, anal, and genital intercourse, with children of different ages, and perpetrated by abusers who have different relationships to the children involved: father, brother, mother, stepparent.

Walters (1975) sees hostility and resentment toward his wife as the father's motivation for incest: "Sexual abuse of a child by a father is the ultimate act of anger toward the wife" (p. 146). By means of this one act, the woman is made to fail as both a mother and a wife.

Some turn the dynamics around and see incest as a result of the female child's efforts to obtain from the father the affection denied by the mother and as an act of hostility on the part of the child toward the mother (Rosenfeld *et al.*, 1977, p. 331).

Reviewing the records of incest referred to the Brooklyn (New York) Society of Prevention for Cruelty to Children, Tormes (1968) sees the wife–mother as a willing, passive, ineffectual "participant" in the incest drama, responding to an unconscious wish for the daughter to assume the mother's role and unable to protect her daughters from their father.

Reviewing some forty-seven research studies that had been done here and abroad on sexual abuse between 1934 and 1977 and adding a study of her own on fifty-eight cases of sexual abuse reported by clients at a mental health clinic, Meiselman (1978) attempted to delineate the distinctive aspects of the abuser. The picture once again is very varied. Few abusers were psychotic; a limited number manifested hypersexuality. Personality disorders and psychopathy were frequent. Alcoholism was associated with sexual abuse in a sizable number of cases. Some abusers were dictatorial and autocratic, dominating the family; others were dependent and shy.

Socioeconomic background was varied, although a large percentage of abusers were of low income and limited education. Background history tended to show poor relationships with their own fathers, but for a sizable percentage of abusers, this was not true. The detailed review of the literature fails to show any clear, distinctive, distinguishing pattern, and many of the identifying factors are not specific to incest.

Many cases were not technically incest because the abuser was a stepparent rather than a biological parent.

Mothers of sexually abused girls often feared their husbands, were frequently themselves uninterested in sexual relations with their husbands, and tended to impose heavy responsibilities for homemaking and child care on the abused daughters, so that they were often perceived as pseudomature and as "little mothers." Illness, death or frequent absence of the wife–mother increases the risk of incest in decreasing the availability of marital sex.

On occasion, the mother did subtly encourage what was going on; more often, she failed to be responsible for protecting the daughter, denying what was happening and maintaining "peace at any price."

Although there was little evidence that the girls involved were especially attractive and/or seductive, some had matured early and were more like women than children. They were not only surrogate mothers but surrogate wives to their fathers. They felt they could not look to their own mother for support and protection. The mothers often had abdicated their responsibility as mothers as well as wives.

Ordinarily abuse does not occur in private, so that other members of the family are aware of it. The fact that the other parental figure is aware of the abuse but unwilling or unable to interfere suggests complicity. If there is a problem of collusion between parents in keeping physical abuse hidden, this is even more likely to be the case with regard to sexual abuse. As is true of abusive families generally, the incestuous family tends to be socially isolated and the secret of the incestuous relationship tends to accentuate such isolation.

Evaluation of Family Modifiability

Diagnosis is followed by an effort to evaluate the parents' capacity to change —to determine the degree of modifiability of the child's environment. If it is clear that change will be minimal, one has to assess the relative dangers, to the child, of remaining in the home as compared with those involved in separation and placement in substitute care.

The agency must also consider the importance of siblings to the child. One survey of 147 families noted that positive relationships in the sibling–sibling subsystem frequently existed side by side with the overwhelmingly negative relationships in the parent–child subsystem (Canadian Welfare Council, 1954, p. 13). Thus the sibling relationship, as a possible source of strength and support to the child, is an important factor in any decision regarding the child.

One must recognize, too, that no home is wholly bad. His parents are the only ones the child has known, and despite neglect and abuse, he has developed some ties to them. Protective agencies have often found—to their surprise and, perhaps, chagrin—that they were attempting to "rescue children who did not want to be rescued." Young, however, found that some children in her sample of abusive and neglectful families were ready and willing to be removed from their homes (p. 99).

There is potential for change in the fact that the parents themselves are unhappy and ambivalent about their situation. The degree of ambivalence present in these situations, which the agency can use in helping the parents, is indicated by the fact that one or another of the parents is, on occasion, the source of complaint to the agency. In fact, Kaufman (1957) cites an instance of a mother calling an agency to report herself as a parent maltreating a child. On the other hand, these are difficult clients to work with generally—not only hard to reach but also hard to change. Frequently others have tried before the client was referred to the protective service agency. Thus "60 percent of the cases which eventually come to the Massachusetts Society for the Prevention of Cruelty to Children had been in contact with a casework or guidance agency at some time or other before the protective service contact" (Rein, 1963, p. 133).

The lack of leverage for therapeutic action that characterizes contact with such families is substantiated by Young (1964):

Neglectful and abusive families show a conspicuous absence of any feelings of guilt about their behavior toward their children; . . . they rarely saw any association between their behavior toward the child and the undesirable behavior in the child, and they showed little awareness of the unacceptability of their behavior until the community intervened [pp. 175–176].

One of the difficulties in working with such families is that they are not responsive to the informal network of social control, which often acts as an ally to the worker in motivating for change:

The social pressures which in other groups compel at least minimum outward conformity have little effect upon the families in this study except as they are officially and specifically implemented. . . . Most of the families in this study had little to lose—social status, economic security, community respect, the good opinion of other people were all lacking and, for most of them, always had been. They may have wished they had some or all of these advantages, but if so, their wishing was a wistful longing for the moon, not a force compelling them to effort. They had no incentive to change their behavior or to limit it—they feared no loss and expected no rewards. Social control had lost its major weapons and relinquished its place to official and legal controls [Young, 1964, p. 84].

Although abusive families are apt to be actively resistive to the offer of help, neglectful families are more often accepting of help but unable to use it effectively or productively.

Treatment Aims and Approach

The core of the agency's work is with the parents, the objective being to prevent further neglect and/or abuse of the child and to alleviate or correct those problems that have led to the situation. The ultimate aim is to preserve the home so that the child can have his needs adequately met within his own natural family.

Protective service clients generally resist social work contacts. A study of intensive services offered such families showed that few families initiated a request for an appointment and that families often failed to keep appointments scheduled by the workers (Baher *et al.*, 1976).

Persistence is required, but overvisiting should be avoided, as it may seem like "hounding" to the parent.

In visits to the home, it may be desirable to focus on the needs of the parents, because meeting the parents' needs results in the parents' greater capacity to meet the child's needs. Also, any attention paid to the child during a visit may alienate the parent, who may feel that his deficiencies in child care are being emphasized by the worker's satisfactory interaction with the child. Furthermore, as a part child himself, the parent's sense of rivalry with his own child for the worker's attention may further excite his animosity toward the child. Workers have to maintain a precarious balance between identifying with the children and thus possibly antagonizing the parents or identifying with the parents at the risk of endangering the children.

Parental behavior concerns the protective service agency only in its effects on the child. The parent is not necessarily asked to change himself; it is the situation detrimental to the child that must be changed. As Kahn (1963) says, the obstacles to thoroughgoing change are so great "that more modest attainments are more common—sustaining the child in his own home without damage, correcting specific defects in parental care, correcting and alleviating the effects on the child of prior parental mishandling" (p. 335). The very presence of the agency may tend to activate latent factors so as to result in a positive change.

The demonstration of community power and concern, expressed in the act of intervention, may itself induce change. The parent, impressed by the community's power as represented by the agency, may become less abusive, less neglectful. This change in behavior, "of which the obvious cause is caution lest legal action be taken, is often discounted as an unimportant indication of a client's likelihood of changing his behavior . . . but it *is* constructive behavior though it is reactive to authority. If no more, it shows that the parent recognizes another standard" (Becker, 1972, p. 87). What has been achieved is compliance in response to the worker's authority (Kelman, 1961). The judicious use of authority by the social worker can help effect change (Studt, 1954; Moss, 1963; Foren, Bailey, 1968; Yelaja, 1971).

The client may accept the social worker's efforts because of his concern over the possible social consequences of his behavior and his desire to avoid certain specific punishments. The new behavior is not adopted because the client believes it to be good or desirable; the new standards remain external; he has learned to do or say what is necessary, but there is no inner conviction in the values followed. Continued supervision is necessary because the client has to be kept constantly aware of the possibility of negative consequences for failure to provide adequate care.

The more desirable goal is to change behavior through the internalization of new standards of child care. To support such a change in values and beliefs, the agency must be certain that the living situation—housing, income, and so on —will allow the parents to act in accordance with a changed attitude toward child care.

Agency intervention imposes a penalty: the loss of privacy. The agency claims the right to know what is going on. Out of a sense of shame and discomfort at exposure, the client may be prompted to change in order to get the agency out of his life.

Families charged with neglect are apt to be multiproblem families facing severe social and physical deprivation, and because of limited education, they are less likely to make effective use of a psychotherapeutic approach to problem situations. The agencies usually have to prove their value to the client by taking concrete steps to alleviate some of the burdens faced by the family.

The most successful approach seems to be one that directs itself to situational changes rather than psychological changes. Neglectful parents appear to be childlike in their dependency, their disorganization, their impulsiveness, their inability to plan, and their lack of judgment regarding the damaging consequences of foolish decisions. They are helped by a casework approach designed to encourage the development of some kind of routine around which they can organize their lives. Like children, they simultaneously welcome and resent being told, in clear, unequivocal terms, what to do. As Young (1964) says, such parents "want borrowed strength, not freedom of choice—a freedom they lacked the strength to use. The authority of the protective caseworker not only protects the children from parents, it protects the parents from themselves" (pp. 125–126). The caseworker acts as a good parent—direct, frank, firm, but nonpunitive. According to Kaufman (1963), "The worker assumes the role of autonomous ego for these parents. He adopts a kindly but firm supportive parental role" (p. 196).

A study by Kelly (1959) of the factors associated with improvement in clients noted that "the problems with which protective service was most often successful were those where what was not being done for the children and what needed to be done for them was made clear and readily understandable to the parent" (p. 25).

Such clients, in short, require a highly structured definition of unambiguous expectations. In reciprocation, the worker has to show the client that he is ready and willing and able to help to effect some improvement, however slight, in the client's living situation. He has to prove, as Overton (1959) says, his "utility value to the client" (p. 50). This may involve taking people to clinics and employment agencies, showing the mother how to shop and cook, and giving direct advice where warranted. The agency may have to take the initiative in doing for the clients some of the things they are incapable of doing for themselves— even such simple things as completing an appplication form for new housing or a new job.

The change in approach is empirically based: some things seem to work. Behind it, however, is the assumption that a therapeutic approach based on a meaningful relationship and dependent for its success on highly developed communication skills between a worker and a client who share some understanding about the psychological causation of problems has not proved to be an effective approach for the kinds of families who make up a considerable segment of the protective service agency's case load.

A relationship of trust in the worker is hard to establish, and initially the client may be a passive recipient of service rather than an active participant in his own treatment. The social worker has to be frank in exercising the authority of his position. Young (1964) suggests that abusive parents respond primarily to authority used without hesitancy or apology, but at the same time without punitiveness:

The caseworker who faces abusing parents cannot be afraid of them. They exploit fear and they deride weakness. Neither can the caseworker afford any illusions about them; with intelligence they can be very convincing and remarkably adept at saying what the caseworker wants to hear. . . . Primarily they respect power, and there is substantial indication that they evaluate any caseworker, or anyone else for that matter, in terms of how much power over them that person has. . . .

By and large, abusing parents were respectful to those they feared, manipulative with those they could use, and indifferent to everyone else. . . .

The greatest asset a caseworker can have in dealing with these families is a deep conviction that no one has the right to abuse the helpless. It is out of such conviction, not anger at the parents, that help is best offered [pp. 95, 127].

Furthermore the structure of contact must be informal, more often in the home rather than in the office. One intensive-casework demonstration project with neglectful parents indicated that it is helpful to plan interviews for the same hour of the same day each week to "establish a pattern that our clients could remember and rely on." The procedure was also designed to help the clients develop a greater sense of planning in their lives (Bishop, 1963, p. 15).

The worker needs to accept the expectation of small gains and limited goals, as well as the initial dependency of the client. The expectations set should be realistic; they should be set with some appreciation of class and ethnic differences in the approach toward child care and should, in no instance, be different from those expected from most parents in the community. Drawing on his experience in helping neglectful mothers in Appalachia, Polansky et al. (1972) note that forming a relationship with such mothers

depends on a worker who has strong convictions about the needs of children and no great need to be popular with every one he meets. . . . The worker can be pretty sure that the mother will be more afraid of him than he is of her. . . . It does not hurt to let the mother save face by expressing her resentment. It is not so necessary to answer an attack as to hear it out. The aim is not to win an argument with her about whether she has a right to be angry, but to win a relationship for the sake of the children. Strength and calmness in the face of attack, even if directed at the worker, usually has [sic] a settling effect, and increases [sic] her respect for one. If one asks how these characteristics are acquired, we can only reply, "The more you do it, the easier it becomes." For after a time, an experienced child welfare worker handles anger like an electrician deals with current. We respect its force and potential for danger, but we are not all that frightened when we believe we know what we are doing [pp. 56–57].

Bandler (1967) aptly summarizes some of the problems in working with such families and the workers' response to these difficulties:

The nature of the families' processes of communication is extremely complicated and requires special attention in achieving involvement. Language is not a familiar vehicle for communication of feelings, or for identifying and categorizing, or conveying information. These families are action-oriented, concrete in their thinking, and not used to introspection or abstract thinking. They have little or no psychological insight into themselves or their behavior and little or no perception of conflict areas or psychological problems. Their solutions of economic, social, and psychological problems are impulsive and for immediate gain. The future is not taken into account. Consequently planning does not enter into their solutions. Problems in communication are compounded by their failure to trust anyone or any institution. Traditional casework methods, which are based on the assumption of trust and which are developed through ordinary avenues of communication, are not adequate. Consequently certain adaptations of casework concepts and techniques were necessary to achieve the initial goal or involvement. Our families had not initiated help or even recognized that they needed it, so the classic setting of the agency was not possible.

Mutual involvement and the gradual establishment of trust in the worker are achieved through the worker's gratification of dependency needs, which need not lead to insatiable demands. During the period of testing the social worker gradually emerges as a constant object and a figure who establishes some order, and a priority of problems, in their chaotic lives. Through such a relationship there appears to develop some enhancement of self-esteem and some improvement in the management of household and children [p. 291].

The worker's acting as a "good parent" in gratifying client dependency needs is based on the idea that maltreatment results from a deprived childhood, resulting in a lack of trust and an inability to love and nurture. A significant element of the protective-service treatment program, then, is concerned with "reparenting" so as to make restitution for a deprived childhood and to help the client "unlearn mistrust."

The worker's display of concern and interest in the client has positive effects in increasing client self-esteem. The investment of the worker's time and energy is perceived as an objective indication to the client that somebody in the community sees him as far from worthless and unimportant.

Helping parents to anticipate problems so they can plan to cope with them rather than reacting impulsively when problems arise, helping them to learn alternative procedures for dealing with child management problems so that they can select a more effect option, listening respectfully to but not supporting nonproductive defenses advanced by the parents, building on the parents' abilities to make the smallest changes in their situation, and mobilizing any sources of support in the group of people associated with the client—all are helpful tactics engaged in by the worker.

The social worker needs to communicate predictability if the client is to develop confidence and trust in the worker. This means that the worker shares honestly and fully with the client, in advance, what it is he plans to do—even if this includes planning court action.

In implementing treatment plans the worker should actively engage the client to the greatest extent possible and should encourage and accept client suggestions. Protective service clients "usually have very little control over their own lives, and when we intervene we threaten what little control they have— specifically, the control they exercise over their children. If we are to help them change, we need to encourage these parents to take charge whenever possible" (Davoren, 1977, p. 113). This might involve encouraging their active participation in implementing any treatment plan and encouraging and accepting client suggestions.

The worker has to be ready to perform a wide variety of roles with these families: adviser, teacher, enabler, intervener, coordinator of treatment, expediter, supporter, and confidant. There must be a constant effort to identify concrete needs and provide concrete services. Professionals who have worked with such parents have remarked on their emotional inaccessibility, the persistence that one has to display in going out to them physically and emotionally, and the difficulty in liking them while aware of what they did to a child (Davoren, 1968).

Another difficulty encountered by many workers dealing with neglect and child abuse is the acceptance of the "banality of evil." One expects the parent who abuses or neglects his child to look and act markedly different from the general run of parents. Instead, such parents are, for the most part, relatively indistinguishable from anyone else.

Workers must also be ready to work with related professional groups: the doctors treating the abused child, the lawyers representing the agency or the parents, and the courts.

The worker has also to consider the treatment needs of the children. Because the child's parents are not providing a good parental model, the worker must present himself to the child as an example of how good parents should act. If the child feels hostile to his parents, he may react with guilt to this feeling of hostility, however justified. He may be anxious about what is going to happen and fearful that the family may break up. He may have been forced to assume responsibility for himself and for younger siblings because of parental default, and he may resent the fact that he is being denied a true childhood. These are some of the problems with which the caseworker can help the child.

It might seem obvious, but the protective service worker should be aware of the need to turn off the lights and lock the door of any home he enters in order to remove a child who has been temporarily abandoned. In transporting a child, he must make certain, lest he himself be accused of neglect, to put seat belts on the child and use the safety latch on the car door.

A protective agency, if it is to do its work effectively, needs a wide variety of resources. The agency may make regular payments to emergency foster families who stand ready to accept any child on short notice. The agency also needs baby-sitters or homemakers who are able to go into homes and care for children temporarily abandoned. It needs access to foster homes in which children may be placed for longer periods of time. The protective service agency may itself provide such services or it may purchase such services from another agency.

A wide variety of treatment resources have been utilized in attempting to meet the needs of this group of clients. One group of innovations involves "shared parenting" to provide the parent with some relief from the stresses and burdens of unremitting child care, which may lead to maltreatment. Among these arrangements are crisis nurseries, drop-in centers, extended-day-care centers and parental surrogates.

The following examples of "shared parenting" through day care involves a father who was abusing his four preschool children:

He explained that he worked at night and tried to sleep and keep his children during the day while his wife worked. He and his wife were having serious marital problems which frequently erupted in verbal and physical attacks upon each other and the children. The father explained that he realized he had whipped the children too hard, but that the problems presented by the conflict between him and his wife, and his inability to get his sleep and watch the children were just too much for his nerves. When the children failed to obey him, he lost his temper and whipped them too hard. Obviously, day care alone is not the answer to this problem but it was one way of reducing the demands made by the children upon their father and of meeting their need for supervision [Medley, 1967, p. 9].

Crisis nurseries operate twenty-four hours a day, seven days a week. They accept children at all hours in order to divert or relieve a potentially damaging crisis situation by providing short-term relief. As emergency shelters, they do not solve an ongoing problem situation and are most effectively used in conjunction with or as a supplement to other services. A crisis nursery may impose a maximum forty-eight- or seventy-two-hour residential stay for a child and may accept a maximum of five to seven children. The danger of parental misuse of the center as a convenience, rather than as a facility for avoidance of abuse, needs to be monitored. "Drop-in" nurseries permit a mother to place children for a few hours "without much explanation or preparation—in moments of great stress—for no other reason than the mother wants relief" (Kempe, Helfer, 1972, p. 48).

Agencies have experimented with providing relief from child care by organizing a "mom's day out." For one day a week over a six-month period, mothers known to the agency's protective service unit are free of child-care responsibilities, which are taken over by students in a social work program.

In San Francisco, the extended-family center provides a "home away from home" for abused children and their parents. The center cares for children between 9 A.M. and 6 P.M., acting as an extended family to relieve the mother while she receives treatment (Ten Broeck, 1974).

Such programs combine a therapeutic nursery facility for children and group therapy and a family-life education program for parents. While the children are cared for, the parents are involved in group activities. The nursery school and its personnel also role-model desirable parental care (Tuszynski, Dowd, 1978). (See also Gardner, 1975.)

Special live-in treatment facilities have also been developed. The New York Foundling Hospital has established a temporary shelter at the Center for Parent and Child Development in an effort to help parents who have abused their children. The program permits mothers and children to live at the hospital for periods ranging from three to six months. During this time, the children are cared for in the hospital nursery or day-care centers, and the mothers receive intensive individual and group therapy from a multidisciplinary team, which includes social workers. The staff provides a model of good mothering by actual demonstrations of desirable child care. Discharge from residence in the hospital is followed up by a year or more of supervision in their own home by "surrogate mothers," who are paraprofessionals selected from the neighborhood in which the mothers live.

During 1973 and 1974, sixty-two families were provided three to four months of in-patient treatment, followed by a one year out-patient follow-up. During the period in residence, each mother is assigned to a social worker who acts as a supportive friend, models appropriate parental behavior, negotiates help in using community resources. Group counseling and psychiatric help are provided (Fontana, Robinson, 1976). A similar program in England is described by Lynch and Ounsted (1976).

Another example of this kind of "engineered community" has been attempted by the District of Columbia Department of Public Welfare: "Women on welfare whose child care seemed substandard were recruited to move into [a specially adapted apartment house] bringing their children with them. In addition to financial help they were offered guidance with housekeeping, health care, child caring . . . even with personal grooming" (Polansky, 1974, p. 128). Parental surrogates or parent aids are paraprofessional "friends" who are available to take over care of the child in the home when some relief is necessary to prevent abuse. In addition, they provide support and friendship, being available to listen to the parent when she wants to talk to some sympathetic mothering person in resolving tension. Parent aids work with the guidance and supervision of the social worker responsible for the family (Lane, Van Dyke, 1978).

Homemakers provide an additional resource for reducing the stress of child care. As supplementary caretakers, homemakers can relieve the frustrated, overburdened mother of some of the load of child care.

As a consequence of the availability of emotional satisfaction and support derived from the relationship with the parent aide, homemaker, and/or supportive day-care personnel, the parent may be able to reduce the demands made on the child for such satisfaction. Such supports tend to diminish the tendency to "role reversal" and the disappointment the parent might feel when the child fails to supply such needs.

Because situations triggering maltreatment sometimes can be resolved only with money, agencies have experimented with emergency relief funds. Such emergency funds have been disbursed as a cash grant to meet emergency housing costs, including those for rent, for restoration of heat and electricity to a home, or for emergency supplies of food. The funds have had the effect of increasing client confidence in the worker's desire and ability to be of help (Horowitz, Wintermute, 1978).

Efforts have been made through the use of such programs as parent effectiveness training to increase the parents' repertoire of disciplinary procedures. The parent is educated to the use of skills in child rearing that emphasize nonpunitive approaches. The assumption is that abusive parents have not had an opportunity to learn desirable parenting procedures because they lacked effective models in their own parents. Further, such parents know little about child development and need both information and training in good parenting. They need training in expanding their repertoire of procedures for child management beyond the almost exclusive use of punishment.

Behavior modification approaches have been used in some child-abuse-control programs directed toward the behaviors of both parents and children. Parents have been trained to use behavior modification procedures based on operant-conditioning concepts in changing the behaviors of their children that stimulate abusive responses. Parents have been trained through the use of behavior modification procedures, such as modeling and role playing, to change their behaviors in response to the child (Reavley, Gilbert, 1976).

Programs have been developed to "package" a comprehensive group of services that might be helpful. Here the treatment innovation relates to a change in the service delivery system. A comprehensive system of services to abused and neglected children pioneered in Nashville by the Tennessee Department of

Public Welfare materially reduced the number of children who had to be removed from their homes (Burt, Balyeat, 1974). The program included twenty-four-hour emergency intake, emergency caretaker service, emergency homemaker service, emergency foster homes, and emergency shelter care for adolescents and families. The program also coordinated the efforts of local public and private agencies on behalf of abused and neglected children.

Because of the availability of such innovative supportive services as emergency caretaker service and emergency homemaker service, in addition to more effective coordination of existing agency services, the number of children placed in substitute care (foster homes and institutions) as a result of neglect and abuse was reduced.

The success of the program led to the establishment in 1975 of a National Center for Comprehensive Emergency Services by the Office of Child Development, Children's Bureau, U.S. Department of Health, Education, and Welfare. The center is designed to provide information, technical assistance, and consultation to communities interested in developing a program of comprehensive emergency services.

The Protective Services Center, established in Chicago by the Juvenile Protective Association but no longer in existence, offered under one roof and under its own administrative control the following services: casework, group work, a day-care center for preschool children, homemaker service, an emergency shelter, temporary foster care, tutoring for children with learning problems, pediatric care, financial aid for special rehabilitative needs, an after-school day-care program, and transportation for children to and from the center. One goal was to help the families establish some predictable routine in their lives. The agency not only had to take children to school but also had to have staff members participate in awakening the children, dressing them, and getting them ready to go. Because of the heavy demands made by the families, only a very limited group could be served by this elaborate program: twenty-six families with a total of 104 children.

Emergency facilities for temporarily "abandoned" children have also been developed. In one California county, a network of "Good Neighbor Homes" was established. These were licensed foster homes that agreed to accept children, at any hour on any day, who needed shelter care. The homes were selected so as to be in the neighborhood of children likely to need such care so that they could remain in familiar surroundings and in the same school while in short-term substitute care (Penner, 1968; Soman, 1967).

A protective service agency in Buffalo, New York, developed a list of "emergency parents" who were available at all times to go into a home and stay with a child who had been left unsupervised and unprotected (Paget, 1967). Each "emergency parent" agrees (for a small fee) to be available for one night of each week. Each is provided with a kit, which includes "blankets, food, cooking equipment, rechargeable flashlight, first-aid kit, light bulbs, disposable diapers, insect spray, and an aluminum folding cot" (p. 128). The work of the emergency parent is as follows:

The police called the agency saying that they had heard from a neighbor that four children were in a home alone, the oldest nine years of age. A caseworker had to enter the home by a window. He found that an unvented gas stove was filling the home with fumes. All children were asleep, one youngster at the very top of the stairs. There was no doubt that a tragedy had been averted. An emergency parent was placed in the home and the sleeping children were guarded from possible accidents. The emergency parent remained all night and part of the morning, when the single parent returned [p. 130].

Emergency caretakers have been used in Chicago to prevent placement of dependent children reported as being without adult supervision in the home (Brown, 1979). Children whose parents were temporarily and unexpectedly absent because of illness, accident, arrest, or drug abuse were cared for up to sixty hours by such emergency caretakers who remained in the home. If the parents did not return within that time, as they frequently did not, homemaker service or foster placement was provided. Because parents were frequently angry and upset to return home and find a stranger caring for their child, protection needed to be afforded emergency caretakers.

A specialized child sexual abuse treatment program developed in San Jose, California (Giaretto, 1976), attempts a personal counseling approach, first separately with the child, the mother, and the father and then with the family as a unit. The personal counseling is supplemented by a self-help group of parents involved with the problem, Parents United. Giaretto notes, without further substantiation, that there has been no "recidivism among the more than 300 families who have received a minimum of 10 hours of treatment and whose cases have been formally terminated" (p. 5). (See also Muenchow, Silver, 1978.)

There are serious possible negative consequences for the daughter's self-perception in bringing a charge of sexual abuse against her father. Since the act in which she participated, however unwillingly, is clearly unacceptable, she tends to be labeled as unacceptable. The rest of the family, facing disruption because of the problems she is raising, is apt to reject her. Consequently, more than most recipients of abuse, the sexually abused need the kind of consistent, dependable support system outside the family that the social agency can provide.

The clear, unequivocal availability and use of court and agency authority is helpful to the sexually abused in reinforcing their determination to say "no" to similar attempts in the future.

Termination

With the family, the agency should plan a target date for termination. The normal family is not one without problems, but one that copes with its problems without the support of a social agency. But because the agency is responsible for seeing that the child is safe, the agency, rather than the family, has the obligation to make the decision regarding termination. When the parents demonstrate that they can function so that the child is no longer in significant danger, it is time for the agency to consider termination. Termination should involve a recapitulation of the changes that have taken place, an explicit expression of commendation and support for the changes made, and a review of some of the difficulties that the parents will inevitably face.

Court Action in Protective Services

The process of assuring more adequate care for the child may involve changes in the child's own home or, if this is impossible, removal to a substitute home. If the parents are unwilling or unable to plan the necessary changes, or if the situation involves so clear and present a danger to the child that he can be protected only by being removed from the home, the agency may have to obtain court action. In taking such action, the principle followed is that "use of the court should be constructive—as a resource, not as a last resort." The court process needs to be seen as "a means of protecting the child rather than prosecuting the parents" (Thomson, 1971, p. 44). The caseworker attempts to exercise his authority in a positive, supportive manner.

The court has the right and the power to *demand*, as against the social worker's entitlement and power to suggest, to persuade, and to influence. Because the court is a powerful resource, its intervention should be initiated appropriately, cautiously, and selectively toward constructive objectives. In every instance, the rights of the parents to the child must be safeguarded, and the abrogation of such rights—however brief—can be sanctioned only by the court.

If the caseworker feels that the children must be removed from the home, he first seeks the parents' voluntary consent. If they refuse, the agency has no alternative but to begin court action. Actually, however, according to the limited statistics available, recourse to legal action is atypical, and most protective service cases are closed without it.

We have already noted that the child continues to remain in his own home in some 80 per cent of the cases reported to protective service agencies. Court action is involved in only a limited number of those 20 per cent of the cases in which the child is removed from the home and placed in substitute care. In many instances, the parents voluntarily agree to the plan for placement. The general estimate is that about 10 per cent of protective service cases actually require the exercise of the court's authority (Mulford, 1956; DeFrancis, 1957; Paget, 1968; Polier, McDonald, 1972).

A study of 250 cases of confirmed abuse attempted to assess the factors that distinguished those cases in which the protective agency sought court action. There was a greater likelihood that court action would be taken in the case of the younger child who sustained serious or multiple injuries, and who lived with a single parent who tended to deny having abused the child (Thomson, 1971, pp. 125–134).

In deciding in favor of court action, the agency is concerned with preventing a recurrence of abuse. This general concern is warranted. Recapitulating the findings of ten studies between 1968 and 1975 that give figures on children reported abused, Maden and Wrench (1977) found that some 51 per cent had been previously abused (p. 204). In many jurisdictions, children who are in imminent danger may be removed from the home by an officer (employees of protective service agency may be invested with this authority) or through an application to the family court for an immediate hearing on the case.

In most jurisdictions, if either a social agency or the police have to remove a child from the home because there is no caretaker available, or because the situation is dangerous, a court hearing must be held within twenty-four hours to determine the appropriateness of the action. Unless the court is satisfied that protection of the child requires his removal from the home, the child must be returned to his parents.

Invoking legal sanction changes the worker, however temporarily, from helper to adversary. The worker should attempt to help the family understand that the use of legal sanction is an effort to motivate the family to mobilize whatever strengths it has in dealing positively with the problem. Many families may find that this sounds much like the "this hurts me more than it hurts you" gambit, and they find it difficult not to see the worker as pitted against them. However, parental hostility supposedly can be mitigated if the worker clearly explains the action he proposes to take and the reasons for it and presents the material in court in such a way as to emphasize the helpfulness of the action to the family. The petition should be presented not as a procedure directed against the parents but as a procedure in behalf of the child (Moss, 1963, p. 387).

The very fact that a legal procedure has been initiated may help the parents to mobilize themselves to make the necessary changes. As Hancock (1958) says, "The agency's authority to insist on more responsible care often induces parents to examine their own situation. . . . While they may protest vigorously, they are actually relieved to find strength in an outside factor that requires something of them" (p. 8). The seriousness of the situation exemplified by the agency's recourse to the court may support and reinforce the positive components of a parent's ambivalence—that part of him that wants to do right by the child.

In those limited number of instances in which court action appears necessary, the agency files a "formal application to invoke the judicial authority of the court." This is different from a complaint that "reports a condition of neglect which needs exploration" (American Humane Society, 1957, p. 19).

The petition, which is a statement to the court of the fact that the child needs protection, should include "evidence concerning the social and family background, specific conditions and frequency of occurrence of neglect as seen by the worker, parents' attitudes toward the children, whether the family used agency help, and, if so, how they used it" (Moss, 1963, pp. 385–386). The material in the petition should be supported by data from schools, medical facilities, other social agencies, law enforcement agencies, and so on.

The petition that initiates the court process is followed by a preliminary hearing within two or three weeks. At the preliminary hearing, the parents indicate whether or not they will consent to or contest the petition. The hearing is also designed to determine whether the allegations of the petition are true and whether the established facts constitute neglect or abuse.

The preliminary hearing is followed by an adjudicatory hearing to determine whether abuse has taken place as defined by state law. At this point, the social worker has to testify as to the facts of the situation and may be subject to cross-examination. The court needs a "preponderance of evidence"—a balance of the evidence indicating abuse—in order to make a determination that abuse has occurred. The adjudicatory hearing is followed by a dispositional hearing, where a determination is made regarding placement of the child or a program of treatment in the child's own home. A date may be set for a future review hearing when progress on the case will be assessed by the court.

At each point in the process, the case may be disposed of. The parents may not contest the proceedings and may agree to some plan acceptable to the court and the agency. Only a limited number of cases actually come to the trial stage, in which the worker may need to testify in the regular adversary process. Throughout the process, the parents are free to hire a lawyer and, in many jurisdictions, to ask for a jury trial, although studies indicate that such rights are less frequently exercised than is desirable (*Columbia Journal of Law and Social Problems*, 1968, p. 230).

Because the judge is concerned with protecting the rights of the parents as well as those of the children and the community, the material presented by the caseworker in support of the petition should follow the rules of evidence generally deemed admissible by courts of law. The material presented must be relevant, based on actual knowledge rather than hearsay, and supported by sufficient facts. A worker's "certainty" that he "feels" a child is neglected or abused finds little sympathetic response in a court of law; the burden of proof rests with the social worker (Sheridan, Mancini, 1962). "Social workers have a habit of using such words as *seem, appear,* and *wonder* as if they were not sure of what they are saying. . . . The court respects the confidence of a worker who *is* rather than *appears,* who *says* rather than *implies,* and who *tells* rather than *shares*" (Schmidt, 1963, p. 119). In filing a petition, the social worker accepts a responsibility—to the court, the community, the child, and the parents—to prepare the material in a manner that will withstand challenge. The same suggestions apply to the social worker's approach in testifying in court.

Social workers need to recognize that courts operate in terms of their own standards and procedures, with a decided orientation to fact and objective evidence. Without clear, well-organized, and specific evidence of maltreatment, social workers are perceived as poor investigators and inadequate witnesses. Lack of precise, objective evidence in support of their recommendations limits court confidence in the worker's planning suggestions.

Social workers are cautioned to avoid casual attire for a court appearance and to prepare in advance by organizing the material for presentation. In testifying, it is suggested that they speak slowly and distinctly, avoid professional jargon and nonverbal responses that cannot be recorded, and refrain from advocacy of a particular outcome, sticking closely to the facts to enhance credibility (Caulfield, 1978, pp. 49–57).

In making a disposition of the case, the judge may decide that there is not sufficient evidence to warrant any action by the court. If, however, he decides that there is sufficient evidence, the judge may make one of several decisions. He can permit the child to remain in his own home but place the family under the supervision of the court. Responsibility for supervision may be delegated to the probation department of the court or to a public or private social agency. The agency has a continuing responsibility to report to the court regarding the conditions under which the child is living. The parents' refusal to make necessary changes can be brought to the immediate attention of the court. As Beck says, the value of protective supervision is that "the agency's legal responsibility to the court, in reference to the family, is brought into focus and made specific for all concerned" (Beck, 1955, Part II, p. 17).

The judge can also place the child under protective legal custody. The child may be permitted to remain in his own home but under the legal custody of a social agency. This is a step beyond protective supervision because the agency given protective legal custody has the "right to care, custody, and control of the child." The agency may remove the child to another home if the parents refuse to make the changes necessary to mitigate the dangers the child faces.

The agency can also terminate parental rights and order the child removed from the home and placed under its own guardianship. Legislation has broadened the options that are available to the agency and the court in seeking to terminate parental rights so that the child can be made available for adoption. Such action can, in some states, be taken (1) if the child has been "abandoned," as evidenced by the fact that the parents have not visited him on a regular basis without good cause for at least six months; (2) if the child has been "permanently neglected," evidenced by failure for more than a year to "substantially and continuously or repeatedly maintain contact with the child or to plan for his or her future, although physically and financially able to do so"; or (3) if the parent is presently, and for the foreseeable future, unable to provide proper and adequate care for the child by reason of mental illness or mental retardation.

The requirement of the New York statute that termination cannot be granted if the agency has not demonstrated diligent efforts to help the family speaks to the responsibility of the community as a partner with the parents to make the home fit for the child.

All these procedures are designed to prevent hasty or arbitrary action and to make certain that any action taken is in accordance with due process. The court's decision also gives legal sanction to a desirable casework plan and reinforces the authority of the worker or the agency. Legal sanctions can do little to help a child other than to reduce the probability of his being injured. The law can dissolve a child's family relationship; it cannot preserve or rebuild it. This is the responsibility and the capability of the social services.

It might be noted that criminal proceedings are rarely initiated with maltreating parents. Criminal prosecution in cases of child abuse is difficult and often ineffective. The child is frequently too young to testify; the parents cannot be made to testify against themselves; and the incident has generally taken place without eyewitnesses. Consequently proof "beyond reasonable doubt" is difficult to obtain.

The probability of criminal action is greater in sexual abuse cases than in cases of either physical abuse or neglect. Community reaction is stronger in the case of sexual abuse. However, the trial may have more damaging emotional consequences for the child required to testify than the sexual abuse itself. The imprisonment of the father may be the culminating act that breaks up an already-fractured family, which might otherwise have been helped to regain its health. Despite these considerations, it is felt that the possibility of legal action is helpful in motivating families to change. In addition, the clear statement regarding the illegality of incestuous sexual abuse communicates society's expectations unequivocally.

The need to use the victim to prosecute the offender leads to the danger that the process of intervention, unless carefully and compassionately handled, may represent as much of a hazard to the child as the sexual abuse itself. The medical examination, the diagnostic study, and the legal questioning may accentuate the sense of guilt, betrayal, and shame the child might feel.

Use of Group Approach

Contacts with individual families may be supplemented by group meetings of parents to discuss child-rearing problems and marital difficulties that affect their handling of children (McFerran, 1957, 1958; Belluci, 1972; Paulsen *et al.*, 1974). Workers planning such meetings have to consider not only lack of motivation but financial problems, which may "make it impossible for prospective participants to hire babysitters and pay for transportation" so that they can attend meetings (1957, p. 31). The agency, therefore, may have to pay for both sitters and transportation.

Parents' attendance at group meetings is interpreted as a demonstration of cooperation with the agency. The agency, however, must be prepared to "require" attendance. Although the size of the group should be limited, many of the members benefit from the knowledge they acquire and are stimulated "to examine their methods of handling their children and to look at themselves critically." The meetings have, in addition, a "social value for many of the members, especially for some husbands and wives who rarely, if ever, had shared an activity of mutual interest" (McFerran, 1957, p. 33).

Group programs have been developed through the cooperative efforts of the courts, social agencies, and educational institutions. In one instance, the court ordered parents adjudged to be neglectful to attend group sessions devoted to family life education. Failure to attend was regarded as contempt of court. Some of the group meetings were devoted to a didactic presentation of material about children's needs and child development, family finances and budgeting, and health care of children. Other meetings were structured to permit a general nondirective discussion among the parents of problems they were having in rearing their children.

A self-help group of abusive parents has been organized and provides an effective adjunctive group treatment resource. Parents Anonymous (PA) was organized in California in 1971 with the help of a social worker. Membership requires that the mother make an open admission of child abuse and express a desire to change.

The organization's bulletins indicate that meetings are designed to help members share their feelings about incidents of child abuse and to express their fears of parenthood or their inability to handle the parental role in a constructive and healthy way. As a result of sharing their feelings and attitudes, members begin to understand themselves better and can start suggesting alternatives and answers for themselves and others. A description of the general orientation of group meetings suggests that it "is not a confrontation group, not sensitivity training, not Freudian analysis. I guess you might call it layman's reality therapy. We just don't let people moan about how they were beaten when they were three; we say, 'You're thirty-three now. The problem is to stop doing what you're doing to your children.'"

By sharing "positive behavior alternatives" to abuse, PA educates its members to more acceptable patterns of parenting. As one member said:

> Parents Anonymous gives you something to do besides abusing. It gives you alternatives; instead of hitting, instead of name-calling, it gives you something to do.

Instead of throwing a child, you throw a cup or a plate. Instead of responding to a temper tantrum with a temper tantrum of your own, you lock yourself in a bedroom until it's over. Something to do instead of abusing [Collins, 1978, p. 91].

The organization is involved in socializing the abusive parent in terms of parental role behaviors that are socially acceptable.

"Support," "caring," and "giving" are repeatedly emphasized in PA meetings and reinforce the ideology of mutual self-help, which is the basic therapeutic factor in the program. The group combines nurturance with an accepting firmness in its unequivocal rejection of child abuse.

Tape-recorded structured interviews with PA members concerning the reasons that prompted them to join indicated that the decisive fact was that the group was perceived as offering the probability of problem-focused help in a context of nonjudgmental acceptance. This was reinforced by the lack of alternative options and a fear of professionals (Powell, 1979). Despite the advantages, many spoke of the threat to personal esteem involved in accepting the label of "Parents Anonymous group member."

As is true in other self-help groups, being accountable to the group is an added factor in contributing to self-control. One PA member said that she knew she would be asked at each meeting, "How did your week go?" "Just thinking about what her answer would be—and knowing it would be difficult to pretend with other parents—was an important factor in controlling her abusive behavior" (Starkweather, Turner, 1975, p. 156).

PA makes a great point of protecting members' anonymity and confidentiality. This protection permits the members to discuss their experiences without risk of public disclosure. The fact that they are sharing their experiences with other parents who have abused children guarantees their being able to "confess" without danger of rejection, recrimination, or humiliation.

Unlike the traditional therapeutic relationship, which sets limits on the extent of personal involvement between the helper and the person being helped, PA deliberately fosters the personal involvement of members with each other. This personalization of interaction is an important component of membership satisfaction in affiliation with the organization, ensuring the availability of an effective social support system. The groups developed through PA meetings act as "surrogate families." Each group member is given the phone numbers of all others in the group and is advised to "reach for the phone instead of the child" when feeling stressed (Holmes, 1978).

In analyzing the dynamics of change experienced by Parents Anonymous participants, Collins (1978) concluded that it involves acceptance of the label of child abuser and transformation of the descriptive label into a positive image. Members are gradually transformed into "lay professionals" who perceive themselves as able to help other child abusers because they themselves have, at one time, been child abusers. By 1978 PA was developing a training program for professionals and was involving abusive parents in the education of the professionals (*Parents Anonymous Frontiers*, 1978).

Social workers do not act as group leaders but as "professional sponsors" to local groups. The group leader or chapter chairperson is always a parent who at one time abused a child. Members can identify more readily with such a person than they can with a "professional therapist whose 'experience of abuse' is deemed vicarious at best and voyeuristic at worst" (Collins, 1978, p. 39). The professional sponsor is a resource person rather than a group member or leader. The professional sponsor's responsibility is to offer some specialized expert knowledge, as it may be required; to be a neutral observer; to resolve conflicts, to act as a role model, and to act as a referral liaison with community services that might be required by PA members.

As is true in any group situation, not all abusive parents can be appropriately referred to Parents Anonymous. The withdrawn parent, the parent who has difficulty in communicating, the parent who is aggressive, impulsive, and disruptive, or the parent who is defensive, frightened, and anxious about "coming out" as an abusive parent is not likely to be able to use PA as a treatment resource.

In June 1978 Parents Anonymous was estimated to have about eight thousand members in some eight hundred chapters. It is defined as a self-help organization providing a "nurturing and therapeutic service" (MacFarlane, Lieber, 1978).

Parents Anonymous membership is primarily white, middle-class, young, and female. In 1977, of some five hundred chapters in the country, only two were identifiably black and three Hispanic. Overall membership was about 4 per cent black (Mohamoud, 1978).

Affiliation with and participation in Parents Anonymous is involuntary for some 7 per cent of parents and is mandated by the court. However, beyond the stage of initial resistance, those who come to Parents Anonymous through this route are indistinguishable from those who are self-referred (Collins, 1978, p. 8).

The national organization has received grants of support from the federal government, acts as cosponsor to an annual national conference on child abuse, and publishes a semimonthly newsletter, *Parents Anonymous Frontiers*.

All of the treatment interventions that bring abusive parents together in a group—Parents Anonymous, group therapy, family therapy, parent education programs, living-in programs—have as one of their goals diminishing the social isolation of abusive parents and providing them with social supports.

EVALUATION OF OUTCOME

Studies concerned with determining whether protective service programs actually achieve their objectives and accomplish the goal of reducing maltreatment of children might be divided into the period that preceded the recent "rediscovery" of the problem and the period of the late 1960s and 1970s, which followed the rediscovery.

The second edition of this text reviewed the earlier evaluation research and concluded that there were no well-designed research studies to establish the degree of success achieved by protective services. The studies by Kelly (1959), Johnson (1960), Scherer (1960), Merrill *et al.* (1962), Bourke (1963), Varon (1964), Young (1964, 1966), Rein (1964), and Johnson and Morse (1968) were reviewed at that time. The general overall conclusion was that the agencies have apparently achieved some modest measure of success.

In bringing the review up to date, we might say that outcome evaluation research relating to protective services has not changed significantly since the earlier review. A consultant's report to the National Institute of Mental Health reviewing child abuse and neglect programs in 1977 notes that "The impact of various treatment approaches and programs has not been measured in any systematic way to date" (Holmes, 1977, p. 167). A recent study of protective services that reviews the evaluation literature notes that "evaluation of treatment services for abusive and neglectful parents constitutes a major gap in the child abuse and neglect literature" (Berkeley Planning Associates, 1977, p. 62).

Statements of levels of success are frequently made with the most limited, if any, substantiating detail. Typical of such statements is the following, made by Steele and Pollock (1968).* It relates to the outcome of treatment of the sixty families included in their study group:

> In the great majority of patients treatment was successful, highly so in some, moderately so in others. Criteria of success were multiple. Of primary importance was a change in the style of parent–child interaction to a degree which eliminated the danger of physical harm to the child and lessened the chance of serious emotional damage [p. 138].

No details are presented of the evaluation procedures employed in arriving at these conclusions. Similarly, Helfer (1975) notes "we should be able to help 70–75 percent with our present understanding and treatment programs" (p. 41). The basis for such an estimate is not detailed.

Such statements of the anticipated successful outcome of treatment are frequently repeated and then supplemented by similarly general statements without further substantiation. Thus Green (1976) says, "Pollock and Steele estimate that 80 percent of these [abusing] parents can be treated with satisfactory results under optimal conditions. Our own treatment program at the DownState Medical Center, operating with limited resources, has helped the majority of the families involved" (p. 427).

The same kinds of general statements of positive outcome, without further substantiation, are frequently made with regard to special programs of intervention. Thus Bean (1975), discussing the use of a specialized day-care program in treating child abuse, notes that "To date 36 families have been involved in the Parents Center with 59 children between the ages of 3 months and 4 years. The results of our treatment approach with both parents and children have been most gratifying. . . . The results have confirmed our premise that parents can change if given the opportunity with certain environmental and emotional supports made available" (p. 139).

Reincidence of subsequent abuse has often been used as a measure of successful intervention. Although reincidence rates assume, with some hazard, that all subsequent incidents have been reported, they are a rough, useful measure of the achievement of the major objective of intervention, namely, that the child not be subsequently maltreated. Reincidence rates vary widely from study to study.

Describing a child abuse treatment program at a hospital based facility, Holmes (1977) notes that "therapeutic services are intensive and tend to continue for a period of two years or more. The payoff is the reinjury rate of 2.2 per-

---

* The same statement, without change, is repeated in the second edition (1974) of the book (p. 124).

cent which is extremely low" (p. 24). Seventy-two families had been treated at this facility by the time of the report.

Gladston (1975) presents an account of forty-six families with seventy-three children treated at a combined facility: a therapeutic day-care center supplemented by a parents' group, providing a correlated treatment of parents and children. The only explicit evaluation material provided is that "over an average period of seven-plus months of attendance in the project, there have been but two known instances of recurring abuse of children" (p. 380). It might be noted that the parents treated were the most motivated of a much larger number of families originally referred to the project (Gladston, 1975, p. 374).

A report (National Center on Child Abuse and Neglect, 1975) on the work of the Child Protective Services Unit of Hennepin County (Minneapolis), regarded as one of the best in the country, notes that "It is of course difficult to measure effectiveness in the field of child protection. But Child Protective Services (Hennepin County, Minnesota) officials believe the Unit's philosophy has worked. As one indication, the recidivism rate between 1963 and 1973 averaged less than 9 percent in cases of physical abuse and 17 percent in cases of neglect" (p. 20).

Other studies have shown higher recidivism rates, however.

Johnson (1977) provides a detailed study of reincidence based on a careful analysis of the records of all families offered protective services in two cities (Nashville, Tennessee, and Savannah, Georgia) between August 1971 and April 1974. The records were reviewed for the reincidence of maltreatment, the length of time between the repeated events of maltreatment, the severity of subsequent injury as compared with the first injury, and the action taken by the agency. The study concluded that approximately 60 per cent of the reported children had been previously abused; that the more recent incidents had a relatively high probability of being more serious in nature than previous incidents; that reentry into the system occurred in a short period of time in a high percentage of the cases; and that "efforts to rehabilitate parents and prevent further abuse and/or neglect have generally failed" (p. 162).

Studies that evaluate outcomes in terms of changes in parental attitudes and behavior also show variable, but generally modest, positive effects. In a follow-up study of fifty-eight abused children completed by Martin, Beezley, Conway, and Kempe (1974):

> the children were evaluated at a mean of 4.5 years after abuse had first been documented. It was disheartening to note the current behavior of the parents toward the previously abused child. Parents of 21 of the children had had psychotherapy as part of their treatment program; 90 percent of the children of these parents were still in the biologic home. Even though the children were no longer being battered in the technical or legal sense, 68 percent of them at follow-up were still experiencing hostile rejection and/or excessive physical punishment. It should be noted that these children were faring much better than those whose parents had received no formal treatment [p. 256].

The Comptroller General's office conducted a study (1976) of protective service outcomes. Selecting ten public welfare agencies in six states, they drew a sample of records in each location for each of three periods between June 1972 and June 1973 for a total of 724 cases overall. Case records were examined, and some evaluation was made as to whether the child's circumstances were (1) "critical" (child in imminent personal danger); (2) "serious" (child provided minimal care); (3) "fragile" (potential for danger but not actual danger); or (4) "satisfactory" (suitable parental and social supports being provided to the child). Similar levels of assessment were made from the record material on the child's physical and emotional well-being.

Analysis of the information from the 714 usable records showed that a child was generally in a "serious" or "critical" situation at case opening and that the child's situation generally improved after case opening, the percentage of younger children achieving improvement being significantly greater than that of older children (p. 17). At opening, only 36 per cent of the children were in "fragile" or "satisfactory" situations. At the end of the study, 73 per cent were in a "fragile" or a "satisfactory" situation, indicating improvement in the situation for some 37 per cent of the children served.

Baher *et al.* (1976) report the effects of an intensive relationship approach to twenty-three families with a history of the abuse of a child under four. The worker was in contact with the family for at least eighteen months, and during the first three months of the contact, he scheduled two interviews a week with the client. Detailed process recordings were kept of all contacts as well as the results of decision-making conferences regarding clients. The workers had very limited case loads and were in every instance professionally qualified. The worker evaluated the outcome by comparing the recorded details of his first contact with the client's functioning at the end of eighteen months of service. The service was primarily a therapeutic, supportive, and accepting personal counseling intervention designed to meet dependency needs, to offer a positive reparenting experience, and to demonstrate concern in attitude and behavior. Despite the considerable effort expended, the changes in the parents' care of the child were minimal:

> The results . . . relating primarily to the interaction between the mothers and the battered children were disappointing. Only slight positive changes were noted in most aspects of these relationships, leaving many doubts about the effectiveness of our treatment service in improving the quality of mothering. . . . The majority of mothers could not be termed even fairly accepting of the battered children after twenty-one months of treatment. . . . It is our impression that some positive changes did occur in the quality of the relationships between mothers and the battered children. The degree of change, however, was generally minimal, and diffused over several items. During the three-year period after referral, twenty-two children were available for possible injury in the home. Of these, twelve (54%) received injuries for which there was no adequate explanation [pp. 171–172; see also Bedger *et al.*, 1976, pp. 206–207 for similar findings].

The Berkeley Planning Associates (1977) recently completed the first large scale comparative child abuse and neglect treatment-outcome study available. It covered 1,724 parents treated in eleven different protective service demonstration projects throughout the nation. Despite the care and detail with which the study was conducted, the study itself notes its principal research deficiencies: there was no control group, the workers provided the data used in the outcome study, the clients were neither observed nor contacted directly, and there was no provision for follow-up.

The workers in the most direct contact with the client in the demonstration project filled out a series of forms developed by the researchers in consultation with practitioners. Data were collected from the time of intake to service termination for 1,724 adult clients during 1975–1976. The forms completed included an intake form, a goals-of-treatment form, and a client follow-up form. A form listing the services provided to the client and a client functioning form were completed at the end of each calendar month. A client impact form provided information on the client at the start of service, and the same form was completed at termination of service.

With reincidence used as an outcome measure, it was found that 30 per cent of the clients served by the demonstration projects abused their children severely or neglected them while in treatment. An evaluation of changes in specific client behaviors, client attitudes, or situational changes showed that in every instance, fewer than 30 per cent of the clients exhibited significant improvement. Less than 40 per cent of the clients improved in at least one third of those areas identified as problems at intake (p. 58).

Treatment interventions that seemed to provide a greater measure of success included lay therapy programs, group parent-education programs, and self-help programs such as Parents Anonymous, perhaps partly because such services were more frequently used voluntarily by motivated clients capable of making effective use of the service. Clients who were treated for longer periods of time showed greater positive change, a result that suggests the value of treatment.

Fitch (1977) studied 140 infants hospitalized in Denver because of child abuse. The children were randomly assigned to a control group and two experimental groups. The first was provided with a limited treatment program; the second group was provided with more extensive treatment programs. In addition, a matched group of nonabused children was studied. All children were given a variety of intelligence and physical and social developmental tests at various intervals. Mothers were given a standard questionnaire to determine changes in their perception of the child and his behavior. The treatment program offered one of the experimental groups consisted of close medical and child counseling service by a group of three pediatricians assigned to the family on a 24-hour on-call basis and of other services by community agencies who were involved in helping the family with its problems. These included marital, educational, and financial counseling; family planning services; individual psychotherapy; anticipatory guidance; role modeling; assertiveness training; socialization group programs; and foster care.

Impact of intervention was measured by comparative changes in child development and by recurrence of abuse over a 30-month period of testing and retesting. The child development scores of the abused nontreated children and those of the treated group were the same (pp. 64–66). However, although 8.7 per cent of the previously abused but untreated group had been reabused, only 2.7 per cent of the abused and treated group had been reabused (p. 169).

Tracy, Ballard, and Clark (1975) provide evaluation outcome data on families with whom behavior modification approaches to child management procedures were attempted. The interventions were provided by "family health workers," whose professional background is not given in the report: "The parents' verbal report was used to assess behavioral changes," although this report was further augmented by "direct observation in the home, clinical reports and verbal reports of others." Forty-one treated families provided a pool of 129 kinds of behavior that needed changing. Of these, 84 percent were rated improved or very improved, while 9 percent were rated worse or the same. Rating of changes was made by the health workers and project coordinator on the basis of some observable indicator. The group studied was composed of families of abused children and families at high risk for abuse. The results are not broken down, so that it is impossible to tell outcomes for the abused families alone.

Additionally, case reports of successful treatment through the use of behavior modification procedures are available in the literature (Polakow, Peabody, 1975; Reavley, Gilbert, 1976; Mastria, Mastria, Harkins, 1979).

A limited number of outcome evaluation reports are available on special approaches to maltreating families: group therapy, day care, coordinated services, engineered environments, and team approaches.

Justice and Justice (1976) used goal attainment scaling in determining the outcome of their group therapy programs with abusive parents. Goal attainment scaling involves specifying a series of explicit, behaviorally objectifiable goals and then determining the level at which the goal has been achieved in therapy, for which a change score is computed. The average length of group treatment ran four or five months, one and one-half hours once a week. At the last report (1976), "abuse has not reoccurred among the 15 couples who have completed group therapy since May, 1973. Furthermore, six months follow-ups show that expected levels of outcome . . . are holding up" (p. 119). The change scores were based on self-reports of changed behavior presented by the parents, who had a considerable investment in presenting themselves as changed. All couples in the parents' group were referred by the county child welfare agency. In 75 per cent of the cases, the child had been removed from the home by order of the court. The couples were told that their chances of getting their child back were likely to be greatly enhanced if they accepted therapy. Furthermore the group leader's report back to the county agency was an important determinant of whether the child was to be returned home. There was considerable incentive, then, for the parents to report progress.

Stephenson (1977) describes the results of a preschool enrichment program for abused children and their families, with preschool teachers acting as the primary therapists. There was considerable turnover, and only ten families appear to have remained in the program for more than a year. The children in the program for more than a year "showed a mean IQ increase of 14 compared to a mean gain of 2 for children less than a year and control children. In 55 percent of the one year plus families, a parent had moved from social assistance, usually via educational upgrading, to permanent employment" (p. 133). The researchers note that "like other workers in this field, we have found it difficult to evaluate our project statistically. Many of the tests were invalid. For instance, we administered the Parental Attitude Research Inventory but discovered that several parents could not read and a number complained they could not understand the questions" (p. 314).

The Bowen project, conducted between 1965 and 1971 by the Juvenile Protective Association of Chicago, attempted to provide under the auspices of a single agency a comprehensive package of treatment interventions to a limited number of abusive and neglectful families. Over the five-year period, an average of twenty-five workers delivered an average of ten different services to a total of thirty-five disorganized families, which included 162 children. The final report of the project notes that it is possible to describe the treatment but difficult to provide any research evidence on outcomes: "The question of results must of necessity be answered in terms of clinical judgment and case description" (Juvenile Protective Association, 1975, p. 88).

Without providing specific statistical details, the report notes that:

> all of the mothers, except those with psychotic conditions, made considerable progress. They took more interest in themselves, became more interested in the life around them, and were able to achieve some gratification from their children. The most visible outward changes were with respect to their self concepts. Since they were closed to their feelings, most were able to be a little more empathic with their children, with a resulting improvement in the quality of the parent child relationships.
>
> In spite of these achievements, for most, there still remained major deficits in sustaining independence in the assumption of parental responsibility. They needed continued help in these areas although at a different level in quantity and quality of input. A few by the end of the project, had achieved greatly improved stability in managing their homes and caring for their children [pp. 139–140].
>
> a small number of families made substantial improvement in both parental functioning and the progress of the children [p. 159]. . . .
>
> By the time the project terminated, most of the parents were functioning at an improved level and the nature and amount of services needed had changed. They had more security, self-esteem and the neglecting symptoms had been ameliorated to some degree. However, they were still somewhat shaky in independent functioning [p. 160].

A measure of the success is the fact that removal of children by the court had to be initiated for only eight of the Bowen Center's thirty-five families.

The New York City Foundling Hospital is an "engineered environment" providing living quarters for mothers and children. During their residence there, both are involved in an intensive program of rehabilitation. Initiated in October 1972, by January 1974 it had treated thirty-eight families, two of which were subsequently child abuse recidivists. However, in 30–35 per cent of the cases, the child was placed in foster care because the mother did not make sufficient progress (American Academy of Pediatrics, 1974).

Lynch and Ounsted (1976) provide some outcome data on fifty families treated in a similar live-in facility in England. In 20 per cent of the cases, the child was still perceived as in danger after treatment, and the child was placed in foster care. Of the families treated, 80 per cent returned home with their children, and there was no subsequent serious abuse except in two cases (p. 206).

The successful use of foster family care to remove the child from any possibility of danger and the subsequent healthy development of children placed in such substitute care are reported by Kent (1976). He studied the physical and emotional development of 219 abused and neglected children. Obtaining data from the schools and the social workers assigned to the case, he compared the child's functioning at the point of the agency's first contact with the child and a year later. In each agency, intervention had resulted in the placement of the child in substitute care, most frequently in a foster family home. During the year in placement, the child made substantial gains in weight and height and "improved on nearly all the problem behaviors" (p. 28) and in I.Q. score, academic performance, and school peer relationships (p. 29). Kent concludes that "intervention in the form of removal of the child from the abusive environment had beneficial results" (p. 28).

Attempts have been made at early identification of parents who are high risk for maltreatment of their children (Lynch, Roberts, 1977; Knight, Disbrow, Doerr, 1978). A treatment program is then offered such parents as a primary prevention procedure, and the effects of such intervention are subsequently evaluated. On the basis of interviews, a questionnaire administered before and after the birth of the child and observation by hospital staff of the mother's reaction to and handling of the infant, 100 mothers were identified as high risk for abuse (Gray et al., 1978). Fifty of the mothers were randomly assigned to a program of intervention services. This consisted of frequent contacts by a pediatrician assigned to the family, weekly home visits by a public health nurse, and ready availability of help to the family whenever indicated. The additional high risk mothers were not offered this service. In addition, there was a control group of fifty "low-risk-for-abuse" mothers identified by the interview, questionnaire, and observation procedures. At the end of seventeen months, the children in twenty-five families in each of the three groups—high risk, special service; high risk, no service; and low risk controls—were randomly selected for analysis. The special intervention program had little impact on outcomes. "There were no significant statistical differences on the basis of Central Child Abuse Registry, indications of 'abnormal parenting practices,' accidents, immunizations or Denver Developmental Screening Test scores" between the high-risk special-treatment group and the high-risk no-treatment group (p. 249).

However, no child in the high-risk special-treatment group "suffered an injury . . . that was serious enough to require hospitalization." On the other hand, five children in the high-risk no-treatment group required in-patient treatment for serious injuries thought to be associated with "abnormal parenting practices." The difference between the two groups with regard to this is statistically significant (p. 250).

In summary, the evaluation studies suggest that the agencies have achieved some modest measure of success. The amount of change one might reasonably expect the agencies to effect must be assessed against the great social and personal deprivation characteristic of the client families. Even the modest success achieved may have been more than could have been expected initially.

The resources available to treat these families are limited. The technology available to the worker in trying to effect change in such families is blunt and imprecise. The low level of confidence in the technology available to treat problems of child maltreatment is indicated by the fact that 39 per cent of some one thousand seven hundred human services personnel interviewed by Nagi (1977) agreed that "we just don't know enough to deal effectively with problems of child mistreatment" (p. 15).

Scarce resources backed by a weak technology applied to a group of involuntary, disturbed clients resistive to change and living in seriously deprived circumstances would seem to guarantee the likelihood of limited success.

EFFECTS ON CHILD DEVELOPMENT

Several studies have attempted to study the effects of maltreatment on the child's development.

Studies of the emotional, physical, language, and cognitive development of abused children tend to show that they lag behind the norms for children at their age levels (Martin, 1976; Jones, 1978). However, the studies lack a comparison with matched controls, and there is a difficulty in evaluating which developmental lags are the results of the abuse and which are the consequence of other factors. The one study that attempts to match the development over a period of time of abused children with nonabused controls tends to show surprisingly little difference between the two groups (Elmer, 1977).

In this study, in which the children were followed up for a period of eight years subsequent to abuse in infancy, seventeen abused children were compared with seventeen nonabused children hospitalized because of accidents. Accident children were matched with the abused children on the basis of age, race, sex, and socioeconomic status. In addition, an "untraumatized, nonaccident" group of thirty-four similarly matched children were included for study. Data were obtained from interviews with mothers and clinicians and from school records, medical records, teachers' questionnaires, and records from other agencies. Groups were compared in terms of health, cognitive development, language development, nervous mannerisms, neurological problems, school achievement, self-concept levels, impulsivity, aggression, and empathy. In general, the findings indicated that the abused children were not significantly different from their nonabused, matched peers. The researchers "had hypothesized that the abused children would score lower than the nonabused children in height and weight, language development, and intellectual functioning. However, few overall differences were found between the abused children, the accident children and their respective comparison groups" (p. 757). There was little difference in self-concept or level of control of aggression. The researchers go on to say that:

> when the followup study was completed, we were at a loss to explain the lack of significant results in differentiating between the abused, accident, and comparison groups or any of the subgroups. Across the board there were very few differences between the groups, and these were relatively minor. The followup staff was astonished and disbelieving [p. 80].
>
> It was impossible to avoid the conclusion that abuse as one method of deviant child care did not appear to make a significant difference at least in the population under study [p. 83].

In reviewing the data, it was concluded that all of the children studied were doing poorly, although the abused children were doing worse than the others. The factor determining the results seems to have been "membership of the majority in the lower social classes, which connotes poverty and its well-known companions—poor education, menial jobs, inadequate housing, undernutrition, poor health and environmental violence" (p. 84). "We come to the conclusion that the results of child abuse are less potent for the child's development than class membership" (p. 110).

Community neglect in failing to provide what the family needs for adequately doing the job of child rearing is as important a concern as attempting to change the behavior of the family involved in maltreatment.

PROBLEMS

1. The problem of establishing explicit standards in determining neglect has not yet been solved by protective agencies. Acceptable minimum levels of parental adequacy vary from community to community and among different groups within the same community. For the agency this means that "since criteria for evaluation of family adequacy have not yet been clearly defined, it is extremely difficult to formulate standards of minimum levels of adequacy in child care below which no child shall be allowed to continue" (Boehm, 1962, p. 12). Actually such standards tend to become established empirically in legal norms as the courts are forced to make definite decisions in particular situations.

State statutes, of course, include a legal definition of neglect, but this definition merely sets broad limits within which each community may define the specifics of neglect. As Meier notes, "The paradox of neglect laws is that they teem with adjectives and adverbs—*properly, improper, necessary, unfit, insufficient, inadequate*—thus requiring a judgment to be made by the court in each specific instance of alleged neglect to determine whether the child is indeed neglected" (p. 158).

The problem of ambiguous definition is frequently expressed as a conflict between the social worker and the community. Not atypical is the case of what appears to be physical neglect ("children are dirty, clothes all torn and ragged; they never have a bath") in a home in which the parent–child relationship is emotionally and socially wholesome; or the case of a loving mother who is somewhat casual in her sexual relations. Although the community may press for action in such cases, the social worker may believe that the situation does not require intervention.

The problem may be expressed as a conflict between the court and the social worker. Situations that appear to the social worker to be clear-cut cases of emotional neglect may be rejected by the court because no evidence of physical damage is available.

If it is difficult to establish a basis for justified intervention in cases of physical neglect and abuse, it is even more difficult in cases of emotional neglect and abuse. A broken arm is a broken arm, but a damaged psyche is more difficult to establish unequivocally. This elusiveness of definition is a problem for the protective service agency because it is not always clear how much, or in what situations, intervention will be supported by the community (Nettler, 1958; Boehm, 1964).

The problem of defining *abuse* and *neglect* is difficult because different norms have to be respected. Involved in every definition is some cultural standard, norm, or expectation of parental behavior, duties, and obligations that are not met or that are implemented in a nonsanctioned manner. But *norms, duties, and obligations* may be defined differently by different groups in our society.

The need to define *child abuse* in terms of its cultural context is noted by Korbin (1977). Cutting a child's face and rubbing charcoal into the lacerations is regarded as child abuse in the United States, but not among the Yoruba of Africa, who practice scarification and among whom a child without such scars would be rejected by his peers. This, for the Yoruba, is the equivalent of painful orthodontia, which we "inflict" upon a child in order to improve his appearance, a procedure we do not regard as child abuse. Nor do we define infant circumcision as child abuse.

Indian children are frequently deliberately left in the care of older siblings; this practice does not constitute neglect. Chicano fathers may demand obedience and overt respect from their children, whereas in white middle-class families, there may be a greater emphasis on democracy.

Kagan (1977) recognizes this dilemma in his observation of

> an uneducated black mother who slaps her 4 year old child across the face when he does not come to the table on time. The intensity of the act tempts our observer to conclude that the mother resents her child. However, during a half-hour conversation, the mother indicates her warm feelings for the boy. She hit him because she does not want him to become a "bad boy" and she believes physical punishment is the most effective socialization procedure. Now her behavior seems to be issued in the service of affection rather than hostility [pp. 40–41].

This example suggests the different norms held by different groups regarding the use of physical punishment in child rearing (Blumenthal *et al.*, 1975, pp. 170–174).

More general norms may be involved as well:

> If parents feel that the natural oils of the body should be preserved and therefore bathe their child only once a week, with the consequence that severe diaper rash develops—is that to be defined as neglect, or simply "different" parenting? If parents choose not to use their food stamps for vegetables, fruits, milk, etc., and instead feed their children nothing but "junk" food, or if they refuse to immunize their children—is that considered neglect, or the exercise of parental rights? If a mother insists on sending her 10-year-old daughter to school in antiquated lace and organdy instead of in a pair of blue jeans, and the daughter is consequently laughed at and isolated by the other children—is that emotional abuse, or parental rights? [Holmes, 1977, p. 116].

The definition of abuse changes not only with the social–cultural context but with the age of the child: the same parental action might be abuse for an infant and not for an adolescent. It is not, therefore, surprising that in interviewing some one thousand seven hundred respondents affiliated with hospitals, schools, courts and social agencies, Nagi (1977) found that 69 per cent agreed with the statement that "It is difficult to say what is and what is not child mistreatment" (p. 15).

A number of different studies confirm the fact that there are differences in the definitions of child abuse and neglect among different sections of the general public and also among members of the different professions concerned with mistreatment of the child (Nettler, 1958; Boehm, 1964; Giovannoni, Becerra, 1977). Despite the differences, there is a core of consensus about what is minimally acceptable child care. The responses of a sample of middle-class and lower-class mothers to a standard-of-living scale identifying specific items related to the adequacy of child care showed considerable unanimity on the part of the mothers. The responses refuted the contention that protective services were imposing middle-class values on lower-class families (Polansky, Williams, 1978). There is also a general acceptance of the idea that social work intervention to help the family is preferred to punitive action against the family (Polansky *et al.*, 1978).

Although there may be consensual agreement on a minimally expected standard of child care, these standards may be applied differently to different groups in the community. Katz (1968, 1971) points to a double standard: the parental fitness of the poor is examined, and the parental fitness of the wealthy parent is assumed. These situational and class differences are also suggested by Walters (1975) in outlining three different "happenings":

> Mrs. A., a welfare client, enters a tavern at 11 P.M., leaving her three children asleep in the car. She is reported to the police, and Mrs. A. is charged with neglect.
>
> Mrs. A., a welfare client, enters a tavern at 11 P.M., leaving her three children asleep in the car. The temperature is −20°, and the police find the children nearly frozen. Mrs. A. is charged with abuse.
>
> Mrs. N., wife of an up-and-coming bank employee, leaves her son in the car in the parking lot of a suburban shopping center for "a few minutes." The car windows are rolled up, and the inside temperature reaches 120°. On her return, Mrs. N. finds the boy unconscious and rushes him to a hospital. The child quickly recovers. Mrs. N. is "in shock" and is comforted by her husband and sedated by her physician. No charges are filed [p. 25].

The problem of defining minimally acceptable standards of care is related to the problem of defining the respective rights of parents and children. The balance between the two differs from community to community, as Maas (1959) found, in a study of child care in nine different communities throughout the country. Earlier in the nation's history, the law jealously guarded the rights of parents while according little attention to the rights of children. This attitude is still a strong influence in our current approach to the problems of abuse, neglect, and exploitation. The protective service agency has to move with considerable circumspection and with clear evidence of harmful conduct, lest it be accused of unwarranted meddling: "The rights of parents are protected by tradition and precedent" (Downs, 1963, p. 133), a tradition and precedent older and more firmly established than any tradition or precedent in favor of the child.

As concepts of children's needs and the context for child rearing change, the protective service agency may be faced with some difficult questions. Is a parent who fails to provide psychiatric treatment for an emotionally disturbed child guilty of neglect? Is provision of orthodontia or plastic surgery required of the parent when the child's emotional and social adjustment may be materially improved as a consequence? Is a child cared for in a hippie commune where marijuana may be frequently used or a child living with a lesbian couple in need of protective service intervention? In 1974 two lesbian mothers won a court decision permitting them to retain custody of their natural children and to maintain a common residence. However, in December 1975, in another case, a jury of ten men and two women "decided that the 9 year old son of a self-described lesbian should be taken from his mother and placed in the custody of the father" (*The New York Times*, December 24, 1975).

Neglect statutes presuppose that we know the nature of the favorable child-rearing context. But given the wider variety of ways children are being cared for currently, on what basis does the agency decide which ways are deleterious to the child? How far may the state intrude into what is an essentially private relationship between parents and child? However benevolent the intention, such intrusion, unless clearly limited, may pose a danger to freedom.

The liberalization of abortion and birth control laws is based on the premise that these decisions are private family matters that should be free from community control. The development of a more active role for protective services is a move toward the broadening of community responsibility for intervention in private matters. Consequently, it is argued that clearly deleterious effects on the child of the parents' behavior rather than the parents' behavior itself should be the basis for a neglect action. If the parents' circumspect promiscuity or discreet alcoholism has no damaging effects on the child, the state should not intervene. More frequently, parental "fitness," rather than demonstrated danger to the child, seems the criterion for intervention.

It has been noted, however, that the reluctance to interfere with parental rights leads to reluctance to report instances of neglect or abuse. Consequently such cases come to the attention of the protective service agency only when the neglect and abuse have become extreme. The reluctance may ultimately have tragic consequences.

In 1953 a boy of thirteen was referred to a children's court because of chronic truancy. A psychiatric examination established the fact that the boy was "drawn to violence" and represented "a serious danger to himself and to others." Psychiatric treatment was recommended by the psychiatrist and the social workers concerned with the boy's situation. The mother refused to accept the recommendation and refused to bring the boy back for treatment. Should the mother have been forced to accept treatment for the boy? This is the question of limits of protective intervention. Nothing was done. Ten years later the boy, Lee Harvey Oswald, assassinated President Kennedy.

2. Legislation mandating reporting by professionals of cases of child mal-treatment and the development of central registries for such reports presents problems for the protective service field (Gibelman, Grant, 1978).

There is a growing disjunction between an increasingly successful reporting system that brings more and more families to the attention of the community and the resources available to help the families identified. The potential for effective service delivery decreases as the size of the clientele grows.

Florida's experience is often cited as a prime example of the potential for an increase in the case load as a consequence of a well-organized reporting system. Seventeen child abuse cases were reported in Florida in 1970. Following the inauguration of a twenty-four-hour WATS hot line in all parts of the state, backed by a program of education, Florida reported 19,120 cases of child abuse in 1971.

Without a commensurate increase in serve personnel, however, many reported cases remained uninvestigated, and even fewer were provided treatment (Cohen, Sussman, 1975).

There is some complaint that reporting laws are counterproductive. The knowledge that a doctor or a hospital is required to report abuse may make some abusive parents reluctant to bring a child for needed medical treatment. The considerable increase in maltreatment reports that follows the effective implementation of reporting laws imposes a very heavy investigatory burden on protective service agencies. Considerable staff time is involved in checking reports, many of which are not substantiated. This work reduces the staff time available for actually helping those families who need and can use help.

Because many reports are not substantiated (as already noted, nationally some 40 per cent are invalid), a sizable number of families are subjected to an agency intervention that proves ultimately to have been unwarranted.

Although it might be said that it is better to make some mistakes than to leave any abused children unidentified, the investigation itself is not a benign experience for those families who are unjustifiably reported. A family that is even temporarily labeled as possibly child abusing has to live with the anxieties provoked by the investigation, anxieties that are not easily expunged from the mind. Furthermore, even if the family name is deleted from the central registry, whatever suspicions are aroused in the neighborhood, if a protective service investigation becomes known, may affect the family's relationship with its neighbors.

The fact that reporting and subsequent intervention sometimes do not lead to treatment, even where the report is valid, limits the justification of intervention. The fact that treatment, even when provided, is often not helpful further reduces the justification for intervention.

Professional selectivity in reporting presents a problem. The national data available indicate that school personnel and social workers are the source of a sizable percentage of maltreatment reports. Doctors provide fewer reports, perhaps because only a small percentage of maltreated children may require medical attention. On the other hand, doctors have limited motivation to report. Although the laws generally provide immunity from any prosecution resulting from reporting, many doctors may be reluctant to accuse their patients of abuse or may see reporting as an infringement on the confidentiality of the doctor–patient relationship. More significantly, given the time and effort involved in reporting and the attendant risks, many doctors are not convinced that reporting serves any valid purpose. There is a general complaint that if they do report, they rarely get feedback on what has been done and that very often nothing is done that significantly alters the situation.

Although reporting laws make professionals who are required to report subject to prosecution if they fail to report cases of maltreatment, such prosecutions have been rare. However, successful suits have been filed against physicians, social workers, and police officers who were aware of a case of child abuse and their obligation to report it but failed to do so (Kohlman, 1974).

Most states have made provision for some kind of registry of child abuse and neglect reports. Such registries serve a variety of functions. They provide basic statistical information regarding child abuse and neglect. They provide reports on any given children, often through a source that is accessible twenty-four hours a day, seven days a week, so that doctors, social workers, or school administrators encountering any evidence of maltreatment can have information on previous incidents as a diagnostic aid.

However, the establishment of state registries has also presented a series of problems. The principal one is that a sizable percentage of the maltreatment reports are not subsequently substantiated. This means that the names of many people are initially included in the registry without justification. A procedure, then, needs to be established and, more importantly, consistently implemented for expunging those names from the record. Second, care must be taken to determine who should have access to such records, which contain sensitive, confidential information. Third, some think that knowing the past history of maltreatment may influence the clinician's diagnostic assessment of the situation he is currently facing.

3. Protective service agencies face a problem in differentiating their area of activity from that of agencies providing general services to children in their own home. Children who require protective services generally come from families with a great variety of problems. All social services to families with children at home are designed to prevent neglect and to protect the child from harm. The dilemma within the profession has been solved somewhat by the merging of protective service agencies with the child welfare agencies offering a general service.

4. There is a problem of overlapping concern in situations calling for protective service not only within the family of social work agencies but also between social work and other professional groups. Law enforcement agencies—the police, the courts—are also involved in protective service situations. Neglect, abuse, and exploitation are not only social problems but legal problems. Many communities have not yet clearly outlined the respective areas of responsibility of the police and the social agencies in protective cases or defined the procedure for effective coordination of the activities of these different agencies in such cases.

The police are also involved in receiving and investigating complaints of neglect and in verifying and evaluating complaints. In some communities, the police become involved in neglect cases because no protective service social agency is available, or none is available around the clock, as are the police.

Attempts have been made to promote cooperation between the police and the existing protective social agencies: the respective appropriate roles and administrative liaison are defined; referral procedures are spelled out; a police officer may be assigned to a social agency; or a police officer and a social worker may jointly investigate a complaint. But because of the lack of clear-cut assignment of responsibility in many communities, there are no "clearly defined channels of communication that enable responsible citizens to know how and where to take action" if they become aware of a situation requiring action (Young, 1964, p. 137).

Maltreatment is often a medical problem as well as a legal and social problem. Consequently there may be possible points of confusion between the responsibilities of doctors and nurses and those of social workers.

Coordination and cooperation are required in situations where there is possible conflict as to who does what for the client.

5. Although all child welfare agencies face the problem of personnel shortages and high turnover rates, the protective service agencies face particular problems in recruiting staff, especially professionally trained social workers. The problem results partly from the nature of the clientele served and the problem situations for which protective service agencies have responsibility. Because the clients do not initiate the request for service themselves, the social workers may, and do, encounter a great measure of critical hostility and resistance. These require of the worker a great deal of patience, strength, and persistence.

Also, many of the clients have been referred to the protective service agency before. As one protective service worker notes:

Most cases which eventually land with the protective agency have been "around the horn" of community services. They display amazing consistency in their "inability to use help" but the protective agency must do something with them! Thus it finds itself with a large and concentrated load of seriously pathological case situations [Philbrick, 1960, p. 7].

Given the same expenditure of effort, the worker is more likely to be rewarded by gratifying client change in contact with the more voluntary client of the family service agency or the child guidance clinic. Noting the great turnover of workers who were assigned to neglectful families, Young (1964) reports that "a good number of the workers said that the apparent futility of their efforts was one of the chief causes of change for them" (p. 114).

In addition to the emotional discomfort involved in working with resistant, seemingly unappreciative clients, there is the physical discomfort and the occasional revulsion experienced by the worker in his encounter with the stink and dirt and disorder characteristic of many neglect cases.

Another aspect of the problem lies in the fact that the social workers in a protective service agency face a conflict between their professional image and the demands of the job. In a study of 110 social workers, Billingsley (1964a) concluded that this discrepancy between the realities of practice and the preferences of workers "is significantly more prevalent among social workers in a child protective agency than among their counterparts in the family counseling agency" (p. 477). The worker's professional orientation emphasizes voluntarism and self-determination, but the job frequently requires him to seek legal sanctions and other action that is in opposition to the parents' wishes.

The job is characterized by a high level of role strain. One aspect of the job requires interventions that are contradicted by other job demands: "Thus, with a given client, the social worker in a child protective agency is required to be a kindly, understanding, nonjudgmental, and accepting therapist; and, at the same time, a firm, resolute, and determined representative of the formal authority of community norms" (Billingsley, 1964b, pp. 17–18).

In dealing with this conflict, workers noted that they "often found the mental and emotional gymnastics necessary (in separating the therapeutic and investigatory responsibilities) a source of strain and guilt and at times our position was quite untenable" (Baher et al., 1976, p. 115).

The characteristics associated with the successful protective-service worker suggest the difficulty of the assignment. Such workers should have a "high tolerance for anger, a relative absence of fear in the face of rage, a willingness to act as a sponge for anger and an ability to use their authority while conveying sympathy and understanding" (Holmes, 1977, p. 160). They should be able to accept hostility from the client without a need to retaliate and to accept rejection without being immobilized. They need to accept client dependence without threatening client independence. They should be able to maintain their morale and convictions in the face of client complaints and ingratitude, frequent failures, and limited success.

As a consequence of these difficult demands, "burn-out" (see pp. 692–694) is more frequently encountered among protective service workers than in other child welfare services.

These, then, are some of the factors that affect recruitment and turnover in protective service agencies.

TRENDS

We have already noted some of the recent trends in protective services: the "rediscovery" of child abuse, the greater involvement of the medical profession in this area of concern, federal support for research demonstration projects, the education of personnel, the passage of state reporting laws, the broadening of the focus of concern to include emotional maltreatment, the greater involvement of public agencies in protective services, and a relative reduction in private agency effort.

Some long-term trends and additional short-term trends might also be noted.

1. The most significant long-term trend in protective services has been the move from a punitive approach to a cooperative one. At one time, the tendency was to remove the child from the home; now much more emphasis is being placed on constructive efforts to rehabilitate the family. The neglectful parent is now less frequently viewed as a willful criminal who should be punished and from whom the child needs to be rescued; he is seen as a troubled person needing help. The trend is to view neglect as a defect, not a vice. The focus of protective service is not protection of the child from the parent but protection of the child from neglect. As Moss (1963) notes, "Children are best protected by adequately functioning parents" (p. 386). Thus the approach now involves identifying and treating the factors that underlie parental neglect as against a previous focus on investigation, adjudication, and punishment.

2. There is increasing recognition that child neglect and abuse, despite their legal aspects, are the concern of social work. Legal sanctions can do little beyond restraining the parents from inflicting harm and damage on the child, and the major problem involves providing for the child's adequate continuing care and custody. As the best protection for a child is an adequately functioning family in which parental roles are effectively implemented, this is a problem for child welfare agencies, not for the police and the courts.

3. There has been a trend toward attempting preventive services. Preventive child-abuse-treatment programs involve the identification of parents who are at high risk for abuse. This is done through a questionnaire, the answers to which supposedly distinguish between mothers who show an attitudinal acceptance of their recently born child and those who indicate a rejection of the child. The questionnaire responses may be supplemented by staff observation of mother–infant interaction shortly after birth.

Negative "nesting" behavior and "claiming" behavior of mothers are noted as indicative of high risk for abuse. If the mother has made little preparation for the child's care on leaving the hospital or if the mother is hesitant about naming the baby, holding the baby, and feeding the baby while in the hospital, this behavior is suggestive of rejection. If the mother is actively repelled by the child's odor, drooling, excrement, or regurgitation, this reaction supposedly points to later difficulty. The preventive program provides education and support of the mother, the active involvement of community agencies that might be of help, and explicit follow-up.

4. Because of the complexity of diagnosis and because of the variety of treatment programs and resources that might be needed in treatment, child protection teams have been developed as a service delivery innovation (Schmitt, 1978). This approach permits a more comprehensive and valid diagnostic assessment,

with contributions from professionals having expertise in different areas. A team approach also permits a more effective coordination of the many agencies that may be involved in a program of treatment. The team serves a supportive function in that it permits sharing responsibility for difficult decisions, hence limiting the anxiety and guilt of any one member. A team also provides an opportunity for approbation from peers—a gratifying reward in an area of service where the rewards are few and limited.

The basic team includes a social worker, a physician, a psychiatrist or psychologist, and a team coordinator or case manager. Additional team members might include an attorney, a child development specialist, a law enforcement representative, and a public health nurse.

Child abuse teams may operate under the auspices of a local child protective services unit or may be based in a hospital with a pediatric service.

Some states have specifically mandated the creation of multidisciplinary child-protection teams in their reporting legislation.

Teams have a variety of names with dramatic acronyms: SCAN (Suspected Child Abuse and Neglect Team); DART (Detection, Admission, Reporting, Treatment Team) (National Center on Child Abuse and Neglect, 1978a).

SUMMARY

Protective services are organized in response to the community's responsibility to protect the child from neglect, abuse, exploitation, and the dangers of living in a morally hazardous environment. Protective services have some distinctive attributes:

1. The client is generally involuntary; agency action is initiated by a person other than the client or by a community agency.
2. The agency is obligated to offer the service to protect the child and to remain in the situation until satisfied that the child is no longer in danger.
3. The agency operates with legal authority delegated by the community and can invoke legal sanctions to protect the child.

Neglect is the most common kind of complaint requiring protective service. This may manifest itself as neglect of the child's needs for adequate food, shelter, clothing, medical care, or education. Less frequently, neglect of the child's emotional needs is the cause of a complaint. Abuse, although dramatic in nature and serious in consequences, accounts for a more limited percentage of the protective service cases.

Neglect appears to be a response to social stress. More often than not, the neglectful mother has no husband, is living on a marginal income and in substandard housing, and is responsible for the care of an atypically large family of children.

Abuse appears to be a response to psychological stress. The parent is reacting to internal conflicts, selects one child in the family as a victim, and responds to his misbehavior in a disproportionate manner. Families referred for protective service are generally living under socially stressful situations.

Protective services have become more generally available with recent increasing interest in child abuse and neglect. Public welfare agencies are accepting responsibility for the service as part of their general services to children, and Title XX funds provide support for such services.

Although the child is the client, the parent is the focus of service. The general social-work orientation that views the client, despite his defects, as someone who should be approached with an attitude of understanding and acceptance is applicable, with modifications, in protective service cases. Here, however, the worker needs to be free to exercise authority in order to protect the child and needs to make unambiguously explicit to the family the nature of agency expectations regarding more adequate care of the child.

The few studies available on the evaluation of protective services suggest that the program is effective in ensuring more adequate care for children in danger. Among the problems noted were the following:

1. The lack of norms regarding standards of adequate parental care that would permit identification of those situations warranting community intervention.
2. The lack of consensus regarding the respective rights of parents and children so that it is clear when the child's rights are being violated.
3. The difficulty in clearly differentiating protective services from general child welfare services to children in their own homes.
4. The difficulties in recruiting protective service workers because of the resistant, multiproblem clientele served and the conflict, for the worker, between professional ideology and the requirements of the service.

Among the new trends noted were the following:

1. The move from a punitive law-enforcement orientation to an approach centered on working cooperatively with the family to effect change.
2. The diminishing extent of voluntary agency responsibility for protective services, and the increasing public agency responsibility for the service.
3. The development of more active case-finding procedures, as exemplified by the "aggressive" or "assertive" social-work approach to multiproblem families.
4. The modification of the traditional psychotherapeutic approach to the client to include a greater emphasis on sociotherapy and a more directive approach.
5. The concern with child abuse and the widespread adoption of legislation to permit identification of and action with abusive parents.
6. The growing acceptance of protective services as primarily a social work function and the development of new resources and innovations such as good-neighbor homes, emergency parents, and client organizations such as Parents Anonymous.

BIBLIOGRAPHY

ALLEN, ANNE, and ARTHUR MORTON. *This Is Your Child.* London: Kegan Paul, Trench, Trubner & Co., 1961.

ALLEN, LETITIA S. "Child Abuse: A Critical Review of the Research and Theory," pp.

43–79, in *Violence and the Family*. Ed. by J. P. Martin. New York: John Wiley & Sons, Inc., 1978.

AMERICAN ACADEMY OF PEDIATRICS. *A Descriptive Study of Nine Health-Based Programs in Child Abuse and Neglect*. Evanston, Ill.: American Academy of Pediatrics, April 1974.

AMERICAN HUMANE SOCIETY. *Report of National Agencies Workshop on Child Protective Services*, Part I. Denver: American Humane Association, 1957.

——. *Protecting the Battered Child*. Denver: American Humane Association, 1963.

——. *National Analysis of Official Child Neglect and Abuse Reporting*. Denver: American Humane Society, 1978.

AMERICAN MEDICAL ASSOCIATION. "The Battered Child Syndrome—Editorial." *Journal of the American Medical Association*, **181** (1962).

AMERICAN PUBLIC WELFARE ASSOCIATION. *Preventive and Protective Services to Children: A Responsibility of the Public Welfare Agency*. Chicago: American Public Welfare Association, 1958.

ANTLER, STEPHEN. "Child Abuse: An Emerging Social Priority." *Social Work*, **23**, 1 (January 1978), 58–61.

ARNOLD, MILDRED. *Termination of Parental Rights*. Denver: American Humane Association, 1962.

ARVANIAN, ANN L. "Treatment of Abusive Parents," pp. 93–101, in *Child Abuse—Intervention and Treatment*. Ed. by Nancy B. Ebeling and Deborah A. Hill. Acton, Mass.: Publishing Sciences Group, Inc., 1975.

BAHER, EDWINA. *At Risk: An Account of the Work of the Battered Child Research Department. National Society for Prevention of Cruelty to Children*. Boston: Routledge, Kegan Paul, 1976.

BAKAN, DAVID. *Slaughter of the Innocents*. San Francisco: Jossey-Bass, Inc., 1971.

BANDLER, LOUISE S. "Casework, a Process of Socialization: Gains, Limitations, and Conclusions," in *The Drifters, Children of Disorganized Lower-Class Families*. Ed. by Eleanor Pavenstedt. Boston: Little, Brown and Company, 1967.

BEAN, SHIRLEY L. "The Use of Specialized Daycare in Preventing Child Abuse," pp. 137–142, in *Child Abuse: Treatment and Intervention*. Ed. by Nancy B. Ebeling and Deborah A. Hill. Acton, Mass.: Publishing Sciences Group, Inc., 1975.

BECK, BERTRAM. "Protective Services Revitalized." *Child Welfare*, **34** (November–December 1955).

BECKER, THOMAS T. *Due Process and Child Protective Proceedings—State Intervention in Family Relations on Behalf of Neglected Children*. Denver: American Humane Society, 1972.

BEDGER, JEAN, et al. *Child Abuse and Neglect—An Explanatory Study of Factors Related to the Mistreatment of Children*. Chicago: Council for Community Services, 1976.

BEEZLEY, PATRICIA, HAROLD MARTIN, and HELEN ALEXANDER. "Comprehensive Family Oriented Therapy," pp. 169–194, in *Child Abuse and Neglect—The Family and the Community*. Ed. by Ray E. Helfer and C. Henry Kempe. Cambridge, Mass.: Ballinger Publishing Co., 1976.

BELL, CYNTHIA, and WALLACE S. MYLNIEC. "Preparing for Neglect Proceedings: A Guide for the Social Worker." *Public Welfare*, **32** (Fall 1974), 26–37.

BELLUCCI, MATILDA T. "Group Treatment of Mothers in Child Protection Cases." *Child Welfare*, **41**, 2 (February 1972), 110–116.

BENJAMIN, LISELOTTE. *Protective Services: A Guide to Its Concepts and Principles*. Pennsylvania Department of Welfare, Bureau of Children's Services, May 1958. Mimeo.

BERKELEY PLANNING ASSOCIATES. *Evaluation, National Demonstration Program in Child Abuse and Neglect*. Berkeley, California: Berkeley Planning Associates, 1977.

BETTER HOMES AND GARDENS. *What's Happening to the American Family—Attitudes and Opinions of 302,602 Respondents.* New York: Meredith Corporation, April 1978.

BILLINGSLEY, ANDREW. "The Role of the Social Worker in a Child Protective Agency." *Child Welfare,* 43 (November 1964a).

———. *The Role of the Social Worker in a Child Protective Agency: A Comparative Analysis.* Boston: Massachusetts Society for the Prevention of Cruelty to Children, January 1964b.

———, et al. *Studies in Child Protective Service: Final Report to the Children's Bureau,* September 1969. Mimeo.

———, and JEANNE M. GIOVANNONI. "Child Neglect Among the Poor: A Study of Parental Adequacy in Families of Three Ethnic Groups." *Child Welfare,* 49, 4 (April 1970), 196–203.

BISHOP, JULIA ANN. *An Intensive Casework Project in Child Protective Services.* Denver: American Humane Association, 1963.

———. "Helping Neglectful Parents." *Programs and Problems in Child Welfare. Annals of the American Academy of Political and Social Science,* 355 (September 1964).

BLUMENTHAL, MONICA D., et al. *More about Justifying Violence—Methodological Studies of Attitudes and Behavior.* Ann Arbor: University of Michigan Institute for Social Research, 1975.

BOARDMAN, HELEN E. "A Project to Rescue Children from Inflicted Injuries." *Social Work,* 7 (January 1962).

BOEHM, BERNICE. "An Assessment of Family Adequacy in Protective Cases." *Child Welfare,* 41 (January 1962).

———. "The Community and the Social Agency Define Neglect." *Child Welfare,* 43 (November 1964).

———. "Protective Services for Neglected Children." *Social Work Practice.* New York: Columbia University Press, 1968.

BOURKE, WILLIAM. "The Overview Study—Purpose, Method, and Basic Findings," in *An Intensive Casework Project in Child Protective Services.* Denver: American Humane Association, 1963.

BROMBAUGH, OLIVE. "Discussion." *Child Welfare,* 36 (February 1957).

BROWN, H. FREDERICK. *Treatment Strategies in the Deployment of Emergency Care-takers in Child Abuse and Neglect Cases.* Chicago, Illinois: University of Illinois at Chicago Circle, April 1979.

BRYANT, HAROLD D., et al. "Physical Abuse of Children: An Agency Study." *Child Welfare,* 42 (March 1963).

BURGESS, ANN W., LYNDA L. HOLSTROM, and MAREEN P. MCCAUSLAND. "Child Sexual Assault by a Family Member: Decisions Following Disclosure." *Victimology,* 2, 2 (Summer 1977), 236–245.

BURT, MARVIN, and RALPH BALYEAT. "A New System for Improving the Care of Neglected and Abused Children." *Child Welfare,* 53 (March 1974), 167–169.

———. *A Comprehensive Emergency Services System for Neglected and Abused Children.* New York: Vantage Press, 1977.

CANADIAN WELFARE COUNCIL. *Child Protection in Canada.* Ottawa: Canadian Welfare Council, 1954.

CAULFIELD, BARBARA. *The Legal Aspects of Protective Services for Abused and Neglected Children.* Washington, D.C.: U.S. Government Printing Office, 1978.

COHEN, STEPHEN S., and ALAN SUSSMAN. "The Incidence of Child Abuse in the United States." *Child Welfare,* 44 (June 1975), 432–443.

COLLINS, MARILYN C. *Child Abuser—A Study of Child Abusers in Self-help Group Therapy.* Littleton, Mass.: PSG Publishing Co., 1978.

COLUMBIA JOURNAL OF LAW AND SOCIAL PROBLEMS. "Representation in Child Neglect Cases: Are Parents Neglected?" *Columbia Journal of Law and Social Problems*, **4**, 2 (July 1968), 230–254.

COOMBES, PHYLLIS, MAUREEN McCORMACK, MARY CHIPLEY, and BEVERLY ARCHER. "The INCADEX Approach to Evaluating Problems and Evaluating Impact in Child Protective Services." *Child Welfare*, **57**, 1 (January 1978), 35–44.

DAVOREN, ELIZABETH. "Services to Multi-Problem Families," pp. 111–113, in *Child Abuse and Neglect—3rd National Conference, April 1977*. Washington, D.C.: U.S. Printing Office, 1978.

———. "The Role of the Social Worker," in *The Battered Child*. Ed. by Ray E. Helfer and C. Henry Kempe. Chicago: University of Chicago Press, 1968.

DeFRANCIS, VINCENT. *The Fundamentals of Child Protection*. Denver: American Humane Association, 1955.

———. *Special Skills in Child Protective Services*. Denver: American Humane Association, 1958.

———. *Child Abuse: Preview of a Nationwide Survey*. Denver: American Humane Association, 1963.

———. *Child Protective Services in the United States: A Nationwide Survey*. Denver: American Humane Association, 1967.

DELSORDO, JAMES. "Protective Casework for Abused Children." *Children*, **10** (November–December 1963).

DE MAUSE, LLOYD (Ed.). *The History of Childhood*. New York: The Psychohistory Press, 1974.

DOWNS, WILLIAM T. "The Meaning and Handling of Child Neglect: A Legal View." *Child Welfare*, **42** (March 1963).

EDUCATION COMMISSION OF THE STATES. *Trends in Child Abuse and Neglect Reporting Statutes*. Denver: Education Commission of the States, Child Abuse Project, January 1977.

ELMER, ELIZABETH. "A Follow-up Study of Traumatized Children." *Pediatrics*, **59**, 2 (February 1977), 273–314.

———. *Fragile Families, Troubled Children—The Aftermath of Infant Trauma*. Pittsburgh: The University of Pittsburgh Press, 1977.

ERLANGER, HOWARD S. "Social Class Differences in Parents' Use of Physical Punishment," pp. 150–158 in *Violence in the Family*, eds. Suzanne K. Steimmetz and Murry A. Strauss. New York: Dodd, Mead, 1974.

FERGUSSON, DAVID M., JOAN FLEMING and DAVID P. O'NEILL. *Child Abuse in New Zealand*. Wellington, New Zealand: A. R. Shearer, 1972.

FINKELHOR, DAVID. "Psychological, Cultural and Family Factors in Incest and Family Sexual Abuses." *Journal of Marriage and Family Counseling* (October 1978), 41–49.

FITCH, MICHAEL J., et al. *Prospective Study in Child Abuse: The Child Study Program*. Denver: Developmental Evaluation Center, 1977.

FOLKS, HOMER. *The Care of Destitute, Neglected, and Delinquent Children*. New York: The Macmillan Company, 1902.

FONTANA, VINCENT S. *The Maltreated Child*, 2nd ed. Springfield, Ill.: Charles C Thomas, Publishers, 1971.

FONTANA, VINCENT, and ESTHER ROBESON. "A Multidisciplinary Approach to the Treatment of Child Abuse," *Pediatrics*, **57**, 5 (May 1976), 760–764.

FOREN, ROBERT, and ROYSTON BAILEY. *Authority in Social Casework*. New York: Pergamon Press, 1968.

FRIEDMAN, R. "Child Abuse: A Review of the Psychosocial Research," in *Four Perspectives on the Status of Child Abuse and Neglect Research*. Washington, D.C.: National Center on Child Abuse and Neglect, 1976.

FRIEDRICH, WILLIAM N., and JERRY A. BORISKIN. "The Role of the Child in Abuse: A Review of the Literature." *American Journal of Orthopsychiatry*, 46, 4 (October 1976), 580–590.

GARBARINO, S. "Some Ecological Correlates of Child Abuse: The Impact of Socioeconomic Stress on Mothers." *Child Development*, 47 (1976), 178–185.

GARBARINO, JAMES. "The Price of Privacy in the Social Dynamics of Child Abuse." *Child Welfare*, 56, 9 (November 1977), 565–575.

GARDNER, LESLIE. "The Gildoy Center: A Method of Intervention for Child Abuse," pp. 143–150, in *Child Abuse Treatment and Intervention*. Ed. by Nancy B. Ebeling and Deborah A. Hill. Acton, Mass.: Sciences Publishing Group, Inc., 1975.

GELLES, RICHARD J. *The Violent Home*. Beverly Hills, Calif.: Sage Publications, 1972.

———. "Child Abuse as Psychopathology: A Sociological Critique and Reformulation." *American Journal of Orthopsychiatry*, 43 (July 1973), 611–621.

———. "Violence Toward Children in the United States." *American Journal of Orthopsychiatry*, 48, 4 (October 1978), 580–592.

GESMONDE, J. "Emotional Neglect in Connecticut." *Connecticut Law Review*, 5 (Summer 1972), 100–116.

GIARRETTO, HENRY. "The Treatment of Father–Daughter Incest—A Psychosocial Approach." *Children Today*, 5 (July–August 1976), 2–5.

GIBELMAN, MARGARET, and STUART GRANT. "The Uses and Misuses of Central Registries in Child Protective Services." *Child Welfare*, 57, 7 (July–August 1978), 405–413.

GIL, DAVID G. *Violence Against Children: Physical Child Abuse in the United States*. Cambridge, Mass.: Harvard University Press, 1970.

GILLESPIE, DAVID F., JAMES R. SEABERG, and SHARON BERLIN. "Observed Causes of Child Abuse." *Victimology*, 2, 2 (Summer 1977), 342–349.

GIOVANNONI, JEANNE M. "Parental Mistreatment: Perpetrators and Victims." *Journal of Marriage and the Family*, 33 (November 1971), 649–657.

GLADSTON, RICHARD. "Preventing the Abuse of Little Children—The Parents Center Project for the Study and Prevention of Child Abuse." *American Journal of Orthopsychiatry*, 45 (1975), 372–380.

GORDON, HENRIETTA. "Protective Services for Children." *Child Welfare*, 25 (May 1946).

———. "Emotional Neglect." *Child Welfare*, 38 (February 1959).

GRAY, JANE, CHRISTY CUTLER, JANET DEAN, and C. HENRY KEMPE. "Perinatal Assessment of Mother–Baby Interaction," pp. 377–388, in *Child Abuse and Neglect: The Family and the Community*. Ed. by R. E. Helfer and C. H. Kempe. Cambridge, Mass.: Ballinger, 1976.

GRAY, JANE D., CHRISTY A. CUTLER, JANET G. DEAN and C. HENRY KEMPE. "Prediction and Prevention of Child Abuse and Neglect," pp. 246–254 in *Proceedings of the 2nd National Conference on Child Abuse and Neglect*, Vol. 2. Washington, D.C.: U.S. Government Printing Office, 1978.

GREEN, ARTHUR, RICHARD W. GAINES, and ALICE SANDGRAND. "Child Abuse: Pathological Syndrome of Family Interaction." *American Journal of Psychiatry*, 131 (August 1974), 882–886.

GREEN, ARTHUR. "A Psychodynamic Approach to the Study and Treatment of Child Abusing Parents." *Journal of the American Academy of Child Psychiatry*, 15 (Summer 1976), 414–429.

GROENVELD, LYLE P., and JEANNE M. GIOVANNONI. "Disposition of Child Abuse and Neglect Cases." *Social Work Research and Abstracts*, 13 (Summer 1977), 24–31.

HANCOCK, CLAIR. *Digest of a Study of Protective Services and the Problem of Neglect of Children in New Jersey*. Trenton, N.J.: State Board of Child Welfare, 1958.

————. *Children and Neglect—Hazardous Home Conditions.* Washington, D.C.: Government Printing Office, 1963.

HELFER, RAY. *Diagnostic Process and Treatment Programs.* Washington, D.C.: Government Printing Office, 1975.

HELFER, RAY, CAROL SCHNEIDER, and JAMES HOFFMEISTER. *Report on Research Using the Michigan Screening Profile of Parenting.* East Lansing: Michigan State University, May 1978.

HENRY, CHARLOTTE. *Hand-to-Reach Clients.* Cleveland, Ohio, May 1958. Mimeo.

HENRY, JULES. *Culture Against Man.* New York: Random House, Inc., 1963.

HOLLIDAY, KATE. "Dial-a-Family." *This Week* (August 4, 1968).

HOLMES, MONICA. *Child Abuse and Neglect Programs: Practice and Theory.* Rockville, Md.: National Institute of Mental Health, 1977.

HOLMES, SALLY. "Parents Anonymous: A Treatment Method for Child Abuse." *Social Work,* 23, 2 (May 1978), 245–247.

HOLTER, JOAN C., and STANFORD B. FRIEDMAN. "Principles of Management in Child Abuse Cases." *American Journal of Orthopsychiatry,* 38, 1 (January 1968), 127–135.

HOROWITZ, BERNARD, and WENDY WINTERMUTE. "Use of an Emergency Fund in Protective Services Casework." *Child Welfare,* 57, 7 (July–August 1978), 432–437.

HOUSDEN, L. G. *The Prevention of Cruelty to Children.* London: Jonathan Cape, Ltd., 1955.

HUNT, DAVID. *Parents and Children in History.* New York: Basic Books, Inc., 1970.

HUNTER, ROSEMARY, NANCY KILSTROM, ERNEST KRAYBILL, and FRANK LODA. "Antecedents of Child Abuse and Neglect in Premature Infants: A Prospective Study in a Newborn Intensive Unit." *Pediatrics,* 61, 4 (April 1978), 629–635.

HYMAN, IRWIN A., ANTHONY BONGIOVANNI, ROBERT H. FRIEDMAN, and EILEEN McDOMILL. "Paddling, Punishing and Force: Where Do We Go From Here." *Children Today* (September–October 1977), 19–23.

JAMES, HOWARD. *Children in Trouble.* New York: David McKay Co., Inc., 1970.

JAYARATNE, SRINIKA. "Child Abusers as Parents and Children: A Review." *Social Work,* 22, 1 (January 1977), 5–9.

JOHNSON, BETTY, and HAROLD MORSE. "Injured Children and Their Parents." *Children,* 15, 4 (July–August 1968), 147–152.

JOHNSON, CLARA. *Two Community Protective Service Systems: Nature and Effectiveness of Service Intervention.* Athens, Ga.: Regional Institute of Social Welfare Research, 1977.

JONES, CAROLYN O. "The Fate of Abused Children," pp. 108–121, in *The Challenge of Child Abuse.* Ed. by Alfred W. Franklin. New York: Grune & Stratton, Inc., 1978.

JUSTICE, BLAIR, and RITA JUSTICE. *The Abusing Family.* New York: Human Services Press, 1976.

JUVENILE PROTECTIVE ASSOCIATION. *The Bowen Center Project—A Report of a Demonstration in Child Protective Services, 1965–1971.* Chicago: Juvenile Protective Association, 1975.

KAGAN, JEROME. "The Child in the Family." *Daedalus,* 106, 2 (Spring 1977), 33–56.

KAHN, ALFRED. *Planning Community Services for Children in Trouble.* New York: Columbia University Press, 1963.

KALISCH, BEATRICE J. *Child Abuse and Neglect—An Annotated Bibliography.* Westport, Conn.: Greenwood Press, 1978.

KATZ, SANFORD. "The Legal Basis for Child Protection," in *Proceedings of Institutes on Protective and Related Community Services.* Richmond, Va.: Richmond School of Social Work, 1968.

————. *When Parents Fail—The Law's Response to Family Breakdown.* Boston: The Beacon Press, Inc., 1971.

————, RUTH-ARLENE W. HOWE, and MELBA MCGRATH. "Child Neglect Laws in America." *Family Law Quarterly,* 9, 1 (Spring 1975), entire issue.

KAUFMAN, IRVING. "The Contribution of Protective Services." *Child Welfare,* 36 (February 1957).

————. "Psychodynamics of Protective Casework," in *Ego-Oriented Casework.* Ed. by Howard Varad and Roger Muller. New York: Family Service Association of America, 1963.

KELLY, JOSEPH B. "What Protective Services Can Do." *Child Welfare,* 38 (April 1959).

KELMAN, HERBERT E. "Processes of Opinion Change." *Public Opinion Quarterly* (Spring 1961).

KEMPE, C. HENRY, et al. "The Battered Child Syndrome." *Journal of the American Medical Association,* 181 (1962).

————, and RAY E. HELFER (Eds.). *The Battered Child.* Chicago: University of Chicago Press, 1968. 2nd Edition, 1974.

———— (Eds.). *Helping the Battered Child and His Family.* Philadelphia: J. B. Lippincott Co., 1972.

KENT, J. T. "A Followup Study of Abused Children." *Journal of Pediatric Psychology,* 1 (Spring 1976), 25–31.

KNIGHT, MAUREEN, MILDRED DISBROW, and HANS DOERR. "Prediction of Child Abuse and Neglect Measures to Identify Parents' Potential," pp. 259–269, in *Proceedings of 2nd National Conference on Child Abuse and Neglect,* Vol. 2. Washington, D.C.: U.S. Government Printing Office, 1978.

KOHLMAN, R. "Malpractice Liability for Failing to Report Child Abuse." *Western Journal of Medicine,* 21 (1974), 244–248.

KORBIN, JILL. "Anthropological Contributions to the Study of Child Abuse." *International Child Welfare Review,* 35 (December 1977), 23–31.

KORSCH, BARBARA, JEWELL CHRISTIAN, ETHEL K. GOZZI, and PAUL V. CARLSON. "Infant Care and Punishment: A Pilot Study." *American Journal of Public Health,* 55, 12 (December 1965), 1880–1888.

LANE, LIONEL. "Aggressive Approach in Preventive Work with Children's Problems." *Social Casework,* 33 (February 1952).

LANE, SYLVIA, and VICKI VAN DYKE. "Lay Therapy: Intimacy as a Form of Treatment for Abusive Parents," pp. 162–167, in *Proceedings of the Second National Conference on Child Abuse and Neglect,* Vol. 2. Washington, D.C.: U.S. Government Printing Office, 1978.

LAUER, BRIAN, ELSA TEN BROECK, and MOSES GROSSMAN. "Battered Child Syndrome: A Review of 130 Patients with Controls." *Pediatrics,* 54 (July 1974), 67–76.

LIGHT, R. "Abused and Neglected Children in America: A Study of Alternative Policies." *Harvard Educational Review,* 43 (November 1973), 556–598.

LYNCH, MARGARET. "Risk Factors in the Child: A Study of Abused Children and Their Siblings," pp. 43–56, in *The Abused Child.* Ed. by Harold Martin. Cambridge, Mass.: Ballinger Publishing Co., 1976.

————, and CHRISTOPHER OUNSTED. "Residential Therapy—A Place of Safety," pp. 195–207, in *Child Abuse and Neglect.* Ed. by Ray E. Helfer and C. Henry Kempe. Cambridge, Mass.: Ballinger Publishing Co., 1976.

————, and JACQUELINE ROBERTS. "Predicting Child Abuse: Signs of Bonding Failure in the Maternity Hospital." *British Medical Journal* (March 5, 1977), 624–626.

LYSTAD, MARY H. "Violence at Home: A Review of the Literature." *American Journal of Orthopsychiatry,* 45 (April 1975), 328–344.

MAAS, HENRY, and RICHARD ENGLER. *Children in Need of Parents.* New York: Columbia University Press, 1959.

MACFARLANE, KEE, and LEONARD LIEBER. "Parents Anonymous: The Growth of an Idea," in *Child Abuse and Neglect*, June 1978. Washington, D.C.: National Center on Child Abuse and Neglect, 1978.

MADEN, MARC F., and DAVID F. WRENCH. "Significant Findings on Child Abuse Research." *Victimology*, **2**, 2 (Summer 1977), 196–224.

MARTIN, HAROLD P. *The Abused Child—A Multidisciplinary Approach to Developmental Issues and Treatment*. Cambridge, Mass.: Ballinger Publishing Co., 1976.

MARTIN, HAROLD, PATRICIA BEEZLEY, ESTHER F. CONWAY, et al. "The Development of Abused Children, Part I. A Review of the Literature; Part II, Physical, Neurological and Intellectual Outcome." *Advances in Pediatrics*, **21** (1974), pp. 25–73.

MARTIN, MARY P. *1977 Analysis of Child Abuse and Neglect Research*. Washington, D.C.: Government Printing Office, January 1978.

MASTRIA, ERNESTO, MARIE A. MASTRIA, and JEAN C. HARKINS. "Treatment of Child Abuse by Behavioral Intervention: A Case Report." *Child Welfare*, **58** (April 1979), 253–261.

MAURER, A. "Corporal Punishment." *American Psychologist*, **29**, 8 (August 1974), 614–626.

McCREA, ROSWELL. *The Humane Movement*. New York: Columbia University Press, 1910.

McFERRAN, JANE. "Parents' Discussion Meetings: A Protective Service Agency's Experience." *Child Welfare*, **36**, 7 (July 1957), 31–33.

————. "Parents' Groups in Protective Services." *Children*, **5** (November–December 1958).

McHENRY, THOMAS, et al. "Unsuspected Trauma with Multiple Skeletal Injuries During Infancy and Childhood." *Pediatrics*, **31** (June 1963).

MEDLEY, H. EARL. *A New Approach in Public Welfare in Serving Families with Abused or Neglected Children*. Nashville, Tenn.: Department of Public Welfare, May 25, 1967.

MEIER, ELIZABETH G. *Former Foster Children as Adult Citizens*. Unpublished Ph.D. Thesis. Columbia University, New York, April 1962.

————. "Child Neglect," in *Social Work and Social Problems*. Ed. by Nathan Cohen. New York: National Association of Social Workers, 1964.

MEISELMAN, KARIN C. *Incest—A Psychological Study of Causes and Effects with Treatment Recommendations*. San Francisco: Jossey-Bass, Inc., 1978.

MELNICK, BARRY, and JOHN R. HURLEY. "Distinctive Personality Attributes of Child-Abusing Mothers." *Journal of Consulting and Clinical Psychology*, **33**, 3 (March 1969), 746–749.

MERRILL, EDGAR J., et al. *Protecting the Battered Child*. Denver: American Humane Association, 1962.

MOHAMOUD, JOYCE. "Parents Anonymous in Minority Communities." *Protective Services Research Institute Report*, **2**, 7 (August–September 1977), pp. 5–6.

MOORE, CAROL W., et al. "A Three-Year Follow-Up Study of Abused and Neglected Children." *American Journal of Diseases of Children*, **120**, 5 (November 1970), 439–446.

MORRIS, MARIAN, and ROBERT GOULD. "Role Reversal: A Concept in Dealing with the Neglected–Battered Child Syndrome," in *The Neglected–Battered Child Syndrome*. New York: Child Welfare League of America, July 1963.

MOSS, SIDNEY. "Authority—An Enabling Factor in Casework with Neglected Parents." *Child Welfare*, **42** (October 1963), 385–391.

MUENHOW, ANN, and EDWARD SLATER. "Help for Families Coping with Incest: Rebuilding Families After Sexual Abuse of Children." *Social Work Practice Digest*, **1**, 2 (September 1978), 19–25.

MULFORD, ROBERT. "Emotional Neglect of Children." *Child Welfare*, 37 (January 1958).

———, *et al. Caseworker and Judge in Neglect Cases.* New York: Child Welfare League of America, 1956.

NAGI, SAAD Z. "Child Abuse and Neglect Programs: A National Overview." *Children Today*, 4, 3 (May 1975), 13–18.

———. *Child Maltreatment in the United States.* New York: Columbia University Press, 1977.

NATIONAL CENTER ON CHILD ABUSE AND NEGLECT. *Child Abuse and Neglect in Residential Institutions.* Washington, D.C.: Government Printing Office, 1978b.

———. *Multidisciplinary Teams in Child Abuse and Neglect Programs.* Washington, D.C.: Government Printing Office, 1978a.

NATIONAL EDUCATION ASSOCIATION. *Report of the Task Force on Corporal Punishment.* Washington, D.C.: National Education Association, 1972.

NETTLER, GWYNNE. *A Study of Opinions on Child Welfare in Harris County.* Houston, Tex.: Community Council of Houston and Harris County, October 1958.

NURSE, SHIRLEY M. "Familial Patterns of Parents Who Abuse Their Children." *Smith College Studies in Social Work*, 35 (October 1964).

OFFICE OF COMPTROLLER GENERAL OF THE UNITED STATES. *More Can Be Learned and Done About the Wellbeing of Children.* Washington, D.C.: Comptroller General's Office, April 1976.

———. *Children in Foster Care Institutions—Steps Government Can Take to Improve Their Care.* Washington, D.C.: Comptroller General's Office, 1977.

OLIVER, JACK. "Some Studies of Families in Which Children Suffer Maltreatment," pp. 16–37, in *The Challenge of Child Abuse.* Ed. by Alfred W. Franklin. New York: Grune & Stratton, Inc., 1977.

OVERTON, ALICE, and KATHERINE TINKER. *Casework Notebook*, 2nd ed. St. Paul, Minn.: Family-Centered Project, Greater St. Paul Community Chests and Councils, Inc., March 1959.

PAGET, NORMAN K. "Emergency Parents—A Protective Service to Children in Crises," *Child Welfare*, 46, 7 (July 1967).

PARKE, ROSS D., and CANDANCE W. COLLMER. "Child Abuse: An Interdisciplinary Analysis," pp. 509–90, in *Review of Child Development Research*, Vol. V. Chicago: University of Chicago Press, 1975.

PAULSON, MONRAD. "Legal Protection Against Child Abuse." *Children*, 13 (1966), 42–48.

PAULSON, MORRIS, *et al.* "Parents of the Battered Child." *Life Threatening Behavior*, 4, 1 (Spring 1974), 18–32.

PELTON, LEROY. "Child Abuse and Neglect—The Myth of Classlessness." *American Journal of Orthopsychiatry*, 48, 4 (October 1978), 608–616.

PENNER, LEWIS G. *The Protective Services Center—An Integrated Program to Protect Children.* Denver: American Humane Association, 1968.

PFOHL, STEPHEN. "The 'discovery' of Child Abuse." *Social Problems*, 24, 3 (February 1977), 310–323.

PHILBRICK, ELIZABETH. *Treating Parental Pathology—Through Child Protective Services.* Denver: American Humane Association, 1960.

PINCHBECK, IVY, and MARGARET HEWITT. *Children in English Society*, Vol. 1: *From Tudor Times to the Enlightenment Century.* London: Kegan Paul, Trench, Trubner & Co., 1969.

POLAKOW, ROBERT L., and DIXIE L. PEABODY. "Behavioral Treatment of Child Abuse." *International Journal of Offender Therapy and Comparative Criminology*, 19, 1 (1975), 100–113.

POLANSKY, NORMAN, et al. "Two Modes of Maternal Immaturity and Their Consequences." *Child Welfare*, **49**, 6 (June 1970), 312–323.
————, et al. "Verbal Accessibility in the Treatment of Child Neglect." *Child Welfare*,
50, 6 (June 1971), 349–356.
————, et al. *Child Neglect: Understanding and Reaching the Parent*. New York:
Child Welfare League of America, 1972.
————, et al. "Public Opinion and Intervention in Child Neglect." *Social Work Research and Abstracts*, **14** (Fall 1978), 11–15.
————, and DAVID WILLIAMS. "Class Orientations to Child Neglect." *Social Work*, **23**
(September 1978), 397–405.
————, R. D. BORGMAN, and C. DE SAIX. *Roots of Futility*. San Francisco: Jossey-Bass,
Inc., 1972.
————, MARY A. CHALMERS, ELIZABETH BUTTENWEIESER, and DAVID WILLIAMS.
"Assessing Adequacy of Child Caring in an Urban Scale." *Child Welfare*, **57**,
7 (July–August 1978), 439–449.
————, CHRISTIAN DESAIX, and SHLOMO SHARLIN. *Child Neglect: Understanding and
Reaching the Parent*. New York: Child Welfare League of America, 1972.
————, CAROLYN HALLY, and NANCY F. POLANSKY. *Child Neglect: State of Knowl-
edge*. Athens, Ga.: Regional Institute of Social Welfare Research, July 1974.
————, and LEONARD POLLANE. "Measuring Adequacy of Child Caring: Further De-
velopment." *Child Welfare*, **54** (May 1975), 354–359.
POLIER, JUSTINE W., and KAY MCDONALD. "The Family Court in an Urban Setting,"
in *Helping the Battered Child and His Family*. Ed. by C. Henry Kempe and
Ray E. Helfer. Philadelphia: J. B. Lippincott Co., 1972.
POWELL, THOMAS J. "Interpreting Parents Anonymous as a Source of Help for Those
with Child Abuse Problems." *Child Welfare*, **58**, 2 (February 1979), 105–113.
REAVLEY, WILLIAM, and MARIE THERESE GILBERT. "The Behavioral Treatment Ap-
proach to Potential Child Abuse: Two Illustrative Case Reports." *Social Work
Today*, **7**, 6 (1976), 166–68.
REIDY, THOMAS J. *The Aggressive Characteristics of Abused and Neglected Children*.
Chicago: Rehabilitation Institute of Chicago, 1975. Mimeo, 13 pp.
REIN, MARTIN. *Child Protective Services in Massachusetts*. Papers in Social Welfare,
No. 6. Waltham, Mass.: Florence Heller Graduate School for Advanced Studies
in Social Welfare, November 1963.
RINDFLEISCH, NOLAN. *Does Maltreatment of Children Exist in Child Welfare Institu-
tions?* Columbus: Ohio State University, May 1978, mimeo, 17 pp.
ROSENFELD, ALVIN A. "Incest and the Sexual Abuse of Children." *Journal of the
American Academy of Child Psychiatry*, **16** (1977), 334–336.
————. "Sexual Misuse and the Family." *Victimology*, **2**, 2 (Summer 1977), 226–235.
SANDUSKY, ANNIE L. "Protective Services," in *Encyclopedia of Social Work*. New York:
National Association of Social Workers, 1964.
————. "Services to Neglected Children." *Children*, **7** (January–February 1960).
SARAFINO, EDWARD. "An Estimate of Nationwide Incidence of Sexual Offenses Against
Chi'dren." *Child Welfare*, **58**, 2 (February 1979), 127–133.
SCHERER, LORENA. "Facilities and Services for Neglected Children in Missouri." *Crime
and Delinquency*, **6** (January 1960).
SCHMIDT, DOLORES M. "The Protective Service Caseworker: How Does He Survive
Job Pressures?" *Child Welfare*, **42** (March 1963).
SCHMITT, BARTON D. *The Child Protection Team Handbook—A Multidisciplinary Ap-
proach to Managing Child Abuse and Neglect*. New York: Garland STPM Press,
1978.
SCHULTZ, LEROY S. "The Child Sex Victim: Social, Psychological and Legal Prospectus."
Child Welfare, **52**, 3 (March 1973), 147–157.

SGROI, SUZANNE M. "Sexual Molestation of Children." *Children Today*, 4 (May–June 1975), 18–21.

SHERIDAN, WILLIAM, and PAT MANCINI. *A Social Worker Takes a Case into Court.* Washington, D.C.: Government Printing Office, 1962.

SILVER, LARRY, et al. "Does Violence Breed Violence? Contribution from a Study of the Child-Abuse Syndrome." *American Journal of Psychiatry*, 126, 3 (September 1969), 404–407.

SIMPSON, HELEN. "The Unfit Parent." *University of Detroit Law Review*, 39 (February 1962).

SMITH, DAVID H., and JAMES STERNFIELD. "The Hippie Communal Movement: Effects of Childbirth and Development." *American Journal of Orthopsychiatry*, 40, 3 (April 1970), 527–30.

SMITH, SELWYN H. *The Battered Child Syndrome Syndrome.* London: Thornton Butterworth, Ltd., 1975.

SOMAN, SHIRLEY C. "Emergency Parents." *Parade* (January 29, 1967).

SPINETTA, JOHN J., and DAVID RIGLER. "The Child Abusing Parent—A Psychological Review." *Psychological Bulletin*, 77, 4 (1972), 296–304.

STARK, RODNEY, and JAMES McEVOY. "Middleclass Violence." *Psychology Today* (November 1970), pp. 52–54, 111–112.

STARKWEATHER, CASSIE L., and S. MICHAEL TURNER. "Parents Anonymous: Reflection on the Development of a Self-help Group," pp. 151–157, in *Child Abuse Intervention and Treatment.* Ed. by Nancy B. Ebeling and Deborah A. Hill. Acton, Mass.: Publishing Sciences Group, Inc., 1975.

STEELE, BRANDT F. *Working with Abusive Parents from a Psychiatric Point of View.* National Center on Child Abuse and Neglect. Washington, D.C.: Government Printing Office, 1975.

————. "Violence within the Family," pp. 3–23, in *Child Abuse and Neglect—The Family and the Community.* Ed. by Ray E. Helfer and C. Henry Kempe. Cambridge, Mass.: Ballinger Publishing Co., 1976.

————, and CARL B. POLLOCK. "A Psychiatric Study of Parents Who Abuse Infants and Small Children," in *The Battered Child.* Ed. by Ray E. Helfer and C. Henry Kempe. Chicago: University of Chicago Press, 1968.

STEPHANSON, P. SUSAN. "Reaching Child Abusers Through Target Toddlers." *Victimology*, 2, 2 (Summer 1977), 310–316.

STOETZER, J. B. "The Juvenile Court and Emotional Neglect of Children." *University of Michigan Journal of Law Reform*, 8 (Winter 1975), 351–374.

STUDT, ELLIOT. "An Outline for Study of Social Authority Factors in Casework." *Social Casework*, 35, 6 (June 1954).

SUSSMAN, ALAN, and STEPHEN S. COHEN. *Reporting Child Abuse and Neglect: Guidelines for Legislation.* Cambridge, Mass.: Ballinger Publishing Co., 1975.

SWANSON, LYNN D. "Role of the Police in the Protection of Children from Neglect and Abuse." *Federal Probation*, 25 (March 1961).

TEN BROECK, ELSA. "The Extended Family Center: A House Away from Home for Abused Children and Their Parents." *Children Today*, 3 (March–April, 1974), 2–6.

THOMAS, A., H. G. BIRCH, and STELLA CHESS. *Behavioral Individuality in Early Childhood.* New York: New York University Press, 1963.

THOMSON, ELLEN M., and NORMAN PAGET. *Child Abuse—A Community Challenge.* Buffalo, N.Y.: Henry Stewart, 1971.

TORMES, YVONNE M. *Child Victims of Incest.* Denver: American Humane Association, Children's Division, 1963.

TRACY, JAMES J., CAROLYN BALLARD, and ELIZABETH H. CLARK. "Child Abuse Project: A Followup." *Social Work*, 20 (September 1975), 398–399.

TUSZYNSKI, ANN, and JAMES DOWD. "An Alternative Approach to the Treatment of Protective Services Families." *Social Casework,* **59,** 3 (March 1978), 175–179.

UNITED STATES DEPARTMENT OF HEALTH, EDUCATION and WELFARE. *Child Sexual Abuse—Incest, Assault and Sexual Exploitation.* Washington, D.C.: Government Printing Office, 1979.

VARON, EDITH. "Communication: Client, Community and Agency." *Social Work,* 9 (April 1964).

WALD, MICHAEL. "State Intervention on Behalf of 'Neglected' Children: A Search for Realistic Standards." *Stanford Law Review,* **27** (April 1975), 985–1039.

WALTERS, DAVID R. *Physical and Sexual Abuse of Children—Causes and Treatment.* Bloomington: Indiana University Press, 1975.

WILSON, THELMA GARRETT. *Ventura Ventures into Child Protective Service.* Denver: American Humane Association, 1960.

WOODEN, KENNETH. *Weeping in the Playtime of Others.* New York: McGraw-Hill Book Company, 1976.

YELAJA, SHAN KAR. *Authority and Social Work: Concept and Use.* Toronto: University of Toronto Press, 1971.

YOUNG, LEON R. "An Interim Report on an Experimental Program of Protective Service." *Child Welfare,* **45,** 7 (July 1966), 373–381.

YOUNG, LEONTINE. *Wednesday's Child.* New York: McGraw-Hill Book Company, 1964.

———. "The Preventive Nature of Protective Services," in *Proceedings of Institute on Protective and Related Community Services.* Richmond, Va.: Richmond School of Social Work, 1968.

ZALBA, SERAPIO R. "The Abused Child—A Survey of the Problem." *Social Work,* **11,** 4 (October 1966).

ADDENDUM

After this chapter was set in type, the national study report on maltreatment for 1978 became available (American Humane Association, *Official Child Neglect and Abuse Reporting, 1978;* Englewood, Colorado; October 1979). It indicated an increase in reports between 1977 and 1978, for a total of 575,506 reports for abuse and neglect in 1978. The report noted that since "not all incidents of maltreatment are reported," it is currently impossible to provide incidence data. Although the study reports provide the best national data base available, "what can be conclusively stated is that reporting statistics underrepresent the actual incidence of maltreatment on a national basis" (p. 8). The 1978 study confirmed once again that single-parent households, lower-income families, and nonwhites are overrepresented in maltreatment reports. Neglect is more frequent than abuse, and most maltreatment does not involve major physical trauma ["only 1.9 percent of involved children suffered injuries such as fractures or brain damage" (p. 42)]. The largest percentage of abused children are of school age, and "deprivation of necessities" is the most frequent maltreatment suffered. Mothers are more frequently involved in neglect and fathers more frequently involved in abuse. Parents are the most frequent perpetrators of abuse, and the educational achievement of such parents is below the national average. "When families involved in abuse and those involved in neglect are viewed separately, two distinct profiles emerge" (p. 45). Abuse families had higher incomes, were more likely to be two-parent families, and had fewer children than did neglect families. On the other hand, they were more likely to show intolerance for child behavior and loss of control during discipline. Environmental stress was more characteristic of neglect families, family interpersonal dynamics more characteristic of abuse families.

6 HOMEMAKER SERVICES

INTRODUCTION

The social insurance and social assistance programs are designed primarily to meet the needs presented by the fatherless family. Homemaker service is designed primarily to meet the needs of the motherless family, to provide for those crucial aspects of the mother's role—child care and maintenance of the home—when the mother cannot perform these functions adequately.

Historical Background

These services, under another name, were being offered as early as 1903, when the Family Service Bureau of the Association for the Improvement of the Conditions of the Poor in New York City employed a number of visiting cleaners who supplemented nursing services by "lifting temporarily the simple everyday domestic burdens from sick mothers." These women were later given the title *visiting housewives*. The Association's Annual Report listed their functions: helping in the renovation and restoration of homes; washing, cleaning, and sometimes preparing meals when the condition of the mother prevented her doing so; and demonstrating the art of good housekeeping. After 1918, care of the children, which was to be the principal reason for such services during many years of homemaker development, begins to be stated in these reports as the purpose of assignments. Although this was always a small service—no more than four visiting housekeepers were employed at any one time from 1903 to 1924—it had much in common with present-day homemaker service (U.S. Department of Health, Education, and Welfare, 1960, p. 1).

Although Breckinridge and Abbott (1912), in a study of the delinquent child, list "visiting housekeepers" as a service provided to families whose children were in danger of becoming delinquent (p. 173), the first organized homemaker program in the country is generally regarded as that established by the Jewish Family Welfare Society of Philadelphia in 1923. The purpose of the program was to provide housekeeper services to families during the temporary absence of the mother. The Jewish Home-Finding Society of Chicago inaugurated its housekeeper service in November 1924. This agency, on the basis of a standing arrangement with family welfare agencies and other welfare organizations of the community, had previously assumed responsibility for the care of children during the mother's absence from home. Prior to the introduction of housekeeping services, all such children had been placed with foster families. Because many of these children required only temporary care during the hospitalization of the mother for observation, surgery, or childbirth, approximately 40 per cent of the total volume of the work of the agency consisted of short-term foster placements (Kepecs, 1939). This proved to be an unsatisfactory method of meeting the situation because of the continual need to find foster homes and the emotional harm the children suffered by removal from their homes. Home-maker services seemed to be a logical alternative.

Goodwin (1939) describes some of the experiences that prompted the Associated Charities of Cincinnati to institute a visiting housekeeping service in 1933:

> As family caseworkers, we had witnessed the turmoil in homes that had to be temporarily broken up because of the mother's illness, and had sensed the anxiety which so frequently resulted from this step for both children and husband. Caseworkers had seen, too, a great many of our mothers postpone much-needed operations or periods of complete rest away from home because they could not face the threat of a broken home. Our experience in attempting to meet these situations on an individual basis, through a neighbor's help, or through employment of another client, had not been satisfactory because we felt that in these situations they had undertaken too great a responsibility without sufficient system of supervision and follow-up [p. 281].

The Housekeeping Aid Program, as it was then called, received considerable impetus during the Great Depresssion under the auspices of the Works Progress Administration (WPA). Women in need of financial assistance were assigned to families in which the mother's illness or temporary absence required supplementation of the maternal role. Although fewer than a dozen family agencies were sponsoring any form of housekeeper services in 1937, almost five hundred projects were operating under the WPA at that time (Goodwin, 1939, p. 279).

Kepecs (1939) notes (p. 267) that in Chicago alone in 1938 about 150 motherless families were kept together through housekeepers furnished by WPA. The final report on the WPA (1944) notes that housekeeping aide projects

> furnished assistance in housekeeping, care of children, and elementary care of the sick in the homes of needy families in times of illness or other emergency. . . . The services of the housekeeping aides not only provided assistance in emergency situations, but also helped to establish the social principle that services can be extended to needy people in their homes in a more satisfactory and economical manner than through institutional care. . . . Through June 30, 1943, women employed on housekeeping aide projects had made more than 32 million visits into homes where the homemaker was ill or where some other emergency existed [p. 69].

As a result of the developing interest in this service, the Children's Bureau sponsored a conference on housekeeper services in Washington, D.C., in November 1937. The conference had the stated purpose of "thinking through the possibilities for the future development of housekeeper services in terms of the fundamental principles of organization and satisfactory standards of services and . . . consider[ing] the various means by which the development of such services might be guided along sound lines." Participating in the conference were representatives of public and private agencies in the field of social work, public health nursing, home economics, vocational training, and the employment of women workers.

In 1939 a national committee was organized to promote homemaker services. By 1971 this had developed into an independent national organization, the National Council for Homemaker–Home Health Aide Services. It promotes the cause of homemaker service by sponsoring national meetings; developing, collecting, and exchanging information regarding homemaker services; establishing standards and accrediting agencies; publishing a newsletter, as well as books and pamphlets; and providing consultation to communities interested in developing homemaker services.

Reasons which have been advanced explaining the rapid growth of homemaker services in the United States include the following:

1. The continuing trend toward a nuclear family system, which arises from the continuing mobility of our population. As a result, fewer members of the extended family are readily available to substitute for the mother when she is incapacitated or absent.
2. The reduced availability of foster homes, which requires that other resources be developed to meet the children's needs when the mother is not available.
3. The cost of placement for large sibling groups, even if foster homes were available.
4. The growth of hospital insurance programs, which results in increased use of hospital resources—by mothers, among others.
5. Improved techniques for treatment of illness, which permit early return of the mother from the hospital and her rehabilitation at home. Once the mother might have been discharged only when she was ready to resume her functions in the family; now she is encouraged to convalesce at home.
6. The growing appreciation of the value to a child of his own home, even one with some limitations, and of the emotional consequences that accompany his separation from his family and his placement in a foster home. Homemaker service is perceived as a significant component in the configuration of home-based services mobilized to increase the probability of maintaining the child in his own home.

Definition

The National Council for Homemaker–Home Health Aide Services defines homemaker service as follows:

Homemaker–Home Health Aide Service is an organized community program provided through a public or voluntary nonprofit agency. Qualified persons— homemaker–home health aides—are employed, trained, and assigned by this agency to help maintain, strengthen, and safeguard the care of children and the functioning of dependent, physically or emotionally ill or handicapped children and adults in their own homes where no responsible person is available for this purpose. The appropriate professional staff of the agency establishes with applicants their need for the service, develops a suitable plan to meet it, assigns and supervises the homemaker–home health aides and continually evaluates whether the help given meets the diagnosed need of its recipients [National Council, 1965, p. 5].

Beatt (1957) emphasizes the fact that homemaker service is essentially a casework service:

> Homemaker service, as a social service to children, is offered by an agency to give casework help and provide the necessary direct care of children through a supervised homemaker. It makes it possible for parents to keep children in their homes. It is offered where parents, whose ability to provide home care and guidance has been impaired by some crisis, will with this help be able to function effectively and the children will be assured a proper home. Its goal is to strengthen, support, supplement, and/or restore parental capacity to care for children and to prevent the unnecessary and/or precipitous removal of children from their own homes. As in any other tangible social service, casework helps the family and children to use the homemaker's direct care constructively, and to deal better with the problem that has necessitated the service [p. 8].

As the definitions indicate, homemaking service differs from maid service or housekeeping service in at least two important respects:

1. The homemaker goes beyond merely doing the housework and feeding the family. She accepts some responsibility for meeting the emotional needs of the children, minimizing their anxiety and maximizing their feeling of security.
2. The homemaker is, in effect, a member of a team charged with the responsibility of implementing a casework plan "to help restore and strengthen parental functioning or otherwise assure that the child has the care he needs." As a member of the team, the homemaker is supervised by the social agency, to ensure coordination of her activities with the overall treatment plan.

Homemaker service is one of the services funded under Title XX of the Federal Social Security Act. A distinction is made between homemaker service, chore service, and home health aide service. Homemaker service is offered by a trained homemaker and involves child care in addition to routine household care. Chore service is home maintenance activity by an untrained person, and home health aide service is focused on medical care.

Homemaker service is based on the premise that the best place for the child is in his own home, that this is the most favorable environment for the development of a healthy personality. Tied to this premise is the conviction that society has the responsibility of assisting the parents to fulfill their role to the best of their ability and that services should be provided by society to enable the parents to care for their children in their own home.

ADMINISTRATION OF HOMEMAKER SERVICE

Recruitment

Many methods have been used to recruit homemakers. The public welfare agencies do most of their recruiting through the merit system. Homemaker positions are generally civil service positions, and some kind of examination is given to interested applicants.

All the mass communication media are employed to acquaint possible recruits with the positions available, and appeals are made to groups in close contact with women who might be interested in such a job. In Fort Wayne, Indiana, for instance, a homemaker agency contacts local industrial concerns that retire their women employees at fifty-five. Once homemaker service has been established and a homemaker staff has been recruited, the staff and the clients are significant sources of contact with potential recruits. Commercial employment agencies have also been used as a source of recruitment. Although most public welfare agencies have no real difficulty in securing well-qualified women for normal full-time service, homemakers with special qualifications—the ability to speak a foreign language, the willingness to work for twenty-four-hour periods or at long distances from home—are somewhat more difficult to find. The 1967 amendments to the Social Security Act, which require the use in welfare programs of subprofessional staff and volunteers, recruited if possible from recipient groups, have given considerable impetus to the development of homemaker service. In almost every state, the poor, the near-poor, and the welfare recipients have been recruited to fill the position of homemaker.

A large-scale community action program in New York City employed indigenous homemakers who, because they lived in the neighborhood and were familiar with the language, background, and lifestyle of the families they were serving, were able to form quick and firm relationships with the families (Goldberg, 1967). Their intimate knowledge of how to cope with the family's problems was of great value—particularly in the teaching of more efficient homemaking and child care on a low-income budget.

One report on the work of a group of indigenous homemakers notes:

> [They] were untrained, but they were not unskilled. They had considerable ability to cope with their environment, and therefore much to offer clients who were less resourceful than they. They knew how to live on a low income, how to stretch leftovers, how to use surplus foods (including powdered skim milk and canned meat, which must have the preservative removed before it is edible), where to buy inexpensive material, and how to sew an attractive garment with it, how to recognize a bargain. They knew which detergents would best clean an icebox or a stove and which made sense on a low income. They knew their neighborhood, which stores were good, and where bargains could be found. They also had learned how to deal with the local merchants. They were familiar with the neighborhood clinics, the welfare center, the child health stations, and the schools, and they could show a client how to fend with these institutions—not in the manner of a professional, who relies partly on the agency's power and partly on his polish, but the way a lower-class person does it for himself. Most of them had taken care of a large family and had planned their schedules well enough to have some time for themselves. They were both skilled and experienced in caring for young children [Goldberg, 1967, p. 191].

The indigenous homemakers were also of help to the staff in educating them to the realities of slum living and to the perceptions and viewpoints of low-income families.

Because heavy physical demands are often made on the homemaker, good health—including freedom from contagious diseases and disabling handicaps—is an important qualification. Agencies also prefer somewhat older women, perhaps because such women are easier to recruit and are more likely to have had experience in child care and home maintenance.

Personality attributes are also important. Social agencies stress maturity, emotional stability, and a liking for children, in several detailed statements of the homemaker service literature (Fitzsimmons, 1951; Brodsky, 1957; Giles, 1957). Educational requirements for homemakers are more flexible: most have a grade-school education (U.S. Department of Health, Education, and Welfare, 1958, p. 30).

Training and Duties

Once the homemakers have been hired, most agencies make provisions for training them. One of the most elaborate of such programs was conducted by the Visiting Homemaker Association of New Jersey in cooperation with Rutgers University. The University Extension Division offered a course to homemakers consisting of some twenty-two hours of instruction. The faculty consisted of social workers, nutritionists, home economists, nurses, occupational therapists, and supervisors of homemaker services. The course included material on child care and development, child psychology, agency policies and procedures, the responsibilities of the homemaker, people's reaction to illness, the purchase and preparation of food, and home management (United States Department of Health, 1960). A similar course has been offered by the University of Illinois School of Social Work (University of Illinois, 1960).

The training of homemakers is accepted by most agencies as a continuing responsibility. Before new homemakers join the staff, provisions are generally made for group meetings at which they discuss with agency social work supervisors the problems encountered on the job. Individual supervision by the caseworker is an additional form of training offered to the homemaker.

The National Council for Homemaker/Home Health Aide Services has formulated a detailed training manual for homemakers.

The homemaker's duties are frequently described as "those of the usual feminine head of the household": care and supervision of the children, family laundry, planning and preparation of meals, cleaning and maintenance of the house, shopping, and so on. They may also include the care of a sick member of the family when no actual nursing is involved. Many agencies protect the homemaker by limiting the amount of heavy work that might be required of her (U.S. Department of Health, Education, and Welfare, 1958, p. 25). An effort has also been made to define the limits of the homemaker's activities as they relate to the nursing of the ill mother at home.

Because homemaker service is offered the family to supplement, rather than substitute for, an inadequately implemented maternal role, the nature of the service varies with the family. In general, the homemaker does not fulfill those duties that the family can perform for itself without undue stress. But, unlike a housekeeper, the homemaker must—if the situation demands it—supplement all components of the parental role: maintenance of the home, socialization of the children, and so on (Child Welfare League of America, 1959, p. 9).

Organization

Homemaker service units are most frequently organized within the agency's administrative structure. Because homemaker service is closely related to the agency's casework functions, it is generally located in, or coordinated with, the unit of the agency offering such service.

A supervisor of homemaker service is assigned full-time responsibility for the administration of the service, and the person so assigned frequently has the title Supervisor of Homemaker Services, Homemaker Supervisor, or Director of Homemaker Services and is charged with recruiting, training, and supervising the activities of the homemakers. If the number of homemakers is too small to warrant the appointment of a full-time supervisor, responsibility for administration of the program may be delegated to a staff member, in addition to his other duties. And in large organizations with a substantial homemaker service program, the caseworker working with a particular family may supervise the homemaker assigned to the family.

Agencies that have an organized homemaker service program may make this service available to clients of other social agencies, a charge being made to the agency with which the client is associated. Also, homemaker service has, on occasion, been organized as a separate social agency that furnishes homemaker service independently to clients of all of the community social agencies.

SCOPE

A 1958 nationwide study found that there were 143 agencies employing 1,700 homemakers providing homemaker service to about 2,200 families during the week the study was conducted.

A national survey of the service indicated that by 1976 there were 3,732 agency units offering homemaker services. As contrasted with the estimated 1,700 homemakers in 1958, the 1976 survey estimated approximately 82,000 homemaker–health aides. It was calculated that service had been growing at the rapid rate of 20 per cent per year during the 1970s (Humphry, 1978; National Council, 1978).

Despite the rapid growth of the service in this country, we still lag behind many other countries. The International Council on Home Help Services estimated that the United States had 29 home-helpers per 100,000 population in December 1976. By contrast, Sweden had 923, Norway 840, and the Netherlands 599 per 100,000 population (Little, 1978, p. 284).

The 1976 survey confirmed a longtime trend toward an increasing proportion of the service's being offered by public agencies. Of the units offering homemaker services, 51 per cent were public agencies, as contrasted with 1958, when 75 per cent of all service units were under the auspices of voluntary agencies. The most rapid growth was in the proprietary (for-profit) sector. By 1977, 15 per cent of the homemaker units were under such auspices, and an additional 5 per cent were privately owned "nonprofit" units.

In developing homemaker service as a profit-making enterprise, a nationwide group, Avail-Ability, has begun to provide local homemaker services operation under the name Avail-a-Care. They advertise the availability of reference-checked, insured, and bonded personnel for nursing tasks and for homemaking and home management tasks.

Here, as in day care, private-enterprise market factors are beginning to influence developments in the field (Reichert, 1977). It is anticipated that the proprietary sector will continue to grow because governmental funding regulations make payments to such units posssible.

Homemaker unit affiliation with the nonprofit public and voluntary agencies was evenly divided in 1976 between social work agencies and health-care agencies. Each represents some 40 per cent of the home-care field. Most homemaker–home health aide service units were relatively small, 50 per cent employing five or fewer aides and only 4 per cent employing one hundred or more aides.

Throughout the 1970s, there was a clear trend in the redistribution of homemaker service efforts away from families with children and nonaged adults to greater concern with the homemaker needs of the aged. The 1976 survey indicated that "relatively little service is given to families with children . . . Over three-fourths of all homemaker–home health aide services are now serving the elderly" (Humphry, 1978, p. 3; see also Moore, 1977, p. 31).

There are no census data available in 1980 that would indicate the number of children receiving this service. The fact that there is a smaller percentage of more recent references in this chapter, as compared with other chapters, reflects the reduction in the relative use of and concern with homemaker service as a child welfare service.

SITUATIONS IN WHICH HOMEMAKER SERVICE IS APPROPRIATE

Unlike foster care or institutionalization, which involve temporary substitution of one set of parents for the biological parents, the situations in which homemaker service is thought to be applicable and appropriate are those that are responsive to some degree of role reallocation within the child's own family. The principal aim in providing such service is to enable the family to remain structurally intact during the period when an essential aspect of the role functions performed by the parental pair is being inadequately implemented.

The role that most frequently needs to be supplemented by homemaker service is that of the mother. Homemaker service may be offered when the mother is temporarily absent because of physical or mental illness or convalescence. Generally the father is called upon to cover the role functions of the mother, but sometimes they are allocated to the older child or children. What may also happen is that some less significant, less essential aspect of the mother's role is neglected, while the activities that must be performed if the family is to continue to function successfully are performed with the expenditure of additional energy and time on the part of incumbents of other positions: father, daughter, student. Because their own primary roles make heavy demands on their time and energy, and because they may never have learned the skills required for the effective discharge of the maternal role functions, considerable tension may be generated. The presence of a homemaker permits a continuation of the usual pattern of role functions in the family, and helps to maintain family stability:

Mr. A's wife was committed to a mental hospital and he came to the home-maker agency when he had to cope alone with the problem of caring for his three small children. An elderly relative had tried to take over while he was at work, but the situation became too much for her. Mr. A., a factory worker, could not afford to hire help nor could he bring himself to put the children in foster homes. A homemaker was sent to give day care to the youngsters during the months that Mrs. A. must remain hospitalized. The assignment to the family will continue during Mrs. A.'s subsequent period of adjustment and psycho-therapy [U.S. Department of Health, Education, and Welfare, 1958, p. 43].

Homemaker service may be appropriately offered when the mother is physically present but has lowered capacity to cope with the ordinary demands of her position because of "physical or mental illness, disabilities, convalescence, residuals of illness, [or] complications of pregnancy" (Child Welfare League of America, 1959, p. 5):

A young mother suffered a postpartum psychosis following delivery of the third child. In this situation, the father was able, by taking his vacation and availing himself of the offers of help made by neighbors, to manage care of the two other children, aged five and two, until his wife was ready for discharge from a psychiatric hospital where she had responded quickly to treatment which relieved the acute phase of her illness. However, the psychiatrist stipulated that she could not assume the responsibility or the pressure of care of her children, and would require further out-patient therapy before she could function adequately as a mother again. Homemaker service made it possible for this mother to return home, where she could oversee her children without assuming full responsibility for their care [New Jersey State Department of Health, 1961, p. 31].

The homemaker service may be offered to help the mother develop more adequate skills in child care and home maintenance. In such cases, role implementation is inadequate because of lack of preparation, training, or knowledge regarding the requirements of the role. The homemaker service has an educational focus in such cases, in areas such as household organization, meal planning and preparation, maintenance of clothing, child rearing, health care and use of health resources, and money management (Grant, Pancyr, 1970; National Council, 1970).

In other cases, the problem of inadequate role implementation may arise from the mother's ambivalence regarding her role. Here the homemaker, in her behavior toward the children, offers herself as an example of the "good mother," which the client may emulate. The following illustrates the use of a homemaker in a teaching capacity:

Mrs. Harvey's situation was referred to the agency by the police, who alleged that she was a neglectful mother and recommended that her children "be taken away from her and placed in foster homes at once." The police had been called to her home the previous night, upon complaint of neighbors that Mrs. Harvey's six children, ranging in ages from one to six years, were alone in the apartment and were not being cared for. The landlord claimed that this was a frequent occurrence. The police described Mrs. Harvey's children as dirty and unkempt.

The two-year-old twins were unclothed except for undershirts. They had remnants of feces on their bodies, and were sleeping in a bed with a worn-out dirty mattress. The baby was nursing a bottle of curdled milk. All of the children seemed to be underweight and malnourished.

Over a period of months, a caseworker–homemaker team worked closely with Mrs. Harvey and accomplished the following:

(1) The homemaker, through her close contacts in the home, learned exactly what basic essentials in clothing, bedding, cleaning equipment, and cooking utensils were needed by this family and the caseworker tapped community resources to meet these needs, which required large immediate outlays of money. (2) Mrs. Harvey learned, by the homemaker's example, to give better care to the children, giving attention to their diet, hygiene, rest, and supervised play. The caseworker helped Mrs. Harvey to secure medical care, as needed. Mrs. Harvey also learned to intervene in the children's quarrels calmly, and was able to give up her past screaming, ineffective efforts at discipline. (3) The homemaker helped Mrs. Harvey to learn better to shop and to plan expenditures now that she had a predictable, though still limited, income. They watched the newspapers for bargains, budgeted, and went shopping together [National Council, 1968, p. 47–48].

In some instances, the use of the homemaker fulfills all the purposes previously mentioned:

Mrs. M. came to the Family Service Agency to request homemaker service because she was expecting to be hospitalized for surgery in the near future.

Homemaker service was provided to the M.'s because it was felt that Marian, sixteen, could not assume major responsibility for caring for her six younger brothers and sisters, which she would have had to do because of Mr. M.'s long hours of work. Because of the emotional problems which two of the children, Dorothy, ten, and Victoria, nine, were displaying in their behavior, it was also felt that a homemaker would be needed to help give the children—and particularly these two—a feeling of security during the time their mother was away. It was expected that the homemaker's observations of the children would give the worker a better understanding of each child and his needs, and would also give the caseworker a clearer picture of inter- and intra-family relationships.

The homemaker was with this family for thirteen weeks. At first it was difficult for the children to accept a stranger in their home, and they directed much of their hostility because of their mother's absence against the homemaker by not speaking to her. It was not very long, however, before they responded to her warmth and interest. After Mrs. M. returned home, she had to be completely immobilized so that it was still necessary for the homemaker to continue to assume most of the care needed by the children. However, as Mrs. M. gained strength, the homemaker gradually returned this responsibility to her. During Mrs. M.'s hospitalization, the homemaker had been able to feed the family more adequately on less money than the family used to spend. Mrs. M. asked the homemaker to help her with menu planning and shopping lists. By the time the homemaker left, Mrs. M. had learned a great deal in this area. To help keep Mrs. M. occupied during her convalescent period, the homemaker also taught her how to mend and darn [Community Service Society, 1958, pp. 1, 2, Appendix 3].

Homemaker service may be offered to supplement the mother's activities when she is so burdened by the demands of a handicapped or sick child as to neglect the needs of her other children. This is an instance of inadequate role implementation in relation to the care of the normal siblings due to the excessive demands of the sick child: "The homemaker can share in the care of the handicapped child or, by assuming some responsibility for the other children and the home, will free the mother so that she can give more time to the handicapped child" (U.S. Department of Health, Education, and Welfare, 1958, p. 4). The homemaker and the caseworker can also help the family develop a more understanding attitude toward the handicapped or ill child. In some instances, handicapped children themselves have been helped by the supervised homemaker to develop greater facility in feeding, dressing, and toileting (Soyka, 1976).

A middle-aged mother applied [for help] at the suggestion of a friend who knew about homemaker service. The mother said she was physically exhausted and going to pieces from the demands of caring for her three-year-old son. He had been born prematurely and weighed only one and one-half pounds at birth. When he was a year old, it was discovered that he was blind. He has been in and out of hospitals for a respiratory ailment; he whines and wheezes even while he is asleep. Recently there has been a diagnosis of cerebral palsy. . . . He cannot sit up and becomes fretful lying in one position. He shrieks in panic when he cannot hear his mother's voice. The father, an artist, had to travel on his job, but took a job as a laborer to be at home. The father made a device to prop up Eddie, but his balance is poor and he topples over. The mother has to reprop him and reprop him. The mother was told that Eddie would never speak, but she patiently taught him to say a few words. The child has to be taken to the clinic three times a week, and the mother was traveling three hours a day to take him there. The mother was troubled about their neglect of Betty, aged seven. . . . Lately Betty is overeating, stealing money, slashing her dresses, and being openly resentful of her brother. . . . The mother said she had closed out Betty and her husband and concentrated her whole life on the handicapped child.

The homemaker in this family is gradually establishing herself with Eddie, who formerly would not let anyone but his mother touch him. The homemaker persuades the mother to rest. The homemaker admires the mother's courage and is helping her to take short cuts in housework so that she can spend more time with Betty. The aim of the homemaker service is to relieve the pressures on both parents and on Betty, to help Eddie be less fearful, and to achieve better balance in their lives [U.S. Department of Health, Education, and Welfare, 1958, p. 4].

Homemaker service may be offered when the mother's role is left permanently vacant. In these instances, the mother has died, deserted, or divorced, and custody of the children has been awarded to the father. The aim in such cases is not to effect a permanent reorganization of the family group with the homemaker as a mother substitute but to relieve stress and pressure on the father so as to permit a reasoned discussion of his long-range plans. Stressful situations may precipitate a decision made on the basis of expediency; with the intervention of the homemaker, the stress is mitigated and the situation is stabilized long enough to permit formulation of an acceptable plan.

Such use of homemaker service may also permit more adequate preparation for the placement of children in a more-or-less permanent substitute family arrangement:

> Mr. L., age thirty-nine, his son, age twelve, and his daughter, age five, lived in an adequately furnished apartment in a public housing project. Mrs. L. had died giving birth to a third child which had also died. . . . Relatives and neighbors had been helping to care for the children since his wife's death, but they could not go on doing so indefinitely. . . . Mr. L. did not want to give up his children, but he did not know how to care for them properly and manage his home. His daughter, who had been happily attending a nursery school before her mother's death, no longer wanted to go to school. His son missed his mother a great deal and stayed alone in his room much of the time. . . . The services of the homemaker were provided to the L. family for twenty-three weeks to stabilize the home situation for Mr. L. and his children while the father and the caseworker considered plans for their future welfare and care. It was also hoped that, during the homemaker's stay with the family, the caseworker would be able to get a better understanding of the children and their reaction to their mother's loss. Such information would contribute greatly in deciding the kind of care that would be best for them [Community Service Society, 1958, pp. 32, 33].

Homemaker service may also be offered as a diagnostic aid in determining the best plan for a handicapped child or in evaluating possible neglect in homes where child care is reputed to be marginal, as well as in testing parents' ability to modify homemaking standards and parent–child relationship patterns.

Less frequently, homemaker service has been offered in the following circumstances:

1. As an alternative to the placement of a child in a detention home or shelter while suitable arrangements for caring are being explored (Johnson, 1956). New York City has been considering "establishment of an auxiliary corps of homemakers who will be available to the police when children are deserted by their parents" (U.S. Department of Health, Education and Welfare, 1960, p. 166; Burt, Balyeat, 1977).
2. As a supplement to day care, when the employed mother cannot remain at home to care for a temporarily ill child, or when day care for the child of a working mother is inappropriate or unacceptable.
3. To supplement the mother's activities "during the summer months for families of migrant farm workers" (U.S. Department of Health, Education and Welfare, 1955, p. 6).
4. To help adoptive parents make the difficult transition to parenthood. This "crisis of parenthood" is a problem of role transition, during which supplementation in adjusting to the new, unfamiliar role is helpful. Similarly homemaker help is offered to parents after the birth of their first child (Brodsky, 1958, p. 11).
5. To permit a mother to attend a clinic on a regular basis or to receive hospital outpatient treatment.
6. To supplement the mother's unfilled role when she must be absent from home because of the illness or death of close relatives, or for educational reasons. For instance, in June 1971 about 500 children under six whose mothers were enrolled in the Aid to Families of Dependent Children (AFDC) Work Incentive Program were cared for by homemakers.

7. Homemakers have been selectively used as a re̲ glect and abuse situations, giving a harassed motl̲ rehabilitation time away from the children.

Although homemaker service, if imaginatively exploited, is appropriate resource in a variety of problem situations, statistics ̲ service is most frequently used in limited kinds of situations. A ̲ of 1,183 cases of families with children indicates that homemaker requested in some 88 per cent of these cases because of the illness of ̲ mother or because of her absence from the home because of illness (U.S. Department of Health, Education, and Welfare, 1958a, p. 67). Currently homemaker service is most frequently offered to families with young children to cover emergency situations of limited duration in which the mother is incapacitated or hospitalized.

The Casework Process in Homemaker Service

The most distinctive aspect of homemaker service is that it is generally offered under agency auspices in a casework context, as part of an overall treatment plan, and that the homemaker is under agency supervision to ensure that her activity will contribute to the fulfillment of the treatment plan.

Referrals to the homemaker service unit of an agency often come from caseworkers within the agency aware of a family situation requiring the service. Frequently referrrals also come from hospitals and doctors. The largest single referring source consists of family, neighbors, and friends.

Intake

Intake in homemaker service achieves the same general purposes as in any agency setting. The worker must help the client articulate his problem and must make clear to the client the kinds of services the agency has available. The worker also tries to make clear the conditions under which the service can be offered, that is, the conditions of client eligibility. He then tries to help the client decide whether or not he wants to use the services available and explores with him the alternative solutions to his problem. Because agency resources are limited, the worker has to be sure that the client not only wants the service but can effectively use it.

There might also be discussion of the question of payment for the service. Private agencies require the client to pay something toward the cost of the service, the amount being determined by the client's income and the number of members in the family. At intake, the client must show readiness to "share financial information including verification of income and to pay toward the service in accordance with his ability" (Chambers, 1955, p. 113).

The family's expectation regarding the homemaker is also discussed, as well as the agency's expectation regarding the adjustments that might be required of the family members in assisting the homemaker to fulfill the functions of the missing mother. The structure of service needs to be agreed upon—who does what and when—and an explicit effort is made to help the client understand

...he distinction between homemaker service and maid service. Also, because in most cases the need for homemaker service is related to the illness of the mother, an attempt is made to obtain a clear picture of the mother's medical condition and the prognosis, her own and the family's attitude toward the illness, and their adjustment to it.

Some specific, clear preparation has to be made for transition to the next step in the process: continuing with the agency, referral to a more appropriate resource, and so on.

Not all problem situations that might be helped by homemaker service are regarded as appropriate for homemaker service. Certain additional factors are significant in the agency's decision to offer service. Because the aim of homemaker service is to preserve the family unit, the worker must determine whether the family can and should actually be preserved. Although the general assumption is that the child's own family offers the best environment for healthy development, in some instances the family situation is so damaging that a substitute family would offer the child a better chance for growth.

"The homemaker cannot create a home—but merely sustain what is there." Thus the worker evaluates the family's emotional, structural, and physical resources. The level of family cohesiveness and stability should be such as to make it likely that it will not fall apart. The service must be given with the expectation that the family will again function normally sometime in the future.

An experienced executive director of a homemaker service agency sets the program in realistic perspective:

> Those of us who have worked for some years in homemaker service must sadly admit that it is quite rare that we are asked to come into a family situation in which everything is normal in the relationship, in which the standards of living are somewhat middle-class or approaching middle-class, and in which temporary illness or dislocation threatens an already intact family life which we can protect and preserve with the simple addition of this one very good service. I say we rarely see it, although I admit that it occasionally does happen [National Council, 1968, p. 74].

The agency also must be sure that the client clearly understands and accepts the service. Here the term *client* refers not only to the individual formally representing the family but to all members of the family who have significant power in determining family decisions and whose patterns of life will be significantly affected by the service. Homemaker service may fail if the father accepts the service without consulting the mother or the older siblings, who may be unprepared for the plan or actually opposed to it. The worker also needs to assess the client's willingness and capacity to work with the agency. The agency selects the homemaker to be assigned and determines some of the conditions under which she will work. Thus, through the homemaker, the agency will be in constant contact with the client. In a study of forty-seven unselected clients who were given homemaker service by well-trained and experienced homemakers, the most important single predictive factor relating to successful use of the service was found to be the applicant's attitude toward the part played by the agency in providing and supervising the homemaker: "In 83 percent of the cases using the service successfully, the family was accepting the agency, whereas

92 percent of the families using the service unsuccessfully were resistive, or in-different, to the agency" (Santulli, 1945, p. 345).

Many agencies, however, specifically point out that the willingness or ability of parents to accept help with personal problems is not necessarily a condition for providing homemaker service for children. The worker must also determine whether or not the client has explored other possible resources: a nondamaging reallocation of responsibilities among family members, the help of available rela-tives, and so on. If resources that might be exploited do exist, the caseworker has the responsibility of helping the client to plan their effective use.

Unless a twenty-four-hour, seven-day-a-week service is contemplated, the agency must have some assurance that there will be a responsible person avail-able, generally the father, to take over during the time that the homemaker is not on duty. Although most agencies prefer that there be a father available in the home to which homemaker service is being offered, Watkins (1958) has shown that homemaker service can be effectively offered to the fatherless AFDC family.

The interview, or series of interviews, may end with an offer of service or with the refusal of service. The most important single reason for the decision not to offer service is actually a tribute to casework efforts at intake. For instance, in a 1958 nationwide study, 21 per cent of the families not accepted for home-maker service had been helped by the caseworker to use their own resources to move toward a solution of the problem (U.S. Department of Health, Education, and Welfare, 1958a, p. 81). And in another study of homemaker service in New York City in 1959, the Community Council (1961) found that 22 per cent of the requests for service were not accepted because the family had been helped by the caseworker to use other resources (p. 11).

The second most frequently cited reason is the tragic shortage of personnel. In two studies cited, 17 per cent and 20 per cent, respectively, of the requests for service had to be denied because a homemaker was not available.

Despite all the concern in the social work literature with the capacity to make profitable use of the service, this .does not show up in any of the studies as the reason for denial of service in a sufficiently large number of cases to be claimed as a special category.

If homemaker service is offered, contact between the client and the case-worker is maintained. One important reason is that introduction of the home-maker into the family creates a unique situation: the temporary introduction into the family system of an adult who has no legal ties to the family, and who sub-stitutes only in clearly defined areas for a key member of the family. The home-maker has a clearly delineated, restricted relationship with the total family system, but one that involves intimate contact and a sharing of parental prerogatives. The caseworker, working with the family and the homemaker, is often helpful in pre-venting problems and minimizing tensions if they arise.

The introduction of a stranger into the family's social system poses the prob-lem of her acceptance by family members both as a person in her own right and as a mother substitute. The homemaker, in turn, faces the problem of accepting the members of the family. An additional problem is that the family may have one idea of the way the assigned role of homemaker is to be enacted and the agency and the homemaker may have another. The caseworker operates as a resource person who facilitates the process of mutual accommodation and helps both the family and the homemaker to cope with failures in understanding.

Still another problem is the danger that a competitive situation will develop between homemaker and mother: "The mother may feel her position in the home challenged by the homemaker" (Gordon, 1955, p. 14). Because the homemaker may care for the children and manage the home somewhat more efficiently, the mother might fear "that this may make her husband critical of her management" (Langer, 1945, p. 185). In a study of families receiving extended homemaker service care, it was noticed that:

> Initially, many of the mothers, including the more adequate ones, evidenced great anxiety about their own displacement and fearfulness around the homemaker's role and function in the home. . . . In the more disturbed and deteriorated family situations . . . the adequacy of the homemakers seemed to threaten these mothers. Competition with the homemaker was increased by the positive reports they received from thoughtless, or malicious, relatives or from friends who told them how much calmer and better behaved their children were and how much better organized their households were now that the homemaker was in charge. Not infrequently, these mothers attempted to alienate their children from the homemaker [Children's Aid Society, 1962, p. 103].

Thus the mother may react to the threat to her position by seeking to frustrate the purpose of the service. The mother may press to "give up the homemaker before her physical condition warrants it" (Leach, 1958, p. 135) or overexert herself by assuming functions beyond her physical capacity even while the homemaker is present.

In some cases, problems arise because homemaker and mother have different conceptions of how the mother's role is to be performed:

> The homemaker and Mrs. F. complained of feeling uncomfortable with each other. The homemaker felt that Mrs. F. was a dominating kind of person who had outbursts of anger. The caseworker thought that one of the problems was that, with Mrs. F.'s improvement and the encouragement given her to take over little parts of the household management, the very different orientations toward household management in the homemaker and Mrs. F. came to the fore and caused, or helped support, some tensions between the two. The homemaker tended toward a high degree of organization and efficient economies. Mrs. F.'s tendency in household management was toward haphazard, less organized methods. In respective individual contacts with the homemaker and Mrs. F., these differences in household management were discussed; an attempt was made to remove any emphasis on one way being better than another and to help each of them accept the fact that there were different, equally acceptable ways of managing a household.

The children may find it difficult to accept the homemaker without feeling conflict over their "disloyalty" to their own mother. The situation poses a problem for the children regarding their response to a woman who acts as a mother without at the same time being a mother. The child might feel conflict about accepting discipline from such a person because disciplining is clearly a prerogative of the true parent. As Baldwin (1953) says, "Children feel suspicion and mistrust of the woman who tries to replace, even in part, the mother" (p. 125). In such situations, the caseworker may discuss with the children their anxieties about what is happening to the family, helping them to understand and accept the mother's limited capacity for child care while she is ill.

The situation also poses problems for the father. As Gordon (1955) notes, "The father may feel his position as provider of the family threatened because the agency selects the homemaker, pays her—at least in part—and it is to the agency that she is responsible" (p. 14). The father may also be threatened by the necessity of taking over some of the mother's functions. Acting as a mother, even in a limited way, may create anxiety for the man who is tenuously holding on to his sense of masculinity, as shown in the following case record:

> We discussed, at some length, the duties Mr. F. expected of a homemaker. He was somewhat embarrassed at going over these details such as ironing and so forth. When I mentioned that, as a man, he might be unaccustomed to some of this "business" but that illness in the family often changed people's roles, he was reassured.

The father may also have difficulty in accepting the assumption of certain aspects of the maternal role by the homemaker:

> Mr. B. had always depended upon his wife to discipline the children, but he resented the homemaker doing it and he would not do it himself [Justiss, 1960, p. 292].

The inability of the father to work cooperatively and effectively with the homemaker may result from feelings and attitudes toward women and mother surrogates stemming from his own developmental experience:

> Mr. Madison, a widower of thirty-five with three children under four years of age, could not get along with homemakers. He was surly, curt, and critical. He was unable to show any appreciation of what was being done for the children. Homemakers tried hard to accept his inability to show any graciousness, but none of them cared to remain long in the home. Gradually, as he and the caseworker discussed the needs in his home and the way he handled these, he was able to talk about some of the experiences that had made him distrustful of women. As he gained some understanding, he found ways to handle more satisfactorily his feelings about women and to find pleasure in friendly, warm relationships with them [Baldwin, 1953, p. 127].

The father and the children may be reluctant to permit any changes in the house, out of "loyalty" to the sick mother. The family may feel that its privacy is being violated by the intrusion of the homemaker into the family and may feel anxious about the possibility that she will disapprove of their ways of rearing the children or managing the home. In the course of one demonstration project, it became clear that some of the more disorganized parents "were fearful that the homemaker would learn too much about some aspect of the family's life that they preferred to keep hidden—such as the whereabouts of the children's father, an illegal source of income, an extramarital affair, or the extent of disturbance in their children" (Children's Aid Society, 1962, p. 103).

Because the request for homemaker service results from some crisis in the family's life, the caseworker may be needed to help with the social and emotional consequences of the crisis situation:

> Mr. K. called the agency for homemaker help in caring for his two children, Mary, eleven, and Raymond, eight and one-half. He was upset about his wife's hospitalization in the middle of the night because of an acute psychotic break. He was overwhelmed with guilt about his wife's hospitalization, thinking that he had contributed to it because he had been unable to face the beginning signs of her disturbance despite his knowledge of a former psychotic break [Community Service Society, 1958, pp. 26, 27].

The father may need help in facing a new, threatening situation occasioned by the change in family structure:

> In the E. family, with four children, twenty-four-hour service was necessitated by the hospitalization of the mother and the long and irregular working hours of the father. Mr. E. was overwhelmed and became agitated when the caseworker or the homemaker tried to enlist his help in planning for the family. He had been overly dependent on his wife and had never participated in the management of the household or the children. With encouragement from the homemaker and the caseworker during the two months his wife remained in the hospital, he gradually assumed a more positive and meaningful place in his family [Children's Aid Society, 1962, p. 103].

The availability of the caseworker is of special importance when the introduction of the homemaker leads to an intensification of the family's difficulties:

> In working with Mr. S., the caseworker learned that he needed to feel totally responsible and to be the only giving person in his family. He had a pathological need to assume both the female and male roles in the family, which made it difficult for him to accept a woman in the home. With his lessened responsibility because of the homemaker's presence, his control weakened so he began drinking, staying out late, and buying for the family in ways which threatened the health and nutrition of the children. The presence of a responsible and efficient woman relieved him of the need to be responsible, while at the same time it threatened his own adequacy [Community Service Society, 1958, p. 45, Appendix].

The caseworker, aware of the underlying problems that may make the service a pathogenic rather than a therapeutic agent, can work toward effecting a more positive use of the homemaker.

Work with the Homemaker

In response to the conflicting reactions to the presence of the homemaker in the home, the caseworker has regularly scheduled conferences with the home-maker as well as with members of the family. This is a service to the family, although an indirect one, for it enables the homemaker to work more effectively with the family.

The social worker is generally responsible for the supervision of eight to ten homemakers. The caseworker sees that the homemaker is assigned to a family and that the assignment is responsibly covered. He sees that each homemaker has an equitable and diversified case load and that assignments coincide with the special competencies and interests of the individual homemakers.

The caseworker helps the homemaker move into the family situation as unobtrusively as possible, "to fit into the family as a source of strength with the least possible threat to the status of any member of the family" (U.S. Department of Health, Education, and Welfare, 1961, p. 9). In order to be able to prepare the homemaker for working with the family, the caseworker has to explore the details of family schedule and routine, the pattern of family activities, the special needs and preferences of the various children, and specific family problems of which the homemaker might need to be aware. The Cook County Department of Public Welfare assigns

> the homemaker prior to the date of expected confinement or hospitalization in order to give the mother and children a better chance to get acquainted with her. . . . This alleviates the fears of the mother as to the care her children will receive during her absence and [helps] the children to adjust to the presence of a stranger [Woldman, 1940, p. 30].

The caseworker also helps the homemaker with her struggle to accept the different ways people may organize their homes and their routines; he helps the homemaker accept the difference between these children, who "belong" to other parents, and her own children:

> Mrs. C., the homemaker placed with a family of four school-age children while the mother was in the hospital, felt puzzled and unsure as to how to handle the problem of discipline. She had, in raising her own children, successfully resorted to reasoning with the child and deprivation of privileges as the means of maintaining discipline. This approach did not seem to work with the R. children. They refused to obey her, saying she was not their mother, and no amount of talking to them seemed to be of help. She wondered what to do next and brought this question for discussion to her conference with the caseworker.

Because the homemaker directly encounters many situations that tend to activate strong emotional reactions—mental illness, a neglectful mother—she needs to have someone with whom she can talk over her feelings. An opportunity for catharsis may allow the homemaker to return to the family ready to work more comfortably in the situation. The caseworker offers this opportunity as well as an emotionally supportive relationship to the homemaker so as to dissipate feelings of discouragement and anxiety regarding her competence. Equally important, the caseworker helps the homemaker to become aware of any "projection of expectations of herself upon the mother or her attitude toward her own husband on the father of the family" (Gordon, 1956, p. 368). He also helps her to keep from overidentifying with, or rejecting, any one member of the family (Clough, Wood, 1958, p. 2). He helps the homemaker to counter any tendency to take sides with a child against the parent, or with the family against the agency, to compete with the natural parents for the love and respect of the children, or to compete with the mother for the affection of the father.

The caseworker also helps the homemaker understand and modify some aspect of her behavior that may be having a deleterious effect on family relationships:

> Mrs. Emmons, twenty-eight years old, was hospitalized for a postpartum depression shortly after her second child was born. She left behind a dirty home, a frightened seven-year-old, the three-week-old baby, and a depressed husband. A homemaker about the same age as Mrs. Emmons was placed in the home. This was one of her first assignments and she was eager to make a good impression. She performed many extra chores as well as restoring order, cleanliness, and regularity in the household. Soon glowing reports came to Mrs. Emmons from her husband of the homemaker's skill and many achievements. Mrs. Emmons' depression increased and she showed much apprehension.
> Through counseling with her supervisor the homemaker came to understand the effects of her actions on the absent mother. She telephoned Mrs. Emmons at the hospital to ask for advice instead of waiting for Mrs. Emmons to telephone the home. The homemaker sent notes and pictures of the children to the mother. When the mother came home six weeks later, the two women were able to work well together, with homemaker's services gradually diminished to two half-days each week until termination some months later [National Council, 1968, p. 125].

Finally, the caseworker helps the homemaker to become aware of any behavior on the part of members of the client family that may be symptomatic of emotional stress: withdrawal, enuresis, thumb sucking, temper tantrums, and so on. Through the homemaker, the caseworker keeps informed of any significant changes in the family situation that might require the help of the caseworker. He helps the homemaker to understand and meet the needs of the children.

Although the homemaker and the caseworker ideally cooperatively complement each other, there is potential for friction. The homemaker is concerned with the immediate practical needs of the family; the caseworker is more apt to focus on long-range psychological goals. The homemaker knows the family intimately and has the allegiance of the family, which may cause the caseworker to feel resentment (Cassert, 1970). The caseworker acts as a "consultant" rather than a "doer," as an infrequent visitor rather than a temporary "member" of the family. The homemaker may feel that she has greater familiarity with the situation and may tend to discount much of the caseworker's advice.

Termination

Eventually the homemaker and the caseworker work together to help the family accept termination of the service, with the homemaker gradually doing less and less for the family while the family does more and more for itself. The caseworker helps the family with problems attendant upon the homemaker's leaving:

> Mrs. H., who had trouble with her back so that she could not lift her baby, had been referred for some special orthopedic exercises to strengthen the affected muscles. She resisted working on them and seemed to be slipping into a pattern of letting the homemaker do all the work, while she sat by giving orders and criticizing the homemaker.

Mrs. H. had to be helped to consider whether she wanted to get well and to face the fact that the homemaker was placed to afford her the chance to try to recover [Gordon, 1955, p. 18].

The caseworker helps the homemaker change, as the situation changes, by gradually taking less direct responsibility for the care of the children and the home as the mother is able to assume more of her normal role.

EVALUATION

Homemaker service has a number of advantages over alternative plans for dealing with the problems presented by the motherless family. The most important single advantage is that it permits the child to remain at home during the time that the mother is incapable of fully implementing her role. Homemaker service imposes a far smaller burden of adjustment on the child than foster care, for the child adjusts to the homemaker in the comforting familiarity of his own home, his one family, his own neighborhood. The homemaker might be regarded as a "traveling foster mother" who comes to the child.

As the New York City Department of Public Welfare notes:

[Since the] inception of the program in 1945, Department of Welfare homemakers have cared for over 30,000 children in their own homes, thus avoiding placement and the consequent breakdown of family life that so often results from the separation of children and parents [Snyder, 1962, p. 1].

In 1967 Homemaker Service of the Children's Aid Society of New York served 138 families, enabling "109 children to remain in their own homes during periods when parents were faced with illness or some other crises that would otherwise have propelled the children into placement in foster homes."

More methodologically rigorous studies of family situations that resulted in child placement show that in the worker's judgment, homemaker service might have prevented placement in some of the cases (Jenkins, Sauber, 1966; Shyne, 1969).

The studies, however, point to the need for greater flexibility in work schedules for homemaker service, and for the recruitment of "persons whose own background provides them with a familiarity and an understanding not only of the language, but also of the customs and mores of the families they are called upon to assist" [Jenkins, Sauper, 1966, p. 189].

Studies of the prevention of placement of children identified as being at high risk for foster care show that homemaker service is associated with increasing the child's chances of remaining in his own home (Sherman *et al.*, 1973, p. 46; Jones, Neuman, Shyne, 1976, p. 58; Burt, Balyeat, 1977, p. 65).

The larger the number of children in the family, the more economical homemaker service is for the community, for "homemaker costs are relatively fixed, regardless of the number of children in the family, while costs for foster care rise in direct proportion to the number of children in the family" (Brooklyn Bureau, 1958, p. 18). Every assessment of comparative costs indicates that homemaker–health aide service is less costly than any of the out-of-the-home alternatives (Robinson *et al.*, 1974, p. 12).

The availability of a homemaker on a twenty-four-hour basis materially reduces the number of children who might previously have been taken to children's shelters when parents were suddenly taken ill at night.

Homemaker service also provides greater assurance that the solidarity of the family will be maintained. The children remain at home and the father continues to carry full, direct responsibility for the discharge of his role vis-à-vis his children.

Homemaker services also contribute to the efficiency and effectiveness of available medical services. Mothers are more likely to accept the necessity for hospitalization if they have assurances regarding the care of their children. Once hospitalized, they are likely to remain as long as is medically necessary, and when they return home, they are likely to follow a prescribed medical regimen rather than attempting to take on too much too soon. Furthermore, because homemaker service permits earlier discharge of many hospital patients, it makes possible a more efficient use of available hospital bed space. According to Justiss (1960):

> Homemaker service provides a type of care which the ill mother can accept more readily and thus it permits her to accept hospitalization. Many mothers have told us that they would rather stay in their own home and die rather than see their children "sent away" to some stranger's home. Offering such service in a rural county in Texas "where, because of inadequate diet, lack of medical care, overwork, and poor health standards, incidence of tuberculosis is extremely high" has resulted in amelioration of a previously dangerous practice. It is reported that "there has not been a single instance of a mother returning home from a hospital against medical advice since the homemaker program has become well established" [pp. 291, 294].

Brodsky (1961) notes that "homemaker service might make it possible for a not too severely mentally ill mother to have hospital day-care treatment service" (p. 15) and a number of unpublished research reports, cited in a review by Sieder and Califf (1976), indicate the successful use of homemakers in maintaining the family unit in cases where the mother was mentally ill but did not require hospitalization.

Equally important, homemaker service reduces the danger of the damaging effects of role reallocation. Without homemaker service, fathers may miss many days of work in an effort to hold the family together. Even in those instances where the father remains on the job, his enactment of the wage-earner role may be impaired because of anxiety about what is happening at home. Homemaker service permits the father to devote himself to the demands of his job with less anxiety. Furthermore, if older siblings are forced to assume the responsibility for performing the functions previously allocated the mother, their enactment of their own student role is impaired through reduced attendance and inadequate preparation. Thus homemaker service reduces the tendency for family members to assume a burden of responsibilities that impairs effective enactment of their central roles.

Another advantage of homemaker service lies in the fact that it may make a family more amenable to needed casework help with other problems. As Johnson (1956) notes, "giving families a tangible service of immediate practical value often makes them more receptive toward help with less obvious problems" (p. 10).

Some of the values of homemaker service may be illustrated by the problem situations that develop in its absence. A study by the Almeda Council of Social Agencies of how a sample of families managed in the absence of the mother and the lack of available homemaker service indicates that the older children were kept out of school to care for the younger children; one parent took an unpaid vacation from work; one parent took his younger children to work; children were left with relatives at a distance from home; and children were left at home without supervision of any kind (Federation of Community Services, 1959).

Follow-up interviews with homemaker service clients indicated their positive evaluation of and satisfaction with the service (Community Service Society, New York, 1958).

PROBLEMS

1. A controversy exists as to the most appropriate auspices for homemaker service. Because the need for the service is almost always precipitated by a health problem, there is some argument for tying the service to health, rather than welfare, agencies. In 1976 about 40 per cent of all homemaker services agencies were operating under the auspices of health agencies or visiting-nurse organizations. The current name of the national organization that has accepted responsibility for advancing the cause of homemaker service—the National Council for Homemaker–Health Aide Services—symbolizes the dual allegiance of the service to both health and welfare. On the other hand, the service is designed to deal not with the health problem but with the social consequences of illness. It is further argued that tying the service to health agencies might tend to foster a narrow view of the appropriateness of the service and might tend to keep it restricted to situations involving illness. If viewed from the point of view of illness, homemaker service becomes focused on the patient; if viewed from the point of view of social dislocation, the service is more frequently directed in terms of the needs of children and it is more legitimately classified as a child welfare service. This ambiguity of emphasis may create a problem during the course of offering the service. When a homemaker enters a family because the mother is ill, "Who should be the homemaker's primary concern, the incapacitated adult or the insecure child?"

2. A second controversial question arises: "Is casework an essential part of homemaker service?" If so, it seems logical that homemaker service should be offered primarily, as it is now, by social agencies. Some point out that the selective, appropriate offering of a resource, supported by community funds, requires an intake casework interview; that the effective use of the service requires the kind of coordination and ongoing help provided by the caseworker; and that in all instances, families needing homemaker services are facing some crisis and the caseworker can be helpful in dealing with its consequences (Baldwin, 1953; Brodsky, 1957, 1958). Aldrich (1956) points out that even seemingly uncomplicated situations actually require the caseworker's continuing help. This point

receives some empirical support from one nationwide study, which indicates that "about six out of every seven families served in the study were provided casework services as well as homemaker service" (U.S. Department of Health, Education, and Welfare, 1958a, p. 65).

Others, however, suggest that, although casework service is needed to determine if the situation calls for a homemaker as an appropriate resource, "this is quite different from requiring a family to be engaged in a continuing casework relationship. If the public gets the idea that, in order to obtain a homemaker, it is necessary to be involved in a continuing casework relationship, the service either will not be used or will be obtained through auspices other than a social agency." Richman points to the "advisability of accepting families who wish to meet their personal needs through homemaker service but who may not need, or want, help with personal problems" (U.S. Department of Health, Education, and Welfare, 1952). "In many cases the family's only need is for the help of a homemaker in an emergency. They neither require nor want counseling or casework. To add such families to the load of the caseworker is not only burdensome but unrealistic" (U.S. Department of Health, Education, and Welfare, 1960, p. p. 21).

3. Another problem derives from the fact that the essential differences between homemaker and housekeeper services are very often blurred in the minds of the layman and, on occasion, in the minds of professionals. In offering the service, this problem of distinction and definition sometimes arises as the agency strives to keep the service from degenerating into a routine, mechanical housekeeping service. A detailed study of home help services in Great Britain, in which extensive interviews were conducted with homemakers, clients, and the public, made clear that the public and the clients had difficulty in perceiving homemaker services as differentiated from maid service (Hunt, 1970).

4. There is also a question as to the proper allocation of the limited homemaker-service resources. Many of the agencies offer the service to the aged as well as to families with young children. Which group can legitimately claim priority when decisions must be made regarding service limitations?

5. Agencies are "frequently insufficiently flexible" in the number of hours per day and the length of time for which homemaker service is offered (Community Council, 1961, p. 5). Some agencies will not provide service if the homemaker is required for more than eight or ten hours a day; others will refuse service if the homemaker is likely to be required for more than three months. National organizations interested in homemaker service have urged that family need, rather than arbitrary limitations, should determine the way the service is offered.

6. Another problem involves lack of public knowledge and acceptance of homemaker service. A study of homemaker service in New York City in 1959 revealed that approximately two thirds of a group of people identified as needing some kind of a home aide because of illness "had neither contacted an agency nor had been referred to one" (Community Council, 1961, p. 5).

An English study of motherless families indicated that relatives and friends were the principal source of help (George, Wilding, 1972). The relevant social services, such as homemaker service, were a source of help in only a small percentage of cases, mostly to lower-class families and for a limited period. Many of the fathers indicated that they would have preferred homemaker services if these had been more readily available. Accepting the help of friends and relatives incurs an obligation, and one may not be able to reciprocate the favor. A Dutch interview study of some sixty families who received homemaker services indicated that they preferred them to the help of relatives and/or friends and neighbors (Netherlands Institute, 1972, p. 75).

7. Recruitment is a problem. The prestige of the homemaker is not high enough to permit easy recruiting of competent personnel, and the limited availability of professionally trained casework supervisors makes difficult the expansion of service to meet the growing demand. Furthermore the service has limited prestige within the agency. Social workers are oriented to thinking in terms of the better-established resources, such as foster care, for dealing with the kinds of problem situations in which a homemaker might be appropriately employed. This tends to the neglect and derogation of homemaker service (U.S. Department of Health, Education, and Welfare, 1960, pp. 5–6).

8. Funding of homemaker service is an ongoing problem. The service has low visibility and low priority for community support either through community chest funds or tax funds. There are some sources of funding available, but these are far from adequate. Although there is some possibility of federal reimbursement for the expense of providing homemaker service to families receiving public assistance, the service is not specifically identified in federal legislation as an essential, mandated service, as are, for instance, protective services and family planning.

There are a variety of sources of support for homemaker services: Medicare, Medicaid, Title XX of the Social Security Act, and others. Lack of coordination among the variety of sources of support result in a continuing problem for agencies (Moore, 1977).

9. With the growth of service offered by private individuals and proprietary agencies, there is an increasing concern with standards. The National Council for Homemaker–Home Health Aide Services has established standards and is acting to accredit agencies that meet the standards. This is a difficult task, however, so that by 1978, there were only 124 agencies that were accredited by the council. There is concern that homemaker service, like nursing-home service, may present opportunities for unscrupulous operators. Reports of such substandard services have already been published (*The New York Times*, December 13, 1977).

TRENDS

We have already noted some of the recent trends: the continuing rapid growth of the services; the increased proportion of service offered by public agencies; the increasing proprietary-entrepreneurial interest in homemaker service; the decrease in service offered children and families; and the increasing proportion of services offered the aged. There follow some additional trends.

1. One trend in homemaker service is toward an expansion of the service and broader definition of situations in which the service might be used. Families that required extended homemaker service once found it difficult to obtain. As a result of special projects illustrating the value of extended homemaker service and the growing recognition of the clear need for such service, more agencies may make homemakers available either over a longer period of time or for more

hours each day. It is likely that the present trend toward an expansion of home-maker service will continue. Growing difficulties in finding foster homes and growing dissatisfaction with the program of foster care will continue to provide an impetus to explore alternative means of meeting the needs of the motherless family.

Developments in other areas are likely to reinforce the need for home-maker service. For instance, the trend toward community-centered psychiatric services, which help to keep more and more of the mentally ill in the community, requires—for its success—supplementary services such as homemaker service.

2. There is also a trend toward a more imaginative use of homemaker service. For instance, California has used funds available through the Children's Bureau Crippled Children's Program to provide homemakers for the mothers of handicapped children so as to relieve them for a few hours a day. Homemakers have also been used with families charged with neglect "in homes in which standards of household management was [sic] so poor as to seriously jeopardize the health and welfare of children in the family" (Shames, 1972, p. 12). The homemaker assisted these mothers in the care of their children and instructed them in better methods of child care. The reports of homemakers have also been found to be of great help in determining actual conditions in families suspected of child abuse (National Council, 1965a, p. 59). And in families with very young retarded children, homemaker service has been used to relieve family pressures and tensions. It has been hoped that as a result, "energies might be released to work out not only appropriate planning for the retarded child, but also to ex-amine and work through family problems created or aggravated by a retarded child" (Retarded Infants Service, 1965, p. 10). Homemakers have also been used effectively with families threatened with eviction from public housing because of poor housekeeping standards, as well as with migrant workers and American Indian families on the reservations (National Council, 1965, pp. 61–62).

3. Homemakers have been taught the essentials of behavior modification approaches and have been given responsibility for observing, recording, and reporting behavior and implementing techniques for changing maladaptive be-havior: "In essence the homemaker serves as the agent through whom the be-havior change program is implemented" (Talsma, 1970, p. 4; See also Steeno, Moorehead, Smits, 1977).

SUMMARY

Homemaker service is a supplementary service that originated in response to the need to assume some aspects of the mother's role for a limited period when she was ill at home or in the hospital. Homemaker service obviates the necessity of placing children in a foster home or institution for short periods and prevents family disintegration during a crisis.

Homemaker service is appropriately offered when:

1. The mother is temporarily hospitalized.
2. The mother is in the home but is ill or convalescing.
3. The mother needs tutorial help in developing homemaker skills.
4. The mother needs assistance in caring for a handicapped child.

5. The mother has died or deserted and the father needs time to make adequate, more permanent plans for the care of the children.

Despite the diverse situations in which homemaker service may be appropriate, its greatest use involves situations in which the mother is ill.

The distinguishing aspects of homemaker service are that the responsibility assumed by the homemaker goes beyond the mechanics of housekeeping to include concern with the social and interpersonal effects of the mother's inability to discharge her role, and that homemaker service is offered as part of a total social-work plan for the family.

Homemakers are generally older women of limited education who have raised their own children and whose skills center on home management and child care. In October 1972 there were about 30,000 homemakers employed by 3,000 agencies offering service to an indeterminate number of families, some percentage of which included children. The number of children affected by the program is very small compared with programs such as OASDI and AFDC.

The caseworker helps prepare the family and the homemaker for each other and works with the homemaker and the family on any problems that might result from her introduction into the family.

Evaluations of homemaker service indicate that:

1. It has been successful in preventing the need for short-term foster care for many children.
2. It has permitted the care of the child in his own home at a more limited expense to the community than would otherwise have been the case if the service were not available.
3. It increases the efficiency and effectiveness of medical service for mothers.

Problems regarding homemaker service include the following:

1. The controversy as to auspices.
2. The necessity for casework as an accompaniment to the service.
3. The confusion between homemaker service and housekeeping service.
4. The limited public knowledge of the program.
5. The low status of the program both in the mind of the public and within the social work profession.

Among the trends identified were the following:

1. A greater flexibility in the use of homemakers for situations requiring twenty-four-hour-a-day coverage and a seven-day week.
2. The continued rapid expansion of the program.
3. The increasing interest of public welfare agencies in homemaker service.
4. A greater diversification of sources of financing for such service.
5. A greater diversification of situations in which homemaker service has been found to be appropriate.
6. The decreasing availability of homemaker services for children and families with increasing use of service by the aged.

BIBLIOGRAPHY

ALDRICH, C. KNIGHT. "A Psychiatrist Looks at Homemaker Service." *Child Welfare*, 35 (October 1956).

BALDWIN, RUTH M. "Values in Long-Time Homemaker Service." *Social Casework*, 34 (March 1953).

BEATT, EARL J. "Community Organization to Meet Homemaker Service Need." *Child Welfare*, 36 (July 1957).

BRECKINRIDGE, SOPHONISBA, and EDITH ABBOTT. *The Delinquent Child and the Home.* New York: Russell Sage Foundation, 1912.

BRODSKY, ROSE. *Homemaker Service: Under Whose Auspices and for What Purpose?* Jamaica, N.Y.: Jewish Community Service of Long Island, September 1957.

———. "Philosophy and Practices in Homemaker Service." *Child Welfare*, 37 (July 1958).

BROOKLYN BUREAU OF SOCIAL SERVICE AND CHILDREN'S AID SOCIETY. *Long-term Homemaker Service—Project Report.* New York, September 1958.

BURT, MARVIN R., and RALPH R. BALYEAT. *A Comprehensive Emergency Services System for Neglected and Abused Children.* New York: Vantage Press, 1977.

CASSERT, HILDA P. "Homemaker Service as a Component of Casework." *Social Casework*, 51, 9 (November 1970), 533–544.

CHAMBERS, KATHERINE N. "First Steps in Homemaker Service: A Study of Applications." *Social Casework*, 35 (March 1954).

———. "The Intake Process in Homemaker Service Cases." *Social Casework*, 36 (May 1955).

CHILDREN'S AID SOCIETY OF NEW YORK CITY. "Nine- to Twenty-four-Hour Homemaker Service Project." *Child Welfare*, 41 (March 1962); 41 (April 1962).

CHILD WELFARE LEAGUE OF AMERICA. *Standards for Homemaker Service for Children.* New York, 1959.

CLOUGH, TRACY C., and JANET C. WOOD. "Homemaker Service to Children in a Multiple-Function Agency." *Child Welfare*, 37 (December 1958).

COMMUNITY COUNCIL OF GREATER NEW YORK. *Homemaker Services Programs in New York City: 1959.* New York, December 1959.

———. *Home Aid Service-Needs of Health Agency Clientele.* New York, June 1961.

COMMUNITY SERVICE SOCIETY OF NEW YORK. *Report of the Extended Homemaker Service Project*, prepared by Adelaide Werner. New York, June 1958.

FEDERATION OF COMMUNITY SERVICES. *Report of the Need for Homemaker Service.* Almeda County, Tex.: Federation of Community Services, January 1959. Mimeo.

FITZSIMMONS, MARGARET. "Homemaker Service as a Method of Serving Children." *National Conference on Social Welfare.* New York: Columbia University Press, 1951.

———. "Homemaker Service: Current Practice and Future Planning." *Social Casework*, 38 (June 1957).

GEORGE, VICTOR, and PAUL WILDING. *Motherless Families.* London: Kegan Paul, Trench, Trubner & Co., 1972.

GOLDBERG, GERTRUDE. "Nonprofessional Helpers: The Visiting Homemakers," in *Community Action Against Poverty.* Ed. by George A. Brager and Frances P. Purcell. West Haven, Conn.: New Haven College and University Press, 1967.

GOODWIN, MARION SCHMADEL. "Housekeeper Service in Family Welfare," in *Proceedings of the National Conference of Social Work, 1938.* Chicago: University of Chicago Press, 1939.

GORDON, HENRIETTA. "Homemaker Service as a Children's Casework Service." *Child Welfare*, 34 (January 1955).

————. *Casework Services for Children—Practices and Principles.* Boston: Houghton Mifflin Company, 1956.

GRANT, JEAN, and LUCILLE PANCYR. "The Teaching–Homemaker Service of a Welfare Department." *The Social Worker,* 38, 2 (May 1970).

HUMPHRY, GILBERT W. (Mrs.). *Shaping the Future of Homemaker–Home Health Aide Services.* Regional Institute Paper. March 1978. Mimeo, 5 pp. New York: National Council for Homemaker–Home Health Aide Services.

HUNT, AUDREY. *The Home Help Service in England and Wales.* London: Her Majesty's Stationery Office, 1970.

JENKINS, SHIRLEY, and MIGNON SAUBER. *Paths to Child Placement.* New York: The Community Council of Greater New York, 1966.

JOHNSON, NORA PHILLIPS. "Creative Uses of Homemaker Service." *Child Welfare,* 35 (January 1956).

————. "Homemaker Service for Children with Psychiatric Disorders." *Child Welfare,* 40 (November 1961).

JONES, MARY A., RENEE NEUMAN, and ANN W. SHYNE. *A Second Chance for Families: Evaluation of a Program to Reduce Foster Care.* New York: Child Welfare League of America, 1976.

JUSTISS, HOWARD. "Hidalgo County Homemaker Program." *Public Health Reports,* 75 (April 1960).

KEPECS, JACOB. "Housekeeper Service for Motherless Families," in *Proceedings of the National Conference of Social Work, 1938.* Chicago: University of Chicago Press, 1939.

LANGER, MARIAN. "A Visiting Homekeeper's Program." *The Family,* 26 (July 1945).

LEACH, JEAN M. "Homemaker Service as a Way of Strengthening Families During Illness," in *National Conference on Social Welfare: Casework Papers, 1958.* New York: Family Service Association of America, 1958.

LITTLE, VIRGINIA. "Open Care for the Aged—Swedish Model." *Social Work,* 23 (July 1978), 282–284.

MOORE, FLORENCE M. "New Issues for In-Home Service." *Public Welfare* (Spring 1977), 26–37.

NATIONAL COUNCIL FOR HOMEMAKER–HOME HEALTH AIDE SERVICES, INC. *Report of the 1965 National Conference on Homemaker Services.* New York, 1965a.

————. *Standards for Homemaker–Home Health Aide Services.* New York, 1965b.

————. *Homemaker–Home Health Aide Services for Families with a Mentally Retarded Member.* New York, 1966.

————. *A Unit of Learning About Homemaker–Home Health Aide Services: Teachers Source Book.* New York, 1968.

————. *Readings in Homemaker Service.* New York, 1969.

————. *Homemaker Service to Strengthen Individual and Family Life—A Focus on the Teaching Role of the Homemaker.* New York, 1970.

————. *Growth, Change, Challenge: 15th Annual Report, 1977.* New York: National Council for Homemaker–Home Health Aide Services, 1978.

NETHERLANDS INSTITUTE FOR SOCIAL WELFARE RESEARCH. *Some Selected Studies.* The Hague, June 1972.

NEW JERSEY STATE DEPARTMENT OF HEALTH. *Homemaker Service Training Course: A Cooperative Project,* rev. ed. New Brunswick, N.J.: Rutgers, The State University, December 1, 1960.

————. *New Jersey Visiting Homemakers—Proceedings of Homemaker Development Seminar.* Princeton, N.J., April 1961. Supplement to *Public Health News* (July 1961).

REICHERT, KURT. "The Drift toward Entrepreneurialism in Health and Social Welfare:

Implications for Social Work Education." *Administration in Social Work,* **1**, 2 (Summer 1977), 123–133.

RETARDED INFANTS' SERVICE, AND ASSOCIATION FOR HOMEMAKER SERVICE. *The Value of Homemaker Service in the Family with the Retarded Child Under Five—Final Report.* New York, November 1965.

ROBINSON, NANCY, EUGENE SHINN, ESTHER ADAMS, and FLORENCE MOORE. *Costs of Homemaker–Home Health Aide and Alternative Forms of Service.* New York: National Council for Homemaker–Home Health Aide Service, 1974.

SANTULLI, MARY. "Criteria for Selection of Families for Housekeeper Service." *Smith College Studies in Social Work,* **15** (1944–1945).

SHAMES, MIRIAM. "Use of Homemaker Service in Families that Neglect Their Children." *Social Work,* **9** (January 1964).

SHERMAN, EDMUND A., MICHAEL H. PHILLIPS, BARBARA L. HARING, and ANN W. SHYNE. *Service to Children in Their Own Homes—Its Nature and Outcome.* New York: Child Welfare League of America, 1973.

SHINN, EUGENE, and NANCY ROBINSON. "Trends in Homemaker–Home Health Aide Services." *Social Work Abstracts,* **10** (1974), 2–9.

SHYNE, ANN. *The Need for Foster Care.* New York: Child Welfare League of America, 1969.

SIEDER, VIOLET, and CHARLOTTE CALIFF. *Homemaker Home Health Aide Service to the Mentally Ill and Emotionally Disturbed: A Monograph.* New York: National Council for Homemaker Home Health Aide Service, 1976.

SNYDER, RUTH. *Homemaker Service—A Supportive and Protective Service for Children and Adults.* New York: New York City Department of Welfare, May 1962. Mimeo.

SOYKA, PATRICIA. "Homemaker–Home Health Aide Services for Handicapped Children." *Child Welfare,* **55**, 4 (April 1976), 241–251.

STEENO, T., R. MOOREHEAD, and J. SMITS. "Homemakers as Change Agents." *Social Casework,* **58**, 5 (May 1977), 286–293.

TALSMA, EUGENE. "The Homemaker Carries Key Role in Child Behavior Modification." Paper presented at National Council for Homemaker Service, May 1970.

TAYLOR, ELEANOR. "Integrating Homemaker Service into Agency Program." *Child Welfare,* **34** (January 1955).

TRAGER, BRAHNA. *Homemaker/Home Health Aide Service in the United States.* Washington, D.C.: Government Printing Office, 1973.

U.S. DEPARTMENT OF HEALTH, EDUCATION, AND WELFARE. *Homemaker Services: A Preventative to Placement of Children in Foster Care.* Washington, D.C.: Government Printing Office, 1952. Mimeo.

———. *Homemaker Services in the United States: A Directory of Agencies, 1954.* Washington, D.C.: Government Printing Office, 1955.

———. *Homemaker Services: A Nationwide Study.* Washington, D.C.: Government Printing Office, 1958a.

———. *Homemaker Services: Twelve Descriptive Statements.* Washington, D.C.: Government Printing Office, 1958b.

———.*Homemaker Services in the United States: Report of the 1959 Conference.* Washington, D.C.: Government Printing Office, 1960.

———. *Children.* Washington, D.C.: Government Printing Office, March–April 1961a.

———. *Homemaker Services in Public Welfare: The North Carolina Experience.* Washington, D.C.: Government Printing Office, 1961b.

UNIVERSITY OF ILLINOIS SCHOOL OF SOCIAL WORK. *Training Course for Homemakers.* Chicago, 1960.

WATKINS, ELIZABETH G. "So That Children May Remain in Their Own Homes: Homemaker Service Strengthens Aid to Dependent Children Program." *The Child*, 18 (October 1953).

———, and LAURA TURTT. "Short-term Homemaker Service." *Child Welfare*, 37 (May 1958).

WOLDMAN, ELINORE R. "Care of Children in Their Own Homes Through Supervised Homemaker Service." *The Child*, 5 (September 1940).

WORKS PROGRESS ADMINISTRATION. *Final Report on the W.P.A. Program, 1935–43.* Washington, D.C.: Government Printing Office, 1944.

7 DAY-CARE SERVICE

INTRODUCTION

Day care is a child welfare service employed when family care for the child must be supplemented for some part of the day. It is designed to permit the child to be maintained in his own home. It also operates to strengthen and support positive parental role enactment. Like homemaker service, day care is primarily concerned with helping the temporarily motherless family—motherless because the mother is working.

Definition: Day Care and Nursery School

According to the Women's Bureau of the U.S. Department of Labor (1953):

A day nursery or day-care center has as its primary function the provision of good group care and supervision of supplemental parental care during the day because . . . parents are unable to care for [their children] due to employment, sickness, or for some other reason [p. 6].

A United Nations (1956) report defines day care as "an organized service for the care of children away from their own homes during some part of the day when circumstances call for normal care in the home to be supplemented." This definition is based on the conception of day care "as a supplement to, but not as a substitute for, parental care" (p. 18).

In each case, these definitions are followed by some discussion of the differences between day care (a child welfare service) and nursery school (an educational service). Despite any overlap, the central purposes of these programs are essentially distinguishable.

The emphasis in day-care programs is on the primary provision of care and protection: food, shelter, adult supervision, and supplementation of primary parental roles. The day-care facility may, incidentally, educate. In fact, the good day-care facility uses its time with the child to further his development, but care and protection are the first responsibilities of day care. By contrast, "the true nursery school, unencumbered as it is by the need to aid the mitigation of the child's deprivation of normal maternal care, can concentrate on its proper role of preschool education" (United Nations, 1953, p. 9). As Moustakas (1955) says, "Parents usually send children to nursery school because they wish to do so; they often send children to a child care center because they must" (p. 154).

Consequently the clientele of the day-care center is more apt to come from lower socioeconomic groups; that of the nursery school, from a college-educated, middle-class group. The day-care center schedule is apt to be congruent with a normal working day; the nursery school schedule is apt to be for a more limited period. The nursery school, growing out of the movement for childhood education, is more likely to have trained professional teachers on the staff than the day-care center, which grew out of a child-protective orientation.

The distinction is clearly made by the Children's Bureau, which, in a report of a 1962 national survey of licensed day-care facilities, defined their principal purpose as the provision of

> care and protection for children either during the parents' working day or for part of the day and for reasons not necessarily connected with parental employment. . . . Nursery schools and kindergartens were not to be considered day-care facilities within the meaning of this definition since the chief purpose of these facilities is education [Low, 1962, p. 29].

There has been a steady movement, however, toward reducing these distinctions, partly because it is believed that all children, having similar needs, should be provided with similar advantageous developmental experiences during the crucial years of early childhood. Thus the Child Welfare League of America, in its 1969 revisions of standards for day-care service, notes:

> Day care as a child welfare service [is] . . . designed to supplement . . . daily care, health supervision, and developmental experience needed for optimum development. Any form of day care should be designed as a developmental service that fosters the child's potentialities for physical, emotional, intellectual, and social development [pp. 9–10].

Similarly the Day Care and Child Development Council of America (1970) defines day care as

> a service which provides essential care and protection to children outside their homes for a major part of the day on a regular basis. Good day care assures opportunities for physical, emotional, and intellectual growth to the maximum of the child's capacity through group programs for preschool and school-age children as well as through family day care.

It should be noted further that there are two types of programs in addition to day care and nursery school that provide both care and education to children under six. One is the compensatory educational Head Start program initiated in 1965 as part of the "war on poverty." The second is the preschool programs that, in some states, enroll children between three and five in prekindergarten as well as kindergarten programs. Both serve a very sizable number of children without reference to their mothers' employment. In October 1976 some 4.8 million three- to five-year-old children (49 per cent of all children in this age group) were enrolled in nursery school and prekindergarten (U.S. Department of Commerce, 1978, p. 15).

Congregate and Family Day Care

A desirable aspect of a good program of day care is the availability of diversified facilities. Day care may be given in a group setting (a center), or it may be given in a home. The latter is sometimes called *foster day care* or *family day care*.

In some situations, individual family day care is the more desirable alternative. If, for instance, the child is less than two years old, he has not progressed to the point where he can effectively operate in a group situation. He is less capable of contributing to or profiting from a group experience. In addition, the child is not capable of handling, without assistance, many of the simple routines of self-care—feeding himself, dressing himself, and so on—so that he requires more individual attention than is often available in a group situation. Being more vulnerable, both physically and emotionally, the younger child requires the special attention and "mothering" that can be more adequately provided by individual day care (Freud, 1949, p. 69). It is often argued, too, that children two years of age or younger are more likely to encounter increased danger of infection in a group setting.

Individual care is also desirable for the older child who is emotionally disturbed. The child may be three or four years of age, but he may still be exhibiting the emotional needs of a child one or two years old. He is not, therefore, ready for a group situation and needs the support available through family day care.

It is also desirable to keep a group of siblings together. Rather than breaking up the sibling group and denying them the support of familiar and possibly well-liked faces, the group might better be provided with a foster mother for the day.

In addition, there are some practical, situational considerations that may dictate the desirability of family day care over group day care. A day-care center requires a sizable population of working mothers in a community to make operation feasible. Family day care is a more flexible arrangement; it can be expanded or contracted according to need. It also permits more individualization. However flexible a day-care center may be, it must maintain a schedule of one kind or another. In rural areas, or where the mother's working day begins or ends at some unusual time, family day care may offer the necessary flexibility.

As a matter of fact, the origin of family day care lay in its greater potential for meeting the individualized needs of particular situations: "Early in 1927 a survey made by the Philadelphia Association of Day Nurseries had shown that care in a day nursery did not meet the requirements of the mothers due to inflexibility of hours, quarantine problems, and exclusion of children suffering from minor illness" (Trout, Bradbury, 1946, p. 3). Individual day care was suggested as a solution and was first used in Philadelphia in late 1927.

HISTORICAL BACKGROUND

It is difficult to know where the first day-care center was established. Jean Frederick Oberlin, a Swiss minister, opened a *garderie,* or day nursery, in 1767 for children whose mothers worked in the fields. Robert Owen is sometimes given credit for an early nursery established in 1816 in response to a recognition of the need for child care and protection resulting from the employment of mothers (National Society for the Study of Education, 1929, p. 11).

One of the first day-care centers in the United States was established in

1854 at the Nursery and Child's Hospital, New York City. Employed mothers who had been patients at the hospital left their children under the care of the nurses when they returned to work. But the first permanent day nursery in the United States was established in 1863, to care "for the children of women needed to manufacture soldiers' clothing and to clean in hospitals" (National Society, 1929, p. 91). By 1898 the service was so well established that a National Federation of Day Nurseries was founded. By 1900 it was estimated that some 175 such centers had been organized in cities throughout the United States, many of them under the auspices of neighborhood settlement houses.

The 1920s were characterized by important changes. The parallel growth of the nursery school movement during this period accentuated the educational needs of the preschool child and resulted in a growing shift in day-care programs from a purely protective emphasis to one that included a concern for education. Furthermore the increasing acceptance of mental hygiene principles in casework and the professionalization of casework itself resulted in more frequent efforts to include casework services as integral elements in day care.

The Great Depression initially had an adverse effect on the day-care-center movement. Increasing unemployment returned many mothers to full-time homemaker status, and limited funds forced the closing of many centers. Ultimately, however, the Depression, through the Works Progress Administration (WPA), provided a large-scale demonstration of some of the values of day care. Such centers were established by the program throughout the country to provide employment for teachers, nurses, nutritionists, and so on. The service they offered was primarily designed not to meet the child-care needs of the working mother but to provide a healthier environment for children from low-income families. Only children of parents who could not afford the tuition of privately operated nursery schools were eligible for admission to the WPA centers. As the final report on the WPA program notes:

> Many young children from low-income families were cared for in WPA nursery schools. The children were given a daily health inspection and necessary medical services in addition to well-balanced meals, play, and rest in an environment conducive to normal development. . . . These nursery schools everywhere demonstrated their value as an efficient and beneficial mode of child care [Works Progress Administration, 1944, p. 62].

Some idea of the scope of the program established is suggested by the fact that in 1937, forty thousand children were in attendance in the WPA nursery schools during a one-month study period.

This program, established under federal impetus and support, was continued during World War II. With the start of the war and the tremendous increase in the need for manpower, the day-care program became part of a systematic national effort to shift women from homes into factories. More than 3 million married women entered the labor force between 1940 and 1944, many of them mothers of preschool children. The care of the children of working mothers became a problem of concern to many communities. "Increased juvenile delinquency in some communities and high absenteeism in some war manufacturing plants often were attributed to a lack of adequate child-care services" (U.S. Department of Labor, 1953, p. 16).

A national conference convened in July 1941, and this was followed by the formation of statewide child-care committees in many states. In July 1942, a sum of $400,000 was allocated to the U.S. Office of Education and the Children's Bureau; grants were made available to states to help establish programs for extended school service and to public welfare agencies to set up day-care centers and other services for children of working mothers.

In further support of this explicit public policy, $6 million, allocated in July 1942 to the WPA, was designated for use in reorganizing its nursery school program in order to meet the needs of employed mothers. When the WPA was abolished by presidential order at the end of 1942, this project was maintained with federal funds made available through the Lanham Act. This Act, concerned primarily with defense housing and public works for defense, was reinterpreted so as to permit the allocation of funds to communities in support of child-care facilities and service. Public programs for day care were supplemented, in some instances, by large industrial firms engaged in war work. The Curtiss-Wright plane factory in Buffalo and the Kaiser shipyards established day-care centers for their employees.

> At its peak, the wartime program of day-care centers for children of working mothers had an enrollment of 129,357 children (July 1944) in 3102 units. By the end of the war, every state, except New Mexico, had submitted request for and received Federal funds under the Lanham act for operation and maintenance of child care programs and some $52 million of Federal funds had been expended for this purpose. . . .
>
> It has been estimated that between 550,000 and 600,000 children received care, at one time or another, under the auspices established through the help of the Lanham act. This, despite the serious handicaps which the program faced due to lack of suitable physical accommodations in many communities and shortages of adequately trained personnel [U.S. Department of Labor, 1953, pp. 9, 19].

Despite urging, on the part of the Children's Bureau, that local communities establish planning groups to ensure the continuation and development of day-care facilities, and despite the fact that mothers using the centers organized to agitate for a long-range program that—unlike the emergency one, which was based on the needs of industry—was planned to meet the needs of children, the end of the war saw a sharp contraction of facilities. The principal factor was the withdrawal of federal funds through termination of Lanham Act support in February 1946. The shortage of trained personnel, the high costs of operation, and the reduction in the number of working mothers also contributed to this change.

The federal government, in justifying termination of its support, noted that assistance under the Lanham Act for child care had been based on the recruitment and retention of workers for war production and essential supporting services.

For a period of time after World War II, there was little change in the day-care picture. During the 1960s, as a consequence of some of the factors to be detailed below (pp. 275–276), there was a resurgence of interest in day care. The high-water mark of such concerns was achieved in 1971, when a very extensive child-care development bill was passed by both houses of Congress (but vetoed by President Nixon). Since that time, no similar measure, such as the Child and

Family Services Act sponsored by Senators Mondale and Brademus in 1975, has achieved enough support to pass Congress. Despite this failure, however, there has been a steady expansion of both public and private day-care facilities in response to the increased demand. The 1962 and 1967 amendments to the Social Security Act, which provided funding for day care for current, past, and potential welfare recipients on a match of $75 of federal funds for every $25 of state funds, helped to fuel this expansion. Since 1975, Title XX—the Social Services Reorganization Amendment—has provided funding to states for day-care funding.

In 1975 state use of Title XX funds for day care generally included custodial care, social development activities, educational and recreational activities, an entrance health examination, ongoing health care, and meals and snacks. Some twenty-three states offered limited programs of day-care services to mentally retarded, physically handicapped, and/or emotionally disturbed children. A smaller number of states offered day-care services to migrant children.

By 1980 the federal government provided some $2.2 billion for child care services through a variety of direct and indirect mechanisms. Child care is the largest single category of expenditures in the Title XX social services program. Through grants to the states it provided, in 1978, care in day-care centers and family-based arrangements to some 800,000 children from low- and moderate-income families. Approximately 2.7 million families received tax credits of up to $800 as reimbursement for child care expenditures.

In recapitulating the history of day care in the United States, it is significant that widespread support of day-care facilities did not result primarily in response to the needs of children but in response to the needs and demands of adult society: to increase job possibilities during the Great Depression and to increase the availability of women during periods of critical labor shortage in World War II.

AN EXPLANATION

During the earlier history of day care, social workers were very much involved in day care—screening applicants for limited day-care resources and counseling with families who wanted to use the service (Steinfels, 1973, pp. 59–64; Greenblatt, 1977). A mother working outside the home was atypical, and in almost every instance, employment was not a matter of choice. Unlike the current situation, the families requesting day care were very likely to be families presenting serious social problems for which social work had been given some responsibility. Because of the nature of the client group to which the service was then directed, day care was closely tied to social work. An unfortunate consequence, however, was that day care, family disorganization, and welfare came to be associated in the mind of the community. The nature of the clientele requesting day care has changed markedly since that period prior to the 1930s, and the day-care field has been making efforts to modify the image.

A major controversy revolves around the question of whether day care is a social utility (like public schools and parks), which every family might need and use at some time, or whether the need and use of day care imply a "problem." Ruderman's (1968) survey of day care in the United States led her to conclude that:

great numbers of normal, middle class, intact, responsible families with working mothers need day-care services and even greater numbers of such families want it. In fact, as we get away from the problem situations cited in welfare documents [it becomes clear that] day care is primarily a child care program on all levels of society for normal children and normal families [p. 341].

It is becoming more widely accepted that day care is a "normal" arrangement required by "normal" families. Why, then, the illustrative material here that emphasizes "problem" situations? This follows from the fact that our primary focus in this chapter is really *not* with day care as a recently developed social utility to meet the needs of the contemporary family. The primary focus *is* on the special functions of the child-welfare social worker in day care and the kinds of help he can offer to those limited number of families who may have problems in effectively utilizing a social service available to all. One may accept an "institutional" orientation toward day care as such and at the same time hold a "residual" orientation toward the particular functions of the child-welfare social worker in day care.

Consequently our concern in this chapter is not with the greatest majority of families, who effectively utilize day care without requiring the intervention of the social worker. Our concern is with those limited number of families who come to day care as a result of some problem situation and with those parents and children whose use of day care produces, or exacerbates, social problems.

Although day care might become a universal social utility, the personal care services provided by the social worker should be available to the limited number of day-care families who might need and want this option.

THE SOCIAL CONTEXT OF DAY CARE: THE WORKING MOTHER

Because the question of the working mother is so intimately related to the question of the need for and the use of day-care facilities, it would be helpful to present some of the more important data concerning the working mother in the United States today.

Over the past eighty years, we have experienced a trend toward an increase of women in the labor force. In 1890 only 18 per cent of all women were in the labor force, and they constituted 17 per cent of all workers; in 1977 48 per cent of all women over sixteen were in the labor force, and they constituted 40 per cent of all workers.

Although the proportion of women workers has increased, it is of greater significance that the number of working mothers with preschool children has increased, too. The numbers change from year to year, but the trend is constant. In 1976 about 5.4 million working women were mothers of children under six years, and about 2.5 million of such mothers had children under three. One out of every three working mothers had a preschool child at home. The number of working mothers with children under six rose rapidly between 1950 and 1977. In 1977 there were 6.4 million children under six whose mothers were employed: "Between 1940 and 1976 the labor force participation rate of mothers increased more than fivefold, the most significant change in the labor force the country has ever experienced" (United States Department of Labor, 1977, p. 4). All women, including mothers of preschool children, are increasing their commitment to work, and the labor market behavior of mothers is becoming more like that of women in general as the labor market behavior of women in general becomes more like that of men. The trend appears to be irreversible. By 1978 husband-wife joint wage-earner families had become the dominant family type.

The problem for parents of role conflict between the time required for adequate child care and the time required for work needs to be resolved. Alternative child caretaking through relatives, family day care, day-care centers, and prekindergarten is one response to the problem. Extended paid maternity leave, shared work, part-time work, and paternity leave are additional possibilities being discussed here and implemented abroad (see Chapter 12).

A number of historical developments help explain women's changed relationship to the labor force. Once the mother contributed to family income by producing goods and performing services in the home. The shift to an industrial economy brought the demand for a cash income, which can be acquired only outside the home in a factory, a store, or an office. As Ogburn and Nimkoff (1955) note, "whereas the farmer and his wife jointly produce food and other goods, the trend is for husbands and wives to produce a joint income, although not from a joint enterprise" (p. 144).

The changing nature of jobs has increased the likelihood of women's working. In 1919 about two thirds of the labor force was centered in the production industries: acriculture, mining, manufacturing, and construction. In general, such industries offer few employment opportunities for women. Since 1919, however, the sharp increase in the relative number of workers employed in wholesale and retail trades, transportation and communication, government agencies, and service industries has provided a very considerable increase in the employment opportunities for women. The rationalization of industrial production so that each job is broken up into small, manageable components has also helped to increase employment opportunities for women. Also, a greater percentage of women currently have the educational background that permits them to take advantage of employment opportunities.

Changed childbearing patterns have also resulted in an increase in the number of women working. In 1890 the last child born was likely to enter school when the mother was about forty years old; in 1973 this was more likely to happen when the mother was about thirty-one.

With her children in school, the mother is more likely to seek employment. Also, increases in rates of illegitimacy, divorce, and family disruptions of all kinds have resulted in an increase in the number of families headed by a woman. There is considerable pressure for such a woman to find day care for her children and to seek employment for herself.

Two world wars in a period of twenty-five years also affected the pattern of changing employment of women: on both occasions, women were encouraged to accept paid employment. Although many of the women returned to the home at the end of the war, employment for women continued to be higher than at prewar levels. The actual experience with women employees changed many fixed ideas about the capacity of women as workers. It also gave many women a more positive acceptance, for themselves, of the role of employee. The civil rights movement has intensified concern with women as a minority group, impelling legislation defending womens' rights to employment opportunities. The women's movement has increased the political power of women and resulted in expanded job opportunities. And "The proportion of women with four years or more of college has doubled since 1952. Generally, the more education women have, the more likely they are to be in the labor force" (U.S. Department of Labor, 1977, p. 29).

The fact that so many goods and services previously produced in the home are now available commercially not only opens up employment opportunities for women but also provides the time for such employment. Labor-saving equipment and the lessened burden of housework free women for outside employment. Finally, the ever-rising standard of living, coupled with a long period of inflation, exerts pressure for an increase in family income. The more things a family needs or wants to buy, the greater the need for supplementation of the income of the principal wage earner.

But the probability that the mother will be working is related to a number of variables, such as the age of her children, the family income, and the family composition. The younger the child at home, the less likely it is that the mother will work. Because economic necessity is the major reason women work, labor-force participation rates decrease as family income increases. Women with husbands are less likely to work than mothers in fatherless families. Because non-white mothers are more likely to be living in low-income families and are more likely to be without husbands, the rate of labor force participation of nonwhite mothers is higher than that of white mothers.

Although the data suggest very clearly that most mothers work because they have to work, it must be remembered that some mothers work primarily because they find a greater sense of self-fulfillment in employment, because they dislike housework and child care, because they have questions about their adequacy as homemakers and mothers, or because they are stimulated by the social contact a job provides.

Because of the steady, sharp increase in working mothers of children under six years of age, increasing numbers of mothers are potentially interested in day care. "At the same time that more mothers have gone to work, the number of adults in the home who can care for children has decreased," intensifying the need for day-care services.

The considerable interest in day care that developed during the 1960s resulted from a number of other factors as well:

1. Increasing costs of the Aid to Families of Dependent Children (AFDC) program have sparked interest in day care. The effort to reduce welfare rolls by requiring work and training has, as a corollary, provision of day-care services for the dependent children of the AFDC mother. The Work Incentive (WIN) program provides special day-care funding to enable AFDC mothers to accept work or training.

2. Recent research on the educability of young children and pressure from the civil rights movement have generated an interest in day care as a compensatory educational experience. Developmental day care could be provided for children of low-income families whether or not the mothers are working. Here the interest in day care derives from a concern with enriching the supposedly limited educational stimulation available in low-income homes in order to prepare the child for school. This is the intent of the Head Start program.

3. Child care increases the number of jobs available to human services para-professionals. It is potentially one of the most productive areas for the implementation of the concept of new careers for the poor. The day-care center can utilize the qualifications of many lower-class women who seek employment but whose only marketable skill is experience in caring for children, and many have been recruited as aides of one kind or another.

4. Advocates of participatory democracy and community control see day care as an excellent vehicle for politicizing local residents. Parents are concerned with and responsive to the needs of their children, so day-care centers can often be organized by the action of community volunteers. As a matter of fact, a study of the Head Start program suggests that its effects on parents and community may be as great as the effects on children: a sizable percentage of Head Start programs have increased the involvement of the poor with local institutions, "particularly at decision-making levels and in decision-making capacities" (Kirshner, 1970, p. 6). Consequently community action groups of one kind or another have contributed to the growing support for day care.

5. For women's groups, day care is crucial in freeing women from their "primary identification as mothers and from the sole responsibility for child rearing." The community, it is argued, shares with the parents the responsibility for child rearing. Consequently such groups are actively supporting the development of day-care centers available to all mothers, employed or not.

SCOPE

Statistics on the scope of day-care facilities are based on the licensing requirements that allow such facilities to be located and counted. The accuracy of these statistics depends, then, on the adequacy of licensing procedures.

In 1979 a total of 18,300 day-care centers were licensed with an aggregate capacity of 900,000 children. It has been noted that in 1977 some 6.4 million children whose mothers worked were under six years of age. Consequently the licensed day-care center facilities available were capable of offering care to about 14 per cent of the total population of risk.

Calculating the need for day-care services by noting the gap between the numbers of preschool children of employed mothers and the places available is a faulty procedure. The immediate family and the extended family are very much a part of the caretaking picture. Most children are adequately cared for in or out of the home by relatives. Many families have no need for day-care services. Many families make their own informal arrangements for care when it is not possible within the family, which is the highest preference. There is considerable ambivalence about the use of day-care facilities. Demonstration projects that have offered cost-free quality day-care service have had fewer takers than anticipated (Woolsey, 1977, p. 135).

However, the fact that close to 50 per cent of all three- to five-year-old children were, in 1978, enrolled by their parents in some kind of primary formal school or day-care program would indicate a considerable acceptance of, and demand for, such programs. The question of hesitance about the use of such programs may apply primarily to the younger child in the case of some families and may be related to cost factors for the three- to five-year-olds in other families (Kamerman, Kahn, 1979).

Although care by relatives is the predominant arrangement for all groups, minority families are even more likely to use such arrangements. This was particularly true of Hispanic families. This suggests the greater availability of the extended family among minority groups.

In 1970 about half of the day-care centers and about 90 per cent of the family-day-care homes were offered under proprietary auspices for profit. Some 35 per cent of day-care-center facilities were under the auspices of voluntary nonprofit agencies, and about 15 per cent were under public auspices. This distribution did not change very significantly over the 1970–1980 decade.

Despite all the talk about day care as a "social service," then, more than half of all such facilities are operated as a business venture. Many of those operating under voluntary auspices are organized by women's clubs, professional women's groups, patriotic organizations, and church organizations. Only a limited percentage of all licensed facilities under voluntary auspices are administered by what might be regarded as social work agencies, such as settlement houses or community centers and child welfare or family welfare agencies.

Effects on the Child

There is considerable research available regarding the effects of mothers' employment on children. Reviews of such research tend to come to very similar conclusions, particularly with regard to the three- to five-year-old child—namely, that if the mother is satisfied with her job and the provision for child care is reasonably good and stable, there is no adverse effect on the child's development. A 1974 review of the research regarding the "consequences for wife, husband and child" of the mother's employment concludes that "the results disprove the theory that maternal employment fosters deprivation of the child" (Hoffman, Nye, 1974). A 1977 review notes that "no consistent differences between preschool children of working and nonworking mothers have been found when potentially confounding variables (such as socioeconomic status, mother's age, child's age, mother's attitude toward work, stability of the home, presence of the father and alternative child care arrangements) have been controlled" (Clarke-Stewart, 1977, p. 34). Analogous conclusions are drawn regarding the effects of the mother's employment on older school-aged children: neither school achievement nor general development appears to be adversely affected (Clarke-Stewart, 1977, pp. 47–48).

It might be noted that research tends to show some positive consequences of the mother's employment: relief from financial strain, increased sharing of responsibility in family life by the father and the children, widening of the mother's interests, and increased independence of the children.

There is less unanimity, or perhaps more uneasiness, about the effects of mothers' employment and the need for surrogate care for children younger than two to three years of age. Reports of carefully conducted studies comparing the development of very young children cared for in a day-care center for part of the day over a period of time with that of children cared for at home indicate little difference (Caldwell, 1964; Kagan, Kearsley, Zelazo, 1977). The children appear to be equally "attached" to their mothers and seem to develop normally. In each instance, however, the experiments were conducted in a carefully designed day-care facility, "well run, nurturant, responsible," guaranteeing high-quality care that is not often available for infants. (See also Bronfenbrenner, 1976.)

Clinicians are somewhat suspicious of the research results and tend to advocate child care by the mother herself during the early years, recognizing the reality that this might not be possible in some families (Fraiberg, 1977).

Licensing

"Day care licensing refers to the requirement by law that a license, permit, or certification be secured before a person, agency, or corporation takes on the care of children away from their own home during the day" (U.S. Senate, 1971, p. 27). It may include registration, licensing, and inspection. The licensing procedure rests on a delegation of legislative power to an administrative agency. The required standards for care become, in effect, "little laws." Licensing ensures the maintenance of some minimum standards of day care and reflects the community's concern for the physical and psychosocial safety of its children (Class, 1958; Day Care Child Development Council, 1970; Granato, Lynch, 1972). By 1970 almost all states had made licensing of day-care centers mandatory.

Fewer states, however, had made licensing of day-care homes mandatory. Whereas 90 per cent of the day-care centers are licensed, fewer than 2 per cent of the family-day-care homes are subject to licensing, because most states do not require licensing if such homes offer care to fewer than three children: "Family day-care homes, then, are generally unregulated and unsupervised by any governmental or social agency. Hundreds of thousands of children, including those whose fees are paid by government funds, are cared for in these homes, about which very little is known" (U.S. Senate, 1971, p. 89; see also Keyserling, 1972).

Licensing regulations are likely to cover such factors as physical facilities, safety standards, health standards, provisions for adequate number and training of personnel, and educational facilities and equipment. They may also indicate the special kinds of provisions to be made for special kinds of children; for instance, a higher ratio of caretakers to children may be required in day-care facilities serving the handicapped (Child Welfare League of America, 1960).

In the discussion of quality of child care within day care, there are repeated references to adult–child ratios. The ratio itself is no certain measure of the level of warmth, maturity, concern, interest, and so on with which a caretaker may interact with a child. However, whereas we find it difficult, if not impossible, to measure such qualities with confidence, we can and do measure adult–child ratios. They do, in a rough way, suggest the necessary, if not the sufficient, condition for quality child care. The ratio has become the objective indicator operationally defining the quality of child care.

Although most licensing statements have emphasized a desirable child–caretaker ratio of one caretaker for six to nine three- to four-year-old children, a national study of the operation of day-care centers showed that the size of the group was an even more crucial variable. If the group is too large, increasing the number of caretakers assigned to the group does not result in a positive outcome. Small numbers of children interacting with small numbers of adults is most effective (Abt Associates, 1978).

There are differences, from state to state, with regard to the specificity of the regulations, the nature of the penalties for violations, the kinds of facilities covered, the regularity and frequency of inspection, and the provisions available for consultation and assistance. There have been some efforts to develop national standards in a model licensing code. Currently the federal government sets the guidelines for a day-care facility if it is to be eligible to receive federal funds.

The state departments of public welfare are generally given responsibility for implementing licensing legislation; less frequently, such responsibility rests with the state department of health or the state department of education. In any case, the office responsible for licensing may provide supervision and consultation and arrange educational programs, institutes, and workshops to help agencies reach, and maintain, an acceptable level of service.

Social workers who implement the state day-care licensing procedures for the state departments of public welfare thus have two major responsibilities: a supervisory–regulatory function and a consultation function. The supervisory–regulatory function assures the parent and the community that conditions at the day-care center are satisfactory. In discharging the consultation responsibility, the social worker helps the day-care center maintain and, if possible, improve conditions for the children at the center.

Generally licenses, once issued, must be renewed every year. Consequently there is provision for a periodic reevaluation of the day-care center. In many localities, however, the licensing staff is too small to do more than keep up with complaints received and has little power to impose adequate penalties for violations. In addition, licensing laws frequently exclude from the licensing requirement sizable groups of centers, such as those run by religious organizations and public school systems.

Licensing procedure involves considerable administrative discretion on the part of the social-worker licensing agent. Basic standards for the group care of children must be applied sensibly and with some flexibility. The licensing social worker attempts to apply the regulations in a spirit of cooperative mutuality, rather than in a spirit of evaluative assessment. The stance should not be the use of regulations to deny a license, but rather the use of regulations to educate toward the desirability of standards and to motivate their acceptance. Licensing standards should be applied fairly, uniformly, and promptly. A day-care applicant should know what the decision is as soon as possible and should be clearly informed of the reasons for the decision.

Day-care administrators frequently challenge the social worker to justify the standards he is attempting to enforce. They question the validity of required child-care ratios and of the credentials demanded of the various day-care-center personnel. They are also keenly aware of inequities in licensing resulting from differences in the application of administrative discretion. Objections frequently come from groups of ghetto residents who have organized a day-care center on their own initiative. The director of one such center comments on licensing requirements:

The center can help to upgrade the community by giving jobs or on-the-job training to persons among the poor who want to work in day care. They could be people who are qualified and talented with children even though they do not necessarily meet the formal licensing requirements. What does a credential or degree tell you about how good a teacher is? [Lynden, 1970, p. 72].

Despite the questions that are often raised about educational credentials, it might be noted that a nationwide study of day-care centers showed that quality care was associated with "staff specialization in child-related fields" (Abt Associates, 1978).

Different agencies involved in licensing different aspects of a day-care center may fail to coordinate their activities or may even set contradictory standards. One center was criticized by the fire department because the yard-door latch was too high for the children to reach in case of fire. Another department then criticized the center because the yard-door latch was so low that the children could open it and run into the street.

Each of the requirements for a license, designed to protect the children, makes establishment of a center more difficult and more expensive. At what point does the need for adequate care and adequate facilities seriously limit the availability of day care? What specific standards, flexibly enforced, are the minimums that are acceptable to the community? This is still a matter for discussion. Licensing regulations that demand too high a standard substitute a problem of low quantity for a problem of low quality.

Questions have been raised about the jurisdiction and effectiveness of licensing. Operators of commercial centers note that they offer a service to parents of children who pay for the cost of care. They contend that this is a transaction between the parents and the day-care center in which government should not interfere. Licensing suggests that the parents are not fully capable of making a competent decision about what is best for their child and need the state's protection in making a choice.

Effectiveness of licensing is also questioned. Once a facility obtains a license, it can act in defiance of licensing regulations with some impunity. Very rarely is a license revoked, suspended, or not renewed. The burden of proof in obtaining a license rests with the applicant; the burden of proof rests with the state in revoking, suspending, or failing to renew a license. Fairly strong proof of the abuse of licensing regulations is needed if the agency has any hopes that court action will sustain its decision not to renew a license, if challenged by the center.

Because many states have found it difficult to monitor the licensing of family day care, they have been shifting to registration as the procedure of choice. Under registration, inspection of the homes is not required. The caretaker lists the names of the children in her home and the regulatory agency provides the home with a statement of mandatory standards. Consultation is provided by the regulatory agency to upgrade the skills of the family day caretaker.

Effective implementation by social workers of the licensing responsibility is impeded by the fact that because "licensing is a specialized service and its functions are not included in the curriculum of a master's degree social work program, virtually no one coming into the job is equipped by previous experience to handle its varied responsibilities" (Prescott *et al.,* 1972, p. 70).

SITUATIONS IN WHICH DAY CARE IS AN APPROPRIATE RESOURCE

The very largest percentage of children in day care are there because their mothers need to work or both need and want to work. The family is intact, the children present no special problems, and the situation is "normal."

Because our concern in this chapter is sharply focused on the specialized contribution that the child-welfare social worker can make to increase the effectiveness of day care, the illustrative material and citations are highly selective.

Day care is most frequently used by the working mother. Day care assumes the role functions relinquished by the mother while she is working. This is a problem of role implementation that results from interrole conflict:

A harassed young mother of twenty-four asked to have her two little boys—Johnnie, aged four, and Jimmie, aged three—enrolled in the nursery so that she might look for a job. She was anxious and pushed by the strain of trying to make ends meet. "We had big doctor bills when Johnnie was born and we have never caught up. How can you have a good family life if you can never pay your bills?" [Merriam, 1959, p. 23].

The S.'s have one child, age three months. Mr. S. is a medical student; Mrs. S. is employed as a secretary. In order for Mr. S. to remain in medical school, mother will continue to work until husband's education is completed [Yudkin, Holme, 1963, p. 43].

Psychological desire, preference, and need may be the determinant of the mother's working in some instances. This is true in the case

of a bright little boy of two whose mother, a compulsive neurotic, found herself unable to adjust to the new duties of a parent. A highly creative, extremely intelligent woman, this young mother was advised to work, thus giving constructive outlet to her compulsive pattern, and to forestall a complete breakdown. Working seemed one way to achieve satisfaction from the drudgeries of home plus the burden of motherhood, yet partially functioning as a mother. In this case, making day care available served to sustain this mother as well as the artistic father, and contributed greatly to the stability of this family [Gordon, 1957, p. 303].

More often, however, children in day-care programs are likely to be members of a family headed by a woman who works because she has to.

Mr. G. died of a sudden heart attack. The family had no savings, limited life insurance, and the OASDI payments do not permit Mrs. G. to support her two children—Jane, three, and Bill, four and a half—without supplementation. She is returning to a job she held before marriage as a typist and placing both children in day care.

Day care may also be provided in situations where the child, because of mental, physical, or emotional handicap, presents an unusually heavy burden. Relief to the overburdened mother during part of the day may be sufficient to obviate the necessity for institutionalizing the child. The need for specialized knowledge in dealing with children who are different may be provided by the day-care facility, staffed by people with specialized education. Daily, time-limited group care also provides an opportunity for normal contact with peers for those children who, because of their handicap, might otherwise be isolated from such normal activities.

The Community Welfare Council of the Greater Sacramento area undertook a survey, in 1960, of parents' attitudes toward the possible use of day care for their retarded children; of 199 questionnaires mailed, 66 were returned, 47 of which indicated a positive response to the use of day care. The need for day care was felt by the parents for reasons that related to the needs of the family and the needs of the retarded child (National Association of Retarded Children, n.d.):

> Most parents feel the need for relief from the demands of constant supervision of their handicapped child in order to meet some of their own personal needs, provide more adequate attention to other children in the family, find employment, and reduce emotional tension within the family.
>
> Parents see the value of day-care services as providing essential social experiences for their children as well as training, therapy, and education that they, as parents, are unable to provide.

The two sets of reasons are related. One parent said, in talking about his retarded daughter:

> The few children in the neighborhood recognize the "difference" and do not want to play with her. The lack of companionship and play affects her to such an extent that she is becoming extremely irritable. This, with the hyperactive personality, is such a burden on my nervous system that I, in turn, cannot always be as objective as I know I should be. A service such as this would be a great help and aid to parents like us with similar problems. It would afford us the relaxation from these tensions, just as I'm certain it would be beneficial to my little girl.

Another parent said:

> The important thing about the program for my child was the opportunity to play with other retarded children as the neighborhood children ignore him. We have been unable to get a babysitter because of his retardation, and some feel he is catching—people just refuse. I need some time away from him so that I can get some of my work done.

Some day-care centers have been organized as a special therapeutic facility for emotionally disturbed children (Faddis, 1956; Selligman, 1958; Chazin, 1969; Bloch, 1970; Lovatt, 1972). The Virginia Frank Child Development Center in Chicago, for instance, describes itself as "a specialized therapeutic nursery and kindergarten for children three to five years of age who are showing signs of emotional and behavioral problems." The center supplements individual therapy by making available a therapeutic environment for part of the day. Actually, however, very limited day-care facilities are available to serve the physically, mentally, or emotionally handicapped child.

In some cases, day care may offer temporary relief when the parent–child relationship is disturbed. The mitigation of constant stress permits reorganization of psychic forces so that the interaction may be turned in a more positive direction. Day care supports the parents' ability to care for the child and reduces tension and conflict, increasing the possibility that the child may be maintained in his own home:

> The S. family presented a picture of serious emotional disturbances for which they have sought counseling in a family agency for some time. Both parents, threatened by their own pathological background, were showing unrealistic fears and anxieties over their two-and-a-half-year-old son's "wild" behavior and his refusal to speak. On psychiatric exams, the child was found essentially normal and his behavior not inappropriate to his age. Both parents genuinely rejected any thought of full-time placement but, with help, could accept the partial separation of day placement which would lessen the heavy burden of living with their youngster [Gordon, 1957, p. 301].

The following situation illustrates the complexity of interaction in a difficult situation for which day care can be a helpful resource:

> J., five-and-one-half, was referred to the [center] by the Riley Hospital Child Guidance Clinic. She had been blind since birth as the result of oxygen exposure. Although both parents were medical students, the mother was regarded as an emotionally and mentally disturbed person. She resisted enrolling J. in the Nursery and did so only at the insistence of the Clinic. The psychiatrist felt it extremely important for the child to be separated from her mother and to have a normal group experience. She made a fine adjustment in our group and will eventually attend the State Blind School. The mother's attitude also improved [Jackson, n.d., p. 31].

Day care may also be used as an alternative to homemaker service when the mother has died or deserted or when her hospitalization will be prolonged:

> One mother who is suffering from phlebitis is not able to give her active three-year-old son full-time care but, with sufficient rest while he is away from home during the day, she can be relaxed and carry on well for the rest of the time. Her husband brings the child to the center [Yeomans, 1951, p. 7].

The day-care staff, like the homemaker who is assigned to a family to help educate the parents to more adequate child-rearing methods, attempts to communicate knowledge about feeding, discipline, child protection, and so on:

> [When the mother] came to observe the children in the day care center, she noted with some relief that Joe was not the only child who threw things. She has seen that there are other children who "can't cut on the line," as she has tried to force Joe to do. Mrs. B. was most interested to learn from the teacher that Joe is too young to be expected to cut "on the line." Since her anxiety over unrealistic expectations for her children has been relieved, the neighbors report that Mrs. B. doesn't spank her children as much as before [Hansen, Pemberton, 1963].

Day-care facilities have also been used as a remedial measure for a seriously deprived home environment. A United Nations (1956) report points out that, where "shortage or inadequacy of housing leads to overcrowding and to unhealthy living conditions," where "sufficient play space is not available," where there is, "concern about child health and a desire to improve the nutrition of certain categories of children," day-care centers may play a role in child protection, "in combating child morbidity and mortality . . . in improving the conditioning of underweight children" (p. 23). In such situations the day-care service assures the children "better care than they would receive if they remained at home" (Hansen, Pemberton, 1963, p. 180). Here inadequate parental role implementation results from deficiencies in the environment: lack of adequate living space, play space, toys, food, and the like.

As Merriam (1959) says, "A mother living on the third floor of an apartment building with a four-year-old child and two younger children may be up against a very real problem of being unable to supervise the older child for any outdoor play while also meeting the demands for the care of the young ones" (p. 22).

Of growing importance is the use of day care to prevent the placement of children in substitute care and as a "respite" resource in protective services (see pp. 194–195).

> The oldest of Mrs. B.'s four children was four when this family came to the attention of the Seven Hills Neighborhood House in Cincinnati. Mrs. B. felt that she was going to have to resort to desperate measures to solve her problems, and she told the agency director that she had decided to place her children in foster care. Beset by an inadequate welfare allotment, substandard housing (four children and herself in two rooms), marital difficulties, and full-time care of the children, Mrs. B. was finding life "too much" for her. The day-care center was suggested as a means of relieving some of her child care burdens so that she could re-establish herself [Hansen, Pemberton, 1963, p. 181].

Some day-care facilities suggest other uses of such resources. Large transatlantic liners provide day-care centers that free the traveling parents of the care of the child during the day. Large department stores and shopping centers provide such resources to permit the parents to shop freely. Similar resources might also be used to permit parents to take part in educational or cultural programs or to take advantage of regular medical or psychiatric treatment programs as outpatients. In each instance, the day-care facilities might, by permitting the parent a greater measure of freedom, contribute to a reduction of parental resentment and parent–child friction and might enhance the parent–child relationship.

Illustrating the use of day care in more normal situations is the following news report:

> The YMCA of Eastern Union County will start a curb service "Mothers Service" on wheels in Linden next month. The YMCA has acquired a thirty-five-foot mobile housetrailer and converted it into a "Jack and Jill" playmobile. The playmobile will set up shop in three different locations in Linden to give mothers two to three hours relief from their youngsters, aged three to five, and time to do some much-needed shopping or other chores [New York Sunday News, November 18, 1962].

Such use of day care suggests its appropriateness for keeping tensions within the family at a manageable level by providing periodic relief from the burdens of child care. Of even greater potential importance is the value of such a service to the single parent, who must be mother, father, nurse, teacher, disciplinarian, provider, and housekeeper without possibility of a break.

EVALUATION

There is a very voluminous literature evaluating the effects of day-care, nursery school, Head Start, and prekindergarten programs on the social, emotional, and especially the cognitive development of the children enrolled. The material is not relevant to our concerns here, which are focused on one component of the program, namely, the social services.

The most important value of day care is that, like other supplementary services, it increases the probability that the child may be maintained in his own home. The mother who must work can do so without finding a substitute home for the child; the handicapped child may not have to be institutionalized; the family facing a crisis may find sufficient relief and support in day care so that it can be held together for the child.

Some 2 million children of working mothers, who might otherwise need public assistance, are supported independently of the assistance program. The mother's salary, either as a sole wage in a female-headed family or as a supplementary wage in a family headed by her husband, lifts these families out of poverty.

Studies by Shyne (1969) and Jenkins (1966) indicate that the need for foster care might have been prevented in some instances if adequate day care had been available.

A study of a demonstration project by a private agency of the value of family day care to forty-two families noted:

> In ten instances—before day-care service was requested—application for full-time care placement had appeared imminent. In nine other situations—though difficult to establish with absolute certainty—from the prevailing evidence of uneasy parent–child relationships and fear of overwhelming responsibilities, it would appear that full-time placement might have eventuated.
>
> In fourteen situations an application to public relief was prevented [Foster Family Day Care, 1962, p. 14].

The director of a day nursery details the cooperative action between her agency and a family service agency in holding a family together:

> The mentally ill mother and the four-year-old child were in such a constant state of friction that the father was afraid his wife would do some harm to the child in his absence at work. We were able to arrange for the father to bring the little girl in the morning and call for her on his way home from work in the evening. On week-ends he is able to act as a "buffer" between mother and child. With the continuing work of the Jewish Family Service with the mother, the home has remained together [Goddard, 1957, p. 32].

Some family problems are related to income deficiency. The mother might provide the necessary increment of income necessary to maintain family stability. Day care, which ensures adequate care of the children, allows this solution to be sensibly considered and comfortably accepted. Thus some families, the exact number being difficult to ascertain, are able to maintain themselves independently of public assistance, because the mother is able to go to work where adequate provision for child care is available.

Conversely, the lack of day-care services can jeopardize the success of efforts being made to help people who are currently receiving assistance to achieve independence. The federal government reported that in June 1971, four thousand AFDC mothers could not be enrolled in the Work Incentive program "for the sole reason that child care was not available" (U.S. Dept. of H.E.W., 1972).

Day care also is a resource that permits a more natural, more acceptable route to help for families with problems: "Parents who are unlikely to seek professional services on their own initiative often respond to help when it is offered along with day care for their children" (Gilfillan, 1962, p. 416). Some families that might not otherwise have obtained treatment for problems adversely affecting their children are, through day care, more accessible to such help.

Children who might not otherwise have a safe, stimulating place to play are provided such a facility; children who might otherwise be deprived of an experience in group interaction under guided supervision are provided with this kind of enriching experience; and children who might otherwise be left to care for themselves, or left to haphazard, uncertain arrangements for care, are more adequately, more safely cared for as a result of the availability of day-care facilities.

Although the following reported incidents may be atypical, they illustrate the possible dangers to which children might be exposed if the mother has to work and cannot make adequate provisions for child care:

> In a small city in Ohio, an eight-year-old girl was burned to death and her six-year-old brother was severely burned in the roominghouse in which the family lived. Their parents were at work. As a result of the death of a five-year-old girl, burned to death in a Connecticut city while her mother was working, labor leaders made plans for the establishment of additional day nurseries for the care of children of employed mothers.
>
> Too great responsibility is often given to the oldest child in a family. An eight-year-old, left in charge of three younger children until midnight while her mother worked on the swing shift and her father was taking a training course, was unable to give proper aid when one of the younger children was injured.
>
> . . . [In one Iowa] city, when a child was hurt in a playground accident, it was discovered that no member of her family was at home all day. The child, too young for school, was just packed off to the playground with a lunch [Fredrickson, 1943, pp. 165–166].

Day care as a supplementary service, then, has great preventive value. It acts to prevent breakup of families, separation of children from their parents, increased dependency on public aid, and dangers and hazards to children.

THE SOCIAL WORKER AND DAY CARE

An adequate day-care program requires a team approach, because it involves a partnership of three professions: education, health, and social work

(Child Welfare League of America, 1946). Some families who seek day-care service know very clearly what they want, why they want it, and how to use it. In such instances, the social worker's only responsibility is to see that the community makes the necessary services available and that the potential applicant is aware of their existence. For some families, however, the decision to use day care is reached only after many interrelated questions have been resolved. In such instances, casework services can be of help.

It is not always clear to the applicant that the mother's employment is the most desirable—or, in fact, the only—solution to the family's problems. For the widow, the divorced mother, or the unmarried mother, AFDC may not have been seriously considered as an alternative or, having been considered, may have been rejected without a full knowledge of the program. The opportunity to talk it over with a social worker having detailed knowledge of the program may result in a decision to stay at home and apply for such assistance rather than to seek employment.

If it is decided that some alternative plan is more desirable, the caseworker can help the applicant in implementing such alternative plans—in making application for AFDC, for instance, or in dealing with the problem of role reallocation in the family so that the child can be cared for at home, or with budgeting so that the mother may not have to work. The caseworker acts as the link between the day-care applicant and resources in the community.

On occasion, when a family has an opportunity to explore the additional expenses involved in employment and to estimate the exact additional net income that employment is likely to yield, they may decide that it isn't worth the trouble. Or once they have decided that it is advisable, the discussion has at least prepared them for the reality they encounter.

Even when the mother is convinced that employment is the preferable alternative, she may still be ambivalent and anxious about the step she is about to take. Such a mother welcomes the opportunity, if available, to discuss her doubts and fears with a caseworker. The caseworker helps her to clarify exactly what effects she thinks her employment will have on the children; he shares with the mother the knowledge that research has made available regarding the specific effects of mothers' employment on children in different situations and discusses with her what precautions might be taken to mitigate any negative effects. Frequently mothers are less explicitly aware that employment affects not only the younger preschool children but also the older children in the family. Sibling–sibling relations might also be affected. The caseworker helps the mother to become aware of the changes that her working will entail for all her children.

The mother's employment also has effects on the marital-pair subsystem. The change from mother–wife to mother–wife–employee necessitates some reallocation of role responsibilities in the family. Both the father and the mother are involved, by the worker, in exploring the changes that might be made in order to accommodate the mother's plans for employment, the degree of acceptance of such changes on the part of both parents, and the possible dangers and advantages of alternative modes of accommodation to the wife's working. In addition, he helps the family to determine whether the mother's employment, with day care, is the most appropriate solution to the problems faced by the family and to explore the availability, feasibility, and acceptability of alternative solutions.

If the mother's employment is the only feasible plan, she may have doubts about her capacity to meet the test of job demands. For women who have been out of the labor market for some time—and especially for women who have never been in it—self-doubt about adequacy may act as a block to performance. They may use discussions with the social worker to reassure themselves and to test the demands they may have to face. Such discussions take the form of anticipatory socialization to the new role of employee.

The discussions, which attempt to help the family to clarify the decision regarding day care, indirectly have value for the child. They tend to reduce the rate of turnover and assure the child a continuity of experience; they reduce the difficulties the child may have in moving into the day-care situation, because the child's feelings about the program reflect, in some measure, those of his parents. "It is only as the parent's anxieties are relieved and she is reassured that her plan to work and use day care is in the best interest of herself and child that the mother is able to use day care to the best advantage" (Golton, 1945, p. 58). The family's feeling of comfort with their decision is an important factor in determining the child's capacity to adjust positively to any kind of care.

The application for day care, as is true for similar services, has generally been prompted by some problem in family living—low income, disruption, illness, death, inadequate housing—and the family may need help in dealing with these problems.

For some mothers, the use of day care and the acceptance of employment may be the first step in establishing independence with the anticipation that this will culminate in divorce. The anxiety and the doubts about day care reflect questions regarding the advisability of breaking up the marriage. The mother may use the day-care application to discuss this more significant decision.

> Mrs. M. applied for day care for Harry, four years old, after an argument with her husband. She had threatened a divorce and he had taunted her with the statement that she could never support herself. She had been employed as a file clerk before marriage and she wondered if she could find a job now. "Maybe," she said, "if I could really prove to myself that I can get a job, I wouldn't have to take all that stuff from my husband. I would really mean it when I say I am walking out."

The decision to use day-care services results in another series of problems with which families may need help. The child who is being enrolled begins the first formal prolonged separation from the family. The caseworker helps the mother to prepare the child for the transition by discussing with her how the child might react and how the mother might respond to the child's ambivalence and resistance and by reassuring her of the "normality" of the child's anxiety.

The child faces the problem of multiple adjustments. He is separated from the mother and expected to accept the care of adults who are strangers to him. He is placed in unfamiliar physical surroundings, generally far from his own neighborhood. Frequently the behavior expected of him may be different from or in conflict with what has been demanded of him at home. Therefore the mother must be prepared for some regression on the part of the child, who may temporarily display more infantile behavior. The need for such preparation is confirmed by Thenaud (1945), who, in a study of requests for day-care service, noted that the mothers showed a general lack of understanding of the possible reactions of the children.

The caseworker tries to help the mother understand that children might feel rejected and not altogether certain that the mother will return. It takes repeated experiences of separation and return for confident assurance to develop that the mother will be back. Time sense is so poorly developed in children that for the mother to say she will be back "in a few hours" may mean little to the child. This knowledge supposedly helps the mother to accept, without undue embarrassment, the child's crying when she leaves. It also helps to clarify the day-center staff's suggestion that the mother explain repeatedly to the child why she is going, what is going to happen, and that she will be back.

Generally the family applies for day-care service when the mother and the father are ready. The child's readiness for the experience, a most important factor in assuring the success of the plan, is often not given explicit consideration. The social worker has to make some evaluation of the child's readiness, based on observation of his behavior and on information provided by the family. It is suggested that if the child has recently undergone some difficult change (the birth of a sibling, a recent operation, a serious illness in the family), entrance into the day-care situation be delayed. This reduces the imposition on the child of too many difficult adjustments at once.

But the decision to enroll the child also produces a variety of conflicts for the mother. She may have questions about the child's negative reaction to her because she is leaving him. She may have questions about her adequacy as a mother for giving up the care of her child to strangers, however temporarily. She may be concerned about the transfer of the child's affection to the "mothers" in the day-care center. She may have some anxieties about the child's adequacy as a reflection of the family's previous care of the child. This anxiety derives from the fact that now, for the first time, the child is performing publicly in a uniform test situation and is being measured by professionals, however informally, vis-à-vis his age mates.

The mother reflects some of the general ambivalence toward day care and needs reassurance that she is not a "bad" mother for leaving the care of her child temporarily to others. She may feel happy at being relieved of some of the burden of child care and feel guilty about her reaction:

Mrs. M., a friendly, intelligent mother, wanted to place Charles, aged five, and Peter, aged two, so that she could go to work. Mr. M. was employed full-time but his earnings were marginal. . . . The arrangements for her job were practically completed when she applied. The carrying out of the total family plan hinged entirely, however, on the admission of the children to the day-care center. Although working meant a great deal to Mrs. M., she expressed many anxieties about leaving her children. She spoke with emotion as she told the worker, "I want to feel sure that the people taking care of my children are responsible. It's been a hard decision to make, even to consider leaving them for two days a week; but five whole days is even more difficult. . . . Maybe in a year's time I'll be able to take them away from you and go back to being a mother again."

Mrs. M.'s concern about leaving the children was real, and yet she was eager to relieve the financial stress. At the end of the first interview, she was not certain that Charles and Peter were to come to the day-care center. Within a few days she talked with the worker again and at this time she said, "I've thought it over.

I am giving them up for a while but I am not really losing them" [Voiland, 1942, p. 101].

Especially for the mother of the very young child, there should be some preparation for the fact that she will be missing much of the gratification of experiencing the development of the child. One working mother whose friend looked after her eighteen-month-old child said, "After a couple of months I find that my friend can understand what my baby is saying; I cannot. He learns new things from her and I feel I am beginning not to know him" (Yudkin, Holme, 1963, p. 131).

Even if day care is desirable, there must be some discussion of the optimum choice of day care for the particular child. Is group day care the best alternative, or may family day care be better?

The social worker attempts to obtain from the parents a comprehensive picture of the child's level of functioning: his likes and dislikes, his physical status, his aptitudes and limitations, his habitual modes of reacting to stress, the most effective ways of motivating the child and of disciplining him, his reaction to adults outside the family, and his reaction to care by them. All this information helps the staff to work with the child in the way that is best for him and for the peer group into which he will be moving. It helps the staff to estimate the difficulty that the child will have in accepting this initial separation.

Some time at intake is devoted to discussing the structure of service and the questions the mother may have about it: fees, family responsibility for bringing and picking up the child on time, care of the child if he becomes ill, health examinations, the schedule of periodic conferences with various members of the staff, the nature of day-care routines, and the things the child should and should not bring.

Arrangements are made for preadmission visits to the center and for preliminary acquaintanceships with the people on the staff who will be working with the child. The contacts between the family and the caseworker, the family and the teacher, help to identify day care with the family in the mind of the child and help him to see it as an extension of the home situation. For some children, arrangements need to be made for gradual desensitization to and acceptance of separation from the mother. The child may be made to come for only a few hours initially, and gradually the length of his stay is increased. It may help to have the mother remain with the child for progressively shorter periods of time after his enrollment in the program.

The visit to the center permits the parent to see for herself what is done there for children and tends to eliminate any fears or illusions she may have regarding the operation of the center. The visit to the center also has diagnostic value for the staff:

The way the child leaves the mother and takes to the teacher and to the [day care] environment, and the mother's reaction to this, begins to indicate to the worker what value the child has to the mother, the kind of relationship there is between them, and how ready she is to turn him over to another person . . . to use the . . . [day care] for his benefit. Sometimes, if her tie to him is weak, just seeing that he takes to the [day care] . . . and can bear separation from her will make her decide that she is in danger of losing him and that she must not let him go. In a surer relationship, however, this experience may be the very thing to settle her doubts about how he will take day care and separation and reassure her that it is all right to go ahead [Rawley, 1943, p. 20].

Later the caseworker can be helpful to the family in working out any situations that adversely affect the child's adjustment to the center. Paradoxically even the child's positive adjustment to day care may create a problem for the mother:

Bobby got along unusually well for a child of his age in making the adjustment to the changed surroundings. Mrs. R. was seeing the caseworker at regular intervals and gradually she told us that Bobby liked the nursery so well that he was making a nuisance of himself week-ends because he was constantly asking if this was the day to go to the nursery. She could not understand this attitude on the part of any child. With much concern she said, "It makes me feel that maybe my home is not as good as it should be. Otherwise Bobby would not seem to prefer the nursery" [Voiland, 1942, p. 100].

The necessity of carrying multiple burdensome roles—wife, mother, and employee—may produce cumulative stress that the mother may wish to discuss. The difficulties of doing justice to all of her responsibilities without feeling guilty and/or inadequate may require the opportunity for periodic discussions with a sympathetic, understanding person.

Problems may arise because of differences between the expectations of the parents and the day-care personnel in regard to the child's behavior. If the child has learned to dress himself and to feed himself more adequately at the center, the parents should be encouraged to expect the same independent behavior at home. This may create a problem for the mother who finds satisfaction in the child's dependency and feels threatened by his developing independence. Sometimes the family sets no limitations on the child's behavior and the day-care center institutes some controls.

Social workers in day care need to be aware of some of the general disadvantages of congregate day care for children. The sizable number of children dealt with requires some regulation of behavior. Some kinds of behavior must be encouraged by day-care personnel and other kinds of behavior discouraged if they are to retain control and their sanity. Studies by Prescott and Jones (1971) indicate that "programs in day-care centers are marked by an absence of strong feelings and of activities that might evoke them. Many staff members appear to be afraid that open expression of strong desires in the form of anger, dependency, or abandoned exuberance would lead to behavioral contagion and chaos" (p. 55). There is less access to adults, less opportunity to meet highly individual needs in privacy away from the group, less possibility of contact with a wider range of age mates, more scheduling, and more control than is experienced in the home.

Throughout the contact with the family, the caseworker tried to help the parents with problems in child rearing that, in time, would be likely to affect the child's adjustment to day care:

A mother of a three-year-old had been finding his thumb-sucking a problem. She first taped the child's thumb to the rest of his hand and, when that failed, applied a bitter chemical which had been recommended by the drugstore. When she learned more about the meaning of thumb-sucking to the child, she was able to deal with it with less rigidity, and could feel less guilty and tense about the behavior, which she had thought was an indication of her failure as a mother [Merriam, 1959, p. 25].

Changes in the home situation may be reflected in changes in the child's behavior in day care. Discussing such changes with the parents helps them to understand how changes in the home are affecting the child. A father may have recently lost his job and may be acting more impatiently toward the child at home, resulting in the child's becoming more withdrawn. A grandparent may have died, making the child appear depressed or anxious in the center.

Here, as in other child welfare services, casework acts to help the client learn what is expected behavior in a new and unfamiliar social role: for the mother and father, the role of partial parent; for the child, the role of member of a day-care group. Once having accepted the designated role, the parents and the child are helped to enact it effectively. Part of the caseworker's responsibility lies in service to the staff in contact with the child, as well as to the family (Eckstein, 1962). Rather than being directly involved in service to day-school children or their parents, social workers often act as consultants to the staff in identifying children with emotional disorders, in managing difficult children, and in interacting with resistant parents. As a consultant, one social worker may serve a number of different day-care programs (Radin, Jordan, 1977).

In liaison between the day-care programs and the community, social workers can make available and activate needed resources, interpret the service and its needs to the community, and help generate and mobilize the support of a pro-day-care constituency.

What seems to be a much needed and desirable service, in line with the responsibility of social work to link people with resources, is an information and referral service, which would provide a family with an overview of the various kinds of day-care resources in the community: location, price range, facilities, size of staff, number of children in the group, and so on.

Casework can also contribute to the successful termination of service. Termination may result from situational factors, such as the family's moving, the mother's remarriage, or the mother's return to the home as a full-time mother. It may come as a result of the child's growing beyond the age when family day care or group day care is appropriate. It may come because it seems clear that either the child or the family is not able to use the service effectively.

Withdrawal from the service is often relatively easy, especially if the child is leaving, along with other children in his group, at the end of a semester. On occasion, however, the reorganization in the life of the child and the family occasioned by termination of service may require some preparation and discussion. If the contact has been satisfactory, the child is likely to have developed relationships of some intensity with the teacher or the family-day-care mother and the peer group of which he has been a part. It is not easy to give this up without some sense of loss.

Much of what has been said relates both to group day care and to family day care. There are some special features of social work in family day care that must be recognized, however.

Family day care shares many similarities with foster care, generally. It involves, as does foster care, a process of recruitment, evaluation, and selection of day-care parents. The sources of recruitment and the process of selection are similar. Some agencies find that with few exceptions, their "foster family home and family day-care home are really interchangeable" (Jackson, n.d., p. 4).

Some special aspects of family day care, however, evolve because the child returns to his own home every night. Thus contact between the day-care parent and the child's own parent is frequent and regular, so that although the day-care mother is less deeply involved with the child than is the foster mother, she has a tendency to be more deeply involved with the child's mother. And because the child experiences separation every day and lives, in effect, in two homes, he might need help in integrating the two major experiences in his life.

Casework with child and mother is similar to that in group day care in that the family is helped to resolve problems that might reduce satisfactory use of the resource:

> Johnny, aged twenty-two months, was a relatively easy child to get along with after his mother left him in the day-care home. He ate and slept well and played contentedly with the toys. As soon as his mother appeared on the scene, however, he ran rampant—jumping on furniture, touching things on tables which had been prohibited, and so on. So serious was his behavior when the mother brought and called for him that the day-care mother didn't feel she could continue to care for him unless the mother began taking some responsibility for disciplining him. It was her impression that the mother never said "no" to him, and never corrected him. There was no question but what Johnny was making life difficult for her but she did nothing about it.
>
> Contact with the mother revealed that because she felt so guilty about leaving Johnny (her relatives all disapproved of her plan to work even though father was in service), she tried to make it up to him by keeping the time they were together free of restrictions and discipline. She wanted it to be a happy, carefree period. Of course it was not. Not only was Johnny's behavior at home upsetting, but he was sleeping poorly and was chronically constipated. It had not occurred to the mother that her indulgence was confusing the child.
>
> With the help of the caseworker, she was able to see how important it was that what was expected of the child in each of his two homes be as consistent as possible. She was helped to see, too, for the first time, perhaps, that parenthood carries with it the responsibility for setting the "do's" and "don't's" which are the basis of habit and character formation in children [Golton, 1945, p. 58].

Informal, private arrangements may result in dissatisfaction that might be resolved by an intermediary. Family caregivers may be resentful and disdainful of the mother's decision to work. They may see the working mother as irresponsible: "Delayed payments, inattention to scheduled pickup time" (Wattenberg, 1977, p. 223), and lack of appreciation of the caregiver's function may result in friction.

Social workers have been active in recruiting and training family day-care providers, in providing a support system, and in making the community aware of their availability (Emlen, 1971; Sulby, Diodati, 1975; Collins, Watson, 1976; Wattenberg, 1977).

Such efforts have been stimulated by the recognition that the family-day-care system is a private entrepreneurial system, largely unlicensed and largely unsupervised, offered by isolated caregivers. Community responsibility toward families would suggest a need for some accountability as to standards and performance.

The fact that specialized social work functions are an important component of day care for the *limited* number of families who *might* need it is recognized in the Federal Interagency Day Care Requirements, which state that in order to be eligible for support, a day-care center should offer social services. The Department of Health, Education, and Welfare (1978) defines social services in day care as "any supportive services apart from actually caring for the child that serve to enhance the functioning of the family as a unit as well as the individuals within it." Although such services are not regarded as a core component of day care, the department argues for their inclusion, since "many child care experts believe no short-term intervention program, regardless of its superiority, can succeed in supporting the age-appropriate cognitive, social, emotional and physical development of a child whose family is overwhelmed by its socioeconomic plight" or other problems. "A comprehensive Social Services component that supports family functioning is necessary to promote the well-being of this child" (p. 82).

In empirical support of its recommendation, the department cites a case study of 450 day-care families conducted in nineteen states in 1977. "Interviews with these clients indicated that approximately one-fourth needed help in (1) getting medical care, (2) getting a better job, (3) getting job training or schooling, (4) getting information on services offered in the community and (5) finding a caseworker or psychiatrist. About three-fourths of these individuals sought help from a social service office" (pp. 82–83).

In recommending a social service component in day-care facilities that receive any federal funds, some specific tasks are assigned. These include (1) "counseling and guidance to the family in helping it determine the appropriateness of day care, the best facility for a particular child, and the possibility of alternative plans for care"; (2) "coordination and cooperation with other organizations offering these resources which may be required by the child and his family" and providing the information and referral which would enable the the family effectively to use such resources; (3) "continuing assessment with the parents of the child's adjustment in the day care program and of the family situation"; (4) objective determination "of the ability of families to pay for part or all of the cost of day care and for payment" (pp. 241–42).

The provision of social services should be under the supervision of a staff member trained or experienced in social work, although federal regulations further require that nonprofessionals must be used in providing the services.

Although federal guidelines tend to establish explicit standards for day-care centers generally, they are actually applicable only with reference to those centers that are federally supported in whole or in part. It was estimated that in 1978 only 8,000 of the 18,300 centers received federal funds and needed to be responsible to the guidelines.

Similarly Head Start guidelines indicate that every Head Start program have a social service program to link the center with the family and the related community services and resources. The social worker in Head Start is charged with the responsibility of being a "strong advocate in obtaining services from local agencies and in referring families to them." Where needed services do not exist, he should "work to develop more effective social services" (U.S. Department of Health, Education and, Welfare, 1967).

The social worker in the day-care center thus acts as liaison between the center and the family, the center and the community, and the family and the community. He helps inform the families about relevant community programs and refers them to services they may need, as well as counseling parents on family planning, nutrition, health care, and family budgeting, and providing them with information about food stamp programs, Medicaid, employment, housing, and public assistance (Archinard, 1971). (See also Strathy, Heinicke, and Hauer, 1974.)

A study of the interpersonal relationships between parents and caregivers in twelve Detroit area day-care centers indicates the need for social services (Powell, 1978). The study indicated that "much interpersonal exchange between parents and caregivers is superficial in content . . . family-related topics are discussed infrequently . . . with few attempts to coordinate children's" experiences in the home and the center (p. 687). About half of the parents felt that "family problems should be discussed with center staff as a general principle" (p. 685), but some 40 per cent of the parents perceived the caregivers as reluctant to discuss parent-initiated topics.

In a follow-up study of forty-two families involved in a demonstration project in family day care, twenty-nine clients indicated that they were helped by the caseworker in "understanding the child's behavior . . . relieving strain . . . adjusting to [the client's] new life . . . [and] getting . . . [the] child established in nursery school" (Foster Family Day Care, 1962, p. 11). A detailed study of the need for casework services in a California day-care center indicated that of the 197 families using the center, about 70 families acknowledged concern over some family problem, though only 23 families actually asked for help. The parents who sought help were concerned about "children's aggressiveness, hyperactivity, temper, excessive demands, [and] attention-getting behavior" (Rapoport, Consweet, 1969, p. 11).

The social work component in day care, as described in *Standards for Day-Care Service*, published by the Child Welfare League of America (1969), and as reviewed in this chapter, exists in only a limited percentage of day-care centers. There is a wide gap between the literature and the actuality. Prescott *et al.* (1972), who did an intensive study of day-care centers in California, note that the "social work component as described in the Child Welfare League of America Standards for Day Care is virtually nonexistent. . . . The literature on day care has been concerned primarily with day care as it ought to be or as it has been assumed to exist."

Only a limited number of social workers are employed in day care. Ruderman (1968) notes in her study that "only 7 percent of the day-care centers have the regular services of a social worker" (p. 102). If Ruderman's estimate were applied to the 167,000 licensed day-care centers throughout the country in 1970, one might estimate about 1,200 full-time social workers employed by day-care centers. Ruderman's findings are confirmed by a study of ninety-eight hospitals operating child-care facilities for use of their personnel: "Only 7 percent indicated they provided any type of social service for the family" (p. 13).

On the other hand, a national survey of some three hundred day-care facilities by the National Council of Jewish Women found that 68 per cent of non-union profit centers and 21 per cent of the proprietary centers surveyed claimed that they employed a social worker (Keyserling, 1972, Table 26, p. 112). It appears that although social workers can make a specific contribution to more effective use of day-care services, they are currently found in only a limited percentage of day-care facilities.

Day-care centers that receive some part of their support from federal funding are more apt to have social workers on the staff. Day-care centers rated as "developmental" because they have the most complete program sometimes include a social worker on the staff. However, only 25 per cent of all day-care centers are rated as "developmental."

The limited number of social services in day-care programs derives from a variety of factors. The programs are operated on limited funds. The first priority is necessarily personnel with training and experience in child development and preschool education who work directly with the children. Social work is an adjunctive service, and although day-care programs operate better with it, they can operate without it. The social worker, as a noncaregiver specialist, is regarded as dispensable. Only a limited number of programs have enough funds to permit inclusion of the social services. Teachers often attempt to do social work themselves or seek consultation with a social worker serving a number of programs.

Despite the formal allocation of some responsibilities to social workers, day-care-center teachers do a good deal of informal social work. Because they are in contact with parents when they bring and pick up the child, the teachers establish a relationship that sometimes includes support and counseling (Joffe, 1977, pp. 60–61). Whereas all children in the program need the services of day-care teachers and attendants, only a limited number of children and families need the social services. Where a sizable percentage of the families need them, there has been a tendency to see indigenous paraprofessionals—people from the local community employed by the center—as capable of providing them (Radin, Jordan, 1977, p. 168).

PROBLEMS

1. Although the percentage of working mothers with young children will continue to increase, there is limited, though growing, public support for the development of day-care resources. An intensive study by the Child Welfare League of America (1962) of leaders in selected communities throughout the United States shows that "most respondents assigned day care moderate rather than high—or low—priority" (p.33).

In part, the priority accorded day care is a reflection of the general lack of knowledge about day-care needs and facilities and the low visibility such problems have, in contrast to the dramatic impact of juvenile delinquency and the problems of emotionally disturbed children.

Day care is primarily a preventive program; the children served do not yet have any problems that are disturbing to the parents or the community, though these may develop later as a result of inadequate child care while the mother is working.

The Child Welfare League study (1962) suggests that the reluctance to support day-care services is also related to a negative view of the working mother —the view that she is working because she chooses to do so and/or because she is not primarily concerned with or interested in the care of her children. One respondent said, "Nothing should be done to encourage any further tendency for mothers to find excuses for avoiding the responsibilities of caring for their children." Another said, "I am strongly opposed to any measure aimed at making private or government agencies devices to have mothers unload their responsibility for their children so they can work" (p. 83).

Although there is a gradual erosion of such attitudes as more women work and the ideology of affirmative action and undifferentiated sex roles gain currency, powerful residuals of this attitude still remain. The hesitancy and ambivalence generated by this attitude act as a brake on the expansion of day care.

Some people question publicly funded day care because they think public policy should support the mothering needs of preschool children by encouraging mothers to remain at home—the original purpose of the AFDC program. Some question it because it does not make much economic sense in the use of public dollars. Recognizing that good, comprehensive day care may cost at least $2,000 per child,

> it may make more economic sense to pay this to parents to be good child rearers rather than to ask them to surrender the care of their children to others. It would seem that the burden rests on those favoring effective day care to show that children are made better off by being placed in high-quality, high-cost, developmental day care rather than being kept at home with parents to whom are transferred the resources that otherwise would be used in that day care. Parental love is hard to buy [Krashinsky, 1973, p. 168].

Public support of day care involves a number of complicated policy issues. There are questions about what kinds of day-care arrangements should be supported, what groups in the community should get such support, and how such support should be offered. Should public support be given to the informal network of family day care that currently supplies a large percentage of out-of-home care for the children of working mothers? If so, how is it to be regulated? Should subsidies be given to all families with children in day care, to public-assistance families only, or to poverty-level families and the working poor as well? Should the purpose of day care be primarily to reduce the number of AFDC recipients, to provide compensatory education, to further women's rights to determine their lifestyles, or a combination of all of these? Should support be in the form of subsidies to day-care operators, of vouchers to parents for use at a day-care facility of their choice, or of tax credits?

There is only limited consensus among the groups supporting day care because they have different motivations (Steiner, 1976), and there is considerable public opposition to government-funded day care (Bruce-Briggs, 1977).

2. The Child Welfare League (1962) also found that most respondents preferred some form of in-home individual care by a relative, reducing support for day care:

> Child care has always been a family responsibility and if the child's own mother is unable to care for him the traditional solution has always been an approximation of maternal care . . . in the child's own home, involving other members of the

family. This is customary and seems natural. Other arrangements, perhaps, especially organized ones, have been less common and therefore may seem strange or unnatural [p. 49].

Paying for child care makes people uneasy because it contradicts the usual family arrangement of child care out of concern and love. The private family-day-care arrangement, which the mother organizes for herself with some neighboring person, although it has contractual and financial elements, resembles the mutual aid system of an extended family. Hence it is ideologically a more acceptable arrangement to many mothers. Additional reasons for opposition were the lack of personal attention they anticipated for their children, the fact that it was likely to be excessively structured and too much like a school, the danger to a child's health of group care, and the fact that their child was likely to be in contact with children from "less adequate families" (Ruderman, 1968, pp. 315–317).

3. There is a problem in deciding the desirable balance of investment and effort in a day-care center and the informal, but much more extensive, system of the individually operated family day care. Agencies and professionals in the field favor an expansion of day-care centers because they control these facilities and they can implement a program for which their training has prepared them. Family day care is controlled by amateurs and eludes supervision and regulation, but it is and will continue to be used by many families.

Emlen (1971), closely studying family day care over a number of years, found that mothers prefer child care "within three blocks of home," "within five minutes of home," "within easy walking distance of home," "in the immediate neighborhood," "near enough so that my older children can join the little ones after school." He reports that many of the mothers also prefer family day care "not only because it was physically convenient, flexibly accommodating, socially approachable, and consumer controllable, but also because it is perceived, and correctly so, as a comfortable and familiar setting in which the working mother finds a responsible, nurturant caregiver who is capable of providing love and comfort as well as new social learning" (pp. 178–179). Still, many of the mothers would prefer group day care, if it were available, because of its greater continuity and its provision of better learning opportunities (Ruderman, 1968; Willner, 1969; Keyserling, 1972).

Family day care is frequently brought to the family's attention through a newspaper advertisement or a notice tacked up on the local supermarket bulletin board. Although professionals may tend to deplore such informal arrangements, Emlen (1971) found that the majority are not so bad as people suppose, and the sample reported in this study reveals an environment for children the potentialities of which are favorable enough to justify an organized effort to strengthen this type of care as a major resource for day care" (p. 3; see also Willner, 1969; 1971). The researchers note "that it is fallacious to assume that family day care is inevitably poor if it is not supervised by a social agency" (Collins, Watson, 1969, p. 528). Despite some clearly hazardous examples, many of the family-day-care mothers are personally adequate and capable of meeting the needs of children.

Because informal family day care will continue to be used by working mothers, professionals concerned with child care are making efforts to help improve it. The Neighborhood Day Care Exchange Project in Portland, Oregon, locates women interested in providing day care in their homes, offers them training and consultation in child care, and puts them in touch with mothers needing day care for their children (Collins, Watson, 1976).

Recent efforts also include special publications and newsletters developed by state departments of public welfare for distribution to day-care mothers, special training programs developed by community colleges in cooperation with public welfare agencies, and the development of day-care homes as satellites of day-care centers, with training of the day-care mothers by the day-care center.

4. Following from the view that the family should provide care for the child in his own home, day care is often perceived as an exceptional procedure. One might point once again to the results of the Child Welfare League (1962) study of community attitudes toward day care, which suggests that respondents generally saw the service as needed by those families who were "different": the low-income family and the "broken family headed by the mother" (p. 93).

This image of the day-care center is reinforced by the fact that because public day-care resources are in short supply, they are currently reserved (through eligibility requirements) for low-income families, single-parent families, and families on public assistance. Socioeconomic segregation often means racial segregation as well. Thus public day-care programs tend to serve children of low-income nonwhite families, while proprietary day-care centers, supported by fees from parents, tend to serve middle-class white families. Whereas middle-income families are "defined" out of publicly supported facilities, low-income families are "priced" out of proprietary facilities. Minority-group children and children of single-parent households are, in fact, heavily overrepresented in nonproprietary day-care centers.

The association between day care and welfare led to a reluctance on the part of some families, noted during World War II, to apply for day care if this had to be done through a social agency (Guyler, 1942). It has been suggested that information about and application for day care should be handled by some agency with more neutral connotations for the public, an agency that is more directly related to the situation that usually prompts the needs for day care, such as the employment services.

5. Another problem is posed by the question of responsibility for day care. Day care meets the definition of a child welfare service. It is an institution organized in response to a social problem, and the social role changes in relation to it. Yet the profession of social work is not certain that it has responsibility for day care. As Host (1963) says, "Too often the recent social work graduate has expressed surprise when day care is described as a child welfare service" (p. 3). And Kuhlmann (1955) notes, "Day care has not yet arrived at the place in the child welfare field where it is viewed as an essential social work program" (p. 23). Although this was written in 1955, it appears to be essentially true today.

Some argue that responsibility for day care should be delegated to the educational institutions rather than to the social service organizations. They note that the school is accepted in all communities as a center for child care; that the school district has an established administrative organization and the housing and the playground space for such centers; that it has available personnel who can assist in the organization, the supervision, and the training of staff; that, in effect, the day-care center merely extends the educational system downward (to include a younger group) and outward (to lengthen the school day of older children).

The problem of responsibility for day care is compounded by other considerations. Although day care meets the criteria for inclusion in any listing of child welfare services, it requires the joint cooperative activity of three professions —health, education, and social work—for effective implementation. Each of these, consequently, has a vested interest in the service. As it stands, however, day care currently belongs more to the commercial-proprietary group than it does to any of the professions. This raises a problem of social policy.

It is argued that the care and the concomitant education of children (because all care involves some education, however informal) should be matters of public concern and support; that permitting day care to develop largely in the hands of proprietary-commercial interests is irresponsible; and that child-care centers ought to represent a community investment in its families rather than a business venture.

The fact that day care has a variety of different possible goals presents a problem of identification. Industry sees day care as desirable in providing a larger and more dependable female labor force; government officials see day care as helpful in moving people off welfare and into employment; educators see day care as early compensatory education that will prepare disadvantaged children more adequately for school; health officials see day care as a case-finding procedure that will bring to light health deficiencies in young children; women's groups see day care as providing women more alternative options in lifestyles; social workers see day care as insuring adequate care and protection for the child of the working mother. The working mother sees child care as a dependable, stable source of care for her child, giving him the opportunity of playing with his age-mates under the supervision of people who are competent to offer some education and training as well. This diversity has resulted in attempts by the different professions involved to incorporate day care within their own particular spheres of influence. As a supplementary parental care facility, it has a social work goal; as a supplementary or compensatory educational program, it belongs to education; as a facility for the physically or mentally handicapped, it can be viewed as a public health resource. Consequently not only are there differences in orientation among health workers, educators, and social workers as to what is important in day care, but there is competitive disagreement concerning who should control the day-care "turf."

6. A problem that has been generally slighted is the need for supervision and care of the school-aged child of the working mother (Harris, 1977). Studies show that the mother often has to leave for work before the child has breakfasted and is ready for school, and that she is not available to the child during lunch or between the time school lets out and the end of the work day. School holidays and vacations are a problem, for they do not always coincide with work holidays and vacations. When the child is ill and out of school, most mothers absent themselves from work—at an anxiety-provoking loss of pay for the mother who is the head of a family.

These problems raise the question of public policy with reference to an extended school day. Such measures have been advocated in some communities where there is considerable concern about "latchkey" children: school-aged children who wear a latchkey on a cord, which symbolizes their responsibility for themselves while their mothers are at work.

7. Ideally day care should be available to any mother who needs to work, wants to work, or merely wants to share the care of her child. The facility should be of high quality, conveniently located, and low in cost. Personnel should be professionally trained and sufficiently numerous to permit individual attention for the child. But the actual situation is far different.

A 1971 national study conducted by the Westinghouse Learning Corporation for the Office of Economic Opportunity (1971) concludes:

> Day care for young children in the United States today is an institution lagging far behind the social change that has brought about the need for it. It is an unorganized, largely unregulated and unlicensed service provided in ways that range from excellent to shockingly poor and yet it is indispensable to a growing number of people in present-day America: the force of working women of child-bearing age [p. 95].

The family that has the greatest difficulty is the one whose income is just high enough to render it ineligible for publicly supported day care but too low to permit proprietary day care. For this family, the working poor, the mother's employment is often a clear economic necessity.

Shortage of trained staff is endemic. Low salaries make difficult the recruitment of adequate numbers of adequately trained people.

Frequently care is not available when the mother needs it. Many women —hospital nurses, waitresses, hotel maids, telephone operators, saleswomen—work weekends or evenings. Yet very few centers are open seven days a week, twenty-four hours a day.

To meet the needs for personnel anticipated by increases in day care in the near future, the Federal Office of Child Development is actively sponsoring the development of a new profession, the child development associate, who, after a two-year program in a junior or senior college and a fieldwork internship, will act to assist day-care-center teachers.

8. There is a bewildering array of sources of government support for day care. Manpower development and training legislation makes funds available to increase the supply of personnel; educational legislation makes funds available to provide compensatory education; social security legislation provides funds to reduce dependence on welfare; housing and urban development legislation and model cities legislation make funds available to achieve the purpose of urban change. Community groups seeking sources of support need considerable expertise in merely knowing where and how to apply for funds. The multiplicity of sources of funding and aims creates a problem for the day-care services.

There is a problem regarding who should be eligible to apply for federal funds in support of day care. Community-action groups argue that they should be eligible to initiate applications for such funds. Direct access by each community-based group is opposed by others because they regard such a procedure as administratively difficult and inefficient. It could mean that the federal government would have to deal with thousands of different community groups to which it might grant funds directly. Consequently it is argued that only state or city governments should be permitted to act as "prime sponsors" in applications for and distribution of such funds. Community-action groups argue in rebuttal that such a procedure may be administratively more efficient but that it also permits tighter control of funds so that the more militant social-action groups can be "frozen out."

TRENDS

1. The change in women's employment situation has been revolutionary, but cultural attitudes are changing more slowly. However, there is a growing acceptance of the fact that mothers' employment is "normal," that in most cases it is necessary, that it does not reflect child neglect, and that it is not necessarily harmful to the child. All this suggests a trend toward greater concern with the need for day care and a greater acceptance of day care. The 1970 White House Conference on Children (1971) recommended that:

> a diverse national network of comprehensive developmental child care services be established to accommodate approximately 5.6 million children by 1980 through consolidated Federal efforts via legislation and funding as well as through coordinated planning and operation involving state, local, and private efforts. . . . The ultimate goal is to make high-quality care available to all families who seek it and all children who need it [p. 283].

There is growing recognition that failure to build an adequate number of day-care centers does not result in a reduction of the number of mothers working but merely leads to less adequate arrangements for the care of children. The sentiment that determined President Nixon's veto, in 1971, of a bill that would have substantially expanded day-care resources—namely, that it "would commit the vast moral authority of the National Government to the side of communal approaches to a child rearing over against the family centered approach" (*The New York Times,* December 10, 1971)—is still prevalent.

In opposition to this feeling that day care might "undermine the American family," there is growing acceptance of the idea that day care might, in fact, help to strengthen the family by facilitating mothers' employment, by intervening to prevent the development of problems in parent–child relationships, and by providing the possibility of maintaining children in the community who might otherwise have to be institutionalized.

It is easy, however, to exaggerate the depth of this trend. Public funding of day care for all families who want and can use it would signal a major shift in the relative distribution of responsibility between parents and community for the care and the socialization of America's children. Traditionally, and currently, the principal responsibility for the care and the socialization of the preschool child has rested with the family. Even for the older child, communal responsibility has been narrowly defined as being concerned with his education during a limited segment of each day. As a consequence of an extensive public day-care program, the community would begin to share with the parent earlier and more extensive responsibility for the child.

2. Professionals are increasingly accepting group day care for very young

children. This trend is stimulated and supported by special projects that have yielded reassuring results. Because care outside the home involves special hazards for the young child, many of the licensing regulations have forbidden group care for children younger than two. Preliminary reports indicate that the needs of infants can be adequately met through group-care arrangements if these entail sensible precautions and a high caretaker–child ratio.

There is official support for and sanction of such a trend. The Office of Child Development, U.S. Department of Health, Education, and Welfare, has published a pamphlet that reviews the question of day care for infants (Huntington *et al.*, 1971). It notes that:

> that for many years professional health and welfare organizations concerned with standards for day care and with organized programs for children have urged that children younger than three years not be in group care. . . . Research has now shown that it is the inadequacy of care frequently suffered in such settings that harms the child and probably not the fact of the brief separation itself.

The pamphlet concludes that caring for infants and toddlers in a group arrangement is acceptable if the center provides continuity of care by one caretaker for every three children and if the caretakers are warm, consistent, sensitive, and respectful of the child's individuality. Under such conditions, the consequences of "multiple mothering," "separation," and "maternal deprivation" are not likely to be encountered. This prescription is a difficult one to fill, and it is difficult to develop centers that provide, and continue to provide, these desirable conditions.

Although there has been continued diversification of day-care facilities in the direction of serving a younger age group, less has been done in the development of services for the school-aged child. There are 21 million school-aged children whose mothers are working. Attention has been called to the needs for care of many of the children during the time between the end of the school day and the mother's return from work and during those periods when school is not in session. A report by the Department of Health, Education, and Welfare published in 1972 notes that "facilities and programs for the care of [these] children are so few as to be practically insignificant" (Hoffman, 1974).

3. There is a trend toward a diversification of the auspices under which day care is offered. Employers have indicated interest in offering day care for the children of their employees because such a service might increase the recruitment of female workers, reduce absenteeism and job turnover, and improve labor relations. For the employee, it means being closer to the child during the day, reducing her anxiety and problems about finding day care, and providing continuity of care for the child. The children have contact with the world of work, the opportunity of seeing their parents in the work role, and a greater likelihood of contacts with males. Frequently hospitals operate such facilities for the use of their personnel. The U.S. Departments of Labor, of Agriculture, and of Health, Education, and Welfare have provided similar facilities. The Ford Foundation has provided up to $15 a week as a child-care allowance for their employees with young children.

The franchise operation and employer-sponsored day care sometimes come together. Ohio Bell Telephone and Western Electric contracted with Singer Learning Centers, a franchise operation, to establish and operate day-care centers for their employees.

Sponsorship of work-place day care by employers at a location close to the place of employment is getting a mixed reaction, however. Employers are still interested but are more skeptical about the results. A sizable number of firms that had made well-planned attempts to provide such service have backed off, most noticeably Tioga Sportswear and KLH, two employers that sponsored widely publicized programs. One study notes that "the dollar benefits of employer subsidized child care are, at best, uncertain. . . . Our analysis suggests that, except under unusual circumstances, savings from employer turnover and absenteeism are likely to be relatively small" (Lewis, 1973).

It is estimated that in 1972 a center at the work site for sixty to seventy children would require a work force of at least one thousand women (Woolsey, 1977, p. 135). A survey by the Ford Foundation in 1971 found that there were about 150–200 employer-supported day-care centers providing care for 6,000 children. An updated estimate in 1977 indicated that little change had occurred (*New York Times,* September 11, 1978).

There was a trend toward making day care a franchise operation. For instance, E. C. K. Chivers and Associates, which handles the franchise for such national operations as Black Angus Steak Houses and Lums, also handles the franchise of what it hoped would become a national network of Kindercare day-care centers. Similarly franchises are available nationwide for Mary Moppet day-care schools. By 1980 some of the steam had gone out of this trend.

Some real estate developers have included day-care centers in new housing areas as an additional incentive to young couples to rent or buy. The day-care center, like the community swimming pool, becomes part of the package of "amenities."

A number of books are available that encourage cooperative day care, organized by mothers themselves for themselves and their children, such as:

1. *The Day Care Book* by Vicki Brietbart (New York; Alfred Knopf, 1974).
2. *Day Care: How to Plan, Develop and Operate a Day Care Center* by E. Evans, B. Shub, and M. Weinstein (Boston; Beacon Press, 1971).

There are suggestions that two mothers fill one job, alternating in the care of their children, and that more jobs be organized so that mothers can work at home.

4. There is a trend toward a greater explicit diversification of day-care facilities. Previously the literature made distinctions primarily between a day-care center and family day care and between nursery care with a primarily educational purpose and day care oriented more toward care and protection. Currently the literature identifies a "child-development center," a "play-group facility," a "preschool-child-care center," a "school-age–child-care center," a "family-day-care home," a "group-day-care home," a "family school-age–day-care home," and a "group school-age–day-care home." Distinctions revolve around the age and the size of the group offered service and the primary orientation of the facility.

Day-care networks or systems have been developed. They involve a systematic combination of different kinds of day-care facilities under some central administration. Thus a day-care center might develop a series of satellite family-day-care homes as part of its operation by recruiting, training, and offering consultation to the family-day-care mothers.

Diversification involves not only the different kinds of day-care facilities providing care for groups of different ages and sizes, but also timing. Because many women work at night, day-care centers in large cities have developed night-care centers and family-night-care homes.

5. There is a trend toward the employment of welfare recipients as family-day-care mothers. The New York City Department of Social Services established the Family Day Care-Career Program. For the children of welfare mothers interested in a job or in job training (called *career mothers*), the program provides care in the home of other welfare recipients (called *day-care mothers*). The exchange frees the career mother to obtain or prepare for employment while providing extra income for the day-care mothers. The homes are selected and approved by the Department of Social Services, and the money earned is not included in the computation of welfare benefits. A training program and follow-up consultation provide child development education for the day-care mothers. Milwaukee (Wade, 1970) and Baltimore (Edwards, 1968) report similar programs.

6. The Head Start program confirmed and intensified the trend toward parental involvement in day-care-center activity. It also tended to enlarge the focus of such involvement. Head Start guidelines require the employment of parents as paraprofessionals and aides in the program whenever possible, and they require parent participation in day-care decision-making and administration. Similarly Federal Interagency Day Care Guidelines require that whenever an agency provides day care for fifteen or more children, there must be a policy advisory committee or its equivalent at the administrative level where most decisions are made. The committee membership should include not less than 50 per cent parents or parent representatives, selected by the parents in a democratic fashion (Cohen, Zigler, 1977).

There are a number of considerations advanced in support of this emphasis on parent participation. It tends to reduce the separation between home and center for the child. If what is taught in the day-care center is substantially similar to what is taught at home, there is less change and greater continuity for the child in moving from the home to the center every day. This is particularly true if there are, to begin with, cultural and ethnic differences between the home and the day-care center. Through parent participation, involvement, and control, the service potentially strengthens the family rather than separating parent and child. Parent participation reduces the risks of alienating the parents and the center staff. It reduces the danger that parents will feel excluded from an important experience that affects their children, and it reduces the feeling on the part of staff that the children are being dumped. With greater parent participation, it is hoped that day care will strengthen rather than undermine the nuclear family. It might be seen as an extension of the family rather than competition—as another kind of extended-family support system.

Parents can be involved as board members of centers, as members of policy advisory councils, as volunteer workers, as employed paraprofessionals, or through regularly scheduled conferences with the center's staff. They should be encouraged to visit the center and observe its activities when they have an opportunity.

Even if the center staff sincerely desires to get the parents involved, this is often difficult. Parents have to allocate scarce time and energy to this activity. They have to find baby-sitters and transportation for evening meetings.

7. There is a growing interest in developing day care for special groups: emotionally disturbed children, mentally handicapped children, and children of migrant workers. The care of such children requires special equipment and personnel with special training who are willing to devote extra time and energy to the children. Such day-care centers also make an explicit effort to involve the parents so that the training and/or the therapy achieved in the center is sustained and supported by the parents in the home. The National Association for Retarded Children has been very active and successful in extending day-care services to such children.

SUMMARY

Day care is a supplementary service designed to provide care for the child during the part of the day when the mother is unavailable. Day care, concerned first with the care and the protection of the child, is distinguished from nursery school, which has a more explicit educational focus.

There are two principal kinds of day care: group day care and day care offered in the family-day-care home. Family day care is the more appropriate resource for the child younger than two years old.

Day care is an appropriate resource for the child whose mother is working, for the handicapped child who does not need institutionalization, for the child living in a deprived environment, and in cases of parent–child conflict when the parent needs some relief from care of the child.

In reality, day care is used most frequently to care for the child of the working mother. The problem of day care is thus closely related to the problem of the working mother. The trend is toward an increase in the number of working mothers. This trend is related to (1) a change in the family from a producing to a consuming unit; (2) the family need for a cash income; (3) changes in the nature of the jobs available; and (4) changes in the life cycle of the family.

In 1977 there were about 6.4 million children under six years of age whose mothers were employed. The probability that a woman will work is related to the age of her children, the presence of a husband in the home, and the level of the husband's earnings.

But despite the sharp increase in the number of working mothers, only a limited number of day-care center places were available: about 900,000 in 1978. Most often, children of working mothers were cared for in their own home by the father or by older siblings. Thus, a small percentage of the children six years of age or under of working mothers were cared for in formal day-care arrangements.

Social workers form part of the day-care-center team, which includes teachers and health personnel as well. Social workers help to prepare the child and the family for the movement into day care, help them with the social and emotional consequences of the use of day care, and act as the liaison between the family and the child in the center.

Problems related to day care include:

1. The low priority given to day care as compared with other child welfare services.
2. Negative attitudes toward the working mother and toward day care as a supplementary-care arrangement.
3. Family day care versus the day-care center as the arrangement of priority.
4. The association of day care with public welfare.
5. The confusion over the professional identity of day care.
6. The problem of neglected age groups.
7. The inadequacy of current resources.
8. Multiple funding sources.

Among the trends identified were the following:

1. A growing acceptance of day care.
2. Increased public support of the availability of day care to all families.
3. A growing acceptance of day care for infants.
4. A diversification of the kinds of day-care arrangements and their auspices.
5. The employment of welfare mothers as caretakers.
6. An increase in parental involvement.
7. An increase in day care for children with special needs.

BIBLIOGRAPHY

ABT ASSOCIATES. *National Daycare Study—Preliminary Findings and Their Implications.* Cambridge, Mass.: Abt Associates, January 1978.

ALLEN, WINIFRED, and DORIS CAMPBELL. *The Creative Nursery Center: A Unified Service for Children and Parents.* New York: Family Service Association of America, 1948.

ARCHINARD, ENOLIA, et al. "Social Work and Supplementary Services," in *Day Care: Resources for Decisions.* Ed. by Edith H. Grotberg. Washington, D.C.: Day Care and Child Development Council of America, 1971.

BLOCH, JUDITH. "A Preschool Workshop for Emotionally Disturbed Children." *Children,* 17, 1 (January–February 1970), 10–14.

BRONFENBRENNER, URIE. "Research on the Effects of Daycare on Child Development." In *Toward a National Policy for Children and Families.* Washington, D.C.: National Academy of Sciences, 1976.

BRUCE-BRIGGS, B. "Child Care: The Fiscal Time Bomb." *Public Interest,* 43 (Fall 1977), 88–102.

CALDWELL, BETTYE. "The Effects of Infant Care," pp. 9–87, in *Review of Child Development Research.* Ed. by M. L. Hoffman and L. W. Hoffman. New York: Russell Sage Foundation, 1964.

———. "What Does Research Teach Us About Day Care for Children Under Three?" *Children Today,* 1, 1 (January–February 1972), 6–11.

———, et al. "Infant Care and Attachment." *American Journal of Orthopsychiatry,* 40, 3 (April 1970), 397–412.

CHAZIN, ROBERT M. "Day Treatment of Emotionally Disturbed Children." *Child Welfare,* 48, 4 (April 1969), 212–218.

CHILD WELFARE LEAGUE OF AMERICA. *Tri-Profession Conference on Day Care—Daytime Care: A Partnership of Three Professions.* New York, 1946.

———. *Standards for Day Care Service.* New York, 1960.

————.*Day Care Report.* New York, September 1962.

————. *Standards for Day-Care Services: Revised 1969.* New York, 1969.

CLARKE-STEWART, ALLISON. *Child Care in the Family.* New York: Academic Press, 1977.

CLASS, NORRIS E. "Licensing of Child Care Facilities by State Welfare Departments." *Children's Bureau Publication, No. 462.* Washington, D.C.: Government Printing Office, 1968.

COHEN, DONALD, and EDWARD ZIGLER. "Federal Daycare Standards—Rationale and Recommendations." *American Journal of Orthopsychiatry,* **47,** 3 (July 1977), 456–465.

COLLINS, ALICE N., and EUNICE L. WATSON. *Family Day Care.* Boston: Beacon Press, 1976.

DAY CARE AND CHILD DEVELOPMENT COUNCIL OF AMERICA. *Basic Facts About Licensing of Day Care.* Washington, D.C., October 1970.

ECKSTEIN, ESTHER. "The Function of the Caseworkers in Day Care Centers." *Child Welfare,* **41,** 1 (January 1962).

EDWARDS, ELVA. "Family Day Care in a Community Action Program." *Children,* **15,** 2 (March–April 1968), 55–58.

EMLEN, ARTHUR. "Slogans, Slots and Slanders: The Myth of Daycare Need." *American Journal of Orthopsychiatry,* **43** (January 1973), 23–37.

————*et al. Child Care by Kith: A Study of the Family Day Care Relationships of Working Mothers and Neighborhood Caregivers.* Portland, Ore.: DCE Books, 1971.

FADDIS, GABRIELLE. "Interaction Between a Nursery School for Disturbed Children and a Nursery School for Normal Children in a Child Guidance Clinic Setting." *National Association for Nursery Centers Bulletin* (Spring 1956).

FOSTER FAMILY DAY CARE SERVICE. *Follow-up Study of Foster Family Day Care.* New York: November 1962. Mimeo.

FRAIBERG, SELMA. *Every Child's Birth Right: In Defense of Mothering.* New York: Basic Books, Inc., 1977.

FREDRICKSON, H. "The Problem of Taking Care of Children of Employed Mothers." *Social Service Review,* **17** (1943).

FREUD, ANNA. "Nursery School Education—Its Uses and Dangers." *Child Study,* **26** (Spring 1949).

GILFILLAN, VIOLA. "Day Care as a Therapeutic Service to Preschool Children and Its Potential as a Preventive Service." *Child Welfare,* **41,** 9 (November 1962).

GODDARD, GLADYS. "Potentialities of Day Care." *Child Welfare,* **36,** 10 (December 1957).

GOLDEN ANNIVERSARY WHITE HOUSE CONFERENCE ON CHILDREN AND YOUTH. *Focus on Children and Youth.* Washington, D.C.: Government Printing Office, 1960.

GOLTEN, MARGARET. "Family Day Care: What It Means for the Parent." *The Family,* **26,** 4 (April 1945).

GORDON, BERTEL. "Criteria for Determining Type of Placement." *Journal of Jewish Communal Service* (Spring 1957).

GRANATO, SAM J., and E. DOLLIE LYNCH. "Day-Care Licensing." *Children Today* (January–February 1972), 23–24.

GREENBLATT, BERNARD. *Responsibility for Child Care.* San Francisco: Jossey-Bass, Inc., 1977.

GUYLER, CATHRYN. "Social Responsibility for the Development of Day Care," in *Proceedings of the National Conference of Social Welfare.* New York: Columbia University Press, 1942.

HANSAN, J., and K. PEMBERTON. "Day-Care Services for Families with Mothers Working at Home." *Child Welfare,* **42** (April 1963).

HARRIS, OLIVER C. "Daycare: Have We Forgotten the School Age Child?" *Child Welfare*, **56**, 7 (July 1977), 440–448.

HOFFMAN, LOIS W., and IVAN F. NYE. *Working Mothers—An Evaluative Review of the Consequences for Wife, Husband and Child*. San Francisco: Jossey-Bass, Inc., 1974.

HOST, MALCOLM, and PATRICIA HASSETT. "Day-Care Services and the Social Work Profession." *Social Work Education*, **11** (April 1963).

HOWARD, MARION. *Group Infant Care Programs—A Study*. Washington, D.C.: Cyesis Program Consortium, February 1971.

HUNTINGTON, DOROTHY S., SALLY PROVENCE, and RONALD R. PARKER. *Daycare—Serving Infants*. Washington, D.C.: Government Printing Office, 1971.

JACKSON, THERESA. *Day-Care Services as Administered Under Various Auspices*. New York: Child Welfare League of America, n.d.

JENKINS, SHIRLEY, and MIGNON SAUBER. *Paths to Child Placement*. New York: Community Council of Greater New York, 1966.

JOFFE, CAROLE E. *Friendly Intruders—Child Care Professionals and Family Life*. Berkeley: University of California Press, 1977.

KAGAN, JEROME, RICHARD B. KEARSLEY, and PHILIP R. ZELAZO. "The Effects of Infant Day Care on Psychological Development." *Evaluation Quarterly*, **1**, 1 (February 1977), 109–141.

KAMERMAN, SHEILA B. and ALFRED J. KAHN. "The Day Care Debate: A Wider View." *The Public Interest* **54** (Winter 1979), 76–93.

KEYSERLING, MARY D. *Windows on Day Care*. New York: National Council of Jewish Women, 1972.

KIRSHNER ASSOCIATES, INC. *A National Survey of the Impacts of Head Start Centers on Community Institutions, Summary Report*. Washington, D.C.: U.S. Department of Health, Education, and Welfare, May 1970.

KRASHINSKY, MICHAEL. "Daycare and Welfare," in *Issues in the Coordination of Public Welfare Programs, Paper No. 7*. Subcommittee on Fiscal Policy. U.S. Congress Joint Economic Committee. Washington, D.C.: Government Printing Office, 1973.

KUHLMANN, FRIEDA M. "Casework Supervision in the Day Nursery." *Child Welfare*, **34** (March 1955).

LEWIS, VIVIAN. "Daycare Costs Benefits Alternatives," in *Issues in the Coordination of Public Welfare Programs, Paper No. 7*. Subcommittee on Fiscal Policy. U.S. Congress Joint Economic Committee. Washington, D.C.: Government Printing Office, 1973.

LOVATT, MARGARET. "Autistic Children in a Day Nursery." *Children*, **9** (May–June 1962).

LOW, SETH. *Licensed Day-Care Facilities for Children: A Report of a National Survey of Departments of State Governments Responsible for Licensing Day Care Facilities*. Washington, D.C.: Government Printing Office, 1962.

LYNDEN, PATRICIA. "What Does Day Care Mean to the Children, the Parents, the Teachers, the Community, the President?" *The New York Times Magazine* (February 15, 1970).

MERRIAM, ALICE H. "Day Care of the Young Child: A Community Challenge." *Child Welfare*, **38** (October 1959).

MOUSTAKAS, CLARK E., and MINNIE P. BENSON. *The Nursery School and Child-Care Center*. New York: William Morrow & Co., Inc., 1955.

NATIONAL ASSOCIATION FOR RETARDED CHILDREN. Leaflet DR741. New York, n.d.

NATIONAL SOCIETY FOR THE STUDY OF EDUCATION. *Preschool and Parental Education, 28th Yearbook*. Bloomington, Ind.: Public School Publishing Co., 1929.

OGBURN, WILLIAM, and MEYER NIMKOFF. *Technology and the Changing Family*. Boston: Houghton Mifflin Company, 1955.

POWELL, DOUGLAS R. "The Interpersonal Relationship Between Parents and Care-givers in Daycare." *American Journal of Orthopsychiatry*, **48**, 4 (October 1978), 680–689.

PRESCOTT, ELIZABETH, and ELIZABETH JONES. "Day Care for Children—Assets and Liabilities." *Children* **18**, 2 (March–April 1971), 54–58.

———, CYNTHIA MILICH, and ELIZABETH JAMES. *The Politics of Daycare*. Washington, D.C.: National Association for the Education of Young Children, 1972.

RADIN, NORMA, and BONNIE C. JORDAN. "Child Welfare: Preschool Programs," pp. 156–169, in *Encyclopedia of Social Work*, 17th issue. Ed. by John B. Turner. New York: National Association of Social Workers.

RAPOPORT, LYDIA, and DONNA M. CORNSWEET. "Preventive Intervention Potentials in Public Child Care Centers." *Child Welfare*, **48**, 1 (January 1969), 6–13.

RAWLEY, CALLMAN. "Casework and Day Care—Beginnings of a Municipal Program." *The Family*, **24** (March 1943).

RUDERMAN, FLORENCE A. *Child Care and the Working Mother: A Study of Arrangements Made for Daytime Care of Children*. New York: Child Welfare League of America, 1968.

SEIFERT, KEVIN. "The Best Men for Child Care Work." *Child Care Quarterly*, **4** (Fall 1975), 188–193.

SELLIGMAN, AUGUSTA. "A Day Residential Program for the Disturbed Pre-School Child." *Child Welfare*, **37** (July 1958).

SHYNE, ANN W. *The Need for Foster Care*. New York: Child Welfare League of America, 1969.

STEINER, GILBERT Y. *The Children's Cause*. Washington, D.C.: The Brookings Institution, 1976.

STEINFELS, MARGARET. *Who's Minding the Children? The History and Politics of Day Care in America*. New York: Simon & Schuster, Inc., 1973.

STRATHY, ESTHER, CHRISTOPHER HEINICKE, and KAYLA HAUER. "The Role of the Social Worker in a Day Care Center." *Ries Davis Clinic Bulletin*, Spring 1974, pp. 25–37.

SULBY, ARNOLD, and ANTHONY DIODATI. "Family Day Care: No Longer Day Care's Neglected Child." *Young Children* (May 1975), 239–247.

THENAUD, AGNES. "Survey of Requests for Day Nursery Care with Reference to Post-war Planning." *Smith College Studies in Social Work*, **15** (1945).

TROUT, BESSIE, and DOROTHY E. BRADBURY. *Mothers for a Day. The Care of Children in Families Other Than Their Own*. Washington, D.C.: Government Printing Office, 1946.

UNITED NATIONS. *Mental Hygiene in the Nursery School*. New York: UNESCO, 1953.

———. "Day Care Services for Children." *International Social Service Review*, **1** (January 1956).

U.S. DEPARTMENT OF COMMERCE, CENSUS BUREAU. *Characteristics of American Children and Youth: 1976*. Washington, D.C.: Government Printing Office, January 1978.

U.S. DEPARTMENT OF HEALTH, EDUCATION, AND WELFARE. *Guide Specifications for Positions in Day Care Centers*. Washington, D.C.: Social and Rehabilitation Services, 1967.

———. *Federal Interagency Day Care Requirements*. Washington, D.C.: Government Printing Office, September, 1968.

———. *Child Care Arrangements of AFDC Recipients Under the Work Incentive Program—Quarter Ended June 30, 1971*. Washington, D.C.: National Center for Social Statistics, February 1972.

———. *The Appropriateness of the Federal Interagency Day Care Requirements:*

Report of Findings and Recommendations. Washington, D.C.: Government Printing Office, 1978.

U.S. DEPARTMENT OF LABOR. *Employed Mothers and Child Care.* Washington, D.C.: Government Printing Office, 1953.

———. *Working Mothers and Their Children.* Washington, D.C.: Government Printing Office, 1977.

U.S. SENATE, COMMITTEE OF FINANCE. *Child Care Data and Materials, June 16, 1971.* Washington, D.C.: Government Printing Office, 1971.

VOILAND, ALICE P. "Casework in a Day Nursery." *The Family,* **23** (May 1942).

WADE, CAMILLE. "The Family Day-Care Program in Milwaukee." *Child Welfare,* **49, 6** (June 1970), 336–341.

WATTENBERG, ESTHER. "Characteristics of Family Day Care Providers: Implications for Training." *Child Welfare,* **56, 4** (April 1977), 211–229.

WESTINGHOUSE LEARNING CORPORATION AND WESTAT RESEARCH. *Day Care Survey 1970: Summary Report and Analysis.* Washington, D.C.: Evaluation Division, Office of Economic Opportunity, 1971.

WHITE, BENJAMIN, and ELLA BEATTIE. "Day Care for the Mentally Retarded as Part of Local Health Services in Maryland." *American Journal of Public Health,* **56,** 11 (November 1966).

WHITE HOUSE CONFERENCE ON CHILDREN. *Report to the President.* Washington, D.C.: Government Printing Office, 1971.

WILLNER, MILTON. "Unsupervised Family Day Care in New York City." *Child Welfare,* **43, 6** (June 1969), 342–347.

———. "Family Day Care: An Escape from Poverty." *Social Work,* **52, 4** (April 1971), 30–35.

WITTLES, GLORIA, and NORMA RADIN. "Two Approaches to Group Work with Parents in a Compensatory School Program." *Social Work,* **16** (January 1971), 42–50.

WOOLSEY, SUZANNE H. "Pied Piper Politics and the Child Care Debate." *Daedalus,* **16** (Spring 1977), 27–45.

WORKS PROGRESS ADMINISTRATION. *Final Report on the WPA, 1935–43.* Washington, D.C.: Government Printing Office, 1944.

YEOMANS, ALFREDA. "Day Care—An Alternative to Placement Away from Home." *Child Welfare,* **32** (October 1953).

YUDKIN, SIMON, and ALTHEA HOLME. *Working Mothers and Their Children.* London: Michael Joseph Ltd., 1963.

8 SUBSTITUTE CARE: FOSTER-FAMILY CARE

INTRODUCTION

Foster-family care, institutional care, and adoption involve substituting another family for the child's own family, so that someone else takes over all aspects of the parental role.

Such a drastic change is necessary when the child's own home presents deficiencies so serious that it cannot provide the child with minimally adequate social, emotional, and physical care. It involves, for the child, not only temporary total separation (except for visits) from his own family and adjustment to a new family, but also a change of location, a change of school, and a change of peer and sibling group.

Because of the pervasiveness of the change in the child's life, substitute care is regarded as the third line of defense in caring for the child. The stipulation that follows from the need to avoid such drastic social surgery is that every effort be made to keep the home intact for the child and to keep the child in the home.

Substitute care in foster families or institutions involves a change in legal custody of the child. Adoption involves going beyond a change in legal custody to a change in legal guardianship. Legal custody is concerned with the rights and duties of the person (usually the parent) having custody to provide for the child's daily needs—to feed him, clothe him, provide shelter, put him to bed, send him to school, see that he washes his face and brushes his teeth. It permits the person or the agency having custody to determine where and with whom the child shall live. Consequently the agency having legal custody of the child can move him from one foster home to another. But although the agency usually obtains legal custody in foster-family care, the child still legally "belongs" to the parent and the parent retains guardianship. This means that, for some crucial aspects of the child's life, the agency has no authority to act. Only the parent can consent to surgery for the child, or consent to his marriage, or permit his enlistment in the armed forces, or represent him at law. Only with a change of guardianship is the natural parents' tie to the child completely severed.

Actually many long-term foster-family placements become *de facto* adoptions. But the fact that legal guardianship of the child—actual legal ownership of the child—has not been transferred from the natural parents to the foster parents has very considerable implications for the nature of the relationship established between foster child and foster family, and it does permit the return of the child to his natural home at any time.

Definition

The term *foster care* is often applied to any type of substitute care facility—boarding home, adoptive home, or institution. However, the Child Welfare League of America's (1959) definition is "A child welfare service which provides substitute family care for a planned period for a child when his own family cannot care for him for a temporary or extended period and when adoption is neither desirable nor possible" (p. 5).

Note that according to the CWLA, it is care in a *family*, it is noninstitutional substitute care, and it is for a *planned* period—either temporary or extended. Thus it is unlike adoptive placement, which implies a *permanent* substitution of one home for another, one family for another. To distinguish this use of the term *foster care* from other kinds of foster-care arrangements, we will refer to it in this chapter as *foster-family care*.

Historical Background

Foster-family care was probably practiced on a limited basis in antiquity: "Under ancient Jewish laws and customs, children lacking parental care became members of the household of other relatives, if such there were, who reared them for adult life" (Slingerland, 1919, p. 27). The early Church boarded destitute children with "worthy widows."

Indenture was an early form of foster-family care that was extensively employed. The Elizabethan Poor Laws provided for the apprenticing of dependent children until their twenty-first year. The master accepted the dependent child into his home; provided him with food, clothing, and the necessities of life; and accepted the responsibility for teaching him a craft or trade. In addition, provision was usually made for some extra payment in the form of clothes and/or money at the termination of the indenture. In return, the child was to work for the master around the house and in the craft or trade as an "employee." Indenture was recognized as a "business deal from which the person accepting a poor child on indenture was expected to receive from the child, a full equivalent in work for the expenses of his support, care and teaching" (Thurston, 1930, p. 10). This is set forth clearly in the following indenture contract:

> By the Massachusetts indenture the selectmen of the township of Leicester bind Moses Love, a poor child two years and eight months old, to Matthew Scott until the boy shall become twenty-one years old, and dwell with as an apprentice during the term of eighteen years and four months (*viz.*) until he shall arrive to the age of twenty-one years—he being a poor child and his parents not being well able to support it. Dureing all which the sd apprentice his sd Master his heirs Execvtors & Adminrs shall faithfully serve at such Lawfull imployment & Labovr as he shall from time to time Dureing sd term be Capable of doing and performing & not absent himself from his or their service without Leave & In all things behave himself as a good & faithfull apprentice ought to do and the sd Matthew Scott for himself his heirs Execvtors & Adminrs do Couenant promise . . . that he the sd Matthew Scott his heirs Execvtors & Adminrs shall & will Dureing the term aforsd find and provide for the sd apprentice sufficient Cloathing meet drink Warshing and Lodging both in Sickness & in health & that he will teach

him or cavse him to be tavght to read & write & siffer fiting his degree if he be Capable of Learning and at the Expiration of the term to Dismiss him with two suits of apparril one to be fitt for Lords day [Thurston, 1930, pp. 15–16].

The preamble of an eighteenth-century Maryland statute on indenture illustrates the relationship between indenture and the problem of child care:

Whereas, it has been found by experience that poor children, orphans, and illegitimate, for want of some efficient system have been left destitute of support and have become useless or depraved members of society; and, Whereas it would greatly conduce to the good of the public in general and of such children in particular that necessary instruction in trades and useful arts should be afforded them, therefore, the justices of the orphans' courts were authorized to bind out orphans, and such children as are suffering through the extreme indigence or poverty of their parents, also the children of beggars, and also illegitimate children, and the children of persons out of this state where a sufficient sustenance is not afforded [Bremner, 1970, p. 266].

Despite the fact that the indenture permitted all sorts of abuses and exploitation, that "it is morally certain that the experiences of indentured children varied all the way from that of being virtual slaves to that of being real foster sons or daughters" (Thurstone, 1930, p. 17), and that there was little guarantee of protection for the child other than public indignation or the foster parents' desire to keep the good opinion of their neighbors, indenture persisted in the United States until the first decade of the twentieth century. It did provide for many children a family life and at least the minimum of regular care.

A number of factors accounted for the gradual decline of the indenture as a means of foster-family care. It was not always profitable for the foster family because children, if taken young, had to be supported for a period of time before they could make a return on their investment. With growing industrialization and the movement of crafts and trades out of the home, the idea of an apprenticeship located in the family became less feasible. But perhaps of greater importance was the impact on indenture of the abolition of slavery, after which it was hard to justify an indenture that required the apprehension and return to the master of a runaway apprentice and that had some of the characteristics of bondage arrangements. In fact, Folks (1902) notes, "It has been seriously suggested that, with the adoption of the Constitutional Amendment in 1865, forbidding 'involuntary servitude,' the indenture system became unconstitutional" (p. 42).

The real origin of modern foster-family care lies with Charles Loring Brace and The Placing Out System of the New York Children's Aid Society. In the middle of the nineteenth century, New York City faced a problem of dealing with a large number of vagrant children who existed with minimal adult care, protection, and support. In 1849 the New York City Chief of Police called attention to the fact that:

ORIGIN

there was a constantly increasing number of vagrant, idle, and vicious children of both sexes who infest our public thoroughfares, hotels, docks, etc., children who are growing up in ignorance and profligacy, only destined to a life of misery, shame, and crime and ultimately to a felon's doom. . . . Their number[s] are almost incredible and to those whose business and habits do not permit them a searching scrutiny, the degrading and disgusting practices of these almost infants in the school of vice, prostitution, and rowdyism, would certainly be beyond belief [quoted in Langsam, 1964, pp. 1–2].

At about this time the Chief of Police reported ten thousand vagrant children in New York City (Thurston, 1930, p. 97).

Brace, a young minister who became the first secretary of the New York Children's Aid Society upon its organization in 1853, developed a new and distinctive method of dealing with the problem presented by these children. The society would "drain the city of these children by communicating with farmers, manufacturers, or families in the country who may have need of such for employment." The appeal was to Christian charity and to the need for labor on the farms. It involved relocating children from the pernicious influences of urban areas, where there was little for them to do, to rural areas, where there was much for them to do and where the environment was regarded as morally sounder. There evolved a particular program of group emigration and placement that resulted in finding foster-family care in free foster-family homes for about 100,000 children between 1854 and 1929 (Langsam, 1964, p. 27).

The procedure was first to collect a group of children in New York City. Many of the children were known to be orphans; some had been abandoned, so that the status of their parents was unknown. But many of the children were half-orphans or children with both parents living. In the latter cases, an attempt was made to obtain parental consent to the child's relocation. The largest numbers of children were provided by institutions in the city, but the society's agents also had responsibility for locating vagrant, uncared-for children. As Folks (1902) says, "The children were received from the newsboys' lodging houses, from orphan and infant asylums, and directly from the parents" (p. 67).

In forming the group, some effort was made to eliminate the physically ill, the mentally handicapped, and the incorrigible. After a group was formed, the children set out for the West or the South in the company of one of the society's workers. The community to which the children were to be sent was encouraged by the society to set up a committee of prominent citizens. The committee had the responsibility of arranging temporary care for the children upon their arrival. Of greater importance was the committee's responsibility to publicize the coming of the children, to encourage families to take them in, and to evaluate the suitability of those families who indicated interest. Upon the arrival in town of the group of children, arrangements were made for their distribution to homes in accordance with the preliminary work done by the local committee.

A report by a pioneer child-welfare worker, Dr. Hastings Hart, to the National Conference of Charities and Corrections in 1884 describes the "placement" procedure:

I was a witness of the distribution of forty children in ——— County, Minnesota. . . . The children arrived at about half-past three P.M. and were taken directly from the train to the Court House, where a large crowd was gathered. Mr. Matthews set the children, one by one, before the company, and in his stentorian voice gave a brief account of each. Applicants for children were then admitted in order behind the railing and rapidly made their selection. Then, if the child gave assent, the bargain was concluded on the spot. It was a pathetic sight, not soon to be forgotten, to see those children, tired young people, weary, travel-strained, confused by the excitement and the unwonted surroundings, peering into those strange faces, and trying to choose wisely for themselves. And it was surprising how many happy selections were made under such circumstances. In a little more than three hours nearly all those forty children were disposed of. Some who had not previously applied selected children. There was little time for consultation, and refusal would be embarrassing; and I know that the Committee consented to some assignments against their better judgment.

The Committee usually consists of a minister, an editor, and a doctor, lawyer, or a businessman. The merchant dislikes to offend a customer, or the doctor a patient, and the minister fears to have it thought that his refusal is because the applicant does not belong to his church. Thus unsuitable applications sometimes succeed. Committee men and officers of the Society complain of this difficulty. The evil is proved by the fact that, while the younger children are taken from motives of benevolence and are uniformly well treated, the older ones are, in the majority of cases, taken from motives of profit, and are expected to earn their way from the start [Hart, 1884].

Although it did not involve a formal contractual arrangement, and the society retained control of the child's custody and could remove the child if it was felt that he was being unfairly treated, the free foster-family arrangement was still based on the exchange of child labor for child care. As Thurston (1930) says in summarizing the program, "It is the wolf of the old indenture philosophy of child labor in the sheepskin disguise of a so-called good or Christian home" (p. 136).

Factors contributing to the decline of this procedure were the opposition of Western states to the "extraditing" and "dumping" of dependent children in their area, the opposition of the Catholic Church to what was regarded as an attempt by a Protestant organization to wean children from their Catholic heritage by their placement in non-Catholic homes, the decline in the number of orphans, and the closing of the frontier, which reduced the need for such labor as the "emigrant" children could profitably provide. Of considerable influence in effecting a decline in the program was the increasing criticism by the growing number of child welfare professionals. The proceedings of the Annual National Conference of Charities and Corrections frequently included attacks on the dangers involved in the method of selecting free foster homes for children and the looseness and infrequency of supervision following placement. Although Brace sought to meet these attacks by reports of "research" by agency workers indicating that only a limited number of children were maltreated or turned out poorly, the criticism was never adequately met. The data of much of Brace's research leave much to be desired in terms of their objectivity, the nature of sampling methods employed, and the somewhat haphazard way in which they were obtained. The distances over which the society operated and the limited number of workers employed precluded any careful selection or supervision of homes.

The first annual report of the Massachusetts State Board of Charities states the core of the problem succinctly:

As a general rule, the persons who now take children into their families from the State institutions do so primarily for their own advantage, and only secondarily, if at all, for the good of the child; but it frequently happens that the child who was taken as a servant secures a place in the affections of the family taking him, and so the connection ceases to be a mercenary one. These cases, however, do not form the rule, it is to be feared.

The system exacted a price from natural parents as well. "Placing out" at a distance meant a kind of pseudoadoption, and the intent actually was to prevent the return of the child to his own home—this, despite the fact that a considerable number of such children did have two living parents. As Thurston (1930) notes, "It does not seem fair to the relatives that they be compelled to surrender a child permanently in order to get whatever care he may need temporarily" (p. 135).

Before a change took place, however, the program stimulated the development of similar programs of foster-family placement in free homes by organizations established to do this within particular states. Such State Children's Home Societies, as they were called, originated with the work of Martin Van Buren Van Arsdale in 1883 in Indiana and Illinois. (Van Arsdale, like Brace, was a minister.) The purpose of the State Children's Home Societies was

> to seek the homeless, neglected, and destitute children and to become their friend and protector, to find homes for them in well-to-do families and to place them wisely; to look occasionally with discretion into the homes, and thus prevent abuse and neglect, and to replace children, when necessary; to make it possible for persons (without children of their own) to adopt a child; to minister, in comforting assurance to parents in fear of leaving their children penniless and homeless; to protect society by guaranteeing proper home training and education to the unfortunate little ones against its greatest enemies, ignorance and vice; to extend our organization into sister states [quoted in Thurstone, 1930, p. 156].

By 1923 there were thirty-four states in which such State Children's Home Societies had been established. The activities of these agencies were, and continue to be, supplemented by sectarian agencies in larger cities, such as the Jewish Child Care Association in New York City and nonsectarian agencies such as the Boston Children's Aid Society.

At the same time, the public agencies were pioneering other alternatives. The Michigan State Public School (in reality, an orphanage) opened in 1874; it was created to be a temporary home for all destitute children who had become public charges, until the children could be placed in foster family homes. Some nineteen other states soon adopted the same plan.

In the late 1860s, Massachusetts pioneered in paying board money to foster families for the maintenance of children who might otherwise have been placed in institutions and who were too young to be profitably indentured. This state also pioneered in more careful supervision of those children who had been indentured by the state.

The Boston Children's Aid Society, under the leadership of Charles Birtwell between 1886 and 1911, carried foster-family care a step further. For each child, Birtwell asked, "What does the child really need?" rather than "Where shall we put the child?" The aim, Birtwell said, "will be in each instance to suit the action to the real need, heeding the teachings of experience, still to study the conditions with a freedom from assumptions and a directness and freshness of view as complete as though the case in hand stood absolutely alone" (Thurstone, 1930, p. 200). This approach required individual study of the child and a variety of different kinds of substitute care—an individualization of need and diversification of services. Such a procedure, when followed, might mean that no substitute service would, indeed, be offered. The study might show that, with some help, the child could be maintained in his own home. Birtwell showed an appreciation of the potentialities of the preventive placement aspects of supportive and supplementary services. Until such an approach gained acceptance, as it did following its affirmation by the First White House Conference on Children in 1909, foster-family care was offered to "rescue" the child from his family.

For Brace, the long-time placement suggested that the foster parent was, in fact, replacing the natural parent in a pseudoadoptive situation. Given Birtwell's approach, the foster parent–foster child relationship becomes something distinctively different—a means through which the child is ultimately restored to his parents.

Birtwell developed a systematic plan for studying foster-home applicant families and a systematic plan of supervision once the child was placed. An effort was made to keep detailed records and to develop principles of action. He was, in effect, attempting to build a science of foster-family care and to professionalize practice.

These ideas resulted in a changed emphasis in foster-family care. Brace and Van Arsdale depended primarily on free foster homes, which meant that the agency did not pay any of the cost of boarding the child; the expense was assumed by the foster home. The gradual acceptance of boarding foster-family care, in which the agency pays for the support of the child, gave the agency greater freedom in selection and less discomfort in closer supervision of the home. A greater acceptance of the need to individualize the child led to a diversification of foster-care facilities and less exclusive reliance on the free foster-family home. Furthermore the growing recognition of foster-family care as a temporary substitute-care facility, an interim provision while the child's own home was being reorganized to reaccept him, meant that the agency worked to keep intact the relationship between the child and the natural parents.

The history of substitute care in institutions and that of substitute care in foster-family homes are interrelated. The mixed almshouses (see Chapter 11) were at one time a frequently employed resource for the institutional care of children. When, toward the end of the nineteenth century, one state after another began to pass laws prohibiting the use of mixed almshouses for children, they recommended that such children be placed in foster homes instead. Thus the closing of mixed almshouses for children increased the tendency to resort to foster-family care (Folks, 1902, pp. 74–80).

Orphanages frequently used foster-family care as a supplementary resource, both in the early years of the life of the child and then again as the child moved toward greater independence. In taking responsibility for infants, before the advent of pasteurized milk and formula feeding, the institution had to provide nursing care. Consequently orphanages would often place the infant in a foster family for wet-nursing.

When the child reached early adolescence, the institutions, in preparing the child for independence, once again placed the children in foster-family homes. As Slingerland (1919) says, "All child-caring institutions must at some age dismiss their wards and the usual method when that age arrives is to obtain a place for a child in a private home as an accepted inmate or paid worker before withdrawing institutional care and support" (p. 39).

Throughout the nineteenth century and the early part of the twentieth century, controversy raged between the advocates of institutional care and the supporters of foster-family care over which was the more desirable method. Foster-family care was given official sanction in 1899 by the National Conference of Correction and Charities. At that meeting, a report was presented by J. M. Mulrey (1900) in behalf of a special committee of prominent child-welfare workers appointed to study the problems of the dependent child and to make recommendations. The report adopted by the conference stated that when a child needed substitute care, consideration should first be given to a foster-family arrangement (p. 167). The First White House Conference on Children in 1909 stated that "the carefully selected foster home is, for the normal child, the best substitute for the natural home." Thus foster-family care was given a clear preference.

It might be noted that the history of foster care echoes with the cry that has accompanied many child welfare innovations. The contention was that providing adequate substitute care for the child would encourage parents to desert or neglect their children because they need not feel guilty that their dereliction would deprive the child of care. As a matter of fact, it was argued that some poor parents would feel it their duty to desert the child in order that he might be given more adequate care in a foster-family home (George, 1970, p. 10).

SCOPE

Current national statistics are not available regarding children in foster-family care. The most recent *national* data made available in 1974 are for March 1972. At that time reports collected from all states indicated that there were 248,512 children in foster-family homes, and an additional 6,598 children in group homes (National Center for Social Statistics, 1974). Subsequent reports in the statistical series concerned with foster care offer selective state statistics but, as in the case of adoption, no national totals (National Center for Social Statistics, 1976).

The rate of children in substitute care of all kinds had declined sharply after the passage of the Social Security Act in 1935, a confirmation of the potency of the social insurance and public assistance programs in maintaining children in their own homes. However since 1960 there has been a steady growth in substitute care as a result of increases in family disruption from all causes.

Although no national figures are available, some other data confirm an increase in the rate of children going into foster care through 1977. Claburn and Magura (1977) note that between 1972 and 1976 the rate of children in foster-family care in New Jersey increased from 4.4 to 5.2 per 1,000 children (Table 1–13).

Based on an analysis of a carefully selected sample of the 1.8 million children being offered social services, Shyne and Schroeder (1978) estimated that in March 1977, 395,000 children were in foster-family homes (p. 112). This would be a rate of 6 per 1,000 children, the highest rate of foster-family care since we began collecting national statistics on foster care,

The number of children in foster care is, in some ways, deceptive. It denotes the number of children living in foster-family homes on a given day as reported by agencies licensing foster homes. It does not, generally, include informal, nonlicensed foster-family-care arrangements made by parents with relatives and friends. It does not, additionally, give consideration to the turnover factor—the flow of children in and out of foster care. In any one year, then, the number of children served by the foster-family-care system is likely to be higher than the official figures—how much higher nobody really knows.

The trend is toward a clear increase in preference for the use of foster-family care as compared with institutional care for those children needing substitute care. In 1933, 47.2 per cent of the dependent, neglected, and emotionally disturbed children needing substitute care were living in foster-family homes, and 52.8 per cent were placed in institutions. In 1972, 80 per cent of children in substitute care were in foster families or group homes and only 20 per cent in institutions. The trend has been away from institutional care to foster care, and this relative difference in the utilization of these two services is expected to continue throughout the 1980s. (See Table 8–1.)

The group home, defined as a residential facility providing twenty-four-hour care in a group setting for six to twelve children or adolescents, is the most rapidly growing foster-care facility. Whereas foster-family-care homes reported a 3 per cent decrease in capacity in 1971–1972, group homes reported a 19 per cent increase in combined capacity during the same period. Despite this rapid increase, only about 7 per cent of children in foster care were living in group homes in 1977 (Shyne, Schroeder, 1978, p. 112).

The relative distribution of auspices under which foster-family-care programs are offered also underwent marked change. In 1933 the voluntary agencies were responsible for 53.3 per cent of the children in foster-family care.

By 1972, 84 per cent of foster-family and group homes placements were made under public-welfare-agency auspices. Group-home facilities, however limited, had much greater voluntary agency input in 1972, 52 per cent of such services being provided either exclusively by voluntary agencies or by voluntary agencies with financial aid from public agencies.

Rates of children in foster-family care differ widely from one jurisdiction to another, leading to the suspicion that the system is responding to many extraneous factors other than the needs and the best interests of children.

Parents are the principal source of referral for children coming into foster-family care, followed by social agencies and the police and the courts. Although white children are the clear majority of those receiving foster-family care, the proportion of nonwhite children is higher as compared with their percentage in

TABLE 8–1. Children in Foster-Family Care and in Child Welfare Institutions for the Neglected, Dependent, and Emotionally Disturbed (National Center for Social Statistics)

Year	Children in Substitute Care (rate per 1,000 children)	Children in Foster-Family Care (rate per 1,000 children)	Children in Institutions (rate per 1,000 children)
1933	5.9	2.5	3.4
1960	3.7	2.4	1.3
1965	4.0	2.9	1.1
1972	5	3.6	1.3

the general population. There are relatively few black children living in group foster homes. There is a slightly greater percentage of males in the foster-care population.

The median age of children in foster family care is higher now than previously, and most of the children in such care are 10 years of age or older (Bernstein *et al.*, 1975; Vasaly, 1975; Thomas *et al.*, 1977; Shyne, Schroeder, 1978). Data presented by Catalano (1974) on children in the New York State foster-care program shows that the median age increased from 8.3 in 1969 to 11 years of age in 1973 (p. 3).

The median age of children in foster family care is, however, younger than those in other forms of substitute care, namely, group homes and institutions where the median age is closer to 14 years.

Children coming into substitute care currently are perceived as more disturbed and more difficult to care for than were their counterparts earlier in the century.

Predicting trends in the scope of foster care is difficult because there are forces moving in opposite directions. The reduction in birthrates experienced since the 1960s has resulted in a smaller population of children under ten and consequently a reduction in the total population at risk for foster-family or group care. However, a continuation of increases in marital disruption and out-of-wedlock pregnancies would suggest that a larger percentage of this small population of children may need substitute care. In addition, the trend toward deinstitutionalization in both mental health and corrections and the trend toward providing community-based programs for children who might earlier have been cared for in institutions, will increase the need for foster-family facilities. This is particularly true for older and emotionally disturbed children.

SITUATIONS IN WHICH FOSTER-FAMILY CARE IS AN APPROPRIATE RESOURCE

Foster-family care is appropriate when the child's own parents are unable and/or unwilling to care for the child at home, even when supplementary services—income maintenance, day care, and homemaker service—are made available.

With the development and increased availability of supportive services, some families who formerly might have required foster-family care can now, through the intervention of such services, maintain their children in their own homes. The children in the foster-family network are consequently the ones whose families cannot or will not respond to such services or for whom adequate supplementary services are not available.

Studies of the reasons that precipitate the need for foster care show that the problems fall into three general categories: parent-related problems, child-related problems, and environmental circumstances (Sauber, Jenkins, 1966; Shyne, 1969; Vasaly, 1975; Shyne, Schroeder, 1978). Parent-related problems are the precipitating factor in some 75–80 per cent of the cases. These include parental neglect and abuse of children, abandonment, physical or mental illness, marital conflict, alcoholism and drug abuse, emotional problems, imprisonment, and "unwillingness to care for child." Child-related problems account for the need to place the child in 15–20 per cent of the cases. These include mental retardation, deviant delinquent behavior, physical handicaps, emotional disturbance, and aggressive behavior in the home, school, or community. Environmental stress and deprivation are the primary precipitating factors in a more limited number of instances (3–5 per cent) and are generally associated with parental and/or child problems. These include such factors as serious financial need or inadequate housing and chronic unemployment.

Most studies indicate that the identification of the primary problem comes from the worker's assessment of the situation. The parents' perception of the primary problem, in the limited number of studies where this is available, tends to differ from that of the worker. Much more frequently, parents see the child's behavior and situational stress as the primary problems requiring placement. Parents see as the major difficulty their own emotional problems, neglect, and abuse much less frequently than the workers (Phillips, Shyne, Sherman, Haring, 1971, p. 10; Jones, Neuman, Shyne, 1976, p. 32).

The precipitating situation, such as the mother's illness, requires placement of the child, in most instances, because the underlying family situation is highly problematic. Family disruption, marginal economic circumstances, and poor health consistently emerge as factors associated with the need for foster-family placement: "Although it is usually a specific crisis that brings children into social agency foster care, during the year prior to placement these families, by and large, were functioning marginally and had experienced difficulties so severe that it might have been anticipated that further stress could not be tolerated" (Sauber, Jenkins, 1966, p. 111). "The over-all picture of the retrospective year prior to placement shows marginal families without sufficient resources to sustain themselves in the community when additional pressures or problems are added to their pre-existing burdens" (p. 61).

A disproportionate number of children in care come from one-parent, non-white families on public assistance.

The precipitating problem in the context of a deprived structural and economic family situation cannot be solved by mobilization of any resources available to the family: neither friends nor relatives are available who are willing and able to care for the children.

Some typical statements of parent-related placement situations follow:

I felt very tired and sick, and I went to a hospital in my neighborhood where they told me I need to be hospitalized immediately since I had hepatitis. I told them I had no one to take care of my children and the doctor took me to Social Service, and the children were placed. I have no friends here in New York, and the only one to take care of my children was my mother-in-law and she was in Puerto Rico [Sauber, Jenkins, 1966, p. 82].

The mother was going out a lot to beer gardens, leaving the children alone most of the time, neglecting them. She would stay out all night. The Court investigated the house; they found the place filthy and just terrible and then decided it wasn't livable for the children. The mother didn't care for them. All the kids ate was canned food, crackers, pretzels and stuff like that. They didn't eat good food. They were left alone and not given affection [p. 156]

Dona, who is 12, came into foster care after her father was put in prison. Her mother had died six years before, and Dona had been living with first one relative and then another since her mother's death. When Dona's father was convicted of armed robbery, she was living with friends of her father. They were not able to care for her during her father's imprisonment, so they asked the agency to find a foster placement for her [Marr, 1976, p. 40].

A child-related problem resulting in the need for foster-family care follows:

Timmy came into foster care at age five. He was the youngest child in a family of seven children. Timmy's father rarely had a steady job but took odd jobs around the community, which usually lasted for short periods of time. Timmy's mother recognized that Timmy had special needs even when he was a small baby, but she had little time or resources to spend providing for those special needs. By the time he was five, Timmy was a difficult child to manage because of his hyperactive behavior that kept him constantly moving from one activity to another. He hardly could speak and usually had to be helped to eat and dress. Most of the time the other children ignored or taunted Timmy, for he was often in their way.

The social service agency became aware of the problem when Timmy's father applied for financial assistance. After investigating the home situation, the case-worker suggested that Timmy might need special help and asked that his parents agree to place him in a foster home. As both parents could no longer manage or cope with his behavior, they readily agreed [Marr, 1976, p. 41].

The families requiring foster-family care because of child-related problems came from a wider range of socioeconomic backgrounds, are more apt to be intact, and are more apt to be white. The child's behavior had exhausted the emotional resources of the family and other relatives are unwilling to undertake the burden of caring for such a child.

Referrals come from a variety of sources and are related to the nature of the difficulty. The most frequent initiators of foster care are the parents themselves and/or close relatives in instances of parents' physical or mental illness or inability to care for the child because of social stress, and when the child's behavior makes it difficult for him to live at home. The police and the courts more frequently initiate placement in cases of neglect and/or abuse.

The nature of foster-family care suggests that it is a feasible resource for the child who has the capacity to participate in and contribute to normal family living. Such care would be inappropriate in the following cases:

1. When a child presents problems of behavior that would not be tolerated in the community, or when he presents problems of behavior that militate against his living in a family group.
2. In the case of a child whose handicap requires some special care and/or training beyond that which can be offered by the family or the community.
3. When the natural parents are persistent in their objections to the child's care in a foster family. The objection may be based on the threat of another family's succeeding where they have failed; the institution is sufficiently different from the normal family setup so as to pose less of a threat to such parents.
4. Similarly, when a child is very much threatened by the divided loyalty to parental figures that is engendered in his placement in another family.
5. When it is desirable to keep a large group of siblings together and finding

a foster family willing to take such a group is unlikely, or when substitute care is necessary for a very limited emergency period.

The present feeling is that all children under six requiring substitute care should be offered foster-family care. The need for continuous close mothering supposedly dictates this. On the other hand, foster-family care is less desirable for the adolescent. Here the demands made for integration into a foster family conflict with one of the significant developmental tasks of adolescence: achieving independence from the family group. Placement of children of this age in a more impersonal setting might be advisable. Although such a decision is perhaps desirable and advisable, the increase in the average age of children coming into and being maintained in substitute care indicates the need for foster-family care for this age group. Studies of the adjustment of adolescents in foster-family care suggest that placement can be successful for this age group (Rosenblum, 1977).

Whether or not to offer foster-family care if the client requests the service is one of the most difficult decisions with which a worker is faced. Efforts have been made to spell out the criteria that should guide the worker in making such a decision (Phillips, Haring, Shyne, 1972; Paul, 1975). Requests for foster-care service on the part of clients are generally referred for further study by agencies, and such requests are more frequently rejected by child welfare agencies than requests for other child welfare services (Haring, 1975, Table 16).

Studies of the decision-making processes of agencies offering child welfare services further suggest their hesitancy in offering placement. The Child Welfare League conducted a study that involved completion by workers in four agencies of detailed intake and decision schedules on new cases during 1970 (Phillips, Shyne, Sherman, Haring, 1971). The object was to identify the variables associated with the decision either to place the child or to provide own-home service. Schedules on 216 cases involving 455 children judged to be in need of service provided data for the study. In almost three quarters of the cases (73 per cent), the decision was made to offer the child service in his own home, with placement being offered in only 16 per cent of the cases coming to the agency for help with a parent–child problem during the study period (p. 12).

The placement-decision families, as compared with the own-home service families, were more seriously disadvantaged and had fewer friends or neighbors to whom they could turn. Mothers in placement families were more often diagnosed as mentally ill and were more often emotionally disturbed, impulsive, and less affectionate and concerned about their children. Where fathers were present in the placement families, they were more frequently seen as inadequate parents. Client placement families "evidenced greater social and psychological pathology than own home cases" (p. 51), so that "placement children were more likely to receive *grossly* inadequate care in the areas of feeding, supervision and guidance, warmth and affection, protection from abuse and concern regarding schooling" (p. 44) if care in their own home was continued. The decision to place seems to have been a considered, deliberate decision in terms of the best interests of the child. The researchers concluded that "the drastic step of separating a child from his family is likely to be taken only if there is evidence of considerable deviance or pathology in the child, his parents or his living conditions" (p. 87).

Other studies comparing the mothers of children in foster care with mothers in comparable circumstances who are caring for their children at home show the greater emotional disturbance in the mothers of placed children (O'Rourke, 1976). Mothers whose children were placed were much more likely to be overwhelmed by responsibility for the family, to show emotional disturbance and low impulse control, and to lack the motivation or the desire to keep the family together (Shinn, 1968, p. 119). Inability to provide adequate care and the mother's pathology were the most frequently cited factors determining placement decisions (Shinn, 1968, p. 222). There were also likely to be fewer interpersonal resources such as relatives, friends, or neighbors to whom the families could turn for help. Placement was less likely when the mother was concerned about the child and motivated to attempt to change. Placement was more likely when the child was receiving "*grossly* inadequate care in the area of feeding, supervision and guidance, warmth and affection, protection from abuse, and concern regarding schooling" (Phillips *et al.*, 1971, p. 44).

The placement decision requires an assessment of (1) the danger to the child's biological, social, and emotional development of the current living situation; (2) the competence of the parents and their motivation and capacity to make necessary changes; (3) the formal and informal support system that might be mobilized to help in maintaining the child in the home without damage; and (4) the strengths and the vulnerability of the child that determine the level of stress with which he can cope without adverse effects.

The difficulties in making "correct" decisions in alternatives of such complexity are illustrated by the low level of agreement among highly experienced practitioners. Three such judges were offered detailed protocols of families at risk for placement and asked to decide independently on the choice of placing the child or offering in-home service to the family. Although the level of agreement between the three judges was considerably better than chance, there was "far from complete agreement"; complete agreement was achieved on request in under half the decisions. (Phillips, Shyne, Sherman, Haring, 1971, p. 83).

Removing a child from his home is a decision that is often open to considerable debate. It can be argued that if more intensive effort had been applied, if alternative options were more actively explored, if additional supplementary care resources had been brought to bear, the removal of the child might have been prevented (Sauber, Jenkins, 1966; Shyne, 1969; Gambrill, Wiltse, 1974; Gruber, 1978). The movement of children into substitute care is sometimes perceived as a political act "to rescue poor children from their parents, as opposed to providing money and social services to children in their own home" (Mandell, 1973, p. 36).

Some empirical attempts have been made to test the contention that a more concerned and focused effort to salvage the home for the child would substantially reduce the rate of placements. The Child Welfare League of America study, *A Second Chance for Families*, attempted to test this hypothesis (Jones, Neuman, Shyne, 1976). The study compares the typical day-to-day efforts of child welfare workers with those of a special unit of workers given access to special resources, such as day care and homemaker service, and working with a limited case load. Both the regular workers and the special-unit workers faced the task of serving children who had been identified as at high risk for foster-care placement. Some 549 families and 992 children were involved in the study. The outcome, of interest to us at this point, is whether or not the special efforts and special resources were able to salvage more homes for children. If placements are, as it is claimed, made without much effort to save the homes, then a special unit, charged with just this function and given the necessary resources and time, would make considerably fewer placements.

The effort did make a difference, but although statistically significant, the difference was very modest. In 60 per cent of the cases, children identified as being at high risk for foster care were actually removed from the home by the regular workers with the usual resources at their command. The special intensive unit working with similar children, with lower case loads and with special resources at their command, were forced to place 52 per cent of their children. The difference between 60 per cent and 52 per cent is a difference that one must respect. But it does indicate that there may be only relatively modest give in the situation and that even with the best efforts and resources, a high percentage of the homes—52 per cent—could not be salvaged (p. 80) and the children had to be removed.

An intensive, multifaceted, prolonged treatment program by the child-placing agency may indeed prevent separation. Goldstein (1973), for example, describes such a program. Less than 5 per cent of children served by the "Placement Prevention Service" have actually required placement. It is noted, however, that this is a long-term program, with many children remaining in the program three to five years.

Intensive contact programs have been developed to prevent the placement of children from families at high risk for placement. The Homebuilders Project in Tacoma, Washington, keeps in contact with such families every day during the first week after referral and in almost equally intense contact over a six-week period. Case loads are limited to two to three families, and a high rate of prevention of placement is claimed (Kinny et al., 1977; Slater, Harris, 1978). There are other reports of preventive placement projects with claims of success that are more often asserted, rather than validated, by evaluation research (Annual Report, 1977). The Federal Administration for Children, Youth and Families has funded a series of demonstration projects focused on innovative use of intensive support services to prevent separation of children from "families-at-risk."

It is often noted, in criticism of the foster-care program, that little effort is made to provide service to children in their own homes and that families are often offered foster-care service inappropriately. However, most of the children, by far, receiving child welfare services are receiving such services in their own home, and studies tend to show that the decision to place is most frequently made appropriately.

Detailed case-by-case analysis of a sample of 1,000 records of the 1.8 million children offered public social services in March 1977, showed that two thirds of the group were receiving service in their own home. The goal of this service that was most frequently reported was "strengthening of the family to lessen need for placement" (Shyne, Schroeder, 1978, p. 60). Most of the children receiving in-home service were receiving income maintenance and other supportive services under the Aid to Families of Dependent Children (AFDC) program. As Jenkins and Norman (1975) note in summarizing their finding on the families of children in foster care, "The much maligned AFDC support probably is the most successful preventive program for keeping children out of foster care" (p. 133).

Jenkins and Norman posed the following question to 128 mothers of children in foster-family care: "Looking back at everything that has happened would you say that placement of your child was absolutely necessary, very necessary, somewhat necessary, or not necessary at all?" Forty-seven per cent considered the placement to be "absolutely necessary," 17 per cent said it was "very necessary," 13 per cent "somewhat necessary," and 23 per cent said placement was "not necessary at all" (p. 111). The negative responses were primarily contributed by those mothers for whom the placement was involuntary (p. 52). In many of these instances, although the mother might have regarded the placement as unnecessary, the community, as represented by both the social agency and the courts, perceived it as necessary to protect the child because of parental neglect or abuse, alcoholism, drug addiction, or criminal activity.

A review by experienced child-welfare workers of the record material in 1,250 cases representing a sample of 29,000 in substitute care in New York City found that in 92.7 per cent of the cases, the record reader supported the decision to place the child (Bernstein, Snider, Meezin, 1975). A "large majority of the workers . . . closest to the actual decision" interviewed in a longitudinal study of 624 children entering placement in 1966 "thought the placement absolutely or very necessary" (Shapiro, 1976, p. 58). When interviewed regarding their perception of the experience, foster children themselves thought the placement was a desirable alternative to their own home situation (Jacobson, Cockerum, 1976).

In some instances, the worker has no choice in making the decision to place: the child may have been abandoned, the mother may have been suddenly hospitalized, the child might have been injured as a result of abuse or neglect. In other instances, the family comes for placement or referral from other agencies that have made efforts to prevent such a step but have failed (Williams, 1972; Goldstein, 1973).

There is no question, however, that in some percentage of cases, greater commitment to retaining the child in the home or the availability of more adequate resources could have prevented placement for some children.

There is a residual group of children, however, who would still need placement if even the best and most adequate of such services were available.

RECRUITMENT, ASSESSMENT, AND SELECTION OF FOSTER-FAMILY HOMES

The essential resource of the program is, of course, the foster home. Such homes have to be recruited, assessed, and ultimately selected for a particular child. A great deal of agency work is devoted to each of these steps.

Recruitment

Recruitment involves a program of interpretation to the public of the need for foster homes for children and the satisfactions to be derived from fostering a child. All mass communication media have been used by agencies in recruitment efforts: newspaper ads, radio, television, billboards, and placards in buses and subway trains. On occasion, such advertisements have been supplemented by making speakers available to church groups, PTA groups, women's clubs, and so on. Experienced foster parents are asked to participate in campaigns and to speak to local groups. They are effective recruiters, and they are apt to convey a realistic conception of foster care.

Such activity is reinforced by the visible enhancement of the symbol of the foster parent. The mayor proclaims a Foster Parent Week, and an award is given to a couple selected as the Foster Parents of the Year. All of this activity develops a "climate of awareness" of the need for foster parents in the community.

The literature on foster-family recruitment suggests, however, that continuous rather than sporadic, intense recruitment drives yield the best results. Some larger child-welfare agencies have their own central home-finding departments with special workers assigned to this task. In other agencies, all workers take responsibility for finding and evaluating foster homes. And usually, for greater effectiveness, several agencies in a community conduct their recruitment efforts jointly. In fact, some communities have developed a central home-finding service under the aegis of the community welfare council (Radinsky, 1963).

Studies of the outcome of foster-care recruitment show a great attrition rate among the families that express initial interest. The largest percentage of those who inquire about foster care withdraw voluntarily; a smaller percentage are rejected, often for very clear and unambiguous reasons, such as overage or poor health. Often less than 10 per cent of the original group are licensed, and very rarely more than 20 per cent (Oughletree, 1957; DeCocq, 1962; Glassberg, 1965; Vick, 1967).

In one instance, a special television program on foster care in Chicago, "The Children Are Waiting," provided viewers with a battery of fifty phones manned by volunteers ready to accept inquiries following the telecast. Some 5,850 people called in response to the program to inquire about foster care, but fewer than 500 families were recruited.

Why do so few apply, and why do so many withdraw their applications? Interviews with a randomly selected sample of one hundred people in St. Louis regarding their attitude toward foster care indicated that many people did not "perceive" the agency's publicized need for foster families (Dick, 1961). There was little prior interest in fostering, so the publicity was largely ignored. Outside employment competes with foster care as a possible satisfying activity for women with limited or no child-care responsibilities; in 40 per cent of the families interviewed, the woman was employed outside the home.

Wakeford's (1963) study of foster parents in England suggests that motivation is related to class differences regarding the role of the mother. Interviews with 66 foster parents and a group of 148 controls selected at random from among nonfostering married couples showed that the relationship between socioeconomic class and foster parenthood is not related to income but to the higher value and prestige accorded the maternal role in working-class families. The foster mother accepts fostering "as an alternative to maximizing income" by working outside the home: "She is more family-oriented than average. She values the home; there she finds most of her satisfactions and employs most of her skills. There she is in her element." This preference is reinforced by the working-class setting, which offers the mother fewer alternative sources of prestige than are available to her middle-class sister. The working-class mother needs children to give significance to the one role that is given prestige according to working-class standards. If she has fewer than an average number of children (and foster mothers had smaller families than average), she can add to their number by fostering. Foster parent-hood thus primarily fills a sociopsychological need rather than an economic one.

Both Fanshel (1960) and Babcock (1965) found, in their detailed studies, that many of the foster mothers came from families with many children, had highly developed homemaking skills, and were positively oriented toward child care and home-centered activities. Babcock notes that foster mothers "regarded the role of mothering as a main task in life, a task they expect to enjoy" (p. 373). They had little interest in a paid job outside the home. Adamson (1973) also found that foster mothers were home- and child-care-oriented, "house proud," and preferred domestic activities, belonging to few, if any, outside organizations.

Appeals from members of the prospective applicant's own ethnic group have greatest credibility for the applicant. Efforts have been made to enlist the coop-eration of the black, Hispanic (Delgado, 1978), or American Indian community in recruiting foster homes for minority-group children. Bilingual staff and staff identified with the community enhances recruitment possibilities. People who have "been there" have greater credibility for the applicant, so that active foster parents are used in recruiting foster parents.

Friends and relatives who are foster parents develop a social network con-cerned with interests around fostering and raise the consciousness of others about foster care. Very often, foster-parent applicants have heard of the program from friends and relatives who stimulated their interest. Social agency publicity has more impact then because people have developed some receptivity to such an appeal.

Because people are reluctant to identify themselves with a program that is negatively perceived, the general public image of the foster-care program af-fects recruitment.

Passive, impersonal strategies that are directed toward a general, unselected public and that involve public informational appeals need to be supplemented by more active, personalized approaches. These involve direct contact with mem-bers of the public who have indicated or might be expected to indicate an inter-est in fostering some particular kinds of children. Personal contact, with minimum delay, of any presumably eligible applicant is vital in sustaining and intensifying interest in fostering.

All methods of recruitment have been found useful, but different methods serve different purposes. Mass media methods serve the purpose of informing and educating; the more personal recruitment procedures serve the purpose of persuading toward, and supporting, a decision to participate in the program.

The idea for foster-family care perhaps originates more frequently with the foster mother and is generally engaged in to satisfy her needs. For the foster fa-thers, "pleasing their wives rather than satisfying pressing internal needs was an important element in the decision of these men to become foster parents" (Fanshe, 1966, p. 156). Satisfaction for the father in providing a masculine model for the foster child is also a prominent theme (Davids, 1968).

The question of motivation becomes even more complex when we recognize that children of different ages may appeal to different patterns of motivation.

This is confirmed by Fanshel's (1961) study, based on interviews with 101 foster couples, data derived from the Parent Attitude Research Instrument (PARI), and ratings by social workers. "A rather basic dichotomy appeared in the study between those foster parents who cared primarily for infants and those who cared for older children": those who cared for infants were more oriented to private gratifications ("enjoying the presence of a cuddly baby in our home"; "I like the affection I get from children"); those who took older children were oriented toward social gratifications ("knowing I am doing something useful for the community"; "I like helping the unfortunate, downtrodden people") (Fanshel, 1961, p. 18).

Such a dichotomy is less evident in a more recent study of foster parents of adolescents (Rosenblum, 1977). Although some community-oriented satisfactions are cited as motives for fostering, the principal, more frequently emphasized motives related to knowing that one was able to help a particular child, satisfactions in the affection one received from the children, and the opportunity of being able to meet the challenge of a difficult task through the use of homemaker skills.

The most potent motivational attraction to foster parenting revolves around the gratifications in the personal, affectionate relationship with children and the rewards of implementing the satisfying role of parent.

Increasing family income through in-home employment in a "job" that calls for homemaker skills in preference to out-of-home, alternative job activities, or in the absence of employment skills, is a secondary contributing motive.

The readiness to accept a child for foster-family care is likely to stem from multiple reasons. Furthermore a motive that is inappropriate in one family may, expressed somewhat differently, have positive implications in another. Josselyn (1952) points this out very clearly in a cogent analysis of the implications of motives for foster family care. Even the desire to find a "replacement" or a companion for one's own child does not necessarily imply failure. A study by Jenkins (1965) of ninety-seven foster homes showed that parents expressing these motives were frequently successful (p. 212).

This suggests that applicants respond to the agencies' appeal out of some need of their own: "In the wish to serve there is the need to serve." This in no way implies a derogation of foster parents' readiness to accept a child or their capacity to do a good job. If their needs are complementary to those of the child, they can be, in fact, the best kind of foster parents. It does indicate, as is true of all behavior, that only those people who anticipate some compensation—emotional, social, or economic—will be prompted to apply for foster parenthood.

Requirements for foster parents may legitimately differ from those for adoptive parents. There need be less concern with the age and income of foster parents than is true for adoptive parents. Foster parents are generally recruited from upper-lower- or lower-middle-class groups, are frequently blue-collar workers, and are generally older than the child's biological parents. Foster parents may be capable of accepting and loving only children of a particular age. (This would pose a problem for adoptive care, where the need to love the child through all stages of development is necessary.) Foster parents must be able to use an ongoing relationship with the agency. (The adoptive parent–agency relationship terminates.) Foster parents must be able to accept the child into the family and to adjust to the loss of the child when he leaves.

The availability of foster-home care is increased not only by recruiting more homes but also by reducing the turnover of the homes already in the system. Jones (1975) interviewed parents in fifty-five homes that had stopped fostering children. He found that there was a core group of foster parents who were retained in the system for long periods of time and that these homes were supplemented by another group of short-stay parents. The long-stay foster homes tended to be the homes of older, working-class people. Among the reasons for giving up fostering over which the agency had some control were the lack of support in the role by the caseworker and the lack of worker help in preparing the parents for the role.

The great extent of turnover, and the problem it might pose for the pool of foster homes available for use, is noted in the finding that "Of all licensed foster homes in San Francisco in 1970, less than one fifth were still active three years later" (Boyd, Remy, 1978, p. 276).

Assessment

The agency has the grave responsibility of finding the best possible substitute home for the child needing care. A detailed study of all applicants is necessary, not only because the agency feels an ethical and professional responsibility to children and their natural parents but also because it has a legal responsibility to the community. Foster homes are licensed in most states, and the agency must certify that the home meets the license requirements.

Some preliminary screening and selection usually proceed on the basis of the objective criteria outlined in state licensing standards. The state normally requires that there be both a father and a mother in the home, that they be young enough and healthy enough to provide adequate care, and that they have an income adequate to meet their own needs. The state also stipulates that the home must provide adequate space for the child, that it must meet adequate sanitary and safety standards, and that it must be located in a community that offers adequate school, health, church, and recreational facilities. Preliminary investigation indicates whether or not the family can meet these basic requirements.

The more difficult aspects of assessment involve the socioemotional factors that are thought to be desirable in a foster home. These are assessed on the basis of a series of interviews with the prospective foster parents, conducted both in the office and in the home. If there are children in the home, some effort is made to obtain their reaction to the parents' plan to accept foster children. An effort is also made to determine the origin of the applicants' interest in foster care, their expectations concerning foster care, and their experience as parents or (if childless) with children generally. Also of interest are the satisfactions and problems they experienced in rearing their own children and the ways in which the introduction of a foster child might require modification in their child-rearing practices, the developmental history of both husband and wife, the history of their marriage and their current marital interaction, the changes they anticipate in the organization of the home and in the interpersonal relationships of family members as a result of the introduction of another child, and their preferences in foster children.

The social worker also explores with the applicants their attitudes regarding visits by the child's natural parents, their attitude toward parents who place their children in substitute care, and their probable reaction to the child's eventual departure. And because the agency has a continuing responsibility for the child, some attempt is made to assess the applicants' willingness to work cooperatively with the agency.

The assessment is designed to inform the applicant about the agency, as well as to inform the agency about the applicant. The applicant is given the opportunity of assessing foster care so that he may decide whether or not he wants it. After learning what is involved in becoming a foster parent, some applicants voluntarily withdraw.

Foster-family care poses a paradox for the applicant. The foster family must want a child very much in order to be motivated to engage in foster-family care, yet they must feel comfortable in giving up the child placed with them. Not only does the foster parent have to accept the possibility of the removal of the child, but he is asked by the agency to participate in a plan that would ensure the probability of the child's removal.

In addition to the interviews and home visits, agencies ask for and contact references provided by the applicant in aiding the worker to make a decision.

Group meetings are used as a screening device. As a consequence of communicating the essential, minimal requirements and expectations of the foster-parent program, agencies can filter out applicants whose situation is inappropriate. Applicants, on learning more about the specifics, can elect not to continue (Gross, Bussard, 1970).

Attempts have been made to explicate the image of the "good" foster parent, a concept used by workers as a generalized standard against which applicants are assessed (Wolins, 1963). The image incorporates many of the middle-class virtues of "planfulness" and responsibility and tends to reflect attitudes similar to those held by the social worker making the assessment (Dingman *et al.*, 1962).

Another approach to developing valid criteria for assessment lies in attempting to study the factors that distinguish the "successful" foster parent from the less successful one, or that distinguish the accepted applicant from the rejected applicant (Parker, 1966; George, 1970; Napier, 1972).

Neither age nor socioeconomic situation seems to be a sensitive indication of "success," although regular income at a level that permits care of the child without strain is desirable. The developmental history of "successful" foster parents shows wide variation (Cautley *et al.*, 1966).

Studies showed that the more acceptable foster homes tended to be more child-centered and concerned with understanding the child (Colvin, 1962; Kinter, Otto, 1964), were able to maintain a desired balance between permissiveness and control, and were able to maintain better relationships with the natural parents (Shapiro, 1976, p. 55).

This combination of assurance in dealing with the stress and strain of child rearing, confidence in the exercise of such skills, and a disciplined, no-nonsense, mother-knows-best approach to child rearing is noted in the research comparing foster mothers' child-rearing attitudes with those of nonfoster mothers (Paulson, Grossman, Schapiro, 1974).

Cautley and Aldridge (1975) followed the experience of 145 first-time foster parents over an eighteen-month period after placement. Ratings of foster-parent success were associated with the "ability of foster parents to cope with the common problems of school age children—prompt and appropriate handling of problems without harshness or excessive discipline and with an understanding of the reasons for such behavior" (p. 53). In general, familiarity with and competence in child-care and child-rearing tasks were associated with success. The foster father's readiness to accept and cooperate with the agency's ongoing participation in the placement, his flexibility, and his concern for the foster child's needs as against his own needs were positively related to the success of the placement, as were the foster mother's ability to individualize the child and her having been the oldest of a number of siblings. High formal religiosity on the part of the parents correlated negatively with success.

A study of sixty foster homes showed that "successful" foster homes, as defined by the social workers assigned to the home, were those that were more accepting of the child's behavior and more tolerant of the child's failings (Rowe, 1976). This finding is further confirmed by responses of a sample of some one hundred children in foster care to questions about their reactions to their placements (Bush, Gordon, LeBailly, 1977). The good foster home, as described by these children, was one that provided love, care, understanding, and respect for their freedom laced with concerned control.

Foster children describe the good foster parent as "a good-hearted person, one who would let you speak how you feel. Someone who would sit down and find out what you want"; "People who care and would like to help you. There are a lot of times when I goof off bad and they could send me away, but they didn't"; "A good foster parent is someone who shows you the same kind of affection a real parent would"; "someone who is strict enough so you won't get into trouble but lenient so you could have some fun." The standard of material comfort in the foster home, which was generally better than that available in the child's own home, was also a source of satisfaction.

In general, the research supports the sensible suppositions that it is good to select people who have familiarity with children and who have developed parenting skills; who can empathize with, understand, accept, and individualize the child; who have some tolerance for child behavior that is somewhat different from the behavior the parents are familiar with; and who have a family life with sufficient stability and internal strength to withstand the burden that the foster child imposes, particularly at the beginning of the placement. Some warnings come up frequently: more attention needs to be paid to foster fathers because they are more significant determinants of placement outcome than we had thought; the foster fathers selected should be receptive toward agency supervision of the foster home and flexible in their response to the child. Ultimately, however, some of foster placement success or failure depends on the particular child: his or her responsiveness, age, adjustive capacity, and behavior and the nature of the particular interaction established with the foster parents. As Krause (1971) notes in summarizing his research, "successful" placement does not depend on the presence of single characteristics but on the interaction of a number of different factors.

Fanshel (1966) supports the contention that the "good" foster parent is difficult to identify as a separate, identifiable entity:

In the research reported here and in other studies of parent behavior, it has become clear that parenthood cannot be studied in isolation from children. . . . Many of the foster parents in this study showed a fairly broad range of behavior with the foster children placed with them. One kind of child could evoke a positive, nurturing kind of response; a child with different characteristics could bring forth almost rejecting behavior from the same foster parent. Although one would expect foster parents who reveal strong ego structures and sound superego values to do uniformly with most children placed with them, their parental capacity must nonetheless be seen as a variable phenomenon. The aim of high-level child welfare practice should be to maximize the parental potential of foster parents through the placement of children who can evoke a positive response in them and the provision of professional casework support to foster parents in order to help them withstand the negative and often seemingly unchangeable behavior of upset foster children [p. 162].

Accepted applicants are generally required to take a medical examination to establish that they are physically capable of caring for a child and have no infectious diseases. Then a license is issued that certifies that this home is authorized to accept children for foster care. The license, in many states, indicates the specific number of children that the home may accept at any one time. Generally, not more than four older children are allowed at one time and not more than two children under two years of age. A license is usually issued for a one-year period, at the end of which the agency must review the situation and re-license the home.

Efforts have been made to develop systematic procedures for more objective assessment of foster-parent applicants. Touliatos and Lindholm (1977) have developed a Potential for Foster Parenthood Scale distributed by the National Foster Parents' Association. The scale includes items regarding the health, employment, and income of foster parents; the time they have available for child care; the opportunities they might provide for the cultural, intellectual, and spiritual development of the child; the nature of their marital relationship; and their parenting ability and foster-parent motivation, flexibility in child rearing, and attitudes toward working with the agency and the foster child's parents. The worker is faced with the difficult job of applying items that require considerable sophisticated interpretation—items such as "gives impression of being a caring person," "is adaptable in expectations of children," "has capacity to undertake the responsibilities entailed in working with a social agency."

Somewhat more attuned to the realities of the assessment procedure as experienced by the worker, Cautley and Lichenstein (1974) have developed a manual concerned with the selection of foster parents. This manual provides an interview outline for separate interviews with the mother and the father, covering most of the essential items already noted. In addition, however, vignettes of typical foster-parent problems are presented for applicant reaction and discussion. The manual provides a coding outline to help the worker interpret applicant responses to the questions raised in the interviews. This code enables the worker to assess whether a response does indicate, for instance, whether a parent is likely to be child-centered, supportive, and flexible in child rearing and whether the marital interaction indicates a good relationship.

Assessment standards need to be flexibly applied and adapted so that they fit the circumstances of the applicant. To require that the home provide a separate room for the foster child or that the mother not work or that the home be a two-parent home may be at variance with the reality of the living situation of minority-group applicants and applicants from disadvantaged communities. Such applicants may need the active help of the agency in meeting minimum standards, even to the point of agency support in improving their homes so that more and safer space is available.

Agencies make an effort to be flexible in assessing applicants and in applying licensing requirements. Foster-parent licensing requirements regarding the mother's employment, the age of the foster parents, and the need for religious affiliations are the ones most frequently waived in practice. There is currently a greater willingness to place foster children in a one-parent home and to accept low-income couples as foster parents. However, the picture of the typical family that continues to guide the social-agency foster-parent selection procedure is a two-parent, independent, nuclear, heterosexual, intraracial family. Although agencies do select other kinds of families—single-parent, homosexual, communal, interracial—they do so infrequently, with some reluctance and anxiety (Thomas, 1977; Petersen, Pierce, 1974).

Some agencies, facing the need for a sizable additional number of foster homes, have experimented with self-approval methods (SAM). All foster-parent applicants are automatically approved and licensed after participating in five mandatory training sessions and one home visit. Interviews with foster-care workers and a comparison of foster parents recruited through SAM and more traditional procedures found that the self-approved method recruits were of "high quality" and in some respects more adequately prepared for the role than traditionally recruited parents (Freund, 1975).

Rather than seeing foster-parent applicants as an undifferentiated group, there is a growing conviction that there needs to be a refinement of perception of and a more deliberate match between the needs of different applicant subgroups and the different kinds of children needing placement. Some foster parents reflect the more traditional picture of a home-centered family seeking the temporary care of a child to continue gratification previously experienced in raising their own children, with little need to see foster payments as income supplements. Other foster parents do not see foster care in temporary terms but are interested in "long-term, quasi-adoptive placement." Other foster parents are interested in placements of variable permanence but one where economic returns for fostering are important complementary considerations to gratification in child care. There are other different configurations of motivations and needs. The group of children needing foster care is also differentiated, with some needing short-term care, some needing long-term care, some requiring greater agency payments to compensate foster parents, and some needing only agency payment covering maintenance. Appeals to different groups may focus on the kinds of children available that most squarely meets their needs.

Applicant withdrawal rather than agency rejection ultimately accounts for the largest percentage of attrition between application and licensing of the home (Festinger, 1966, p. 104). Applicant attrition—whether from rejection or, more frequently, withdrawal—is related to (1) family-centered factors (family disagreements about applying, changes in the family situation as a result of illness, housing, employment changes, the stress of other responsibilities) and (2) social circumstances (difficulty in providing care in a one-parent family, age, limited housing space, police record).

Following recruitment, assessment, and approval, an agreement is signed with the agency as part of the licensing procedure. A study (Festinger, 1974) of such agreements used by state departments of social services throughout the United States notes some uniformities regarding what is included. The agreement generally includes a statement of the foster parents' responsibilities for caring for the foster child, helping with the agency's plan for the child, and keeping the agency informed of accidents, illnesses, or changes in the child's location, such as during vacation. It restricts the rights of the foster parents to accept other children or to take action for the adoption of the foster child without agency permission. Procedures regarding the biological parents' visits are spelled out. A key aspect of the agreement, appearing in almost all contracts, is the requirement that foster parents agree to the removal of the child at the request of the agency and the relinquishment of contact with the child.

The value of agency recruitment, assessment, and selection of foster homes as contrasted with an unregulated system in which parents themselves seek and find substitute care for their children was substantiated by a recent English study of the two procedures. Holman (1973) studied the outcomes of privately arranged foster care in the case of some 143 children in England. The foster homes found by the biological parents for their children generally gave the children reasonably good care, and the foster parents were conscientiously concerned with the needs of the children. However, they had less understanding of the needs of the children, and there was considerable discrepancy between the foster parents' and the biological parents' conception of the purposes of foster care. There was a much higher incidence of school behavior problems on the part of these children, contrasted with children whose placement had been arranged by social agencies. However, the parents who chose the foster home visited the children in the foster home more regularly.

Selection

The placement of a child involves the selection of a particular home for a particular child: "The focus has shifted from choosing the 'best adjusted parents' to selecting foster parents whose needs meet the needs of the child to be placed" (Kinter, Otto, 1964, p. 361). Selection, then, is on the basis of complementarity of needs.

This is not entirely a new idea. In 1867 the Massachusetts Board of State Charities recommended "that a child of passionate temper should not be placed in a family where the master or mistress is of a similar disposition. When such instances do occur there is apt to be trouble pretty soon." Placements of children evacuated from London during the war indicated that "nervous children were best placed in quiet, conventional types of home while the active, aggressive children were best in free and easy homes with companions" (Bowlby, 1951, p. 127).

Colvin (1962) reports on an investigation of the extent to which the foster parent–foster child relationship was "growth-producing and mutually satisfying":

With regard to the success of the mothers with children of different temperaments, our findings indicated that mothers showing a high need for play did best with children of low impulse control. Similarly, mothers with a high need for order did best with children showing high withdrawal, whereas mothers with a high need for play and nurturance did best with children showing a low degree of withdrawal.

In general, both for mothers and fathers the study indicated that "parents with specific needs do relatively well or poorly with children showing specific personality characteristics" (Colvin, 1962, pp. 45–46).

The home that might be good for a child early in life might become unsuitable later. Jenkins (1965), in the course of studying ninety-seven foster homes, noted that in one group of five homes, the mothers took young children for short periods of time and were uniformly successful with them. If the children stayed to the point where they were growing in independence, these mothers found that they were developing difficulties in relation to the child (p. 217).

The age and sex of the foster parents' own children are also significant. Several studies (Bowlby, 1951, p. 129; Trasler, 1960, p. 223) have shown that failures in foster placement, which result in the child's removal from the home, are associated with the fact that the foster parents had a child of the same sex and age as the foster child. The explanation is that such a situation sets up undesirable competition.

Foster-family care of an emotionally disturbed child may require greater impersonality, less involvement—a relationship that approximates, in some essential ways, the professional relationship. Thus the foster parent who can maintain more emotional reserve may be selected for such a child.

It must be noted that the selection of a home is not always a conscious, deliberate process. It is often a "search, seek, find" operation of expediency rather than an exercise of professional judgment.

The desirable prescription is for the social worker to match the child needing a foster home with the available foster parents identified as being best able to deal with the special qualities of that child. In reality, however, it is questionable whether such matching is feasible. One of the few attempts to test the frequency with which matching takes place was done by Fanshel and Grundy (1971), who studied some 152 foster homes in New York City. Having available a rating of the Child's Behavioral Characteristics and the workers' responses to a Foster Parent Appraisal Form, they assessed the extent to which "the characteristics of the child were matched with foster parents' special general capabilities." The results tended to "suggest that, for the most part, placements seem to be based upon administrative expediency—children are placed where vacancies exist with little attention on psychological grounds" (p. 28).

Workers are faced with providing the child with "the best plan possible rather than the best possible plan." Inappropriate placements are often the result of the lack of availability of appropriate placement facilities rather than a consequence of a worker's faulty decision. Data from a variety of studies done in different states showed that "The major reasons for inappropriate placements was the great shortage of foster care facilities for teens and special needs children" (Vasaly, 1976, p. 47). Children who should be in a group foster home, a specialized foster-family home, or a residential treatment center may be placed elsewhere because such resources are in very short supply.

Types of Foster Care

The process of selection requires a decision on the part of the agency as to the kind of foster-family care it should offer the child. The agency may choose from among the following kinds of noninstitutional, twenty-four-hour-a-day arrangements:

1. *Receiving homes*—specialized boarding homes designed to care for children on short notice for limited periods of time. This service is offered primarily to babies and younger children for whom an institutional arrangement is felt to be undesirable even for a short period of time (MacMahon, 1958) and in situations requiring emergency removal of a child from a home.
2. *Free, work, or wage homes*—the child is placed in a free home, in which the agency pays no board rates, when it is anticipated that the child will be adopted by the family. Work or wage homes may be appropriate for the older child who can make a contribution in recompense for care.
3. *Boarding homes*—the agency and/or the natural parents pay the foster parents a board rate. This is, by far, the most common type of foster-family-care arrangement.
4. *Group homes*—may be viewed as a large foster-family unit or a small institution. It is a living facility within the normal community simulating a family for a small group of unrelated children. The group home requires more extended discussion, not because it offers service currently to any significant number of the children in foster-family care but because it is likely to be an increasingly significant facility in the foster-care field.

The group home may be that of a private family whose members have been recruited because of their understanding of and willingness to work with a large group of children. More frequently, it is a single home or apartment owned or rented by the agency and staffed by "foster parents" who are employed by the agency (Miller, 1954; Greenberg, 1963). It is established in a residential community and is indistinguishable from neighboring units. A married couple is employed on a free-rent-and-board basis, plus a board rate for each child, or on the basis of a straight monthly salary. The "foster parents" work around the clock, much as they would if these were their own children.

The Child Welfare League of America Group Home Standards Statement (1978) suggests that group homes "should not be used for fewer than five children or more than twelve. A group of six to eight children is optimum because it is small enough to allow for individualization and large enough to remain a group even if a member is (temporarily) absent" (p. 27). It is further recommended that both boys and girls under twelve be included together in a group home. For older children, careful planning is necessary in relation to facilities and supervision. The children should participate with staff in the development and implementation of house rules.

Group home houseparent turnover is very high, with one study showing only 17 per cent of the houseparents holding the job for more than a year (Shostak, 1978, p. 315). Long workdays, and long workweeks, coupled with a lack of insulation from group home problems even during office hours and lack of privacy, made for dissatisfaction with the job.

Regular houseparent staff is assisted by shift workers—frequently college students without prior experience. Turnover of shift workers was also high.

Children selected for group homes must be able to live with the group without endangering themselves and others. The children need to be well enough to attend school regularly. An attempt is made to preserve some balance in the group, so that some aggressive youngsters are tempered by some quieter ones and some relatively normal adolescents. Gula (1964) estimates that group homes, "accepting referrals from a wide range of referral agencies, admit less than half" (p. 13).

The group home, whether owned and operated by an agency or by a private family licensed to accommodate a large group of children, is an intermediary facility. It offers some of the personalization of family living typical of family care, yet permits some of the distance from adults possible in an institution. It provides the normal community environment found in the foster-family home, yet, like the institution, it offers the "opportunity to form peer relationships which are not as threatening as sibling relationships or as different as relationships between foster children and the natural children of the foster parents" (Gula, 1964, p. 28). This permits the child to feel less threatened and less guilty about establishing a competitive relationship with his foster parents and reduces the threat to biological parents that is posed by another set of "parents" who may succeed where they failed. Consequently the group home is selected for "emotionally detached youngsters who are either too fearful to risk exposure of their feelings in close relationships or simply do not know how to find their way in close relationships" but who can operate without difficulty in the normal community (Schwartz, Kaplan, 1961, p. 10). It is also selected for adolescents because their principal developmental tasks revolve around establishing independence from parents and parental surrogates and it is desirable to offer the kind of diluted, attenuated parental relationships characteristic of the family group home.

The group home has greater therapeutic potential than the foster-family home, particularly for the adolescent. Therapeutic changes in the child's behavior in the foster-family home depend on what the foster parents can make available in terms of relationships with the child and models of acceptable behavior. The group home makes these available, but it also provides a peer group, interaction with which helps to control and modify undesirable behavior.

The group home owned and staffed by the agency offers additional advantages to emotionally disturbed children. The pay may be high enough to permit the employment of foster parents with some professional training; the fact that it is operated by the agency may allow heavier demands on the "foster-parent" staff in meeting the special needs of emotionally disturbed children and in providing the scheduling necessary for special classes, appointments with psychotherapists, and so on. The group home owned and operated by the agency has the additional advantage of permitting the foster parents to be somewhat more relaxed, tolerant, and accepting of the inevitable minor destructiveness of emotionally disturbed children.

The group home may be selected for some emotionally disturbed children for whom the agency does not want to risk the possibility of removal and replacement. Such children are frequently difficult for the normal foster family to keep. In the usual foster home, the foster parents share in the decision on whether or not the child stays. In the agency-owned home, the agency alone makes this decision. Thus the group home provides the feeling of permanence and continuity for the child who needs this security.

The group home may also serve as a "halfway house" for children who are ready to be discharged from an institution but who are not yet ready to return to their own families. It permits the orderly, progressive reintroduction of the child back into the community. And it has been used as a service following the treatment of emotionally disturbed children in residential care (Naughton, 1957).

Some of the thinking involved in making a decision regarding the selection of the appropriate kind of care is illustrated in the following case:

> The conflict between Sarah W., age eleven and one-half, and her mother had become too difficult for Mrs. W. to stand. The father had deserted them several years prior to the present request. Sarah felt that both she and her mother had been abused and rejected by the father.
>
> Sarah responded with extreme rage to her mother, who subtly provoked these outbursts. But she got along well at school with her teachers and classmates and was able to establish a good relationship with the girls and the leader in her Girl Scout troop, even though she was not able to reach out to and initiate a personal friendship with children individually. Sarah was, indeed, a very lonely child and had no intimate friends.
>
> The mother became ill from cancer, and a homemaker was placed in the home. Sarah got along well with the homemaker although whenever she tried to approach her in a motherly way, Sarah would remark irritably, "Now don't start mothering me!"
>
> The child welfare worker concluded that a foster home did not seem wise for Sarah at this time. To be placed in a family would be too threatening for Sarah since she was clinging so tenaciously to her mother now that separation was pending. Sarah could respond positively to adults only when the relationship was not too intense or personal and spread over many children, as with her teachers and the scout leader. . . .
>
> A group home would offer Sarah the advantages of group living and the support of a group. All of the girls in the home would have been placed there for many of the same reasons as Sarah and some, if not all, would have difficulties in the parent–child relationship. She would have a relationship with a house mother, yet this would not be highly personal. She would have the advantage of living in the community and continuing to meet the demands of community life. At the same time, because of the smallness of the group, she would have an opportunity to develop personal relationships with individual girls—and the intimate climate of the group home would help Sarah come to grips with the basic problem affecting her relationship with her mother [U.S. Department of Health, Education, and Welfare, pp. 52–53].

In summary, then, foster parents need to be recruited, assessed, and then selected. A constant recruitment effort is necessary to provide the field with the number of families it needs. Foster care appeals to a limited group of families —generally to families at the upper-lower and lower-middle socioeconomic level who feel some social or emotional imbalance.

The worker, in assessing the family, uses as a guide the licensing regulations, which require certain minimum levels of physical adequacy of the home and the neighboring community. In addition, workers have a clear image of the "good" parent, which generally follows the middle-class mental health image. However, workers do not always apply the image in assessing foster parents because of the pressure for homes. Selection is made in terms of the complementary needs of the children and the foster parents, and the placement has to be individualized so that a good "fit" is obtained.

PROCESS

Intake

Children come into foster care through two principal routes:

1. Parents may make application to the agency for such service.
2. The child may be committed to the agency for foster care after having been adjudged abused, neglected, dependent, or delinquent.

Neglect is a frequently encountered contingency, so many children come into care via this second route (see Chapter 5). In such cases, there is no application for service; the decision concerning the children is sometimes made over the parents' opposition or with their passive acquiescence. But for parents who come to the agency of their own volition, there is more of a possibility for casework help in coming to a decision. The very availability of supplementary and supportive services intensifies the problem of decision by increasing the range of choices. Of course, the parents may not be aware of the services—or, being aware, may have some objection to using them. If so, the social worker informs them of the availability of such services and helps them to resolve some of their negative feelings about the services:

> Mrs. M., a mother of two preschool children, has recently been deserted by her husband after years of marital conflict. The family had only limited savings since Mr. M. was a semiskilled punch press operator who had earned little more than a marginal income. Mrs. M. had some experience as a beautician before she was married six years ago. She wanted to place the children, go back to school, upgrade her skills, and then have the children come live with her. She had heard about AFDC but was reluctant to consider it. The worker helped her to feel somewhat more accepting about being "on welfare" particularly because a plan was worked out for part-time day care for the children while Mrs. M. enrolled in a beautician course. As a result, she withdrew her request for placement.

If there are some strengths in the client or the client's situation that might permit the child to remain at home, the worker explores them with the client. However, if it is clear that the child's own home is "predominantly injurious to the child" and that the family situation is "unmodifiable," or if the parents insist that the child be placed, the agency works with the parents toward the placement of the child. A parent may express a desire for placement but not necessarily accept it. Successful placement needs the continuing active participation of the natural parent and his conviction that this decision is the correct one.

Bowlby (1951), quoting a study done at the Maryland Children's Aid Society in 1942, notes that where both the child and the natural parent accepted placement, the chances of success for the foster placement were very great. In few cases was the child able to show an accepting attitude toward placement if his parents did not themselves hold and sanction such an attitude (p. 119).

If the social worker, in collaboration with the parents, has decided that placement is indeed the best and most feasible choice, he must then make clear to the parents that foster care does not relieve them of the burden of parenthood indefinitely and that such care is, ideally, temporary. Foster family placement is, in effect, a sociotherapeutic resource permitting a temporary reduction in whatever stress is imposed on the parent by his need to care for the child. Like any treatment resource, it is best used either as a means of effecting change or as increasing the possibility of effecting change, following a clear diagnostic evaluation of the total situation. Responsible placement requires that the parents be helped to plan the necessary changes that will ultimately permit the child to return. Ideally, planning for the child's return begins at the same time as planning for the child's placement.

Although it may be clear to both parents that placement is designed to allow them to work toward achieving the changes that will permit the child to return home, placement of a child relieves the crisis; there may consequently be less motivation to do anything about anything, particularly if doing something involves some effort on the part of the parents to effect changes in themselves. To keep participation and motivation high, and to maintain parent–child ties, the agency involves the natural parents in what has been called the *structure of service.*

However limited their contribution may be, the agency seeks to have the natural parents pay for some of the board rate of the child. Even a limited amount symbolizes the parents' responsibility for the child. Actually, however, relatively few parents pay any part of the cost of such care: payment comes primarily from county or state funds, in the case of public agencies, and agency funds, in the case of the voluntary agency. The agency encourages parental visits to the child in the foster-family home, and all forms of communication for continuing contact.

The agency encourages the parents to share as much information as possible about the child so that the agency will be able to select the optimum foster family. The agency also involves the parents in preparing the child for placement, helping them to deal with the child's reaction to placement. The act of separation itself is used to maintain the parents' sense of responsibility to the child. The agency helps the parent to feel that in helping the child to make a comfortable adjustment to separation, he is fulfilling his obligation to the child and demonstrating his concern for the child. The agency may even ask parents to visit the prospective foster home so that they will be assured of the adequacy of the care the child will receive. All of these activities serve to keep parental participation and responsibility at a high level.

It is suggested that the process of separation from the child is easier for the biological parents if they can visit the foster home and meet the foster parents. Seeing the reality of the foster home is reassuring, and the parents' sense of participation and involvement in the process is also intensified.

Thus far, we have discussed two different ways in which the agency seeks to help the child through casework with the parent:

1. It helps the parent come to the decision that placement will be of greatest benefit to the child.
2. It helps the parent to maintain intact his responsibility to the child and his contact with the child, and it plans with the parent from the start for the child's return.

The agency also seeks to help the parent directly by helping him to deal with some of the disturbing feelings that may result from the necessity of placing the child. Although all parents fail at one time or another, the failure is usually limited and private—a family affair. Here, however, the extent of failure is almost total, and knowledge of it has to be shared with the agency and, ultimately, with the foster parents. This involves a loss of self-esteem, an anticipation of rejection and censure, and an intensification of feelings of inadequacy and shame. This feeling is apt to be intensified with placement and with the pressure to recognize that the foster parents are daily demonstrating more adequacy in the care of the child than the natural parents themselves.

For some parents, the placement of the child is an enactment of their desire to get rid of him. The parents feel great anxiety and guilt as a consequence of those desires and as a result of the sense of relief and release they feel in having someone else accept the burden of responsibility for the care of the child. For other parents, placement might be a gratifying way of punishing the child, and once again, this gratification might engender guilt. Relieving guilt while keeping the sense of responsibility high seems like a delicate task for the worker—and it is.

Acceptance of foster-family care by the natural parents involves acceptance of an anomalous position. They retain the status of parents, but they no longer practice directly the daily responsibilities of the role. They have to relinquish some of the prerogatives of parenthood to another set of parents. They may fear that, in doing so, they might lose the child's affection and respect to the foster parents. The agency has to help the parents in their struggle with these fears.

Finally, although placement relieves the parent of the burden of care for the child and the loss of some prerogatives regarding his control, it also involves the loss of gratification. Filial deprivation for parents is a process paralleling parental deprivation for children (Jenkins, 1967, 1969; Jenkins, Norman, 1972). As part of a larger study, some 430 parents were asked, "How did you feel the day your child was placed?" (Jenkins, Norman, 1972). Reactions identified included sadness, anger, bitterness, relief, thankfulness, worry, nervousness, guilt, shame, emptiness: 88 per cent reported a feeling of sadness, followed, frequently, by nervousness and worry; 30–39 per cent reported feelings of guilt (usually mothers) and shame (usually fathers). These feelings were directed against themselves. About half the parents reported feelings of anger and bitterness, of thankfulness and relief; in most instances, such feelings were directed toward the agency. Anger and bitterness were likely to be felt when separation resulted from neglect and/or abuse; thankfulness, when it resulted from the physical illness of the mother; relief and guilt, when it resulted from the child's behavioral maladjustment. Unless some of these feelings are resolved, the success of the placement might be jeopardized and the child's adjustment to foster care made more difficult (see also Aldgate, 1976).

The different primary reasons that bring children into foster care are associated with the kinds of families from which the children come and the reactions of the parents to the placement experience. Children who come into care because of the physical or mental illness of the mother come disproportionately from nonwhite, single-parent, marginal-income homes. The parents are more inclined to accept the service, to see it as facilitative, and to be satisfied with the service. Where the primary reason for entry into care is the child's disturbed behavior, the family involved is more apt to be a white, intact, middle-income family. The family is likewise accepting of the service and inclined to perceive it as helpful. Children who come into care because of abuse or neglect or because of severe family disruption (alcoholism, drug abuse, crime, family conflicts) are likely to be disproportionately from nonwhite, single-parent, marginal-income families. Such families are opposed to the service, see the agency as usurpers of parental rights, and are dissatisfied with the service.

Without an awareness of his feelings, the biological parent may find it very difficult to be honest with the child if this involves an open confession that his return home is not likely. The tendency is to tell the child the good news he wants to hear rather than the bad news he has to hear. The biological parents may demand obedience, even in absentia, to themselves rather than to the foster parent. They may force the child to behave in allegiance to themselves rather than to the foster parents and thus use the child in their resentment against the foster parents, the "better" parents. Developing an awareness of such feelings is the caseworker's responsibility.

The statistics on discharge outcome, which confirm that the largest percentage of children in foster care return to their own homes, justify an agency orientation that clearly says to the biological parent, "Even though your child is in foster care, you are still the most important person in your child's life. Your child needs you. He or she needs to know that you love and care about him or her even though you are not directly caring for him or her. Your child needs to keep in close contact with you" (New York City Department of Social Services, 1977).

Because foster family care is designed to be temporary substitute care, the agency has the obligation of working with the biological parents to effect the changes necessary to permit the child to return home.

However, in actuality, studies show that little direct rehabilitative service is offered the biological parent (Stone, 1969; George, 1970; Fanshel, Maas, 1972). Summarizing the findings of a national study on foster care, Maas concluded that "Agency relationships with most fathers and mothers of the children in care are such that if parental conditions are to be modified, the process will have to be one of self-healing without any assistance of casework service" (Maas, 1959, p. 5).

In response to these persistent criticisms, and as a result of the fact that such inaction increases the risk of a child's remaining inappropriately in foster care for long periods, alternative procedures have been recommended. There is currently a greater emphasis on systematic case planning with the parents of children in foster care. *Systematic case planning* is defined as the identification of the specific changes necessary for a child to return home; the setting of time limits for achieving these changes; and careful work to bring about such changes, including help and support to the natural parents as required (Wiltse, Gambrill, 1974a, p. 14).

At the level of worker–client contact, what is proposed is a greater specification of expectations and responsibilities through the use of contracts that clearly spell out these considerations so that both the worker and the client know what might be expected of them and what changes need to be made within a given period of time. The details of such systematic planning procedures, including contracting, are carefully spelled out in several manuals (Stein, Gambrill, 1976; Pike *et al.*, 1977).

Contracting is recommended by Gambrill and Wiltse (1974) as one of the conclusions in their study of foster care. The recommendation is being implemented in foster-care programs that make use of contracts negotiated between the agency and the biological parents (Stein *et al.*, 1974).

A *contract* is defined as a working agreement between client and worker concerning the purpose of their interaction and the processes through which that purpose is to be achieved. Contracts identify not only the problem to be worked on but the roles of the participants in the interaction, the objectives to be achieved, and the time limits. Written contracts are more desirable than verbal contracts, and the more specific, concrete, and behaviorally oriented the language of the contract, the greater the likelihood that it will be understood, accepted, and achieved. There should be considerable mutuality in the formulation of contracts, so that there should be some preliminary interaction before a contract is drawn up. Once drawn up, it should be open to renegotiation and change.

Such contracts list objectives in specific measurable terms ("Mother will visit child in care one hour a week for the next three months; father will apply for three jobs in the next week; the family will contact three rental agencies in a two-day period to find housing with more space").

The contracts specify not only what the client will do but also what the worker is obligated to do to help the client—the agencies he will contact, the number of appointments he will make with the client, the resources he will provide.

An example of a short-term contract between a client and a worker follows:

I, (Client), have stated my interest in regaining custody of _____ (Child), and in order to work toward that goal, I agree to the following conditions:

1. I agree to visit _____ (Child), every Wednesday from 1:00 P.M. to 3:00 P.M. in the (Child Welfare Agency) office.
2. I agree to meet with _____ (Caseworker), every Wednesday at 3:00 P.M. in the (Child Welfare Agency) office to discuss my visits with my child, to review planning concerning my child, and to discuss changes in my situation as well as any other relevant matters.
3. I agree to participate in weekly meetings with a counselor from the County Mental Health Clinic.
4. I agree to keep (Caseworker) of (Child Welfare Agency) informed at all times of my whereabouts and home address.

I, (Client), understand that failure to meet the terms of this agreement may result in a petition for termination of parental rights to my child, (Child).

       (signed)   (date)
       (Client)

I, (Caseworker), acting on behalf of (Child Welfare Agency), agree to assist (Client) in her efforts to regain custody of her child, (Child), and, in order to work toward that goal, agree to the following conditions:

1. I agree to have (Child) at the (Child Welfare Agency) office every Wednesday at 1:00 P.M. for visit with her mother, (Client).
2. I agree to meet with (Client) each Wednesday at 3:00 P.M. in the (Child Welfare Agency) office.
3. I agree to arrange transportation, upon request, for (Client) so that she can attend weekly meetings with the mental health clinic counselor.
4. I agree to maintain (Child) in foster care until a permanent plan can be accomplished for her.
5. I agree to keep (Client) informed of any significant matters relating to her child, (Child), such as illnesses, school progress, etc.

       (signed)   (date)
     (Caseworker)

It is jointly understood and agreed between (Client) and (Caseworker) that this agreement will continue in effect for a period of ninety days (unless jointly modified) and will be reviewed by (date), to evaluate progress toward meeting the stated goals. [Pike *et al.*, 1977, pp. 50–51].

Contracts have the advantage of giving clear focus to casework efforts with the client and reducing misunderstandings and discrepant expectations between worker and client. They require of the client an active interest in being helped and some clear notion of what he wants to happen with the worker's help.

Often there are few significant sanctions that the agency can apply if the client does not adhere to the contract. In foster care, there is such a penalty. In contracting with the biological parents of children in foster care, it is often clearly indicated that failure to work toward change will result in having the agency move toward the termination of parental rights so as to achieve permanence for the child through adoption. Thus one supposedly prime condition of good contracting—that it be honestly entered into without coercion—is at variance with another aspect of contracting with the parents of children in foster care. The consequences of the failure to follow and implement the contract are made explicit, namely, that the child may not be returned home. A widely distributed "Guide for Parents of Children in Foster Care" (New York City Department of Social Services, 1977) notes clearly that, "Your parental rights and responsibilities go together. If you do not carry out your parental responsibilities, you may lose or endanger your parental rights. . . . You can lose your parental rights to your child without your consent if you do not carry out your parental responsibilities while your child is in placement."

As a matter of fact, one value of contracting is that it provides documentation of parental failure to respond to efforts on the part of the agency to help the parent effect changes in those conditions that would make possible the child's return home. The documentation of such service and the lack of response provide the explicit evidence needed to support a petition to the court for the termination of parental rights (Pike *et al.*, 1977, p. 38).

Here, as in protective services, the worker is faced with implementing a multiple role as helper–facilitator–supporter of the client in planning to change and as evaluator of the outcomes of such efforts. The obligation to the client is to make clear these different responsibilities: "We will work together so that you are no longer alcoholic, or drug addicted, or abusively rejecting of your child, but if within (some specified period of time) the situation has not changed, we will recommend to the court the termination of your parental rights." Service programs involved in such unwelcome dilemmas express confidence that clients can distinguish between a "threat and a clear explanation of realistic alternatives" and that parents respond to such frankness (Pike *et al.*, 1977, p. 43).

Achieving is difficult for the worker because of the kinds of families the agency is called upon to help. Profiling the biological parents from data provided by foster-care studies in five different states, Vasaly (1976) says that:

> As a group they tend to be maritally unstable. Most report having several children: few of the children live with the parents. The parents are generally poorly educated. Many are unemployed and those that are employed are apt to be employed at unskilled or semi-skilled work. Most are below poverty level income, and many are receiving public assistance [p. 21].

A random sample of 210 workers' rating of the parental adequacy of parents of children in foster care in Oregon in 1975 rated 73 per cent of the biological mothers and 74 per cent of the biological fathers, when present, as presenting either "major" or "severe" problems in child care. *Major* was defined as follows: "parental problems necessitating the child's placement in foster care are serious and probably chronic." *Severe* is defined thus: "parental problems necessitating the child's placement in foster care are serious, chronic and this parent is unresponsive to efforts to change the situation" (Emlen, 1976, p. 7.3). The parents who need to place a child frequently have such limited strengths that even the best service may not result in rehabilitation. If, as the relevant studies indicate, lack of motivation to change is one of the factors in the behavior of the biological parents that determine the worker's decision to place the child, we can expect that this same lack of motivation would continue, after placement, to make rehabilitation of the home more difficult.

Some parents who place their children move or disappear shortly afterwards and are no longer available. The worker is obligated to attempt to follow up, locate, and reinvolve the parent if at all possible. Some parents are institutionalized as mentally ill and are not physically and/or emotionally available for planning. Some parents clearly indicate that agency intervention is unwelcome and reject the agency's efforts to work with them.

In some cases, the worker who is making an honest and determined effort and achieving little in the way of results gets discouraged and stops trying. He allocates the limited time available to working with other, more receptive families.

The intervention most frequently employed by workers in counseling with the biological parents is support: emotional reassurance and encouragement (Sherman, Neuman, Shyne, 1973, p. 45; Gambrill, Wiltse, 1974, p. 14).

In refutation of the tendency to derogate "soft" services, it might be noted that "the most positive feelings about agency operations" expressed by mothers in follow-up interviews "were in relation to the individualized and personalized services" (Jenkins, Norman, 1975, p. 93).

Workers' helpfulness is a function of the support system available: where the social supports that the worker can tap into are strong (income maintenance, health, legal aid), the workers are perceived as helpful; where the support systems are weak (jobs, housing), the workers are apt to be perceived as less helpful. Group services are also used in helping the parents. Murphy (1976) describes a program of group meetings focusing on the problems faced by such parents.

The Child in Placement

The movement of the child from his own home to the foster home involves the process of separation, transition, and incorporation. The anticipation of separation elicits strong emotional reactions in the child, so that considerable preparation is required. The child supposedly struggles with the following kinds of reactions, many of them unconscious (Littner, 1950; Charnley, 1955; Gordon, 1956; Glickman, 1957):

1. Feelings of rejection ("My parents don't want me"), which engender feelings of worthlessness.
2. Guilt ("I am so bad that they had to get rid of me"), which leads the child to feel that he has contributed to breaking up the home.
3. Hostility ("I hope they get hurt for having rejected me"), which reinforces the guilt, because hostile feelings, particularly against one's own parents, are a punishable offense.
4. Fear of abandonment ("Will my parents want me back? What will happen to them while I am away?")
5. Fear of the unknown ("Where am I going? Will they like me?").
6. Shame ("Why can't my parents, like other parents, take care of me?").

The sense that he is responsible for his placement is particularly acute for the child in care whose siblings are still at home. "Why me?" may be a difficult question to answer to the child's satisfaction.

Almost all social work literature contends that separation from the parents for placement in substitute care engenders these feelings in the child, but there is very little, except sparse anecdotal clinical excerpts, to confirm this contention. Such anecdotal material is not in the form of raw data and tends to be the reporter's interpretation of the child's feelings. All this, however, may be practice wisdom based on the worker's accurate perception of the child's feelings, which are below the level of the child's awareness and so incapable of being articulated, except indirectly.

Of interest here is the fact that Meier (1962), after lengthy interviews with sixty-one young adults who had spent considerable time in foster care, notes: "Current perception of most of the subjects as to why they could not remain with their own families is based on realistic appraisal of their home situation rather than an unrealistic self-blame" (p. 149). Most of the children in placement come from grossly deprived environments, in most cases from broken homes, and may have recognized their parents' inability to care for them.

Weinstein (1960), in interviews with sixty-one children in foster care, asked about the reasons that brought them there. He found that the age of the child at the time of placement and at the time of the research was an important factor in determining the child's realism in assessing the situation. Most reasons given were external to the child and centered on the inability of his parents to care for him. It is significant, however, that there was considerable distortion in the child's memory of his home situation, indicating the operation of repressive factors (pp. 32–33). Some of the contingencies requiring placement seem to be easier for the child to accept. Death—clear, unequivocal, and a matter of fate—is perhaps the easiest to accept. Mental illness is more difficult because the parent is apparently physically well, yet is unable to care for the child.

Thomas (1967) hypothesized that placement involves separation from and loss of objects that afforded the child gratification. This loss initiates a process of grief and mourning through which the child removes cathexis from the libidinal objects from which he is now separated so as to make psychic energy available for investment in new objects, namely, the foster parents. The process of mourning is supposedly reflected in a series of clearly identifiable behaviors: preprotest, protest, despair, and detachment. In studying the reactions to placement of thirty-five white school-aged children (through detailed interviews with their foster parents), Thomas found that the children did experience some process of mourning, although its stages were not as clearly demarcated as he had hypothesized. Separation and object loss seemed less difficult for those children who had some clear idea as to what would happen to them. Surprisingly there was little difference in the process between those children who were visited very rarely by their natural parents and those children who received frequent visits.

There is far less discussion of the loss the child faces in being separated from siblings, though Meier (1962), in her study of former foster children, found that sibling deprivation was keenly felt and keenly remembered.

Because separation is difficult and because the agency is active in implementing separation, the agency often becomes the target of the child's hostility. An older foster child, in discussing her memory of separation with her caseworker, said, "You can't help being afraid and you have to hate someone. When I first met you I hated you because you were associated with the break-up of my home" (Kastell, 1962, p. 101).

Bowlby (1951) suggests joint interviews with the parents and the children "in which the whole situation is exhaustively reviewed and a common plan reached" (p. 120). This approach would make it more difficult for the child to support the fantasy that the agency is responsible for his placement and would help him to form a realistic understanding. Current interest in family interviewing reinforces Bowlby's suggested approach.

The social worker encourages the child to share his feelings, to be open with himself regarding his reactions to his natural parents and his foster parents, and to talk about his disappointments and hostilities as well as his satisfaction in the placement. The worker helps the child to express his feelings, because unless these feelings are expressed and clarified in open discussion, they will create difficulties in adjustment.

These discussions are also designed to help the child correct any distortions he may have about the reasons for his being placed in foster family care—to let him know as clearly as possible what is going to happen next, to help him anticipate the experience, and to permit him to meet the experience "in small doses" so that he can assimilate it emotionally. Throughout, the worker presents the situation as honestly and objectively as possible on a level that the child can understand, on a level that is meaningful to him. The worker includes the child as actively as possible as a participant in the entire process.

After a home has been selected, the child makes brief visits to his prospective home, accompanied by the worker, who acts as a supporting figure during the time the child is separating from one home but is not yet incorporated in another. Sooner or later, however, the child has to make the transition. Supposedly the best time to move a child into a foster home is early on Friday afternoon: he has time to get acquainted with the home before night, and the weekend permits contact with the whole foster family before the child (if he is old enough) is off to school on Monday. Nevertheless the change is a radical one for the child:

> Everything the child has known in the past disappears. Everything he experiences is strange—the bed he sleeps in, the location of the bathroom and the closet for his clothes, the food, the family routine, the toys, the yard, the school, the people in close proximity to him. Nothing which happens from day to night is the same and there is no person to look to for a familiar response [Hill, 1957, p. 3].

In his anxiety at the strangeness and the change, the child might regress: the toilet-trained child may become enuretic, the child who had begun to speak may stop speaking or may speak haltingly, the child who was establishing some independence may begin to cling. These are the behavioral manifestations of inner tension.

Even after the move, there is a transitional period during which the child lives physically in the foster home but psychologically, to some extent, in the home he left behind. It is said that the child lives in one home and loves in another. During this transitional period, the child is adjusting to his changed relationship to his biological parents and his new relationship to his foster parents. He is making some shift in his loyalties and affection. He is shedding old ways of doing things and learning new ones.

If the foster child is to fit into the foster family, he has to be socialized to its mores and daily customs, which may conflict with those of his natural family. Patterns of eating, recreation, toileting, dressing, speaking, thinking may be different. To learn one set of patterns is to unlearn another; to adhere to one is to be disloyal to the other. There is a period of transitional confusion, during which the child is trying to establish himself in this rather strange and demanding role of foster child.

The foster child has a dual family status: he belongs, in part, to both his foster family and his biological family. His "belonging" in the biological family may be purely formal and legalistic, but by name and by kinship affiliation he is still part of that family system. As one foster child said to the foster mother, "I am my mother's daughter but your child."

The confusion is evident in the following excerpt from a case record:

> Pauline is continuing to make her adjustment, at a quicker rate than expected. At first she was unable to call the foster parents anything—neither *Aunt* and *Uncle* nor *Mother* and *Father,* admitting to her worker a feeling of great strangeness, since they were really not her relatives, and it seemed confusing to her to have two mothers. She thought it might be easier to call them just simply by their first names, something the worker could quite understand. Subsequently, however, there was a change in this and Pauline took the initiative in asking the foster mother whether she could call them *Mother* and *Father.* When assured that anything she would like to call them would be all right, she immediately started calling her foster parents *Mother* and *Father* [Juliusberger, 1961, p. 5].

The worker alleviates the child's anxiety by displaying an understanding acceptance of the child's ambivalent love–hate feelings toward his biological parents and by sanctioning his divided loyalties.

During the early period in the foster home, the child may be on his best behavior—the so-called honeymoon period of foster placement. This may give way to a period of testing, in which the child probes the limits of behavior the foster parents will accept. If separation symbolizes rejection for these children, then rejection is something they have actually experienced and are fearful of encountering again. Testing is the child's plea for reassurance that he is wanted in this home.

If the child remains in the home for some time and if the foster parents accept him and his behavior, he ultimately becomes incorporated in the new status. He has some clear idea of who he is, what is expected of him, and what he can expect of others. He makes some adjustment to the foster home and to himself as a foster child.

Throughout this process of separation, transition, and incorporation, the worker makes periodic visits to interview the child in the home. The purpose of these contacts is to help the child with any problems that he may be having in adjusting to the foster parents, the siblings in the home, the new community, or the new school. The visits are also designed to help the child come to grips with the consequences of his status as foster child, which is different from the status of his peers. Because the child brings his past into his present home, the worker tries to help him deal with the residuals of the emotional and social difficulties that most of these children have experienced in their own homes.

Because foster family care status is, as we have noted, an unusual one involving simultaneous membership in two family systems, the worker helps the child to understand the meaning of foster care. As is true for any role, clear understanding of the placement situation is an important precondition of the child's adjustment to it. Thorpe (1974), like Weinstein (1960), found that the level of well-being of a child in foster care was related to the child's clear understanding of the situation. Thorpe interviewed 122 foster children all over five years of age who had been in the same home for at least a year. Objective measures of the child's adjustment were obtained through completion by both teacher and foster parents of the Rutter Behavior Scale, rating the child's behavior.

Children with a good knowledge of their own background and good understanding of the foster care situation showed better adjustment on the rating scales. Knowledge and understanding were related, as might be expected, to the age at which the child entered foster care, older children being more knowledgeable.

Contact with his own parents was positively related to the child's adjustment in foster care. Children were able to identify successfully with two sets of parents, and even children who had been in the foster homes for many years, identified with the foster parents, and wished to remain there wanted to maintain contact with their biological parents.

Ideally the worker represents continuity for the child—the one stable relationship in a world of changing relationships. The worker was with the child before he met the foster parents and will be with him after he leaves them.

The child may experience conflict about sharing his problems with the worker. He may feel disloyal to the foster parents if he discloses their shortcomings, and he may fear repercussions. He may feel that his relationship to the worker, too, is at stake. Because the worker chose the foster home, the child feels that any complaints will be viewed as a reflection on the wisdom of that choice. The child may use the worker as a shield against the foster parents and as a weapon against them. He may try to induce the worker to intercede in his behalf to obtain concessions from the foster parents.

The worker's conception of the purpose of these contacts may not be adequately communicated to the foster child. Weinstein (1960) undertook to interview sixty-one children in foster care. The children selected for interviewing were over five years of age and had been in a secure placement for some time. The interviews were designed to elicit the child's definition of the situation and his locus of identification. They included such questions as "What does *foster* mean?"; "What do you call your own parents? Your foster parents?"; "If you had some trouble or were worried whom would you like to talk to about it?" In Weinstein's study, none of the children perceived the social worker as having a responsibility to facilitate his return to his own parents (p. 44). In only two cases did the answer to such questions as "If you had some trouble or were worried, whom would you like to talk to about it?" or "If you could pick anyone in the world to live with, whom would you pick?" indicate a predominant identification with the social worker (p. 48). Similarly Gottesfeld (1970), in a study concerned in part with foster children's reactions to foster care, found that "While social workers should be ideal agents for helping the foster child to deal with the conflicts and problems of foster home care, the foster child does not perceive the social worker in this way. Less than half the foster children [in the study group] expressed a need to call their social workers about a problem" (p. 28).

Foster children complain that they see social workers infrequently and that the workers change so often that it is difficult for the children to get to feel comfortable with any one of them. Workers generally approach foster children with a problem-oriented attitude, so that the child comes to feel that contact is unnecessary unless there is something actually or potentially troublesome (Gottesfeld, 1970, p. 26).

Children's eligibility for AFDC assistance is carried with them when they are removed from their own home. Such payments are then made to the foster-family home or the institution in which the child is placed. This is known as AFDC–FC (*FC* for "foster care"). In December of 1977, about 107,000 children, the majority in foster-family homes, were receiving such assistance totaling $32.218 million. The child's relatives are entitled to receive AFDC–FC if they take responsibility for his care.

The Foster Family in the Placement Process

The foster family is prepared for the child's placement in the home by the caseworker, who shares with the family the background information he has gathered: the reasons for the child's placement, his developmental history, his peculiarities and preferences, his special fears and special pleasures, his weaknesses and strengths. Yet foster parents sometimes complain that the agency does not provide them with sufficient background information—perhaps because in his desire to find a place for the child, the social worker might tend to describe the child as less disturbed than he actually is.

The worker should, whenever possible, actively involve the foster parents in the planning process. They are the principal ingredients of a successful placement, and their thoughts and feelings should be given serious and continuous consideration. Because the pattern of the relationship is set in the early contacts, it is during these contacts that the worker needs to actively solicit the participation of the foster parents and make certain that they are acquainted with what is going on and what the agency expects, and that any promises and requests are scrupulously made and acted upon.

The child's visits to the foster home help to prepare him to move in and help to prepare the foster parents for his coming. A room has to be made ready. Preparation for placement also involves the caseworker's sharing information about the natural parents and their visitation rights and privileges and discussing with the foster parents a convenient schedule for visiting.

In preparation for placement and in helping the family with the critical adjustment to the child's entrance into the family, contacts with both foster father and foster mother are more likely to lead to the success of the placement than contact with the mother only.

Whatever the foster parent knows or has been told about foster care and about child rearing in general, the worker has to translate at this time into relevance to this particular placement. It is better to repeat details than to assume that the foster parents know.

Foster parents need help in assisting the child to understand and accept the reasons for his or her placement. To do this effectively, the foster parents themselves need a clear understanding of the reasons, which the worker must provide.

The foster parents' perception of the child tends to shape the way they relate to the child. The worker needs to help the foster parents understand and respond empathetically to the child's actual or anticipated behavior. This should be done descriptively rather than through labeling. Using a diagnostic or psychiatric label tends to brand the child, encouraging misperception of the child's behavior so that it is seen in line with the label, and in general tends to accelerate the development of a self-fulfilling prophecy. Children labeled and perceived as "emotionally disturbed" are responded to as though they were "emotionally disturbed" and respond, in turn, to this persistent reaction to them.

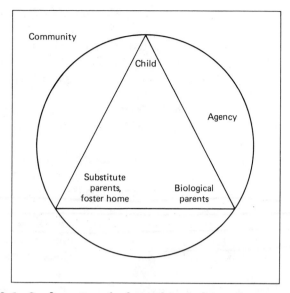

FIGURE 8–1. Configuration of relationships in foster care.

With the inclusion of the foster parents, the nature of the triangular relationships in foster care becomes clear. The foster parents have a relationship with both the child and the biological parents; the biological parents, with both the child and the foster parents; the child, with both sets of parents. The triangle, in uneasy equilibrium, is bound together by the agency, which serves the child, the biological parents, and the foster parents, and provides continuity in the process. With placement, there is a redistribution of parental roles, which are now shared among biological parent, foster parent, and agency worker. The process is affected by the distinctive attributes of the surrounding community. The configuration is illustrated in Figure 8–1.

FOSTER PARENT ROLE: DISTINCTIVE ASPECTS

The foster-parent role presents a number of problems, some of which derive from the crucial differences between foster parenthood and biological parenthood. The foster parents enact the parental role in their day-to-day contact with the child, yet they do not have the full rights of the true parents. Because they are acting for the child's biological parents, not replacing them, and because they receive the child through the agency, they are only partial parents; they share control of the child with both the biological parents and the agency.

The foster parents want a child to board. Yet, in getting a child, they find they get an agency as well. The agency sets limits and advances directives as to how the foster parents are to behave toward the child—a situation not normally encountered by biological parents. The shared control and responsibility for the child are clearly set forth in the instruction pamphlets issued to foster parents. As one such pamphlet points out: "Disciplining a child must be done with kindness and understanding. Corporal punishment, which includes striking, whipping, slapping, or any other form of discipline that inflicts the child with physical pain, is prohibited. Don't forget that *prohibited* means *not allowed.* Disobeying the regulation is cause for cancellation of the foster home license." Another pamphlet says, "You are expected to give each child six years old and and over a monthly allowance. We insist on this as a means of teaching the child the value of money." No change in the sleeping arrangements of the child may be made without the approval of the agency, nor may the child be taken out of the state on a vacation trip without the prior approval of the agency. The foster parent is obligated to discuss the child's behavioral difficulties with the agency.

Limited control implies limited responsibility as well. The fact that the agency is responsible for the basic cost of maintenance of the child indicates an essential difference between foster parenthood and biological parenthood. Furthermore the foster parents are responsible for the child for only a limited segment of his life span. And because the duration of their contact with the foster child is indefinite, the foster parents cannot plan for the child's future, nor can they legitimately expect to share in the child's future achievements (McCoy, 1962).

Although all parents are accountable in a general way to society, there are no formal channels that periodically take a measure of their performance. The foster parents, however, are accountable to an agency, and the yearly relicensing is the procedure by which an accounting is explicitly made. The decision as to whether the child remains or goes rests with the agency. The state license usually includes a clause stipulating that the foster parents must agree to the removal of the child upon the request of the agency. Removal of a child from the biological parents' home can be effected only after due process of law. Removal of the foster child from the foster-family home can be undertaken merely on the basis of the agency's decision. The foster parents' relationship with the child has very limited legal protection. If the foster parents value this relationship, this situation must of necessity make them anxious and desirous of pleasing —and sometimes even of placating—the agency.

The foster parents do not "own" the child; they are merely borrowing him for a time. Because the child belongs ultimately to the biological parents, the foster parents cannot encourage him to make a full emotional investment in themselves, nor can they permit themselves unrestrained expressions of affection for the child because they must give him up at some point. In fact, the more the foster parents make the child "truly their own," the more guilt they might feel at "stealing" the child from his own family. The foster parents have to be able to let the child into the family easily, and out again just as easily.

All this suggests another difference between foster parenthood and biological parenthood. The biological parents expect to be rewarded for their care and and affection by full, reciprocal affection from the child. Because full expression of emotional responsiveness must be inhibited in foster care, other sources of satisfaction need to be enhanced. One source of satisfaction is from a job well done—a successful job of parenting. Another source of satisfaction lies in the approbation and appreciation of the agency and in joint participation with the agency in a socially significant undertaking. Another legitimate source of satisfaction is the more adequate financial return. These kinds of satisfactions tend to distinguish the foster parent from the biological parent.

Although explicit differences between foster parenthood and biological parenthood exist, foster parenthood remains an ambiguously defined role, and its enactment is likely to occasion difficulty. The foster parent is not always certain what is expected of him, and his definition of the situation may conflict with that of the public, the agency, the biological parents, or the child.

Wolins (1963) attempted to define the role of the foster parent empirically by interviews with nineteen child welfare workers, ninety-three foster parents, and seventy-eight close neighbors of foster parents. The study showed that the foster parents and their neighbors tended to define the foster parents' role as an approximation of the biological parents' role. Few of the respondents defined the role in any unique or distinctive way: "More than three-fourths of our foster parents perceived themselves as most like a natural parent. For them, confusion is resolved when they understand others' expectations of them to be no different from those of a natural parent" (Watson, 1968, p. 30).

Ambinder *et al.* (1962) attempted to elicit foster parents' conception of their role. With regard to foster parents' perception of their own role, the "most clear-cut category" elicited was that of "natural parent surrogate." This attitude is typified in the response "caring for these children would be like bringing up my own." Foster parents saw the caseworker as

> an ongoing contact person, supervising and helping with problems of the child. The emphasis is on the supervisory component of the caseworker's function and there is less perception and acceptance of the helping function. The foster parents' perception of their role and their perception of the caseworker's role are logically consistent.

The data suggest that many of the foster parents wish to exclude the caseworker from significant involvement in the life of the foster home—a further manifestation of their desire to act as real parent surrogates, jealously guarding the prerogatives of this role from outside interference. As Weinstein (1960) points out:

> There is little in the way of clean-cut formulations of the limits of responsibility and power to initiate or veto decisions associated with each of the positions in the [placement] system. In consequence, relationships develop in which there are disagreements about the rights and responsibilities of each of the parties. The child may be confronted with three sets of adults, all of whom have some stake in caring for him and planning for his future. In the absence of clearly structured role expectations, both power and responsibility may sometimes be shared, sometimes competed for, and sometimes denied by one or more of the three [p. 15].

Holman (1975) distinguishes between "exclusive" and "inclusive" foster families. Exclusive foster parents attempt to make the child their own and exclude other relationships. They see foster care as a quasi-adoptive situation. Exclusive foster parents see the child as "their own." The biological parent is an unwelcome visitor; the social worker is perceived as a "friend" rather than an agency representative with some responsibility for the child.

Inclusive foster parents, on the other hand, do not identify themselves as the "real" parents of the child, welcome the biological parents' visits, and see the social worker as a colleague.

Holman notes that success in fostering is more likely to be achieved with the inclusive concept because, being more closely aligned with the realities of the situation, such an orientation occasions less conflict for the foster parent. Long-term foster homes are, however, in less conflict with an exclusive conception of parenthood, and more long-term foster parents see their role in more exclusive terms.

A study by McWhinnie (1978) of some ninety English foster homes indicated that the majority saw foster care in inclusive terms. They preferred limited visits on the part of the biological parents and saw themselves as having responsibility for most of the significant problems in foster care, so that they, rather than the worker, would explain to the child the reasons for his foster-care status (see also Adamson, 1973).

Role conflict is engendered when the foster parent acts as a biological parent to his own child and as a foster parent to the foster child. Similarly it is difficult for a foster child to learn that appropriate behavior for the role of foster child is different from appropriate behavior for the role of biological child. Children who have had previous experience in foster homes, where they have had the opportunity to learn to be a foster child, tend to make more successful subsequent adjustments to the role.

Working with the Foster Parent

Because foster parenthood is difficult and easily misunderstood, the agency seeks to help the foster parent in caring for the child. The worker visits regularly, discussing with the foster parents the child's adjustment and the family's reaction to the child. He acts, in these contacts, as an adviser–teacher, a counselor, and a source of psychological support, trying to allay anxiety, reduce guilt, and provide reassurance.

It is often difficult for the foster parents to understand the child's behavior. Although they have learned something of the child's past, which helps to explain his behavior, they need to experience it in order to appreciate the psychodynamic logic of what appears to be inappropriate behavior. The general interpretation given by the worker, in preparation for placement, as to what to expect has limited meaning. It comes to life as the foster parents actually see the child behaving in the ways that were anticipated. At these times, discussions with the caseworker are more likely to develop the kind of understanding the child needs from the foster parents.

It is hard for foster parents to understand how a child might still feel some affection for the natural parents, given the nature of the negative treatment he has received from them. The fact that the child continues to miss the natural parents and continues to talk about them might be seen by the foster parents as a rejection of themselves or a comment on the adequacy of their care. The worker reassures the foster parent that this is not the case.

The arrival of a foster child means a reworking of the old family configuration. The family's interactional pattern grows more complex with the inclusion of another person, and although this may be a source of satisfaction and pleasure, it also may create problems in interpersonal relationships with which the caseworker attempts to help. The worker has to be readily available and willing to help, make an effort to answer questions, and be appropriately reassuring, particularly during the critical transitional period of the first weeks following placement. Patterns of interaction between foster parents and child are established shortly after placement. It is easier to establish a good pattern than to reverse a negative interaction. Attitudes toward the worker and the agency are likewise established during this early period. The worker needs to make the extra effort during this period to ensure a positive orientation toward himself and the agency and to establish a cooperative relationship.

The early period in placement is apt to be a high-risk period. Foster parents feel a sense of frustration and anxiety when there is no sign of positive change in the child.

The foster parents may find it difficult to behave in an appropriately different way toward their own children and toward the foster child. Their status is different, yet to treat the foster child differently may occasion resentment and rebellion on the part of the foster child; to treat him as the others may cause difficulties with their own children.

As a consequence of his power to give and remove a child, the foster parents tend to see the caseworker as a parent figure. Technically, then, the situation presumably evokes transference reactions in which the foster parents act toward the worker as though he were their parent. This reaction would then give the caseworker considerable influence with the foster parents (Kline, Overstreet, 1956).

The foster mother knows the foster child better than the caseworker ever can, but the caseworker knows foster children and general reactions to foster care situations and can bring to the foster mother a perspective on foster care that is helpful:

> . . . [The caseworker] knows that fostering is largely a matter of trial and error, and that if a fostering fails it may be because he has not selected the right child or the right foster home, or that the child was not yet ready for a fostering experience, or that the interference of the real parents has made the success of the fostering impossible. But the foster parent does not have this experience of fostering as a guide. The foster parent . . . tends to feel that the success or failure of the fostering rests entirely on what the foster home has to offer to the child. To learn that this is not so will relieve the burden on the foster parents [Rastell, 1962, p. 116].

One of the most important contributions that the caseworker makes to the psychic comfort of the foster parents is his assurance that their occasional negative feelings toward the foster child are understandable, acceptable, and entirely normal; that an occasional failure in dealing with the foster child is inevitable; and that negative behavior on the part of the child is not a reflection of any inadequacy on their part as parents. Such reassurance, coming from a representative of the agency that has had experience with many foster placements, is often an effective antidote to the compulsive self-doubt that affects many foster parents as they encounter problems that they had not anticipated in being surrogate parents to troubled children from troubled homes.

Furthermore the caseworker's recognition, in the name of the agency, which represents the community, that they are doing an important job satisfactorily helps to compensate foster parents for the frequent disappointments felt in the slight emotional return they get from the child in response to the considerable emotional energies they invest.

Foster parents more frequently ask for support and sanction than for instruction or advice. They recognize what the social worker recognizes but rarely makes explicit—that living day by day, all day, with the child, they know far more about his behavior than the social worker, who visits briefly and infrequently. Consequently they are aware that social workers may not be able to provide them with magical answers that will change a difficult child into an angelic child. What they do want, and keenly appreciate, is a caseworker who does listen with empathy, sympathy, and interest, and who gives them the commendation of the agency for their efforts. Foster parents want and respond warmly to the worker's availability, interest, concern, and willingness to discuss their problems with them in a joint effort to find possible solutions. The worker has greater experience with foster care compared with the foster parents' experience, a wider perspective on foster care, and a structured, problem-solving approach to child-care problems. These are helpful even if the worker may lack a ready, easy answer to questions raised.

Although some studies suggest that the worker is seen primarily as performing administrative functions—that is, linking the child and the placement and supervising the placement—other studies indicate that the worker is perceived as a source of understanding and help, a role the worker is more interested in and more prepared to implement.

Interviews with 219 foster parents indicated that "overall the foster parents were highly positive in their view of the agencies" (Rosenblum, 1977, p. 57). Foster parents responded positively to the fact that the worker had a "good understanding of a child or a child's problems," that "the worker treated them with respect and/or like fully capable adults and/or *not* like clients" (p. 57). "Attempting a therapy role with them and their family" is considered disrespectful, an intrusion into private concerns unrelated to their fostering role. It is rejected also on the basis that it is perceived as moving the worker's principal concern away from a cooperative arrangement focused on helping the child, to working with the foster family.

English foster mothers had a generally positive view of the social worker, less than 1 per cent clearly expressing a negative view. Although most found the workers to be interested and considerate, this doesn't necessarily mean that they found the workers helpful. Some 37 per cent of 122 foster mothers interviewed found the workers "hardly" or "not at all" helpful (Holman, 1973, p. 225). Jenkins and Norman (1976) also found that workers were rated higher on interest and understanding than they were on helpfulness (p. 64).

English foster mothers saw the role of the social worker as primarily concerned with inspection rather than with problem solving. An analysis of the content of child-care workers' interviews with foster parents shows that most items were, in fact, concerned with inspection and an assessment of how the placement was going. Of the 997 content items identified, only 15 per cent were devoted to "supportive-discussion of problems, ventilation and reassurance," and 6 per cent to "education: advice and information; developing self-awareness" (Holman, 1973, p. 239).

The caseworker brings a more professional knowledge of foster care and—equally important—the support of the agency's resources. The agency, in addition to providing board payments, makes available all the resources of the community. It takes care of medical and dental treatment; it provides glasses, orthopedic appliances, and prescription medicine; it makes available psychological testing and psychotherapy for the child.

The caseworker's visits, then, are designed to help the foster family in discharging the joint agency–foster family responsibility for the care of the child. The foster family may see the worker's role differently, however:

> The worker may define the situation as one of consultation where he assists in the development of the child through advice based upon his professional knowledge. The foster mother may define the situation quite differently. What to the worker may be guidance, can be constructed by the foster mother as an implicit attack on her adequacy as a parent. There may be an attempt on the part of the foster mother to curtail her relationship with the worker; in effect, to shut the agency out [Weinstein, 1960, p. 11].

Therefore the mother may share with the agency only information that suggests that everything is fine.

Visits by the caseworker to the home are also designed to discharge the supervisory responsibility of the agency. As Kline *et al.* (1972) say, "The foster parents' primary role is that of surrogate parents to the child within their own family setting under the supervision of an agency that is responsible and accountable for the child's care" (p. 220). The caseworker visits to see how the child is getting along, what more needs to be done, and whether or not the child is adequately cared for. The supervisory components may be threatening to the foster mother and are apt to make her defensive. Some mitigation of the threat comes from the fact that the caseworker attempts to see the foster parents as persons in their own right, rather than as an "environment" for the child. He approaches the foster parents with some consideration for their needs and anxieties, assuming that they are not solely interested in justifying themselves and concealing their failings and difficulties but, rather, that they are eager to do a creditable job and to understand the child and whatever difficulties he has. The worker also appreciates that the foster parents have a direct and personal stake in the child's behavior and that they face direct and personal consequences of his behavior.

Agencies have supplemented periodic visits with experimental family sessions: meetings with foster parents, their own children, and the foster child, all at the same time (Lindberg, Wosreck, 1963). Such an approach has the advantage of including the father and the siblings, permits the worker to observe family interaction directly, and permits all the family members to know what the foster child is sharing with the social worker. In contrast to such an approach, one foster parent said, "He [the foster child] called the worker [and said] that I was overprotecting him. They came to see him and talked to him in the car" (Ambinder *et al.*, 1962).

The foster parent may perceive the worker as child-oriented rather than neutral and consequently may feel some resentment. The following statement by a foster parent reflects his perception of the situation:

> It has seemed to me that the uh . . . welfare workers have more or less taken the attitude that the children are always right . . . It impressed me that the children

kind of have that idea that, well, the children are right and no matter what the foster parents do to try and correct it, well they're being biased. . . . They're not giving the child a fair chance . . . and I think that's wrong in a way. . . . Well I know it was in our case . . . 'cause . . . [the worker] thought that we should not punish him . . . by spanking him . . . and uh . . . well last time I wanted to ask her if she wanted to take him to live with her for a couple of weeks and see what she would do. . . . Now maybe that's just . . . one worker. . . . She said that she had kind of felt that way too . . . that she tries to see things from the child's point of view rather than the parents. . . .

Foster fathers tend not to be the passive partners they are generally perceived to be by caseworkers. Their apparent passivity derives from the fact that they see the child-rearing role as primarily the responsibility of the foster mother. Their peripheral relationship to the social worker is reinforced by a "value system which precludes discussions of child-rearing problems with women who are not related to them" (Davids, 1968, p. 164). The foster fathers, Fanshel (1966) notes, are "quite strong and firm in the areas they perceive to be within their proper area of functioning" (p. 151). A special study of forty-one foster fathers tended to confirm Fanshel's findings (Davids, 1968).

Continued contact with the foster father is both helpful and desirable. If trouble is developing, indications may come first from the foster father. The mother may be more reluctant to share incipient problems because, as the principal child-care parent, she may feel that they reflect on her adequacy. The foster father is often less hesitant about speaking up.

The population of younger foster parents demonstrates a greater involvement of the father in child rearing and child care. The current increasing tendency toward overlap in maternal and paternal roles may be advantageous for the foster-care system.

The phone might be more frequently, expeditiously, and economically employed to keep in contact with foster families. Phone interviews can be as helpful as visits. In the scheduling of phone interviews, consideration should be given to whether the foster father might be available to talk.

Visits

The periodic visits by the social worker call attention to an additional penalty of foster parenthood: some loss of privacy. The agency has the right and the obligation to intrude upon the foster parent–foster child relationship. Furthermore acceptance of the foster child involves acceptance of visitation rights by the natural parents. In getting a child, the foster parent not only gets an agency, he gets the child's family as well.

Ideally the relationship between foster parent and biological parent should be one of mutual cooperation toward achieving what is best for the child. Each should recognize and accept the different responsibilities and the different contributions of the other toward making placement the least damaging to the child. Yet there is apt to be considerable deviation from the ideal relationship. As Weinstein (1960) notes:

The foster mother may define the status of the natural mother as inferior in the relationship. She may be unwilling to entertain suggestions made by the natural mother on the grounds that she is inadequate by virtue of the child's being in placement. Any attempts on the part of the natural mother to participate may be resisted as unwelcome interference. The natural mother may see herself as superior in the relationship, according the foster mother a position similar to that of a "hired servant." She may see her position as the child's natural parent as entitling her to the right of unlimited critical review of the foster mother's actions. Such conflicting definitions of the situation may lead to open hostility [p. 13].

Throughout the process, the worker encourages contacts between the foster child and the biological parent through visits, letters, and phone calls. Such contacts help the child to make a positive adjustment to the foster home. The available research shows that the adjustment of the child in the foster home and the likelihood of returning home is positively related to continuing visits of the biological parents to the child (Weinstein, 1960; Pringle, 1965; Sherman, Neuman, Shyne, 1973; Holman, 1973; Thorp, 1974). The difference that visiting makes in the adjustment of the child to the foster home suggests that the biological parents, although absent, continue to affect the life of the child. The biological parent cannot so easily abdicate his influence, and the ties that bind the child to the biological parent are not easily dissolved.

A study of visiting patterns as related to discharge from care indicated that there was a "strong association" between the two, demonstrating the "centrality of visiting as a key element in the return of foster children to their own homes" (Fanshel, 1975, p. 502).

Despite the difficulties inherent in the situation, the visits of the biological parents are important to the child because:

1. He identifies with his parents and perceives rejection of his parents, manifested by limited visiting privileges, as a rejection of himself.
2. He needs to see his parents occasionally, lest he develop ideal fantasies about them.
3. He misses them and mourns their absence.
4. He is helped by their visits to adjust to the realities of separation and to remember the objective reasons that required his separation from his parents (Littner, 1971, pp. 18–19).
5. If the intent of foster care is temporary, substitute care visits between the child and his biological parents are required to maintain the continuity of the relationship.

However, studies confirm that visits are a source of considerable dissatisfaction and difficulty to the foster parents (Gray, Parr, 1957; Swindell, 1961; Wolins, 1963; Littner, 1971). Foster parents may resent the biological parents because:

1. They visit at inconvenient times and are sometimes upset and demanding, sometimes drunk and argumentative.
2. The child might be upset by the parents' visits and may become more difficult for the foster parents to handle.
3. Foster parents are threatened by the competition of the biological parents for

the love and affection of the child or because they feel guilty about not having done enough for the foster child.

4. The parents' visit may present the child with an opportunity to pit foster parent and biological parent against each other.

5. Out of strong feelings of sympathy for the foster child, foster parents may dislike the biological parents for the harm their physical and/or emotional neglect has caused the child.

Sometimes the relationship is characterized by troublesome dependency. The biological mother in her visits seeks to act like a child toward the foster parent, discussing her troubles and seeking support and reassurance, thus perverting the foster-care situation.

Biological parents have complained that foster parents intrude on their visits with their children, make significant decisions about the child's life without consulting them, and fail to notify them of special events in the child's life in which they might like to participate. Differences in living standards between foster homes and biological homes create problems for the biological parent in competitive adequacy of child care (Murphy, 1976).

Coming frequently from different worlds, foster parents and biological parents often have little in common—except for the child, with whom both may be competitively concerned.

In the following material, some of the reasons for conflict between the foster parents and the biological parents are illustrated, as is the caseworker's approach to the problem:

Mrs. G. expressed her very strong disapproval of Mrs. S. as a mother and as a person. She was able to come out and say in no uncertain terms that she disliked Mrs. S. and thought she was a "hateful person." When I tried to discover some of the reasons for the foster mother's feelings, she told me that Mrs. S. had "no respect." I asked her what she meant by this and she said, "She didn't respect me or my home." She told me how she would come into her house smelling of alcohol and how she used to come in and bring men with her and about how she would smoke while she was there, even though Mrs. G. had told her that Theresa was allergic to smoke and that she did not like to have anyone smoke in the same room with Theresa. She said that Mrs. S. would complain about the care she was giving Theresa and told Theresa she was not being well cared for.

The foster mother said she knew Mrs. S. did not like her either and after this last incident, Mrs. S. had never been there again to visit Theresa. Mrs. G. felt that she had tried to be fair about it and had done as much as she could be expected to in allowing Mrs. S. to come into her home; that she felt she had to put up with just too much to let the mother come in and act the way she did. I asked Mrs. G. if she could think of any reason why the mother might act this way, and she said that she could not. She could not understand why people should find fault with someone who had taken care of their children whom they were not able to care for themselves, especially when the care she was giving to Theresa was good and she was feeding and clothing her well. I said these complaints were not surprising to me because we had found that many times parents could come into a foster home and complain about the way the foster mother cared for their children. We have found that the reason the parents did this was mostly because they felt guilty about not being able to care for their children and resented the fact that someone else was able to give them good care. Foster mother said she thought this was true and could see why they would feel that way. The foster mother went on to say she thought if the mother had really wanted to take care of her children, she would find a way to do it, using the old expression "where there's a will, there is a way." I laughingly replied that if all parents could take care of their own children we would be out of business * [Wires, 1954, p. 9].

The visits look different from the point of view of the biological parent. According to Mrs. McAdams, a mother of six children who were placed when she became mentally ill:

The fact that you are visiting your child in a foster home is a reminder that you are, at least for the time being, a failure as a parent. You are very sensitive, especially during the first visits. Sometimes a foster parent, in a well-meaning effort to let you know that your child is doing well in a foster home, will make comments on how well the child is eating, how neat he keeps himself and his room, how happy he is, etc. To me, this type of remark was just an implied criticism of the care I had given my child, and was a verbal slap in the face. . . .

The foster parent who gives you orders and instructions in the presence of your child is another problem. You are told that you should have the child back in the foster home at 5 o'clock, and admonished not to be late, or you are told to be sure little Tommy doesn't go outside without his sweater, as he has just recovered from a cold. These instructions may be necessary, but your kid, no matter how young, is already aware of the fact that you have little authority at this time, and this only increases the child's concern as to how responsible you are. If it is necessary to give the natural parent instructions about taking the child away from the foster home on an outing, it would be better to do so out of the child's presence. . . .

I think it is possible for foster parents and natural parents to have mutual respect for each other, but the very nature of their relationship makes it impossible to avoid elements of jealousy and competition. In the case of my children, finding themselves in the position of having foster parents whom they loved and admired and yet having to cope with me trying to strengthen their love for me and regain their trust was almost too much. This problem took a lot of effort at all levels, before they accepted the fact that love for one set of parents did not imply disloyalty to the other. . . .

I know quite often children return from visits with the natural parents with all sorts of plans and promises given them during the visit. It is very difficult to deny a child any hope when the immediate situation seems to be pretty bleak. My kids were able to extract tentative promises of when we would all be reunited, because my pride was killing me and I didn't have the heart to say that I had no home, no money, and no definite time when I would have sufficient emotional and financial resources for getting these things [McAdams, 1972, p. 52].

In this instance, the children were returned home after several years of having been provided, the mother notes, with "a stable home environment and parental supervision at a time of crisis and emotional turmoil."

Recognizing their importance, the agency encourages visits and requires that

* From Emily Wires, "Some Factors in the Worker–Foster Parent Relationship," *Child Welfare* (October 1954). By permission of Child Welfare League of America, Inc.

the foster parents permit them. However, the agency also attempts to control the timing and the frequency of visits. If visiting in the home is too upsetting to the foster family and the child, the agency arranges for such visits to take place in the office.

The worker has to prevent any hostility between the biological parents and the foster parents from affecting the child. Any derogation of the biological parent to the child as a consequence of such hostility is likely to be perceived by the child as a derogation of himself because he is identified with his parents. The agency seeks to mediate between the two sets of parents, maintaining some equilibrium between conflicting needs so that the situation does not harm the child's adjustment to the placement.

The child's behavior may increase his parents' hesitancy to visit. If the child is angry at the rejecting parent, perhaps because of the placement, the parent's discomfort in response to the child's behavior discourages visiting. If the child makes the parent feel guilty about the placement, subsequent visiting is more painful (Aldgate, 1976). If the child does not seem to welcome the parent's visits and appears unappreciative and difficult to talk with, visits are likely to drop off. Jenkins and Norman (1975, p. 67) note that mothers of children in foster care are aware that visits might be upsetting to them and to their children.

Infrequent, irregular visiting is regarded as the least desirable alternative. The uncertainty creates anxiety, the sporadic nature makes planning difficult, and the child's expectations are often raised and frustrated (Holman, 1973, p. 201).

Once visits have stopped, for whatever reason, they are difficult to renew and require special encouragement on the part of the worker and clear receptivity on the part of foster parents.

The data available seem to demonstrate clearly that despite the importance of visits, the majority of children in care longer than two years are infrequently or never visited by parents (Gruber, 1973; Fanshel, 1975, 1977; Vasaly, 1976).

Although Gruber (1970), George (1970), and Thorp (1974) report that in some varying percentage of cases social workers have discouraged parents from visiting children in care, Claburn and Magura (1977) found that agency prohibition of parents' visiting is the principal reason in only a very limited number of cases (6 per cent) where the reasons for no visiting or limited visiting have been ascertained. "Much more frequently, the cause is that parents have either disappeared, are unable to visit, or, if able, are unwilling to visit!"

A content analysis of interviews between child-care workers and sixty-five parents of children in foster care further showed that 39 per cent of the items identified were concerned with encouragement of visiting. This was the largest single item of discussion identified (Holman, 1973, p. 244). Festinger's (1974) study of typical placement agreements between agencies and foster homes in some forty states shows that one of the most frequently included sections in such agreements relates to visiting between the biological parents and the child in the foster home.

It is argued that visiting is sufficiently important in maintaining the biological parent–foster child relationship so that visiting should be given special encouragement and effort on the part of the worker and in agency procedures. In interviews with the parent, the worker should communicate the importance of visits and the agency's concern about the regularity of such contacts. Visiting schedules should be included in contracts formulated between the agency worker and the biological parents. When a regular schedule of visits is maintained, the parents might be sent letters of commendation. Failures to visit might prompt a special delivery letter or a telegram from the agency as a reminder. The worker might bring the child for a visit to a hospitalized parent.

Workers can actively encourage visiting by supporting the parent's decision, reinforcing it by praise and approval, by discussing the nature and source of parental hesitancy and ambivalence about visiting, by reassuring the parent of the critical importance of the visits to the child, by reassuring the parents that they are entitled to visits in line with agency policy, and by acting as an understanding intermediary between parent and child and parent and foster parent in cases of conflict.

Agencies can and are moving toward the elimination of such restrictive policies as prohibition of visiting "during the early part of the placement" to give the child a chance to "settle" and as limitations on the frequency of visits and the time available to the parent during each visit. Volunteers are recruited to provide transportation to parents interested in visiting.

Parental visits may be particularly disruptive to the foster home and unsatisfactory for the placed child if the parent is accompanied by other children in the family. Agency payments for baby-sitters to permit the parent to visit alone are advisable.

Visiting might be encouraged through a more active involvement of the parents in the ongoing life of the child while he is in placement so that they continue some part-time parenting: signing the report card, participating in open-school day, taking the child for dental or medical appointments.

It is suggested that maintenance of a parent's visitation log be mandatory for all agencies because it is such a sensitive indicator of the long-term fate of the child in care. In addition, such a log would provide documentation of parental failure in support of a petition to terminate parental rights.

Despite exhortations by agencies to workers to actively encourage visiting by such procedures and despite the progressive elimination of restrictive visiting policies, there is some ambivalence about visiting that derives from competing considerations. The pressure to maintain children in a stable situation free from the trauma and damage that visits sometimes create and the pressure to keep foster homes in the systems by minimizing impositions on the foster parents related to visiting act to dampen workers' enthusiasm about visiting. It is felt that giving clear priority to the biological parents' desires and convenience may jeopardize the retention of some foster homes.

The investment of time in casework service with the biological parents, as measured by frequency of contact, is associated with higher levels of visiting. Higher levels of visiting are associated with the greater likelihood of return home. The chances for the child's return home are greatest during the first year of placement. Social workers with five or more years of experience combined with some advanced training were likely to be more successful in achieving the child's return home (Shapiro, 1976). These considerations argue for a determined effort, by experienced and trained workers, toward initiating and sustaining a frequent and consistent pattern of parental visitation early in the child's placement.

Replacement

The most desirable placement is one that permits the child to remain in the same home during the entire period of foster care. Removal from one foster home and replacement in another imposes on the child the emotional burden of repeated separation and change. Every replacement reactivates, and hence reinforces, previous separation and rejection experiences and tends to confirm for the child any predisposition he may have to regard himself as unacceptable to others. It increases the child's difficulty in determining who he is and where he belongs and in establishing a stable sense of identification. It is likely to increase his lack of trust in parental figures. The child is afraid to invest himself in relationships with others because of the experience of hurt, and his relationships are maintained at a shallow level. Frequent replacement makes it more likely that the child will manifest emotional problems and that subsequent placement will fail (Eisenberg, 1965).

A child may be moved from a foster home if the situation there is not conducive to his best interests, or if his behavior (or that of his parents) makes it very difficult for the foster parents to keep him, or if a change has taken place in the foster family situation—if a foster parent becomes ill or dies, if the foster family moves, and so on. Sometimes the move is a result of a deliberate plan on the part of the agency—perhaps from a receiving home to an appropriate foster home. It is difficult to know the frequency with which each of these contingencies "causes" the removal of the child.

Frequently, causative factors are compounded. An emotionally disturbed child behaves in a way too difficult for the foster parent to tolerate and cope with, so that they take advantage of a situational change to request the child's removal. Disturbed behavior, then, is as often the cause of replacement as it is a result of it.

In one study, 44 per cent of placement terminations had to do with changes in the foster-home situation; 50 per cent of the terminations were related to foster-child problems (particularly acting-out problems, such as stealing, promiscuity, and truancy) and the foster child's relationship with the foster parents. Only 6 per cent were related to problems with the child welfare agency (Rosenblum, 1977, p. 87).

Some foster parents contemplating termination are less likely actually to terminate if they have ties to other foster parents or foster-parent organizations. An even more potent factor in reducing the number of actual terminations is the relationship with the social worker. Foster parents who have worked closely with a social worker in trying to deal with the foster child's problems were less likely to terminate (Rosenblum, 1977, p. 92).

Foster parents derive their principal gratification from their interpersonal, affectionate relationship with the foster child and from evidence that he is responding to their care and efforts. On the other hand, difficulties in foster care and risk of placement termination are associated with a negative relationship between the child and the foster parents and with expectations for change that are not being achieved. Foster care turnover is likely to be greater if foster parents have unrealistically high expectations of the changes they hope to achieve in the foster child's behavior. Such expectations lead to the absence of reward and the increased possibility of failure. The worker does best by keeping expectations realistic and supporting and reassuring the parents in their efforts.

Difficulties between the foster child and other children already in the home and difficulties between the child's foster parents and his biological parents have been associated with high risk for placement termination (Shaw, Lebans, 1977).

Given the problems for the child in discontinuous living experiences, in the perception of adults as hurtful figures and of himself as unacceptable, the caseworker has a difficult decision to make. Are the dangers in the home so great and the advantages of the next available foster home so unquestionable as to warrant replacement? Often, of course, the decision is made for the social worker by foster parents who insist upon the child's removal. However, in those cases, the worker should have been aware of the deteriorating situation and should have been discussing the foster parents' reactions to the difficulties. A precipitous removal made in the heat of a crisis is to be avoided.

When replacement must be made, it should be planned and as a result of the participation of the social worker, child, parents, and foster parents. If possible, it should have the acceptance of the foster parents, so that they can help the child to move. This is difficult if the move is a result of the failure of the foster parents to cope adequately with the child's behavior, because the move itself is a symbol of their failure. Throughout the replacement procedure, the caseworker must be sensitive to the feelings of the foster parents and must attempt to help them feel less anxious, less guilty, less threatened by the experience. As Herstein (1957) says, the caseworker should "present the reasons for replacement in terms which would be both realistic and within the boundaries of what the foster parents can emotionally and objectively accept" (p. 24).

The caseworker should also encourage the child's expression of feeling regarding the replacement and should help to interpret it in such a way that the child does not perceive the experience as another personal failure.

It would be helpful to both the child and the foster parents if they saw one another occasionally after the child has been replaced, so that the child's memory of the foster parents will not be distorted by anxiety-provoking fantasies and the foster parents will be reassured that the child is adequately cared for and does not hate them.

The foster-care system is often charged with burdening the children in care with the discontinuity and disruption resulting from frequent changes in placement while in care. The impression given, in discussions of the failings of the system, is that a large percentage of children are repeatedly placed and replaced.

A recapitulation of eleven studies since 1970 covering the experience of some sixteen thousand children in care an average of two years or longer showed that some 75 per cent of the group had two or fewer placements (Kadushin, 1978, p. 101).

Even this more favorable picture of placement stability and continuity does not entirely do justice to the system. In many instances where children were placed more than once, one of the two or more placements was inevitable and/or consciously and deliberately planned. The first deliberately temporary placement is often made because of an emergency and gives the agency an opportunity to select an appropriate home for the child and to prepare the home for the child's coming while providing temporary care for the child who is unable to be cared for in his own home. It may be necessary for the child to be removed from the home immediately because of some acute crisis situation in the home or because of imminent personal risk to the child. Consequently the first placement, of necessity, is unplanned and deliberately temporary.

As a matter of fact, discontinuity in the foster care child's significant relationships may, more often, be a factor of worker turnover rather than foster-home replacement.

A nationwide study of children in foster family care in 1977 (Shyne, Schroeder, 1978) showed that 78 per cent had no more than two placements (p. 218). On the other hand, the same study showed that only 68 per cent of the children had no more than two different workers (p. 80).

Termination

Ideally, once the child is in foster care, a plan should be formulated among three basic alternatives:

1. Planning for the child's return home by working with the biological parents and the child toward modification of those conditions that necessitated placement.
2. Planning for the termination of parental rights and permanent parental substitution, when there is little likelihood that the home situation can be sufficiently modified. This involves working with the biological parents so that they consent to the child's release and placement for adoption.
3. Planning for long-term foster care when it is not likely that the child will ever be able to return to his own home and there is little likelihood that he can be placed for adoption.

Actually many of the key factors in the agency's choice of alternatives are shrouded in ambiguity and subject to change. The modifiability of the child's own home situation may not be clear at first, and the child's adoptability changes with the passage of time.

The first alternative terminates, of course, with the child's return home; the second, with adoption of the child; the third, with the child's achievement of independence.

With more older children coming into foster care, a more frequent termination now is "discharge to self." The child reaches majority and becomes independent of foster care. In a very limited number of cases, a child who has made clear by his behavior that foster-family care is inappropriate is discharged to institutional care.

Identifying the nature of the discharge of some eighty-six hundred children who left foster care in New York City in 1977, Fanshel (1978) found that the biological parents were by far the most important source of permanence for children, most children being discharged to their parents within the first two years of placement. Even after the second year, children continued to be discharged to their parents, although at a lower rate. Adoption by foster parents or adoption by others was not a significant source of permanence for children until after they had been in care for five or more years. Some 10 per cent of discharges were for adoption. Some 13–16 per cent of children achieved separation from the system by reaching majority and being discharged to their own care. Only about 1 per cent of the children were discharged to institutional care. "Discharge destinations tend, in aggregate, to shift from natural parents to foster parents to own responsibility as time in care becomes extended" (p. 480).

A study of the stability of the situation following the discharge of child from foster care showed returned-to-parent discharge the least stable alternative and discharge to adoptions most stable (Lahti et al., 1978, p. 4.3). Children who return home from foster-care placement are sometimes replaced in foster care after a short period of time (Claburn, Magura, Chizeck, 1977). Although it is, on the face of it, desirable for the agency to provide every opportunity for return home, more consideration may need to be given to the possibility that the return home may lead to more discontinuity and placement recycling.

Foster-family care is best terminated when the biological parents want the child home and can make a home for him. The parent may seek to terminate placement prematurely out of guilt, or in response to the child's insistence that he be permitted to come home, or out of a fear that the child will forget him or reject him. These are reasons that make the success of the child's return home problematic.

White children are more likely to return home from care than nonwhite children. Children who come into care because of physical illness of a parent or because of situational stress are more likely to return home than children who come into care because they are neglected or abused, because their parents are drug abusers, or because they have been abandoned (Sherman et al., 1976; Fanshel, 1975a). The worker's perception of the foster child's mother is related to rate of return home. "A mother who was perceived by the worker as generally adequate, not too severely disturbed, one who could be 'worked with,' who was unlikely to drift away from agency contact while the child continued in care, who visited as much as possible, who resented or felt guilty about continued separation from her child, who had positive attitudes toward the worker and the agency," and in whose case the worker was perceived as being interested and supportive was more likely to have her child discharged in her care (p. 94).

The composite picture of the child who is most likely to leave care within a reasonably short period of time is apt to be a white child, visited regularly by his parents (who are in frequent contact with their social worker), and who perceives his parents in positive terms (Fanshel, 1975a). Frequent intensive contact by skilled, experienced workers is related to earlier discharge (Shapiro, 1975).

The most frequent events related to return home are in line with the intent of foster care: the mother has recovered from a mental illness, the mother has recovered from a physical illness, the parent had received time-limited placement to work out personal plans that are now implemented, the mother has been released from imprisonment, the child has made gains in foster care permitting him to return home (Fanshel, Shinn, 1978, p. 150). In some 73 per cent of the cases in Fanshel's study, what was involved was a change in the family's capacity to care for the child or a change in the child that made it possible for the family to care for him (p. 152).

The following case situations are examples of the most frequent discharge disposition, return of the child to his own home:

Miss R. is an unmarried Black mother supported by public assistance since the birth of her first child. She was 24 years old at the time her three infant children were placed. Miss R. required emergency hospitalization for jaundice and hepatitis, and the Department of Social Services arranged for temporary placement in a foster home. Miss R. was hospitalized for a month. The children were returned to her home several months later when she was able to care for them. She felt that the children had been well cared for and were "healthy and happy." She was grateful for the placement, as it allowed her to regain her health and strength.

Mrs. R. is a Puerto Rican, Catholic, 24-year-old mother of three who was deserted by the children's father. Her Department of Social Services worker suggested she visit an outpatient clinic at Metropolitan Hospital when she complained of being depressed and nervous. She said she hit the children for the slightest thing. Afraid that she might lose control and hurt her children, she made arrangements to have the children placed. They were still in placement two years later. Mrs. R. continued in treatment, went to work and began living with a new common-law husband with whom she shortly had a child. By the time of the last study interview, five years after entry, the placed children were discharged home. Mrs. R. said, "I learned I couldn't live without the kids."

Mrs. T. is a 40-year-old white, Jewish mother, separated from her addicted husband after a stormy marriage, overwhelmed by depression and unable at the time of placement to care for her four children. She was not able to send them off to school. Previous to the placement there was a homemaker in the home for almost two years. Mrs. T. had been hospitalized and in treatment in the past, although she was not hospitalized at the time of placement and during the five-year study period. She did, however, continue to receive psychiatric care. She said her family thought she was a "bad mother" for placing the children, but she thinks she "did them a favor." Five years after the placement, three of her children were home. One remained in care, and she felt he was doing well, improving in school, and getting advantages like medical care, music lessons, and camp. Mrs. T. is visited weekly by the placement agency social worker and is more optimistic about the future. She has gotten better housing, which had been a severe problem for her.

Miss K. is a 42-year-old, Black, Protestant, unmarried mother of five children. Miss K. had a drinking problem and apparently often left the children alone. She stated that the placement was due to her drinking and "neglect" of the children. She said that an aunt who lived next door called the police "to scare me." "I was out drinking and having a good time when I should have been home with the children." After the placement, Miss K. noted, "The only thing on my mind was to get my children back. I had to prove myself [to the court probation officer]." She stopped drinking, and within a year her children were discharged home. At the time of the last study interview, four years after the discharge, she had not gone back to drinking. "The placement," she said, "made me a better mother. It taught me a lesson. It really straightened me out."

The children of this 28-year-old Black Catholic mother were placed while she served a short jail sentence for "running numbers." She blames her husband for placing the children. The father's story was different. He said the mother was with another man and he had been paying someone to care for the children and couldn't afford it anymore. The children were discharged to the mother after three years in care. She had gotten out of jail, divorced her husband, remarried, and received "help in getting back" at a mental health clinic. She spoke warmly of the support and interest of the social worker [Jenkins, Norman, 1975, pp. 34–40].

Foster care, when successful, provides an acceptable level of care for children who would otherwise have been deprived of such care. It provides a benign opportunity for continued actualization of the child's potentialities. It is less successful in resolving the family problem that caused the child to go into care in the first place.

Evaluating the experience of some 260 families in foster care, Jenkins (1975) notes that:

> Although undoubtedly preventive and community services could have made it possible for a percentage of these children to remain at home, the review of the changes in family circumstances over five years tends to support the need for foster care as an institution that can take total responsibility for children during a period of parental incapacity and severe family crisis. It is, however, a partial service not effective in preventing further placement or resolving the problems that brought children into care [p. 42].

Children very often return to relatively unchanged, disadvantaged one-parent families still receiving public assistance.

Cross-sectional studies of a population of children in care show that the average length of time in care is generally four years or longer. A small percentage (10–15 per cent) are in care for ten years or more (Bryce, Ehlert, 1971; Gruber, 1973; Rowe, Lambert, 1973, p. 37; Catalano, 1974, p. 5; Gambrill, 1974, p. 12; Vasaly, 1975; Fanshel, Grundy, 1975, p. 10; Hargrave et al., 1975). Although valid, these findings tend, for a variety of reasons, to give a distorted picture of the operation of foster-care systems. The essential difficulty is that such studies review the situation of children living in foster care at one particular period of time, when the study was being done. Such a procedure tends to exaggerate the impact of the backlog of all the children who, over the years, have been unable to move out of foster care, and it underestimates the impact of turnover—the impact of those children not in the study because they have left foster care.

A study based on a cross-sectional population of the current caseload biases the findings in the direction of including a disproportionately high percentage of children in long-term care.

Cross-sectional studies of a foster-care population tend to do an injustice to the foster-care system because, heavily weighted as they are with an accumulated residual group of children who have remained in care, they picture foster care as less temporary than it is for many children.

A longitudinal study that follows the experiences of the same group of children in foster care over time gives a different picture of the foster-care system. Jenkins (1967) follows 891 New York City children placed over a two-year period. Of this group, 54 per cent had been discharged from care after three months in placement. At the end of two years, 75 per cent of the group had been discharged from care (p. 451). This longitudinal analysis showed foster care to be a temporary arrangement for most of the children accepted into care.

A five-year logitudinal study by Fanshel and Shinn (1978) of over six hundred children in foster care in New York City showed a lower rate of discharge. At the end of five years, 64 per cent of the group had returned home. However, if white children were analyzed separately, 77 per cent of this group had been returned home by the end of five years. About 60 per cent of the children who remained in care—white and black—came into care because they had been abandoned or deserted, so that there was no home for them to which they could conceivably return.

A longitudinal study in England presents strikingly similar results: "At the end of five years, nearly two-thirds of the underfives admitted to the voluntary societies in 1962 had been either adopted or returned to their parents. . . . However, this satisfactory outcome applied to less than half of the colored children (47 percent) compared with 70 percent of the white children" (Tizard, Joseph, 1970, p. 585).

It is estimated that following the career of a group of children entering foster care would show that 25 per cent are likely to remain in care for long periods of time (Regional Research Institute, 1976). Some of these children have no home to which they might return, are not freed for adoption, or if freed for adoption, are not placeable because they are too old or too handicapped or are older and nonwhite. Some are in stable, long-term foster-care arrangements. Some are free for adoption and are placeable but are the victims of agency drift and failure to plan effectively. The problem of this residual group of children in unplanned foster care for longer than is justifiable is discussed more fully under "Problems" (pp. 382–389).

Group Methods and Education in Foster-Family Care

Group methods have been used in working with foster parents. Membership in these groups is voluntary and the groups are small. In one instance, however, attendance was required as part of the responsibility that parents assumed in caring for foster children (Thomas, 1961, p. 220). Sometimes the meetings are directed to foster mothers only, but more frequently they are designed for both foster parents. Although the groups often start with a didactic instructional format, they move to a more informal pattern in which the content for discussion is decided on by the group members. Group activities include an annual foster parents' "recognition" party sponsored by the agency and highlighted by awards to foster parents.

Foster parents' groups have discussed such topics as:

1. The feelings and problems that the child brings into placement.
2. The meaning of separation.
3. Child development
4. The common problems of children in foster care, particularly enuresis and disobedience.
5. The differences in disciplining foster children and one's own children.
6. The attitudes of the community toward foster parents and foster children.
7. How to help children leave foster care.
8. The roles of the agency and the social worker in foster care.
9. The foster child with special needs.
10. Attitudes toward the biological parents.

Group meetings with foster parents conducted by agency personnel have the following purposes and advantages:

1. To heighten the foster parents' identification with the agency and its program and to develop loyalty to the program.
2. To widen the foster parents' concern and interest from their own foster child to all the children offered service by the agency.
3. To increase their knowledge and skills of foster parenthood and to improve their relationship with the foster child through increasing tolerance and understanding of the child's behavior.
4. To offer the foster parents an opportunity to discuss problems of mutual concern with other foster parents.
5. To enhance the status and, hence, the satisfactions of foster parents. They see themselves as a group specially chosen by the agency for a significant function.
6. To enable the agency to have a better understanding of the experiences encountered by foster parents in their day-to-day dealings with the child and their reactions to these experiences.
7. To enable foster parents to gain an appreciation of what is involved for the biological parent and the child in the experience of separation. There is an opportunity for foster parents to develop a greater tolerance toward the natural parent as they learn something about the difficult life situations such parents face.
8. To enable the foster parents to gain a better appreciation of the agency's difficulties and problems. One father in one of the groups said, "I used to think the agency shouldn't make it so easy for parents to place a child. I thought it was like taking off an overcoat and saying, 'Here, take care of it,' but I see it isn't so easy."
9. To develop a consensus about the role of the foster parent and the relative rights and obligations of the agency and the foster parents vis-à-vis the foster child and the biological parents.
10. To help the foster parents realize that in some instances, they may fail despite their best efforts and that failure in foster care may result from the child's deficiencies rather than from any shortcomings on their part. They appreciate the truth of this as they listen to other foster parents discussing some of the problems they have encountered. It relieves the foster parents of a private evaluation of failure and guilt and feelings of frustration and discouragement.
11. To permit, in the safety of numbers, foster parents' expression of dissatisfaction with agency policy, although some caseworkers fear the development of a foster parents' trade union that would bargain with the agency for better rates for foster parents (Roberts, 1962).
12. To permit a more expeditious discussion, with a large number of parents, of agency policy as it affects foster parents, and to obtain their help in formulating or reviewing policy.
13. To spark and plan recruitment programs for the agency and to help increase the supply of foster homes by reducing turnover (MacDonald, Ferguson, 1964).
14. To give prospective applicants a clearer idea of what is involved in

foster parenthood and to help them to come to a decision. This permits judicious self-screening by some who find that the correction of their misconceptions has left them with no desire to continue. Such group meetings help prepare those who decide to continue for the home study so that they are in a better position to participate effectively.

The general objectives of group meetings are a lower rate of foster-parent turnover, fewer replacements of children, and more capable foster parenting for the child during the time he is in placement.

A nationwide survey of 173 foster-care agencies showed that 38 per cent offered some kind of group service to foster parents (Weinbach, Edwards, Levy, 1977). Family-life education programs, group intake programs, and parent orientation programs were among the most frequently offered group services.

Education in foster parents' role enactment provided by agency-sponsored group discussions (Goldstein, Dall, 1967; Mills *et al.*, 1967) is supplemented by specialized courses offered by schools of social work in cooperation with child-placing agencies. Such a course might meet for ten to fifteen weekly sessions and cover material on the basic developmental needs of children, the meaning of separation, the problem of adjustment to the foster home, and the place of the biological parents and the agency in foster care (Appleberg, 1968; Reistroffer, 1968; Hanwell *et al.*, 1969).

The Child Welfare League of America has developed a basic curriculum for foster-parent education that includes training materials and a variety of audio-visual aids. In addition to the curriculum on foster-care training developed by the Child Welfare League, curricula are available from a number of universities that have developed such programs (Heinritz, Frey, 1975; Marr, 1976; Guerney, 1976; Ryan, Warren, McFadden, 1977).

Foster-care training programs tend to be oriented toward behavioral modification. Positive changes in the behavior of foster children are noted as a consequence of the foster parents' application of techniques learned in the training programs (Penn, 1978).

A two-year follow-up of a behaviorally oriented foster-parent training program offered to 105 foster families showed such training to be effective in reducing foster-parent turnover (Boyd, Remy, 1978). Such training tended to compensate for inexperience in foster care and "tempered" stress in the foster parent–child relationship.

Foster parent training is regarded as a necessity in the preparation of parents for what has been termed "treatment fostering"—the fostering of emotionally disturbed or handicapped children requiring special knowledge and skills. Foster parents may be eligible for special additional payments for "treatment fostering" only upon completion of special foster-care education.

EVALUATION OF THE CONSEQUENCES OF FOSTER-FAMILY CARE

The nineteenth-century controversy over the "placing out" of large numbers of children from metropolitan areas in the East to rural areas in the West and the South produced a rash of evaluation studies, many of which were somewhat haphazard and biased. Some of the more respectable of these early studies have little relevance now because of the changed nature of the foster-family-care program. We will attempt, therefore, to review only the more recent studies.

In the early 1920s, the State Charities Aid Association in New York City evaluated all those children who had been under foster-family care through the agency for at least one year and were, at the time of the study, at least eighteen years old (Thies, 1924). This study was, as the agency contends, "the first serious effort to collect, at first hand, on a considerable scale, the facts as to the careers of an unselected group of foster chidren" (p. 6). Information was obtained from interviews by social workers with the foster child himself or with the foster parents or relatives. The foster children were categorized by "experienced supervisors" as "capable" (subjects who were law-abiding, who managed their affairs with good sense, and who were living in accordance with the moral standards of their communities) or "incapable" (subjects who were unable or unwilling to support themselves adequately, who were shiftless, or who defied the accepted standards of morality or order of their communities). Of 562 foster children in the group who were not subsequently adopted and on whom sufficient data for judging were available, 73 per cent were judged "capable" and 27 per cent "incapable" at the time of follow-up. Age at placement was significantly related to outcome: children who were five or younger when placed were more likely to be judged "capable." Outcome was not related to the socioeconomic level of the home but was related to the quality of foster parent–foster child relationships.

Baylor and Monachesi (1939) did a follow-up study of 478 children after discharge from foster care. For most of the children, the research was conducted four to six years after discharge. The Social Service Exchange was used to obtain follow-up information and "visits were made, sometimes several, in the homes of people concerned; employers were visited or sought by correspondence" (p. 414). The material assembled by field-workers was evaluated independently by each of the authors. Of the 478 children for whom a "behavior evaluation" was attempted, 67.4 per cent were found to be "behaving favorably" at the time of the follow-up. Children who had been placed for health reasons, because of a "broken home," or because of dependency and neglect showed a much lower percentage of "unfavorable behavior" than children placed because of behavioral difficulties and/or delinquency (p. 417).

The Dutch Child Caring Agency, Tot Steun, did a follow-up interview study in 1952–1954 of 160 former foster children born between 1903 and 1920 who had been in the care of the agency at one time for a "considerable length of time" (Van der Walls, 1960). Interviews conducted by social workers ran for two or three hours. It was found that "more than half of all the respondents expressed strong negative feelings toward their foster parents" and most of these had severed "every contact with the foster parents after coming of age," as they had with their own parents (p. 30). Those who had contact with their own families during foster-family care and felt accepted by their own mothers were more accepting of the foster parents: "The feeling of being loved by their own mothers evidently helped their relationship with the foster parents," for these respondents "tended to speak kindly of their foster parents." This reinforces the findings of Weinstein (1960) and Cowan and Stout (1939) that positive contacts with the natural parents assist in the child's adjustment in the foster home. In summation, the report notes that "the situation of many of these former foster children at the time of the inquiry left much to be desired. Socially, many were rather well established. Only a few were unemployed or antisocial or had lost the parental rights to their own children. However, many felt unsuccessful, dissatisfied, and distressed" (p. 33).

Gil (1964) conducted follow-up interviews with twenty-five former foster children or their relatives, five to six years after the termination of agency service. Judgments were made regarding the extent to which these foster children had realized their "developmental potential," previously evaluated on the basis of a critical analysis of the significant data in the foster child's agency record. Twelve of the twenty-five subjects showed "considerable realization of preadmission developmental potential"; thirteen showed limited realization of such potential (p. 235). The degree of realization was not related to the number of replacement experiences but was "markedly associated" with the quality of the foster home in which the subject had been placed. Tinker, too, found that when the foster-family home meets the emotional needs of children, they tend to develop normally and healthily (Tinker, 1952a,b,c). Murphy (1964), reviewing the records of a Canadian agency, selected the records of mentally normal children who had been in continuous foster-family care for more than five years, whose cases were closed at the time of the study, and who were at least eleven years of age at the time the case was closed. Two senior social workers, who had been with the agency throughout and who had "unusually complete memories," made available their knowledge of the outcome of each of the 316 cases selected for study. This was supplemented by agency records, which included postclosure contacts with foster child, foster parents, and "courts, hospitals, family agencies, and some employers in the city." The two senior officers divided the 316 former foster children into three categories:

1. Outcome satisfactory ("A") in terms of the child's social milieu.
2. Outcome less satisfactory ("B"), but without signs of pathology or open disturbance.
3. Outcome unsatisfactory ("C"), usually with signs of pathology or disturbance. C ratings were given if there was a record of admission to a mental hospital or involvement with the courts on other than a trivial charge.

Of the 316 cases, 61, or 19.3 per cent, were given a C rating; 151, or about 50 per cent, received an A rating (p. 392). Murphy also found that the sex of the foster child is a significant factor in outcome: if placement was the result of illegitimate births, the likelihood of failure in later life was significantly greater for a female child than for a male child.

Ferguson (1966) did a follow-up study of some 140 young adults who had been cared for in foster-family homes during childhood in Scotland. At age twenty, 96 per cent of the group were employed or in training and were independently responsible for their own support. The rate of delinquency was high, however, 17 per cent having been convicted of some crime before age twenty. It must be noted, however, that more than 50 per cent of this group had tested IQ scores below 90.

Meier (1962) did a follow-up interview study of sixty-one adults between the ages of twenty-eight and thirty-two who had been in foster care in Minnesota for a period of at least five years. The criteria for outcome were based on the interviewers' ratings of the respondents' level of social effectiveness (employment and economic circumstances, care of the home and of the children, social relationships outside the home) and their feeling of well-being (feeling of adequacy, capacity to experience pleasure). Fifteen men and twenty-four women —some 64 per cent of the total sample—had positive ratings in all areas of social functioning; the rest had a negative rating in at least one area; and three respondents have negative ratings in three areas. In summary, Meier notes:

> Current circumstances of these young adults as a group contrast sharply with family circumstances at the time of their placement; with few exceptions they are self-supporting individuals, living in conformity with the social standards of their communities. The children of most of them are well cared for. . . . In most areas of adaptation, current functioning compares favorably with that of the general population [p. 2].

Age at first placement and the number of placements were not found to be significantly related to overall social effectiveness and sense of well-being, but they were related to specific aspects of functioning. Like Murphy, Meier found that the sex of the foster child was a very important variable in determining response to foster care. The data suggested that being reared away from his own family in itself damaged the male's self-concept, whereas for the female, the content and quality of the experience were of greater importance.

Children who were in foster care for long periods have in 70–80 per cent of the cases grown up satisfactorily. Some of the associations usually thought to be related to outcome, such as age at placement and number of replacements, are not unequivocally supported in the studies. Outcome seems to be differentially related to the sex of the child and directly related to the interpersonal quality of the foster home.

The studies cited were concerned with the long-range effects of foster-family care. There is also a concern with the more immediate consequences for the child of the foster-care experience during the time that the child is in foster care.

There is a conviction, repeatedly expressed in articles on foster care, that except for a very short stay, foster care must, on the face of it, be destructive to the child. Not "belonging" to anyone on a clearly defined basis, the child is denied the assurance of continuity, and continuity in a relationship with loving, accepting caretakers is considered an essential prerequisite to healthy development. Neither the child nor the foster parent can emotionally invest himself fully in a relationship whose permanence is tenuous. The child is denied the possibility of a healthy sense of identification with the foster family, and the foster parents, uncertain of their entitlement and prerogatives, cannot act decisively in making child-rearing decisions.

There is the further supposition that the experience of separation, as well as the system itself, is psychologically unhealthy. Separation poses for the child the loss of established relationships with parental figures, however unsatisfactory, with siblings, and with a familiar environment. Coming into an unfamiliar family and an unfamiliar environment, the child has to build a new way of life. The child further has to come to terms with the reasons for his removal from the biological home and with the stigmatized and atypical status of a foster child. As a consequence of the separation itself and the lack of assured permanence inherent in the foster-care situation, it is hypothesized that there is considerable risk that the foster child will be developmentally damaged and that the likelihood of such damage will increase with time in care.

It is generally conceded that the physical development of the child in care is good. On the other hand, children in foster care supposedly manifest many emotional problems (Vasaly, 1975, Tables 24, 25, 26, pp. 53–63). More recent studies mirror the results of earlier studies (Boehm, 1958), showing a relationship between length of time in care and an increasing percentage of children with emotional problems (Holman, 1973, p. 121; Rome, Lambert, 1973, p. 154; Canning, 1974; Hargrave, Shireman, Connor, 1975; Vassaly, 1975, p. 63). On the other hand, some studies show that the physical, intellectual, and emotional adjustment of most children in long-term foster care is satisfactory (Kadushin, 1958; Madison, Schapiro, 1969, 1970).

The essential problem with all of this research, either favoring or damning foster care, is that these are studies of children at one point in time, generally after the child has been in care for some time. Without baseline data giving the children's functioning at admittance into care, it is difficult to know whether the problems are the result of the children's longer time in care or if the length of time in care results from the children's problems. Problem children are more difficult to move out of foster care, so that one might expect a greater proportion of such children to appear in any long-term-stay group.

The possibility throughout of confounding concomitance with cause is great. There is no way of knowing whether or not children came into the system maladjusted or whether they developed such behavior while in foster care.

Follow-up interviews with foster parents and children in foster care about a year after placement emphasize the importance of baseline entering data in determining the effects of foster care (Lahti et al., 1978). Data in this study were available on some 490 children over a four-year period before and after foster-care placement. The study showed that children who got along well when they first entered placement were more likely to do well in placement: "The past was a good predictor of the present" (p. 9.4).

Furthermore, more often than not, there is no comparison available regarding the level of behavioral and emotional problems manifested by children living with their own parents. All children, as developing organisms, have limited ego strength and are subject to age-specific disorders, normal developmental lags, and a heightened response to transitory stress situations. Because all children manifest problems, we would need to know if the number and intensity of problems manifested by foster children is atypical. More specifically, in order to most validly assess the effects of living in foster care on the child's development, we would need a more refined base of comparison than the general population of children. Because the foster-care child population is heavily weighted with children who are socioeconomically deprived, the basis for comparing developmental deficits is not the population of children at large but a population of socioeconomically deprived children.

Fanshel and Shinn (1978) completed a longitudinal study that compares the child's adjustment when he came into the system with adjustment after he had been in foster care. They rigorously obtained elaborate baseline data on the children's social, emotional, and cognitive functioning on entrance into care and then, at periodic intervals during a five-year period while the child was in care, assessed the child's development during time in care. A number of indexes were developed to document carefully the children's bio-psycho-social functioning. These included a Health Status Index, an Emotional Problems Indicator, and a Developmental Problems Index. Information regarding the children's preplacement development, social–emotional adjustment, and behavioral disciplinary problems was obtained from interviews with the biological mother shortly after the child's admission to care.

Depending on the child's age, either the Cattell, the Minnesota Preschool Scale, or the Wechsler Intelligence Scale was used to obtain a measure of the child's intelligence shortly after entrance into care and at stated intervals during the time in care. Following testing, on each occasion the clinical psychologist was asked to record a clinical assessment of the child's emotional functioning.

Caseworkers assigned to the case were required to complete a specially devised Child Behavior Characteristics form at the end of the first ninety days in placement, at the end of two and one-half years, and at the end of five years. Information for form completion was derived from the worker's own observation of the child and from interviews with his foster parents. The information obtained permitted an assignment of scores measuring such items as the child's likability, agreeableness, emotionality-tension, and withdrawal. Other forms completed by the caseworker provided more information regarding emotional maturity, psychosomatic reactions, aggressiveness, and fears. Additional information was obtained from the child's teachers on such forms as the Rating Scale for Pupil Adjustment.

It can be said with some confidence that this study is the most elaborate and carefully designed and executed study currently available regarding the development of the child in foster care.

Summarizing the most significant conclusions of the research, Fanshel and Shinn note that "We do not find that the longer a child spends in foster care the more likely he is to show signs of deterioration" (p. 490); "Our findings do not show that children who remained in foster care fared less well with respect to intellectual abilities, school performance and personal and social adjustment compared to those who returned to their own homes" (p. 479); "Continued tenure in foster care is not demonstrably deleterious with respect to IQ change, school performance or measures of emotional adjustment" (p. 491).

Another, less rigorous, longitudinal study comparing baseline placement entrance data with data obtained after a period in care was conducted by Palmer (1976). She studied changes in the adjustment of two hundred children who entered foster care after age three and remained in care for at least five years. An assessment of the changes between time of placement and time of last entry was made by two readers who independently read the complete record material. Behavior problems and emotional problems were defined and categorized. Record data at time of placement served as a baseline. The results are as good as the record data and the perceptivity of the record readers. With this caveat in mind, the report showed that behavior problems from point of entry over the five-year period decreased. Over one half of the children who began with serious emotional problems had less serious problems at the end. Although a five-year stay in foster care might not have been helpful, it does not appear to have been harmful for this group of children.

The importance of an appropriate comparison group in interpreting the data is illustrated by a study evaluating the physical and mental health of children in foster care. Swire and Kaveler (1977) studied a sample of 668 children drawn from the population of children in foster-family care in New York City in 1973–1974. Evaluations were conducted by a team of pediatricians and other professionals associated with the Cornell Medical School hospital in New York City. The results of the evaluation showed that a considerable percentage of the children in foster care had physical and emotional problems and conditions that required attention and correction.

When the researchers compared the results with other studies available of similar populations of disadvantaged children in the general community, the levels of physical and psychiatric impairment seemed roughly comparable. The findings would seem to be attributable, they note, to "the greater health risks associated with poor inner-city minority group living" (p. 350) rather than to the foster-care experience.

The general conclusion that might be drawn from these studies of the immediate and long-range effects of foster-family care is that with reasonable caution in the selection of such placements, followed by agency support of the placement, the substitute care is not injurious to the child's development and does not prejudice his chances for successful adult adjustment. Although the research cited does not directly address this question, it would seem that the child who is removed from a potentially injurious situation has a better chance for healthy development in a foster home than if he had remained in his own home.

This supposition is empirically confirmed in a study by Kent (1976) that, comparing the level of development of abused children at the point of their removal from the home with their functioning after one to two years in foster care, found that they had made improvements physically, cognitively, and emotionally.

PROBLEMS

1. One of the most serious problems faced by the foster-home program is that it fails to fulfill its purpose for some children. The distinguishing aspect of foster care is that it is designed to be a temporary arrangement. Currently, however, some children moving into foster care never return to their own homes.

These are the children who are likely to grow up in foster care, "orphans of the living," unvisited and unwanted by their parents, yet not fully "belonging" to the foster family, and living in a placement that goes on and on without termination but also without assurance of permanence.

Studies show that the longer a child has been in placement, the greater is the likelihood that he will continue in placement (Mass, Engler, 1959; Jenkins, 1967; Mass, 1969; Fanshel, 1971; Shapiro, 1972; Fanshel, Shinn, 1978). Although parents have strong reactions to placement, their motivation to see the child returned home diminishes with time. Their sense of responsibility for the child, not being actively exercised, atrophies. Many gradually reorient their lives to the reality that they are no longer actually parents caring for their children and accept employment and move into smaller apartments. Having reorganized their lives in ways that do not include the child, they find that his return would be disruptive and increasingly resist it. The separation becomes total—except in legal terms. Many of these children, however, although they no longer have much relationship or contact with their own parents, nevertheless legally "belong" to them and are not free for adoption. Of necessity, then, they live in an inbetween world: between a family that does not want them and a family that cannot fully have them. These children should be provided with an adoptive home or with permanence in contractual long-term foster care.

More recently, this situation has been the subject of increased discussion, concern, and examination. A number of factors have converged to give increased visibility to the sizable number of foster children "in limbo." Concern with the rights of children has made us sensitive to the entitlement of such children to some regularization of their status. The decreasing number of white, nonhandicapped infants available for adoption has prompted reexamination of the status of all children in substitute care in an effort to determine if some of those children could be made available for adoption, thus increasing the supply of adoptable children. The growth and the increasing power of foster-parent organizations has heightened concern with this question because foster parents are often anxious to obtain some clearer definition of their own status in these ambiguous situations. Increasing public resentment in the 1970s against being taxed to support social programs added concern about program costs and impelled an effort to free more children for adoption.

These considerations provided the very receptive ground for a book by several prestigious authors (Freud, Goldstein, Solnit, 1973). The principal thesis of the book, which is relevant to and reinforces concern with the child "in limbo," is that children need a sense of permanence for healthy development. Earlier, agencies had been asked to provide adequate care for the child in a healthy physical, social, and emotional environment. The foster-care system is currently being required also to assure the child permanence in living arrangements and continuity of relationships.

Nationwide reviews of the performance of the system, by two different child advocacy groups, indicted the system for its failure in meeting children's need for permanence (Children's Defense Fund, 1978; National Commission for Children in Need of Parents, 1979). Violation of the obligation to provide a permanent situation seems most serious in the case of many children who entered the system when very young and were optimally placeable for adoption (Fanshel, 1979). A variety of solutions have been proposed and implemented to deal with the barriers to the achievement of permanence. One set of solutions relates to changes in the laws regarding the termination of parental rights so that the foster child who is unlikely to return to his own home can be freed for adoption. The termination of parental rights is more frequently possible now for the child who is "permanently neglected," whose parents fail, despite the diligent efforts of the agency, to maintain any kind of meaningful contact with the child. However, a number of difficulties stand in the way of freeing the child for adoption. Organizational barriers in both the child welfare agency and the court system relate to the personnel time available to implement the termination of parental rights, legal experience in handling such petitions, and attitudinal barriers regarding parents' rights, which intensify reluctance to undertake such procedures. The child's age, race, and handicaps that reduce the child's placeability if freed lead to a hesitancy to attempt an effort that, if successful, would leave the agency as parent to the child. The child himself may be opposed to adoption and well adjusted to the foster home. Lack of knowledge of the whereabouts of the parents, active or anticipated opposition by the parents to termination, and the continuing interest of the parents in the child, however vague or intermittent, make action to free the child difficult. Consequently it is suggested that changes in values and attitudes need to accompany the changes in legal procedures. The worker needs to have convictions about the clear priority of the rights of the children when they are in conflict with the rights of the biological parents, about the value of achieving permanence for the child as early as possible, about the adoptive acceptability of the children regardless of age, race, or handicap, and about the acceptability for adoption of a wider variety of family forms: single parents, working parents, and older parents. The worker needs to develop greater skill in identifying the children who might be freed for adoption and in implementing the legal procedures that will accomplish adoption. These changes would need to be supplemented by an effective program of subsidized adoption to increase the possibility of adoption by the child's foster parents (see Chapter 10).

Other efforts are directed toward agency barriers to achieving permanence, through adoption or alternative resources. Agency inefficiency in monitoring the "drift" of children in foster care is addressed in a set of proposed solutions. In general, these involve (1) more explicit intra-agency efforts to monitor plans for the child and to implement more intensive efforts to achieve permanence and (2) arrangements for extra-agency monitoring, by courts and citizens review boards, of agency efforts toward permanence. The intent of both internal and external review procedures is to introduce more systematic planning and accountability into the system. In general, what is suggested is more explicit planning, monitoring, and review of worker activity in response to the central problem of deficiencies in case management. The proposed solutions are directed toward achieving more systematic, structured, goal-oriented performance on the part of the work force.

Agencies have reported on special efforts to review their case loads to identify, with varied success, those children for whom more adequate plans for permanence are warranted and to implement such plans. (Fellner, Solomon, 1973; Chestang, Heymann, 1973; Atherton, 1974; Rothschild, 1974). Larger agencies have experimented with the administrative review of planning for foster children on the part of units within the agency as a way of preventing "drift" (Claburn, Magura, 1977).

To implement external review procedures, legislation has been adopted to require court review of children in foster care at periodic intervals, such as twelve months or eighteen months. The Children in Placement project (CIP) sponsored by the National Council of Juvenile and Family Court Judges is another example of the use of the court setting to monitor postplacement planning toward permanence. Volunteers are recruited and trained to review the court records of children who are in foster care as a consequence of court-ordered placement. The objective of the record review by the volunteers is to identify those children who might be returned home or freed for adoption (Steketee, 1977; 1978). Efforts are being made to have the program adopted by juvenile and family courts throughout the country.

Another external agency-review system, by local citizens' boards, is reported by Chappell (1975). To stimulate more definite decision-making in each case, a statewide foster-care review-board system was legislated in South Carolina in 1974. Review boards, consisting of unsalaried residents of the area, were established in each of the sixteen state judicial circuits. They were to review the case of each child in their area who had been in public or private foster care for a period of six months to determine what effort had been made, or might be made, to find a permanent arrangement for the child. If the review board and the agency disagreed on the best plan for the child, a judicial review of the situation could be requested.

Although these procedures are relatively recent innovations, by 1976 a surprisingly large number of child welfare decisions were subject to such review. Claburn, Magura, and Resnick (1976) obtained information from state agencies in forty-seven states, the District of Columbia, and Puerto Rico concerning provisions for the periodic case review of children in foster care. Twenty-four per cent of the responding jurisdictions indicated that they required a full court review involving "statewide statutory requirements for agencies to submit periodic reports to the judiciary justifying the status of children in out of home placements" (p. 397). An additional 29 per cent had developed a "centralized administrative system for regular mandatory reviews of the status of foster children" (p. 397). Thus over half the states had some systematic, mandatory, periodic review that went beyond traditional case supervision.

There is some debate on the net effects of such formal legal requirements in reducing the extent of "drift" in the foster-care system and the number of children "in limbo." Some agencies claim that such laws merely ask the agencies to do what they are already doing, while burdening them with a considerable amount of additional work in routinely preparing cases for court action and appearing in court, all of which robs time and effort from needed services. Others claim, however, that the legal requirement for periodic court review of the status of children in foster care gets the agencies to do what they otherwise would not have done, or would not have done as promptly or conscientiously.

Festinger (1975, 1976), reviewing the effects of such procedures in New York courts on achieving permanence for children, notes that they have the effect of moving the agencies toward more expeditious, systematic planning for children. In some instances, court review resulted in the child's being freed for adoption; in a smaller percentage of cases, the child was ordered returned to his own home. In 45 per cent of the cases, the child was continued in foster care. The extent to which the required court review actually facilitated more rapid, more decisive action on the part of the agencies in making a definite plan for the child is difficult to determine because there is no valid basis for comparison with truly comparable situations. Festinger feels that court review did have a modest catalytic, "facilitating impact" on agency decision-making. What is perhaps of equal interest is that the court depended heavily on agency recommendations and that the court's decision was most often in line with agencies' recommendations, suggesting confidence in the agencies' assessment of the foster-care situation.

Although court or citizen board reviews "force foster care agencies to sharpen up ambiguous plans for individual children and defend these plans" (Young, Fiske, 1977, p. 68), such review systems require that the reviewer—court, review board, central administrator—make decisions based on summarized information provided by the caseworker responsible for the case. It is difficult to see on what basis the reviewer could consistently make decisions that improve on those achieved by the worker in direct contact with the case. It is likely that as a result of more explicit periodic review of cases, fewer children will be without a worker assigned to their case (as happens now), more biological parents will have more regular contacts with the agency, and some additional percentage of children will face less delay in moving toward adoption.

The evidence currently available would suggest that although case review systems and case systemization procedures can be helpful, their potentiality for improving the foster-family-care program might be limited. The deficiencies in the system that they are directed to correct may not be the most significant factors in determining outcomes. More systematic, structured case management by the worker, although helpful, is not as important as other factors not directly addressed by internal or external case-review procedures. These problems include, among others, the limited strengths and the deprived circumstances in the biological family, making the situation resistive to change; the characteristics of the child in care and the attitude of adoptive applicants toward such children; the limited technology available to the worker in bringing about intra- and interpersonal changes; and the high case loads, limited training, and turnover rates of direct-service workers.

A series of large-scale demonstration programs have been established to explore different approaches to achieving permanence for children "in limbo." The procedures of such demonstrations have subsequently been employed by specially established programs throughout the country with the support of federal funding. The most notable examples of such projects are the Alameda Project in California (Stein, 1976; Stein, Gambrill, 1977) and the Oregon Project (Pike, 1976; Emlen et al., 1977).

The Alameda Project was a two-year experiment during which three specially assigned workers with a limited case load (twenty cases "defined as families") "offered intensive service to the natural parents using behavioral methods of treatment while county child welfare workers provided their usual services to the child in the foster home" (Stein 1976, p. 39). Case outcomes in the units to which the special workers were assigned were compared with cases in a designated control unit in the same agency. Although the control and the experimental families were well matched in terms of ethnicity, structure, and the reasons that brought the children into care, the two groups were different in terms of the ages of the children—the control group children being significantly older ($p < .001$) than the children in the experimental group. At the end of two years of effort, comparisons were made between the status of 145 children in the experimental group and 148 children in the control group. A significantly greater percentage ($p < .001$) of the experimental group children had been returned home or had achieved or were headed for adoption than was true for the control-group children. The researchers attribute the greater success in achieving permanent outcomes for the experimental group to early systematic planning by the demonstration workers, facilitating early decision-making on the part of the parents. Contracts provided the specific framework and content for worker–client interaction. They also provided the evidence needed for active steps taken to terminate parental rights in planning for adoption.

The Oregon Project (Pike, 1976) employed a somewhat different set of procedures in dealing with problems of the foster-care system. The project emphasized intensive, systematic casework in achieving permanent planning for children and active, aggressive pursuit of the termination of parental rights to free children for adoption. The project design involved limited case loads (twenty-five children per worker as opposed to the usual case load of fifty to sixty children in Oregon) and full-time legal assistance to free children for adoption. Social workers were trained to develop expertise in the tasks required to achieve termination. The project accepted 509 children for the project from the total (2,283) foster-care case load. The children selected had been in care one year or more, were twelve years of age or younger, were not likely, in the worker's judgment, to return home, and were considered adoptable. At the end of the three-year period (November 1973–October 1976), an impressive 79 per cent of the children were out of foster-family care: 27 per cent had been returned home, and an additional 52 per cent either were in adoptive homes or their adoption was being actively planned (Emlen et al., 1977, p. 5).

The factors contributing to success, as explicated by the researchers, are somewhat different from those identified in the Alameda Project. For one thing, the researchers note that "project cases were not randomly selected. The project's success should be interpreted in part as success in selecting the most likely candidate for permanent planning" (p. 6), no small achievement in itself.

When an attempt was made to compare the outcome for the project's children with that for a control group handled in accordance with routine agency procedures, the project's results are somewhat less impressive. Nine months after the project children were placed, a follow-up study was conducted to determine the stability of placements and the child's adjustment. An attempt was made at this time to compare project outcomes with the record of case dispositions and stability of placement achieved by the regular children's service division with standard case loads. Whereas 66 per cent of the project children were in permanent placements in the follow-up study period, smaller percentages of children in two comparison groups who had received regular routine service had achieved permanence: 43 and 46 per cent. However, the average age of the children in the three groups differed because the project group had been deliberately restricted to children under twelve years of age. When children in the project group were compared with children of similar ages in the comparison group, the difference between outcomes decreased: "The overall effect was that the project placed approximately the same number in permanent placements in this age group as did routine activity" (Lahti et al., 1978, p. 4.2). The level of stability of the project placement group and of the placements achieved by routine casework was the same.

There are apparently no easy solutions to the question of permanent planning for children in foster care. The Child Welfare League of America conducted an experiment testing two frequently suggested approaches (Sherman, Neuman, Shyne, 1973). One approach involved a monitoring system in which the workers would be held accountable for the status of the children, would have to develop specific plans for more permanent care, and would have to report periodically on their efforts to implement the plans. The second approach was the assignment of a special worker for intensive casework with the biological parents, helping them with the problems that had led to the need for foster care. The League obtained the cooperation of an agency with a sizable foster-family program. The foster-care case load was divided into three groups. One group included foster-care cases monitored for permanent planning; the second group of cases was provided with intensive casework; the third group of cases was designated as a control group and no special services were offered. The special monitoring and intensive casework services were continued over a period of four months with a total of 413 children involved in the three groups. The point of the experiment was to determine whether both or either one of the special strategies—monitoring and intensive casework—had significant effects on permanence, compared with the traditional approaches offered the control group. The result was that neither of the experimental approaches had the significant effect anticipated. Children were not returned to parents more frequently, nor were permanent plans for the child likely to be made more frequently under either of the two experimental conditions, contrasted with regular practice (p. 54). However, although there was no significant increase in the number of children returned home as a consequence of special planning, when children in the special planning group did return home, they were more likely to remain at home. This is obviously important. More of the children in the control group who went home were subsequently returned to foster care. Although special service did not speed up the process, it reduced errors.

It is claimed that as a consequence of special efforts such as those previously detailed, a larger percentage of children have achieved permanence either through return home or adoption than would otherwise have been the case. Statistics from states that developed well-organized programs whose explicit objective is permanence show a drop in total foster care caseloads following initiation of such efforts—in South Carolina, from 4,000 to 3,500; in Virginia, from 11,876 to 10,369 over a two-year period; in Oregon, from 4,400 in 1972 to 3,600 in 1976. Some part of this reduction was a result of the reduction in the general population of children; some was a consequence of the growing unavailability of infants for adoption, making possible adoptive placement of a larger number of older foster children. Some percentage of the reduction is, however, a result of permanent planning programs. In general, it would seem that explicit case planning and case monitoring, backed by special training on process and procedures relevant to permanence and supported by leadership at the supervisory and administrative levels committed to the desirability of permanence, reduce the possibility of drift and increase the probability of the earliest provision of permanent care.

The studies suggest however that achieving permanence for children who have been in foster care for some time either by return home or by adoption may not be easy, and that many children might continue to remain in foster-family care. The supposition is that such a situation has negative effects on the child's adjustment. However, the limited empirical data do not support this conclusion. Apparently, many children perceive long-term foster care as being as permanent as other kinds of arrangements.

Lahti et al. (1978) studied the effect of permanence on the child's adjustment based on interviews with parents and children. Permanence was strongly related to positive child adjustment, children with better ratings tending to have "parents who viewed the placement as a permanent one." But although it might seem evident that perception of permanence would be highly correlated with categories of placement (i.e., whether the child was in his own home, in an adoptive home, or in a foster-care placement), this supposition was not sustained by the data. In summarizing, Lahti *et al.* note that their

> single most important finding was that a sense of permanence was one of the best predictors of a child's well being. However, sense of permanence was not necessarily related to the legal permanence of the placement. Perception of permanence happens without legal sanctions. And it may be absent even when legal sanctions are there—whether the child was in a legally permanent placement, adoption, or returned home or was in a legally temporary foster care made very little difference in his level of adjustment and health at the time of the interview. Perception of permanence was the key [p. 9.3].

What little difference there was tended to favor the adoption group.

The fact that foster care did provide a sense of permanence was evident from the findings: "We have not found foster care to be characterized by unstable placements affording children limited chance for satisfactory adjustment and growth in secure surroundings as we might have expected. While the foster care placements did not equal the adoptive placements in terms of sense of permanence, scores in these areas were surprisingly high" (p. 8.11). "Children in foster care were getting along surprisingly well" (p. 9.6).

These findings confirm the findings of a similar earlier study by Lawder *et al.* (1971). This study, comparing children in long-term foster care with a group of children in adoptive homes, showed that "there were no statistically significant differences in the functioning of the two groups of parents nor in that of the two groups of children" (p.74).

More recently, Fanshel (1979) found that for the majority of children who had been in foster homes for an average of 6 years, this had become their "real home." Accepted by the foster parents and attached to, identified with, and integrated into the foster family, most were "at peace with the current arrangements" (p. 63).

The findings point to the fact that explicit, planned long-term placements in a quasi-adoptive situation in which foster parents are granted considerable autonomy may be an acceptable alternative for those children who cannot return home and who are not placeable for adoption. Such long-term care would involve a contractual agreement between the agency and the foster family: the agency agrees not to remove the child, and the family agrees to accept the responsibility for his continued care. The arrangement is achieved through deliberate planning rather than as a result of drift and default in decision making. Despite these findings the logic is convincing that an adoptive placement, which combines legal and perceived permanence, is likely to offer the child a greater probability of stability than a long-term foster home not reinforced by legal sanctions, even if the intent is for the foster home to be permanent. A "marriage" through adoption has more factors conducive to permanence than "living together" in foster care.

In recapitulation, achieving permanence for each child in foster-family care or in danger of foster care placement is a principal problem for the system. Various procedures are being tried in an effort to resolve this problem.

2. There is a continuous problem in finding a sufficient number of adequate foster homes.

A 1968 nationwide study of foster-care agencies showed that the most important factor "adversely affecting quality of care" was "lack of facilities—both foster homes and group care resources" (Stone, 1969, p. 14). The shortage of homes limits the deliberate care with which the social worker can select a home for a particular child. Despite the practice view that priority should be given to the child's needs, in actuality not need but resources available often determine the decisions.

The difficulty of finding adequate foster-family homes is likely to become progressively more severe. Women's liberation, zero population growth, the increasing percentage of working mothers—all contribute to the devaluation of parenthood and the child-rearing functions. The competition of the employment market, for which many more women can now qualify, and its substantially higher economic returns will further reduce the number of women likely to be interested in foster care. The large families that once served as the training ground for many foster mothers are a thing of the past, and limited house space makes the addition of another family member difficult. The more open, working-class family, from which foster parents traditionally come, is being replaced by the middle-class family, a compact nuclear group that discourages the entry of newcomers (George, 1970, p. 85). The fact is that there are, and probably always have been, relatively few people who are willing to accept the burden and the responsibility of rearing someone else's child.

The need for additional family income, a second wage-earner, means that some potential foster mothers cannot afford to foster. Combining part-time work and fostering may increase the number of families recruited. Helping applicants find part-time work and offering the freedom to work as one of the advantages of fostering older children may contribute to recruitment.

Foster homes are not only difficult to recruit but, once recruited, are difficult to retain. The average length of service by foster parents is four to six years. The single most frequent reason for giving up a foster-care license was that the parents "were no longer interested" (Stone, 1969, p. 33).

If foster-family care is in short supply for young children without physical or emotional handicaps, facilities are even more seriously limited for older or handicapped children. Foster families have been found for physically handicapped, mentally retarded, emotionally disturbed children, but many more are needed (DeVizia, 1974; O'Regan, 1974; Bauer, Heinke, 1976; Moore, 1976; Barker, Buffe, Zaretsky, 1978; Freeman, 1978; Coyne, 1978). Special placement programs have resulted in successfully placing physically handicapped or mentally disabled children in foster homes. For instance, the special placement unit of the Rancho Los Amigos Hospital, a rehabilitation facility in Los Angeles, has placed some two hundred physically handicapped children in foster homes (Soeffing, 1975). The success of special programs in recruiting family care for handicapped children relates to careful selection of the family, education of the parents regarding the special care needed by such children, and the level of staff support offered the family.

Arkava and Mueller (1978) studied forty-three foster homes caring for handicapped children and compared them with an equal number of homes caring for nonhandicapped children. The handicapped children, most of whom were mentally retarded, were younger, had been in foster care longer, and had experienced more replacements than the other children. Foster parents had to spend more time and energy caring for the handicapped children, who were more dependent. They were more confined and restricted in family activities because of the children's limitations and because baby-sitters were hard to get, and the care of such children was more expensive because of more frequent breakage. The need for and the willingness to take special training in the care of the handicapped, the need for support services, and the difficulties in recruitment were noted. There are greater problems for the family in having their own children accept the handicapped child and the need for additional care he imposes, as well as greater problems in the neighbors' acceptance of the child. The availability of schools that have the resources for education of the handicapped child needs to be considered as well.

Agencies have to make a special effort to provide periodic, sanctioned "time off" to foster parents caring for the handicapped child.

Foster parents are currently liable, in many jurisdictions, for any damage resulting from the actions of their foster children. Agencies should provide insurance to protect the foster parent. The fact that Freeman (1978), in reporting on the placement of retarded children, notes that "Two foster homes were set on fire, a neighbor's house was set on fire, two neighbors' houses were broken into" (p. 116) indicates the need for such insurance, particularly in fostering emotionally disturbed children. In order to encourage foster families to take emotionally disturbed children, New Jersey became the first state to finance liability insurance coverage for foster homes and foster parents. Foster parents were insured by the state for up to $300,000 for personal and bodily injury and property damage. This legislation, adopted in 1973, was designed to deal with foster applicants' hesitancy because of the possible damage that might be caused by an emotionally disturbed child. Despite the difficulties, agencies that have developed foster-care programs for such children have noted success in the continued good care and the enhanced development of the children (Jewish Child Care Association of New York, 1965; Bauer, Heinke, 1976; Freeman, 1976).

Given the increasing age of children coming into foster care, the anticipated increasing gap between the number and kinds of children needing foster-family care, and the number of families ready to take the kinds of children available, a question can be raised as to whether other kinds of community-based care should not be more actively considered. Community-based group care rather than family care may be a feasible alternative.

Foster care poses special problems for some particular groups in the population. The placement rate of American Indian children is considerably higher than that of white children, and almost all such children have been placed in Caucasian homes. Preventive services are in even shorter supply for the American Indian population as compared with the general population, and the extent of poverty is greater. Few American Indian foster homes are available, and many families, among the limited number of applicants, have difficulty in meeting the licensing requirements (Center for Social Research and Development, 1976; American Academy of Child Psychiatry, 1977). It is suggested that social agencies do not, as yet, have a clear appreciation of American Indian parenting patterns and the involvement of siblings in the care of younger children. This lack of understanding leads them to perceive the need for intervention and placement where it is not valid (Ishisaka, 1978).

Recruitment of an adequate supply of foster family homes for black children also presents a problem. The disadvantaged economic situation of the black community contributes to this difficulty. However, other factors are also involved.

One of the barriers to the recruitment of black homes identified by Royster (1975) was the fact that the informal foster-care system was competing with the formal system under agency auspices. Because a larger percentage of black families than white families were already caring for both related and nonrelated children for whom they had accepted responsibility, fewer black families were available for formal foster-care recruitment. In 1970, black families in Pennsylvania, where Royster did his study, "cared for 12.5 percent of children under 19 who are not members of the nuclear family; whites care for 3.6 per cent" (pp. 3–4). There is a marked difference between black and white informal foster care. Whereas 7.3 per cent of black children in 1970 were living with "neither parent in families," this was true for only 1.5 per cent of white children.

3. The problem of recruitment is related to the problem of finances. Defining the role of the foster parent primarily as the equivalent of biological parents, foster parents are uneasy about the question of compensation because biological parents are not paid for being parents. There is "an inherent antagonism in our value system between remuneration and being parents. Families are not market places, and the personal relations offered to foster children are not up for sale" (Rosenblum, 1977, p. 108).

Foster parents most frequently see an acceptable rate as one that adequately meets the cost of maintaining the child in care without requiring any additional contribution from their own pocket. They tend to reject the idea of foster-care payment as an increment to family income or as a payment in recognition of services rendered (McWhinnie, 1978, p. 17). As it is, however, foster parents tend to have to use their own funds to pay for a variety of expenses incidental to the activities of the foster child—expenses that are necessary if the child is to be participate as an equal among his peers (Thomas, 1977, pp. 50–51). These include expenses for clothing above the agency allowance, transportation, recreational activity, parties, toys, games, personal grooming needs, and school expenses. Foster parents, in effect, rather than being adequately supported by the foster-care system, tend, in fact, to subsidize the system.

That compensation is not an academic matter is confirmed by a statistical analysis of the number of foster homes in various states as related to the level of payments in these states. The conclusion indicates that "the effect of the payment level" on the number of homes "is indeed substantial" (Simon, 1975, p. 406).

Monthly base rates in late 1975 (Cully, Healy, Settles, VanName, 1977) ranged from a minimum of $65 a month for a seven-year-old child in New Mexico to $187 for the same-aged child in Alaska, with a national average of about $113 a month. This payment generally covers food, room, and recreational and personal expenses. There are initial one-time payments in most states for start-up costs, including a wardrobe and some needed furniture. The standard consumer price index or the Bureau of Labor Statistics budget for estimates may be used to determine costs (DeJong, 1975). At best, however, these methods compute only the direct costs of maintaining a child.

A variety of different methods used to compute indirect costs—the cost of parental time and effort in child care—all resulted in an estimate that indicated that indirect costs, which are not reimbursed, exceed the costs of direct care (Cully, Settles, VanName, 1975; Settles, VanName, Cully, 1976, 1977).

Increases in maintenance rates have generally lagged behind increases in the cost of living. Consequently, in a time of rapid increases in cost of living, foster parents are asked to accept even less in real income than previously. Board rates are not regarded as taxable income and are not generally regarded as income in determining public assistance grants. But there is no payment for the time and energy devoted to the care of the child.

The Child Welfare League is frank and direct in calling for higher board rates. *Child Welfare*, the official organ of the League, calls attention to the fact that "children are 'stacked up' in temporary shelters awaiting more appropriate placement," while boarding rates are far lower than the rates usually received by baby-sitters and, in "most cities in the country, a cleaning woman can earn in two days more than foster parents receive in a week" (Glover, 1964, p. 56).

Foster-family-home placements have always been recruited on the basis of a quid pro quo. The nature of return for the foster parent has changed, however, with changing circumstances. At one time, almost all foster homes were free homes. Payment was the labor contributed by the child to the family. Urbanization required a money payment and put a new stress on the psychic satisfactions derived from fostering children.

Efforts have been made to study the effects on foster care of the payment of a fee or a salary to foster parents for the time and effort devoted to child care (Jaffee, Kline, 1970). In one experiment, a salary of $200 a month was paid (in addition to the usual basic maintenance allowance), and the foster parents were viewed as agency employees. In a second experiment, a $100 service fee was paid. In general, the effects of such payments were positive:

1. The agencies were less defensive and apologetic in their relationship with the foster parents. The agency felt freer about making task assignments. One agency required that "the foster parents submit a brief monthly report on the child's adjustment." The requirement was met with regularity by most of the foster homes.
2. Agencies were less defensive in presenting the realities of the foster children's difficulties. The workers were less anxious about sharing the details of a child's behavioral difficulties for fear that the foster parents would reject the request for placement.
3. Payment for child care did not adversely affect the quality of care given: "Caseworkers gauged the over-all quality of foster parent functioning to be excellent or good in almost seven of ten cases" (Jaffee, Kline, 1970, p. 82).
4. The payments highlighted and made explicit the value to the agency and the community of the service performed by the foster parents.
5. The foster parents felt a greater sense of identification with the agency and perceived agency staff members as peers and colleagues.

It had been feared that such an arrangement might render foster parents vulnerable to the charge that they were mercenary in accepting a salary for the care of a child, and that the children might react negatively to the fact that they were a source of income. Neither effect was confirmed by the studies.

In another experiment, which focused on a group foster home, foster parents were retained as salaried employees of the agency: "There was no evidence of incompatibility between the employee status and the parenting role" (Pratt, 1968, p. 27). Nor was there any evidence that care of the children was adversely affected by the greater financial returns offered.

It is not certain that such procedures would lead to easier recruitment and longer retention of more foster homes. The limited empirical material available, however, suggests that a modest increment of homes might result. More adequate financial payments do enhance and support foster-family-care functioning. And for some, the financial supports make possible the realization of a desire to become foster parents. Compassion and altruism, reinforced by an affective bond between foster parents and foster child and by some psychic recompense to the foster parent in meeting his own emotional needs, enable the foster parent to accept with more equanimity the burdens of foster parenthood. However, compassion and altruism, reinforced by psychic return and *adequate* financial reward, may provide a larger pool of foster homes than is currently available.

Providing special payments to compensate foster parents for the additional effort of caring for an emotionally, physically, or mentally handicapped child is a special problem. It requires clear definition of different levels of difficulty and a determination of who sets such special allowances, how they are set, and when they are set, before or after the child is placed (Specht, 1975). The problem of reducing special rates if the child improves in care as a result of the efforts of the foster parents is a difficult decision because discontinuance penalizes parents for their success. Foster parents should be given the right to appeal special rate decisions.

4. The problem of board rate payments is related to the problem of the agency's definition of its relationship to the foster parents. In one sense, foster parents are "clients" of the agency because the agency has a resource—foster children—that can help to meet some of the foster parents' needs. In another sense, they are nonprofessional volunteer members of an agency staff, offering their homes and their services to meet the needs of children. In one sense, they stand in a supervisee relationship to the supervisor–worker assigned to the home (Glickman, 1957, p. 201). In another sense, they are colleagues cooperatively engaged with the worker in helping the child, each providing different kinds of help, offering skills at different professional levels.

Differences in definition imply different interpretations of the appropriate agency–foster parent relationship. Those who define the foster parent as a client suggest that it is appropriate for the caseworker to offer casework treatment to the foster parent. In asking for a child, the foster parents "are unconsciously seeking help with their own needs." "Asking for a child may serve as a ticket of admission to the agency to enable the family to get its own needs met" (Glickman, 1975, p. 199). In this view, the child is a therapeutic resource offered to the family by the agency.

If the foster parents are volunteer helpers, then any board rate payment is inappropriate. If they are paid employees and colleagues, then the level of board rate payment is inadequate.

There are recurrent suggestions that adequate levels of board rate payments would ensure a larger supply of applicants and resolve the confusion in the agency–foster parent relationship. It is suggested that foster parenthood be clearly established as a job title, that the agency pay adequate compensation, and that the foster parent be clearly recognized as an employee of the agency. This approach would further help to differentiate more clearly the foster parent role from the biological parent role. The foster parent would be defined as a person offering full-time physical, social, and emotional care to nonrelated children in a family setting as an employee of a child welfare agency.

If the foster parent is considered a trusted employee, then much of what is detailed in the literature regarding the contact between the caseworker and the foster family parallels the material on good employer–employee relationships: the need for recognition and appreciation of work well done; the need for support, reassurance, and understanding when the worker is facing some difficulty on the job; and the need for maintaining a high level of morale.

As is true for any job, there are necessary elements of administrative supervision to assure the agency that the job is being competently performed. Caseworker visits to determine how the child is being cared for are also in line with the employee–employer relationship. The agency has to take some responsibility for developing skills, for educating the employee to meet the demands of the job. The educational–advising component in the caseworker's visits coincides with this aspect of the employer–employee relationship.

The agency employee concept makes more understandable, and more acceptable, an extensive evaluation study in selecting foster parents. As would be true for any job situation, the employing agency should have the right to assure itself that the applicant has the necessary qualifications for the position.

Opponents of this conception of the foster parent's role maintain that it would complicate and demean the foster child–foster parent relationship. If the foster parent is an employee, then the child can view his stay in the foster home as a business transaction, himself as a source of income, and any acceptance of himself as a person predicated on the desire for such income. He can use this as a lever to threaten foster parents with the loss of their job. In response, however, it is pointed out that teachers, psychiatrists, and caseworkers ask for adequate compensation for services performed and yet present themselves as accepting children for their own sake and are deeply concerned with helping them. The interrelated problems of adequate recruitment, board payments, and the definition of the foster parents' relationship to the agency remain currently unresolved.

Foster parents themselves are very ambivalent about employee status. As expressed in discussions at meetings of foster parents' organizations, the conflict between the humanitarian motive and the monetization of the child care becomes clear (Rosendorf, 1972). As has already been noted, foster parents most often see themselves as acting as parents to the child in their care, as contrasted with the agency conception of foster parents as a special kind of status. In any case, it is clear that lack of a coherent, consensually accepted definition of the role of foster parents presents a problem. The development of a clear role model might make a notable contribution to increasing the effectiveness of the service, as Thomas (1977, p. 49) notes.

5. The field of social work also faces a problem in that it does not have clear title to the function of foster-family placement. Children may be placed in an independent foster-family home directly by their own parents. It is not known how many children are placed independently in foster homes. Parents do

have the privilege of planning for their own children; the decision to place, when and where, rests primarily with the parents. Parents with money make this decision without controversy—by sending their children to boarding schools, camps, and so on. It is felt that people without money should have the same privilege. Yet the possibilities of abuse do exist, and because society does have a stake in what happens to the child, it has the right to regulate placements.

TRENDS

We have already noted the trend toward an increasing rate of children coming into foster-family care; the fact that such children, on entrance into the system, currently are likely to be older than previously; the continued shift in the greater use of foster-family care as against the institution for children needing substitute care; the increasing use of group homes as against foster-family homes for older children, and the continued shift of responsibility for substitute care from private to public agencies. We have also noted the trend toward greater concern with helping the foster child achieve permanence as soon as possible.

1. The changing nature of the foster child places a heavier burden on the foster-family home. This suggests a trend toward an explicit recognition of foster-family care as a treatment resource. The more benign, more therapeutic environment of a good foster family, in itself, has treatment potential. It permits the actualization of the recuperative capacities of the child and permits the psyche an opportunity to mend itself. Just as many illnesses yield to rest, good food, and the reduction of outer stress, so a healthy emotional environment may encourage and support the health-striving tendencies within a child. There is a trend, then, toward actively enlisting the foster parents, wherever possible, in the treatment plan. The caseworker may instruct the foster parents to behave in such a manner, to respond in a particular way to the child, so as to reinforce and support casework efforts.

2. There has been a trend toward greater diversification of foster homes. In addition to the development of a variety of different kinds of group homes, there has been an attempt to develop specialized foster homes to offer care for special groups of children and youth: the mentally defective child, the physically handicapped child, the delinquent child, the unmarried mother.

Innovative efforts have been made to develop programs that are midway between full day care and full foster-family care. Five-day foster care is such a compromise (Loewe, Hanrahan, 1975). The child lives with his foster parents during the week but returns to his own home for weekends, holidays, and vacations. Such a facility is appropriate in those instances in which the biological parents are capable of part-time parenting. It maintains the child's relationship with his parents and their continuing responsibility for him, increasing the feasibility and probability of planning for the child's return home. This program is part of a general effort to provide a wider choice of foster-home arrangements to meet the variety of needs presented by different groups of children coming into foster care.

3. Foster parents have begun to organize nationally, and the First National

Conference of Foster Parents met in Chicago in 1971. By 1972 some two hundred foster-parent associations had been formed across the country (Rosendorf, 1972). In their local association meetings and at the national convention, foster parents expressed gratification at the support and help they received from social workers. Yet dissatisfactions with social workers' activities are also expressed by foster parents. Foster parents want more specific help in dealing with children's problems and often feel that workers are not equipped to offer such help. They tend to feel exploited by workers who visit irregularly and who are not readily available. They think that workers do not always frankly share with them the extent of the children's difficulties or of the biological parents' pathology. They are chagrined that workers often do not sufficiently credit the knowledge they have about the child, and they resent the agency's power to place and remove the child. Foster parents generally want more autonomy and the right to participate in plans and decisions regarding the child (Kennedy, 1970; Close, 1971).

Foster parents recommend that some kind of review procedure be established to handle disagreements between the foster home and the agency; that foster parenting be given a career line so that experienced foster parents are utilized in the training and supervision of foster-parent recruits; that, in addition to more adequate compensation, fringe benefits (social security, liability insurance, and so on) be provided (Fanshel, 1970; Reistroffer, 1968).

Specialized foster care, the increased availability of special education and training for foster parents, the development of an organizational superstructure by foster parents that sponsors publications, an annual convention, and lobbying and advocacy activities—all speak to the growing "professionalization" of foster parents.

The First National Conference of Foster Parents held in 1971 has been followed by annual conferences each year. The national conferences are well established by now and get a large and enthusiastic turnout. Foster parents are organized on the community level in action for foster-children programs, lobbying in support of legislative programs beneficial to foster care (Zellner, 1974). There is an annual national Action for Foster Children Week in May.

To some extent this trend has generated a problem of potential conflict between foster parents and child welfare agencies and between foster parents and biological parents. Foster parents have successfully organized to obtain greater rights in making decisions with regard to a child in their care beyond the usual informal discussion with their worker or case conference procedures. They have pressed for the right to notice and a hearing before a child is removed by the agency; to petition for the termination of rights of the parents of a child in their care; to priority in adoption if the child becomes free for adoption; and to be recognized as parties at child custody hearings. A foster-parent organization—Organization of Foster Families for Equality and Reform (OFFER)—scored a significant victory for such rights in the case of OFFER v. Dumpson when a federal court found that after one year in the foster home, a child could not be removed without the protection of an impartial hearing with the foster child, the foster parents, and the biological parents participating. This decision protected the rights of the child who did want to be returned to his biological parents and also provided due process for the foster parent contesting the agency's decision. In July 1977 the U.S. Supreme Court reversed the lower court decision and ruled that the agency could remove a child from a foster home without a hearing. A hearing must be granted only if the foster family requests it and only if the child has been in the foster home for at least eighteen months. However, the very fact that the case came to trial indicated the seriousness with which the foster parents' right to dispute agency decisions is regarded.

The most frequent reason for such disputes between foster parents and the agency revolves around the agency's removing a child for the purpose of placement for adoption. The agency may have found an adoptive home that they regard as a more desirable permanent placement than the foster family. In some cases where the decision to remove has been disputed, the parents were older, the foster family was a single-parent family, the foster family had three or more children of their own and childless couples were waiting, or the foster family needed a subsidy to adopt and, in accordance with subsidy legislation, an adoptive home that did not require subsidy was being given priority. Sometimes the foster home had been selected reluctantly because of pressure to provide a home for a child, but marital problems or questionable emotional stability precluded acceptance of the home for permanent adoptive care. In some instances, the agency has taken action to remove a black child from a white foster home in order to place the child in a black foster or adoptive home. The rights of the foster parent to retain the child, supported by the claim of psychological parenthood, have conflicted with the assertions by some members of the black community that the best place for a black child is in a black home, if one is available.

Currently, in response to a recognition of such potential conflict, many agencies provide clear prior notice in writing of the intent to remove the child, and others go beyond this and provide a hearing; some have a procedure for preremoval case-review appeals at the request of the foster parent. Another interesting procedure is the appointment of experienced social workers with child welfare experience from agencies other than the one involved in the dispute to act as neutral peer reviewers and decision makers (Albert, 1978).

In addition to the increased possibilities of conflict between foster parents and agencies resulting from the growing professionalization and organizational power of foster parents, there is a potential for conflict between foster parents and biological parents.

Previously the claims of the biological parent to the child were unquestionably preeminent. Now such blood ties compete with the bonds of affection that may have developed between foster parent and foster child as a result of daily care and concern over a period of time. Even the fit parent may be denied the return of his or her child if it is decided that the child, temporarily given up for foster care, now regards the foster parent as the psychological parent. Psychological parenthood is regarded as taking precedence over blood ties, and the rights of the child to continuity are regarded as having priority over the rights of the parents to the child.

There has been a series of court cases that indicate a tendency to shift the emphasis from the requirement that the court establish the biological parents' unfitness in terminating parental rights to an emphasis that requires the parent to prove that termination is not in the child's best interests. The child's entitlement to continuity in the established relationship with the foster parent and the foster parents investment in that relationship are given some priority over the biological parents' rights to have the child restored to them (Whitten, 1973; McCarty, 1974; Egginton, Hibbs, 1975–1976). Having established psychological parenthood, foster parents can legitimately claim that it is possibly damaging to the child to remove him for return to his own home despite the fact that his parents want him and can care for him. This "tug-of-love" conflict is clearly seen in the decision of a federal judge to permit the adoption of a seven-year-old boy by foster parents who had cared for him over a two-year period. The mother had originally accepted foster care for the child because she was handicapped by multiple sclerosis. Subsequently her illness improved to the point where she could care adequately for the child. At the time the mother requested the child's return, she was maintaining a viable, if marginal, home for her two older children. The judge refused the return and sanctioned the adoption on the basis of the foster parents' development of a relationship of psychological parenthood with the child and because of the "severely shortened life expectancy of the mother" (*Washington Star*, July 7, 1974). Biological parents can no longer regard foster parents as a helpful convenience; they may conceivably become a potential threat to the biological parents.

Although the needs of the individual child may be more clearly protected by such a shift, there is a possible danger to children generally in the insult to the integrity of foster care as an institution resulting from such a reorientation. The danger is that biological parents may become more hesitant to use the foster-care system if it involves the risk of losing the child. Alternative makeshift arrangements may be made for the temporary care of children in crisis situations because of anxieties associated with the use of the foster-care system. These arrangements might be damaging to the children generally.

Although the recognition of the foster parents' claims is responsive to the rights of the child and the foster parents, it represents a potential danger. In many subtle ways, foster parents can discourage visiting on the part of the biological parents and then point to the visiting pattern of the biological parents as evidence of disinterest in the child, justifying the termination of parental rights. Establishing "psychological parenthood" and alienating the child from the biological parent may become, for some, the procedure for increasing the probability of adoption of the child—a "back door" to adoption.

Along with growing concern about the rights of foster parents has been increasing efforts to protect the rights of biological parents. Ombudsman advocacy units have been established to act on appeals by biological parents against agency decisions. Most often the appeal was concerned with getting the child returned home or changes in visiting schedules (Citizens Committee for Children, 1975).

Protection of rights has also been extended to other groups involved with foster care. In response to a concern by native Americans about the disproportionate frequency of foster care placement of Indian children, Congress passed and the president signed an Indian Child Welfare Act in 1978. The law gave Indian tribes greater control over the disposition of Indian children. Placement with members of the child's tribe was to be given priority over placement with non-Indian families.

4. Because it is difficult for large public agencies to keep accurate track of children in foster care, efforts are being made to use computers to assure the responsible and continuous assignment of every child in care.

5. There is a trend toward increasing the interest in and the development of group foster homes, but there is neighborhood opposition to such facilities.

The New York Times (July 16, 1972) reported that "a plan to use a private house as a group home for nine children from New York City has thrown this middle-class mostly white neighborhood [in a city suburb] into an uproar." Neighborhood opposition is based not only on antipathy to lower-class, possibly disturbed, children, but also on the fact that many of the children to be placed in group homes might be black.

An attempt to establish a group foster home for retarded children in Scarsdale, a New York City suburb, also evoked considerable controversy (*New York Times*, July 22, 1978). In response, some communities are developing zoning regulations that require every area of a community to accept their fair share of responsibility for such homes. This action is meant to preclude the larger concentration of such homes in one section of a community, generally the more disadvantageous area where the neighborhood may have less political clout (see also pp. 614–615).

SUMMARY

Foster-family care is substitute care in which the role of the biological parent is implemented by another set of parents. Unlike other forms of substitute care—institutional child care and adoption—foster-family care is designed to be temporary and to offer the child care in a family setting. In general, children for whom foster-family care is appropriate are those who cannot be cared for in their own home, even if supportive and supplementary services are provided, and who can make use of and contribute to family life.

The children usually come from chronically deprived lower-class families facing crisis situations. Although most of the children are white, there is a disproportionate number of nonwhite children.

The situation that most frequently precipitates the need for short-term foster care is the illness of the mother. Problems in parental role implementation due to death, divorce, desertion, and inadequate income, manifested frequently in neglect and/or abuse, bring a sizable group of children into long-term care. The child's disturbed behavior or physical and mental handicaps may also give rise to the need for long-term care.

Although there are several different kinds of foster-family homes, the foster-family boarding home accounts for some 95 per cent of all foster-family placements.

Foster families must be recruited, evaluated, and ultimately selected for a particular child. Agencies operate a constant recruitment service, assisted by special recruiting drives. Relatively few of those who indicate interest in foster-family care ultimately become foster parents. Withdrawal of application accounts for the greatest percentage of such attrition. Rigorous, selective standards are of considerably less importance in eliminating applicants.

Foster families tend to come from the upper-lower- and the lower-middle-class segments of the community. The mothers in such families regard child rearing as an important role, one from which they derive considerable satisfaction.

Casework with the biological parents is directed toward helping them with the feelings that are likely to accompany placement: guilt, shame, anxiety, sadness, and loneliness. It is also designed to help them keep intact a relationship with the child and to resolve their problems in order to permit the child to return home.

Casework with the child is directed toward helping him make the physical and emotional separation from his own home and the transition to the foster home. It is also designed to help him deal with his fears of abandonment, his feeling of rejection, his hostility toward his own parents, and his anxiety over acceptance by his foster parents. It also helps him to resolve the conflict of feeling toward his own parents and his foster parents and to define his role as a foster child.

Casework with the foster parents is directed toward preparing them for placement, helping them to accept the child, and helping them with problems regarding the child's adjustment in the home. It is also designed to help them in their relationship with the child's biological parents and to deal with the differences between the role of foster parent and that of biological parent. Group methods have also been used to supplement and support the casework approach in working with foster parents.

Evaluation studies of foster-family care indicate that many children who have experienced such care grow up satisfactorily.

The following problems were identified as being of current concern:

1. Foster-family care tends to become permanent for a sizable number of children.
2. A shortage of trained personnel and the pathology in the families from which the foster children come make the rehabilitation of the natural families unlikely.
3. Although many children remain in substitute care, their legal ties to their biological parents make them unavailable for adoption.
4. There is great difficulty in recruiting a sufficiently large number of desirable foster homes.
5. Board payments for foster care are inadequate.
6. There is no clear-cut definition of the foster parents' relationship to the agency, so that the parents are sometimes regarded as clients, sometimes as colleagues, sometimes as paid employees.
7. Personnel shortages and personnel turnover affect the recruitment of foster parents and the continuity of caseworker–child relationships.

Among the trends identified were the following:

1. An increase in the rate of children coming into foster care and increased public-welfare responsibility for such placements.
2. Greater pathology in the families placing children and in the children placed.
3. More explicit recognition of the potential of the foster family as a treatment resource, in addition to its potential as a resource for child care.
4. A greater diversification of foster-family homes and of the groups of children for whom such a resource might be used.
5. A greater professionalization of the foster-parent role, the increased organizational power of foster-parent groups, and the growing possi-

bilities of conflict between foster parents and agencies and foster parents and biological parents.

6. Computerization of agency case-load data.
7. Increased concern with zoning changes to accommodate to the needs of more community-based group-home facilities.

BIBLIOGRAPHY

ADAMSON, GILVARY. *The Caretakers*. London, England: Bookstall Publishers, 1973.

ALBERT, MARILYN. "Preremoval Appeal Procedures in Foster Family Care: A Connecticut Example." *Child Welfare*, 57, 5 (May 1978), 285–297.

ALDGATE, JANE. "The Child in Care and His Parents." *Adoption and Fostering*, 84 (No. 2, 1976), 29–39.

ALDRIDGE, MARTHA, and PATRICIA W. CAUTLEY. "The Importance of Worker Availability in the Functioning of New Foster Homes." *Child Welfare*, 54 (June 1975), 444–453.

AMBINDER, WALTER, et al. "Role Phenomena and Foster Care for Disturbed Children." *American Journal of Orthopsychiatry*, 32 (January 1962).

——, and DOUGLAS SARGENT. "Foster Parents' Techniques of Management of Preadolescent Boys, Deviant Behavior." *Child Welfare*, 44 (February 1965).

AMERICAN ACADEMY OF CHILD PSYCHIATRY. *Supportive Care, Custody Placement and Adoption of Indian Children*. Bottle Hollow, Utah: American Academy of Child Psychiatry Conference, April 1977.

AMERICAN CIVIL LIBERTIES UNION. "Conflict of Rights Among Children, Foster Parents and the State." Children's Rights Report (January, February, March 1977).

ANNUAL REPORT. New York: Lower East Side Family Union, October 1977.

APPLEBERG, ESTHER. *A Foster Family Workshop Report*. New York: Wurzweiler School of Social Work, Yeshiva University, 1968.

——. "The Dependent Child and the Changing Worker." *Child Welfare*, 48, 7 (July 1969), 407–412.

ARKAVA, MORTON L., and DAVID N. MUELLER. "Components of Foster Care for Handicapped Children." *Child Welfare*, 57, 6 (June 1978), 339–345.

ATHERTON, CHARLES F. "Acting Decisively in Foster Care." *Social Work*, 19 (November 1974), 658–659.

BABCOCK, CHARLOTTE. "Some Psychodynamic Factors in Foster Parenthood—Parts I and II." *Child Welfare*, 44, 9, 10 (November, December 1965).

BARKER, PHILIP, CAROLE BUFFE, and RUTH ZERETSKY. "Providing a Family Alternative for the Disturbed Child." *Child Welfare*, 57, 6 (June 1978), 373–738.

BAUER, JOHN E., and WARREN HEINKE. "Treatment Family Care Homes for Disturbed Foster Children." *Child Welfare*, 45 (July-August 1976), 478–490.

BAYLOR, EDITH, and ELIO MONACHESI. *The Rehabilitation of Children*. New York: Harper & Row, Publishers, 1939.

BERNSTEIN, BLANCHE, DONALD A. SNIDER, and WILLIAM MEEZIN. *Foster Care Needs and Alternatives to Placement—A Projection 1975–1985*. New York: New York State Board of Social Welfare, November 1975.

BOEHM, BERNICE. *Deterrents to the Adoption of Children in Foster Care*. New York: Child Welfare League of America, 1958.

BOWLBY, JOHN. *Maternal Care and Mental Health*. Geneva: World Health Organization, 1951.

BOYD, LAWRENCE H., and LINDA L. REMY. "Is Foster-Parent Training Worthwhile?" *Social Service Review* (June 1978), 275–296.

BREMNER, ROBERT H. *Children and Youth in America, A Documentary History,* Vol. 1: *1600–1865.* Cambridge, Mass.: Harvard University Press, 1970.

BRYCE, MARTIN, and ROGER EHLERT. "144 Foster Children." *Child Welfare,* **50,** 9 (November 1974), 499–503.

BURT, MARVIN, and RALPH R. BALYEAT. *A Comprehensive Emergency Services System for Neglected and Abused Children.* New York: Vantage Press, 1977.

BUSH, MALCOLM, ANDREW C. GORDON, and ROBERT LE BAILLY. "Evaluating Child Welfare Services: A Contribution from Clients." *Social Service Review,* **51** (September 1977), 491–501.

CANNING, REBECCA. "School Experiences of Foster Children." *Child Welfare,* **53** (November 1974), 582–587.

CATALANO, ROBERT. *Research Report on New York State Foster Care.* Albany, N.Y.: State Department of Social Services, October 1974.

CAUTLEY, PATRICIA W., *et al. Successful Foster Homes—An Exploratory Study of Their Characteristics.* Madison: Wisconsin Department of Public Welfare, June 1966.

———, and DIANE P. LICHTENSTEIN. *Manual for Homefinders—The Selection of Foster Parents.* Madison: University of Wisconsin Extension, Center for Social Services, 1974.

———, and MARTHA ALDRIDGE. "Predicting Success for New Foster Parents." *Social Work,* **20,** 1 (January 1975), 48–53.

CENTER FOR SOCIAL RESEARCH AND DEVELOPMENT. *Indian Child Welfare: A State of the Field Study.* Denver: University of Denver, Center for Social Research and Development, 1976.

CHAPPELL, BARBARA. "One Agency's Periodic Review in Foster Care—The South Carolina Story." *Child Welfare,* **54** (July 1975), 477–486.

CHARNLEY, JEAN. *The Art of Child Placement.* Minneapolis: University of Minnesota Press, 1955.

CHESTANG, LEON, and IRMGARD HEYMANN. "Reducing the Length of Foster Care." *Social Work,* **18** (January 1973), 88–92.

CHILD WELFARE LEAGUE OF AMERICA. *Standards for Foster Family Care.* New York, 1959.

CHILDREN'S DEFENSE FUND. *Children Without Homes.* Washington, D.C.: Children's Defense Fund, 1978.

CITIZENS COMMITTEE FOR CHILDREN OF NEW YORK CITY. THE PARENTS' RIGHTS UNIT. *Responding to Grievances of Parents with Children in Foster Care.* New York: Citizens Committee, 1978.

CLABURN, W. EUGENE. *Some Informal Notes on the Comptroller's Recent Audit of New York City Foster Care.* Trenton, N.J.: State Department of Human Services, June 13, 1977.

———, and STEPHAN MAGURA. *Foster Care Case Review in New Jersey: An Evaluation of Its Implementation and Effects.* Trenton, N.J.: State of New Jersey Foster Care Research Project, 1977.

———, STEPHEN MAGURA, and SUSAN P. CHIZECK. "Case Reopening: An Emerging Issue in Child Welfare Services." *Child Welfare,* **56** (December 1977), 655–663.

———, STEPHAN MAGURA, and WILLIAM RESNICK. "Periodic Review of Foster Care: A Brief National Assessment." *Child Welfare,* **55** (June 1976), 395–405.

CLOSE, KATHRYN. "An Encounter with Foster Parents." *Children,* **18,** 4 (July–August 1971), 138–142.

COLVIN, R. "Toward the Development of a Foster Parent Attitude Test," in *Quantitative Approaches to Parent Selection.* New York: Child Welfare League of America, January 1962

COWAN, EDWINA, and EVA STOUT. "A Comparative Study of the Adjustment Made by Foster Children After Complete and Partial Breaks in Continuity of Home Environment." *American Journal of Orthopsychiatry,* **9** (1939).

COYNE, ANN. "Techniques for Recruiting Foster Homes for Mentally Retarded Children." *Child Welfare,* **57,** 2 (February 1978), 123–131.

CULLY, JAMES D., DENIS F. HEALY, BARBARA H. SETTLES, and JUDITH VAN NAME. "Public Payments for Foster Care." *Social Work,* **22** (May 1977), 219–233.

———, BARBARA H. SETTLES, and JUDITH B. VAN NAME. *Understanding and Measuring the Cost of Foster Care.* Newark: University of Delaware, 1975.

———, JUDITH B. VAN NAME, and BARBARA H. SETTLES. "Measuring the Indirect Costs of Child Care." *Public Welfare,* **34** (Fall 1976), 6–16.

DAVIDS, LEO. *The Foster Father Role.* Unpublished Ph.D. thesis. New York University, New York, 1968.

DAVIES, LINDA S., and DAVID BLAND. "The Use of Foster Parents as Role Models for Parents." *Child Welfare,* **57,** 6 (June 1978), 580–586.

DE COCQ, GUSTAVE. *The Withdrawal of Foster Parent Applicants.* San Francisco: United Community Fund of San Francisco, June 1962.

DE JONG, GERBER, and C. SPECHT. "Setting Foster Care Rates. I: Basic Considerations; II: Special Cases." *Public Welfare,* **33** (Fall 1975), 37–46.

DELGADO, MELVIN. "A Hispanic Foster Parents Program." *Child Welfare,* **57,** 7 (July–August, 1976), 428–431.

DEVIZIA, JOSEPH. "Success in a Foster Home Program for Mentally Retarded Children." *Child Welfare,* **53** (February 1974), 121–125.

DICK, KENNETH. "What People Think About Foster Care." *Children* (March–April 1961).

DINGMAN, HARVEY F., et al. "Prediction of Child-Rearing Attitude." *Child Welfare,* **41** (1962).

DINNAGE, ROSEMARY, et al. *Foster Home Care—Facts and Fallacies.* London: Longman Group Ltd., 1967.

EGGINTON, MARGARET L., and RICHARD E. HIBBS. "Termination of Parental Rights in Adoption Cases: Focusing on the Child." *Journal of Family Law,* **14** (1975–1976), 547–580.

EISENBERG, LEON. "Deprivation and Foster Care." *Journal of American Academy of Child Psychiatry,* **4** (1965), 243–248.

EMLEN, ARTHUR. *Barriers to Planning for Children in Foster Care,* Vol. 1. Portland, Oregon: Regional Research Institute for Human Services, Portland State University, 1976.

———, et al. *Overcoming Barriers to Planning for Children in Foster Care.* Portland, Ore: Regional Research Institute for Human Services, Portland State University, 1977.

FANSHEL, DAVID. "Parental Failure and Consequences for Children—The Drug Abusing Mother Whose Children are in Foster Care." *American Journal of Public Health,* **65** (June 1975), 604–612.

———. "Specialization Within the Foster Parent Role. I: Difference Between Foster Parents of Infants and Foster Parents of Older Children." *Child Welfare,* **40** (March 1961a).

———. "Studying the Role Performance of Foster Parents." *Social Work,* **6** (January 1961b).

———. *Foster Parenthood—A Role Analysis.* Minneapolis: University of Minnesota Press, 1966.

———. "Role of Foster Parents in the Future," in *Foster Care in Question.* Ed. by Helen D. Stone. New York: Child Welfare League of America, 1970.

———. "The Exit of Children from Foster Care: An Interim Research Report." *Child Welfare*, **50**, 2 (February 1971), 65–81.

———. "Children Discharged from Foster Care in New York City: Where to—When— At What Age." *Child Welfare*, **57**, 11 (September–October 1978), 467–483.

———. "Preschoolers Entering Foster Care in New York City: The Need to Stress Plans for Permanency." *Child Welfare*, **58** (February 1979), 67–87.

———. *Computerized Information for Child Welfare: Foster Children and Their Foster Parents*. New York: Columbia University School of Social Work, March 1979.

———. "Parental Visiting of Children in Foster Care: Key to Discharge." *Social Service Review*, **49** (December 1975b), 493–514.

———. "Parental Visiting of Foster Children: A Computerized Study." *Social Work Research and Abstracts*, **1** (Fall 1977), 2–10.

———. "Status Changes of Children in Foster Care. Final Results of the Columbia University Longitudinal Study." *Child Welfare*, **55** (March 1976b), 143–171.

———. "Foster Parenthood: A Replication and Extension of Prior Studies." New York: Child Welfare Research Program, School of Social Work, Columbia University, April 1971. Mimeo.

———, and JOHN GRUNDY. *Computerized Data for Children in Foster Care: First Analysis from a Management Information Service in New York City*. New York: Child Welfare Information Service, November 1975.

———, and H. MAAS. "Factorial Dimensions of the Characteristics of Children in Placements and Their Families." *Child Development*, **33** (1962).

———, and EUGENE B. SHINN. *Dollars and Sense in the Foster Care of Children: A Look at Cost Factors*. New York: Child Welfare League of America, 1972.

———, and EUGENE B. SHINN. *Children in Foster Care: A Longitudinal Investigation*. New York: Columbia University Press, 1978.

FELLNER, IRVING, and CHARLES SOLOMON. "Achieving Permanent Solutions for Children in Foster Home Care." *Child Welfare*, **42** (March 1973), 178–187.

FERGUSON, THOMAS. *Children in Care and After*. New York: Oxford University Press, 1966.

FESTINGER, TRUDY B. "Placement Agreements with Boarding Homes: A Survey." *Child Welfare*, **53**, 10 (December 1974), 643–652.

———. "The Impact of the New York Court Review of Children in Foster Care: A Follow Up Report." *Child Welfare*, **55** (September–October 1976), 516–544.

———. "The New York Court Review of Children in Foster Care." *Child Welfare*, **54** (April 1975), 211–245.

FOLKS, HOMER. *The Care of the Destitute, Neglected, and Delinquent Children*. New York: The Macmillan Company, 1902.

FREELING, NELSON W., STANLEY KISSEL, and LOUIS SARGENT. "Parenting for Foster Parents." *Child Psychiatry and Human Development* (Summer 1976), 244–250.

FREEMAN, HENRY. "Foster Home Care for Mentally Retarded Children: Can It Work?" *Child Welfare* **57**, 2 (February 1978), 113–121.

FREUD, ANNA, JOSEPH GOLDSTEIN, and ALBERT SOLNIT. *Beyond the Best Interests of the Child*. New York: The Free Press, 1973.

GALAWAY, B. "Contracting: A Means of Clarifying Roles in Foster Family Services." *Children Today*, **5** (1976), 20–23.

GAMBRILL, EILEEN D. "Facilitating Decision Making in Foster Care." *Social Service Review*, **5** (September 1977), 502–513.

GAMBRILL, EILEEN D., and WILTSE, KERMIT T. "Foster Care: Prescriptions for Change." *Public Welfare*, **32** (Summer 1974), pp. 39–47.

————, and KERMIT T. WILTSE. "Contracts and Outcome in Foster Care." *Social Work,* **22** (March 1977), 148–149.

————. "Foster Care: The Use of Contracts." *Public Welfare,* **32** (Fall 1974), 20–25.

GEORGE, VICTOR. *Foster Care: Theory and Practice.* London: Kegan Paul, Trench, Trubner & Co., 1970.

GIL, DAVID. "Developing Routine Follow-up Procedures for Child Welfare Services." *Child Welfare,* **43** (May 1964).

GLASSBERG, EUDICE. "Are Foster Homes Hard to Find?" *Child Welfare,* **44** (October 1965).

GLICKMAN, ESTHER. *Child Placement Through Clinically Oriented Casework.* New York: Columbia University Press, 1957.

GLOVER, E. ELIZABETH. "Is Child-Caring Important?" *Child Welfare,* **42** (February 1964).

GOLDSTEIN, HARRIET. "Providing Services to Children in Their Own Homes," *Children Today,* 2 (July–August 1973), pp. 2–7.

————, and ADOLINE DALL. "Group Learning for Foster Parents. I: In a Voluntary Agency; II: In a Public Agency." *Children,* **14,** 5 (September–October 1967).

GORDON, HENRIETTA. *Casework Services for Children.* Boston: Houghton Mifflin Company, 1956.

GOTTESFELD, HARRY. *In Loco Parentis—A Study of Perceived Role Values in Foster Home Care.* New York: Jewish Child Care Association of New York, 1970.

GRAY, P. G., and E. A. PARR. *Children in Care and the Recruitment of Foster Parents.* London: Social Survey, 1957.

GREENBERG, ARTHUR. "Agency Owned and Operated Group Foster Home for Adolescents." *Child Welfare,* **42** (April 1963).

GROSS, P., and F. BUSSARD. "A Group Method for Finding and Developing Foster Homes." *Child Welfare,* **55,** 9 (November 1970), 521–524.

GRUBER, ALAN R. *A Study of Children, Their Biological and Foster Parents.* Springfield, Mass.: Governor's Commission on Adoption & Foster Care, 1973.

————. *Children in Foster Care—Destitute, Neglected, Betrayed.* New York: Human Sciences Press, 1978.

GUERNEY, LOUISE F. *Foster Parent Training Prospect.* University Park, Penna: 1976.

GULA, MARTIN. *Agency-Operated Group Homes.* Washington, D.C.: Government Printing Office, 1964.

HANWELL, ALBERT F., et al. *A Guide for Foster Parent Group Education.* Boston: Boston College Graduate School of Social Work, 1969.

HARGRAVE, VIVIAN; JOAN SHIREMAN; and PETER CONNOR. *Where Love and Need Are One.* Chicago: Illinois Department of Social Services, 1975.

HARING, BARBARA L. *1975 Census of Requests for Child Welfare Services.* New York: Child Welfare League of America, September 1975.

HART, HASTING H. "Annual Report," in *Proceedings of the National Conference of Charities and Correction.* Boston: George H. Ellis, 1884.

HEINRITZ, GRETCHEN, and LOUISE A. FREY. *Foster Care: How to Develop an Educational Program for Staff or Foster Parents.* Boston: Boston University School of Social Work, 1975.

HERSTEIN, NORMAN. "The Replacement of Children from Foster Homes." *Child Welfare,* **36** (July 1957).

HILL, ESTHER. "Is Foster Care the Answer?" *Public Welfare,* **15** (April 1957).

HOLMAN, ROBERT. *Trading in Children: A Study of Private Fostering.* London, England: Routledge & Kegan Paul, 1973.

————. "The Place of Fostering in Social Work." *British Journal of Social Work,* **5** (Spring 1975), 3–29.

HUNT, ELIZABETH. "Foster Care for Delinquent Girls." *Children,* 19 (September–October 1962).

ISHISAKA, HIDEKI. "American Indians and Foster Care: Cultural Factors and Separation." *Child Welfare,* 57, 5 (May 1978), 299–307.

JACOBSON, ELINOR, and COCKERUM, JOANNE. "As Foster Children See It." *Children Today,* 5 (November–December 1976), pp. 32–36.

JAFFEE, BENSON, and DRAZA KLINE. *New Payment Pattern and the Foster Parent Role.* New York: Child Welfare League of America, 1970.

JENKINS, RACHEL. "The Needs of Foster Parents." *Case Conference,* 11 (January 1965).

JENKINS, SHIRLEY. "Duration of Foster Care—Some Relevant Antecedent Variables." *Child Welfare,* 46, 8 (October 1967a), 450–456.

———. "Filial Deprivation in Parents of Children in Foster Care." *Children,* 14, 1 (January–February 1967), 8–12.

———. "Separation Experiences of Parents Whose Children Are in Foster Care." *Child Welfare,* 48, 6 (June 1969), 334–341.

———, and ELAINE NORMAN. *Filial Deprivation and Foster Care.* New York: Columbia University Press, 1972.

JENKINS, SHIRLEY, and SAUBER, MIGNON. *Paths to Child Placement.* New York: Community Council of Greater New York, 1966.

JONES, EVAN O. "A Study of Those Who Cease to Foster," *British Journal of Social Work,* 5 (Spring 1975), pp. 31–41.

JONES, MARY, RENEE NEUMAN and ANNE W. SHYNE. *A Second Chance for Families: Evaluation of a Program to Reduce Foster Care.* New York: Child Welfare League of America, 1976.

JOSSELYN, IRENE. "Evaluating Motives of Foster Parents." *Child Welfare,* 31 (February 1952).

JULIUSBERGER, ERIKA. *Phases of Adjustment in a Typical Foster Home Placement.* New York: Jewish Child Care Association of New York, 1961.

KADUSHIN, ALFRED. "The Legally Adoptable, Unadopted Child." *Child Welfare,* 37 (December 1958), pp. 19–25.

———. "Children in Foster Families and Institutions" in *Social Service Research: Review of Studies.* Ed. by Henry Maas. New York: National Association of Social Workers, 1978.

KASTELL, JEAN. *Casework in Child Care.* London: Kegan Paul, Trench, Trubner & Co., 1962.

KENNEDY, RUBY. "A Foster Parent Looks at Foster Care," in *Foster Care in Question.* Ed. by Helen D. Stone. New York: Child Welfare League of America, 1970.

KENT, JAMES T. "A Follow-up Study of Abused Children." *Journal of Pediatric Psychology,* 1 (Spring 1976), 25–31.

KINNY, JILL, BARBARA MADSEN, THOMAS FLEMING, and DAVID A. ITAAPALA. "Home Builders: Keeping Families Together." *Journal of Consulting and Clinical Psychology,* 45 (1977), 667–73.

KINTER, RICHARD H., and HERBERT OTTO. "The Family Strength Concept and Foster Care Selection." *Child Welfare,* 43 (July 1964).

KLINE, DRAZA, and HELEN OVERSTREET. *Casework with Foster Parents.* New York: Child Welfare League of America, 1956.

———, HELEN OVERSTREET, and MARY FORBUSH. *Foster Care of Children—Nurture and Treatment.* New York: Columbia University Press, 1972.

KRAUS, JONATHAN. "Predicting Success of Foster Placements for School-Age Children." *Social Work* (January 1971), 63–71.

LAHTI, JANET, *et al. A Follow-up Study of the Oregon Project.* Portland, Ore.: Regional Research Institute for Human Services, Portland State University, August 1978.

LANGSAM, MIRIAM. *Children West*, Logmark ed. Madison: The State Historical Society of Wisconsin, 1964.

LEE, JUDITH. "Group Work with Mentally Retarded Foster Adolescents." *Social Casework* (March 1977), 164–173.

LEWIS, MARY. "Long-Time and Temporary Placement of Children," in *Selected Papers in Casework*. Raleigh, N.C.: Health Publications Institute, 1951.

LINDBERG, DWAINE, and ANNE WOSREK. "The Use of Family Sessions in Foster Home Care." *Social Casework*, **44** (March 1963).

LINDHOLM, BYRON, and JOHN TOULIATOS. "Characteristics of Foster Families." *Social Thought*, **5**, 1 (Winter 1978), 45–56.

———. "The Art of Being a Foster Parent." *Child Welfare*, **57**, 1 (January 1978), 3–12.

LITTNER, NER. *Some Traumatic Effects of Separation and Placement*. New York: Child Welfare League of America, October 1950.

———. "The Importance of the Natural Parents to the Child in Placement," in *Preliminary Conference Report First National Conference of Foster Parents*. Publication No. 72-5. Washington, D.C.: Department of Health, Education, and Welfare, 1971.

LOEWE, BESSIE, and THOMAS E. HANRAHAN. "Five-Day Foster Care." *Child Welfare*, **54** (January 1975), pp. 7–18.

MAAS, HENRY. "Highlights of the Foster Care Project: Introduction." *Child Welfare*, **38** (July 1959).

———. "Children in Long-term Foster Care." *Child Welfare*, **48**, 6 (June 1969), 321–333.

———, and RICHARD ENGLER. *Children in Need of Parents*. New York: Columbia University Press, 1959.

MacDONALD, MARY, and MARJORIE FERGUSON. "Selecting Foster Parents: An Essay Review." *Social Service Review* (September 1964).

MADISON, BERNICE, and MICHAEL SCHAPIRO. "Long-term Foster Family Care: What Is Its Potential for Minority-Group Children?" *Public Welfare*, **27** (April 1969), 167–194.

MANDELL, BETTY R. *Where Are the Children?* Lexington, Mass.: Lexington Books, D. C. Heath Co., 1973.

MARR, PAM. *Introduction to Foster Parenting*, Vols. 1, 2. Manhattan: Kansas State University, Department of Family and Child Development, 1976.

McADAMS, MRS. "The Parent in the Shadows." *Child Welfare*, **51**, 1 (January 1972), 51–55.

McCARTY, DAVID C. "The Foster Parents' Dilemma: 'Who Can I Turn to When Somebody Needs Me?'" *San Diego Law Review*, **11**, 2 (February 1974), 376–414.

McCOY, JACQUELINE. "The Application of Role Concept to Foster Parenthood." *Social Casework*, **43** (May 1962a).

McWHINNIE, ALEXINA. "Support for Foster Parents." *Adoption and Fostering*, **92**, 2 (1978), 15–21.

MEIER, ELIZABETH G. *Former Foster Children as Adult Citizens*. Unpublished Ph.D. thesis, Columbia University, New York, April 1962.

MILLER, CLARA. "The Agency Owned Foster Home." *Child Welfare*, **33** (November 1954).

MILLS, ROBERT B., *et al.* "Introducing Foster Mother Training Groups in a Voluntary Child Welfare Agency." *Child Welfare*, **46**, 10 (December 1967).

MOORE, PAULENE M. "Foster Family Care for Visually Impaired Children." *Children Today* (July–August 1976), 11–15.

MULREY, J. M. "The Care of Destitute and Neglected Children—Report of One Committee." *National Conference of Charities and Correction, 1899.* Boston: George Ellis, 1900.

MURPHY, H. B. M. *Foster Home Variables and Adult Outcome.* Mimeo. 1964.

———. "Natural Family Pointers to Foster Care Outcome." *Mental Hygiene,* 48 (July 1964).

———. "Predicting Duration of Foster Care." *Child Welfare,* 47, 2 (February 1968), 76–84.

NAPIER, HARRY. "Success and Failure in Foster Care." *British Journal of Social Work,* 2, 2 (Summer 1972), 187–203.

NATIONAL COMMISSION FOR CHILDREN IN NEED OF PARENTS. *Who Knows? Who Cares? Forgotten Children in Foster Care.* New York: National Commission for Children, 1979.

NATIONAL CENTER FOR SOCIAL STATISTICS. *Children Served by Public Welfare Agencies and Voluntary Child Welfare Agencies and Institutions, March 1972.* Washington, D.C.: Government Printing Office, January 1974.

———. *Children Served by Public Welfare Agencies and Voluntary Child Welfare Agencies and Institutions, March 1975.* Washington, D.C.: Government Printing Office, March 1976.

NAUGHTON, FRANCIS X. "Foster Home Placement as an Adjunct to Treatment." *Social Casework,* 38 (1957).

NEW YORK CITY DEPARTMENT OF SOCIAL SERVICES. *The Parents' Handbook—A Guide for Parents of Children in Foster Care.* New York City: Department of Social Services, January 1977.

O'REGAN, GERARD W. "Foster Family Care for Children with Mental Retardation." *Children Today,* 3 (January–February 1974), 20–22.

O'ROURKE, ALICE M. "The Psychological Characteristics of Mothers Whose Children Are in Foster Boarding Home Care Compared with Mothers Whose Children Are at Home with Them." Unpublished Ph.D. thesis, National Catholic School of Social Service, Catholic University of America, 1976.

OUGHELTREE, CORNELIA. *Finding Foster Homes.* New York: Child Welfare League of America, 1957.

PALMER, SALLY. *Children in Long-term Care: Their Experiences and Progress.* Canada: Family and Children's Services of London & Middlesex, August 1976.

PARKER, ROY. *Decision in Child Care.* London: George Allen & Unwin, Ltd., 1966.

PAUL, SISTER MARY. *Criteria for Foster Placement and Alternatives to Foster Care.* Albany: New York State Board of Social Welfare, May 1975.

PAULOS, SUSAN. *Foster Care Study—Factors Associated with Placement Stability.* Vancouver, B.C.: Children and Society, December 1972.

PAULSON, MORRIS J., SYLVIA GROSSMAN, and GARY SHAPIRO. "Child Rearing Attitudes of Foster Home Mothers." *Journal of Community Psychology,* 2 (January 1974), 11–14.

PENN, JOHN V. "A Model for Training Foster Parents in Behavior Modification Techniques." *Child Welfare,* 57, 3 (March 1978), 175–180.

PETERSEN, JAMES, and A. DEAN PIERCE. "Socioeconomic Characteristics of Foster Parents." *Child Welfare,* 53 (May 1974), 295–304.

PHILLIPS, MICHAEL H., ANN W. SHYNE, EDWARD A. SHERMAN, and BARBARA L. HARING. *Factors Associated with Placement Decisions in Child Welfare.* New York: Child Welfare League of America, 1971.

———, et al. *A Model for Intake Decisions in Child Welfare.* New York: Child Welfare League of America, 1972.

———. *Permanent Planning for Children in Foster Care: A Handbook for Social Workers.* Portland, Ore.: Regional Research Institute for Human Services, Portland State University, March 1977.

————. "Permanent Planning for Foster Children." *Children Today,* 5 (November–December 1976), 22–25.

POLIER, SHAD. "Amendments to New York's Adoption Law–the Permanently Neglected Child." *Child Welfare,* 38 (July 1959).

RADINSKY, ELIZABETH, *et al.* "Recruiting and Serving Foster Parents." *Child Welfare,* 42 (January 1963).

RAPP, CHARLES A. and JOHN POERTNER. "Reducing Foster Care: Critical Factors and Administrative Strategies." *Administration in Social Work,* 2 (Fall 1978), 335–346.

REGIONAL INSTITUTE OF SOCIAL WELFARE RESEARCH. *Barriers to Planning for Children in Foster Care.* Portland, Ore.: Portland State University, February 1976.

REISTROFFER, MARY. "A University Extension Course for Foster Parents." *Children,* 15 1 (January–February 1968).

————. "Participation of Foster Parents in Decision-Making–The Concept of Collegiality." *Child Welfare,* 41, 1 (January 1972).

ROBERTS, V. K. "An Experiment in Group Work with Foster Parents." *Case Conference,* 9 (November 1962).

ROSENBLUM, BARBARA. *Foster Homes for Adolescents.* Hamilton, Ont.: Children's Aid Society of Hamilton-Wentworth, 1977.

ROSENDORF, SIDNEY. "Joining Together to Help Foster Children–Foster Parents Form a Natural Association." *Children Today,* 1, 4 (July–August 1972), 2–7.

ROTHSCHILD, ANN M. "An Agency Evaluates Its Foster Home Study." *Child Welfare,* 53 (January 1974), 42–50.

ROWE, DAVID C. "Attitudes, Social Class and the Quality of Foster Care." *Social Service Review,* 50 (September 1976), 506–514.

ROWE, JANE. "Fostering in the Seventies." *Adoption and Fostering,* 90, 4 (1977), 15–20.

ROWE, JEAN, and LYDIA LAMBERT. *Children Who Wait–A Study of Children Needing Substitute Families.* London, England: Association of British Adoption Agencies, 1973.

ROYSTER, EUGENE C. *Barriers to Foster Care in the Black Community.* Lincoln University, Lincoln University, Pa: Department of Sociology, Lincoln University, 1975.

RYAN, PATRICIA, BRUCE WARREN, and EMILY J. McFADDEN. *Course Outlines–Foster Parent Training Project.* Ypsilanti: Eastern Michigan University, April 1977.

SARASON, IRWIN. *A Guide for Foster Parents.* New York: Human Sciences Press, 1975.

SAUBER, MIGNON. "Preplacement Situations of Families: Data for Planning Services." *Child Welfare,* 46, 8 (October 1967), 443–449.

————, and SHIRLEY JENKINS. *Paths to Child Placement.* New York: Community Council of Greater New York, 1966.

————. *Child Care and the Family.* Occasional Papers on Social Administration No. 25. London: George Bell & Sons, Ltd., 1968.

SCHWARTZ, MIRIAM, and ISADORE KAPLAN. "Small Homes–Placement Choice for Adolescents." *Child Welfare,* 40 (November 1961).

SHAPIRO, DEBORAH. *Agencies and Foster Children.* New York: Columbia University Press, 1975.

————. "Agency Investment in Foster Care: A Study." *Social Work,* 17, 3 (July 1972), 20–28.

SHAW, MARTIN, and KATHRYN LEBANS. "Foster Parents Talking." *Adoption and Fostering,* 88, 2 (1977), 11–16.

SHERMAN, EDWARD, RENEE NEUMAN, and ANN W. SHYNE. *Children Adrift in Foster Care–A Study of Alternative Approaches.* New York: Child Welfare League of America, 1973.

SHINN, EUGENE B. *Is Placement Necessary? An Experimental Study of Agreement*

Among Caseworkers in Making Foster Care Decisions. Unpublished doctor of social work thesis. Columbia University, New York, 1968.

SHOSTAK, ALBERT L. "Staffing Patterns in Group Homes for Teenagers." *Child Welfare,* 57, 5 (May 1978), 309–319.

SHYNE, ANN. *The Need for Foster Care.* New York: Child Welfare League of America, 1969.

———, and ANITA W. SCHROEDER. *National Study of Social Services to Children and Their Families.* Rockville, Md.: Westat Inc., 1978.

SIMON, JULIAN L. "The Effect of Foster Care Payment Levels on the Number of Foster Children Given Homes." *Social Service Review,* 49 (September 1975), 405–411.

SLATER, EDWARD P., and WILLIAM HARRIS. "Therapy at Home." *Practice Digest,* 1 (1978), 20–21.

SLINGERLAND, W. H. *Child-Placing in Families.* New York: Russell Sage Foundation, 1919.

SMITH, MICHAEL J. "A Question about Parental Visiting and Foster Care." *Social Service Review* (September 1976), 522–523.

SOEFFING, MARYLANE. "Families for Handicapped Children: Foster and Adoptive Placement Programs." *Exceptional Children,* 41, 8 (May 1975), 537–543.

SPECHT, CAROL. "Selecting Foster Care Rates. II: Special Cases." *Public Welfare,* 33 (Fall 1975), 42–46.

STEIN, THEODORE J. "Early Intervention in Foster Care." *Public Welfare,* 34 (Spring 1976), 39–44.

———, and EILEEN GAMBRILL. *Decisionmaking in Foster Care—A Training Manual.* Berkeley, Calif.: University Extension Publications, 1976.

STEKETEE, JOHN P. "The CIP Story." *Juvenile Justice,* 28, 2 (May 1977), 4–11.

———. "Concern for Children in Placement—The CIP Story." *Child Welfare,* 57, 6 (June 1978), 387–393.

STONE, HELEN D. *Reflections on Foster Care—A Report of a National Survey of Attitudes and Practices.* New York: Child Welfare League of America, 1969.

SWINDELL, BERTHA E. "The Function and Role of the Natural Parent in the Foster Family Constellation." *Child Welfare,* 45 (February 1961).

SWIRE, MARGARET R., and FLORENCE KAVALER. "The Health Status of Foster Children." *Child Welfare,* 56 (December 1977), 635–650.

THIES, S. VAN S. *How Foster Children Turn Out.* New York: State Charities Aid Association, 1924.

———. "The Resolution of Object Loss Following Foster Home Placement." *Smith College Studies in Social Work,* 36, 3 (June 1967).

THOMAS, GEORGE. *A Community Oriented Evaluation of the Effectiveness of Child Caring Institutions.* Athens, Ga.: Regional Institute of Social Welfare Research, 1975a.

———, LEONARD POLLAND. ROBERT BRANSFORD, and SHRIKANT PARCHURE. *Supply and Demand for Child Foster Family Care in the Southeast.* Athens, Ga.: Regional Institute of Social Welfare Research, January 1977.

THORPE, ROSAMUNDE. "Mum and Mrs. So and So." *Social Work Today,* 4 (February 1974), 691–695.

THURSTON, HENRY W. *The Dependent Child.* New York: Columbia University Press, 1930.

TINKER, KATHERINE. "Do Children in Foster Care Outgrow Behavior Problems?" *Minnesota Welfare,* 8, 4 (October 1952c).

———. "Children in Foster Care Who Have Outgrown Problems." *Minnesota Welfare,* 8, 5 (November 1952a).

———. "Children in Foster Care Who Remained Disturbed." *Minnesota Welfare,* 8, 6 (December 1952b).

TIZARD, BARBARA, and ANNE JOSEPH. "Today's Foundlings." *New Society,* 35, No. 418 (October 1970), pp. 584–585.

TOULIATOS, JOHN, and BYRON W. LINDHOLM. "Development of a Scale Measuring Potential for Foster Parenthood." *Psychological Reports,* 40 (1977), 1190.

TRASLER, GORDON. *In Place of Parents.* New York: Humanities Press, 1960.

U.S. DEPARTMENT OF HEALTH, EDUCATION, AND WELFARE. *Child Welfare Services. How They Help Children and Their Parents.* Washington, D.C.: Government Printing Office, 1957.

———. *Children Served by Public Welfare Agencies and Voluntary Child Welfare Agencies and Institutions. March 1972.* Washington, D.C.: National Center for Social Statistics, March 1974.

U.S. OFFICE OF THE COMPTROLLER GENERAL. *Children in Foster Care Institutions— Steps Government Can Take to Improve Their Care.* Washington, D.C.: Government Printing Office, February 1977.

VAN DER WAALS, PAULER. "Former Foster Children Reflect on Their Childhood." *Children,* 7 (January–February 1960).

VAN NAME, JUDITH B., BARBARA M. SETTLES, and JAMES D. CULLY. "Measuring the Cost of Caring for a Child in Foster Care." *Child Welfare,* 56 (July 1977), 432–438.

VASALY, SHIRLEY M. *Foster Care in Five States: A Synthesis and Analysis of Studies from Arizona, California, Iowa, Massachusetts, and Vermont.* Washington, D.C.: Social Work Research Group, George Washington University, June 1976.

VICK, J. E. "Recruiting and Retaining Foster Homes." *Public Welfare,* 25, 3 (July 1967), 229–234.

WAKEFORD, JOHN. "Fostering—A Sociological Perspective." *British Journal of Sociology,* 14 (December 1963).

WEINBACH, ROBERT W., MARTHA JANE EDWARDS, and REBECCA F. LEVY. "Innovations in Group Services to Foster Parents: A Survey of Agencies." *Children Today* (January–February 1977), 18–20.

WEINSTEIN, EUGENE. *The Self-Image of the Foster Child.* New York: Russell Sage Foundation, 1960.

WHITTEN, PATRICIA. "The Rights of Foster Parents to Children in Their Care." Chicago Kent Law Review 86 (1973), 86–112.

WILLIAMS, CAROL J. "Helping Parents to Help the Children in Placement." *Child Welfare,* 51 (May 1972), 297–303.

WILTSE, KERMIT T. "Decision Making Needs in Foster Care." *Children Today,* 5 (November–December 1976), 2–6.

———, and EILEEN D. GAMBRILL. "Foster Care, 1973: A Reappraisal." *Public Welfare,* 32 (Winter 1974a).

———. "Foster Care Plans and Alternatives." *Public Welfare,* 32 (Spring 1974b), 12–21.

WIRES, EMILY M. "Some Factors in the Worker-Foster Parent Relationship." *Child Welfare,* 33 (October 1954).

WOLINS, MARTIN. *Selecting Foster Parents.* New York: Columbia University Press, 1963.

YOUNG, DENNIS, and STEPHEN FINCH. *Foster Care and the Non-Profit Agencies.* Lexington, Mass.: D. C. Heath & Company, Lexington Press, 1977.

9 THE UNMARRIED MOTHER AND THE OUT-OF-WEDLOCK CHILD

INTRODUCTION

Children born out of wedlock account for some 90 per cent of adoptions by nonrelatives. Consequently many of the agencies that offer adoptive services also offer services to the unmarried mother. The discussion of adoption services in Chapter 10 is, then, logically preceded by a discussion of out-of-wedlock pregnancy and services to the unwed mother.

Aside from the relationship to adoption, the unmarried mother and the out-of-wedlock child present a situation in itself requiring the intervention of child welfare services. It is a parent–child relationship in which one of the significant roles, that of the father, is not covered, thus increasing the risk that the needs of the child will not be fully met. Consequently child welfare agencies offering adoptive and other services are heavily involved with the unmarried mother and the out-of-wedlock child.

Historical Background

The attitude toward illegitimacy is related to family structure. Negative attitudes toward illegitimacy are designed to protect the monogamous family and the associated marital ties. Polygamous societies make little of technical illegitimacy. The Christian attitude toward monogamy and extramarital sexuality resulted in the development of a more punitive attitude toward illegitimacy. Religious sanctions were reinforced by secular motives during the Middle Ages to solidify such an attitude. As Krause (1971) notes:

> It was natural that men, as legislators, would have limited their accidental offsprings' claims against them both economically and in terms of a family relationship, especially since the social status of the illegitimate mother often did not equal their own. Moreover, their legitimate wives had an interest in denying the illegitimate's claim on their husbands, since any such claim could be allowed only

at the expense of the legitimate family. Against these forces have stood only the illegitimate mother and the helpless child, and thus it is not surprising that our laws are inconsiderate of the child's interest.

Under English common law, the illegitimate child was "son of no one" (*filius nullius*) or "son of the people" (*filius populi*)—without name, without a right to support or inheritance. Yet the illegitimate child was not socially stigmatized in pre-Puritan England:

> until the sixteenth century bastardry had not been thought any great shame. Men took care of their bastards, were indeed often proud of them, and in many cases brought them home to their wives or mothers to be brought up. Children born out of wedlock were thus to be found growing up in their father's house with their half-brothers and sisters without a hint of disgrace either to themselves or to their natural parents [Pinchbeck, Hewitt, 1969, p. 201].

The gradual hardening of attitudes arose not only from concern for the sanctity of the family but perhaps, more significantly, from concern for the burden on the community posed by illegitimate children. Nobody was seriously concerned about the fourteen illegitimate children fathered by Charles II, but there was widespread concern about the indigent illegitimate child.

The Poor Law Act of 1576

> made the first legislative provision for illegitimate children so many of whom were abandoned by their parents and left to be maintained from charitable or public sources. The preamble of the Act indicates the spirit in which this problem was approached. "Firste, concerning Bastards begotten and borne out of lawful Matrimony (an Offence againste Gods lawe and Mans Lawe) the said Bastards being now lefte to bee kepte at the chardge of the Parishe where They been borne, to the greate Burden of the same Parishe and in defrauding of the Reliefe of the impotente and aged true Poore of the same Parishe, and to the evill Example and Encouradgement of lewde Lyef: It ys ordeyned and enacted . . ." [Pinchbeck, Hewitt, 1969, pp. 206–220].

The legislation indicated that the mother and the putative father might be punished and both were responsible for support of the child.

> The main concern of Parliament was the relief of public expenditure and the exposure of the moral failure of those who were responsible for bringing the child into the world. . . . Legal sanctions were to be employed against men and women whose bastards became a charge on the community; there were no legal penalties for those who could afford to support the fruits of their own indiscretions [Pinchbeck, Hewitt, 1969, p. 207].

The principal ground of concern then, and one might add, now, "were the economics of maintenance rather than the circumstances of conception" (Pinchbeck, Hewitt, 1969, p. 220).

The English Poor Laws formed the basis for the even more punitive attitudes of Puritan colonists, who punished extramarital fornication and required the parents to support the child who was the result of fornication. Thus Anne Williams, in 1658, petitioned the court for maintenance from Richard Smith "for a child the defendant hath got by her." The court "ordered that the said Richard Smith maintain the child and that the woman for her act committed, be whipped and have thirty lashes well laid on" (Bremner, 1970, p. 52).

Throughout the nineteenth century, the resources available to the out-of-wedlock child for maintenance were the same as those available to any other child who needed help from the community. This included binding out in apprenticeship, and indoor and outdoor relief.

Over the last hundred years, there has developed a more compassionate attitude toward the illegitimate child, a lessening of the distinctions between the legitimate and the illegitimate child, and a reduction in the discriminations against the illegitimate child. Changing attitudes are reflected in changing terminology—from *bastard* to *illegitimate child* to *child born out of wedlock* or the less frequently employed *extramarital child* and *love child*. There are frequent citations of illustrious out-of-wedlock children: William the Conqueror, Erasmus, Leonardo da Vinci, Alexander Hamilton, Aleksandr Borodin, Willy Brandt.

The legal status of the child born out of wedlock differs from state to state, but more frequently now such a child has a right to inherit from his mother and, where paternity is acknowledged, the right to inherit from his father. Many states have acknowledged the illegitimate child's rights to benefits under workmen's compensation laws in case the father is injured or killed. Federal legislation has recognized the illegitimate child's rights to veteran's benefits and Old Age and Survivor's Insurance benefits from his father's account.

In 1972 the U.S. Supreme Court, granting the entitlement of an out-of-wedlock child to workmen's compensation benefits on the death of the child's father, noted that "No child is responsible for his birth" and that equal protection under the Fourteenth Amendment should not be denied. But out-of-wedlock children still face substantial legal disadvantages in some states (Krause, 1966, 1967, 1971).

The child's status is not indicated on the short-form birth certificate used for such purposes as school registration or job application, which merely lists name and time and place of birth.

Legitimation of the child can now be achieved by marriage of the parents after the child's birth, by petition to the court if the parents are not married, and by the father's acknowledgment of paternity. With legitimation, birth records are changed so as to delete any indication of the child's previous illegitimate status. If the father voluntarily acknowledges paternity, he is obligated to support the child. Bastardy proceedings or paternity proceedings can be instituted to establish the paternity of the child and to force the father to support the child. This is a civil procedure that often, however, resembles a criminal action. If a man is judged to be the father but fails to make support payments, he can be prosecuted. But it is difficult to prove that a particular man is the father of the child. Blood tests merely exclude the possibility; they do not establish certainty. Paternity proceedings are usually instituted by the mother (often required in order to establish eligibility for Aid to Families of Dependent Children [AFDC] assistance) but may be instituted by the state.

The mother is regarded as guardian of her child and as such has the right to custody, care, and control of the child and a right to the child's earnings. Currently there is increasing concern about the rights of the father. In the case of Stanley *v.* Illinois in April 1972, the U.S. Supreme Court decided that the unwed fathers "who desire and claim competence to care for their children" have a right to a hearing before plans can be made for the child. What had been previously primarily the mother's prerogative is now extended to the unwed father and his "entitlement" to the child he fathered is legally recognized. The father's consent to adoption had been required if paternity had been acknowledged or legitimation established. *Stanley* v. *Illinois* required that some effort be made to contact the father even if there had been no acknowledgment of paternity and to provide him the opportunity for some say in the disposition of the child. (The effects of this and related judicial decisions on adoption are discussed in more detail later.) Whether the putative father's consent to abortion must be obtained is an additional, as yet largely unresolved, question. Some states require consent to either abortion or adoption by the parents of the mother-to-be if she is a minor.

In our society, an out-of-wedlock child is one born to a woman who is not legally married to the father at the time of birth. The fact is that a considerable number of pregnancies are conceived prior to marriage, but the subsequent marriage of the couple before the birth of the child legitimizes the conception. This occurrence does not create a serious social problem. Society is less concerned with illicit coition than with illicit births. Less frequently, a child may be legally illegitimate but not socially illegitimate because the father is living in a stable, although not legal, relationship with the mother and accepts responsibility for the care of the child.

SCOPE

The latest national statistics available at the time of this writing (1979) indicate that there were 468,000 births among unmarried women in 1976 among the 3.168 million total live births. Out-of-wedlock births thus made up 14.8 per cent of all live births in that year. In 1970 there had been 399,000 out-of-wedlock births, making up 10.7 per cent of all live births. Numbers are important because they indicate the total population of children at risk for services to the unmarried mother–out-of-wedlock child pair.

Rates per 1,000 fecund women aged fifteen to forty-four are more sensitive indicators of trends, however. Although the number of births out of wedlock has been increasing steadily since World War II, the illegitimacy rate (live births per 1,000 unmarried women fifteen to forty-four years of age) has leveled off since 1968. The increase in the number of out-of-wedlock births is primarily a result of the larger number of fecund women aged fifteen to forty-four in the population. Whereas the total population of the country between 1960 and 1970 increased by 13 per cent, the number of Americans aged fifteen to nineteen jumped by 46 per cent, providing a disproportionate increase of fecund women who risk out-of-wedlock pregnancies.

Between 1970 and 1975, illegitimacy rates for every age group except the fifteen-to-nineteen age group went down—and within this age group it went up only for the white teenager: between 1970 and 1975, the illegitimacy rate for black teenagers went down from 96.9 to 95.1, whereas it went up from 10.9 to 12.1 for white teenagers (see Table 9–1).

TABLE 9–1. Estimated Illegitimacy Rates by Age of Mother and Race: 1970–1975

Race and Age of Mother	Rate per 1,000 Unmarried Women	
	1970	*1975*
All races:		
All ages 15–44	26.4	24.8
15–19	22.4	24.2
20–24	38.4	31.6
25–29	37.0	28.0
30–34	27.1	18.1
White:		
All ages 15–44	13.9	12.6
15–19	10.9	12.1
20–24	22.5	15.7
25–29	21.1	15.1
30–34	14.2	10.0
Black:		
All ages 15–44	95.5	85.6
15–19	96.9	95.1
20–24	131.5	109.9
25–29	100.9	78.1
30–34	71.8	51.0

* Public Health Service, National Center for Health Statistics, Series 21, No. 30. Sept. 1978, p. 23.

The fact that the rate of teenage pregnancies was continuing to go up while for all other age groups it was going down, the fact that teenage out-of-wedlock births constituted slightly more than half of all out-of-wedlock births in 1976, and the fact that this age group of women was more vulnerable and less prepared to respond to the problem than might be true of her older unmarried sister—all pointed to the teenage out-of-wedlock pregnancies as a focus for service.

Viewing the statistics from another, perhaps more optimistic perspective, it might be noted that only 2 per cent of white fifteen- to nineteen-year-olds and less than 10 per cent of black adolescents gave birth to out-of-wedlock infants in 1975.

A number of factors other than the increase in the population of fecund women have been cited to explain the increase in out-of-wedlock births despite increased family planning and abortion services.

Although open to controversy, there does seem to be some basis for the contention that more unmarried women are sexually active than previously and that premarital sexual activity begins at an earlier age, increasing the risk of an out-of-wedlock pregnancy. Thus Zelnick and Kantner (1978) calculate on the basis of interviews with a probability sample of some 4,400 fifteen- to nineteen-year-old women that whereas in 1971 three out of every ten women had experienced premarital sexual intercourse, this number had increased by 1976 to four out of ten (p. 11). In 1971, 47 per cent of unmarried nineteen-year-old women had had sexual intercourse; by 1976 this number had increased to 55 per cent (Zelnick, Kantner, 1977, p. 56).

Sexual activity by an increasingly large percentage of the unmarried population has overcome the effects of the increased availability of contraception and abortion.

As a consequence of better health conditions, women are becoming capable of having children at an earlier age than they could previously, thus lowering the age at which they risk a first pregnancy. The mean age at menarche, indicating the onset of fertility, was about 16.5 years in 1870. By 1950 it was estimated to be 13.5 (Cutright, 1975, p. 18).

Better nutrition and health conditions also diminish the number of spontaneous abortions, increasing the likelihood that more of the children conceived will actually be born (Cutright, 1975).

The current increasing tendency to delay marriage also increases the amount of the time during which an out-of-wedlock pregnancy is risked.

With increasing prolongation of education for a larger percentage of young people, the reduction of job opportunities for teenagers, and a recognition that early marriages are a high risk for divorce, a larger percentage of young people are postponing marriage.

With sexual maturation taking place earlier and the age of marriage later, the period of nonmarital fecundity is increased, exposing more people to more years at risk of an unwanted, premarital pregnancy.

All of these factors favor a probable increase in the number of children born out of wedlock.

On the other side of the equation, opposing the probability of such an increase, is the greater knowledge about and availability of contraceptive devices and the greater availability of abortion on demand. No matter what numbers of fecund nonmarried women increasingly engage in extramarital intercourse, the combination of contraception and abortion will tend to dampen the increase of children born out of wedlock.

As a consequence of the availability and the use of contraceptives by teenagers, an estimated 680,000 premarital pregnancies were avoided in 1976. This statistic suggests that many sexually active teenagers were using contraceptives effectively. However, an additional 313,000 pregnancies might have been avoided if those teenagers who did not want to become pregnant had consistently used effective contraceptives.

Between 1973, when the U.S. Supreme Court decision made abortion in the first trimester legal, and 1976, 5 million abortions were performed in the United States. Of the 1.3 million abortions performed in 1976, one third were obtained by women under twenty years of age, three fourths of the abortions were to unmarried women, and two thirds of the pregnant women were white. A substantial number of out-of-wedlock births were thus averted by abortion, many of them to teenagers (Forrest, Tietze, Sullivan, 1978). Between 1973 and 1976, the percentage of black abortions increased, as did the percentage of unmarried aborters.

White and Nonwhite Out-of-Wedlock Births

A disproportionate number of out-of-wedlock births are nonwhite. Although the difference lessened somewhat between 1970 and 1975, the black out-of-wedlock rate in 1975 was seven times higher than the white rate. Of the 448,000 out-of-wedlock births in 1975, 262,000 were to black mothers, and 186,000 to white mothers. Because a greater percentage of unmarried black women are sexually active and at earlier ages than white women, a larger percentage are at risk for premarital pregnancy for a longer period of time. In 1976 31 per cent of unmarried white women and 63 per cent of unmarried black women fifteen to nineteen years old had had intercourse. By age fifteen, 38 per cent of black women were sexually active, as against 14 per cent of white fifteen-year-olds (Zelnick, Kantner, 1977, p. 56).

Although black out-of-wedlock children are more often incorporated into the extended family structure than are such white children, most black unmarried mothers did not intend to get pregnant. Interviews with some 340 single black pregnant adolescents revealed that "two-thirds of the girls were shocked and extremely upset when they first discovered they were pregnant" and that 80 per cent wished they were not pregnant (Furstenberg, 1976). However, although the largest percentage did not intend the pregnancy, a larger percentage of black unmarried mothers in a 1976 national survey intended pregnancy (29 per cent) than did white respondents (19 per cent) (Zelnick, Kantner, 1978, p. 14).

Between 1971 and 1976 there was an increase in the percentage of both black and white sexually active, unmarried females who used contraceptives. This percentage was smaller, however, for black women than for white women in 1976 (Zelnick, Kantner, 1977, p. 62).

A variety of other factors help to explain the wide, although diminishing, differences between white and nonwhite illegitimacy rates.

1. The historical experience of the blacks under a slave system that had little regard for marriage and a high regard for black children, however fathered, is sometimes presented as a component of the cultural "causes" of the problem in the present. Southern law did not recognize slave marriages, so that all slave children were, by law, illegitimate. Children fathered by a white but born of a slave mother inherited her status. It is suggested, then, that the historical experience in slavery is antithetical to the development of a concern that the child be born in wedlock.

2. An increase in illegitimacy rates has generally accompanied large-scale migrations. Families are temporarily disorganized and husbands and wives are separated for long periods of time. Recently blacks have experienced a large-scale internal migration, from the South to the North and the West and from rural to urban locations.

3. Out-of-wedlock statistics imperfectly reflect the extent of extramarital coition. Between coition and illegitimate birth one can counterpose, in succession, contraception, abortion, or marriage before birth of the child. Each procedure reduces the number of children born out of wedlock, and each is less easily available to the nonwhite unmarried girl.

An effort is being made to provide more information about the use of contraception and the possibility of abortion and to increase the availability and the accessibility of such services in the black community. There is increasing use of such services, which accounts for some of the reduction of black illegitimacy rates between 1970 and 1975. However, a substantial difference in services still remains.

4. Differences in out-of-wedlock birthrates are also the result of differences in access to, and motivation toward, the use of alternative resolutions of out-of-wedlock pregnancies. A study of the resolution of teenage pregnancies in a national sample of women fifteen to nineteen years old in 1971 clearly showed these differences in disposition: "Whites are about six times more likely than blacks to marry before the outcome of the premarital first pregnancy," thus legitimizing the pregnancy (Zelnik, Kantner, 1974, p. 79). (See also Bowerman, Pope, 1969; McCarthy, Menken 1979.)

As Garland (1966) notes, "the middle or upper class white woman who becomes an out-of-wedlock mother biologically has greater opportunities of becoming an in-wedlock mother socially" (p. 85). The higher unemployment rate among black males and the more limited, lower-paying employment opportunities available to them understandably make many black single pregnant girls reluctant to "solve" a difficult situation by contracting a hazardous marriage. The objective situation perhaps favors the decision that "no marriage is bad; but no marriage is better than a bad marriage." Hasty marriages in response to a premarital pregnancy have low survival rates generally, but this is particularly true in the case of such marriages by young black couples (McCarthy, Menken, 1979, p. 23).

There are also racial differences in the use of abortion and adoption: "White teenagers who do not marry prior to the outcome of a premarital first pregnancy are seven times more likely to terminate the pregnancy by induced abortion than blacks." Of those carrying the child to term and not marrying, "Among whites 18 percent gave up their child for adoption compared to only two percent of Blacks" (Zelnik, Kantner, 1974, p. 79). This is partly in response to the fact that there are fewer opportunities for the adoptive placement of the black child.

Each one of these alternative outcomes of the same out-of-wedlock pregnancy is heavily weighted in favor of the white mother. Consequently, when statistics are collected on the number of out-of-wedlock children in the community, many more black children than white children are counted (Zelnik, Kantner, 1974).

In effect, the number of illegitimate births is related to the number of women of childbearing age in the community, reduced by the number of those not sexually active, reduced by the number who use contraceptives consistently and who don't conceive, reduced by the number who conceive but choose abortion, and further reduced by the number of pregnant, unmarried women who choose marriage before birth (Hartley, 1975).

5. In all of this discussion, the question of socioeconomic class intrudes as a contaminating factor, so that part of the racial difference in illegitimacy rates is a function of differences in the class distribution of members of the two racial groups.

The Governmental National Center for Health Statistics Study on Illegitimacy notes that "There is considerable evidence that socioeconomic composition is an important factor contributing to the white–nonwhite differential in illegitimacy.

It is likely that if it were possible to control for social class, much of the difference between those two groups would disappear" (U.S. Department of Health, Education, and Welfare, 1968, p. 16). Herzog (1964) similarly notes that if "illegitimacy estimates were related to income as well as color, the Negro–white difference would be drastically reduced" (p. 121).

Recent trends suggest that black and white unmarried women are becoming more alike. The percentage of increase of unmarried white women becoming sexually active is greater than for blacks, more blacks are using contraceptives and having abortions than formerly, fewer white women are marrying to legitimize a pregnancy than formerly, and fewer are giving their child up for adoption.

DETERMINANTS OF OUT-OF-WEDLOCK PREGNANCY

The social work approach to the single pregnant girl reflects the profession's thinking about the origin of the problem. This has undergone some changes over time. Before the Great Depression, the emphasis on personal and moral inadequacy led to the perception of the unmarried mother as morally promiscuous and/or mentally deficient. During the 1930s, the blame was placed on the socially deficient environment: the broken home and the poverty-stricken home were the factors that "explained" unwed motherhood. Studies of out-of-wedlock births focused on class and color as factors determining attitudes toward extramarital intercourse and contraception.

After World War II, the emphasis shifted to psychological determinism. Out-of-wedlock pregnancy was seen as a symptom of some psychological need—conflict with a dominant mother, lack of response from a passive father, a desire for self-punishment, a search for a dependable love object, an attempt at self-assertion and independence.

Young (1954) noted that "Although a girl would obviously not plan consciously and deliberately to bear an out-of-wedlock child, she does act in such a way that this becomes the almost inevitable result" (p. 22). Out-of-wedlock pregnancy was seen as not only a symptom of individual disturbance but as a symptom of family pathology.

The continuing search for causes has generated a series of studies of personality differences between the single pregnant woman and her single unpregnant sister. Results vary, some demonstrating personality disturbance in the unmarried mothers, some finding them essentially normal (Pauker, 1969, pp. 47–54).

Perhaps one of the most comprehensive and carefully controlled of these studies was that conducted by Vincent (1961). One hundred young unwed mothers were matched in terms of crucial variables with an equal number of single girls who had never been pregnant. In psychological tests, the latter scored consistently at a more positive level of personality functioning, but differences between the two groups were smaller than anticipated and most of the scales showed no difference in the *"direction"* and *"pattern"* (italics in original) of the responses (p. 119). When compared in terms of developmental background, the groups showed an "absence of any statistically significant familial differences" (p. 117). Vincent concluded that "unwed motherhood is not the result of any one personality type, intrafamilial relationship, or social situation" (p. 179).

Furthermore, any personality differences that are revealed may be the response to the pregnancy rather than the cause of it. Pauker (1969), who asked, "Are they pregnant because they are different or are they different because they are pregnant?" examined the personality profiles obtained *before* conception for a group of unmarried mothers and those of a matched group of nonpregnant peers and found them to be "very similar in shape and elevation" (p. 60). The unwed mothers' group showed no "striking personality difference from other girls," though it included a significantly larger number of girls who came from homes broken by separation or divorce (p. 63).

A careful analysis by Cutright (1971) showed that such factors as level of religiosity, level of secularization of a society, divorce rates, decline of the authoritarian family, and levels of assistance granted the unmarried mother are unrelated to the changes in the illegitimacy rate. In response to Young's contention that illegitimate pregnancy is, consciously or unconsciously, deliberately desired, Cutright (1971), reviewing the relevant research, concluded that "there is substantial evidence that most unwed mothers would prefer to avoid the status" (p. 26). As someone has said, "Unmarried motherhood is a social status, not a psychiatric diagnosis."

Currently it is recognized that unmarried motherhood is too complex a phenomenon to yield a particular set of "explanations." There is a growing acceptance of the supposition that just as there is no juvenile delinquency but rather a series of different kinds of juvenile delinquents, there is no unmarried motherhood but rather a series of different kinds of unmarried mothers who come to the experience through many different routes (Plionis, 1975). Causation may differ with age, with social or racial background, and with personal experience. The determinants are cultural, personal, environmental, and—in some instances—accidental: contraceptives do fail and abortions are not always available. Even with the consistent use of contraceptives, the anticipated failure rate, which varies from 2 to 5 per cent for the pill to 30 per cent for foam and 35 per cent for rhythm, would result in a sizable number of out-of-wedlock pregnancies.

Currently social workers tend to emphasize factors such as psychosocial disturbances in the family (disturbed parent–child relationship, disturbed marital relationship, lack of parental affection and understanding, lack of communication among family members) and emotional disturbance in the individual (impulsivity, defective superego development, self-rejection, desire to punish parents, anxiety about sexuality, loneliness), but there is also serious consideration given to the general social situation (changing sex norms, changing attitudes in the relationship between the sexes and toward marriage, the effects of socioeconomic conditions on establishing and maintaining a viable marriage). And as Perlman (1954) points out, the psychological explanation is more frequently applied to white unmarried mothers; the cultural explanation, to the nonwhite unmarried mothers. The white unmarried mother is seen as acting out a personal conflict; the nonwhite unmarried mother is seen as responding to a deprived socioeconomic environment.

Whereas previously the attempt to understand the unmarried mother focused on differences between those women who were premaritally active and those who refrained from intercourse, more attention is given now to differences among subgroups of the large percentage of unmarried women who are sexually active. What explains the fact that some of the sexually active group consistently and effectively use contraceptive protection, whereas others remain at high risk for pregnancy? What explains the difference between those who, when they find they are pregnant, obtain an abortion and those who do not? What explains the difference between those who, having carried a child to term, keep the child, and those who surrender the child for adoption? Each fork in the road separates one group from another in a highly involved decision.

The birth of a child out of wedlock is the consequence of a series of sequential decisions. At each point in the decision making, an alternative choice would have prevented this outcome.

The first decision is to become sexually active or to refrain from premarital sex. If the woman is sexually active, her second preventive decision is to use an effective contraceptive consistently or to insist that her partner provide contraceptive protection.

Although a minority, some percentage of sexually active single women fail to use contraception because consciously or unconsciously they want to become pregnant. Studies show that 20–30 per cent of the women who experienced a premarital pregnancy indicated that it had been wanted at the time it occurred (David, 1972, p. 439). But despite the fact that 70–80 per cent had not wanted to become pregnant, most not intending pregnancy failed to use a contraceptive. One national study of unwed teenagers showed that "the overwhelming majority of those who became pregnant indicated that the pregnancy had been unintended but only 13% of these reported that they used any kind of contraceptive to prevent it" (Shah, Zelnik, Kantner, 1975, p. 34). (See also Furstenberg, 1976, p. 15.)

Advocates of sex education and family planning suggest that out-of-wedlock pregnancies result from a lack of adequate knowledge about human sexuality and/or a lack of knowledge of or access to contraceptives. There are relatively few who are as uninformed as the woman who said, "My Pap smear was negative. How could I get pregnant?" But a high percentage do not know the time during their menstrual cycle when they are at highest risk for becoming pregnant. However, Chilman (1977), reviewing some twelve studies relating to this question, indicates that "most of them show that there is little, if any, relationship between levels of measured knowledge and contraceptive behavior" (p. 245). Nonavailability ("didn't have it with me," "don't know where to get it," "too expensive") accounts for a limited percentage of reasons for failure to use contraceptives (Zelnik, Kantner, 1975). More frequently, risk taking resulted from discounting the possibility that they could or would get pregnant. Unprotected intercourse frequently does not result in pregnancy, which justifies the response so frequently encountered in studies when the unmarried mother who is aware of contraceptives is asked why she did not use them: "I didn't think I would become pregnant." She sees it as an unfortunate accident, something that just happened. She feels victimized by an unlucky stroke of fate that her friends, engaging in the same behavior with the same lack of precaution, have escaped.

There may also be shame and embarrassment in the overt planning for sex required for effective contraception. For the unmarried women, sex relations are apt to be intermittent, unpredictable, and unplanned. The use of contraception implies the opposite: planned predictability. Planning for, obtaining, and using contraception clearly define the user as a sexually active person. This, rather than actually engaging in intercourse, is the more self-defining action. While engaging in intercourse, one can still deny that one is "that kind of girl." The process of seeking and obtaining contraceptives (coital preparedness) makes such denial more difficult (Rains, 1971; Lindemann, 1974). This presents a woman with a conflict, "for she cannot maintain her self-image as a 'nice girl' through rationally planning possibly 'not to be one'" (Bowerman, 1966, p. 391). Guilt in engaging in what is perceived as an immoral act may be diminished by assuming the risk of punishment through possible pregnancy. The woman may have disguised hostility toward her parents; toward her sexual partner, who would be discomfitted and upset if pregnancy resulted; or toward herself and masochistically seeks punishment. There is an ambiguity as to who is responsible for being prepared, the woman or her partner. Each might assume that the other is taking precautions or may feel resentful about the responsibility. There may be heightened pleasure in the thrill of risks taken, in sex that is planlessly spontaneous, unencumbered by the possible side effects of any contraceptive device. There is "coital gamesmanship" reflecting a power struggle in the relationship and manipulation of sex for the purpose of ensuring a marriage. There may be a desire for confirmation of one's fecundity or potency in conceiving a child. There may be a depressed, apathetic, passive submission to fate with little confidence that conception can be controlled. There may be an inability to control one's life consciously, an impulsive, irresponsible lack of mature self-discipline to prevent the occurrence of events that would have serious negative consequences for oneself. There may be an inability to imagine the difficult consequences of an out-of-wedlock pregnancy, a childish yielding to the needs of the moment, and a failure to use contraceptives because it involves some inconvenience.

Resistance to the use of contraceptives may include fears that they may harm any child conceived, that they will reduce the possibility of having children at a later time when pregnancy is wanted, and that those who advocate the use of contraceptives are doing so in order to ensure a lower black birthrate and guarantee continuing white supremacy.

Lack of contraceptive use because the woman "wanted to get pregnant" or "wouldn't mind if I became pregnant" was frequently associated with imminent and definite decisions to marry (Shah, Zelnik, Kantner, 1975).

Although not always effective and in some instances not even actively wanted, pregnancy does include the possibility of converting a tenuous, indefinite commitment on the part of the male partner into a definite commitment.

Contraceptive use increases with age, with frequency of intercourse, with the increasing stability of a relationship, and with increased commitment to possible marriage. An active attitude toward the control of their fate on the part of women, high self-evaluation, and personal competence are associated with the use of contraceptives. "Fatalism, passivity, a sense of powerlessness, feelings of incompetence and risk-taking" (Chilman, 1977, p. 234) are negatively associated with contraceptive use.

Lindemann (1975) attempts to define different stages in contraceptive use in a longitudinal analysis. The first stage is an amateurish, inconsistent, hesitant use of contraceptives when sexual activity has just been initiated, intercourse is sporadic, there is confidence that pregnancy cannot happen, and the self-image as a sexually active human being is not yet crystallized. With more frequent, more consistent sexual activity, the woman has a greater willingness to accept her identity as a sexually active woman, a greater openness to sharing this identity with her peers, and a greater deliberateness in seeking information and advice from peers and partners. This "peer perception" stage is followed by the "expert stage," in which the woman becomes more assured in the use of contraceptives and seeks the help of professionals in obtaining the most effective contraceptives. These formulations are based on research interviews with unmarried, sexually active women.

Pregnancy, abortion, and childbirth, rather than the initiation of sexual activity, are for many women the route to effective and motivated contraception, because these events, unlike intercourse, put them in touch with knowledgeable, professional service-providers.

Sexually active women in the early teens are especially vulnerable to unwanted pregnancies. They are moving from a status of low fecundity, when they were not capable of having a child and are naturally contraceptively protected, to a status of increasingly greater fecundity. Their image of themselves has to change in accordance with this gradual change in fecundity, accompanied by active contraceptive use.

Luker (1975) also based her conclusions on interviews with unmarried, sexually active women. She concluded that the woman who knows about contraceptives and has access to them may still fail to use them as a consequence of a personal risk-taking calculus that can be perceived as rational. Pregnancy risk-taking is seen as no less rational than the risk taken in "failing to fasten safety belts in cars, cigarette smoking," or engaging in sports activities with a high percentage of injuries such as skiing. What is involved is a cost–benefit analysis balancing the future probable but uncertain risk of becoming pregnant and the consequences of pregnancy against the more immediate and certain costs of contraception. For many, there is still considerable "cost" in contraceptive use, varying somewhat with different kinds of contraceptives. The pill requires a confession to a doctor about nonmarital sex, it has possible side effects, and it requires consistent use, implying a commitment to and anticipation of future sexual involvement and resulting in questions related to self-image. A diaphragm requires the embarrassment of a medical fitting, manual vaginal contact, the patience and cooperation of the male partner, and so on. Each procedure requires some measure of embarrassment, inconvenience, monetary cost, and diminution of maximum pleasure. The consequence, and there are often no consequences, is a pregnancy that can be undone by abortion or that results in an out-of-wedlock child. The latter outcome has advantages that counterbalance the disadvantages.

Based perhaps on previous experiences with unprotected intercourse that did not result in pregnancy, the risk taker may argue, "I actually have a high chance of not getting pregnant from any one sexual act. If I do get pregnant, I can get an abortion. If I decide against an abortion, becoming a mother may not be so bad and it has some advantages, but I probably won't get pregnant anyhow." It is the certainty of paying present, actual, immediate costs against ambiguous, imagined, possible, tolerable costs.

Having become pregnant as a result of a decision to become sexually active and a failure to use contraception effectively, the single pregnant woman can still avoid becoming a single pregnant mother through abortion.

Abortion users, like contraceptive users, are more likely to have high educational/occupational aspirations and to be doing well in school, to come from more advantaged families, to value control over their lives, and to see themselves as competitive people. They are more likely to "have hope for their futures as self determining, achieving individuals and do not want their lives burdened by an unwanted out-of-marriage pregnancy or by a forced marriage" (Chilman, 1977, p. 279; see also Kane, Lachenbruch, 1973; Bracken, Klerman, Bracken, 1977).

Carrying the baby to term has more unequivocal community sanction. Those who choose to abort have to contend with the residue of previous nonaccepting attitudes toward abortion held by themselves as well as others. Nonaborters are more likely to have strong ethical reservations about abortion than aborters.

In comparing unmarried black adolescent women who had their babies with those who chose to have an abortion, Fishman and Pally (1978) found that nearly half of those who delivered their babies had made this decision because they wanted to have a child. "The girls were very happy about the pregnancy" (p. 38). Similarly another study found that the decision not to abort was frequently associated with a desire for a child (Zelnick, Kantner, 1978, p. 14).

There is positive incentive to become a mother, even out of wedlock. Given the approbation accorded motherhood, the lack of strong alternative sources of satisfaction in life for some women, the reduced stigma associated with unmarried motherhood, and the social support available in terms of medical and public assistance, day care, and continuing-education programs, those who feel some desire to have a child or "did not mind" becoming pregnant may tend to see the unmarried-mother situation as not seriously disadvantaged.

Fishman and Palley (1978) note that "Young women who carried their pregnancies to term tended to find their schoolwork difficult, and the vast majority of them disliked school. The pregnancy per se did not cause many of them to leave school; rather, they often became pregnant because of their dissatisfaction with school" (p. 37). As a consequence of becoming a mother, a woman gains a sanctioned excuse to drop out of a school situation in which she feels defeated and inadequate, to leave a job that is dissatisfying and meaningless, or to give up a living arrangement that is a source of tension and conflict. As a consequence of becoming a mother, she finds a meaningful and socially valued focus around which she can organize an identity and her life; a sense of self-worth, self-esteem, and self-fulfillment; and a gratifying interpersonal relationship with another human being. Motherhood leads to an acceptable and assured means of financial support and medical care that provides the possibility of independent living without parental interference:

> When an adolescent girl feels that not enough which is meaningful and which promotes security is occurring at home within her family, when she feels the school curriculum is irrelevant to her interests, when she is dissatisfied with her relatives, and when she does not feel her life is going in a definite positive direction, it is often then that she does not care if she becomes pregnant [Shouse, 1975, p. 185].

Often the child is not wanted for his own sake but at least partially as a means of achieving another objective: to achieve adult status, to get married, to find a sanctioned opportunity to move out of the parents' home, to have "something of my own," or to use as a "passport to freedom and independence."

Some of this presentation suggests the effect of the availability of income maintenance support and medical and education programs on the decisional process. There is no evidence to suggest, however, that AFDC "causes" out-of-wedlock pregnancies. Analyzing the relationship between the levels of grant payments and the access barriers to AFDC as these relate to legitimacy rates to 1965, Cutright (1970) found that AFDC was not an incentive to an out-of-wedlock pregnancy. Janowitz (1976), analyzing somewhat similar factors for a later period, found that for nonwhite younger women, larger welfare payments were associated with higher illegitimacy rates. Moore and Caldwell (1976), analyzing a 1971 national probability sample of fifteen- to nineteen-year-old women, found that "high state AFDC benefit levels and acceptance rates were not found to be associated with greater probability of pregnancy." They concluded that benefits did not "increase the likelihood that an unmarried virgin would have intercourse" and that "there was no evidence that AFDC benefits serve as an evident incentive to child-rearing outside marriage" (pp. 2, 3).

Many of these findings are the result of large-group statistics involving crude measurement-of-policy variables. The decision-making process at the individual level may be somewhat different. At this level, income support programs and the associated benefits may influence some of the decisions being made, as Sklar and Berkov (1974) note in analyzing the relevant data: "Although it does not seem likely that teenagers purposely become pregnant in order to take advantage of these benefits, the benefits do lessen the penalties of illegitimate childbearing and childrearing outside of marriage" (p. 90).

A study of the Joint Economic Committee, U.S. Congress (1974), concluded "that there was a sizeable financial gain for a single woman to have her first child" and "that in all cases studied it was clear that welfare tended to neutralize those child-bearing decisions that are influenced by costs" (p. 80).

Availability of benefits makes it possible for mothers to avoid marriages that have low probability for success because they lack a sound social, emotional, or financial basis and to care for the child outside of a marriage. The availability of benefits may influence some women not to have an abortion or not to place the child for adoption because there is a source of support for caring for the child: "The availability of public assistance appears not to cause out-of-wedlock pregnancy, but it may affect what a young woman does about this pregnancy" (Chilman, 1977, p. 308).

The continued increase in the number of out-of-wedlock births, despite a very large increase in family-planning and abortion services, indicates that this problem is more complex than being merely a question of contraceptive technology, education, accessibility, and availability. "Solving" the "problem" of unmarried motherhood requires attention to ideological, sociological, psychological, and motivational factors as well. Simple, acceptable, widely available, safe, low-cost procedures about which all fecund males and females were knowledgeable, backed by readily accessible elective abortion, would undoubtedly help, but it is likely that children would still continue to be conceived and born out of wedlock.

The complexity of the social, psychological, situational, and idiosyncratic interpersonal factors relating to out-of-wedlock pregnancy would suggest that it is a problem that promises no easy solution.

SERVICES FOR THE SINGLE PREGNANT WOMAN

Social workers are involved in services to prevent out-of-wedlock pregnancies. In 1976 some 40 percent of metropolitan family planning agencies and 20 percent of non-metropolitan agencies employed social workers (Torres, 1979, p. 111).

The large majority of social workers feel that teenagers should have access to birth control information and that social workers have a responsibility to disseminate it (Meyer, Stone, 1974; Reichelt, Werley, Ager, 1977). Realistically recognizing their current limited training regarding the specifics of birth control procedures, they defer to nurses and doctors to instruct and demonstrate regarding this. In addition, social workers accept the responsibility of counseling with and providing information to those seeking an abortion.

With regard to birth control and abortion, social workers primarily provide information and referral service and counseling around attitudes and feelings regarding the use of such services.

Outreach programs bring information and services to adolescents where they congregate: street corners, discos, record stores, fast-food outlets, and so on. Further, information is provided and group discussions are conducted in the argot of the adolescent group, for example, the use of *screw* and *ball* instead of *intercourse*.

The principal service, however, is to the woman who is pregnant out of wedlock. There are many different contexts for an out-of-wedlock pregnancy. The woman might be married, but to someone other than the father of the child she is carrying. The mother may be living with the father but may not be legally married to him. The woman may have been married and is now separated, widowed, or divorced, or the woman may be single and never-married. The context for illegitimacy that the social agency most frequently encounters is the last: the single, pregnant, never-married woman.

The unmarried mother who receives service from a social agency is the exception rather than the rule. A 1960 nationwide study concluded that "about one out of six mothers who have illegitimate children in a year receive service either in public or voluntary agencies near the time of the pregnancy" (Adams, 1962, p. 43). The younger the unmarried mother, the more likely she is to have contact with a social agency. White unmarried mothers are more likely to make contact with voluntary agencies; nonwhite mothers, with a local department of public assistance. A disproportionate amount of the total available social service time and energy has been directed toward white girls above the poverty level who are interested in placing their out-of-wedlock child for adoption (Rashbaum *et al.*, 1963).

Because many unmarried mothers, although needing such service, either may not know of its availability or may be reluctant to use it, some states require hospitals to report all illegitimate births to the local department of public welfare. A social worker then visits the mother, informs her of the services available, and helps her to decide whether or not she wants to use them.

Wisconsin requires that all hospitals "report illegitimate pregnancies" to the State Division of Family Services, "so that social service might be offered the mother." Despite these efforts, the four-year period of 1973 through 1976 showed a decline in unmarried mothers' use of social services—from 67 percent to 41 percent. The younger unmarried mothers were more likely to accept service. By far the greatest majority of those accepting service were being aided by a county social-service department, only 15 per cent receiving service from a voluntary agency (Wisconsin Department of Health and Social Services, 1977).

Pregnancy is a crisis situation. The urgency of coming to a decision about the child and the highly emotional responses that an out-of-wedlock pregnancy is likely to evoke make the client temporarily more willing to accept help.

The unmarried mother needs two kinds of service from the agency: sociotherapy and psychotherapy. Sociotherapy includes income maintenance, housing (in some instances away from the family, in a maternity home or a foster home), prenatal and obstetrical medical care, legal counseling, vocational counseling, and educational counseling. The psychotherapeutic services are intended to help with the emotional disturbance, conflict, and tensions occasioned by the illegitimate pregnancy. The services include counseling and emotional support in regard to the woman's changing relationship with her own family, her relationship with the putative father, her changing relationship to peers, her reaction to the pregnancy and the anticipated birth experience, her plans for the child, her changes in self-concept, and the total emotional configuration that might have motivated the girl to become pregnant.

In general, the single pregnant girl is likely to be more interested in sociotherapy than in psychotherapy. Most of the unmarried mothers to whom service is offered are likely to be more concerned with the specific, immediate problems posed by the pregnancy and the birth of the child.

A study of the services offered fifty "young, poor, uneducated" unmarried mothers indicated that although both clients and workers often identified similar problems as needing attention, there was a difference in emphasis (Rubenstein, Bloch, 1978). Both identified problems of housing and financial assistance and of establishing paternity, the relationship with the alleged father, the relationship with the woman's parents, and the decision about the baby as being among those most frequently requiring assistance. However, "workers gave relatively more emphasis to intra and interpersonal factors than to lack of tangible goods and social services . . . clients tended to emphasize their lack of resources and interpersonal rather than intrapersonal problems. Clients rarely spoke of their own behavior as contributing to their problems" (p. 74). However, although the workers had some bias about the intrapersonal nature and sources of the clients' problems, they gave priority to the clients' perception of need rather than to their own preferences. A good deal of the help offered was centered on providing concrete services rather than "therapy." As a consequence, most of the clients were satisfied with the service, felt that they had been helped, and would recommend the service to others, whereas the workers themselves assessed the results as "mildly positive."

Arranging for adequate medical care is an immediate consideration. The unmarried mother, in contrast to the married mother, tends to seek medical care later in the pregnancy and to get less adequate care. She is therefore more likely to have some complications during delivery and runs a greater risk of dying. The younger the unwed mother, the more she is apt to delay in obtaining medical services (Pakter, Nelson, 1965). The tendency to deny the pregnancy, a common reaction in many unwed mothers, is particularly pronounced among teenagers and causes a delay in going for help. Higher infant morality rates, low birth weight, prolonged labor, hypertension, anemia, and toxemia are more likely to be associated with teenage pregnancies (Stepto, Keith, Keigh, 1975, p. 89). Teenage pregnant women are likely to start going for medical care later in the pregnancy, to get less adequate care, and to suffer from a poorer diet during pregnancy. The factor of conception out-of-wedlock is complicated by factors of the class, race, and age of the mother. Many unwed mothers are lower-class nonwhites, which makes adequate medical and nutritional care difficult to obtain in any circumstances.

Medical care for unmarried mothers with limited resources can be financed through Medicaid. The older unwed mother may obtain financial assistance under the AFDC program, if she is willing to file a complaint against the putative father. If paternity is established, the father will be required to contribute monthly toward the support of the child. If the father is not known, not located, or not able to pay, financial assistance through AFDC is available in some states even before the birth of the child. (The pregnant single woman is not eligible for unemployment insurance because she is not eligible for employment.) If employed when she became pregnant, she may be eligible, however, for medical care through the health insurance policy of the employing organization.

Housing is available in maternity homes and foster homes. The latter are often "wage" homes, in which the girl receives room and board in exchange for baby-sitting and light housework.

The legal status of the teenage unmarried mother complicates the planning situation. She often needs her parents' legal permission to receive medical care, to enter a maternity home, or to give up the child for adoption. The teenager may also find it difficult to obtain financial assistance unless her parents can satisfy the agency that they cannot support their daughter and that they are willing to apply for aid in her behalf.

The single pregnant woman faces not only the practical problems of medical care, finances, housing, and so on, but emotional problems as well. For the married woman, pregnancy is a joyful occasion, and she is applauded and supported by those who are close to her; for the single girl, it is occasion for regret, dejection, worry, and social disapproval. Although society is currently more accepting, or at least less openly punitive, in its response to the unmarried mother, she is still considered somewhat atypical and deviant.

Guilt and shame, if manifested at all, are more likely to be evoked by the pregnancy rather than by the sexual activity that caused it (Taylor, 1965), but the general situation in which the single pregnant girl finds herself is apt to evoke strong feelings of anxiety and panic. Denial and distortion of reality are understandable when the reality involves "having to acknowledge that she has been abandoned by the baby's father, that she is in social and economic jeopardy, and that she will either have to relinquish a baby she may love or . . . keep a baby she is not sure she is going to love" (Bernstein, 1971, p. 31). The social worker can help the unmarried mother deal with her feelings about her situation.

The social worker may help initially by referring the woman to services to determine whether she is actually pregnant. If pregnancy is definite, the woman might need help in deciding whom she wants to tell: parents, male friends, woman friends.

The social worker might help to prepare the woman to share this information through role playing and might act as convener and mediator in a meeting between the woman and significant others where the information about the pregnancy is shared and discussed.

Perhaps the first question that needs discussion is whether or not to tell the parents about the pregnancy, and, if so, how to do it. Parents frequently hate to be told, yet want to be told. Although learning about the pregnancy may make them feel that they have failed as parents, they often offer emotional support and concrete help. The girl wants to conceal the pregnancy lest she hurt her parents, yet she is relieved and comforted when they rally to her support.

The initial reaction of parents may be negative: shock, disbelief, rejection, disappointment, chagrin, guilt, and so on. However, most families seem to resolve these negative attitudes, if not during the pregnancy, very often after the birth of the baby. More often than not, parents offer their emotional support and share their resources with the unmarried mother.

Although there is much in the situation that creates conflict between daughter and parents, there is much that moves them toward reconciliation. The parents' guilt and compassion and the daughter's desire to make amends for the pain she may be causing them may move them toward reconciliation. The worker reinforces those tendencies that move parents and child toward mutual forgiveness and attempts to resolve or mitigate the divisive elements in the situation.

For some girls, the pregnancy may precipitate maturity. As a pregnant woman, the girl is perceived as an adult engaging in an adult experience. As a consequence, she may decide to move away from home and establish greater independence, or she may find that she is now emotionally ready for marriage.

Most pressing is the need to discuss and resolve her feelings about the child and to make plans for the child. Innocent though it may be, the child has occasioned considerable difficulty for the mother, which may make the mother feel resentment, and guilt and shame about her resentment.

The social worker can help the mother to distinguish her feelings about plans for the child from those of her family and/or of the child's father. If a woman has a strong emotional need for the child but is persuaded or coerced to give it up, she may incur another illegitimate pregnancy in search of the lost child. The worker can also help the mother to distinguish between what is desirable for the child and what is desirable for herself. As Crockett (1960) says, "Not only is it important that the unmarried mother reach the right decision but also that she reach it in a way that leaves her convinced that she has chosen wisely" (p. 77).

The decision to marry the putative father is usually a decision to keep the baby, starting with considerable economic, social, and emotional burdens, because the marital choice is being made under some duress. Marriages contracted while the woman is pregnant are much more likely to end in divorce than marriages in which no pregnancy is involved.

The unmarried woman who wants to keep her child must be helped to assess her capacity to care for the child as a single parent. If she seriously overestimates her capacity, she may later regret the decision. She may need clarification of the problems that she is likely to face and information about the resources in the community that might be able to help her with those problems.

The woman who gives up her child must be helped to give up motherhood as well and to resolve her feelings of loss. In most instances, despite a difficult period of transition, she resumes her place in society and in her own mind as a single, childless woman.

A woman who has decided to give up her baby may feel threatened by and may guard herself against feeling tender toward the child, as this feeling may make implementing her decision more difficult. The girl who gives up her child may be haunted at intervals by thoughts of the child, wondering—without being able to find out—what is happening to him. She also has the problem of deciding whether or not to tell the man she may plan to marry about this incident in her life.

The worker helps the mother to anticipate these feelings so that she is less likely to be overwhelmed by them and is better prepared to accept and resolve them.

In helping with these decisions, the social worker is inevitably involved with significant others in the client's life who also influence the decision. The decision to abort or to keep the child often involves the client's parents and sometimes the putative father. The decision to adopt involves the putative father, as does any decision to legitimize the child through marriage. The client's mother is very often an influential factor in these decisions (Young, Beckman, Rehr, 1975). The worker must often obtain the parents' and the boyfriend's cooperation in implementing these key decisions.

In working with the single pregnant woman, the worker has to know about human sexuality, contraceptive information and procedures, abortion procedures, adoption procedures, the legal procedures regarding establishing paternity and relinquishment, and the anticipated consequences and problems associated with keeping the child. The worker has to be knowledgeable about income maintenance, day care, educational housing, and health services in the community.

The social worker provides an opportunity for an exploration of the multiple problematic decisions that the unmarried mother needs to resolve in a context of objective acceptance. Based on her knowledge of probable consequences associated with alternatives and options, the social worker can help the unmarried mother make a decision that has a chance of being individualized and comfortably acceptable.

Maternity Home

The maternity home is a specialized institutional facility developed to meet the needs of single pregnant women. The most recent survey showed that there were 201 such institutions (60 per cent of them under denominational auspices) in the United States in 1966 offering service to about twenty-five thousand women. (Pappenfort, Kilpatrick, 1970).

Eligibility requirements are such that, until recently, they tended to restrict the use of maternity homes to young, never married, not previously pregnant girls interested in placing their children for adoption. Until very recently, fewer than 10 per cent of all residents of such homes were nonwhite, although a large percentage of all single pregnant women are nonwhite. Rules and regulations, which frequently include a curfew, tend to exclude the older pregnant woman. Casework service and attendance at weekly group-therapy sessions are mandatory in many maternity homes.

Such homes were established in the United States as early as 1836, but most were founded in the late nineteenth and early twentieth centuries (Pappenfort, Kilpatrick, 1970). The largest network of such homes was operated by the Florence Crittenton Association of America (now part of the Child Welfare League of America) founded in 1890 by a wealthy businessman, Charles Crittenton, in memory of his daughter. The early philosophy of the homes is expressed in the names they took: "House of Refuge," "Door of Hope," "Rescue Home," "House of Mercy," "Sheltering Arms."

Another large group of maternity homes is operated by the Salvation Army, whose mission is to rescue "fallen women" and "betrayed young girls."

Maternity homes provide care and rehabilitation as well as sanctuary (Rains, 1970). Many still rigorously protect their clients' identities.

Some homes have their own maternity units, and others arrange for delivery to take place at a local hospital. Some have nursery facilities so that the mother can care for the child for a short time after delivery.

The maternity home staff is concerned with helping the mother to prepare for the birth of the baby and for the decision she must make for the future. Individual and group counseling and educational and recreational activity are included as part of the program. One of the desirable therapeutic aspects of the homes, that a group of unmarried mothers are living together, affords each woman a great measure of comfort and support as she compares notes and discusses common problems with others in the residence. It also makes possible the sharing of living experiences in group therapy sessions as a supplement to the casework interview (Kaltreider, Lenkoski, 1970; Steinmetz, 1964).

Because the stay in a maternity home is relatively short, and because different residents are at different points in their pregnancies, people join and leave the group constantly. However, as all members share a common, highly affective experience, they rapidly get caught up in group discussions.

Maternity homes face a crisis: for the first time in their history, they are facing a decline in applications, possibly because single pregnant women no longer want, or need, the concealment that the maternity home offers. Many homes are making a more decided effort to attract black unmarried mothers, and have attempted to offer service on an outpatient basis to unmarried mothers.

In 1970 there were forty-six Florence Crittenton homes in different locations. By 1975 they had been reduced to thirty-six such programs. The nature of the service had changed, and most were now called *residential services*. For instance, the Crittenton Maternity Home in Detroit was closed, and a comprehensive service center offering assistance to adolescent unmarried mothers was opened in the inner city named after a black pediatric cardiologist, Lula Belle Stewart.

Multiservice Centers for Single Pregnant School-aged Girls and Group Programs

In the 1960s, there was a rapid development of multiservice, comprehensive, interdisciplinary programs for single pregnant women—from 35 such centers in 1968 to 375 programs of this kind in 1975. The multiservice centers seek to provide, or coordinate, a comprehensive program of health, educational, and social services for pregnant school-aged girls living at home. In meeting these needs, the local board of education works together with the local department of health and the local department of public welfare.

One pioneer program of this nature—the Webster School in the District of Columbia—was organized in 1963 (Howard, 1968). It enrolls only teenage pregnant girls and offers a program of educational, health, and welfare services provided by an interdisciplinary team of teachers, psychologists, social workers, doctors, public health nurses, and nutritionists. Another such program, the Oakland, California, Interagency Cyesis Program, involves the participation of the departments of welfare, health, education, and recreation; the YWCA; community action groups; and voluntary agencies. Through such projects, the girls continue their high school studies with teachers provided by the local board of education. In addition, there are special classes in child care, health care during pregnancy, and home economics. Individual and group counseling is provided by social workers, who also help the girls make use of local social-agency programs. Maternity care is provided by health personnel. Some of the projects offer pediatric care, family-planning information, adoption placement, vocational training, and psychological diagnostic evaluation. Service is offered to the putative father and the girl's own family. But few of these programs provide continuing contact with the mother and child. Most girls, after they give birth, return to their regular school setting (Wright 1966; Boykin, 1968; Goodman, 1968; Howard, 1968; Osofsky, 1968; Zober, 1969; McMurray, 1970).

The most comprehensive programs provide services in vocational counseling, training, and placement; prenatal, postpartum, and pediatric care; birth control counseling and services; abortion counseling and services; adoption counseling and services; legal counseling and services; casework and group work; psychological testing and psychiatric treatment; child development; parent and consumer education; financial assistance and budget counseling; leisure-time activities; day-care counseling and services; and housing counseling and services.

Such services were developed in response to a growing sensitivity to the educational consequences of teenage pregnancy. Many school systems had previously required that the pregnant teenager leave school. Separated from her peers if expelled during the pregnancy and having lost a year of school, the girl is understandably reluctant to return to school after the birth of the child. As a result, most of the girls never complete their education and are trapped in a cycle of low-paying jobs and limited income. School systems did attempt to provide continuing education for the pregnant teenager through instruction in the family home or through educational programs in the maternity home, but such resources were available to only a limited number of girls.

Pregnant students now have the option in many school districts either to remain in their regular school program or to transfer to a special school program for pregnant women. Federal government policy withholds federal funds from any school that discriminates against pregnant teenagers by expelling them. The objective of the government is to help such women complete their education so that they can obtain better employment and achieve self-support.

A national study of programs offered to pregnant teenagers showed that most often they were under the auspices of local departments of education and departments of health (Wallace *et al.*, 1973). Such programs were less frequently offered under the auspices of departments of welfare, although voluntary United Fund agencies and YWCAs often sponsored such programs. Most of the programs offered counseling, health, education, employment, and adoption services. They less frequently offered legal advice, special work with fathers, or day-care services.

In multiple service centers social workers are responsible for the coordination and planning of counseling services, developing working relationships with community health and welfare agencies, and formulating effective referral procedures. They also assist with interpretation of the program to the general public and develop outreach efforts to inform and interest eligible clients in the use of the service. In addition, they formulate social data record forms and maintain appropriate social data records, recruit, train, and supervise volunteers, and provide individual and group counseling with young fathers.

Multiservice programs have achieved, at least on a short-term basis, the greater probability of return to school after childbirth, continuing education, an improved health outcome for mother and child, and a modest decrease in the likelihood of a second out-of-wedlock pregnancy.

Group work programs in the community have been attempted. The groups are formed around the common problems faced by the single pregnant girl (Barclay, 1969). Group work has been offered the unmarried mothers in the community both before and after confinement (Johnson, 1969; Bracken, 1971; Danforth *et al.*, 1971; Kolodny, Willow, 1972). Group programs conducted jointly by public health nurses and social workers and focused on the medical and social aspects of pregnancy and preparation for confinement seem to have the greatest interest.

EVALUATION

A study of the effectiveness of different approaches to the treatment of unwed mothers in a traditional child-welfare agency concluded that the methods "felt to be most effective are environmental manipulation, both direct and indirect, and sustaining, *i.e.*, offering encouragement and reassurance and fewer instances in which reflective discussion or consideration is involved" (Power, De Chirico, 1969, p. 8).

The research included the random assignment of ninety-one single pregnant women to one of three different treatment conditions: tangible environmental supportive service, intensive individual casework services, or intensive group counseling. Differences in functioning at the end of treatment were assessed by a casework research interviewer one month, six months, one year, and two years following delivery and were compared with an assessment of functioning at intake based on interviews and psychological tests. Although environmental manipulation and sustaining were most successful, service generally did not effect any change in most clients: "Relatively few girls have grown through the experience. . . . The large majority resume their previous pattern of functioning as well as previous modes of adaptation" (Power, De Chirico, 1969, p. 8).

Another study conducted in a similar kind of agency obtained its principal data from the unmarried mothers, whose responses to a checklist indicated that they perceived the agency as offering important services:

> They confirmed that their caseworkers had helped them get through the experience as soon as possible, had helped them keep their pregnancies secret, had helped them know how to answer questions about their absence from the community during their pregnancies, had helped them obtain vocational guidance, had helped those clients who wanted to keep their babies to make a suitable plan to do so, had helped those who wanted to place their child for adoption to sign the permanent surrender, had helped school-age girls get back into school and had helped some of the young girls to get back into their own homes [O'Rourke, 1968, p. 473].

Some 32 per cent of the respondents indicated that they had been helped by casework services to develop a greater understanding of themselves and their behavior.

A comprehensive program of services (casework, group work, medical and educational services) to a group of 240 teenage unmarried mothers and their families was evaluated by Bedger (1969). Five key areas of functioning—the client's relationship with her family, her relationship with the putative father, the adequacy of her plans for the baby, her plans for her own future, and environmental stress—were rated at intake by the interviewer–caseworker and at closing by the caseworker assigned to the case. The rating at closing showed greatest improvement in the client's relationships with her own parents and in the general family interaction. Overall, "55 percent of the cases studied were rated [at closing] more positive in functioning on the five areas utilized. In 34.6 percent of the cases change was negative and in 9.6 percent of the cases there was no evidence of change" (p. 43). But as there was no control group, it is not clear that the positive results were ascribable to the comprehensive program offered.

A postpartum intensive group-therapy project involving forty-seven weekly sessions for a limited number of unwed mothers showed participants manifesting a "significant increase in self-esteem," improved impulse control, and increased feminine identification as a result of the experience. Assessment was made on the basis of social work and psychiatric interviews and psychological tests before and after treatment. By contrast, a control group of nonparticipant unwed mothers showed fewer positive changes during this period (Busfield et al., 1969).

There have been few serious attempts to evaluate the multiservice programs. One such evaluation of the Webster School indicated that it was very successful in its principal aim of continuing the girls' education throughout their pregnancy so that they were able to return after childbirth to the regular school at the same level as their nonpregnant peers. It was successful in bringing the girls under prenatal care early in the pregnancy and ensured their receiving such care consistently. As a consequence "the proportion of low-birth-weight infants, the infant mortality rates, and other indices were better for Webster girls than for various Negro populations in the District" (Howard,

1968, p. 40). However, "repetition of pregnancy among the girls was not reduced as a result of participation in the Webster program. Many girls had second babies within a relatively short period of time" (Howard, 1968, p. 57).

A six-year study compared the outcomes of school-aged pregnant women receiving comprehensive care programs with a control group matched for age and socioeconomic status who received only obstetric clinic service with no continuity of care (Klerman, Jeckel, 1975). The children of mothers in the comprehensive care program were more likely to be full-term and healthier newborns. For at least the first two years of service, more of the experimental group completed high school. The positive effects of the comprehensive program tended to decline with time despite the important advantages in the early period of service (see also Bennet, Bardon, 1977).

Attenuation of short-term effects of program intervention has resulted in follow-up procedures. Illustratively, one multiple-service agency to adolescent unmarried mothers in Boston found that while program intervention was initially successful, "two years after participation in the program almost half of the mothers have dropped out of school and half have experienced at least one more unintended pregnancy" (Cartoof, 1978, p. 662). As a consequence, the program developed continuing support procedures that included a follow-up visit to each mother on the average of once every three months after the birth of the child. Such continued contact resulted in lowering the rate of school dropouts and reducing the percentage of subsequent unintended pregnancies.

The current situation with regard to the effectiveness of service in response to the problem of illegitimacy is aptly summarized by researchers who studied 134 black and white unwed mothers receiving agency service and concluded that:

> field observation and the response of the clients in the study raised little question about the capacity of the voluntary social agency to meet the *immediate* needs of the illegitimately pregnant girls who come or are brought for help. Plans are made, medical care is given and babies are placed for adoption when this is desired. . . . There seemed to be ample recognition of the value of agency services. . . . Difficulties in giving help arise in large measure from the fact that social agencies and the professionals they employ impose complex goals on themselves which usually go far beyond the goal of meeting a crisis situation. Most agencies aim to give the client an experience of lasting value to bring about long-run changes that are presumed to be constructive [Shapiro, 1970, p. 64].

They are apt to be least successful with regard to these more ambitious objectives.

THE PUTATIVE FATHER

For each out-of-wedlock child being carried by a single pregnant girl, there is, of course, a putative father. The putative father was once ignored or regarded only as a source of financial support for the unwed mother and her child. This was followed by a period during which contact was attempted with the putative father because of what he could contribute toward the emotional as well as the financial support of the unwed mother and because knowledge of the putative father was helpful in adoptive planning for the child. Currently contact with the putative father is predicated on the recognition that he might want help in his own right with the problems he faces relating to the out-of-wedlock pregnancy.

The movement has been from seeing the putative father solely as a resource of help to the unmarried mother to perceiving him as a person in his own right who might be troubled about a difficult situation in which he is a principal participant.

The current focus is on father–mother–child rather than exclusively on the mother.

Characteristics

Studies of the background of the unmarried father indicate that he is generally of the same age, social class, and educational level as the single pregnant girl, and that he has known the girl for some time prior to the onset of the pregnancy (Sauber, 1966; Grow, 1967; Pope, 1967; Pannor *et al.*, 1971). He is usually not promiscuous: "Relationships between unwed mothers and unwed fathers are much more meaningful than popularly supposed and . . . unwed fathers have more concern for their offspring than is generally realized" (Pannor *et al.*, 1971, p. 85). The relationship of the unmarried father to the mother cannot validly be characterized as either deviant or exploitative.

Only a small minority of pregnancies result from short-time contact with casually encountered strangers. In most instances, the unwed father is far from the phantom figure one might expect if the mother were motivated to become pregnant in response to her own private needs and needed a man only for his biological contribution.

Social workers have tended to favor a psychological "explanation" for unwed fatherhood. The supposition is that, like unwed motherhood, unwed fatherhood is a symptom of some psychological need. The unwed father, it is believed, acts out of hostility toward woman, or out of a desire to confirm his virility, or in rejection of authority and the core culture, or in reaction to fears of latent homosexuality.

Males manifesting highly aggressive sexual activity are apt to be manipulative and exploitive. Poor users of contraceptives are more apt to be socially irresponsible and more oriented toward risk taking (Cvetkovich *et al.*, 1975) and see their female partners as having the primary responsibility for contraception. The responses of a group of unmarried fathers to the California Psychological Inventory substantially mirrors the standard profile. Modest deviations indicated less social maturity and responsibility and more self-centeredness (Pannor, *et al.*, 1971, p. 103–106). This lack of clear-cut differentiation between putative fathers and males in general is confirmed by other comparisons of the two groups (Pauker, 1968).

As Caughlan (1960) notes, the "act which initiates pregnancy" may range from "nothing more than a witless discharge of physiological tension" to the "fullest expression of the most mature relationship. . . . A great variety of psychosocial predisposing and precipitating factors can lead to the onset of this condition" (p. 29).

Services to the Unwed Father

The agencies that have made a special effort to offer service to the unmarried father have found that he is available, troubled, concerned, and frequently anxious to be of help (Burgess, 1968; Platts, 1968; Pannor *et al.*, 1971).

Perhaps the agency that has most actively and consistently attempted such a service is the Vista Del Mar Child Care Service in Los Angeles, which serves a predominantly urban, middle-class, white clientele. The agency notes that about 80 per cent of the fathers whom they contact are seen and that the majority of those have four or more interviews with the male caseworker (Pannor *et al.*, 1971, p. 59, Table 17).

A public agency that attempted a program of service to unmarried fathers found that in at least 70 per cent of the cases he was "available for interviews and frequently anxious to help in planning for his baby" (Platts, 1968, p. 537).

At least one agency requires that the unmarried mother accepted for service be willing to have the agency contact the unmarried father "for cooperation in giving history and consent to adoption" (Burgess, 1968, p. 72). The agency found that 83 per cent of the fathers whom they attempted to reach "made themselves available for an interview" (Burgess, 1968, p. 72).

A nationwide study of services offered by voluntary agencies to twenty thousand unwed mothers in 1966, however, indicated that only about 7 per cent of the putative fathers were interviewed by the social agencies (Grow, 1967, p. 46). If the putative father was a teenager, there was greater likelihood that he would be seen by the agency.

The failure to make active efforts to include the putative father may be functional. As Barber (1975) notes in a study of unmarried fathers, "The presence of an involved father does complicate the situation. He represents a third opinion which the decision makers have to take into consideration. . . . His exclusion has the advantage of convenience but is fundamentally unrealistic" (p. 20).

The unmarried father's fear that admission of paternity may make him legally responsible for continuing support of mother and child might lead him to refuse the invitation of the agency or to support a decision for adoption, as adoption settles any question of the need for continuing financial support. Putative fathers who are married and have legitimate children are reluctant to contact the agency out of the desire to protect their own families.

At the Vista Del Mar Agency, permission to contact the father is first obtained from the mother, and if possible, the mother arranges to bring the father for his first contact with the agency. A separate male worker is assigned to the father. Where the agency finds it necessary to make a direct contact with the father, it attempts to motivate his participation by stressing his importance in planning for mother and child and by stressing the help the agency can offer the father himself. If this fails to evoke his interest, "legal implication, such as statutory rape, etc. *may* have to be explained, at the worker's discretion, to impress upon the unmarried father the importance of his becoming involved with the agency" (Pannor *et al.*, 1971, p. 55). Many fathers, however, do come when offered the opportunity.

Although follow-up studies show that most of the unwed mothers who keep their child receive AFDC, the child's biological father is a source of some support for a sizable minority of the group (Pozonyi, 1973; Clapp, Raab, 1978). At least for the first year or two after the birth of the child, contact is often maintained with the father, although this gradually phases out. This contact is a source of continuing emotional as well as financial support.

The relationship with the child's father is often sufficiently stable so that many mothers have given consideration to marriage. They are seriously ambivalent about or clearly reject marriage because they objectively assess it as a less desirable alternative. They see the putative father as "irresponsible," "immature," prone to "get into trouble," or "not a suitable father" or feel that they are "better off without him" (Hopkinson, 1976, p. 41). Sometimes, however, it is the father who "backs out" and rejects marriage. With the birth of the baby, the relationship between the partners changes, and the men are assessed by the women not only in terms of their relationship to themselves but also in terms of their feelings toward the child, their sense of responsibility and attachment to the child, and their relationship with the child as a father. If there is a clear feeling that marriage would be a mistake, the mother is less ready to continue to involve the father through pressing for support payments.

The norms and values of the core culture require that a man protect and support the female he has impregnated and their child. There are, of course, many different ways in which the unmarried father mitigates any feeling of responsibility, guilt, or remorse. These range from "It may have been somebody else, not me," to "She didn't have to do it if she didn't want to and she should have taken proper precautions." Yet many men do feel remorse and shame if they fail to come to the support and assistance of the mother and child. Unlike the unmarried mother, the unmarried father does not have the physical and social discomfort of nine months of pregnancy and the pain of delivery through which some "atonement" is achieved.

The agency offering service to the putative father hopes to help him directly in the following ways:

1. By clarifying his attitude toward and relationship with the child, the agency may help him achieve a feeling of psychological fatherhood. This requires a reorientation of his self-concept and is more complex, of course, than the unthinking achievement of physical fatherhood. Without such help, the child remains for the father a shadowy fantasy rather than a living reality.
2. By clarifying his feelings of guilt and responsibility toward the mother and child, the agency may help him come to some decision about what he plans to do in discharging any responsibility he may feel. Contact with the agency can help the unmarried father clarify his financial responsibility to the mother and child and has resulted in substantial contributions toward both (Pannor et al., 1971, p. 95).
3. Contact with the agency can help the unmarried father clarify his relationship with the mother so that he can either dissolve it without excessive guilt or resolve his indecision about marriage.
4. Contact with the agency can help the father to resolve any emotional problem that may have contributed to his becoming a putative father and to reduce the possibility of recurrence.
5. The agency can offer information about any possible legal action against him as well as information regarding his entitlement to the child.

6. The agency helps the unmarried father clarify his indecision about whether or not to share with his own parents the problem he faces so as to obtain their support and help.

The agency is also interested in the indirect service to mother and child that might result from contact with the putative father. Discussion with the unmarried mother of the question of permitting contact with the unmarried father helps her clarify her relationship with him, what she hopes for from him, and what she can realistically expect. Joint sessions among the unwed mother, the father, and the social worker can be helpful in dispelling any romantic, unrealistic fantasies the pair may have about each other and the nature of their relationship. The very fact that the father is taking some responsibility for the decision regarding the child is reassuring and supportive to the mother. As a consequence of sharing this responsibility, the mother may feel more confident and less anxious.

For effective adoptive planning, it is desirable to have detailed information regarding the child's paternal and maternal background. Contact with the putative father can provide more complete information of this nature. (Anglim, 1965). Such knowledge might subsequently be communicated to the adopted child to give him a more complete sense of identity. The father's involvement is important to the child in other ways as well. Consent to the registration of paternity permits the child to claim and obtain benefits from the social security account of the father.

The legal position of the unwed father has been an unenviable one. He has been responsible for support, but the disposition of the child has been decided by the mother. Recently agencies have supported changes so as to make paternity hearings more like civil proceedings and to grant the unwed father some legal entitlement in plans made for the child.

The trend in recent legal decisions has been to give the putative father a greater entitlement in the plans for his out-of-wedlock child. The decisions indicate that the putative father has entitlement to the child and cannot be deprived of it without due process. The decisions do not grant the unwed father custody of his children, nor do they place him wholly on an equal footing with the unmarried mother (see pp. 509–510).

THE DECISION TO KEEP OR PLACE

There are three possible decisions when one is pregnant: to abort, to carry the child to term and keep it, and to carry the child to term and place it for adoption. Having carried the child to term, the mother has two alternatives: to keep it or to place it for adoption.

Although a very high percentage of nonrelative adopted children are born out-of-wedlock, only a small percentage of children born out-of-wedlock are adopted. Most such children are kept and raised by the unmarried mother and/or her family. Whatever the reasons, the recent trend has been for a greater proportion of unmarried mothers to keep their babies rather than surrendering them for adoption.

Sklar and Berkov (1974) estimate on the basis of a detailed study of the relevant statistics that the proportion of out-of-wedlock children adopted in California declined from about 30 per cent in 1967 and 1968 to about 15 per cent in 1971 and 1972. Reports from specific child-welfare agencies support this statistic. For instance, among the unmarried mothers who received counseling from the Family and Children's Service of London and Middlesex, Canada, in 1966, 26 per cent kept their children; in 1971, 62 per cent kept their children. There is, of course, an immediate effect on the number of children available for adoption.

A social worker in a maternity home notes that "whereas in the past one out of every five women in the residence elected to keep their babies, now more than half keep them" (Friedman, 1975, p. 322). And they "are keeping their babies because they want to."

In one study of decision making by five hundred pregnant single women, in only 5 per cent of the cases was the adoption decision ever considered: "Professional advice about adoption was almost never sought" (Bracken, Klerman, Bracken, 1978).

Whereas many women who previously gave up the baby for adoption did so either because they could not care for it or did not want baby care to interfere with other life plans—education, career, marriage, travel—currently the same women would more likely obtain an abortion rather than give birth to a baby they did not want and were not planning to keep. Consequently a much greater percentage of the women who currently carry their children to term are likely to have decided that they want the child and can care for the child. It is not so much that a higher percentage of women are deciding to keep their children once born, but that fewer children destined to be given up for adoption are being born.

Abortion does everything adoption does for the single pregnant women— and more. It eliminates the risk of having the responsibility for care of a child in a single-parent family, it permits the continuation of education and career, and it eliminates the danger of reduced marriage possibilities and the negative sanctions, however attenuated, associated with unwed parenthood. In addition, abortion eliminates the inconvenience and danger of delivery and the trauma of having to give up a child carried to term. Adoption provides a way out of an unwanted birth; abortion provides a way out both of an unwanted pregnancy and of an unwanted birth.

Among adolescents, adoption is now more frequently perceived as an unfashionable, unacceptable cop-out. If the girl has decided to have the baby rather than having an abortion, there is a sense that she is obligated to care for the child.

The tendency to keep rather than to place the child receives additional impetus from the fact that an increasing percentage of children are growing up in single-parent homes. Having experienced this kind of child-rearing context, the mother may be more likely to accept it as a viable possibility for her own child in rejecting adoption.

Research efforts have been devoted to determining the distinguishing characteristics differentiating the group of mothers keeping the child from those surrendering the child (Meyer et al., 1956; Jones et al., 1962; Yelloly, 1965, 1966; Gil, 1969; Festinger, 1971; Grow, 1979).

The factor of race is clearly associated with the decision to keep or surrender the child. More white unmarried mothers give up their children for adoption as compared with black unmarried mothers. There is some controversy as to whether the decision of the black unmarried mother is freely made or a consequence of the more limited adoption opportunities available to black children.

Until recently, many maternity homes (which serve as channels for adoptive placement) were not open to nonwhite women, and most of the adoptive agencies served white adoptive parents. But even now, when more adequate services are available to nonwhites, relatively few nonwhite children achieve adoption, because there is disproportionately a greater supply of such children. Recognition of this reality may have shaped the preference of the nonwhite unmarried mother.

Preference may have been shaped, too, by the historical antecedents of slave culture and subsequent rural living, both of which provide a tradition of extended family care of the black out-of-wedlock child in preference to giving him up. Whatever the determining factors, research reveals that black unmarried mothers express a stronger preference for keeping their children than do white unmarried mothers. Shapiro (1970) found that one of the strongest and clearest differences in racial attitudes related to the adoption of the out-of-wedlock child: black unmarried women "heavily favored keeping children born out-of-wedlock" (p. 59).

The context in which the decision to keep or surrender the child for adoption is made has been changing rapidly as attitudes toward single parenthood change and as services for single parents change. Consequently, some of the earlier research on this question may not accurately reflect the more recent situation. A study of 210 white unmarried mothers in 1973–74 by Grow (1979) may be more relevant. Comparing those who kept their child with the limited number in the group who surrendered their child for adoption, Grow found, in contrast with earlier research, that there was no difference in the mental health functions of the two groups. The women who kept their children more often came from parental homes broken by divorce or separation, so that they had had some experience with single parenthood. They were more likely to be younger and less well educated than women who surrendered their child, knew the putative father longer and were more likely to maintain continuing contact with him, and lived with parents or relatives during pregnancy. There was, consequently, more assurance of a support system available to provide help in keeping the child. Fewer of the mothers who kept their child were attending school and motherhood represented less of a change in life-style and career planning than was the case for mothers surrendering the child for adoption.

Timing

The timing and firmness of the mother's decision are important variables. The sooner the mother decides, the sooner the agency can begin to make definite plans for disposition. If she decides upon adoption, the child can be placed in an adoptive home directly from the hospital in which he has been delivered. This reduces the possibility of discontinuity of mothering for the child, the problem of adjusting to a number of different mothers, and the trauma of separation after becoming adjusted to some mothering person.

It may be argued that an early decision is in the best interests of the mother as well. If giving up the child is an act of major psychic surgery, it might be less difficult before the mother builds a strong affectional relationship with the child. However, it is also argued that the mother needs some time in contact with the child to resolve whatever decision she has made. A hurried decision entails the risk of subsequent regret and of attempts to reverse the decisions, with disruptive consequences for the adoptive parent and the child. Hence the firmness of the decision is as important as its promptness.

Perhaps a two-stage process is desirable: a tentative conclusion before the baby is born and a final ratification afterward.

The agency's principal tenet is to encourage flexibility in decision making, which permits each mother to come to her own decision in her own time. In general, research indicates that most mothers come to a firm, consistent decision either before or shortly after birth of the child. A study of 221 unmarried mothers showed that "four out of every five single mothers reached their decision within a week after confinement" (Triseliotis, 1969, p. 35).

Interviews with 116 mothers in Scotland who carried their out-of-wedlock children to term despite the availability of a publicly subsidized abortion program indicated that most of the mothers decided they wanted to keep the child from the time they realized they were pregnant (Hopkinson, 1976, p. 33). For some, this was a consequence of their continued relationship with the putative father; for some, guilt and a sense of responsibility toward the child were factors. For most of the mothers, however, the decision was based on their emotional involvement with the child and a desire to be a mother to the child. If they had given any consideration to adoption as an alternative outcome, it was not self-initiated but in response to parental pressure. Pannor *et al.* (1971) and Bowerman (1966) also found that the women they studied had also made an early decision.

The factors that appear to be related to the decision to place or keep the baby and the findings regarding the timing and the consistency of the decision feed into each other. The decision to place or keep the child is most strongly associated with situational circumstances—age, educational level, socioeconomic position—which are assessable even before birth of the child and act as principal constraints on the mother, limiting her options. The emotional relationship with the child and attachment to the child are not generally as important a factor in the decision. Realistically recognizing and evaluating her situation even before delivery, the mother generally comes to a decision about what she can do and has to do. Contact with the child only infrequently results in a change of decision. Thus Yelloly (1965, 1966) found that of 160 unmarried mothers, 68 per cent made a decision very early in the pregnancy—a decision to which they held with consistency and upon which they finally acted. In most instances, the decision was based on strong objective considerations, such as the presence of other children of the mother, the married status of the putative father, and the attitude of the mother's parents.

In follow-up interviews with unmarried mothers who kept their children, Reed and Latimer (1962) found that "72 percent of all mothers decided before the birth of the baby to keep the baby." Most were lower-class nonwhites. However, more than "half of the middle-class girls did not decide to keep the baby until after the birth of the baby" (p. 90). Mothers who had few choices made a decision early; mothers with more options made the decision later. The research further notes that mothers with prolonged ambivalence and strong conflicts about the decision are apt to be less emotionally stable and ultimately more likely to keep the child. This finding would suggest that these mothers are less responsive to the constraints of external reality and act more in response to internal emotional needs.

Of interest to social workers is the mother's perception of who helped her make the decision. In the overwhelming percentage of instances, the mothers studied by Bowerman (1966) said they turned to their parents for help—most frequently to their own mothers. Female relatives (sisters, aunts, grandmothers) were also frequently consulted: "The alleged father is brought into these considerations relatively rarely . . . [and] it is very clear that the counsel of physicians, social workers, and other professionals (attorneys, clergymen, teachers) is sought by (or 'urged upon') but a small fraction of the respondents, almost all of whom are white" (pp. 197–99). Only about 1 per cent indicated that a social worker had been most important in influencing the decision. It thus appears that in most instances, the caseworker is faced with helping the mother to confirm and implement a decision rather than helping the mother to make it. Raynor (1971) came to the same conclusion in a study of British unwed mothers; 70 per cent of the mothers made their decision before the baby was born. Fewer than two out of five had discussed their decision with a social worker before making it, although the social worker was instrumental in implementing a plan that had already been made.

Stating the data another way, however, accentuates the service need. The studies cited earlier show that 20–30 per cent of the unwed mothers are undecided about their decision, often up to and beyond the birth of the baby. It is this group—a sizable group in terms of numbers—who need and may welcome the help of the social worker in clarifying a difficult, significant decision.

Of interest to social workers is the fact that seeing the child and caring for the child after birth made the decision to give up the child easier for some but more difficult for most of the mothers studied. The preference was to make a firm decision and act on it as early as possible. Most of the mothers indicated that delaying the final implementation of the decision created conflict for them.

Even if, as is so often the case, the mother has made a clear decision about what she plans to do about the pregnancy before meeting the social worker, the worker can still make a significant contribution. He can mediate between the client and the pressures of others who might want the client to accept their own solution. In addition, the worker may help the client resolve any additional ambivalence about her decision and increase her satisfaction with it. The worker may also mobilize resources to implement the choice decided on by the client.

Keeping the Child

The unmarried mother who places her child for adoption has been the primary concern of child welfare agencies. Yet it is recognized that a larger percentage of unmarried mothers keep their children and that frequently child welfare problems derive from this fact. However, there are few specific services directed primarily to this segment of the single-parent population.

It may be unwise and unhelpful to attempt to provide services during and immediately after pregnancy and to abandon the client once she has become established as a parent.

Because unmarried mothers continue to have problems, with which they struggle more or less successfully, while contact with the social worker tapers off, perhaps the worker should seriously consider follow-up visits at periodic intervals. Although such visits might be construed as an unwelcome intrusion and invasion of privacy, one follow-up research interviewer "found little to support this objection in the mother's attitudes toward my visits. The fact that the mothers did not seek out assistance or advice was not an indication that it was not needed, nor that it would not be welcomed if offered" (Hopkinson, 1976, p. 227).

For many unmarried mothers who keep their child, the critical period is likely to come at the end of the first year. By then, it is clear that some of the more optimistic plans are not going to be achieved; the romanticism of parenthood has worn off and the confining drudgery of reality has become apparent; the good intentions of support from parents, relatives, friends, and the child's father have worn thin or have been exhausted; and possibilities for real change appear more limited. More adequate financial assistance and child care and housing are among the most frequently identified in unmet needs of this group.

It is estimated that about 60 per cent of all out-of-wedlock children eventually receive public aid at one time or another (Moore, Caldwell, 1976). In 1969 some 29 per cent of all children on AFDC were born out of wedlock; by 1975 the number had increased to 31 per cent and was the largest single contingency occasioning the need for assistance.

Living with parents solves the housing problem, some of the problems of loneliness, the availability of an emotional support system, and some of the problems of helping with child care. These advantages, however, are obtained at a price that often results in a decision to establish an independent household. There may be disagreements about the care of the child and generational conflicts about the nature of the mother's social life and expectations. The mother may be dissatisfied with her continuing dependent-child status, and the unwed mother may, in her parents' eyes, become an older sibling to her own child. The parents may resent the overcrowding and finding themselves involved in child care at a time in their lives when they thought they would be free of it. As a consequence of these problems, there is a gradual tendency for more mothers to establish independent living situations and fewer to continue to live with their parents (Hopkinson, 1976; Clapp, Raab, 1978).

Although many unwed mothers date and continue to be sexually active, loneliness and social isolation are still a problem, particularly for those living independently and not working; work provides meaningful social contacts as well as income. The desire for counseling and group service is highest among nonworking mothers in independent living situations (Clapp, Raab, 1978).

Teenage parenthood may be particularly difficult for mother and child. Becoming a parent in adolescence increases the the risk of the disruption of education, with consequent effects on employment opportunities and income. Becoming a parent to a child out of wedlock in adolescence reduces the options available:

The girl who has an illegitimate child at the age of 16 suddenly has 90 percent of her life's script written for her. She will probably drop out of school; even if someone else in her family helps to take care of the baby, she will probably not be able to find a steady job that pays enough to provide for herself and her child, she may feel impelled to marry someone she might not otherwise have chosen. Her life chances are few [Campbell, 1968, p. 238].

Furstenberg states that there is a normative schedule of developmental tasks that need to be completed before one moves to the next life stage. Early parenthood, especially when it occurs out of wedlock, is a significant departure from the normative sequence. Adolescence is a time for establishing social, emotional, and economic independence from one's parents. It is a stage of preparation through education for a job and a career. The role of parent is incompatible with the role of student. The demands of a dependent baby force the adolescent parent to seek emotional and economic support from her own parents instead of attempting to achieve independence. Adolescence is a time for experimenting with and establishing an identity; early parenthood imposes an identity. Some of the most significant life choices, for which adolescence should be the preparation, are prematurely preempted or foreclosed, choices relating to a career, a mate, and the decision to become a parent. "Unscheduled parenthood" thus has the effect of accelerated "premature status transition, propelling people into positions (parenthood) they are unready or unprepared to assume, and forcing them to relinquish statuses that they currently enjoy (adolescence)" (Furstenberg, 1976, p. 4).

The consequence is a higher risk of failure to complete education; premature entrance into the job market, with access only to repetitive, uninteresting jobs that pay marginal wages; early, rapid childbearing; and limitations on the normal opportunities for social development.

The empirical research seems to support the hypothesis. Follow-up studies of adolescent unmarried parents show that they were behind their peers in terms of educational achievement, employment and career opportunities, and income (Furstenberg, 1976; Trussell, 1976; Moore, Waite, 1977; Card, Wise, 1978). Two things need to be noted. First, it is not clear that the disadvantaged outcomes are primarily related to out-of-wedlock pregnancies. Many of these adolescents were doing poorly in school prior to the pregnancy and might have dropped out in any case; many came from disadvantaged backgrounds that presented difficulties even without a pregnancy, for successfully completing the normative sequence of tasks. Second, many adolescent mothers do not conform to the typical "outcome." Furstenberg (1976) says in his analysis of lower-class black unwed mothers, "One of the most impressive findings was the diversity of responses to a common event" (the out-of-wedlock pregnancy); "The outcome of the five year follow-up was enormously varied" (p. 218).

There is little specific follow-up service to unmarried mothers who keep their children, but there have been studies that are concerned with what happens to the mother and the out-of-wedlock child who stay together (Reed, Latimer, 1962; Pakter, Nelson, 1965; Sauber, 1965; Wright, 1965; Crumidy, Jacobziner, 1966; Opel, 1969; Corrigan, 1970; Sauber, Corrigan, 1970; Crellin *et al.*, 1971).

The results generally are a tribute to the heterogeneity of the unmarried mother group and a confirmation of the fact that no stereotype is applicable to this group as Furstenberg validly noted.

As Sauber and Corrigan (1970) say, "although these women shared the common experience of bearing a child out-of-wedlock and rearing that child, their lives as mothers followed many different paths" (p. 145). Many get married and merge into the two-parent family group; many remain single. Many have additional out-of-wedlock children; some do not. Some are employed full-time and self-supporting; some are employed part-time and receive supplementary help from relatives; some are wholly supported by relatives (including continuing contributions from the putative father); some are supported by public assistance. Some are living with relatives; some with friends; many alone. For most mothers, recreational and social life and involvement in community activity are limited and meager, but most resume their place among an accepting group of friends and relatives. A few have continued their education or have received further vocational training; most, however, have not. A substantial minority face financial difficulty and live in substandard housing. A very high percentage indicated that given the opportunity, they would decide once again to keep the child (Bernstein, 1966, 1971).

In almost all instances, they appear to be reasonably adequate, concerned mothers who are doing a creditable job in rearing their children. Very few of the children are placed in foster homes or with relatives; even fewer are neglected and/or abused.

One of the earliest follow-up studies of unmarried mothers, which involved interviews with fifty-four women some eight years after their confinement, concluded that "adoption was not necessarily the only desirable solution, as evidenced by the fact that some mothers who kept their children seemed to have done well by both the children and themselves" (Levy, 1955, p. 33).

A study by Reed and Latimer published in 1962 reviewed the situation for 118 mothers, both black and white. Physical and psychological examinations of the children showed the largest majority of them to be "developing normally physically, mentally, and emotionally" (p. 107). Similarly Wright's (1965) interview study of eighty unmarried mothers who kept their babies concludes that "contrary to the original hypothesis, a majority of the children were judged to be faring well" (p. 52).

The child-rearing practices of unmarried mothers who keep their children are not essentially different from those of comparative samples of low-income black and white mothers, although unmarried mothers are more concerned about restricting aggressive behavior and more likely to stress the importance of doing well in school (Corrigan, 1970).

Oppel (1969) compared the care and development of black illegitimate children with a matched group of legitimate children. The findings did not support the "contentions that mothers of illegitimate children are more likely to give poor care to their children than are mothers of legitimate children" (p. 133). Nor was there any significant difference in development of the two groups of children.

A careful follow-up study of unmarried mothers who kept their babies was conducted by Sauber for the Community Council of New York. The study reported on the adjustment of mother and child one and a half years after birth (Sauber, 1965) and then again six years after birth (Sauber and Corrigan, 1970). Some 90 per cent of the 205 women still in the study when the child was six were black or Puerto Rican. A comparison between these children and legitimate children in the community studied by the Manhattan Survey of Psychiatric Impairment of Urban Children showed that they were essentially similar in emotional functioning (Sauber and Corrigan, 1970, p. 138).

The report echoes the implications of the studies already cited—that "more recognition should be given to the *strengths* of one-parent families rather than too hasty an attribution of pathology to them" (p. 45). The report concludes:

> The study findings clearly challenge many myths about women who have had a child out of wedlock. For the great majority, this experience has not been the beginning of a life of promiscuity, instability, and dependency. Although some have suffered, the majority have coped very well, pursuing their lives in different ways, with the result that, six years after their first child was born, they have, in most respects, blended into the general population of mothers and children and exhibit the wide range of life styles and life situations found among families in the population generally. Perhaps the greatest service that could be rendered to this group is that they no longer be labeled "unwed mothers" but that they be viewed as parents, often single parents, of young children, and that they be provided with the respect and the social and economic supports necessary for them to carry out these roles [p. 157].

A study in Scotland of 116 unwed mothers who kept their child showed the great resourcefulness and determination of these mothers against considerable odds (Hopkinson, 1976). Coming from disadvantaged family backgrounds and having left school at the minimum legal age, they provided good care to their children on limited incomes. They requested social work assistance during crisis periods and the help provided was in the nature of practical assistance.

Contrary to these general positive findings, however, are the results of a careful follow-up study in England that compared the development of out-of-wedlock children placed in adoptive homes with the progress made by out-of-wedlock children who remained in a single-parent home with the mother. On the basis of most of the criteria employed in the study, the adoptive child's adjustment and development were in advance of his nonadopted out-of-wedlock peer (Crellin *et al.*, 1971).

A five-year follow-up of children of adolescent unmarried mothers, as contrasted with a comparison group of children, showed that the children of the unmarried mothers "were less well-equipped in terms of cognitive skills than their counterparts in the other samples." However, "there was no clear indication that children of adolescent parents are more socially maladjusted" (Furstenberg, 1976, p. 214).

The unmarried mother, parents, extended family, and friends are very often the most potent source of support services that can be mobilized to help in making the adjustments required by single parenthood (Furstenberg, Crawford, 1978). They provide child care to enable the mother to complete her education or to work, and they provide food, clothing, housing, financial aid, child-rearing advice, and emotional support. Unmarried mothers who continue to live with their parents are more likely to receive such help than women living alone. A high proportion of unmarried mothers and their parents continue to maintain positive, supportive relationships. "The assistance rendered by family members significantly alters the life chances of the young mother" (Furstenberg, Crawford, 1978, p. 333). This support system is an important resource that the social worker might help to mobilize.

The mother who keeps her child takes her place in the community along with all other single mothers who are rearing their children without benefit of a husband–father, because of death, desertion, divorce, or separation. The problems encountered by the single parent who comes to single parenthood through an out-of-wedlock birth are not significantly different from those encountered by other single parents. The services required by the unwed mother who keeps her child are, in essence, those required by all single parents: income maintenance, help with housing, day care, vocational education, job referral, help in finding adult companionship, help in making contacts with eligible males, and and help in finding satisfying leisure activity. Ultimately these mothers do face a special difficult problem: explaining to the child the whereabouts of the father.

Only occasionally, as in AFDC application or housing project application, is any distinction made between out-of-wedlock single parenthood and other kinds of single parenthood, to the disadvantage of the former. In making application for AFDC, the mother has to name and initiate action against the putative father for support of the child. Housing projects frequently discriminate against unmarried mothers. But in general, public policies and socioeconomic conditions helpful to the single-parent family headed by a woman are also helpful to the unmarried mother who keeps her child.

Here, as in adoption, the significant factor that differentiates this family from other single-parent families headed by a woman lies in the nature of the genesis of the particular family. Once past genesis, however, the essential points of similarity between all single-parent families headed by a woman are overwhelmingly greater than any differences.

In exemplification of this change in orientation, the National Council for the Unmarried Mother and her Child (established in 1918 in England) changed its name to National Council for One Parent Families in 1974. Nevertheless there is some persistence of the idea that the social and economic situation is, or should be, different for the single parent with an out-of-wedlock child. An effort is made to preserve the subjective perception of the difference between having a child in the context of marriage and outside this context. If this were not the case, we would just as actively accept adoption as an option for the separated, divorced, or widowed single parent as for the never-married single parent (MacIntyre, 1977, pp. 185–187).

PROBLEMS

1. Providing adequate services to the unmarried mother and her child involves a very understandable ambivalence. Agencies can be, and are, criticized for doing "too much" by those whose concern is with conservatively maintaining social institutions and who see any help to the unmarried mother as an encouragement of illegitimacy; agencies are also criticized for doing "too little" by those who are concerned with the needs of the unmarried mother and her child. The threat to the mores conflicts with compassion for the child. This is the classic dilemma that has consistently made difficult the offering of help needed by the unwed mother and her child.

A permissive attitude toward illegitimacy would suggest that society attaches no great significance to marriage as the context for child rearing.

The question is whether or not such a conflict is as true as it is seemingly obvious. Certainly more punitive attitudes toward the unmarried mother and her child have not discouraged increases in illegitimacy rates, nor have more liberal public policies invariably resulted in sharp increases in illegitimacy rates (Wimperis, 1960, pp. 323–324).

In an article comparing worldwide illegitimacy rates, the 1957 edition of the Encyclopaedia Britannica comments that "the policies regarding illegitimate children have been especially liberal in the Scandinavian countries, and studies conducted in these countries have produced no evidence that such a liberal policy promoted illegitimacy" (Vol. 12, p. 85).

The persistent myth of a relationship between the adequacy of welfare programs available to the unmarried mother and increases in illegitimacy is very carefully examined both nationally (as it affects the AFDC program) and internationally, by Cutright (1971), who found it to have no basis in fact. Apparently illegitimacy rates are not very responsive to positive changes in the level of such services and assistance.

Nor are they responsive to punitive measures, such as voluntary or compulsory sterilization, denial of public assistance, and criminal prosecution. In general, where such measures (particularly restriction of financial assistance) have been implemented, they have not resulted in any reduction in illegitimacy rates. They have, however, resulted in more deprived living conditions for the children affected by such policies.

2. There is a problem in developing procedures and approaches for reducing the illegitimacy rate. The illegitimacy rate is reflective of many pervasive aspects of the culture. Prominent public figures, such as actresses Vanessa Redgrave and Mia Farrow, and a member of the British Parliament, Bernadette Devlin, have proudly, openly, and without apology borne children out of wedlock. Such examples both reflect and encourage a more matter-of-fact attitude toward unwed parenthood.

A popular seventeen-year-old character in the Mary Worth comic strip, syndicated nationwide, discovered, in 1978, that she was pregnant out of wedlock shortly after winning a national scholarship. She goes on, in the cartoon strip, to sort out the options open to a pregnant, unwed teenager with Mary Worth's help. There is no imputation of moral stigma associated with the pregnancy in the cartoon story.

In reducing the negative sanctions against sexual activity, outside of the exclusive confines of a marital relationship, as exemplified by group sex and the more casual acceptance of extramarital sex, society has also reduced some of the negative sanctions against premarital sex. There is a growing acceptance, particularly among younger people, that sexual behavior among consenting participants is a matter of personal choice rather than of morality, although young women are still somewhat more conservative than young men in this matter. There is an acceptance of sex as an egalitarian, nonexploitive experience that is recreational as well as relational in nature. It is seen as an expression of open, honest intimacy representing emotional freedom and promoting individual growth.

We have never had a tradition of rigid separation of the sexes during adolescence, of chaperonage, or of compulsory marriage in the event of premarital pregnancy. But premarital chastity, particularly in females, was the norm to which adherence was expected—despite contrary actual behavior. The current norm is less hypocritical, and there is greater congruence between our expressed attitudes and our actual behavior. However, it would be naive to expect that a changing attitude toward sex behavior does not affect the level of premarital sexual activity, increasing the risk of out-of-wedlock pregnancies.

3. There is continued public ambivalence about countermeasures that might reduce the number of out-of-wedlock pregnancies, and there is hesitant support for such measures. There is some basis for the contention that concerted efforts to provide information and services to all fecund women of whatever age or marital status do result in a modest reduction in first out-of-wedlock pregnancies and repeated out-of-wedlock pregnancies (Furstenberg, 1970; Yurdin, 1970) and that freer access to elective abortion does result in a decline in out-of-wedlock births (Hartly, 1970, p. 87; Cartright, 1971, p. 33).

However, compulsory school-based sex education, contraceptive services, and abortion services are still a matter of public controversy and far from universally available.

In 1975 some 4 million teenage women, most of them unmarried, were sexually active and not intending to get pregnant. Of this group, 60 per cent were receiving contraceptive services from 340 hospitals, 1,500 health departments, 170 Planned Parenthood affiliates, and 500 "other" agencies, such as neighborhood health centers and community action programs (Alan Guttmacher Institute, 1978). Organized contraceptive services for adolescents were available in most parts of the United States. However, the fact that 40 per cent of sexually active, unmarried teenagers had not received family-planning services from any organized facility in 1975 is a cause for concern. We have yet to resolve our ambivalence about advertising family-planning services on billboards, TV, buses, and T-shirts and in newspapers and magazines.

Some 30 per cent of women estimated to want abortion in 1976 were unable to obtain it, primarily because it was not available. In 1975, two years after the U.S. Supreme Court ruling on abortions, it was estimated that as "many as 770,000 women who needed abortions—mostly the young, the poor and the rural —could not get them" (*The New York Times*, January 2, 1977). In 1976 eight out of ten counties in the United States had no abortion service.

Many disadvantaged, young, rural, nonwhite women thus had to find the time, the money, and the sophistication required to go to an unfamiliar community to obtain an abortion (Forrest, Tietze, Sullivan, 1978).

The financing of abortions for low-income women is a growing problem. Medicaid funds had earlier been available to pay for abortions for women who could not afford them. In 1976, however, Congress legislated to restrict federal contributions to Medicaid payments for abortion. The states could continue on their own to pay all of the charges for an abortion under Medicaid. However, as a consequence of the financial burden this would impose, many states restricted access to abortion for low-income women who could not afford an abortion without such help.

In 1977, before the passage of such restrictive legislation, an estimated 300,000 poor American women obtained a publicly subsidized abortion; approximately 85,000 of such subsidized abortions involved teenagers. Access to abortion was made more difficult by additional legislation adopted by some states, including the restrictive regulation of clinics offering abortion, the requirement of parental and spouse consent before the mother could get an abortion, and "informed-consent" laws that required that the woman be told explicitly about the viability of the fetus to be aborted. In pressing for the adoption of all these various legislative and judicial procedures, the prolife, antiabortion groups were pitted against the prochoice, proabortion groups.

In addition to the inadequacies in programs of sex education, contraceptive services, and abortion, access to income maintenance services and medical services are a problem for women pregnant out of wedlock. In some states, neither maintenance payments nor medical services under the AFDC program are available until after the birth of the child.

4. There is a problem regarding the accessibility to contraceptives and abortion services for minors without notification to or consent of parents. All barriers to nonprescriptive contraceptives—vaginal foams, jellies, condoms—have been generally removed. The problem relates to contraceptives requiring medical prescriptions and procedures, such as the pill, the diaphragm, and the IUD. Here the constitutional right of minors to privacy conflicts with the fact that physicians are liable to a civil suit if they treat minors without parental permission. A U.S. Supreme Court decision in 1976 (in the Danforth case) did give minors the right to an elective abortion without prior parental permission, although nothing was settled about possible notification of the parents.

Minors have already won the right to treatment of venereal disease and drug and alcohol abuse without parental consent.

Social security regulations require that the AFDC program make family-planning services available to all sexually active recipients of public assistance and Medicaid, whether they are minors or not.

The argument in favor of privacy is that the requirement of consent or even notification deters minors from using family-planning or abortion services. The adolescent may continue to remain sexually active, although failing to use the service, and risk the possibility of pregnancy rather than deal with parental reaction to the knowledge that she is having intercourse.

The request for contraceptive information and service generally follows, rather than preceding, the initiation of sexual activity, so that the availability of contraception is not the stimulus for such activity (Settlage, Boroff, Cooper, 1973).

The argument in favor of parental notification and/or consent rests on the fact that parents have a "compelling interest" in what is happening to their child, for whom they still have primary responsibility; that providing such options as contraceptives and abortion without parental consent weakens family ties and erodes parental authority; that knowledge about a crucial aspect of their child's life may permit them greater opportunity for counsel and advice; and that the family need to know about the use of a drug such as the pill if they are to deal with the health needs of their children. In addition, it is felt that making family-planning services available to teenagers without parental knowledge or consent is tantamount to community sanction of premarital sex. Although advocates of parental notification and/or consent grant that there is no evidence of any direct link between the availability of services and the decision to engage in sexual activity, they point to the general climate of permissiveness sanctioned by the availability of such programs to minors.

A recapitulation in 1975 showed that some twenty-six states permitted access to contraceptives and abortion without parental consent for those fifteen years of age and older.

A study in 1978 (Torres, 1978) of some fifteen hundred unmarried adolescents seventeen years of age and younger indicated that 55 per cent of the adolescents receiving family-planning services had themselves notified their parents. An additional 9 per cent said that their parents did not know but that even if they had been informed, the teenager would have used the service. A group of 20 per cent would have decided not to come if their parents had had to be informed, but this group would have resorted to the nonmedical contraceptive procedures available without consent. In 12 per cent of the cases, the teenager would have continued to have sex and would not have used the service or any protection. Only 4 per cent of the group said that as a consequence of the notification requirement, they would have stopped having sex. The study suggests that the net effect of notification and/or consent laws is likely to result not in a reduction in sexual activity but in continued activity with less effective protection or no protection at all for a substantial percentage of current service users.

TRENDS

We have already noted some of the trends relating to this area of service: an increase in the number of children born out-of-wedlock but a decrease in the out-of-wedlock birthrate for all groups except white teenagers; a decrease in the number of women who, carrying the child to term, surrender the child for adoption; a decrease in maternity home service and an increase in the development of community-based, multi-service agencies targeted on school-aged single pregnant women; and increasing efforts to reduce the legal disadvantages of out-of-wedlock status. Some additional trends follow.

1. There is increasing public recognition of, and concern with, the problem. There is public concern over the increasing percentage of children supported by AFDC who are born out-of-wedlock. By 1978 out-of-wedlock birth was unequivocally in first place as the reason for need. Illegitimacy is thus imposing an increasing financial burden on the community.

But there is another element in the recent concern: the white middle-class community has gradually become aware that illegitimacy involves a growing percentage of its own sons and daughters. No longer is it a condition confined to blacks or to the "promiscuous," the "feebleminded," or the "products of broken homes": "The middle and upper social strata [now] feel threatened because of their growing sense that their own children are engaging in precisely the kinds of activities which they once thought were the exclusive properties of the lower class" (Goode, 1967, p. 272).

There is particular concern with the continued increasing rate of teenage out-of-wedlock births. Special organizational and legislative efforts have been targeted on this group.

The Consortium on Early Child Bearing and Child Rearing, affiliated with the Child Welfare League of America, and the National Alliance Concerned with School Age Parents are among the organizations concerned with education and service regarding early parenting.

The Adolescent Health Services, Pregnancy Prevention and Care Act of 1978 proposes a five-year program with federal matching funds to supplement existing services and to coordinate existing services, with some limited funds for new services. The objective of the bill "is to prevent unwanted initial and repeat pregnancies among adolescents and decrease the likelihood that they will become dependent on welfare." An Office of Adolescent Pregnancy Programs has been established in the Department of Health, Education and Welfare.

2. Despite the fact that males become sexually active at an earlier age than females, little family-planning effort has been specifically directed to them. The experimental distribution of free condoms at places where males generally hang out has been attempted, and some group rap-session programs have been attempted. A study of high school males showed that although they had knowledge of contraception, usage appeared to be haphazard and inconsistent. More than half of the 420 respondents to a questionnaire agreed that "only the female should use birth control" (Finkel, 1975, p. 257), indicating a limited commitment to the consistent use of male-controlled methods of contraception, such as withdrawal and the condom.

We have already noted that greater efforts have been made to involve the putative father in the decisions regarding his child. This is one aspect of a more general trend pressing for changes in attitude and services that make contraception, abortion, pregnancy, child care, and support a matter of shared concern. There is increasing recognition that at each point in the process, both the male and female have to accept responsibility for the decision and contribute what they can to implementing the decision.

3. Social agencies are beginning to face the effective competition of many other organizations in offering services of prime interest to many unmarried mothers: agencies established by clergy, women's liberation organizations, and grass-roots organizations representing the youth counterculture. Every college newspaper and every underground press publication carries ads or notices about the availability of contraceptive information and abortion counseling. Such groups, which have no official connection with social work, provide access to and sometimes financial aid for abortion and contraception to all women, no matter what their age or marital status.

A testimonial to the growing number of recently developed services is the special listing "Problem Pregnancies" in the Yellow Pages of some phone books.

4. Agencies are beginning to note that they are receiving more requests from unmarried mothers who have kept their children but who are finding, after a year or two of struggle, that they need help. There is a shift then to greater concern with postnatal services. These include the development of services for the unmarried mother and her child for some time after the birth of the child. For instance, the Louise Wise Agency in New York City, an adoption agency, runs a postnatal residence for unmarried mothers, where some twenty women may stay as long as six months after the birth of their babies (Benas, 1975; Kreech, 1975).

The single-parent program in Omaha, Nebraska, serves a block of apartments in a housing development for single parents (Heger, 1977). In addition to low-cost housing, the agency provides job training or schooling, social services, and day care in a center located in the housing unit. The program is coordinated by social workers. Individual counseling is supplemented by group sessions. Contracts are developed in line with goals selected by the mothers in consultation

with the social workers. The agency has found a low-keyed approach most helpful, teaching child care, for instance, not in a didactic fashion but at a point
where a mother has difficulty in child discipline.

SUMMARY

Out-of-wedlock births are the principal source of children for adoption. Consequently adoption agencies are very much involved with the problem of the
single pregnant woman.

Although the number of illegitimacies has increased over the 1960s, the rate
of increase has diminished. The rate among nonwhites is considerably higher
than that among whites, largely for historical and socioeconomic reasons.

The single pregnant woman needs medical, housing, and financial help as
well as help in preparing for the birth of the child and in deciding whether
to keep the child or to give it up for adoption. The agency provides a variety
of services to meet these needs and also attempts to help the putative father.

Studies show that the woman who keeps her child is more apt to be nonwhite, lower-class, and limited in education. There is limited support for the contention that she is likely to be somewhat less mature than the woman who gives
up the child.

Follow-up studies of the mothers who keep their children show that care is
adequate and child development generally normal. However, such children are
at a developmental disadvantage when compared with children who have been
placed for adoption. The mother who keeps her child faces essentially the same
problems as mothers who have lost their husbands.

Among the problems noted were

1. The continuing ambivalence about offering the necessary help and
   services to the unmarried mother and the out-of-wedlock child.
2. The changing sex norms, which increase the risk of such pregnancies.
3. The lack of services for some groups of women, particularly the nonwhite and the poor.
4. Problems concerning parental consent for services to teesage women.

Among the trends noted were

1. The increasing number of out-of-wedlock births but the decreasing rates
   for all groups except white teenage women.
2. The decreasing number of children born out of wedlock surrendered for
   adoption.
3. The increasing concern with the problem of teenage pregnancy.
4. The greater involvement of the putative father in decisions regarding the
   child and greater concern about his responsibility throughout.
5. The proliferation of agencies outside of social work concerned with this
   problem.
6. The development of multiservice centers to meet the needs of the
   teenage unmarried mother and services to the unmarried mother who
   keeps her child and the decrease in maternity home service.

BIBLIOGRAPHY

ADAMS, HANNAH. *Social Services for Unmarried Mothers and Their Children Provided Through Public and Voluntary Child Welfare Agencies,* Child Welfare Report No. 12. Washington, D.C.: Government Printing Office, 1962.

ALAN GUTMACHER INSTITUTE. *Contraceptive Services for Adolescents: United States and County, 1975.* New York: Alan Gutmacher Institute, 1978.

ANGLIM, ELIZABETH. "The Adopted Child's Heritage—Two Natural Parents." *Child Welfare,* 44, 6 (June 1965).

BARBER, DULAN. *Unmarried Fathers.* London: Hutchinson Co., 1975.

BARCLAY, LILLIAN E. "A Group Approach to Young Unwed Mothers." *Social Casework,* 50, 7 (July 1969), 379–384.

BEDGER, JEAN E. *The Crittenton Study—An Assessment of Client Functioning Before and After Services.* Chicago: Crittenton Comprehensive Care Center, April 1969.

BENAS, EVELYN. "Residential Care of the Child Mother and Her Infant—An Extended Family Concept." *Child Welfare,* 54, 4 (April 1975), 291–294.

BENNET, VIRGINIA C., and JACK I. BARDON. "The Effects of School Programs on Teenage Mothers and Their Children." *American Journal of Orthopsychiatry,* 47, 4 (1977), 671–678.

BERNSTEIN, ROSE. "Unmarried Parents and Their Families." *Child Welfare,* 45, 4 (April 1966), 185–193.

———. *Helping Unmarried Mothers.* New York: Association Press, 1971.

BOWERMAN, CHARLES E., et al. *Unwed Motherhood: Personal and Social Consequences.* Chapel Hill, N.C.: Institute for Research in Social Science, University of North Carolina, 1966.

BOYKIN, NANCY M. "A School-Centered Multidiscipline Approach to the Problems of Teen-Age Pregnancy." *Child Welfare,* 47, 8 (October 1968), 478–487.

BRACKEN, MARCH. "Lessons Learned from a Baby Care Club for Unmarried Mothers." *Children,* 18, 4 (July–August 1971), 133–137.

BRACKEN, MICHAEL, LORRAINE KLERMAN, and MARYANN BRACKEN. "Coping with Pregnancy Resolution Among Never Married Women." *American Journal of Orthopsychiatry,* 48, 2 (April 1978), 320–332.

BREMNER, ROBERT H. *Children and Youth in America—A Documentary History,* Vol. 1: *1600–1865.* Cambridge, Mass.: Harvard University Press, 1970.

BURGESS, LINDA. "The Unmarried Father in Adoption Planning." *Children,* 15, 2 (March–April 1968), 71–74.

BUSFIELD, BERNARD L., et al. *Out-of-Wedlock Pregnancy—What Happens Next: An In-depth Survey of Postnatal Unwed Mothers Treated by Long-term Group Therapy.* Boston: Crittenton Hastings House, 1969.

CAMPBELL, ARTHUR. "The Role of Family Planning in the Reduction of Poverty." *Journal of Marriage and the Family,* 30, 2 (1968), 236–245.

CARD, JOSEFINA J., and LAUREN L. WISE. "Teenage Mothers and Teenage Fathers: The Impact of Early Child Bearing on the Parents' Personal and Professional Lives." *Family Planning Perspectives,* 10, 4 (July–August, 1978), 199–207.

CARTOOF, VIRGINIA G. "Post Partum Services for Adolescent Mothers." *Child Welfare,* 57 (December 1978), 660–666.

CAUGHLIN, JEANNE. "Psychic Hazards of Unwed Paternity." *Social Work,* 5, 3 (July 1960), 29–35.

CHEETHAM, JULIET. *Unwanted Pregnancy and Counseling.* London: Routledge, Kegan Paul, 1977.

CHILMAN, CATHERINE. *Social and Psychological Aspects of Adolescent Sexuality—An Analytic Overview of Research and Theory.* Milwaukee: Center for Advanced Studies in Human Services, University of Wisconsin—Milwaukee.

CLAPP, DOUGLAS F., and REBECCA S. RAAB. "Followup of Unmarried Adolescent Mothers." *Social Work* (March 1978), 149–153.

CORRIGAN, EILEEN M. "The Child at Home: Child-Rearing Practices of Unwed Mothers Compared to Other Mothers," in *Illegitimacy: Changing Services for Changing Times.* New York: National Council on Illegitimacy, 1970.

CRELIN, EILEEN, M. L. KELLMER PRINGLE, and PATRICK WEST. *Born Illegitimate—Social and Educational Implications.* London: National Children's Bureau, 1971.

CROCKETT, MARY L. "Examination of Services to the Unmarried Mother in Relation to Age of Adoptive Placement of the Baby," in *Casework Papers.* New York: Family Service Association of America, 1960.

CRUMIDY, PEARL M., and HAROLD JACOBZINER. "A Study of Young Unmarried Mothers Who Kept Their Babies." *American Journal of Public Health,* **56,** 8 (August 1966), 1242–1251.

CUTRIGHT, PHILLIPS. "The Rise of Teenage Illegitimacy in the United States, 1940–1971," pp. 3–4, of *The Teenage Pregnant Girl.* Ed. by Jack Zackler and Wayne Brandstadt. Springfield, Ill.: Charles C Thomas, 1975.

———. "Illegitimacy: Myths, Causes, and Cures." *Family Planning Perspectives,* **3,** 1 (January 1971), 26–48.

CVETKOVICH, GEORGE, *et al.* "On the Psychology of Adolescent Use of Contraceptives." *Journal of Sex Research,* **1,** 3 (August 1975), 256–270.

DANFORTH, JOYCE, *et al.* "Group Services for Unmarried Mothers—An Interdisciplinary Approach." *Children,* **18,** 2 (March–April 1971), 59–64.

DAVID, H. P. "Unwanted Pregnancies, Costs and Alternatives." *Demographic and Social Aspects of Population Growth.* Ed. by C. F. Westoff and R. Parke. Washington, D.C.: Government Printing Office, 1972.

FESTINGER, TRUDY BRADLEY. "Unwed Mothers and Their Decision to Keep or Surrender Children." *Child Welfare,* **50,** 5 (May 1971), 253–263.

FINCK, GEORGE H., *et al.* "Group Counseling with Unmarried Mothers." *Journal of Marriage and the Family,* **27,** 2 (May 1965), 224–229.

FINKEL, MADELON L., and DAVID J. FINKEL. "Sexual and Contraceptive Knowledge and Attitudes and Behavior in Male Adolescents." *Family Planning Perspectives,* **7,** 6 (November–December 1975), 256–260.

FISCHMAN, SUSAN H., and HOWARD A. PALLEY. "Adolescent Unwed Motherhood—Implications for a National Family Policy." *Health and Social Work,* **3,** 1 (February 1978), 31–46.

FORREST, JACQUELINE D., CHRISTOPHER TIETZE, and ELLEN SULLIVAN. "Abortion in the U.S., 1976–77." *Family Planning Perspectives,* **10,** 5 (September–October 1978), 271–279.

FRIEDMAN, HELEN L. "Why Are They Keeping Their Babies?" *Social Work* (July 1975), 322–323.

FURSTENBERG, FRANK F. "The Social Consequences of Teenage Parenthood." *Family Planning Perspectives,* **8,** 4 (July–August, 1976a), 150–164.

———. *Unplanned Parenthood—The Social Consequences of Teenage Childbearing.* New York: The Free Press, 1976b.

———, and ALBERT G. CRAWFORD. "Family Support: Helping Teenage Mothers to Cope." *Family Planning Perspectives,* **10** (November–December 1978), 322–333.

GARLAND, PATRICIA. "Illegitimacy—A Special Minority-Group Problem in Urban Areas—New Social Welfare Perspectives." *Child Welfare,* **45,** 2 (February 1966), 81–88.

GIL, D. G. "Illegitimacy and Adoption—Its Socioeconomic Correlates: A Preliminary Report." *Child Adoption,* No. 1 (1969), 25–37.

GOODMAN, ELIZABETH M. "Trends and Goals in Schooling for Pregnant Girls and Teenage Mothers," in *Effective Services for Unmarried Parents and Their Chil-*

dren—Innovative Community Approaches. New York: National Council on Illegitimacy, 1968.

GROW, LUCILLE. *Unwed Mothers Served by the Voluntary Agencies.* New York: Data Collection Project for Agencies Serving Unmarried Mothers, 1967.

————. "Today's Unmarried Mothers: The Choices Have Changed." *Child Welfare,* **58** (June 1979), 363–371.

HARTLEY, SHIRLEY. "The Decline of Illegitimacy in Japan." *Social Problems,* **18,** 1 (Summer 1970), 78–91.

————. *Illegitimacy.* Berkeley: University of California Press, 1975.

HEGER, DONNA T. "A Supportive Service to Single Mothers and Their Children." *Children Today,* **6,** 5 (September–October 1977), 2–4.

HERZOG, ELIZABETH. "Unwed Motherhood: Personal and Social Consequences." *Welfare in Review,* **2,** 8 (August 1964).

HOPKINSON, ANGELA. *Single Mothers: The First Year.* Edinburgh: Scottish Council for Single Parents, 1976.

HOWARD, MARION. "Comprehensive Service Programs for School Age Pregnant Girls." *Children,* **15,** 5 (September–October 1968a), 193–196.

————. *Multiservice Programs for Pregnant School Girls.* Washington, D.C.: U.S. Department of Health, Education, and Welfare, Social Rehabilitation Service, Children's Bureau, 1968b.

————. *The Webster School—A District of Columbia Program for Pregnant Girls.* Children's Bureau Research Report No. 2. Washington, D.C.: Government Printing Office, 1968c.

————. "Improving Services to Young Fathers." *Sharing* (Spring 1975), 10–22.

"Illegitimacy," in *Encyclopaedia Britannica,* XII. Chicago, 1957, pp. 84–85.

JOHNSON, BETTY. "The Unwed AFDC Mother and Child Welfare Services," in *The Double Jeopardy: The Triple Crises—Illegitimacy Today.* New York: National Council on Illegitimacy, 1969.

JONES, WYATT C., et al. "Social and Psychological Factors in Status Decisions of Unmarried Mothers." *Journal of Marriage and the Family,* **25,** 3 (August 1962), 224–230.

KALTREIDER, NANCY, and L. DOUGLAS LENKOSKI. "Effective Use of Group Techniques in a Maternity Home." *Child Welfare,* **50,** 3 (March 1970), 146–152.

KANE, FRANCES, and PETER LACHENBRUCH. "Adolescent Pregnancy: A Study of Abortions and Non Abortions." *American Journal of Orthopsychiatry,* **43** (October 1973), 796–803.

KLERMAN, LORRAINE, and JAMES JEKEL. "School Age Mothers: Problems, Programs, Policy," in *Studies in Maternal Health.* H.E.W. Public Health Service. Washington, D.C.: Government Printing Office, 1975.

KOLODNY, RALPH, and WILLOW V. REILLY. "Group Work with Today's Unmarried Mothers." *Social Casework,* **53,** 10 (December 1972).

KRAUSE, HARRY D. "Bringing the Bastard into the Great Society—A Proposed Uniform Act on Legitimacy." *Texas Law Review,* **44,** 5 (April 1966), 829–859.

————. *Illegitimacy: Law and Social Policy.* Indianapolis: The Bobbs-Merrill Co., Inc., 1971.

————. "Equal Protection for the Illegitimate." *Michigan Law Review,* **65,** 3 (January 1967), 477–505.

KREECH, FLORENCE. "A Residence for Mothers and Their Babies." *Child Welfare,* **54,** 8 (September–October 1975), 581–592.

LINDEMANN, CONSTANCE. *Birth Control and Unmarried Young Women.* New York: Springer Publishing Co., Inc., 1975.

LUKER, KRISTIN. *Taking Chances: Abortion and the Decision Not to Contracept.* Berkeley: University of California Press, 1975.

MacIntyre, Sally. *Single and Pregnant.* New York: Prodist, 1977.

McCarthy, James, and Jane Menken. "Marriage, Remarriage, Marital Disruption and Age at First Birth," *Family Planning Perspectives,* 11 (January–February 1979), 21–29.

McMurray, Georgia L. "Community Action on Behalf of Pregnant School-Age Girls: Educational Policies and Beyond." *Child Welfare,* 49, 6 (June 1970), 342–436.

Meyer, Henry J., et al. "The Decision of Unmarried Mothers to Keep or Surrender Their Babies." *Social Casework,* 39, 4 (April 1956), 103–109.

——, et al. "Unwed Mothers' Decisions About Their Babies—An Interim Replication Study." *Child Welfare,* 38, 2 (February 1959), 1–6.

Meyer, H. J., and J. Stone. "Family Planning in the Practice of Social Workers." *Family Planning Perspectives,* 6 (1974), 176–183.

Moore, Kristin A., and Steven B. Caldwell. *Out of Wedlock Pregnancy and Childbearing.* Washington, D.C.: The Urban Institute, 1976.

——, and Linda J. Waite. "Early Childbearing and Educational Attainment." *Family Planning Perspectives,* 9, 5 (September– October 1977), 220–225.

Nicholson, Jill. *Mother and Baby Homes.* London: George Allen & Unwin, Ltd., 1968.

Oppel, Wallace C. *Illegitimacy—A Comparative Follow-up Study.* Unpublished Ph.D. thesis. National Catholic School of Social Services, Catholic University. Washington, D.C., 1969.

O'Rourke, Helen A. "The Agency as Seen Through the Eyes of Its Clients." *Child Welfare,* 47, 8 (October 1968), 470–477.

Pakter, Jean, and Frieda Nelson. "The Unmarried Mother and Her Child—The Problems and the Challenges," in *Illegitimacy: Data and Findings for Prevention, Treatment, and Policy Formulation.* New York: National Council on Illegitimacy, 1965.

Pannor, Reuben, et al. *The Unmarried Father—New Approach to Helping Unmarried Young Parents.* New York: Springer-Verlag New York, Inc., 1971.

Pappenfort, Donnell M., and Dee M. Kilpatrick. *A Census of Children's Residential Institutions in the U.S., Puerto Rico and the Virgin Islands: 1966,* Vol. 6: *Maternity Homes.* Social Service Monographs, 2nd series. Chicago: University of Chicago, School of Social Service Administration, 1970.

Pauker, Jerome. "Girls Pregnant Out of Wedlock," in *The Double Jeopardy: The Triple Crises—Illegitimacy Today.* New York: National Council on Illegitimacy, 1969.

Paul, Eve W., Harriet Pilpel, and Nancy F. Wechsler. "Pregnancy, Teenagers and the Law of 1974." *Family Planning Perspectives,* 6 (Summer 1974), 142–147.

Perlman, Helen Harris. "Unmarried Mothers," in *Social Work and Social Problems.* Ed. by Nathan E. Cohen. New York: National Association of Social Workers, 1954.

Pierce, Ruth I. *Single and Pregnant.* Boston: Beacon Press, Inc., 1970.

Pinchbeck, Ivey, and Margaret Hewitt. *Children in English Society,* Vol. 1: *From Tudor Times to the Eighteenth Century.* London: Kegan Paul, Trench, Trubner & Co., 1969.

Platts, Hal. "A Public Adoption Agency's Approach to Natural Fathers." *Child Welfare,* 47, 9 (November 1968), 530–537.

Plionis, Betty M. "Adolescent Pregnancy: A Review of the Literature." *Social Work* (July 1975), 302–307.

Pochin, Jean. *Without a Wedding Ring—Casework with Unmarried Parents.* London: Constable & Company, Ltd., 1969.

Pope, Hallowell. "Unwed Mothers and Their Sex Partners." *Journal of Marriage and the Family,* 29, 3 (August 1967), 555–567.

————. "Negro–White Differences in Decisions Regarding Illegitimate Children." *Journal of Marriage and the Family*, 31, 4 (November 1969), 756–764.

POWER, EDWARD, and MATHEW DE CHIRICO. *The Treatment of Unwed Parents—How Determined? How Effective?* Paper presented at Regional Annual Conference, Child Welfare League of America, March 1969, Pittsburgh. Mimeo.

PUBLIC HEALTH SERVICE, NATIONAL CENTER FOR HEALTH STATISTICS. *Characteristics of Live Births, 1973–1975.* Washington, D.C.: Government Printing Office, September 1978.

RAINS, PRUDENCE M. "Moral Reinstatement—The Characteristics of Maternity Homes." *American Behavioral Scientist*, 14, 2 (November–December 1970), 222–235.

————. *Becoming an Unwed Mother—A Sociological Account.* New York: Aldine Atherton, 1971.

RASHBAUM, M., et al. "Use of Social Services by Unmarried Mothers." *Children*, 10, 1 (January–February 1963), 11–16.

RAYNOR, LOIS. *Giving Up a Baby for Adoption.* London: Association of British Adoption Agencies, November 1971.

REED, ELLERY F., and RUTH LATIMER. *A Study of Unmarried Mothers Who Kept Their Babies.* Cincinnati, Ohio: Social Welfare Research, Inc., 1962.

REICHEIT, PAUL, HARRIET WERLEY, and JOEL AGER. "Social Work Attitudes Toward Birth Control for Teenagers." *Community Mental Health Journal*, 13, 4 (1977), 352–359.

ROBERTS, ROBERT W. (Ed.). *The Unwed Mother.* New York: Harper & Row, Publishers, 1966.

RUBENSTEIN, HIASAURA, and MARY H. BLOCK. "Helping Clients Who Are Poor: Worker and Client Perceptions of Problems, Activities and Outcomes." *Social Service Review*, 52, 1 (March 1978), 69–84.

SANDBERG, EUGENE C., and RALPH I. JACOBS. "Psychology of the Misuse and Rejection of Contraception." *American Journal of Obstetrics and Gynecology*, 110 (1971), 227–242.

SAUBER, MIGNON. *Experiences of the Unwed Mother as Parent.* New York: Community Council of Greater New York, 1965.

————. "The Role of the Unmarried Father." *Welfare in Review*, 4, 9 (November 1966), 15–18.

————, and EILEEN M. CORRIGAN. *The Six-Year Experience of Unwed Mothers as Parents.* New York: Community Council of Greater New York, 1970.

SETTLAGE, DIANE S., SHELDON BOROFF, and DONNA COOPER. "Sexual Experience of Young Teenage Girls Seeking Contraceptive Assistance for the First Time." *Family Planning Perspectives*, 5, 4 (Fall 1973), 223ff.

SHAH, F., ZELNIK, MELVIN, and KANTNER, JOHN. "Unprotected Intercourse Among Unwed Teenagers." *Family Planning Perspectives*, 7 (1975), 39–43.

SHAPIRO, DEBORAH. "Attitudes, Values, and Unmarried Motherhood," in *Unmarried Parenthood—Clues to Agency and Community Action.* New York: National Council on Illegitimacy, 1967.

————. *Social Distance and Illegitimacy—Report of a Pilot Study.* New York: Research Center, Columbia University, School of Social Work, 1970.

SHOUSE, JUDITH. "Psychological and Emotional Problems of Pregnancy in Adolescence," pp. 161–186, in *The Teenage Pregnant Girl.* Ed. by Jack Zackler and Wayne Brandstadt. Springfield, Ill.: Charles C Thomas, 1975.

SKLAR, JUNE, and BETH BERKOV. "Teenage Family Formation in Postwar America." *Family Planning Perspectives*, 6, 2 (Spring 1974), 80–90.

STEINMETZ, MARTHA A. "Role-Playing in a Maternity Home." *Children*, 11, 2 (March–April 1964), 61–64.

STEPTO, ROBERT C., LOUIS KEITH, and DONALD KEITH. "Obstetrical and Medical Problems of Teen-age Pregnancy," pp. 83–133, in *The Teenage Pregnant Girl*. Ed. by Jack Zackler and Wayne Brandstedt. Springfield, Ill.: Charles C Thomas, 1975.

STEVENSON, NICHOLOS, and RITA DUKETTE. "The Legal Rights of Unmarried Fathers." *Social Service Review*, **47**, 1 (March 1973), 1–15.

TAYLOR, LILLIAN E. "Social Attitudes Toward Sexual Behavior and Illegitimacy," in *Illegitimacy: Data and Findings for Prevention, Treatment, and Policy Formulation*. New York: National Council on Illegitimacy, October 1965.

TEELE, J. E., *et al*. "Factors Related to Social Work Services for Babies of Mothers Born Out of Wedlock." *American Journal of Public Health*, **57**, 8 (August 1967), 1300–1307.

TORRES, AIDA. "Does Your Mother Know . . . ?" *Family Planning Perspectives*, **10**, 5 (September–October 1978), 280–282.

———. "Rural and Urban Family Planning Services in the United States." *Family Planning Perspective*, **11** (March–April 1979), 109–114.

TRISELIOTIS, JOHN. "The Timing of the Single Mother's Decision in Relation to Adoption Agency Practice." *Child Adoption*, No. 3 (1969), 29–35.

TRUSSELL, T. JAMES. "Economic Consequences of Teenage Child Bearing." *Family Planning Perspectives*, **8**, 4 (July–August 1976), 184–190.

ULLMAN, A. "Social Work Service to Abortion Patients." *Social Casework*, **53** (1972), 481–487.

U.S. CONGRESS, JOINT ECONOMICS COMMITTEE. *Income Security for Americans: Recommendations of the Public Welfare Study*. Washington, D.C.: Government Printing Office, 1974.

U.S. DEPARTMENT OF HEALTH, EDUCATION, AND WELFARE, PUBLIC HEALTH SERVICE. *Trends in Illegitimacy—United States: 1940–1966*. National Center for Health Statistics, Series 21, No. 5. Washington, D.C.: Government Printing Office, 1968.

VINCENT, CLARK. *Unmarried Mother*. New York: The Free Press, 1961.

WALLACE, HELEN, *et al*. "A Study of Services and Needs of Teenage Pregnant Girls in the Large Cities of the United States." *American Journal of Public Health*, **63**, 1 (January 1973), 5–16.

WATSON, J. A., and VINCENT RUE. "Problem Pregnancies: Analyzing the Counselor's Role." *Sharing* (Spring 1974), 15–17.

WIMPERIS, VIRGINIA. *The Unmarried Mother and Her Child*. London: George Allen & Unwin, Ltd., 1960.

WISCONSIN DEPARTMENT OF HEALTH AND SOCIAL SERVICES. *Unmarried Mothers in Wisconsin 1976*. Madison: Wisconsin Department of Health and Social Services, 1977.

WRIGHT, HELEN R. *Eighty Unmarried Mothers Who Kept Their Babies*. Department of Social Welfare, State of California, May 1965.

WRIGHT, MATTIE K. "Comprehensive Service for Adolescent Unwed Mothers." *Children*, **13**, 5 (September–October 1966), 171–176.

YELLOLY, MARGARET. "Factors Relating to an Adoption Decision by the Mothers of Illegitimate Infants." *Sociological Review*, **13**, 1, New Series (March 1965).

———. "Adoption and the Natural Mother." *Case Conference*, 13 (December 1966), 270–277.

YOUNG, ALMA T., BARBARA BECKMAN, and HELEN REHR. "Parental Influence on Pregnant Adolescents," *Social Work* (September 1975), 387–391.

YOUNG, LEONTINE. *Out of Wedlock*. New York: McGraw-Hill Book Company, 1954.

YURDIN, MAZY O. "Recent Trends in Illegitimacy—Implications for Practice." *Child Welfare*, **49**, 7 (July 1970), 373–375.

ZELNIK, MELVIN, and JOHN F. KANTNER. "The Resolution of Teenage First Pregnancies." *Family Planning Perspective*, **6** (Spring 1974), 74–80.

————. "Sexual and Contraceptive Experience of Young Unmarried Women in the U.S., 1976 and 1971." *Family Planning Perspectives,* **9,** 2 (March–April 1977), 55–63.

————. "First Pregnancies to Women 15–19: 1976 and 1971." *Family Planning Perspective,* **10,** 1 (January–February 1978), 11–20.

ZOBER, EDITH. "The Pregnant School Girl." *Child Welfare,* **48,** 6 (June 1969), 362–366.

10 SUBSTITUTE CARE: ADOPTION

INTRODUCTION

Adoption involves becoming a parent through a legal and social process rather than through a biological process. For the child, adoption involves a *permanent* change in family affiliation. It is an ancient process of providing children for childless parents and parents for parentless children. Adoption provides permanent substitute care for the child when his natural parents are unable or unwilling to care for him and have been legally freed of any ties to the child. The effect of adoption is to create a new parent–child unit. According to the old Roman legal code, "Adoption imitates nature." According to the Greeks, "Adoption is a method of demanding from religion and law that which nature had denied" (Hastings, 1908, p. 107). A more formal definition of *adoption* suggests that "It entails the extinction of all present or future rights and obligations of the natural parents of the child and the transfer, by administrative or legal authority, of all these rights and obligations to a married couple who have no blood relationship with the child" (Toussieng, 1960, p. 63).

Biological parenthood cannot be shared. Psychosocial parenthood, however, is a complex of rights and obligations that can be "shared, acceded to, delegated, surrendered, or otherwise circulated among [different people] according to specific rules" (Carroll, 1970, p. 8).

Historical Background

All of the ancient peoples—the Egyptians, the Babylonians, the Greeks, the Romans—sanctioned adoption. The Bible speaks of it. Pharaoh's daughter adopted Moses and Mordecai adopted Esther. The Code of Hammurabi mentions adoption and the protection that should be given the adoptive parent. Sargon, King of Babylonia, circa 2800 B.C., was adopted. The inscription that tells his story reads:

> Sargon, the mighty king, King of Akkad, am I. My mother was a vestal, my father I knew not. . . . In my city, Azupirani, which is situated on the bank of the Euphrates, my mother, the vestal, bore me. In a hidden place she brought me forth. She laid me in a vessel made of reeds, closed my door with pitch, and dropped me down into the river, which did not drown me. The river carried me to Akki, the water carrier. Akki the water carrier lifted me up in the kindness of

his heart. Akki the water carrier raised me as his own son. Akki the water carrier made of me his gardener. In my work as gardener I was beloved by Istar, I became the king, and for forty-five years I held kingly sway [Quoted in Clothier, 1939, p. 598].

In earlier periods, adoption was not so frequently resorted to in solution of the problem of childlessness, because a simpler solution was socially acceptable. If a wife was infertile, the husband took another woman to bear him children. Thus Sarah, who was childless, urged Abraham to take Hagar, her maid, as a concubine, with whom he then had a child. In ancient Greece and Rome, adoptions were arranged so as to acquire an heir to perpetuate the family or to manage extensive family property. Thus Solon, in Greece, sanctioned adoption as a means of providing continuity for a family line.

In early Rome, one function of adoption was to permit a candidate for office to qualify under the provision "that a candidate who had children, or who had more children, was to be preferred to one who had none or fewer" (Hastings, 1908, p. 113).

In India, adoptions were arranged so as to provide a male heir in order to meet the demands of religious ceremonials. Among the Hindus, the adopting father declared to the adoptive son, "I accept thee for the fulfillment of religion; I take thee for the continuation of lineage" (Hastings, 1908, p. 110). Among the Hindus, as among the Chinese, the need in adoption was specifically for a male child, because "Heaven awaits not one who has no male issue." The childless couple might adopt children so as to be sure of having care in their old age. This is the attitude expressed in a Hawaiian saying, "Feed human beings, for they can be sent on errands" (Carroll, 1970, p. 27).

In some cultures, adoptions might be informally arranged between people who knew each other well and who were tied by bonds of mutual obligation. Parents who had too many children gave some to relatives or friends who had none or too few. In such arrangements, there might be continuing and frequent contact between the two families, creating an additional parental relationship rather than a substitute parental relationship (Carroll, 1970; Benet, 1976).

The focus of earlier adoptions is suggested by the medieval definition of adoption "as a legitimate act imitating nature for the solace and comfort of those who have no children."

In earlier periods of man's history, then, adoption served to meet the needs of adults; today it is supported primarily because it meets the needs of parentless children. There is no body of common law regarding adoption. Consequently there was little precedent for adoption procedures in Colonial America. Abbott (1937) notes that "provision for care of dependent children by means of adoption was probably delayed by the development of the relation between master and apprentice" so that orphans and children of indigent parents could be bound out to obtain care in this way (p. 461).

Orphan asylums continued to use such indentures as one of the principal forms of placing their children until some years after the Civil War. The contract, made between the institution in behalf of the child and the family accepting the child, obligated the family to maintain the child until the age of eighteen "with proper meat drink washing and lodging and all other necessaries fit and convenient for a child of his/her age and condition and to teach the child reading writing and arithmetic as well as some trade; to rear the child in such a way as that he/she may be useful to himself/herself and the community" (Mc-Causland, 1976, p. 23).

After the Civil War the words "doth bind" gave way to such phrases as "treated in every way as if the child were the natural child" of the parents.

Prior to the passage of general adoption laws, state legislatures followed the practice of "passing special acts providing for the adoption of particular children by particular adults" (Witmer, 1963, p. 29).

There is some question about whether Massachusetts or Texas was the first state to pass an adoption law. Nevertheless it is clear that the Massachusetts statute enacted in 1851 became the model for many of the other state adoption laws passed during or shortly after the Civil War. It provided for

1. The written consent of the child's biological parent.
2. Joint petition by both the adoptive mother and father.
3. A decree by the judge if he was satisfied that the adoption was "fit and proper."
4. Legal and complete severance of the relationship between child and biological parents.

By 1929 every state had passed some kind of adoption legislation. The adoption laws indicate that "From the outset, most laws [at least as interpreted judicially] have had the welfare of the children as their main purpose" (Witmer, 1963, p. 43). Although the laws of the different states varied in effectiveness, the history of adoption has been a movement toward a greater emphasis on the protection of the principals affected by adoption: the biological parents, the adoptive parents, the community, and the child.

The early statutes were intended primarily to "provide evidence of the legal transfer of a child by the biological parents to the adopting parents and provision for a public record of the transfer" (Abbott, 1938, p. 165). The judge's decision that the adoption was "fit and proper" was based only on his contact with the parties to the adoption. Recognizing that this was not sufficient to prevent adoption by unsuitable or unscrupulous parents, some states provided for more extensive inquiry regarding the adoptive parents. Thus in 1891 Michigan began to require that the judge make an investigation before finalizing an adoption. This law was later amended to provide for a social investigation by an agency that was, generally, in a better position to conduct such a study. In 1917 Minnesota passed the first law requiring detailed investigation by a local agency or the state department of public welfare and a written recommendation to the court regarding the advisability of permitting the adoption.

Responses to the "application-for-adoption" form used by the Chicago Orphan Asylum in the 1880s and 1890s reflected the adopters' preferences and motivations:

> The blue-eyed, golden-haired little girl was the desire of many; a few wanted a black-eyed brunette; or one "not too homely," definitely "not a redhead." One woman didn't care too much about "looks" but wanted assurance that the child "had not one drop of Irish blood." Disposition and health are defined: "clean, healthy, sensible and good dispositioned"; a "strict Christian, well dispositioned";

"light complexion, well disposed"; "a sunny German girl who can sing." One man requested a boy "possessing some force of character . . . it would be a home where no tobacco nor whiskey would be tolerated. Please send five photographs."

Why they wanted a child was often expressed in terms of work; to wash dishes and run errands, to be a companion for an only child or an elderly person living in the family; to "herd cattle, bring in coal, and take care of the cow" (that applicant was turned down immediately); to do light housework; to act as nursemaid. But there were those who loved children and had none, or who wished to extend their love to an orphan. There is only one instance of a woman wanting a child to make a little noise, she couldn't bear the silence when her daughter left home to be married! [McCausland, 1976, p. 64].

Before the introduction of community controls, advertisements such as the following, which appeared in the *Chicago Tribune*, were not uncommon:

PERSONAL—Wanted—Healthy Twins or Baby girl under 6 months, by couple able to give children wonderful home and future. Address KH 385, Tribune. (December 21, 1919)

PERSONAL—Wanted for adoption by wealthy Chicago couple, infant girl or boy. Address KH 386, Tribune. (December 21, 1919)

PERSONAL—Wanted to Adopt Baby month old, by responsible couple; good home. Address B 599, Tribune. (December 21, 1919) [Quoted in Bremner, 1970, p. 139]

Some of the unfortunate situations that might result were reported to a 1925 Commission appointed to study and revise the Pennsylvania statutes relating to children:

CASE VII.
Frances, aged thirteen, recently made a personal application to a social agency stating that her foster father had been having sexual relations with her for the last two years. Upon investigation living conditions were found to be very bad. The foster mother corroborated the child's statements. Frances had been legally adopted in May 1918. She was sold to her foster parents by her mother for a quart of whisky [Quoted in Bremner, 1970, p. 142].

Attempts to provide additional protection for the child included the introduction of a trial period between the time the child was placed in the adoptive home and the time the adoption was legally consummated. Also an increasing number of states required that records of the adoption proceedings, once completed, be closed and sealed and that a new birth certificate for the child be issued at that time. All these changes indicated a shift from emphasis on the purely legal aspects of transfer of the child to a growing appreciation of the human aspects of adoption.

Even though the legal structure for formalizing adoptions had been established, adoptions had low priority as a substitute-care alternative. The movement began to develop some momentum between 1910 and 1920. Special adoption agencies were established at that time that devoted full time and energy to this particular service. The moving forces behind the establishment of some of the principal private agencies concerned with adoption—Louise Wise, Spence Adoption Agency, and Chapin Adoptions Agency in New York, and The Cradle in Chicago—were women volunteers from prominent and wealthy backgrounds (Romanofsky, 1974).

The tradition of the "amateur" with interest in and commitment to adoption is still very much part of the picture today, as we shall note later on.

SCOPE

Adoptions are generally broken down into two principal groups: related and nonrelated. In related adoptions, the child is adopted by a stepfather, a stepmother, a grandparent, an uncle, and so on. Social agencies are not so directly concerned with such adoptions. In nonrelated adoptions, the child is adopted by persons who have no family ties to him. Social agencies are directly concerned in finding the home, evaluating it, and supervising it for a period of time after the child has been placed. Our interest, therefore, is primarily with nonrelated adoptions.

Until 1973 national statistics on adoption were made available through the National Center for Social Statistics. Although no national statistics are available subsequent to 1973, there are statistics available of the reports of a limited number of individual states. The latest such listing available in 1978 covered the situation in 1975 for some thirty-one states. Recognizing the need for detailed national statistics on adoption, the Adoption Reform Act of 1978 provides that the U.S. Department of Health, Education, and Welfare create a system for gathering national statistics regarding adoption and foster care.

The number of children adopted increased from 57,000 in 1957 to 175,000 in 1970—about half of the group in 1970 consisting of nonrelative adoptions. The year 1970 was the high-water mark of adoptions in the United States. Since 1970, there has been a slow, steady decline in adoptions.

It is possible to get a clearer idea of the sharp decrease in adoptive activity by comparing the figures on "children adopted by unrelated petitioners" for individual states in 1970 and 1975: 1970 is the year in which the largest number of adoptions has ever been recorded; 1975 is the year for which the most recent statistics were available at the time of this writing (June 1979). Selecting twenty representative states for which statistics are available in both years, it is noted that in 1970, 48,744 children were adopted by unrelated petitioners. In 1975, the same twenty states yielded a total of only 29,528 such adoptions (National Center for Social Statistics, 1972, 1977).

In the absence of national statistics available from the federal government, the Child Welfare League of America has accepted the responsibility for collecting statistics semiannually from a sample of its voluntary and public member agencies. The earlier reports from the Child Welfare League of America from 1971 through 1975 indicated "a decrease of 50 percent in the number of children accepted for adoptive placement and of 57 percent in the number of adoptive homes approved" (Haring, 1976, p. 501).

The latest report available in the series published by the Child Welfare League of America shows a continuing "downward trend in the number of children accepted for adoption and the number of adoptive homes approved by the voluntary agencies participating in the study" (Shyne, 1977).

Statistics of specific agencies and of particular states exemplify the downward trend. The Los Angeles County Department of Adoptions, the largest public agency of its kind in the United States, placed 1,100 children in 1973 in contrast to the 2,500 children placed in the late 1960s. Spence Chapin in New York City, one of the largest voluntary adoption agencies, decreased its placements from 476 in 1967 to 110 in 1973. In 1972 there were 1,785 nonrelated adoptions completed in Wisconsin. In 1977 only 985 such adoptions were completed.

Agencies throughout the country began, in 1975, to stop taking applications for white, unhandicapped infants or to slow down applications. Prospective adoptive parents were explicitly informed that there was likely to be a three- to five-year wait for such a child.

The trend has been toward an increase in the percentage of nonrelative adoptions made under the auspices of social agencies. Although voluntary agencies still account for the greatest proportion of such placements, there has been a gradual increase of public agency activity. However, the Child Welfare League reports that the composition of the child population accepted for adoption differs markedly between the voluntary and the public agency. Whereas the very young, healthy child predominates among the children available through the voluntary agencies, albeit in reduced numbers, more than 60 per cent of the public agency children are over one year of age and nearly a third are handicapped by physical disability, mental retardation, and other disabling conditions. Both types of agencies accept a disproportionate number of black children, such children making up some 25 per cent of the total number of children accepted for adoption in 1976. These children continued to be placed more slowly, so that a higher proportion of the accepted black children continued to await placement as compared with accepted white children.

The number of black children placed has decreased somewhat since 1970, but the decline has apparently stabilized recently (Opportunity, 1976). Agencies in 1974 reported that black children made up 40 per cent of the backlog of children waiting for adoption, clearly in excess of the percentage of black children in the population.

Although most of the children are less than three months old at placement, because more older children are being placed the median age at placement has moved up slowly.

The percentage of unrelated adoptions is decreasing as compared to related adoptions. Unrelated adoptions are currently a smaller part of the total adoption statistic than was true in 1970.

SOURCES OF CHILDREN FOR ADOPTION

The sources of children for nonrelated adoptions are listed in descending order of importance:

1. Children born out of wedlock.
2. Abandoned, neglected children.
3. Foreign-born children.
4. Orphans.
5. Legitimate children voluntarily surrendered for adoption by their parents.

The principal source, by far, of nonrelated children available to adoptive parents are the children born out of wedlock. According to the Children's Bureau, in 1971 about 87 per cent of all children adopted by nonrelatives were born out of wedlock.

The social "orphans"—children whose parents have rejected, neglected, or deserted them—form a sizable group of the children available for nonrelated adoption. In such cases, society has to intervene to terminate the rights of the biological parents and to free the child for adoption (see Chapter 8).

Although children born out of wedlock continue to provide the largest percentage of children available for nonrelative adoptions, their number is declining. There has been a gradual increase of the percentage of in-wedlock children becoming available for adoption.

Children in foster care are being freed for adoption more frequently and are becoming a growing source of children for adoption. This is particularly true of the large number of children who have been in foster care for some time and have been virtually abandoned by their parents. Concern about permanence for such children has resulted in increasing frequent efforts to terminate parental rights and place the child for adoption.

The full orphans—the children whose parents have died—form a smaller number of children available for adoption. Although in 1920 1.9 per cent of all children were full orphans, in 1977 only 0.1 per cent of all children were so deprived—a very limited segment of the child population.

Little is known about married couples who voluntarily give up their children for adoption. It is the impression of social workers in contact with such parents that conditions such as "economic pressures, unsatisfactory housing, unwillingness to accept family responsibilities . . . [and] emotional problems involving rejection of the child" account for such voluntary relinquishment (Citizens' Adoption Committee, 1952, p. 8). Agency studies confirm that only a small number of mothers relinquish for adoption a child fathered by their own husband with whom they are still living (Platts, 1970).

A final source for adoption are foreign children. Some are adopted abroad by U.S. citizens; others are brought into the country for purposes of adoption. These are children who have been orphaned or abandoned in their home country and who, for one reason or another, could not have been adopted there.

During the time between 1968 and 1975, when the total number of adoptions in the United States first rose and then declined, the adoption of foreign children continued steadily upward—from 1,612 children in 1968 to 5,633 in 1975. Although this figure for intercountry adoptions is a small percentage of the total children placed, it is somewhat more than 10 per cent of the unrelated adoptive placements estimated for 1976.

The list of sources of children available for adoption suggests that adoption is appropriate under the following conditions:

1. When the biological parents are unable to care for the child because the family was never completely organized—as in the case of the illegitimate child, who never had a father.
2. When the biological parents are unable to care for the child and are not likely to be able to do so in the future—as in the case of the child whose parents have died or have deserted him.

3. When the biological parents have proved unable and/or unwilling to care adequately for the child.
4. When the parents voluntarily relinquish their rights to the child.

Adoption is not appropriate under the following conditions:

1. When the child with close family ties has parents and/or relatives who might be helped to care for the child adequately in his own family home.
2. When the child is so physically, mentally, or emotionally handicapped that he cannot live in a normal family setting, develop normal relationships with parental figures, and function adequately in a family.

Child-Applicant Ratio

The principal source of adoptive parents is the infertile couple. Less frequently, the applicants have a child, or children, of their own, cannot have additional children, and are interested in increasing the size of the family through adoption. Not all infertile couples are interested in adoption. As a matter of fact, one study of couples who had come to a hospital infertility clinic showed that only about half of those who were infertile resorted to adoption (Humphrey, 1969).

Some fertile couples concerned about population growth have deliberately chosen to adopt a child already born rather than giving birth to one of their own.

Adoptions by applicants who are fertile but elect to add to their family by adoption have been termed *preferential adoptions* (Feigelman, Silverman, 1979). As compared with more traditional adopters, such applicants tend to be older, better educated, and more liberal in orientation. The ability to select the sex of the adopted child was an important motive in giving preference to adoption over biology as a procedure for adding a child to the family.

One of the most significant statistics determining agency practice and procedure is the ratio of adoptive applicants to children available for adoption. When this ratio is high, the agency can be highly selective; when it is low, the agency tends to modify, relax, or eliminate various eligibility requirements.

The ratio of adoptive applicants to available children has varied widely over the past twenty years. During some periods there were almost as many infants as applicants. More recently there have been decidedly more applicants than infants available.

One of the principal factors in the decrease of white, nonhandicapped children available for adoption is the greater availability of contraception and abortion, as a consequence of which the rise in illegitimate birth rates has been slowed. More significantly, fewer unmarried mothers give up their babies for adoption, because more adequate social services enable more of them to keep and raise their children, and the stigma attached to unmarried motherhood is fading.

Sklar and Berkov (1974) estimate, on the basis of a detailed study of the relevant statistics, that the proportion of out-of-wedlock children placed for adoption declined from about 30 per cent in 1967–1968 to about 15 per cent in 1971–1972. A report on unmarried mothers in Wisconsin notes that whereas 61.5 per cent of white mothers in Milwaukee County kept the child in 1971, by 1976, 91.4 per cent were keeping the child (Wisconsin Department of Health and Social Services, 1977, Table C; see also Friedman, 1975; Bonham, 1977).

REQUIREMENTS OF ADOPTIVE PARENTHOOD

In order to adopt a child through a social agency, the applicant must meet certain requirements set by the agency. In 1954 the Child Welfare League of America made a nationwide study of the practices of adoption agencies, devoting a major section of the study to eligibility standards. The study was updated by a less extensive review by Brieland (1959) in 1958. The eligibility requirements for adoption through social agencies, as reviewed in such studies, are reflected in the recommended standards established by the Child Welfare League of America (1973) and form the basis for this discussion. Actual adherence to these requirements differs with the agency, the circumstance, and the particular applicant. The requirements themselves change with time and with changes in the adoption picture.

In the context of a ratio that is favorable to the adoptive applicant, agencies can move, as they have, toward a shift in emphasis in their relationship to the applicant from assessment and evaluation to facilitation and enabling. Where the ratio of applicants to children is such that almost all applicants can be provided with a child, the social worker can be concerned with helping the applicants accept and prepare for adoptive parenthood rather than focusing on determining which applicant is the most acceptable. The tendency, then, is to broaden the definition of the "adoptable" parent and to "screen people in" rather than "screen people out." When the number of infants is limited, however, "requirements" are employed not only, as is usually the case, for the primary purpose of the interests of the child but also to limit the backlog of successful applicants waiting for children. A high ratio of applicants to children available not only makes selectivity possible, it requires greater selectivity.

Some of the criteria considered important and given emphasis are definite and objective (e.g., age, physical health, marital status); some are ambiguous and subjective (e.g., emotional health, capacity for parenthood, motive for adoption).

Age

The desirable age of adoptive parents for adoption of an infant lies between thirty-five and forty-five. There are several reasons for this requirement. First, it increases the probability that the parent will be alive throughout the sixteen to eighteen years of the adoptive child's dependency. Having lost one set of parents, the adoptive child would be doubly deprived if the adoptive parents died before he was ready to assume independence. The age requirement follows the folk saying "Late child, early orphaned." Furthermore too great an age spread between the adoptive parents and the child increases the possibility of intergenerational difficulties in understanding. The older adoptive parent would be too far removed in time to empathize with the child. Too great a difference in age also limits the energy available for the physically burdensome demands of child care and decreases the possibility of parental participation in the activities of the adopted youngster. Finally, too great an age spread between parents and child is discrepant with the normal family situation. The atypicality calls attention to the fact that this family is different from others.

In the case of the older child being proposed for adoption, however, the desirable age of the applicant can be raised while a constant difference in age between parent and child is still maintained.

Physical Health

The agencies also require some assurance of good physical health—again, to ensure the child against the loss of another set of parents. It also assures the agency that the applicants have the requisite physical capacity to care for the child adequately. It prevents the possibility of infection of the child if the applicant suffers from an infectious condition. In the case of the father, poor health or a disability raises some question about employment security and the ability to provide for the child's economic needs.

Marital Status

The applicants for adoption should be married. Most agencies require that the marriage have been in existence for some minimum period—generally from three to five years. Thus the marriage has had a chance to prove itself and to achieve some stability, and there has also been an opportunity for the couple to achieve parenthood by natural means. The divorce rate is highest during the first five years of marriage. Requiring this minimum time lapse gives the child greater assurance that the family into which he is moving will remain intact.

Infertility

The couple must have medical proof that achievement of parenthood through natural means is doubtful. If the couple is fertile but has deliberately chosen to complete the family through a legal procedure, one might legitimately question the degree of their acceptance of parenthood. There is, furthermore, some concern about the differences in treatment of the adopted child and a natural child that might be born to fertile parents after completing adoption. Permitting a fertile couple to adopt an infant when other, less fortunate, couples are competing for such a child might be regarded as an inequitable disposition of available resources.

In many instances, infertility can be established on the basis of medical examination. In some cases, however, a history of unsuccessful experience in trying to conceive or a series of miscarriages establishes the fact of infertility. Furthermore childlessness for reasons other than sterility is a justification for completing a family through adoption. When pregnancy clearly represents a hazard to the health of the mother, or when there is a strong likelihood that a hereditary difficulty will be transmitted, the applicants are likely to be considered.

Religion

In many states, the law specifies that, whenever practical, a child be placed in a home of the same religious persuasion as that of his biological parents. In line with this requirement, applicants must have some religious affiliation, even if merely of a *pro forma* nature.

Financial Stability

Financial stability, rather than any minimum income, is a requirement set by most adoptive agencies. The agency would like some assurance that the family can count on a steady, even if limited, income and that it will be able to carry the extra burden of child care without imposing a strain on the stability of family relationships.

Emotional Health

Although the agencies are looking for "emotionally healthy" parents, the term itself is open to considerable differences in definition. Even if clearly defined, it would be difficult to measure. Emotional health, as stated in the adoption literature, implies, among other things, a clear understanding of oneself, a relaxed acceptance of all one's weaknesses and strengths, a minimum of unresolved developmental conflicts, adequate enactment of principal social roles, an ability to postpone gratification and to deny self-gratification out of consideration for the needs of others, a flexible conscience that can accept some failure, some occasional sinfulness without crippling guilt, a capacity to form satisfying and permanent interpersonal relationships, and the ability to be independent and yet be capable of dependency if it is objectively justified. It is said that in order to be a happy parent, one must first be a happy person.

Capacity for Parenthood

The capacity for parenthood is tied to the factor of emotional health, because the emotionally healthy person supposedly possesses the essential prerequisites for competent parenthood. Yet capacity for parenthood goes beyond emotional health; it includes the capacity to love, accept, and offer emotional security to children; the capacity to permit them to grow in terms of their own individuality; and a readiness to accept, understand, and meet the inevitable behavioral problems of children. The good parent is flexible in his expectations and is realistic in accepting the child's limitations; he/she accepts children as an end in themselves rather than as a means toward some parent-defined end; she/he likes children and enjoys them.

Some idea is given about the applicant's attitude toward children in his statement regarding the kind of child he would like to have. The question of expressed preference itself is not as significant as the tenacity and rigidity with which the statement of preference is held. This suggests that the applicant has a strongly preconceived idea of what the child should be like and that unless the child comes up to such expectations, he faces the danger of rejection.

In assessing the capacity for parenthood, the agency explores with the applicants their own experiences as children. Such background information is important because this experience materially affects their enactment of the parental role. If they have had a satisfactory experience, they are likely to have developed positive patterns of identification with a good parent. A negative experience may imply not only the absence of such patterns of identification but also residual problems in the parent–child relationship that are likely to be reactivated when they themselves become parents.

Adjustment to Sterility

Because the problem that brings the applicants to the adoptive agency is most frequently the inability—for whatever reason—to have children biologically, at the time of application, the nature of the applicants' adjustment to this deprivation is an important consideration. The adoptive child is a constant living reminder of the adoptive parents' deficiency. If the problem has not been adequately resolved, it is likely to result in difficulties in the parent–child relationship. The applicants' reaction to the agency's request for medical certification of their fertility status might be regarded as indicative of their attitude toward their infertility. If they resist the medical examination strongly, or if they are made excessively anxious by the requirement, one might question how successfully they have accepted the condition.

Quality of the Marital Relationship

Although the length of time the couple has been married says something about the quality of the marriage, more than this needs to be assessed. Because the child is likely to be affected by the dynamics of marital interaction, the agency would like to assess the degree of mutual emotional satisfaction the applicants derive from their marriage. Factors such as mutual participation in decision making (particularly with reference to the decision to adopt), the extent to which each of the partners comfortably accepts his sexual identification, the degree of mutual sexual satisfaction, the acceptance of allocated roles within the family—all are regarded as important considerations. A happy family starts with a happy marriage.

Motives for Adoption

The agency is also interested in the motives that have prompted the applicant to apply for adoption. Some motives are regarded by the agency as less desirable and more indicative of possible future difficulty. In general, motives that focus on the needs of the adoptive parents are regarded as less acceptable and more suspect than those that center on the needs of the child. However, the same expressed motive can have a positive meaning in the life configuration of one couple and a negative meaning when viewed in terms of another couple's situation. A desire to help a child grow may have positive connotations as expressed by an accepting, understanding couple; but in the case of a rigid, self-centered couple, it may indicate a desire to push the child to fulfill the prospective parents' needs and ambitions.

Couples who wish to adopt a child for the purpose of stabilizing a shaky marriage or as a "replacement" for a recently deceased child are classically suspect, although some may be acceptable.

One important dimension is the extent to which the applicants consciously recognize their motivations. An "undesirable" motivation of which the applicant has some awareness is subject to modification and change; consequently even undesirable motives of which the applicant is aware are likely to be acceptable to the agency.

Natural parenthood can be achieved without one's giving any explicit thought to why he wants children. The adoptive couple's decision to become parents is a voluntary, deliberate step that requires that motives for parenthood be made explicit because they must be shared with the agency.

The records of successful adoptive parents give some idea of the varied motivations for parenthood.

Mrs. M., who could not conceive a child because of the congenital absence of the uterus, said that both she and her husband had come from large families. "There always had been many nieces and nephews running in and out of the home. She felt that a home was rather lonesome or just too quiet without children. She compares the way the house is when her nieces and nephews are visiting and after they leave. It's so enjoyable having the children around and it's pretty lonesome when the children leave, so that it makes them want to have their own all the worse. It's very lonesome with just the two of them in the house."

Mrs. W. and her husband, a machinist, could not have children because of an insufficiency of sperm. She said she had always wanted a child. "Playing with a child, dressing it up, teaching it right from wrong, was about the best life that one could imagine. She felt that there are so many little things she loves to do, such as sewing, making lampshades, decorating, collecting things out of doors, that she would like to do with a child. Things don't seem to be quite complete without a child to share it with. Children fill up a home."

A manufacturer of electrical equipment, whose wife had three miscarriages, said that "raising children would give them a purpose in life. There would be more to life than just having fun and having one's own selfish gratification. If they were able to provide satisfying home experiences to children and could help them to grow into healthy normal adulthood, to be good citizens, they would feel that there was some purpose to their lives. Living as a married couple without children was just too selfish a way of life. He felt, too, that what he and his wife had earned and accumulated for themselves should be passed on."

Mr. A., a lawyer, and somewhat older than most adoptive applicants, said that "having a child would keep them from getting in a rut. Both he and his wife had observed this tendency in other couples who are childless. They become selfish, self-centered, and self-satisfied when they get to be fifty. The become smug and sufficient unto themselves. They have a great deal of love that is going to waste and which will be wasted if they wait much longer to try to adopt a child."

Some of the typical responses of would-be parents who were asked to tell why they decided they wanted children include companionship, a significant goal, interest and purpose in life, pleasure in helping a child to grow and develop, pleasure in seeing the world fresh again through sharing a child's experience, a bridge into the future, satisfaction in a duty to be performed, the opportunity to share one of life's more significant experiences with friends, and the desire to share affection with a child and receive affection from a child were among the reasons for desiring children.

Paradoxically even the penalties are sought as pleasures: the noise, the work, the activity, the anxiety that comes with rearing children. These seem to be an antidote to boredom, an insurance against selfish overconcern with one's own narrow desires.

Attitudes Toward Nonmarital Parenthood

Because most of the children available for adoption are born out of wedlock, the applicants' attitude toward nonmarital parenthood is significant. A negative, punitive attitude might condition the parents' response to the adopted child.

Attitude of Significant Others

It is also important for the agency to get some idea of reactions to the idea of adoption on the part of people who are close to the applicants. If the applicants' parents, for instance, are strongly opposed to the idea of adoption, this might increase problems in adjustment to the adoption on the part of the applicant.

Table 10–1 lists some of the less categorical factors that are involved in the agency's decision regarding an applicant's eligibility.

It might be noted that stability is a recurrent criterion—physical stability, emotional stability, financial stability, marital stability. The agency is responsible for acting for the community in behalf of the child too young to choose wisely for himself. The agency needs to guarantee the child a permanent home. Stability presupposes continuity and the likelihood of permanence.

But what confirmation is there that the agency can make a reliable decision regarding such criteria? Brieland (1959) designed a study to determine the reliability with which social workers make decisions regarding adoptive applicants. He taped the intake interviews that one caseworker conducted with five different adoptive applicant couples. Brieland then played the tape of these interviews to 182 caseworkers in twenty-eight different agencies in thirteen states. Each worker was given a transcript of the interviews to follow while listening to the tapes. Having heard the tape, each worker was asked to decide whether or not the agency should continue contact with the couple. The percentage of agreement among the 184 workers varied from couple to couple, ranging from 89.1 per cent agreement in the case of one couple to 61.4 per cent agreement in

TABLE 10–1. Rating Sheet for Prospective Parents

Some Criteria in Evaluating Couples Who Wish to Adopt a Child

Total personality

Family relationships
Work adjustment
Relationship with friends
Activity in community

Emotional maturity

Capacity to give and receive love
Acceptance of sex roles
Ability to assume responsibility for care,
  guidance, and protection of another
  person
Reasonable emotional stability
Flexibility
Self-respect
Ability to cope with problems, disap-
  pointments, and frustrations

Quality of marital relationship

Successful continuance of marriage not
  dependent on children
Respect for each other
Capacity to accept a child born to other
  parents

Feelings about children

Basic love for children
Ability to deal with developmental
  problems
Sensitivity to and understanding and
  tolerance of children's difficulties
Ability to individualize child

*Feelings about childlessness
and readiness to adopt*

Absence of guilt regarding infertility
Mutual decision to adopt
Ability to tell child he is adopted
Attitudes toward biological parents and
  illegitimacy

Motivation

Desire to have more nearly complete
  life
Desire to accept parental responsibility
Desire to contribute to development of
  another human being
Desire to love and be loved

---

the case of another couple. Overall agreement for the total of the five cases was 73.6 percent, so that, for the total sample, the percentage of agreement was at a statistically significant level. Although these results suggest some general tendency toward agreement between worker and worker as to how they evaluated each couple, they also indicate some considerable percentage of disagreement. Brieland (1961) himself has offered a critical analysis of the research problem of such a study and the limitations of the results.

In 1970 Brown (1970) replicated Brieland's study, using videotapes of interviews for presentation to eighty-four workers in adoptive agencies. There was 72 per cent agreement regarding decisions on the five couples—but again substantial deviation from the consensus.

The social worker is called upon to assess ambiguously defined entities such as the applicants' maturity, their marital relationship, their reaction to infertility, their attitude toward children, and their capacity for rearing a child. The behavioral criteria by which these factors are measured are nowhere adequately delineated. Furthermore the worker is asked to predict their behavior in the future, in complex interaction with some unknown child. Ripple (1968), in a follow-up study of adoption, found "little evidence that potential for good parenting can be assessed with confidence" (p. 494).

Even applicants who want to be honest and open with the worker may not be able to evaluate accurately how they will react to adoptive parenthood. The following is the case record of an adoptive home from which a school-aged boy was removed:

> Mrs. R. shared with the worker how terribly upset and guilty she was feeling. . . . She commented that she had always thought of herself as having more patience than most people and it was a great surprise to her to learn that she was not patient. . . . She was very critical of herself, feeling that she should have been able to accept John and work with him longer than she did. She continues to be surprised to learn that she does not have the patience she thought she did and that she can get so nervous and upset.

Mrs. R. had presented herself in the application interview as patient and accepting, which she honestly perceived herself to be.

Many applicants, knowing what the agency worker is looking for, try to project the image of acceptable adoptive parents. Isaac (1965) suggests how to produce a favorable impression:

> Use the pronoun *we* not *I;* share the fact that you have problems but that you have "handled" them maturely; while on good terms with own parents indicate that you are not on such good terms so as to seem dependent; if the wife works she should indicate that she is happy on the job—but not too happy so that she is ready to give it up for motherhood; indicate that the marriage is a satisfying one, that there are, however, disagreements and conflicts, but these are satisfactorily resolved [p. 6].

Such efforts on the part of applicants to act the role of acceptable applicants further confounds the worker's attempt to make an accurate assessment.

However, despite these difficulties, which need to be explicitly acknowledged, the fact is that workers in both the Brieland and Brown studies cited agreed with each other on the selection of applicants at a level that was statistically significant. This consistency reflects some consensus on the selection criteria employed and some consensus on the assessment of applicants and confirms the findings of an earlier study (Maas, 1960).

The topic will be discussed in greater detail later, but it needs to be noted here that factors reviewed by the agency as already defined are most applicable to the application for white, unhandicapped infants.

Agency experience in recruiting homes for children with special needs—older children, minority group children, handicapped children—who are more difficult to place has resulted in a reassessment of the criteria for adoption. In trying to reach out for adoptive applicants for children with special needs, agencies have been willing to accept applicants who do not, in some ways, meet the criteria previously listed. In doing so, workers have begun to question the justification for each of the criteria in terms of its functional utility in the performance of the job of adoptive parenthood.

It has become more and more clear that the essential overriding criterion is the ability of the parents to accept and love and nurture a child, to understand and individualize a child, and to have both the capacity and the competence to deal successfully with the problems of rearing a child. All else is commentary, and some of the criteria listed are now seen as having less importance.

The criteria, additionally, serve the administrative function of providing a basis for keeping applications at a manageable level. With many more applicants for healthy white infants than there are such children available, some reasonably defensible procedure must be applied to "screen out" some applicants.

Where there is a need for more applicants than there are children available, as in the case of special needs children, agencies can comfortably adopt a stance of seeing all applicants having an average capacity for parenthood. The effort is to "screen in" all applicants, to salvage all applicants by helping them to resolve any ambivalence about adopting and to solve any problems that stand in the way of adopting. The orientation is "educative" rather than "investigative," and the agency concerned with placing children with special needs can administratively afford such an orientation.

Not only are criteria differently applied as the nature of the child needing adoption is different, but they are also applied differently in terms of the nature of the applicant. Some of the criteria are clearly inapplicable to the applicant who is able to achieve parenthood biologically but elects to adopt instead, and they are inappropriate to the single-parent applicant.

Although the possible significance of the criteria listed is recognized, there is currently less rigid adherence to the requirements and greater flexibility in assessing the criteria in relation to the applicants' total situation.

PROCESS IN ADOPTION

From Application to Placement

The agency seeks to obtain from a variety of sources the information it needs in making a decision. The principal source, of course, is the adoptive applicants themselves. The agency caseworker schedules office interviews with the couple and with each member of the marital pair separately. The interviews generally include discussion of the following:

1. How the interest in adoption developed.
2. Motivation for adoption.
3. Attitude toward childlessness and infertility.
4. Understanding of children and experiences with children.
5. History of the marriage and current patterns of marital interaction.
6. Developmental history.
7. Educational and employment history.
8. Patterns of social participation.
9. Attitude of the extended family toward adoption.
10. Attitude toward illegitimacy and the out-of-wedlock child.
11. Problems anticipated in adoption and how they must be handled.
12. Attitudes toward working with the agency.

If all goes well, the interviews are followed by a series of home visits, during which the caseworker has an opportunity of seeing the couple react in an informal, familiar setting. The worker is also able to obtain some information about the physical resources of the home and the neighborhood. References, submitted by the applicant, are contacted for whatever additional information they can provide. They not only help the caseworker to see the applicant through the eyes of other people but also indicate the extent to which the applicants are integrated into the community and the attitude of the community toward adoption.

Throughout all of these contacts, the agency, acting for the child, is assuring itself that these applicants will provide an adequate, stable home for the child. It is also helping the adoptive applicants to decide that this is what they really want to do and helping them to adjust to the idea of impending parenthood. The nine months of pregnancy provide the opportunity to biological parents for adjusting to the idea of the significant changes in their lives that will follow the birth of their child. The study period provides an opportunity for thoughtful self-examination, anxious anticipation, and hopeful delay that entails the kind of emotional reorganization that is involved in actual pregnancy. It helps prepare the applicant, emotionally, for parenthood. It is highly desirable that the adoptive parents be active participants in this process of mutual exploration because, as Campbell (1957) says, "For successful adoption, children need to be 'taken' by the adoptive parents, not merely given by the agency" (p. 184).

A letter from one adoptive parent regarding the study experience notes:

> By the end of our interviews we felt that, even if we were not accepted by the agency, we had gained a valuable experience that would enable us to approach adoption from other sources with a much greater understanding of its problems and difficulties than we had before.

An adoptive mother, in a retrospective analysis of her experience, said:

> In our thoughts about adoption, my husband and I had raised many questions and hypothetical situations to each other concerning an adopted child. Two of these neither of us could answer satisfactorily. One dealt with the discipline of an adopted child who might remind you that since you are not their real parent they do not have to obey you, and how to cope with an adopted child's curiosity about his natural parents. By answering these questions, the social worker made us feel that at this point the interview really began. We began to see the social worker's role as a dual one. The interviews are not only to serve the purpose of finding out about you, but are there to help you and answer any doubts that you may have in regard to an adopted child.

How does the application and study process actually work out in practice? Bradley (1966) studied the processing of some four hundred applicants in eight agencies. The process was completed within four or five interviews, indicating that it is not a prolonged, elaborate procedure. The median amount of time between application for and placement of a child was seven to nine months, closely approximating the usual pregnancy time lapse.

Of the applicants, 26 per cent were rejected by the agencies; another 6 per cent might have been encouraged to withdraw but withdrew voluntarily. Interestingly the most highly professionalized agencies had the lowest percentage of rejection; the least professionalized, the highest (p. 110).

Bradley checked the social workers' assessments against the decisions actually made in order to determine the factors associated with selection. Those factors having the highest association with acceptance were "positive qualities of couple interaction in their marriage, flexible and outgoing characteristics of both husband's and wife's personalities, the couples' openness, their nonneurotic motivation for adoption, their adequate marital role performance, and their acceptance of infertility" (p. 22). However, applicants were also accepted who "tended to be marginal couples who were considered more suitable for marginal children"—hard-to-place children (p. 188). In other words, there were two alternative but nonsimultaneous routes that led to a positive impression of couples as adoptive prospects, with the "better" couple seen as suitable for the "better" child and the marginal couple seen as more suitable for the marginal child (p. 189). This finding confirms an earlier study, which indicated that applicants who presented qualifications that differed from those generally accepted by the agency sought to improve their chances by indicating a willingness to accept a hard-to-place child (Kadushin, 1962). A more recent study of the application process in English agencies showed that "in the case of hard-to-place children, agencies compromised considerably in their expectations of adoptive applicants" (Triseliotis, 1970, p. 88).

Once the applicants have been approved for adoption, the agency is faced with the problem of selecting a child for them. Some effort is made to match child and parents in terms of ethnic background, physical appearance, temperament, and intelligence potential. Having been selected as adoptive parents, at this point they are selected as adoptive parents for a particular child.

The period between the completion of the study and the actual placement of the child is perceived as a very stressful time. There is the feeling of being in limbo, a fear that the agency may forget or overlook the application, a sense of being unable to control one's destiny, and unnerving uncertainty about when the adoption will be made—if ever. Some repeated brief contacts during this period by the agency might be reassuring.

When the agency has determined on a mutually advantageous selection of child and parents, the adoptive parents are called in and given background information on the child. Any questions or doubts they may have are discussed and, if possible, resolved. If all goes well on the verbal presentation, the parents meet the child and a decision is made.

One study of this point in the process notes:

> One factor which increases the anxiety and discomfort of adoptive parents during the placement process is that, unlike natural parents, they can "back out" if they choose. When parents are having their own children, however worried they may feel, they have no choice but to accept it; therefore they have no decision to make [McCormick, 1948, p. 145].

In the case of older children, aware of what is going on, an effort may be made to have the prospective parents meet the child by arranged "accident" in the park, supermarket, and so on. This gives the adoptive parents an opportunity to see the child without his feeling rejected if they decide against taking him.

The caseworker is also involved in working with the child. If the child is an infant, little preparation for the impending change is possible. However, the agency arranges for a thorough physical check of the child and informs the adoptive parents of the results. With older children, an effort is made to prepare them for the change by discussing with them the meaning of adoption and some of the problems they will experience in moving into a new home with a new set of permanent parents. For the older child, a gradual process of placement can be arranged. This might involve an overnight visit to the adoptive parents or a series of such visits before the final move is made (Andrews, 1961).

From Placement to Adoption

After the child is placed in the home, there is a trial period, usually six months to a year, during which the child is still under the legal guardianship of the agency. At the end of the trial period, if it is agreeable to both the agency and the adoptive parents, the final adoption takes place through appropriate court action.

The trial period or postplacement service, as it is sometimes more neutrally designated, is based on the recognition that not even the most acute, perceptive study can confidently predict how the adoptive parents will actually feel when confronted with rearing the adopted child. At best, the study "can differentiate between the potentially good prospects and more or less poor risks." This period, then, can be viewed as an extension of the home study. At this point, the parent is actually performing as a parent rather than talking about, imagining, or anticipating parenthood. The period thus serves a protective function, ensuring that the child has, in fact, been placed in a desirable home. This time is, consequently, a threat to the adoptive parents, for the agency might decide to remove the child if problems become serious. Actually, only rarely is a child likely to be removed after placement and before final adoption. Studies (see pp. 544–547) indicate that removal occurs in only about 2 per cent of the cases.

The trial period protects the adoptive parent as well. If the child is not developing normally, if a physical or mental handicap has become manifest, the parent has a right to reconsider before the adoption is made final.

The agency, however, would like to emphasize that this period is one of helping the parents and the adopted child develop a sense of kinship and of helping them with the inevitable problems that arise as a result of such a radical change in their life situation. The agencies see this supportive function as taking precedence over the protective function.

Here the perception of adoptive parents seems to be at variance with the intent of the agency. An interview study of fifty-seven adoptive couples in Minnesota indicated "that they rated the 'probation' function as their opinion of the primary purpose of the continued contact by the agency," whereas caseworkers unanimously regarded help in successful integration of the adoptive family as the primary purpose. Of these families, 40 per cent felt that postplacement interviews had not been particularly helpful; 19 percent felt that the visits had been of "substantial" help (Gochros, 1962, p. 9). The clients' view of postplacement service as primarily protective is confirmed by another, more limited, study of client reaction (Zober, 1961).

Few of the parents felt that a clear, unambiguous statement of the purpose of the trial period had been communicated by the agency. When it had been, the parents were more likely to feel that the contacts were helpful—especially in two general areas: "reassurance (such as reassurance that they were doing a good job, that their child was developing properly or that the agency would not take the child away) and problem solving (such as provision of child care and developmental information and legal procedural information or help with specific adoption problems such as how to tell their child about adoption)" (Gochros, 1967, p. 322). "The single area of service that the greatest number of adoptive parents considered the most helpful was reassurance that they were doing a good job as parents" (Gochros, 1962, p. 10).

Studies indicate that the actual contacts between the agency and the family during this period are generally infrequent. Gochros (1962) found that visits were made about once every three months, and Triseliotis (1970) found that an average number of 1.6 visits were "paid to each case during the average six months probationary period" (p. 106).

Some adoptive parents might resent the implication that they cannot be adequate parents without agency help. Continuing contact serves to remind them that they are not biological parents and that the child is not yet their own.

Although most adoptive parents feel that adoption services are helpful in preparing them for their adoptive role, few have voluntary contact with the agency after adoption, preferring to turn to family, friends, and their pediatrician for help with parent–child problems (Starr, 1970, pp. 499–500).

PROBLEMS OF ADOPTIVE FAMILIES

The Adoptive Parent

Once the child is adopted, the family is like all other families—yet different. Consequently they have the same problems all other families face but, in addition, some unique problems that derive from the fact of adoption. Biological parents require no intermediary in achieving parenthood; adoptive parents require the agency. Biological parents pass no test of adequacy; adoptive parents must satisfy the agency of their adequacy. Biological parents can count on the child's arrival within a given period of time; adoptive parents do not know when —or if—the child will come. Adoptive parenthood, unlike biological parenthood, cannot be achieved in private in a moment of impulse; it requires a deliberate process in which motivation must be made explicit and shared with others. Adoptive parents can control the sex of the child, can ensure that the child is without serious defect, and can avoid the discomforts of pregnancy and childbirth; at the same time, they miss the experience of unity with the child in developing life and giving birth.

Once past the point of genesis, the differences between adoptive and biological families grow smaller and the similarities grow larger. Even the most perceptive observer would be hard put to distinguish an adoptive family from a biological family in a restaurant, at the beach, in a department store.

Parenthood is primarily a social role, and title to the status *parent* should be reserved for those who actually perform its functions. The Talmud says, "He who raises up the child is called 'father'; not he who begot the child." The playwright Schiller noted, "It is not flesh and blood, but the heart, which makes us fathers and sons." Krugman (1964) observes, "The differentiation to be made is not between two sets of parents ('natural' and 'adoptive') but between *parents* and those who *give birth* to the child" (p. 357).

As *parents,* then, adoptive parents face all of the problems of adjustment and change in accepting the child into the home that all other parents face with the birth of a child. And they continue to face those problems encountered by all parents in conscientiously trying to raise a biologically, socially, and emotionally healthy child.

But society is ambivalent about granting full endorsement to the adoptive parent. The very words *natural mother* or *real mother* suggest that the adoptive parent is "unnatural" and/or "unreal," reflecting society's attitude that biological relationships are more important than social relationships, that "giving birth" is more important than "caring for," and that we are obliged to honor biological relationships for their own sake. Our vocabulary, reflecting our thinking, our mores, and our legal procedures, suggests that adoption is a second-best route to parenthood. More recently, adoptive parents' organizations have been suggesting the use of the term *biomother* or *bioparents* to distinguish the birth parents from the adoptive parents.

At any rate, adoptive parents do have some particular problems that derive from their unique status. They are members of a minority group who have achieved parenthood in a special way (Kirk, 1964). Given a choice, adoptive parents would have preferred to conceive as well as rear their children. They usually come to adoption out of necessity, not by choice.

There are no readily available role models of adoptive parenthood that would help socialize adoptive parents to their status. Whereas the biological parent role almost uniformly elicits from others comments indicating support and approbation, the adoptive parent role frequently elicits comments that contain components of hostility, derision, and rejection.

With adoption, the parent faces the problem of accepting his status publicly. Application for adoption may be kept secret, but with the arrival of the child, the extended family and the immediate neighbors become aware of the adoption. The loss of anonymity raises such questions as what to tell friends and relatives about the child's background. But of somewhat greater difficulty is the fact that the adoptive parents now risk public recognition of their infertility. Questions will be raised about why they needed to resort to adoption.

Adoptive parents may bring to parenthood some special feelings about the child. Because adoptive parenthood is achieved with the consent of the community through selection by a community agency, adoptive parents may feel a greater sense of accountability for their performance as parents. They may, on occasion, feel guilty that they are not living up to the expectations of the community, that better parents might have been chosen for the children. As one adoptive parent said, "The yardstick by which the adoptive parent, as a parent, is measured is a longer one." They may feel that because the child has once been deprived, they have an obligation to be more indulgent with him. They may feel that because some part of the child belongs irrevocably to the natural parent, they cannot be as firm in disciplining him—that he might reject them. The adoptive parent is aware that he shares the child, at least in fantasy, with the biological parents. He may be concerned that the child will ultimately seek out and make contact with the biological parents.

The adoptive parent may be concerned about his entitlement to the child, possibly feeling somewhat equivocal about the completeness of his relationship to the child. There is a feeling that a social–emotional relationship is less binding, more fragile, than the relationship between biological parent and child, in which the social–emotional component is reinforced by the mutual bond of blood. The problem for the adoptive parents is that of really feeling that the child "belongs" to them.

Raleigh (1954), in a study of adoptive families at a child guidance clinic, noted that adoptive mothers "tended to be more overanxious about their children's problems and were more overprotective in their attitudes," which suggests "that the adoptive mothers tended to feel more insecure in their parental role" and had a greater need to appear concerned (p. 70). Adoptive mothers were also more inconsistent in their disciplining than natural mothers and felt less secure in coping with their children's unacceptable behavior (p. 69).

However much the adoptive parent may have moved toward the conviction that environment is the more important component in the child's development, there are still some residual feelings about the unknown hereditary elements behind the child's behavior. Because most of the children are illegitimate, uneasy feelings about "bad blood" and the child's destructive impulses may make the parents anxious.

Although in their day-to-day living most adoptive parents do not feel different from other parents, the adoptive experience "leaves something like an old surgical scar—it is there if you look hard enough, it doesn't hurt until something knocks against it" (Timms, 1973, p. 38).

Problems of Adoptive Children

The adopted child faces all the general problems of development encountered by his nonadoptive peers. In this sense, he is a child among other children. But, in addition, like the adoptive parents, he faces some special problems that are related to the fact that he is an adopted child.

The fact that the "birth parents" of the adoptive child are different from the "bread parents," those who actually perform the role of parents, presents the child with special problems. The child faces the problem of "genealogical bewilderment," of accepting the fact that he is the biological product of parents whom he does not know and never will know. Who are the people who gave him birth? What were they like? The process of self-identification is a more difficult one for the adopted child.

Freud (1950) points out that every child, when faced with the reality of some rejection by his parents, imagines that he is really a stepchild or an adopted child and that his real parents are all-loving and all-permissive.

Sooner or later, however, the child accepts the fact that his parents are both loving and rejecting. However, because the adopted child does, in fact, have two sets of parents, he can separate the components of this ambivalence by letting one set of parents embody the negative, rejecting component and the other set of parents represent all that is loving and accepting. The task of fusing the two aspects of the parental image is consequently more difficult for the adopted child, and the tendency to idealize the unknown biological parent is great. Yet the very fact that the first set of parents gave him up for adoption raises doubts in the child's mind about his acceptability, posing a difficulty for the development of a positive self-image.

As the child grows older, he may want to know why his own parents could not care for him. The significant question, for the child, is whether or not he was so bad, so unacceptable, that his parents needed to reject him. Some assurance must be given to the child that his placement for adoption did not result from any wrongdoing on his part: "Just as parents need to feel that they are worthy of parenthood, so too the most important question in any child's mind is not 'How did I get here' but 'Are you glad I am here?'" (LeShan, 1958, p. 274).

With adolescence, another problem arises. Many adopted children are aware that they are illegitimate. Identified, to whatever limited degree, with natural parents who engaged in illicit sex, of which they are the living evidence, the child faces the problem of resolving any predisposition to think, "Like father, like son; like mother, like daughter." The child also may have greater difficulty in establishing independence because of feelings of gratitude and obligation toward the adoptive parents that conflict with the need to break away from them.

Although these are the special problems that might be faced by adoptive parents and children, there is little empirical evidence to show how frequently such problems actually do arise. Kadushin (1971) found that adoptive parents perceived the differences between themselves and biological parents but rarely considered such differences to be problems. Research on the emotional problems of adopted children reveals that the psychosocial development of such children is, in most instances, indistinguishable from that of their peers.

Telling

The most difficult, most troublesome, unique aspect of adoption is the problem of "telling." "Telling" involves the process of gradually sharing with the child the information that he is adopted and helping him to understand and emotionally accept the fact. This proves to be a problem for adoptive parents as well as for their children. Many of the problems already discussed are activated or exacerbated by the necessity for telling.

The question "How shall I tell my child he is adopted?" contains within it a second question: "How do I accept myself as an adoptive parent?" Telling makes explicit the fact of infertility; telling makes explicit the fact that the child had other biological parents; telling introduces the natural parents' image into the family system and threatens the exclusiveness of the relationship between adoptive parents and child. Comfortable telling thus requires not only that the adoptive parents resolve their feelings about their infertility but also that they be sufficiently confident of the strength of the child's emotional kinship with them so that it is not threatened by the fact of a biological kinship with others. As Kirk (1959) puts it, telling conflicts with the requirement for "integrating" the child into the family because it "differentiates" the child from the family (p. 319). Telling also is anxiety-provoking because it raises the whole question of sexuality: how babies are conceived, how babies are born. Parents may be diffident about telling because they feel uncomfortable with such questions.

Telling forces both adoptive parent and child into an explicit recognition of their adoptive status. Parents may be reluctant to impose the burden of this atypicality on the child, the knowledge of this difference from his peers. They

may be anxious to spare the child the knowledge that he was born out of wedlock or that his parents were neglectful.

Telling also raises questions relating to an additional "public" not in the picture when the placement was made. What if the child's friends ask about his
being adopted? Should the school be informed when he is first enrolled? Should
neighbors be told when the family moves to a new neighborhood?

There is some clinical support for the supposition that adoptive children contend with these feelings and questions. Schechter (1960), drawing on his experience with adopted children in private psychiatric practice, notes that the
child made aware of his adoption has to "cope with the knowledge of the rejection by the original parents, representing a severe narcissistic injury" (p. 31).
This gives rise to recurrent anxiety in the children, for "having been given up
once for undetermined reasons, they may be given up again at some future time,
also for undetermined fantasied reasons" (p. 31).

Despite the difficulties involved, it is generally agreed that it is desirable
for the adoptive parent to tell the child that he is adopted. Aside from the fact
that not telling falsifies the relationship and requires that the adoptive parents
live a lie, it is possible that the child might discover, through other sources, that
he is adopted. The parents' silence, then, might be taken to mean that there is
something bad about the fact of adoption.

Adoptive children who accidentally learned of their adoption or who learned
of it precipitously in some crisis situation described their reaction as that of
"panic," "profound hurt," "rejection," "having been deceived" (Hagen, 1968;
Paton, 1954).

Telling is desirable because it requires adoptive parents and children to
clarify between themselves the nature of their relationship. Not only is it prag-
matically expedient because of the great risk of exposure, but it is also ethical:
The child is entitled to know his true origins. Furthermore, rather than
threatening the relationship, telling may intensify positive feeling between parents and child as they acknowledge their "shared fate." Some research findings
suggest that those adoptive families that openly accept the idea of adoption, implied in telling, are apt to be better adjusted to adoption (Kirk, 1964, pp. 95–99).

There is some controversy, however, over when telling should take place.
The agencies recommend that telling begin early in the child's life and be rein-
troduced for discussion at progressively higher levels of complexity. Parents are
advised to introduce the word early, to apply the word and the concept in appropriate situations, and to tell the child about adoption simply and directly as
one of the facts of life that the child needs to know.

More recently, some psychoanalysts have advised that telling should be delayed until the child is beyond the Oedipal stage in development. Telling the
younger child supposedly feeds his fantasies and makes more difficult the resolution of the Oedipal conflict. It is suggested that when the child is between six
and twelve, he has a better grasp of reality and can develop a more realistic
image of the adoptive situation (Ansfield, 1971; Peller, 1961). The material in
support of this view is very limited, restricted to isolated clinical examples, and
contradicted by Witmer's (1963) study, which showed that a delay in telling was
associated with heightened negative reactions on the part of the child (p. 392).

The level of interest in adoptive status is not uniform throughout the child's
life. There is a peak period around eight or nine when his peers become explicitly

aware of and raise questions about adoptive status. When the adolescent is struggling with self-definition, questions about his origins become more insistent.
And at each level, there is progressively deeper understanding of the meaning of
adoption as it is explained in a different context. To the young person approaching marriage, it might be explained that marriage is, in effect, a procedure
through which husband and wife "adopt" each other and develop a relationship
more intense than any blood relationship. Perhaps, however, full understanding
is not achieved until the adopted child becomes a parent himself. One adoptee
said, "I never saw anybody of my own flesh and blood until I held my baby in
my arms."

There are also suggestions on how to tell. The general advice is that the
parents should share the information confidently, realistically, and positively,
without anxiety or apology, suggesting that the parents themselves have to feel
very comfortable with the idea of adoption.

Overemphasis is as much an indication of discomfort with the idea as vigorous avoidance. The adoptive parents of the child who said, "I knew. They knew
I knew. I even told them I knew. But they still refused to talk about it" are
clearly uncomfortable with the fact of adoption. But discomfort is also present in
the case of the family of the adopted child who said, "It was good to know that I
was adopted, but I wished that they would stop talking about it."

As McWhinnie (1967) notes, in summarizing the reaction of adopted adults
whom she interviewed:

> None of these adopted children wanted their adoptive status shrouded in com-
> plete secrecy. . . . Equally they did not want constant reference to it. They
> wanted something in between, where their adopted status was acknowledged
> without embarrassment and then overtly forgotten so that they were treated
> exactly as if they were the biological sons and daughters of their adopted
> parents. . . . Thus they were emphatic that they did not want to be introduced
> as an "adopted son" or an "adopted daughter." They wanted to feel they belonged
> in the family and were completely accepted there as a son or daughter [p. 249].

Emphasis in telling might be more productively placed on what the child
has gained, a home with accepting parents, rather than on loss of the biological
parents.

Adoptive parents must feel, and communicate to the child, that adoptive
parenthood and adoptive childhood are, in essence, the same as biological parent–
child relationships; that the adopted child belongs just as certainly and securely
in the adoptive family as the biological child does in his family.

Telling at its best can be an expression of love and acceptance of the child.
The account of how he came to be adopted can reinforce feelings of belonging
and identity. However, telling can also be used as a weapon. Depending on the
spirit of the communication, it may be designed to make the child feel obligated
for all the adoptive parents have done for him or as a threat that the child
might be "returned" if he does not give satisfaction.

Adoptive parents have to accept responsibility for telling. Earlier studies
indicated that adopted children were indifferent toward adoption. Apparently
the children studied rarely took the initiative of asking questions. More recent
studies suggest, however, that children are eager to know but, despite their

curiosity, feel that they cannot initiate discussion about origins, that the information has to come from the adoptive parents on the initiative of the adoptive parents. As adopted children, they feel hesitant about taking responsibility for raising these questions, out of fear of hurting, or upsetting, or appearing disloyal to the parents (Jaffee, 1974). However, although retrospectively adult adoptees may state that they were anxious to know about their past when younger, Tizard (1977, pp. 141–143) notes that some of the child's resistance to telling is real. The child, as a child, has difficulty in integrating the idea that he had another parent who surrendered him for adoption with the idea that there is another set of parents to whom he somehow has some attachment. The reluctance on the part of the child, often noted by adoptive parents, to discuss the matter of adoption freely in response to the parents' invitation might be self-protective.

Agencies generally recommend that parents introduce the child early and gradually to the idea of adoption, through the judicious use of such books as *The Chosen Baby* (Wasson, 1939), *The Family That Grew* (Rondell, 1951), or *Why Was I Adopted?* (Livingston, 1978). Announcement cards, used to inform others of adoption, tend to emphasize the "chosen-baby" motif. One of the more popular ones runs

> We have a brand new baby,
> And there isn't any doubt
> We got just what we wanted—
> Because we picked our baby out!

However, the "chosen-child" concept places a great burden on the child of living up to some great expectations. It is clearly inappropriate in those situations where there is a biochild in the family. Furthermore the chosen-child explanation is essentially false. As one adopted child said, "I was not chosen as an individual; my parents just wanted a child." The idea of being "wanted" rather than "chosen" is closer to the realities of the adoptive situation.

A more difficult question, of more pressing concern to the adopted child, is "Why did his biological parents give him up?" Frequently the answer is "Because they could not care for you and loved you so much that they wanted the best for you." But the idea that "they loved you so much" is rejected by adopted adults. One woman said:

> First of all I don't think it is possible to feel true potential love for a newborn or growing child. This comes from living together. Also if my real parents loved me so much, why did they give me up? I used to think, "Are my adoptive parents going to give me up, too, because I know they love me?" It is more honest to say that there are circumstances which make it necessary to place the child for adoption. It is a question of the ability to be a parent, not a question of love [Hagen, 1968, p. 27].

Another difficult question concerns the kinds of information about the biological parents that should be shared with the child. The agency, too, must determine how much of its knowledge about the bioparents should be shared with the adoptive parents.

Generally the agency provides only information that would help the adoptive parents in their child-rearing responsibilities or that has bearing on the child's development. Information given adoptive parents might therefore include medical information about the child's birth, immunization history, special health problems, sleeping patterns, and food preferences; information about the biological parents' ages, education, and general appearance, and the nature of the relationship between the child's father and mother. Many agencies prefer not to burden the adoptive parents with too many details of the child's background so that they can truthfully tell the child that they do not know much about the biological parents. However, what can be truthfully pointed out is that whatever reason occasioned the inability of the natural parent to care for the child, he showed enough concern for the needs and welfare of the child to give him up for adoption.

It is difficult to discuss adoption without implying that the child has been rescued from inadequate parents, yet to imply this may make it difficult for the child, who is to some extent identified with his biological parents. The adoptive parents must therefore communicate background information in an accepting, understanding tone. This in itself may be difficult for many adoptive parents: having been highly motivated to have a child, they find it difficult to empathize with or understand a mother who has given up her baby. A follow-up study showed that there "appeared to be a link between the adoptive parents' attitudes to the natural parents and the difficulty they found in telling the child he was adopted. Though none considered telling to be easy, those who actually disapproved of the natural parents found it to be more difficult" (Seglow, 1972, p. 149). For all, there is the problem of conveying understanding and acceptance of the unmarried mother without implying the moral and practical acceptability of out-of-wedlock pregnancy.

Relevant research involves interviews with adult adoptees who shared, retrospectively, their experience in the telling process (McWhinnie, 1967). Another study was based on small group meetings of adult adoptees who met over a period of six months to discuss their experiences in adoption (Hagen, 1968). To a considerable extent the adoptees agreed that it was crucial for the parent to share with the child the fact that he was adopted, that integration of the meaning of adoption takes place gradually and that real understanding is not achieved until adolescence or even early adulthood, and that although it is necessary to reiterate the fact of adoption, it should be referred to only on those occasions when the situation calls attention to adoptive status.

The principles of "telling" might be summarized as follows:

1. The child's receptivity to the fact of his adoptive status is best assured if the parents themselves accept it and are convinced of the importance of telling.
2. The child need be told at any one time only as much as he can understand, so that telling is a gradual process.
3. There will be many different opportunities to tell the child, and repetition in different contexts is useful. Everyday use of the word, when appropriate, helps make it comfortably acceptable.
4. Overemphasis, like avoidance, has some dangers. Telling the child he was chosen may burden him with the need to live up to excessive expectations.
5. The parent must take the initiative in offering information about adoption.

6. Sharing of such information is not likely to threaten the relationship between adoptive parents and children if the relationship is an essentially positive one.

The Question of Search

The concern with telling is related to concern with another aspect of adoption, the search of adoptive children for more detailed knowledge of their roots and for possible contact with their biological parents. _Search_ is defined as the efforts of either the adult adoptee or the birth parent to secure identifying information that might possibly lead to locating the other party. The need to search derives from the fact that in most jurisdictions, once a child is legally adopted, the record of how the child came to be adopted is sealed, and information from the record about his biological parents is not available to the adopted child. It also means that information about the adoptive family in which the child has been placed is not available to the biological parent. The purpose is to protect the biological mother from any possibility of subsequent intrusion on her life by the child she has surrendered and to protect the adoptive parents and the child from interference from the biological mother. It also reinforces the idea that the adoptive parents are the true parents of the child and that there are no parents other than the adoptive parents.

The intent of the sealed records is to symbolize the dissolution of the relationship between adoptee and birth parents and to substitute for it the adoptive parent–adoptive child relationship. Anonymity "helps the adoptive family establish itself as a social unit, free from outside interference and provide an environment in which the child is encouraged to identify with his adoptive home" without competitive ties and pulls (Burke, 1975, p. 1200). Sealing the record also protects the out-of-wedlock child from the stigmatization that might result from a revelation of his status.

The question of opening adoptive records does potentially affect the lives of the biological parent and the adoptive parents as well as the life of the adoptee. Social and emotional constraints operate to condition the behavior of all parties in the triangle and to condition their attitude toward the search. The adoptee may be constrained from any impulse to seek out further information about the birth parent by a sense of loyalty to the adoptive parents and a desire not to hurt them by the seeming ingratitude implied in the search. The adopted child might feel this is an "unspoken debt to be paid with acquiescence and silence: it is a form of emotional indenture even though it is made in the name of love" (Lifton, 1975, p. 5). To deny the debt is to act as a traitor.

In addition, there is the constraint from intruding on the life of the birth parent. The birth parent may be constrained by a respect for the privacy of the adoptive family and the disruption such an intrusion may occasion for them and the adopted child. When finally contacted as a consequence of the efforts of the adoptee, the birth parent may be constrained to accept the contact whatever the private preference rather than overtly rejecting the child a second time. The adoptive parents may discourage the search not only because of the threat to their image as the child's true parents but also out of concern for the possible hurt to their child that might result from the revelation of embarrassing background material or a possible negative reception by the birth parent.

The search is regarded by some adoptive parents as posing a potential threat not only to the adoptive parent–adoptive child relationship but also to the integrity of adoption services. Many child welfare workers offering service to unmarried mothers know that they often are willing to place the child through an agency because of the assurance of confidentiality and anonymity. Not being able to provide such assurance decreases the advantages of agency placement as compared with black- or gray-market placements of the child by the parents or the guarantee of anonymity through child abandonment. The anxiety about the possibility of subsequent contact may intensify the biological mother's hesitancy about surrendering the child for adoption, decreasing the number of adoptable infants available. A final decision becomes more difficult for the birth mother to live with if she anticipates that at some unpredictable time in the future, the child might reenter her life. It may also intensify the potential adoptive applicant's ambivalence about moving into adoption, thus reducing the number of applicants. Providing identifying information is also regarded by agencies as a violation of their promise of confidentiality and anonymity to the biological mother and the adoptive parents.

If unsealing records is a violation of promises of confidentiality and anonymity made to both the birth and the adoptive parents, if it permits an invasion of privacy of the birth parents' current life and an intrusion of the birth parent into the adoptive family, it also has its advantages. There are possible gains for all parties in the relationship as a consequence of the search. The adoptees have the opportunity of learning what they want and need to know about their roots and their heritage, and they can feel a sense of continuity with the past, can come to grips more surely with problems of identity, and can, through the experience with reality, correct their fantasies. The birth parent can resolve old guilt feelings and resolve nagging questions about what happened to the relinquished child. The adoptive parents can lay to rest all of the anxieties about the effects on their relationship with their child of a contact with the birth parent. A secretive cloud may be dissipated, and the relationship may be continued with greater honesty and openness.

The claim is made that the sealed record and the consequent interdiction of access to such background information runs counter to the psychological needs of the adoptee in adolescence and young adulthood. All adolescents, of course, face the difficult problem of identification, that is, defining their uniqueness as a separate individual and developing a coherent, stable self-image. For the adopted adolescent, the problem of self-identification is made more difficult because she needs to incorporate the image of two sets of parents and to do it in the face of vague and limited knowledge about her biological antecedents (Sorosky, Baran, Pannor, 1975).

It is said that adoptees are like amnesia victims who cannot remember some part of their lives; they feel that an important piece of their life story is missing. There is a sense of psychological amputation in the absence of knowledge of their beginnings, a sense of partial identity, a gap in the self-image, a sense of "genealogical bewilderment" (Sants, 1965). Lacking continuity and connectedness to his or her origins, the adoptee can be capable of only partial self-identification.

Having reviewed the relevant literature relating to adoption and identity conflicts, Sorosky, Baran, and Pannor (1975b) conclude that "adoptees are more vulnerable than the population at large to the development of identity problems in late adolescence and young adulthood" (p. 25). Proponents of open records contend that open records would help the adoptee to resolve this difficult problem because he or she would have access to information about hereditary background. Genealogical information is available from three sources: agency files, records of the court that approved the petition for adoption, and the birth record.

Scotland, Finland, and Israel have for some time permitted the adoptee's access to birth records. This change was legislated in England in 1975, and in 1977 Canada was seriously considering similar legislation. In the United States prior to 1971, Alabama and Kansas permitted adoptees access to birth records, and Virginia permitted access to adoption-court record material. Access to adoptive records can currently be obtained in most states on a petition to the courts for "good cause." The problem is that *good cause* has not been clearly defined, and judges, therefore, have considerable discretion in making such decisions. Matters of health, possible genetic defects, and controversial inheritance situations have been among the "good causes" for opening adoption records. A general desire for more knowledge about one's background, or, the need to resolve problems of identity, have not been accepted as "good cause" for such a procedure.

If a social agency made the placement these records may also be available, but here again the adoptee must prove to the agency worker that there is good and sufficient reason for his obtaining the desired information. As a result, adoptees have been arguing that their constitutional rights to significant information about their own background are denied to them. The sealed-record procedure is viewed as a violation of the Fourteenth Amendment, because it denies adoptees "equal protection of the laws," and of the First Amendment, which can be construed to include not only the right to speak but the right to receive information (Anderson, 1977; Burke, 1975; Prager, Rothstein, 1973). Equal protection of the law is claimed because the sealing of the records causes adoptees psychological pain, suffering, and damage not experienced by nonadopted persons. The contention is that adoptees, as a group, are discriminated against because they are denied information contained in the birth record that is freely available to every other citizen. The agreement made between the agency, the birth parent, and the adoptive parent for anonymity and confidentiality, was, it is said, made without the consent of the adoptee, who is a coequal partner to the information held secret.

Groups of adoptees, and some biological parents whose children were adopted, have organized to press their claim for open records. Orphan Voyage was established in 1954 by an adopted social worker, Jean Paton, to call attention to this problem. More recently, ALMA (Adoptees Liberty Movement Association) was established by Florence Fisher. ALMA publishes a handbook written by a professional genealogist giving advice on procedures to be employed in searching out records. Search committee workshops are conducted to help members with problems relating to search. In 1977 ALMA claimed a membership of ten thousand around the country.

The Association for the Protection of the Adoptive Triangle (APAT), composed primarily of adoptive parents, has been organized in support of the sealed record.

Biological parents have organized their own group, Concerned United

Parents, to press their concerns (*The New York Times,* January 23, 1978). They are asking that the biological mother actively participate with the agency in reviewing the applications of adoptive parents and in selecting the parents for their child. Detailed interviews with thirty-eight mothers who earlier in their lives had surrendered a child for adoption indicated that they frequently thought about the adopted child with considerable mixed feelings of guilt, pain, loss, and mourning (Baran, Pannor, Sorosky, 1977; Sorosky, Baran, Pannor, 1978). In addition to whatever guilt or shame the birth parent feels about having had a child out of wedlock, there is the additional burden of guilt and shame related to having surrendered the child. Many birth parents continue to feel discomfort over the relinquishment, even though most recognize it as inevitable and desirable and in line with wanting to provide an intact family for the child. They are interested in knowing how the child has developed and want to explain to the child what prompted their decision. A desire for expiation and absolution also seems to be common.

It might be pointed out that the problem of search is not limited to the adoptees. It is also of concern to out-of-wedlock children raised by their mother who might be interested in meeting their father. Rod McKuen (1976), the poet, details just such a chronicle in his book *Finding My Father—One Man's Search for Identity.* The child who is a product of artificial insemination may also be interested in finding his father. In each case, one half of the child's genealogy is missing for him.

The Child Welfare League of America, in its *Standards for Adoption Service* (1973), supports the sealed record. It notes that services to the different parties in the adoptive situation involve a pledge of confidentiality, that the biological and the adoptive parents should not be identified to each other, and that the biological parents "should not be reinvolved after the relinquishment of the child; and that the child should be protected . . . from the intervention of the natural parents after his placement." The League, in recognition of a need to reexamine its policy with regard to sealed records, solicited questionnaire responses from 163 member agencies in 1976. The report of this study (Jones, 1976) noted that assurances of anonymity and confidentiality were being made to birth parents and adoptive parents by most adoptive agencies. Of the agencies queried, 27 per cent indicated that they would be willing to enter a waiver of anonymity into the record if this was requested by the birth parent, but most agencies indicated that the question of such a waiver had never been raised.

The agencies indicated that it was their practice to share a great deal of the information they had available regarding the birth parents with the adoptive parents and recommended that the adoptive parents share it with the child. This information included the age, race, ethnic and religious affiliation, education and occupation, physical description, personality and temperament, medical and psychiatric history, and intellectual capacity of the birth parents. Information was shared regarding siblings and the circumstances of birth if the child was born out of wedlock. The circumstances of birth were less frequently shared if it was the result of rape or incest. Reasons for the child's relinquishment were also shared if they involved abuse, neglect, parental mental illness or retardation, alcoholism, or drug addiction. Imprisonment was less frequently shared if this was the principal reason for the child's relinquishment. The name and residence of the birth parent were almost never shared with the adoptive parents

(Jones, 1976, p. 9). The information is most frequently shared verbally except for medical information, which is often put in writing.

Agencies have occasionally conducted a search for the biological parent at the request of an adoptee, although the number of such searches has been quite limited, averaging about six per agency per year. The search is conducted primarily by telephone, and each search involves an average of six hours of staff time: two hours for a thorough reading of the record, two hours for interviewing the adoptee, and two hours for the search itself. About half of the total of 246 searches undertaken by 163 responding agencies during 1975 resulted in an actual reunion. In the majority of instances in which the birth parents were located and contacted, they were agreeable to meeting with the adult adoptee, and 87 per cent of the meetings were defined as successful: "all parties involved were glad they had met" (Jones, 1976, p. 19).

The agencies had also received requests from birth parents about children relinquished for adoption. These were fewer in number than the requests from adoptees for information about their birth parents. Most of these requests were for nonidentifying information. Only 37 per cent of the birth parents contacting the agency sought help in locating their children. The agencies cooperated in undertaking such searches at the request of the birth parents.

Agency opinion very definitely supported the idea that the searches were caused by a natural, nonneurotic desire for information of significance to the adoptee. Only one tenth of the social agency respondents regarded searches as a manifestation of poor emotional adjustment or as evidence of an unsatisfying adoptive experience.

The general feeling of adoption agencies in 1976, as reflected in the Child Welfare League of America questionnaire study, was that the sealed-record controversy had opened a question that would continue to be debated and needed to be resolved. However, agency opinion was that because of the dangers for all parties concerned, identifying information should be made available case by case rather than by legislative revision in favor of blanket accessibility of records. As a corollary, the agencies felt that although anonymity and confidentiality still should be respected, agency information should be more accessible to the adoptee and that agencies should be flexible in sharing what was available.

The Children's Home Society of California (1977), a large voluntary agency, received questionnaire responses about searches from some 300 adult adoptees, 100 birth parents, and about 1,000 adoptive parents, most of whom had been clients of the agency. About 49 per cent of the adult adoptees were either "partially" or "totally dissatisfied" with the information they had regarding their birth parents. This information had been provided, in most instances by their adoptive parents and, in some 19 per cent of the cases, directly by the agency. Although 31.7 per cent of these 300 adoptees reported that they thought of searching for their birth parents "all the time" or "often," 38 per cent of the respondents "rarely" or "never" gave this a thought (Children's Home Society, 1977, p. 20). Those who were interested in searching were motivated by a desire to know about their heritage, their health history, and their siblings and "because they feel that without this knowledge 'a part of myself is missing.'" Those who were uninterested in the search were "satisfied with their life" and felt that "their adopted family is their" true family. Of the limited group of adopted children who had actively engaged in a search, 65 per cent felt that their adoptive parents felt totally comfortable or more-or-less comfortable about what they were doing. Some 32 per cent felt that their adoptive parents were "quite uncomfortable" or "totally opposed" to the search.

Birth parents were also very much divided on this question. Whereas 28 per cent of the birth parents said that they were interested in making contact with the child they had placed for adoption, 26 per cent said that they did not intend to attempt this because "they have made their decision," it was not fair to intrude, and it was an invasion of the privacy of the adoptive home.

In general adult adoptees were more favorably disposed toward an open-records policy, birth parents somewhat less so, and adoptive parents least favorably disposed. However, it should be noted that although adoptive parents were least enthusiastic as compared with the other groups involved, some 73 per cent of adoptive parents were in favor of open records.

What is involved in unsealing the records are two separate, but related, questions. The first is concerned with making more detailed information about his or her biological background available to the adoptee. This might be satisfactorily accomplished by making the adoption records available. But beyond this, there is the second question of identifying the biological parent to the adoptee and thus making it possible for one to find the other. Access to information about background may or may not lead to reunion with the biological parent.

Taking advantage of the fact that Scotland does permit access to adoptive records, Triseliotis (1973) interviewed the limited number of adoptees who requested such information in 1969 and 1970. During the two-year period, 98 adoptees made such a request and 70 were interviewed. These 70 broke down into two rather distinct groups differentiated by their principal motive in wanting to see the records: a group that wanted to "meet the natural parents" (42 adoptees) and a group that wanted "background information only" (26).

A detailed review of their adoptive experience tended to show that for the most part, the adoptive parents of these adoptees seeking access to their records violated the prescriptions of good adoptive practice regarding telling. Most of the adoptees had been informed quite late in childhood that they were adopted. Over one half learned about it, when they did find out, from somebody other than their adoptive parents. Upon learning about their adoptive status, most were given little or no detailed information about their biological parents, and even the limited sharing was rarely followed by joint discussion.

The group that was interested in a reunion with the biological parents were characterized by a poor sense of identity and lack of a positive self-image. They were generally more dissatisfied with their relationship with their adoptive parents, according to Triseliotis: "There was hope that the natural parents (if found) would make up to them what they missed from other relationships" (p. 159). The group interested in information only were generally more satisfied with their relationship with their adoptive parents. They were interested in obtaining information "that would help them complete themselves and tie up loose ends."

It was during adolescence that most of the group felt the greatest sense of curiosity about their origins. However, most of them did not act on their desire for additional information until later. The formal request for access to the records was triggered by significant experiences related to the human life cycle of accession and abandonment: death of the adoptive parent, an impending marriage, birth of a child, divorce. Some situational factors prompted the move: need for a birth certification for the armed forces, a civil service exam, a life insurance application.

Sorosky, Baran, and Pannor (1947a,b,c; 1975a,b; 1976; 1978) studied reunions that became known to them by contacts solicited through newspaper reports of their interest in such events. As was true of Triseliotis's group, many of these adoptees experienced a late, disruptive revelation of adoption: the median age at which the group learned of their adoptive status was seven years, much later than is recommended by the agencies, and the fact of adoption was, in 32 per cent of the cases, learned from somebody other than the adoptive parent.

When adoptees meet with their biological parents, in 80 per cent of the cases or better, the meeting proves to be successful and satisfying to the participants (Jones, 1976; Triseliotis, 1973; Stevenson, 1976; Ehrlich, 1977; Lifton 1978; Sorosky, Baran, Pannor, 1978).

Most adoptees who engaged in a search find the outcomes were helpful. They reported a "sense of closeness," of "knowing better where they stood." Despite adoptive parents' anxiety, in very few cases did a search result in damage to their relationship with the adopted child. More often the adopted child reported a deeper sense of appreciation for the adoptive parents.

This information is augmented by single case studies of reunions (Lindemann, 1969; Dalsheimer, 1973; Kiester, 1974; Howard, 1975; Freedman, 1977), some of which are very detailed (Fisher, 1973; Lifton, 1975).

In almost every study done, female adoptees are much more desirous than male adoptees of learning more about their birth parents and more about their biological heritage and are more anxious to make contacts with the birth parents. The search and the pressure for open records appear to be sex-related.

Detailing her own experience as a member of an organization concerned with the rights of adoptees, Lifton (1975) notes that the "majority of those searching were women" (p. 179). Of the 154 applications for birth information received from adoptees by the Scotch Registers Office between June 1975 and July 1976, twice as many were received from female applicants as from males. The samples in the Stevenson, Triseliotis, and Sorosky *et al.* studies were heavily weighted with females.

It is suggested that women, as child bearers, are more sensitive than males to problems of biological continuity, are more concerned with their genetic heritage, are freer to acknowledge the complex of feelings associated with adoptive status, are more likely to define themselves in terms of family, and may have more identity conflicts in our society.

In view of the greater sensitization of the agencies, as well as the public, to the need to share more complete information on background with the adoption agencies, the Child Welfare League of America is recommending some changes in agency procedure. Not only is it necessary to collect and record more detailed factual and descriptive data on biological parents, but the agencies have to state more clearly that they will make this information available to adoptees as well as to the adoptive parents. Firm guarantees of confidentiality of identity may no longer be made to biological parents and adoptive parents because the state laws regarding confidentiality are subject to change. Biological parents, on surrender of the child, may be asked to note in writing their willingness to have the agency identify them to the adopted child if she requests their identification on attaining majority.

The movement is toward the idea that neither the biological parents nor the adoptee has absolute rights to either confidentiality or access and that freer access to nonidentifying background information should be granted. This approach would satisfy the need of the adoptee without threatening anonymity of the biological parent.

It is recommended by adoptee organizations that, in addition to an unsealing of the records, regional reunion registries be established. Both birth parents and adoptive parents would contribute relevant current information. When the adoptees achieve adulthood and were interested in filling in knowledge of origins, there would be an up-to-date file available. A similar updated file would be available about the adoptee for the interested birth parent. The reunion file would make it easier for birth parent and adoptee to find each other.

It is further recommended that the adoptee's birth certificate list the name of the agency responsible for the adoption so that the adoptee would have a point of contact for beginning a search. Agencies can also act as communication mediators—transmitting information between adoptees and biological parents without identifying one to the other.

In recapitulating her own experiences in finding her bioparents, an experience which involved its share of pain and guilt and ambivalence, Lifton (1975) feels that it is a high-risk venture. The search leads to a very difficult encounter and presents problems in resolving an atypical relationship for which society provides little, if any, preparation. What kind of ongoing relationship should or can one establish with a bioparent late in life? How does one deal with the almost inevitable discrepancy between the fantasy biomother and the reality?

Here the agency can provide a continuing service. Accepting without equivocation the rights of adoptees to search, the agency can provide help in implementing search procedures and guidelines for conducting a search. The agency can provide preparation for the initial shock of contact based on the experience of others who have searched and found their biological parents. The agency can help resolve the problems of the continuing relationship after contact.

Some agencies have already begun to give greater emphasis to the problems that face the adoptive triad—birth parents, adoptive parents, and adopted child—long after adoptive placement. The Children's Home Society of Minnesota, for instance, provides postlegal adoption service relating to the search and its implications. Open birth-record legislation was signed into law in Minnesota in 1977. When a request by an adoptee for information on his birth parents is received by the Bureau of Vital Statistics, the request is referred to the agency that made the original adoptive placement. The agency is obligated to attempt a contact with the birth parent within six months. The agency must make contact in a personal and confidential manner rather than by mail. Upon contact, the birth parent can agree to the disclosure of information on the birth record to the adoptee or can decline such consent, in which case the information is not released. A waiting period is also provided before disclosure in case the adoptee wants counseling during this time. For adoptions that follow passage of the law, the birth parents are notified at the time of the termination of parental rights that they may sign an affidavit of consent or refusal of disclosure to be attached to the adoptee's new birth certificate. This affidavit will determine the adoptee's access to information in the future.

A word of caution; this discussion of changes with regard to search applies generally to the child surrendered more or less voluntarily by the birth mother. However, change in policy would also apply to those adoptions made as a result of the involuntary termination of parental rights over the clear opposition of the birth parents. In these instances, the birth parents may not feel so friendly toward the adoptive family and may actively seek to disrupt the relationship between adoptee and adoptive parents. Further, in these instances, which are apt to be characterized by severe neglect and abuse and greater pathology in the birth family, the information about origins may be more difficult for the adoptee to handle.

Extending the advocacy of open records one step further leads to a consideration of "open adoption": "An open adoption is one in which the birth parents participate in the separation, placement process, relinquish all legal, moral and nurturing rights to the child, but retain the right to continuing contact and to knowledge of the child's whereabouts and welfare" (Baran, Pannor, Sorosky, 1976, p. 97). If birth parent and adoptee are in contact some years after the adoption, why not continue the contact during the entire adoption process? The open adoption is one in which the birth parent(s) and the adoptive parents jointly and continuously have responsibility, if unequal, for the rearing of the child. It is advanced as a desirable alternative when the single unmarried parent cannot rear the child but cannot bring herself to the finality of total relinquishment. Open adoption is an acceptable compromise.

Open adoption involves a different conception of the allocation of parental responsibilities, which are shared by two sets of parents rather than being totally invested in one set of parents.

GROUP APPROACHES IN ADOPTION

Group methods have been used effectively in adoptions. Some agencies arrange for a group meeting of applicants to review some general ideas about adoption and agency procedure in processing an application. The content of these meetings tends to be primarily "factual, and the method of presentation instructional," although the aim is partly to reduce an applicant's anxiety (Stumpf, 1963, p. 88).

As a result of these orientation meetings, couples who are interested in continuing contact with the agency are better informed about what to expect and about what is expected of them (Springer, 1956). Some decide not to submit an application—couples who are very ambivalent about adoption or who clearly cannot meet the eligibility requirements (Vieregge, 1963, p. 102).

Attempts have been made to use group meetings for getting to know the applicants (Dillow, 1968; Wingfield, 1969; Kaplan, 1970; Wiehe, 1972). It has been hypothesized that use of group meetings for the home study "would make it possible to neutralize the study so that fear of the power of the worker would be diminished, defensiveness lessened . . . and preparation for parenthood enhanced" (Kaplan, 1970, p. 128). As Biskind (1966) notes, "Parents in the group situation are freer to acknowledge their perplexities and fears" (p. 145).

Groups permit the use of some interpretive material and procedures that would not be feasible in interviews with a couple alone. Some agencies arrange for group meetings between parents who have completed adoption and new applicants. The adoptive parents act as resource persons, answering questions and sharing their experiences with the group. Visual aid material explaining adoption procedures and the current adoptive situation can be profitably used with a group. One agency shows a series of slide programs and relevant movies over its period of contact with a group of adoptive applicants. These include slide programs such as "Introduction to Adoption" and "What Are We Waiting For?" produced by the Council on Adoptable Children in Michigan, and "Who Cares About Jamie?" produced by the Massachusetts Adoption Resource Exchange; and movies such as "One of the Family," produced by the Los Angeles Bureau of Adoptions (Goodridge, 1975).

Group meetings permit more expeditious schedules of first contact so that applicants do not have to wait very long before they are seen.

Group application and group study can have the additional advantage of providing a support system for members subsequent to adoption. Having shared over time a common experience related to adoption, members of the group can maintain contact with each other in the postplacement period.

Groups have generally included from four to six adoptive couples; some agencies give applicants the option of choosing individual or group approaches.

Group meetings have also been used during the period between placement and adoption and after final adoption. Conklin (1962) found that one of the advantages of the use of groups between placement and final adoption lay in countering the defensiveness of workers in contact with the family during this period. The caseworkers who had made the placement and, for purposes of continuity, were assigned responsibility for contact with the family during this period, tended to defend the correctness of their decision to place the child by failing to recognize incipient problems. The opportunity to observe the adoptive couples in group meetings permitted the agency to get a more objective picture of their reaction to adoption.

Group support may help to overcome the diffidence and anxiety new adoptive parents feel in the period immediately after placement—precisely when they feel least free to share doubts and misgivings and difficulties with the workers (Chappelear, 1967; Schwartz, 1968; Pettigrew, 1969).

One agency arranges a group meeting shortly before final legal adoption as a sort of graduation exercise. Other agencies have experimented with group meetings after final adoption (Campbell, 1957; Collier, 1960; Sandgrund, 1962; McWhinnie, 1968).

Most legal adoptions take place before the children are two years of age. Some of the most difficult problems of adoptive parenthood are only theoretical at this point. When adoptive parents actually encounter the full impact of the child's questions about adoption—when he is five or six—they might want then to discuss them with the agency and with other adoptive parents.

Bellucci (1975) and Pannor and Nerlove (1975) report the use of groups for the purpose of counseling with parents and older adopted children. In one instance, the children's and parents' groups met separately, and a summary of what had been discussed in the children's group was shared with the parents. The problems that the children were encountering in adjusting to adoption and the expectations of their adoptive parents became clearer to the parents. Sibling rivalry and the confusions associated with being identified with two sets of parents were additional focuses of discussion. Pannor and Nerlove (1975) conducted separate meetings of parents and children followed by joint meetings of the two groups. The group meetings had the effect of freeing up communication between adoptive parents and children about questions related to the child's past, which, because they created anxiety, had not been adequately discussed.

The number of adoptive couples engaged in such postadoptive meetings is, as yet, small, partly because postplacement contact is a process that differentiates adoptive parents from other parents and is consequently resisted by adoptive parents.

The Rejected Applicant

Not all applicants are successful in becoming adoptive parents. As Michaels (1947) notes, "If it is occasionally necessary to choose between a possible injustice to a family and possible injustice to a child, the agency must, by virtue of its essential responsibility, protect the child" (p. 370).

The agency, however, has a responsibility to deny the applicants in a way that results in minimal damage to their psychic health. The applicants are generally vulnerable: they have applied because of a condition—the inability to have a child by natural means—that, in itself, is a deep narcissistic wound. However the agency handles the situation, "there is no softness that can remove entirely the sting of being denied parenthood for the second time—first by life, and then by society" (Michaels, 1947, p. 372).

The agency strives to help the applicants come, on their own, to the same conclusion reached by the agency—that they are not ready for adoption and that in pressing their application, they are doing themselves a disservice. If the agency is successful, the applicants withdraw their application as a matter of choice and the agency has performed a helpful service both to the adoptive applicants and to its pool of adoptable children. The following is an example of such a situation:

> Mr. and Mrs. W. came about the adoption of an infant. It had not been absolutely determined that they could not have their own child, although the chances were slim and Mrs. W. felt that she did not want to wait any longer for a child. Mr. W. brought out many questions about the effects of heredity on a child and how adopted children turn out.
>
> The worker commented that evidently Mr. W. was not sure he could feel comfortable about being a parent to a child strangers had borne. He enlarged on his own question and fear. The worker told them about the shortage of children, and the need of the agency to limit applications drastically, saying that one of the things the agency needed to know in deciding which families to add to the long waiting list was which were most likely to feel like parents to children placed with them, and that it would be hard for us to know when the W.'s did not know it themselves. The worker suggested that perhaps this was something they needed to settle for themselves first.

Mr. W. seemed very relieved, and Mrs. W. agreed that they should withdraw their request for the present, and explore the possibilities of having their own baby [Michaels, 1947, p. 373].

Frequently the applicants dispute, rather than consider, their lack of readiness for adoption or their failure to meet the agency's requirements. This problem is met more easily when the agency can honestly point to the large number of applicants and hide behind assertions that it is "being forced to turn down even very fine families because of the shortage of children" (Michaels, 1947, p. 375). The objective situation, rather than any applicant deficiency, is stressed. As Michaels (1947) notes, "As far as possible the onus of failure to obtain a child should be placed on the external adoption situation beyond the . . . [applicants'] control and the agency's" (p. 375). A second line of defense is to explain the rejection, wherever possible, in terms of the applicants' failure to meet certain specific requirements: age, housing, religion, and so on. Applicants who do not meet specific minimum requirements are weeded out early in the process. Some applicants are rejected because they are judged by the agency to have "limited capacity for parenthood," because of "immaturity" or psychosocial deficiencies. These are, of course, as real and as important as specific requirements of age, health, and income. Having decided, however, that the applicants do not meet agency standards in these regards, the agency must interpret this decision to the client. The problem has not been entirely resolved. Aronson (1960) notes that the key to the approach "lies in awareness of the fact that telling the whole truth may, instead of being a virtue, actually be an act of the crassest cruelty and may throw into disequilibrium a situation which has some stability. . . . [Under] these circumstances we must not only permit but encourage rationalization" (pp. 23, 33), by which the applicants can explain—acceptably, to themselves—the agency's rejection. The principle dictates that the agency leave helpful psychic defenses intact. Accordingly Brown (1951) suggests that the agency interpret rejection so as to direct the applicants' hostility toward the agency rather than against each other (p. 160). It is helpful to stress the acceptability of the applicants as individuals despite the fact that the agency questions their acceptability for a particular social role—that of parenthood. At the same time, the agency can point to their competence in many other social roles: as husband or wife, as employee, as friend. The negatives that have prompted the agency's decision are related to one particular sector of their lives, and there is no imputation of their adequacy in terms of other roles.

Rejection of an application may be easier if the agency shares some of its doubts and misgivings with the couple as they arise (Kasporwicz, 1964). The final decision is then something for which they have been partially prepared.

It is difficult to distinguish the applicants rejected by the agency from those who withdraw voluntarily. Agencies responsible for placing children with special needs, who have a smaller applicant pool from which to select, may strive to retain every applicant. However, every agency is responsible for rejecting those applicants who in their best judgment would harm a child placed in their care.

Even agencies specializing in the placement of children with special needs find that only a limited number of those interviewed go on to adopt (39 per cent), despite the fact that agency "eligibility" requirements are limited in number and flexibly applied (Unger, Dwarshuis, Johnson, 1977, p. 148).

INTERNATIONAL ADOPTIONS

In response to a humanitarian concern for the many children abroad who have been displaced, abandoned, or orphaned as a result of postwar upheaval, and because there have been for some time more adoptive applicants than adoptive infants available in this country, an increased interest has developed in the adoption of foreign children. Such interest has also been stimulated by the mobility of American families, many of whom have lived abroad for extended periods with the armed forces or in the employ of foreign branches of American concerns.

There are several social agencies with international affiliates that handle such adoptions. The principal officially recognized agency is Travelers Aid International Social Service, a voluntary, nonsectarian social welfare agency with headquarters in Geneva, Switzerland. It has branches in many countries, the American branch of TAISS having been established about forty years ago. Each of the branches is staffed and supported by the country in which it is located.

Before a child is moved for adoption from his country of origin, ISS establishes the fact that the child is "an orphan or deprived of normal family life and that there is no prospect for him to be adopted unless he comes to the United States" (Hochfield, 1963, p. 4). The preadoption requirements of the state of the child's proposed residence must be met and assurance received from an "appropriate social welfare agency that the social investigations have been satisfactorily completed in both countries, that the prospective adoptive home is recommended, and that the child has been found suitable for adoption" before the U.S. Immigration and Naturalization Service will process the child's immigration (Hochfield, 1963, p. 4). The child has to be certified as free for adoption, a passport and exit visa need to be obtained for the child, and an entry visa to the United States has to be cleared.

These requirements suggest that the international adoption program has reasonable built-in safeguards, that it is not likely to be exploited as a procedure to "dump" foreign children, and that it offers the American child seeking adoption only limited competition.

Currently intercountry adoptions are an additional resource for meeting the demands of adoptive parents. As Adams and Kim (1971) note in reviewing intercountry adoption statistics, "With the developing shortage of 'adoptable' white infants in the United States, American parents are beginning to look overseas for children" (p. 218).

The new language that must be learned, the new foods to which the child must become accustomed, the new customs and new ways that must be assimilated—all complicate the process of adjustment for the adopted foreign child. In addition, most of these children are older, so that they face the general problems that older children encounter in becoming truly integrated into a new family. Despite this combination of problems, and despite the greatly deprived early developmental experiences faced by these children, many of whom were abandoned, follow-up studies reveal good adjustment to American homes and adoption success (Colville, 1957; DiViglio, 1956; Graham, 1957; Valk, 1957; Welter, 1965; Kim, Reid, 1975; Kim, 1977).

Despite the existence of international agencies, such adoptions are hampered because of the differences in the adoption laws of various countries. As a consequence, the first World Congress on Adoption and Foster Placement held in Italy in 1971 petitioned the United Nations to convene an international conference for the purpose of establishing a World Convention on Adoption Law and formulating a uniform code.

Some of the more controversial aspects of international adoptions were more sharply defined as a consequence of Operation Babylift at the end of the war in Vietnam (see Joe, 1978). With the collapse of South Vietnam, the U.S. government sponsored and supported an effort to "rescue" children from South Vietnam for adoptive placement in the United States. As a consequence of Operation Babylift, some two thousand Vietnamese children were flown to the United States for adoption here. Groups that had, over a period of time, been engaged in the placement of children from Korea and South Vietnam—Holt International Children's Fund and Travelers Aid International Social Service of America (TAISSA)—were enlisted in the effort.

Opponents of the airlift pointed to the disadvantage to these children of removing them from their familiar sociocultural surroundings, to the loss of their cultural heritage, and to the problems that they were likely to encounter in adjusting to a "racist" society. The Child Welfare League policy on overseas adoption was that "adoptions outside the child's own country should be considered only when suitable plans cannot be made for him in his own country." The League pointed to the fact that overseas adoption programs inhibited the development of child welfare services in other countries and that the development of such services to meet the needs of all children in these countries should have priority. It was noted that after the civil war in Nigeria in the 1960s, which left fifty thousand children homeless, offers were made by the United States, among several countries, to place many of these children for adoption abroad. The Nigerian government refused the offer and made efforts to meet the needs of those children with outside assistance that might otherwise have been expended in an overseas adoption program. As a consequence, some years later all but a handful of such children were being cared for by their immediate or extended families in their native land.

In empathy with the Vietnamese, nonwhite groups indicated that the airlift could be insultingly interpreted as an unwillingness or an inability on the part of the Vietnamese people to care for their own children. It was seen as a deprivation to them of their most valuable resources, future Vietnamese citizens. Black organizations empathized with the Vietnamese dislike of transracial placements of children but in addition felt resentment that the time and energy involved in international adoptions was misplaced. The effort, they felt, should have been devoted to the placement of American black children.

Since the airlift, there has been continuing agitation about these adoptions because some of the children proved not to have been legally available for adoption. A class-action suit was brought against the government in behalf of the parents of the airlifted children. Bitter custody battles were fought, and in about twenty-five instances, the children were removed from the adoptive homes and returned to the parents (Johnston, 1976). Because of the haste with which the airlift had been organized, the children involved had not been processed through the regular agency procedure, which safeguards adoptive parents from such contingencies.

A considerable body of helpful literature became available to parents who had adopted Asian children. The government published a pamphlet providing tips on the adjustment of Asian children (Children Bureau, 1975), and one of the adoptive parents' organizations published a reader concerned with international adoptions (Kramer, 1975). These materials provide Korean and Vietnamese recipes, short vocabulary word lists, a listing of relevant books and films, and so on.

By 1977 Korea and other Asian countries had taken active steps to reduce the number of their children available for adoption abroad. With the Far East becoming less active as a source of supply of children for adoption, interest is beginning to shift to other areas. OURS (Organization for a United Response), the Minnesota-based agency of parents who have adopted from abroad, has worked out arrangements with orphanages and agencies in Colombia and Mexico in developing an active program of adoption from these countries.

Laws relating to permitting entrance of children into the country for adoption were amended in 1975 to permit intercountry adoption by single-parent applicants.

Single applicants unable to obtain younger children for adoption in the United States have made successful efforts to adopt children from abroad. However, not all foreign countries permit adoption of their children by single applicants.

LEGAL ASPECTS OF ADOPTION

Adoption is regulated by state law (Brieland, Lemmon, 1977). As a consequence, there is considerable variation from state to state in the legal procedure and philosophy associated with adoption. Although a national adoption law has been proposed, there is little active support for it.

The legal procedure for adoption is initiated by the filing of a court petition. The court responsible for handling adoption proceedings might be the probate court in one state, the juvenile court in another, and the superior court in still another. The petition, generally filed in the county in which the adoptive parents live, includes the pertinent information regarding the child, the adoptive parents, and the biological parents. Consent to adoption must be obtained from the biological parents. In many instances, the agency has obtained guardianship of the child, and it is the agency that gives consent to adoption. In other instances, it has obtained a signed "surrender" of the child by the biological parents, which authorizes the agency to place the child for adoption. But parental surrender or relinquishment of the child is more ambiguous than the clear termination of parental rights through judicial action: "Only with such judicial termination is there a complete divestment of all legal rights, privileges, duties, and obligations of the parent and the child with respect to each other" (U.S. Department of Health, Education, and Welfare, 1961, p. 10). When the child is fourteen years of age—in some states, as young as ten years of age—his consent to adoption is also required.

The petition having been filed, a notice of proceeding is given to alert those people affected by the adoption. An official investigation of the circumstances regarding the adoption is then ordered by the court and is usually carried out by the public welfare agencies. When the child has been placed by an agency, the agency adoption study is the relevant material offered the court. The investigating agency makes a recommendation to the court based on the information it has obtained.

A hearing is then held, usually in a closed court, at which time the court meets with the adoptive parents, the child, and any witnesses it deems should be heard. The court then makes a decision based on the material made available during the hearing and on the report from the agency authorized to study the adoption. The decision is made in terms of the best interests of the child. The adoption petition may be approved or denied, or a decision may be deferred to some later date.

This order is usually temporary or interlocutory. The final order is not granted until after the passage of some time, six months to a year. During this time, the child lives in the home of the adoptive parents but does not yet legally belong to them. At the end of the trial period, the final order for adoption is approved. Before issuing the final order, the court generally asks for a recommendation from the supervising agency. Once the final decree has been issued, there is the possibility of annulment, but this is rare: the child is the legal child of the adoptive parents.

In many states there is no provision for an interlocutory order, but it is necessary for the child to have lived in the home of the petitioner for some time, usually six months to a year, before a petition for adoption can be initiated. Because in such instances the investigations are made after the child has been living with the adoptive couple for some time, the court is likely to decide adversely only in unequivocally disadvantageous situations. Registration with a public welfare agency *before* taking a child into the home, as is currently required by some states, permits the agency to make an investigation of the desirability of the home before such a relationship is established.

The effect of a final decree is to establish a parent–child relationship between the petitioner and the adopted child and to terminate all relationships between the child and the biological parents. When the final adoption order is granted, the child legally assumes the surname of his adoptive parents. A new birth certificate may be issued in this new name, and the record of the adoptive proceedings is sealed.

For the most part, with the final decree, the legal rights, duties, privileges, and obligations of biological parents and child exist between the adoptive parents and child. But although the child may inherit from the adoptive parents, the child does not, if an alien, gain their citizenship. This has created a special problem in international adoptions, requiring special legislation by Congress to provide for the issuance of nonquota visas to permit "eligible" foreign children to come to the United States for adoption even though the immigration quota of their native country is oversubscribed.

When the child and the adoptive parents are not residents of the same state, the petition for adoption may be initiated in the state where the child lives, but it is more desirable if the action is initiated in the state in which the adoptive parents reside. This procedure expedites the social study of the adoptive applicants, upon which rests the decision of the court to grant or deny the petition. However, bringing the child into the state in which the adoptive parents reside also presents a problem. Most states require the permission of the state department of public welfare before a child is permitted to enter the state for the purpose of adoption. This requirement is meant to protect the state from the necessity of supporting a dependent child if the adoption is not consummated.

Since adoptions are regulated by state laws and since laws differ from state to state, placing children across state lines presents problems. An interstate compact on the placement of children has been developed to expedite such placement. By 1980, forty-three states had enacted uniform interstate compact legislation. The compact agreement provides protection for children placed across state levels, coordinates the activities of agencies in different states dealing with the same adoptive family, provides for supervision and periodic reports on each interstate placement, and guarantees children financial and legal protection as they are moved from one state to another.

Two recent U.S. Supreme Court decisions concerned with the rights of the unmarried father of the child being considered for adoption have created serious problems for the agency. Hitherto surrender by the mother of the right to the child or termination of the mother's parental rights was sufficient to free the child for adoption. Care, custody, and control of an out-of-wedlock child resided exclusively with the mother, and the birth father was not regarded as having any entitlement in the decision regarding the disposition of his child. In *Stanley* v. *Illinois*, 1972, the U.S. Supreme Court declared that unwed fathers were entitled to notice of custody and adoption proceedings concerning their children. Stanley, an unwed father, had lived with and had supported the children whose custody was being transferred to the Illinois Department of Public Welfare following the death of their mother.

The practical implication of this decision was that the agency could not place a child for adoption without challenge if it had the consent of only the mother. The father now needed to be located, informed that adoption was being planned, and given an opportunity to petition the court for custody of the child or asked for his legal surrender if this was his decision (Glen, 1974; Dukette, Stevenson, 1975; Bodenheimer, 1975; Barron, 1975).

Previously agencies had not totally ignored the father but, whenever practicable, had attempted to encourage the participation of the unwed father in the decision regarding adoption. Rather than being an optional procedure implemented out of concern and consideration, such attempts involving the father have now become mandatory.

The earliest possible adoptive placement of the child is delayed until due process has been accorded the father; consequently, the agency is faced with the problem of notifying the father and responding to his plans and adoptive parents face an additional possible challenge to their entitlement to the child. Agency efforts to adhere to procedures that guarantee promptness of placement to the child and finality of the decision to the biological mother and the adoptive parents are made more difficult by the necessity of giving sincere consideration to the biological father's rights.

The situation was mitigated somewhat by a U.S. Supreme Court decision in 1978 that upheld a Georgia law giving fathers of children born out of wedlock no legal rights to challenge their children's adoption (*Quilloin* v. *Walcott*). The distinction made here, as against *Stanley* v. *Illinois,* was that the father in this instance had never accepted any responsibility with respect to the "daily supervision, education, protection or care of the child."

This suggests that due process in respecting the rights of out-of-wedlock fathers may apply only to the limited groups of such fathers who acknowledged paternity by a legal statement or by their behavior in support of the child.

INDEPENDENT ADOPTIONS

The adoption process described pertains to only a limited number of the nonrelated adoptive placements consummated each year. Sizable proportions of nonrelated adoptive placements are achieved each year outside this route. These are the independent adoptions. In 1971, the last year for which we have national statistics of the total of about 83,000 children adopted by unrelated persons, 65,000 (79 per cent) were placed by social agencies; 17,000 (21 per cent) were placed independently. There has been a steady change in the proportion of children placed through agencies and those placed independently with unrelated persons. In 1944, of the 26,000 adoptive children placed, 12,700 (49 per cent) were placed through agencies, and 13,300 (51 per cent) were placed independently. Despite the steady change in favor of the agency placement, the fact that in 1971 some 21 per cent of the children placed for adoption with unrelated persons were placed independently indicates that this was still an important route to adoption.

The term *independent adoption* applies to a number of different procedures. The natural parents may make their own contact with a person whom they know, through one source or another, wants to adopt a child. Or a doctor or lawyer may know of parents unable or unwilling to care for a child, and a childless couple seeking a child, and he or she may act as the intermediary. This is sometimes termed the *gray market* in adoptions. A third kind of independent placement involves an actual business transaction. In this case, a "black marketeer" undertakes to sell a baby to a couple eager to adopt. No statistics are available that indicate how many of the independent placements are of one type or another.

Independent placement involves dangers and disadvantages to the child, to the adoptive parents, to the biological parents, and ultimately to the community.

The rights of the child to a good home are not as securely guaranteed in independent placement. The gray market and the black market are oriented to the needs and desires of the adoptive couple rather than to the needs of the child. The agency makes the best effort, however fallible, to find a good set of parents for the child. The couple with whom the child is independently placed has been subject to no assessment process. The only eligibility requirement, in many instances, is ability to pay, which bears little direct relationship to capacity for parenthood and is no guarantee of an emotionally healthy environment for the child.

It might seem, from the adoptive parents' point of view, that there are obvious advantages in independent adoption: no "red tape," no elaborate interviews, no need to meet what are perceived as restrictive agency eligibility requirements, and no need to satisfy a social worker of their capacity for parenthood. Yet the seeming advantages may, in fact, be disadvantages. Becoming a parent is not an unmitigated pleasure, nor is the desire for parenthood unequivocal. The agency's interviews with prospective adoptive parents are designed as much to help the applicants clarify for themselves their decision about parenthood as they are to satisfy the agency that their home will be a good one for a child. Frequently, on the basis of the exploration in which the agency procedure involves the adoptive couple, they decide they do not really want to adopt a baby.

The independent adoption procedure gives the couple no explicit opportunity to discuss with someone experienced in such matters the problems involved in adoption, the burdens they are undertaking, and the changes adoption will occasion in their lives—problems, burdens, and changes they may choose not to accept once they are made evident.

The supposed advantages of getting a child without agency entanglements is also a disadvantage during the period between placement and final adoption. The adoptive parents are, in some respects, different from biological parents, and there are many unique aspects in the adopted child–adopted parent relationship. The independent adopter's freedom from agency entanglements also means "freedom" from agency help in dealing with the social and emotional consequences of adoption—the problems attendant upon the assumption of this unique role.

Assurance of confidentiality of the adoption may be less firm in independent adoptions than in agency adoptions. Contact between natural parents and adoptive parents, which is deliberately broken in agency adoption, is a greater possibility in the independent adoption. When the natural parents themselves have arranged for placement, they know the identity and, in all likelihood, the whereabouts of the adopters. In adoptions through the gray or black market, the identity of the adoptive parents may be kept secret, but the degree to which such secrets are maintained depends on the intermediary's moral and ethical standards.

Social-agency adoption procedures generally involve the agency's obtaining clear title to the child so that it is in a position to assure the prospective adoptive parents that there will be no difficulty in their legal title to the child. Some independent placements occasion great anxiety for the adoptive couple because they may not be sure that the natural parents will consent to adoption.

Finally, because in some independent placements the sole concern is providing the adoptive parents with a child at a price, any information that is likely to increase the adoptive parents' hesitancy to accept the child may be falsified.

Independent placements involve disadvantages for the unmarried mother as well. Instead of being helped to arrive at her own decision regarding the disposition of the child, she is pressured to make one decision—to surrender the child for adoption. She is also deprived of help with the personal and/or social difficulties that might be related to the out-of-wedlock pregnancy. Nor is there, of course, any effort made either to contact or to help the father.

Social workers point out that providing families for parentless children is too important to the community to be left unregulated. Social agencies are keenly aware of the dangers cited. Their procedures are designed to protect the child in getting the best possible home and the best possible care while waiting for a home. They are also designed to protect the adoptive parents by freely disclosing any of the child's shortcomings, by assuring confidentiality, by making certain of the legal availability of a child, by helping the parents to make a reasoned decision regarding adoption, and to resolve those problems that might endanger the adoption. They are also designed to protect the unmarried mother by giving her support, care, and protection during her pregnancy; by helping her come to a firm decision regarding disposition of the baby; and by helping her with those problems that may have led to her pregnancy. In addition, agency adoptions offer the following advantages:

1. A professional staff with a special knowledge of adoption problems.
2. A pool of adoptive homes from which to select the one that meets the needs of a particular child.
3. Consultants—psychiatrists, psychologists, geneticists, pediatricians—who aid the agency staff in dealing with special problems.
4. Uniform records of all transactions in line with the agency's accountability to the community.
5. Alternative resources—foster homes, institutions, and so on—that are available to care for the child while he is awaiting adoption, if the placement fails, or if the child proves to be unplaceable.

And only the social agency discharges another important community function; it actively seeks to find homes for children who are hard to place.

The reduction in the number of white, unhandicapped infants available for adoption resulted in the reactivation of independent gray- and black-market adoptions in the 1970s (Baker, 1978), a problem that had been a concern of a congressional investigation in 1956 (U.S. Senate, 1956).

Newspaper accounts of special investigative reports for such papers as the *Christian Science Monitor, The New York Times, New York Daily News,* and the *Cleveland Plain Dealer,* during 1974–1975, called national attention to the revival of the black market in adoption. Reporters posing as a husband and wife couple interested in "buying" a child approached dealers claiming access to children adoptable at a price. On other occasions, reporters posed as pregnant unmarried women interested in "selling" their child. During the mid-1970s, prosecutors in Los Angeles; Washington; Bergen County, New Jersey; and New York City investigated and, in some instances, indicted participants in black-market adoptions (*The New York Times,* June 28, 1977).

These revelations, among other considerations, prompted a congressional hearing on "baby selling" by the Subcommittee of Children and Youth, Senate Committee on Labor and Public Welfare (U.S. Congress, 1975). Testimony indicated that unwed mothers were pressured, misled, and sometimes coerced to surrender the baby for adoption; that birth records were falsified so as to indicate that the adoptive mother, rather than the unmarried mother, gave birth to the child; and that payments of up to $25,000 were made in obtaining a child. There was testimony that some parents, very anxious to adopt, went heavily into debt to pay the price of adoption.

Although the testimony repeated some of the hazards and quasi legalities uncovered by a previous congressional investigation of black-market practice conducted by Senator Kefauver in the 1950s (U.S. Senate, 1956), there were some differences in the 1970s. Abortion clinics were regularly monitored by black-market operations as an avenue of access to unmarried mothers. There were reports of a file of young men and women who were on call to "make" a baby for a prospective adoptive couple. There were reports of pressures exerted on young unmarried mothers to surrender the child for adoption, of procurers waiting for expectant mothers outside pregnancy clinics and abortion facilities, and of "baby farms" where young women were paid to become pregnant or to carry through their pregnancies if they agreed, in return, to place the child for adoption.

It was difficult for those offering testimony at the hearings to estimate the extent of this black market because such transactions are not a matter of record. However, educated guesses resulted in an "unsolid" estimate of some five thousand children involved in such transactions.

A national study of independent adoptions involved questionnaires to 91 social agencies and personal interviews with 131 couples who adopted through independent placement, 115 mothers who relinquished their children for independent adoption, and 75 "facilitators," mostly lawyers and doctors, who helped arrange such transactions (Meezan, Katz, Russo, 1977).

The motivation that prompts the applicant to resort to independent adoptive resources is primarily to maximize the possibility of obtaining the kind of child they prefer—a white, healthy infant—with a minimum of delay, inconvenience, and outside control of their decision. A large majority of the group (84 per cent) had had prior contact with a social agency in exploring the possibilities of adoption. Most frequently, they were discouraged because of closed intake or long waiting lists and, additionally, in some cases (15 per cent), because they already had children or because of maximum age and religious matching requirements. However, in actuality, the eligibility requirements were not much of a deterrent because of those in the sample who did apply to adopt, only one was rejected. But, rather than wait the two to three years that seemed to be necessary before receiving a child, they resorted to independent adoption. In 62 per cent of the cases, a white, healthy infant was placed within six months after contact with a child-placing intermediary. Almost 90 per cent of the children were younger than two weeks old at placement, and consequently younger than most agency-placed children.

Agency procedure and/or worker performance did not make a significant contribution to the applicant's decision to resort to independent adoption, although this was a factor in some instances. Those who had had contact liked the agency for the most part and accepted the need for such agency procedures as requests for references and assessment interviews.

The parents did recognize some elements of risk in the independent adoptive situation. The principal worry was the possibility that the biological mother would change her mind about relinquishment and interfere with the adoption. Anxiety was expressed by 37 per cent of the couples that the child might have a physical problem of which they were unaware. Only a limited number (18 per cent) of adoptive couples were concerned about possible interference by the biological mother who might know of their identity.

The study staff, reviewing all relevant data, judged 13 per cent of the adoptions to be legally questionable.

Most adopters were satisfied with the adoption and the children placed with them, whom they reported, in the greatest number of instances, to be developing normally.

The biological mother is drawn to independent adoptive auspices for equally understandable, eminently practical reasons. In many instances (about 50 per cent), she was unaware of an agency service available to meet her problems. But even when the mother is aware of such service, she knows, or soon finds out, that the agency has no option but to provide the needed help under considerations that make it difficult for the mother to accept. Money is available only through application for public assistance; medical help is available only through a clinic; adoption can be pursued only if the father is contacted or, when the mother is a minor, if her parents are informed. If the mother, like most, prefers private medical care and nonstigmatized financial assistance without the involvement of significant others and without administrative red tape, independent adoptive channels provide this kind of care. Mothers see other advantages in independent adoptions, such as greater ability to control the selection of the adopters of their child and the fact that the child will never be placed in foster care, for however limited a period of time.

Private-care medical expenses are, in fact, paid by the adopter in most instances, along with housing and maintenance costs in a more limited number of cases.

About 30 per cent of "the total sample stated that provision of financial aid was influential in their decision to relinquish the child independently" (Meezan, Katz, Russo, 1977, p. 108).

Converging data from the 321 interviews with the participants in independent adoption—the adopters, the biological mothers, and the intermediary "facilitators"—confirmed the fact that the hypothesized dangers of such adoptions did, in fact, exist, albeit at modest levels of frequency.

Illustrations of some of the risks uncovered by the study follow (Meezan, Katz, Russo, 1978, pp. 28–35).

1. Unmarried mothers fail to receive the counseling that might be needed:

A disturbed, 16-year-old unmarried mother was referred for counseling after delivery and surrender. She felt she had been forced into the adoption, primarily by her mother. No one had helped her understand her situation, alternatives or consequences. None of her feelings had been dealt with.

2. The adopted child may be placed in a problematic home because there is no obligation in independent adoption to screen applicants in accordance with some criteria which protect the best interests of the child.

Child was placed through a doctor when family agency refused because of severe medical problems including cancer in one of the spouses. While application was in the process of being turned down, the couple adopted independently.

3. Because the confidentiality and the anonymity of the participants are not as carefully safeguarded in independent adoption, there is a greater possibility of the biological parent's intrusion into the adoptive family's life.

Experience with a biological mother who, during the first year after placement placed pressure on adoptive parents by calling them for "loans" of money when she was in economic difficulties.

Mother of child "changed her mind" but the court termination was final—so she called and tried to visit the adopting family. They are planning to move out of state in order to avoid further contact.

4. The legal entitlements of adoptive parents may be in greater jeopardy in independent adoptions.

Biological parents were divorced. Mother had custody of the child. She placed infant with couple who wished to adopt. Biological father filed custody suit, claiming that his rights were not terminated and that he had remarried and could now care for the child. Child was returned to biological father.

5. The adoptive couple may be denied information that might significantly influence their decision and/or the child's health situation.

Adoptive parents were not informed that the biological mother and others in her family were severely diabetic. The adoptive parents were under the impression that the biological mother was free of health problems.

Legal reviews of the independent adoptive situation confirm the independent adopter's uneasiness about the legal aspects of such adoptions. Revocation of consent is more frequently attempted in independent than in agency placements because the natural mother is often not psychologically prepared when she signs the consent forms (*Rutgers Law Review*, 1973, p. 712). The probability of successful challenge by the biological mother of the placement is greater in independent adoptions than in agency adoptions:

Some states distinguish between consents given in private-placement adoptions and those executed in agency-placement adoptions. These states have concluded that a mother who has the help of an agency does not require as much protection as a mother who privately places the child herself. Since the adoption agency counsels and helps the mother arrive at an enlightened decision it may not be inequitable to stop her from challenging a consent [*Columbia Journal of Law and Social Problems*, 1972, p. 167].

An earlier, large-scale follow-up study of children placed independently showed that the success rates of such placements were generally high, although not as advantageous as agency placements (Witmer *et al.*, 1963). More recently, less extensive follow-up studies tend to suggest the same general conclusion.

Furlough (1974) randomly selected a sample of thirty agency adoptions and thirty independent adoptions made during 1965–1967 and involving children placed before the end of their first year. Studying child-rearing practices, the physical, social and emotional environment of the adoptive home, the adoptive child's adjustment, and the process of "telling," Furlough found that there was little difference between the two sets of homes on 322 factors analyzed for levels of significant difference. He concluded that children placed for adoption independently can have the same opportunities for healthy, normal emotional development as those placed by agencies. Despite the essential similarities between the two groups, whatever differences were noted tended to favor the agency placements. Whereas all of the agency homes were intact by the time of the follow-up, only 66 per cent of the children in the independent adoptive homes had a father living with them. In 20 per cent of the cases, the father had died, and in 15 per cent, the father was divorced or separated. Apparently agency homes had been selected with greater care to provide the continuity of a two-parent family for the child. When present, more independent fathers than agency fathers "planned their activities so that they spent all of their time away from the children" (p. 67).

McMahan (1974) studied twenty-three socioeconomic characteristics of all independent and agency adoptions in three counties of Arkansas over a five-year period; 97 agency placements were compared with 131 independent placements. Quantifiable socio-economic characteristics such as living accommodations, length of marriage, age, employment, and income did not significantly distinguish agency from independent adopters.

In general, both groups were more alike than they were different in terms of socioeconomic considerations. Independent adopters were more likely to have difficulty in meeting agency requirements regarding the age of the husband and the number of children in the home at the time of application.

Although objectively the child, in each case, is provided with very much the same kind of home, from a subjective point of view agency families were more open and relaxed, had a secure feeling legally, and were unafraid and cooperative. On the other hand, independent families were suspicious, cautious, secretive, and afraid and, in many instances, uncooperative: "This tends to indicate that, for the most part, couples who adopt through a licensed child placing agency feel more secure about the whole process and have greater peace of mind than do couples who adopt a child from other sources" (p. 84). (See pp. 517–522 for additional comment on this comparison.)

The potential hazards in independent adoptions and the advantages of agency adoptions have stimulated pressure to give the agencies exclusive control over adoptive placement. Giving the agency the exclusive right to make adoptions is resisted on a number of grounds, namely, that the superiority of agency adoption as compared with independent adoption is not unequivocally established; that competition with independent adoption has forced agencies to make desirable changes; that people in many sections of the country do not have available an agency that meets licensing standards and has a staff of trained competent workers; that such exclusivity tends to discourage adoptions; that the biological mother would be denied the opportunity of selecting parents for her child; and that legislation giving exclusive control to agencies has not, in fact, resulted in effectively eliminating the gray and black markets. Agency critics recognize, however, that adoptions are of too great a concern to the community to permit haphazard placement. The argument, then, is not between the independent adoptions and the agency but between a social agency monopoly of adoption and some reasonable regulation of independent adoptions (Podelski, 1976; Turano, 1976).

In 1978 Connecticut, Delaware, Minnesota, and Michigan were the only four states that clearly prohibited independent adoptions. Although independent adoptions were permitted in other states, state law regulated such adoptions in some states more carefully than in others. Careful regulation of independent adoptions requires some review of the situation by the Department of Social Services before the placement of the child; all fees associated with the birth placement and adoption of the child need to be itemized and reported, and there are provisions for court supervision of every aspect of the process. There is support for pending federal legislation making it a federal crime to transport children across state lines for black market placement.

Both the gray and the black markets are difficult to police because those involved are not likely to claim that any crime is being committed and the child is too young to initiate action.

The very considerable variations in state laws make it possible to maneuver through the loopholes. Attempts to close such loopholes through compacts between states have not been successful, and there seems little likelihood that a uniform nationwide adoption act will be legislated (Hunt, 1972).

The Adoption Reform Act of 1978 directed the Secretary of Health, Education, and Welfare to make a study of independent adoptions and to provide Congress with a report. This report is not yet available at the time of this writing.

EVALUATION

Many studies have attempted to answer questions regarding the "success" of adoptive placements. The available studies have been summarized in Table 10–2.* Only those studies are included in which definite information is presented regarding sources of data and criteria of outcome and in which some attempt was made at a statistical analysis of data. The studies cited vary in the level of methodological precision with which they were conducted, in the nature and detail of the data obtained, in the criteria of outcome employed, in the procedure used in making judgments of outcome, and in the statistical rigor with which the data were analyzed. The study population of the research cited in Table 10–2 is almost exclusively that of white, nonhandicapped, infant adoptive placements.

The recapitulation (Table 10–3) indicates that 66 per cent of the adoptions were judged unequivocally successful; an additional 18 per cent were judged to be of fair, moderate, or average success; 16 per cent were judged to be failures. It would seem, therefore, that adoptions are most frequently successful.

But how do agency placements compare with independent placements? And how does the success of adoptive families compare with the success of biofamilies? In the absence of normative data regarding the "success" rate of biofamilies, the latter question is impossible to answer at this time. The material in Table 10–2, however, permits some tentative answers to the first question.

Only Witmer's (1963) study is exclusively concerned with nonagency placements, though the studies by Armatruda (1951) and by Kornitzer (1968) offer some additional material. Armatruda's study, although frequently cited to show the superiority of agency placements, is not a true follow-up study because as-

* Bibliographical citations provide information about the source of the material included in Table 10–2 for the convenience of those readers interested in reviewing the studies directly.

TABLE 10–2. Adoptive Outcome Studies

Study and Date	Size of Study Group and Lapse of Time Between Placement and Study	Outcome		Data Used for Follow-up Assessment	Auspices
		Outcome Criteria for Categorization	Number and Percentages		
Van Theis (1924)	235 (adults) 12–18 years after placement	"Capable" "Incapable"	207 (88.1%) 28 (11.9%)	Interviews with adoptive children, adoptive parents, and "other persons" by project interviewer	Agency
Morrison (1950)	24 (children) 10–17 years after placement	"Getting along satisfactorily" "Unsatisfactory adjustment"	18 (75%) 6 (25%)	Interview with adoptive parents by agency workers	Agency
Brenner (1951)	50 (families) median of 4.4 years after placement	"Successful" "Fairly successful" "Unsuccessful"	26 (52%) 18 (36%) 6 (12%)	Observation of children in home, interviews with adoptive mothers by agency workers, psychological tests of children	Agency
Neiden (1951)	138 (adults) 15–20 years after placement	"Very good" "Good" "Indifferent" "Bad"	35 (25%) 62 (45%) 29 (21%) 12 (9%)	Records and interviews with adoptive parents by agency social workers	Agency
Armatruda (1951)	100 (children) at time of placement	"Good" "Questionable" "Poor"	76 (76%) 16 (16%) 8 (8%)	Agency study of adoptive home, study of child by Yale development clinic	Agency

Study	Sample	Outcome (N, %)	Outcome category	Method of data collection	Source
Fairwether (1952)	18 (children) 3–4 years after placement	18 (100%)	"Good"	Interviews with adoptive mothers by agency workers, psychological tests of children	Agency
Edwards (1954)	79 (children) 5 years after placement	69 (87%) 9 (12%) 1 (1%)	"Very happy" "Some problems" "Serious problems"	Information not available	Agency
National Association for Mental Health, England (Estimated 1954)	163 (children) minimum of 2 years after placement	142 (87.1%) 21 (12.9%)	"Satisfactory" "Unsatisfactory"	Agency records	Agency
Davis and Douck (1955)	396 (children) 1 year after placement	371 (93.7%) 25 (6.3%)	Not removed Removed	Agency records	Agency
Fradkin and Krugman (1956)	37 (children) during first year after placement	27 (73%) 6 (16%) 4 (11%)	"Good" "Intermediate" "Poor"	Ongoing contact with parents during first year of supervision, tests of infant	Agency
Witmer et al. (1963)	484 (children) most 9 years after placement	324 (67%) 39 (8%) 121 (25%)	"Excellent to fair" "Not definitely unsatisfactory" "Definitely unsatisfactory"	Interviews with parents and teachers by project interviewers, psychological tests of children	Independent
McWhinnie (1967)	52 (adults) 16–66 years after placement	21 (40.5%) 21 (40.5%) 10 (9%)	"Good" and "Fairly good" "Adjustment in all areas" "Reasonable adjustment in some fundamental areas" "Adjustment poor in many areas"	Interviews with adoptive children as adults	Independent

TABLE 10–2. (Continued)

Study and Date	Size of Study Group and Lapse of Time Between Placement and Study	Number and Percentages	Outcome Criteria for Categorization	Data Used for Follow-up Assessment	Auspices
Ripple (1968)	160 (children) 9–10 years after placement	75 (47%) 47 (29%) 38 (24%)	"Within the normal range" "Some problems in adjustment" "Serious emotional or behavioral problems"	Agency records, interviews with father, mother, child	Agency
Kornitzer (1968)	233 children and adults (time lapse varied)	96 (41.2%) 85 (36.5%) 45 (19.3%) 7 (3.0%)	"Success" "Average" "Problems" "Bad"	Interviews with mother by researcher, some fathers interviewed	Agency and independent
Lawder et al. (1969)	200 (families) 8–15 years after placement	29 (14%) 98 (49%) 53 (27%) 20 (10%)	"Superior" "Good" "Fair" "Poor"	Interviews with fathers and mothers together and alone	Agency
Jaffee and Fanshel (1970)	100 (adults) 20–30 years after placement	33 (33%) 34 (34%) 33 (33%)	"Low problems" "Middle range" "High problems"	Interviews with father and mother separately, questionnaire completed independently by parents	Agency
Bohman (1970)	122 (children) 10–11 years after placement	34 (28%) 28 (23%) 33 (27%) 25 (20%) 2 (2%)	"No symptoms" "Slight symptoms" "Moderate symptoms" "Problem child" "Requiring institutional care"	Interviews with father and mother together and alone	Agency

Study	Sample	Results	Adjustment categories	Method	Source
Seglow et al. (1972)	145 (children) 9 years after placement	19 (82%) 23 (16%) 3 (2%)	"Very well" "Not well adjusted" "Disturbed"	Interviews with adoptive mothers, some adoptive fathers	Agency
Kolmenick (1976)	100 (children) 5 years after adoption	83 (83%) 17 (17%)	"Average to good social adjustment" "Poor adjustment"	Adoption records; court files; clinical interviews; observation; IQ tests	Agency
Raynor (1977)	105 adoptees, 15–18 years after placement	73 (70%) 26 (25%) 6 (5%)	"Excellent to good" "Barely adequate or marginal adjustment" "Poor adjustment"	Individual taped interviews	Agency

TABLE 10–3. Recapitulation of Adoptive Outcome Studies

Outcome	Number	Percent
Unequivocally successful	1,739	65.7
"Satisfactory"		
"Very good"		
"Good"		
"Successful"		
"Superior"		
"Low problems"		
"No symptoms or slight symptoms"		
"Excellent to fair"		
"Within normal range"		
"Very well adjusted"		
Intermediate success	482	18.2
"Not definitely unsatisfactory"		
"Fairly successful"		
"Indifferent"		
"Questionable"		
"Some problems"		
"Intermediate"		
"Average"		
"Moderate symptoms"		
"Not well adjusted"		
Unsuccessful	424	16.1
"Unsatisfactory"		
"Poor," "low"		
"Problematic"		
"Unsuccessful"		
"Incapable"		
"High problems"		
"Problem child"		
"Disturbed"		
Total	2,645	100.0

sessment of the home was made at the time of placement. Kornitzer's study shows that only 14.4 per cent of agency placements, but 25.6 per cent of "third-party and direct placements," were categorized as problems or failures (p. 159). Witmer's study shows a failure rate of 25 per cent for nonagency adoptions.

If the data from Witmer's study, and those from the Kornitzer and Arma-truda studies concerning children independently placed, are deleted from Table 10–2, the failure rate for agency placements becomes 14.8 per cent—considerably lower than the 25 per cent failure rate in Witmer's study and the 25.6 per cent failure rate of independent placements in Kornitzer's study. Any conclusions must remain tentative because of the differing levels of validity of the data used in the different studies. Justifying the cautionary note is the fact that the infor-mation in Table 10–7 (below) indicates that adoptive children who are referred for psychiatric treatment are just as likely to have been placed through a social agency as to have been independently placed.

Another series of outcome studies (summarized in Tables 10–4, 10–5) focus on such children who "were hard to place" or, more euphemistically, "children with special needs": older children, handicapped children, nonwhite children, and foreign-born children. All placements were made by social agencies.

Table 10–4 indicates that even problem placements are likely to be successful. The general conclusion, then, that can be derived from the studies summarized in Tables 10–2, 10–3, 10–4, 10–5, and 10–6 is that most adoptions turn out well and that adoptions under agency auspices are somewhat more likely to succeed than independent adoptions.

Emotional Disturbance in Adopted Children

Another series of studies focuses on the frequency of referral of adopted children to guidance clinics or psychiatric services. A higher rate of referral for emotionally disturbed behavior among adopted children would suggest that child rearing is less successful in the adoptive family than in the biofamily. Tables 10–6 and 10–7 list the relevant studies and summarize the findings.

The research data show that 4.6 per cent of the patients at the facilities studied were nonrelative adoptees. Because it is estimated that only about 1 per cent of all children are nonrelative adoptees, it would appear that such children are clearly overrepresented in the clinic population. The rate is higher than the rate for children from biofamilies. It may, however, be lower than that which we have a right to expect, given the insults to psychic health that the adoptive family has encountered. As Fanshel says, "The controversy revolves around the question whether adoptive children and natural-born children have the same odds working for them with respect to the opportunity to develop stable personalities and successful life adjustments."

It is argued, in explanation, that the adoptive family population is more apt to seek professional help for solving problems. Having resorted to an agency for adoption, they are more likely than other families to resort to agencies again. But Schechter (1964) sought to test this theory by examining the tendency of adoptive couples to use pediatric clinics; he concluded that adoptive parents were no more "agency-prone" than bioparents.

Some specific characteristics of the adoptive family may create special stresses for the adoptive child. Most adoptive parents receive their first child in their early thirties, whereas most biological parents have their first child in their early twenties. Patterns of marital interaction and family ritual may have become less flexible with time and may be difficult to change in response to the incorporation of a child in the family system. The adoptive child is more apt to be a first child of older parents and more likely to be an only child. Furthermore adoption is still an atypical procedure for achieving parenthood, and the family may react to the stress of minority-group status.

The child must deal with the "rejection" by his biological parents, some "genealogical bewilderment" over his origin, and the problem of fusing "good" and "bad" parental images. Adoptive parents must resolve their feelings about

TABLE 10–4. Adoptive Outcome Studies of Special-Needs Children

Study and Date	Nature of Placement Difficulty	Size of Study Group and Lapse of Time Between Placement and Study	Outcome		Data Used for Follow-up Assessment
			Number and Percentages	Outcome Criteria for Categorization	
Graham (1957)	Foreign-born children (transracial adoption)	50 children (2–10 years after placement)	32 (64%) 13 (26%) 5 (10%)	"Satisfactory positive adjustment" "Only fair" "Poor or very poor adjustment"	Interviews with parents and teachers
Rathbun et al. (1964)	Foreign-born children (transracial adoption)	33 children (6 years after placement)	5 (15%) 16 (49%) 10 (30%) 2 (6%)	"Superior" "Adequate" "Problematic" "Disturbed"	Joint interviews with parents
Franklin-Massarik (1969)	Moderate to severe handicap	71 children (4–12 years after placement)	26 (37%) 29 (41%) 16 (22%)	"Excellent" "Good" "Doubtful"	Joint interviews with parents, unstructured observation of child
Kadushin (1970)	Older–age 5–12 at placement	91 children (4–10 years after placement)	67 (73%) 8 (9%) 18 (16%)	"High ratio of parental satisfactions to dissatisfactions" "Balance between satisfactions–dissatisfactions" "Low ratio of satisfactions to dissatisfactions"	Joint interviews with parents, questionnaire responses

Zastrow (1971)	Nonwhite children (transracial adoption)	44 children (1–6 years after placement)	"Extremely satisfying" — 36 (88%) "More satisfying than dissatisfying" — 5 (11%) "Half and half" — 1 (1%)	Interview with parents
Fanshel (1972)	Nonwhite children (transracial adoption)	97 children (starting with placement, repeated annual interviews for 5 years)	"Problem-free" — 51 (53%) "Adequate" — 24 (25%) "Adequate but guarded" — 10 (10%) "Poor" — 11 (11%)	Joint interviews with parents, interviews with father–mother alone (repeated over 5-year period)
Jackson (1975)	Nonwhite children (transracial adoption)	49 (6 years after placement)	"Highly satisfactory" — 35 (72%) "Satisfactory" — 10 (20%) "Problematic" — 4 (8%)	Group discussions; individual, taped interviews; questionnaires
Kim, Reid (1975)	Foreign-born children (transracial adoption)	72 (1–4 years after placement)	"Adjusting very well" — 45 (62.5%) "Good adjustment" — 24 (33%) "Fair or poor adjustment" — 3 (4%)	Mail questionnaire
Tizard (1977)	Two years of age or older at placement after institutional care during infancy	30 (2½ years after placement and 6 years after placement)	"Parents satisfied"; "Mutual attachments strong" — 24 (84%)	Individual taped interviews; observation of children; teacher reports

TABLE 10–5. Recapitulation of Table 10–4

Outcome	Number	Percentage
Unequivocally successful	385	72
"Satisfactory"		
"Positive adjustment"		
"Superior"		
"Adequate"		
"Problem-free"		
"High ratio parent satisfaction to dissatisfaction"		
"Extremely satisfactory"		
Intermediate success	88	16
"Only fair"		
"Adequate but guarded"		
"More satisfying than dissatisfying"		
Unsuccessful	64	12
"Poor or very poor adjustment"		
"Doubtful"		
"Problematic"		
"Poor"		
"Disturbed"		
"Low ratio of satisfaction to dissatisfaction"		
Total	537	100

infertility and fear of competition from the child's biological parents. Further, however short the period between birth and adoption, every adoptive child faces some experience of early separation and some discontinuity in mothering. All these factors impose possible stresses on the adoptive family.

Research suggests that congenital factors may contribute to the problem. Most adopted children are born out of wedlock to young women for whom this is the first pregnancy. Such a pregnancy is apt to be highly stressful, and some of the mother's tension and anxiety might adversely affect the fetus. Furthermore such mothers are apt to get less adequate nutritional and medical care during pregnancy and less emotional support. The higher mortality rate, the higher congenital anomaly rate, and the lower birth weight associated with such pregnancies, cited in Chapter 9 is confirmation of the stressful context of such a pregnancy for the child. One study of the patients at a pediatric hospital unit showed that a disproportionate percentage of adopted children had "minimal brain damage." A review of the developmental records led to the conclusion that "indifferent prenatal medical care may have been crucial in determining brain injury" (Kenny *et al.*, 1967, p. 29). Electroencephalographs of adopted and nonadopted children suggest that "adopted children as a group, due to various biosocial deprivation and insults, sustain a high percentage of neurological damage" (Losbough, 1965, p. 4). This may be related to the finding, confirmed by a number of different studies, that when adopted children are disturbed, they are more apt to demonstrate aggressive, hostile, hyperactive behavior than other kinds of disturbed behavior.

The emphasis placed on the emotional difficulties of adoptive children requires some correction in perspective. Despite the overrepresentation of adopted children in psychiatric facilities, for whatever explainable reasons, the fact of the matter is that relatively few adopted children receive treatment for emotional disturbance. After reviewing the relevant material, Kadushin (1966, 1967) notes that about 98 per cent of the adopted children in the community apparently have never been referred for psychiatric treatment. As Humphrey (1963) notes, "Since only a small proportion of adoptive parents ever seek psychiatric advice, it seems that most adoptions work out happily for both parents and children" (p. 607).

Another series of studies can be cited that confirm this conclusion and further tend to confirm that emotional disturbance in adopted children is the exception rather than the rule. The studies listed in Table 10–6 are studies of selected samples of adopted children identified by their referral to a psychiatric facility. Comparisons of a random sampling of adopted children with a random sampling of a matched group of nonadopted peers reveal—with a few exceptions—that adopted children develop as healthily, physically and emotionally, as their nonadopted peers.

One of the earliest studies, by Nemovicher (1960) is one of the few exceptions: in comparing thirty adopted children with thirty nonadopted classmates, he found that adoptive children were apt to be significantly more "hostile," "fearful," and "tense."

Repeating psychological tests of adopted children when they were eight months old, four years old, and seven years old and comparing the results with a carefully matched group of nonadopted children similarly tested, Fisch *et al.* (1976) found that the adopted children were more dependent and socially immature. The researchers suggest in explanation that "many adoptive parents, because of their anxiety and concern, tend to overcompensate for a lack of a 'blood relationship' (with the child) by a neurotically exaggerated closeness that interferes with the child's development of independence and social maturity" (p. 499).

However, a number of other studies using larger groups of adopted and nonadopted children matched for comparison and basing their conclusions on personality tests, sociometric measures, school achievement, teacher observations, and parents' reports found little significant difference between the development of adopted and nonadopted children (Witmer, 1963; Mikawa, 1968; Elonen, Schwartz, 1969; Bohman, 1970; Hoopes *et al.*, 1970; Seglow, Pringle, Wedge, 1972; Breetz, Taylor, 1975). There were indications in two studies (Bohman, 1970; Seglow, Pringle, Wedge, 1972) that the adjustment of adopted boys was somewhat more problematic than the adjustment of their nonadopted peers.

Thus, though adopted children are significantly overrepresented in the clientele of psychiatric facilities, adopted children are, on the whole, very similar to their nonadopted peers in terms of development and adjustment. This is a tribute to the adoptive parent–child relationship, for adopted children start life with some initial handicaps, and adoptive families must struggle with some unique problems.

Another kind of "success" criterion, of interest to the community taxpayers, might be cited. Every child placed for adoption in infancy saves the taxpayers some $122,000, which the community would have had to expend if the child continued in foster care through his dependency. "It might be economical to

TABLE 10–6. Studies of Adopted Children Referred for Psychiatric Treatment

Study	Total Number in Study Group	Number of Adoptees in Study Group	Percentage of Adoptive Children Referred for Service	Percentage of Referred Adoptees Placed by Agency	Adoption Status— Relative or Nonrelative
Stonesifer (1942)	2,000	48	2.4%	—	Both
Holman (1953)	100	7	7.0%	—	Nonrelative
Pringle (1961)	2,593	210	8.3%	—	Both
National Association of Mental Health, England (1954)	1,152	17	1.5%	—	Both
Schechter (1962)	120	16	13.3%	50% [e]	Nonrelative
Toussieng (1962)	357	39	10.9%	51%	Nonrelative
Humphrey, Ounsted (1963)	2,700	80	2.9%	50%	Nonrelative
Sweeny (1963)	292	21	7.2%	—	Nonrelative
Goodman (1963)	593	14	2.4%	50%	Nonrelative
Ketchum (1964)	196	20	10.7%	"Most often"	Both
Screchter (1964)	—	159 [c] (41 adults 118 children)	6.6% [d] (average from three psychiatric facilities)	46%	Nonrelative

Borgatta, Fanshel (1965)	2,281	123	5.5%	—	Nonrelative
Menlove (1965)	1,314	59	4.6%	—	Nonrelative
Simon Senturia (1966)	1,371	35[b] (29 children, 6 adults)	2.6%	—	Nonrelative
Kirk et al. (1966)[a]	2,117	132	6.2%	—	Both
Jameson (1967)	390	42	10.8%	55%	Nonrelative
Reece, Levin (1968)	1,017	30	2.95%	56%	Nonrelative
Work, Anderson (1971)	1,282 (outpatients) 363 (inpatients)	56 34	4.3% 9.3%	— —	— —
Silver (1970)	80	10	12.5%	90%	Nonrelative
Harper, Williams (1976)	191	21	11%	100%	Nonrelative

[a] The table includes only those tabulations from Kirk's study that were presented by the author as having high or medium reliability. [See Kirk, Jonassohn, Fish, 1966, Table 5, p. 297]

[b] This figure includes 29 children and 6 adults.

[c] This figure includes 118 children and 41 adults.

[d] This percentage represents an average from three psychiatric facilities.

[e] These data were given in the 1964 study.

TABLE 10–7. Recapitulation of Table 10–6

Study	Total Number in Study Group	Number of Adoptees in Study Group	Percentage of Adoptive Children Referred for Service	Percentage of Referred Adoptees Placed by Agency
Total relative and nonrelative adoptions (excluding Schechter, 1964)	20,238	983	4.8%	—
Total nonrelative adoptions	10,806	497	4.6%	53%

assign a caseload of only 5 children to an (adoptive) homefinder, since success in finding a suitable adoptive family for only one child would more than compensate for the worker's annual salary" (Fanshel, Shinn, 1972, p. 25).

Factors Associated with Adoption Outcome

Extensive research has provided information on the success of adoption and has helped to determine the relationship among the various factors that influence outcome. Such research was designed to test the validity of the criteria traditionally applied in selecting adoptive homes.

In general, background factors of both the child and the parents appear to have little relation to adoptive outcome. This finding runs contrary to the premise that developmental history needs to be carefully reviewed in adoptive interviews. The number of placements experienced by the child, his history of institutional placement, his socioeconomic background, and his history of preadoptive deprivation do not appear to be related to adoptive outcome. Age at placement is generally negatively related to outcome, but a very high percentage of older children are successfully adopted.

The child's background variables seem to have less and less significance as prognostic factors from placement to follow-up. This is a tribute to the resilience of children in surmounting earlier developmental deficiencies, to the coping capacity of the adoptive parents, and to the rehabilitative potential of a good adoptive home.

Similarly parental background is of questionable significance. Starr *et al.* (1970) attempted to test the relationship of developmental experience to adoptive outcome. On the basis of social history data obtained through self-report questionnaires and inventories, they selected two groups of adoptive parents: one was composed of applicants who had experienced a happy, loving childhood in a harmonious, affectionate home; the other consisted of applicants who had experienced some rejection or neglect in homes in which there were marital conflict and psychic stress. Forty-three adoptive couples in each group were interviewed at follow-up to evaluate their functioning as adoptive parents. "The findings indi-

cated that early life experiences were only minimally associated with performance as adoptive parents" (p. 494).

The age of adoptive parents, the length of their marriage, their religious
affiliation, and the number and status of the other children in the home show
little relation to outcome. Assessments of parents' motivation for adoption are of
questionable significance as a predictor of adoptive success, as are their attitudes
toward infertility and childlessness. Socioeconomic status, education, and income
are only feebly related to positive outcome.

None of the research shows matching between adoptive parents and children to be a factor in adoptive outcome. The general factors most clearly related to adopted success are the attitude of the parents toward the child and
the nature of their relationship with the child. Acceptance of and satisfaction
in adoptive parenthood—coupled with warmth toward and acceptance of the
child—were invariably associated with adoptive success. Conversely, the factor
most clearly related to difficulty was parental rejection, although it is not clear
whether the rejection causes the difficulty or the difficulty causes the rejection.

The child's sex is clearly related to outcome. Adoptive boys seem to be more
likely to be maladjusted than either adoptive girls or nonadoptive peers.

Although we have attempted to list and assess the effect of the discrete
factors on adoptive outcome in any particular situation, the various factors interact with each other so as to modify the effects of the contribution of any one
factor to the overall result. Ultimately it is the configuration of factors that determines outcome.

CHILDREN WITH SPECIAL NEEDS

The Nonwhite Child

One of the most serious problems in the field of adoption concerns the children who are or who might be legally free for adoption, who could benefit from
and contribute to normal family living, but who are difficult to place because
they belong to minority groups (black, Chicano, American Indian, and so on);
because they are older; because they are physically, mentally, or emotionally
handicapped; or because they are a part of a group of three or four siblings who
should be placed together. This group of children, previously termed hard to
place, are now more frequently called children with special needs or children
who wait.

Minority group children constitute one large group of children for whom
adoptive placements are not readily available. This is particularly true for black
children. Statistics collected by the Child Welfare League of America from a
nationwide sample of adoption agencies indicated that, in 1976, "nonwhite homes
are still in very short supply in relation to the number of nonwhite children
accepted for adoption" (Shyne, 1977, p. 3). A more comprehensive nationwide
survey of children receiving child welfare services from public agencies found
that, of the children legally free for adoption and receiving service, "home finding was more successful for white children than for Black children" (Shyne,
Schroeder, 1978, p. 125).

Various studies have attempted to identify deterrents to adoption on the part of nonwhites (Herzog *et al.*, 1971a; 1971b). Parent-centered reasons were related to lack of knowledge about the magnitude of the problem; anxieties about undesirable traits in the child or damage as a result of early developmental experience; and anxiety about economic insecurity. Agency-centered reasons were related to a perception of the agency as being evaluative, threatening, and demanding in its approach to applicants. The agency was perceived as having a middle-class bias, a white-racist orientation, and a readiness to reject. Agency "red tape," requirements, procedures, and length of time between application and placement were mentioned as agency-centered deterrents, the applicant being "overevaluated" and "overinterviewed."

The most frequently reported deterrent was economic insecurity: "Again and again it is pointed out that black families have lower incomes, less job security, fewer economic reserves than most white families, and that the incomes, though generally lower, more often represent two wage-earners" (Herzog, Bernstein, 1965, p. 8). This conclusion is supported by those of other studies (Fanshel, 1957; Deasy, Quinn, 1962; Foote, Putnam, 1965; Fowler, 1966). Detailed interviews with 129 middle-class black families in Hartford, Connecticut, revealed that "overwhelmingly our informants attributed the problem [shortage of black adoptive homes] to the prevalence of low income, poor employment, and inadequate housing among blacks" (Foote, Putnam, 1965, p. 48).

The reality is that adoption is a low-priority problem in the black community as compared with other problems, that the deterrent of economic insecurity and anxiety is still a powerful reality, and that the black community of two-parent families above the poverty line is, and has been, adopting at about the same rate as white parents (Herzog, Bernstein, 1965; Bonham, 1977).

Some agencies have succeeded in placing an increasing number of black children in black homes. A review of the procedures that are related to their greater effectiveness in meeting the problem indicates the following (Sandusky *et al.*, 1972). These agencies made a definite effort to involve members of the black community in the development of programs, policies, and procedures, as board members, workers, volunteers, and interpreters of agency need and service. They actively cooperated with local departments of public welfare and conducted continuous mass-media campaigns to "present" children needing adoption. District offices were opened in the black community. Changes in agency procedure permitted the scheduling of evening interviews in the home immediately after application. Agency requirements relating to age, length of marriage, number of children in the family, income, infertility, and mother's employment were relaxed in an effort to "screen in" rather than "screen out" applicants. The time between application and placement was reduced, so that some of the agencies completed home studies and placed children within two to four months after application.

Earlier research had suggested that the dropout rate, once application had been made to an agency, was higher for blacks than for white applicants (Bradley, 1966; Fanshel, 1957; Fowler, 1966). However, a more recent study showed that this was not the case (Festinger, 1972, p. 24).

In order to see what might be done to lower the withdrawal rate of blacks who applied for adoption, Festinger (1972) conducted telephone interviews with desirable applicants—eighty black women and eighty-six white women—

who had withdrawn. Black applicants more often than white applicants attributed their withdrawals to agency rules and procedures—the "number of forms, interviews, and questions." Yet this was a major reason in 17.5 per cent of the cases. Factors over which the agency had little or no control accounted for 51.6 per cent of the major reasons for the withdrawal of black applicants: pregnancy following application, financial difficulty, unanticipated circumstances (illness, job transfer, and the like), and ambivalence about adoption. Interestingly enough, although some of the black applicants had been seen by white workers, this was never listed as a factor in withdrawal. The researcher concluded that the black withdrawal rate might be reduced if the agency was clearer and more direct about its expectations and procedures. The results of the study parallel the findings of Shireman's (1970) similar study in Chicago.

A study by Wachtel (1972) of adoptions of black children shows a strong correlation between the frequency of agency placement of such children and the proportion of the agency's social workers who are black (p. 6). In line with this finding, agencies have attempted to reduce social and physical distance between themselves and the black client group they seek to serve by decentralizing service and locating the service in the neighborhoods where the clients live, involving members of the client group in agency activities as volunteers and/or board members, increasing the number of staff members identified with the client group as professional or paraprofessional employees, and using newspapers and radio stations representing the client group. Public agencies have experimented with special outreach programs organized and staffed by black social workers and located in the black community. The Tayari office of the San Diego Department of Public Welfare is an example (Neilson, 1976). *Tayari*, a Swahili word meaning "family and tribal unity," focused on finding black homes for black children.

Black families who do adopt are similar in significant respects to white adoptive families. Scott (1976) reviewed the results of a special nationwide interagency effort to find black adoptive homes for black children. Agencies involved included black administered adoption agencies such as Homes for Black Children (Detroit), Afro-American Family and Community Services (Chicago), and Harlem-Dawling Children's Service (New York City). Over the course of a year of active operations, the project succeeded in placing 111 children across the country in black families. The characteristics of the black applicants to the project mirrored those of the usual white adoptive applicants, being clearly middle class. Most were married and had family incomes of over $14,000. About 40 per cent had at least some college education (pp. 28–29). Most of the children placed were under five years of age (p. 47). Only a small percentage of applicants (most frequently single adoptive applicants) was willing to accept handicapped children.

Transracial Adoptions

Transracial adoptions—the placement of nonwhite children in white adoptive homes—is one resource developed to meet the adoptive needs of such children. Attempts at such placements were initiated in the 1950s and continue today. New York City set up an Adopt-a-Child program in 1955; San Francisco organized MARCH (Minority Adoption Recruitment of Children's Homes) in 1955; Minneapolis set up PAMY (Parents to Adopt Minority Youngsters) in 1961; the U.S. Bureau of Indian Affairs and the Child Welfare League of America sponsored a nationwide Indian Adoption Project in 1958. These projects have been reviewed by Billingsley and Giovannini (1972).

Statistics indicate that transracial adoptions increased sharply during the latter part of the 1960s, tripling between 1968 (700) and 1971 (2,574) (Opportunity, 1971). By 1971 there were an estimated 10,000 transracial adoptive families in the United States and Canada involving black, American Indian, or Oriental children.

As Billingsley (1969) notes, interracial adoption follows a "continuum based on skin color," as well as a continuum reflecting community attitude toward a particular racial minority. It is easier to place the lighter-skinned child; it is easier to place black children in Canada, where they form a small proportion of the population, but harder to place American Indian children in those sections of Canada where there are many Indians; Oriental children are easier to place than blacks. Transracial adoptions most frequently involve children of mixed racial black–white background.

Researchers have attempted to identify the special characteristics of parents who accept children of another race (Pepper, 1966; Falk, 1969, 1970; Sellers, 1969; St. Dennis, 1969; Raynor, 1970; Priddy, Kirgan, 1971; Zastrow, 1971; Fanshel, 1972; Grow, Shapiro, 1974; Simon, Alstein, 1977). Such parents are likely to have higher occupational levels and higher educational attainment than adoptive families generally; they are more distant socially and geographically from their relatives; they are more likely to be fertile and to have had children in the family prior to adoption; their motive is more likely to be that of providing a home for a child who might otherwise not be adopted; they tend to be somewhat more individualistic and inner-directed and to have a higher self-concept. As Fanshel (1972) notes, "Repeatedly, the element that has been most noteworthy in the self-descriptions of the [parents] . . . has been a certain independence, often self-referred to as a 'stubborn streak.' . . . It is not that they would not care what their neighbors think; it is rather that they would not allow themselves to be guided in their actions by such considerations" (p. 322).

They are not necessarily without prejudice, as some who have accepted American Indian children made it clear that they would not accept a black child, and some of those who accepted a child of black–white parentage would not have accepted a full-blooded black child. Their voting habits and political ideologies reflect diverse convictions; only a minority viewed transracial adoptions as a gesture expressing their conviction about an integrated society.

Some were prompted to accept transracial adoptions in order to ensure that the agency would place a child with them as soon as possible. As is true of the placement of all hard-to-place children, agencies have been ready to relax standards and make concessions in order to increase the number of applicants willing to adopt transracially.

Frequently it appears that the applicant who has accepted a hard-to-place child was initially solely interested in adopting a child; only later, after some discussion of the situation with the agency, did he consider a minority-group child, an older child, or a handicapped child.

Ladner (1977) notes that of the 136 transracially adoptive couples she interviewed, "There were numerous cases in which the parents would have adopted a white child rather than a black one had a white child been available" (p. 49).

However, there are a limited number of people who were initially and specifically interested in adopting transracially, "to help," to be of "some service," to do "some good."

Available research clearly indicates that applicants interested in such adoptions are not meeting some neurotic need or expressing a sense of rebelliousness. It further suggests that the worker's attitude toward the feasibility and desirability of transracial adoptions is an important determinant of the applicants' response. Applicants are sensitive to the worker's attitudes and are more likely to respond positively when transracial adoptions are presented in a flexible, nondefensive manner.

The trend toward transracial adoptions has created a countertrend: an active opposition on the part of nonwhites to the placement of their children in white homes (Carroll, 1970; Chestang, 1972; Herzog *et al.*, 1971; Jones, 1972; Chimezie, 1975; Jones, Else, 1979). Blacks who oppose such placements say that:

> Black families build in mechanisms to handle living in a racist society. White families could not provide these for a black child. . . . Identity is all-important and no white family can provide this for a black child. . . . I question the ability of white parents—no matter how deeply imbued with good will—to grasp the totality of the problem of being black in our society—I question their ability to create what I believe is crucial for these youngsters—a black identity [Jones, 1972, pp. 40–41, 157].

It is feared that the child might be perceived "as an alien in the white community and a traitor in the black community" (Madison, Schapiro, 1973, p. 543), lacking security in one and solidarity with the other.

Ideas of racial integration and assimilation clash with the ideas of cultural pluralism, black autonomy, and black separatism. The idea that a white home is better than no home at all clashes with the contention that "a home and love are not enough to pay for loss of identity" (Ladner, 1977, p. 86).

Transracial adoption suggests white paternalism, a rejection of black values and life-style, and a rejection of racial roots. In addition to the charge that transracial adoption results in a loss of the child's identification with the black community, there is the further accusation that transracial adoption is a procedure designed primarily to meet the needs of white adoptive applicants who lack white children to adopt rather than to meet the needs of nonwhite children, and that a more concerted effort could be made to find nonwhite homes. Transracial adoptions would then be only one approach—and a limited one at that—of a more comprehensive campaign involving a number of different procedures to find homes for nonwhite children.

In April 1972, the National Association of Black Social Workers went on record as being in "vehement opposition" to the placement of black children with white families and called transracial adoptions "a growing threat to the preservation of the black family" (*The New York Times,* April 12, 1972).

American Indian groups also complain of some of the same problems in offering service to Indian children (U.S. Department of Health, Education, and Welfare, Children's Bureau, 1976, p. 18).

Perhaps we need to be reminded that this position is not very different from the position of denominational agencies. Catholic adoption agencies were long committed to the principle that any Catholic child could be placed for adoption only in a Catholic home (Bowers, 1956). The "child-saving" activity of one group is perceived as a "child-snatching" activity by another group. One of the most vehement controversies in the history of child welfare took place in late nineteenth-century America, when Catholic organizations charged that placement agencies such as the Children's Aid Society were "maintained for the purpose of bribing poor destitute Catholics to abandon their faith." Placing Catholic children in Protestant homes was not charity, it was claimed, but sectarian zeal designed to destroy a child's faith in the religion of his parents (Langsam, 1964, pp. 48–50).

Around the turn of the century, Jewish communal organizations were very much concerned about the Jewish children being cared for in Catholic institutions, "where the risk of conversion was greatest." In 1903, of 447 dependent Jewish children in non-Jewish institutions, 403 were in Catholic institutions. In response to this concern, strenuous efforts were made to remove the children and place them in the care of agencies that were under Jewish auspices (Romanofsky, 1974).

The opposition to transracial adoption on the part of nonwhite groups and the ambivalence of the social work profession regarding its ultimate desirability have had a decidedly inhibiting effect on such programs. By 1977 transracial adoption as a program for meeting the adoptive needs of nonwhite children had been sharply curtailed. Even those agencies that had pioneered and had the greatest conviction in such placements were making progressively fewer of them.

Although there has been a consistent decline in the number of black children placed with white families since the high point in 1972, when 468 agencies reported that 2,574 such placements had been made, transracial placements continue to be made. In 1975, with a larger number of agencies reporting, there were 831 such placements, accounting for 20 per cent of all black children placed in nonrelative homes in that year (Opportunity, 1976). It is estimated that between 1961 and 1975, fifteen thousand black children were adopted by white families.

The adoption standards recommended by the Child Welfare League followed the shifting sentiment. The 1958 edition of the standards suggested the discouragement of transracial placement: "Physical resemblances should not be a determining factor in the selection of a home, with the possible exception of such racial characteristics as color." The 1968 edition, however, noted that "racial background should not determine the selection of the home for the child. . . . It should not be assumed that difficulties will necessarily arise if adoptive parents and children are of different racial origin." In 1972 this standard was amended: "It is preferable to place children in families of their own racial background."

A limited number of transracial placements are still being made, but there is more effort now to determine if the adoptive applicants are clearly aware of their own attitudes toward race and to accept only those who have a strong biracial orientation and ties to and in the black community (Katz, 1974).

The controversy regarding transracial adoption raised a series of researchable questions. Efforts have been made to answer some of them.

The question of the representativeness of the negative response to transracial adoptions advanced by the National Association of Black Social Workers has often been raised. Harvard, Royse, and Skerl (1977) attempted to answer this question by interviews with a systematically selected random sample of black families living in a Dayton, Ohio, black ghetto community. The interviewers were black, and 150 people were interviewed. The researchers summarized their findings by noting that "The data suggest that the majority of blacks do not oppose the idea of transracial adoptions and a large majority could be described as favorable to this alternative under certain conditions" (p. 188).

The most intriguing and significant questions raised by such adoptions relate to their outcome generally—and specifically with regard to the problem of the adopted child's sense of racial identification.

In attempting to answer the question of transracial adoptive outcome, the Child Welfare League in 1971 studied 125 children in transracial adoptive placements (Grow, Shapiro, 1974). At the time of the study, the children were at least six years of age and had been in their adopted home for three years or longer. On the average, the children were actually nine years of age and at the time had been in their adoptive homes for over seven years. The study was done in seven different cities throughout the United States and Canada. Two in-depth interviews were held with the adoptive parents by experienced social workers not connected with the adoption agencies. The two interviews were held a year apart. In addition, the children were given some standard psychological tests and reports were obtained from their teachers. Grow and Shapiro concluded that the success rate of transracial adoptions (about 77 per cent) compared favorably with the success rate noted in studies of adoption by white families of white, nonhandicapped infants. Relatively little evidence was detected of problems of confusion or denial of racial background in the children studied, most of whom were pre-adolescent (Grow, Shapiro, 1975, p. iii). Most of the children were doing well in the home, in school, and in the community. Their scores on the California Test of Personality compared favorably with those of white adoptive children in white families (see also Jackson, 1976).

Chimezie criticized the Grow and Shapiro (1974) study for contributing little to settling the question of the effects of transracial adoption on the black child's sense of racial identity. In replying, these researchers point out that the focus of the study was on the adequacy of the child's development in such a situation rather than on the question of racial identity per se (Chimezie, 1977; Shapiro, Grow 1977).

The question of racial identity was, however, the direct focus of a study of transracially adopted children conducted by Simon and Alstein (1977). They interviewed and employed projective techniques with 120 black children in white homes. The children ranged from three to eight years in age, the mean age being 4.4 (Table 6.3, p. 40). The procedures employed were a replication of those previously used in a variety of studies by others concerned with the perception of racial identity of black and white children living with their biological parents.

The transracially adopted child living in a white family showed little bias in favor of whites. The black child's identification of himself was as accurate as the white child's identification of himself, which might not have been the case if the back children were rejecting of their blackness and preferred whiteness: "It appears that black children reared in the special setting of multiracial families do not acquire the ambivalence to their own race reported in all other studies involving black children" (p. 158). However, the fact that the mean age of the black children in the study group was 4.4, the age at which the sense of racial identity is just beginning to emerge, raises questions about the stability of the study results.

Fanshel's (1972) study of transracial placements is perhaps the most comprehensive and rigorous of such research. As a result of a cooperative effort of the U.S. Bureau of Indian Affairs and the Child Welfare League of America, 395 Indian children were placed with white families over a ten-year period. Annual interviews were conducted with the families of ninety-seven of these children for five years after placement. The fathers and the mothers were interviewed jointly and separately, and the adjustment of the child was studied in detail. The overall conclusion "was that the children are doing remarkably well as a group." Health and cognitive development were normal:

> . . . In personality and behavior patterns there are more incipient signs of difficulties than in other areas, [but] this is true of only 30 percent of the children, and most of these are seen to have moderate rather than serious problems. The children appear to be well-imbedded within their adoptive families and the relationships appear to be as close and devoted as one would find in other kinds of adoptive families or in biological family units [p. 323].

It seems clear that whatever problems might be encountered in the future, the transracial adoptive experience is less problematic than had been anticipated during childhood and latency.

Despite the controversy about the ultimate desirability of transracial adoption, it is regarded as more desirable than foster-home care or institutional care. Still, questions about the advisability of transracial adoption derive from the special problems that such adoptions present to the adoptive children and parents: acceptance of the child by siblings, playmates, peers, relatives, and neighbors, and, most difficult of all, the problems related to the resolution of racial identification. Being Oriental, or American Indian, or black, and living with Caucasian parents in a Caucasian environment, how can the child be helped to develop a stable, secure concept of racial identification? How will the white community react when the child reaches adolescence and begins dating? The child's affectional ties are with the white world of his parents, which constitutes his reference group for socialization. However, the world outside the family responds to the child in terms of the child's visible racial affiliation.

Agencies and parents, dealing with these problems in anticipation, adhere to general principles of mental health: "All children have problems of identification in adolescence, this is just more of the same"; "if the child can be helped, through love and acceptance, to resolve his identity as a human being, she will then be able to resolve his racial identity"; "building a good self-concept through parental trust, love, and acceptance will provide the necessary secure foundation for healthy resolution of the problem."

In addition, parents have been advised to learn something about the art, literature, history, and lifestyle of the child's race and to attempt to convey these to the child so that she can develop some pride in her heritage. Further, it is recommended that the family develop social and professional contacts with people of the child's racial background or move to a racially mixed neighborhood so that the child may play with children of her own race. It has also been suggested that the parents attempt to identify and resolve any racist feelings they may have that might intrude upon their relationship with the child.

If "telling" involves a discussion of sex, "telling" by transracial adoptive parents involves a discussion of race as well. To say, "God made people differently. . . . All people are colored; some people are colored white, some black. . . . Just as people have different color hair and eyes, they have different skin colors" may be sufficient for the young child. Parents and agencies indicate that the seriousness of the problems that will be encountered by these children is a function, in a large measure, of the state of race relations when they reach adolescence.

One resource, developed by the parents themselves, may be helpful: associations of transracial adoptive families, which meet to discuss common problems and share solutions. The meetings permit the sharing of a common experience, and members provide social and emotional support for each other. The Open Door Society of Montreal was the earliest of such organizations. There are now Open Door Societies in Indiana, Missouri, Illinois, and Wisconsin. Other organizations include The East–West Society, the Council on Adoptable Children, Families for Interracial Adoption, and the Interracial Family Association. In 1969 such organizations began sponsoring an annual North American Conference on Adoptable Children, devoted in large measure to problems of transracial adoption.

Transracial adoptions are recent, and the children are still quite young. Follow-up research available at this point indicates that sibling acceptance is not much of a problem; grandparents are more resistive at first but later appear to welcome the children; young playmates and peers accept such children readily; the negative reaction of neighbors is private, as yet not public; explicitly manifested prejudice is unfashionable and infrequent. Parents frequently encounter stares of curiosity, but rarely overt hostility. As a matter of fact, parents note that it is more embarrassing to have to cope with gushing comments of approbation. Transracially adopted children who are old enough to be in school have experienced heckling and teasing, but this has been neither frequent nor persistent, although such experiences may not be consistently shared with adoptive parents.

Zastrow (1971), in a study comparing the responses of in-race and transracial adoptive parents, found the levels of satisfaction in the adoption, for both groups, to be equally high, although Falk (1970) found transracial adoptive parents to have lower levels of satisfaction and to be somewhat less likely to say that they would repeat the experience.

In general, then, it might be said that transracial adoptions, as one option for nonwhite children awaiting adoption, need to be given serious consideration. It is an alternative that offers the child the advantages of permanence in place of long-term foster care or institutional living. Until we can make available a nonwhite adoptive home for every nonwhite child who needs one, it is a resource that might need to be used.

The Older Child

Another sizable group of adoptable but hard-to-place children is composed of older children. The general difficulties in the adoptive placement of the older child have been discussed in articles (Hallinan, 1952; Starr, 1955; Schapiro, 1957; Leatherman, 1957; Lawder, 1958; Boehm, 1958; Bell, 1959; McCoy, 1961; Epstein, Heymann, 1962; Chema, 1970; Sharrar, 1970; Neilson, 1971, 1972; Bayley, 1975; Edwards, 1975; Biggert, 1976; Chestang, 1976; Belken, 1977; Katz, 1977; Jones, 1979) and in books (Kadushin, 1970; Carney, 1976; Jewett, 1978).

In 1970 it might have been said, with some justification, that a child over two years of age was difficult to place for adoption. With the continuing shortage of adoptable infants, the age at which a child presents difficulty for adoption has increased. By 1980 white, nonhandicapped children up to seven or eight years of age were being placed for adoption with relatively little difficulty. However, a nationwide study of children being offered adoptive services by public child welfare agencies indicated that, in 1977, adoptive homes could be found for only 36 per cent of the children 11–14 years of age and 13 per cent of 15–17-year-olds (Shyne, Schroeder, 1978, p. 131).

Any initial deterrent to placeability ultimately results in additional deterrents. Because the minority-group child or the handicapped child is initially hard to place, the delay results in his becoming an older child who is now harder to place because of age. Because placeability is greatest at earlier ages, the most effective service to the special-needs child is to make special efforts to place him as early as possible.

Adoption of older children presents the agency, the child, and the adoptive parents with some special problems. Because older children placed for adoption have already developed some characteristic ways of reacting to parental figures and to family life, "matching" comes up again as a consideration of significance. Unlike the physical "matching" of the past, which adoption agencies have rejected, this kind of "matching" involves a concern for a good fit between adopter and adoptee in terms of temperamental compatibility: Do they tend to like similar kinds of activities? Are they organized, neat, and punctual? Or are they loosely structured, fast or slow in reacting to events, highly emotional or emotionally bland? (Boyne, 1978).

The selection of an adoptive home for an older child requires his active participation, for he is consciously and explicitly aware of the experience. Unlike the infant, the older child measures the acceptability of the prospective adoptive couple, and any doubts or hesitancies he may have must be given consideration.

The dynamics identified as related to grieving at the loss of contact with people with whom the child has had an affectionate relationship have been applied to the placement of the older child. In the move from foster home, in which the older child may have lived for some time, to the new, unfamiliar adoptive home setting, workers may be impelled to overprotect the child from the inevitable suffering that the move might occasion. Rather than being unduly and unhelpfully comforting, the worker needs to permit the child to feel the sense of mourning and grief that may be evoked. During this time of transition, feelings about the birth parent may be reactivated, and the child may need help in re-resolving these feelings. For such a child, adoption involves the loss not only of the biological parents but also of the foster parents.

The foster parents with whom the older child has lived are enlisted in helping the child and the adoptive parents to make the transition.

In helping the older child to get a coherent picture of himself and his life as a preparation for placement, agencies have developed the life-story book procedure, the "Story of Me" scrapbook. The worker helps the child to put together a scrapbook of his life: a written account of who she is, where she has been, and the people she knows and their relationship with her, all illustrated with pictures.

Separation is gradual, consisting of a series of overnight and/or weekend visits to give the child the "chance to let go of his old life before losing it" (Jewett, 1978, p. 10). However, such preparation can be unduly prolonged, intensifying anxiety about the impending change.

By the time a child is five years old, he has already developed some relationship, of which he is explicitly aware, with parents, parent substitutes, siblings, and other relatives. He has a vivid memory of a life lived with other people in other places. The adoptive parents have to establish themselves in the child's life either in addition to or in opposition to such memories. Thus parents who adopt an older child can less easily fantasize that the child is truly their own.

An older child is therefore apt to face a problem of competing or conflicting loyalties. Having developed emotional ties of some intensity to either his biological parents or his foster parents, he cannot permit himself to "belong" unconditionally to the adoptive parents without betraying his love for the adults to whom he previously felt some allegiance.

Adopting an older child deprives the adoptive parents of the affectional contact with an infant and the satisfactions in shaping the child's life during the time when he is most malleable. The older child comes to adoptive parents with an established name and with an established way of dealing with the problems of daily living that may or may not fit into the adoptive family's way of doing things. The adoptive parents must, in some measure, accept the child as he is; they are deprived of the opportunity of socializing the child, from the start, in terms that are acceptable to them.

The older child is more likely to be a "damaged" child. Having lived for some years under conditions that are not generally conducive to stable emotional development, he is likely to have developed some emotional disturbances. The older the child, the older the problem and the less susceptible it is to therapy. This is less likely to have happened to infants available for adoption, who have had, by virtue of their age, only limited exposure to pathogenic conditions.

Having overtly experienced rejection, older children are apt to anticipate rejection. They are likely, then, to be reticent about allowing themselves to feel love for the adoptive parents or to express affection. They are more likely to test the adoptive parents' patience and endurance in order to prove their acceptability. The adoptive parents, thus, are in for a harder time and, at least initially, fewer satisfactions. Adoptive parents need to be advised of the need for patience, the slow growth of love and affection, and the slow pace of mutual adjustment.

However, there are advantages. The older child can participate in family activities, communicate with parents, and be talked to. There is less of the drudgery in training and caring for a totally dependent child, and there is less anxiety about "telling" because the child has experienced the placement and knows that he is adopted. Parents who have adopted older children stress these advantages:

> Father: You can build rapport more easily, I think. You have a youngster who can talk and you got a youngster who can do things. . . . I mean . . . you get a tiny infant in the home and they lay in the basket or you take them out and give them a bath and dress them and feed them and that's just about the extent of it. Where you take the six- to eleven-year-old, these youngsters already have interests and you can cultivate those interests, you can even build new interests. And this, I think to me, was the . . . was one of the nicest factors in adopting an older child.
>
> Mother: Babies are so routine and you don't get much enjoyment out of them . . . you know just sterilizing bottles and washing diapers whereas I think someone older is much more interesting. Older people if they would take an older child would find it more enjoyable.
>
> Father: You have a child that wants to be adopted . . . and that's one thing in your favor . . . and he knows it. . . . I mean he's aware of it . . . that his folks can't keep him. He's already trying to adjust, because he wants to and he's old enough to understand . . . to realize.
>
> Father: We adopted an older child so that we didn't have to go through this diaper wash, two o'clock feeding, walk the floor bit.
>
> Father: I think that's one advantage . . . of adopting an older child . . . The child knows it's being adopted . . . with an infant you . . . you'd always have to wonder—well, gee—when should I tell her or should I ever tell her . . . and with the older child . . . it's just a fact when she comes. . . .

Kadushin (1970) interviewed ninety-one families with children who had been placed for adoption at five years of age or older. The greatest majority of such placements were successful and the children appeared to be adjusting well. Yet all these children had spent their infancy and early childhood under very deprived circumstances. In almost all instances, the biological parents' rights to the child had been terminated by the courts as a consequence of neglect and/or abuse. The study shows that the older children, despite memories of earlier attachments, do develop strong relationships with their adoptive parents and learn and accept the ways of the new family. In the recuperative environment of a healthy, permanent family, old emotional wounds are healed.

Both the adoptive parents and the social workers who have written about this subject agree that although difficult, adoptions of older children are possible and ultimately very rewarding. As a consequence, although previously the increased frequency of the adoption of older children was to a considerable extent a consequence of the lack of availability of younger children, currently such placements are somewhat more frequently made out of the conviction that they are the best kinds of placement choices for some families. The agencies' slogan stimulating interest in the adoption of the older child is "Have a child; it's as beautiful as having a baby."

The Handicapped Child

That the existence of a physical, emotional, or mental handicap should make a child difficult to place for adoption is almost self-evident (Taft, 1953;

Lake, 1954; Beaven, 1956; Colville, 1957; Fowler, 1957; Schapiro, 1957; Fradkin, 1958; Hornecker, 1962; Gallagher, 1968; Franklin, Massarik, 1969; Knight, 1970; Ferman, Warren, 1974).

Children who are physically handicapped or mentally retarded require more than the normal amount of parental time and energy; they require specialized knowledge and facilities; they are apt to impose a greater burden of medical expense as well as medical care; they are less likely than the normal child to enable the adoptive parents to derive satisfactions from their achievements; and they are likely to remain dependent for a longer period.

Children with such medical conditions as cleft palate, hernia, asthma, crossed eyes, deafness, blindness, congenital heart defects, or mild cerebral palsy can be, and have been, successfully placed for adoption. In most instances, however, the physical handicap has been mild or correctable. Less frequently, mildly retarded children have been placed for adoption.

Franklin and Massarik (1969), who conducted intensive follow-up interviews with 169 families who adopted handicapped children, concluded that "children with medical conditions of all degrees of severity and correctability can be successfully placed and reared in adoptive homes" (p. 399). Most of the children were between five and twelve years of age at the time of the interview. Although the families ultimately proved adaptive and resilient in meeting the handicapped child's special needs, a majority of the parents had expressed some concern at the time the child was presented to them. Only a small minority of the couples had themselves initiated a request for a handicapped child; in most instances, the agency initiated discussion of the possibility of placement for such a child. The agency, in finding homes for such children, tended to be more flexible in applying eligibility criteria and to move more expeditiously in processing applications (Franklin, Massarik, 1969, p. 463). Some of the adoptive parents had originally been foster parents to the handicapped child. An attachment to and a relationship with the child had developed, and adoption resulted. Initial placement for foster care may be a desirable procedure in the case of the hard-to-place child. It permits the parents to develop a commitment to the child without initially feeling an obligation to make the child a full member of the family.

A questionnaire study of administrators and workers of ninety public and private adoption agencies in a six-state area focused on the adoption of physically handicapped children (Ferman, Warren, 1974). The study showed that workers in these agencies had placed 178 children with such disabilities as Down's syndrome, congenital heart disease, cleft palate, epilepsy, muscular dystropy, and sickle-cell anemia. The adoptive families of such children most frequently fell into three groups: foster parents who had lived with the child for some time, parents who had had personal and/or professional experience with physical and mental disabilities, and parents whose application for the adoption of a white, normal infant was not likely to be accepted because of age, the number of children already in the family, and so on. Experience with a disability as a factor motivating the acceptance of a handicapped child prompted the suggestion that the organizations for parents of handicapped children might be a fruitful source of recruitment.

In widening the criteria for acceptability of adoptive applicants for children with special needs, agencies have accepted persons with stable heart and diabetic conditions, handicapped polio victims, and applicants who were deaf.

The adoption of handicapped children requires close liaison between the agency, the parents, and the medical personnel treating the condition. Knowledge of rehabilitative, educational, and counseling resources in the community specializing in work with the particular handicap is also necessary. The support of medical subsidies for rehabilitative services and close postplacement contact between family and agency are essential.

In the studies of handicapped adopted children, as in other studies of adopted children with special needs, the parents interviewed frequently urge the researchers to stress two points: first, many of the problems for which the agency had prepared them, and which they had anticipated, did not occur; second, there was decided pleasure in having these children, some special rewards in the feeling of performing a useful, significant function, and some special understandings to be derived. Anderson (1971), who wrote about his own experiences in adopting three transracial children, sees these children "as children of special value who enrich and deepen human experience in uncommon ways" (p. 181). He is seconded in this way by the novelist Jan deHartog (1969), who perceptively recounts his own experiences in adopting Asian children.

ADOPTION DISRUPTION

In addition to those studies previously cited regarding the outcomes of adoptive placements, studies regarding adoptive failure might be cited as evidence of the overall success of the adoption system. The studies cited in this section employ a standard objective criterion for identifying failure in adoption: removal of the child from the home at any time between placement and legal adoption (in most states, a period of a year). It might be noted that many of the children who are removed from a home before legally adopted are successfully replaced in another adoptive home. As a consequence, the term *adoption disruption* is thought to be more accurate than *adoption failure*.

Table 10–8 lists the studies up to 1970 providing data on disruptions.

All the studies cited in Table 10–8 are concerned overwhelmingly with children who were white, very young, and without handicaps at placement. Of the 34,499 placements, only 648, or 1.87 per cent, resulted in disruption.

More recent studies presenting data on disruption are more frequently concerned with older, minority group, or handicapped children, and the rate of disruption for these adoptive placements is higher.

The Children's Home Society of North Carolina placed 410 special-needs children over the eight-year period 1967–1974. Twenty-four children, some subsequently successfully replaced, needed to be removed, which showed an initial failure rate of 8 per cent (U.S. Congress, 1975, p. 401). In 1970, 2.7 per cent of children placed for adoption in California through public welfare agencies were returned to the agency. By 1973 this figure had increased to 7.6 per cent (Bass, 1975, p. 50). Although there is no breakdown to suggest the characteristics of the children returned to the agency, the rate of failure increased as agency placements of children with special needs increased.

TABLE 10–8. Summary of Studies Relating to Failed Adoptive Placements

Study	Agency Auspices	Period Covered by Study	Children Placed	Children Returned to Agency	Failure Rate
Davis, Douck (1955)	Public	3 years (1951–53)	396	25	6.3%
Calif. Citizens' Adoptions Comm. (1965)	Public-voluntary	1 year (1962)	4,470	85	1.9%
Kornitzer, Rowe (1968)	Voluntary	1 year (1966)	9,614	109	1.1%
Edmonton, Canada (1969)	Public	2 years (1967–68)	3,086	43	1.4%
Kornitzer (1968)	Public-voluntary	Unclear	664	15	2.2%
L.A. County Dept. Adoption (1967)	Public	2 years (1965–66)	4,910	129	2.6%
Lefkowitz (1969)	Voluntary	5 years (1965–69)	8,040	82	1.0%
Kadushin, Seidl (1971)	Public	8 years (1960–68)	2,945	85	2.8%
Goldring, Tutleman (1970)	Public	1 year (1968–69)	2,384	75	3.1%
TOTAL			34,499	648	1.87%

One agency devoted to placement of children with special needs indicated a disruption rate of 11 per cent over a follow-up period (Welfare Research, Inc., 1977, p. 22). Spaulding for Children, another agency that specialized in the placement of special-needs children and that, between 1968 and 1976, placed 199 older and/or handicapped children, found that its "disruption" rate was about 10.6 per cent (Unger, Dwarshuis, Johnson, 1977, p. 67).

This recapitulation of studies on adoption disruptions necessitates a modest revision of the summary statement made earlier in this chapter (p. 517) about adoption outcomes. The generally low disruption rate is a confirmation of the fact that, although most adoptions are successful, adoptions under agency auspices are somewhat more likely to be successful than independent adoptions. But adoptive placements of children with special needs, although generally successful, are likely to be more problematic, with placements of older and handicapped children being somewhat more difficult than those involving transracial or international adoptions. However, most of the children returned to the agency after adoptive placement were subsequently placed successfully in other homes. As a consequence of subsequent successful replacement of children after the first adoptive disruption, only 2 per cent of the two hundred children placed by Spaulding have had to be returned to foster care or an institution.

The fact that children have been successfully placed following a disrupted adoption indicates the desirability of terminating a difficult placement rather than struggling against heavy odds to salvage it. This fact also suggests the complexity of variables that result in a successful placement and the futility of assigning blame for the disruption. Both the worker and the family are likely to feel a sense of failure and guilt. If the worker is to be helpful to the family in this situation, he has to recognize, given the background of special-needs children, that some failures are to be expected, that compatibility between family and child cannot always be predicted in advance even with the most perceptive diagnostic skill, and that some problems emerge only in the test of the living situation following placement. The worker can seek support from peers and supervisor, the adoptive family from other families in the adoptive organization with which they may be associated. The agency takes the point of view that "disruptions" must be accepted as just another step in the process through which the agency understands more clearly what the child needs and through which the adoptive family understands more clearly the kind of child it can accept and care for. Disruptions are seen as "a logical and mutual conclusion" to a complex experience in living together, not as an exercise in blame. If the worker is able to resolve immobilizing feelings of guilt and/or failure, the adoptive child and family can be helped toward a subsequently more successful experience. There must be an acceptance of the increased probability of adoptive placement failures as we seek to find homes for children who present more severe problems for placement (Unger, Dwarshuis, Johnson, 1977, pp. 195–232).

Once disruption takes place and the child needs to be removed, the worker's responsibility is to minimize the possible damage to the participants and to work for alternatives. The disappointment to the child needs to be recognized, and the extent to which the worker thinks he contributed to the disruption needs to be discussed. The worker can review the experience with the child to identify the factors that caused difficulty in this placement and that would need to be explicitly avoided in the next possible placement. The worker should share with the child the fact that the agency is still ready and willing to find another home for him.

The family, in reacting to failure, may blame the agency for ineptitude in placing the child and for failure to be sufficiently helpful to prevent disruption. The worker has to be ready to accept his contribution to the event and, in discussing it with the family, may learn how to handle a similar situation more successfully in the future.

The worker has to act as a bridge between the child and the family so that they can understand what has happened and divert energy devoted to blaming each other into more productive channels. The worker might help the family to assist the child in the move he now must make.

If there are other children in the family, their guilt, disappointment, and anxiety may also warrant some discussion (Donley, 1978).

Disruptions have some advantages in that they clarify the particular placement needs of the particular child. We now know more clearly the placement situations that need to be avoided.

Adopting parents, adopted children, and adoption workers may each contribute to disruption. Adopting parents may misjudge their ability to accept a child with special needs; they may fear failure and feel threatened by inevitable initial difficulties; they may expect too much of themselves and the child and not be sufficiently flexible in modifying expectations. Adoptees may still be emotionally tied to biological or foster parents and may be unable to accept the adoptive parents. Opposed to adoption, adoptees may manifest problems that are beyond the capacity of most parents. Workers may oversell a child, soft-pedaling the problem the adoptive parents will face; they may "stretch the family" by pressuring them to accept a child with special needs beyond the parents' preference; in their strong motivation to place a child, they may fail to heed the danger signs that might make them dubious about the wisdom of the decision.

PROBLEMS IN ADOPTION

We have noted some of the problems that are of concern to adoption agencies—the question of declining numbers of children surrendered for adoption, the problem of independent adoption, the problem of insufficient placements for special-needs children, the problem of adoptive disruptions, the problem of adoptees' rights and the "search." Some additional problems are discussed below.

1. Despite our discussion of the increased possibilities of adoptive placement for children with special needs—the minority-group child, the older child, the handicapped child—finding sufficient adoptive placements for such children continues to present a problem. This is particularly true for the children with multiple deterrents to placement: older minority-group children, minority-group children with handicaps, older children with handicaps, and so on.

There is clearly a hierarchy of preferences in the minds of adoptive applicants, the white unhandicapped infant being at the top of the ladder and the older, mentally retarded, physically disabled, minority-group child being toward the bottom. As children become increasingly scarce at the top of the hierarchy ladder, adoptive applicants, move down to a child who has lower preference for them. As a consequence of the siphoning off of children who were only yesterday regarded as being unplaceable because of lower preference, the children who remain behind and who are currently available for adoption are characterized by more serious problems. They generally present more than one kind of special need.

For instance, the Massachusetts Adoption Resource Exchange, in a letter to subscribers to whom they periodically send pictures and descriptions of the children available, tells the readers that:

> the ages and special needs of the children registered with the Exchange have changed over the past two years. The children who were waiting for homes in 1980 are as follows: white children 9 years old and younger children with serious physical disorders, emotional problems and serious intellectual needs (Down's Syndrome, cerebral palsy and blindness); school age brother and sister groups of 2, 3 and 4 children who should be placed together; black and mixed black and white children of all ages, some also having physical, emotional and intellectual needs.

Following are short descriptions of children with special needs waiting for adoptive placements in 1978 and listed with an adoption exchange. In each case, a picture of the child accompanies the description:

Donald is an active thirteen-year-old boy who is now in the seventh grade. He wears a hearing aid and as a younger child was operated on for a cleft palate and a harelip. The operation was successful. Donald loves baseball and outdoor activities in general.

Ricky is an eight-year-old mixed-racial boy with curly brown hair, brown eyes, and an olive complexion. He has above-average intelligence but he doesn't always work up to his potential. He was rejected from an adoptive home recently. This has caused a sense of insecurity in Ricky. This boy does very well in artwork and seems to have musical and dramatic potential. He is emotionally immature but a patient and giving family could give him the self-assurance he needs.

Walter has been in foster care for four years and has experienced many tantrums in the past. Therapy is recommended after placement; subsidy should be available for this. Walter is shy and apprehensive with strangers, but he likes to give and receive affection from those he knows. Although he has average intellectual ability, he is functioning slowly in school. Walter does have a tendency to develop respiratory problems and he is currently enuretic.

William is an eleven-year-old black child, shy and quiet. He is attending a special-education class, and it is felt that he will perform better in areas requiring manual dexterity rather than verbal skills.

Justine and William are brother and sister. . . . Justine is an eleven-year-old girl with blond hair and blue eyes. She has learning deficits . . . but can attend public school if she is enrolled in a special-education class. . . . William is twelve . . . has progressed very well in a special school and now is ready to attend public school. He is sometimes prone to exhibit aggressive behavior at school; however, he responds well to those he knows.

Ronald is an eighteen-month-old boy. Ronald is a mongoloid child, his development thus far has been slow; however, he does respond playfully to affection.

Joey is a six-year-old boy. He is perceptually handicapped and will need special classes to deal with the learning disabilities that have arisen because of this. Joey will also need a corrective operation because one of his eyes turns out. Though this young boy has been diagnosed to have bronchial asthma, he does enjoy playing ball and exploring new things.

Jimmy is a seven-year-old black child. He is blind and currently living at the state school for the blind. He has average potential in school. Hs is difficult to control but responds to warm firmness.

With the continuing shortage of white, unhandicapped infants, the definition of *hard-to-place* tends to be revised in the direction of greater difficulty. In 1978 the hard-to-place child was over eight years of age, of minority race, moderately retarded, or physically handicapped.

In 1978 ARENA (Adoption Resource Exchange of North America) had about one thousand children registered with them, 46 per cent of whom were described as slow or retarded; 55 per cent of the children needing homes were school-aged black children, seven years of age or older. It is probably true that no child can or should be identified as "unadoptable," yet it is true that some children are more difficult to place or are less adoptable than other children. The reality is that many more people than are needed come to the agency to offer their homes to white, unhandicapped infants. Very few applicants offer their homes to the mentally retarded or the physical handicapped child needing placement.

Chambers (1970) asked 175 adoptive applicants to indicate their willingness or unwillingness to adopt different kinds of special-needs children. Although slightly more than half indicated a willingness to consider physically handicapped or Spanish-American children, only 10 per cent would consider a child over five and less than 10 per cent were willing to consider the adoption of an emotionally disturbed child or a black child. The study notes that "willingness" is specific to a particular kind of child, and the couple who may be willing to accept an older child may not be willing to accept a black child.

Simon and Altstein (1977) substantiate the fact that the willingness to accept one kind of child with special needs does not necessarily suggest willingness to accept another kind of hard-to-place child. Although the parents in their study had all adopted a child of a different race, only 14 per cent indicated a willingness to accept a child as old as five years of age. The mentally retarded child was acceptable to only 1 per cent of the group, and only 8 per cent indicated that they would have been willing to adopt a child with a physical handicap "if they could not have obtained the child they did" (p. 86).

A study of the operations of the New York State adoption exchange indicated the limited interest in the special-needs children available for adoption (Grossman, Epstein, Neilson, 1976). The exchange was legislated in 1971 as a service that compelled the listing of every child legally freed for adoption for whom no home had been found after six months and of every family approved for adoption with whom no child had been placed for six months. "However there was little match between the children registered, largely older, non-white and handicapped and the families registered, most of whom wanted healthy white babies and cuddlers." In January 1975, of the 1,346 families listed, 94 per cent "would accept only a white child under 4 without a handicap. Only 5 per cent were interested in adopting a black child" (p. 1).

Although it is true that some applicants have an initial preference for a special-needs child because of ideology, political orientation, a heightened sense of civic responsibility, or some personal experience, this group of adopters is decidedly a minority. It would be unrealistic to expect that the problem of adoption of special-needs children could even begin to be resolved by the preferences of this small group of applicants. Here the agency has to educate the community to the availability of such children; actively seek homes through outreach; actively motivate prospective adoptive parents to accept such children; remove disincentives to such adoption by modifying requirements, by prompt home studies, and by immediate placement; and intensify incentives by offering support subsidies for maintenance and medical care.

Despite the attention and concern given to the placement of children with special needs and the reiterated emphasis on the changing definition of the adoptable child, the fact is that the largest percentage of children currently placed for adoption still conform to the traditional picture: the white, unhandicapped, infant child. For instance, some states reported statistics on the number of handicapped children adopted in 1976 and the number of normal children adopted. Michigan, which placed a total of 1,895 normal children in 1974, placed 107 physically, mentally, or emotionally handicapped children—about .05 per cent of the children placed. Minnesota placed 1,508 normal children and 14 handicapped children, 0.01 per cent of the total. Massachusetts placed 854 normal children and 72 handicapped, 0.08 per cent of the total. During the same year, 70 per cent of all adoptees in Massachusetts, 69 per cent in Michigan, and 74 per cent in Minnesota were under two years of age at the time of placement. The median age of children at the time of placement in these three states was about five months, indicating that most children placed were infants (National Center for Social Statistics, 1976, Tables 4, 9, 10, 11).

As the pressure to free those children who have remained in foster care for some time intensifies, the likelihood is that a larger number of older minority-group children will require agency service in finding homes. This presents a problem for the agencies because placement of special-needs children requires considerable time, effort, and skill. The Los Angeles Department of Adoptions, based on its considerable experience with such placements, estimates that it takes two and one half times as long to place older children as it does to place infants (Larsen, 1978, p. 33).

Adoption agencies have frequently been accused of being reluctant to attempt the placement of children with special needs. This may have been true at an earlier period, but more recently the data tend to dispute this. Seidl (1972) arranged for calls to adoptive agencies inquiring about placement of white and minority group children and taped workers' responses. The responses "strongly suggest that caseworkers responded more favorably to requests for transracial adoption than to requests about adopting a white child" (p. 120), indicating the receptivity of workers to such adoptions. A nationwide questionnaire study of agency attitudes and practice toward adoptive placement of retarded children (Krisheff, 1977) indicated that the largest percentage of agencies were favorably oriented toward attempting such placements and were making efforts in that direction. Meezin, Katz, and Russo (1978) found that two-thirds of the couples who finally resorted to black market adoptions because unhandicapped white infants were not available through the agencies reported that the worker had discussed with them the availability of special-needs children. They were not interested (p. 84). The fact is that adoption agencies have been routinely placing older, nonwhite, and handicapped children in adoptive homes. Shyne and Schroeder (1978) estimated that at the time of their nationwide survey in 1977, of the 102,000 needing adoption service, public child welfare agencies had placed for adoption 29,000 children older than six years of age and 10,000 black children (pp. 131–32).

2. Although there is a trend toward greater public acceptance of adoption, there are still residues of derogatory community attitudes regarding adoption. Kirk (1964) notes that in a study of comments encountered by adoptive parents, some 32 per cent had been told, "How lucky you are that you didn't have to go through all the trouble of pregnancy and birth as I did"; 22 per cent had encountered such comments as "How well you care for the child, just like a real mother"; 82 per cent heard "Tell me, do you know anything about the child's background?" All these comments are subtle devaluations of adoptive parenthood (p. 30). Even the seemingly complimentary comments ("Isn't it wonderful of you to have taken this child") encountered by 92 per cent of the respondents tended to differentiate the adoptive parent from the biological parent.

Another aspect of this problem is that the public is still not fully aware of, and does not fully accept, the viewpoint of social agencies regarding adoption. Adoption workers are still often accused of being arbitrary, of "playing God," of unnecessarily withholding children from adoptive parents, and so on. It is partly because of this feeling that the public has not more vigorously supported efforts to legislate against independent placement, and there is still considerable controversy as to whether social workers should be given primary control of adoptions. Adoption concerns social relationships. Adoption "creates" parent–child relationships and directly affects the marriage. Clearly, then, according to our definition of *child welfare*, it is within the professional responsibilities of the social work profession. Yet social workers have not succeeded in convincing the public that they should be primarily, if not exclusively, responsible for bringing parentless children and childless "parents" together.

3. The religious requirement in adoption is the subject of considerable controversy and hence another problem for the field of adoption (National Council of Churches, 1965). One aspect of the problem results in a decided imbalance between supply and demand for some religious groups. Because there are relatively few illegitimate Jewish children available, the ratio of Jewish adoptive applicants to Jewish adoptable children is higher than for other religious groups, forcing the Jewish applicant into the gray or black adoption market. Thus, at a time when the median ratio was three adoptive couples to every white infant, the ratio in agencies serving Jewish couples was eight adoptive couples to every white infant (Brieland, 1959, p. 24).

An even more significant and more general difficulty is related to the inequity imposed on the nonreligious applicant. He is penalized for his agnosticism by his inability to qualify as an adoptive applicant. The American Ethical Union, a society of humanists, expresses the dilemma and point of view of this group of potential adopters. Because Ethical Culture is not a religion, there are "literally no babies for them to adopt." They comment:

> Americans, providing that they meet all other standards, deserve equal opportunity to adopt children openly, without having to profess a religion to which they do not honestly subscribe, through legitimate adoption channels. In this area, as in any other, there should be no discrimination on the basis of religious beliefs [*The New York Times*, October 11, 1959].

The Child Welfare League of America (1973) suggests that although the religious faith of the natural parents should be respected and—wherever possible—followed in the selection of an adoptive home for the child, "placement of children should not be restricted, in general, to homes with formal church affiliation" (p. 25). This point of view is rejected by the National Conference of Catholic Charities, which has been the most active organization in advocating the retention and the extension of the religious requirements in adoption. The Conference feels that "Among the factors that play a part in successful adoption, the weightiest, although not the sole element, is the religious status" [of prospective adopters].

A third aspect of the problem is that, supposedly, the adoption of children is denied or delayed if there are no coreligionist applicants available at the time they are released for adoption. There is no study that substantiates such denial of adoption, except in some few instances (Cawley, 1957; *Columbia Law Review*, 1954).

But there is the question of the right of the relinquishing parent to determine this aspect of the child's future life. If the parent's power to determine where the child shall live, how he will be raised, educated, and cared for is terminated, why not the control of religious affiliation? Religious matching of adoptive applicants and child "wherever practicable" (as most state laws require) involves, in effect, the determination of the child's religious affiliation by the bioparent (Ramsey, 1959).

The more recent trend has been toward an easing of the religious qualification in adoption. In 1971 the New Jersey Supreme Court overturned a lower court ruling that denied an adoption petition in the case of parents who were professed atheists (Gollub, 1974). In 1970 Massachusetts and Maryland revised their legislation so as to permit adoption without reference to the child's religious background. A New York State revision permits the biomother to express her lack of preference for a particular religion for her child's future home. A mother who professes no religious preference usually signs a waiver giving the agency the power to decide on the religious factor in placement.

With the current deemphasis on matching as a necessary or even a desirable criterion for placement, some of the rationale for the religious protection requirement loses force. Giving greater priority to the child's needs has led to a more stringent definition of "whenever practicable." A delay of more than a month or two in the child's placement to satisfy the religious requirement may be regarded as impractical because it denies the child the speediest permanent placement decision. Religion is now more frequently a significant but not a controlling factor in adoption decisions.

4. With the decrease in the number of children available for adoption, adoptive agencies are beginning to face a question of survival. In the early 1970s, such agencies were beginning to diversify their functions, moving out from adoption to family counseling and family-life education. Such diversification provides the agency with a useful service to occupy staff. A small percentage of agencies have chosen to discontinue their adoption service altogether. Other agencies have reduced staff. The Los Angeles County Department of Adoption, which employed 277 caseworkers in March of 1970, had only 115 such workers in July, 1978 (Larsen, 1978, p. 17).

It is likely that the next two decades will see a reduction in the demand for adoptive services. Low birthrates after 1955–1960 in North America and Europe will result in a smaller group of adopters in the near future. The twenty-five to thirty-five age group, which supplies the largest number of adoptive applicants, is likely to be smaller than it has been during the 1970s.

Technological and ideological factors may also decrease the level of adoptive demand. Remedies for infertility and sterility have steadily eroded the number of couples who have to resort to adoption. Greater control over the childhood diseases that once caused sterility and the venereal diseases that once resulted in miscarriages and stillbirths has increased the ability of some women to conceive children and carry them to term. The perfection of artificial insemination techniques and the growing acceptance of this procedure may further reduce the number of couples who seek to meet the problem of childlessness through adoption (Brandon, Warner, 1977). A nationwide survey of obstetricians and gynecologists, for example, yielded an estimate of 6,000 to 10,000 children who are born annually in the United States as a result of artificial insemination (Curie-Cohen et al., 1979, p. 588). Thus, a fairly substantial number of possible adoptive applicants have resorted to an alternative procedure in response to problems of fertility.

The successful implantation, in 1978, of an ovum fertilized in the laboratory promises another alternative for a large number of women who might otherwise have had to resort to adoption.

Childlessness has been increasingly accepted as an optional lifestyle. The decision not to become a parent no longer requires an apology nor occasions as much discomfort as it previously did. The concern regarding population growth and the ideology of the women's movement contribute toward the growing acceptance of childlessness. As a consequence, more infertile couples may choose to adjust to their situation by accepting their childlessness rather than attempting to change their situation through adoption.

On the supply side there may be a continued long-term reduction in the number of children available for adoption. The single-mother–out-of-wedlock-child family is only one type of single-parent female-headed family. Any policy changes to the advantage of the growing number of single-parent female-headed families generally will be an advantage to the never-married mother as well. Special measures such as housing for single-parent families, increases in day-care facilities, and special maintenance allowances for single-parent families will reduce the difficulties of keeping and caring for the child of the unmarried mother as well as of other single parents. Consequently such mothers are likely to be in a better position in the future to raise their own child rather than surrendering the child for adoption. Policy changes are likely to move in the direction of reducing disincentives to surrender the child for adoption.

The general climate of social attitudes has changed in a direction that makes it easier for the unmarried mother to keep and raise her child. Less stigma and social rejection are associated with the status of unmarried mother. An increasingly neutral, less punitive attitude toward the unmarried mother attenuates the incentives toward surrender.

Demographic changes during the next decade will also result in a probable reduction in the number of children available for adoption. The low birthrates of 1965–1975 project a smaller group of adolescents and young adults in the near future. This is the age group for which the rate of illegitimacy is highest and for whom the difficulties in keeping and raising the child are greatest. The pressure of circumstances predisposing to surrender are great for this group, as well as the pressure from significant others, such as parents, on whom the adolescent is likely to be dependent. A decrease in the size of this group will decrease the number of children available for adoption.

The lowering of the age at which a child is regarded as a minor and legally dependent on parents may likewise result in a reduction of the number of children available for adoption. The trend is toward a reduction in the age of emancipation from twenty-one to eighteen. A larger number of single pregnant adolescents will be in a position to make independent decisions regarding abortion and keeping their child without involving the consent of their parents. The greater weight of such parental pressure has been in the direction of surrender of the out-of-wedlock child. Earlier emancipation will tend to reduce the potency of pressure in this direction.

It is not likely that with reductions in the number of white, unhandicapped infants available, a continuing high number of nonrelatives adoptions will be made. There are currently a sizable number of older, handicapped, minority-group children available for adoption. The number of such children available is likely to increase as foster-care agencies review their case loads and move more actively toward the termination of parental rights of those parents who have manifested little, if any, consistent continuing interest in their child. But if past experience in the shortage of white, unhandicapped infants is suggestive, only a small percentage of potential adopters are likely to move to adopt their newly released children. A larger percentage of potential adopters, moving down their hierarchy of preferences, soon reach a point where the decision not to adopt at all is more acceptable than the decision to adopt the kind of child who is available.

All of these changes move in the same direction. Reductions in both supply of and demand for adoptable children suggest some leveling off, if not a continuation, of the reduction in the number of adoptions completed each year. Adoption services may be less significant in the future.

Mitigating the effect of these changes is the increased emphasis on the child's entitlement to permanence. This intensifies efforts at finding adoptive placements for a larger percentage of the children in foster care and increases the significance of adoptive services. Staff time no longer needed for a reduced number of infant placements can be shifted to a more concerted focus on special-needs adoption.

TRENDS

We have previously noted some trends in adoption that may now be summarized. There has been a decrease in nonrelative adoptions since 1970. Children are being placed more often under agency auspices and increasingly under public child-welfare-agency auspices. There are fewer white, healthy infants available for adoption, so efforts have increased to place nonwhite, older, and handicapped children. One aspect of this trend is the interest in transracial adoptions. Other innovative procedures include a greater variety in recruitment approaches, the acceptance of single-parent adoptions, the development of a national adoptive exchange program, and the use of adoptive subsidies.

1. There is a trend toward greater flexibility in recruitment procedures in order to develop interest in the hard-to-place child. One approach involves a vigorous program of publicity. This has required some reevaluation of confidentiality that kept children from being identified publicly but had the unintended effect of concealing their need. The Louise Wise Adoption Service, in deciding on a program of publicity for adoptable physically handicapped children, said, "We believe it is more important for . . . [the children] to find loving, permanent homes of their own than to go unphotographed, unpublicized, and homeless." Brief descriptions of each of six physically handicapped children, as well as photographs, were made available to newspapers. The response to this particular campaign was immediate and overwhelming: over five hundred couples responded. The agency evaluated the applicants immediately, and within three months, four of the six children were placed. Weingarten (1958), the public relations consultant who supervised the campaign, argues that confidentiality implies that the "agency will use information responsibly in the client's behalf, that this responsibility involves not only protection against improper

disclosure but sharing appropriate information with appropriate persons at appropriate times in order to provide the client with the best possible service."

The Los Angeles County Bureau of Adoption at one time published a quarterly bulletin, *The Top Ten Tots,* about hard-to-place children. In Canada over 130 Ontario newspapers carry a syndicated column called "Today's Child," which presents children needing adoption. The *Detroit Sunday News* has had a special feature entitled "A Child Is Waiting" since 1968. As a consequence of this publicity, homes have been found for a total of 236 children over a six-year period. "Adoption Day in Court" is a procedure used in Los Angeles to publicize adoptions. Media representatives interview and film families waiting in court to finalize their adoptions.

The pioneer use of television by the Minnesota Division of Child Welfare as an aid in recruiting homes for hard-to-place children has now become standard procedure (Fricke, 1956). The Los Angeles County Department of Adoptions "shows" adoptable children each week as part of a regularly scheduled television program. In almost all cases, these are hard-to-place children. Children under two years of age are personally presented; pictures of older children are shown. There is no indication that the children are hurt by this procedure, although some object to what they call the commercial sale of children.

Some agencies have used closed-circuit television and one-way mirrors to present adoptable children to parents without their being aware that they are being observed for possible placement. Videotape has also been used to "show" a child who lives in one section of the country to prospective parents living elsewhere (Paget, 1969).

Some cities have arranged an Adoption Week to promote adoption (Sarmiento, 1969). An Adoptive Father of the Year is selected, and all the babies available for adoption are brought to a picnic arranged at a local park for all adoptive families in the area. Agencies have experimented with an "adoption party" sponsored by the agency (Edgar, 1975). Fourteen or fifteen children meet an equal number of adoptive couples in an informal get-together where they can mingle freely, play games, talk, and get to know each other.

Agencies have used parents who have adopted children with special needs in outreach programs to help find and then share their experience with prospective adopters. They have used classified ads to recruit adoptive parents, have provided special feature stories to newspapers on special-needs children, and have used spot announcements on radio stations with a minority-group audience.

There is a much more explicit and active attempt to involve interested, experienced adoptive parents in the process of selecting and preparing new adopters. This is particularly true for the placement of children with special needs (Shireman, Watson, 1972; Middlestadt, 1977). Experienced adoptive parents meet with applicants on a "family-to-family" basis, attend group meetings as resource people to share their experiences and know-how, and become part of the "support system" available to the adoptive parent following the placement of a child.

2. There is a trend toward the expansion and computerization of adoption resource exchanges. *Adoption resource exchange* has been defined by the Child Welfare League as "an organized means of exchanging information among agen-

cies about children for whom they have difficulty in finding appropriate homes and about adoptive applicants for whom they have no suitable children" (Felton, 1953, p. 26). Ohio was the first to originate a statewide exchange, and most tend to be an intrastate resource. However, such a resource can be extended to a regional level and, ultimately, to a national level.

The adoption exchange has the advantage of increasing the opportunities for placement because it makes available a larger pool of potential adopters for the child, and a larger pool of children for the applicant (Jacquith, 1962). Agencies list the children available for placement with a central adoption-resource exchange. A summary of the essential descriptive data accompanies each name. At the same time, the agencies send summaries of data on adoptive parents who are waiting for children and who have expressed an interest in and a capacity for accepting hard-to-place children.

Adoption exchanges are of the greatest immediate benefit to the hard-to-place child. Schapiro (1957) notes that "state experience with adoption clearance services shows that almost all of the children placed through them are children of minority groups and mixed racial parentage [and] those who are older [or] handicapped" (p. 46). Leatherman (1957) cites the Texas Adoption Exchange as an important factor in the adoptive placement of a sizable number of older children.

In 1967 the Child Welfare League of America established a national adoption-resource exchange that includes Canadian agencies and is known as ARENA (Adoption Resource Exchange of North America).

Between 1967, when it was organized, and 1976, ARENA placed a total of 1,760 children. This is an average of somewhat less than 200 children each year. Although the results are modest given the number of children supposedly awaiting placement, the achievements are notable from the point of view of the kind of children for whom homes were found. A sizable number of the placements were of older children, children who were mentally retarded or physically handicapped, minority-group children, and siblings placed together. Often the children were hard to place for more than one reason.

The California Department of Social Welfare's Adoptions Resource Referral Center was the first adoption exchange in the country to computerize its operations. The Adoption Reform Act of 1978 provides for a government-sponsored national adoption-information exchange using computers and data-processing methods to identify children waiting for adoptive homes and applicants interested in adopting.

3. Adoption maintenance subsidy is another incentive designed to increase adoptive placements for special-needs children. Based on their nationwide survey of children receiving public child welfare service, Shyne and Schroeder (1978) estimated that a total of 102,000 children were legally free for adoption but that one-third of the group required an adoption subsidy if they were to be placed (p. 125). Most of these were children older than nine years of age. The Child Welfare League of America adoption standards recommended consideration of subsidized adoptions as early as 1958. In 1968 New York became the first state to enact such legislation. Within the next ten years, a total of forty-one states and the District of Columbia adopted such a program.

Advocates back the subsidy because it is cost-effective, being more economical for the community than either foster care or institutionalization, and because it offers the child the guarantee of continuity, stability, permanence, and the identity of a family name.

Adoption subsidies are employed as a recruitment device and as an inducement to foster parents who are already caring for a child to adopt that child. Adoption subsidies assist in recruiting families for adoption who might not otherwise consider adoption because of limited income or who might not consider the adoption of a child with special problems without some additional financial assistance.

In subsidized adoption, the agency continues to make financial contributions to the adoptive family after the legal adoption of the child. Agencies have for some time subsidized the adoption of physically handicapped children by continuing to pay for the medical care of the child. Agencies have also subsidized the joint placement of a group of siblings. In special instances, agencies have subsidized adoptive parents for a limited period so that psychiatric treatment might be provided for an adoptive child.

Special-service subsidies may also be made available to cover the legal and court costs of adoption, remedial education, speech and hearing therapy, physiotherapy, wheelchairs, and braces.

An agency might agree to a time-limited subsidy to permit a family to adjust to the loss of a wife's earnings when she leaves her job upon placement of the child. These are special, time-limited transitional uses of subsidy to ensure the success of the placement (Sternay, 1959; Wheeler, 1969).

Subsidized adoption maintenance is quite different. The community makes a monthly grant to the adoptive family to meet the routine expenses of rearing the adopted child. It thus makes adoption possible for low-income families that could not otherwise afford to adopt a child. The legislation is designed to make more adoptive homes available for hard-to-place children. For instance, the Illinois State Department of Children and Family Services may provide subsidies to "persons who adopt physically or mentally handicapped, older, and other hard-to-place children." The California legislation is designed to encourage the adoption of children for whom "permanent homes were not readily available because of age, physical handicap, or ethnic background."

In addition to subsidized adoption for the usual groups of special-needs children, some states have included those children "not placed within six months of the time they became legally available for adoption." The six-month delay in placement is regarded as ipso facto confirmation that the children are hard to place.

Some legislation restricts subsidization to adoptive parents who have previously cared for the child in foster care. This permits the foster parent to adopt the child without loss of board-care support. Many of the children adopted as a result of the availability of subsidization were. in fact, formerly foster children in the home.

Subsidized adoption has, in fact, achieved the objective of increasing the adoption opportunities of children with special needs. For instance, in 1975, 561 subsidized adoptions were completed in New York City, 416 of nonwhite children, 145 of white children (Dall, 1977, p. 35). A recapitulation of subsidized adoptions in six states—Connecticut, Illinois, Iowa, New Jersey, New York, and Vermont—indicated that "the largest proportion of children adopted were over 6 in every state" (Jones, 1975, p. 738). Many were physically handicapped, mentally retarded, or emotional disturbed, and a disproportionate percentage were black. Almost 90 per cent of the children adopted through the subsidized adoption program were adopted by their foster parents.

An analysis of comparative costs indicates that subsidized adoptions do result in substantial savings to the community (Jones, 1975, pp. 723, 740, 742).

A special direct-service demonstration project conducted in Chicago in 1972–1974 indicates the value of and the problems associated with subsidized adoption (Hargrave, Shireman, Connor, 1975). One hundred and twelve black children in foster care in Chicago were identified as being appropriate for adoption, more than half (54.5 per cent) being, in fact, legally freed for adoption. The evidence of the demonstration project is clear. Over a period of sixteen to eighteen months, project workers were able to obtain adoption for 75 of the 112 children—about 70 per cent of the group. About 75 per cent of these children (56 children) were adopted by their foster parents, and subsidy was the factor that permitted 7 out of 8 foster-parent adoptions. The project established the "adoptability of black children in foster care," and "subsidy was clearly a casework tool of considerable importance" in making this possible (p. 45). A group of physically handicapped children also achieved adoption with the help of subsidies.

Some children were not accepted as adoptees by the foster parents with whom they were living, and the project, despite determined efforts at recruitment, was unable to find adoptive homes for them. Retarded and emotionally disturbed children were the most difficult to place.

The change of status holds dubious advantages for the long-term foster parents. Although they gain a greater guarantee that the child will remain with them, the removal of the child is not actually a serious threat. Caring for a child with special needs in a stable, ongoing situation, they recognize that the chances of removal of the child are not very great and that the agency will keep the placement intact if this is the foster parents' preference. Changing to adoptive status does not mean any change for the better in the maintenance allowance, and the foster parents may be anxious about losing the allowance if their income increases above a given level, if state policy should change, or if they move to another state.

The adoptive family is not eligible for subsidy in most states if the family income exceeds certain limits. For instance, in March 1976, the income eligibility criterion in New York State for a family of four, including the adopted child, was $14,549. This eligibility criterion required an annual review of the family's financial status in order to determine continuing eligibility for subsidy. Foster families close to the eligibility maximum may be hesitant to move into subsidized adoption because of uncertainty about continuing support—a support that would not be jeopardized if they continued as foster families (Dall, 1977).

An additional concern of serious significance to these foster parents, many of whom are past middle age, is the indefinite legal commitment to the care of the child. They lose the freedom of exercising their options to give up the care of the child in case of serious illness or the death of one of the foster parents. Changing from foster care to adoptive status means providing for some alternative guardianship for the child within the family in case of illness or death, as the agency is no longer guardian. Older foster parents may also be hesitant about the inheritance implications of change of status because adoption makes the child entitled to such benefits.

In some instances, the foster parents risk the loss of free medical care and educational benefits for the child that are available with certainty in long-term foster care but are dubiously available to the adoptive parent. There is a further risk in the loss of supportive services from the agency, obligatory in the case of foster care and less certain in the case of adoption. In addition, the foster family must be willing to share the details of its financial situation with the agency in order to qualify for adoptive subsidy.

Given these considerations, it is not surprising that workers associated with Chicago's subsidized-adoption demonstration project found foster parents suspicious of subsidization and mistrustful of agency intentions (Hargrove, Shireman, Connor, 1975).

Some foster parents can be induced, with the help of subsidies, to adopt the child placed with them; others cannot. Some 40 per cent of the foster families approached by workers in the Chicago demonstration project decided not to adopt the children in their care. What distinguished this group of foster families from the group that decided to adopt? The child in care was more often severely handicapped or of adolescent age. The foster mother who decided to adopt, as contrasted with her nonadopting sister, was more strongly child-centered and more strongly attached to the child and enjoyed the child more unequivocally (Hargrove, Shireman, Connor, 1975, pp. 64–68).

In raising the question of subsidized adoption, the worker is challenging the foster parents to make explicit their level of commitment to the foster child. The challenge also contains the implicit threat of possible removal of the child. If the foster parents refuse to consider adoption and the worker has strong convictions about the greater desirability of a subsidized adoption, the worker has the obligation of making efforts to find an alternative home for the child. If the search for a home is unsuccessful, as it might be because of problems that many of these children present, the worker has to fall back to the position of maintaining the child in the foster home. The entire process, from challenge or threat, to the maintenance of the status quo, is apt, however, to sour relations between the foster family and the agency.

There is a further problem for the worker of violating the older child's need for stability and continuity by replacement for adoption, if the foster home in which he has lived continuously for some time is not interested in adoption. The worker faces the decision of disrupting a well-established relationship in the expectation that providing a permanent home for the child will ultimately be more beneficial. The risk for the child is a temporary discontinuity in the hope of achieving greater permanence, with some possibility that the changeover may fail.

There are no national totals available regarding children placed for adoption as a consequence of the availability of a subsidy. Although the system is new and growing in most states, the number of such adoptions is still limited.

In some states, funds for the program are minimal. The situations in which subsidy is available are, in some instances, very limited, and the eligibility requirements are often ambiguous.

The U.S. Children's Bureau has formulated a model state-subsidized Adoption Act and Regulations as a guide to the states (Katz, Gallagher, 1975). Although the model act takes the position that the needs of the child for an adoptive home are the basis for subsidy and that the financial condition of the adopting family is not a consideration, every state, except Michigan, applies a means test as a qualification. The family has to establish, and continue to certify each year, that its income is below a state-established level in order to continue to be eligible for subsidy.

Because the subsidy program requires a yearly review of income for subsidy adjustment, it continues the involvement of the adoptive family with the agency. Agencies and some adoptive parents see this continuing contact as reassuring and helpful (Goldman, Linde, 1969). Some contend that such periodic checks are not necessary. Maryland's program, for instance, requires "no annual reporting on income" (Polk, 1970, p. 58). As Watson (1972) says, "The task is to devise a system of fiscal accountability for subsidized adoptions that does not insist on the casework involvement of the family, that does not give the impression of checking up to see how the adoption is working out, and that does not imply that the agency has any continuing responsibility" (p. 228). An annual affidavit from the family as to its financial situation may be the answer.

4. Widening the pool of adoptive applicants by accepting single parents is part of the effort to increase placement opportunities for special-needs children. Applications from nonmarried adults are accepted only when two-parent families are not available. Agency policy generally states that such applicants will be considered only for the placement of special-needs children. Price (1975) raises questions about such a policy in reviewing the general question of single-parent adoptions. He notes that "if a single parent is not deemed suitable to care for a normal child, there should generally be no consideration of him or her as a potential parent to a problem child" (p. 13). Such placements have been made with single, divorced, or widowed women and, occasionally, with single men (Branham, 1970; Costin, 1970; Kadushin, 1970a). The single applicant, to be acceptable, must have close contact with an extended family (to provide help and male relatives as surrogate fathers) and a healthy sexual identification without hostility toward the opposite sex. She must also have good health, because illness would rob the child of his one parent; the financial capacity to care for the child without working; or a reasonably permanent, viable plan for child care. She must be a mature, stable person whose motive for adoption is primarily oriented toward the child's needs.

The registration with ARENA of single parents approved for adoption increased from 33 in 1970 to 209 in 1975. Actual placements of adoptees with single parents through the exchange increased much more modestly, from 5 such placements in 1970 to 14 in 1975. However, the Los Angeles County Department of Adoption, which pioneered such placements, has increased this service more markedly. Whereas single-parent adoptions accounted for 0.5 per cent of all children placed by the agency in 1966–1967, such placements accounted for 9 per cent of all adoptions in 1975 (Anderson, 1976, pp. 8–10). Between 1965 and 1975, this agency made 289 single-parent adoptive placements.

A committee for single adoptive parents was formed in Washington, D.C., in 1973. It acts as an information service to prospective single adoptive parents and publishes a "Handbook for Prospective Single Parents."

A study (Shireman, Johnson, 1976) of thirty-one single adopters showed that they were generally women of moderate income engaged in professional occupations such as teaching and nursing. Although noted as mature with a high capacity for nurturing a child, many were still not completely emancipated from their parents: "They were strongly tied to and had much interaction with parents and siblings with a corresponding lack of involvement with friends" (p. 107). This may have reflected the agencies' attempts to select single applicants who did have contact with an extended family that could serve as "backup" for care of the child and as a source of male identification. Fifty per cent of these parents had lived in a single-parent home during some time in their childhood, so that they were not strangers to the single-parent family.

A follow-up study of eighteen single-parent adoptions three to four years after placement showed most of the children to be adjusting well; in only two cases was there some question about the child's emotional adjustment (Shireman, Johnson, 1976). Some 60 per cent of the parents had not told the child of adoption at age four, indicating that "telling" was problematic for the group. Most frequently day care or kindergarten was used for child care during the time the single parent was working; care by relatives was the resource of choice of a smaller number of parents.

Feigelman and Silverman (1977) compared mail questionnaire responses received from 58 single adoptive parents with some 650 responses obtained to the same questionnaires from adoptive couples. Single adopters were much more likely to live in an urban residence as compared with the suburban living situation of couple adopters. They were generally older and more highly educated than couples and were more likely to be nonwhite. The typical single adopter was a black women living in an urban area and employed in either education or social work. Single adopters "showed substantially greater willingness to adopt hard-to-place children and their attitudes were reflected in the kinds of children they actually adopted" (p. 422)—more frequently older, nonwhite children.

Single adoptive parents were just as likely to report that their child's overall adjustment was either "excellent" or "good," as did the adoptive couples, in subjectively assessing the adjustment of their children. In both cases, the overwhelming majority of adoptive children were reported as presenting no problems. Controlling for the age of children at the time of placement, single adopters were just as likely to indicate that they would encourage others to adopt as were couples. However, both single and couple adopters of older children were more reserved in their encouragement as compared with single and couple adopters of younger children.

The presumed danger of single-parent adoption—that the parent might become overly devoted to and overprotective of the child because there are no competitive strong affective attachments, as might be the case if there was a spouse in the picture—does not seem to be substantiated by the current limited data available.

Friends and community were less supportive of single adopters than they were of couples, and the lowest level of support was perceived by single male adopters. It is presumed that single-parent adoptions will gain in acceptance as the single-parent family comes to be perceived not as a deviant family form but as an alternative family form.

The agency might have to help the single parent develop some response to the feelings the child might have about having been denied a two-parent home.

Single-parent adoption also requires some change in the counseling of the unmarried mother. Currently social workers help the unmarried mother deal with her guilt and hesitancy in giving up the baby by assuring her that she is making it possible for the child to have a "normal" two parent family. Greater emphasis needs to be given to the fact that some single women are in a better position to provide adequate child care and that these are the women the agency would select.

Although single-parent applicants were previously perceived in terms of increasing the pool of adoptive parents for special-needs children, they are beginning to be seen as the applicants of choice for some kinds of children. Not having to divide affectional supplies and attention with a mate enables the single-parent adopter to focus on the needs of the adopted children. Some older disturbed children find it easier to cope with one parent than with two.

The one-parent life-style is an increasingly common option. The community support systems that have developed to assist single parents generally are important resources assisting the single-parent adopter in adjusting to single parenthood.

5. There is a trend toward an attenuation of the previously clear distinctions between foster care and adoption.

Earlier in the history of substitute care, foster-family care and adoptions were clearly separate and distinguishable services. There were identifiable differences between the nature of the children offered the two different services, the nature of the problems that occasioned the need for their care, the kinds of parents who were recruited for the two different services, the criteria employed in their selection, and their subsequent relationship to the agency. Currently, however, there is a more frequent interpretation of the two services so that they are less clearly distinguishable. The foster-family child today is the adoptive child tomorrow; the foster family often opts to adopt. There is less of a tendency to recruit foster families in terms of criteria that are different from those employed in adoptive family recruitment. The adoptive family receiving a subsidy is paid in the same way as the foster family for the care of the child. Long-term foster care is indistinguishable from adoption and might be regarded as a social adoption.

The recently enacted state laws that give foster parents priority if and when their foster child becomes legally available for adoption tend to vitiate differences between adoptive-parent applicants and foster-parent applicants. This tends to make foster and adoptive homes less distinctively different and more conceptually interchangeable. In line with this one agency avoids labeling applicants for the care of a child as either foster-care *or* adoptive applicants, seeing all as family resources and assessing all applicants in terms of the same criteria and the same standards in determining the decision to place or not to place a child (Hegarty, 1973).

Another agency places children who need foster care now but who might be available for adoption in the future with adoptive applicants who can accept the indefiniteness of such an arrangement (Gill 1975). The agency sees the program as "straddling" the traditional differences between foster care and adoptive placement.

The overlap between what were previously two relatively separate systems results not only from the fact that more foster parents are becoming adoptive parents but also from the fact that more foster children are being freed and placed for adoption.

The gradual merging of foster care and adoption means that these previously clearly separate units in an agency have to work more closely together (O'Neill, 1977; Dooley, La Franco, 1974). Because children placed for fostering may end up being adopted, the adoption unit has to be more concerned with all children who come to the agency for service, not only those explicitly referred for adoption. Standards for substitute-home selection methods and the goals of foster care and adoptive services have to be brought more into harmony with each other. The centralization of home finding for foster care and adoptive homes becomes desirable.

It might be noted that agencies have, for some time, been permitting foster parents to adopt, and the 1973 Child Welfare League Revised Adoption Standards notes the acceptability of this procedure. Several follow-up studies showed that children adopted by foster parents did as well as children adopted by parents who had been selected for adoption. Foster-parent adoption thus proves to be a viable permanent-placement option (Tizard, 1977; Lahti, 1978).

6. The sealed-record controversy and the search movement suggest a trend toward an orientation that gives greater consideration to the biological inheritance that the child brings to the adoptive situation. The influential report by Goldstein, A. Freud, and Solnit (1973) gives unequivocal emphasis to the primary importance of the "psychological parent," the "bread" parent who actually cares for the child, as compared with the birth parent. The movement for open records, on the other hand, points to the importance of the birth parents, of blood ties, of biological continuity, of origins and genealogy, and of genetics.

The emphasis given to background information and the search for the birth parent derives from an orientation that has been previously muted, if not expressly rejected, by the adoption field. It suggests the significance of genetic inheritance and biological factors that might contribute to shaping the development of the adoptee. By implication, it suggests that the environment of the adoptive home and the relationship with the adoptive parents are not the sole determinant in the life of the adoptee. The search gives greater visibility and significance to components contributed by nature in the nature–nurture configuration that makes the adoptee what he is and will be. This is quite a different orientation from the one that has general acceptance by the field, namely, that genetic–constitutional factors are of limited, clearly secondary importance and that the interpersonal environment of the adoptive home is the primary influence determining the adoptee's development.

Recent research conducted with sizable samples of adoptees, separated from birth parents in infancy, and compared with carefully matched controls may require some reconsideration of emphasis and a more respectful consideration of the influence of genetic inheritance as a determinant of the adoptive child's development. These include the detailed studies of adoptees in Denmark by Rosenthal, Wender, Kety, et al. (1968a, b, c, 1971, 1975), Rosenthal (1972), Wender (1972), Schulsinger (1972), Goodwin et al. (1973), and Hutchings and Mednick (1975); studies of children placed for adoption by agencies in St. Louis by Cunningham, Cadoret, Loftus, and Edwards (1975a, b); of children placed by agencies in Oregon by Heston (1966); of children born to women offenders while in reformatories or state training schools by Crowe (1972, 1974); of hyperactive adopted children by Morrison and Stewart (1973); and studies of the cognitive development of adoptees by Munsinger (1975a, b), Fisch (1976), and Scarr and Weinberg (1975, 1978).

The overall conclusions of these various research studies indicate that although the adoptive home can and does have the effect of maximizing potential, there is considerable resemblance between the adopted child and the birth parent from whom the child was early separated, in terms of a variety of significant factors.

7. There has been a trend toward organizing adoptive parents on local and and national levels. Adoptive-parent groups have advocacy functions, educative functions, and social and support functions. They provide a friendship group for people with a significant interest in common and provide the opportunity of discussing common problems. In some instances, they publish their own paper, as does the Organization for a United Response (OURS) in Minneapolis, an organization of adoptive parents who have adopted interracially or internationally.

National leadership for adoptive parents' organizations is provided by the North American Council on Adoptable Children, which publishes *Adoptalk*. Opposed to exclusive control of adoptions by social agencies, the organization distributes bumper stickers that proclaim, "Room for one more? Adopt."

The North American Center on Adoptions, organized in the mid 1970s as a division of the Child Welfare League of America, provides assistance to such organizations and engages in educational and advocacy activities concerning adoption. The center publishes a quarterly, *Adoption Report,* and along with adoptive parents' organizations and other groups, sponsors an annual North American Conference on Adoptable Children.

8. There is a trend toward ensuring greater parity between adoptive parenthood and bioparenthood. Some firms that provide maternity allowance benefits to the biomother are granting similar allowances to adoptive mothers. Civil service regulations permit the use of sick leave and vacation time so that an expectant mother can take paid leave before and after delivery. She may continue on unpaid leave for a time without jeopardizing her job. There is a growing demand to permit an adoptive mother to remain at home with the child for a short period of time after placement without jeopardizing her position. Exemplifying this trend, in 1977 Oregon passed a law permitting taxpayers to deduct the expenses involved in adoption, including attorney's fees, court costs, adoption filing fees, social agency fees, or doctor's fees. Since 1972 the I.B.M. Corporation has assisted with expenses incurred when an employee adopts a child.

9. There has been a trend toward the development of single-purpose specialized agencies within the adoption field. For some time, we have had agencies that specialized in international adoptions, such as Holt International Children's Service, the Pearl Buck Foundation, and International Social Services. More recently, however, special agencies have been organized to offer exclusive service to special-needs children for whom adoptive homes are hard to find. Spaulding for Children was among the first of such agencies. Earlier, short-lived precedents for this kind of effort had been established in the 1950s, Parents to Adopt Minority

Youngsters (PAMY) and Minority Adoption Recruitment of Children's Homes (MARCH) being examples.

Starting in Michigan, Spaulding units have been established in Ohio, New Jersey, and New York. Other agencies, specializing in the placement of "children who wait" (a term they prefer instead of "children with special needs") joined with Spaulding in 1975 to develop a national network calling themselves Family Builders Agencies. The network is coordinated by the North American Center on Adoption.

SUMMARY

Adoption, a second form of substitute care, involves the legal and permanent transfer of parental rights and obligations from the biological parent to the adoptive parent.

Adoptive parents may be related to the child, or they may be people who were formerly total strangers to the child. The latter are termed *nonrelative adoptions* and constitute about half of the total adoptions consummated.

Children available for nonrelative adoption are most frequently (80–85 per cent) born out of wedlock. Children of parents whose parental rights have been terminated by the courts because of neglect constitute another important source of adoptive children. Infertile married couples form the majority of nonrelative adoptive parents.

The agency, in selecting among adoptive applicants for the children available, takes the following factors into consideration:

1. The age of the parents in relation to the age of the child.
2. Adequate physical health.
3. The stability of the marriage.
4. Fertility status.
5. Religious affiliation.
6. Emotional health and maturity.
7. Capacity for parenthood.
8. Adjustment to sterility.
9. Motivation for adoption.
10. The reaction of significant others in the applicant's family.

Interviews with the couple are followed by individual interviews with husband and wife, home visits, and contact with references. After the study, a child is selected; the applicants are informed, and arrangements are made for a meeting between the applicants and the child. If the reactions of both the agency and the applicants are positive, the child is placed. After a period of six months or a year, legal steps are initiated to make the adoptive couple the legal parents of the child. During this period, the agency helps the parents and the child to make the adjustment to this socially established parent–child relationship.

Some of the recurrent problems related to adoption are the following:

1. Desirable procedures for sharing with the child the knowledge that he is adopted.

2. The parents' acceptance of their status as adoptive parents.
3. The special difficulties adoptive parents may have in child rearing.
4. Legal procedures in completing the adoption.

Group approaches have been effectively used at different points in the process of adoption: at intake, during the interim period between placement and legal completion of the adoption, and after legal adoption.

Nonrelative adoptions may also take place outside agency channels—in the gray market, in which doctors and lawyers act as intermediaries, often without fee, and in the black market, in which children are "sold" for a profit. These independent adoptions carry certain potential dangers to the child, the biological parents, the adoptive parents, and the community.

A recapitulation of evaluation studies of completed adoptions indicates that about 65 per cent are unequivocally successful and that an additional 18 per cent achieve some intermediate level of success; 17 per cent are deemed unsuccessful. The overall success rate of agency adoptions is computed at about 85.2 per cent, as contrasted with a success rate of 75 per cent for independent adoptions.

A recapitulation of studies of adoptive children receiving service at guidance clinics and psychiatric facilities shows a rate of 4 per cent of nonrelative adoptees at such agencies as compared with an estimated rate of 1 per cent of such children in the general population. However, adoptive children do not tend to show any unique symptoms—except, perhaps, greater aggressiveness—and it would appear that such children are no more disturbed than nonadopted children.

The following problems regarding adoptive services were identified and discussed:

1. The problem of the hard-to-place child.
2. Problems regarding transracial adoptions.
3. The controversy over agency control of adoption and independent placement.
4. The problem of religious qualifications for applicants.
5. The problem of the possible declining importance of adoption services.
6. The problem of the adoptee's "search."

The following trends were identified and discussed:

1. The trend toward increased numbers of adoptions, particularly under agency auspices, although the adoption rate remains steady.
2. The trend toward a decrease in the availability of white, nonhandicapped infants and a changing applicant-to-child ratio.
3. The trend toward increasing concern with and placement of nonwhite, older, or handicapped children.
4. The trend toward innovative procedures in recruiting adoptive parents, the development of adoption exchanges, the subsidization of adoptive families, and the acceptance of the single applicant.
5. A trend toward greater parity between adoptive parents and bioparents.
6. The trend toward a reduction in differences between foster-family care and adoption.

7. The trend toward specialized adoption agencies.

8. The trend toward a greater active involvement of adoptive parents in organizational activities relating to adoption.

9. The trend toward a greater consideration of genetic–constitutional factors in adoption.

BIBLIOGRAPHY

ABBOTT, GRACE. "Adoptions." *Encyclopedia of Social Science*. Ed. by Edwin R. Seligman. New York: The Macmillan Company, 1937.

———. *The Child and the State*, Vol. I. Chicago: University of Chicago Press, 1938.

ADAMS, JOHN E., and HYUNG KIM. "A Fresh Look at Intercountry Adoptions." *Children*, 18, 6 (November–December 1971), 214–21.

ADOPTION AND FOSTERING. "Telephone Advice Service." *Adoption and Fostering*, 85, 3 (1976), 29–30.

———. "Adoption Statistics." *Adoption and Fostering*, 88, 2 (1977), 62–64.

ANDERSON, C. WILSON. "Single Parent Adoption: The Viewpoints of Law and Social Work." Unpublished mimeograph, May 1976.

———. "The Sealed Record in Adoption Controversy." *Social Service Review*, 51, 2 (March 1977), 141–154.

ANDERSON, DAVID C. *Children of Special Value—Interracial Adoption in America*. New York: St. Martin's Press, Inc., 1971.

ANDREWS, ROBERTA. "The Transitional Method in the Adoption Placement of Older Infants and Young Toddlers." *Child Welfare*, 40 (May 1961).

ANSFIELD, JOSEPH G. *The Adopted Child*. Springfield, Ill.: Charles C Thomas, Publishers, 1971.

ARMATRUDA, CATHERINE, and JOSEPH BALDWIN. "Current Adoption Practices." *Journal of Pediatrics*, 38 (February 1951).

ARONSON, HOWARD. "The Problem of Rejection of Adoptive Applicants." *Child Welfare*, 39 (October 1960).

BAKER, NANCY C. *Baby Selling—The Scandal of Black Market Adoptions*. New York: Vanguard Press, 1978.

BARAN, ANNETTE, REUBEN PANNOR, and ARTHUR D. SOROSKY. "Open Adoption." *Social Work*, 21, 2 (March 1976), 97–100.

———, REUBEN PANNOR, and ARTHUR D. SOROSKY. "The Lingering Pain of Surrendering a Child." *Psychology Today* (June 1977), 58–60, 88.

———, ARTHUR SOROSKY, and REUBEN PANNOR. "The Dilemma of Our Adoptees." *Psychology Today* (December 1975), 38–42, 497–98.

BARRON, JEROME A. "Notice to the Unwed Father and Termination of Parental Rights Implementing Stanley vs. Illinois." *Family Law Quarterly*, 9 (1975), 527–546.

BASS, C. "Matchmaker, Match Matter—Older Child Adoption Failures." *Child Welfare*, 54, 7 (July 1975), 505–512.

BAYLEY, NESSIE. "Homefinding for Older Children and the Use of Groups." *Child Adoption*, 81, 3 (1975).

BEAVEN, PAUL. "The Adoption of Retarded Children." *Child Welfare*, 35 (April 1956).

BELKIN, ALICE. "Placing Older Children." *Adoption and Fostering*, 87, 1 (1977), 15–18.

BELL, VELMA. "Special Considerations in the Adoption of the Older Child." *Social Casework* (June 1959).

BELLUCCI, MATILDA T. "Treatment of Latency-Age Adopted Children and Parents." *Social Casework*, 56, 5 (May 1975), 297–301.

BENET, MARY K. *The Politics of Adoption*. New York: The Free Press, 1970.

BIGGERT, LINDA. "Some Observations on Placement of Older Children." *Adoption and Fostering*, No. 4 (1976), 21–24.

BILLINGSLEY, ANDREW, and JEANNE GIOVANNINI. "Research Perspectives on Interracial Adoption," in *Race Research and Reason: Social Work Perspectives*. Ed. by Roger Willer. New York: National Association of Social Workers, 1969.

———. *Children of the Storm—Black Children and American Child Welfare*. New York: Harcourt Brace Jovanovich, Inc., 1972.

BISKIND, SYLVIA. "The Group Method in Services to Adoptive Families." *Child Welfare*, **45**, 10 (December 1966), 561–564.

BODENHEIMER, BRIGITTE M. "New Trends and Requirements in Adoption Law and Proposals for Legislative Changes." *Southern California Law Review*, **49** (1975), 11–109.

BOEHM, BERNICE. *Deterrents to the Adoption of Children—Foster Care*. New York: Child Welfare League of America, December 1958.

BOHMAN, MICHAEL. *Adopted Children and Their Families—A Follow-up Study of Adopted Children, Their Background Environment and Adjustment*. Stockholm: Proprius, 1970.

BONHAM, GORDON S. "Who Adopts: The Relationship of Adoption and Social–Demographic Characteristics of Women." *Journal of Marriage and the Family*, **39** (May 1977), 295–306.

BORGOTTA, EDGAR F., and DAVID FANSHEL. *Behavioral Characteristics of Children Known to Psychiatric Outpatient Clinics*. New York: Child Welfare League of America, 1965.

BOWERS, SWITHEN. "The Child's Heritage—From a Catholic Point of View," in *A Study of Adoption Practice*, Vol. 12. Ed. by M. Schapiro. New York: Child Welfare League of America, 1956.

BOYNE, JOHN. "A Mental Health Note in Adoption of School-age and Teen-age Children." *Child Welfare*, **52**, 3 (March 1978), 196–199.

BRADLEY, TRUDY. *An Exploration of Case Workers' Perceptions of Adoptive Applicants*. New York: Child Welfare League of America, 1966.

BRANDON, JOAN, and JILL WARNER. "Artificial Insemination Donated and Adoption: Some Comparisons." *British Journal of Social Work*, **7** (Autumn 1977), 335–41.

BRANHAM, ETHEL. "One-Parent Adoptions." *Children*, **17**, 3 (May–June 1970), 103–106.

BRATFOS, OLE, et al. "Mental Illness and Crime in Adopted Children and Adoptive Parents." *Acta Psychiatrica Scandinavica*, **44**, 4 (1968), 376–384.

BREETZ, SHERYL L., and DELORES A. TAYLOR. *Helping Services Used by Adoptive and Natural Parents*. Hartford: Child and Family Services of Connecticut, August 1975, 20 pp.

BREMNER, ROBERT H. (Ed.). *Children and Youth in America: A Documentary History*, Vol. 2: 1866–1932, Parts 1–6. Cambridge, Mass.: Harvard University Press, 1970.

BRENNER, RUTH. "A Follow-up Study of Adoptive Families." *Child Adoption Research Committee* (March 1951).

BRIELAND, DONALD. *An Experimental Study of the Selection of Adoptive Parents at Intake*. New York: Child Welfare League of America, 1959a.

———. "Practices in Selecting Adoptive Parents." *Child Welfare*, **38** (May 1959b).

———. "The Selection of Adoptive Parents at Intake." *Casework Papers, NCSW—1960*. New York: Columbia University Press, 1961.

———, and JOHN LEMMON. *Social Work and the Law*. St. Paul, Minn.: West Publishing Co., 1977.

BROWDER, ALBERT J. "Adoption and Foster Care of Handicapped Children in the United States." *Developmental Medicine and Child Neurology*, **17** (1975), 614–620.

BROWN, COLIN. "Scottish Experience on Access to Birth Records." *Adoption and Fostering*, No. 4 (1976), 27–28.

BROWN, EDWIN G. *Selection of Adoptive Parents—A Videotape Study*. Unpublished Ph.D. thesis, School of Social Service Administration, University of Chicago, August 1970.

———, and DONALD BRIELAND. "Adoptive Screening—New Data, New Dilemmas." *Social Work*, **20**, 4 (July 1975), 291–295.

BROWN, FLORENCE. "What Do We Seek in Adoptive Parents?" *Social Casework*, **32** (April 1951).

BURKE, CAROLYN. "Adult Adoptee's Constitutional Right to Know His Origins." *Southern California Law Review*, **48** (May 1975), 1199–1211.

CALIFORNIA CITIZENS' ADOPTIONS COMMITTEE. *Serving Children in Need of Adoption*. Los Angeles, June 1965.

CAMPBELL, ANNE. "Principles of Social Work Applied to Adoption Practice, Policy and Procedure," in *Social Work and the Preservation of Human Values*. Ed. by William Diton. London: J. M. Dent & Sons, Ltd. 1957.

CARNEY, ANN. *No More Here and There—Adopting the Older Child*. Chapel Hill: University of North Carolina Press, 1976.

CARROLL, JEROME. "Adoption by Whites of Children of Afro-American Heritage— Some Issues for Consideration." *Adoptalk*, **6** (March–April, May–June 1970).

CARROLL, VERN (Ed.). *Adoption in Eastern Oceania*. Honolulu: University of Hawaii Press, 1970.

CAWLEY, C. C. "The Outlaws." *The Christian Century* (April 3, 1957).

CHAMBERS, DONALD. "Willingness to Adopt Atypical Children." *Child Welfare*, **49**, 5 (May 1970), 275–279.

CHAPPELEAR, EDITH, and JOYCE FRIED. "Helping Adopting Couples Come to Grips with Their New Parental Roles." *Children*, **14**, 6 (November–December 1967), 223–226.

CHEMA, REGINA, *et al*. "Adoptive Placement of the Older Child." *Child Welfare*, **49**, 8 (October 1970), 450–458.

CHESTANG, LEON. "The Dilemma of Biracial Adoption." *Social Work*, **17**, 3 (May 1972), 100–105.

———, and IRMGARD HEYMANN. "Preparing Older Children for Adoption." *Public Welfare*, **34**, 1 (Winter 1976), 35–40.

CHILDREN'S HOME SOCIETY OF CALIFORNIA. "Report of a Research Project." *The Changing Face of Adoption*, March 1977.

CHILD WELFARE LEAGUE OF AMERICA. *Adoption of Oriental Children by American White Families—An Interdisciplinary Symposium*. New York, 1960.

———. *Supply and Demand in ARENA—An Analysis of the Relation of Characteristics of Children Registered with ARENA and the Characteristics Acceptable to Families Registered*. New York: Child Welfare League of America, May 1972.

———. *Standards for Adoption Service*. New York, 1973.

CHIMEZE, AMUZIE. "Transracial Adoption of Black Children." *Social Work*, **20**, 4 (July 1975), 296–301.

———. "Bold but Irrelevant: Grow and Shapiro on Transracial Adoption." *Child Welfare*, **56**, 2 (February 1977), 75–86.

CITIZENS' ADOPTION COMMITTEE OF LOS ANGELES COUNTY. *Natural Parents Who Relinquish Children for Adoption*. Los Angeles, June 1952.

CLOTHIER, FLORENCE. "Some Aspects of the Problem of Adoption." *American Journal of Orthopsychiatry*, **9** (1939).

COLLIER, CATHERINE. "A Postadoption Discussion Series." *Social Casework*, **41** (April 1960).

COLUMBIA JOURNAL OF LAW AND SOCIAL PROBLEMS. "Revocation of Parental Consent in Adoption Proceedings, Recent Developments." *Columbia Journal of Law and Social Problems* (1977), 105–109.

COLUMBIA LAW REVIEW. "Religion as a Factor in Adoption." *Columbia Law Review,* **54** (1954), 376–403.

COLVILLE, ANITA. "Adoption for the Handicapped Child." *Child Welfare,* **36** (October 1957).

CONKLIN, LLOYD, *et al.* "Use of Groups During the Adoptive Post-Placement Period." *Social Work,* **7** (April 1962).

COSTIN, LELA B. "Adoption of Children by Single Parents." *Child Adoption* (November 1970), 31–33.

CROWE, RAYMOND. "An Adoption Study of Antisocial Personality." *Archives of General Psychiatry,* **31** (1974), 785–791.

CUNNINGHAM, LYNN, REMI J. CADORET, ROSEMARY LOFTUS, and JAMES E. EDWARDS. "Studies of Adoptees from Psychiatrically Disturbed Biological Parents. I: Psychiatric Conditions in Childhood and Adolescence." *British Journal of Psychiatry,* **126** (1975a), 534–549.

————. "Studies of Adoptees from Psychiatrically Disturbed Biological Parents. II: Temperamental, Hyperactive, Antisocial and Developmental Variables." *Journal of Pediatrics,* **87** (1975b), 301–306.

CURIE-COHEN, MARTIN, LESLEIGH LUTTRELL, and SANDER SHAPIRO. "Current Practice of Artificial Insemination by Donors in the United States." *New England Journal of Medicine,* **300** (March 15, 1979), 585–590.

DALL, ADOLIN. "Subsidized Adoption in New York City," in *Adoption of the Older Foster Child.* New York: New York State Council of Voluntary Child Care Agencies, February 1977.

DALSHEIMER, BABETTE. "Adoption Runs in My Family." *MS* (August 1973), 82–83, 112–113.

DAVIS, RUTH, and POLLY DOUCK. "Crucial Importance of Adoption Home Study." *Child Welfare,* **34** (March 1955).

DEASY, FEILA C., and OLIVE W. QUINN. "The Urban Negro and Adoption of Children." *Child Welfare,* **41** (November 1962).

DEHARTOG, JAN. *The Children—A Personal Record for the Use of Adoptive Parents.* New York: Antheneum Publishers, 1969.

DEPARTMENT OF PUBLIC WELFARE. *Report on Adoptions.* Edmonton, Alberta, Canada, 1969. Mimeo.

DILLOW, LOUISE. "The Group Process in Adoptive Home Finding." *Children,* **15,** 4 (July–August 1968), 153–157.

DIVIGLIO, LETITIA. "Adjustment of Foreign Children in Their Adoptive Homes." *Child Welfare,* **35** (November 1956).

DONLEY, KAY. "The Dynamics of Disruption." *Adoption and Fostering,* **92,** 2 (1978).

DOOLEY, DOROTHY, and ROBERT LA FANCO. "Implementing a Plan for Permanence at the New York Foundling Hospital." *Catholic Charities Review,* **58** (October 1974), 5–13.

DOTY, ROSEMARIE, and RICHARD MERWIN. "Parents Relinquishing Rights to First-Born Legitimate Children." *Child Welfare,* **48,** 2 (February 1969), 100.

DOUGHERTY, SHARON A. "Single Adoptive Mothers and Their Children." *Social Work,* **23** (July 1978), 311–314.

DUKETTE, RITA. "Perspectives for Agency Response to the Adoption-Record Controversy." *Child Welfare,* **54,** 8 (September–October 1975), 545–554.

————, and STEVENSON, NICHOLAS. "The Legal Rights of Unmarried Fathers: The Impact of Recent Court Decisions." *Social Service Review,* **47,** 7 (1973), 1–15.

EDGAR, MARGARET. "The Adoption Party." *Child Adoption,* **79,** 1 (1975), 45–50.

EDWARDS, MARGARET. "Adoption for the Older Child." *Child Adoption,* No. 4 (1975), 22–27.

EHRLICH, HENRY. *A Time to Search.* New York: Paddington Press, 1977.

ELDRED, CAROLYN A., *et al.* "Some Aspects of Adoption in Selected Samples or Adult Adoptees." *American Journal of Orthopsychiatry,* Vol. 42 (April 1976), 279–90.

ELONEN, ANNE, and EDWARD SCHWARTZ. "A Longitudinal Study of Emotional, Social and Academic Functioning of Adoptive Children." *Child Welfare,* 48, 2 (February 1969), 72–78.

EPSTEIN, LAURA, and IRMGARD HEYMANN. "Some Decisive Process in Adoption Planning for the Older Child." *Child Welfare,* 46, 1 (January 1967), 5–9.

FAIRWEATHER, O. E. "Early Placement in Adoption." *Child Welfare,* 31 (1952).

FALK, LAWRENCE L. "A Comparative Study of Trans-racial and In-racial Adoptions." *Child Welfare,* 49, 2 (February 1970), 82–88.

———. "Identity and the Transracially Adopted Child." *Lutheran Social Welfare,* 9 (Summer 1969), 18–25.

FANSHEL, DAVID. *A Study in Negro Adoption.* New York: Child Welfare League of America, January 1957.

———. *Far from the Reservation: The Transracial Adoption of American Indian Children.* Metuchen, N.J.: Scarecrow Press, Inc., 1972.

———, and EUGENE B. SHINN. *Dollars and Sense in the Foster Care of Children—A Look at Cost Factors.* New York: Child Welfare League of America, 1972.

FEIGELMAN, WILLIAM, and ARNOLD R. SILVERMAN. "Single Parent Adoptions." *Social Casework,* 58, 7 (July 1977), 418–425.

———. "Preferential Adoption: A New Mode of Family Formation." *Social Casework: The Journal of Contemporary Social Work,* 60 (May 1979), 296–305.

FERMAN, PATRICIA R., and WARREN, BRUCE L. *Finding Families for the Children.* Ypsilanti, Mich.: Eastern University Press, 1974.

FESTINGER, TRUDY BRADLEY. *Why Some Choose Not to Adopt Through Agencies.* New York: Metropolitan Applied Research Center, Inc., 1972.

FISCH, ROBERT, *et al.* "Growth Behavior and Psychological Measurements of Adopted Children—The Influence of Genetic and Socio-Economic Factors in a Prospective Study." *Journal of Pediatrics,* 89 (September 1976), 494–500.

FISCHER, CLARENCE D. "Homes for Black Children." *Child Welfare,* 50, 2 (February 1971), 108–111.

FISHER, FLORENCE. *The Search for Anna Fisher.* Greenwich, Conn.: Fawcett Crest, 1973.

FOOTE, GWENDOLYN, and ROSALIND L. PUTNAM. *Negro Attitudes Toward Adoption in Hartford.* New Haven: The Connecticut Child Welfare Association, September 1965.

FOSTER, H. H. "Adoption and Child Custody: Best Interests of the Child." *Buffalo Law Review,* 22 (1972), 1–16.

FOWLER, IRVING. "The Urban Middle-Class Negro and Adoption: Two Series of Studies and Their Implications for Action." *Child Welfare,* 45, 9 (November 1966), 522–524.

FOWLER, LOWA. "Problem of Adoption Placement in British Columbia." *Social Welfare and the Preservation of Human Values.* Ed. by William Diton. London: J. M. Dent & Sons, Inc., 1957.

FRADKIN, HELEN. "Adoptive Parents for Children with Special Needs." Discussion by Ruth Taft. *Child Welfare,* 37 (January 1958).

FRANKL, ANNI W. "Work with Adoptive Parents." *Child Welfare,* 38 (April 1959).

FRANKLIN, DAVID S., and FRED MASSARIK. "The Adoption of Children with Medical Conditions. Part I: Process and Outcome; Part II: The Families Today; Part III: Discussion and Conclusions." *Child Welfare,* 48, 8, 9, 10 (October–November–December 1969), 459–467, 533–539, 595–601.

FRANKLIN, HELEN, and DOROTHY KRUGMAN. "Program of Adoptive Placements for Infants Under Three Months." *American Journal of Orthopsychiatry*, **26** (1956), 577–93.

FREEDMAN, JOEL. "An Adoptee in Search of Identity." *Social Work*, **22**, 3 (May 1977), 227–228.

FREEMAN, NORA L. "Remodeling Adoption Statutes after Stanley Versus Illinois." *Journal of Family Law*, **15** (1976–1977), 385–422.

FREUD, SIGMUND. "Family Romances," *Collected Papers*, Vol. 5. London: Hogarth Press, Ltd., 1950.

FRICKE, HARRIET. "T.V. or Not T.V.—Minnesota Settles the Question." *Child Welfare*, **35** (November 1956).

FRIEDMAN, HELEN. "Why Are They Keeping Their Babies?" *Social Work*, **20**, 4 (July 1975), 322–323.

FURLOUGH, ROBERT. "Agency Adoptions Compared with Independent Adoptions." Unpublished Ph.D. thesis, Florida State University, Tallahassee, 1974.

GALLAGHER, URSULA M. "The Adoption of Mentally Retarded Children." *Children*, **15**, 1 (January–February 1968), 17–21.

———. "Adoption Resources for Black Children." *Children*, **18**, 2 (March–April 1971), 49–51.

GAYLORD, C. L. "The Adoptable Child's Right to Know." *Case and Comment* (March–April 1976), 8.

GILL, MARGARET H. "The Foster Care/Adoptive Family: Adoption for Children Not Legally Free." *Child Welfare*, **54** (December 1975), 712–20.

———. "Adoption of Older Children: Problems Faced." *Social Casework*, **59**, 3 (May 1978), 272–278.

GLEN, GEORGE S. "Adoption: An Added Ingredient." *Ohio Northern Law Review*, 1 (1974), 462–479.

GOCHROS, HARVEY. *Not Parents Yet—A Study of the Postplacement Period in Adoption.* Minneapolis, Minn.: Division of Child Welfare, Department of Public Welfare, 1962.

———. "A Study of the Caseworker–Adoptive Parent Relationship in Postplacement Service." *Child Welfare*, **46**, 6 (June 1967), 317–325.

GOLDBERG, HARRIET L., and LEWELLYN H. LINDE. "The Case for Subsidized Adoptions." *Child Welfare*, **48**, 2 (February 1969), 96–99.

GOLDRING, HOWARD, and JANIE TUTLEMAN. *Adoption Failures at the Los Angeles County Department of Adoptions.* Unpublished master's thesis, University of Southern California, School of Social Work, June 1970.

GOLDSTEIN, JOSEPH, ANNA FREUD, and ALBERT SOLNIT. *Beyond the Best Interests of the Child.* New York: The Free Press, 1973.

GOODMAN, JEROME. "Adopted Children Brought to Child Psychiatric Clinics." *Archives of General Psychiatry*, 9 (November 1963).

GOODWIN, DONALD W. "Drinking Problems in Adopted and Non-adopted Sons of Alcoholics." *Archives of General Psychiatry*, **31**, 2 (August 1974), 164–169.

———, et al. "Alcoholic Problems in Adoptees Raised Apart from Alcoholic Biological Parents." *Archives of General Psychiatry*, **28** (1973), 238–243.

GRAHAM, LLOYD. "Children from Japan in American Adoptive Homes," in *Casework Papers*. New York: Family Service Association of America, 1957.

GROSSMAN, HANNA, DOREE EPSTEIN, and ANNE NELSON. *An Evaluation of the New York State Adoption Exchange.* Albany, N.Y.: Welfare Research, Inc., 1976.

GROW, LUCILLE J., and DEBORAH SHAPIRO. *Black Children—White Parents—A Study of Transracial Adoption.* New York: Child Welfare League of America, 1974.

———. *Transracial Adoption Today—Views of Adoptive Parents and Social Workers.* New York: Child Welfare League of America, 1975.

HAGEN, CLAYTON, et al. The Adopted Adult Discusses Adoption as a Life Experience. Minneapolis: Lutheran Social Service of Minnesota, 1968.

HALLINAN, HELEN. "Adoption for Older Childlren." Social Casework, 33 (July 1952).

HARGRAVE, VIVIAN, JOAN SHIREMAN, and PETER CONNOR. Where Love and Need Are One. Chicago: Illinois Department of Children and Family Services, 1975.

HARING, BARBARA L. "Adoption Trends, 1971–1975." Child Welfare, 55, 7 (July–August, 1976), 501–503.

HARPER, JULIET, and SARA WILLIAMS. "Adopted Children Admitted to Residential Psychiatric Care." Australian Journal of Social Issues (1976), 43–52.

HASTINGS, JAMES (Ed.). Encyclopedia of Religion and Ethics. New York: Charles Scribner's Sons, 1908.

HEGARTY, CORNELIUS. "The Family Resources Program: One Coin, Two Sides of Adoption and Foster Family Care." Child Welfare, 52 (February 1973), 91–99.

HERZOG, ELIZABETH, and ROSE BERNSTEIN. "Why So Few Negro Adoptions?" Children, 12 (January–February 1965).

———, et al. Families for Black Children: The Search for Adoptive Parents. I: An Experience Survey. Washington, D.C.: Government Printing Office, 1971a.

———, et al. "Some Opinion on Finding Families for Black Children." Children, 18, 4 (July–August 1971b), 143–148.

HESTON, LEONARD N. "Psychiatric Disorders in Foster Home Reared Children of Schizophrenic Mothers." British Journal of Psychiatry, 112 (1966), 819–825.

HOCHFIELD, EUGENIE. "Across National Boundaries." Juvenile Court Judge Journal, 14 (October 1963).

HOLMAN, ROBERT. Trading in Children: A Study of Private Fostering. London: Routledge and Kegan Paul, 1973.

HOME OFFICE AND SOCIAL WORK SERVICES GROUP, SCOTLAND. A Guide to Adoption Practice. London: Her Majesty's Stationery Office, 1970.

HOOPES, JANET, et al. A Follow-up Study of Adoptions, Vol. 2: Postplacement Functioning of Adopted Children. New York: Child Welfare League of America, 1970.

HORNECKER, ALICE. "Adoption Opportunities for the Handicapped." Children, 9 (July–August 1962).

HOWARD, ALICIA, DAVID D. ROYSE, and JOHN A. SKERL. "Transracial Adoption: The Black Community Perspective." Social Work, 22, 3 (May 1977), 184–189.

HOWARD, MARY. "An Adoptee's Personal Search for Her Natural Parents—I Take After Somebody; I Have Real Relatives; I Possess a Real Name." Psychology Today (December 1975), 33–37.

HUMPHREY, MICHAEL. The Hostage Seekers. Essex, England: Longmans Group Ltd., 1969.

———, and CHRISTOPHER OUNSTED. "Adoptive Families Referred for Psychiatric Advice. I: The Children." British Journal of Psychiatry, 109 (1963).

HUNT, ROBERTA. Obstacles to Interstate Adoption. New York: Child Welfare League of America, 1972.

HUTCHINGS, B., and S. MEDNICK. "Registered Criminality in the Adoptive and Biological Parents of Registered Male Criminal Adoptees," in Genetic Research in Psychiatry. Ed. by R. R. Fieve, H. Brill, and D. Rosenthal. Baltimore: Johns Hopkins University Press, 1975.

ISAAC, RAEL J. Adopting a Child Today. New York: Harper & Row, Publishers, 1965.

JACKSON, BARBARA. Family Experiences of Inter-racial Adoption. London: The Association of British Adoption and Fostering Agencies, 1976.

JAFFEE, BENSON. "Adoption Outcome: A Two Generation View." Child Welfare, 53, 4 (April 1974), 211–224.

———, and DAVID FANSHEL. How They Fared in Adoption: A Follow-up Study. New York: Columbia University Press, 1970.

JAMESON, GRACE. "Psychiatric Disorders in Adopted Children in Texas." *Texas Medicine,* **63,** 4 (April 1967), 83–88.

JAQUITH, ESTHER. "An Adoptive Resource Exchange Under Private Auspices." *Child Welfare,* **41** (May 1962).

JEWETT, CLAUDIA S. *Adopting an Older Child.* Boston: Open Door Society of Massachusetts, 1978.

JOE, BARBARA. "In Defense of Intercountry Adoption." *Social Service Review,* **52** (March 1978), 1–20.

JONES, CHARLES E., and JOHN F. ELSE. "Racial and Cultural Issues in Adoption." *Child Welfare,* **58** (June 1979), 373–82.

JONES, EDMOND D. "On Transracial Adoption of Black Children." *Child Welfare,* **5,** 3 (March 1972), 156–164.

JONES, JEAN Y. "Subsidized Adoption." *United States Congress Adoptions and Foster Care Hearings.* Subcommittee on Children and Youth, Committee on Labor Public Welfare, U.S. Senate. Washington, D.C.: Government Printing Office, 1975.

JONES, MARTHA. "Preparing the School Age Child for Adoption." *Child Welfare,* **58** (January 1979), 27–34.

JONES, MARY ANN. *The Sealed Adoption Record Controversy: Report of a Survey of Agency Policy, Practice and Opinions.* New York: Child Welfare League of America, 1976.

KADUSHIN, ALFRED. "The Legally Adoptable, Unadopted Child." Child Welfare, **37** (December 1958).

––––––. "A Study of Adoptive Parents of Hard-to-Place Children." *Social Casework,* **43** (May 1962).

––––––. "Adoptive Parenthood: A Hazardous Adventure." *Social Work,* **11,** 3 (July 1966).

––––––. "Letter to the Editor." *Social Work,* **12,** 1 (January 1967), 127–128.

––––––. "Single-Parent Adopters: An Overview and Relevant Research." *Social Service Review,* **44,** 3 (September 1970a).

––––––. *Adopting Older Children.* New York: Columbia University Press, 1970b.

––––––. "Adoptive Status—Birth Parents vs. Bread Parents." *Child Care Quarterly Review,* **25,** 3 (July 1971), 10–14.

––––––, and FREDERICK SEIDL. "Adoption Failure: A Social Work Postmortem." *Social Work,* **16,** 3 (July 1971), 32–37.

KAPLAN, IRVING H. "A Group Approach to Adoptive Study." *Journal of Jewish Communal Services,* **47,** 2 (Winter 1970), 127–135.

KASPORWICZ, ALFRED. "Interpreting Rejection to Adoptive Applicants." *Social Work,* **9** (January 1964).

KATZ, LINDA. "Older Child Adoptive Placement: A Time of Family Crisis." *Child Welfare,* **56,** 3 (March 1977), 165–171.

KATZ, SANFORD N., and URSULA M. GALLAGHER. "Subsidized Adoption in America." *Family Law Quarterly,* **10** (Spring 1976), 3–54.

KENNY, THOMAS, *et al.* "Incidence of Minimal Brain Injury in Adopted Children." *Child Welfare,* **46,** 1 (January 1967), 24–29.

KETCHUM, B. "Reports on Study of Adopted Children." *Child Welfare,* **43** (1964), 249.

KETY, SEYMOUR S. "Studies Designed to Disentangle Genetic and Environmental Variables in Schizophrenia: Some Epistemological Questions and Answers." *American Journal of Psychiatry,* **133,** 10 (October 1976), 1134–1136.

––––––, *et al.* "Mental Illness in the Biological and Adoptive Families of Adopted Schizophrenics." *American Journal of Psychiatry,* **128,** 3 (September 1971), 302–306.

––––––, DAVID ROSENTHAL, PAUL WENDER, and FINI SCHULSINGER. "Studies Based on a Total Sample of Adopted Individuals and Their Relatives—Why They Were

Necessary, What They Demonstrated and Failed to Demonstrate." *Schizophrenia Bulletin,* **2,** 3 (1976), 413–428.

KIM, DONG S. "How They Fared in American Homes—A Follow Up Study of Adopted Korean Children in the U.S." *Children Today* (March–April 1977), 2–6.

KIM, H. T., and ELAINE REID. "After a Long Journey," pp. 307–427, in *The Unbroken Circle.* Ed. by Betty Kramer. Minneapolis: Organization of United Response, 1975.

KIRK, H. D. "A Dilemma of Adoptive Parenthood—Incongruous Role Obligation." *Marriage and Family Living,* **21** (November 1959).

———. *Shared Fate.* New York: The Free Press, 1964.

———, KURT JONASSOHN, and ANN FISH. "Are Adopted Children Especially Vulnerable to Stress?" *Archives of General Psychiatry,* **14** (March 1966).

KLOMINECK, WANDA. "The Development of Adoptive Children in Their New Family Environment." *International Child Welfare Review,* **28** (March 1976), 43–51.

KNIGHT, IRIS. "Placing the Handicapped Child for Adoption." *Child Adoption,* **62,** 4 (1970), 27–35.

KORNITZER, MARGARET. *Adoption and Family Life.* New York: Humanities Press, Inc., 1968.

———, and JANE ROWE. *Some Casework Implications in the Study of Children Reclaimed or Returned Before Final Adoption.* Surrey, England: Standing Conference of Societies Registered for Adoption, May 1968. Mimeo.

KRUGMAN, DOROTHY. "Reality in Adoption." *Child Welfare,* **43,** 7 (July 1964).

LADNER, JOYCE. *Mixed Families—Adopting Across Racial Boundaries.* Garden City, N.Y.: Doubleday & Company, Inc., 1977.

LAHTI, JANET, *et al. A Follow-up Study of the Oregon Project.* Portland, Ore.: Regional Research Institute for Human Services, Portland State University, August 1978.

LAKE, ALICE. "Babies for the Brave." *Saturday Evening Post* (July 31, 1954).

LANGSAM, MIRIAM Z. *Children West.* Madison: State Historical Society of Wisconsin, 1964.

LAWDER, ELIZABETH, *et al.* "A Limited Number of Older Children in Adoption—A Brief Survey." *Child Welfare,* **37** (November 1958).

———. *A Follow-up Study of Adoptions: Postplacement Functioning of Adoption Families.* New York: Child Welfare League of America, 1969.

LEATHERMAN, ANNE. "Placing the Older Child for Adoption." *Children* (May–June 1957).

LEEDING, ALFRED. "Access to Birth Records." *Adoption and Fostering,* **89,** 3 (1977), 19–25.

LEFKOWITZ, MORRIS. Director of Services, Children's Home Society of California. Personal communication, December 12, 1969.

LE SHAN, EDA. *You and Your Adopted Child.* New York: Public Affairs Committee, 1958.

LIFTON, BETTY. *Twice Born—Memoirs of an Adopted Daughter.* New York: McGraw-Hill Book Company, 1975.

———. *Lost and Found—The Adoption Experience.* New York: Dial Press, 1978.

LINDE, LLEWELLYN H. "The Search for Mom and Dad." *Minnesota Welfare,* **19,** 2 (Summer 1967), 7–12.

LINDEMANN, BARD. *The Twins Who Found Each Other.* New York: William Morrow & Co., 1969.

LIVINGSTON, CAROLE. *Why Was I Adopted?* Secaucus, N.J.: Lyle Stuart, 1978.

LOS ANGELES COUNTY DEPARTMENT OF ADOPTIONS. *Biennial Report 1965–67.* Los Angeles, October 1967.

LOSBOUGH, BILIE. "Relationship of E.E.G. Neurological and Psychological Findings in

Adopted Children (75 cases)." *A Medical Journal of E.E.G. Technology*, **5**, 1 (January 1965), 1–4.

MAAS, HENRY. "The Successful Adoptive Parent Applicants." *Social Work*, **5** (January 1960).

McCAUSLAND, CLARE L. *Children of Circumstance—A History of the First 125 Years of the Chicago Child Care Society*. Chicago: Chicago Child Care Society, 1976.

McCORMICK, REA. "The Adopting Parents See the Child," in *Studies of Children*. Ed. by Gladys Meger. New York: King's Crown Press, 1948.

McCOY, JACQUELINE. "Identity as a Factor in the Adoptive Placement of the Older Child." *Child Welfare*, **40** (September 1961).

McMAHAN, RALPH S. "An Investigation into the Socio-Economic Characteristics of Child Adopters in Relation to Methods of Distributing Adoptable Children." Unpublished doctoral dissertation, University of Arkansas, Little Rock, 1974.

McWHINNIE, ALEXINA M. *Adopted Children—How They Grow Up*. London: Kegan, Paul, 1967.

———. "Group Counselling with Seventy-Eight Adoptive Families." *Case Conference*, **14**, 11–12 (March–April 1968).

———. "Who Am I?" *Child Adoption*, **62** (November 1970), 36–39.

MADISON, BERNICE, and MICHAEL SHAPIRO. "Black Adoption—Issues and Policies: Review of the Literature." *Social Service Review*, **47** (December 1973), 531–560.

MECH, EDMUND V. "Adoption: A Policy Perspective," Chapter 8, in *Review of Child Development Research*. Ed. by Bettye M. Caldwell and Henry N. Ricciuti. Chicago: University of Chicago Press, 1973, pp. 467–508.

MEEZAN, WILLIAM, SANFORD KATZ, and EVA RUSSO. *Adoptions without Agencies: A Study of Independent Adoptions*. New York: Child Welfare League of America, 1977.

MENLOVE, FRANCES L. "Aggressive Symptoms in Emotionally Disturbed Adopted Children." *Child Development*, **36** (June 1965).

MICHAELS, RUTH. "Casework Considerations in Rejecting the Adoption Application." *Social Casework*, **28** (December 1947).

MIDDLESTADT, EVELYN. "Facilitating the Adoption of Older Children." *Children Today*, **6**, 3 (May–June 1977), 10–13.

MIKAWA, JAMES, and JOHN BOSTON. "Psychological Characteristics of Adopted Children." *Psychiatric Quarterly Supplement*, **42**, 2 (July 1968), 274–281.

MORRISON, HAZEL. "Research Study in Adoption." *Child Welfare*, **29** (1950).

MORRISON, JAMES R., and MARK A. STEWART. "The Psychiatric Status of the Legal Families of Adopted Hyperactive Children." *Archives of General Psychiatry*, **28**, 6 (June 1973), 888–891.

MOTT, PAUL E. *Foster Care and Adoptions: Some Key Policy Issues*. Prepared for the Subcommittee on Children and Youth of the Committee on Labor and Public Welfare. Washington, D.C.: Government Printing Office, 1975.

MULREY, J. M. "The Care of Destitute and Neglected Children." National Conference of Charities and Correction, 1899. Boston: George Ellis, 1900.

MUNSINGER, HARRY. "The Adopted Child's I.Q.: A Critical Review." *Psychological Bulletin*, **82** (September 1975a), 623–659.

———. "Children's Resemblance to Their Biological and Adopting Parents in Two Ethnic Groups." *Behavior Genetics*, **5** (1975b), 239–253.

NATIONAL ASSOCIATION FOR MENTAL HEALTH, ENGLAND. *A Survey Based on Adoption Case Reviews*. London: National Association for Mental Health, 1954.

NATIONAL CENTER FOR SOCIAL STATISTICS. Office of Information Systems. S.R.S. H.E.W., *Adoptions in 1970*, June 1972.

———. *Adoptions in 1975*. Washington, D.C.: Government Printing Office, April 1977.

NATIONAL CONFERENCE OF CATHOLIC CHARITIES. *Adoption Practices in Catholic Agencies.* Washington, D.C., 1957.

NATIONAL COUNCIL OF CHURCHES°OF CHRIST IN THE UNITED STATES. "Religious Factors in Child Adoptions—A Study Document." *Lutheran Social Welfare Quarterly,* 5 (March 1965).

NEILSON, J. "Placing Older Children In Adoptive Homes." *Children Today,* 1, 6 (November–December 1972), 7–13.

———. "Tayari: Black Homes for Black Children." *Child Welfare,* 55, 1 (January 1976), 41–50.

NEMOVICHER, JOSEPH. *A Comparative Study of Adopted Boys and Nonadopted Boys in Respect to Specific Personality Characteristics.* Unpublished Ph.D. thesis, New York University, 1960.

NEW YORK STATE COMMISSION ON CHILD WELFARE. *Barriers to the Freeing of Children for Adoption.* New York: New York State Department of Social Services, March 1976.

NIEDEN, MARGARETE Z. "The Influence of Constitution and Environment Upon the Development of Adopted Children." *Journal of Psychology,* 31 (1951).

OFFORD, D. R., *et al.* "Presenting Symptomatology of Adopted Children." *Archives of General Psychiatry,* 20, 1 (January 1969), 110–116.

OHIO DISTRICT 11. *Adoption Project. Final Report,* Warren, Ohio: Trumbull County Children's Services Board, 1977.

O'NEILL, M. M. "Adoption—Identification and Service." *Child Welfare,* 51, 5 (May 1972), 314–317.

OPPORTUNITY. *National Survey of Black Chilldren Adopted in 1975.* Portland, Ore.: Boys and Girls Society of Oregon, December 30, 1976.

PAGET, NORMAN. "Use of Video Equipment in a Child Welfare Agency." *Child Welfare,* 48, 5 (May 1969), 296–300.

PANNOR, REUBEN, *et al. The Unmarried Father—New Approaches in Helping Unmarried Young Parents.* New York: Springer-Verlag, 1971.

———, and EVELYN A. NERLOE. "Fostering Understanding Between Adolescents and Adoptive Parents Through Group Experience." *Child Welfare,* 56, 8 (September–October 1977), 537–545.

PATON, JEAN M. *The Adopted Break Silence.* Philadelphia: Life History Study Center, 1954.

PELLER, L. "About 'Telling the Child' of His Adoption." *Bulletin of the Philadelphia Association of Psychoanalysis,* 11 (1961), 145–154.

PEPPER, GERALD W. *Interracial Adoptions: Family Profile, Motivation, and Coping Methods.* Unpublished Ph.D. thesis, University of Southern California, 1966.

PETTIGREW, BRENDA. "Group Discussions with Adoptive Parents." *Child Adoption,* 1 (1969), 39–42.

PLATTS, HAL K. "Facts Against Impressions—Mothers Seeking to Relinquish Children for Adoption." *Children,* 17, 1 (January–February 1970), 27–30.

PODOLSKI, ALFRED L. "Abolishing Baby Buying: Limiting Independent Adoption Placement." *Family Law Quarterly,* 9 (Fall 1975), 547–554.

POLK, MARY. "Maryland's Program of Subsidized Adoptions." *Child Welfare,* 49, 10 (December 1970), 581–583.

PRAGER, BARBARA, and STANLEY A. ROTHSTEIN. "The Adoptee's Right to Know His Natural Heritage." *New York Law Forum,* 19 (Summer 1973), 137–156.

PRIDDY, DREW, and DORIS KIRGAN. "Characteristics of White Couples Who Adopt Black–White Children." *Social Work,* 16, 3 (July 1971), 105–107.

RALEIGH, BARBARA. "Adoption as a Factor in Child Guidance." *Smith College Studies in Social Work,* 25 (October 1954).

RAMSEY, PAUL. "The Legal Imputation of Religion to an Infant in Adoption Proceedings." *N.Y.U. Law Review,* **34** (April 1959), 649–690.

RATHBUN, CONSTANCE, *et al. Later Adjustments of Children Following Radical Separation from Family and Culture.* Paper presented at the Annual Meeting, American Orthopsychiatric Association, Chicago, 1964.

RAUTENAN, ALINA. "Work with Adopted Adolescents and Adults—The Experience of a Finnish Adoption Agency," in *The Adopted Person's Need for Information About His Background.* London: Association of British Adoption Agencies, 1971.

RAYNOR, LOIS. *Adoptions of Nonwhite Children—The Experience of the British Adoption Project.* London: George Allen & Unwin, Ltd., 1970.

———. "Twenty One Plus and Adopted." *Adoption and Fostering,* **87,** 1 (1977), 38–46.

REECE, SHIRLEY, and BARBARA LEVIN. "Psychiatric Disturbances in Adopted Children: A Descriptive Study." *Social Work,* **13,** 1 (January 1968), 101–111.

REEVES, B. "Protecting the Putative Father's Rights after Stanley v. Illinois, Problems in Implementation." *Journal of Family Law,* **13,** 115.

RIDAY, EDWIN. "Supply and Demand in Adoption." *Child Welfare,* **48,** 8 (October 1969), 489–492.

RIPPLE, LILLIAN. "A Follow-up Study of Adopted Children." *Social Service Review,* **42,** 4 (December 1968), 479–497.

ROMANOFSKY, PETER. " 'To Save . . . Their Souls': The Care of Dependent Jewish Children in New York City 1900–1905." *Jewish Social Studies* (1974), 253–61.

RONDELL, FLORENCE, and RUTH MICHAELS. *The Family That Grew.* New York: Crown Publishers, Inc., 1951.

ROSENTHAL, DAVID. "Three Adoption Studies of Heredity in Schizophrenia." *International Journal of Mental Health,* **1,** 1–2 (1972), 63–75.

———, *et al.* "The Types and Prevalence of Mental Illness in the Biological and Adoptive Families of Adopted Schizophrenics," pp. 345–362, in *The Transmission of Schizophrenia.* Ed. by David Rosenthal and Seymour S. Kety. London: Pergamon Press, 1968a.

———. "Schizophrenics' Offspring Reared in Adoptive Homes," pp. 377–391, in *The Transmission of Schizophrenia.* Ed. by David Rosenthal and Seymour Kety. London: Pergamon Press, 1968b.

———. "Parent Child Relationships and Psychopathological Disorder in the Child." *Archives of General Psychiatry,* **32,** 4 (April 1975), 466–476.

———, WENDER, PAUL H., and SEYMOUR KETY. "A Psychiatric Assessment of the Adoptive Parents of Schizophrenics," in *The Transmission of Schizophrenia.* Ed. by David Rosenthal and Seymour Kety. London: Pergamon Press, 1968.

ROWE, JEAN, and LYDIA LAMBERT. *Children Who Wait—A Study of Children Needing Substitute Families.* London: Association of British Adoption Agencies, 1973.

RUTGERS LAW REVIEW. "Adoption Psychological Parenthood as the Controlling Factor in Determining Best Interests of the Child." *Rutgers Law Review,* **26** (1973), 693–712.

ST. DENNIS, GERALD. *Interracial Adoptions in Minnesota: Self Concept and Child Rearing Attitudes of Caucasian Parents Who Have Adopted Negro Children.* Unpublished Ph.D. thesis, University of Minnesota, 1969.

SANDGRUND, GERTRUDE. "Group Counseling with Adoptive Families After Legal Adoption." *Child Welfare,* **41** (June 1962).

SANDUSKY, ANNIE LEE, *et al. Families for Black Children—The Search for Adoptive Parents. II: Program and Projects.* Washington, D.C.: Government Printing Office, 1972.

SANTS, H. J. "Geneological Bewilderment in Children with Substitute Parents." *Child Adoption,* **47** (1965), 32–42.

SARMIENTO, J. M. "Adoption Week: A Publicity Project in Adoptive Recruitment." *Child Welfare*, **48**, 3 (March 1969), 166–169.

SCARR, SANDRA, and RICHARD A. WEINBERG. "IQ Test Performance of Black Children Adopted by White Families." *American Psychologist* (October 1976), 726–739.

———. "Attitudes, Interests and I.Q." *Human Nature*, **1**, 4 (April 1978), 29–36.

SCARR-SALAPATECK, SANDRA, and RICHARD A. WEINBERG. "When Black Children Grow Up in White Homes." *Psychology Today* (December 1975), 80–82.

SCHAPIRO, MICHAEL. *A Study of Adoption Practice*, Vol. 3: *Adoption of Children with Special Needs*. New York: Child Welfare League of America, April 1957.

SCHECHTER, MARSHALL. "Observation on Adopted Children." *AMA Archives of General Psychiatry*, **3** (July 1960).

———, et al. "Emotional Problems in the Adoptee." *General Archives of Psychiatry*, **10** (February 1964).

SCHULSINGER, FINI. "Psychopathy: Heredity and Environment." *International Journal of Mental Health*, **1** (1972), 190–206.

SCHWARTZ, WILLIAM. "Group Work in Public Welfare." *Public Welfare*, **26** (October 1968), 348–356.

SCOTT, DELLA B. *A Report on Characteristics of Registrants for Adoption, Children Placed and Services Rendered by Adoption Agencies*. New York: Travelers Aid International Social Services, 1976.

SEELIG, GEORGE B. "The Implementation of Subsidized Adoption Programs: A Preliminary Survey." *Journal of Family Law*, **15**, 4 (1976–1977), 732–769.

SEGLOW, JEAN, MIA-KELLMER PRINGLE, and PETER WEDGE. *Growing Up Adopted—A Long Term National Study of Adopted Children and Their Families*. Windsor, England: National Foundation for Education in England and Wales, 1972.

SEIDL, FREDERICK. "Transracial Adoption: Agency Response to Applicant Calls." *Social Work*, **17**, 3 (May 1972), 119–120.

SELLERS, MARTHA. "Transracial Adoption." *Child Welfare*, **48**, 6 (June 1969), 355–356.

SHAPIRO, DEBORAH, and LUCILLE J. GROW. "Not So Bold and Not So Irrelevant. A Reply to Chimezie." *Child Welfare*, **56**, 2 (February 1977), 86–91.

SHARRAR, MARY L. "Attitude of Black Natural Parents Regarding Adoption." *Child Welfare*, **50**, 5 (May 1971), 286–289.

———. "Some Helpful Techniques When Placing Older Children for Adoption." *Child Welfare*, **49**, 8 (October 1970), 459–463.

SHAW, MARTIN, and KATHRYN LEBANS. "Children Between Families." *Adoption and Fostering*, **84**, 2 (1976), 17–27.

SHIREMAN, JOAN F. *Subsidized Adoption: A Study of Use and Need in Four Agencies*. Chicago: Chicago Region Child Care Association of Illinois, 1969. Mimeo.

———. "Adoptive Applicants Who Withdrew." *Social Service Review*, **44**, 3 (September 1970), 285–292.

———, and PENNY R. JOHNSON. "Single Persons as Adoptive Parents." *Social Service Review*, **50**, 1 (March 1976), 103–116.

———, and KENNETH WATSON. "Adoption of Real Children." *Social Work*, **17**, 3 (July 1972), 29–38.

SHYNE, ANN W. *Adoption Statistics 1976*. New York: Child Welfare League of America, May 1977.

———, and ANITA W. SCHROEDER. *National Study of Social Services to Children and Their Families*. Rockville, Md.: Westat, Inc., 1978.

SILVER, LARRY. "Frequency of Adoption in Children with Neurological Learning Disability Syndrome." *Journal of Learning Disabilities*, **3**, 6 (June 1970), 306–310.

SILVERMAN, ARNOLD R., and WILLIAM FEIGELMAN. "Some Factors Affecting the Adoption of Minority Children." *Social Casework*, **58**, 9 (November 1977) PP 554-61.

SIMON, NATHAN, and AUDREY SENTURIA. "Adoption and Psychiatric Illness." *American Journal of Psychiatry*, **122** (February 1966).

SIMON, RITA A., and HOWARD ALSTEIN. *Transracial Adoption*. New York: John Wiley & Sons, Inc., 1977.

SKEELS, H. S. *Adult Status of Children with Contrasting Early Life Experiences*. Monographs, Society for Research Child Development, Vol. 31, No. 3 (1966).

——, and I. HARMS. "Children with Inferior Social Histories: Their Mental Development in Adoptive Homes." *Journal of Genetic Psychology*, **72** (1948), 283–293.

——, and M. SKODAK. "A Final Follow Up Study of One Hundred Adopted Children." *Journal of Genetic Psychology* (1949), 85–125.

SKLAR, JUNE, and BETH BERKOV. "Teenage Family Formation in Post War America." *Family Planning Perspective*, **6** (Spring 1974), 80–90.

SMITH, CAROLE R. "Adoption Advice: A New Service." *British Journal of Social Work*, **6**, 2 (1976), 158–175.

SMITH, REBECCA. "The Sealed Adoption Record Controversy and Agency Response." *Child Welfare*, **55**, 2 (February 1976), 73–74.

——. "Adoptive Parents and the Sealed Record Controversy." *Social Casework*, **55**, 9 (November 1974a), 531–536.

——. "Opening the Sealed Record in Adoption." *Journal of Jewish Communal Services* (1974b), 188–196.

——. "The Reunion of Adoptees and Birth Relatives." *Journal of Youth and Adolescence*, **3** (1974c), 195–206.

——. *The Effects of Sealed Records in Adoption*. Paper presented at American Psychiatric Association meeting, May 6, 1975a, in Anaheim, California. Mimeo, 7 pp.

——. "Identity Conflicts in Adoptees." *American Journal of Orthopsychiatry*, **45**, 1 (January 1975b), 18–27.

——. The Effects of the Sealed Record in Adoption." *American Journal of Psychiatry*, **133**, 8 (August 1976), 900–904.

SOROSKY, ARTHUR D., ANNETTE BARAN, and REUBEN PANNOR. *The Adoption Triangle— The Effects of the Sealed Record on Adoptees, Birth Parents and Adoptive Parents*. Garden City, N.Y.: Anchor/Doubleday, 1978.

SPAULDING FOR CHILDREN. *Older and Handicapped Children Are Adoptable: The Spaulding Approach*. Chelsea, Mich., 1975.

SPRINGER, HELEN. "Sharing Responsibility with Applicants to Adopt." *Child Welfare*, **35** (March 1956).

STARR, J. "Adoptive Placement of the Older Child." *Casework Papers*. New York: Columbia University Press, 1954.

STARR, PHILIP, et al. "Early Life Experiences and Adoptive Parenting." *Social Casework*, **51** (October 1970), 491–500.

STERNAU, AMELIA. "Short-Term Financial Aid for Adoptive Parents." *Child Welfare*, **38** (October 1959).

STEVENSON, P. S. "The Evaluation of Adoption Reunions in British Columbia." *The Social Worker*, **44**, 1 (Spring 1976), 9–12.

STONESIFER, ELSIE. "The Behavior Difficulties of Adopted and Own Children." *Smith College Studies in Social Work*, **13** (1942).

STUMPF, MARGARET. "Group Meetings for Prospective Adoptive Applicants," in *Group Methods in the Public Welfare Program*. Ed. by Norman Fenton and Kermit Wiltse. Palo Alto, Calif.: Pacific Books, Publishers, 1963.

SWEENY, DOLORES, et al. "A Descriptive Study of Adoptive Children Seen in a Child Guidance Clinic." *Child Welfare*, **42** (November 1963).

TAFT, RUTH. "Adoptive Families for 'Unadoptable' Children." *Child Welfare*, **32** (June 1953).

THEIS, SOPHIE VAN SENDEN. *How Foster Children Turn Out.* New York: State Charities Aid Association, 1924.

THOMAS, MORLAIS. "Foster/Adoptive Home Breakdowns." *Child Adoption,* 66 (1971), 29–33.

THUNEN, MARGARET. "Ending Contact with Adoptive Parents—The Group Meeting." *Child Welfare,* 37 (November 1958).

TIMMS, NOEL (Ed.). *The Receiving End—Consumer Accounts of Social Help with Children.* London: Routledge and Kegan Paul, 1973.

TIZARD, BARBARA. *Adoption—A Second Chance.* New York: The Free Press, 1977.

TOLOR, ALEXANDER, and JOHN S. TAMERIN. "The Question of a Genetic Base for Alcoholism: Comment on the Study by Goodwin et al. and a Response." *Quarterly Journal of Studies on Alcohol,* 34 (December 1973), 1341–1347.

TOUSSIENG, POVL. *European Seminar on Inter-Country Adoptions. Lysin, Switzerland, May 1960.* Geneva: United Nations Technical Assistance Office.

——. "Thoughts Regarding the Etiology of Psychological Differences in Adopted Children." *Child Welfare,* 41 (February 1962).

TRISELIOTIS, J. P. *Evaluation of Adoption Policy and Practice.* Edinburgh University, Department of Social Administration, 1970.

——. *In Search of Origins.* London: Routledge and Kegan Paul, 1973.

——. "Identity and Adoption." *Child Adoption,* No. 4 (1974), P27.

TURANO, MARGARET. "Black Market Adoptions." *Catholic Lawyer* (Winter 1976), 48–69.

TVENSTRUP, ULF, and JORGEN HANSEN. *Tendencies in Development During Recent Years Within Danish Child and Youth Care, with a Special View to Changes in Number and Kind of Placements Outside Parental Home.* Copenhagen: National Board of Social Welfare, Child and Youth Services, 1974.

UNGER, CHRISTOPHER, GLADYS DWARSHUIS, and ELIZABETH JOHNSON. *Chaos, Madness and Unpredictability.* Chelsea, Mich.: Spaulding for Children, 1977.

U.S. CONGRESS. *Adoption and Foster Care 1975. Hearings Before the Subcommittee on Children and Youth of the Committee on Labor and Public Welfare.* U.S. Senate, April, July 1975. Washington, D.C.: Government Printing Office, 1975.

U.S. SENATE. *Hearing Before the Subcommittee to Investigate Juvenile Delinquency of the Committee on the Judiciary.* Washington, D.C.: Government Printing Office, 1956.

VALK, MARGARET. *Korean-American Children in American Adoptive Homes.* New York: Child Welfare League of America. September 1957.

VIEREGGE, ELIZABETH. "Experience with Applicants in a Single Preadoption Group Meeting," in *Group Methods in the Public Welfare Program.* Ed. by Norman Fenton and Kermit Wiltse. Palo Alto, Calif.: Pacific Books, Publishers, 1963.

WACHTEL, DAWN D. *Adoption Agencies and the Adoption of Black Children.* Washington, D.C.: Adoptions Research Project, 1972.

WASSON, VOLINTINA. *The Chosen Baby.* New York: Cormick and Evans, 1939.

WATSON, KENNETH. "Subsidized Adoption: A Crucial Investment." *Child Welfare,* 51, 4 (April 1972), 220–230.

WEINGARTEN, VICTOR. "Breaking the Barrier of Confidentiality." *Child Welfare,* 37 (April 1958).

WELFARE RESEARCH, INC. *Regional Adoption Program.* Albany, N.Y.: Welfare Research Inc., 1977.

WELTER, MARIANNE. *Comparison of Adopted Older Foreign Born and American Children.* New York: International Social Service, 1965.

WENDER, PAUL H. "Adopted Children and Their Families in the Evaluation of Nature-Nurture Interaction in the Schizophrenic Disorders." *Annals Review of Medicine,* 23 (1972), 355–372.

WHEELER, KATHERINE B. "The Use of Adoptive Subsidies." *Child Welfare,* **48,** 9 (November 1969), 557–559.

WIEHE, VERNON. "The Group Adoptive Study." *Child Welfare,* **51,** 10 (December 1972), 645–649.

WINGFIELD, F. "Prospective Adopters Groups: An Experiment." *Social Work,* **26,** 4 (October 1969), 14–16.

WISCONSIN DEPARTMENT OF HEALTH AND SOCIAL SERVICES. *Unmarried Mothers in Wisconsin—1974.* Madison, Wis.: Division of Family Services, 1975.

WITMER, HELEN, *et al. Independent Adoptions.* New York: Russell Sage Foundation, 1963.

WORK, HENRY H., and HANS ANDERSON. "Studies in Adoption: Requests for Psychiatric Treatment." *American Journal of Psychiatry,* **127,** 7 (January 1971), 948–950.

ZASTROW, CHARLES. *Outcome of Negro Children—Caucasian Parents' Transracial Adoptions.* Unpublished Ph.D. thesis, University of Wisconsin, Madison, 1971.

ZOBER, EDITH. "Postplacement Service for Adoptive Families." *Child Welfare,* **40** (April 1961).

11 THE CHILD-CARING INSTITUTION

INTRODUCTION

The child-caring institution is a third facility that offers total substitute care for the child whose parents cannot and/or will not implement their parental role. The foster home is a temporary facility; the adoptive home, a permanent one. Both provide the child with family care. The institution, like the foster home, provides temporary substitute care; like the adoptive home, it can offer permanent care; but unlike either, it offers group care rather than family care.

A *children's institution* is defined as a twenty-four-hour residential facility in which a group of unrelated children live together in the care of a group of unrelated adults.

Mayer, Richman, Balcerzak (1977) define an *institution* as "one or more buildings especially established for the purpose of housing and caring for groups of children (fifteen or more) who cannot live with their families. It may be located either within or without a residential community" (p. 52). This definition helps distinguish an institution from a group home, which generally has not been specifically established to care for children, generally houses less than fifteen children (more frequently six to twelve), and is always located in a residential community.

There are many different kinds of institutions serving different kinds of children. Among them are the following:

1. Institutions for normal but dependent and neglected children. This is the closest modern analogy to the old orphan asylum.
2. Institutions for physically handicapped children. These are separate institutions for children who are blind, deaf, crippled, asthmatic, and so on.
3. Institutions for mentally retarded or mentally defective children.
4. Institutions for the confinement and rehabilitation of juvenile delinquents. These are often called *training schools*.
5. Institutions for emotionally disturbed children; these are known as *residential treatment centers*.

There are other institutions that do not necessarily serve a special population of children but that are distinguished by their special purpose. These include:

1. Emergency facilities that accept children on a short-term basis while a study is made of the situation to determine the best plan for their care. Such a facility might also be used for children who need short-term care.
2. Diagnostic or observation centers to which a child is referred for the explicit purpose of undergoing a detailed physical, psychological, and social study.

Although institutions deal with the child who faces some problem in the parent–child relationship, many institutions are not under social-work child-welfare auspices, perhaps because the central problem is perceived as a medical problem in the case of the physically handicapped child; as a problem of law enforcement in the case of the juvenile delinquent; or as a medical, educational, or vocational problem in the case of the mentally deficient child. Hence institutions operate under the auspices of many groups.

The heterogeneous responsibility for the child-caring institutions stems also from the fact that well into the 1920s, the social work profession saw the child-caring institution as a somewhat disreputable last resort. Only after World War II did professional social work "accept" the institution as a specialized service to be selectively and appropriately used for some groups of children.

The different institutions serving different groups of children are, of course, apt to differ in many essential details. All have in common the fact that they are group-care facilities that provide total substitution for the biological parents' care of the child. This implies, then, that many significant elements are common to all institutions. Our concern in this chapter is with those general factors that are characteristic of all institutions. However, whenever we do encounter the more particular practice of institutions, we will focus on institutions for the dependent and neglected and on residential treatment centers for emotionally disturbed children. These institutions employ the bulk of social workers working in institutional child care.

Historical Background

The institution has a long history. The *xenodocheion* established by the Council of Nicaea in 325 to give shelter to the sick and the poor became asylums for abandoned children as well. In 787 Datheus, Archbishop of Milan, established an institution to care for children. Concerned about the abandonment of children, he noted: "These horrors would not take place if there existed an asylum where the adulterer could hide her shame but now they throw the infants in the sewers or the rivers and many are the murders committed on the new-born children" (Payne, 1916, p. 294). Similarly the pitiful condition of the many abandoned children in fifteenth-century France attracted the sympathy of St. Vincent de Paul, who established homes for *enfants trouvés* in 1633.

But although there existed a limited number of institutions exclusively concerned with caring for children, the more typical pattern was to have the children share an institution with other deprived groups in the population. Admission records of the New York City Almshouse note that some 15 per cent of the admissions between 1736 and 1746 involved "young and parentless children—the orphaned and the deserted—who would remain until the beginning of their apprenticeship" (Rothman, 1971, p. 39). Only a few institutions for dependent children had been established by the end of the eighteenth century. One had been established in New Orleans as a result of the need to care for a large number of children orphaned by an Indian massacre at Natchez. Another was established as a result of a yellow fever epidemic in Philadelphia. More frequently, however, children requiring institutional care were consigned to mixed almshouses "to live with the aged, the insane, the feebleminded, and the diseased. They were usually cared for by the ignorant employees; their physical needs were neglected. . . . Those who survived knew only the life and routine of a pauper institution" (Abbott, 1938, p. 4). Some almshouses did make an effort to see that children's needs were met, however. The Rules and Orders for the Management of the Work House in Boston, dated 1739, noted:

> That when any children shall be received into the House, there shall be some suitable women appointed to attend them; Who are to take care that they be wash'd, com'b and dress'd every morning, and be taught to Read and be instructed in the Holy Scriptures . . . and that the rest of their time be employ'd in such work as shall be assigned them [quoted in Whittaker, Trieschman, 1972, p. 397].

Although additional institutions for children were built early in the nineteenth century, the number of children in mixed almshouses continued to grow. As investigation after investigation confirmed the undesirable conditions under which the children lived, a growing dissatisfaction led to increasingly insistent demands that this method of caring for children be prohibited. Thus the Board of Public Charities for the State of Ohio, in its report for 1869, declared:

> Nearly one thousand children in the poor-houses of Ohio! What is to be done with them? Think of their surroundings. The raving of the maniac, the frightful contortions of the epileptic, the driveling and senseless sputtering of the idiot, the garrulous temper of the decrepit, neglected old age, the peevishness of the infirm, the accumulated filth of all these; then add the moral degeneracy of such as, for idleness or dissipation, seek a refuge from honest toil in the tithed industry of the county, and you have a faint outline of the surroundings of these little boys and girls, all more or less intelligent, many of them bright and beautiful, in such homes as these. How deeply must every human sympathy be touched with the reflection, that to these little children the poor-house is "all the world" [Abbott, 1938, p. 52].

There were some attempts at compromise by making separate institutional facilities available to children on almshouse grounds, but these attempts were few and unsatisfactory.

During the latter part of the nineteenth century, many states prohibited almshouse care for children. Thus New York State, in 1875, declared that children should "be removed from almshouses and provided for in families, asylums or other appropriate institutions." This meant that alternative forms of care had to be provided for the literally tens of thousands of children who had to be removed from almshouse care in one state after another. By this time, both foster care and institutions exclusively concerned with children, such as orphanages, had been developed. And, as Thurston (1969) notes, "as children were withdrawn or refused admission to almshouses, the tendency to build orphan asylums—already strong—was stimulated" (p. 90). The rapid use of the orphan asylum is exemplified by New York State, which had only two such institutions in 1825 but more than sixty in 1866.

The asylum was seen as shelter, sanctuary, and training school for the child. Moralism dictated the routine, and the orientation put a premium on order, obedience, and character development through work. Institutions were developed under the auspices of benevolent organizations, charitable individuals, and religious groups. An early history of social work notes:

> Institutions are in favor with the benevolent because the work done is so manifest. . . . Buildings are obvious and the money that goes into them takes a concrete form gratifying to contributors. The churches prefer such life for the children dependent on them because the children can be so easily isolated from teachings other than their own and there is opportunity for catechetical instruction [Warner, 1942, p. 134].

Public institutions were also developed under municipal, county, and state auspices. The first state institution was established by Massachusetts in 1866, and many states followed the pattern of housing dependent children in one central institution and placing them in families as soon as possible. The nineteenth century also witnessed the development of special institutions for the care of the physically handicapped, the deaf, the blind, the mentally retarded, and the delinquent. Thus, by 1923 the U.S. Census on Children Under Institutional Care listed 1,558 "orphan asylums" (Thurston, 1930, p. 39).

But even while the special institution for children was superseding the almshouse, serious questions were being raised about the advisability of any kind of institutional care for children. The late nineteenth and early twentieth centuries witnessed a continuous, prolonged, and often acrimonious debate in child welfare circles between the proponents of institutional care for children and the advocates of family foster care (Wolins, Piliavin, 1964).

A growing recognition of the importance of the family to the child's healthy psychosocial development resulted in a growing preference for family foster care. The prevailing negative attitude toward the institution was supported, and strongly reinforced, by a United Nations report, *Maternal Care and Mental Health*, by John Bowlby (1951), which provided a detailed review of a considerable body of research showing the deleterious effects of institutional care on child development.

Child welfare workers developed a hierarchy of preferences: the child's own home, even if inadequate, was felt to be better than the best foster home; a foster home, even if inadequate, was felt to be better than the best institution. More recently, however, the controversy regarding the relative merits of the boarding home and the institution has been redefined in different terms. The institution is no longer viewed in terms of a hierarchy of preferences but, rather, in terms of its appropriateness for certain groups of children who cannot be served by any other kind of facility. Institutions and foster homes have come to be seen as complementary, rather than competitive, resources. Each is necessary and appropriate for different groups of children, and each has a particular place in the total pattern of child-care services.

The institution is retained as an option, one component of the continuum of services available, to be used when it best meets the needs of the child and the family and after less restrictive alternatives have been either unsuccessfully attempted or considered but found to be inappropriate. As an option, the institution is linked with other components in the continuum of services. There is reluctant acceptance of the idea that institutional care may be an exceptional but nevertheless necessary and potentially helpful form of placement.

The resolution of the controversy resulted not only from the redefinition of the problem but also from a more critical attitude toward Bowlby's major thesis—that institutional care was likely to be harmful to the child. More recent research has softened the negative attitude toward the institution and contributed to the growing readiness to use it when it meets the needs of the child (Cusler, 1961; World Health Organization, 1962; Witmer, Gershenson, 1968; Wolins, 1968a, b, 1974; Moyles, Wolins, 1971; Child Welfare League of America, 1972; Rutter, 1974; Langmeier, Matejcek, 1975; Tizard, 1977).

THE "UNIQUENESS" OF THE INSTITUTION

The fact that institutional care is group care in a separate, twenty-four-hour, residential, physically defined community gives it some unique advantages that can be exploited to meet the special needs of some groups of children.

1. The institutions offer opportunities for a diluted emotional relationship with parental figures. Because the child in the institution has to share the houseparents with many other children, his relationship with them is apt to be attenuated. This permits the child to maintain a certain "safe" psychological distance from the parental figure and to modulate his contact in accordance with his emotional needs. Just as the child may want less from institutional parent figures, they, in turn, make fewer demands on the child. Specific portions of the houseparents' "time and energy have been purchased in relation to therapeutic purposes" (Simon, 1956, p. 2). As employees, they are less apt than foster parents to demand psychic repayment from the child.

2. The institution provides the child with a greater variety and choice of parental figures. If the child feels uncomfortable with the houseparent, he may develop a relationship with the resident teacher, or the resident social worker, or the resident maintenance man. There is a greater chance in the institution that the child will find the kind of person with whom he wants to identify.

3. The institution offers greater tolerance for all sorts of behavior that could not and would not be accepted in the community: "The greater symptom tolerance in an institution applies not only to acting-out behavior, but to withdrawn or bizarre behavior—for example, a child who sits by himself and will not talk or one who refuses to bathe for weeks" (Lerner, 1952, p. 107). A child can also be permitted a greater range of destructive behavior in an institution than in a normal home. None of the staff "owns" the institution, so that destructive behavior, although deplored, does not arouse the intense reaction it might evoke from foster parents whose furniture was being ruined. The institution is in a better position than a private home to "absorb" such losses. By the same token, "the diffusion of the child's hostility among many adults makes it easier for any one staff member to take" (Child Welfare League of America, 1964, p. 7).

4. The fact that institutional living requires rules, regulations, and a certain routine may be an advantage to many children who need the tight structure of

precise routine to reinforce their own efforts at self-control. The regularity, consistency, and stability of the institutional structure and the routines of orderly living provide the kind of support some children need. Many have experienced the anxiety that comes from living in an uncertain situation. Many of these children have never had a pattern of regularity in their daily routine. The explicit structure of regulation relieves the child of the responsibility for making decisions regarding his behavior, decisions that may occasion anxiety. Routine simplifies the child's life and permits him to know, with some assurance, what to expect.

5. Also, the institution is allied with those components of the child's ambivalence that strive to maintain control and to manifest acceptable behavior. Internal controls, which are weak in the child's own character structure, are built into the institution to help the child control himself. The child recognizes that the staff will support him in his efforts to refrain from impulsive, unacceptable behavior. Those kinds of behavior that the child might manifest in the open community—running away, truancy, sexual promiscuity, and so on—are not permitted in the more controlled, closed environment of the institution. Furthermore, unlike parental controls, institutional controls have the force of law, and because they are impersonal, uniform, and imposed on every member of the group, they are more difficult for the child to fight (Hechler, 1956). The institution carries the stamp of authority, and unlike parental controls, institutional controls are less likely to be seen as a personal attack.

6. The fact that the child lives his daily life as a member of a peer group means that the group has power to control his behavior. Group pressure can be applied to motivate the child to change his behavior so as to be less deviant, more conforming. Intimate daily living with a peer group provides the possibility of exploitation of group interaction as a catalyst for change. Through identification with the peer group, the child is able to accept and want what the peer group accepts and wants. For instance, one boy at first resented contact with the institutional social worker. The worker, consequently, delayed scheduling an appointment:

> All of H.'s group went to their regular appointments with their workers and H. became increasingly annoyed by this "neglect" when he received no appointments. After two months, he finally asked, "What the hell is the matter with that jerk of a social worker? Can't that guy write? Why doesn't he send me a pass for an appointment?" The worker, at this point, finally sent H. his appointment. The boy immediately was involved in an intensive treatment relationship [Shulman, 1954, p. 322].

7. Of great importance is the fact that residential group care permits the institution to plan the child's daily living experience so that it will be optimally therapeutic. It can provide the child with an environment that is planned and controlled so as to help the child. A child who is having difficulty with peers in one cottage can be moved to another cottage and another peer group within the same institution. An institutional staff can deliberately select children for a cottage group in accordance with some explicit considerations as to what kinds of friends each of the children needs. The institution can regulate the demands it enforces on the child in line with the child's inadequacies. It can particularize the details of his living situation, and within limits, it structures his reality to meet his clinical needs:

[It can provide] a flexible low-pressure environment for the deeply disturbed sensitive child, a clearly defined, more rigidly organized environment for the acting-out aggressive child who needs help in controlling his impulses. The environment for the young impulse-driven schizophrenic child with little personality structure must give greater weight to such considerations as the use of space, the allotment and scheduling of time. It might provide for greater emphasis on order and regularity and movement in personal routine [Alt, 1960, p. 131].

Also, because many institutions control the child's educational program, they can provide a more individualized curriculum, permitting a slower pace with more intensive personal tutoring.

8. Because the institution has specially trained personnel and special facilities, it can meet the unusual needs of the blind, the mentally defective, the emotionally disturbed, and so on. The institution, with its professional staff, can provide special physical rehabilitation programs, special medical treatments, and special remedial educational programs. The institution makes the child available and accessible to treatment—contact with personnel offering therapy is facilitated by virtue of the fact that the child is living on the grounds. The child is available for diagnostic study as well. The staff can observe his behavior at firsthand rather than having to depend on reports from parents, teachers, and so on.

SITUATIONS IN WHICH INSTITUTIONAL CARE IS THE APPROPRIATE RESOURCE

Institutional care is appropriate in many of the situations in which the child must be removed from his own home and placed under substitute care for some indefinite period (see Chapters 8 and 9). Those children referred for institutional care are more likely to have been removed from their homes as a result of their inadequacy in implementing their roles, primarily because of emotional, physical, or mental handicaps. Children who are removed from the home because of parental inadequacy are more likely to be placed in a foster family or made available for adoption. Despite this difference, the primary decision is whether to remove the child from his own home. Referral to a foster family or institutional care is a secondary decision.

The choice of institutional care may be predicated on what the child brings or fails to bring to the situation. The child, for one reason or another, may be unable to make use of the substitute-family situation found in boarding or adoptive care. He may be emotionally incapable of developing a satisfactory relationship with parental figures, neither accepting them nor responding to them with affection. Trasler (1960) notes the reactions of such children to the foster care that had been inappropriately selected for them:

The foster parents complained that M., the illegitimate child of a feeble-minded woman, "showed no signs of affection for them and appeared to be indifferent to their demonstrations of affection for her. They felt that she would never be able to adjust herself to their family group" [p. 21].

S.'s mother had been committed to a mental hospital and she had been shuttled from one home to another. Her foster parents asked that she be removed from the home because of her "apparent lack of real affection for them." They told the social worker "how often they had been hurt and grieved by S.'s complete lack of loyalty or any positive feeling for them. She does not harmonize with them at all and they feel quite unable to regard her as a member of the family" [p. 37].

Such children need, for a time, the kind of parent–child relationship provided by the institution: attenuated relationships, emotional distance, and limited involvement.

This same advantage of the institution may make it the most appropriate placement for a child who is very closely tied to his natural parents. Placement in a foster-family home for such a child would excite a conflict of loyalties between allegiance to his own parents and affection for the foster parents. Placed in an institution, without obligation to respond to a close relationship with parental figures, the child is spared the problem of competitive allegiances.

This aspect of institutional life also makes it an appropriate placement for the adolescent. The adolescent is faced with the problem of emancipating himself from close family ties, reducing his emotional investment in the family, and increasing his emotional investment in the peer group. For the adolescent, the institution offers a less intense relationship with parental figures and easy access to a peer group.

The institution is also appropriate for the child whose behavior makes him difficult to live with in a normal family setting. If the child is very aggressive and/or destructive, he cannot live satisfactorily in the close give-and-take of the normal family. Furthermore the community might find it difficult to tolerate his behavior; his aggressiveness may present a danger to other children and to community property. The child who set fires or engages in repeated acts of vandalism and who is beyond the control of parents needs an institution. The child who masturbates constantly and openly, who soils himself, who demonstrates extreme withdrawal behavior and unrelieved apathy is not likely to be acceptable in a boarding home. Such children, in fact, have often been rejected by a succession of foster parents and need the temporary permanence of an institution. The acting-out child needs the controls, limits, structure, and orderliness of the institution. The child manifesting bizarre, neurotic behavior needs the greater tolerance of deviation that the institution can provide.

The following are descriptive statements of children who were referred to a residential treatment center:

"Screaming fits and unmanageable at home"; "timid, fearful and withdrawn, screaming and fear of adults"; "found to be carrying out 'an under-cover reign of terror' in the school"; "picks fingers raw, frightful temper"; "mother at wits' end— boy has violent temper, antagonistic to everyone"; "soiling, enuresis, destructive behaviors"; "unaccountable bursts of sobbing; preoccupied with fire; a considerable danger in the home"; "sleeps badly, screams at night, night terrors"; "never spoke in the house; 'used to cry if you looked at him,' no life, no spontaneity, no interests"; "destructive, unruly, disobedient, spiteful, and uncontrollable"; "restless, completely uninhibited, acting on strong instinctive impulses, very difficult, and has terrible rages in which he kicks and bites and nothing is safe from him"; "truancy and unwillingness to go to school, suffers from sudden and extreme panics and anxieties" [Balbernie, 1966, pp. 137–67].

The problems presented at admission at another residential treatment center suggest the difficulty of community living for the group. More than a third of the group "were aggressive, violent and given to attacking others"; "hyperactive"; "prone to stealing, lying and setting fires" (Oxley, 1977b, p. 494).

Mayer, Richman, and Balcerzak (1977) point out that decisions regarding institutionalization depend on the child's ability to control his impulses. If the child tends to distort reality and live in the world of fantasy and cannot postpone gratification and manage his impulses, then the protection and control provided by the institution may be a necessary and appropriate setting.

The agency is under pressure to institutionalize some children, not in response to the needs of the child but in response to the community's demand for protection from his deviant behavior.

Mayer, Richman, and Balcerzak (1977) further note that referral for residential treatment is often made because other facilities have been eliminated. If a child is too disturbed to live in the family and in the community, he is too disturbed to live in a foster-family home or a group home, so that by the process of elimination only the residential treatment center is left.

For the child who is clearly psychotic or suicidal, the psychiatric hospital rather than the institution may be the facility of choice.

Children who cannot tolerate group life and are consistently disruptive in a group setting are dubious candidates for institutional care. In summary, the child admitted to an institution is a school-aged or older child who is sufficiently emotionally disturbed so that he cannot be maintained in the community even when community-based treatment is available, but is not so disturbed as a homicidal or suicidal patient, who might be a danger to himself and others. The typical child in this kind of center is difficult to control at home, his or her behavior is not tolerated well by the parents, and the child's relationship with the parents is unsatisfactory. The school finds it difficult to handle the child and the community rejects him. Parents either prefer or are willing to accept institutional placement, and the agency sees both parents and children as capable of making some change. This is the configuration presented by the institutional staff when outlining their admissions criteria.

The decision to offer institutional care may be based not on what the child brings or fails to bring to the situation but on the parents' responses. The natural parent who is greatly threatened by the loss of his child's affection to foster parents may be better able to accept his child's placement in an institution. The fact that the child has to share the institutional parent figures with a group of children reduces the natural parent's anxiety. Furthermore the institution is perceived as being sufficiently different from family living so that the parent may feel less guilty if the institution succeeds where he has failed with the child. The parent can attribute such success to the special facilities and the professional staff of the institution.

One study found that parents with a child in an institution were more likely to "tell others honestly where the [children] were than were parents whose child was in a foster home" (Aldgate, 1978, p. 29). This finding suggests that parents feel that greater stigma and shame are associated with foster-family placement than with institutional placement.

Choice of an institution may also be predicated on the need for short-term care. As Lerner says, "The institution, because it demands less in terms of emotional involvement, protects the child from making ties that must soon be broken" (Lerner, 1952, p. 108).

Also, a large group of siblings who want to be and should be kept together have found this to be possible only through institutional placement:

> Eight of nine children in one family orphaned by an auto accident will shortly pile into two automobiles for the seventy-mile ride to Kannapolis where they will enter an orphanage in answer to their plea to remain together.
>
> The children, who range in age from four to fourteen, now are in five foster homes. A ten-month-old infant is still in another home. The orphanage won't accept him until he is two.
>
> "I talked to them as a group," said the social worker. "I explained to them this may be the only way they could remain together." * (Capital Times, Madison, Wisconsin June 1963).

Institutional placement is supposedly contraindicated for infants and very young children. Such children are too young to profit from group living and require the more intensive relationship and mothering that are more likely to be available in a family setting.

Ideally, then, institutional placement is offered the child and the family after some considered assessment of the situation. Ideally the child should not end up in an institution simply because more desirable alternatives are not available. Institutional care should be "treatment by choice rather than treatment by default" (Shulman, 1954, p. 319). It appears, however, that here, as elsewhere, there is a gap between the ideal and reality. Studies of children in care reveal wide variations from community to community in the relative proportions of children placed in foster care and in institutions (Maas, Engler, 1959, p. 15; Wolins, Piliavin, 1964). In 1970 some 50 per cent of all children in substitute care in Kentucky and Nebraska were cared for in institutions. In Maryland and Nevada, however, only about 8 per cent of the children in substitute care were in institutions. Variations in per capita income, per capita taxes, unemployment rates, and the racial composition of the state population did not account for a significant amount of the variation, according to the preliminary analysis conducted by the Urban Institute, Washington, D.C. (Koshel, 1973, p. 36). Because it is not likely that there are wide variations in the children's situations, the differences in the frequency with which the institution is used are attributed to community attitudes toward the different kinds of substitute care, to expediency, and to the lack of availability of alternative resources (Wolins, Piliavin, 1964, p. 43).

A national survey of two thousand children's institutions indicated that 36,000 children had been accepted or retained because this was the only expedient and feasible plan, though not the best (Pappenfont, Kilpatrick, 1966, p. 457). At the same time, the institutions did not have room for some 54,000 children that they felt needed and should have gained admittance. In summary, over a "one-year period, directors of children's institutions reported that they made 126,829 decisions about children in need that they personally considered contrary to the best interests of the child in question, simply because of administrative

---

* From Associated Press dispatch from Lenoir, N.C., printed in *The Capital Times*, Madison, Wis., June 1963. By permission of The Associated Press, New York.

problems or because the appropriate resource was not available" (Pappenfont, Kilpatrick, 1969, p. 458).

Maluccio and Marlow (1972), after reviewing the relevant literature, concluded:

> The decision to place a child in residential treatment is presently a highly individualized matter based on a complex set of idiosyncratic factors defying categorization. The literature does not indicate agreement on consistent criteria or universal guidelines and it is not certain whether institutions diverse in origin, philosophy, policy, and clientele can agree on a basic set of premises [Maluccio, Marlow, 1972, p. 239; see also Hill, 1976, p. 31].

It is repeatedly noted in social work journals that referral to the institution should be based on diagnostic study of the child. Nevertheless a study of the records of five hundred children admitted into residential treatment showed that less than 10 per cent had a "complete psychiatric evaluation" and that about 60 per cent were referred on the basis of psychological testing alone (Bedford, Hybertson, 1975).

Like some decisions in foster care, the decision to refer a child to a residential treatment center may be often "more a decision of desperation than of deliberation," of chance rather than choice.

Rather than placement's being a haphazard phenomenon, there is a general consensus regarding which kind of child belongs in what kind of facility, but reality keeps the worker from making placement decisions based exclusively on defensible criteria. For instance, the most pressing need identified in a study of a two thousand-case sample of some twenty-nine thousand children in substitute care in New York City was in the area of institutional care and group homes. Children were inappropriately placed in other facilities because there was no space available in residential treatment centers and in group homes and residences (Bernstein et al., 1976).

Briar (1963) attempted an experimental study of how social workers go about making the decision to offer the child an institution or foster care. Study findings indicated that social workers do take into consideration the extent of the child's emotional disturbance and the preferences of the biological parents. Greater emotional disturbance in the child and opposition by the biological parents to foster care were associated with choice of the institution rather than a foster home. This finding is clearly in line with a decision based on diagnostic assessment. However, the study also showed that social workers in an agency that stressed foster care tended to recommend such care, whereas workers in agencies committed to institutional care tended to recommend this kind of care. This, then, is another factor influencing the decision process that violates the principle that decisions regarding the use of the institution should be based on diagnostic considerations.

As in the case of foster-family care, institutional child care is rarely offered without some prior preventive efforts (Hylton, 1964, p. 126). In an examination of forty-five referrals to a residential treatment program, randomly chosen over a four-week period, Martin, Pozdnjakoff, and Wilding (1976) found that in 85 per cent of the cases a variety of services had been offered in an attempt to retain the child in the community. "Placement was not sought lightly or offered as a reflex" (p. 271).

In studying the placement history of 215 children placed in residential treatment care, Maluccio's (1974) findings were similar. Institutional care was not the first choice but followed an attempt to deal with the problem in the community, "nearly all of the children and their parents having been active with at least one community agency." The decision to refer the child for institutional care was made "after a prolonged period of services to the child in his own home" (p. 230; see also Bloch, Behrens, 1955; Oxley, 1977, p. 495).

For some children, institutional care may not be the least restrictive setting, but it may be the least detrimental alternative—better than continued living in a family that rejects caring for him or better than multiple placements in foster-family homes that cannot cope with his behavior. In many cases, a less restrictive program in a foster-family home has been attempted for the child and has failed.

More frequently now than ever before, children coming into residential care are a residual group who have not been responsive to efforts made to treat them at home and in the community.

And as in the case of foster-family care, special efforts have often been successful in preventing institutional placements. Bedford and Hybertson (1975) describe a special Treatment Alternative Project (TAP) that achieved this objective. Children between the ages of four and ten living in the Greater Boston area and scheduled for residential treatment were diverted instead to the project. The project workers, assigned a limited case load of ten families, made an explicit effort to help the parents achieve a "thorough understanding of their part in the process" and to identify "parental stress points and reduce tension." Of forty-one active cases, only three children originally slated for residential center care were sent into such care, the others "being treated in their own homes or in foster homes with various kinds of special supports" not otherwise identified (p. 110).

Outreach efforts offering an intensive multiservice program attempt to divert institutional placement and to keep the child in the home. Cohen and Ewalt (1975) describe such a program offered to children whose behavior made them likely candidates for institutionalization. A task-centered approach was employed with the client family, and consultation was offered to community systems in contact with the child. The effort to retain in the community the total of eight children served by the program was very labor-intensive: The expense "to the agencies for supportive services was far more costly than for the general run of cases . . . moreover within one year, despite the effort of families, school personnel and workers, three of the eight children had been placed in residence" (p. 341). On balance, however, the program, despite the atypical effort and expense required, was more economical than would have been the case if the eight children had been placed initially.

Linnehan (1977) and Gordon (1978) also detail programs that have been able, by dint of great effort and extraordinary commitment on the part of the staff, to maintain severely disturbed and even psychotic adolescents in the community in a group setting.

SCOPE

In 1976 there were some 152,000 children in noncorrectional institutions. This includes children in institutions for the dependent and neglected, physically handicapped, mentally handicapped, and emotionally and psychiatrically impaired. The statistic does not include children in correctional institutions—training schools, prisons, reformatories, local jails, and detention homes (United States Bureau of the Census, 1978, p. 83). Our concern in this chapter is with two particular kinds of institutions—institutions for the dependent child and residential treatment centers for emotionally disturbed children—that are generally regarded as the responsibility of the child welfare service system. Children in correctional institutions are the responsibility of the juvenile justice system; physically and mentally handicapped children are perceived as the responsibility of the health care system.

In 1976 there were about 40,000 children in institutions for dependent children. These institutions have been defined by the U.S. Bureau of the Census as follows:

> This class of homes covers orphanages and other institutions which provide long-term care for children; it also covers institutions generally known as receiving homes or shelters which provide temporary care primarily to children whose homes have been broken by illness, desertion, death, and social crises.

Most of these institutions are under private—usually denominational—auspices. In fact, twenty-three states listed no public institution for the dependent and neglected in 1966 (Pappenfont et al., 1970b, Table 1, p. 2). The mean age of children living in these institutions in 1970 was about twelve or thirteen. Only 4 per cent of the population of these institutions was four years of age or younger (U.S. Department of Commerce, 1973). In institutions for the dependent and neglected, the population was 59.3 per cent male and 40.7 per cent female, but in residential treatment centers it was 70 per cent male and only 30 per cent female. Black children made up 15 per cent of the population of institutions for the dependent in 1970, and an additional 9 per cent of children were of Spanish origin.

Statistics show that such institutional placement is not long-term substitute care. The average stay in homes for the dependent and neglected is likely to be two-and-a-half to three years (Pappenfont et al., 1970, Table 23, p. 29). Institutions for dependent and neglected children are thus temporary care facilities, with children ultimately returning to their own homes or leaving at eighteen in their own care.

The changing composition of the population of children's institutions is reflected in the fact that 75 per cent of the children in "children's homes" in 1923 were full orphans. In 1957 only 8 per cent of such children were full orphans (Kieth-Lucas, Sanford, 1977, p. 8).

The residential treatment center, defined by the Children's Bureau as an "institution for the treatment of emotionally disturbed children in which planning is based on clinical study and in which treatment is carried out according to recommendations emerging from such a clinical study," serves only a small percentage of children in institutional care (Pappenfont et al., 1970c). The term is generally applied to facilities that provide a total therapeutic program for children whose emotional problems are sufficiently serious so that outpatient treatment is not regarded as a suitable alternative. The structure, staffing, and programs provide a planned and controlled therapeutic living situation.

As of January 1974, there were 340 residential treatment centers in the

United States, providing a total of 19,000 beds, but with an actual total of 17,700 residents. Of these facilities, 64 per cent had fewer than 50 beds, 8 per cent having 100 beds or more. Some 97 per cent of the facilities were under private auspices (Witkin, 1976).

There were wide variations in such facilities available to children in different states. Wisconsin provided 94 residential-treatment-center beds per each 100,000 children under eighteen in the state, as compared with 10 beds per 100,000 in Indiana and zero spaces available in Alabama and Montana (Witken, 1976, p. 13). The average length of stay of the child in care was about one-and-a-half years. The length of stay was shorter in smaller institutions as compared with larger ones. Social workers constituted 83 per cent of the full-time clinical staff (social workers, psychologists, psychiatrists) in the residential treatment centers. About 2,000 social workers were employed in such facilities in 1974 (Witken, 1976, Table 11).

SOCIAL WORK AND INSTITUTIONAL CARE

Preparation for Placement

Before the agency can seriously consider the institution as a resource in any particular instance, it has to study the child and the family. The parent is helped to explore the nature of the situation requiring substitute care for the child, and to discuss possible alternatives. Intake discussions with parents considering the institutionalization of a child may result in decisions to keep the child in the home. Hagen (1958) reports, without further amplification, that, "at a certain small multiple-service children's agency that has a strong casework service, 80 per cent of the parents applying for institutional service decided they would keep their children with them and work out their problems within the home" (p. 4).

This finding was confirmed by an experiment in Israel in which "two local public welfare offices were operated for a period of eighteen months by a university-guided team of social workers to test the effects of innovative work, on rate of institutional placements for dependent children" (Jaffe, 1970, p. 7). The two experimental offices emphasized explorations of solutions other than institutional care. Two control offices, which accepted the clients' initial requests for institutional care, showed a significantly larger proportion of institutional placements than the two experimental offices.

In many instances, the decision to institutionalize the child has come after frustration and disappointment in attempts to use supportive and supplementary services to maintain the child at home. Many emotionally disturbed children have received treatment at child guidance clinics or by psychiatrists in private practice before being committed, as noted above.

If institutionalization is the only feasible alternative, the parents need help in coping with their possible sense of failure and guilt at their inability to care for their child and in accepting surrender of their child. They have to be prepared to accept the fact that the substitute parents in the institution may succeed in helping the child make the kinds of changes that he was not able to make at home. At the same time, helping the parents to resolve doubts about the plan for placement is helpful to the child. The child can better accept the placement if his parents do so.

It is hoped that many children will return home after temporary institutionalization. Consequently an effort must be made to maintain the ties between the natural parents and the child. Discussion of the structure of service-visiting procedures, support of the child while institutionalized, and so on helps to accomplish this by stressing the continuing responsibility of the parents for the child. As Gula (1958) says, "The institution should be an interim, not a terminal, resource" (p. 20).

Conceptually the institution is seen as part of a continuum of help offered the child and the family. Rather than isolating this event in the life of the child from what precedes and follows it, the objective is to see the institution as part of the total support system to the family and the child. The institution attempts to change the child and the family in which he was and will be imbedded, and to develop linkages between the institution and all other systems of significance to the child's development.

Although it provides temporary substitute care of the child, the institution is not intended to supplant the family. It is, temporarily, part of the support system that helps the family to make those changes that will enable it to care for the child (Whittaker, 1978).

Placement here, as in the foster home, breaks the cycle of negative parent–child interaction and gives parents and children an opportunity for a "psychological" breather so that some change can take place.

The concern currently is with co-planning with parents. Work with parents increases the likelihood that the child will perceive his placement as a family decision rather than as an agency decision. Work with parents may be oriented not only toward helping them change to become more adequate parents but toward obtaining their full support of the placement decision.

At this point, parents are asked to sign a board agreement statement indicating what regular payments they will be making for support of the child. The payments are set according to their capacity to pay. At the same time, unless the child is being sent to an institution by order of the court, a written consent is obtained from the parents for institutionalization of the child.

The parents are also involved in the social study of the child conducted by the agency in preparation for placement. The institution, if it is to do its job effectively, must know something about the child's developmental history, his particular difficulties, his particular pattern of response to his parents and his peers, and so on. The parents are the principal source of such information. When the child to be placed is older, he, too, is involved in the social study. A report summarizing the background information on the child is sent to the institution for the guidance of the personnel.

Preparation for placement involves a visit to the institution by both the child and his parents before admission. During this visit, the child might meet with the housemother and some members of the group with whom he will be living. Frequently these institutions make available literature specially prepared for the child, which answers some of the most frequent questions children are likely to ask about living in an institution.

Preparation *with* the child, rather than merely *for* the child, involves more than providing reading material or arranging for a visit. It requires active discussion between caseworker and child of the fears and doubts that are aroused by separation from the parents and placement in the institution. It requires discussion of why institutionalization is necessary, what is going to happen, and when and under what circumstances the child will be returning home.

The institutional staff should be prepared for the child's arrival, and they, in turn, should have prepared the group with which the child is to live. The social worker and the institutional staff should discuss how the child is likely to affect the group to which he is assigned and how the members of the group are likely to affect him. This implies that the group has been selected with some thought as to how its composition will further the treatment plans for this child. Also, "some institutions have a 'Welcome Committee' of two or three children in each cottage or section to introduce the new child and help him to feel at home" (United Nations, 1956, p. 38).

The importance of preparing the child is based on the recognition that institutional placement is a very radical change in the child's life. As Beedell (1970) says, "The variety of new contacts with adults and other children which face a child joining a residential unit are almost comparable to those an adult would face who moved to a new town, changed her job, broke an engagement to marry, and contemplated another all on the same day" (p. 34). More difficult yet is the fact that the child is asked to live with peers whom he has no say in choosing: "Each child had to adjust in some way to children he has never seen before, who may or may not like him, and whom he may or may not like and with whom he will be constantly thrown" (Konopka, 1968, p. 34).

The Child in Care

The social worker is currently given greater responsibility for initiating overall planning with the parent, the child, and the institution and for coordinating and monitoring the implementation of the plan. The social worker has a knowledge of the "road map" that charts the course through the institutional experience.

Caseworkers have a continuing responsibility to work with the child once he is moved to the institution. They must help him adjust to the setting and make optimum use of what the institution has to offer. At the same time, they act as a bridge between the child's past—his own home and parents—and his present life in the institution. The social worker seeks to help the child deal with the problems of separation from his old life and integration into the life of the institution, of adjustment to institutional regulations and demands, and of interaction with the peer group and the institutional staff.

The treatment rationale of the institution in helping the child to change has traditionally been predicated on two complementary approaches. In delineating these approaches we are using the residential treatment center as a model because, although it currently serves only a limited number of the children in institutional placement, it serves as the prototype for the more progressive institutions of all kinds. The two complementary approaches involve individual psychotherapy and the structuring of a total therapeutic environment through which the child can be helped to change.

On the basis of a significant relationship with the caseworker, the child is helped to explore the dynamic basis for his behavior, to understand why he behaves as he does, and to change his behavior. Psychotherapy in the institution is more likely to center on the dynamics of present behavior rather than on material out of the child's past. This, as a matter of fact, is an advantage to the caseworker because he can reach the child at a time of emotional stress to discuss conflicts through which the child is living. Treatment moves out of the office into the child's world and his immediate reality for on-the-spot therapy:

> When S., a thirteen-year-old youngster, was adamant in refusing to return to her group and marched up and down the institution's "campus," it was her [case] worker who joined her in the march. The material handled during this time was not at all dissimilar to the content of their interviews: the child's feeling that she was too sick to be helped, that her rejection by the family was devastating and motivated these overwhelming feelings of hopelessness. When she marched past the gate, she said she could not control herself and not even the worker could control her. On the ensuing three-mile hike through neighboring towns and the final return to the grounds of the institution, the child received not only the demonstration of the worker's ability to control her, which diminished her feelings of anxiety, but also some insight into her current concern about her mother's illness and its relationship to the incident [Shulman, 1954, p. 322].

But individual psychotherapy is only one way in which the institution hopes to effect change in the child—and for those children whose ability to develop an emotionally involved relationship with any therapist is limited, it is not the most effective way. The second approach lies in a procedure unique to institutional living. Because the administration has the possibility of controlling the nature of the child's world, an explicit effort is made to structure his daily experiences so that all aspects of his environment have a therapeutic intent and impact: "Residential treatment differs significantly from outpatient and other treatment methods by taking responsibility for total management of the child's current experience-in-living. It attempts to monitor and modify, for therapeutic gain, all facets of the child's life" (Child Welfare League of America, 1972, p. 37). Thus treatment infiltrates all areas of a child's life. Food, recreation, education, allowances, chores, peer grouping, discipline, personal hygiene, visiting—all the daily activities have, in addition to their manifest meaning, some psychological meaning for the child.

For example, food is a physiological necessity and a source of pleasure. Beyond this, however, feeding is a symbol of the parents' acceptance of the child, of their willingness to care for him, and of the child's dependence on them. It is a bridge to a relationship between the child being fed and the adult doing the feeding. Food is food, but it also signifies love. It can be used, therefore, to help a child toward emotional health as well as physical health. Thus snacks, extra portions, sweets, the regularity of mealtimes, and special permission to dawdle over food might be employed as a part of an explicit design to give the child the kind of experience he needs.

By the same token, play is a physiological necessity and a source of pleasure. It releases tension and hostility, permits the acting out of unresolved experiences, relieves anxiety, and helps develop a feeling of self-confidence and a more acceptable concept of self. It results in a more positive relationship with peers and with the adults who supervise play. Play can be explicitly employed to provide the child with a corrective living experience.

These daily activities, then, are structured to induce, encourage, and support positive changes in behavior. The living situation is the therapeutic tool, and in an environment conditioned to meet his needs, the child lives therapy. Clinical reports confirm the contention that the therapeutic milieu itself, even without accompanying psychotherapy, is capable of effecting considerable change in the behavior of disturbed children (Lander, Schulman, 1960). Psychotherapy and the therapeutic milieu are complementary aspects of the total treatment program:

> We conceive of the residential treatment settings as a psychodynamically determined environment in which the total living experiences of the child are contrived and integrated with individual treatment comprising a unified therapeutic plan. The total life of the child, including his group living experiences, relationships with adults and children, school classes, work assignments, and recreational activities, becomes part of the therapeutic experiences of the child. . . . The experimental aspects of the child's life are consistent, parallel, and intermesh with the process of individual treatment [Shulman, 1954, p. 319].

However, here, as elsewhere in the child-care services, there has been a gradual shift in the basic orientation of the rationale of treatment programs. Those based on psychoanalytical psychology have less acceptance currently, whereas behavior modification approaches are gaining ascendancy.

More and more frequently, the literature reports experiences with incentive systems, conduct points, therapy points, goal-attainment scaling, and behavior contracting. There is a clear delineation of the privileges and rewards that follow from behavior changed in a positive and desirable direction and loss of privileges and withholding of rewards for failures to comply (Browning, Stover, 1971; Meyer, Odom, Wax, 1973; Crenshaw, 1976; McInnis, Marholm, 1977; Johnson et al., 1976). Such procedures clearly communicate expectations and provide opportunities for the children to assume responsibility for their own behavior (Dimock, 1977).

Rather than attempting an explanation of the intrapsychic conflicts that resulted in the child's emotional difficulties and then providing the opportunity for reexperiencing and resolving those conflicts in the therapeutic interaction, institutions oriented toward reeducation and behavior modification adopt an alternative hypothesis as to what needs to be done: "We prefer to say that the children we work with have learned bad habits. They have acquired new adaptive ways of relating to adults and children" (Hobbs, 1974). With greater use of behavior modification procedures has come a shift in the focus of intervention. Rather than being primarily concerned with the resolution of intrapersonal and interpersonal problems, the focus more frequently is on teaching specific social skills that would improve the child's ability to cope in relating to others (Whittaker, 1979).

In general, social workers in institutions are involved in individual treatment, consultation, and in-service education with the child care staff and take part in family therapy and liaison work with community agencies at intake and discharge.

Treatment in the institution is largely a responsibility of the casework staff. A study of over 600 residential treatment centers notes that they employed over 1,600 full-time social workers, the greatest majority of whom had a master's degree: "Social workers along with school teachers were employed more universally in residential treatment centers than other types of professional personnel. . . . and were utilized to a greater extent than [members of] any other professional discipline" (HEW, NIMH, 1971, pp. 11–12). A 1966 nationwide study of children's institutions in general revealed that psychiatrists were seeing 10,000 children for treatment or counseling, and social workers were offering service to 65,000 children (Pappenfont, Kilpatrick, 1969, p. 453).

If social workers and psychiatrists share total responsibility for individual psychotherapy, the entire staff shares responsibility for creating and maintaining the therapeutic environment. Although all share in this task, it is the particular responsibility of the child-care worker. These workers go under different names in different institutions: *cottage parent, houseparent, group parent, counselor, group counselor, residential worker, group living staff*. Whatever the title, the principal task is the same: the day-to-day care of the child. He is the nearest thing to a full-time parent assigned to the child. He lives with a small group of children in a cottage or in a circumscribed section of a building. He sees to the children's feeding and eats with them; he gets them to bed on time and wakes them up; he is concerned with their personal hygiene and their clothing needs; he settles fights and disputes among them and disciplines those needing discipline; he cares for and comforts them when they are sick; he gets them off to school and is there to greet them when they come home; he makes sure they do their homework and often helps with it. He is responsible for the daily living arrangements for the individual child, for the needs of the group as a group, and for the maintenance of the living quarters. The Child Welfare League (1964) indicates that "the child care staff is the heart of the program in an institution for children" (p. 61).

Behavior modification procedures increase the importance of the child-care worker's position. The child-care worker is more directly responsible for the "clinical" program when behavior modification is employed. He or she charts behavior changes, keeps "points" cards and token banks, and distributes rewards and reinforcements: "The child care worker now has free access to resources as well as power to dispense them—be they points, tokens, candy or material awards the [children] have to turn to him" (Maier, 1975, p. 417).

A rich literature is being developed directed toward the education of houseparents. Manuals and detailed accounts of institutional child care point to particularly sensitive times in the day's routine (wake-up time, meals, going to bed) and to recurrent types of problems (stealing, wetting and soiling, running away, sexual activity, disruptive and destructive behavior on the grounds and in the cottage) (Lambert, 1977; Adler, 1976; Klein, 1975; Baker *et al.*, 1972; Trieschman, Whittaker, Brendtro, 1969; Mayer, 1965, 1963). These books further offer suggestions on how to deal with such events and such problems in a therapeutic manner.

Kamerman and Kahn (1976) give a good description of the operation of a variety of group homes and institutions (pp. 273–299).

The professional clinical staff—the social worker, the psychiatrist, the psychologist—have ultimate responsibility for diagnosing the child's problem and planning his treatment. But the child-care worker—in direct, intimate, continuous contact with the child—has the primary responsibility for implementing the treatment plan. It is he who, in disciplining the child and arranging for his daily needs and activities, organizes the child's life in accordance with the treatment plan and provides the content of the therapeutic living experience.

The social worker consults with the child-care worker, explaining what the child needs, getting feedback information about how the child is behaving from day to day in reaction to the treatment plan, and soliciting the help of the child-care worker in reformulating the treatment plan.

The social worker has a similar relationship with other institutional personnel who may be playing a significant part in the child's life. This requires a cooperative relationship of respect among all members of the institutional staff. The need for such a relationship between child-care worker and social worker is particularly important. It is somewhat disappointing, then, to note that studies on the relationship between social workers and cottage parents indicate a relationship often characterized by resentment, differences of opinion, and lack of mutual respect (Piliavin, 1963). The caseworkers resented the cottage parents' emphasis on control, their intrusions into the caseworker's counseling responsibilities, and their failure to carry out treatment plans developed by clinic workers and agreed upon in case conferences. The cottage parents, on the other hand, felt that the caseworkers were either unrealistic in their treatment of the children or in their appraisal of the possibilities of program implementation within the cottages.

Child-care workers and social workers, having different responsibilities, necessarily have different perspectives on what they regard as important. In studying the residential treatment center, Polsky (1968) found that child-care workers emphasized activities concerned with meeting institutional demands: cottage housekeeping, maintaining the institutional standards regarding language or dress, and regulating the child's relationship to subsystems in the institution, such as school, work, and appointments with therapists (Polsky, Claster, 1968). Social workers concerned with therapy emphasize individualization and flexible interpretation of institution regulations in terms of the need of the particular child. The child-care worker, more concerned with smooth cottage management and functioning, sees such an orientation as destructive of the orderly housekeeping job he is requested to do. The child-care worker is apt to be oriented to the cottage group as the unit of treatment and concern; the social worker, to the individual child. Both are concerned with seeing that the children adhere to institutional norms, and both discourage behavior that is disruptive of the social system of the institution, but social workers are more likely to give precedence, where there is a conflict, to those activities that presumably facilitate the child's therapy, change, and psychological development (Dick, 1971).

Differing expectations lead to conflict. The child-care worker may expect that the social worker will provide clear and explicit "solutions" for coping with behaviors that disrupt cottage life. The social worker finds it difficult to communicate the fact that there are often no ready-made "solutions."

On the other hand, the social worker expects the child-care worker to implement a treatment program in the cottage, and the child-care worker may find it difficult to communicate the disruptive consequences of the social worker's recommendations. Confidence and respect between the two groups are eroded and conflict develops. As one houseparent said, "I can't get through to the social worker what the kid is like in the cottage." (See also Kieth-Lucas, 1977).

Some institutions have developed a team approach in dealing with such staff problems. Social workers visit each cottage and take part in the deliberations of each cottage team. The team—the teacher, the social worker, the cottage parents, the recreation leader—meet to plan and coordinate their efforts and direct them toward an agreed objective. For example, the child in question is shy, withdrawn, isolated: the social worker helps him express his feelings and explains the motives for his behavior; the teacher helps him establish contact with the children in the classroom; the recreation leader plans activities that might involve the child; the cottage parents utilize living situations to build a bridge between the child and other children.

The size of the cottage group varies, but it is rarely under eight and rarely more than fifteen. This is the primary group, the family of peers with whom the child lives. In the area or cottage assigned to the group, the child is allotted a private place, his own bed, his own furniture for his clothes. He eats with his group in the dining area in the cottage. He may attend the regular community schools, or he may be assigned to the school on the institutional grounds organized in accordance with a curriculum approved by the local board of education and staffed by licensed teachers. The institution provides recreational facilities—television in the cottage, playing fields, scheduled movies—and, in addition, the child might be involved in the recreational programs of community agencies, such as the YM- and YWCA, the Boy and Girl Scouts, and the Little League. The children are also given an allowance and are expected to perform the kinds of chores normally demanded of a child in the family: making their beds, helping with the dishes, and so on. Older children may be paid for the performance of institutional maintenance tasks: working in the yard, cutting wood, assisting in the library and in the canteen, and so on.

While the child is in the institution, the caseworker continues to work with the parents to prepare for the child's return home. Parents are advised of the child's progress and are encouraged to visit him regularly. Visits can assist the child in making progress, for they indicate the parents' concern for and attachment to him and assure him that he has not been abandoned.

Parental visits tend to reinforce the parents' commitment. At the same time, they present difficulties because, for many children, their relationship with the parents is a source of conflict, and the visits reactivate such conflicts. The caseworker tries to structure the visits so that they have an optimum beneficial effect. The caseworker might, for the good of the child, control the timing, frequency, and length of such visits (Addessa, 1972). The visits may be restricted to institutional grounds, or the parents may be encouraged to visit with the child away from the institution. Workers may help the parents to plan the visits and suggest things to do with the child for those parents who seem at a loss after the first few minutes of contact.

Parental visits can be dealt with more therapeutically in the institution than in the foster family. Because the staff with whom the parent comes into contact on such visits is either professionally trained or under professional supervision, the response to parents' behavior—even that which is disruptive to the child's placement—is more likely to be accepting and understanding. The child-care worker is less apt to feel that he is a rival of the natural parents for the child's affection and hence is less apt to feel threatened by their visits. As Mayer (1958) says, parents on visits "frequently try to show the child-care worker that he is not so perfect either. They may find the living room disorderly, the tablecloth torn, the floor dirty, and may become unduly upset about it, even though they may be poor housekeepers themselves" (p. 146). Social workers help the child-care worker to accept with understanding some of the critical reactions that parents exhibit as an expression of their guilt at having others care for their child. Furthermore institutional rules and regulations can be applied to control parents' visits without their feeling that such limitations are a personal attack.

Aldgate (1978) points out that a study of children in different substitute-care situations showed that children in residential care were actually more frequently and more consistently visited than children in foster-family homes. Although one component of the difference might be those children with stronger family ties may originally have been selected for institutional rather than foster care, the data show other factors operating. Parents feel more encouragement to visit children in institutions, there are fewer constraints and greater flexibility in when and how they may visit without fear of disrupting the child's living situation, they feel less competition from the institutional staff for the affection and loyalty of their children, and the institution provides greater opportunity to be alone with the child when parents visit.

Some institutions previously sought to reduce contact between the child and his parents, because the parents had "done enough harm already." The child was fenced in and the parent was fenced out. The institution now sees itself as the ally of the parents in helping the child; consequently it encourages their active involvement in the life of the child and the services of the institution. As Mayer (1958) says, "Child care workers must always remember the adage that one can take children away from parents but one cannot take parents away from children" (p. 145).

Currently many institutions have moved from rejection to toleration, to passive acceptance, and to active encouragement of parent participation in treatment plans with the child. Parents may even help to care for the child in the institution for limited periods, participate in institutionally sponsored children's outings, and be included in periodic evaluation of the child's progress (Kemp, 1971; Magnus, 1974).

In order to encourage the continuing involvement of the parents with their children in the institution, some agencies have encouraged phone calls between them and have paid for such calls. There is a recognition that the greater the involvement of the family in preplacement and placement planning and the greater the involvement with the child during the period of residence, the more likely the child will be to accept the placement and the more likely it will be that he will return home (Criss, Goodwin, 1970; Mora *et al.*, 1969).

The adjustment of children returned from a residential treatment center is related, as might be expected, to parental pathology and difficulties in the parent–child relationship. The prognosis is unfavorable for a child returning to a family in which little change has occurred in the parent–child relationship. Recognizing that placement has profound effects on the family as well as on the child, social workers employed by the institution are taking greater direct responsibility for working with the child's family rather than working through the social worker in the local agency. They have organized discussion groups and counseling groups for parents and have offered sociobehavioral training programs in child management techniques (Heiting, 1971).

Contact with parents varies with the institutional setting. Because many children in institutions for the dependent and neglected come from broken, multiproblem homes, fewer of these parents are seen by the agencies as being amenable to treatment, and 47 per cent of the institutions for the dependent and neglected did not provide casework or therapy with the families (Pappenfont *et al.,* 1970b, p. 267). However, of the residential treatment centers, 83.7 per cent provided casework or therapy with parents (Pappenfont, 1970c, Table 250, p. 267).

Where a child in residential treatment has lost contact with a family, efforts have been made to find a "resource family"—a family that might visit the child and take him away from the institution on an occasional outing (Moran, Niedz, Sampson, 1975).

Group workers have been assigned special functions in the child-caring institutions (Konopka, 1970; Schulze, 1951). Most frequently, they are concerned with the supervision and coordination of special recreational services. In the more advanced institutions, they might be asked to develop programs of group psychotherapy or to organize meetings of cottage groups offering guided group interaction. Groups have been used not only as a therapeutic corrective device to aid in the child's normal development, but also as an aid in management of the institution (Maier, 1965; Mayer, 1972). The cottage unit meets to decide on cottage living rules. "Campus councils," representing the child population of the institution, meet as a group to help legislate for the institution as a whole (Baxter, 1963). There are also reports of group psychotherapy with parents of children in a residential treatment center (Winder *et al.,* 1965).

Termination

Once a child has been in an institution for some time, a periodic review of the situation is advisable. This will reduce the child's chances of being "overlooked" and remaining in the institution longer than is necessary. Termination should come when the child has received maximum benefits from institutional care. To hold him beyond that point is to deny him some measure of a more normal life. Just as the social worker helps the child to make the transition into the institution, so he should help the child to make the transition into the community. Services before placement may reduce the need for placement; the availability of services following placement may reduce the time in placement.

Intake, life in the institution, and discharge from institutional care are all different steps in a single process. Preparation for and help with the return to the community are an important unit in the process. As Kahn (1960) says: "Rehabilitation must ultimately take place in the community. Institutionalization is, at best, a successful period of removal from the community in order to help the individual equip, and prepare himself for his return" (p. 14). Service needs to be provided to help in making the transition from institution back into the community.

Vocational counseling and job-placement training for adolescents being prepared for discharge from an institution for dependent and neglected children have been combined with a program for locating entry-level jobs in the community (Barchi, 1977).

Efforts to help the child make the transition from the institution to the community involve follow-up services to the child in his own home or on an outpatient basis, foster care, group homes, or halfway houses.

A nationwide survey indicated that about half of the institutions were providing some kind of aftercare service to former residents (Pappenfont, Kilpatrick, 1969, p. 455). Institutions for emotionally disturbed children were among those most likely to have established some specific provisions for such service.

Termination may involve an intermediate stage between the institution and the return home. In some cases, foster-family care is indicated for the child as further preparation for living in the normal family setting. Some children cannot go home because they have no home to go to or because their parents are still not ready to accept them. They, too, might need foster care. However, foster care is not always available for these children or, if available, may not be desirable because the child is in late adolescence.

For such children, transitional residence clubs have been established. These are extensions of the institution, located in the city. The child lives in the residence club, as he might live in a large hotel. He has greater freedom, more autonomy, and more responsibility for organizing his life than he had in the institution. In addition, the residence club staff stands ready to assist the child with personal, vocational, and educational guidance. Staff members are assigned to every floor of the residence and are readily available for interviews. Bellefaire, a residential treatment center in Cleveland, operates a number of group homes accommodating four or five children (Greenberg, Mayer, 1972). The homes are "one-family dwellings in a middle-class suburban area and are indistinguishable from other homes on the street" (p. 423).

It has been suggested that institutions coordinate the need of institutional children for contact with some interested adult with the need for aftercare. Thus foster parents could be selected a year in advance of the child's planned discharge. They might visit the child at the institution and have the child visit with them on weekends and holidays. They would be paid on a standby basis even before the child is placed in their home.

Residential treatment centers are developing a postdischarge foster-care program of their own. For instance, the Astor Home for Children in New York has licensed foster homes that the institution has recruited for care of its children.

The institution, or the parent agency administering the institution, takes responsibility for aftercare follow-up of those children who can return to their own homes. The contact enables the family and the child to have the continued support and help of the agency as the child is reincorporated into his own home. If all goes well, fewer and fewer interviews are scheduled, and ultimately contact is terminated. The emphasis should be on a continuum of care from services to the child and family before institutionalization of the child through the institutional experiences and during the period following discharge from the institution.

EVALUATION

Evaluation of the work of the child-caring institution is complicated by the fact that the term covers many different kinds of facilities serving distinctively different groups. The criteria for the assessment of outcome for the residential treatment institution for emotionally disturbed children are different from the criteria for assessing the outcome of a training school for delinquents—and these, again, are different from the criteria applicable to an institution serving the blind.

Social workers have a greater professional investment and interest in some child-caring institutions than in others. It is clear that the residential treatment center is one such kind of institution. We will therefore focus on evaluation studies of the residential treatment center.

Johnson and Reid (1947) studied the outcome of the treatment of 339 children accepted for treatment at the Ryther Child Center in Seattle, Washington, during the period 1936–1945. Treatment was categorized as "successful" if the child was subsequently able to adjust to his own home or a foster home, if he was getting along well in school or at work, and if he was living in accordance with community legal standards. Seventy-five percent of the group were rated "satisfactory" by these criteria. There was limited information available for assessment in some cases, but in general, children who were younger at the time of admission to care were more likely to have been successfully treated.

Rausch (1959) conducted a detailed observational study of a small group of six emotionally disturbed children in residential treatment. The behavior of each of these children "was characterized by such overwhelming aggressiveness that they could not be tolerated by community, schools, foster parents, or parents" (p. 10). Trained observers taped details of a particular child's behavior in six different kinds of interactional situations. The observational protocols were coded by at least two coders working together to categorize the nature of the behavior that had been observed. Observations were repeated after the child had been in residential treatment for eighteen months:

> Over a year and a half, the interpersonal behavior of the children shifted considerably. The major changes were in the relations of the children with adults. Here there was primarily a decrease in hostile, dominant behavior and an increase in passive, friendly behavior. The appropriateness of the behavior increased both in relations with children and adults. The patterns of change were consistent with treatment aims, and they seemed, at least in part, a function of the treatment program [p. 25].

Black and Glick (1952) used the Glueck Prediction Scale to evaluate the success of the treatment program at Hawthorne Center. Applying the scale to one hundred delinquent boys, they determined "that the relative chances of the Hawthorne boys for making a good community adjustment," if they had not received treatment, "were slight." In only eight of the one hundred cases "was there an even chance of not recidivating." Follow-up study of the group five years after discharge revealed that 74 per cent of the boys had not committed any offense for which they might have been arrested (p. 39). The difference between the high prediction and the actual rate is attributed to treatment received at Hawthorne. The validity of the results depends, of course, on the validity of the Glueck Prediction Scale.

Silver (1961) reports on a study of fifty-four children placed by the Jewish Family and Children's Service of Detroit in two different residential treatment centers. He notes that 60 per cent evidenced some positive change in behavior as a result of their stay at the residential treatment center, 20 per cent showed no change, and an additional 20 per cent showed a negative change. There is no indication in the report as to how the judgment was made. Success in treatment was related to the diagnosis: Silver states that, "in the neurotic group, there was a preponderance of positive outcome; on the other hand, in the combined category of character disorder and psychotic," (p. 201) there were fewer children who had positive outcome. Success in treatment was related to time in treatment, but not to whether the children and/or the parents had an awareness of their need for treatment.

Allerhand (1966) conducted a follow-up study of fifty boys discharged from Bellefaire, a residential treatment institution in Cleveland. Data for the study included a two-hour taped interview with each boy, interviews with his parents, and psychometric examinations of the boys. Included among the eleven different areas of social functioning assessed by the researchers were participation in family life, dating patterns, stability of school or work situation, and presence or absence of disciplinary actions in the community with regard to the boy. On the basis of the assessment, 64 per cent of the fifty children were manifesting successful social performance at the time of the follow-up study. One of the more significant findings is confirmation of the fact that adaptation at point of discharge is not in itself indicative of adaptation at follow-up. The incongruence between expectations at discharge and actual performance at follow-up was related to the level of stress or support provided by the living situation to which the boy returned: "It is the supportive or stressful nature of the post-institutional milieu that appears to be the critical factor in success, without regard to the within-institution career pattern" (p. 142). Only at the extreme end of the continuum were the boys' adaptations at discharge impervious to the effects of the post-discharge environment. For some, the capacity for adaptation had been so strengthened by the institutional experience that they could successfully cope with postdischarge stress; for others, who had been unable to respond even to the benign environment of the institution, no amount of postdischarge support seemed sufficient to enable them to adapt with adequacy. Postdischarge levels of adaptation were also a function of the extent to which the recommendations of the Bellefaire staff for aftercare living had been implemented. The researcher points out that institutional living prepares the child for institutional living but because the child ultimately needs to take his place in the community, the institution needs to provide the opportunity for more direct exposure to community demands.

The results of this study receive support from a follow-up of children who had been treated at Children's Village, a residential treatment center in Connecticut. The researchers found that "continuity and support following residential treatment was essential to postdischarge adaptation" and that "the greater the degree of support in the postdischarge environment the greater the degree of the child's adaptation to the environment" (Taylor, Alpert, 1973, pp. 50–51). Work with the child's family is clearly indicated. Of the seventy-five children studied, 31 per cent were judged to have achieved significant change in both self-esteem and behavioral functioning, 47 per cent were thought to have achieved significant change, and 22 per cent were felt to have made no change or to have regressed during their stay in treatment.

Maluccio (1974) studied the outcome of 215 children placed in residential treatment programs by the state departments of Rhode Island. The case records were used as the basic source of data, supplemented by mail questionnaires completed by the treatment institutions. The records varied in completeness of detail.

Because of the limited residential-treatment facilities in Rhode Island, many of the children had to be placed out-of-state, which adversely affected continuing contact between the child and his family and the efforts made by agencies to offer treatment services to the family.

Although discharge from residential care after an average of two years resulted from "successful treatment" in two thirds of the cases, in one third of the cases the treatment center confessed its "inability to help the child." The institution's own ratings of the change achieved by the child, which were obtained through the mail questionnaire without any substantiation, indicated "substantial" or "moderate" improvement in 48 per cent of the 76 children for whom such data were obtained.

The Children's Reeducation Center in Greenville, South Carolina, treating mildly or moderately disturbed children from six to twelve years old, had a 90 per cent success rate in returning children to public school. The program is based on reality therapy and behavioral modification and involves frequent parental visiting and a program of postrelease support (Hobbs, 1970, p. 202). (See also Weinstein, 1974.)

Millman and Schaefer (1975) report on the use of the Devereux Child Behavior Rating Scale by child-care counselors and the Devereux Elementary School Behavior Rating Scale by teachers and teachers' aides at Children's Village, a residential treatment center for emotionally disturbed boys. The counselor who knew the boys in the cottage and the teachers who knew the boys in the classroom periodically completed the forms, which assessed observable behavior. Ratings for over one hundred boys over the period of a year showed most significant changes in "social isolation," "coordination," "need for adult contact," "impulsivity," and "emotional detachment." There was less change in "social aggression" and "unethical behavior" (p. 696). "According to staff ratings, the deviant behavior of a group of preadolescent boys in residential treatment tended to show a slow, steady and often significant improvement over a 12 month period" (Schaefer, Millman, 1973, p. 160). "Behavioral competence" scores (personal hygiene, social functioning) improved more readily than "behavior control" factors (impulse control, acting out).

A follow-up mail survey of parents of children served at this residential treatment center asked about the child's adjustment after discharge and the parents' assessment of the help offered by the center (Schaefer, 1976). Responses from thirty-five parents indicated marked or slight improvements in functioning in about two thirds of the cases.

A follow-up study was done on seventy boys who had been admitted to a residential treatment center at an average age of eight-and-a-half years and who remained in the institution about three years (Oxley, 1977a, b). The follow-up, four years after discharge, showed that some 83 per cent of the group had made positive changes from admission to follow-up. Improvement was associated with greater parental involvement in the treatment program and was attributed to the agency's explicit requirement of such parental involvement.

More descriptive studies that present clinical accounts of success in residential treatment are those by Redl and Wineman (1951, 1953) and by Bettelheim (1951, 1955).

In recapitulation, then, the few studies available do support one another in suggesting that residential treatment in an institution does have positive effects on the child's behavior.

There are fewer recent evaluations of the effects of the other institutions of particular concern to social workers, namely, institutions for the dependent and the neglected.

Thomas (1975) in one of the few reports available on the effects of institutional care of the dependent and neglected child studied thirty-six such institutions with a total resident population of some 1,750 children. Careful testing in this study of the effects of such institutional care on the children's cognitive (verbal learning performance ability), social (task and social relations competence), and affective (sense of self-direction in daily life activities) development showed that the institutions were neither as harmful as had been feared nor as helpful as had been hoped. The report concludes that:

> an assessment of institutional environments is obtainable by evaluating the development patterns of institutionalized children over time in residence and comparing these patterns with those evidenced by a noninstitutionalized cohort. The evaluations that we conducted along these lines produced a body of evidence that suggests the prescribed effects of institutional care on child development to be over-rated in terms of both negative and positive consequences. For the most part the competency levels of institutionalized children do not differ radically from those demonstrated by non-institutionalized children. . . . By and large the institutional experience does not prove to be potent enough to produce gross deviations in child development for good or ill [Thomas, 1975, p. 206].

From a positive point of view, however, the institution did provide, for the children placed, a safe, healthy, caring environment in which the child had the unhindered opportunity to grow and to develop his potential.

PROBLEMS

1. A significant aspect of evaluation is concerned with the deficiencies inherent in institutional care. The earlier concern that institutionalization traumatizes the child because it imposes maternal deprivation and stimulus deprivation seems to have given way to a more critical analysis of the problem, as already noted. It is currently conceded that a reasonably well-organized institution with a decent child–staff ratio can provide the child with the affectionate care and stimulation he needs for adequate growth (Witmer, Gershenson, 1968, p. 81). The research on infant deprivation, which was the basis of so much of the concern, is not applicable to most institutional populations, which are composed largely of children between ten and twelve years of age—well beyond the critical period for maternal deprivation.

It is difficult, however, even for those institutions with a low child–staff ratio and adequate resources, to provide continuity of care, which requires a relationship with a nurturing adult who has primary responsibility for care of the child over a significantly long period in the child's development. Discontinuity in care in the institution results from the fact that a twenty-four-hour caretaking day is likely to require three sets of different parents, that caretakers need days off and vacations, and that all institutions have a very high staff turnover. A constant problem for institutional management is the shortage of trained staff and the associated problem of high staff turnover. Many, particularly younger, workers view the position as a temporary one.

A review of the limited material available on the child-care worker suggests that such a person is "young, highly mobile in an occupational sense, of moderate education, and with limited experience" (Toigo, 1975, p. 9). As Mayer says, they are hired for a job rather than for a career and for a particular agency rather than for an occupational field. Given their low status in the institution, the low pay, the lack of a career line and promotional possibilities, the lack of an occupational reference group with which they can identify, and the emotionally stressful nature of the job, it is easy to understand why 30–40 per cent of child-care workers quit within a year. When directors of child-care institutions were asked in a nationwide study to list their recommendations for change, the one most frequently listed was for "raising the quality of the child care staff through recruitment at higher salaries and/or increasing in-service training" (Pappenfont, Kilpatrick, 1969, p. 458).

2. The distinctive features of the institution present problems as well as advantages. One of the most distinctive features of institutional care is that it is a group situation. In constant, intimate interaction with one another, the children themselves informally assign social roles to members of their group, so that it has a definite social structure: leaders and followers, exploiters and exploited. The group also develops its own code of behavior, to which it expects members to conform if they want to be accepted by and included in the group.

It is to be remembered that most of the children served by the institution are teenagers. Distrust of and hostility toward adults are at their height at this time, even among teenagers who have not experienced difficulty—and these children have known little except hurt and pain from the adults they have encountered. Furthermore the need for acceptance by the peer group and dependence on the peer group are very great during adolescence. The peer group can, therefore, exercise considerable control over those who refuse to conform to its code by threatening to reject them.

Given these considerations, it is not unusual to find that the social structure and the code of the group are developed without consultation with adults on the staff and that children in the institution feel a strong pressure to accept them. As long as the social structure and the code of the group reinforce the aims of the official structure of the institution, the group is an additional powerful resource that helps the child to change in the desired direction.

The problem is, however, that this informally developed social subsystem might operate to encourage and support behavior that is in opposition to that officially sanctioned by the institution. In such a case, group living—the distinctive feature of the institution—provides the basis for a serious problem of competition between the formal, official system and the often incompatible, informal subsystem (Polsky, 1962).

The group code generally discourages the kind of intimate, psychologically open relationship with institutional staff that is necessary to the achievement of the therapeutic aims of the institution. According to Ohlin and Lawrence (1959), "Under existing circumstances, the inmate as a client must run the risk of social rejection by his peers to gain full advantage of the treatment experience" (p. 9). Furthermore the social structure of the group is built along autocratic lines, leaders and followers having markedly unequal status and interpersonal relationships being characterized by the exploitation of the weak by the strong. This, too, is in contravention to what the institution is trying to teach about democratic group living characterized by understanding and acceptance.

A problem inherent in group homes as well as in institutions is the contagious effect that children have on each other. Whatever differences there are from child to child, they share the stigmatized fate of referral to the facility, most frequently because of some behavioral emotional problems. The peer group, which supposedly is a principal agent of therapeutic change, is often made up of a heavy concentration of disturbed children. Healthy, well-adjusted children coming from a stable, wholesome background are a missing ingredient in group composition. The peer culture established by such a one-sided mix of children can work to impede rather than to accelerate desirable changes in the children. Inherent in the nature of the group is the risk of the development of what has been termed *secondary deviance* in response to stigmatized labeling and peer-group contagion.

As a congregate-care facility dealing with a sizable group of children, the institution needs regulations and rules. Thus a conflict arises between the need for some regimentation and the therapeutic need to individualize the situation for each child. Individualizing regulations in response to the therapeutic needs of a particular child results in conflict in the institution. Children are confused and upset when they see one child treated one way for an infraction of the rules and another child treated another way for an infraction of the same rules. The problem is to reconcile regulations and individualization in a situation where the procedure is open to the scrutiny of the client group.

The institution is currently faced with a dilemma that arises from greater sensitivity to children's rights. The child has the right to treatment in the least restrictive setting and without any coercion. As a consequence of attempting to adhere to granting such rights, institutions need to resolve difficult conflicts between children's rights and children's needs, and the rights of the individual child versus the rights of the group of children in the institution. The dilemma is that in satisfying children's rights, we may be denying children's needs. This dilemma arises clearly in institutional care, as explicated in an article by Mayer and Pearson (1975). What if, in order to help the adolescent, the most desirable prescription is a controlled environment, and the adolescent, in claiming his rights, rejects this alternative? Respecting his rights denies him access to what he needs in order to have a more satisfying life.

Living with children inevitably involves problems of discipline, setting limits and establishing controls. This is especially true in a group context composed of children who are there in the first place because they have difficulties in behavior control. Institutional child-care workers employ all of the procedures traditionally utilized by parents in attempting to get the child to act in a socially acceptable manner: appeals to reason, use of the power of the relationship and the risk the child runs of alienating the workers, the withholding of privileges or the providing of extra privileges, and so on. In addition, group living provides an opportunity for appealing to the need of the group and the group's judgment of the child's behavior as a leverage for control.

However, all of these procedures may fail. Even in the most accepting of settings, restraints may occasionally be necessary (Linnihan, 1977, p. 686), in apparent contradiction to the rights of the child. Protection of the child, the child-care worker, institutional property, and the rights of the other children may ultimately dictate the exercise of authority and the use of physical restraint, "time-out" facilities, "control rooms," or "quiet rooms" (Endres, Goke, 1973; Drisko, 1976). Physical punishment implies action out of consideration for the needs of the child, not in response to anger and a desire to hurt. It involves the least amount of use of force to accomplish its objectives and is always a procedure of last resort. However euphemistically phrased, the use of such procedures involves a difficult conflict for the staff.

One advantage of the institution—the fact that the social worker is directly aware of the child's problems and, in fact, injects himself into the child's reality—also serves to create a problem. The workers are called upon to make recommendations that directly affect the lives of the children—recommendations regarding a child's visit home or a parent's visit to the institution, recommendations regarding a child's discharge from the institution, recommendations regarding the disciplining of the child when he breaks the rules. The worker is, then, no longer a neutral figure to whom the children can freely confide all. The child becomes aware of some of the real-life consequences of his sharing. The problem is reconciling the power of the worker over the child's life and the therapeutic neutrality needed for the best worker–child contact.

Another advantage of the institution—the variety of adults available from among whom the child can select an object for identification—may cause conflict. The adults might be working at cross-purposes with one another, each teaching and advocating different things. The problem is to integrate the activities of the different adults in contact with the child so that their different contributions to the child reinforce, rather than conflict with, one another.

3. Another problem faced by the institution is that the people who have the greatest responsibility for therapy and who have the greatest functional power for therapy have the least education and status (Simon, 1956). Mayer (1965) points out that "while the child-care workers have far less professional education and experience than other people on the staff, they spend more time with the child than anyone else. They are exposed more acutely to his pathology and have to deal with it more directly than any other member of the staff" (p. 83). Despite their responsibility for dealing with the day-to-day and hour-to-hour reactions of the children and despite their responsibility for structuring the details of the therapeutic situation, the child-care workers are under the direction of others and must, because of their more limited education, defer to the professional clinical staff of social workers, psychiatrists, and psychologists.

4. Another of the current problems of the institution is one we tend to associate with a past period in our history. In 1950 Albert Deutsch published a detailed, and shocking, nationwide report of child-caring institutions that were guilty of neglect and exploitation of the children living in them. He described training schools in which the housing was dilapidated and overcrowded; the food scanty, monotonous, and inedible; the educational and recreational resources primitive or nonexistent; and the care of the children, at best, indifferent, and at worst, clearly irresponsible. A report published in 1970 of conditions in children's institutions around the country mirrored the 1950 findings (James, 1970). A report in 1976 (Wooden, 1976) repeated the 1970 findings, which had repeated the 1950 exposé.

A survey of a sample of eighteen institutions in five states caring for children receiving Aid to Families of Dependent Children (AFDC) support payments was conducted in 1976 by the Office of the Comptroller General (U.S. Office of Comptroller General, 1977). Deficiencies in seven of the eighteen institutions were noted, primarily with regard to physical facilities: "children sleeping on mattresses on the floor in cramped and dingy rooms"; "broken and dirty bathroom facilities which were cited by two health agencies as inadequate" (p. 25). Licensing did not guarantee "that institutions maintained their facilities at acceptable levels" (p. 27). Although defects were found in the facilities, there were no findings regarding neglect and abuse of the children in the institutions surveyed.

Ensuring adequate physical care, let alone healthy social and emotional care, for children in institutions appears to be a recurrent problem. It might be noted, however, that for the most part, the horrendous examples cited by Deutsch, James, and Wooden concern facilities for delinquents. The institutions for which child-welfare social work has some responsibility—the residential treatment center and institutions for the dependent and neglected—are not as frequently indicated, although there are deficiencies.

A conference on child abuse and neglect in residential institutions sponsored by the Children's Bureau in 1977 agreed that all placements in institutions for treatment should be voluntary, that no corporal punishment should be permitted, and that any restraints, isolation, or seclusion should be used only as a last resort. The Child Welfare League of America statement of standards on group homes notes that "corporal punishment, solitary confinement and deprivation of food are not acceptable means of discipline" (p. 24). By 1977 most states had procedures for reporting abuse and neglect in institutions and provisions for an independent investigation of any reports of maltreatment.

5. Another problem is the uneven distribution of residential treatment institutions so that many sections of the country are without such a facility. Other communities do not have temporary shelters or detention homes. The result is that some children, who clearly do not belong there, are committed to adult wards of psychiatric hospitals or are held in prisons. Also many institutions are understaffed, lacking social workers and other professionally trained people. As a result, such institutions see custody as the only service they can offer.

Some states do not have sufficient institutional placement for emotionally disturbed children, but in other instances, the institution is reluctant to take some of the children referred to them because they are likely to be a disruption and a threat to the institutional community (Gordon, 1978, p. 302). As a consequence, some states have been sending children to institutions outside the state that are willing to take them, or even to institutions outside the country. For instance, Illinois has sent children needing institutional care to Canada (*Chicago Tribune*, July 27, 1975). (See Children's Defense Fund 1978, pp. 57–74.)

The shortage of residential treatment center facilities is chronic and growing. The Joint Commission on the Mental Health of Children identified this shortage in 1970 as dictating one of the more pressing service needs. Along with escalating expenses, the number of children identified as needing such a frequently unavailable resource is growing. Part of the increase in demand may stem from the effort to divert children from correctional programs and to redefine delinquent behavior in mental health terms.

6. Institutions and group homes face a problem of public acceptance when

they attempt to locate in a community. Group-home staff reports indicate that at best group homes are tolerated rather than fully accepted. There is often organized opposition in terms of petitions, testimony at zoning- or planning-board meetings, picketing, and court action. There is on occasion destruction of group-home property and facilities and harassment and scapegoating of group-home children.

In addition to the fact that group-home neighbors are fearful about decline in property values and the possible deviant behavior of group-home children, plus the fact that group homes often bring nonwhite children into a white neighborhood, there is also concern about "saturation." The deinstitutionalization of a variety of kinds of institutions has resulted in an influx into some neighborhoods of the mentally ill and mentally disabled, drug users, and ex-offenders. Until there is a more equitable distribution of group homes, some neighborhoods will find themselves "saturated" by such homes.

The tolerance quotient of the community and the community schools for deviance varies, but it is rarely very high. Whatever the level of acceptance of deviant behavior within the group home itself, the fact that it is located in the community and that the children live "in" the community a good part of the time sets limits on the kinds of children the group home can include: difficulties in getting zoning, the fearful antagonisms of many neighborhoods, and the needs of the children for acceptance in the community make it necessary to set certain behavior expectations (Mayer, Richman, Balcerzak, 1977).

Faced with the problem of community opposition to group homes, one group of agencies attempted an interorganizational effort (Stickney, Capaivolo, 1976). The Community Resident Information Services Program assists in locating sites for group homes, provides consultation on zoning and community relations, works with citizens' groups, and serves as an information exchange and a resource bank for relevant studies and reports. Based on their experience, they suggest a thorough study of the community and its residential pattern, a slow low-profile approach, and the involvement of community leaders in planning for the institution or group home. Selecting an appropriate neighborhood that is likely to be receptive, or at least not strongly opposed; preparing the neighborhood for the opening of the group home; gradually bringing the home up to a full complement of children; and sharing group-home facilities with the neighborhood whenever possible—these have been among the tactics that make it easier for the neighborhood to accept the group home.

Weber (1978) has identified the different neighborhood variables that the group-home developer needs to be aware of in deciding on a strategy for entry into the community. He suggests, among other things, educating neighbors through one-to-one contacts by the house parents of the projected group home, being frank about possible problems but indicating procedures for keeping them to a minimum, and being clear about the legal basis that gives the group home the right to open.

TRENDS

We have previously noted some of the trends in institutional child care: the change in the relative distribution of children between foster-family care and the institution for children needing substitute care; the increased efforts to include the participation of parents in the treatment program; the increased concern with aftercare programs; and the greater use of behavior modification procedures.

1. A principal trend in institutional care is the change in the nature of the population served. The development of supportive and supplementary services has reduced the number of children requiring substitute care. Now the children who require it are more frequently those who are so disturbed or who come from a situation so disorganized that even supportive and supplementary care would not permit them to be kept in their own homes or in foster homes. And even if the situation is so precarious as to require substitute care, the foster home is usually the first choice. Thus the institution receives those children who not only require substitute care but who are unable to use family-type substitute care. The institution, then, tends to serve the most difficult of the most difficult cases.

Gula (1958) cites this trend when he states:

> the more severely disturbed, aggressive[ly] delinquent, and severely retarded children are squeezed to the top and referred to institutions. Since these children have more complex treatment needs, institutions are being asked to provide more specialized care and treatment [p. 4].

The change is noted by Jonsson (1972), who says:

> The nice children that we used to get . . . pale, with sorrowful faces and shy, quiet manners . . . [have been replaced by] unhappy children who express their longing for understanding and tenderness in a language which is natural to them; swearing, and pestering and using foul language, kicking and punching and stealing, playing truant, bad table manners, sex talk, smoking, and boasting [p. 42].

2. With the diversification of child welfare services and the changes in the nature of the children institutionalized, there has been a change in the nature and the purpose of the institution. From a general placement setting for children needing substitute care, the institution has become a specialized kind of agency serving a special population. The trend is to modify the essential purpose of the institution from custody to treatment. The modern institution is said to be a "filling station, not a parking lot." Yesterday's "inmate" is today's "patient":

> There is hardly a children's institution today that will not say that providing treatment is its primary responsibility. This has become such a fashionable cliché that it is not uncommon for some children's institutions called a home, a school, a village, or a farm to be described as "analytically oriented," as "a clinical setting," or as "a residential treatment center" (Browne, 1963, p. 77). But this trend is more a result of a change in the nature of the children served than a result of a desire for increased status on the part of the institution.

3. This change in the program of the institution has resulted in the increased professionalization of staff. Custody and care do not require professional services; treatment does. Hence there is a trend toward an increase in the number of social workers, psychiatrists, psychologists, and remedial teachers working in the institution. This change corresponds with a trend toward upgrading the nonprofessional staff in the institution, particularly the crucially important house-

parent staff. Many schools of social work have developed special, noncredit courses for houseparents, generally covering such topics as normal child development, the meaning of separation, the impact of institutional living on children, the use of living routines in meeting children's needs, discipline in the institution, the child and his relatives, and the dynamics of group living. The Child Welfare League of America acts as a clearing house of information about such programs (Berman, 1970). By 1970 institutions of higher learning in twenty-one states were offering courses in preparation for child-care work, many at the junior college level (Mayer, Marsushima, 1969).

An association of child-care workers has been organized, and a journal devoted to residential child-care practice, *Child Care Quarterly,* was started in 1972. A curriculum for the certification of child-care workers has been formulated. At the beginning of the 1980s, however, the training of child-care workers is seen as a beneficial but not yet essential prerequisite qualification for the position.

4. "Deinstitutionalization" is a steady, long-term trend in child care. Statistics regarding the relative distribution of children in foster-family homes as compared with children in institutions show a steady drop in the use of institutions in favor of foster-family care. Between 1928 and 1940, three hundred institutions were closed in the United States and many more have been closed since (Reid, 1975).

Although there has been almost a complete cessation of the building of new institutions, community-based group homes had an explosive growth in the early 1970s. New York City, which had 158 group homes for 1,500 children in 1973, had 230 group homes by June 1974 (Citizens Committee for Children of New York, 1976).

The press toward "mainstreaming," "normalization," and "a least-restrictive environment" with regard to the developmentally disabled and the physically handicapped gives additional current impetus and acceleration to this long-term trend.

Federal policy also gives clout to deinstitutionalization. Title XX of the Social Security Act Amendments recognizes the selective need for the institution as a useful component in the continuum of services. Although it makes federal funds available for "preventing or reducing inappropriate institutional care," funds are also provided for "securing referral or admission to institutional care when other means of care are not appropriate" and for "providing services to individuals in institutions."

However, Title XX is not neutral with reference to the institution. The regulations are decidedly biased in pressing toward deinstitutionalization wherever possible. Funding is made available under fewer restrictions and more liberal conditions to group-home facilities as contrasted with institutions.

It might be noted that the long-term trend toward deinstitutionalization involves two different aspects. One is the reduction in the number of children referred to institutions and the closing of institutions. Second, it involves the deinstitutionalization of the institution itself. The attempt has been made, whenever possible, to make the institution more "familylike."

As it applies to changes in the institution, deinstitutionalization involves a redesign of the institution toward a less restrictive environment. This new design includes changes from larger to smaller facilities, from larger to smaller living units, from group to individual living and sleeping quarters, from segregation from the surrounding community to greater integration with the community, and a reduction in the more structured aspects of the institutional living situation. All of this permits the child an experience that more closely approximates noninstitutional living. In the old institution, children slept in dormitories, ate in large mess halls, wore uniforms, and marched in line. In the new institution, children live in small cottage units, have their own rooms, eat with a small group in the cottage dining room, and dress according to their individual taste. Children now move from the institution into the community, attend community schools, use local recreational facilities, join in local activities, shop in community stores, use the local library, and so on. Community volunteers act as special tutors for the children, serve as scout leaders, take children to swimming lessons in the community, and the like.

If the words we use suggest the nature of our perceptions, then the changing vocabulary of the institution connotes a "normalization" of the institution. As Whittaker (1976) points out, institutional *grounds* have now become a *campus*, the *patient* becomes a *student*, the *cottage* becomes a *dormitory*, *discharge* is now *graduation*, and a *treatment center* is now a *residential school*.

Most children's institutions are not "total institutions" in the sense that all life-supporting functions are carried by the institution in isolation from any contact with the outside world. Most are "mediatory" institutions, oriented to and interacting with the surrounding community (Seidl, 1974).

These efforts to deinstitutionalize the institution are quite different from the intent of the current deinstitutionalization social movement. The two principal forms of deinstitutionalization, while moving in the same general direction, have two distinctively different objectives. One form of deinstitutionalization is designed to improve the institution; the objective of the most recent deinstitutionalization drive is to eliminate the institution. Improving the institution by changing its potentially damaging aspects recognizes the utility of the institution as a child-care service. Deinstitutionalization efforts that seek to eliminate the institution imply in effect that the institution, as a part of the child welfare spectrum, is beyond salvaging.

The most dramatic example of the move toward deinstitutionalization was the closing by Massachusetts in 1972 of all of its seven state-administered institutions for juvenile offenders. This is, of course, the most drastic procedure for deinstitutionalization. Other states have attempted a more gradual program of deinstitutionalization. This involves reducing the number of children sent to institutions and making explicit efforts to review the population of institutions in order to send as many children as possible back to their home community. Concomitant with such efforts is a gradual development of alternative community resources, such as specialized foster-family homes, agency owned and operated group homes, and the purchase of service from proprietary group homes (Bakal, 1973; Ohlin, Coates, Miller, 1974).

Although there is a decided trend toward deinstitutionalization, particularly with regard to the "normal" neglected and dependent child, there is a demand for a growing number of spaces in the institution for the emotionally disturbed, as already noted. This may not be entirely contradictory because the residential treatment center is likely to be perceived as more therapeutic than custodial and hence to have "corrected" the worst features of institutional care.

Although the general trend is clearly in the direction of a reduction in institutional care and an increase in community-based care, this is still a matter of some controversy. Unions feel the responsibility for protecting the jobs of members employed in institutions; the communities in which the institutions are located resist the loss of community income if the institutional payroll is eliminated. Some of the anticipated advantages of community-based care are found to be more difficult to achieve, and some of the disadvantages are becoming more apparent.

The promise of large savings in the difference between institutional costs and group-home costs is proving to be somewhat illusory. Group-home costs creep up to within stalking distance of institutional costs. Part of the costs are shifted to the general community. Because the group homes use many of the services in the community that the institution provides for out of its budget, group homes appear to be more economical. An audit report of the New York City Comptroller's Office (1977), which provides the funds for most of the children in substitute care in New York City, noted that the cost of care of the child in a foster-family home in June 1977 was $4,904 on an annual basis, of institutional care $13,408, and of group-home care only slightly less, at $13,140 (pp. 3–4). Youth Services of Philadelphia computed their cost of maintenance of adolescents in community-based group homes as $15,000 per year per child in 1975–1976 (Levine, 1977, p. 145).

Although group homes are located in the community and are thus closer to the child's family, they have not been any more successful than the institutions in sustaining continued contact between parents and children (Citizens Committee for Children of New York, 1976, pp. 33–34).

Community group-home living provides opportunities that a more sheltered institutional environment can control: "Any 'action' these youngsters want is available to them in the streets. The pull of street culture and the promise of hustles are strong. [The community group home] has to deal with gangs, with pushers, with bars," with pimps, and so on (Levine, 1977, p. 147).

There is very limited research regarding the outcomes of community-based group-home facilities and nothing comparing the outcomes of such programs with those of institutional care for the kinds of children who have been the primary concern of this chapter.

Taylor et al. (1976) did a follow-up study of twenty-four girls who had lived for an extended period of time in a group home in Philadelphia. The girls had entered the home at an average age of fifteen and were discharged after an average stay of two-and-a-half years at seventeen and a half. At the time of follow-up, the average age of the girls studied was twenty-two and a half.

The girls had been accepted in the group home after unsuccessful efforts had been made to treat them in their own home and in foster-family homes. The girls were either seriously emotionally disturbed or schizophrenic. They required a controlled, structured, therapeutically oriented milieu. The group home, a brick house in a residential neighborhood, provided care, caseworkers, psychiatric treatment, an educational program, a group program, and a corps of volunteers who acted as big sisters. The therapeutic mix was cemented by "caring," which was defined as "giving of oneself even when the response and visible progress of children are discouraging, as they usually are in residential treatment . . . ; ignoring personal inconvenience, as when the director or caseworker would spend a whole night looking for a runaway girl or when child care staff would sit up all night with a girl in acute distress" (p. 53).

Although making positive changes in functioning, cautiously attributable to the intervention of the group-home program, the actual performance at follow-up of the girls was marginal. Having entered the program with "extremely limited emotional, personal and social resources, the girls were making their way in the world with some effectiveness" (p. 82). They had achieved reasonable independence and were working out their lives without having been arrested, hospitalized, or, for the most part, being dependent on welfare.

Koshal (1973) summarizes the research regarding deinstitutionalization for dependent and neglected children by noting that:

> With regard to dependent and neglected children there is widespread presumption that the living environment provided by a foster family home or group home is better than that provided by a residential institution. As we have shown above [in the body of the review] the empirical evidence for that position is incomplete [p. 53].

Concluding a similar kind of review of available evidence, Thomas (1975) says that "There is very little in the way of research findings demonstrating clearly the advantage of either half-way houses or group treatment homes—we simply do not know whether the group treatment home is superior to institutionalization or not" (p. 21).

The ideological gains in terms of the normalization and the least-restrictive environment of community-based facilities are, however, clear advantages.

5. Parallel with deinstitutionalization there has been a trend toward *partial institutionalization*.

Day treatment for the emotionally disturbed child is a partial institutionalization, between outpatient treatment and residential care. The children referred present the same kinds of behavioral problems presented by children in residential treatment centers: lack of impulse control, aggressiveness, and disordered perception. The difference in the service offered relates to the availability, the willingness, and the ability of the parents to care for the child in the evening and on weekends and their acceptance of their own involvement in the program of treatment. The child is in care during the day Monday through Friday. The parents attend parents' group meeting every other week and meet weekly with a worker (Ross, Schreiber, 1975). Day treatment has been used to supplement residential treatment rather than as an alternative to it. Following residential treatment, children have been referred to continuing help through day treatment (Marshall, Stewart, 1969).

Another kind of partial institutionalization involves twenty-four-hour care of the child during the week and out-care of the child in his own home on weekends and during vacations (Astrachan, 1975). This kind of program requires that the parent pick up the child for weekend care and deliver the child to the institution at the end of the weekend. At both these times, the parent, in contact with the institution's staff, has the opportunity of discussing the family's and child's experiences. Weekend visiting of the child from the institution has a number of advantages in addition to keeping the parents involved and maintaining the relationship between parents and children. It permits the child to test some of his changed behavior in a real-life context, it permits the parents to practice a changed attitude toward the child under reduced stress, and it prepares the child for the transition from the treatment center back into the family (Weisfeld, Laser, 1976). The child is clearly a continuing member of the family, and the parents have continuing responsibility for his care.

Some settings have formalized such joint responsibility. Oxley (1977) describes a residential-treatment-center program that requires that "parents must agree to be actively involved in their children's treatment; children must return home on weekends and for a summer vacation lasting one month" (p. 493). Reports on such programs indicate that there is less pressure to succeed if the child gradually becomes involved with the family through weekend visits and "if placement fails at this stage it is not devastating to either partner." It permits the child gradually to "test the gains made in personal therapy in a real life setting. It is the [child's] equivalent of field work for the social worker" (Huffman, 1975, p. 353). There is an additional advantage in that it is easier to retain child-care staff in a program that provides weekends off and some respite from contact with the children.

6. New experiments are being attempted in order to meet the problems of staff shortages. One imaginative effort, the foster-grandparent program, initiated and supported by funds from the Office of Economic Opportunity, involves hiring older people on an hourly basis to come into the institutions and care for the children. This program permits an increased ratio of staff to children and more personalized care for each child. The greatest help has been provided to institutions for mentally deficient and physically handicapped children, which house many younger children who need to be fed and played with and to have their clothes and bedding changed.

7. There has been a move toward the racial integration of children's institutions. The fact that segregated institutions could be denied public funds acted as an effective stimulus for desegregation (Gula, 1966). Desegregation has meant not only acceptance of minority-group children but a change in staffing pattern so as to open employment in institutions, at all levels, to minority-group applicants.

Desegregation has been complicated by the fact that some institutional charters were written to exclude racial-minority-group children; some communities with which institutions have interpenetrated were segregated. Black children residing at the institution might be going to all-white schools, pools, theaters, and so on. Parents of white children in the institution might object to their children living in such close, intimate association with minority-group children. Despite these difficulties, many institutions have successfully integrated both staff and children.

SUMMARY

The child-caring institution is a third form of substitute care, which provides congregate-group care rather than substitute-family care. The group care it offers permits some unique advantages:

1. The child is not pressured or obligated to develop a close relationship with parental figures.

2. The peer group itself can be used as a catalyst for helping the child to change.
3. The routine required in group living and the regulations that the institution is required to enforce offer security to the child and support him in controlling his impulses.
4. The institution can tolerate a wider range of behavior than is acceptable in the community.
5. Special facilities for care, treatment, rehabilitation, and vocational training can be made available to a group of youngsters burdened by the same disability.

The distinctive attributes of institutional living suggest the kind of child to whom institutional care might be selectively offered when substitute care is needed:

1. The child who, because of previous negative emotional experiences with parents, is unable to relate positively to them and hence cannot make effective use of family care.
2. The adolescent, who faces the developmental task of dissolving ties to parents and for whom a situation permitting attenuated parent–child relationships is therefore desirable.
3. Youngsters requiring special facilities or programs: emotionally handicapped, impulsive, delinquent youngsters requiring the structure of controls rather than open community living, the physically handicapped, and the mentally deficient.
4. Youngsters whose behavior is a danger to themselves and the community, or whose behavior cannot be tolerated by the community.
5. Youngsters whose parents are threatened by the thought of another family's succeeding where they failed, but who can accept the institution as a form of substitute care.

In helping the child, the institution also takes advantage of the unique properties of group living. In addition to individual psychotherapy, the institution attempts to structure the child's daily living experience so that it encourages and supports healthy change. This can be done in the institution because the staff controls the nature of the child's environment: whom he lives with; where and how he eats, sleeps, plays, and goes to school; and so on.

Problems faced by the institutions include the following:

1. The difficulty in providing continuity of care because of great staff turnover.
2. The potentially negative effects of group living. Children living in groups set up their own social system and code of behavior, which may oppose, rather than support, the aims of the institution.
3. The contradiction between the need for regulations and the need to individualize; the conflict between the needs of the individual child and the needs of the group.
4. The disparity between the education and the status of the child-caring staff and their therapeutic significance to the child.

5. The public's ambivalent attitude toward the institution and the children it serves.

Among the major trends noted were the following:

1. The increased use of the institution as a special resource for special children.
2. The change in the rate of children referred to institutions, but the increased severity of the problems presented by the children referred.
3. The movement from custody to treatment as the major service offered, and the diversification of treatment approaches.
4. The increased professionalization and upgrading of staff, including houseparents, and the increased diversification of institutions.
5. The attempt to deinstitutionalize and desegregate the institution, the increasing tendency to involve the parents in the treatment program, and the trend toward partial institutionalization.
6. Increasing concern with aftercare programs.
7. Continued attempts to find alternatives for institutionalization.

BIBLIOGRAPHY

ABBOTT, GRACE. *The Child and the State,* Vol. 2. Chicago: University of Chicago Press, 1938.

ADLER, JACK. *The Child Care Worker 1975.* New York: Brunner/Mazel, 1976.

ALDGATE, JANE. "Advantages of Residential Care." *Adoption and Fostering,* 92, 2 (1978), 29–33.

ALLERHAND, MELVIN E., et al. *Adaptation and Adaptability: The Bellefaire Follow-up Study.* New York: Child Welfare League of America, 1966.

ALT, HERSCHEL. *Residential Treatment of the Disturbed Child.* New York: International Universities Press, Inc., 1960.

ASTRAHAN, MYRTLE. "The Five Day Week: An Alternative Model in Residential Treatment Centers." *Child Welfare,* 54, 1 (January 1975), 21–26.

BAKAL, YIZHAK. *Closing Correctional Institutions.* Lexington, Mass.: D. C. Heath & Company, 1973.

BALBERNIE, RICHARD. *Residential Work with Children.* Elmsford, N.Y.: Pergamon Press, Inc., 1966.

BARCHI, CARL F. "A Community Reentry Model." *Child Welfare,* 56, 9 (November 1977), 593–600.

BAXTER, MARY JANE. "House Council—An Integral Part of Residential Treatment for Disturbed Children." *Catholic Charities Review* (May 1963), 46–47.

BEDFORD, LINDA, and LARRY D. HYBERTSON. "Emotionally Disturbed Children: A Program of Alternatives to Residential Treatment." *Child Welfare,* 54 (February 1975), 109–115.

BEEDELL, CHRISTOPHER. *Residential Life with Children.* New York: Humanities Press, Inc., 1970.

BERMAN, SAMUEL P. "A Report on a Child Welfare League of America Pilot Project to Train Child Care Workers." *Child Welfare,* 49, 3 (March 1970), 156–160.

BERNSTEIN, BLANCHE, DONALD A. SNIDER, and WILLIAM MEEZIN. *Foster Care Needs and Alternatives to Placement.* New York: New York State Board of Social Welfare, November 1975.

BETTELHEIM, BRUNO. *Love Is Not Enough*. New York: The Free Press, 1951.

———. *Truants from Life*. New York: The Free Press, 1955.

BLACK, BERTRAM, and SELMA GLICK. *Recividism at the Hawthorne-Cedar Knolls Schools*. New York: Jewish Board of Guardians, 1952.

BLOCH, DONALD, and MARJORIE BEHRENS. *A Study of Children Referred for Residential Treatment in New York State*. New York: New York State Interdepartmental Health Resources Board, 1955. Mimeo.

BOWLBY, JOHN. *Maternal Care and Mental Health*. Geneva: World Health Organization, 1951.

BREMNER, ROBERT H. (Ed.). *Children and Youth in America—A Documentary History*, Vol. 1: *1600–1865*. Cambridge, Mass.: Harvard University Press, 1970.

BRIAR, SCOTT. "Clinical Judgment in Foster Care Placement." *Child Welfare*, 42 (April 1963a).

BROTEN, ALTON M. *House Parents in Children's Institutions—A Discussion Guide*. Chapel Hill: University of North Carolina Press, 1962.

BROWNE, CLIFTON T. "Some Problem of Children's Institutions in Achieving Maturity." *Child Welfare*, 42, 2 (February 1963).

BROWNING, ROBERT M., and DONALD O. STOVER. *Behvaior Modification in Child Treatment*. New York: Aldine Publishing Company, 1971.

BUREAU OF THE CENSUS, U.S. DEPARTMENT OF COMMERCE. *1976 Survey of Institutionalized Persons—Current Population Reports*, p. 23, No. 69. Washington, D.C.: Government Printing Office, 1978.

———. *1970 Census of Population—Persons in Institutions and Other Group Quarters*. Subject Reports PC(2)–4 E. Washington, D.C.: Government Printing Office, 1972.

CASLER, LAWRENCE. "Maternal Deprivation—A Critical Review of the Literature." *Monograph of the Society for Research in Child Development*, 26 (1961).

CHILD WELFARE LEAGUE OF AMERICA. *Maternal Deprivation*. New York, January 1962.

———. *Standards for Services of Child Welfare Institutions*. New York, 1964.

———. *From Chaos to Order: A Collective View of the Residential Treatment of Children*. New York, 1972.

———. *Standards for Group Home Service for Children*. New York: Child Welfare League of America, 1978.

CHILDREN'S DEFENSE FUND. *Children Without Homes*. Washington, D.C.: Children's Defense Fund, 1978.

CITIZENS COMMITTEE FOR CHILDREN OF NEW YORK. *Group Home for New York City Children*. New York: Citizens Committee for Children, December 1976.

COHEN, MARGRIT, and PATRICIA EWALT. "An Intensive Program for Severely Disturbed Children." *Social Casework*, 56 (June 1975), 337–342.

CRENSHAW, DAVID J. "Teaching Adaptive Interpersonal Behavior: Group Techniques in Residential Treatment." *Child Care Quarterly*, 5, 3 (Fall 1976), 6–16.

CRISS, FLORENCE L., and RAY C. GOODWIN. "Short-Term Group Counseling for Parents of Children in Residential Treatment." *Child Welfare*, 49, 1 (January 1970), 45–48.

DEUTSCH, ALBERT. *Our Rejected Children*. Boston: Little, Brown and Company, 1950.

DICK, HARRY. "Nature and Significance of Changes in the Houseparents' Role in Institutions for Children." *Journal of Health and Human Behavior*, 12, 4 (December 1971).

DIMOCK, EDMUND T. "Youth Crises Service: Short term Community Based Residential Treatment." *Child Welfare*, 56 (March 1977), 187–195.

DRISKO, JAMES W. "Memo to Institution Staff: Physical Involvement with Children—A Therapeutic Intervention." *Child Welfare*, 55, 7 (July–August 1976), 469–477.

ENDRES, V. JOSEPH, and DOUGLAS H. GOKE. "Time Out in Residential Treatment Centers." *Child Welfare*, 52, 6 (June 1973), 559–563.

FINKELSTEIN, NADIA E. "Family Participation in Residential Treatment." *Child Welfare*, 53, 9 (November 1974), 570–575.

FLEISCHER, LAWRENCE. *Analysis of the Need for Long Term Residential Child Care.* New York: Human Resources Administration, Department of Social Services, 1976.

GORDON, JAMES S. "Alternative Group Foster Homes: A New Place for Young People to Live." *Psychiatry*, 39 (November 1976), 339–354.

———. "Group Homes: Alternative to Institutions." *Social Work* (July 1978), 300–305.

GREENBERG, ARTHUR, and MORRIS F. MAYER. "Group Home Care as an Adjunct to Residential Treatment." *Child Welfare*, 51, 7 (July–August 1972), 423–435.

GROUP CHILD CARE CONSULTANT SERVICES. *The Basic Course for Residential Child Care Workers.* Chapel Hill: University of North Carolina, 1978.

GULA, MARTIN. *Child-Caring Institutions.* Washington, D.C.: Government Printing Office, 1958.

HAGEN, HELEN. *The Institution as a Casework Agency.* New York: Child Welfare League of America, February 1958.

HECHLER, JACOB. "Social Controls in Institutional Treatment." *Social Work*, 1 (April 1956).

HEITING, KENNETH H. "Involving Parents in Residential Treatment of Children." *Children*, 18, 5 (September–October 1971), 163–167.

HILL, ALICE. *Toward an Evaluation of the Use of Residential Group Facilities by Local Child Welfare Agencies.* Washington, D.C.: The Urban Institute, September 1976.

HOBBS, NICHOLAS. "Project Re-Ed. New Ways of Helping Emotionally Disturbed Children," in *Crisis in Child Mental Health: Challenge for the Seventies.* Joint Commission on Mental Health of Children. New York: Harper & Row, Publishers, 1970.

HUFFMAN, STUART. "Some Observations on Weekend Foster Home Visitation as a Step Out of the Institution." *Child Welfare*, 54 (May 1975), 351–353.

HUGES, DAVE S. "Supporting the Child During Wake-up Time." *Child Care Quarterly*, 2, 4 (1973), 277–281.

HYLTON, LYDIA. *Residential Treatment Center, Children Program Costs.* New York: Child Welfare League of America, 1964.

JAFFE, E. D. "The Impact of Experimental Services on Dependent Children Referred for Institutional Care." *Social Work Today*, 1, 2 (May 1970a), 5–8.

JAMES, HOWARD. *Children in Trouble—A National Scandal.* New York: David McKay Co., Inc., 1970.

JEWETT, DAVIS R. "The Group Home—A Neighborhood Based Treatment Facility." *Children Today* (May–June 1973), 16–20.

JOHNSON, LILLIAN, and JOSEPH REID. *An Evaluation of Ten Years Work with Emotionally Disturbed Children.* Seattle: Ryther Child Center, 1947.

JONSSON, GUSTAV. "Introduction to New Staff," in *Children Away from Home—A Sourcebook of Residential Treatment.* Ed. by James K. Whittaker and Albert E. Trieschman. New York: Aldine Publishing Company, 1972.

KAHN, ALFRED. *When Children Must Be Committed.* New York: Citizens' Committee for Children of New York, June 1960.

KAMERMAN, SHEILA B., and ALFRED S. KAHN. *Social Services in the United States—Policies and Programs.* Philadelphia: Temple University Press, 1976.

KEMP, CLAIRE J. "Family Treatment Within the Milieu of a Residential Treatment Center." *Child Welfare*, 50, 4 (April 1971), 239–242.

KIETH-LUCAS, ALAN, and CLIFFORD W. SANFORD. *Group Child Care as a Family Service*. Chapel Hill: University of North Carolina Press, 1977.

KLEIN, ALAN F. *The Professional Child Care Worker—A Guide to Skills, Knowledge, Techniques and Attitudes*. New York: Association Press, 1975.

KONOPKA, GISELA. *Group Work in the Institution*, revised. New York: Association Press, 1970.

———. "What Houseparents Should Know," in *Children in Care*. Ed. by J. N. Tod. Essex, England: Longman Group Ltd., 1968.

KOSHEL, JEFFREY. *Deinstitutionalization—Dependent and Neglected Children*. Washington, D.C.: The Urban Institute, December 1973.

LAMBERT, PAUL. *The ABC's of Child Care Work in a Residential Setting*. New York: Child Welfare League of America, 1977.

LANGMEIER, JOSEF, and Z. MATEJCEK. *Psychological Deprivation in Childhood*, 3rd ed. Ed. by G. L. Mangan. New York: John Wiley & Sons, Inc., 1975.

LERNER, SAMUEL. "The Diagnostic Basis of Institutional Care for Children." *Social Casework*, **33** (March 1952).

LEVINE, THEODORE. "Community-Based Treatment for Adolescents: Myths and Realities." *Social Work*, **22** (March 1977), 144–147.

LINNIHAN, PATRICIA. "Adolescent Day Treatment: A Community Alternative to Institutionalization of the Emotionally Disturbed Adolescent." *American Journal of Orthopsychiatry*, **47**, 4 (October 1977), 679–688.

LOEWE, BESSIE, and THOMAS E. HANRAHAN. "Five Day Foster Care." *Child Welfare*, **54**, 1 (January 1975), 7–18.

MAAS, HENRY, and RICHARD ENGLER. *Children in Need of Care*. New York: Columbia University Press, 1959.

MAGNUS, RALPH A. "Teaching Parents to Parent: Parent Involvement in Residential Treatment Programs." *Children Today*, **3**, 1 (January–February 1974), 25–27.

MAIER, HENRY W. "Learning to Learn and Living to Live in Residential Treatment." *Child Welfare*, **54** (June 1975), 406–420.

——— (ed.). *Group Work as Part of Residential Treatment*. New York: National Association of Social Workers, 1965.

MALUCCIO, ANTHONY N., and WILMA D. MARLOW. "Residential Treatment of Emotionally Disturbed Children: A Review of the Literature." *Social Service Review*, **46**, 2 (June 1972), 230–250.

———. "Residential Treatment of Disturbed Children." *Child Welfare*, **43**, 4 (April 1974), 225–235.

MARSHALL, K., and M. F. STEWART. "Day Treatment as a Complementary Adjunct to Residential Treatment." *Child Welfare*, **48** (1969), 40–44.

MARTIN, LAWRENCE, IJA POZDNJAKOFF, and JOYCE WILDING. "The Use of Residential Care." *Child Welfare*, **55**, 4 (April 1976), 269–278.

MAYER, GOETZ, and JAMES PEARSON. "Social Control in the Treatment of Adolescents in Residential Care: A Dilemma." *Child Welfare*, **54**, 4 (April 1975), 246–256.

MAYER, MORRIS F. "The Group in Residential Treatment of Adolescents." *Child Welfare*, **51**, 8 (October 1972), 482–493.

———, and JOHN MARSUSHIMA. *A Guide for Child Care Workers*. New York: Child Welfare League of America, 1958.

———. *Supervision of Houseparents*. New York: Child Welfare League of America, 1965.

———. "Training for Child Care Work: A Report on a National Conference." *Child Welfare*, **48**, 9 (November 1969), 525–532.

MAYER, MORRIS F., LEON H. RICHMAN, and EDWIN A. BALCERZAK. *Group Care in North America*. New York: Child Welfare League of America, 1977.

McInnis, Elizabeth T., and David Marholin. "Individualizing Behavior Therapy for Children in Group Settings." *Child Welfare,* 56, 7 (July 1977).

Meyer, Margaret. "Family Ties and the Institutional Child." *Children,* 16, 6 (November–December 1969), 226–231.

Meyer, Margit, E. E. Odom, and Bernice S. Wax. "Birth and Life of an Incentive System in a Residential Institution for Adolescents." *Child Welfare,* 52, 8 (October 1973), 503–509.

Miller, Jerome, and Lloyd E. Ohlin. "The New Corrections—The Case of Massachusetts," pp. 154–176, in *Pursuing Justice for the Child.* Ed. by Margaret K. Rosenheim. Chicago: University of Chicago Press, 1976.

Millman, Howard L., and Charles E. Schaefer. "Behavioral Change: Program Evaluation and Staff Feedback." *Child Welfare,* 54, 10 (December 1975), 692–702.

Montrose, M. Wolf, *et al.* "Achievement Place—The Teaching Family Model." *Child Care Quarterly,* 5, 2 (Summer 1976), 92–101.

Mora, George, *et al.* "A Residential Treatment Center Moves Toward the Community Mental Health Model." *Child Welfare,* 48, 10 (December 1969), 585–590.

Moran, Michael S., Barbara Niedz, and Gregory Simpson. "The Resource Family: Helping Emotionally Disturbed Children in Residential Treatment." *Children Today* (November–December 1975), 26–29.

Moyles, William E., and Martin Wolins. "Group Care and Intellectual Development." *Developmental Psychology,* 4, 3 (1971), 370–380.

New York City Comptroller's Office. *Audit Report on Foster Care Agencies' Achievement of Permanent Homes for Children in Their Care.* New York: City Comptroller's Office, June 1977. Mimeographed, 81 pp.

Ohlin, Lloyd, and William Lawrence. "Social Interaction Among Clients as a Treatment Problem." *Social Work,* 4 (April 1959).

———, Robert B. Coates, and Alden D. Miller. "Radical Correctional Reform: A Case Study of the Massachusetts Youth Correctional System." *Harvard Educational Review,* 44 (February 1974), 74–111.

Oxley, Genevieve B. "Involuntary Clients' Responses to a Treatment Experience." *Social Casework,* 58, 10 (December 1977a), 607–614.

———. "A Modified Form of Residential Treatment and Its Impact on Behavioral Adjustment." *Social Work,* 22 (November 1977b), 493–498.

Pappenfont, Donnell, *et al.* *A Census of Children's Residential Institutions in the U.S., Puerto Rico and the Virgin Islands: 1966: Vol. 1: Seven Types of Institutions.* Chicago: University of Chicago School of Social Service Administration, 1970a.

———, *et al.* *A Census of Children's Residential Institutions in the U.S., Puerto Rico and the Virgin Islands: 1966, Vol. 2: Institutions for Dependent and Neglected Children.* Chicago: University of Chicago, School of Social Service Administration, 1970b.

———, *et al.* *A Census of Children's Residential Institutions in the U.S., Puerto Rico and the Virgin Islands: 1966, Vol. 4: Institutions for the Emotionally Disturbed Children.* Chicago: University of Chicago School of Social Service Administration, 1970c.

———, and Dee Morgan Kilpatrick. "Child Caring Institutions 1966: Selected Findings from the First National Survey of Children's Residential Institutions." *Social Service Review,* 43, 4 (December 1969), 448–459.

Paul, James L., Donald J. Stedman, and G. Ronald Neufeld (Eds.). *Deinstitutionalization—Program and Policy Development.* Syracuse, N.Y.: Syracuse University Press, 1977.

PAUL, SISTER MARY. *Criteria for Foster Placement and Alternatives to Foster Care.* Albany: New York State Board of Social Welfare, 1975, pp. 56–57.

PAYNE, GEORGE H. *The Child in Human Progress.* New York: G. P. Putnam's Sons, 1916.

PILIAVIN, IRVING. "Conflict Between Cottage Parents and Caseworkers." *Social Science Review,* 37 (March 1963).

PIZZAT, FRANK. *Behavior Modification in Residential Treatment of Children.* New York: Behavioral Publications, February 1972.

POLSKY, HOWARD. "Changing Delinquents' Subculture: A Social Psychological Approach." *Social Work,* 4 (October 1959).

———. *Cottage Six—The Social System of Delinquent Boys in Residential Treatment.* New York: Russell Sage Foundation, 1962.

———, and DANIEL S. CLOSTER. *The Dynamics of Residential Treatment—A Social Systems Analysis.* Chapel Hill: University of North Carolina Press, 1968a.

———. *Social Systems Perspectives in Residential Institutions.* East Lansing: Michigan State University Press, 1968b.

PROSSER, HILARY. *Perspective on Residential Child Care: An Annotated Bibliography.* Atlantic Highland, N.J.: Humanities Press, 1976.

RAUSCH, HAROLD. "The Interpersonal Behavior of Children in Residential Treatment." *Journal of Abnormal and Social Psychology,* 59 (January 1959).

REDL, FRITZ, and DAVID WINEMAN. *Children Who Hate.* New York: The Free Press, 1951.

———. *Controls from Within.* New York: The Free Press, 1953.

REID, JOSEPH H. "On 'Deinstitutionalization.'" *Child Welfare,* 54 (April 1975), 295–297.

RHODES, WARREN. "Problems in the Development of Inventive Programs." *Child Welfare,* 56, 3 (March 1977), 173–179.

ROSS, ANDREW L., and LAWRENCE S. SCHREIBER. "Bellfaire's Day Treatment Program: An Interdisciplinary Approach to Emotionally Disturbed Children." *Child Welfare,* 54, 3 (March 1975), 183–194.

ROTHMAN, DAVID J. *The Discovery of the Asylum.* Boston: Little, Brown and Company, 1971.

RUTTER, MICHAEL. *National Deprivation Reassessed.* Baltimore, Md.: Penguin Books, 1974.

SCHAEFER, CHARLES. "Follow Up Survey by Mail." *Social Work,* 21, 4 (July 1976), 327–328.

———, and HOWARD E. MILLMAN. "The Use of Behavior Ratings in Assessing the Effect of Residential Treatment with Latency-Age Boys." *Child Psychiatry and Human Development,* 3 (1973).

SCHULZE, SUSANNE. *Creative Group Living in Children's Institutions.* New York: Association Press, 1951.

SEIDL, FREDERICK. "Community-oriented Residential Care: The State of the Art." *Child Care Quarterly,* 3 (Fall 1974), 150–163.

SHULMAN, RENA. "Treatment of the Disturbed Child in Placement." *Jewish Social Service Quarterly,* 30 (Spring 1954).

———. "Examples of Adolescent Group Homes in Alliance with Larger Institutions." *Child Welfare,* 54 (May 1975), 341–349.

SILVER, HAROLD. "Residential Treatment of Emotionally Disturbed Children: An Evaluation of Fifteen Years' Experience." *Journal of Jewish Communal Service,* 38 (1961).

SIMON, ABRAHAM. "Residential Treatment of Children." *Social Service Review,* 30 (September 1956).

STICKNEY, PATRICIA, and ANTHONY CAPAIUOLO. "From CRISP: Strategy for Community Residences," *Child Welfare,* **55** (January 1976), 54–58.

TAYLOR, DELORES A., and STUART W. ALPERT. *Continuity and Support Following Residential Treatment.* New York: Child Welfare League of America, 1973.

TAYLOR, JOSEPH L., et al. *A Group Home for Adolescent Girls—Practice and Research.* New York: Child Welfare League of America, 1976.

TAYLOR, SAMUEL. "Institutions with Therapeutic Residential Programs," in *Child Caring: Social Policy and the Institutions.* Ed. by Donnell Pappenfort, Dee M. Kilpatrick, and Robert W. Roberts. Chicago: Aldine Publishing Company, 1973.

THOMAS, GEORGE. *A Community Oriented Evaluation of the Effectiveness of Child Caring Institutions.* Final Report to the Office of Child Development, HEW, Project No. OCD-CB 106. Athens, Ga.: Regional Institute of Social Welfare Research, 1975a.

———. *Is Statewide Deinstitutionalization of Children's Services a Forward of Backward Social Movement?* Urbana-Champaign: School of Social Work, University of Illinois, 1975b.

THURSTON, HENRY. *The Dependent Child.* New York: Columbia University Press, 1930.

TIZARD, BARBARA, and J. REES. "The Effect of Early Institutional Rearing on the Behavioral Problems and Affectional Relationships of 4 Year Old Children." *Journal of Child Psychology and Psychiatry,* **16** (1975), 61–73.

TOIGO, ROMULO. "Child Care Manpower Development: A Literature Review." *Child Care Quarterly,* **4** (Spring 1975), 6–17.

TRASLER, GORDON. *In Place of Parents.* London: Kegan Paul, Trench, Trubner & Co., 1960.

TRIESCHMAN, ALBERT E., et al. *The Other Twenty-three Hours.* Chicago: Aldine Publishing Company, 1969.

UNITED NATIONS. *The Institutional Care of Children.* New York, 1956.

U.S. DEPARTMENT OF HEALTH, EDUCATION, AND WELFARE, National Institute of Mental Health. *Residential Treatment Centers for Emotionally Disturbed Children, 1969–1970.* National Health Statistics Series A, No. 6. Washington, D.C.: Government Printing Office, 1971.

UNITED STATES OFFICE OF COMPTROLLER GENERAL. *Children in Foster Care Institutions—Steps Government Can Take to Improve Their Care.* Washington, D.C.: Government Printing Office, February 1977.

VINCENT, BEN. *Begone Dull Care—An Informal Guide to the Residential Care of Children.* London: Her Majesty's Stationery Office, 1968.

WARNER, AMOS G., et al. *American Charities and Social Work,* 4th ed. New York: Thomas Y. Crowell Company, 1942.

WEBER, DONALD E. "Neighborhood Entry in Group Home Development." *Child Welfare,* **58** (December 1978), 627–642.

WEINSTEIN, L. *Evaluation of a Program for Re-educating Disturbed Children: A Followup Comparison with Untreated Children.* Washington, D.C.: Government Printing Office, 1974.

WEINTROB, ALEX. "Changing Population in Adolescent Residential Treatment. New Problems for Program and Staff." *American Journal of Orthopsychiatry,* **44,** 4 (July 1974), 604–610.

WEISFELD, DAVID, and MARTIN S. LASER. "Residential Treatment and Weekend Visits Home." *Social Work,* **21,** 5 (September 1976), 398–400.

WHITTAKER, JAMES K. "The Changing Character of Residential Child Care: An Ecological Perspective." *Social Service Review* (March 1978), 22–36.

———, and ALBERT E. TRIESCHMAN (Eds.). *Children Away from Home—A Sourcebook of Residential Treatment.* Chicago: Aldine Publishing Company, 1972.

————. "Colonial Child Care Institutions: Our Heritage of Care." *Child Welfare,* **50,** 7 (July 1971), 396–400.

————. *Caring for Troubled Children.* San Francisco: Jossey-Bass, 1979.

WINDER, ALVIN, *et al.* "Group Therapy with Parents of Children in a Residential Treatment Center." *Child Welfare,* **44** (May 1965).

WITKIN, MICHAEL S. *Residential Treatment Centers for Emotionally Disturbed Children—1973–74.* Mental Health Statistical Note 130. Washington, D.C.: National Institute of Mental Health, April 1976.

WITMER, HELEN, and CHARLES P. GERSHENSON. *On Rearing Infants and Young Children in Institutions.* Children's Bureau Research Reports No. 1. Washington, D.C.: Government Printing Office, 1968.

WOLINS, MARTIN, and IRVING PILIAVIN. *Institution or Foster Family—A Century of Debate.* New York: Child Welfare League of America, September 1964.

————. "Group Care: Friend or Foe." *Social Work,* **14,** 1 (January 1969), 35–53.

————. "Young Children in Institutions—Some Additional Evidence." *Developmental Psychology,* **2,** 1 (1969), 99–109.

———— (Ed.). *Successful Group Care: Explorations in the Powerful Environment.* Chicago: Aldine Publishing Company, 1974.

WOODEN, KENNETH. *Weeping in the Playtime of Others.* New York: McGraw-Hill Book Company, 1976.

WORLD HEALTH ORGANIZATION. *Deprivation of Maternal Care—A Reassessment of Its Effects.* Geneva: World Health Organization, 1962.

12 CHILD WELFARE SERVICES IN OTHER COUNTRIES

INTRODUCTION

All countries have child welfare problems that are similar to those encountered in this country. All of the world's children are dependent for a long time and are cared for, primarily, in families. And all over the world parents fall ill, die, desert, have children out of wedlock, struggle with limited resources, and so on. Children who suffer from neglect, abuse, and physical, mental, and emotional handicaps are encountered everywhere in the world.

Madison (1968), after a comprehensive recent review of family and child welfare services in the Soviet Union, concludes that "the Soviet definition of child welfare services would not differ essentially from the definition currently used in the United States" (p. 175). Although child welfare services in all countries are not identical, there are similarities that suggest common problems and analogous solutions. Everywhere "common societal needs seem to generate somewhat similar institutional responses" (Kahn, Kamerman, 1976, pp. 362–363), so that everywhere the same kinds of child welfare services have been developed: supportive, supplementary, and substitute services. And everywhere, the service delivery systems seem to face similar kinds of problems: inadequate financial support, shortages of trained personnel, problems of service integration and coordination, overlap and ambiguous spheres of program responsibility.

The following three case studies from three widely separated countries—Poland, Zambia, and Japan—are a testimonial to the universality of child welfare problems.

Poland

A social inspectress learned, during her supervision of the guardianship of little Mania, that the latter loved her "guardian" so much that she wanted to become her real daughter. Mrs. N. shared the same desire. She had taken in the child when a baby from the hands of her mother, a girl in great despair, who had subsequently disappeared. The guardian had taken preliminary steps with a view of adopting the little girl, but the formalities had seemed too complicated. Mania bore, in fact, the name of her mother, and it was first of all necessary to initiate a long procedure in order to clear up the situation. With the help of the guardianship court and the police, our inspectress had a search carried out in several provinces, and ended up by finding the mother. The latter was married, had three children, and her husband knew nothing of the fourth. The mother at once consented to the adoption of her first illegitimate child, and everyone was happy [Veillard-Cybulska, 1966, pp. 24–25].

Zambia

Joan Mulonga, aged twelve, came to the office and complained she had no school uniform and was not getting enough to eat—all because her father is sick with asthma and out of work; her mother works as a nursemaid but does not earn enough to keep them. Asked her to ask one of her parents or both to come and see me as soon as possible.

Mr. Mulonga came as requested. He knew his daughter had been to see me; he had in fact sent her himself. He had had an attack of asthma and had not been able to come himself. Said he has had asthma for twelve years or so. He is a chef by profession and is married to a Coloured woman from South Africa. Because of his asthma he cannot keep a job—he is always getting attacks and employers say they cannot afford to keep sick men. He has been to many doctors who have failed to cure him. Is now undergoing treatment at . . . Clinic. His wife is working as a nursemaid but does not earn enough for the family. He has considered taking a light job as an office orderly so that his asthma will not bother him but he has not been able to find one yet. Has also thought of returning to his village in the Fort Janeson area but with his Coloured wife who is not accustomed to village life he cannot do this. They are presently short of food and his daughter requires school uniforms. He thought we might help. I said we were prepared to help but would have to look into the situation more fully. Issued him with a voucher for rations pending inquiry [Clifford, 1966, pp. 19–20].

Japan

Mrs. F., age thirty, a graduate of junior high school, has a husband, a university graduate, age thirty-three, a son, five, and a daughter, two. Because Mr. F. is an only son, the couple live with Mr. F.'s mother and are partially dependent on her. Mrs. F. came to our agency saying she could not tolerate the home situation longer because of the over-close relationship between Mr. F. and his mother and the fact that his mother was trying to dominate her. The couple had married for love immediately following Mr. F.'s graduation from university and after he had secured his first job. From the beginning his earnings were insufficient and mother helped financially. Mrs. F. complained that they had no privacy even in the bedroom and that the grandmother not only gave "blind love" to the two grandchildren but also that she insisted on controlling everything in the family, doling out money to Mrs. F., and making her account for what she spent. Mrs. F. felt that her mother-in-law treated her like a maid and when she complained about this Mrs. F., Sr., scolded her for acting superior. We worked with Mr. F. and tried to help him play a more dominant role in the family. But the two women could not get along so the young couple decided to live separately from Mrs. F., Sr., and we closed our case [Dessau, 1968, p. 121].

The Caseworker (1974) was written by a Hungarian novelist, George Konrad, who had been a child welfare worker in Budapest. Originally published in Hungary some twenty-five years after the Communists came to power, the novel details his experiences with child welfare problems in that country. The problems would be familiar and recognizable to any American child welfare worker. They involve the same lugubrious litany of abandoned children, neglected children, parents overwhelmed by the burdens of caring for children on limited resources, the loss of a father or a mother and subsequent parent–child difficulties, and disturbed and handicapped children. The fact that the setting is Hungary and the context is a Communist society does not alter the essentially human problems that the worker needs to resolve.

The growing industrialization and urbanization of more and more of the world results in changes with which we are familiar and which directly and indirectly affect the need for child welfare services: the gradual decline in the family's ability to meet the needs of child care traditionally met through mutual aid from the tribe and members of the immediately available extended family, for example.

Everywhere there are more women in the labor force, including mothers of young children; this has resulted in a reexamination of relative child-rearing responsibilities of men and women. Rates of divorce and out-of-wedlock pregnancies have increased in the communist world and the social democratic countries as they have in the United States. For instance, the divorce rate tripled in the Soviet Union between 1960 and 1976 (*The New York Times,* February 19, 1978), and in 1973 28 per cent of all Swedish births were out of wedlock (Liljestrom, 1978, p. 23). Everywhere there is an increase in single-parent families, and everywhere these families are apt to be economically disadvantaged. For instance, although only 1 per cent of Japanese families are receiving welfare, 23 per cent of female-headed families are receiving such assistance (Nakamura, 1977, p. 205). Everywhere there is an inequitable distribution of wealth and everywhere there is a problem of poverty. In September 1974, the Soviet Union announced a new program offering a public assistance subsidy to 12.5 million children in low-income families (*The New York Times,* September 28, 1974). Every country has its minority groups, and everywhere minorities face some disadvantaging discrimination.

Despite changes and problems, the family is universally regarded as the most desirable context for child rearing. The Soviet Union has not been able to develop a wide-scale program of boarding schools as originally planned, and the communal kibbutz is "home" for only a very small percentage of Israeli children. In neither the Soviet Union nor Israel nor anywhere else has the concept of a nonfamily context for child rearing gained widespread acceptance. There is general consensus that good family welfare is the best child welfare.

In all countries, despite ideological differences, there is acceptance of governmental responsibility for the care of dependent children. The trend is to broaden the contingencies that are defined as requiring community intervention to attempt to provide more adequately for the children involved in these situations, and the community is accepting greater partnership with parents in the responsibility for the rearing of the preschool child.

Despite these impressive similarities, there are differences in the frequency with which different kinds of problems are encountered and in the nature and pattern of services that have been developed to deal with them. Among the factors that determine differences in the programs are the following:

1. Attitudes toward "preventative" solutions: contraception, abortion, abandonment, and so on.
2. Child dependency ratios.

3. Level of economic wealth of the community.
4. Political and administrative development.
5. Prevalent attitude toward women and children.
6. Position of the nuclear family vis-à-vis other social institutions in the community.
7. Historical antecedents in coping with child welfare problems.

Preventive Solutions

Some of the "preventive" solutions to child welfare problems are acceptable in other countries. Contraception is, of course, widespread and has gained great acceptance.

A detailed worldwide review of the status of abortion law and practice (Zimmerman, 1976) indicated that after a quarter of a century of liberalization of abortion legislation, "60 percent of the world's population live in countries where abortion during the first trimester is legal either for social or economic reasons or 'on request' without any specific indication. Another 16 percent live in countries where abortion is permitted on extended medical grounds, for eugenic indication and/or for humanitarian reasons such as those associated with rape and incest" (p. 1). In late 1974, France legalized abortion in the first ten weeks of pregnancy. Earlier that same year, a law on contraception had been passed that provided for the distribution of contraceptive devices through the social security system with fee exceptions for poor women and minors. It eliminated any requirement of parental consent and mandated confidentiality for services to minors.

The trend toward the liberalization of abortion laws continued throughout the 1970s. In February 1977, Israel adopted legislation permitting abortions for a wide variety of reasons on approval of an application by a three-member committee, one of whom had to be a social worker (*The New York Times*, February 1, 1977). In May 1978, Italy adopted a law "permitting state subsidized abortion for women over 18 in the first three months of pregnancy for health, economic, social or psychological reasons" (*The New York Times*, May 18, 1978). For women under eighteen, consent of both parents or a guardian was required. In both Italy and Israel, the change effected by the legislation was expected to be limited, as in both countries, abortion had been widely practiced earlier, despite its technical illegality (*The New York Times*, March 23, 1975).

Although Swiss voters rejected a 1977 referendum proposal permitting abortion on demand in the first trimester of pregnancy (*The New York Times*, September 16, 1977), a liberalized law permitting abortion for specific reasons had been adopted a year earlier. One acceptable condition was certification by a social worker that an abortion was necessary to spare the expectant mother "grave distress."

In some European countries, such as Portugal, Ireland, and Belgium, abortion remained illegal without exceptions through 1978. In the predominantly Muslim Arab countries, abortion remained strictly illegal, as it did in most Central and South American countries. However, in South America, the law does not reflect reality, and millions of illegal abortions are performed in these countries each year (*The New York Times*, March 23, 1975; May 26, 1977).

The International Planned Parenthood Federation estimated that in 1978

30–50 million abortions were performed throughout the world, roughly half of them illegally.

India, which began to permit abortions on demand in 1971, found subsequently that more drastic pressures were necessary to prevent the birth of unwanted children. In 1976 India attempted the first large-scale governmental program of coercive if not actually compulsory population control through enforced sterilization (Landman, 1977). It was proposed that civil service positions, free medical facilities, low-interest government loans, and government-subsidized housing be available to men with more than two children only after they agreed to a vasectomy. Men with two children who agreed to be sterilized were paid 150 rupees, roughly the equivalent of half a month's salary of an urban unskilled worker. As a result of a determined campaign using such incentives and disincentives, it was reported that between April and December in 1976, 7 million sterilizations were performed in India. However, the fall of the government of Premier Indira Gandhi was attributed to the backlash against such rigorous population control measures.

Perhaps the most notably successful effort to prevent excess births has been achieved by the People's Republic of China. The most informed estimates are that the Chinese birthrate per 1,000 population decreased from 35 in 1964 to 14 in 1975 (Brackett, 1976, p. PJ-213). This success is attributed to systematic, comprehensive programs making modern contraceptives, sterilization, and abortion widely accessible with the unequivocal support of government units at all levels. In addition, the active participation of all communal and neighborhood citizen groups was directly enlisted in the effort. The policy, embodied in the slogan, "Late marriage, small families, long intervals between births," was given high priority (Jaffe, Oakley, 1978).

Access to abortion is universal in those countries where abortion is permitted and where a public health program is in operation. Abortion, available to all, is one of the public health services. This is in contrast to our own system, where access to a publicly supported abortion requires meeting a means test. In Poland "women are entitled to temporary disability benefits after an abortion" (Kahn, Kamerman, 1976, p. 198). However, in some countries, France and Yugoslavia being examples, the availability of an abortion requires the acceptance of some counseling about family planning.

Abandonment of children as a solution for the parents, if not for the community, is still prevalent. Acosta (1977) reports that the abandoned and neglected street child is a problem of Bogotá, Colombia: "These children live in the streets 24 hours a day subsisting by stealing, moving in groups called galladas and sleeping on the sidewalks covered with old newspapers. Police estimates give a number of about 9,200 children living under these conditions" (p. 233). And early death due to infanticide or the lack of resources "prevents" many high-risk children from becoming child-welfare-service clients.

The hunger–famine belt above the equator, including such countries as India, Ethiopia, Guatemala, and Bangladesh, experienced severe food shortages in 1974. As a result, death and malnutrition affected a sizable percentage of the children in those areas of the world: "It has been estimated that roughly 15 million children a year die before the age of 5 of the combined effects of infection and malnutrition. This annual toll represents a quarter of all the deaths in the world" (*The New York Times,* October 6, 1974).

Child labor as a solution to child welfare problems is still widespread. In the Latin American countries, for instance, "an appreciable proportion of the labor force is still under fifteen" (United Nations, 1966, p. 48).

Dependency Ratios and Levels of Industrialization

Dependency ratios—the ratios of productive adults to dependent children in the country—vary widely, affecting child welfare needs and resources. It is predicted that by 1985 there will be, in the developed countries, sixty-three adults caring for twenty-six dependent children; in the developing countries, fifty-six adults will be faced with the care of forty dependent children (United Nations, 1970, p. 26).

The dependency ratio is significant because it reflects the burden imposed by the unproductive group on the productive group. Where the relative number of producers is small, production is limited and has to be thinly distributed. The special programs required by the dependent must be funded from these already scarce resources.

The differences for children in the two sectors of the world, resulting from the contrasting dependency ratios, are further exacerbated by a growing maldistribution of wealth between the two sectors. During the 1960s, the world total gross national product increased by some $1,100 billion. About 80 per cent of this increase went to the developed sectors, which contain only one quarter of the world's population; "only 6 percent of the increase went to countries where per capita incomes average $2000 or less, but which contain 60 percent of the world's population" (Titmuss, 1972, p. 3).

The United Nations (1963) notes, "No country can afford to move into programs of social entitlement until its economic resources have reached a point where a substantial amount can be made available for social expenditure" (p. 109).

> The proportion of total governmental expenditure on social services varies directly with per capita gross domestic product. As gross domestic product rise public expenditure on social services also rise. The richest countries spend more than half their budget or nearly 15 percent of their domestic product on social services. In marked contrast the low income developing countries were able to devote only a little more than one quarter of their governmental budget or less than 5 per cent of their domestic product to such services [United Nations, 1979, p. 37].

Not only are developing countries characterized by high dependency ratios and limited resources, but they also face a heavy need for investment capital for economic development. Investment of capital in industry may, in the long run, result in more adequate child-welfare resources and services. In the short run, however, the needs for such resources and services compete with the needs for child welfare services.

The problem is not only one of allocating limited financial resources but also one of allocating limited human resources. When there are few people in the country who have an opportunity for professional training of any kind, social work cannot easily compete with such professions as medicine, teaching, or engineering. As a United Nations (1963) report indicates, the limitations on the social service programs in the underdeveloped countries are dictated by their absolute poverty of resources in money, personnel, and institutional structure (p. 106).

In the last analysis, the wealth of the community is the essential basis for any system of social welfare. And the degree of industrialization is decisive in determining the level of wealth. However, even if sufficient wealth were available, it might be deployed for child welfare services only if there is a favorable attitude toward the needs of the child. Thus, in some developing countries, the emphasis on investment in industry is sometimes balanced by the recognition not only that children are the beneficiaries of economic development programs but that they are themselves an investment. Adequate provisions for children then become part of the national economic strategy. It is as necessary to improve the quality of human resources as it is to increase the supply of capital resources.

Dependency ratios and the level of industrialization of the economy dictate not only the amount that might be made available for social welfare but also the kinds of social problems to which social welfare gives priority. It is not likely that a highly developed program of child welfare services will be given priority in countries where most people live in villages, "where there is little transportation, no telephone, no school, no doctor, only the most primitive housing and few, if any, literate people" (United Nations, 1965, p. 41). Priority in these countries must be given to the most basic needs: keeping the child alive, keeping him fed, and providing him with the beginnings of an education.

In many parts of the world, children suffer from chronic semistarvation (Sicault, 1963). Undernourishment resulting from lack of food is compounded by malnourishment arising from lack of the all-important proteins required by the growing child. Milk is still a luxury food in many underdeveloped countries. *Kwashiorkor,* a widespread diet-deficiency disease of children in such countries, comes from an African word that, literally translated, means "first–second." It connotes "the disease the first child gets when the second is expected" and is associated with weaning and denial of the mother's milk.

Many childhood diseases are widespread in underdeveloped countries, sapping the energy and vitality of the children and reducing their capacity and motivation for learning. Malaria, trachoma, bilharziasis, diarrhea, parasitic infestations, yaws, and chronic hunger make these children dull and apathetic. Despite improvements in health conditions and the resulting reduction in infant mortality rates in the developing countries in recent years, these rates are still, in some instances, four and five times higher than they are in more economically advanced countries. And those countries that are still confronted with the most elementary problems of food needs, health needs, and educational needs for all children can hardly be expected to develop great concern about the services needed by groups of specially deprived children. Where all are deprived, those who are specially deprived lose any claim to special treatment.

Three quarters of the world's children, nearly a billion of them, live in developing countries. Of the hundred children born every half-minute in these areas, twenty will die in their first year; two thirds of the remainder are likely never to see adolescence, and only one in four reaches "old age"—which, in terms of the average length of life in some of these countries, is about thirty-eight years. Of one hundred children born in India and one hundred children born in the

United States, more Ameican children will live to age sixty-five than Indian children will live to age five (Heilbroner, 1959, p. 2).

Only a little more than half of those who survive to age five in the developing countries will ever set foot in a classroom. Fewer than 40 per cent of that half will complete the elementary grades (United Nations, 1970).

Large numbers of children live on the pavements in Bombay and Calcutta or grow up under the most deprived environmental circumstances in the *favelas* or *ranchos* of Latin America or the *bustees* or *shuggies* of India. Makeshift housing in one shantytown or another is "home" for a sizable percentage of the world's population of children—a "home" without water, heat, electricity, sewerage, or a garbage disposal system (United Nations, 1971).

In the mid-1960s the United Nations reported:

> while in North America and western Europe, men and women ate on an average about 3000 calories and eighty to ninety grams of protein a day; in Latin America, with the exception of Argentina, the average fell to 2400 calories and some seventy grams of protein; in Asia, 2100 calories and fifty grams; and in Africa, the protein consumption was lower still [United Nations, 1968, p. 56].

Illegitimacy rates are ten times greater in some countries than in the United States: "In some areas in Latin America the illegitimacy rate is as high as 60 to 70 percent of all births; in these circumstances what is needed is a policy to organize the family rather than one to strengthen it" (United Nations, p. 12–13).

Table 12–1 shows some of the differences between the developed countries and the underdeveloped countries in regard to some essential factors affecting the welfare of the child.

The limited development of general community services for health, education, and welfare in the underdeveloped countries means that a great deal of child welfare is concerned with the problem of inadequate role enactment resulting from deficiencies in community resources. These difficulties lie outside the parent–child relationship network but affect it adversely.

Thus, although child welfare services in the more advanced countries may have to be provided on an individual basis for those children who lack the normal arrangement for care—the child of the broken family, the emotionally disturbed child who cannot make good use of the family that is available—child welfare in the underdeveloped countries is more concerned with providing for all children, on a mass basis, those essential primary conditions necessary for normal, healthy development. Whereas child welfare is concerned in the United States with the handicapped child who cannot use the available schools, the problem for child welfare in the underdeveloped countries is to make schools available in the first place.

Political and Administrative Development

The concept of childhood as a clearly differentiated period in development having special needs and special rights is associated with the development of nation-states. A review of constitutional provisions relating to childhood of 139 nations showed that formal claims for responsibility for children was not asso-

TABLE 12–1. International Comparison of Selective Factors

Economically Advanced Nations		Developing Nations	
Female Life Expectancy at Birth—1975 [a]			
Netherlands	77.2	Algeria	54.8
United States	76.5	Bolivia	47.9
Federal Republic of Germany	75.5	Ethiopia	39.6
Poland	74.2	Bangladesh	35.8

[a] United Nations, *Demographic Yearbook*, 28th issue, 1976 (New York: United Nations, 1977), pp. 130–134.

Economically Advanced Nations		Developing Nations	
Birthrate per 1,000 Population [b]			
England–Wales (1976)	11.9	Bolivia (1975)	44
France (1976)	13.6	Ghana (1975)	48.8
United States (1976)	14.7	Afghanistan (1975)	49.2
USSR (1975)	18.1	Nigeria (1975)	49.3

[b] United Nations, *Demographic Yearbook*, 28th issue, 1976 (New York: United Nations, 1977), pp. 260–265.

Economically Advanced Nations		Developing Nations	
Infant Mortality (Number of Deaths of Infants Under 1 Year of Age Per 1,000 Live Births)—1957 [c]			
Denmark	10.7	Guatemala	75.4
France	12.2	Indonesia	12.5
United States	16.7	Congo	180.0
USSR	27.7	Zambia	259.0

[c] United Nations, *Demographic Yearbook*, 28th issue, 1976 (New York: United Nations, 1977), pp. 305–308.

Economically Advanced Nations		Developing Nations	
Per Capita National Income—1975 [d] *(Expressed in U.S. Dollars)*			
Switzerland	7,810	Colombia	515
Sweden	7,557	Morocco	440
United States	6,236	Philippines	325
Federal Republic of Germany	6,029	Tanzania	162

[d] United Nations, *Statistical Yearbook*, 1976 (New York: United Nations, 1977), pp. 689–691.

Economically Advanced Nations		Developing Nations	
Population Per Physician—1974 [e]			
France	681	Egypt	7,495
Sweden	645	Uganda	20,685
Israel	631	Chad	44,387
United States	622	Upper Volta	59,595

[e] United Nations, *Statistical Yearbook*, 1976, pp. 833–836.

TABLE 12-1. (Continued)

Net Food Supplies—Calories per Day, 1967–1968 [f]

New Zealand	3290	Bolivia (1966)	1980
United States	3200	Iran (1966)	1890
Denmark	3150	Algeria (1966)	1870

[f] United Nations, *Statistical Yearbook*, 23rd issue, 1971 (New York: United Nations, 1972).

Percent of School Age Population (5–19) Enrolled in School—1975 [g]

United States	86%	India	41%
United Kingdom	83%	Saudi Arabia	25%
Netherlands	63%	Somalia	18%
USSR	62%	Afghanistan	11%

[g] *Children in the World* (Washington, D.C.: Population Reference Bureau, 1978), p. 61.

Dependency Ratio—Percentage of Population 0–14 Years of Age and 15–64 Years of Age, Major World Areas, 1965 [h]

Region	0–14	15–64	Region	0–14	15–64
Europe	24	64	Africa	44	53
North America	25	64	South Asia	43	54
USSR	26	65	Latin America	42	54

[h] United Nations, *1978 Report on the World Social Situation* (New York: United Nations, 1979), p. 4.

ciated with differences in level of economic or social development. It is part of a worldwide expansion of state authority over children as a consequence of the needs of nation-states for developing a citizenry committed to the nation. Although the institutional claims are worldwide, the ability to implement responsibility for and control over lives of children varies (Boli-Bennet, Meyer, 1978).

The development of child welfare services and associated social-security programs is dependent on the ability of the country to develop a sophisticated administrative and fiscal apparatus. It requires birth registration procedures to determine how many children there are and where they are located, and it permits the certification of age for social security. Yet a United Nations (1966) report on child welfare services in Africa noted that "only about a third of the nations in the region had birth registration programs in 1964" (p. 23). The provision of services requires the opening of local offices, the establishment of forms and procedures for record keeping, accounting, and a communications system so that people can be reached, checks sent, and appointments made. A workmen's compensation program requires associated medical services; an unemployment insurance program requires associated job-finding and vocational retraining services. A network of social services requires the recruitment, training, and deployment of many workers who possess the necessary skills. An efficient social-insurance program requires the acceptance of a strong central authority so that a uniform program can be administered in a standardized manner throughout a country.

A well-developed social-insurance and income-maintenance program requires a population that can read and write so that forms can be completed; a postal service that efficiently covers the country; an address system so that people can be located for postal deliveries; birth, marriage, and death registry to provide documents related to eligibility; and a banking service if payments are made by check. These programs then require a well-developed network of related institutions and a sophisticated administrative infrastructure, which may be lacking in some countries, particularly in rural areas (Mouton, 1975, pp. 64–67).

The Relationship of the Nuclear Family to the Community

Child welfare services are also affected by the other institutional arrangements available to meet the needs of children. In a relatively simple, localized, self-sufficient society, which until recently characterized Africa, "The family and tribal pattern of relationship and responsibility function to meet the recognized social needs of its members. Not only the parents but the larger family group assumed responsibility for the rearing of children" (United Nations, 1963, p. 105). Family and tribal organizations furnished protection against some of the same risks and difficulties for which social services are organized in the more highly industrialized countries. A United Nations (1966) report on child welfare services in Africa notes:

> The concept of adoption is new in Africa as is also the concept of illegitimacy. By virtue of the extended nature of the family system, adoption has not been necessary in the past and has been looked down upon. Children have been valued in and of themselves and relatives have considered it their obligation to look after orphans and neglected children. For example the response from Sierra Leone comments, "There are no adoption laws, but the family system is such that as a rule there are hardly unwanted children. Children are cared for even by non-relatives" [p. 26].

In more traditional societies, kinship fostering, child lending, and other informal transactions in sharing the responsibilities of parenthood provide substitute care for children. Substitute care takes place not only because parents have died or are ill or working but because one family has too many children to care for and another family has too few. There is a redistribution of children from those who have too many to those who have none.

Such solutions to child welfare problems, however, become progressively less feasible as a society becomes more industrialized. With the movement to urban areas, the extended family disperses and traditional solutions no longer apply. Hasen (1969), discussing social security in India, points out that "the joint family is disintegrating with increasing urbanization" and that the "family is losing both the capacity and the willingness to act as the sole agent responsible for providing social security" (pp. 193–194). A process of "detribalization" takes place. The movement to the city brings a dependence on wage employment, on a money economy. The authority of the father is diminished, for he no longer is head of a family production unit. With this decline in paternal authority comes a painful reallocation of role responsibilities and privileges between the different generations within the family group and between husband and wife. The United Nations notes that in the new industrialized, urbanized society, the family "may have no tie to any group which feels a direct responsibility for its welfare. At the same time, the instability of the urban family results in increasing numbers of deserted mothers and abandoned children" (*International Child Welfare Review*, p. 124). Urbanization, then, increases the likelihood of child welfare problems while it simultaneously denies the structure through which such problems were previously resolved (United Nations, 1955). The network of tribal mutual aid and support weakens and there arises a need for the institutionalization of child welfare services: "In developing societies, social welfare services emerge to meet human needs that can no longer be satisfied exclusively through the traditional institutions of a more static period" (United Nations, 1965, p. 10).

Although adoption was once unknown in Africa and the word did not appear in the language, by the 1970s changing social conditions in Africa dictated the need for such a service. The tribal clan or extended family is no longer available to provide child care. In 1974 in Kenya, 300 people were approved for adoption and 60 children were locally adopted through the work of the Kenyan Child Welfare Society (Miller, 1978, p. 19). Such changes come slowly, however. The United Nations (1974) sent a questionnaire to member nations regarding programs for children in need of substitute care and reported that such programs as foster care and adoption were given low priority in most of the developing countries: "The highest priority indicated is for basic health, nutrition and day care services, especially for the young child . . . very few countries give any priority to services for children in need of substitute care" (p. 4).

Attitude Toward Women and Children

Industrialization and urbanization change the position of women in the family. A changing attitude toward the child is tied to a changing attitude toward the mother. More adequate care for the child requires more adequate education of the mother and a greater concern for her needs. The mother suffering from "maternal depletion syndrome"—resulting from early marriage, frequent pregnancies, inadequate diet, and overwork—can hardly be expected to meet the needs of the child. An important aspect of child welfare in the developing countries, then, is concerned with the child indirectly through concern with the mother. A changing, more positive attitude toward the needs of women is expressed in the establishment of women's clubs and social centers, set up side by side with children's clinics, devoted to the teaching of mothercraft and homemaking and to helping women with the problems they face.

Poverty of resources alone does not always explain the difficulties encountered in providing adequate care for the child. Sometimes cheap, healthy foods, such as peanuts, are available, but it may not be traditional to offer these to children. Up to a point, the improvement of children's health may be more directly affected by educating the parents than by increasing the supply of doctors or medicine. But this often requires programs directed toward the reduction of illiteracy, particularly that of women.

The Influence of Historical Precedent and Ideology

The pattern of child welfare services is determined by the nature of earlier institutionalized approaches to similar problems (United Nations, 1964). Countries previously under British control, in accordance with the British pattern, rely heavily on voluntary agencies; former French colonies associate social service with health and nursing activity and stress family allowances; Latin American countries stress social service offered under the auspices of the Catholic Church.

Countries that, like the United States, value independence, autonomy, individualism, self-reliance, and self-fulfillment are likely to be more resistant to welfare legislation than are countries that value the idea of community responsibility for the welfare of all of their citizens. Different countries also give priority to different groups in the population in allocating welfare resources. France is strongly child-oriented; Denmark is more strongly oriented to its old people.

Ideological differences regarding the respective roles of father and mother, the relative responsibility of the community and the family regarding child care and child rearing, and the extent of legitimate and appropriate interference by the state in family matters, determine, in some measure, differences in child welfare services and policies.

Religious ideology is a factor determining the nature of services developed. Adoption is less acceptable to Islamic law, although it does occur in Islamic countries.

Differences in child welfare services result from differences in the availability of alternative institutions that have sanctioned responsibility for child welfare problems. The kinship group, the extended family, or the tribal organization may perform such services, as is the case in sections of Africa. Trade union organizations in East European countries act to provide child welfare services to families. Where primary group relationships—the family, the neighborhood group, the trade union in the shop, and so on—are strong and effective, there is less need for formal agency assistance in responding to parent–child problems.

SOME SELECTIVE COMPARISONS: CHILD WELFARE SERVICE HERE AND ABROAD

Having discussed some of the factors that affect the development of child welfare programs generally, we shall now review the different categories of services—supportive, supplemental, and substitutive—and point to variations and modifications found in other countries. Because of the possible appropriateness of these variations and modifications to our own child-welfare problems, most of the countries cited are similar to the United States in levels of industrialization and standards of living.

It would be an impossibly lengthy task to review in detail the child welfare programs of even a representative group of countries, so we must be quite selective. Our purpose is to call attention to those aspects of these programs that we might consider in strengthening our own child-welfare programs. Consequently the result is not likely to be a fair comparison. To do justice to our own program, we would have to cite the weakness of the foreign programs to which we call attention. If we were to present a balanced picture, for instance, of the Soviet welfare system as it affects children, we would have to note that the social insurance system does not cover agricultural workers as adequately as it does industrial workers, that there is no unemployment insurance system in the Soviet Union, that political "undesirables" can lose their rights to social security, that there are no statistics available on adoption and no published evaluations of Soviet services, that mothers of young children may be denied financial assistance if they refuse to accept work or work training, that income maintenance programs for divorced or deserted mothers are inadequate, and that the low level of social insurance payments and a very limited program of public assistance payments leave large groups of recipients in poverty (Simanis, 1972; Minkoff, Turgeon, 1976; Madison, 1977; *The New York Times,* November 19, 1978; McCauley, 1979). However, given the aim of stimulating thinking toward a broader, less ethnocentrically based perspective on child welfare services, a selective presentation of alternative approaches appears justified.

It might be noted that in general this country's efforts with regard to welfare programs compares favorably with similar efforts abroad. A nation's political ideology is apparently not the most important factor in determining its level of commitment to social welfare (Wilensky, 1975).

It is very difficult to make valid comparisons in terms of some common baseline of the efforts different countries make in meeting the welfare needs of their population. The most frequently attempted effort is in terms of the proportion of a nation's gross national product devoted to social programs. Unfortunately what is included in the statistics of social programs varies from country to country. In the United States, funds for education are included in the social program budget but are not included in the social program statistics of other countries—Sweden and Great Britain, for instance. Despite such caveats, it is clear that the amount of public funds devoted to social welfare in the United States—which includes all income maintenance, social insurance programs, and the public provision of health, education, housing, and other welfare services—has grown very rapidly since 1965. By 1976 such public expenditures represented 20.6 per cent of the gross national product. In 1912 only 2.5 per cent of the gross national product was devoted to such purposes. "When social welfare expenditures in the private sector are added to those in the public sector," a total of 27.5 per cent of the gross national product was devoted to social programs in 1976 (Skolnik, Dales, 1977, p. 4).

Although the percentage of the U.S. gross national product allocated to such purposes seems to be behind that of Great Britain, Sweden, and West Germany, the gap is smaller than is often perceived. Merriam (1978) notes that in 1978 the most recent reliable international comparison was for the year 1971, when the United States was clearly behind other comparably industrialized countries in the amount of gross national product devoted to welfare. Given the increases in the budgetary allocations for welfare between 1971 and 1977, she indicates that "the gap between us and other countries is certainly not as great in 1977 as it was in 1971" (p. 121; see also Ball, 1978, p. 261).

The additional expenditures for welfare in the United States from the private sector are not matched by any comparable expenditures in European countries. In most West European countries, private charity is not encouraged and there are no tax-deduction incentives for such giving (*The New York Times*, July 2, 1978). The substantial funding of voluntary services through community chests and councils and United Funds, and the absence of such expenditures in European countries, further reduces the gap in the comparable percentage of the gross national product devoted to welfare in the United States and in the European welfare states.

Supportive Services

Great Britain is one of the relatively few countries to have developed a highly professionalized program of supportive services. It has a network of family service agencies, many of which are affiliated with the national council of family casework agencies. Operating under the auspices of some family service agencies are the Family Discussion Bureaus, which offer marital counseling. The government provides grants-in-aid to such organizations.

The work of the Family Service Units in Great Britain started during World War I, when conscientious objectors founded the Pacifist Service Units to care for disorganized, bombed-out families in large English cities. As a result of their contact with the families, and the realization that many of the difficulties presented by the families were not the result of the war, the units began to work toward helping the families resolve some of their basic problems. Although casework is the principal method of aid, the units operate in a distinctive way. The staff lives together in a house in the district they serve, and its members are available to families in the district on a twenty-four-hour basis. The staff attempts to demonstrate, in this home, that standards can be maintained even though the housing is poor. In establishing a relationship with families whom he cannot reach through "talk" alone, the caseworker may go into the home and assist the family directly by scrubbing floors, washing clothes, caring for the children, cooking a meal, and so on (McKie, 1963; Philip, 1963).

Holland has attempted to help the multiproblem family in an even more comprehensive way. It has set up special villages, known as *reeducation centers*, to which the family is moved. Employment for the father is obtained in the neighborhood, and the children go to the village school. Through demonstrations, teaching, and counseling by social workers who visit daily, the families learn how to manage the home, how to budget, and how to live together with less friction.

In 1973 Japan had 149 child guidance centers handling some 244,000 cases: "Each child guidance center has shelter facilities for children who are brought into the center because they have been deserted, their families have broken up or they have run away" (Nakamura, 1977, p. 201). A table of the problems that bring children to the child guidance centers indicates that problems manifested by children in Japan are similar to those encountered in the United States (p. 200).

For many parents seeking help, the complexity of social services is baffling. They need help not only in determining where to go but also in understanding the eligibility requirements and the procedures. The British have established a network of Citizens' Advice Bureaus to help people find their way around the complex world of social services. Simple explanations are offered, information about what is available is given, and referrals are made to the proper agency (Zucker, 1965; Leissner, 1967).

Another supportive service of interest is the subsidized vacation. The Norwegian government provides subsidies to families in order to enable housewives to have an annual two-week vacation, preference being given to housewives with small children. France and Germany maintain family holiday homes—nonprofit establishments designed to permit the family to vacation together. The Swedish government supports, through grants-in-aid, holiday homes for housewives. During their absence, vacationing mothers may arrange for homemakers from the local social-welfare bureau to prepare meals for their husbands and children and to do housecleaning. Such homemaker service is given at community expense if the family of the vacationing mother cannot afford to pay (Uhr, p. 17).

If protective services are included as supportive services, we might note that most countries provide sanctions in the case of neglect by parents of their duties toward their children or in case of child abuse. Perhaps Sweden has the broadest definition of child abuse, and however it is enforced, the law makes illegal petty bodily injury, which includes almost all corporal punishment of children. Although all countries have legislated services protecting the child from neglect and abuse, most do not identify child abuse as an explicit concern. A detailed review of protective services in different countries concludes that except for Canada and England "no other country studied has found it necessary to develop the kinds of specialized programs we have in the United States for identifying such children. The major debate relates to whether or not child abuse represents a phenomenon distinct from maltreatment of children generally and whether it warrants special policies and programs" (Kamerman, 1975, pp. 36–37).

The detection of potential child-welfare problems and efforts at prevention are assisted by programs of periodic visits to the families by health and social work personnel during the child's infancy. France, for instance, has a program of "compulsory medical, psychological and social examination of children at definite intervals between the ages of three months and thirty months" (David, Lezine, 1974, p. 61). Since 1970 these examinations have been made a prerequisite to the payment of family allowances. They supplement the four prenatal obstetrical examinations required of the mother in order to qualify for maternity benefits. A social worker also makes a prenatal visit to the home to become acquainted with the family, to discuss possible problems, and to inform the family of social welfare benefits and services.

In Hungary, the district nurse, who performs social work functions in addition to traditional nursing functions, regularly visits all families with children from birth until six years of age. Visits are made every ten days during the first two months after birth, then once a month until the child is a year old. The child is then visited every two months between the ages of one and three and every four months between three and six years of age (Hermann, Komlosi, 1972, p. 371).

In Sweden, child welfare centers throughout the country check the child's health during the first two years of life through a series of home visits. Recently a special control examination at age four was introduced for all children. The aim was to detect the behavioral and social problems as well as the medical problems of children at this age.

Periodic review of the child's situation by community representatives provides regularly scheduled protection for the child in China also:

> When a mother returns home from a maternity hospital with her new-born infant, health workers from her lane station, accompanied by the doctor working there, call to see how she feels and advise her on child feeding. They visit the baby two or three times during the first month after birth. Whenever it is ill, a doctor can be summoned at any time, providing treatment free of charge. The infant continues to receive check-ups every three months until it is 18 months old. Check-ups are than scheduled at six-month intervals until it reaches the age of three, after which it is examined once a year [Wen, 1977, p. 116].

Countries that provide for periodic examinations of young children may regard child-abuse identification programs as superfluous. The community becomes aware of child abuse as a consequence of such regularly scheduled reexaminations.

Although periodic examinations of all children provide a protection for the potentially abused preschool child and obviate the need for a specific service concerned with child abuse, the school-aged child is offered less protection in most countries. Universal school-health examinations as part of national health insurance programs provide some protection, but these take place at widely dispersed intervals. Perhaps this is why, along with the fact that the largest percentage of abused children are older than six, no country is without reports of child abuse and neglect (Smith, 1975, pp. 28–30). Sweden is most liberal in defining child abuse. In April 1979, Sweden's parliament passed a law saying that parents may not spank their children or treat them in any other humiliating way. Complaints of violation were to be handled by social workers and police with referrals to family courts.

For whatever it's worth in the supportive effect it might have, it is worth noting that whereas the United States celebrates Father's Day and Mother's Day, East Europeans celebrate International Children's Day: in Bulgaria, it is regarded "as a big public event in which it is the duty of all to participate" (Veillard-Cybulska, 1969, p. 13); in Poland, the motto for the day is "The upbringing and the education of children is the responsibility of all" (Veillard-Cybulska, 1966, p. 51).

Supplementary Services: Social Insurance, Homemaker Service, Day Care

The most recent review of social security programs throughout the world (U.S. Department of Health, Education, and Welfare, Research Report 50, 1978), summarizing the programs in 128 countries from Afghanistan to Zambia, indicated that all countries provide some protection to the wage earner and his or her children and family. Workmen's compensation was the program most frequently listed; unemployment insurance was least frequently listed. The countries with the most comprehensive programs of protection, which include many of the industrialized countries, cover old age, disability, work injury, unemployment, and health insurance, including temporary illness, maternity benefits and family allowances. The United States is somewhat exceptional among the highly industrialized nations because it has no national health insurance program, no temporary sickness or maternity assistance program, and no family allowance program.

The Soviet Union does not have a program of unemployment insurance. Because the state takes responsibility for ensuring that all who can and want to work have employment, the lack of such a program is not regarded as a deprivation. It suggests that unemployment insurance is a public policy option made necessary by a system that consistently operates with some percentage of its potential work force unemployed. A job guarantee program might be considered a more desirable alternative approach to providing family income.

The most widespread kind of social insurance of direct interest to children is the family allowance. Originally adopted in France to encourage a higher birth rate, its spread to more than sixty countries was based on the idea that the existence of dependent children should not give rise to undue inequalities in family levels of living. The program provides for the payment of a regular allowance to every family for the support of each child and corrects the imbalance between family income and family need.

Family allowances are sometimes called a social or a moral wage because they make family support needs, as well as the value of labor, a determinant of family income. The allowance is designed for adopted and foster children as well as for natural children. In some countries, allowances are paid to all families with dependent children regardless of employment status or family income. In other countries, they are paid only to families with limited income, only to people in certain occupations, or only upon the birth of the second or a third child.

Family allowances are usually financed by a tax on employers or out of general governmental revenue. Generally there is a cutoff point for eligible children, which ranges between fourteen and eighteen years; however, this cutoff point may be extended for children who are in school or who are sick or handicapped.

Before 1972, "Japan and the United States were the only industrial nations which did not include a national system of cost allowances for children among the social security programs" (Kirkpatrick, 1972, p. 39). In January 1972, after ten years of debate, Japan adopted a family allowance program whose goal is "to lead to the healthy upbringing of children and the stability of life at home." Currently the United States is the only highly industrialized nation without such a program.

One might point to our own income tax reductions for each dependent child as an indirect family allowance program; however, most of the countries that provide family allowances do so in addition to allowing income tax reductions.

Eligibility requirements may restrict access to such allowances. Thus family allowances become available to families in the Soviet Union only after the birth of the fourth child. With an increasing percentage of Soviet families being limited to one or two children, an increasing percentage of families remain ineligible (Madison, 1975, p. 253). In 1971, when the monthly family allowance payment for the fourth child was 4 rubles, the minimum monthly wage was 70 rubles (p. 278). For many Soviet families, then, family allowances may not provide a significant additional income. In other European countries, family allowances do have significant implications for family income. Expressed as a percentage of average industrial earnings, the family allowance for a family with three children in 1972 amounted to 20.8 per cent in Belgium, 14.3 per cent in the Netherlands, and 10.9 per cent in Italy (Kahn, Kamerman, 1976, p. 37).

Adopted children are eligible for payments in most children allowance programs. Such payments would go to all families, rich and poor alike, without a means test, although the rich family would lose much of this amount in some countries through income tax—a loss that the British call "clawback" in their own family allowance program (*The New York Times,* August 7, 1977).

In the many African countries that have a family allowance system, such payments contributed to family income, in 1972, between 8 and 14 per cent of the monthly guaranteed minimum wage (Mouton, 1975, p. 31). Because such programs were employment-related rather than universal, however, only a limited number of families benefited, as only a limited number of African families are tied to the wage-labor force.

In special instances, family allowance grants are increased. For instance, in Czechoslovakia, families taking care of a disabled child who has not been placed in an institution become entitled to double the family allowance for that child (International Social Security Association, 1974, p. 28).

In addition to the actual additional income provided to the family, family allowances provide a sense of security. Guaranteed by the government, they provide a dependable regular income.

Unlike the United States, most European countries have government-operated health insurance programs. The particular significance for child welfare, aside from the increments to family income that result because the insurance pays the family's medical bills, is that it provides prenatal, delivery, and postnatal medical care for every mother and child and guarantees the possibility of adequate medical attention for every child. This may help account for the fact that in 1977 the United States ranked 16th in the world in infant mortality rates. (See Table 2–1, p. 56.) Most of the countries with lower infant mortality rates—Sweden, the Netherlands, Australia, Great Britain, Denmark—have national health insurance programs. However, many countries with socialized medicine programs have higher infant mortality rates than those in the United States. Hungary, Cuba, Rumania, and Poland had infant mortality rates that, in 1976, were substantially higher than that of the U.S. (Council for Mutual Economic Assistant, 1978, p. 13).

Health insurance plans provide medical care, sickness insurance, and substitute income when the wage earner is ill. Although most of the industrialized nations make sickness insurance available as part of the social insurance system, the United States does not. Those countries having social-insurance sickness benefits increase the insurance or provide supplementation when the wage earner has dependent children (United Nations, 1959, pp. 17–18). Sickness allowance is also paid when a working mother is needed at home to care for a sick child (Kakol, 1959, p. 56). For instance, in Bulgaria, should a child under the age of three fall ill, the working mother can obtain paid leave to care for the child (Veillard-Cybulska, 1969, p. 6). In East Germany, single parents who need to care for a sick child receive sick pay during their absence from work (Manpel, Hawk, 1966, p. 91). The benefits provided to wage earners vary with the length of continuous employment. In the Soviet Union, 100 per cent of the salary is provided during the time of illness after eight years of continuous employment

(Minkoff, Turgeon, 1976, p. 38). In West Germany, full wages are provided for the first six weeks of illness and 75 per cent thereafter. Both East Germany and West Germany provide extra sickness benefits for wage earners with children. A two- to seven-day waiting period is imposed in most programs before sick benefits are available, and cash benefits are most frequently set at 50–75 per cent of average earnings.

Although labor force participation is required in most countries as a qualification for receiving sickness benefits, in Sweden housewives who are incapacitated by illness are eligible for such help.

Sickness insurance also covers wages for limited periods during the time a parent has to stay home to care for a sick child. Most frequently such coverage is limited to a period of five to fifteen days and is often restricted so that only the mother is eligible. In Sweden, Norway, and Austria, in an effort to encourage sharing of child-rearing responsibilities, both the father and mother are eligible for such paid leave in caring for a dependent child.

In addition to health insurance, which provides free medical care, many countries protect the working mother and her child by offering maternity benefits (International Labor Office, 1965). Maternity benefits compensate the family for the loss of the mother's wages during pregnancy, enable her to stop work earlier in the pregnancy, and permit her to remain home with the baby for at least a minimum period after birth. Thus the working Soviet mother receives maternity benefits at the rate of 100 per cent of pay for a sixteen-week period —eight weeks before and eight weeks after confinement. Italy's social insurance system provides 80 per cent of earnings up to thirteen weeks before and eight weeks after confinement. In Yugoslavia, "working women are entitled to 133 days of paid maternity leave and subsequently their working day is reduced by four hours until the child reaches three years of age" (Scaberne, 1969, p. 23). Israel grants working women a three-month leave at 75 per cent of salary at the time of confinement. The women may return to work and "be permitted an hour less work per day until the end of the year at the expense of the employer" (Neipris, 1971, p. 298).

As a protection to both mother and child, maternity benefits are frequently made on condition that the mother use the free medical care provided during the pregnancy. For instance, France pays a prenatal allowance with the onset of pregnancy; the nine monthly payments due for the period of pregnancy are divided into three, each being paid after the medical examination and provided that the examination has taken place at the proper time. With this kind of inducement, 95 per cent of all Finnish expectant mothers, for instance, are under medical care (Central Union, 1968, p. 22).

After maternity leave, a woman worker who is breast-feeding her child may have the right to some time off. In the Soviet Union, for example, working mothers are allowed a breast-feeding break of at least half an hour every three-and-a-half hours.

Special additional consideration is given in atypical situations. Thus, in Czechoslovakia, maternity leave is extended from twenty-six weeks to thirty-five weeks at 90 per cent of gross average earnings if the mother gives birth to twins or if she is unmarried. In the Soviet Union, maternity leave is also granted to women who adopt infants (Madison, 1973, p. 103).

Although the United States has no program of maternity leave under government auspices, many women employed in organizations covered by health insurance programs do have maternity benefits.

An amendment to previous civil rights legislation, the Pregnancy Discrimination Act, effective in April of 1979, required that employers treat pregnancy as any other temporary disability with regard to health insurance, disability benefits, and job and seniority protection. Providing such coverage in employee health insurance plans became, in effect, mandatory.

It is estimated that 40 per cent of employed women have such coverage and that benefits amount to two thirds of average wages for periods ranging from thirteen to twenty-six weeks (Kahn, Kamerman, October 1978). As compared with women in many other countries, fewer American women are covered for maternity benefits, and for those eligible, coverage is generally less generous.

A modification of the maternity leave plan in Sweden permits the family to decide whether the father or the mother will stay home to care for the child during a period after birth. Government grants and employers' contributions provide some 95 per cent of the father's salary for a period of up to seven months if he elects to care for the child. The program does not require the husband to use all seven months. If the wife works, the two are free to split the total time available to suit their own needs. In 1976, after the program had been in operation for three years, some 7 per cent of eligible fathers elected to use at least some of the time allocated to them for such a purpose, the average number of days used by fathers being about forty-five, or a month and a half (*The New York Times,* December 7, 1976). Norway has a similar but more limited and more ambivalent eighteen-week maternity leave policy. Only the mother is eligible for the first six weeks after the birth of the baby, but the additional twelve weeks can be split between the father and mother. However, the father can elect to take unpaid paternity leave for up to one year with full job protection (Henriksen, Halter, 1978, p. 62).

France gives some formal recognition of the father's involvement in the birth of the child in a special provision—*congés de naissance*—which provides a three-day holiday with pay for the father within fifteen days before or after the birth.

Many countries pay a birth grant—a lump sum to help the family with the temporary increases in expenses associated with the birth. In 1977 the birth grant in East Germany was $420, in France about $365, in Hungary $125, and in Finland $65. In Argentina, a birth grant, which in 1977 amounted to about $300, was also paid upon the adoption of a child (U.S. Department of Health, Education, and Welfare, Research Report 50, 1978, p. 9).

The People's Republic of China provides maternity benefits of 100 per cent of earnings for up to fifty-six days before confinement and fifty-six days after delivery. In addition, there is a birth-grant lump sum "equal to current value of 5 feet of cloth" (Sidel, 1976, p. 190).

As an alternative to providing day-care services for the very young child so as to permit adequate care of the child while the mother works, some countries provide extended support benefits to the mother in lieu of working. Postpartum maternity benefits are a step in this direction. In replacing wage-earned income, maternity benefits permit the mother to remain at home for a period of time and care for the child without income loss. Extending this concept, some countries provide maternity benefits for the first two or three years of the child's life.

In response to a concern about declining population, East Germany gives mothers a half-year off at full pay after the birth of a child and makes it possible for working mothers to extend their leave of absence up to a year while keeping their jobs and getting monthly stipends (*The New York Times*, April 28, 1978). Hungarian women are entitled to a maternity leave from employment of twenty to twenty-five weeks at full salary. If employed for a year prior to the child's birth they can subsequently elect to stay home and care for the child until the child is three years old. During this period they receive a grant that is almost half of the average salary for women (Ferge, 1978, p. 175). Austria has a more modest program; it permits the mother to receive financial support through unemployment insurance for the first year after the birth of the child (Krebs, Schwartz, 1978, p. 206).

Women employees who opt to stay at home to care for a child for the first two or three years of the child's life are given credit, in these programs, for those years in the computation of pension time. Maternity leave allowances, subsequent support payments, and the continued counting of this period of child care toward pension coverage reduce the pressures on mothers to return to work after childbirth.

The extension of maternity leave is viewed with some ambivalence on the part of some women in other countries where similar measures have been proposed. There is a feeling that such measures may be implemented at the expense of a greater commitment to day care and jobs for women and that the pressure to stay at home to care for the young child will erode options for women (Scott, 1977). Knowing that a woman can leave work with support for two or three years following the birth of the child may make employers more hesitant to hire women. Further, an absence of two or three years from employment may adversely affect a woman's career. The policy comes close to being a "mother's wage," since it involves paying the mother for remaining in the home to care for the child in preference to returning to employment. The fear is that in strengthening the woman's position as mother it weakens her position as a woman, reinforcing the traditional stereotyping of female roles.

Despite extensive social security programs, all countries find the need for a public assistance program. Almost everywhere social insurance is backed up and supplemented by a means-tested public assistance program. In England, these are called *supplementary benefits;* in France, *allocation supplementaire* or *l'aide sociale;* in Sweden, *social hjälp.*

Some countries do far more than we do in advertising the availability of such programs and encouraging people to implement their eligibility. For instance, there is little, if any, advertising of the Aid to Families of Dependent Children (AFDC) program in the United States. On the other hand, there is great concern in Great Britain with what they call *take-up*—the percentage of eligible people who actually apply for the benefits to which they are entitled. To implement this concern and to give the programs visibility, the British post offices and many other public buildings have posters informing people of allowances—including those affecting children—for which they might apply. Government-supported Citizen Advice Bureaus located at the neighborhood level distribute leaflets and offer advice regarding application procedures.

Indirect procedures have also been adopted to help maintain family income at a level that would permit adequate care of the child. Hot school lunches at little or no cost and free distribution of food to low-income families supplement the family budget. Rent allowances go further than subsidies of low-cost housing. Denmark, for example, has a system of differential rents for families with three or more children living in flats built especially for such families. Rent reductions of up to 70 per cent are given according to the number of children, and "about half of all families with two or more children under sixteen years receive rent subsidies" (Henning, 1969, p. 145). In France, housing allowances can range up to 85 per cent of the rent for families with four or more children.

In Denmark, low-income families may also receive textile discount coupons of specified value to be used toward the purchase of children's clothing. In Belgium, Greece, France, and Scandinavia, large families are given special reductions of 50–75 per cent on train and bus fares. Sweden provides free holiday travel, once a year, to a place of rest and recreation for members of low-income families.

Homemaker service is more highly developed in some countries than it is in the United States. In Great Britain, homemaker service is one of the programs offered as part of the National Health Service Act—Britain's socialized-medicine plan. In Finland, legislation requires that there be homemakers available in every public health district to work closely with midwives and public health nurses. As a result, the number of homemakers per capita is much higher than in the United States.

In 1972 the Netherlands had 1 homemaker per 380 population. At that time, the United States had 1 homemaker per 7,000 population (Kahn, Kamerman, 1975, p. 105). Both Sweden and Norway provide temporary "child-care attendant service," a homemaker being available to care for the employed mother's child who, being ill, cannot be cared for in his usual day-care center group. In addition, Germany has a special organization that offers homemaker service to large families, on the theory that giving the mother of a large family an opportunity for a break from unremitting child care is sensible preventive therapy.

Although there is no formally established program of training for homemakers in the United States, several European countries have such a program. Holland has an eighteen-month curriculum; France, which classifies homemaker service as a social profession, offers a seven-month program; Finland has schools offering a two-year course in homemaker training; Sweden offers a fifteen-month homemaker training course in fourteen schools scattered throughout the country (Nordstrom, 1969). In every instance, the courses offer a combination of theoretical material and practical fieldwork in a hospital, a child-care institution, or supervised placement in a family.

Expansion in the employment of married women gives rise everywhere to the problem of the need for day care. Many European countries apparently do not share our reluctance to have a day-care facility associated with the mother's place of work or our reluctance to offer group care to children under three years of age. Consequently, especially in the East European countries, the factory crèche, or infant nursery, is quite common (United Nations, 1956, pp. 18–44). Part of the greater need for and, hence, the acceptability of group care is predicated on the fact that a significantly larger percentage of women in East Europe work outside the home than is true in the United States. In addition, the housing shortage there makes home care less feasible.

All new Soviet apartment buildings are required to reserve a minimum of 5 per cent of their space for a crèche, and "all enterprises employing more than

500 workers must provide nursery and *crèche* facilities" (Radin, 1970, p. 31). Every effort is made to provide adequate care. A "patronage nurse," implementing the role of a social worker, visits the homes of children whose families are applying for day care to help integrate the child's experience in the day-care center and the home (Orlova, 1969). The nurseries that enroll children at three months of age have one "upbringer" for every four children at the younger age levels.

China, too, provides widespread day-care facilities for children and infants. Such services are necessary because almost 90 per cent of all Chinese women are in the work force (Sidel, 1972). Nursery rooms are available in most factories and other work places. There are some full-time nurseries open day and night, and some parents take their children home only on weekends. Approximately 50 per cent of the children between one-and-a-half and three years of age are cared for in communal nurseries; grandparents care for an additional large group of children.

In Japan, the Sony Company operates a day-care center for its many women employees. Twice a year, the children are given complete medical checkups. The children study English from the age of two-and-a-half years through Sony tape recorders (Bayh, 1970).

Other countries, such as France, Belgium, and Israel, provide some kind of day care, at least half-time, for a larger percentage of their three- to five-year-old children than does the United States. An effort is being made to extend kindergarten education downward and universalize such a program for all three- to five-year-olds.

Besides day-care centers and the infant's nursery or *crèche*, Norway has a large number of "park aunts," who look after children of preschool age in parks and playgrounds. The mother who needs to shop or visit a clinic, or who merely wants to catch her psychic breath, may leave the young child with the park aunt for part of the day. In Sweden, " 'afternoon homes' and 'walking tours' are provided in many neighborhoods. Under this arrangement one of the women in the neighborhood takes care of the children of employed mothers and, when the weather will permit, takes them on tours" (Rosenthal, 1967, p. 82).

"Baby parking" in *Haltes-garderies* is provided in France:

> In this institution, during the day, for a limited time, and on an occasional basis, care is given to children ranging from 3 months to 5 years, or 18 months to 5 years. A maximum of 20 children is permitted in such centers. The service is available both to working and to nonworking mothers and provides some freedom for the nonworking mother who may otherwise be completely tied down to home and child care. These centers are usually related either to full-day day care programs or to nursery schools [Kahn, Kamerman, 1976, p. 157].

Substitute Care: Foster Care, Adoptions, Institutions

All industrialized countries find that they are required to provide substitute care for some percentage of their children in foster-family homes, adoptive homes, or institutions.

Hazel (1976), a member of the Council of Europe's Coordinated Research Group, which examined the use of substitute care in seventeen different European countries, summarized her experiences by noting that "In all the industrialized European countries there are children who can no longer remain in their own home with their parents because society is no longer willing to tolerate their conduct or because their parents are ill, separated, have disappeared or have neglected or ill-treated their children" (p. 310).

Given the limited availability of comparable statistics, it is hard to know whether or not the United States tends to employ substitute care more frequently than other similarly industrialized countries.

In England and Wales, the number of children in care on March 31, 1976, was 100,628: "This represents 7.5 per 1,000 estimated population under the age of eighteen in England and 6.4 per 1000 in Wales" (House of Commons, 1977, p. 3). The circumstances of children who came into care paralleled the problems encountered in the United States: abandonment, death, or imprisonment of the parents; short- and long-term parental physical or mental illness; and "unsatisfactory home conditions" (p. 9).

Despite the more adequate homemaker and day-care services available in Sweden, the rate of children in substitute care per 1,000 under the age of sixteen increased from 8.6 in 1971 to 9.4 in 1975 (Sveriges Officiella Statistik, 1977, Table B1, p. 33).

In the case of Britain and Wales and Sweden, the rate of children in substitute care would seem to have been higher than in the United States for the equivalent period.

Early in the century, adoption was of little importance as a child welfare service in Europe. However, as a result of the large number of children orphaned by two world wars, European countries became more interested in adoption. Legislation legalizing adoption was passed in countries where no such legislation had previously existed: in Denmark in 1923, in Britain in 1926, and in Portugal in 1967. Existing adoption laws were revised to give greater protection to the child and the adoptive parent. Current legislation in most European countries is, for the most part, similar to that in the United States (United Nations, 1953, 1956; Gerbler, 1963; Moore, 1968).

Unlike procedures in the United States, however, a foreign child adopted by a British citizen is automatically granted British citizenship. This ensures for the child a greater feeling of identification with the adoptive family and suggests that he has the same status as a natural child.

In an effort to control black- or gray-market adoptions, some countries have national regulations that parallel the legislation passed by some of our states. Great Britain forbids the payment or the acceptance of any payment or reward for arranging an adoption and prohibits the publication of advertisements either offering or seeking children for adoption. Denmark stipulates that before an adoption order is granted, information shall be elicited as to whether a fee has been paid or is to be paid any of the interested parties.

The attitude toward religious preference in adoption tends to be permissive. In Denmark, there is no legal provision in the adoption law concerning the child's religion and no legal bar to placing a child of one religious affiliation with adoptive parents of another. In England, the mother may express a religious preference, which then determines the religious affiliation of the adoptive couple with whom the child is placed, but when unmarried mothers do not indicate a preference, the agency is permitted to place the child with a family of any religious affiliation. An Agnostics Adoption Society is available to offer service to those adoptive couples who are reluctant to declare a religious affiliation or who have none.

The shortage of children available for adoption is even greater in some European countries than in the United States. As a matter of fact, some American children who could not be placed for adoption here have been placed in Sweden. This was true of a black child with a heart defect placed through the help of an American agency (*The New York Times*, August 20, 1972). Sweden and the Netherlands, having very few of their own children available for adoption, have been actively recruiting children for adoption abroad. Sweden has established a special organization, the Council for Intercountry Adoption, to facilitate such adoptions. There were 2,888 petitions for adoption in Sweden in 1975. In 1,380 instances (48 per cent), the child was of Asian descent. In 4 per cent of the cases, the adopter was a single parent (Sveriges Officiella Statistic, 1977, p. 72).

As a consequence of the shortages of adoptable children and the implementation of transracial adoptions in response, opposition to this procedure has developed in other countries. For instance, British Columbia, Canada, legislated a program of subsidized adoption in 1973. It was prompted by concern on the part of Canadian Indians that so many of their children were being placed with Caucasian families. It was felt that more Indian families would be able to adopt if adoption subsidies were made available.

In response to the universal problem of finding adoptive homes for special-needs children, other countries have developed specialized organizations.

And, as in the United States, special efforts have been made to recruit minority-group adoptive homes for racial minority children awaiting adoption. In 1975 nine London boroughs conducted a special project known as "Operation Soul Kids." An agency specializing in the adoptive placement of children with special needs, known as Parents for Children, has also been funded.

Parent to Parent Information of Adoption Services (PPIAS) is a group that was formed in Britain in 1971 by parents who had adopted hard-to-place children. As a self-help and mutual-support group, they act as a resource to prospective adoptive parents considering the adoption of a child with special needs. For instance, one of their members who has adopted an older child or a racial minority-group child might meet and discuss their experience with an applicant considering the adoption of such a child.

Some countries have been in advance of our own in dealing explicitly with the problem of disclosure of background information to adoptees. We previously noted (p. 495) that Finland, Scotland, and Israel permit adoptees to examine their birth records. The British Children Act of 1975 provided that children adopted after 1975 are entitled, on request, to a certified copy of the original birth record at eighteen years of age. A person adopted before 1975 can likewise obtain a copy of the birth document, but only after an interview with a counselor. An English organization called Jig-Saw is the counterpart of the American organization ALMA—concerned with the rights of adopted children and their search.

According to Israeli law, adopted children are allowed to petition the District Court in Tel Aviv to see the registry of adoption in order to learn their real parents' names only. Should they wish to go further and actually meet their biological parents, the court must ask the latter's consent. If they do consent, the meeting is arranged and supervised by an experienced social worker [Barinbaum, 1974, p. 549].

The criteria for adoptive applicants are similar in other countries to the criteria employed here. The following is an example of a "favorable" adoptive placement reported in a study of adoptions in Poland:

Mr. and Mrs. CB are farmers and neither of them received secondary education. When they adopted the child, the wife was 36 and the husband was 43. After 12 years of marriage, they adopted a boy of three who was in an orphanage; at the time of the enquiry, the boy was almost seven years old.

The CB's farm is located at the foot of the mountains, and covers six hectares. It is well equipped with agricultural machines and mechanical appliances, and the main activity is stock-breeding. The house has two rooms and a kitchen, with running hot and cold water and central heating. The kitchen is the best decorated room, and family life is focused there. Mr. and Mrs. CB form a fairly positive couple, solid, stable and founded on their attachment and common place of work where, nonetheless, they do not necessarily have the same interests.

There even seems to be a slight reproachfulness on the part of the wife who sees herself as being overloaded with work in the house in addition to that on the farm. She also has a certain complex with regard to her husband for not having borne him a child and she underestimates herself in relation to other mothers. She constantly repeats that her sister has already had three children since she adopted her son. She only has one child, and in the country, this is not enough.

Both parents are kind and jovial, and relate immediately to others. Husband seems more in control of himself and better balanced than his wife, who is not very sure of herself as a mother, and even less so in her role as a woman. Both show great friendliness in their relationship with the child. Mother is more consistent towards the child than the father, who declares himself to be unable to punish the child, because he feels sorry for him.

The child himself has considerable freedom (too great?), since he passes his time with children of his own age when mother is working in the fields. Her orders are hardly ever respected even though her demands are reasonable. The father's view is that the child has quite simply forgotten his mother's injunction and that he "has every right to do so because he is still small."

The child loves his parents, and is for them a source of pride and joy. The family is on very good terms with the neighbours and often helps them out. The couple is also interested in work of a social nature, and both in turn have been village mayor. At the present time they are active in the Housewives' Circle and the Fathers' Circle.

They experienced a long and difficult period during the child's rehabilitation. When he first came to their house, he posed important problems of upbringing. He was fearful and aggressive in all respects. He searched convulsively for his mother's hand and was mistrustful toward father and men in general. His stay in the orphanages left a mark on him for some time, and during that period he avoided other children.

Parents demonstrated considerable tact and understanding which had not been obtained from books but through their intuition, their experience and the love they feel for the child [Klomineck, 1976, p. 46].

Although the worldwide trend is toward the increasing use of foster-family care in preference to institutional care when substitute care is needed, there are wide differences in the proportion in which different substitute-care facilities are used. In 1973 there were 14,300 children in institutions in Indonesia and 2,000 in foster-family homes, and there were 10,000 children in institutions and 2,000 children in foster-family homes in Israel. In the Netherlands in the same year, there were 10,000 children in institutions and 9,500 in foster-family homes (United Nations, 1974, pp. 12–13).

Sweden, having made a definite effort to reduce the use of institutions for children, has 80 per cent of its children in substitute care either in the homes of relatives or in foster-family care. The effort is made to place even seriously disturbed children and delinquents in foster-family care rather than in institutions. The orientation is toward minimal use of substitute care whenever possible (Hazel, 1974, p. 310).

And, as is true in this country, greater efforts are being made to provide adoptive homes for children in institutions. In Germany, the "popular magazine Brigette runs a series with large colour photographs captioned Holt Die Kinder aus den Heimen—get the children out of the institution"—the children featured being older or handicapped (Benet, 1976, p. 92).

Efforts have been made to use the institution as the locus for treating the whole family rather than the child only. Thus Ska, a "children's village" located not far from Stockholm, reorganized their program in 1972 so as to accommodate whole families rather than individual children. Some of the families in the treatment program include "a mother, father and seven children ages 3–15 years. The family has had extended contact with social welfare and child welfare authorities. A couple of the older children are drug users and the father has an alcohol problem." "Family composed of mother, father and three children ages 10–16 years: crises connected with the children's school truancy, vagabonding, glue sniffing. Father ill." The families, living in their own apartments in the institution, have continuing responsibility for the care of their children. The therapeutic work is with the family as a treatment unit (Borjeson, 1974).

Developing a stronger link between the institution and the community to which the child is being returned has gone further in some European countries than here. In Sweden, the institutional worker "may accompany the child when he returns home and may remain there all day or even overnight until he has settled down" (Hazel, 1975, p. 772). In France the institutional worker may continue to work with the child in the community after his return. In West Germany, the institution is used in deliberate integration with foster-family care:

> Disturbed children in care may first be admitted to a therapeutic institution where the staff seeks to understand and help them. At the same time, the institution acts as a center for the training and support of qualified foster families to whose care the children are gradually transferred. The whole process is carefully planned, the residential staff, the social worker and the foster parents working together as a team of which the child's parents may also be part . . . residential establishments acting like the hub of a wheel from which the [foster family] placements radiate like a series of outposts [Hazel, 1976, p. 324].

Some attempts have been made in Europe to develop distinctive types of institutions for dependent and neglected children. The most notable example is the "children's village," established originally in Austria by Hermann Gmeiner. The village consists of a series of ten to sixteen cottages, each with a "mother" and, ideally, nine children, both boys and girls, of various ages from babyhood to adolescence. Only those children who are healthy enough emotionally and physically to live in a family without receiving special attention are accepted. The "mother" is given a budget for each child and cares for the children as though they were her own. The children attend the local school and are a part of the local community. The mother buys food at the village store and the "family" may supplement the budget by planting and tending a kitchen garden. The mothers are carefully selected, undergo a four-month training period, and either are unmarried or are childless widows (Wachstein, 1963; Wolins, 1969; Dodge, 1972). The *Dorfleiter,* or village manager, provides the only "fathering" that is officially available. Familiar with each child in the village, he has the responsibility for advising the mothers and serving as a combination judge, mediator, and father confessor. Every village has a corps of "family helpers," often cottage mothers in training, who assist the mothers or substitute for them during time off or vacation or when they are ill. There is some evidence that a sense of family develops among the children in a particular cottage and that the movement is successful in achieving its aim of healthy child-rearing for many of the children it accepts.

The SOS Children's Federation, which sponsors the children's villages, has built about 110 such villages throughout the world and by 1976 had facilities in fifty-five countries on five continents.

Institutions for children in Europe include, as a key staff member, a professional known as an *educateur,* who has no counterpart in American institutions. The *educateur* has the responsibility of resocializing the child assigned to the institution, organizing the child's activity in such a way as to ensure changes in the child's behavior (*International Child Welfare Review,* 1971; Linton, 1969). The distinctive difference in the approach of the *educateur,* sometimes called an *orthopedagogue,* lies in the techniques he uses for resocializing the child:

> [This may include use of] ceramics, painting, weaving, woodwork, metal craft, puppets and marionettes, home economics, interior design, music, dance, body movement and expression, hobbies, and physical and vocational re-education. In addition the *educateurs* are trained to use radio, television, and films, cultural events, holidays, birthdays, and sporting events as techniques for activating and re-educating the maladjusted child [Linton, 1969, p. 322].

The idea is to reach the child through meaningful activity that involves interaction between the child and the *educateur.*

Unlike the houseparent in this country, the *educateur* is not responsible for the maintenance of the child's living facilities. In France, some of the *educateurs* work with gangs in the slum areas and are employed in youth centers.

The European *educateur* function, with its emphasis on resocialization, has influenced the development of programs in this country. The Re-Ed (re-educational) experimental programs for disturbed children here are patterned on the *educateur* model.

The Unmarried Mother–The Out-of-Wedlock Child

Some of the legislation regarding the unmarried mother–out-of-wedlock child pair is more humane in the Scandinavian countries than in the United States. In Norway, for instance, the state, rather than the mother herself, takes the responsibility for establishing paternity. In Denmark, once the question of paternity is established and the father's contribution to the care of the child is determined, the mother is entitled to advance payments of the father's contribution from public funds; the authorities then undertake to recover the amount from the father. Such advance payments are also made to the divorced mother when the father defaults in making support payments. In these countries, once paternity has been established, the child's right to inherit from his father is also granted (Morrisey, 1968).

Private agencies in France have been experimenting with housing for the unmarried mother and the illegitimate child. These are known as *hôtels maternelles*. While the mothers are working, infant nurses, and later kindergarten teachers, care for the child. The mothers pay for the child's upkeep and, in general, finance the maintenance of the home.

Britain has developed a somewhat similar arrangement: working mothers' hotels. The mother and the child live at the hotel for a period of a year or two after the birth of the baby. The hotel staff cares for the child while the mother goes out to work. The hotels are open to widowed mothers and deserted wives as well as unmarried mothers. Similar housing is available in Denmark (Wynn, 1964, p. 145).

New Zealand has a statutory provision that a child welfare worker must be notified, in confidence, in every case of illegitimate birth. This gives the social worker the opportunity of making an offer of help to every unmarried mother (Anderson, 1963, p. 4).

Recognizing that from its start in life, the out-of-wedlock child is handicapped by virtue of its lack of a father's protection, European countries provide for the appointment of a public guardian to the child (Wimperes, 1960, pp. 333–340). In Germany, the Local Youth Board provides a guardian at the birth of the child to assist the mother and protect the child through the development of a personal relationship with the family. In Sweden, the child welfare guardian "sees that the child receives the financial benefits to which he is entitled and can start executive proceedings against a father who neglects to pay maintenance" (Wester, 1970, p. 5). As a consequence of the advocacy activities of such guardians, paternity has been established for an estimated 90 per cent of out-of-wedlock children in Sweden. In Finland, a "communal godfather" is appointed for each illegitimate child. Sometimes the appointed guardian is a professional social worker; sometimes he is a lay volunteer selected by the child welfare board. The trend has been toward reducing the guardian's control over the family and making his appointment voluntary rather than automatic.

ORGANIZATION OF CHILD WELFARE SERVICES

One of the most persistent problems faced by American child welfare is the coordination of the work of the many different agencies dealing with various aspects of the child's situation. The social agencies in Paris have been experimenting with a plan to meet this problem. The city is divided into districts. All the public and private agencies in the district offering family service coordinate their efforts under a combined staff. The combined staff, in effect, forms a new agency that represents all of the agencies. The workers in the coordinating group remain staff members of the agencies that employ them, but they form a unified social-work department offering the family services in the district. The workers of the united agency elect a director—usually an outstanding, experienced worker —to coordinate the work of the members of the combined family-service unit (Schort, 1965).

In France, some 25 per cent of all social workers are general, all-purpose workers, similar, perhaps, to our rural social workers. Called *polyvalent social workers*, and sometimes called *family social workers*, they cover all geographic areas: "These social workers, mostly female, are trained in a system which combines basic social work with some elements of public health nursing. The relevant law requires coverage by one polyvalent worker of each sector, a geographic area with a population group of some 5,000" (Kamerman, Kahn, 1976, p. 333).

A comprehensive review of social welfare programs in Britain by the Seebohm Committee (1969) made radical suggestions for total reorganization of the pattern of service. The proposal, adopted by Parliament in 1970, was to unite all government-supported social workers in a community in one department under their own administrative control and supervision. Service would be offered by a team of ten to twelve social workers through area offices serving populations of 50,000–100,000 people. Separate child-welfare services would merge with other personal services to individuals and families to form a comprehensive, community-based, family-oriented agency offering a wide variety of services. The objective of the reorganization of British social services was to meet the total requirements of the individual or family, rather than a limited set of symptoms, by providing community-based and family-oriented services that are available to all.

A similar reorganization of the social service delivery system in Scotland integrated services so that a single local social-work department was charged with administering all programs that "utilize the insights and skills of the profession of social work. The objective was to provide" a single door on which anyone might knock for help with confidence of getting it (Gandy, 1977, p. 47).

It might be noted that the English and Scottish efforts to offer a comprehensive, integrated service through generically oriented social workers have posed some unresolved problems. The specialized kinds of knowledge and skills required in offering particular kinds of services, such as child welfare, have raised questions about the greater efficiency of more specialized approaches (Gandy, 1977; Kahn, Kamerman, 1976, p. 319).

In the Soviet Union, social services are more closely tied to social insurance than they are in the United States, which permits a much wider access to family problems than is true for social insurance agencies in the United States. Similarly, Australia has organized a special casework service within its general social security administration, and "French social security agencies employ social workers to perform *polyvalent* social duties, which include family casework and the handling of problems with which families may be faced" (*International Social Services Review*, 1959, p. 30). France, too, combines social services and the social insurances:

> One of the characteristic features of the French social security system is that it links a program of health and social services to the agencies that administer benefit payments. That means that these organizations are not merely administrative and financial agencies, but that they use part of their resources to activate a true program of services for the benefit of their members [Laroque, 1969, p. 182].

The French family-allowance system, for instance, makes available such services as homemaker service, day care, and family holidays to family allowance recipients (Rodgers, 1968, p. 317).

The Soviet Union and other European countries organize their child welfare services in a pattern different from ours. In these countries, all social service functions are considered ancillary to some other primary concern. Thus family counseling and service for young children are provided by health agencies; those for older children and young people, by educational agencies.

Although no particular, explicitly designated professional social-work group exists in the Soviet Union, the functions that the social worker performs for the child are just as necessary there as elsewhere. In the absence of a profession of social work, these functions are performed principally by the schoolteacher, the nurse, and the trade union (Madison, 1960, 1963, 1964, 1968; United Nations, 1961). The teachers have the responsibility for being aware not only of the educational progress of the child but of his psychosocial development as well. In discharging this responsibility, the Soviet teacher is aided by the fact that he moves with the child through the first four years of schooling. The teacher visits with the parents regularly in the home and in the school to discuss problems and to give advice regarding the upbringing of the child. The schools may recommend to the local district soviet government the removal of children from the care of their parents (in cases of neglect) and may be asked by the local government to consider adoptive homes for children who are available for adoption. The work of the teacher is supplemented by the children's inspector, who is also an employee of the educational system. He is responsible for dealing with truancy and behavior problems, investigating complaints of child neglect, and supervising the placement of children on the very few occasions when foster care is employed.

Child welfare functions are performed by the "patronage" or "social" nurses, operating out of district clinics, each clinic composed of a team of one pediatrician and two patronage nurses responsible for service to 1,000 children: "Since the team serves the same children throughout their childhood and adolescence both in their home and in the clinics, it becomes thoroughly acquainted with them, their families, and their total life situation" (Madison, 1963, p. 322). The nurses are primarily concerned with the health problems of the children, but they also have the responsibility of helping the family with the social and emotional problems encountered by the child as well as with problems of housing, financial assistance, guardianship, and so on: "It is compulsory for a nurse and a doctor attached to the local infant welfare clinic to visit the child in his home on the day he leaves the hospital or on the following day. They examine the state of health and living conditions of the newborn baby and give advice to the mother" (U.S. Department of Health, Education, and Welfare, 1969, p. 103). The district clinic is the central organization to which the family relates in meeting the physical and health needs of the child throughout childhood. This system provides not only integrated care but also continuity of care.

The work of the teacher and the patronage nurse is supplemented by the trade unions, which have been given the responsibility for discharging some of the "helping" functions in connection with social problems faced by families of union members. The trade unions have developed child welfare programs and attempt to involve their members as "patrons" for children who need help:

The "good" trade union committee concern themselves not only with providing summer camps for the children of the employees but also with giving emotional supportive help to the widow who is losing control over her adolescent son or to the unmarried mother who is rearing her youngster single-handedly [Madison, 1964, p. 200].

More emphasis is placed on the use of volunteers in direct work with parents around parent–child problems. A teacher concerned about a child might request that members of the union committee in the plant where the father works talk to the father. The local soviet may ask a "good" mother to make a visit to give advice to the family.

Comradeship courts in factories, housing blocks, or collective farms, with "judges" elected by their peers, use "measures of social pressure" to "help" neglectful or ineffective parents become more competent. The comradeship courts stand behind parents' committees made up of neighbors who take the initial responsibility for seeing that parents adequately care for their children. Parents' committees "are composed of parents who have been successful in raising their own children" (Viellard-Cybulska, 1965, p. 133). They help the parent to relate to the child and offer practical assistance, such as seeing that the children attend school and helping an overburdened mother with child care.

All the child-care manuals emphasize the fact that all citizens have a concern for all children. What might be regarded as meddling in someone else's affairs in the United States is an act of good citizenship in the Soviet Union. It is, in effect, an implementation of the principle of child advocacy.

Many European countries demonstrate a greater willingness to involve local lay leadership and volunteers in the responsibility for child care. For instance, in Sweden, the child welfare boards take the responsibility for major services in the local community. Members of local child-welfare boards are judges, teachers, physicians, and nurses, who serve as citizens rather than in their professional capacity. The board has the right to employ professional social workers to implement its decisions, but it has the ultimate responsibility for seeing that child welfare services are provided to any child in the community who needs them. In Sweden, the social welfare boards have an advocacy–social action function: "They must try first of all to influence children's living conditions in general. They are to see to it that there are playgrounds, day nurseries, leisure time activities and so on" (Elmer, 1975, p. 121).

Other countries make greater use of lay helpers and volunteers than we do in our child welfare programs. Associated with this approach is a greater emphasis on decentralization and consumer participation in service delivery. In Yugoslavia, great emphasis is placed on the principle of "solidarity and mutuality" in social policy making and service delivery in the work place and the neigh-borhood (Smolik, Krikovic, 1977).

Wakumura (1977) reports that there are some 160,000 "volunteer workers in child welfare" in Japan. Commissioned by the Minister of Health and Welfare, they are selected from "among those people who are considered mature, with relevant life experiences" and are expected to serve a term of three years. During the 1972 fiscal year, such "volunteer workers in child welfare" dealt with 4,433,450 family problem situations (p. 199).

As in the Soviet Union, many of the child welfare functions are implemented in China by members of workers' committees at the place of employment or by residents' committees in the neighborhood. *Peking Review* (November 3, 1978) notes that residents' committees elected by neighborhood residents "promote family planning and are smooth hands at mediating in petty squabbles and settling family bickerings." For example:

> An old man was anxious to have a grandson. He was disappointed because his daughter-in-law gave birth to two granddaughters for him. He often found himself locked in one altercation after another with her.
>
> Pien Ai-hua, member of the residents' committee in charge of women's affairs, patiently persuaded the old man to do away with the decrepit idea of looking up to men and down on women. Meanwhile she asked the daughter-in-law to respect the old man and take good care of him. Her mediation paid off: Quarrels between the two began to simmer down.

Intrusions by co-workers and neighbors into parent–child relationships are sanctioned and there is clear rejection of the idea that any special training is required in providing such "help" (see also Sidel, 1977).

In Holland, many dependent and/or delinquent children are placed under the supervision of a family guardian, a private person of good conduct who volunteers to devote his time to helping the child and the family without pay. Organizations of family guardians serve as a link between the volunteer and the juvenile judge and also recruit, train, and supervise family guardians. The family guardian is generally assigned one or two children and their families. Although there is some difficulty in recruiting family guardians, most of the child welfare experts note with surprise that many people still volunteer for such work and are very consistent in discharging their responsibility. As a matter of fact, there is less turnover among family guardians than among professional social workers; families assigned a family guardian have greater continuity of care. A report from the Dutch Ministry of Justice points out that the activity of the volunteer family guardian is "not typical casework. It is rather a matter of pedagogic influencing through a confidential relationship. The family guardian represents a bit of healthy society within the family." The help offered may vary "from practical advice connected with the choice of school or a profession to serious, penetrating talks" (Rood-DeBoer, 1966, p. 22).

In Denmark, volunteers are used as supervising guardians to assist the family with advice and guidance in matters relating to children. And in Poland, "social guardians" are appointed to offer assistance to families in trouble in an effort to "improve the financial, social, and educative condition, cooperate in the fight against alcoholism, hooliganism, prostitution, ill treatment of children, and against all social scourges" (Viellard-Cybulska, 1966). The People's Councils in

Rumania, composed by lay volunteers, perform similar functions, offering "legal and social assistance services taking the form of surveillance, primarily of a preventative nature, which intervene effectively only if and when the physical development, education, upbringing, vocational training of the child are endangered by the improper behavior of the parents or their negligence manifested in its upbringing" (United Nations, 1967, pp. 51–52).

Supranational Child Welfare

There are organizations that offer child welfare services across national boundaries. International Social Service (ISS) conducts an intercountry adoption program; the International Union for Child Welfare, publishers of the *International Child Welfare Review*, conducts international child-welfare seminars and conferences and stimulates child welfare research; the United Nations International Children's Emergency Fund, better known as UNICEF, is active in combating disease and hunger, has equipped maternal and child health centers throughout the world, has inoculated millions of children against a variety of infectious diseases, has distributed billions of pounds of food to hungry children, and has trained thousands of midwives. The United Nations Bureau of Social Affairs collects and disseminates information regarding child welfare problems throughout the world; various agencies of the United Nations offer technical assistance to nations in developing their child welfare services in a demonstration of international mutual aid.

In 1959 the United Nations adopted a Declaration of the Rights of the Child, which explicitly recognizes the right of the child to grow up with affection and acceptance with his own parents in a home that provides adequately for his physical, social, emotional, and spiritual needs. It stipulates, furthermore, that the child should be given special protection by the community against all forms of neglect, abuse, and exploitation. The Declaration of the Rights of the Child stands as an explicit statement of what the people of the world hope they can achieve for their children.

In December 1976, the General Assembly of the United Nations passed a resolution declaring 1979 the International Year of the Child. The International Year of the Child was the twentieth anniversary of the adoption by the United Nations of the Declaration of the Rights of the Child. The objectives in designating 1979 as the International Year of the Child were to heighten the concern about children's needs and intensify efforts to meet these needs. The effort made in behalf of children, as compared with competing priorities, is miniscule, however.

At its annual meeting in June 1978, the executive board of UNICEF allocated $207.5 million for projects in 102 countries and territories. This total budget was the equivalent of the amount that was being spent by the world on armaments in approximately five hours at that time.

SUMMARY

The problems that require child welfare services are universal. The services available in each country to meet children's needs are a function of such factors as the economic resources available for caring for dependents, the ratio of dependents to productive adults, the general attitude toward the child, and the availability of alternative patterns of mutual aid in the primary group.

Developing countries are currently facing some of the same problems in organizing social services that were faced by the more economically advanced nations two or three centuries ago. Child welfare services in such countries are primarily concerned with meeting the basic health, educational, and housing needs of the child population.

A review of the supportive, supplementary, and substitutive child welfare services in nations similar to the United States suggests that the social insurance plans of such countries, as they affect the child, are more comprehensive than our own. They include family allowances, maternity benefits, medical care, and sickness insurance. Some additional details were noted regarding differences between child welfare services here and abroad.

BIBLIOGRAPHY

ACOSTA, JOSEFINA. "Columbian Elites and the Underdevelopment of the Social Welfare System," pp. 221–239, in *Meeting Human Needs*, Vol. 2. Ed. by Daniel Thurz and Joseph Vigilante. Beverly Hills, Calif.: Russell Sage Publications, 1977.

ANDERSON, LEWIS G. "Child Welfare in New Zealand." *Indian Journal of Social Work*, 24, 1 (April 1963).

BALI-BENNETT, JOHN, and JOHN MEYER. "The Ideology of Childhood and the State: Rules Distinguishing Children in National Constitutions." *American Sociological Review*, 43 (December 1978), 797–812.

BALL, ROBERT M. *Social Security—Today and Tomorrow*. New York: Columbia University Press, 1978.

BARINBAUM, LEA. "Identity Crises in Adolescence: The Problems of an Adopted Girl." *Adolescence*, 9 (Winter 1974), 547–564.

BAYH, MARVELLA. "Russians and Japanese Ahead in Day Care." *Voice*, 3, 2 (February 1970), 3–4.

BENET, MARY K. *The Politics of Adoption*. New York: The Free Press, 1976.

BORJESON, BERGT. *Reestablishing an Identity: Family Treatment at Ska Children's Village*. Stockholm: Child Welfare Board, 1974.

BRACKETT, JAMES W. "World Fertility 1976—An Analysis of Data Sources and Trends." *Population Reports*, Series J, No. 12. Washington, D.C.: Department of Medical and Public Affairs, The George Washington University Medical Center, November 1976.

CENTRAL UNION FOR CHILD WELFARE IN FINLAND. *Child Welfare in Finland*. Helsinki: Central Union for Child Welfare, 1968.

CLIFFORD, W. *A Primer of Social Casework in Africa*. New York: Oxford University Press, 1966.

COUNCIL FOR MUTUAL ECONOMIC ASSISTANCE. *Statistical Yearbook*, 1977. London: Industrial Press Ltd., 1978.

DESSAU, DOROTHY. *Glimpses of Social Work in Japan—Revisited*. Kyoto: Social Workers' International Club of Japan, 1968.

DODGE, JAMES. "SOS Children's Villages Throughout the World: Substitute or Superior Service." *Child Welfare*, 5, 6 (June 1972), 344–353.

ELMER, AKE. "Sweden's Model System of Social Service Administration," pp. 196–218, in *Meeting Human Needs*, Vol. 1. Ed. by Daniel Thurz and Joseph Vigilante. Beverly Hills, Calif.: Russell Sage Publications, 1975.

FERGE, ZSUZSA. "Hungary," in *Family Policy*. Ed. by Sheila B. Kamerman and Alfred J. Kahn. New York: Columbia University Press, 1978.

FRIIS, HENNING. "Issues in Social Security Policies in Denmark," in *Social Security in Perspective*. Ed. by Shirley Jenkins. New York: Columbia University Press, 1969.

————, and ANDERS FROM. "Denmark Human Services in the Service State," pp. 111–127, in *Meeting Human Needs*, Vol. 2. Ed. by Daniel Thurz and Joseph Vigilante. Beverly Hills, Calif.: Russell Sage Publications, 1977.

GANDY, JOHN M. "Scottish Governmental Reorganization and Human Service Delivery by Teams," pp. 33–54, in *Meeting Human Needs*, Vol. 2. Ed. by Daniel Thurz and Joseph Vigilante. Beverly Hills, Calif.: Russell Sage Publications, 1977.

GARMEZY, EDITH. "Meeting the Problems of Illegitimacy—The Danish Way," in *Effective Services for Unmarried Parents and Their Innovative Community Approaches*. New York: National Council on Illegitimacy, 1968.

HASAN, SAIYID Z. "Social Security in India: Limited Resources—Unlimited Need," in *Social Security in International Perspective*. Ed. by Shirley Jenkins. New York: Columbia University Press, 1969.

HAZEL, NANCY. "Child Placement Policies in England, Belgium and Sweden." *Social Work Today*, 5 (August 1974), 309–311.

————. "Residential Care as the Key to Fostering—The German Experience." *Social Work Today*, 5 (March 1975), 771–772.

————. "Child Placement Policies: Some European Comparisons." *British Journal of Social Work*, 6, 3 (1976), 315–326.

HEILBRONER, ROBERT L. *Mankind's Children—The Story of UNICEF*. New York: Public Affairs Pamphlet, 1959.

HENRIKSEN, HILDUR VE, and HARIET HOLTER. "Norway," in *Family Policy*. Ed. by Sheila B. Kamerman and Alfred J. Kahn. New York: Columbia University Press, 1978.

HER MAJESTY'S STATIONERY OFFICE. "Adoption of Children—Departmental Committee on the Adoption of Children." Sir William Houghton, Chairman. London, 1970.

HERMANN, ALICE, and SANDOR KOMLOS. "Early Child Care in Hungary." *Early Child Development and Care*, 1 (November 1972), whole issue.

HOUSE OF COMMONS. *Children in Care in England and Wales—March, 1976*. London: Her Majesty's Stationery Office, 1977.

HUSBY, RALPH, and EVA WETZEL. "Public Assistance in Sweden and the United States." *Social Policy* (March–April 1977), 28–31.

International Child Welfare Review. Special Issue—"The *Educateur*" (February 1971).

————. "Born in a Foreign Country; Adopted in Denmark." *International Child Welfare Review* (March 1978).

INTERNATIONAL LABOR OFFICE. *Maternity Protection—A World Survey of National Law and Practice*. Geneva: International Labor Office, 1965.

INTERNATIONAL SOCIAL SECURITY ASSOCIATION. *The Role of Social Services in Social Security: Trends and Perspectives*. Geneva, 1974.

JAFFE, FREDERICK S., and DEBORAH OAKLEY. "Observations on Birth Planning in China." *Family Planning Perspectives*, 10, 2 (March–April 1978), 101–108.

KAHN, ALFRED, et al. *Neighborhood Information Centers—A Study and Some Proposals*. New York: Columbia University School of Social Work, 1966.

————, and SHEILA B. KAMERMAN. *Child Care Programs in Nine Countries*. Washington, D.C.: U.S. Department of Health, Education, and Welfare, Publication No. OUD 30080, 1975a.

————. *Not for the Poor Alone—European Social Services*. Philadelphia: Temple University Press, 1975b.

————. *Social Services in International Perspectives—The Emergence of the Sixth System*. Washington, D.C.: Government Printing Office, 1976.

KAISER, GUNTHER. "Child Abuse in West Germany." *Victimology*, **2**, 2 (Summer 1977), 294–306.

KAKOL, KAIMIERZ. *Social Rights and Facilities in Poland*. Warsaw: Polonia Publishing House, 1959.

KALVESTEN, ARINA-LISA. "Changes in Sweden." *Adoption and Fostering*, **95**, 1 (1979), 41–43.

KAMERMAN, SHEILA B. "Eight Countries: Gross National Perspectives on Child Abuse and Neglect." *Children Today*, 4 (May–June 1975), 34–40.

————, and ALFRED J. KAHN. "Who's Taking Care of Our Children?" New York: Columbia University School of Social Work, October 1978, mimeo, 8 pp.

————. "Work and Family in Industrialized Societies." *Signs: Journal of Women in Culture and Society* (Summer 1979).

KIRKPATRICK, ELIZABETH K. "Children's Allowances in Japan." *Social Security Bulletin*, **35**, 6 (June 1972), 39.

KLOMINECK, WANDA. "The Development of Adoptive Children in Their New Family Environment." *International Child Welfare Review*, **28** (March 1976).

KONRAD, GEORGE. *The Caseworker*. New York: Harcourt Brace Jovanovich, 1974.

KREBS, EDITH, and MARGARETE SCHWARTZ, "Austria," in *Family Policy*. Ed. by Sheila B. Kamerman and Alfred J. Kahn. New York: Columbia University Press, 1978.

LANDMAN, LYNN C. "Birth Control in India: The Carrot and the Rod." *Family Planning Perspectives*, **9**, 3 (May–June, 1977), 101–110.

LAROQUE, PIERRE. "Social Security in France," in *Social Security in International Perspective*. Ed. by Shirley Jenkins. New York: Columbia University Press, 1969.

LEISSNER, ARYEH. *Family Advice Services*. Essex, England: Longman Group Ltd., 1967.

LILJESTROM, RITA. "Sweden," in *Family Policy*. Ed. by Sheila B. Kamerman and Alfred J. Kahn. New York: Columbia University Press, 1978.

LINDSTROM, MARITA V. "Finland: Communal Control of Social Services," pp. 129–150, in *Meeting Human Needs*, Vol. 2. Ed. by Daniel Thurz and Joseph Vigilante. Beverly Hills, Calif.: Russell Sage Publications, 1977.

LINTON, THOMAS E. "The European *Educateur* Model—An Alternative—Effective Approach to the Mental Health of Children." *Journal of Special Education*, **3**, 4 (Winter 1969), 319–327.

MADISON, BERNICE. "Contributions and Problems of Soviet Welfare Institutions." *Social Problems*, **7**, 4 (Spring 1960).

————. "Welfare Services for Children in the Soviet Union, 1945–1963." *Child Welfare*, **42**, 7 (July 1963).

————. "Canadian Family Allowances and Their Major Social Implications." *Journal of Marriage and Family Living*, **26**, 2 (May 1964a).

————. "Social Welfare: Soviet Model." *Social Service Review*, **38**, 2 (June 1964b).

————. *Social Welfare in the Soviet Union*. Stanford, Calif.: Stanford University Press, 1968.

————. "Soviet Income Maintenance Policy for the 1970's." *Journal of Social Policy*, **2**, 2 (April 1973), 97–117.

————. "Social Services for Families and Children in the Soviet Union Since 1967." *Child Welfare*, **53**, 7 (July 1974), 423–434.

————. "Social Services Administration in the U.S.S.R.," pp. 241–280, in *Meeting Human Needs*, Vol. 1. Ed. by Daniel Thurz and Joseph Vigilante. Beverly Hills, Calif.: Russell Sage Publications, 1975.

————. "Social Services for Women: Problems and Priorities," pp. 307–332, in *Women in Russia*. Ed. by Dorothy Atkinson, Alexander Dallin, and Gail W. Lapidus. Stanford, Calif.: Stanford University Press, 1977a.

————. *Soviet Income Maintenance Programs in the Struggle Against Poverty*. Washington, D.C.: Kennan Institute for Advanced Russian Studies, 1977b. Mimeo, 92 pp.

MANPEL, SIEGFRIED, and KANE HAWK. *Social Policy in the Soviet-Occupied Zone of Germany.* Bonn: Federal Ministry of Labour and the Social Structure, 1966.

MCAULEY, ALASTAIR. *Economic Welfare in the Soviet Union—Poverty, Living Standards and Inequality.* Madison: University of Wisconsin Press, 1979.

MCKIE, ERIC. *Venture in Faith.* Liverpool: Liverpool and District Family Service Unit, 1963.

MERRIAM, IDA. "Social Security and Social Welfare Indicators." *The Annals of the American Academy of Political and Social Sciences,* **435** (January 1978), 117–139.

MILLER, BETTE S. "Background Document Prepared for International Union of Child Welfare." Geneva, Switzerland. August 1978. Mimeo unpublished, 39 pp.

MINKOFF, JACK, and LYNN TURGEON. "Income Maintenance in Eastern Europe." *Social Policy* (March–April 1976), 33–45.

MORISEY, PATRICIA GARLAND. "From Scandinavia to the Urban Ghetto—Implication of Scandinavian Welfare Programs for Services to Unwed Mothers," in *Effective Services for Unmarried Parents and Their Children—Innovative Community Approaches.* New York: National Council on Illegitimacy, 1968.

MOUTON, PIERRE. *Social Security in Africa—Trends, Problems and Prospects.* Geneva: International Labor Office, 1975.

NAKAMURA, SUMIKO. "Japan: National Prefectural and Local Social Services," pp. 197–219, in *Meeting Human Needs,* Vol. 2. Ed. by Daniel Thurz and Joseph Vigilante. Beverly Hills, Calif.: Russell Sage Publications, 1977.

NEIPRIS, JOSEPH. "Social Service in Israel—A Review of Programmes and Policies." *Journal of Jewish Communal Services,* **47**, 4 (Summer 1971), 289–315.

NORDISK STATISTISK SKRIFTSERIE. *Social Security in the Nordic Countries.* Copenhagen, 1976.

NORDSTROM, MARGARITA. "Social Home Help Services in Sweden," in *Readings in Homemaker Services.* New York: National Council for Homemaker Services, 1969.

ORLOVA, NINA V. "The Protection of Children's Rights and Interests in the U.S.S.R." *International Child Welfare Review,* **23**, 4 (October 1969), 15–21.

OSBORN, ROBERT J. *Soviet Social Policies—Welfare Equality and Community,* Homewood, Ill.: Dorsey Press, Inc., 1970.

PHILIP, A. F. *Family Failure.* London: Faber & Faber, Ltd., 1963.

POPULATION REFERENCE BUREAU. *Children in the World.* Washington, D.C.: Population Reference Bureau, 1978.

RADIN, NORMA. "Preschool Programs of the U.S.S.R." *Child Welfare,* **49**, 1 (January 1970), 29–36.

RODGERS, BARBARA N., *et al. Comparative Social Administration.* New York: Atherton Press, Inc., 1968.

ROOD-DEBOER, M. *Child Care in the Netherlands.* The Hague: National Foundation for Child Welfare, 1966.

ROSE, ALBERT. "The Canadian Welfare State and Federalism," pp. 9–31, in *Meeting Human Needs,* Vol. 2. Ed. by Daniel Thurz and Joseph Vigilante. Beverly Hills, Calif.: Russell Sage Publications, 1977.

ROSENTHAL, ALBERT H. *The Social Programs of Sweden—A Search for Security in a Free Society.* Minneapolis: University of Minnesota Press, 1967.

SCABERNE, BRONISLAV. "Child and Youth Welfare in Yugoslavia." *International Child Welfare Review,* **23**, 1 (October 1969), 22–35.

SCHAEFER, DIETER. Federal Republic of Germany, Report III. "Cross National Studies of Social Service Systems." New York: Columbia University School of Social Work, 1976.

SCHORR, ALVIN. *Social Security and Social Services in France*. U.S. Department of Health, Education, and Welfare, Social Security Administration Research Report No. 7. Washington, D.C.: Government Printing Office, 1965.

SCOTT, HILDA. "Women's Place in Socialist Society: The Case of Eastern Europe." *Social Policy*, 7 (March–April 1977), 32–85.

SEEBOHM, FREDERIC, Chairman. *Report of the Committee on Local Authority and Allied Personal Social Service*. London: Her Majesty's Stationery Office, 1969.

SICAULT, GEORGE. *The Needs of Children*. New York: The Free Press, 1963.

SIDEL, RUTH. *Women and Child Care in China*. New York: Hill and Wang, 1972.

———, and VICTOR SIDEL. "The Human Services in China." *Social Policy*, 2, 6 (March–April 1972), 25–34.

———. "People Serving People: Human Services in the People's Republic of China," pp. 163–196, in *Meeting Human Needs*, Vol. 2. Ed. by Daniel Thurz and Joseph Vigilante. Beverly Hills, Calif.: Russell Sage Press, 1977.

SIMANIS, JOSEPH. "Recent Changes in Russian Social Security." *Social Security Bulletin*, 35, 12 (October 1972).

———. "Social Welfare Expenditures, Fiscal Year 1976." *Social Security Bulletin* (January 1977), 3–19.

SMITH, SELWYN. *The Battered Child Syndrome*. London: Butterworths, 1975.

SMOLIK-KRKOVIC, NADA. "Yugoslavian Self-managing Communities," pp. 151–161, in *Meeting Human Needs*, Vol. 2. Ed. by Daniel Thurz and Joseph Vigilante. Beverly Hills, Calif.: Russell Sage Publications, 1977.

SPIRO, MELFORD. *Children of the Kibbutz*. New York: Schocken Books, Inc., 1968.

STEIN, HERMAN (Ed.). *Planning for the Needs of Children in the Developing Countries*. New York: United Nations, 1965.

SVERIGES OFFICIELLA STATISTIK. *SociaVarden 1975*. Stockholm: Statistiska Centralbyran, 1976.

SWEDISH INSTITUTE. *Social Benefits in Sweden*. Stockholm: The Swedish Institute, 1966.

THURSZ, DANIEL, and JOSEPH L. VIGILANTE. *Meeting Human Needs*, Vol. 1: *An Overview of Nine Countries*. Beverly Hills, Calif.: Russell Sage Publications, 1975.

———.*Meeting Human Needs*, Vol. 2: *Additional Perspectives from Thirteen Countries*. Beverly Hills, Calif.: Russell Sage Publications, 1977.

TITMUSS, RICHARD. *Developing Social Policy in Conditions of Rapid Change—The Role of Social Work*. 16th International Conference on Social Welfare. The Hague, August 1972, Mimeo.

UHR, CARL G. *Sweden's Social Security System*, U.S. Department of Health, Education, and Welfare, Social Security Administration Research Report No. 14. Washington, D.C.: Government Printing Office, 1966.

UNITED NATIONS. *Study on Adoption of Children*. New York, 1953.

———. *Processes and Problems of Industrialization in Underprivileged Countries*. New York, 1955.

———. *Comparative Analysis of Adoption Laws*. New York, 1956a.

———. "Family and Child Welfare." *International Social Service Review*, 1 (January 1956b).

———. "Objectives in Social Policy for Improving Family Levels of Living." *International Social Service Review*, 5 (September 1959a).

———. "Social Insurance and the Family." *International Social Service Review*, 5 (September 1959b).

———. "Social Security and the Social Services." *International Social Service Review*, 5 (September 1959c).

———. *1963 Report on the World Social Situation*. New York, 1963.

———. *Patterns of Social Welfare Organization and Administration in Africa*. New York, 1964.

——. *Family, Child and Youth Welfare Services.* New York, 1965.

——. *Family, Child and Youth Welfare Services in Africa.* New York, 1966.

——. *Organization and Administration of Social Welfare Programmes—A Series of Country Studies: The Union of Soviet Socialist Republics.* New York, 1967.

UNITED NATIONS DEPARTMENT OF ECONOMIC AND SOCIAL AFFAIRS. *Organization and Administration of Social Welfare Programmes—A Series of Country Studies: Rumania.* New York, 1967.

——. Commission for Social Development. *Trends in the Social Situation of Children—Report of the Secretary-General.* New York, January 8, 1970.

——. Economic and Social Council. *Children and Adolescents in Slums and Shanty-Towns in Developing Countries.* New York, March 1971.

——, ECONOMIC AND SOCIAL COUNCIL, COMMISSION FOR SOCIAL DEVELOPMENT. *Protection and Welfare of Children—Report of the Secretary General.* New York: United Nations, November 15, 1974.

——. *Demographic Yearbook, 28th issue.* New York: United Nations, 1977.

——. *Statistical Yearbook, 1976, 28th issue.* New York: United Nations, 1977.

——, *1978 Report on the World Social Situation.* New York: United Nations, 1979.

UNITED NATIONS CHILDREN'S FUND. *Children and Youth in National Development in Latin America—Report of a Conference.* New York, 1966.

——. *Strategy for Children.* New York, 1968.

U.S. DEPARTMENT OF HEALTH, EDUCATION, AND WELFARE, PUBLIC HEALTH SERVICE. *Special Report: The First U.S. Mission on Mental Health to the U.S.S.R.* Public Health Service Publication No. 1893. Washington, D.C.: Government Printing Office, 1969.

U.S. DEPARTMENT OF HEALTH, EDUCATION AND WELFARE, OFFICE OF RESEARCH AND STATISTICS. *Social Security Program throughout the World—1977.* Research Report No. 50. Washington, D.C.: Government Printing Office, 1978.

VEILLARD-CYBULSKA, HENRYKA. "Aspects of Child Welfare in the People's Democracies. II: Poland." *International Child Welfare Review,* **20,** 1 (1966), 5–61.

——. "Aspects of Child Welfare in the People's Democracies. I: U.S.S.R." *International Child Welfare Review,* **19,** 3 (1965), 101–132.

——. "The Welfare and Protection of Children and Adolescents in Bulgaria." *International Child Welfare Review,* **23,** 4 (October 1969), 3–13.

WACHSTEIN, SONIA. "An Austrian Solution to the Problem of Child Placement." *Child Welfare,* **42,** 2 (February 1963).

WECHSBERG, JOSEPH. "A House Called Peace." *The New Yorker* (December 22, 1962).

WEN, WEI. "Child Care in New China." *Assignment Children,* **39** (July–September, 1977), 115–119.

WESTER, ASTRID. *The Swedish Child.* Stockholm: The Swedish Institute, 1970.

WILENSKY, HAROLD L. *The Welfare State and Equality.* Berkeley: University of California Press, 1975.

WIMPERES, VIRGINIA. *The Unmarried Mother and Her Child.* London: George Allen & Unwin, Ltd., 1960.

WOLINS, MARTIN. *The SOS Kinderdorf: Families in a Village.* 1969. Mimeo.

WOSCHIECHOWSKI, SOPHIE. "Poland's New Priority: Human Welfare," pp. 169–195, in *Meeting Human Needs,* Vol. 1. Ed. by Daniel Thurz and Joseph Vigilante. Beverly Hills, Calif.: Russell Sage Publications, 1975.

WYNN, MARGARET. *Fatherless Families.* London: Michael Joseph Ltd., 1964.

ZIMMERMAN, MARGOT. "Abortion Law and Practice—A Status Report." *Population Reports,* Series E, No. 3. Washington, D.C.: Department of Medical and Public Affairs, George Washington University, 1976.

ZUCKER, MILDRED. "Citizen's Advice Bureaus—The British Way." *Social Work,* **10,** 4 (October 1965), 85–91.

13 THE SOCIOLOGY OF THE CHILD WELFARE WORKER

INTRODUCTION

The sociology of occupations is a well-developed specialization, its justification deriving from the fact that each distinctive occupation is a subculture. It has its own language, its own special patterns of thought, its own special values, its own special ways of relating to the other occupational groups with which it cooperates, its own concerns and problems, its own knowledge and skills, and its own demography. Each occupation has its particular pressures and anxieties and its own particular areas of conflict between the mores of the occupation and the mores of the surrounding culture. Each occupation is a miniature social world, with its own distinctive sociopsychological milieu. One of the principal responsibilities of professional education is the socialization of recruits to the professional subculture, the "community of occupation" (Goode, 1957, p. 195). Greenwood (1957) notes:

> The transformation of a neophyte into a professional is essentially an acculturation process wherein he internalizes the social values, the behavior norms, and the symbols of the occupational group. In its frustrations and rewards, it is fundamentally no different from the acculturation of an immigrant to a relatively strange culture [p. 53].

As is true of a distinctive ethnic group, members of an occupational subculture have a sense of mutual identification, a recognition of their special differences from other people in the wider community. This is sometimes called the *professional self* or the *sense of the professional identity*—the explicit self-awareness on the part of a person that he/she is a social worker and that he/she behaves in accordance with the way people identified as members of this occupational group should behave. Differential association, the need to associate primarily with members of the occupation on the job and often the choice of such associates during leisure time, tends to reinforce the effects of professional education in shaping the occupational identity.

This solidarity is further enhanced by some homogeneity in the kind of people selecting an occupation. The nature of the occupational tasks tends to act as a screening device attracting and selecting people with particular kinds of personality attributes and repelling other kinds of people. However, having selected a profession and having been selected by a profession, the individual finds that those personality characteristics that are useful to the profession are emphasized and reinforced, and other personality attributes are attenuated by disuse or are actively discouraged. In this sense, then, the occupation ultimately tends to shape personality. "If personality is the subjective aspect of culture, then a man's work, to the extent that it provides him a subculture and an identity, becomes an aspect of his personality" (Hughes, 1958, p. 23). Lubove (1965), in reviewing the history of the profession of social work, says, "The profession was not only a career but a way of life which shaped personality by offering it a means of expression" (p. 118).

These statements suggest the basis for a sociological approach to child-welfare social work. The approach sees child-welfare social work as a circumscribed social institution within the larger community and child-welfare social workers as an identifiable, organized subgroup in society.

Child welfare has a specialized language in terms such as *placement, TPR, U-M, home study,* and so on. Child welfare workers have special interests and shared values, a good deal of social interchange, and in-group gossip. Differential association, in-group language, in-group gossip, and humor tend both to reflect and to reinforce the sense of identity as a child welfare worker. Solidarity is further intensified by special publications such as *Child Welfare* and periodic meetings such as the annual regional meetings sponsored by the Child Welfare League of America. As a consequence, practitioners develop a distinctive way of thinking about the problems and the people that are so much a part of their activities. This special point of view becomes part of the subcultural configuration that distinguishes the child welfare worker.

PROFILE OF THE CHILD WELFARE WORKER

Child-welfare social workers constitute a sizable percentage of all social workers. In 1978 it was estimated that overall 350,000 people were holding the job title of social worker. Of these it is estimated that some 25 per cent were involved in offering child welfare services.

Students in schools of social work have a continuing high level of interest in training in this field of practice. In 1978 full-time master's degree students placed in child welfare and family services combined made up one of the largest field-practice concentrations of students. Composing 17 per cent of all students in field placements, they were exceeded only by the students in psychiatric services, who made up 23 per cent (Allen, Whitcomb, 1979).

Social work is classified as a woman's profession. In 1978 some two thirds of all social workers were women, and one third were men. However, the distribution is more skewed in child welfare services, where it is estimated that 80 per cent of all of the workers are women. The sexual distribution of recruits in social work training suggests that the concentration of females is likely to continue. In 1972, 63.5 per cent of students in graduate schools of social work were women; in 1978, this percentage had increased to 72.2 per cent of all students.

The profession is disproportionately white. Despite recent efforts to recruit minorities into social work, the percentage of nonwhites is lower than their proportion in the population generally. Compared to the general population, Jews are overrepresented and Protestants and Catholics are underrepresented in the profession (Loavenbruck, 1973).

A comparison of the socioeconomic status of social workers with that of their parents' status indicates that in becoming social workers the group was upwardly mobile. This is much truer for male social workers, who tend to come from upper-lower-class or lower-middle-class backgrounds, than for female social workers, who are more likely to come from upper-middle-class or lower-upper-class families (National Opinion Research Center, 1966).

The bulk of child welfare workers are employed in public welfare agencies. A study of the educational background of workers providing social services to children in public welfare agencies indicates that most workers have limited education and experience in social work. The typical caseworker offering social services to children in public agencies "emerges as a person with a bachelor's degree in a field other than social work and a little more than three years of experience in social services to children and families" (Shyne, Schroeder, 1978, p. 26). Only 9 per cent of the workers in the study had a graduate degree in social work. Voluntary nonpublic child-welfare agencies employed fewer social workers, but the majority of the staff of such agencies had a graduate degree in social work.

The Employment Situation

Long-term projections by the U.S. Department of Labor (1977), published in their *Occupational Outlook Handbook,* indicated that "employment of social workers is expected to increase faster than the average for all occupations through the mid-1980's." The report goes on to say that if "the number of students graduating from social work programs continues to increase at the same rate as in the 1960's and early 1970's, persons having bachelor's degrees in social work will face increasing job competition. . . . Graduates of master's degree programs . . . qualified for a wider range of jobs . . . are expected to have good opportunities through the 1980's" (p. 565).

Despite these projections, a study in 1977 of the employment situation of some nine thousand members of the National Association of Social Workers confirmed what many members knew (*National Association of Social Workers News,* September 1977, p. 11). It indicated a tighter labor market for social workers. Although the unemployment rate of the social workers polled was comparatively low, a bare 2 per cent, this rate still contrasted with the oversupply of jobs available in earlier years. By 1980 holders of bachelor's degrees were finding it difficult to obtain jobs as social workers, and holders of master's degrees had fewer jobs from which to choose and some difficulty in finding them.

More restrictive government budgets, greater competition for tax dollars, a growing resistance to increasing taxation for publicly supported social-service programs, the trend toward civil service declassification, and the separation of income maintenance and social service programs in public welfare adversely affected the number of jobs available to new recruits to the field.

The difficulty resulted not only from a slowdown in the general rate of increase in the number of jobs, and from an actual decrease in jobs in some areas of social work, but also from the increased number of people seeking employment in social work. Since 1974, the bachelor of social work degree has been recognized as the first professional degree in social work, and an increasingly large number of schools are offering such an accredited program. In the late 1960s and early 1970s, there was a rapid expansion in the number of graduate schools of social work, and consequently an increase in the number of professionally trained graduates. In 1950 all of the schools of social work in the United States enrolled 4,336 full time students; by 1978 the number had increased to 18,500 full time enrollees. As job opportunities for teachers, clinical psychologists, and graduates in several liberal arts areas decreased in the 1970s, more people were attracted to social work because it provided continued, if diminished, vocational opportunities.

The job situation for social workers with training has been adversely affected by the move toward declassification in civil service systems. Declassification eliminates specific educational requirements as a prerequisite for job eligibility. Specifically, many civil service positions that previously required a master's degree in social work or a bachelor's degree with a social work major for application were, as a result of declassification, open to applicants without such qualifications. Declassification was justified on the basis of contributing to affirmative action because it made child welfare jobs available to a wider group of people. The supporting argument was that there was no convincing proof that the educational requirement actually was relevant to subsequent job performance. Reinforcing such arguments was the pressure to hold the line or even to reduce civil service salaries by lowering the educational qualifications for the available social work positions. In confirmation of this trend, a "1975 study of state civil service education requirements for social service positions conducted by the National Association of Social Workers concluded that many state social service agencies do not require specialized training or professional education for most direct service positions in social services" (*National Association of Social Work News,* November 1976).

At the same time, the increase in the number of states with laws regulating social work practice moved in the opposite direction. State regulations had the effect of giving formal and explicit recognition to specialized professional education for social work and of offering greater job protection to people with such credentials. By 1978 twenty-three states and Puerto Rico had some kind of law regulating who could use the title of *social worker.* Some of these statutes include an examination requirement for licensing. Twenty-five additional states had social-work regulatory legislation pending in 1978.

Although the decrease in the number and percentage of children in the population in the 1970s might suggest a decrease in the need for child welfare services in the future, such a conclusion would have validity only if there was a clear linear relationship between numbers and service needs. The demand is elastic, however, responsive to shifts in social policy and to an increase in the number of families facing severe problems as the result of changes in unemployment, inflation, divorce, and so on. An increase in demand for services may, in fact, accompany a decline in the number of children in the population.

Salary

The National Association of Social Workers recommended an annual minimum salary level for social work professionals for 1977 of $11,700 for a worker with a bachelor of social work degree, and $14,600 for a worker with a master's degree in social work. In 1977 federal government starting salaries for social workers with a master's degree but without experience ranged between $11,523 and $14,097.

The 1977 Child Welfare League of America Salary Study (Shyne, 1977), which collated data from 205 member agencies, indicated that the agencies employed 2,605 full-time direct-service child welfare workers, a slight decrease from the number employed in 1976. The percentage of these workers with graduate social work degrees had increased, however, from 61 to 65 per cent. The median salary in 1979 for social work practitioners with a graduate degree was $14,750; for practitioners with no graduate social-work training, the median salary was about $12,000.

Social workers, like nurses and teachers, are responsive to "a dedicatory ethic," which elevates service motives and denigrates material reward as the proper motivation for work. The work is seen not as a "job" but as a "calling." However, there is a growing tendency to see dedication as a form of subsidy to the welfare system, which social workers are no longer willing to grant.

Despite efforts at affirmative action, the research available tends to indicate that women are promoted less rapidly than men in family and children's agencies, and that women are paid less after comparable time on the job and while holding positions of comparable responsibility. Studying the employment history of 132 respondents (77 females and 55 males) in twenty family-service agencies in Michigan, Knapman (1977) found that "females reported a significantly greater average than males of months employed prior to promotion" (p. 462) from one level to another in the agency. Controlling for the factor of length of employment in the agency, the results indicated that "females earn significantly less than males" (see also Belon, Gould, 1977).

Controlling for the size of agency staff, the Child Welfare League reported that female executive directors were paid less than male executive directors. Of the 190 child welfare agencies reporting such data in 1976, 80 per cent had male executive directors (Haring, 1976, p. 12).

The Public Image

The potential for attracting recruits is partly a function of the public's perception of the occupation. In general, studies suggest that the profession is viewed in favorable terms. When asked to select adjectives to describe the social worker, people are apt to choose words such as *sympathetic, understanding, humane, tolerant, patient, generous, likable, warm,* and *friendly* (Bailey, 1959; Timms, 1961; Barlow, 1963). An interview study of attitudes toward welfare programs indicated that child welfare programs were more likely than other programs to elicit strong support (p. 29).

Although the image of social work is now generally positive, the same studies suggest other difficulties (Regional Research Institute, 1971, p. 21). People "are extremely vague about what social work is, what it does, who does it, and with what success. . . . Unlike such fields as medicine and law, and so on, which people can define clearly, social work is amorphous and extremely diverse; hence, very difficult to picture clearly" (Regional Research Institute, 1971, p. 18). Social work is most frequently perceived as being concerned only with the destitute, the needy, and the deprived. The layman sees no relationship between the activities of the profession and any problem he might have. He rejects, in general, any identification of himself as a possible social-work client (Bailey, 1959, p. 66).

An important factor regarding the sociology of an occupational group is its prestige level—the rank in the hierarchy of value that any occupation holds relative to any other occupation. No studies are available to indicate the prestige level of the child welfare worker vis-à-vis other occupational groups, but studies of the prestige level of social work in general might be taken to reflect that of child welfare. In general, such studies show that social work ranks high in prestige when compared with all occupational groupings, but it ranks low when compared with other professions. Its prestige ranking compares favorably with other traditional women's professions—teaching, nursing, librarianship—but, like these, it is considered a minor, if not a marginal, profession (Kadushin, 1958; Etzioni, 1969; Toren, 1972).

The occupational prestige score assigned social work in 1975 was on a par with the scores of accountants, librarians, clergymen, chiropractors, and secondary school teachers. The rating was higher than for nurses, kindergarten teachers, air traffic controllers, actors, painters and sculptors, and radio and television announcers, but lower than for dentists, physicians, engineers, psychologists, political scientists, and architects (Temme, 1975, pp. 270–334).

Social work is ranked high on education and high on contribution to society, but low on financial return. A person interested in coming into social work may be less concerned with the general prestige ranking of social work but specifically concerned with whether or not the particular aspect of the profession that is of concern to him has prestige. Social workers themselves feel that they rate high on their contribution to society and their ability to help people (Polansky, 1953). Many workers have a conviction that social work offers a greater opportunity to be of assistance to people than many other occupations, and that their work is interesting and significant, making a vital contribution to the community. The largest majority of social workers would encourage their children to become social workers, although this response was more positive if the child in question was female rather than male (Clearfield, 1977).

CHILD-WELFARE SOCIAL WORK— A SPECIAL FIELD OF PRACTICE

In the public's perception of social work, the child welfare functions are the most visible and the most frequently identified. Condie *et al.* (1978) interviewed a random sample of people in four different communities in an effort to find out how the public views social work. Given a list of different functions that social workers might perform, "child protector" was the only function identified by more than 50 per cent of the sample as being congruent with their perception of social work. Given a listing of twenty-four settings in which social work might be practiced, once again child welfare services were most clearly visible. The three agencies most frequently identified as employing social workers were welfare departments, agencies concerned with foster children, and adoption agencies (p. 51).

A home interview of 9,346 respondents in seven states asked about their perception of the most acceptable use of the public funds available for social welfare. Programs relating to children had the most unequivocal support: "Four out of five respondents would spend 'however much is necessary' to help welfare children become productive adults" (Carter, Fifield, Shields, 1973, p. 18). The respondents were asked to rank their willingness to support seventeen different social services. Four of the six top-ranked services were child welfare services: foster-home care, protective services, adoption services, and day care (p. 26).

Public attitudes toward a profession are shaped in part by the attitudes toward the client group with which the profession is associated. In the case of social work, the public perception of the primary client group is generally negative. The clientele consists of the physically, emotionally, characterologically, or economically deviant or variant: the handicapped, the legal offender, the dependent, the unemployed, the mentally ill, and so on. But although the orientation toward the general client group is less than enthusiastically accepting, the public makes distinctions within the group on the basis of certain criteria. "Blamability" and "curability" are among the criteria on which such distinctions are made: To what extent is the client responsible for his situation? And to what extent can one expect that the situation will change and that the client will become a productive citizen? On both these counts, children are regarded as "acceptable" clients. The social workers and the social work agencies serving children receive a greater degree of approval than agencies serving other client groups. In studying the reaction of the New York State legislature to bills concerned with the different client groups served by social agencies, Howe (1978) found that the concerns of child welfare agencies were given the highest priority. Bills relating to child abuse, neglect, foster care, and adoption were more likely to be approved than bills concerned with the handicapped, the indigent, the aged, and so on.

The positive perception may often be diminished somewhat by the inclusion of welfare in the designation *child welfare*. "Many people see the welfare and forget the child."

Reviewing the problems of children in foster care, a New York State legislative committee concluded that there was justification for having social work personnel specialized in child welfare. The committee recommended that "child welfare work should be recognized as a specialized professional discipline," and that civil service standards of selection and testing should take such specialized knowledge and skills into consideration (Pisani, 1976, p. 133).

However, despite the favorable general public attitude toward the group of activities designated as child welfare services and the recognized need for specialized knowledge and skills, the organization of public child-welfare-service delivery systems underwent an adverse change during the 1970s. Previous to the 1970s, child welfare services in public welfare agencies were assigned to specially designated child-welfare-service units. Such units had clear identity and visibility and very often included the most highly professionalized staff in the agency. They were perceived as elite units, and association with such a unit was a source of status and pride. The federal government's mandate for separation of public assistance payments and social services in Aid to Families of Dependent Children (AFDC) and the requirement that there be a single organizational entity for all social services, including child welfare services, resulted in the dismantling of such units. Child welfare workers were assigned to social service units offering service to a diversified group of clients, and the special identification with and expertise in child welfare was vitiated. As contrasted with the earlier situation, *child welfare* is less frequently clearly defined in public welfare agencies, and there is a diffusion of administrative responsibility for such services. There is more frequently, now, no agency administrator clearly responsible for and concerned with giving child welfare services a priority as a special agency function. Specialized in-service child-welfare training has frequently been replaced by generic social-work training. The overall conclusion of a detailed study of public child welfare in twenty-five states in 1975 was that such services were less adequately supported and had less visibility, prestige, and professional status than had been true a decade earlier (Childrens Bureau, 1976).

Who Chooses Social Work? When? Why?

An occupation perpetuates itself by attracting and selecting new recruits from the potential candidates for the professions. Whom does child-welfare social work tend to attract? When do they make the decision to select child welfare, and what are the reasons that prompt their decision?

More women than men enter social work because its functions reflect the role responsibilities of women in society. There are, however, additional reasons for the attractiveness of social work to women.

Because many women are either supplementary wage-earners or responsible only for their own support, the matter of relatively low salaries is not a great deterrent to their choice of social work as a profession. The fact that it is a "woman's field," conversely, might tend to attract some men. The National Manpower Council (1957) suggests, "The best way for a man to insure his advancement is to prepare for a field of work in which most employees are women" (p. 240). Men are promoted more rapidly and more frequently to administrative and supervisory positions, earn more for comparable jobs, and are more likely to publish in social work journals (Rosenblatt, 1970). Despite changes toward a reduction in sexism, the reality, as of 1980, is that there are persistent residuals that affect career decisions.

Social workers, including those in child welfare, make their occupational choices relatively late. This is partly a function of the low visibility of social work as a profession (Kadushin, 1958). Although most children encounter teachers and doctors and nurses, relatively few ever see a social worker. The same limited visibility is characteristic of social work in the mass communication media. There has been only one, relatively brief, television series in which a social worker was the central person. The profession lacks distinctive ceremonial garb, insignia, or gadgetry by which it might be clearly identified and remembered.

Another reason for the relatively late selection of social work as a career choice lies in the undifferentiated nature of preparation. Social work does not require a definite commitment either in high school or in college. Students majoring in a wide variety of fields can still obtain social work positions upon graduation from college and can apply for admission to graduate schools of social work. Early specialization and early commitment encourage early crystallization of choice.

A nationwide study of students in schools of social work notes that:

> As a group, social work students become aware of this field at a relatively late state in their education. Direct contact with social work and social workers (in pre-professional employment in social work) as well as college courses and instructors were the major sources of information for students about social work. . . . Social work was not seriously considered or decided on until last year in college or after graduation [Pins, 1963, pp. 31–34; see also Chatterjee, 1973].

For many students, social work is a second occupational choice. These students have initially been interested in other fields of human service: the ministry, teaching, psychology, and so on. Frequently people discover social work when they seek employment after graduation from college. As college students, they may have been interested in sociology or one of the other social sciences, but one needs to tie this to an occupational outlet. Social work is one of few possible occupational expressions of such interest.

In general, intrinsic satisfaction in the work (satisfaction in service, satisfaction in working with people, satisfaction in indulging a technical interest in human behavior) is more frequently stressed by those who choose social work than extrinsic job satisfactions (salary, professional status, job security, and so on). The task rather than the reward is a principal source of attraction (Pins, 1963, p. 138; Pins et al., 1972).

Students interested in social work are more likely than others to emphasize that the "ideal job must permit me to work with people rather than with things" and "give me an opportunity to be helpful to others" (Rosenberg, 1964). The social work group scores very low on the external-reward–oriented value complex, which stresses high earnings, status, and prestige. On a personality typology analysis, social work students show greater concern than others with being liked, wanted, needed, approved of, and appreciated.

In comparing the responses of a sample of clinical psychologists, psychiatrists, and social workers to the Strong Vocational Interest form, Klein (1962) noted that clinical psychologists and psychiatrists were alike but that the social workers differed from both. The social worker had lower scores on scales suggesting "scientific values and interests" and higher scores on scales concerned with "altruistic" values (p. 179).

McCornack and Kidneigh (1954), in a study of approximately twelve hundred social workers, delineated the interests of male and female social workers as distinguished from those of men and women in general. They found that "a strong liking for verbal activities and a dislike of the physical sciences seem to be the distinctive interests of social workers" (p. 163; see also Gockel, 1966, 1967; National Opinion Research Center, 1966; Walther, 1970).

Students see social work as involving the kind of work they would enjoy doing and as an occupation in which they can succeed. They perceive the values and the technical concerns of the profession as being congenial to their personal interests and predispositions. A limited number of students feel that social work can help them "to become a better person, parent, marriage partner" (Pins, 1963, p. 115). There is little empirical support, however, for the contention that social work attracts people who become interested in the profession because they themselves are emotionally disturbed.

In general, then, the typical social worker might be characterized as a white female of urban origin and middle-class background, with strong social service and social interaction interests, who makes the choice rather late in her academic career, often after having seriously considered other alternatives. As reflected in the National Association of Social Workers membership statistics, she is further a "direct service worker who provides casework, perhaps supplemented with group work and some community activities in a psychiatric or medical setting or on a family or children's agency" (Meyer, Siegel, 1977, p 1073).

The Career Line

After one has selected child-welfare social work, how does he obtain a position, and what is likely to be the subsequent course of his career? Currently there are two principal routes into the profession: through civil service examinations for public child-welfare positions following graduation from college; and through professional training in graduate school. Fully trained workers are more likely to work in voluntary child-welfare agencies; workers not fully trained are likely to work in public agencies. However, in agencies in which fully trained workers work side by side with those not fully trained, there is little difference in the tasks assigned to them and little difference in the work they do (Jones, 1966).

The career line of the fully trained worker offers more possibilities. The line of promotion in the profession leads to administration—from direct services in a casework position, to supervision or consultation, to executive duties. The movement away from direct service is characteristic of professions practiced in an organizational setting (teaching, engineering, librarianship, and so on). It is less likely to be true in the entrepreneurial professions: the doctor or lawyer advances by developing a larger, more select, more remunerative practice, so that, while advancing, he stays with direct service. The pressure toward vertical mobility is even greater in social work than in most professions practiced in organizational settings. This is true because only about one-third of all social workers have full professional training. Each fully trained professional, then, has to magnify his potential impact on the client group. One trained child-welfare caseworker can service just so many clients. The same trained worker, acting as supervisor to six or seven child welfare workers, can affect, albeit indirectly, a larger client group.

Vertical mobility is not as easily open to the worker without graduate training. For this worker, advancement is along horizontal lines. While continuing in the same kind of job, the worker with experience and seniority is rewarded with a smaller and more desirable case load, a better office, more autonomy and freedom, more respect and prestige from peers, better secretarial service, and, of course, higher pay. But the limited job openings and promotional possibilities for the workers who are not fully trained prompt many of them eventually to complete a graduate degree.

Studies done in an earlier period tended to show high turnover rates for social work personnel (Tolen, 1960; Podell, 1967; Kermish, Kushin, 1969; U.S. Department of Health, Education and Welfare, 1971). Information on the rate of turnover for the more recent period characterized by a tighter job market is not available.

In general, job turnover studies indicate that the tendency of both men and women with professional training is to remain in social work. If they leave one social work position, it is to accept another social work job.

Women more frequently resign for family-related reasons; men for job-related reasons, such as higher salaries and better opportunities for advancement.

In child welfare, as in other fields, the woman's career pattern is likely to be more discontinuous than a man's. After graduation, the woman moves into the job market and stays until she marries or has her first child, when she resigns from the job. When her last child is no longer dependent, she may return to her career.

The career pattern of the single, professional female child-welfare worker is analogous to that of men, but she is less likely to move frequently from one job to another.

Interviews with people who left social work positions indicate that although situational demands (pregnancy, residential relocation, child-care problems) account for some of the departures, dissatisfaction with the job situation was a more frequent reason. Such dissatisfaction included "overwhelming job demands; poor atmosphere and morale within the agency; inability to be of real help to the client; poor supervision; little respect, encouragement, and support from agency administration; and little opportunity to use one's own initiative and be creative" (Kermish, Kushin, 1969, p. 137). Salary and fringe benefits are rarely the most important reasons for leaving, although these are significant contributing factors in the decision.

Weinberger (1970) found that salary (once this reaches an acceptable level) was not related to job satisfaction, but that autonomy in the work situation, opportunity for direct work with clients, and a more professional agency climate providing more opportunity for interaction with colleagues were. Principal satisfactions on the job come from contact with clients and contact with colleagues. Conversely, the greatest source of dissatisfaction were those unresponsive clients who were withdrawn, hostile, and unable or unwilling to acknowledge their problems and who manifested no desire for a relationship with the worker (Shapiro, 1977, p. 140). Client unresponsiveness was a more significant factor in a worker's defection from a child welfare position than were unsatisfactory job conditions or low salary.

Allocation of time on the job indicates that only about half the time available is devoted to direct contact with clients, despite the fact that this is the principal source of job satisfaction. Paperwork, conference, travel time, and so on take up the remainder of time available (Shapiro, 1977, p. 21), and this is a source of some job dissatisfaction.

Relatively little turnover results from discharge or induced resignations.

OCCUPATIONAL PROBLEMS

Every profession has occupational problems, which grow out of the work it does, the way it does it, and the context in which it does it. This is equally true for child welfare. There tends to be some disparity between the ideology of the child welfare worker and that of the society in which he operates. Rapoport (1960) calls attention to this problem:

> Social work seeks to embrace and implement some principles and values which may be essentially unpopular and uncongenial to the dominant social order. Hence, in some respects, social work seems to be outside the main stream of society. . . . This particular role of the profession gives it the attributes of a minority group in society [p. 63].

It contributes to a feeling of marginality, a feeling of being different, on the part of the worker. The child welfare worker has to resolve the impact of society's ambivalence toward the job it is asking him to do. Two contradictory orientations contend for acceptance in the mind of the public (Szurek, 1942). One orientation is an expression, however modified, of social Darwinism and the Puritan ethos, which suggest that man is the architect of his own destiny, that he is in full rational control of his fate and situation, and that failure is indicative of weakness and inadequacy, of some "unfitness":

> The needy, the poor, the sick, the unemployed, the unemployable, the delinquent, the unadjusted—these are the social analogies of the biologically unfit: the extension of assistance to such groups involves a negation of the natural process and results in the enfeeblement of society. Social Darwinism is exemplified by the rugged individualist with his contempt for failure [Greenwood, 1953, p. 8].

The other orientation is that of the Judeo-Christian ethic of social responsibility for those dependent and in need: the young, the physically handicapped, the mentally handicapped, the mother with young children, the aged. The humanitarian ethos suggests that there are no "strong men," only men who have been spared; that those who have not needed help are taking pride in a self-sufficiency that derives, to a very considerable extent, from a more fortuitous situation. Those who grow up in an unbroken family, blessed with a healthy, normal body and a healthy, normal mind, born with the right color, in the right country at the right time, are counted among the "fit." A change of circumstance —a crippling accident, the sudden death of a parent, the birth of a mentally defective child—and the thin line between self-sufficiency and dependency is wiped out. Because everyone is potentially dependent, the humanitarian ethos is pragmatic. It ensures the obligation of support for ourselves when we need the support of the community. The profession of social work identifies clearly and unequivocally with the humanitarian orientation.

Neither modified social Darwinism nor humanitarianism has won a clear victory in our society. We cannot permit the dependent child of the unmarried mother to die—this is a victory for the humanitarian orientation. However, we grant our support grudgingly, hesitantly, with considerable doubts about the wisdom and morality of what we are doing—this is the victory of the Puritan ethic and social Darwinism. Society asks the child welfare workers to perform certain tasks, and then denies them adequate resources to achieve that goal.

It may be that society is not really concerned about the effectiveness of child welfare services. The mere existence of such services, whatever their effectiveness, acts to assure society that something is being done about social problems that excite the conscience of the group (Nokes, 1967; Pierce, 1970). For such "institutions to be viable it is not, in fact, necessary for them to be efficient" (Nokes, 1960, p. 144).

Society supports social work agencies because they are part of the necessary apparatus for social control. They act to mitigate the effects of situations that might lead to social conflict and to alleviate the most egregious effects of social dysfunction. The limited support given to child welfare agencies allows them to perform this secondary function. The support necessary to carry out their primary functions—to provide adequate measures for prevention and/or rehabilitation—society is not yet willing to grant.

The child welfare worker, therefore, has to implement a policy that reflects society's ambivalence, and has to resolve, within himself and in contact with the client, the behavioral implications of that ambivalence. He has to implement a policy that conflicts, to some degree, with the values of the profession. This conflict creates a stress for the worker in contacts with his peers. Acculturation to the professional ethos means that the social worker is likely to be more understanding of deviancy than is true of the laymen with whom he associates (Polansky, 1953). He finds himself "explaining" the delinquent child, the broken family, the neglectful parent, the unmarried mother to friends and relatives who feel punitive toward such groups.

Yet the worker is a member of that same society from which he differentiates himself in implementing his role as a social worker. As a member of the general society, he holds some of the same attitudes, and he might still not have resolved many of the moral dilemmas encountered in his work—dilemmas posed by the unmarried mother, the self-centered parents who neglect their children, the deserted mother living with a succession of "boyfriends," the AFDC mother who "cheats" on the agency, the unmarried teenager's request for abortion or contraception, the family's request for the institutionalization of a mentally deficient child. The worker thus frequently faces the stress of making decisions and taking action in the face of moral, ethical, and value questions about which he is himself still undecided.

The problems with which child welfare workers are concerned, and the work required of them, also present occupational problems (Babcock, 1951; Shirley, 1954; Littner, 1957). These are problems with which every human being has to contend in growing up: "Living on a job that is so closely allied to life itself makes separation of work from other areas of life exceptionally difficult. Since, in social work, the work task and living are often simultaneously experienced, anxiety is greater than in many other fields of endeavor" (Babcock, p. 417). In this work, more than in many other kinds of work, there is an interpenetration of different areas of one's life.

The worker who has been disappointed in his own parents is predisposed to overidentify with the deprived child. In studying adoptive parents or foster parents for the child, he is likely to be highly critical and demanding. Rejecting the application of couples who apply to become adoptive or foster parents may be a highly satisfying opportunity for the worker to "punish" his own parents symbolically. Conversely, the need to reject clearly unacceptable applicants may conflict with the worker's fear of symbolically rejecting his own parents. Working with the unmarried mother reactivates the woman social worker's own anxiety about the possible failure to control her impulses and desires. Encountering separation experiences, the worker is predisposed to react in terms of his own remembered separation experiences—the hospitalization or death of a parent, the threat of divorce, and so on. The worker might picture himself as a "rescuer" of children from rejecting parents, or as a "superior" parent protecting the victimized child, or as an "avenging angel" acting in the child's behalf.

That such feelings do, in fact, affect the worker's attitudes and activity with a child he is called upon to help is suggested by a study done by Rosen (1963). Although the subjects for the study were child-care workers in a residential treatment program, the conclusions have relevance for social workers. Depth interviews eight to ten hours long were conducted with child-care workers and were concerned with the workers' developmental history and their reactions to the children at the center. It was found that "strong positive feelings toward a child were associated with the worker's perception of that child as being similar to his childhood self. Strong negative feelings toward a child were associated with a worker's perceiving the child as dissimilar to his childhood self," or as having traits that the worker rejected in himself (p. 260).

The fact that the worker is constantly called upon to help in situations that reflect his own experiences requires him to develop a high degree of self-awareness. This is fostered and encouraged by the profession. The child welfare supervisor's responsibility involves helping the worker to examine himself to see how and under what circumstances his own needs and feelings intrude on his handling of a case situation. Some workers delight in such introspective self-examination and the self-awareness to which it leads. Others are made uncomfortable by it and resent it.

Some occupational stress is occasioned by the responsibilities of the job. The decisions the worker is called upon to make generally have great implications for the future of children. This is an awesome responsibility, and conscious awareness of the possible consequences of one's activities is apt to create emotional tensions. Furthermore the child welfare worker deals with people who are living under considerable stress and strain. He encounters them at a time of crisis, when their emotional reactions are overt and strong. The need to deal with a great deal of raw emotion—anxiety, anger, depression, grief—and the constant exposure to highly charged emotional situations, while under the necessity of controlling one's own emotional responses, is highly enervating. As Feldman (1953) notes:

The worker, face to face with the client in the interview, is exposed continually to an onslaught of unrepressed primitive feelings. The avalanche of feeling with which the . . . social worker is confronted is an unusual stress situation peculiar to the task of extending psychological help. It is, in a sense, an occupational hazard [p. 153].

There is an additional stress involved in working with children. The barriers between impulse and behavior, between emotion and acting out, are not as solid for the child as they are for the adult. Hence the worker who deals with children has to face the unnerving prospect of dealing with a greater measure of impulsive behavior, a greater measure of direct, open expression of feeling, (Chethik, 1967). The worker encounters "clients" who have not asked for and do not want agency service and who are hostile and resistive to his efforts to help. Despite such hostility and the worker's own very human reaction of antipathy to some clients, professional practice principles require that he act acceptingly (Mayer, Rosenblatt, 1973).

The self-image that is characteristic of many people who select social work —the image of an accepting, tolerant, understanding, helpful person—increases the probability of job stress. Encountering difficult problems, many workers find that they are, after all, not angelic, but only human. When angry, unkindly or critical feelings about clients begin to surface, a considerable amount of psychic energy is expended in defending against such feelings in an attempt to preserve the more acceptable self-image. This reaction is often intensified when the client is of a different race or sex and accuses the worker of sexism or racism.

A strong need to be liked and a strong need to be helpful are often frustrated by the realities of the job. Workers find that they have to do much that risks client hostility rather than love, and that in many situations they are truly ineffective through no fault of their own.

Uncompleted tasks are frustrating and stressful, and often the worker finds that only partial completion of a task is possible. At some point, cases need to be referred, clients drop out, a case ends in midstream. The satisfaction that comes with the unambiguous solution of a problem and a subsequent follow-through is often denied the worker, who is left with "unfinished business."

Stress results from the demands of the position and the adequacy of skills that workers bring to the job. Almost every article on foster care repeatedly and ritualistically recommends that counseling be offered to the family of a placed child. However, interviews with workers in seven selected county-welfare agencies in New York State offering foster care found that one half "considered themselves unequipped for counseling" (New York State Commission on Child Welfare, 1976, p. 101).

Along with other social workers, child welfare workers face stress related to the current controversy regarding the possible conflict between client rights and client needs. Currently greater emphasis than ever before is being given to clients' rights in stricter adherence to due process of the law. In some instances, child welfare workers face the stress of seeing needs disregarded or unmet in adherence to rights. A child who might need a substitute home or residential treatment may fail to get it because the parent or child refuses to accept the recommendation and has a legal right to nontreatment. "Doing good" is suspect, and regarded as a disguised exercise of power, and the client is perceived as needing protection from the control, however well-meaning, of the worker. The child welfare worker shares, with so many others, the decline in the legitimacy of authority and expertise (Gaylin, Glasser, Marcus, Rothman, 1978).

The occupational danger of emotional exhaustion results also from the constant need to give of oneself emotionally on the job. The flow of emotional supplies goes one way, from the worker to the client, and it may lead to the emotional depletion of the worker.

The most important instrument in the child welfare worker's work is the child welfare worker himself. A worker may view failure in a case not only as a reflection on professional skill but also as a reflection on his competence as a person. More so than in most other jobs, the child welfare worker *is* his work. Failure, then, is apt to be more keenly felt and it is likely to be personalized.

Some of the occupational stress to which the child welfare worker is subject stems from ambiguity about what he should be doing and how he should be doing it. Techniques and approaches for helping the client are not so clearly established as to provide clear-cut guidelines for the worker's behavior. For many situations, there is no validated professional consensus as to the most effective approach. For instance, should the AFDC mother be encouraged to work or to stay home with her children? Should a child be removed from his home, or should an attempt be made to maintain him in a home with neglectful parents? In addition to incomplete or imperfect mastery of available knowledge, the worker has to accept the limitations of professional knowledge itself.

Child-welfare social work shares this problem with other human relations professions. Hughes (1958) states, "In the factory there is at least fair consensus about what the object produced shall be. There is often no such consensus in institutions where things are done for, or to, people" (p. 76). The worker also has to live with the absence of clear and objective standards of performance. As Polansky (1959) says, "This is no field which can count units of production, volume of sales, or even Trendex ratings" (p. 314). The worker, therefore, has to have a high tolerance for ambiguity and an ability to live with the responsibility for acting decisively while uncertain as to aims and outcome.

Many situations encountered by child welfare workers have all the essential elements of the classic Greek tragedies. They involve conflicting but legitimate interests and needs. The justifiable needs of the parents may conflict with the justifiable needs of children; there may be a conflict between the rights and privileges of a foster parent and the rights and privileges of a natural parent. The child welfare worker has to act so as to recognize and understand the conflicting needs of all parties in the situation. Even if the child's needs have priority, it is not always clear how those needs can best be met. Would it be best to keep the child in the home while working with the parents to effect change? When are parents ready to receive a child back from substitute care?

> About a month after Mrs. Y. returned from the state mental hospital she expressed a desire to have her children back. Hospital prognosis was ambiguous. A telephone call to the attending physician was not helpful. Mrs. Y. refused to see a psychiatrist in an outpatient clinic. She clamored for her children. She seemed to be in fairly good shape as far as the worker could tell [Wasserman, 1970, p. 97].

Such stress increases with progressively more intensified, conflicting, and incompatible demands, with the increasingly explicit claims of "rights" being made by the participants in many child welfare situations: rights of children, rights of biological parents, rights of foster parents, rights of adoptees and adopters, rights of the community, and so on. Each of these pulls the worker in a different direction. Taking necessary action without seriously violating the "rights" of any one of the parties to the transaction becomes more and more difficult, if not impossible. The worker has to cope with accusations of injustice from some group in most of the significant decisions that he must make.

And there is the problem of decisions regarding the competing needs of one child client and another child client. Devoting a considerable amount of time to one child's adjustment to his placement may mean that another is left in limbo for a longer period of time without any foster home available. As one worker put it:

> The conflict that I felt was not only between the regulations and the clients but between client and client. If you want to help clients get schooling or job training or discuss personal problems with people who may be very eager to talk to you about them, you do so with the knowledge that you are not using this time to help get basic material things to people who just as desperately need them [Miller, Podell, 1971, p. 24].

Stress resulting from pressures from advocates of various interest groups in behalf of clients' rights is reinforced by the tendency of clients to be critical of the services offered them. There has been, according to Margaret Mead, "a revolt of all the people who are being done good to."

Some difficulties arise from the nature of the problem situations that are the principal concern of child welfare and the specialized expertise that the profession has developed, or has failed to develop, in helping with such problems.

A profession claims a monopoly in providing a particular service on the basis of superior knowledge and skills. They are granted the monopoly when the profession is successful in "persuading society that nobody else can do the job and it is dangerous to let anybody else try" (Goode, 1969, p. 279). The community justifies granting that monopoly on the grounds that only a special group, with special knowledge and special training, has the skills to perform the service effectively and efficiently and without damage to the client: "It is felt that not just anybody can do the job, so the job territory is marked 'off limits' to the amateur, often by law" (Goode, 1969, p. 284). Thus only the lawyer who has been admitted to the bar can practice law; only the licensed physician can practice medicine. Almost anyone, however, is free to use the title of social worker, and everyone claims some expertise in parent–child relationship problems.

Furthermore, there is no clear "manifest disaster criterion" applicable in child welfare, as there is in some other professions. Doctors warn that the patient will die; the engineer can predict that the bridge will collapse; the dentist can assert that the tooth will be lost. Rarely can social workers assert that such immediate disasters will follow from failure to utilize the skills of the profession. Nonqualified performance, then, is accepted by the public with little anxiety about outcome, making it difficult for the profession to establish an exclusive prerogative concerning child-welfare social-work tasks. The lay public cannot recognize the need for special competence in an area where everyone is "expert." As Charles Dollard put it, "Social work has had to fight a constant rear guard action against the pervasive notion that any man with love in his heart can do the job" (quoted in Etzioni, 1969, p. 147). The profession holds that what is needed is "not uninhibited love of humanity, spontaneous sentiment, or undisciplined emotion and compassion, but rather a scientific, trained intelligence and a skillful application of technique" (Lubove, 1965, p. 122). However, society is reluctant to grant child-welfare social workers the legitimacy of such special competence because the workers have, as yet, been unable to demonstrate that they "command esoteric knowledge and skills which enable them to accomplish their task much more efficiently and with better results than any other enthusiastic amateur" (Etzioni, 1969, p. 147).

There is no area of child welfare activity in which the worker has clear monopoly. He shares control of homemaker service with public health nurses, of day care with educators, of protective service with the police, and so on. And in many states adoption is, with public sanction, independently arranged by lawyers and doctors. Such a situation is, in effect, a derogation of the special skill and knowledge possessed by the child welfare worker and, consequently, the occasion for some occupational stress.

The agency context in which child welfare tasks are performed imposes an occupational stress. The worker faces some problems that derive from the conflict between the ideology of the profession and the needs of agency structure, between the professional culture and bureaucratic needs (Vinter, 1959; Billingsley, 1964). An agency is a bureaucracy, with a formal hierarchic organization. Different workers are assigned to the performance of different tasks, and there is a formal chain of command, control, and supervision. In order for any sizable organization to operate efficiently, rules, regulations, and procedures must be formulated and followed. Bureaucratic red tape is inevitable, particularly in social agencies supported by public funds and accountable to the public. The worker desires to devote his energies to service and finds himself enmeshed in red tape; he accepts the profession's broad commitment to help the client and finds that his ability to help is limited by the more restrictive procedures of the agency.

The professional commitment is to individualize the client; bureaucratic efficiency requires that the client be categorized and that his eligibility be judged according to uniorm regulations. Regulations and procedures restrict the professional exercise of autonomous judgment and decision.

The professional orientation emphasizes ends rather than means: offering the best possible service to the client, helping the client to solve his problems, and so on. The bureaucratic orientation emphasizes means rather than ends: offering the service in compliance with rules and regulations, following agency procedures, and so on. Billingsley (1964), who has studied this conflict in child welfare agencies, notes:

> In spite of the social worker's intellectual and emotional commitment to meeting the needs of his client, it is apparent that these needs must be met within the framework of structured approaches imposed by the agency and the profession even over the worker's own estimation of the needs of the client. This is consistent with findings in studies of other professions [p. 403].

The conflict between the two orientations leads to a strain between the agency demand that a given number of units of work be performed and the desire of the professional to do the best possible job. Billingsley identifies this as the conflict between quantitative output and qualitative performance.

Control over the worker's decision in the agency is frequently determined by nonprofessionals: members of the agency board and legislators. The agency regulations they formulate limit the autonomy of the professional worker and are designed to protect the taxpayer, the community, or the agency budget rather than the client.

In the agency, as in any bureaucratic organization, there is an informal structure that exists side by side with the formal structure. The formal organization is "owned" by the professional trained workers who occupy, or who will occupy, the positions of administrative and executive power in the formal structure. Workers without professional training, who remain in direct service, form a well-organized clique. The bureaucracy represents the more orthodox professionalized ideals and seeks to run the agency in accordance with these ideals. The informal clique tends to oppose the aims of the supervisory staff in significant ways and to modify such approaches.

The vertical hierarchy (supervisor, administrator) educates the worker in accepted agency practice while the horizontal hierarchy of peers carries on a program of informal "in-service training" as to what is acceptable practice. A great deal of solidarity develops among clique members—a solidarity permitting the enforcement of sanctions against members who violate acceptable patterns of clique behavior. This can be almost as powerful as the rewards (promotions, raises, and the like) used by the vertical hierarchy (Jacobs, 1969; Zimmerman, 1969). For the many child welfare workers who are not fully trained, there may be occupational stress occasioned by the conflict between the demands made on them by the formal structure of the agency, as represented by the supervisor, and those imposed by the clique (Bogdanoff, Glass, 1964).

In addition, every worker in every profession faces the problem of adjusting to what has been termed *reality shock,* the discrepancy between the norms inculcated by professional training and the actual requirements of practice (Styza, 1972).

Wasserman (1970) followed the careers of twelve graduates of a school of social work who obtained positions in 1966 as child welfare workers in a public agency. The actual work situation encountered was quite different from what they had expected. Instead of handling limited case loads that would permit a leisurely review of a situation and a reasoned professional decision, the workers were constantly faced with emergency situations that required immediate action. Sheer physical and emotional fatigue resulted from "the cumulative impact, perhaps the cumulative terror, of a large number of cases—by the human suffering, deprivation, disorder, ignorance, hostility, and cruelty the worker must face as part of his everyday work situation" (p. 96).

Child welfare workers, particularly those in public agencies, encounter the most extreme and most unacceptable forms of psychopathology in parents: drug addiction, sexual deviations, promiscuity, prostitution, chronic alcoholism, criminal activity, incest, and severe physical abuse of children (Shapiro, 1977, p. 126). Child and adolescent clients exhibit delinquent and/or emotionally disturbed behavior, precocious sexuality, destructiveness, obscene language, and the ability to manipulate others. Unless the worker has a great deal of experience with and tolerance of deviance, "reality shock" is inevitable.

Blau (1960) describes some of the aspects of reality shock encountered by workers in a public assistance agency in Chicago. The new worker, he says:

> encounters clients who are very different from what he had expected and with whom he must establish a working relationship.
>
> They tended to look forward to establishing a warm, although not intimate, relationship with deserving and grateful clients, and considered the caseworker as the agent of society who extended a helping and trusting hand to its unfortunate members. Newcomers generally deplored the "means test" and cared little about protecting public funds by investigating whether clients meet eligibility requirements, feeling that a trusting attitude should accompany financial aid in the best interest of rehabilitation. The attitudes of most new caseworkers toward clients were strongly positive, if somewhat sentimental and idealistic. Contacts with clients put these views to a severe test, which often resulted in disillusion.
>
> Clients in dire need, since the assistance allowance, originally set low, never caught up with the inflationary trend were under strong pressure to conceal what slim resources they might have had and try to get a little more money from the agency, even if this required false statements. People under such deprived conditions tend to look upon government organizations as alien forces that must be tricked into yielding enough money for survival, and consequently some clients, although by no means all, tried to cheat. In fact, the situation in which recipients found themselves made honesty a luxury. The new caseworker was typically full of sympathy for clients' problems, but as he encountered clients who blamed him personally for not helping them enough, even though agency procedure limited him, and clients met his trusting attitude by cheating and lying, the newcomer tended to experience a "reality shock" just as new teachers do whose first assignment is an overcrowded class in a slum [p. 34].*

As a consequence of these different kinds of stresses encountered by the child welfare workers, researchers have explicitly identified a configuration of responses that has been labeled *burnout*. Burnout implies emotional depletion or exhaustion as a result of constant, excessive demands. It is characterized by a sense of hopelessness, despair, and pessimism; a cynical, alienated attitude toward the job; and emotional detachment and distancing from the client (Maslach, 1976; Berkeley Planning Associates, 1977; Maslich, Pines, 1977; Mattingly, 1977; Armstrong 1978; Pines, Kafrey, 1978).

Distancing from clients is manifested by talking about clients as cases rather than as individuals, by avoiding contacts with clients, by more frequent absences and tardiness, by reluctance in scheduling appointments unless imperative, and by spending as much time as possible in office bull sessions. The distancing that effectively enables the worker to be objective while empathic and to identify with the client without being overwhelmed becomes, in burnout, an excessive detachment, which leads to a loss of care and concern for the client.

As a consequence of burnout, service to the client suffers because the worker has less capacity for the patient individualization of clients. He becomes

* From Peter M. Blau, "Orientation Toward Clients in a Public Welfare Agency," *Administrative Science Quarterly* (December 1960). By permission of the author and *Administrative Science Quarterly*.

rigid and stereotypical in response. He works inefficiently and with diminished productivity.

Burnout has a contaminating, depressing effect on the atmosphere of the agency, and one worker's burnout behavior intensifies tendencies toward burnout in others. Some workers quit the job in response to burnout, and the agency is faced with the expenses of recruiting and training new workers.

Researchers studying the problem have suggested a variety of procedures for preventing burnout, or at least for extending the period before it is experienced. A reasonable case load with the careful assignment of only a limited number of difficult cases helps to mitigate against the emotional overloading of the worker. Frequent, sanctioned time-outs for the worker at those points where exhaustion is being most keenly felt are suggested. A day off in the middle of the week or an afternoon off after a difficult morning might be permitted, the time to be made up when the worker feels more in control. A temporary change of assignment from the field to the office, with diminished responsibility for contacts with clients, helps the worker to catch his psychic breath and to "recharge emotional batteries." Reduction in job pressures and sanctioned escape from job pressures help reduce the dangers of burnout.

In-service training meetings and attendance at conferences and workshops not only counter burnout by making workers feel more adequate in coping with job tasks but also permit time away from direct client contact.

Support from the worker's supervisor is particularly helpful. The supervisor, representing the administration, should indicate accepting understanding of the worker's negative feelings toward the job and toward his clients and should encourage the worker to express them openly. Frequent feedback by the supervisor, where objectively warranted by the worker's performance, is helpful.

Peer support in terms of mutual compliments and acknowledgment of each other's good work is helpful. " 'It must have been a tough deal with that new kid last night,' 'you did beautifully with X yesterday,' can go a long way toward diminishing personal disenchantment" (Freudenberger, 1977, p. 95). The peer group as a mutual support system for bitching and griping about clients and the job provides a catharsis for negative feelings.

Service offered through a team rather than by an individual worker tends to reduce the risk of burnout. The responsibility for difficult decisions is shared, and anxiety about failure, and guilt when it occurs, is diffused over a number of workers. The solidarity developed in workers as a team provides the worker with a readily available support system of people who are knowledgeable about and empathic with the problems the worker faces.

An adequate support system on the job deriving from comfortable sharing relationships with peers and supervisors is more potent in preventing burnout than pay or work variety or work autonomy (Pines, Kafray, 1978).

Positive feedback from clients either implicitly in client improvement or explicitly in expressions from the client to the worker that his efforts have been helpful reduce the dangers of burnout.

If stresses diminish intrinsic job satisfaction, then perhaps the agency administration can counterbalance this loss by increasing extrinsic satisfaction. A substantial raise in pay for the workers whose jobs are most stressful and least satisfying may help to reduce burnout.

Perhaps the most effective antidote for burnout is a personally satisfying life off the job, during which time psychic sources of energy can be renewed and where restful recuperation from job stresses is possible. In addition, a clear recognition and acceptance of the fact that failures on the job are inevitable and that there are limits to how much one can give of oneself can further contribute to reducing burnout.

In summary, there are a sizable number of stresses associated with the work of child welfare services, stresses that sometimes result in worker burnout. A candid presentation of this problem is unavoidable if we are to modify counterproductive romantic illusions so that people can be adequately prepared for the realities of practice.

But if the difficulties are great, so are the victories and rewards. Throughout the country, children are more adequately cared for because child welfare workers have helped resolve the conflict between parents and children," problems that might have culminated in the dissolution of the family. Millions of children are able to live with some continuing assurance of having their basic needs for food, shelter, and medical care met because child welfare services are providing income maintenance. Thousands of children are able to continue living in familiar surroundings with people they know and love because child welfare workers have helped obtain needed day-care or homemaker services. Hundreds of thousands of children are protected from possibly recurring abuse and neglect because child welfare workers are available to intervene in their behalf. And additionally, hundreds of thousands of children are provided with a loving, caring substitute living arrangement in a foster family or an institution during the time when their own family cannot provide such care. Each year tens of thousands of children who are denied a family are provided with permanent care in adoptive homes that were recruited and made available through the efforts of child welfare workers. This is an overall impressive record of achievement, to which each worker contributes in her or his small measure. The statistics are the cumulative product of individual workers struggling with helping a limited number of families.

And despite the difficulties, studies show that workers who stay with the job and accept its realities do find considerable satisfaction in the help they offer children and families (Blau, 1960). The content of reality shock, the disenchantment, and the subsequent recovery of "faith" are graphically described by a New York City Youth Board worker assigned to a gang of delinquent girls:

> It's not easy to love a delinquent girl. She's vulgar, she's coarse, she's loud. She denies her girlhood and flaunts her sex. She despises the world, her life, herself.
>
> Offer her love, and she's suspicious. Treat her with respect, she's on guard. Be her friend, and she will use you. Come to her aid, she'll be astonished, but refuse her just once and she'll turn on you.
>
> She will test you, deceive you, disappoint you, exhaust your patience, and shake your resolve. Her demands are endless, her gratitude nonexistent. You try to remember what you really believe, that the noise and bravado and selfishness hide a hungry child. Hungry for love, for attention, for respect, and decency—and, all too often, hungry for food. You will teach and preach, instruct and persuade.
>
> A youth worker's voice can get very tired.
>
> Then one day she'll decide you're for real. You don't have an angle and you're not a kook. She doesn't understand it, but she accepts it. You'll begin to see the signs. She manages to sit next to you in the candy store. She asks you to let her

fix your hair different. You hear familiar words—yours—coming out of her mouth, and you realize she's caught the meaning of what you've been saying.

You'll begin to see little signs of respect—for you and for herself.

It doesn't always happen that way, of course. Not eight times out of ten, or even five times out of ten. But it happens. And when it does, you'll know that even if it happens only one time out of a hundred, it's enough [Hanson, 1958, pp. 20–21].

And, as a psychiatrist once said in reflecting on the realities of his profession, "every once in a while we are, beyond a doubt little saviors: and help weather a crisis, dispel a dread, release a growth, . . . a lasting change for the better" (Lederer, 1967, p. 36).

SUMMARY

Child welfare, as a social institution established by society to perform specific functions in meeting human needs, has a defined structure, designated statuses and roles, an explicit value system, goals, and operational principles. It can, then, like any social system, be described in sociological terms.

The typical child-welfare worker is a white woman of middle-class background working as a caseworker in a public child-welfare agency located in an urban, industrialized area. She made a decision to go into social work during her last years in college, or shortly after graduation, after majoring in social science and attaining average grades. She is not likely to have a master's degree in social work. In one out of four cases, she is likely to leave the agency because of marriage or childbirth or to move with her husband to a new job. In 1979 she was earning about $15,000 a year. She was attracted to social work because she likes to work with people, because it offers an opportunity for service to others, and because she felt she had the attributes and interests that would make for success in the profession. She tends to be less interested in the extrinsic rewards such a position could offer. If she remains with the agency, promotional opportunities are likely to be limited because of her lack of full professional training.

A smaller group of child welfare workers do have a master's degree in social work, and their career line involves promotion upward in the agency hierarchy and away from direct service to the client. Salaries for fully trained workers were some $3000 a year higher than those for holders of bachelor degrees, and salaries for men are generally higher than those for women. Men also advance more rapidly than women to positions of executive responsibility.

The prestige level of social work is high among all occupations but relatively low within the family of the professions. The public image of social work is a positive one, even if there is considerable vagueness as to what social work is and what the social worker does.

The profession has established an organizational apparatus for the promotion of professional interests, the maintenance of standards, the protection of the client, and the induction and training of recruits. The relevant organizations for the child welfare worker are the National Association of Social Workers, the Child Welfare League of America, and the Council on Social Work Education.

Some of the more significant occupational problems faced by the child welfare worker include the following:

1. Conflict between the value orientations of the occupational subculture and the wider community and the failure of the community in providing unequivocal and adequate supports to the child welfare worker.
2. The failure of the child welfare field to obtain control over the qualifications for the title *child welfare worker* and monopolization of child welfare services.
3. The interpenetration of life and work.
4. The responsibility for formative life experiences without a clear consensus as to techniques and aims and without sufficiently definitive knowledge in many areas.
5. The constant exposure to emotionally evocative experiences.
6. The conflict between bureaucratic structure and professional ideology and between the professionalized formal structure and the informal, nonprofessional clique structure.
7. Conflict between the legitimate and incompatible needs of the various participants in child welfare interaction so that meeting the needs of one means denying in some measure the needs of the other.

Burn-out (emotional depletion on the job leading to counterproductive interactions with the clients) was identified and some of the procedures for mitigating it were discussed.

A PERSONAL COMMENT

This is an objective, analytical account of the sociology of the child welfare worker. Yet something is missing—something that eludes the kind of summarization of factors characterizing an occupational subculture.

Throughout the text, the writer has consciously and deliberately refrained from intruding himself into the material. At this point, he is taking the liberty of editorializing. The impulse to make a personal comment stems from a firm commitment to child-welfare social work, the values for which it speaks, and the task it is asked to do. It stems from a conviction that child welfare workers are engaged in one important sector of the most significant task of any community: the task of rearing the next generation. Nothing—not all our building, not all our production, not all our scientific advances—can equal in importance the work of helping, in whatever way, to ensure that our children, who constitute our eternity, grow to adulthood healthy in mind, body, and spirit. Socrates, at his wisest, noted this:

> If I could get to the highest place in Athens, I would lift my voice and say, "What mean ye, fellow citizens, that ye turn every stone to scrape wealth together and take so little care of your children to whom ye must one day relinquish all?"

The most meritorious of societies is the one that welcomes the question, "Is it well with the child?" and answers, truthfully, "All is indeed well."

The Talmud, emphasizing the importance of each individual life, says, "If, during the course of your own life, you have saved one life, it is as if you have saved all mankind." Few occupations give us the opportunity of participating in the saving of a life. The everyday work of the child welfare worker is concerned with just that—reclaiming a child for life. It is to be expected that such a task would be very difficult. It is also to be expected that there are few, if any, tasks that offer the same degree of satisfaction and the same sense of accomplishment.

The task is large and difficult. The aims and hopes have to be commensurately modest. The medieval medical dictum is applicable and appropriate here: "To cure some time, to relieve often, to comfort always."

The red wine of life, the passion in the encounter with children denied a childhood, needs to be included here as an addition to the factual data regarding the child welfare worker. It is included in the child welfare worker's job.

BIBLIOGRAPHY

ALLEN, RUBIN, and G. ROBERT WHITCOMB. *Statistics on Social Work Education in the United States, 1978.* New York: Council on Social Work Education, 1979.

ARMSTRONG, KATHERINE. "How Can We avoid Burn-Out?" *Proceedings of the 2nd National Conference Child Abuse and Neglect* (April 1977). Washington, D.C.: Government Printing Office, 1978.

BABCOCK, CHARLOTTE. "The Social Worker in a World of Stress." *Social Service Review,* 25, 2 (March 1951).

BAILEY, MARGARET. "Community Orientations Toward Social Casework." *Social Work,* 4, 3 (July 1959).

BARLOW, WALTER. *Public Understanding of Social Welfare.* Columbus, Ohio: National Conference on Social Welfare, 1963.

BELON, CYNTHIA J., and KETAYUN H. GOULD. "Not Even Equals: Sex Related Salary Inequities." *Social Work* (November 1977), 466–471.

BERKELEY PLANNING ASSOCIATES. *Project Management and Worker Burnout Report.* Berkeley, Calif.: Berkeley Planning Associates, December 1977.

BILLINGSLEY, ANDREW. "Bureaucratic and Professional Orientation Patterns in Social Casework." *Social Service Review,* 38, 4 (December 1964).

BLAU, PETER M. "Orientation Toward Clients in a Public Welfare Agency." *Administrative Science Quarterly,* 5, 4 (December 1960).

BOGANOFF, EARL, and ARNOLD GLASS. *The Sociology of the Public Assistance Caseworker in an Urban Area.* Unpublished M.S. thesis, University of Chicago, Chicago, March 1964.

CARTER, GENEVIEVE W., LILLENE H. FIFIELD, and HANNAH SHIELDS. *Public Attitudes Toward Welfare—An Opinion Poll.* Los Angeles: Regional Institute in Social Welfare, UCLA, December 1973.

CHATTERJEE, PRENAB. "Recruitment in Law, Medicine and Social Work: Some Comparative Trends." *Social Work Education Reporter,* 21 (December–January 1973), 24–27.

CHETHIK, MORTON. "The Emotional 'Wear and Tear' of Child Therapy." *Smith College Studies in Social Work,* 39 (February 1967), 147–156.

CHILDREN'S BUREAU, OFFICE OF CHILD DEVELOPMENT. *Child Welfare in 25 States— An Overview.* Washington, D.C.: Government Printing Office, 1976.

CLEARFIELD, SIDNEY M. "Professional Self Image of the Social Worker: Implications for Social Work Education." *Journal of Education for Social Work,* 13, 1 (Winter 1977).

CONDIE, C. DAVID, JANET A. HANSON, NANCI E. LANG, DEANNA K. MOSS, and ROSALEE A. KANE. "How the Public Views Social Work." *Social Work* (January 1978), 47–53.

ETZIONI, AMITAI (Ed.). *The Semiprofessions and Their Organization—Nurses, Teachers, Social Workers.* New York: The Free Press, 1969.

FANSHEL, DAVID. "Child Welfare," in *Encyclopedia of Social Work,* 16th Issue. Ed. by Robert Morris. New York: National Association of Social Workers, 1971.

FELDMAN, YONATTA, *et al.* "One Aspect of Casework Training Through Supervision." *Social Casework,* 34, 4 (April 1953).

FREUDENBERGER, HERBERT S. "Burnout: Occupational Hazard of the Child Care Worker." *Child Care Quarterly,* 6, 2 (Summer 1977), 90–99.

GAYLIN, WILLARD, IRA GLASSNER, STEVEN MARCUS, and DAVID ROTHMAN. *Doing Good— The Limits of Benevolence.* New York: Pantheon Books, 1978.

GOCKEL, GALEN L. "Social Work as a Career Choice," in *Manpower in Social Welfare— Research Perspectives.* Ed. by Edward E. Schwartz. New York: National Association of Social Workers, 1966.

———. "Social Work and Recent College Graduates: A Report on Two National Surveys." *Social Work Reporter,* 15, 2 (June 1967).

GOODE, WILLIAM. "Community Within a Community—The Profession." *American Sociological Review,* 22, 2 (April 1957).

———. "The Theoretical Limits of Professionalization," in *The Semiprofessions and Their Organization—Teachers, Nurses, Social Workers.* Ed. by Amitai Etzioni. New York: The Free Press, 1969.

GREENWOOD, ERNEST. *Toward a Sociology of Social Work.* Special Report Series No. 37. Research Department, Welfare Counsel of Metropolitan Los Angeles. Los Angeles, November 1953.

———. "Attributes of a Profession." *Social Work,* 2, 3 (July 1957).

HANSON, KITTY. *Rebels in the Streets.* Englewood Cliffs, N.J.: Prentice-Hall, Inc., 1958.

HARING, BARBARA L. *Salary Study 1976.* New York: Child Welfare League of America, April 1976.

HOWE, ELIZABETH. "Legislative Outcomes in Human Services." *Social Service Review* (June 1978), 173–185.

HUGHES, EVERETT. *Men and Their Work.* New York: The Free Press, 1958.

JACOBS, JERRY. "Symbolic Bureaucracy: A Case Study of a Social Welfare Agency." *Social Forces,* 47, 4 (June 1969), 413–422.

JONES, BETTY L. "Nonprofessional Workers in Professional Foster Family Agencies." *Child Welfare,* 45, 6 (June 1966), 313–325.

KADUSHIN, ALFRED. "Determinants of Career Choice and Their Implications for Social Work." *Recruitment for Social Work Education and Social Work Practice,* 6 (April 1958a).

———. "Prestige of Social Work—Facts and Factors." *Social Work,* 3 (April 1958b).

KERMISH, IRVING, and FRANK KUSHIN. "Why High Turnover? Social Work Staff Losses in a County Welfare Agency." *Public Welfare,* 27, 2 (April 1969), 134–139.

KLEIN, FREDERICK, *et al.* "Strong Vocational Interest Blank Scores of Clinical Psychologists, Psychiatrists and Social Workers." *Journal of Counseling Psychology,* 9 (1962).

KNAPMAN, SHIRLEY K. "Sex Discrimination in Family Agencies." *Social Work* (November 1977), 461–465.

LEDERER, WOLFGANG. "Stalking the Demons." *The Progressive,* 31, 9 (September 1967), 34–37.

LITTNER, NER. *The Strains and Stresses on the Child Welfare Worker.* New York: Child Welfare League of America, 1957.

LOAVENBRUCK, GRANT. "NASW Manpower Survey." *National Association of Social Workers News* (March 1973), 10–11.

LUBOVE, ROY. *The Professional Altruist.* Cambridge, Mass.: Harvard University Press, 1965.

MASLACH, CHRISTINA. "Burned Out." *Human Behavior* (September 1976), 16–21.

———, and AYALA PINES. "The Burn Out Syndrome in the Day Care Setting." *Child Care Quarterly,* 6, 2 (Summer 1977), 100–113.

MATTINGLY, MARTHA A. "Sources of Stress and Burn-out in Professional Child Care Work." *Child Care Quarterly,* 6, 2 (Summer 1977), 127.

MAYER, JOHN E., and AARON ROSENBLATT. *Sources of Stress Among Student Practitioners in Social Work: A Sociological View.* 1973. Mimeo.

McCORNACK, RITA, and JOHN KIDNEIGH. "The Vocational Interest Patterns of Social Workers." *Social Work Journal,* 35, 4 (October 1954).

MEYER, HENRY, and SHELDON SIEGEL. "Profession of Social Work: Contemporary Characteristics," in *Encyclopedia of Social Work,* 17th issue. New York: National Association of Social Workers, 1977.

MILLER, RONALD, and LAWRENCE PODELL. *Role Conflict in Public Social Services.* New York: Office of Community Affairs, Division of Research and Innovation, 1971.

NATIONAL MAN POWER COUNCIL. *Women Power.* New York: Columbia University Press, 1957.

NATIONAL OPINION RESEARCH CENTER. *Silk Stockings and Blue Collars.* Chicago: University of Chicago Press, April 1966.

NOKES, PETER. *The Professional Task in Welfare Practice.* New York: Humanities Press, 1967.

———. "Purpose and Efficiency in Humane Social Institutions." *Human Relations,* 13, 2 (May 1960), 141–155.

PEIRCE, F. P. "A Functional Perspective of Social Work." *Social Work Education Reporter,* 18, 1 (March 1970), 48–61.

PINES, AYALA, and KAFRY DITSA. "Occupational Tedium in the Social Services." *Social Work* (November 1978), 499–450.

PINS, ARNULF M. *Who Chooses Social Work? When? and Why?* New York: Council on Social Work Education, 1963.

———, et al. *Students in Schools of Social Work.* New York: Council on Social Work Education, 1972.

PISANI, JOSEPH R. *Barriers to Freeing Children for Adoption.* Albany, N.Y.: Temporary State Commission on Child Welfare, March 1976.

PODELL, LAWRENCE. "Attrition of First-Line Social Service Staff." *Welfare in Review,* 5, 1 (January 1967), 9–14.

POLANSKY, NORMAN. "The Professional Identity in Social Work," in *Issues in American Social Work.* Ed. by Alfred Kahn. New York: Columbia University Press, 1959.

———. "Social Workers in Society." *Social Work Journal,* 34, 4 (April 1953).

RAPOPORT, LYDIA. "In Defense of Social Work—An Examination of Stress in the Profession." *Social Service Review,* 34, 3 (March 1960).

REGIONAL RESEARCH INSTITUTE OF SOCIAL WELFARE. *Public Opinion Poll of Social Services.* Los Angeles: School of Social Work, University of Southern California, March 1971.

ROSEN, JACQUELINE L. "Personality Factors in the Reaction of Child Care Workers to Emotionally Disturbed Children." *Psychiatry,* 26, 3 (August 1963).

ROSENBERG, MILTON. *Occupational Values and Occupational Choice.* Unpublished Ph.D. Thesis, Columbia University, New York, 1964.

ROSENBLATT, AARON, et al. "Predominance of Male Authors in Social Work Publications." *Social Casework,* 51, 7 (July 1970), 421–430.

SHAPIRO, DEBORAH. *Agencies and Foster Children*. New York: Columbia University Press, 1976.

SHURLEY, JAY T. *Emotional Stresses Encountered in Social Work Practice*. First Annual University of Texas Social Work Conference, May 1954. Mimeo.

SHYNE, ANN W. *Salary Study 1977*. New York: Child Welfare League of America, March 1977.

———, and ANITA G. SCHROEDER. *National Study of Social Services to Children and Their Families*. Washington, D.C.: National Center for Child Advocacy, March 1978.

STYZA, LARRY. "Reality Shock in a Public Welfare Setting." *Public Welfare*, 30, 3 (Fall 1972), 43–46.

SZUREK, S. A. "The Social Plight of the Social Worker." *American Journal of Orthopsychiatry*, 12, 1 (1942).

TEMME, LLOYD. *Occupation Meanings and Measures*. Washington, D.C.: Bureau of Social Science Research, 1975.

TIMMS, NOEL. "Knowledge, Opinion, and the Social Services." *The Sociological Review*, 9, 6 (November 1961).

TOLLEN, WILLIAM B. *Study of Staff Losses in Child Welfare and Family Service Agencies*. Washington, D.C.: Government Printing Office, 1960.

TOREN, NINA. *Social Work: The Case of a Semiprofession*. Beverly Hills, Calif.: Russell Sage Publications, 1972.

U.S. DEPARTMENT OF LABOR. *Occupational Outlook Handbook*, 1978–1979 ed. Washington, D.C.: Government Printing Office, 1978.

VASALY, SHIRLEY. *Foster Care in Five States*. Washington, D.C.: Government Printing Office, 1976.

VINTER, ROBERT. "The Social Structure of Service," in *Issues in American Social Work*. Ed. by Alfred Kahn. New York: Columbia University Press, 1959.

WALTHER, REGISTT, et al. "The Occupation Culture of Policemen and Social Workers." *Experimental Publications System*, Issue Ms. No. 314–256, American Psychological Association, December 1970.

WASSERMAN, HARRY. "Early Careers of Professional Social Workers in a Public Child Welfare Agency." *Social Work*, 15, 3 (July 1970), 93–101.

———. "The Professional Social Worker in a Bureaucracy." *Social Work*, 16, 1 (January 1971), 69–95.

WEINBERGER, PAUL. *Job Satisfaction and Staff Retention in Social Work*. School of Social Work, San Diego State College, January 1970. Mimeo.

ZIMMERMAN, DON. "Tasks and Troubles—The Practical Bases of Work Activities in a Public Assistance Organization," in *Explorations in Sociology and Counseling*. Ed. by Donald A. Hansen. Boston: Houghton Mifflin Company, 1969.

INDEX

Abandonment: and adoption, 470, 471; and foster care, 374; and "Good Neighbor Homes," 197; history of, 34, 35–36, 39–40; and neglect, 158, 161; and role rejection, 17; mentioned, 48, 49, 50, 584, 633

Abortion: after amniocentesis, 55–56; availability of, 55; history of, 34; and illegitimacy, 38, 55, 442; liberalization of laws, 50, 217; and Medicaid, 50, 452; motives for, 37, 38; in other countries, 444, 633, 634–35; use of, 425–26

Abraham, 466

Abuse: and child-care institutions, 613–14; context of, 168–69; defined, 159; effects on child development, 213–14; and foster family care, 342; and indenture, 315; intergenerational, 179–80; investigation of, 172–77; legal definition of, 214–15; problems in treatment of, 214–20; reincidence of, 206–7; reporting of, 160–61, 172; scope of, 171–77; and social isolation, 179, 184, 188; treatment for, 189–98; and parental role unfulfillment, 24, 26, 99, 140, 151, 160, 260, 448, 615

Abusive parents: discussed, 178–79; intergenerational abuse and, 179–80; and social isolation, 179, 184, 188; and therapeutic day care, 207

Action for Foster Children Week, 397

Adam and Eve, 33

Ad litem, 156

Adolescence: adoption during, 442, 488, 494, 498; child-bearing during, 446–47; child guidance clinics during, 80; family services during, 454; and foster-family care during, 319, 325, 340; and institutional child-care during, 589; and vocational counseling during, 605

Adolescent Health Service, Pregnancy Prevention and Care Act, 454–55

Adopt-a-Child, 533

Adoptalk, 564

Adoptee: and access to birth records, 263–64; and emotional disturbance, 523–30;

and OASDI, 119; problems of, 487–88; rights of, in other countries, 656–67; and search for biological parents, 493–501, 656

Adoptees Liberty Movement Association (ALMA), 495, 650

Adoption: of adolescents, 422, 498; in Africa, 641; age at placement, 470, 530; and age of parents, 384, 565; black market in, 551, 566; and child abuse cases, 212; child-applicant ratio of, 472–73; community attitude toward, 550–51; confidentiality and, 514; and contact with putative father, 441; counseling for, 434; criteria for applicants, in other countries, 657–58; de facto, 313; demand for, 552–54; disruption of, 544–57; evaluation of services of, 517–31; exchange programs in, 554, 555–60; failure of, 544; and foster care, 347, 370–71, 374, 383–84, 397, 562–63; gray market in, 551, 565; group methods in, 501–5, 566; of handicapped child, 542–44; history of, 465–69; and illegitimacy, 441–42; independent, 510–17; international, 505–7; legal aspects of, 507–510; motivation for, 476–77, 565; of older children, 483–84, 530, 539–42; open, 501; in other countries, 649, 654, 655–56; preferential, 472; placement, 484–85; problems in services of, 547–54, 566; process in, 481–85; and race, 420; and religious requirements, 551–52; and rejected applicants, 503–5; and right to records, 563–64; requirements of adoptive parents, 473–81; scope of, 469–70; by single parent, 384, 554, 560–62; sources of children for, 470–72; of special needs children, 480–81, 531–44; subsidized, 384, 556–60, 656; success of, 530–31; and "telling," 488–93, 565; transracial, 506, 533–39, 544, 566, 656; trends in, 554–67

Adoption Act and Regulations, 559–60

"Adoption Day in Court," 555

Adoption Reform Act (1978), 469, 517, 556

Adoption Report, 564

Adoption Resource Exchange of North America (ARENA), 548, 556, 560

Adoption Resources Referral Center, 556

Adoption Week, 555

Adoptive care, *vs.* foster care, 314

Adoptive families: problems of, 485–501

Adoptive Father of the Year, 555

Adoptive homes, 4, 314

Adoptive parents: and adjustment to sterility, 476; application for, 481–83; and outreach programs, 555; requirements of, 473–76

Aftercare programs: in institutional child care, 605–6, 616

Affirmative action, 397, 677

Africa, 214, 638, 640, 641, 643, 649

Afro-American Family and Community Services, 533

Agnostics Adoption Society, 656

Aid to Families of Dependent Children (AFDC): and children born out-of-wedlock, 427, 446, 454; costs of, 145; and crises leading to application, 129–30; and day care, 275, 286; and death of father, 118–19; eligibility for, 128–29; and fraud, 143, 145; and institutional child care funding, 614; intake of, 130–34; and low-income groups, 104; and need, 128; number of persons receiving assistance from, 130; and prenatal care, 128; and prevention of placement, 327; problems in service of, 140–45; as supplementary program, 126–40

Aid to Families of Dependent Children-Unemployed, 128

Alameda Project, 386, 387

Alcoholism, 16, 24, 138, 144, 167, 186, 187, 217

Allocation Supplementaire (France), 652

Almeda Council of Social Agencies, 257

Almshouses: mixed, 48, 319, 585

American Bar Association Juvenile Justice, 164

American Civil Liberties Union, 48

American Ethical Union, 551

American Humane Association, Children's Division, 151, 155, 159

American Indians: and adoption, 531, 534, 535, 538; and foster-family care, 330, 391

Amphidroma, 47

Annual National Conference of Charities and Corrections, 317

Apathy: and incidence of abuse, 182

"Apathy-futility syndrome," 185

Apprenticeship, 40, 315, 415, 585. *See also* Child labor; Indenture

Argentina, 658, 651

Aristotle, 34, 38

Arithmetic of child production, 33, 46, 51, 69

Ashley, Lord: Earl of Shaftesbury, 49

Asia, 638, 656

Assertiveness training, 209

Associated Charities of Cincinnati, 236

Association for Improving the Conditions of the Poor, 96

Association for the Improvement of the Conditions of the Poor, 235

Association for the Protection of the Adoptive Triangle (APAT), 495

Astor Home for Children, 606

Australia, 38, 649, 661

Austria, 650, 652, 659

Avail-Ability, 241–42

Avail-a-Care, 241–42

Aversion therapy, 87

"Baby bust," 53

"Baby parking," 654

"Baby selling." *See* Black market

Bangladesh, 635

Barron Ego-Strength Scale, 185

Bastardy. *See* Illegitimacy

"Battered children," 154, 156, 160. *See also* Abuse

Behavior modification: and homemaker service, 260; in institutional child care, 600–1; and intervention outcome, 209–10; evaluated, 100–2; and parents as co-therapists, 88, 89–90; as treatment program, 86–91; and treatment of abusive parents, 196

Bellefaire; residential treatment center, 606, 608

Berkeley Planning Associates, 208–9

Bernado, Dr., 49

Better Jobs and Income Program, 141

"Binding out," 40

Bioparents: defined, 486

Birth control, 50, 54, 217. *See also* Abortion; Contraception; Family planning services
"Birth dearth," 53
Birth grant: in other countries, 651
Birthrate, 46, 52, 53, 55, 67, 552, 639
Birtwell, Charles, 318–19
Blacks: and abortion, 426; and adoption, 470, 506, 531–33; 560; and child care, 49–50, 69, 443; and family income, 64–65; and foster-family care, 322, 330, 372, 391–93; and institutional child care, 595
Black market: in adoption, 510, 512–13, 517, 551, 566
Blake, William, 44
Board money: for foster care, 318
Board of Public Charities for the State of Ohio, 585
Boarding home, 314, 339
Boston, Massachusetts, 154, 437, 585, 594
Boston Children's Aid Society, 318
Bowen Center, 211
Bowen project, 210–11
Brace, Charles Loring, 49, 315, 316, 317, 319
"Bread parents," 487
British Children Act, 656
British Columbia, Canada, 656
Brokerage, 78
Brooklyn Society for Prevention of Cruelty to Children, 187
Brutality, 143. *See also* Abuse; Neglect
Bulgaria, 647, 649
Bureau of Child Guidance, New York City, 77
Bureau of Employment Security of the U.S. Department of Labor, 118
Bureau of Labor Statistics, 392
Bureau of Vital Statistics, 500
Burn-out: of protective service workers, 221, 692–93
Bustees, 638

Cain and Abel, 33
California Department of Social Welfare, 556
California Psychological Inventory, 185
Canada: adoption in, 495, 534; foster-family care in, 378

Canadian Indians, 656
Caretaker service, 130, 197
Carom, Thomas, 49
Casework: and AFDC families, 134–35, 147; and child abuse, 173–77, 199–200; counseling, 99–100, 103, 161; and emergency parents, 197–98; in family therapy, 95–96, 236; in foster-family care, 387–88, 400–1; goals of, 81–82; and homemaker services, 238, 241, 247–55, 257–58, 261; by objectives, 106; in protective services, 190–98; in supportive services, 80–91; task-centered, 90–91
Caseworker-homemaker team, 244
Caseworker, The, 632
Cash relief grants, 76, 196
Cattel Scale, 381
Census of Requests for Child Welfare Services (1975), 62
Center for Parent and Child Development, 195
Central Child Abuse Registry, 212
Central registries: for child abuse reports, 217
Cerebral palsy, 245
Charity, 76, 127, 316
Charity Organization Societies, 76
Chapin Adoption Agency, 468
Chicago Orphan Asylum, 467
Chicanos: and adoption, 531
Child: defined, 44–45, 52; rights of: in adoption, 510; in the Age of Enlightenment, 39; in child abuse cases, 201; in Europe, 47; and foster-family care, 383–84, 398–99; and illegitimacy, 415; and institutional child care, 612; recognition of, 151–52; role of, 11–12, 28; and standards of child care, 216; status of, 33, 45, 47–48, 51, 69, 642–43
Child abuse. *See* Abuse; Neglect
Child Abuse Prevention and Treatment Act (1974), 156, 163–64
Child Advocacy Programs, 1975, 98
Child and Family Services Act, 1975, 272
Child's Behavioral Characteristics, 338, 381
Child Care Quarterly, 617
Child care: homemaker services, 240, 243; standards of, 215–16
Child care experts, 51

Child-dependency ratio, 54, 65, 633, 636–38, 640

Child Development, 43

Child development: child abuse, 179, 196, 213–14; defined, 76–77; foster-family care, 382; homemaker training, 240; intervention outcome, 209

Child guidance clinic: and adoption, 487, 523; approach of, 77; and community, 96; and delinquency, 107; drop out rate, 102–3; and family therapy, 94–96; and group counseling programs, 91; history of, 76–77; scope of, 79–80

Child interrole conflict, 22

Child labor: discussed, 44, 49; and free foster-family care, 317; legislation against, 127. *See also* Apprenticeship; Indenture

Child lending, 641

Child Protective Services Act, 158

Child Protective Services Unit of Hennepin County (Minneapolis), 207

Child-rearing, 5, 43, 68–69, 196, 203

"Child rescue," 155

"Child-saving" movement, 127

Child Welfare, 43, 393, 674

Child welfare: defined, 1–28; as profession, 28, 673–97; services: and changing values, 68; decline in demand for, 54; defined, 6–7; development of, 33; and divorce, 57–58; and minority groups, 66–67; in other countries, 643–66; and single-parent families, 61–62; statistics on, 66–67; supportive services, 70; supranational, 665; and working mothers, 66

Child Welfare League of America: and adoption, 469, 470, 473, 496, 497, 499, 506, 531, 551, 555, 556, 564; and day care, 268, 295, 296–97, 299; definition of child welfare, 5; and education on early parenting, 454; and foster-family care, 314, 325, 326, 376, 387, 393; and institutional child care, 601, 617; and maternity homes, 433; and supportive services, 99; and transracial adoption, 534, 536, 538

Child Welfare League of America Group Home Standards Statement, 339

Child Welfare League of America Revised Adoption Standards, 563

Child Welfare League of America Salary Study, 677

Child welfare worker: characteristics of, 28, 674–78

Childhood: defined, 44–45; "discovery" of, 33, 69; history of, 153–54; in other countries, 638

Childhood Level of Living Scale, 176

Childlessness, 53–54, 68, 70, 533

Children in Placement (CIP), 384

Children's Aid Society, 536

Children's Bureau Crippled Children's Program, 260

Children's Bureau, National Center on Child Abuse and Neglect, 164

Children's Bureau, Office of Child Development, 156

Children's Bureau, U.S. Department of Health, Education, and Welfare, 197, 236, 268, 271, 471, 595, 614

Children's Defense Fund, 48

Children's Home Society: of California, 497; of Minnesota, 500; of North Carolina, 544

Children's Reeducation Center, 609

Children's Rights Report, 48

Children's Village, 608, 609

Children's village, 658–59

Children Today, 43

China. *See* People's Republic of China

"Chiseling," 143

Chore services, 238

"Chosen-child" concept, 491

Christian Science Monitor, 512

Citizens' Advice Bureau, 646, 652

Citizens' review boards: and foster-family care, 384–86

Civil rights, 651

Civil Rights movement, 48, 69, 274, 275

Civil service, 239, 676

Cleveland Plain Dealer, 512

Code of Hammurabi, 39, 465

Cognitive development, 213

Collective bargaining, 124

Collective neglect, 168–69

Commonwealth Fund, 77, 78

Community: and AFDC, 140; and child abuse, 152, 154, 190, 201, 219; and child care, 216; as client, 96; and day care, 276; and homemaker service, 237, 259, 261; and neglect, 168–69, 213–14; as *parens patriae*, 12; and protective services, 12–13, 152–53, 217; responsibility to the child, 11, 12, 69; and sanctioning of out-of-wedlock birth, 426

Community-action groups, 301–2
Community agencies, 209
Community Council, 249
Community Council of New York, 448
Community mental-health, 78
Community Mental Health Centers Act of 1963, 78
Community organization, 25, 91, 108
Community resources: and inadequate role implementation, 22–23
Community Resident Information Services Program, 615
Community Service Agency, 97–98
Community service center, 104, 106
Community Service Agency of New York, 96–97, 107
Community Welfare Council of the Greater Sacramento Area, 282
Comptroller General, 169, 207–8
Concerned United Parents, 495–96
Congés de naissance, 651
Consortium on Early Child Bearing and Child Rearing, 454
Constantine, 39
Consumer Price Index, 124–25
Contraception: acceptance of, 50–51; access to, 56–57; history of, 34; in other countries, 633, 634, 635; and teenagers, 428; use of, 423–25. *See also* Birth control; Family planning services
"Contracting," 106, 346–47
Corporal punishment: and foster parents, 355–56. *See also* Abuse
Cottage groups. *See* Residential treatment center
Council on Adoptable Children, 539
Council of Europe's Coordinated Research Group, 655
Council for Intercountry Adoption, 656
Council of Nicaea, 584
Council on Social Work Education, 695
Counterconditioning, 87
Courier, 43
Courts: and adoption, 495, 507–10; and child abuse, 155, 219; and foster-family care, 321, 323, 384–86; and parental rights, 383, 398; and Parents Anonymous, 205; and protective services, 199–202. *See also* U.S. Supreme Court
Cradle, The, 468
Crisis nurseries, 194–95
Crittenton, Charles, 433
Crittenton Maternity Home, 433

Cuba, 65, 649
Czechoslovakia, 649, 650

Datheus, Archbishop of Milan, Italy, 584
Day care: adult-child ratio in, 278–79; after-school, 197, 300–1, 303; alternative to homemaker service, 283; and child abusers, 161; clientele of, 267–68, 272–73; community responsibility for, 69; congregate, 268–69; congregate *vs.* family, 298–99; defined, 267–68; and deprived home environment, 283–84; and diversification of facilities, 304–5; education in, 299–300; effects on child, 277–78; eligibility for, 129; emotionally disturbed children in, 306; employer-sponsored, 303–4; evaluation of, 285–86; family, 269, 277, 292–94, 305–6; foster, 269; and franchise operations, 303–4; funding for, 301–2; goals of, 300; for handicapped children, 306; history of, 272; and homemaker services; 243; and illness of mother, 283; for infants, 302–3; intake, 290; and intervention outcome, 210; licensing regulations for, 278–80; and mother's anxieties about, 289–90; in other countries, 651, 653–54, 655; parental involvement in, 305; personnel of, 172, 302; problems in, 292–302, 306–7; profit-making, 277; propriety of, 281–85; public image of, 299; public support of, 296–97; purchase-of-service of, 145; and relation to social work, 272–73; role of social worker in, 286–96; scope of, 276–81; shoppers', 284; and social services, 299–300; statistics on, 276–77; termination of, 292; as treatment resource, 190–95; trends in, 302–6, 307; and Work Incentive program, 142; and working mother, 66, 276, 281, 306
Day Care and Child Development Council of America, 268
Death of parent, 24, 28, 126, 142, 245, 261, 350
Declaration of the Rights of the Child, 48, 665
Deinstitutionalization, 322, 617–21
Delaware, 516
Delinquency: and AFDC children, 140; and child guidance clinics, 76, 78, 79;

Delinquency (*cont.*)
  as symptom of emotional disturbance, and need for foster-family care, 342; and homemaker services, 235; and incidence of abuse, 180; prevention of, 127
Delinquent training school, 27
de Montpellier, Guy. *See* Montpellier, Guy de
Denmark, 643, 649, 653, 660, 664
Denver Developmental Screening Test, 212
Dependence: and foster-family care, 321
Dependency ratio, 1970–1976: 54–55
Desegregation: and institutional child care, 621
Desensitization: in treating school phobia, 87–88
Desertion: and dependence, 142; and fatherlessness, 145; and foster-family care, 374, 584; and homemaker service, 245; as parental role rejection, 18; and parental role unfulfillment, 24; statistics on, 58
"Detached workers," 106
Detention home, 246
Detribalization, 641–42
Deutsch, Albert, 613
Developmental Problems Index, 381
Devereux Child Behavior Rating Scale, 609
Devereux Elementary School Behavior Rating Scale, 609
Directory of Psychiatric Clinics for Children, 77
Disability: and dependence, 142
"Discharge to self," 370
Discipline, 10, 12, 153–54, 159, 612–13
Discrimination, 81, 140–41, 169, 183
District of Columbia Department of Public Welfare, 196
Divorce: acceptance of, 58; and dependence, 142; and fatherlessness, 145; and need for homemaker service, 245; no-fault, 58; and OASDI, 119; and parental role unfulfillment, 24; rate of, 57–58, 67, 70
Doctors, medical: and child abuse reporting laws, 218
Dorfleiter, 659
Drop-in center, 105, 195
Dropout rate: in family services, 102–3; in supportive services, 108

Drug addiction, 16, 24, 81, 138, 167, 198
Dutch Child Caring Agency, 377–78

East-West Society, The, 539
East Germany, 649, 650, 651
"Echo baby boom," 53
Educateur, 659
Education: compulsory, 127, 146; effects on child development and, 213; and income, 64–65; level of, and employability, 141; level of, and incidence of child abuse, 160, 183, 187; for pregnant teenage girls, 434
Educational counseling, 209, 429
Educational neglect, 162, 163
Egypt, Ancient, 34
Eighteenth century: child care in, 154, 585
Elderly: use of homemaker services, 242, 258, 559
Elizabethan Poor Laws, 314
Emergency parents, 197–98
Emergency relief fund, 196
Emergency services, 195, 196–97, 584
Emotional abuse. *See* Abuse
Emotional disability, 24
Emotional disturbance: and adopted child, 523–30
Emotional handicap, 20–21
Emotional maltreatment, 221
Emotional needs: of child, 9–10; of parent, 12
Emotional neglect, 163–66, 214
Emotional Problems Indicator, 381
Emotionally disturbed child: and day care, 282; and foster-family care, 321, 338, 340–41, 368, 390–91; and institutional child care, 596–623; population of, 80
Employment: opportunities for, 81; potential, 141; programs, 147; skills, 141, 160; of social workers, 675–77; of women, 273–76
Enfant trouvés, 584
Enfranchisement, 41
England: adoption policies in, 483, 495; and child labor, 44, 49; Elizabethan Age in, 36, 158–59; and foster-family care, 329–30, 337, 358, 360, 374; illegitimacy in, 414; Victorian, 158–59. *See also* Great Britain
English Poor Laws, 414–15
Enlightenment, Age of, 39, 51

Environment, engineered: as treatment facility, 196, 210, 211; and need for foster-family care, 322

Error rate; defined, 143

Ethiopia, 635

Europe: abandonment in, 35–36; birthrate in, 552; child welfare services in, medieval, 39–40; infanticide in, 35; legal status of child in, 47; parent-child relationship in, 46

Euthanasia, 50

Exploitation, 151, 158, 168, 305. *See also* Abuse; Neglect

Exposure, 36, 38, 158

Exposure to unwholesome circumstances, 158, 167–68

Extramarital child, 415. *See also* Illegitimacy; Pregnancy

Factories: and child labor, 154

Factory Acts, 49

Factory *creche*, 653–54

Family: abusive, 160, 177–80, 183, 189; changes in concept of, 316; child's role in, 12; and child development, 586; and childhood dependency, 70; communal, 61, 216; forms of, 68–69; and homemaker services, 255, 258–59; in the Middle Ages, 45–46; nuclear, 43, 45, 46, 68–69, 237, 641–42; sequential monogamous, 61; single-parent, 163, 323, 448–49, 633; status of, 33, 45, 69; as unit of consumption, 51–52; as unit of production, 51; and working mother, 273–76

Family allowance: in other countries, 648–49

Family Assistance Plan, 141

Family Builders Agencies, 565

Family counseling, 104, 105

Family Court, 177

Family Day Care-Career Program, 305

Family Discussion Bureau, 645

Family disruption: and AFDC, 143–44; and divorce, 57–58; and foster-family care, 323

Family, extended: and blacks, 419, 443; and day care, 276; and extended-family center, 195; and illegitimate child, 449; as social institution, 41, 42

Family, fatherless: and AFDC family, 134, 143–44; and day care, 281

Families for Interracial Adoption, 539

Family health workers, 209–10

Family-life education, 91, 95, 105, 138, 195, 376

Family planning services: acceptance of, 51; and AFDC, 135, 453; availability of, 55; for males, 455; and purchase-of-service, 145; support for, 50. *See also* Birth control; Contraception

Family service: and community organization, 96, 97; contact made by, 81; evaluation of, 98–102; and family therapy, 95–96; funding for, 103; and group approach, 91–95; history of, 76–77; process in, 80–98; scope of, 79–80

Family Service Association of America, 76, 79–80, 81–82, 91, 97, 98, 107

Family Service Bureau of the Association for the Improvement of the Conditions of the Poor, 235

Family Service Units, 645

Family therapy, 95–96, 102, 103, 108, 205

Family Welfare Association of America, 76

Family Welfare Association (London), 103

Father, foster. *See* Foster father

Father, putative: discussed, 437–41; unwed, 415–16, 438, 439–41, 509–10

Favelas, 638

Federal Administration for Children, Youth and Families, 7, 327

Federal Interagency Day Care Guideline, 305

Federal Interagency Day Care Requirements, 294

Federal Office of Child Advocacy, 98

Federal Office of Child Development, 301

Federal Standards on the Prevention and Treatment of Child Abuse and Neglect, 164

Female Assistance Society, 49

Female-headed household, 59–60, 62, 120. *See also* Family

Feudal system, 42

Filiocentricity, 52

Filial deprivation, 344

Filial therapy: in behavior modification, 89–90

Filius nullius, 414

Filius populi, 414

Financial assistance, 27, 81, 99, 197. *See also* Public assistance

Finland, 495, 650, 651, 653, 656, 660

First Amendment: access to birth records and, 495
First National Conference of Foster Parents, 396–97
Fisher, Florence, 495
Florence Crittenton Association of America, 433
Food Stamp program, 129, 133, 215
Ford Foundation, 313, 364
Foreign-born children: and adoption, 470, 471. *See also* Adoption
Foster-care agencies, 554
Foster-family care: acceptance of, 309; and adoption, 471, 562–63; *vs.* adoptive care, 314; age at placement and, 377, 379; and board money, 318; in child abuse cases, 161; child in placement in, 349–54; and child-related problems, 324; and contracting, 346–47; costs of, 392–94; defined, 314; and demonstration projects, 386–88; and dependent child, 321; effects on, on payment of a fee, 393–94; and emotionally disturbed child, 321; in England, 374; evaluation of consequences of, 376–82, 401; exclusive and inclusive, defined, 357–58; free, 316–17; and group methods of education, 374–76; of handicapped child, 374; history of, 314–20; and homemaker services, 235–36; impropriety of, 324–25; incorporation of child into, 349, 351–52; *vs.* institutional care, 586–87; intake, 342–49; and intervention outcome, 211–12; length of time in, 373–74; long-term, 389; and neglected children, 321; of nonwhites, 374; and number of homes, 389–92; in other countries, 654, 658; and placement decision, 325–26, 395–96; problems of, 382–96; process of, 342–55; propriety of, 322; public image of, 330; reasons for, 322–23; and replacement, 368–70; and return home, 371; review procedures in, 397; scope of, 320–22; and separation, 375–76; and source of referral, 321; specialized, 396; termination of, 370–74; and termination of institutional child care, 606; trends in, 107, 321–22, 396–402; turnover in, 368–69; types of, 339–41; and visiting parents, 362–69. *See also* Group foster home
Foster-family home: assessment of potential, 332–37; and emergency care, 197;

recruitment of, 328–32; specialized, 338, 618; for unmarried mother, 429
Foster father, 334, 362
Foster-grandparent program, 621
Foster mother, 330
Foster Parent Appraisal Form, 338
Foster Parent Week, 329
Foster parenthood: *vs.* biological parenthood, 335–37
Foster Parents of the Year, 329
Foster parents: and group methods, 374–76; of handicapped child, 543; motivation of, 329–38; organizations for, 396–97; and relationship to agency, 394–95; and resentment of biological parent, 363–64; rights of, 397–98; role of, 355–76; and subsidized adoption, 558–59
France: attitude toward child, 46, 47; discipline of child, 153–54
Free clinics: as alternative agency, 105
Free home: as type of foster care, 339
Freud, Sigmund, 43, 76, 203, 487
Foundling home, 36–37, 40
Foundling Home (Moscow), 37
Fourteenth Amendment: and illegitimacy, 415, 495

Genesis, 33
Genetic birth defects, 55–56
Genetic counseling, 55
Geneva, Switzerland, 505
Gestalt therapy, 95
Glueck Prediction Scale, 607
Gmeiner, Hermann, 659
Goal attainment scaling: and determining intervention outcome, 210
"Good cause": and access to birth records, 495
"Good Neighbor Homes," 197
Government, federal. *See* U.S. government
Government National Center for Health Statistics Study on Illegitimacy, 420–21
Grants-in-aid, 129, 140, 146, 646
Gray market: in adoption, 510–17, 551, 566
Great Britain: child labor in, 154; homemaker service in, 258; Parliament, 661. *See also* England; Scotland
Great Depression: and day care, 270; and family service agencies, 76; and mother's pension program, 128; and social welfare, 146

Greece, Ancient: adoption in, 465, 466; infanticide and exposure in, 34, 38
Greece, modern, 653
Group approach: with AFDC, 136–37; in child abuse treatment, 195, 203; with pregnant teenagers, 435–37
Group counseling programs, 91–95
Group foster home: defined, 321; and emotionally disturbed child, 391; discussed, 339–42; trend toward, 399–400
Group home, for emotionally disturbed child: advantages of, 621–22; community acceptance of, 614–15; costs of, 619; problems of, 619–20; and purchase-of-service, 618; and zoning, 615. See also Institutional child care; Residential treatment center
Group methods: and adoption, 501–5, 565
Guaranteed income, 144
Guardianship, 202
Guatemala, 635
Guidance: anticipatory, 209
Guild: as mutual aid group, 42, 43, 45

Halfway house, 341, 605
Haltes-garderies, 654
Handicapped children: adoption of, 470, 480–81, 534, 540, 544–45, 547–50; and day care, 281–82; and foster-family care, 342, 374, 390–91
"Hansel and Gretel," 36, 154
Harlem-Dawling Children's Service, 533
Hart, Dr. Hastings, 316
Hawthorne Center, 607
Head Start Program, 268, 275, 276, 285, 294–95, 305
Health, 7, 146, 148, 169, 212, 213, 323
Health insurance: in other countries, 649–50
Health Status Index, 381
Healy, Dr. William, 76, 77
Hellenistic Age, 34, 39
Henry IV, 153–54
Hinduism, 466
Hispanics, 66, 205, 277, 330. See also Chicanos; Spanish-speaking Americans
Holland, 645, 647, 653, 656, 658, 664
Holt International Children's Fund, 506
Holt International Children's Fund Service, 564
Home economics, 236, 240
Home health aide service, 238

Home maintenance, 240, 243
Homebuilder's Project: and prevention placement, 327
Homemaker service: administration of, 238–41; casework process, 247–55; costs of, vs. foster-family care, 255–56; evaluation of, 255–57, 261; history of, 235–37; intake in, 247–52; in other countries, 646, 653, 655; problems in, 257–59, 261; propriety of, 242–47; recruitment for, 238–40, 259; scope of, 241–42; summary of, 260–61; termination of, 254–55; trends in, 145, 259–60, 261
Homemaker Service of the Children's Aid Society of New York, 255
Homes for Black Children, 533
Homosexuality: and child care, 216
Hôtels maternelles, 660
Hot-line crisis switchboards, 105
Housekeeping Aid Program, 236
Houseparent: in a child-care institution, 601
Housewife: social services for, in other countries, 646
Housing: inadequate, 163, 183, 213
Humanitarianism, 33, 39, 40, 152
Hungary, 632–33, 646, 649, 651, 652

Illegitimacy: and abortion, 38; and adoption, 441–42; 450, 471; and child, 58, 119, 182; history, 413–16; rate of, 58–59, 66, 67, 70, 472, 638; scope of, 416–21; social services for, 427–35, 456
Immigrants, 49, 51, 60, 142–43
Immigration, 24, 51, 143
Imprisonment, 24, 28, 48, 323–24
Incest, 38, 39, 166–67, 187, 202. See also Sexual abuse
Income: guaranteed, 141; and incidence of abuse and neglect, 160, 163, 183, 187; median, 64, 66, 67; in other countries, 639; redistribution of, and subsidized adoption, 558; and working mother, 65–66
Income maintenance programs, 38–39, 115–18, 126, 138, 144–46, 429
Indenture, 304–15, 466. See also Apprenticeship; Child labor
India, 35, 466, 635, 637, 638, 641
Indian Adoption Project, 534
Indian Child Welfare Act, 399

Indian, American. *See* American Indian

Indian, Canadian. *See* Canadian Indian

Indonesia, 658

Industrial Revolution, 40

Industrialization, 42, 51, 636–38

Infanticide, 34–40, 49, 152

Infant mortality rate, 56, 57, 66, 67, 70, 637–38, 639

Infant nursery, 653

Ingraham *v.* Wright, 169

"In limbo," 383, 385, 386

In loco parentis, 115

Institute for Juvenile Research, 76–77

Institutional child care; advantages of, 587–89, 621–22; child abuse in, 613–14; and deinstitutionalization, 617–20; evaluation of, 606–10; *vs.* foster-family care, 586–87; history of, 584–87; licensing of, 614; neglect in, 613–14; in other countries, 654, 658–59; and parental visits, 603–5; and partial institutionalization, 620–21; placement in, 596–98; population of, 616; problems in, 610–15, 622–23; propriety of, 589–94, 622; purposes of, 616; and racial integration, 621; role of child-care worker in, 601–2; scope of, 594–96; special facilities in, 588–89; staff of, 616–17; summary of, 621–23; termination of, 605–6; and therapeutic milieu, 600; treatment programs in, 598–606; trends in, 615–21, 623

Institutional maltreatment, 169

Intercultural conflict, 24

Intergenerational conflict, 24

International Child Welfare Review, 665

International Children's Day, 647

International Council on Home Help Services, 241

International Journal of Child Welfare, The, 43

International Planned Parenthood Federation, 634–35

International Social Services, 564, 665

International Union for Child Welfare, 665

International Year of the Child, 665

Interracial Family Association, 539

Interrole conflict, 19, 28, 65

Intrarole conflict, 18–19, 28

IQ tests, 185, 212, 378, 381

Ireland, 634

Irish: as immigrant group, 142–43

Islamic law, 643

Israel, 495, 596, 633, 650, 654, 656, 657

Italians: as immigrant group, 142–43

Italy, 506, 634, 650

Japan, 56, 631, 632, 633, 645, 648, 654, 664

Jewish Child Care Association, 318

Jewish Family and Children's Service, 285, 607

Jewish Family Welfare Society of Philadelphia, 235

Jewish Home-Finding Society of Chicago, 235

Jews: and adoption, 536, 551; and social work, 675

Jig-Saw, 656

Job placement, 99, 135, 142; *See also* Employment

Job-placement training: and institutional child care, 605

Joint Commission on the Mental Health of Children, 614

Joint Economic Committee, U.S. Congress, 427

Judaism, 314

Judeo-Christian ethic, 684–85

Justinian Code, 37

Juvenile Court of Cook County, Illinois, 76–77

Juvenile delinquency. *See* Delinquency

Juvenile Protective Association, 197, 210

Juvenile Rights Project of the American Civil Liberties Union, 58

Kefauver, Estes, 513

Kelly, Florence, 49

Kennedy, John F., 217

Kenyan Child Welfare Society, 642

KHL: and employee sponsored day care, 304

Kindercare, 304

Kinship fostering, 641, 643

Know-Nothing movement, 143

Korea, 506

Kwashiorkor: defined, 637

L'aide sociale, 652

Landsmanschaft organizations, 49

Language: development of, and child abuse, 213

Lanham Act: and federal funds for nursery school, 271
"Latchkey" children, 300–1
Latin America, 636, 638, 643
Law enforcement agencies: and reporting of abuse, 160–61, 162, 219. *See also* Police
"Lay professionals," 204
Lay therapy programs, 209
Legal custody, 201–2, 313
Legislation: for adoption, 467–69
Legitimate child: defined, 58; and adoption, 470
"Legitimate violence," 159
Legitimation, 415
Lesbianism, 216
Lettre de cachet, 47
Licensing, state: of foster-family homes, 332, 335, 336
Life expectancy, 57, 67, 68, 70, 639
Living-in program, 205
Local Youth Board, 660
London, England, 337, 656
London Foundling Hospital, 37, 40, 49
Los Angeles Bureau of Adoptions, 502
Los Angeles County Department of Adoption, 470, 552, 555, 560
Los Angeles Department of Adoptions, 550
Louis XIII, 49
Louise Wise Agency, 455, 468, 554
Love child, 415
Lums: and employee-sponsored day care, 304

"Mainstreaming," 617
Malay Peninsula, 38
Malnutrition, 158, 169
Maltreatment, 158, 159, 177–88 *passim*. *See also* Abuse; Neglect
Manhattan Survey of Psychiatric Impairment of Urban Children, 448–49
Marijuana, 216
Marital: child, defined, 58; counseling, 8, 209; disruption, 58, 60, 144; problems, 78, 179, 203, 348; relationship, 476; therapy, 102
Marriage, 53, 57, 143–44, 182, 418
Mary Moppet, 304
Maryland Children's Aid Society, 343
Massachusetts, 314, 318, 467, 549, 552, 586, 618

Massachusetts Adoption Resource Exchange, 547
Massachusetts Board of State Charities, 317, 337
Massachusetts Society for the Prevention of Cruelty to Children, 189
Maternal Care and Mental Health, 586
"Maternal depletion syndrome," 642
Maternal mortality rate, 57, 66, 67, 70
Maternal role: and homemaker service, 240, 242
Maternity benefits, 650–51
Maternity home, 429, 432–34, 442, 456
Medicaid, 50, 132, 259, 452, 453
Medical agencies: and reporting of child abuse, 160–61
Medical care: denial of, 158, 162–63; for unmarried mother, 429, 430
Medicare, 259
Medicine, socialized *See* Health insurance
Mental deficiency, 15–16, 128, 182, 186
Mental health: community clinics, 78, 80
Mental illness, 24, 202, 350
"Mental injury," 164
Mental retardation: and adoption, 470, 542–44; and foster-family care, 390–91; and OASDI benefits, 120
"Mental well-being," 164
"Mercy killing," 50
Merit system, 238–39
Middle Ages, 42, 45, 413–14
Migrant farm workers, 246, 260, 306
Migrations, 419
Minister of Health and Welfare (Japan), 664
Minnesota Division of Child Welfare, 555
Minnesota Multiphasic Inventory, 185
Minnesota Preschool Scale, 381
Minority Adoption Recruitment of Children's Homes (MARCH), 534, 565
Minority groups: and adoption, 40, 480–81, 531–39, 544–45, 547–50; and child welfare services, 66, 70; and day care, 276–77
Model Statute Social Workers' License Act, 2
Modeling: as behavior modification technique, 87
"Mom's day out": as treatment resource, 195
Mondale, Walter, 272
Montpellier, Guy de, 39–40
Moscow Foundling Home, 37

Mother, foster. *See* Foster mother
Mother: disabled, and OASDI, 119–20; illness of, and need for homemaker service, 247; unmarried, 63, 160, 421, 435, 437–41, 448–54, 456, 660; widowed, and OASDI benefits, 121; working, 67, 246. *See also* Working mother
Motherless family: and need for homemaker service, 236
"Mother Service," 284
Mothers' aid, 146
Mothers' pension program, 127, 146
Multiple service center: for pregnant teenagers, 434–35, 436, 456
Munt, 47
Muslim Arab countries, 634
Mutual aid societies, 49

Napoleonic Code, 47
Narcotics addiction, 17, 144, 169. *See also* Drug addiction
National Alliance Concerned with School Age Parents, 454
National Association of Black Social Workers, 535, 537
National Association for Retarded Children, 306
National Association of Social Workers, 2, 675–77 *passim,* 682, 695
National Association of Societies for Organizing Charity, 76
National Center for Child Abuse and Neglect, 156
National Center for Child Advocacy, 98
National Center for Comprehensive Emergency Services, 197
National Center for Social Statistics, 469
National Center for the Prevention and Treatment of Child Abuse and Neglect, 156
National Center on Child Abuse and Neglect, 160, 167, 169
National Committee for Mental Hygiene, 77
National Conference of Catholic Charities, 97, 551
National Conference of Charities and Corrections, 316, 320
National Conference on Social Welfare, 3
National Council for Homemaker-Home Health Aide Services, 237, 240, 257, 259

National Council for One Parent Families, 450
National Council for the Unmarried Mother and Her Child, 450
National Council of Jewish Women, 295–96
National Council of Juvenile and Family Court Judges, 384
National Education Association, 169
National Federation of Day Nurseries, 270
National Foster Parents' Association, 335
National Institute of Mental Health, 206
National Manpower Council, 680
National Organization for Non-Parents, 53
Native American. *See* American Indian
Nazi Germany, 50
Negative claiming behavior: and high risk for abuse, 221
Negative income tax, 144
Negative nesting behavior: and high risk for abuse, 221
Neglect: and foster-family care, 321, 342; and homemaker service, 260; in institutional child care, 613–14; and role rejection, 17, 18, 24, 28
Neighborhood, 41, 42, 43, 81, 140
Neighborhood Day Care Exchange Project, 299
Neighborhood Service Centers, 104
Netherlands, 56, 241, 259. *See also* Holland
New Jersey Supreme Court, 552
New York Children's Aid Society, 316
New York City, Bureau of Child Guidance, 77
New York City Almshouse, 584
New York City Comptroller's Office, 619
New York City Department of Public Welfare, 255
New York City Department of Social Service and Family Day Care-Career Program, 305
New York City Foundling Hospital, 211
New York City Youth Board, 694
New York County Society for the Prevention of Cruelty to Children, 154–55
New York Foundling Hospital, 195
New York School of Social Work, 77
New York Society for the Prevention of Pauperism, 49
New York Times, The, 400, 512
New Zealand, 660
Nigeria, 506

Nixon, Richard M., 141, 271, 302
No-fault divorce. *See* Divorce, no-fault
Nonmarital attitude, 478. *See also* Childlessness
Nonmarital child. *See* Illegitimacy; Pregnancy
Nonwhites: and adoption, 506, 531–39; and child welfare services, 66; and foster-family care, 321–33, 345, 371, 374; and illegitimacy, 66, 419–21; and maternity homes, 443; mortality rate, in U.S., 56, 66; percentage of, living in poverty, 63–66
North American Conference on Adoptable Children, 539, 564
North American Center on Adoptions, 564, 565
Norway, 241, 646, 650, 651, 653, 654, 660
Nursery and Child's Hospital, 270
Nursery school, 267–68

OASDI. *See* Old Age, Survivors', and Disability Insurance
Observation center: and institutional child care, 584
Occupational role: and interrole conflict, 19
Occupational therapy, 240
Oedipal stage, 489
OFFER *vs.* Dumpson, 397–98
Office of Adolescent Pregnancy Programs, 455
Office of Child Development, Children's Bureau, U.S. Department of Health, Education, and Welfare, 105, 156, 197, 303
Office of Economic Opportunity, 105, 621
Old Age, Survivors', and Disability Insurance (OASDI): and death of father, 116; and illegitimate child's benefits, 124; increasing coverage of groups and, 123–24; as social assistance, 115, 118–23, 415
Older child: adoption of, 534, 547–50
One-parent home. *See* Family
Open Door Society of Montreal, 539
Operant conditioning, 87
Operation Babylift, 506–7
Operation Soul Kids, 656
Ordinal position: and incidence of abuse, 183

Oregon Project, 386–87
Organization for a United Response (OURS), 507, 564
Organization of Foster Families for Equality and Reform (OFFER), 397–98
Oriental children: adoption of, 534, 538
Orphans, 57, 470, 471, 584, 595
Orphan asylum, 27, 466, 583, 585–86
Orphan Asylum Society, 49
Orphan Voyage, 495
Orphanages, 319
"Orphans of the living," 382
Orthopedagogue, 659
"Outdoor relief," 40, 48, 127, 415

Pacifist Service Units, 645
Pakistan, 50
Parens patriae, 12, 151, 152
Parent Attitude Research Instrument, 331
Parent-child development center: trend toward, 105
Parent-child dyad, 180–82
Parent-education program: group, 209
Parent Effectiveness Training, 94, 95, 196
Parent-locator service, 145
Parent to Parent Information of Adoption Services (PPIAS), 656
Parental adequacy, 348
Parental aids: as paraprofessional friends, 196
Parental Attitude Research Inventory, 210
Parental consent: and services to teenagers, 456
Parental rights: in abuse cases, 159, 173, 201, 217; and adoption, 507–10, 551–52, 554, 565; defined, 151–52, 215, 313; and foster-family care, 345, 398–99; and standards of child care, 216; termination of, 212, 347, 383
Parental role: expectations of, 9, 24, 28; failure of, 157, 158; inadequacy, 203; rejection of, 17–18, 28, 151, 161; rights and obligations of, 9; unfulfillment of, 14–15, 57–58, 115; unoccupied, 13, 14
Parental surrogates, 194–95, 196
Parents United, 198
Parenthood: adoptive, 473–81, 485–87, 544, 564; psychological, 399, 465
Parents, adoptive. *See* Adoptive parents
Parents Anonymous, 105, 203–5, 209
Parents Anonymous Frontiers, 205

Parents for Children, 656
Parents to Adopt Minority Youngsters (PAMY), 534, 564–65
Parents Without Partners, 105
"Park aunts," 654
Partial institutionalization, 620–21
Patria potestas, 47
Paton, Jean, 495
"Patronage nurse," 654
Pearl Buck Foundation, 564
Peking Review, 664
People's Councils (Rumania), 664–65
People's Republic of China, 35, 366, 635, 647, 651, 654, 664
Permanence: in foster-family care, 388–89
Personality: and relationship to neglect, 186, 187
Philadelphia Association of Day Nurseries,
Physical abuse. *See* Abuse
Physical handicap. *See* Handicapped children
Pinkney, Judge Merritt W., 127
Placement Prevention Service, 327
"Placing out," 318, 376–77
Placing Out System of the New York Children's Aid Society, The, 315
Planned Parenthood, 452. *See also* Family planning services
Plato, 34, 38–39
Pliny, 38
Poland, 631–32, 635, 647, 649, 657–58, 664
Police: and abuse and neglect cases, 162, 198–99, 216, 219; as referral source in foster-family care, 321; mentioned, 221, 246
Politics: relation of, to child welfare, 41
Poor Law Act: and illegitimacy, 414–15
"Poor man's divorce," 58. *See also* Desertion
Population: of the aged *vs.* children, 52, 55; of children, 70; teenage, 54; per physician, in other countries, 639
Portugal, 634, 655
Postnatal care, 56
Postpartum depression, 254
Postpartum psychosis, 243
Postplacement service: and adoption, 484–85
Potential for Foster Parenthood Scale, 335
Poverty, 56, 62–68 *passim,* 70, 97, 140, 213

"Poverty index" level, 132, 146
Pregnancy: out-of-wedlock, 58, 59, 142, 145, 415, 421–28, 633
Pregnancy Discrimination Act, 651
Prekindergarten, 268
Premarital pregnancy. *See* Pregnancy
Premature birth: and high risk of abuse, 182
Prenatal care, 56, 429–30
Preplanned service, 105–6
Preschool enrichment programs. *See* Day care; Head Start Program
President Carter's Commission on Mental Health, 80, 102
Privacy: loss of, and foster parenthood, 362; and protective service agencies, 190–91; right of minors to, and abortion, 453
Prostitution, 168
Protective services: history of, 153–57 *passim;* in other countries, 646; responsibility to the child and, 157–58, 219–21; as a supportive service, 26
Protective Services Center, 197
Protestantism, 317
Protestants: in social work, 675
Psychiatry, 78, 216, 217, 260
Psychoanalytic psychology, 86
Psychologist: clinical, and role in child guidance clinic, 86
Psychosis, 187, 211
Psychotherapy: evaluation of, 90, 99, 100–2; for unmarried mothers, 429; and institutional child care, 598–99; group, 605
Public assistance: history of, 127–29; income maintenance, 126–40; in other countries, 652–53; and OASDI, 115–23; vs. social insurance, 116–17
Public health, 46, 212, 236
Public welfare programs, 130
Pueri alimentarii, 39, 48
Puerto Ricans, 65, 372. *See also* Spanish-speaking Americans
Puerto Rico, 323, 385, 676
Purchase of service: by AFDC, 107–8, 145–47, 618; and day care, 145; in group homes, for emotionally disturbed child, 618
Puritan ethos, 684–85

Quilloin *v.* Walcott, 509–10

Race: and adoption, 442–43, 533–39; and illegitimacy rates, 419–21; and integrated institutional child care, 621; and socioeconomic class, 420–21; identity, and transracial adoptions, 537–38

Ranchos, 638

Rating Scale for Pupil Adjustment, 381

Receiving home: as type of foster care, 339

Recidivism rate: in abuse, 207. *See also* Abuse

Reciprocal inhibition: as behavior modification technique, 87, 88

Reeducation center, 645, 659

"Reparenting," 193, 208

"Rescue Home," 433

Residence clubs, 606

Residential services, 433. *See also* Maternity home

Residential treatment center, 338, 583, 590, 595. *See also* Institutional child care

Residential worker: in a child care institution, 601

Role: inadequate implementation, and homemaker services, 242–45; incapacity, defined, 15–17; modeling, 209; rejection, and abandonment, 17–18, 28; reversal, 196; strain, and social work, 220; unfilled, 14–15. *See also* Social role

Roman Catholic Church, 39, 40, 42, 43, 45, 314, 317, 536, 643, 675

Roman Empire, 34–35, 37, 39, 48, 465

Roman Twelve Tables, 38

Rome, Ancient, 40, 47, 49, 466

Rumania, 649, 664–65

Runaway house, 105

Rutter Behavior Scale, 353

Ryther Child Center, 607

Saint Vincent de Paul, 49, 584

Salary: of social worker, 677

Scandinavia, 451, 653, 660. *See also* Individual countries

Schools, 160–61, 169, 203, 213, 215, 218, 640

Science, 51

Scientific Revolution, 43, 69

Scotch Registers Office, 499

Scotland, 378, 444, 449, 495, 498, 661

Secondary deviance, 612

Seebohm Committee, 661

Self-approval methods (SAM), 336

Self concepts, 211, 213

Self-help group, 105, 198, 203–5, 209

Seneca, 38

Separation: and dependence, 142; and foster-family care, 343, 349–51, 379–80; and parental role unfulfilled, 24

Service, hard, 135

Service delivery: and diagnosis, 221

Settlement house, 106

Seven Hills Neighborhood House, 284

Sexual abuse, 158, 166–67, 187–88, 198

Sex education, 423, 452

Sex norms, 419–21, 451–52, 456

Sex of child: and foster family care, 379

Sex therapy, 95

Sexual promiscuity, 186

"Shared parenting," 194–95

Shelter care, emergency, 197. *See also* Emergency care

"Sheltering Arms," 433

Shuggies, 638

Siblings, 7–8, 42, 188, 324, 350, 592

Sickness allowance: in other countries, 649–50

"Significant others," 88

Single-parent family. *See* Family, single-parent

Single Parent Family Project, 107

Slavery: abolition of, 315

Social class: and acceptable minimum of child care, 215–16; and effects on child development, 213; and foster parenthood, 329–30, 400; and illegitimacy rates, 420–21; and incidence of abuse, 161, 183–84, 187, 215

Social Darwinism, 684–85

Social hjälp (Sweden), 652

Social insurance: eligibility for, 116; OASDI, 118–23; vs. public assistance, 116–17; as supplementary service, 115; trends in, 123–26; and workmen's compensation, 117; and unemployment insurance, 117–18

Social isolation, 161, 178, 179, 184, 188

Social role: of child, 11–12, 20–22; community and, 12–13, 22–25; defined, 8–25; of parent, 9–11, 13–20

Social Security Act of 1935, 7, 118, 128, 139, 145, 146, 259, 320

Social Security Act: 1962 amendment, 155, 272

Social Security Act: 1967 amendment, 104, 156, 238, 239, 272

Social Security Administration, 125

Social security system: in other countries, 647–54

Social Service Exchange, 377

"Social utilities," 135

Social work: and adoption, 536–38, 546–47, 551; child-welfare, 5–8, 678–95; and day care, 272–73, 286–96; and right to foster-care placement, 358–62, 395–96; and institutional child care, 596–606; and out-of-wedlock pregnancy, 429–32; and protective services, 219–20

Social worker: polyvalent, 661; professional, 1–5, 584, 673–97

Social Work, 2

Society for the Relief of Poor Widows with Small Children, 49

Society for the Prevention of Cruelty to Children, 154–55

Sociotherapy, 4, 429

Socrates, 696

Solon, 34

Sony Company, 654

SOS Children's Federation, 659

South America, 634

Soviet Union: child welfare services in, 631, 633, 644, 648, 649, 650, 653–54, 661, 662–63, 664

Spanish-speaking Americans, 65, 80, 163, 595. *See also* Chicanos, Puerto Ricans

Spaulding for Children, 545, 564, 565

Special intensive unit, 326–27

Specialization of social institutions, 33, 104–5

Special needs child: adoption of, 530–45, 547–50, 557–60, 562

Spence Chapin Adoption Agency, 468, 470

Standards for Adoption Service, 496

Standards for Day-Care Service, 295

Stanley *vs.* Illinois, 415–16, 509, 510

State Charities Aid Association, 377

State Division of Family Services, 429

States: and abortion, 452–54; and adoption, 467, 507–10, 516, 517, 562; and AFDC, 129; child's rights in, 151, 415; and corporal punishment in schools, 169; and day care, 272, 279, 301–2; and definition of physical and mental incapacity, 128; and foster-family care,

332, 385; and laws regulating social work, 676; and mixed almshouses, 319; and protective services, 155, 156; responsibility to the child, 45, 157; sexual abuse laws, 166; and support recovery programs, 145; and unemployment, 128

Step-relationship: and child abuse, 166–67, 188

Sterility: and adoptive parents, 476

Sterilization, 54, 635

Stress: and child abuse, 163–64, 183–84, 218–19

Subcommittee of Children and Youth, Senate Committee on Labor and Public Welfare, 512

Substitute service: and adoption, 465–567; defined, 27; and foster-family care, 313–402; statistics on, 320; in other countries, 641–42, 654–60

Supplementary service: and AFDC, 126–40; and day care, 267–307; defined, 27, 115; and homemaker service, 235–61; in other countries, 647–54

Support recovery programs, 145

Supportive service: "boundaries" of, 103; clientele of, 96, 107; community organization and, 96–98; defined, 25–26, 75; evaluation of, 98–102; in other countries, 745–47; problems of, 102–3; process in, 80–88; trends in, 104–7

"Surrogate families": and Parents Anonymous, 204

"Surrogate mothers," 195

Sweden, 241, 644, 646, 647, 649, 650, 651, 652, 653, 654, 655, 656, 658, 660, 663

Switzerland, 634

Systemic case planning, 345–46

"Task-centered casework," 106

Tax: payroll, 125

Tayari: San Diego Department of Public Welfare, 533

"Telling." *See* Adoption

Teenage parenthood, 445–47, 456. *See also* Adolescence

Teenage pregnancy, 59, 417, 420, 429, 434–35, 456

Teenagers: and contraceptive information,

428, 429; and parental consent for services, 456

Termination: and adoption, 370–71; of foster care, 370–74; of parental rights, 370; of protective services, 198

Texas Adoption Exchange, 556

Thalidomide, 50

Thematic Apperception Test (TAT), 182

Title IV. *See* Social Security Act

Title XX. *See* Social Security Act, 1967 amendment

Tot Steun, Dutch Child Caring Agency, 377–78

Trade unions, 42, 662–63

Training schools, 583

Transactional analysis, 95

Travelers Aid International Social Service (TAISS), 505 506

Treatment Alternative Project (TAP), 594

Treatment: in family service agencies and child guidance clinics, 82–86; in institutional child-care, 598–606; procedures of, 108

Trends: in adoption, 554–65; in AFDC, 145–46; in child abuse reporting, 172; in day care, 302–6; in foster-family care, 396–400; in institutional child care, 615–21, 623; in protective services, 221–23; in social insurance, 123–26; in supportive services, 107; for unmarried mother, 454–56

"Triggering context": and stress, 184

Truancy, 22, 158, 217

Underdeveloped countries, 41

Unemployment: defined, 128; statistics on, 53, 63, 66, 67

Unemployment insurance: as social insurance, 115, 117–18; in other countries, 647–48

United Fund, 435, 645

United Kingdom. *See* Great Britain

United Nations: and adoption, 506; and day care, 267; and the Year of the Child, 1979, 48

United Nations Bureau of Social Affairs, 665

United Nations Children's Fund, 41

United Nations General Assembly: and

Declaration of the Rights of the Child, 48

United Nations International Children's Emergency Fund (UNICEF), 665

United Nations Secretariat, 2

United States: adoption in, 469, 471, 508, 534; and AFDC program, 146; and child abuse legislation, 156; and contraceptive services, 452; history of day care in, 269–72; population of children in, 52; and societies for the prevention of cruelty to children in, 155; and status of the child, 51; and women in the labor force, 273–76; and workmen's compensation, 117

U.S. Bureau of the Census, 183, 595

U.S. Bureau of Indian Affairs: and adoption, 534, 538

U.S. Census on Children Under Institutional Care, 586

U.S. Children's Bureau, 559

U.S. Congress: and funding for abortion, 452; and adoption, 508, 512, 517; and child-care development bill, 271; and social services of AFDC, 135; and welfare reform, 141

U.S. Constitution: Eighth Amendment, 169; First Amendment, 495; Fourteenth Amendment, 415, 495

U.S. Department of Agriculture: and day care facilities, 303; and Food Stamp program, 133

U.S. Department of Health, Education, and Welfare, 145, 156, 197, 303, 455, 469

U.S. Department of Labor, 124, 303, 675

U.S. government: and poverty index, 62, 132; and Title XX, 137–39; and Operation Babylift, 506–7

U.S. Immigration and Naturalization Service, 505

U.S. Immunization Survey, 169

U.S. Office of the Comptroller General, 614

U.S. Office of Education, 271

U.S. Supreme Court: and abortion, 50, 418–19, 452, 453; and corporal punishment in schools, 169; and illegitimacy, 415; and OFFER *vs.* Dumpson, 397–98; and rights of unmarried father, 509; and Stanley *vs.* Illinois, 415–16; and the Weisenfeld case, 125

United Way, 103
Unwanted pregnancy, 55, 182. *See also* Illegitimacy; Pregnancy
Unwed father. *See* Putative father

Van Arsdale, Martin Van Buren, 318, 319
Venereal disease, 167
Vietnam, 506–7
Virginia Frank Child Development Center, 238
Visiting Homemaker Association of New Jersey, 240
Vista Del Mar Child Care Service, 439
Vives, 49
Vocational counseling, 429, 434, 605
Vocational training, 99, 236
Volunteer agencies: and foster-family care, 394; and homemaker services, 237, 242; and protective services, 49, 155, 321, 434, 439; and purchase of services, 107; role of, in other countries, 663–65

Wage home, 339
War on poverty, 268
WATS hot line, 207
Wealth redistribution, 140. *See also* Income
Webster School in the District of Columbia: and pregnant teenagers, 434, 436–37
Wechsler Intelligence Scale, 381
Weisenfeld, Stephen, 125
Welfare Branch of the Division of Claims Policy, Bureau of Retirement and Survivors' Insurance, 120
Welfare program: public image of, 142–43
West Germany, 56, 644, 646, 650, 653, 658, 660
Westchester County, New York, 81
Western Electric, 304
Westinghouse Learning Corporation, 301
Whites: illegitimacy and, 419–21; infant mortality of, 56–57; in social work profession, 675
White House Conference on Children: 1909, 319, 320; 1960 Golden Anniversary, 155; 1970, 48, 98, 302
Widowhood, 59, 63
Woman's Bureau of the U.S. Department of Health, Education, and Welfare, 2

Women's Bureau of the U.S. Department of Labor, 267
Women: attitude toward, in other countries, 642–43; divorced, and OASDI benefits, 125; employment of, 65–66, 67, 236, 273–76, 633, 654, 677, 678, 680; status of, 68; in social work profession, 674
Women's movement, 48, 68, 275, 276, 390, 455, 553
Work home, 339
Workhouses, 40
Work Incentive (WIN): and day care, 275, 286
Working mother: and day care, 25, 273–76, 281, 285–86, 300–1, 306; discussed, 65, 66, 67, 70, 390; effects on child of, 277–78; and interrole conflict, 19–20; public image of, 296–97
Working mothers' hotels, 660
Workman's compensation, 115, 117, 118, 124, 647
Works Progress Administration, 236, 270, 271
Workshop, sheltered, 135
Work training: and WIN, 142
World Congress on Adoption and Foster Placement, 506
World Convention on Adoption Law, 506
World Health Organization, 7
World War I, 41, 127, 645
World War II: and day care movement, 270–71, 299; and divorce rate, 57

Xenodocheion, 584

Year of the Child, 1979, 48
Young Men's Christian Association (YMCA), 284, 603
Young Women's Christian Association (YWCA), 434, 603
Youth Services of Philadelphia, 619
Yugoslavia, 635, 650, 663–64

Zambia, 631, 632
Zero population growth, 53, 68, 390
Zoning: and group homes, 615